reverse pg 8

argu 885 - 889

satsy pg 976 & byre

⊗ page 988 — where the disciple
s is not m. Poth

The Gospel of Jesus
In Search of His Original Teachings

"In this work, John Davidson has probed the origins of Christianity in a provocative and illuminating way. By carrying us back to our beginnings, we see both the brilliance of essential Christianity and the distortions through which this tradition has been filtered through the ages. It is a gold-mine of new insights."

Rt. Rev. John Shelby Spong
Bishop of Newark, New Jersey
Author of *Resurrection: Myth or Reality?*

"Only rarely is a work of this nature published which can be instantly recognized as a classic. John Davidson's new book, *The Gospel of Jesus*, will be essential reading for anyone seeking or researching the Jesus of history.

"It is interesting to ask why this book has never been written before. The manuscripts and other texts cited to illustrate the beliefs and understandings of Greeks, Jews and assorted Palestinians of the immediate pre- and post-Christian era are readily available to scholars, but have often been dismissed as worthless, heretical or simply irrelevant. Yet if one wished to study, say, the speeches of Winston Churchill you would first consider the historical situation of the time, the hopes and aspirations of the audience, and the influence of later events and subsequent generations who came to regard him as a super hero. This book does exactly that. It strips away the layers in a unique way and reveals a Jesus who may seem unfamiliar or even unrecognizable to some.

"Every Christian creates or has created for them an image of Jesus that is valid or relevant for them. Some persuade others that their vision has greater validity than others. Possibly John Davidson has created yet another image: Jesus the mystic, the spiritual Master, Jesus the gnostic. An image which fits his understanding of spirituality. What he does do which is so compelling, however, is to provide new interpretations of many parts of the New Testament that were previously difficult to understand.

"Mysticism is little understood by the popular mind, and Jesus the mystic may be a surprising image. But many will be fascinated by the rich and universal spirituality common to all the major world religions. This spirituality must be closer to first-century Palestine than the sanitized version taught in theological colleges today. More importantly, it must be closer to the spirituality taught by Jesus and lost simply because it is so hard for the Western mind to grasp.

"The roads that lead to a true understanding of God may not be so dissimilar after all."

Stephen Broughton MA
Broadcaster and Founder Member of the 'Sea of Faith'

DEDICATION

To the Good Shepherd
Who Waits by the Door

I am the Door:
by me if any man enter in,
he shall be saved,
and shall go in and out,
and find pasture.

John 10:9

O Doorkeeper, open the door to me.
I will not stem my tears, O Powerful One,
unless thou wipe away my sin.

Psalms of Heracleides, MPB p.188

THE GOSPEL

OF

JESUS

In Search of His Original Teachings

Born in 1944, John Davidson has had a life-long interest in mysticism. Graduating in 1966 from Cambridge University with an honours degree in natural sciences, he took a post at the University's Department of Applied Mathematics and Theoretical Physics, where he worked for seventeen years.

In 1984, he left the University to pursue independent interests and since then has written a number of books, including a series on science and mysticism. The present book is his second on the teachings of Jesus and the mysticism of his times.

The author is married and continues to live near Cambridge.

A Note From the Publishers

Due to the nature of this book and in order to make it accessible to as wide a readership as possible, its entire production, up to the printing and binding stage, has been performed as a service, freely given. We are grateful to the many individuals who have given of their time and energy.

The retail price should not exceed £14.95 (UK), $22.95 (USA) and the equivalent in other currencies.

BY THE SAME AUTHOR

On Science and Mysticism

Subtle Energy (1987)
The Web of Life (1988)
The Secret of the Creative Vacuum (1989)
Natural Creation and the Formative Mind (1991)
Natural Creation or Natural Selection? (1992)

On Mysticism in Jesus' Era

The Robe of Glory (1992)

THE GOSPEL OF JESUS

In Search of His Original Teachings

John Davidson M.A. (CANTAB)

ELEMENT

Shaftesbury, Dorset • Rockport, Massachusetts
Brisbane, Queensland

First published in Great Britain in 1995 by
Element Books Limited
Shaftesbury, Dorset SP7 8BP

Published in the USA in 1995 by
Element Books, Inc.
P.O. Box 830, Rockport, MA 01966

Published in Australia in 1995 by
Element Books Limited for
Jacaranda Wiley Limited
33 Park Road, Milton, Brisbane 4064

Designed by Roger Lightfoot & Wayne Caravella
Cover design by Max Fairbrother
Typeset by Wayne Caravella
Printed and bound in India by Thomson Press

British Library Cataloguing in Publication
data available

Library of Congress Cataloging in Publication
data available

ISBN 1–85230–720–X

ACKNOWLEDGEMENTS

I am grateful to the many scholars and publishers whose work has contributed to this book. Many of the passages quoted are no longer restricted by copyright and some are too small to require it. Other extracts are printed by generous copyright permission of E.J. Brill (*The Canonical Prayerbook of the Mandaeans*, E.S. Drower, 1959; *Panarion of Epiphanius of Salamis*, tr. Frank Williams, 1987; *The Books of Jeu and the Untitled Text in the Bruce Codex*, tr. Violet MacDermot, 1978; *The Nag Hammadi Studies* series, volumes XI (1979), XV (1981), XX (1989), XXI (1989), XXII (1985), XXVI (1984), XXVIII (1990), ed. (respectively) D.M. Parrott, B.A. Pearson, B. Layton, B. Layton, H.W. Attridge, S. Emmel, C.W. Hedrick); of E.J. Brill and HarperCollins Publishers Inc. (*The Nag Hammadi Library in English*, ed. J.M. Robinson, 3rd completely revised edn., 1988); of Wm.B. Eerdmans (*The Text of the New Testament*, Kurt and Barbara Aland, 1987); of Penguin Books (*Conversations of Socrates*, Xenophon, tr. H. Tredennick and R.A.H. Waterfield, 1990; *History of the Church*, Eusebius, tr. G.A. Williamson, 1965; *The Dead Sea Scrolls in English*, G. Vermes, 1988; *The Jewish War*, Josephus, tr. G.A. Williamson, 1959 and 1981); of Cambridge University Press (*Origen Contra Celsum*, Origen, tr. Henry Chadwick, 1986); of Methuen (*Life of Richard Rolle*, F.M.M. Comper, 1969); of the Nederland Intitut voor het Nabije Oosten (*The Teachings of Silvanus*, J. Zandee, 1991); of Scholars' Facsimiles & Reprints (*Manichaean Literature*, J.P. Asmussen, 1975); of SPCK (*Studies of the Spanish Mystics*, E.A. Peers, 1928); of the University of London (*Bulletin of the School of Oriental and African Studies* XI and XII, 1943-1946, 1948); of Oxford University Press (*The Apocryphal Old Testament*, ed. H.E.D. Sparks, 1985; *The Manichaean Hymn Cycles in Parthian*, Mary Boyce, 1954); Routledge & Kegan Paul (*Graces of Interior Prayer*, A. Poulain, tr. L.L. Yorke Smith, first edition 1910, enlarged 1950); of the University of Uppsala (*Mesopotamian Elements in Manichaeism*, Geo Widengren, 1946); of the Syndics of Cambridge University Library (a photograph of a page from *Codez Bezae Cantabrigiensis*).

Extracts from the *Authorized Version* of the Bible (*King James Bible*), the rights in which are vested in the Crown, are reproduced by permission of the Crown's Patentee, Cambridge University Press.

Extracts taken from the *Jerusalem Bible*, published and copyright 1966, 1967 and 1968 by Darton, Longman & Todd and Doubleday (a division of Bantam Doubleday Dell Publishing Group Inc.) are reprinted by permission of the publishers.

Thanks are due to Thomas Richman for his insights into the meaning of certain passages from Plato and the Greek mystic philosophers.

I am also grateful to Rt. Rev. Hugh Montefiore, Rev. Robert Philp and Rev. David Torrance for their critical assessment of all or parts of the manuscript, making valuable suggestions, (they were not always in agreement with my point of view!) Thanks, too, go to Dr Penny Gibson who helped substantially with major editorial structuring, to Faith Singh and Dr John Templer who made many helpful recommendations, to Barbara Pindow and Matthew Seal for the copy editing, to Yvette Beigel and her team for the sub-editing and proofreading, to Sandra Castellino for proofreading and making the index (no small task), to Alan Bailey for the map, to Wayne Caravella for the typesetting, and to a large number of other friends who have generously and freely given of their time and expertise, helping in many ways with the research. Lastly, I must express undying gratitude to my own spiritual Master for all his grace and inspiration. He left the body in June 1990 after requesting me, a little more than a year before, to write this book.

Contents

PART I: The Setting

PART III: The Son of God

PART IV: The Return of the Soul

EPILOGUE
MANY MYSTICS

INTRODUCTION

Because of its universal prevalence, mysticism has been called the perennial philosophy, encountered at all times, amongst all peoples and present in all religions. In fact, when one looks with an unprejudiced eye at the religious teachings of the world, one finds that beyond the differences of ritual and culture, almost all are founded upon the same universal spiritual or mystic truths. A study of this universal spiritual basis to religion and the attempt to practise it in everyday life widens one's outlook, making it possible to see past the confines of religion, prejudice and preconception into the free and wide-open spaces of true spirituality. This spirituality is the inheritance of all human beings. Yet it seems to be an innate human characteristic to narrow down the universal into the particular and the parochial.

From my earliest childhood I have been interested in the mystical, though I could not at first put a name to it. But certain feelings and experiences in life and within myself have led me inexorably to a mystical understanding. Prior to embarking upon the research that led to *The Gospel of Jesus*, I had not studied Jesus' teachings in a detailed manner and – other than reading a few books on the subject – had rarely looked further afield than the New Testament. But the last six years have been devoted almost entirely to the study of Jesus' teachings, early Christianity and the history of the New Testament texts, together with an intensive exploration amongst a profusion of fascinating allied literature from around the time of Jesus.

It has been the most interesting and rewarding research project that I have ever undertaken and has repeatedly demonstrated the wealth of mysticism present in the Middle East, Egypt and the Graeco-Roman world, not only during Jesus' time, but for centuries and possibly millennia, both before and since. From this research and from a long-standing study of the mystical and religious literature of the world, I have felt with increasing conviction that Jesus was not an isolated phenomenon, but was one of many who have taught the perennial mystic path. And in a way, although Christianity began as a Middle Eastern religion, for those of us raised in Christian countries, this ancient literature is a part of our rightful heritage. Yet it has largely been lost and forgotten by all but a few diligent scholars.

For those who seek to understand the teachings of Jesus, a knowledge of this ancient literature can illuminate more clearly the meaning of his words. Many people, however, who have grown up in Christian countries have rejected Christianity as having little to offer in a modern world. But when we study the teachings of Jesus, pure and simple, we find that they speak directly to the human heart, whoever and wherever we may be, addressing the everyday problems and vicissitudes of life as well as the far deeper issues of ultimate truth, reality and spiritual enlightenment.

We cannot easily escape our childhood conditioning. If only by reason of exposure, we have a certain cultural background built into us, despite ourselves. Consequently, having almost unconsciously become familiar with the words of Jesus, it comes as a great and often surprising relief to understand the spiritual meaning contained in them and to realize that they are universal in their character. It may also lead us to realize that in rejecting the false and the spurious, we had also rejected what could have been true and helpful. And no honest person would deny that we can all use a little help in our lives, in many ways.

It requires only careful scrutiny and consideration to realize that the teachings of Jesus and those of Christianity are not the same. There are a number of practices and special beliefs in Christianity that are not founded on anything that Jesus actually said or taught. Added as the religion developed, their starting point can often be traced historically to a particular place or period. In addition, many of Jesus' sayings in the gospels and the record of events concerning him are difficult to understand and consequently have been interpreted in a variety of ways by different people, at different times. This divergence between Christianity and the teachings of Jesus is an important factor in our search for what he originally taught.

From a detailed investigation of Jesus' teachings in the gospels and elsewhere, it seems that he taught the mystic path of the Creative Word or the divine *Logos* – a path that many mystics both before and since have taught, a path of great and enduring importance to all those in search of Truth. If this really is the case, then there are indeed great divergencies between Christianity and Jesus' real teachings – often subtle, yet frequently of deep significance.

The present book, therefore, has a number of allied purposes. Firstly, it explores the teachings of Jesus in the light of this ancient and universal mystic teaching. This entails an exposition of the main features of the perennial path, expressed – as far as possible – in the way that Jesus taught it. Specifically, in approaching each aspect of the mystic path, I have generally begun by referring to the teachings of Jesus as found in the four canonical gospels, rather than the tenets, beliefs and theology of later Christianity.

Often, however, the canonical sayings of Jesus on a particular subject are so sparse that what he really taught still remains obscure and open to speculation. That is why the early Christians found it necessary to formulate precisely what it was they believed – and why it was that there was frequently so much disagreement. Furthermore, scholarly research over the last century and a half has led to the realization that the gospels, with the possible exception of a major portion of John, were not compiled by those who knew Jesus. They were almost certainly written between forty and seventy years after the death of Jesus, a lapse of two or more generations, presenting plenty of opportunity for things to have become distorted. It has also become evident that the gospel compilers, although incorporating the teachings of Jesus, had their own individual points of view and in some instances can actually be observed adjusting or presenting Jesus' sayings and teachings to fit these beliefs. The gospels then passed through a period of copying and general editorial tampering that lasted three or four centuries and it is only these edited and often differing versions which have survived to modern times.

As a consequence, in order to better understand the words of Jesus, it is essential to spread a wider net than the canonical gospels in the search for the meaning that lies behind them. Another of the purposes of this book, therefore, has been to place Jesus in his cultural and religious milieu, in particular, the mystical context of his times. To accomplish this, I have drawn extensively upon material from outside the New Testament.

It is fortunate that despite the efforts of earlier 'orthodox' Christianity to destroy the evidence, there is a great wealth of literature now available from early Christian times. Some of it has only been discovered in the last fifty or one hundred years and some translated only in the last two decades. And although it must be only a small fraction of what once existed, in many of these fascinating documents, the sayings, metaphors and parables of Jesus found in the four gospels are used and explained in such a way that considerable light is cast upon them. They also reveal the broad spectrum of belief and understanding that prevailed amongst the early Christians concerning Jesus' teachings.

Because the intention has been to place Jesus in the context of his own times, I have drawn only sparingly from the writings of later Christian mystics and teachers. It is certainly true that there is a great deal of wonderfully inspiring literature written by these mystics, many of whom were accused of heresy in their own time, some even being executed for their beliefs and experiences. Most, if not all, of the key principles of mysticism can be supported and elucidated by reference to their teachings. But, in this book, the idea has been to demonstrate the meaning of Jesus' teachings by reference to his own words and to those of his near contemporaries and, in general, I have only used quotations from Christian mystics to help elucidate the nature of mystic experience.

This book is written primarily for those of a Christian background who find themselves seeking for a higher and deeper understanding than dogma and ritual can impart. Its presentation and style, therefore, are intended to make its contents accessible to the lay person. This is the first time, I believe, that such a wide-ranging study of the mystical and allied writings of Jesus' times has been attempted. On the other hand, though avoiding the use of scholarly footnotes, all excerpts and citations are clearly referenced and can easily be traced to their sources by those pursuing their own research. In fact, the research behind this book has been as thorough as it could be.

Generally, books concerning the mystic literature of early Christianity have been written by professional scholars, often by those with little or no experience of the mystical. But mysticism – being a matter of personal, inner experience rather than intellectual study – will always be misunderstood to a greater or lesser extent by those whose only experience has been intellectual. Since my interest is primarily mystical, this book may help, therefore, to provide another point of view and afford some stimulating reading.

The overall plan is straightforward. The book is divided into four parts. The first chapter of Part One looks at the relationship of religion to spirituality and mysticism, discusses the nature of mysticism and introduces the fundamentals of the perennial mystic teaching. This is equated with the essence of what scholars have termed the 'gnostic myth'. The process by which mystic or spiritual teachings become a religion is also discussed and becomes one of the refrains running throughout this book.

The next four chapters of Part One cover the background to the New Testament and allied ancient literature. The origins and authenticity of the various texts are examined, according to the findings of scholarly research. The little that is known of Jesus' life history is also considered and key characters such as Paul are introduced. The intention, here, is only to provide a background for the understanding of the original teachings of Jesus. No attempt is made to depict the development of Christian dogma or to provide a history of early Christianity.

The main body of the book, divided into three further parts, is then concerned with a systematic study of the teachings of Jesus – considered in the light of the universal mystic path – and the way in which a large number of early Christians understood him. Each chapter takes a topic and explores it thoroughly. The subjects presented in Part Two are those of God, the Creative Word, the creation and the soul, the origin of good, evil and sin, and the part that man is called upon to play. In Part Three, the nature and role of the mystic Saviour or Son of God is discussed, while Part Four focuses on the path of man's return to God. It includes a discussion on the character of mystic baptism, the nature of true prayer and how man may overcome his difficulties in this world. Also considered is the spiritual basis for a true morality and ethics, together with its relationship to mystic teaching and the path of discipleship. The Epilogue then spreads a wider net and provides a very brief overview of some of the mystics prior to Jesus' time who taught the same universal mystic truths.

Though I have endeavoured at all times to keep the content direct and clear, it should be understood that no attempt is being made to convince anyone of anything, nor to shape anybody's thinking, nor to argue about any aspect of the Bible. The quest for Truth is a personal odyssey in which every person has to seek for themselves and to satisfy their own inner self. The question of dogma does not arise. I have only tried to put certain facts – often of an irrefutable historical character – before the reader and then to let him or her judge for themselves. There may be parts of this book where the reader finds himself in disagreement with the author. Fair enough. But if what is written here is found to stimulate and to inspire the reader to clarify his or her own understanding, then its purpose has been achieved.

It has been said that a wise man simply presents the truth as he understands it, without entering into disputes with others. In general, this principle has been adopted throughout, for many of the sayings and parables of Jesus are hedged around with such an ambience of traditional Christian explanation that if it had been taken in hand at every step to deal with all the other possible interpretations, presenting the mystical and Christian points of view alongside each other, and arguing the way through to a conclusion, the book would soon have lost all sense of direction and have never reached an end. Moreover, the conservative and traditional Christian is unlikely to be moved from his position by such an approach and, in any case, many passages frequently have more than one 'traditional' or 'scholarly' interpretation!

Consequently, I have often given an interpretation according to an understanding of universal mysticism and have left it at that. It can be said, therefore, that the exposition is a personal interpretation based upon the principles of the mystic path. It is not that the conventional Christian interpretation is unknown to me, simply that the intention is to present the universal mystic teachings rather than to enter the realm of scholarly, religious and theological debate. To do so would have been to deaden the text, making it thoroughly indigestible, damaging the main purpose of the book. Nevertheless, all the cardinal features of Christian belief – such as resurrection, the virgin birth, the second coming, Jesus' miracles and so on – have all been addressed in their turn and if the reader wonders why so-and-so has not been mentioned at one place, it is probably because it is covered somewhere else.

Regarding the texts used herein, they are all known to scholars as accredited ancient documents and are mentioned, discussed and quoted in scholarly literature. Translations of many of these books and texts have long been out of print, but living only ten or fifteen minutes' drive from the Cambridge University Library has made it very simple to locate and consult them.

Generally, I have used translations as I have found them. In a few instances, however, where more than one translation exists, I have collated them into a new rendering which seemed more accurately to convey the meaning. But the motivation has always been to present the original meaning of the text and to make it clear to the ordinary reader. In an even smaller number of instances, a new translation has been provided.

It is possible, I suppose, that some will think that quotations have been selected out of context to suit my purposes. I have been very careful to avoid such errors. There are so many writings which clearly express perennial mystic truths that one is spoilt for choice. Not all are of the same spiritual calibre, of course, and without going into lengthy details, I have tried to sketch the general character of the texts employed by appropriate introductory comments or in the survey of the various non-canonical sources provided in chapter five.

Since some of these translations are over a hundred years old and usage of the English language has changed to some extent, I have also adjusted punctuation, as well as spelling, and occasionally sentence construction, so as to be consistent with modern times and to communicate the sense more readily to the modern reader. Capitals have also been added or removed to highlight certain meanings and for the sake of consistency. Any significant clarifications or additions to a translation offered by myself or the original translator have been placed in round brackets, while significant conjectured words or phrases, usually provided by the original translator to fill gaps in an original, defective manuscript, appear in square brackets ([ ]). In the interests of readability, some of the square and round brackets of the original translations have been omitted, where the correctness of the bracketed text seems more or less certain. In a very few instances, grammatical construction or other small changes have also been made.

New Testament translations, unless otherwise stated, have been taken from the *King James Version*. Although the Greek text substantiating this translation is by no means the best and oldest available, the translation, despite its archaic character, still conveys – to my mind – the most accurate spiritual and mystic meaning. This choice is discussed more fully at the relevant point in the book. However, I have dispensed with the verse structure, added some modern punctuation and spelling, occasionally used capitals to clarify meaning and sometimes put explanatory words in round brackets. This makes the ancient language much easier to follow. I have also set many of the passages in a poetic form so that the reader may take in the meaning more readily.

As scholars have so frequently pointed out, it is uncertain who wrote the gospels. However, when quoting from them, I have commonly used expressions such as "Matthew says". This should really be read as a shorthand for "the author of this particular section of the gospel attributed to Matthew says". It is not being implied that the disciple Matthew actually wrote the words attributed to him.

Similarly, when it is said that "Jesus says", this is according to the document being quoted, whether from the gospels or other literature. One cannot always preface his sayings with such comments as "in a saying attributed to Jesus". In the majority of cases, however, it is really quite unknown whether or not Jesus actually said words to that effect, though the prior discussion and the context will normally be sufficient to permit the reader to judge the likelihood for him or herself. The same, of course, is true of passages attributed to Peter and others. As the author, I have always weighed in my mind the probable authenticity of all passages. It is something of which one must be constantly aware when dealing with all such ancient texts, though in many instances it does not matter very much since the point at issue is often what those particular early Christians actually believed Jesus to have taught. Putting such beliefs into the mouth of a famous person was a literary habit and style of the times. It was common to many ancient writings, not just to those of Christianity.

It has not been possible to incorporate all of the extant sayings and parables of Jesus from the canonical gospels into the present book. If, therefore, some of the reader's favourite passages have been omitted, I can only offer apologies. But the attempt has been made to include all the more well-known sayings of the great teacher and those considered to be the most significant.

It has also been necessary to make a decision on what to call the two parts of the Bible which Christians know as the Old and the New Testaments. Judaism, of course, does not accept the Christian addition, referring to its own scriptures simply as the Bible. In a Christian context, this is ambiguous and when the reference is specifically to one part, so as to avoid confusion or tortuous phraseology, I have followed the Christian convention with apologies to Jewish readers. In terms of the truth they each contain, I do not believe that the one is any older or newer than the other.

Because of modern attitudes, writers are often faced with a difficulty concerning the use of 'he', 'him' and so forth, when in fact referring to all human beings - men *and* women. In the past, a generalized person or individual was always referred to as a 'he' and that was that. In present times, people are more sensitive. I have tried therefore to pursue a middle path, sometimes using a singular form (*eg.* 'a person') mixed with the colloquial plural form ('they', 'them' or 'themselves'), sometimes using 'he', 'his' or 'himself' and occasionally writing 'he or she'. I am sure that this solution will not please everybody, but I have done my best. As far as I am concerned, all human beings share a common and natural equality, regardless of sex, race, colour, religion, social position or any other external difference. And God, of course, is far beyond all physical attributes, even if it is conventional to speak of that Supreme Power as 'He'.

I have been as thorough as possible, covering all aspects of this ancient path and including a wealth of quotations to support interpretations. In the majority of instances, many more quotations could have been added and the decision to include or exclude has often been difficult. Since a book of this nature has not been previously attempted, there seemed no good reason to omit important and relevant material on the grounds of space alone. Nonetheless, the text is organized, I hope, in a readable and coherent fashion and the reader should find the going easy enough if they have an interest in the subject.

A book such as this could easily have been truncated to a quick and easy read – another debunking of traditional beliefs concerning Jesus, aimed at the popular market. That has never been the intention. It has been written primarily for an altogether deeper kind of reader who is prepared to spend time in the search for truth and meaning, and I hope they will find something here to help them. Many of the quotations have an inspirational value that will never be outlived. Were material to have been omitted at the outset for the sake of a quick read, the book would have lost its value as a source of future inspiration.

No human endeavour is entirely perfect in its execution. In a book of this nature, dealing with ancient texts, often fragmentary, defective or difficult to decipher, subject to a wide array of differing opinions and conflicting data, many of them using languages no longer extant, there will always be room for misunderstandings, misinterpretations and mistakes of one kind or another. All the same, I have diligently done whatever could be done, checking and rechecking facts, interpretations and quotations with the help of an expert and willing team. A number of scholars and other well-informed people have also gone through the manuscript. So with the grace of God, I trust that there will be nothing too outrageous, though any remaining errors can certainly be laid at my door. The details presented of the mystic path, however, do most definitely accord with what has been taught by mystics throughout all ages and even at the present time. And that – I believe – is the main thing.

John Davidson
Cambridge

PART I

The Setting

CHAPTER ONE

Religion, Spirituality & Mysticism

Christianity in the Melting Pot

Many millions of people, over the last two thousand years or so, have professed a belief in the teachings of Jesus. For the most part, they have channelled their religious aspirations – weak or strong – into a belief in certain received tenets without ever questioning their reliability and while understanding still less of their history. It is pertinent, therefore, to question the wisdom of this approach. Is ignorance a safe basis for belief? For ignorance can make such strange presumptions.

The colonial days of recent centuries were noted, amongst other things, for extensive missionary activity in the 'heathen' and 'ignorant' (that is to say, non-Christian) areas of the world. As a consequence, it was suggested that the Bible be translated into a number of 'native' languages like Swahili, the various African dialects, and so on. The matter was publicly debated and the temperature at times ran high. One old lady could not see why it was even necessary and her last word on the subject was unequivocal. "If English was good enough for St Paul," said she, "it should be good enough for them!"

Only in recent times has the massive public ignorance concerning the origins of Christianity and the history of the New Testament writings seen any significant erosion. Indeed, for most of Christianity's history, the entire subject has been ignored. What was lacking was not only an objective and dispassionate approach, but also a desire to know.

The beginnings of a rational and analytical study of the New Testament documents were first published in Germany during the eighteenth century. From this it became clear that things were not as they had always been supposed. But in the face of many centuries of inertia and ingrained belief, research proceeded slowly and new insights were won only with considerable effort. Hence, it was not until the mid-nineteenth century that scholars seriously questioned the historical

13

accuracy of the gospels. Yet the evidence for such concern is present within the gospels themselves, as we shall see.

For the last century and a half, various European and American scholars, particularly from Germany in the earlier years, have increasingly subjected the origins of Christianity and the gospels themselves to an unprecedentedly detailed scrutiny and analysis. And this despite the fact that in the early days such brave and pioneering research and the conclusions to which it led often held back the advancement of individual academic careers.

The years 1835-1836, for instance, saw the publication of *The Life of Jesus Critically Examined*, a two-volume book by Tübingen University tutor, David Friedrich Strauss. Carefully appraising all the discrepancies between the gospels, he argued that they could not have been written by eyewitnesses, but must have been compiled much later, freely constructed out of a wealth of confused early Christian traditions. He also dismissed the miracle stories as fabrications designed to give Jesus greater standing. But whatever his colleagues may have thought of his work, the university authorities were unimpressed. He was dismissed from his tutorship, later failing – for the same reasons – to gain a professorial chair at Zürich.

The discoveries, realizations and opinions of such pioneers are of great interest and importance to every Christian. Yet for a long time the results of their studies remained largely within the scholarly domain. In fact, it has only been in recent decades, with the advent of popular books on the subject, as well as considerable media coverage, that the fruits of their research have really reached the public consciousness. For what has been uncovered represents a considerable challenge to Christian faith which many people are still quite unwilling to address. Even now, there are many who are simply unaware of some of the basic and almost incontestable facts concerning the origins of the New Testament.

The gospels, for example, were compiled in Greek between 35 and 70 years after the death of Jesus from a variety of sources. And while Jesus is presumed to have spoken Aramaic as his mother tongue, not one authentic Aramaic source of his sayings and teachings has ever come to light. Furthermore, scholars have demonstrated many times that the gospel compilers had different cultural backgrounds and individual points of view which they were trying to promote, not necessarily in sympathy with the original teachings of Jesus or even with each other. The presentation of his teachings was therefore coloured from the outset by human opinion and interpretation.

The last few decades have seen an unprecedented intensification in the demand for information on Christian origins. "Have we been misled for the last two thousand years?" is now a question that can be seriously asked. The quest for answers has turned books on the pre-Christian, Dead Sea Scrolls into best sellers, while the teachings of the gnostics, a group once castigated as heretical and persecuted, harassed, exiled and executed by the orthodox Christian clergy, now get treated with great respect for what they can tell us of early Christian beliefs. Scholars around the world devote their lives to the study of the few extant ancient texts. Popular books on the subject are constantly appearing in the bookshops.

The freedom of thought and expression now enjoyed in most western countries, together with a blending of cultures and an exposure to other belief systems, has led many to question the unique character of Christianity and its authority as a vehicle conveying Jesus' teachings. The dissatisfaction is further aggravated by an increasing trend towards materialism, generating a deep division between religious and material life. As a result, Christianity's unique message of the miraculous birth of an only Son of God who died an excruciatingly painful death in order to pay for the 'sins of the world', no longer seems relevant to a modern scientific age. Nor to many – no longer fearful of the stigma of heresy, social ostracism or the conflict of disbelief – does it even seem reasonable.

Long-established opinions concerning early Christian history, asserted to enhance faith rather than present the truth, have been discarded. The overly-romantic picture of early Christian harmony, for example, once unquestioned, is now no longer tenable, for the evidence of controversy, previously overlooked, is readily discernible even in the New Testament itself. From the letters of Paul, for instance, it is evident that he was considerably at odds with Peter and the other disciples in Jerusalem, though none of the New Testament writings present more than Paul's side of the story. Additionally, discoveries during the last two centuries of ancient manuscripts, together with a reappraisal of both the canonical and so-called 'apocryphal' texts, have led to a picture of early Christianity, deeply divided within itself as to doctrine, and probably encompassing an even wider spread of opinion and belief than it does today. It seems that even the earliest Christians were confused as to what Jesus had really taught.

Many of the gnostic Christians, for example, believed that Jesus had taught reincarnation, a belief prevalent at that time throughout Europe, North Africa (particularly Egypt) and the Middle East.

Others rejected a belief in the virgin birth, the physical resurrection of the body and other tenets that are now considered primary Christian doctrine. Origen (*c.*185-254), head of a school for Christians in Alexandria very early in the third century, quoted some gnostics as stating the belief in a physical resurrection to be a "faith of fools"[1] and Origen himself maintained that resurrection was not to be understood literally, but in a figurative and incorporeal sense.[2]

In addition, a great many of the earliest Christians confidently expected the return of Jesus and the end of the world to take place during their own lifetimes. Paul, the writers of Matthew, Mark and Luke's gospels, along with many others, were all awaiting it. As things turned out, it was a mistaken belief which had to be modified when time passed with no hint of any second coming. And the Christian teachers of those times found themselves hard pressed to explain away the delay, for by that time it had been written into the gospels and words proclaiming it had been attributed to Jesus, while other sayings of his had also been interpreted in a similar eschatological light.

All this, however, was before so-called orthodox Christianity had gained Imperial patronage and political power (early in the fourth century) and before Christian belief had been formalized and established, albeit by frequently disharmonious councils of Christian bishops. There was no Nicene creed to be repeated by the faithful and opinion was still a free and loose commodity. After all, Christianity was still a minor cult, one amongst many in the Roman Empire, and had yet to face more than two centuries of intermittent persecution before it was adopted as the state religion.

At the present time, the situation has come full circle, for a number of modern Christians, enjoying a freedom of speech denied their predecessors for more than one and a half millennia, have also felt at liberty to voice contrary opinions, as did their earliest counterparts. Some have even declared that they believe God and religion to be human inventions, though useful nonetheless.

Faced with dissension within the ranks, many of the orthodox – being made to feel acutely uncomfortable by the airing of such doubts in public – have suggested that those who hold such beliefs are no longer Christians and should forthwith leave the Church. Not so long ago, they would simply have been excommunicated, expelled or ostracized. Yet the modern 'doubters' remain within the Christian fold, as they would have done in Christianity's earliest days.

Modern democracy and a freedom of speech permitted not only by law but also sanctioned and championed by society have allowed all those who wish to say something to speak out with little fear of censorship or persecution. Yet it has taken a long time for Christian Europe to emerge from the dark ages of religious persecution and authoritarianism which began when Christianity received the impetus of political power nearly seventeen centuries ago.

And where – in all this manifestly human discussion and dissent – are Jesus' real teachings? What would Jesus have thought of all the bickering, interpretation and dogmatism? An outline of the earliest attempt to translate the Bible into common English will serve to show the extent to which human accretions have surrounded, obscured and often obliterated Jesus' teaching of love for God and one's fellow human beings.

The New Testament was written in the colloquial, conversational Greek of the times, Greek having become widespread as an international language of the Middle East and parts of North Africa and Europe, particularly in the wake of Alexander's conquests in the fourth century BC. By the third and fourth centuries AD, as the native Latin of the Romans supplanted Greek as the *lingua franca* of the period, the New Testament and the entire Bible then became available in Latin, formalized in Jerome's fourth-century *Vulgate* translation.

But as the centuries passed and Christianity spread throughout Europe, Latin also became an increasingly unspoken language until few men and even fewer women could comprehend it. It was a language only of the scholars and even many of the clergy found it difficult to grasp its meaning. Yet, the attitude of the medieval church to circulation of the Bible is epitomized by the edict of the Council of Toulouse, passed in 1229 AD, that no lay person should be permitted to own a copy of any Biblical book, least of all in a translation, except, perhaps, the *Psalms*. To possess any written work containing the teachings of Jesus was illegal.

It was to be expected, therefore, that in 1382 when John Wycliffe, previously master of Baliol College, Oxford, aided by his student Nicholas Hereford, made the first translation of the Bible into English (from the Latin), that the ecclesiastical authorities were significantly disturbed. Before the work was even completed, Hereford had been excommunicated. And for wishing to place before the common people the possibility of reading and judging for themselves the meaning of the Bible, Wycliffe was condemned as a heretic. Hindered, but undeterred, he pursued his vision, completing his translation. Then, employing a team of itinerant preachers trained to read and explain its meaning, he brought it to the attention of ordinary working folk.

The hatred which Wycliffe's activities generated in the minds of those he defied typifies the innate, self-defensive response of a closed mind to maintain its own condition of ignorance. Maybe the few educated Christians and the clergy of those times felt that power was being wrested from their hands, and perhaps, too, they were fearful that their interpretations would be contested or that their lack of understanding would be brought to light. Whatever it may have been and however important were the ecclesiastical protagonists, it was all human 'stuff'. Christianity and Jesus' teachings had long since parted company.

Our purpose, here, is simply to put before the reader some of the historical background to many of the things we take for granted in our present times, so that independent and individual conclusions may be drawn. For there are numerous features of Christian history and the development of the New Testament which may cause surprise, as we proceed. Yet most of these are matters of historical fact, not of interpretation.

A Perennial Message

Six centuries have passed since Wycliffe's struggles and – as in its earliest days – Christianity is once again in the melting pot, a haven for all manner of belief. Yet the religion continues on, fractured and splintered into many sects, groups and points of view. For despite the arguments over doctrine and dogma, there still lies in Jesus' teaching something that appeals to the essentials of the human heart, something that rings true, something universal beyond all the human accretions of religion. Whatever the many generations of Christians may have made of Jesus' teachings, whatever Christianity may have become, whatever anecdotes may have been woven around his life story, however much the gospels have been translated and edited, there still remains something fundamental, beautiful and true, something timeless in their message.

Consider, for example, Jesus' exhortation to turn from the ephemeral world towards the spiritual and eternal:

> Lay not up for yourselves treasures upon earth,
>   where moth and rust doth corrupt,
>   and where thieves break through and steal:
> But lay up for yourselves treasures in heaven,

where neither moth nor rust doth corrupt,
and where thieves do not break through nor steal:
For where your treasure is, there will your heart be also.

Matthew 6:19-21

He points out that to spend one's life chasing the evanescent things of this world is a waste of a life. Attention should be given to the eternal and the spiritual. Such passages are universal in their message, relevant to all mankind, and could have come from the pen of many holy men and mystics, whatever their religious background. Though doubtless beautifully put, his observation is common to many religions. Similarly, Jesus is pointing to a characteristic of the human mind, when he says:

No man can serve two masters:
for either he will hate the one, and love the other;
or else he will hold to the one, and despise the other.
Ye cannot serve God and mammon.

Matthew 6:24

The mind, he says, cannot go in two directions at once. It can either go towards God or towards the world, not both at the same time. Yet this is true of any human being, whatever their era, nationality or religion. Many other spiritual and religious teachers have said the same. Again, it is an attitude and a way of life beyond religious dogma which is indicated when he continues:

Therefore I say unto you, take no thought for your life,
what ye shall eat, or what ye shall drink;
nor yet for your body, what ye shall put on.
Is not the life more than meat, and the body than raiment?

Behold the fowls of the air: for they sow not,
neither do they reap, nor gather into barns;
yet your heavenly Father feedeth them.
Are ye not much better than they?

Which of you by taking thought
can add one cubit unto his stature?

And why take ye thought for raiment?

Consider the lilies of the field, how they grow;
　　they toil not, neither do they spin:
And yet I say unto you,
　　that even Solomon in all his glory
　　was not arrayed like one of these.

Wherefore, if God so clothe the grass of the field,
　　which today is, and tomorrow is cast into the oven,
　　shall he not much more clothe you,
O ye of little faith?

Therefore take no thought, saying,
　　"What shall we eat?" or, "What shall we drink?"
　　or, "Wherewithal shall we be clothed?" ...
　　for your heavenly Father knoweth
　　that ye have need of all these things.
But seek ye first the kingdom of God,
　　and his righteousness;
　　and all these things shall be added unto you.

Take therefore no thought for the morrow:
　　for the morrow shall take thought for the things of itself.
Sufficient unto the day is the evil thereof.

Matthew 6:23-34

Such teachings have a timeless beauty and cannot be paraded as specifically Christian. They are a recommendation of how to live one's life with an awareness of God's presence, not some strange religious doctrine to be believed. They are universal in their outlook. In fact, if the sayings of Jesus are carefully studied, it is found that this is the case with practically everything he says. True, some of the more obscure passages, especially in St John, do require some familiarity with the other literature of the period in order to understand the allusions and analogies, while other gospel passages are confused, having suffered from additions, alterations and deletions. But the underlying trend in all that Jesus says is universal and spiritual, not sectarian or religious.

In conducting a genuine search for the real teachings of Jesus, if one studies only those sayings and teachings that are directly attributed to him, both in the gospels and elsewhere, one is constantly faced with three deeply significant facts. Firstly, much of Christian dogma and theology is not supported by the teachings of Jesus – or at best, his teachings require considerable interpretation before Christian belief can be read into them. Secondly, Christian ritual and ceremony did not originate with nor was it even endorsed by Jesus. Thirdly, on stripping away the overlays of Christian belief and dogma, one finds in Jesus' teachings a simple, universal and spiritual message – a common message which has been given by many mystics who have come into this world.

The difficulty is that the whole of Jesus' teaching did not find its way into the gospels or the New Testament, while things which Jesus did not teach have been added. His teachings in themselves are pure and beautiful. It is only what has been added to them that is being questioned. Keeping an open and discriminating mind, therefore, one has to search through all the literature of early Christian times to arrive at a general understanding of what he really taught.

Even so, the picture is by no means clear. From earliest Christian times, there were differences of opinion and interpretation. This is the nature of the human mind and it is true of any field of human endeavour, whether science, philosophy, politics or religion. The human situation and condition is inherently one of ignorance and in the absence of direct experience man is forced to speculate upon the nature of things. And, naturally, there is disagreement on some issues while others become accepted, even acquiring the status of dogma through the power of habit and repetition. But speculation is only interpretation and much of specifically Christian thought and doctrine would seem to come into this category.

Mysticism and Mystic Experience

It would seem, then, that there is considerable divergence between the teachings of Jesus and those of Christianity, and although these initial chapters are more concerned with the historical aspects of Jesus and the New Testament, the main emphasis of this book is on Jesus' actual teachings. Therefore, since it is suggested that his teachings were those of a mystic, it will be helpful to discuss the nature of mysticism.

The essence of mysticism is generally understood to be a transcendental experience in the sphere of consciousness. As a consequence, it is something that a person *lives*, not a philosophy or doctrine which has been *read* or studied. In its broadest sense, it is an expansion of normal consciousness, an awakening of hidden potential such that understanding beyond that of normal human reasoning and mental

activity becomes inwardly manifest. Those who are fortunate enough
to have such experiences also feel an interior joy and ecstasy, a bliss
that brings them closer to God within themselves. The culmination of
such ecstasy is union with God, within. Mystical writings contain many
descriptions of such experiences, as the following extracts from European Christian mystics indicate.

That the mystic gains access to a source of knowledge and understanding that transcends the intellect becomes clear from an experience related of the Italian Barnabite monk, Francesco Saverio Bianchi[3]
(1743-1815):

> One day when Pater Magno, a doctor, *littérateur*, and distinguished
> philosopher, was delivering himself of an enthusiastic eulogy of these
> sciences to which he was devoted, Francis, in order to make him appreci-
> ate the higher value of the sciences of God, replied: "I also, in my youth,
> ardently pursued these subjects of knowledge, and I even prayed to God
> to help me to attain them in order that I might be more useful to my
> congregation. After this prayer, I once found myself inundated with a
> vivid light; it seemed to me that a veil was lifted up from before my eyes
> of the spirit, and all the truths of human science, even those that I had
> not studied, became manifest to me by an infused knowledge. This state
> of intuition lasted for about twenty-four hours, and then, as if the veil
> had fallen again, I found myself as ignorant as before. At the same time
> an interior voice said to me: 'Such is human knowledge; of what use is it?
> It is I, it is My love that must be studied.'"
>
> *Life of Francis Xavier Bianchi IV (Baravelli), GIP p.279*

A similar experience is related of St Ignatius Loyola (*c.*1491-1556),
founder of the Jesuits:

> He once went from Manresa to a little church distant from thence a
> quarter of a league, to pray; and while he was going, he was suddenly
> transported and elevated in spirit: wherefore he sat himself down by the
> river side. And as he cast the eyes of his body upon the water, those of his
> soul were suddenly filled with a new and extraordinary light. For, in one
> moment, seeing no sensory image or object, he perceived wonderful
> things in a spiritual and sublime manner. By this light, certain things
> pertaining to the mysteries of the faith, together with other truths of natu-
> ral science, were revealed to him, and this so abundantly and so clearly,
> that he himself said that if all the spiritual light which his spirit had re-

ceived from God up to the time when he was more than sixty-two years old, could be collected into one, it seemed to him that all of this knowledge would not equal what was at that moment conveyed to his soul. This vision lasted for a long while.

Life of St Ignatius Loyola I:VII (Ribadeneira), GIP p.279, LSFY p.92

Likewise, it was related of the Rhineland mystic, Blessed Hermann Joseph of Steinfield (*c*.1150-1241):

Once when Brother Joseph was buried in these meditations, he stood at night at the window of the sacristy and gazed at the rising moon and stars. And a great longing seized him that he might see creation as it is in the eyes of God; so he said to the Creator: "O dear Lord, Thou Creator of all things, although, so long as I remain here in Babylon (this world of exile from God), I can only see Thee dimly through a glass, yet wilt Thou give me such a knowledge of Thy creation, by which I may know and love Thee better."

And as he stood there praying, he was suddenly raised above himself in such a wonderful manner, that he could not afterwards account for it, and the Lord revealed to him the whole beauty and glory of the firmament and of every created thing, so that his longing was fully satisfied. But afterwards, when he came to himself, the prior could get nothing out of him than that he had received such an unspeakable rapture from his perfect knowledge of creation, that it was beyond human understanding.

Life of Hermann Joseph (Bolland), GIP p.278

There are a great many descriptions of this kind in the mystic literature of the world. That such knowledge arises from an inward expansion of consciousness is illustrated by an experience recorded by Pope Gregory I (Gregory the Great, *c*.540-604) of the Italian, St Benedict of Nursia (*c*.480-550), where it is described as an enlargement of the "inward soul":

The man of God, Benedict, being diligent in watching, rose up early, before the time of matins (his monks being yet at rest) and came to the window of his chamber, where he offered up his prayers to Almighty God. Standing there, all on a sudden, in the dead of night, as he looked forth, he saw a light which banished away the darkness of the night and glittered with such brightness, that the light which did shine in the midst of darkness was far more clear than the light of day. Upon this sight a marvellous strange thing followed, for as he himself did afterwards report, the whole world, gathered as it were under one beam of the sun, was presented before his eyes.... For by means of that supernatural light, the capacity of the inward soul is enlarged.... But albeit the world was gathered together before his eyes, yet were not the heaven and earth drawn into any lesser room than they be of themselves, but the soul of the beholder was more enlarged.

Gregory the Great, Dialogues II:XXXV, DSGG pp.112-114

Or as the well-known St Teresa of Avila (1515-1582) puts it, in her simple way:

When our Lord suspends the understanding and makes it cease from its activity (when the mind is made motionless), He puts before it that which astonishes it and occupies it; so that without making any reflections (without reasoning) it shall comprehend in a moment more than we could comprehend in many years, with all the efforts in the world.

St Teresa, Life XII:8, LSTJ p.92

And:

In an instant the mind learns so many things at once that if the imagination and intellect spent years in trying to enumerate them, it would be impossible to recall a thousandth part of them.... Although no words are pronounced, the spirit is taught many truths.

St Teresa, Interior Castle VI:V.8-9, ICM pp.202-203

Associated with this experience of mystic understanding is a great joy and inward bliss. As the Italian Angela de Foligno (*c.*1248-1309) wrote, the "soul swimmeth in joy and knowledge":

There is nothing then that the soul understandeth or comprehendeth to be compared with the rapture to which she can inwardly attain. For when the soul is lifted up above herself by the illumination of God's presence, then she understandeth and taketh delight and resteth in those good things of God that she can in no wise describe, for they are above the understanding and above all manner of speech and above all words. But in these the soul swimmeth in joy and knowledge!

Angela of Foligno, Book of Visions and Instructions LVI, VIAF pp.191-192, GIP p.277

The highest relationship of the soul to God during such transport is summarized by St John of the Cross (1542-1591) as "union with God":

It is only a soul in union with God that is capable of this profound, loving knowledge, for it is itself that union.

> *St John of the Cross, Ascent of Mount Carmel II:26.5, AMC p.207*

And again by Marina de Escobar (1554-1633):

> When in a deep ecstasy, God unites the soul suddenly to His essence, and when He fills her with his light, He shows her in a moment of time the sublimest mysteries. And the soul sees a certain immensity and an infinite majesty.... The soul is then plunged, as it were, into a vast ocean which is God and again God. It can neither find a foothold nor touch the bottom. The divine attributes appear as summed up in one whole, so that no one of them can be distinguished separately.
>
> *Marina de Escobar, VMEII II:XXXIV, GIP pp.275-276*

Mystic experiences are clearly of the soul within. Pointing out that the faculties active during such experiences are those of the "soul", Alvarez de Paz (1560-1620) writes:

> In this degree (of contemplation) ... eyes are given unto the soul by which she may see God.... When you see light with the bodily eyes, you do not arrive thereat by a comparison of ideas, as when we say: "Light is not darkness" or "It is a quality". You simply see light.
>
> In the same way, the soul in this degree of contemplation affirms nothing, denies nothing, attributes nothing, avoids nothing, but in complete repose she sees God. It will be said: this is astonishing, or rather unbelievable.... I admit that it is astonishing. The fact, however, is very certain....
>
> In this supernatural manner, the soul knows God in the depths of her being, and she sees Him, so to say, more clearly than she sees the material light with the eyes of the body.... This sight (of God) inflames the soul with a very ardent love.... Neither the senses, nor the imagination, have the least part in this vision; all takes place in the summit of the spirit.
>
> *Alvarez de Paz, IPSO V:III.XIV, GIP p.282*

"Neither the senses, nor the imagination, have the least part in this vision", he says and confirming that such experiences are utterly beyond the sensory and bodily faculties, St Teresa wrote:

> There appear to me two things in this spiritual state (the longing to see God) which might endanger life. One is that of which I have just spoken

(the inward anguish of spiritual longing); ... the other is an excessive gladness and delight, so extreme that the soul appears to swoon away and
seems on the verge of leaving the body, which indeed would bring it no
small joy.

St Teresa, Interior Castle VI:XI.11, GIP p.266, ICM p.259

Similarly, after one of her many experiences, Marina de Escobar
related:

> When back in my cell I found myself wholly changed.... It seemed as
> though my soul were no longer wholly in my body, but that the superior
> part had remained in those heights, inebriated, plunged in the vision of
> God's supreme perfections, and that I retained the inferior part, that
> which gives life to the senses and bodily faculties only.

Marina de Escobar, VMEII I:XLVII, GIP p.276

Now, although such experiences may have only been the beginning of
what is attainable, several things, characteristic of all mystic experience, emerge from them. Firstly, mystics speak with the certainty of
personal experience. The knowledge revealed to them in mystic experience is self-evident and is not acquired through the processes of reason. It is a genuine 'revelation'. Consequently, they do not feel the need
to justify their position, for it is not an intellectual one. They do, however, remain fully aware that other people may find their experiences
very hard to understand and, when they describe them, they try to do
so in as clear a manner as possible. Secondly, mystic experience is of
the mind and soul. The sensory and bodily faculties are held in abey-
ance and the mystic often becomes entirely unconscious of the body
and the physical universe. Thirdly, such experiences are characteristically accompanied by feelings of great inner joy and bliss. Lastly, the
ultimate consummation of such experiences is union with God and
any mystic knowledge gained is essentially secondary to a longing for
that union.

It is also significant that no one who has experienced anything re-
motely mystical has ever considered it to be anything other than a
glimpse of a higher reality. Like awakening from sleep, the experience
carries with it its own innate touchstone of validity. Those who dis-
count mystic experience as simply the product of religious hysteria or
an overheated brain have rarely studied the matter at first hand. For if
they had ever met and conversed with those who had been the frequent recipients of genuine mystic experience, they would have realized

that this had only been accomplished by a balanced self-discipline and a control of the mind and emotions that is quite inconceivable to most people. True mystics are wise, understanding and balanced human beings, not fanatical, self-seeking or emotionally overwrought. In fact, uncontrolled emotion and imagination will actually prevent a soul from concentrating the consciousness within, thereby making true mystic experience impossible.

Since no amount of theology or reasoning can replace mystic experience, it can be readily understood why the true mystic has little time for reason and normal human mental functioning as the primary means of understanding the nature of reality. All the same, by bringing an individual into contact with a higher reality, mystic experience or even a strong feeling for the mystical, has illumined the minds of many of the world's greatest men and women. As C.F.E. Spurgeon comments in *Mysticism in English Literature*:

> Two facts in connection with mysticism are undeniable, whatever it may be, and whatever part it is destined to play in the development of thought and of knowledge. In the first place, it is the leading characteristic of some of the greatest thinkers of the world – of the founders of ... religions, of Plato and Plotinus, of Eckhart and Bruno, of Spinoza, Goethe, and Hegel. Secondly, no one has ever been a lukewarm, an indifferent, or an unhappy mystic. If a man has this particular temperament, his mysticism is the very centre of his being: it is the flame which feeds his whole life; and he is intensely and supremely happy just so far as he is steeped in it.
>
> *C.F.E. Spurgeon, MEL p.2*

The same author also comments on the certainty of the mystic concerning his experience:

> The mystic is somewhat in the position of a man who, in a world of blind men, has suddenly been granted sight, and who, gazing at the sunrise, and overwhelmed by the glory of it, tries, however falteringly, to convey to his fellows what he sees. They, naturally, would be sceptical about it, and would be inclined to say that he is talking foolishly and incoherently.
>
> But the simile is not altogether parallel. There is this difference. The mystic is not alone; all through the ages we have the testimony of men and women to whom this vision has been granted, and the record of what they have seen is amazingly similar, considering the disparity of personality and circumstances. And further, the world is not peopled with totally blind men. The mystics would never hold the audience they do hold,

were it not that the vast majority of people have in themselves what
William James has called a "mystical germ" which makes response to their
message.

C.F.E. Spurgeon, MEL pp.5-6

This is the point – the mystic faculty is the heritage of everyone, whoever they are. Undeveloped as it may be in the majority of us or present
only in its most nascent form, everyone has the capacity to develop
knowledge of the divine. As a result, mystic teachings strike a deep
chord in the hearts of many.

The Mystic Path

With this general understanding of what we mean by mysticism, we
can continue with a more specific synopsis of the ancient and perennial, mystic philosophy, though it will be necessary at this juncture to
take for granted certain things more fully corroborated and explained
in later chapters.

All mystics have said that there is one God, a God beyond all human names, words and religions. He is the source of all creation and
yet His essence is beyond all its diversity and multiplicity. They say
that He is the one Ocean of Being; that He is an Ocean of Light, an
Ocean of Power and an Ocean of Love and that the soul is a drop of
that Ocean. They also point out that the relationship of a drop of love
to an Ocean of Love is naturally one of love. The fundamental and real
relationship of the soul and God is therefore that of love.

God is thus the primary essence of the soul. He is the source or
origin of life and being, and the soul is the life force within every living
being. The essence of life is the soul; that is our real and innermost
nature, our true self. As a consequence, God is to be found at the spiritual heart of every living creature. As Jesus said:

> The kingdom of God is within you.
>
> *Luke 17:21*

The goal of all true mysticism is the soul's direct, personal experience
of God. This has been called God-realization or union with God. Consequently, the mystic path is that path or practice which leads the soul
to God and a mystic is one who has some inner or mystic experience
of that path. The designation is essentially related to a person's inner

condition, not to their outer mode of living, nor to their beliefs. Consequently, although many mystics within the Christian tradition have led solitary or secluded external lives, such a way of life is not essential and may even detract from the highest mystical experience. Jesus himself did not lead a solitary life.

But what is meant by 'within' and 'inner experience'? When we close our eyes, we are automatically within ourselves. Although a person will normally see nothing but darkness within when their eyes are shut, that darkness is actually the starting point of the spiritual journey back to God. It is all a question of the mind's attention. When the mind is scattered in thoughts concerning the outside world, it cannot really be said that a person is within themselves, even if their eyes are shut. But when the attention becomes concentrated upon and interested in what lies within that darkness, then the inner journey can be started.

Now, the highest mystics are those who have reached or realized God within themselves, and amongst them are those who have been called perfect Masters, Saviours, Sons of God, Messengers, Apostles, Teachers and many other names in different languages. They are divinely appointed to take souls back to Him. Hence, Jesus also said:

> Repent: for the kingdom of heaven is at hand.
>
> *Matthew 4:17*

The purpose of the Masters in coming to this world is to awaken human beings to God's immanent presence, to awaken people to the presence of the indwelling Lord so that they may seek to return to Him and to experience His light and power for themselves, within themselves. Jesus was speaking of this personal experience of God when he said:

> Blessed are the pure in heart:
> for they shall see God.
>
> *Matthew 5:8*

One who sees or experiences God within is a mystic and, from a study of his teachings, Jesus can confidently be placed in this category. As he also said:

> I and my Father are one.
>
> *John 10:30*

Such inner experience, however, requires the practice of particular techniques. These have been called contemplation, spiritual practice, interior prayer, mystic prayer, supplication and so on, and they entail something quite different from the set, verbal prayers of religious litany. They are the means which mystics advocate as the only sure method of reaching God within oneself. Jesus is alluding to this entirely inward and spiritual practice when he says:

> The light of the body is the eye:
> if therefore thine eye be single,
> thy whole body shall be full of light.
> *Matthew 6:22*

This *single eye* lies in the forehead, behind and slightly above the two eyes, though it is a mental centre, not a physical one. It is the thinking centre of a human being, the focus or headquarters of the mind and soul, also called the eye centre or third eye. It has often been compared to a door and the early stages of spiritual practice are like knocking at this door. It is the place where the attention is to be withdrawn from the senses and inwardly concentrated. Withdrawing the attention from the external world and from the extremities of the body to this point is the first step on what is called the inner journey – the mystic ascent of the soul. It is the start of the inner journey. And when the attention is concentrated, when one knocks at the door, then the door is opened, a great light is experienced within oneself and the soul commences the inward journey back to God. Hence, Jesus says:

> Ask, and it shall be given you;
> seek, and ye shall find;
> knock, and it shall be opened unto you:
>
> For every one that asketh receiveth;
> and he that seeketh findeth;
> and to him that knocketh it shall be opened.
> *Matthew 7:7-8*

The opening of the inner door, however, is only the beginning. From that point onward the soul travels the path back to God by means of inner light and also – most importantly – inner sound. These are the soul's constant guides and companions, so to speak.

Now mystics have said that God has formed and continuously maintains His creation in existence through a creative Power or emanation from Himself. According to John's gospel, in common with many mystics of his era, Jesus called this Power the Word or *Logos* and many other names. The mystic path that leads the soul back to God is the path of this Word, and the light and sound which the soul hears within are the soul's direct experience of this Power. The soul actually travels upon this great, creative outpouring on its return to God and many mystics have referred to its audible character by calling it the Voice of God. As Jesus said in St John's gospel:

> The dead shall hear the Voice of the Son of God;
> and they that hear shall live.
>
> *John 5:25*

The "dead" are the souls of this world who have forgotten God, their inward source of life. They are spiritually "dead". But when they "hear the Voice of the Son of God" – when they meet a Master who teaches them how to contact the mystic Sound within themselves – then they "shall live". Then their inner consciousness will be expanded and they will truly live. Their inner beings will be filled with light and sound. But for this to take place, a Master must first mystically baptize or initiate a soul. In essence, this is an entirely inward affair and can be likened to the tuning of a radio to a particular wavelength. The radio has the capacity to receive radio signals but must first be tuned. This is the "baptism from heaven"[4] spoken of by Jesus and which is required before a soul can ascend through the heavens and reach the kingdom of heaven, God.

Mystics have repeated many times that the Lord's creation is a vast, multi-storey affair. At the 'bottom' or outermost part lies the physical universe and at the 'top', deep within the heart of everything, is God. In between are many heavens or realms of increasing subtlety, beauty and bliss. These the soul must traverse on its inward journey or mystic ascent to God. As Jesus said:

> In my Father's house are many mansions:
> if it were not so, I would have told you.
>
> *John 14:2*

These heavenly places are not to be considered as being stacked one atop the other like so many bricks in a builder's yard. Human words are inadequate to describe them and the manner of their creation and existence. Words such as 'above' and 'ascent' are used only by way of metaphor. These regions, like God Himself, are within us and can be experienced by withdrawing the attention from the world and focusing it within. This gives rise to an expansion of spiritual consciousness and the heavenly realms are traversed in consciousness, not in space, space being a characteristic of this world.

The ascent through these inner regions does not take place without considerable effort. There is a reason for this. Mystics say that within the hierarchy of creation are various centres of 'power' or 'administration'. These centres have been called the 'rulers' (Greek, *archons*) of these realms. Of these, one ruler is of more significance to us as human beings than all the others. This is the ruler known as Satan, the Devil, the Evil One and a great variety of other names. But he (if such an anthropomorphic epithet may be employed) is not to be considered as an individual, but as a great administrative force within the creation. His power, like all else in creation, is derived from the supreme ruler, God, and his divinely appointed purpose is to keep souls away from their Source.

Now it is clear that this understanding of Satan is at variance with traditional Christian conceptions of the subject. Satan, however, is generally agreed to be the force which keeps souls away from a spiritual life and a more detailed discussion, as with other aspects of this synopsis, is better left to the appropriate place. It may be observed, however, that Satan has also been called the Universal Mind or Negative Power and just as the soul is the drop of the Lord, so is the mind a drop or agent of this Negative Power.

In simple terms, a human being is comprised of body, mind and soul. The body is familiar to everyone; the soul is the real self and the innermost essence of life; and the mind is that which entertains thoughts, desires, emotions, memories and a great deal more. And it is the mind that must be purified, concentrated, stilled and detached from the body and the world before the soul can realize its innate perfection and return to God. Again, Jesus says it succinctly:

> Be ye therefore perfect,
>   even as your Father which is in heaven is perfect.
>
>   *Matthew 5:48*

As preparation for this mystic ascent, the individual must strive to overcome all the human imperfections which originate within the mind. The mystic path, therefore, includes ethics and morality, something which is acceptable and common to all people and all religions. And although mystics have often been amongst the most highly esteemed members of a religion, in the popular mind, the highest aspect of religious practice consists of leading a good human life, according to the highest ethics and morality, of prayer to God, and of having firm faith in a particular system of belief. But in mysticism, leading a good life is only the beginning, the preparation. It is like cleaning a cup. It is contemplation or spiritual practice which fills the cup, thereby making the cleaning process worthwhile. Purity of mind and the good character which results from it are a means, not an end.

Jesus and Christianity

Now it is clear that these basic elements of mystic or spiritual teaching are to be found in practically every religion. The main difference between mysticism and religion would thus appear to be that mysticism – in its purest form – is primarily experience-oriented and interested specifically in the personal relationship of the soul to God, whereas religion is more concerned with external practices and beliefs.

Mysticism is inner, religion is outer – or at least has many outward trappings – most of which have developed after the departure of the founder. It seems reasonable to infer, therefore, that the outward practices and even many of the beliefs which make Christianity a unique religion came into being after the demise of Jesus and his direct disciples. To a large extent, this is historically verifiable and we will be considering the origins of many of these beliefs and practices, as we proceed.

It is generally true that after the departure of any leader or teacher in this world, their followers are unable to maintain the same vision and to continue things in the way in which they began. Adulteration, divergence and even schisms soon result. In the case of religion, this process of dilution, diversification and externalization can take many avenues. Over the centuries, Christianity has diversified in probably more ways than any other religion in known history and it is interesting to consider some of these, in general terms, for to note the trends and reasons for this process may help us to trace Jesus' teachings to their purer origins.

It has been observed that the driving force behind a truly spiritual life is interior, mystic prayer. Being entirely inward, this prayer constitutes a completely personal path. No one else need ever know that an individual is practising it. A person may never even talk about their inward life unless they come across someone who has a deep and genuine interest. Outwardly, they will live a normal, straightforward existence, being good, kind and honest with everyone, without feeling the need to convert others to their own point of view.

Possessing an inner surety far greater than simple belief, such a person is secure within themselves. It is the certainty which stems from direct personal experience, from the practice of interior prayer. Without that, the mind automatically focuses on external matters. The path of one who follows a religion therefore tends towards various external practices and the belief in certain verbally-formulated tenets, for there is no other alternative. And if our minds are not inwardly contained, there will be a tendency to want to tell others what we are doing and to convince them of our beliefs.

This proselytizing and missionary spirit, present in Christianity from very early times, is an approach which true mystics never advocate, for they know that emotional or intellectual conversions from one belief system to another will never take a person back to God nor even do much to change an individual's character. On the contrary, belief without understanding and experience can often lead to bigotry and intolerance, the very opposite of their message of love, harmony and forbearance. Beliefs and dogmas can so often be a crystallization of spiritual or mystic truths.

As the story goes, the Devil and a friend were once taking a walk when they saw a man delightedly stoop down to pick something up. "What did he pick up?" asked the Devil's friend. "A piece of Truth," replied the Devil, casually. "What, aren't you concerned?" exclaimed his friend. "No," responded the Devil, "I'll get him to make a belief out of it!"

The desire for new converts and to increase numbers are amongst the first identifiable trends in the formation of a religion and the drift away from true spirituality. A teacher who takes on students who are genuinely interested and who come to him of their own sincere desire is one thing. This is the attitude of a mystic. But those who actively seek to convert others to their own way of thinking is quite another. The former respects the inward integrity of another, while the latter do not. The one is inner, the other outer.

The same process of externalization also leads to the development of an organizational hierarchy and priesthood. As with all people of like mind, the disciples of a mystic naturally enjoy meeting together, for such meetings can reinforce their desire for spiritual practice and increase their understanding of the path they follow. Generally speaking, they also have great affection for each other and like to share that joy and love, for love shared is love augmented. Moreover, a mystic of the highest order is always with his disciples, inwardly, and his spiritual presence and blessings on such occasions can bring a rich reward of peace, bliss and inspiration. As Jesus said to his disciples:

> Where two or three are gathered together in my name,
> there am I in the midst of them.
>
> *Matthew 18:20*

When people meet together in groups, there is a need for some simple organization, if only to arrange and inform participants of venues. Where numbers warrant the selection of individuals to be responsible for making these arrangements, mystics advise that their attitude towards others should be one of service. Hence, in St Matthew, we find Jesus advising his disciples:

> But Jesus called them unto him, and said,
> "Ye know that the princes of the Gentiles
>   exercise dominion over them,
>   and they that are great exercise authority upon them.
> But it shall not be so among you:
>   but whosoever will be great among you,
>   let him be your minister;
> And whosoever will be chief among you,
>   let him be your servant:
> Even as the Son of man came not to be ministered unto,
>   but to minister, and to give his life a ransom for many."
>
> *Matthew 20:25-28*

To minister is to serve and here Jesus points out that when the Master himself, the "Son of man", comes only as a servant, then those disciples who take on organizational positions should consider themselves to be the servants of the others, not their chiefs or bosses. Yet, when spiritual practice becomes of secondary importance or is entirely forgotten, such positions of service can become opportunities for the expression of egotism and self-importance. Then the 'organizers' become the 'bosses' who very soon expect others to pay respect to them. There is also likely to be a jostling for positions of perceived importance, for in any community there will always be those who like to be in the limelight and to be honoured.

At such meetings, in the absence of the physical presence of their Master, someone also needs to speak about the teachings, to remind others – and themselves – of the path they follow. In early Christian times, speakers on spiritual subjects were known as 'prophets' and there is no reason why this should not have been anyone with a good grasp of the essentials and with the gift of clear expression, for a mystic appoints no priests. Certainly, there were none we know of in the time of Jesus. It would seem that the proper attitude for such 'prophets' or speakers should again be one of service, freely given. But when the Master and his direct disciples are no longer living – or even, sometimes, when they are – it takes only a little time before a few ambitious individuals push their way forward, promoting themselves as authorities and telling others how to behave. And in the process, they may misinterpret or misrepresent the purity and simplicity of the mystic teachings, bending them to their own particular cultural or religious background and individual way of thinking.

Thus, what begins as a practical necessity and an opportunity to serve others can become an external practice and an end in itself. As long as the *raison d'être* is to foster enthusiasm for spiritual practice, the meetings, their organizers and their speakers have a value. But as soon as this is forgotten, then the continuation of such practices increasingly becomes little more than a ritual. The recipe is repeated, faithfully or distortedly, but no one remains who really understands the nature of the cake or even that there is one. In the case of Christianity, as time passed the simple meetings evolved into the complex ceremonial worship of later times. And along with it developed the priesthood whose precursors are clearly discernible in early Christianity, where the organizational structure of deacons, presbyters and bishops has been maintained to this day, with further additions as the religious organization grew in size and complexity.

Like many mystics both before and since, Jesus was somewhat scathing of the role of priests and this is most probably why the Jewish priests of the time brought him before Pontius Pilate, the local Roman governor with the authority to punish him. If the story is authentic, the high priest himself was even present at Jesus' arrest.

The charge they brought against him was political, something that would force the Roman governor into action. They said that he claimed to be the "King of Jews", the Messiah, a potential cause of civil unrest. But from a study of Jesus' sayings, one can well understand the real reasons why they disliked him, for he did not mince his words. In

St Matthew, there is a long passage concerning the priests of those times which contains such unequivocal statements as:

> Woe unto you, scribes and Pharisees, hypocrites!
> for ye shut up the kingdom of heaven against men:
> For ye neither go in yourselves,
> neither suffer ye them that are entering to go in.
>
> *Matthew 23:13*

And in the *Gospel of Thomas*, he says the same thing in equally pithy language:

> Woe to the Pharisees,
> for they are like a dog sleeping in the manger of oxen,
> for neither does he eat nor does he let the oxen eat.
>
> *Gospel of Thomas 102, NHS20 p.89*

In both instances, Jesus means that the priests have the teachings of the past mystics in their hands – in the scriptures and the holy books. But not only do they make no use of what is in front of them, they also prevent others from doing so. They do not really know what the scriptures mean nor do they understand how to follow them, yet – like a dog sleeping on the food of cattle – they prevent the true seekers of spiritual nourishment from finding the sustenance for which they hunger. They may speak learnedly on the meaning of the scriptures, but without really understanding the depth in them, they unknowingly confuse and confound the real seekers of mystic truth. This is generally true even amongst the most well-meaning, humble and sincere of priests, whatever their religion, for unless a person has learnt how to find God within themselves, how can they guide others on that path? Jesus' comments concerning the Pharisees are thus equally applicable to the priests of today, whatever their religion.

Lacking the realization that a mystic's teachings are meant primarily to lead their disciples towards inner experience through the practice of mystic prayer, later followers naturally fall into intellectual disagreement over matters of interpretation. The attempt to understand essentially mystic and esoteric doctrines in the absence of a living mystic inevitably leads to exoteric (outward) interpretations. Hence, schisms and arguments develop, various groups are formed, often around powerful or charismatic personalities, and unity and harmony are lost. Some of the divisions that formed in the early centuries of Christianity still exist today and many others have come into being, too.

The arguments are almost always over doctrine and its interpretation, for in the absence of spiritual practice and dedication to the inner quest, there is little else upon which understanding can be based. In the case of early Christianity, even the written gospels which were claimed as authentic differed from community to community. There was a *Gospel according to the Hebrews*, quoted by Jerome (*c.*347-420) and Origen, that had a Jewish bias; a *Gospel of the Egyptians* with ascetic tendencies favoured by Christians of non-Jewish origin in Egypt and mentioned by the Christian teachers Origen and Clement of Alexandria (*c.*150-215, *fl.*180-200); and a *Gospel of the Ebionites* which demonstrated little liking for the doctrines of Paul and was roundly condemned by Epiphanius (*c.*315-403), a fourth-century Christian heresiologist (one who decries those perceived as 'heretics'). And there were many others, too, some of which have only come to light in recent years and from which we will be quoting in these pages. We have already encountered the *Gospel of Thomas*, one amongst a group of esoteric texts found in the Egyptian sands in 1945, known as the Nag Hammadi codices (of which more, later). Additionally, there were a multitude of other writings proclaiming teachings attributed to Jesus whose contents are often of considerable interest. All of these, and many other early Christian texts, demonstrate the diversity of opinion and interpretation which spread very rapidly after Jesus' death.

Organization, then, and the conveyance of spiritual teaching, once the means to a higher end, become ends in themselves when spiritual practice wanes. A further aspect of this trend is the acquisition of material property. Early Christian groups were known as 'churches' and they met informally in individual homes. Later on, several centuries after the death of Jesus, when their numbers had increased and Christianity had been legalized, they put up special buildings to which they gave the same name. But becoming the focus of external religious activity, it cannot have been long before more importance was given to these places, built of wood, stone and mortar, than to the human beings who frequented them. And whenever that happens, the inspiration that can be derived from simple meetings, devoid of ritual, is lost. Vast sums may even be spent on the erection and maintenance of such places while people starve or live in abject poverty around. The same is true in all world religions.

Again, there is a tendency amongst the advocates of most religions to assert that only their particular Saviour was truly sent from God and that all others are false or inferior. Like Christianity, they may believe that their Saviour was higher than all previous mystics or prophets. Or they may contend, as does Islam, that their Messenger was the last true Messenger, though acknowledging that those who came before may also have been sent from God. The point at issue seems to be that there are perfect mystics, lesser mystics and also charlatans or pseudo-mystics.

Mystics point out that a living teacher is required to teach the living, as will later be discussed. But for a disciple to attain the highest spiritual goal, his Master naturally has to be of the highest order. Mystic teachings can thus degenerate through one who is not perfect proclaiming himself to be so. Jesus is speaking of all such false Masters when he says:

> Beware of false prophets,
> > which come to you in sheep's clothing,
> > but inwardly they are ravening wolves.
> Ye shall know them by their fruits:
> > do men gather grapes of thorns, or figs of thistles?
>
> *Matthew 7:15-16*

They wear "sheep's clothing", Jesus says – they may even give the highest form of teaching and display many outward signs of humility – "but inwardly they are ravening wolves". Within themselves they are full of human passions, just like everybody else. They can be distinguished, he says, by the fruits that are gathered from them; that is, the expected results of spiritual practice and of following their teachings are not forthcoming. The mind does not become gradually purified and true mystic understanding fails to develop.

It is clear from a study of the early Christian period that the relationship of Master and disciple was an accepted part of esoteric teaching, for the later debates concerning the authenticity of a spiritual teacher focused upon whether he had been a true or false teacher and who his own Master had been. In the Hellenistic world of Christianity's earliest years, one of the terms used for mysticism was the Greek word, *gnosis*, meaning 'knowledge', specifically divine knowledge, inwardly revealed. Hence, the mystics were called *gnostics* and accusations of being a false or lesser teacher were levelled at a number of these gnostics, notably the mid-first-century Simon Magus, a Samaritan mentioned in *Acts* and a contemporary of Jesus, Paul and the apostles. But the very fact that this was a point of issue amongst the early

Christians highlights the importance given to the Master-disciple relationship and hence to the esoteric and mystical character of Jesus' teachings.

One of the commonest charges levelled at Jesus, at his disciples and at Simon Magus, too, was that they were 'magicians', lesser mystics, said to resort to the performance of 'lower-order' miracles in order to convince people. Both Jesus and Simon were also, in their turn, accused of being messengers of Satan, rather than the supreme Lord. As we read in the gospels:

> And the scribes which came down from Jerusalem said,
> "He (Jesus) hath Beelzebub, and by the prince of the devils
> casteth he out devils."
>
> *Mark 3:22*

Intriguingly, in the early Christian *Clementine Recognitions* and *Homilies*,[5] although the central character of the work is Peter and the writer is pro-Jesus, it is stated that Simon Magus was the successor of John the Baptist. It is also related that Simon was – for a short while – displaced from this position by the manipulations of a fellow disciple, Dositheus, who took advantage of Simon's absence in Egypt to try and take his place.[6]

In these writings, as well as in the apocryphal *Acts of Peter* and other similar literature, Peter and Simon Magus are frequently portrayed as being in debate or contention with each other. Like the stories of warring Greek gods, familiar to many people of those times, Simon performs extravagant miracles, flying through the air, rolling on burning coals and so on, while Peter derides the use of such miraculous powers. Since these writings promote Peter's point of view, his teachings and behaviour are always depicted as superior to those of Simon, yet Irenaeus informs us that Simon was held by his disciples to have been a Saviour and a Son of God.[7] And from the mid-second-century Christian father, Justin Martyr (*c.*100-165), we learn that Simon had a considerable following in his own time and even a century later was still worshipped as the "first God" by "almost all the Samaritans and a few even of other nations", particularly in Rome.[8]

Irenaeus and other early Christian heresiologists mention a number of such gnostics, many of whom called themselves Christians.[9] Simon's successor, say both Justin Martyr and Irenaeus, was Menander.[10] And from Irenaeus and other early Christian fathers we learn of many other 'heretics' of this period who gave similar teachings, including the second-century Saturninus, Basilides and Valentinus.[11] The fourth-century fathers, Eusebius (*c.*265-340) and Epiphanius, intimate that Saturninus in Syria and Basilides in Egypt had both been the disciples of Menander or at least had come from the same school.[12] All these were known as gnostic or mystic teachers, many said to have had a large following, Basilides and Valentinus being amongst the most well-known Alexandrian gnostics of the second century.

Each one had his own teacher or Master and many claimed that they had received their teaching through one or other of the apostles. Clement of Alexandria writes that Basilides professed "for his Master, Glaucias, an interpreter of Peter"[13] – a somewhat unclear designation. He also adds that Basilides was taught by Matthew, while Hippolytus (*fl.*210-236) has it that

> Basilides ... and Isodorus, the true son and disciple of Basilides, say that Matthias (not Matthew) communicated to them secret discourses, which, being specially instructed, he heard from the Saviour.
>
> *Hippolytus, Refutation of All Heresies VII:VIII, RAH p.273*

Intriguing confirmation of the same tradition of Master and disciple is provided by the oldest surviving gnostic group, the Mandaeans – a gnostic sect of Jewish ancestry who moved to Mesopotamia in the early or perhaps pre-Christian era, yet miraculously managed to survive until the present century in the marshlands of southern Iraq and Iran. The Mandaeans give allegiance to John the Baptist as well as to a number of other mystics or Saviours of the past, many of them clearly mythical. They also assert that Jesus was a not a true Master and are even antithetical to him in two of their many books. And although the origins of this group are cloaked in mystery and no sure inferences can be drawn from their traditional beliefs, the assertion clearly stems from an understanding that there are both false as well as true Saviours – and that a true Saviour is required to attain salvation.

The history of the mystics, the gnostics and the early Christians of this period is by no means clear, but the early second-century father, Hegesippus, wrote that the real splintering began after the martyrdom of James the brother of Jesus (*c.*62 AD), head of the community of disciples at Jerusalem, when different individuals wished to take over the leading position.[14] This confirms our previous observation that the process of dilution and diversification takes place increasingly as the true initiates or disciples of a Master pass away.

Threads such as these run throughout the early Christian tradition, demonstrating that the issue centred around who was a genuine Master and who was not, who was the genuine successor duly appointed by their predecessor and who was not, and which Master could lead their disciples to the highest, rather than to some intermediate, goal. This is a matter to which every seeker of the mystic truth, then as now, must sooner or later address themselves, if they wish to find a teacher. It is very clear therefore that in earliest Christian times Jesus, Peter, Simon Magus, the apostles and the many gnostics were all considered to be teachers of an esoteric and mystic reality, but that this understanding was lost with the passage of time.

The formation of religion, then, is a process of outward diversification, crystallization, externalization and literalization. Without adequate guidance, the inclination of the mind is always to move away from the inner source and out into the world of matter, giving importance to words and material things, rather than the intangible spirit within.

The same principle can be seen at work in the kind of spiritual regimes practised by some of the early Christians, but never described or even hinted at by Jesus in the gospels or elsewhere. The desert fathers, for example, early Christian solitaries who took to a secluded life in the desert, important though they realized interior prayer to be in their search for God, tended to stress the physical rather than the spiritual. In the attempt to transcend the limitations of the body and the senses, they resorted to ascetic practices which highlight a person's physicality, drawing attention to the body rather than providing a means of rising above it in utter forgetfulness of self and matter.

The founding of monasteries and spiritual communities, established long after the time of Jesus, where people could escape from the world in order to attend more diligently to God, is of a similar nature. They are an external expression of what is actually to be achieved within. The higher mystics always teach that the relationship of the soul to the Lord is personal and individual. Mystic prayer is therefore to be practised in solitude rather than in group situations where a person remains conscious of those around them. It is the mind which is to be controlled and simply putting constraints upon the body does not lead to control of the mind within. It is more like beating the kennel to train the dog. Hiding away from the world and its responsibilities in the hope of achieving detachment and godliness is actually more likely to engender suppression of desire than its conquest. Certainly, the corruption and hypocrisy, into which many of the monasteries fell, demonstrate the point that adopting a particular outward way of life or a particular form of dress does not of itself inculcate inner holiness.

Mystics therefore advise their disciples to lead normal lives in the world, fulfilling all their responsibilities without becoming too deeply engrossed or unnecessarily involved. In this way, basic human desires and needs are naturally fulfilled without an issue being made of them and seekers of the mystic reality are less easily lured into the trap of making an external display of their supposed inward holiness.

Confusion and externalization often arise simply over a misunderstanding of mystic terminology. In ancient times, for instance, as we have noted, spiritual practice was known as prayer. Even many of the later Christian mystics, like St Teresa of Avila and St John of the Cross, spoke of 'interior prayer' by which they specifically referred to various forms of spiritual practice or contemplation. To a modern mind, however, unfamiliar with the mystic path, the term is sometimes read as a reference to verbal prayer and the mystic meaning overlooked.

Likewise, the injunction to pray ceaselessly, found in early Christian literature, including the letters of Paul,[15] actually refers to constant inward vigilance and attention towards God. And although this may indeed include the *mental* repetition of certain words, it does not refer to the continuous mumbling or verbal repetition of some prayer or invocation – while the mind wanders elsewhere – that was later practised.

Again, when true interior prayer as the primary focus of spiritual life is forgotten, the simplicity of the mystic teachings becomes overlaid by the intellectual complexities of theology, occultism, astrology, numerology and the many gnostic and theosophical systems, or by the subtle attractions of psychism, clairvoyance and various forms of lower mystic practice or magic. These are subtle yet still external entanglements which divert attention from the simplicity of concentration required to follow the higher mystic path to God. It is certainly true that the complexities of Christian theology were not developed or expounded by Jesus himself.

As we have observed, all such avenues of diversification and decline arise from the outgoing tendencies of the mind. But perhaps the greatest materialization of a mystic's teachings has been their use to justify the mistreatment of fellow human beings, including torture, execution and murder. First, the teachings become enshrined as 'sacred scripture' or inviolable dogma. Then, if anyone speaks ill or disagrees with the received interpretation, he is deemed a heretic. With this justification, people have indulged in much cruelty, bloodshed and violence in the name of religion. Christianity is not the only culprit here. It seems to be a facet of human nature.

True mystics give their teachings but do not advertise, proselytize or coerce. People can take it or leave it, as they please. Yet their later, self-appointed 'followers' have gone to war in the name of their founder, slaughtering thousands of the 'infidel', whoever he may be. Christian and Muslim alike have been guilty of this crime over the last many centuries. And the Jewish historian, Josephus (*c.*37-100 AD), informs us that above the gateway to the Jewish Temple at Jerusalem, the centre of Judaism before its destruction by the Romans in 70 AD, a sign in Greek and Latin forbade all 'heathens' to go further. The Jews, he reports had been given permission by the Romans to kill all trespassers, an unusual dispensation that has been verified by archaeological finds during the last century and a half. The warning read:

> No foreigner is to enter within the balustrade and embankment around the sanctuary. Whoever is caught will have himself to blame for his death which follows.
>
> *Corpus Inscriptionum Iudaicarum II, no.1400, DYKG p.116*

This, of course, is in direct opposition to the teachings of the Jewish patriarch and prophet, Moses:

> Thou shalt not kill.
> *Deuteronomy 5:17, KJV*

And not only did Jesus repeat this Mosaic axiom, he also reminded his followers of another saying from *Deuteronomy*:

> Thou shalt love the Lord thy God with all thine heart,
> and with all thy soul, and with all thy mind.
> *Matthew 22:37; cf. Deuteronomy 6:5, KJV*

And he linked it to one from *Leviticus*:

> Thou shalt love thy neighbour as thyself.
> *Matthew 19:19 & 22:29; Leviticus 19:18, KJV*

In fact, Jesus' philosophy of non-violence and humility in the face of opposition is unequivocal:

Ye have heard that it hath been said,
'An eye for an eye, and a tooth for a tooth:'
But I say unto you, that ye resist not evil:
    but whosoever shall smite thee on thy right cheek,
        turn to him the other also.
And if any man will sue thee at the law,
    and take away thy coat, let him have thy cloak also.
And whosoever shall compel thee to go a mile,
    go with him twain.
Give to him that asketh thee,
    and from him that would borrow of thee turn not thou away.

Ye have heard that it hath been said,
'Thou shalt love thy neighbour, and hate thine enemy.'
But I say unto you, love your enemies,
    bless them that curse you,
    do good to them that hate you,
    and pray for them which despitefully use you,
    and persecute you.

Matthew 5:38-44

It seems clear, then, that Jesus would never have condoned many of the external activities carried out in his name. Indeed, none of those described – though they have made up such an essential part of Christianity for so many centuries – were in existence when he lived. During his lifetime, there was only Jesus and his disciples, with a minimum of organization. Exactly how they lived and precisely what he taught them is unclear. But it is sure that there were no set forms of worship, no churches, no priesthood, no monasteries, no violent defence of doctrine, in fact, none of the ramifications which now constitute such an important part of Christianity.

There appears to be practically no limit to the diversity which the mind can find to occupy itself in the external world, justifying it all in the name of religion. Under the influence of the mind a person will justify, without the slightest qualms, without even noticing the dichotomy, a course of action which is diametrically opposed to the fundamental precepts of the one in whom they profess faith. The mind will let us do almost anything but sit down quietly within ourselves and begin the inner quest.

We have discussed the nature of mysticism, the externalizing character of the mind and some of the processes involved in the formation of religion. It is with this understanding, therefore, that we now approach the New Testament and other early Christian literature. For a great many Christian scholars have demonstrated that the New Testament writings as we have them today do not contain the pure, unadulterated teachings of Jesus nor are they a reliable record of his life. Following the pattern of decline, they are the product of the early Christian religion, compiled some time after the demise of Jesus, containing elements that relate more to the beliefs and interpretations of the early Christians than to the teachings of Jesus. Let us now consider how this has happened.

Notes and References

1. In Origen's *Commentarium in 1 Corinthians, JTS* 10 (1909) pp.46-47, tr. in *GG* p.11.
2. *eg.* Origen, *Against Celsus* VII:32-34, *OCC* pp.420-422.
3. Also known as Francis Xavier Bianchi, not to be confused with Francis Xavier (1506-1552), a founding member of the Jesuits.
4. *Matthew* 21:25.
5. Described in greater detail on p.165*ff.*
6. *Clementine Recognitions* I:LIV, II:VII-XII, *CR* pp.179,196-200; *Clementine Homilies* II:XXIII-XXIV, *CH* pp.42-43.
7. Irenaeus, *Against Heresies* I:XXIII, *AHI* p.86*ff.*
8. Justin Martyr, *First Apology* XXVI, *WJMA* p.29.
9. Justin Martyr, *First Apology* XXVI, *WJMA* p.30; Eusebius, *History of the Church* 3:26, *HC* p.136.
10. Justin Martyr, *First Apology* XXVI, *WJMA* p.29; Irenaeus, *Against Heresies* I:XXIII.4, *AHI* p.89.
11. *eg.* Irenaeus, *Against Heresies* I:XXIII-XXIV, *AHI* pp.89-93; Hippolytus, *Refutation of All Heresies* VII, *RAH* pp.265-307; Hegesippus, in Eusebius, *History of the Church* 4:22, *HC* p.182.
12. Eusebius, *History of the Church* 4:7, *HC* p.158; Epiphanius, *Panarion* II:22-24, *PES* p.55.
13. Clement of Alexandria, *Miscellanies* VII:XVII, *WCAII* p.486.
14. Hegesippus, in Eusebius, *History of the Church* 4:22, *HC* p.182.
15. *1 Thessalonians* 5:17.

CHAPTER TWO

The Story of the New Testament

The Validity of Sacred Writings

To understand how the gospels and other ancient writings have reached us, it is useful to know something of book production techniques in ancient times and how they differed from today. To begin with, there were no print runs consisting of multiple, identical copies of a book, checked over for spelling, grammatical and other errors, and published by permission of the author complete with copyright provisos and royalty agreements.

Every book was a one-off – hand-copied, not necessarily by an accomplished scribe, likely to be as full of mistakes as any hand-written manuscript is today. And the opportunities for pirating, editing, changing, amalgamating, incorporating and generally making free with other people's material, usually unacknowledged and commonly claimed as the author's own, was so great that it was not unusual for a manuscript to end with the threat that dire consequences would befall any who should change it. There is a good example in the *Book of Revelation*, which ends with the warning:

> If any man shall add unto these things,
>   God shall add unto him the plagues
>   that are written in this book:
> And if any man shall take away
>   from the words of the book of this prophecy,
>   God shall take away his part out of the Book of Life,
>   and out of the Holy City,
>   and from the things which are written in this book.
> *Book of Revelation 22:18-19*

47

This is a particularly rich caveat, for scholars are generally agreed that the *Book of Revelation* is itself a composite document, probably based upon a Christianized version of an earlier Jewish apocalypse, with further additions from other sources. Even the terminal threat is unlikely to be completely original!

So familiar was it to the people of those times for writings to get changed by others that there are many direct and indirect references to the problem. There is even a saying of Jesus on the matter, quoted by Clement of Alexandria and several other early writers, though its source has never been determined. Clement is quoting Jesus when he advises the best approach to the study of scriptural writings:

> "Be ye skilful money-changers" (says Jesus),
> rejecting some things, but retaining what is good.
>
> *Clement of Alexandria, Miscellanies I:28, WCAI p.467*

This is a saying quoted in the gnostic tractate, *Pistis Sophia*, as:

> Become like the wise money-changers,
> take what is good, cast away what is evil.
>
> *Pistis Sophia III:134, PS p.348*

A money-changer would always know how to distinguish the counterfeit coin from the real, rejecting the one and retaining the other. In other words, since the scriptures were known to have been changed and edited, they needed to be approached with intelligence and discrimination. And if this was the case two thousand years ago, how much more then is it true today?

Several of the early fathers quoted this saying of Jesus and we also find it in three places in the *Clementine Homilies*. Speaking of the fact that some of the things in the "Scriptures" – which would have meant the Old Testament – are actually incorrect, and referring to one of Jesus' comments recorded in Mark and Matthew, the writer has Peter say:

> If, therefore, some of the Scriptures are true and some false, with good reason said our Master, "Be ye good money-changers", inasmuch as in the Scriptures there are some true sayings and some spurious. And to those who err by reason of the false scriptures he fitly showed the cause of their error, saying, "Ye do therefore err, not knowing the true things of the Scriptures;[1] for this reason ye are ignorant also of the Power of God."
>
> *Clementine Homilies II:LI, CH pp.55-56*

In another place, the writer – again through Peter – even suggests that the scriptural books were written to test the people's understanding and ability to discriminate, pointing out that many of these spurious passages were taken as justification for some of the worst sins of humanity, including murder. In this excerpt, Peter is speaking of those who misunderstand the scriptures, even thinking that God is ignorant or acts unjustly and deceitfully or is appeased by sacrifices. The reference, of course, is to some of the Old Testament stories where God is described as behaving in an angry and vindictive manner:

> For supposing the expressions of the Scriptures which are against God, and are unjust and false, to be true, they did not know His real divinity and power. Therefore, in the belief that He was ignorant and rejoiced in murder, and let off the wicked in consequence of the gifts of sacrifice; yea, moreover, that He deceived and spake falsely, and did everything that is unjust, they themselves did things like to what their God did, and thus sinning, asserted that they were acting piously....
>
> But somewhere also he (Jesus) says, wishing to exhibit the cause of their error more distinctly to them, "On this account ye do err, not knowing the true things of the Scriptures, on which account ye are ignorant also of the Power of God".[2]
>
> Wherefore every man who wishes to be saved must become, as the Teacher (Jesus) said, a judge of the books written to try us. For thus he spake: "Become experienced bankers". Now the need of bankers arises from the circumstance that the spurious is mixed up with the genuine.
>
> *Clementine Homilies XVIII:XIX-XX, CH pp.286-287*

Not only were manuscripts unreliable as regards their authenticity but the people of those days well understood that whatever they might read may not be the words of the one to whom they were ascribed. The late second- and early third-century Christian teacher Origen, comments on this in passing, when quoting a passage attributed to Jesus:

> I have read somewhere that the Saviour said – and I question whether some one has assumed the person of the Saviour, or called the words to memory, or whether it be true that is said – but at any rate the Saviour himself says: "He that is near me is near the fire. He that is far from me is far from the kingdom".
>
> *Origen, on Jeremiah 3:3, ANT p.35*

Note his comment, "I question whether someone has assumed the person of the Saviour ..." We will have occasion to see how writing words in the name of Jesus or anybody else was a common practice in ancient times, both in the New Testament and elsewhere.

Some had an even more radical approach when determining what was authentic and what invented. The mid-second-century gnostic teacher, Marcion, for example, was more than dubious about the provenance of *all* the Christian gospels and writings. Believing that none of the gospels had been written by the apostles and with no canon of orthodox Christian literature yet in existence, Marcion felt able to give himself a free hand. He rejected Matthew and Mark in favour of what seems to have been a significantly slimmed-down and altered version of Luke. He omitted – amongst other things – the first three chapters containing the nativity stories of Jesus and John the Baptist. Only the chronological statement in the first verse of the third chapter is retained. The last chapter containing all the resurrection stories is also omitted and there is some evidence that this section did not exist as a part of Luke's gospel during Marcion's time or at least not in the copy of the text that Marcion had used.

Marcion also accepted the epistles of Paul, whose teachings were central to his beliefs, but he also felt free to make changes to these, too, omitting whatever he thought Paul would not have said and altering other passages, here and there. Whether or not Marcion's many textual 'corrections' were all justifiable is highly debatable, but his actions demonstrate that the people of those times had great difficulty determining what was authentic and what was not, considering it quite acceptable to try and change things back to what they thought it should have been whenever the occasion seemed to warrant it. Such an approach, of course, was likely to create further divergence from the original text whenever prejudice and dogma met with a contrary doctrine. As many scholars have demonstrated, evidence of this process at work in the New Testament is not hard to find, as we shall see.

Ancient Book Production

Two thousand years ago, Middle Eastern documents were mostly written on papyrus, vellum or parchment. Papyrus was largely, though not exclusively, manufactured in Egypt from the pith of the tall aquatic *Cyperus papyrus* plant, an important raw material also used in the manufacture of sails, light skiffs, ropes, shoes and other items. With a range extending from the Middle East into central and North Africa and southern Europe, papyrus flourished in the Nile Valley and Delta and was also found along the Euphrates and in Syria. Nowadays, its habitat is confined to the banks of the Blue and White Niles, and also Sicily, where it was probably introduced during the Arabic occupation. The ornamental papyrus sometimes grown today is a smaller cousin of its wild counterpart which could grow to a height of over ten feet and whose triangular stalk could attain the thickness of a man's wrist.

To prepare a suitable writing material, its stem was cut into sections and these were then sliced with sharp cutting blades into wafer thin slices. The resulting strips were laid side by side with the plant fibres running in parallel and a second layer was laid on top with the fibres running at right angles to the layer beneath. The two layers were then moistened, pressed flat and smoothed down. Finally, any projecting fibres and rough edges were trimmed off and the resulting papyrus sheet cut to the desired size.

Though the samples of papyrus seen today in museums have usually discoloured to a darkish brown due to centuries of burial or concealment, fresh papyrus was of a light grey or yellowish hue. Unlike surviving fragments, the material was by no means fragile. In fact, it was quite strong enough to be made into rolls more than thirty feet long and to have a useful library life of several decades.

Papyrus rolls were arranged with the fibres running horizontally on the uppermost layer, forming natural guides for straight writing. The papyrus roll, however, only provided a one-sided sheet of paper and the majority of early Christian texts used the *codex*, a format similar to modern books, which permitted writing on both sides.

To make a codex, one or more sheets of papyrus were taken and folded down the middle, a single sheet producing four sides and four sheets providing sixteen. These sets of folded sheets, known as a quire, were then bound and stitched, with or without a cover, to form a book or codex. This had the advantage of freeing the second side, though writing horizontally across the vertical fibres of the papyrus was not as easy. In addition to economy, the advantages of this arrangement were that longer texts could thereby be accommodated in one document and the difficulty of winding through a long roll to find a place was also overcome. A codex was also easier to conceal.

With the exception of a third-century copy of the *Epistle to the Hebrews*, written on the reverse of a vellum roll, all the most ancient Christian documents are found on papyrus. Vellum, prepared from the skin of a calf, kid or lamb, and parchment, made from the hide of older animals, was expensive and perhaps objectionable to some people, for it is almost unknown as a material for Christian documents before the fourth and fifth centuries.

Parchment or vellum, however, had the advantage of being a more durable material than papyrus. The hair and flesh were first removed from the hide using a solution of lime mordant. The material was then trimmed to size and the surface polished and smoothed flat with pumice stone and chalk. Parchment was formed into codices, like the later papyrus books, and since the hair side was usually darker than the flesh side, the pages were normally arranged so that all the sides of one hue faced in the same direction. Unlike papyrus, leather materials had no natural lines to guide the writer's hand. Consequently, ruled lines were commonly drawn with a metal stylus, usually on the hair side, forming a raised ridge on the other side. These impressions can still be seen on many ancient manuscripts.

Parchment must have been a far more expensive material to use. With full sheet sizes of approximately 10" x 15", folded to make a book size of 10" x 7"", only two sheets could have been prepared from one sheep or goat, one from each of its sides. As a result, a selection of New Testament writings, taking an average of 200 to 250 full sheets, would have required the hides of a good-sized flock. Add to this the cost of preparing the parchment, together with the fees of a professional scribe, and the total expense can be well imagined.

Some ancient manuscripts, particularly from the sixth century, used parchment dyed purple, were inscribed with silver and gold lettering, sported illumined initials and contained miniature drawings. Clearly, they were a luxury of the wealthy alone, to be used as showpieces, and it is noticeable that the quality and authenticity of the text used in such fancy manuscripts is generally inferior. As observed earlier, the more importance is given to externals, the less concern is given to spirituality.

Until the third century, the ink used for ancient texts was almost invariably based upon soot or lampblack, after which it was increasingly replaced by nut-gall and iron sulphate inks. And just as we re-use scrap paper today by writing upon the reverse side, so too were ancient manuscripts recycled. In fact, some of the most important manuscripts known to modern scholars are *palimpsests* in which an earlier writing has been washed and rubbed off, to be overwritten with a later text. To scholars and antiquarians, it is usually the earlier text which is of interest, and painstaking scientific techniques have been devised for deciphering the scarcely legible remains, tantalizingly concealed beneath a later text.

Although paper was invented by the Chinese during the first century AD, its use only spread into the Middle East during the eighth century, during the great expansion of culture and education in the Arab and Islamic worlds of that time. And in Europe and the West, paper only began to gain in popularity during the twelfth century.

This means of book production, one at a time, prevailed for Christianity's first fifteen centuries. The first printed Bible, Johann Gutenberg's forty-two line Bible, was a Latin version, produced in the 1450s. Gutenberg had invented the system of printing by means of movable type, and he brought into print what he must have realized would become the most enduring best seller of all time, the Bible. Today, only a few dozen copies remain of his original print run, valued in the market at several million pounds apiece.

Now the significance to our theme of this brief survey of ancient book production techniques is this. Firstly, papyrus and leather, indeed, even paper, are organic, compostable materials and it is only in consistently arid areas of the world, with low or zero rainfall, that manuscripts from the distant past have ever survived intact. Only in the libraries of the most ancient desert monasteries, buried in the desert sands or shielded from occasional rainfall in desert caves, can we ever hope to find early manuscripts of any kind, including those documents we now call the New Testament. It is an odd fact, therefore, that one of the key factors in determining which ancient writings have survived until the present day has been the weather.

This is one of the main reasons, for example, why we know considerably more about the beliefs and documents of the early Egyptian Christians than we do of their counterparts who lived in Rome, Corinth, Antioch, Damascus, Edessa or Jerusalem, where the moister climate has long since returned all ancient documents to the earth. And incidentally, this is one of the reasons why it is a practical impossibility for really ancient manuscripts to be secreted away in the Vatican library, as occasionally alleged or hoped. In Italy's temperate climate, they would almost certainly have long since suffered irreparable damage due to mould, decay and other factors. Besides, scholars seeking previously unknown manuscripts have covered the ground so many times that there is little likelihood of anything significant still lying undiscovered in such an obvious depository.

The second reason why ancient book production techniques have an important relevance to our theme is centred around the fact that every book was a one-off. Each one being hand-copied, it invariably contained unintentional errors, just as letters, manuscripts and type-scripts do today. At the most, a professional scriptorium might produce a number of copies of the same original text with one man dictating while a group of scribes wrote it down. But individual errors were still bound to occur, perhaps even more so when scribes were unable to proceed at their own speed. And dictation is liable to introduce its own kind of errors when words with different meanings and spellings sound the same.

One might think that many of these mistakes would be obvious to a reader or future copyist, but this is not necessarily true, for errors can still make sense, even though the original meaning has been changed. Moreover, writing in those days had a feature which to us must seem very odd. Not only were no upper and lower case letters used in Greek until the ninth century – everything was written in capital letters – but there were no punctuation marks, no spaces between words, no de-finitive endings to sentences and no paragraphs. In fact, there were virtually none of the reading aids which we take for granted. A glance at *figure 1* will demonstrate the point.

In Semitic languages such as Hebrew and Aramaic, the situation was further exacerbated by the fact that there were no vowels either. Even today, modern Semitic languages such as Hebrew and Arabic have no letters representing vowels. Vowel sounds are indicated by means of small points and accents, a system whose origins stem from about the fifth century AD. In old, handwritten manuscripts, therefore, the presence of a tiny dot or dash, like the dot on an 'i', could very easily be confused. An itinerant fly walking unconcernedly across a page could leave a mark that would change the meaning!

Furthermore, there were no verse or chapter numbers in the Bible, these being a much later addition to the text. The division into our familiar chapters did not take place until about 1200 AD, and verses were not added until 1557. Many people have pointed out, however, that though useful for reference purposes, the breaking of the text into verses of equal weight has had the effect of losing all natural paragraphing and has also encouraged the practice of extracting verses at random from their context in order to prove some point or other, when the verse itself, in context, may mean something entirely differ-ent. For these reasons, many modern translations of the Bible have relegated the verse numbers to the margins or dispensed with them altogether.

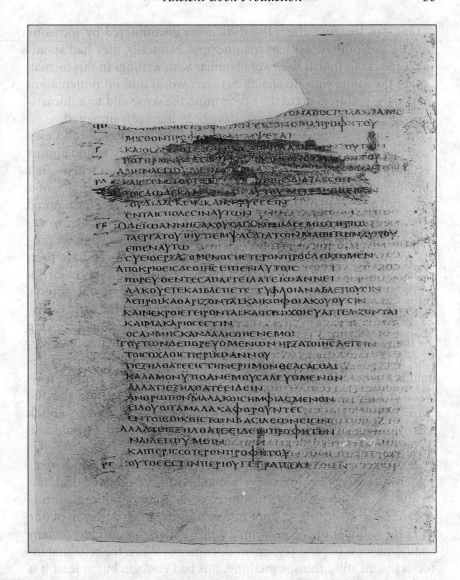

Figure 1. One of less well-preserved pages from Codex Bezae Cantabrigiensis. Many other ancient New Testament texts have not fared so well. Note the absence of punctuation marks, spacing between words, as well as upper and lower cases. *(Reproduced by permission of the Syndics of Cambridge University Library.)*

One can imagine, then, the difficulties encountered by someone reading one of these ancient manuscripts. Naturally, they had an advantage over us in that they were familiar with writings in this format, but all the same, with no spaces between words and no punctuation marks, the ability to accurately determine the sense and to automatically correct scribal errors would have been markedly impaired.

It is unlikely that even the original copy of any book would ever have been perfect and the production of the first copy would almost certainly have introduced variants to the original text. But with its first copying, its history had only just begun. These days, all copies of a new book are printed from one set of masters, which have been pored over and corrected, as far as may be. But in those days, each copy was likely to be used as the master from which a further copy was produced. An alert scribe, as he went along, would no doubt have been expected to do his best to correct the errors of his predecessor(s), while at the same time attempting to minimize his own. Copyists, however, especially amongst the minority groups like the early Christians, were not necessarily professionals, but were often only copying for themselves, a friend or their community, in their spare time, perhaps at night when the day's work was done. And working by candlelight is not the best way to produce error-free copies. As a result, mistakes in the source text might never be noticed, nor could they be corrected with any degree of certainty unless a second copy of a book was available, taken from another source. And new errors would also be introduced.

Textual scholars, in their attempts to reconstruct ancient and error-ridden documents have extensively analyzed and categorized the kinds of mistake most frequently encountered. As in modern times, untidy or careless handwriting was not uncommon and the confusion of one letter for a similar one, even amongst tidy writers, has produced many textual variants in New Testament documents. When the resulting incorrect word still means something, it is bad enough, but at least it is likely to be copied onward in the same way, and might get corrected at a later date, or at least the mistake would spread no further. But when the result of an error was meaningless, then succeeding scribes would all try in their own ways to correct the text, adding a profusion of variants. As one scholar has put it, a meaningless variant scatters in successive manuscripts like farmyard chickens invaded by a hungry dog. This phenomenon is also common amongst New Testament texts.

Further, with no spaces between the letters, different combinations of words could sometimes be formed out of a string of letters, again adding to the confusion. And if the different variants all made sense, it then became impossible to determine the meaning intended by the original author.

Mistakes found commonly amongst modern copy typists are also encountered in these ancient texts and a tired scribe – like a tired typist – was more error-prone, especially when copying a long continuous text. While repeatedly moving the eye back and forth between a text and the page under production, one or more paragraphs, sentences, letters, syllables or words can get accidentally repeated – or omitted. Modern typists have solved the problem of losing their place by learning to type without looking at the keyboard, enabling them to keep their eyes on the manuscript being copied. But without a typewriter to ensure that letters are correctly formed and positioned, the scribe would have had to move his eye between the old work and the new. In this way, sometimes whole blocks of text got omitted – or repeated – especially when there was a phrase or group of letters that was repeated in the source.

Matthew chapter 5, verses 19 and 20, for example, have commonly suffered in this way. In the *King James Version*, the translation reads:

(19) Whosoever therefore shall break
    one of these least commandments, and shall teach men so,
    he shall be called the least in the kingdom of heaven:
But whosoever shall do and teach them,
    the same shall be called great in the kingdom of heaven.
(20) For I say unto you, that except your righteousness
    shall exceed the righteousness of the scribes and Pharisees,
    ye shall in no case enter into the kingdom of heaven.

Matthew 5:19-20

The first and the second sentences of verse 19, as well as verse 20, all end with the phrase "in the kingdom of heaven". There are very few ancient manuscripts of the New Testament and in two of these, the scribes omit the second sentence of verse 19, passing straight from the first occurrence of "the kingdom of heaven" to the start of verse 20. The scribe of another manuscript, confusing the third with the first occurrence of the phrase, went straight from the end of the first sentence in verse 19 to the start of verse 21.

Even with the best of intentions, therefore, all ancient books had mistakes in them. Indeed, there are very few modern printed books which are error-free. Usually, the first thing that an author or a publisher sees upon picking up a newly printed book is an error, sometimes significant!

But not all copyists of the past were simply scribes. Many of them had literary aspirations of their own or held particular personal points of view. Consequently, when copying a book, a scribe was likely – to a greater or lesser extent, depending upon the individual – to become an editor. Explanatory phrases or sentences, for example, might be added according to the individual's own understanding. Scholars call these a 'gloss' and the gospels contain many of them. In some cases, it may never have been the intention that they should have been incorporated into the text, being placed by the original scribe only as marginal notes. But a later copyist included them in the main text, all the same.

There is a good example of this kind of editorial change in one of the miracle stories recounted in John's gospel. The *King James Version*, translated from a fifteenth-century Greek manuscript, reads:

> (3)   ... in these lay a great multitude of impotent folk,
>   of blind, halt, withered, waiting for the moving of the water.
> (4)   For an angel went down at a certain season into the pool,
>   and troubled the water: whosoever then first
>   after the troubling of the water stepped in
>   was made whole of whatsoever disease he had.
> (5)   And a certain man was there,
>   which had an infirmity thirty and eight years....
>
> *John 5:3-5*

Referring to the more ancient manuscripts, however, we discover that the explanatory comment at the end of verse 3, as well as the whole of verse 4, are later editorial explanations and additions, for they are not found in the earliest texts. Moreover, the addition to verse 3 and the entire verse 4 supplement appeared in later texts from different hands and at different times, for different manuscripts contain varying combinations of the addition. What makes the additions seem plausible is that they explain a later comment in verse 7, which reads:

> (7)   ... the impotent man answered him,
>   "Sir, I have no man, when the water is troubled,
>   to put me into the pool:
>   but while I am coming, another steppeth down before me."
>
> *John 5:7*

So the addition of the angel, as the one who stirs the water, is not that of the original gospel writer, but of a much later Christian with an ingenious turn of mind as well as a belief in angelic intervention in the affairs of men. As it stood in the original, the pool was probably an intermittent underground stream or maybe a natural hot spring through which gases would sometimes bubble, bringing relief to sufferers from certain ailments. An editorial 'explanation' has added a supernatural overtone to a natural phenomenon.

Not only were phrases added and deleted from the gospels and other New Testament writings, but major revisions and editorial work were also undertaken at various times and for various reasons. These, together with variants due to scribal mistakes and attempted error correction have produced identifiable families and family trees amongst the ancient New Testament texts.

Early New Testament Manuscripts

The earliest known papyrus fragment of any canonical gospel, now preserved in the John Rylands Library at Manchester University, was first published in 1935, discovered amongst the ruins of an ancient provincial town along the Nile. From the style of its handwriting, it has been dated to around 125 AD. The text, written on the front and back, though fragmentary, can be identified as part of Jesus' conversation with Pilate as recorded in *John 18:31-34* and *18:37-38*, and it is commonly assumed that this passage came from a copy of St John's gospel, though how much the entire text would have resembled the gospel we know is, of course, unknown.

Such a fragment, however, though compelling because of its date, tells us nothing of Jesus' teaching nor of the authenticity of the gospels, and though other early fragments of canonical texts have been found, some with greater and some with lesser content, the earliest more or less complete manuscripts of the gospels and other New and Old Testament books, date from the fourth and fifth centuries. Significantly, all these come from the period after the time of the Emperor Constantine and the acquisition of political power by the so-called orthodox church, early in the fourth century.

Amongst these ancient texts is the fourth-century *Codex Sinaiticus*, discovered in May 1844 at the Monastery of St Catherine, Sinai, by the German ancient language specialist, Constantin Tischendorf. It now resides in the British Library in London, having been bought from an impoverished Soviet government in 1933 for £100,000. *Codex Sinaiticus* has numerous unique readings, as well as many careless errors, and comes from the same textual family as *Codex Vaticanus*, a fourth-century manuscript of unknown provenance which appears in a Vatican inventory of 1475. Still residing in the Vatican, with photographic facsimile copies available for scholars, this latter codex is considered to be the most significant and reliable of all the early Greek manuscripts.

The gospel text of the fourth-century *Codex Vaticanus* is largely supported by that found in an early third-century papyrus containing fragments of Luke and most of John up to chapter fourteen, and this papyrus has in many ways undermined the previously maintained belief that all the New Testament texts available to us had undergone a thorough revision during the fourth century. Of course, the existence of the earlier papyrus does not preclude the possibility that that document had not already received considerable editorial attention.

Codex Bezae Cantabrigiensis, for example, stems from the fifth century and now has its home in the Cambridge University Library. Its text represents a different family of texts to *Codex Vaticanus* and *Codex Sinaiticus* and, like them, has earlier relatives amongst some of the third- and fourth-century papyri. But the internationally known German scholars, Kurt and Barbara Aland of the Institute for New Testament Studies Textual Research in Münster, comment that

> the additions, omissions, and alterations of the text, especially in Luke
> and Acts, betray the touch of a significant theologian.
>
> *Kurt and Barbara Aland, TNT p.108*

Two further manuscripts complete the meagre tally of full Bible codices that have survived from the fourth and fifth centuries. First is the fifth-century, *Codex Alexandrinus*, now in the British Library, which came from the Patriarchal Library of Alexandria in the seventeenth century as a gift to Charles I of England. Second is *Codex Ephraemi Syri Rescriptus*, a fifth-century palimpsest with significant *lacunae*, these being actual holes or areas of illegibility in the manuscript.

There are, then, only five of these more or less complete Bible codices, and of these only one, *Codex Vaticanus*, is considered tolerably reliable, though the others provide further readings of interest and importance from a textual point of view. This contrasts with the fragmentary remains of over 80 other papyri spanning the period up to the eighth century, of which the majority (50-60) come from the period up to the fifth century. It is from this mixed bag of manuscripts that scholars have pieced together what they consider to be the most accurate versions they can produce of the gospels and the rest of the New Testament.

Scholars make a great deal of these manuscripts in preparing what they call a 'critical text', that is, a text formed by the careful deliberation and evaluation of all available versions of a particular passage. There is, of course, frequent difference of opinion as to the correct reading, and out of seven such 'critical editions' of the Greek New Testament prepared during the twentieth century, one-third of the verses have variations in more than one word, some insignificant, some significant. But this by no means indicates that two-thirds of the New Testament is as it was when first written. It only means that two-thirds of it is true to one particular lineage or family of texts, as that lineage stood at the beginning of the fourth century, when Christianity became a state religion. Prior to this, in the words of Kurt and Barbara Aland:

> Until the beginning of the fourth century the text of the New Testament developed freely. It was a 'living text', unlike the text of the Hebrew Old Testament, which was subject to strict controls.... And the New Testament continued to be a 'living text' as long as it remained a manuscript tradition, even when the Byzantine church moulded it to the procrustean bed of an ecclesiastically standardized and officially prescribed text. Even for later scribes, for example, the parallel passages of the gospels were so familiar that they would adapt the text of one gospel to that of another. They also felt themselves free to make corrections in the text, improving it by their own standards of correctness, whether grammatically, stylistically, or more substantively. This was all the more true of the early period when the text had not yet attained canonical status, especially in the early period when the Christians considered themselves filled with the Spirit. As a consequence, the 'Early text' was many-faceted, and each manuscript had its own particular character.
>
> *Kurt and Barbara Aland, TNT p.69*

It is interesting to examine some of these variants, of differing significance. For instance, following a centuries-old tradition, *Luke 2:14* in the *King James Version,* reads:

> On earth peace, good will toward men.
>
> *Luke 2:14*

But the *English Revised Standard Version,* finding corroboration for its text of this passage in all of the early codices named above, as well as other manuscripts, reads:

> On earth peace among men with whom he is pleased.
>
> *Luke 2:14, RSV*

The difference in the *King James Version* arose from the loss of one letter from the end of one Greek word. In this instance, it is unclear whether the change was intentional or otherwise, nor is it particularly significant. In other passages, however, it is very clear that alterations have been made to suit the point of view of the copyist, the commonest change being the addition of a word, a phrase or even some more substantial passage. In fact, one of the general guidelines used by scholars seeking to establish the most authentic Greek text of the New Testament is that the shorter reading is usually more likely to be the original, for the text had a marked tendency to expand by addition, as time went by.

Changes were also made to improve the rough Greek of the original or to correct the gospel compiler himself. Mark's gospel, for example, has numerous small errors of various kinds, geographical, historical and otherwise, as we will shortly see, and later copyists attempted to smooth out the mistakes. In *Mark 1:2-3,* for instance, in the more original manuscripts such as *Codex Vaticanus* and *Codex Sinaiticus,* the text reads:

> As it is written in Isaiah the prophet:
> "Behold, I send my messenger before thy face;
>   who shall prepare the way.
> The voice of one crying in the wilderness:
>   prepare the way of the Lord,
>   make his paths straight."
>
> *Mark 1:2-3, RSV*

But actually, the text attributed by Mark to Isaiah is a composite. Only the second sentence comes from *Isaiah* (*40:3*), the first sentence being from *Malachi 3:1.* Later manuscripts have therefore corrected the line to read:

> As it is written in the prophets: ...
>
> *Mark 1:2, KJV*

And this is the way it appears in the *King James Version*. Interestingly, a number of scholars have pointed out that the same 'proof' quotations occur in a similar order in a number of writings, suggesting that the early Christians circulated a book of Old Testament 'proofs' or 'testimonies' from which they copied without consulting the original Bible texts, for the same errors consistently recur in otherwise unconnected writings.

Matthew, copying from Mark, corrects the error simply by omitting the first sentence from *Malachi*, while Luke does the same, adding the two succeeding verses from *Isaiah*. Matthew and Luke do use the *Malachi* quote, but at other places (*Matthew 11:10* and *Luke 7:27*), though all three of the gospel compilers agree in using both quotes in reference to John the Baptist. The original context of the sentence, however, by no means suggests a prophecy concerning John the Baptist, though it has become associated with him through centuries of repetition.

Other changes were introduced to harmonize the different texts, Mark's gospel being particularly prone to augmentation from the others because of its sparse character and reliance on anecdotal rather than spiritual material. Some of the Greek manuscripts have such additions and 'corrections' on every page. An inattentive or tired scribe, familiar with all the gospel texts, knowing much of them by heart, might inadvertently – from his memory – add words belonging to similar passages in the other gospels. But in many instances, the alterations were probably quite intentional. Following the principle that 'holy scripture' could not admit of variations, the copyist would attempt to make Jesus say the same thing, in the same words, in all the gospels, despite the contrary indication of his sources.

Amongst the most significant of these alterations and additions is the ending to Mark's gospel, consisting of chapter 16, verses 9-20, which is found in almost all the later Greek manuscripts as well as all but the more recent English translations. The story up to verse 8 relates that Mary Magdalene, Mary (Jesus' mother) and Salome (the wife of Zebedee and mother of James and John) had gone to the sepulchre and found a young man sitting there who tells them that Jesus has risen. There is then an abrupt change of direction and verses 9-20 recount Jesus' resurrection appearances and his ascension, together with a far more radical command to evangelize than is found in Matthew.

The problem is that in most of the really ancient manuscripts, including *Codex Vaticanus* and *Codex Sinaiticus*, Mark's gospel ends at verse 8. And since the fourth-century Christian fathers, Eusebius of Caesarea and Jerome, make statements which confirm this, we may be assured that in the earlier version of Mark, verses 9-20 did not exist. Further evidence of Mark's original gospel having ended at verse 8 is seen in the proliferation of *different* endings which have appeared in later manuscripts after verse 8. People wanted an ending that complied with Christian teaching – and supplied it out of their own imagination.

In one instance, not only does the new ending carry the conventional addition of verses 9-20, but between verses 14 and 15 there is a further significant interpolation to the conversation between Jesus and his disciples:

> And they (the eleven disciples) defended themselves thus:
> "This age of lawlessness and unbelief is under the sway of Satan,
>   who does not allow those under the yoke of unclean spirits
>   to understand God's truth and power.
> Now, therefore, reveal your righteousness."
>
> This is what they said to Christ, and Christ answered,
> "The number of years allowed for Satan's authority has been reached,
>   but other terrible things draw near.
> I was handed over to be killed for those who have sinned,
>   so that they might turn to the truth and sin no more,
>   and so inherit the spiritual and incorruptible glory
>   of righteousness which is in heaven."
>
> *Mark, JB, footnote 16.c, p.89*

These endings demonstrate a common literary habit of the times – the practice of putting words into the mouths of others. And crediting Jesus with words that he never spoke is a characteristic not only of later New Testament manuscripts, but also of far earlier Christian literature, including the original gospels themselves.

A school teacher, aware that his students have been cheating, can – by a careful analysis of their work – ascertain to some extent which of his pupils has been copying from whom. Similarly, despite all the changes which have undoubtedly occurred in the New Testament documents, it is often possible for honest scholars to determine which of all the available readings is the most authentic. But this technique can only go back as far as the earliest available documents, certainly no earlier than the fourth century in most instances. The Alands write:

> There are certainly instances of major disturbances in the New Testament text caused by theological as well as by pastoral motives, because many

expressions in the original text were not easily adapted to later needs....

From the very beginning, the tradition of the New Testament books was as broad as the spectrum of Christian churches and theologians. Even in the first, and especially in the second century, their numbers were remarkably large. This tradition could not be closely controlled because there was no centre which could provide such a control. Church centres were not developed until the third/fourth century, and even then their influence was limited to their respective provinces.

Furthermore, not only every church but each individual Christian felt a 'direct relationship to God'. Well into the second century Christians still regarded themselves as possessing inspiration equal to that of the New Testament writings which they read in worship services.

Kurt and Barbara Aland, TNT pp.289-290

In other words, during the early centuries, the text of the New Testament was not considered 'sacred scripture', like the Old Testament, and people felt at ease in making free with it. They "regarded themselves as possessing inspiration *equal* to that of the New Testament writings." Perhaps it was because of these differences in the text that references by Christian writers to collections of the four gospels are not found until well into the second century, for they sat uneasily beside each other. They were also written for different communities, each gospel compiler having a different intention in mind, and there was a marked tendency for the community in each particular area to have its own gospel, to which it adhered, to the exclusion of others. As we have seen, there was the *Gospel According to the Hebrews*, the *Gospel of the Ebionites* and the *Gospel of the Egyptians*. There were also gospels of Peter, Matthias, Barnabas, James, Thomas, Bartholomew, Andrew and others, too, each of which were used by certain groups and not others, though not always exclusively.

Some of the early Christian writers, particularly those of a more open-minded nature, such as the late second-century Christian teacher, Clement of Alexandria, cite these texts without giving any impression that they considered them in any way unacceptable. And Origen, Clement's pupil and successor, clearly suggesting early controversy over gospel authenticity, prefaces a quotation from the *Gospel according to the Hebrews* with:

And if any accept the *Gospel according to the Hebrews*, where the Saviour Himself saith: ...

Origen, Commentary on John (2:12), ANT p.2

All the same, by careful comparison of manuscripts, numerous alterations and additions can be eliminated. But, as we have said, the best that could ever be achieved is a version of the gospels something like it was during the third, fourth and fifth centuries, two to four hundred years after the death of Jesus. For only from this period have anything appreciable by way of gospel texts and fragments ever been recovered.

Now scholars are generally agreed that the actual composition of the gospels themselves is dated at something like thirty-five to seventy years after the death of Jesus, while the letters from Paul, Peter, James and the others – if they are authentic – must have been written even earlier. So if the majority of the New Testament documents were written by 100 AD, there would have been a period of two or three hundred years in which the original text of the gospels and the rest of the New Testament could have been edited, with our hardly being able to determine the extent. And given the circumstances and attitudes described, there is little doubt that they did so evolve. As a result, even with the best available Greek texts before us, we are still unsure how much they really represent Jesus' actual words.

Many of the early Christians simply did not consider the gospels as divinely revealed or they had distinct reservations about it. They must have understood only too well the processes by which books got about. Certainly, none of the New Testament documents themselves claim to be a direct revelation from God, except perhaps the *Book of Revelation*. In the process of gradual crystallization, therefore, it was not until the end of the second century that anything like a canon of New Testament books came into being, though both then and for several centuries that followed, there remained considerable disagreement over which books should be included. The Eastern churches, even at the beginning of the fourth century, rejected the *Book of Revelation*, for example, and it is absent from many Greek texts of the New Testament. There was also controversy over the authenticity of John. And Irenaeus, the late second-century Bishop of Lyons, gave it as his considered opinion that there could only be four gospels. "It is not possible", he wrote, "that the gospels can be either more or fewer in number than they are", for they correspond to the "four zones in the world in which we live, and four principal winds". Just as the wind – like the Spirit – breathes vitality on all, so too, he reasoned, does the gospel, for "the church is scattered throughout all the world, and the 'pillar and ground' of the church is the gospel and the spirit of life".[3] Consequently, he argued, there must be precisely four gospels, no more and no less. A dubious piece of logic, to say the least.

New Testament Greek

Until a hundred years ago, the Greek language of the New Testament had puzzled scholars, for it did not seem like the Greek of classical literature, nor was it of any other known form. Prior to the latter years of the nineteenth century, therefore, it had generally been assumed that New Testament Greek was of a special character, probably devised by the Holy Spirit for the transmission of his special message. A few scholars suspected otherwise and various papyri were unearthed in Egypt which could have confirmed their suspicions. The first recorded find was in 1778 when a collection of forty or fifty papyrus rolls were dug up – probably in the Fayum (a fertile area in northern Egypt, south of Cairo) – by a group of native Egyptians. But having no idea of the value of their find, they are said to have burned the rolls. Only one was preserved, now in the Naples Museum, proving to be a document dated to 191 AD, concerning work upon the Nile embankments.

During the nineteenth century, further important papyrus finds were made in Egypt, many of the documents being of a private nature and written in everyday Greek. Remarkable discoveries were also made of long-lost Greek classics, some papyri dating as far back as the third century BC. Then in 1897, two young British archaeologists from Oxford, Bernard Grenfell and Arthur Hunt, discovered a multitude of papyri from the second century AD in the rubbish heaps of the ancient Egyptian town of Oxyrhynchus. Amongst these were fragments of previously unknown sayings attributed to Jesus.

The thought of unknown gospels in the everyday use of people who lived so close to Jesus' time caught both the public as well as scholarly imagination and prompted an intensive period of Egyptian excavation. Over the ensuing years a vast number of papyri were unearthed from various sites and, from a study of these documents, it became clear that the language of the New Testament was not the Greek of the Holy Spirit. It was the Greek of the common people.

Ancient urban rubbish dumps are favourite hunting grounds for archaeologists, if they can find them, for rubbish is a window into the lives of the depositors, and far more was found at Oxyrhynchus than New Testament fragments. Of the great mass of papyri discovered only two or three percent are literary. The vast majority are private documents – "letters, invitations, petitions, contracts, deeds, leases, lists, tickets, accounts, birth notices, death notices, complaints, reports, accounts, receipts, wills, marriage agreements, divorces, legal proceedings, questions to the oracles and so on".[4] All aspects of everyday life are represented, including the contents of the Roman record office which appears to have undergone a thorough clear-out in early Christian times. The old records had been carried out to the rubbish heap in baskets and set alight. But supervision must have been scant, for the fire went out before they were all consumed and the sand blew over the remains, burying and preserving them for maybe eighteen hundred years. Some of these papyri were even carried into Grenfell's camp in the same baskets in which they had been taken out to the city limits, so many centuries before.

Many of the letters have a personal touch that reaches across the centuries through the familiar human feelings they express. One small boy who had clearly been left behind against his will when his father had embarked upon a trip to Alexandria, wrote thus:

> Theon to his father Theon, greeting. It was a fine thing of you not to take
> me with you to the city! If you won't take me along with you to Alexandria,
> I won't write you a letter, or speak to you, or say goodbye to you, and if
> you go to Alexandria, I won't take your hand or ever greet you again!
> That is what will happen if you don't take me! And my mother said to
> Archelaus, "He upsets me! Take him away!" It was fine of you to send me
> presents! great ones! shucks! They fooled us there, on the twelfth, the day
> you sailed. Well, send for me, I implore you! If you don't, I won't eat, I
> won't drink! There!
>
> *Oxyrhynchus Papyri, MENT p.101*

These documents from daily usage clearly demonstrate that not only is the Greek of the New Testament ordinary conversational Greek, but that much of it is of a decidedly poor quality. Scholars have described it as "barbarous Greek", "Jewish Greek" and other less than complimentary terms. It is certain, therefore, that those who wrote the gospels were not literary people, though the author of Luke and *Acts* certainly had literary aspirations.

That Greek was the language in which the New Testament books were written down is now generally accepted. Even though it is presumed that the sayings, discourses and parables of Jesus must at one time have been in Aramaic, unless they did not originate with Jesus at all, there is no evidence to support the idea that the other gospel material is of anything other than Greek origin. The fact that all the Old Testament quotations occurring in the New Testament are taken, not from the Hebrew, but from the Greek *Septuagint,* the Greek translation of the Old Testament prevalent at that time, lends further weight to Greek having been the original language.

English Translations

Until recent decades, the English translation with which most people were familiar was the *Authorized King James Version* or one of its Revised Versions. Commissioned in 1604 by King James I, the Bible text was divided up among six groups of scholars – four for the Old Testament and two for the New. Their brief – as it says in the preface – was not to create a new translation, but to revise what already existed:

> Truly (good Christian reader), wee never thought from the beginning, that we should neede to make a new Translation, nor yet to make of a bad one a good one.... but to make a good one better, or out of many good ones, one principall good one, not justly to be excepted against.

There had been a number of earlier English versions. We have already mentioned Wycliffe's 1382 translation from the Latin. This had set the scene for Tyndale's first translation from the Greek, published in 1526. Born on the Welsh borders in the 1490s, William Tyndale received his Master's degree at Oxford in 1515, going on to Cambridge for further study. In 1516, the first printed edition of the New Testament in Greek was published by the Dutch scholar, Erasmus, and there is little doubt that it would have come to Tyndale's notice. Ordained as a priest during his time at university, some time after leaving Cambridge, around 1521 he took a post as chaplain and tutor in the home of Sir John Walsh, in Gloucestershire.

It must have been some time during this period that the thought grew upon him that if lay people were to understand Christianity, they would have to be able to read the Bible for themselves. This alone, he later wrote, was his motivation in deciding to translate the New Testament into English. And though he probably began his translation while in London in 1524, he was unable to find suitable patronage in England while he completed the task. He therefore went to Hamburg where his work must have continued, for in the following year, 1525, he was ready to begin printing.

Like Wycliffe, Tyndale had to translate in secret. He also had to find a place where he could get the printing done without discovery. For this reason, he moved on to Cologne, in Germany. But there, with only ten sheets of a quarto edition printed, he was discovered by Cochlaeus, a powerful force of authoritarian conservatism within the church. Remaining in Germany, he fled with his assistant to Worms, taking with them the material that had already been completed. There, they continued their work, assisted financially by a number of English businessmen who were interested in the Reformation. Within the year they had finished the printing of an octavo edition, followed by the quarto edition in the following year.

The church authorities, however, alerted by Tyndale's discovery at Cologne, did their best to suppress the book. Cuthbert Tunstall, the Bishop of London at that time, preached a sermon in which he denounced the new translation, proclaiming that anyone in possession of a copy should hand it over to the church authorities or be excommunicated. At the close of his tirade, a copy was publicly burnt. Large numbers of the book were also bought up by the church authorities and put to the flames, with the result that only one quarto and one octavo edition, together with parts of another octavo, have survived.

Cochlaeus maintained that the Latin Vulgate was the only correct form of the Bible and he poured out vitriol upon Tyndale's work:

> The New Testament, translated into the vulgar tongue is in truth the food of death, the fuel of sin, the veil of malice, the pretext of false liberty, the protection of disobedience, the corruption of discipline, the depravity of morals, the termination of concord, the death of honesty, the well-spring of vices, the disease of virtues, the instigation of rebellion, the milk of pride, the nourishment of contempt, the death of peace, the destruction of charity, the enemy of unity, the murderer of truth!
>
> *Cochlaeus, MENT p.8*

But Cochlaeus seemed to have forgotten, like the old lady with whom we began, that the *Vulgate* was itself a translation "into the vulgar tongue" of the times, made by Jerome under instructions from Pope Damascus. Moreover, it too had been just as vehemently attacked, amongst its castigators being St Augustine. In fact, the original Greek in which the gospels had first been written was of a particularly "vulgar" variety, though it would be several centuries more before this was realized.

Despite fierce opposition, Tyndale bravely continued with his work, revising his earlier translations and starting work on a translation of the Hebrew Old Testament into English. But he lived the life of a fugitive. In 1535, residing with English business friends at Antwerp, he brought out what were to be his last revisions of the New Testament and the Pentateuch.[5] Soon after, he was betrayed by a friend, arrested by officers of Emperor Charles V and imprisoned in Vilvorde Castle, near Brussels. A year or so later, he was condemned as a heretic, strangled and burned.

But Tyndale had opened up a new pathway, and though he made a considerable impact upon the thinking of his time, it was little compared to his influence on posterity. Within fifteen years, his translation, at first suppressed and condemned, had become the basis of an Authorized New Testament of the Church of England. And more than a flavour of his terse and sturdy Anglo-Saxon translation is apparent in all the versions which followed. The editions of Coverdale (1535) and Rogers (1537), the *Great Bible* (1539), the *Geneva Bible* (1560) (often called the *'Breeches Bible'* for its translation of *Genesis 3:7*, "they sewed figge tree leaves together, and made themselves breeches"), the *Bishop's Bible* (1568) and the *King James Version* (1611) were all more like revisions of his work than new translations. Indeed, Rogers' edition of 1537 was actually Tyndale's last revision of 1535, produced in the year before his death.

The original 1611 edition of the *King James Version* had many misprints and spelling mistakes, many of which were corrected in a second edition which came out in 1613. But one typographical error has never been corrected, making it the world's longest lived 'typo'. *Matthew 23:24* speaks of the "Pharisees" as "ye blind guides, which strain *at* a gnat, and swallow a camel", while the correct rendering should be to "strain *out* a gnat" – presumably from food or drink. It may have been a common idiom of Jesus' times akin to "penny wise, pound foolish".

The *King James Version* itself was almost immediately revised in 1615, 1629 and 1638, then again in 1762 and finally in 1769, most of these revisions being undertaken in order to bring the language and the spelling up to date, few serious corrections being deemed necessary.

However, despite the significant breakthrough in returning the Bible to the common language of the people, the Greek text from which the original *King James Version* had been made, possessed all the faults and few of the virtues of the modern, critical editions of the Greek New Testament text. Of the earlier manuscripts now known, only *Codex Vaticanus* had at that time been discovered, but – locked away in the Vatican library – there was little chance of Tyndale gaining access to it, even if he knew of it, and his translation was made from the third edition of Erasmus' Greek New Testament, while the King James revisers consulted a 1589 edition of Erasmus' text produced by Beza, a notable scholar of the times.

Desiderius Erasmus (*c*.1466-1536), a Dutch scholar whose real name was Gerhard Gerhards, was a leader of the Renaissance in northern Europe. Erasmus must have had the production of a Greek New Testament in mind, for when he heard of an edition of the Greek text being prepared in Spain, under pressure of competition, he rushed through his first edition of 1516, based upon five Greek manuscripts of the Bible he had been able to locate in Basel. But these were of very late date, stemming from the eleventh to the fifteenth centuries, and not one of them contained the entire New Testament. As a result, his text was derived mostly from one fifteenth-century manuscript containing the gospels and from a thirteenth-century text in which he had found *Acts* and the various Epistles. Of the *Book of Revelation*, all he had was a single incomplete copy whose small gaps he ingeniously filled by retranslating the missing portions from the Latin *Vulgate*. Within a year, Erasmus had 'edited' an entire text of the Bible and rushed it into print. And though he later corrected many of the misprints in second and third editions, he never substantially improved the text.

Thus the original *King James Version* remained, despite the gradual discovery of more authentic texts. Indeed, it was in 1628, less than twenty years after the publication of the *King James Version*, that the fifth-century *Codex Alexandrinus* was given to the English monarch by Cyril Lucar, the Patriarch of Constantinople, previously Patriarch of Alexandria, from where this codex had probably originated. This manuscript was the very first of the early Greek texts to become readily accessible to Western scholars, but it came too late to be of use to the King James translators.

With the passing of the centuries, as other early codices came to light, it became increasingly apparent that the *King James Version*, though it had acquired the respect of tradition, had many imperfections and required revision. It had been left unchanged for so long, however, that it had taken on an air of permanency and unchangeability and there was a reluctance on the part of Christian authorities to update it. Increasingly, therefore, especially during the eighteenth and nineteenth centuries, a wide variety of private translations were made and published, many of them relating to the more ancient Greek texts.

It was not until Tischendorf's momentous discovery, in 1864, of the *Codex Sinaiticus*, highlighting the imperfections of the *King James Version* from yet another text, that it was decided by British and

American ecclesiastical authorities that the *King James Version* should undergo a full revision in the light of the ancient texts, at the same time bringing the language up to date.

The translators had the benefit of help from Westcott and Hort, a team of scholars who had been working for many years on what was later to be the first critical text of the Greek New Testament prepared according to modern methods. The fruit of their endeavours they generously made available to the translating teams before the publication of their own work.

There was, however, considerable disagreement over the extent of the revision. Perhaps predictably, the American team wanted many more changes than their more conservative English counterparts, but the Americans had given an assurance that they would not publish a separate edition of the Bible until fourteen years after the publication of the new English edition. The *Revised English Version* of the New Testament was thus published in 1881, with that of the Old Testament following in 1885. True to their promise, the *Revised American Version* did not appear until 1901.

Considering the Greek texts then available, the *Revised English Version* in particular is notable for its conservatism. Indeed, the overriding concern was "to introduce as few alterations as possible into the text of the *Authorized Version* consistently with faithfulness." The group of English-speaking reviewers, usually numbering twenty-four, met for periods of usually four days at a stretch, doing six hours work per day. They read through the entire text twice and by the time they had finished they had clocked up 407 sessions. All suggested changes had to be carried by a majority on the first reading and by a two-thirds majority on the second. And with many of the reviewers being more concerned with retaining the original text rather than updating it according to the requirements of the earliest textual witnesses, rather less was changed than more.

The *Revised English Version* of 1881-1885 was not copyrighted. As a consequence, since editorial tampering is a habit that dies hard even in the days of printing, in the two decades between 1881 and 1901, a number of unauthorized American publications were made in which the text was altered in the supposed interests of the American public. The *Revised American Version* of 1901 was therefore copyrighted, the copyright eventually being acquired in 1928 by the International Council of Religious Education which effectively meant the American and Canadian churches. This Council appointed a committee of scholars to take charge of the text of the *Revised American Version*.

The revisers of the 1870s had access to all the major Greek texts which we have today, but they still laboured under the impression that the Greek of the New Testament was a special "Biblical Greek". Without access to the wealth of Greek in the Egyptian papyri, the meaning of some expressions remained obscure to them and, as time passed, more modern scholars felt that they had made considerable advances both as to the meaning of the 'Scriptures' as well as in textual and source criticism. Furthermore, there were a number of words in the *King James Version* which had either dropped out of common English usage or had changed their meaning. The word 'let', for instance, is used in the sense of 'hinder', 'take no thought' for 'be not anxious' and 'ghost' for 'spirit'. Many of these words still remained in the *Revised English* and *American Versions*. As a result of these factors, in 1937, the Council authorized a new revision which would

> embody the best results of modern scholarship as to the meaning of the Scriptures, and express this meaning in English diction which is designed for use in public and private worship and preserves those qualities which have given to the *King James Version* a supreme place in English literature.
>
> *Preface, RSV*

All suggested changes were submitted by the thirty-two members of the committee of scholars to an Advisory Board of fifty representatives from the various co-operating Christian denominations for advice and counsel. Additionally, all changes had once again to be agreed by a two-thirds majority of the committee members. In this manner, the *Revised Standard Version* was produced, the New Testament being published in 1946, followed by the Old Testament in 1952. But such was the strength of Tyndale's original translation, that even the revisions of 1881-1901 and 1946-1952 still retained the character and vitality of his great work.

In more recent times, a large number of New Testament translations have appeared, including a further *New Revised Version* published in 1989. But the quality of all translation, however well-intentioned, will always reflect one common feature: the translators' understanding of the text. No one who did not fully understand the subject would ever try to translate a scientific paper, for what is really being translated is meaning, rather than words. An accurate rendition of meaning cannot be conveyed by one who does not fully understand it, however literal their translation may be. And it is over the meaning that Christianity has been so divided throughout the last two thousand years. So even if the Greek text used were the best critical edition available and even if it accurately represented Jesus' teachings, conveying his exact words, even then the problem of accurate translation would still exist.

Just as one with a scientific training is required to translate scientific writings, so too with mystic literature. For only a mystic will really understand the mystic meaning and the import behind the words. The rest of us, at best, will only catch a hint of the meaning, depending upon our spiritual perspicacity. In *Luke 17:21*, for instance, the *King James Version* reads, "Behold, the kingdom of God is within you!" Now, all mystics, whatever their creed or faith and whatever their level of attainment, would agree that God is within. So indeed do many other people, Christian or otherwise. However, not all translators of the New Testament share this simple, essential understanding. Hence, Hugh Schonfield, in the *Authentic New Testament*, renders it, "the kingdom of God is right beside you". The *New English Bible* and the *Jerusalem Bible* have Jesus say that "the kingdom of God is among you", the *Revised Standard Version* reads, "in the midst of you" and the *New Testament in Modern English* and the *Unvarnished Gospels* have it as being "inside you".

"Inside you" has the same meaning as "within you", but "among you", "beside you" and "in the midst of you" have different meanings, certainly from a mystic point of view. Now God being within oneself is something readily grasped by most spiritually-minded people, and if such a fundamental mystic truth as this cannot be adequately grasped and translated by New Testament scholars, then it can readily be imagined how easily more esoteric matters could be misunderstood and mistranslated.

For example, only one who is actively seeking mystic experience of God can really understand the meaning of the Greek words translated in the *King James Version* as, "Blessed are the pure in heart: for they shall see God". Most other translations follow this meaning more or less, but the *New Testament in Modern English* strikes out on its own with: "Happy are the utterly sincere, for they will see God."

From a mystical point of view, purity of heart implies not only a complete absence of human imperfection, but complete transcendence of all division and separateness from God. This is a very high mystic state, far beyond that of simply being a tolerably good human being. And though one who is pure is also "utterly sincere", it is clear that the meanings of "pure in heart" and "utterly sincere" are different. Sincerity alone will not bring a soul into the state of mystic union with God, where the soul can be said to see Him. But when a soul is utterly pure, "perfect, even as your Father which is in heaven is perfect", then that soul automatically attains union with God.

Similarly, the "thou shalt not kill"[6] of *Deuteronomy*, mirrored in the "do not kill" of Mark and Luke[7] becomes a prohibition against "murder" in the *New English Bible*, the *New International Version*, the *New Testament in Modern English* and the *Authentic New Testament*. But interestingly, the *Revised Standard Version* and the *Jerusalem Bible* keep to "kill" in all instances. Even the "thou shalt do no murder"[8] of the *King James Version* of Matthew is rendered as "you shall not kill". The phraseology, of course, is significant, as all the translators must have been aware, since 'killing' refers to all life, 'murder' only to human beings. 'Kill', like the statement in *Deuteronomy*, is ambiguous; 'murder' is not.

Browsing through the different translations, then, many such variations can be noted and one sometimes wonders how much the various scholars have knitted their brows purely for the sake of finding individual ways of saying what they conceive the meaning to be, even if their rendering drifts away from the meaning of the Greek text. Simply having the best available Greek text, therefore, does not imply that the translation genuinely reflects its meaning.

There is another side to this discussion. As we have said, the gospels were written in the common Greek of the time and scholars inform us that the gospel Greek is often rough. Now, if any of the sayings and discourses of Jesus given in the gospels are authentic, one assumes that they were originally spoken in Aramaic. 'Rough Greek', therefore, is an observation concerning the Greek translation, not the original words of Jesus.

Masters always communicate in simple language, but that does not mean that their words are without beauty. Simplicity, profundity, wisdom and character are the hallmark of a mystic's manner of speaking, for their aim is to communicate with ordinary people. They are natural poets, with a great gift for conveying things in straightforward yet penetrating language. It seems most unlikely, therefore, that in Jesus' original Aramaic tongue his words would have been as uncouth as some of the modern translations have made them out to be. They would have had a rhythm and beauty to them. It could thus be argued that Tyndale actually restored some of their original charm and poetry.

The matter has a bearing upon the difficult choice of a translation to which this book should turn for the words of Jesus and despite the problems with its underlying Greek text, the *King James Version* has generally been used for New Testament translations, though keeping a careful eye upon the *Revised* and other versions. Generally speaking, the words attributed to Jesus have fared better in transmission than the remainder of the New Testament text, and most importantly, to my mind, the translation of the *King James Version* usually captures the spiritual meaning more beautifully and more precisely than the majority of the modern language versions, some of which are almost grotesque. And when you take away the poetry, you take away much of the ability to convey meaning. Tyndale's English, of course, obscures the stylistic differences between and within the various Biblical documents, but for our present purposes, meaning must be afforded the highest importance and it is also doubtful whether any of the attempts to convey the varying character of the gospels in English translation have actually been successful. For the Old Testament, various versions have been used, particularly the *Jerusalem Bible* for its use of authentic texts and its simple, poetic style.

The Teachings of Jesus and the New Testament

We have come a long way from the earliest days of Christianity and further still from the time and teaching of Jesus himself. We have seen that the early tradition of the gospels, supposed to represent the teachings of Jesus as written down by his disciples, was actually in constant flux and that a question mark hangs over almost everything we read. We have observed how the church authorities have fought over the Bible, have made it illegal for others even to own a copy, and have even killed and murdered in order to assert their own opinions about it. We have noted how the Bible has moved through a multitude of versions and translations, each produced at different times by different people with differing motivations. We have sketched a world where the teachings of a divine Master have receded into the background as human, political, theological, ecclesiastical and every other kind of consideration have gained prominence.

The history of the New Testament would seem to be a microcosm of what has happened in Christianity itself, for this has been the pattern from the very earliest days. It is, as we have pointed out, the result of the human mind moving outward from its inner centre. Moving into external affairs, far away from Jesus' simple yet profound teachings, everything but the personal, inward and truly spiritual search for God has assumed importance. Surely, then, it cannot be maintained that the content of the Bible has been guided by the Holy Spirit, when the imprint of man is so easily discernible? Surely it is begging the question to admit that although formulated by imperfect human be-ings, Christian dogma is still divinely revealed by the Holy Spirit? For where, in all of this manifestly human history, is Jesus' teaching? What relationship does it bear to what he taught?

From all the evidence, it does not seem that the greatest damage to Jesus' teaching took place during the period of flux before the fourth and fifth centuries. Nor are the multitude of copies and translations to be found too much at fault in the dilution of his teachings. It seems more likely that it was those who compiled the gospels who did the initial damage, preserving some while distorting other parts of his teachings, according to their own personal beliefs and understanding. And since much of the evidence for this comes from within the gospels and other New Testament documents themselves, it is time we studied them in greater detail.

NOTES AND REFERENCES

1. *cf. Matthew* 22:29, *Mark* 12:24.
2. *Mark* 12:24.
3. Irenaeus, *Against Heresies* III:XI.8, *AHI* p.293, quoting *1 Timothy* 3:15.
4. E.J. Goodspeed, *MENT* p.101.
5. The first five books of the Old Testament (from *Genesis* to *Deuteronomy*), tradition-ally ascribed to Moses.
6. *Deuteronomy* 5:17, *KJV*.
7. *Mark* 10:19, *Luke* 18:20.
8. *Matthew* 19:18.

CHAPTER THREE

Who Wrote the Gospels?

Cultural Conditioning

It is only when it is accepted that the gospels have passed through the hands of many imperfect human beings like ourselves, with a variety of motivations and interpretations, that it becomes clear that to reach an understanding of what Jesus really taught requires careful and honest sifting. To effectively study the New Testament documents, it is necessary to divest the mind of all feelings concerning their inviolable sanctity. Their meaning may certainly point to something sacred, but no words or documents in themselves are sacred or exhibit perfection. All notions that these texts are inherently perfect and sacred must be put aside.

After centuries of cultural conditioning, this is more easily said than done. One may reject them unconditionally or, at the other extreme, accept them unthinkingly and 'completely'. These attitudes are the easiest. But to study them in detail, retaining one's impartiality, is the most difficult of all, for then one's best discriminative and critical faculties must be used, overcoming the influence of the last two millennia of indoctrination that lurks within the cultural psyche.

To perceive the New Testament in its true perspective, it is also helpful to know something of the social, religious, political and general milieu – the cultural context – of the Graeco-Roman-Judaic world of that period. The international, intellectual atmosphere of Alexandria, the intense and fervent Judaic mood of Jerusalem and Palestine, the mystical and mystery cults of Egypt, Syria, Asia Minor, Mesopotamia, Greece and Rome, the traditional worship of a pantheon of gods, the continual political strife within the Roman Empire – each of these was a world in itself, containing many sub-worlds of thought, belief and feeling. Innumerable crosscurrents continuously interacted and coalesced and it requires considerable effort, as well as flexibility, empathy and objectivity, to enter impartially into the mental atmosphere of those times.

As it was then, so it is now. People are different everywhere and every home is almost a different world. So to study the documents of this period – Biblical or otherwise – with no attempt to understand the manifold strands comprising the atmosphere of the times is an almost meaningless task. Familiarity with the words of the New Testament, translated into any kind of English – modern or antique – does not provide us with a true perception of the context. Rather, over-familiarity blinds us to the need for such an understanding.

Yet, if we are to place our faith in an authority we have never investigated, are we not stretching gullibility to the extreme? Are we sure that simply following the herd will ensure the salvation of our souls? We make a full investigation into matters of this world, in order to form our own opinions and make our own decisions. Yet in matters of the spirit, we hand over the enquiry to others. Is this wise? Does our experience of human nature, past and present, justify such a faith in others? We do not purchase a chair for our house except by personal choice. Yet in matters of the soul and its salvation, we have a deep-rooted tendency to believe whatever is taught to us as children and in many cases hardly give it any further thought at all.

It is true that no cultural or literary research of the past is required in the quest for mystic truth, for such truth lies within oneself. Nevertheless, since so many people in the West are born into a Christian atmosphere and have grown up with these beliefs around them, it can be greatly liberating to one's thought to understand something of one's cultural origins. In search, then, of our religious roots and to help us understand something of the character of the texts containing Jesus' teachings, we consider in this chapter the origins of the four canonical gospels.

Mark, the Roman Gospel

It had always been assumed, on traditional grounds, that the earliest gospel had been Matthew. It is a measure of the power of belief over rationality and observation, then, that it was not until the mid-nineteenth century that scholars, noting that there were many passages in Mark which also appeared in Luke and Matthew, began to suspect that the compilers of Matthew and Luke had both used Mark as a source. That being the case, Mark must have been written before either of them.

Observing, furthermore, that Luke and Matthew also shared many of Jesus' sayings and parables in common, often word for word, they further postulated the existence of a document comprised of Jesus' teachings from which both Luke and Matthew had independently copied. This was called Q, from the German *Quelle* meaning source, Germany being the country from which the first gospel analysts of the eighteenth and nineteenth centuries came.

It is this simple technique of studying parallel passages side by side that has led to some remarkable insights into the origins and interrelationships of these three gospels. In fact, it was because of their similarity and in places their identical wording that scholars coined the term 'the synoptic gospels', meaning those that can been seen from a single viewpoint. Like a teacher faced with evidence that his examination pupils have copied answers from each other, it is possible, with patience, to slowly unravel some sort of a picture of who has been copying what from whom. It is safe to say, however, that no one theory or picture is accepted by all scholars, for there is too much information, too many possibilities and too much tension between faith and rational observation. Moreover, the three or four hundred years of editing, collating and shuffling of the texts which intervened between the original writings and the earliest extant manuscripts have helped to confuse the picture even more. Mark, for example, gained passages from Luke and Matthew, as time went by. It is not surprising, therefore, that there are a number of conflicting scholarly theories and points of view.

Traditionally, it had always been held that Mark had been written in Rome and, in general, scholarly opinion supports this view. The gospel is thought to have been penned by an unknown Roman Christian for his own community, the majority of whom were Greek-speaking, sometime between 65 and 80 AD. That is 35 to 50 years, roughly two generations, after the death of Jesus. But the tradition that it was written by John Mark, described in *Acts* as the companion of Paul and later said to have been an interpreter to Peter, has no historical support, though it is mentioned by a number of the early church fathers. Marcus was, after all, a very common Roman name.

One of the most remarkable aspects of Mark is that it is composed almost entirely of narrative material, much of it miraculous. The writer was clearly a lover of miracle stories for he records very little of Jesus' actual teaching. His simple and direct message is of Jesus the Son of God – demonstrated through his signs and miracles – who was persecuted and crucified for the sins of mankind. Man must repent and be baptized for Jesus would soon be coming again to judge the world. The followers of Jesus would then be saved and the rest would be condemned to hellfire. Observing this simple theme, scholars have conjectured that Mark was written to bolster the faith of an unlettered community of Roman disciples during a period of hardship, perhaps during or after the persecutions of Nero following the great fire of Rome in 64 AD and when it began to seem as if the second coming would never come.

Strangely, Mark makes no mention of any supposed virgin birth. The nativity stories found in Luke and Matthew are completely absent, as in John's gospel. Mark begins as he continues with an abrupt entry into his account of the ministry of John the Baptist (of whom, too, no biographical information is given). Moreover, he ends with an empty tomb – there are no resurrection stories either; these are later additions, as we have already discussed.

For one who was such a lover of the miraculous, these two omissions are surprising, for they would have made good material. It can only be presumed, therefore, that either Mark had not heard of or he did not believe in the virgin birth and the various nativity stories. His omission of the resurrection stories, however, is curious and it has been suggested that the original version did have an ending, but that it was lost early on. It is also possible that the stories which Mark did relate of the period after the crucifixion were unacceptable to other Christian groups and therefore got deleted soon after they were written.

Where Mark got his information is largely a mystery, but some scholars think that they can identify up to seven separate sources from which he drew material,[1] and the structure of the gospel provides considerable evidence for Mark's use of a variety of written and oral sources. For instance, he gives two accounts of the feeding of a multitude,[2] though a study of these anecdotes reveals that they are really variants of the same story.

The significant clues to Mark's Roman origins come mostly from a study of the language, style, content and bias of the gospel itself, some evidence being more abstruse than others. For a start, its Greek is arguably the least polished in the New Testament and is clearly not the work of a natural Greek speaker. It also contains a number of Latinisms and Latin forms of Greek words. It is explained, for example, that Pilate's courtroom is the *praetorium*.[3] The Greek term would have been perfectly clear, but the Latin word makes it more understandable to Roman readers. Again, when explaining that two *lepta* make one *quadrans*, Mark converts the currency unit to that of Rome for the benefit of his local readers ("And there came a certain poor widow, and she threw in two mites (*lepta*), which make a farthing (*quadrans*)"[4]). Likewise, the rank of the Roman soldier present at Jesus' crucifixion is given as *kentyrion*,[5] a simple transliteration of the Latin term into Greek letters. But both Luke and Matthew, though copying from Mark, are more conversant with Greek, and use the Greek *hekatontarkes* to indicate his rank.[6]

It is unsure, however, whether Mark was a native Roman or whether he came from one of the many ethnic communities who lived there, as is common in all international cities. Either way, there is a general scholarly consensus which considers it most unlikely that Mark's gospel was compiled by someone who knew Palestine, for it has some geographical errors which no one who knew the country would ever have made. In chapter seven, for example, Mark reports:

> Returning from the district of Tyre, he (Jesus) went by way of Sidon towards the Sea of Galilee, right through the Decapolis region.
>
> *Mark 7:31, JB*

But while the Sea of Galilee lies some thirty miles to the southeast of Tyre, Sidon lies about 30 miles due north! To have gone to Galilee via Sidon would have meant setting off in entirely the wrong direction (see *figure 2, next page*). And since there was no road from Sidon to Galilee in those days, even if Jesus had gone to Sidon after Tyre, he would have needed to return through Tyre. Moreover, since the region of the Decapolis lay to the south of the Sea of Galilee, he would have had to go to Galilee *before* going to the Decapolis – not *after*! He could not have gone to Galilee *via* the Decapolis as Mark indicates.

Again, there is considerable confusion over the location of the "country of the Gerasenes", where Mark sets his story of Jesus' cure of a man "with an unclean spirit".[7] It will be recalled that the herd of about two thousand pigs into which Jesus is said to have sent the devil (whose name, suggestively, was "Legion") were feeding on a mountainside and subsequently ran down a cliff into the Sea of Galilee and were drowned. The difficulty here is that the town of Gerasa (now Jerash) lies more than thirty miles to the southeast of the southernmost tip of the Sea of Galilee! Matthew, who clearly had a Jewish and probably Palestinian background, changes the name to Gadarenes, derived from Gadara, quite another town altogether, while, in Luke, some ancient manuscripts read Gerasenes and other Gadarenes.

But even this does not really solve the problem, for although Gadara

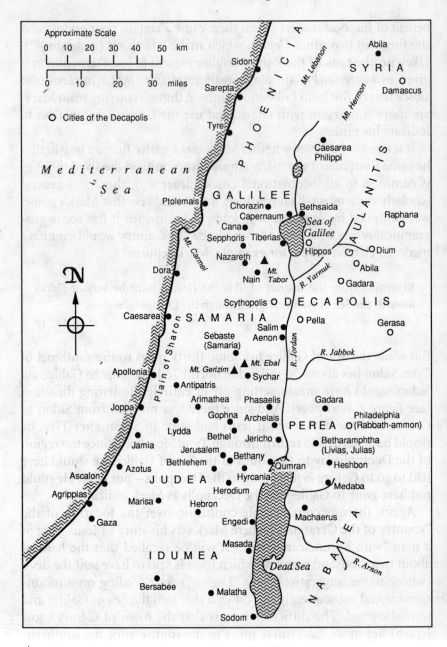

Figure 2. Palestine and the surrounding areas in the time of Jesus.

– one of the cities of the Decapolis and an important town with Greek and Roman traditions – seems to be the city that Mark has in mind, being located on an isolated spur of rock with steep slopes on all sides except the east, it is actually situated some eight miles to the southeast of the Sea of Galilee! Like Gerasa, it is simply too far away.

The Sea of Galilee is certainly enclosed to the east and west by volcanic mountains sloping steeply down either to the water or to a narrow strip of shoreline on the west, but Mark's story cannot easily be accommodated to the terrain, even if it were conceded that the region was named after the town of Gadara. And it is unthinkable that the area was named after the town of Gerasa for it is simply too far away and there were other sizeable towns in between, notably Salim and Pella.

Incidentally, the *King James Version* reads "Gadarenes" in all versions, which is another way of 'solving' the problem. It must also be pointed out that a herd of two thousand pigs would surely be a farmer's nightmare and must be well-nigh unmanageable.

There is also a generally accepted scholarly opinion that the compiler of Mark is unlikely to have been Jewish for, in addition to a marked anti-Jewish tone common to all the gospels, he exhibits a deficient as well as insensitive knowledge of Judaism and Jewish customs. He relates an incident, for example, which he uses as a setting for a selection of Jesus' sayings concerning the difference between spiritual and bodily purity:

> Then came together unto him the Pharisees, and certain of the scribes, which came from Jerusalem. And when they saw some of his disciples eat bread with defiled, that is to say, with unwashen, hands, they found fault. For the Pharisees, and all the Jews, except they wash their hands oft, eat not, holding the tradition of the elders. And when they come from the market, except they wash, they eat not. And many other things there be, which they have received to hold, as the washing of cups, and pots, brazen vessels, and of tables.
>
> *Mark 7:1-4*

Really, the narrative is little more than the record of a complaint made by the Pharisees concerning the fact that Jesus' disciples sat down to eat without washing their hands. This gives Mark a lead-in to Jesus' sayings. The Pharisees, however, are not complaining about matters of domestic hygiene, but of ritual cleanliness according to Jewish custom. Mark informs his reader, "for the Pharisees, *and all the Jews,* except they wash their hands oft, eat not, holding the tradition of the elders. And when they come from the market, except they wash, they eat not." Mark explains the Jewish custom for the benefit of his readers. But he is wrong, for in the time of Jesus such ritual washing was *only* mandatory for the Pharisees and priests – *not* for lay people like Jesus and his disciples.

So although there is no reason from the setting to doubt the authenticity of Jesus' sayings, the events as Mark relates them do not stand up under scrutiny and are unlikely to have taken place. They therefore demonstrate both the fictitious character of the anecdote as well as a deficiency in Mark's knowledge. Furthermore, that Mark feels it necessary to explain Jewish customs presumes he is writing for a non-Jewish readership, and that he sometimes gets it wrong proves his own unfamiliarity with Palestinian Judaism.

Mark also changes material where it suits his purpose. For example, Jesus' teaching on divorce as given by Mark cannot be authentic for it only makes sense in a Roman setting. According to Mark, Jesus says:

> Whosoever shall put away (divorce) his wife,
>   and marry another, committeth adultery against her.
> If a woman shall put away (divorce) her husband,
>   and be married to another, she committeth adultery.
>
> *Mark 10:11-12*

The latter comment, however, would have been irrelevant and incongruous in a Jewish setting, at least in Palestine, where women had no rights of divorce over their husbands. That the saying seemed unlikely to its readers more familiar with Palestine is witnessed by the treatment given it by Luke and Matthew when incorporating it into their own compilations. Luke corrects the mistake by simply omitting the second sentence,[8] while Matthew adds to the saying, providing an excuse for a man to divorce his wife, also changing the second sentence altogether to bring it into line with Jewish custom:

> Whosoever shall put away his wife,
>   saving for the cause of fornication,
>   causeth her to commit adultery:
> And whosoever shall marry her that is divorced
>   committeth adultery.
>
> *Matthew 5:32*

Mark's error thus leads to two further variants of Jesus' teaching on the matter and, in this instance, we cannot be sure what Jesus actually taught.

There is also the curious timing in Mark's description of Jesus' last two days, something which has been a source of Christian controversy for centuries. Mark describes how "the chief priests and the scribes" wanted to avoid arresting Jesus during the Passover festival, "lest there be an uproar of the people":

> After two days was the feast of the Passover, and of unleavened bread: and the chief priests and the scribes sought how they might take him by craft, and put him to death. But they said, "Not on the feast day, lest there be an uproar of the people".
>
> *Mark 14:1-2*

Passover, or the feast of the unleavened bread, is an eight-day festival beginning with the ritual killing and eating of the Passover or Paschal Lamb on the evening of the "first day of unleavened bread". Following this, according to Jewish tradition, "none of you shall go out at the door of his house until the morning".[9] But Mark describes Jesus as having the last supper with his disciples arranged on that day:

> And the first day of unleavened bread, when they killed the Passover, his disciples said unto him, "Where wilt thou that we go and prepare that thou mayest eat the Passover?"
>
> *Mark 14:12*

There would have been nothing unusual in that, but later that evening, Jesus and his disciples all go to the Garden of Gethsemane where Jesus is arrested. Subsequently, during the same night, he is tried before the Sanhedrin, and on the following morning he is taken to Pilate, examined, sentenced and crucified. So, according to Mark, not only would Jesus have been executed at the very time the Jewish authorities wished to avoid, but there would have been repeated violations of the Passover night by everyone involved in the nocturnal arrest and trial of Jesus, including the chief priests and the members of the Sanhedrin. Whatever the truth of the events concerning Jesus' crucifixion, it is evident that Mark's account is either self-contradictory or indicates an ignorance of Jewish custom, and scholars have come up with a variety of scenarios to try to explain these contradictions, none of which is entirely satisfactory.

Part of the difficulty in reconciling Mark to Jewish custom is that Matthew is clearly uncomfortable with Mark's account. He copies over Mark's story, but omits the explanatory "when they killed the Passover":

> Now the first day of the feast of unleavened bread the disciples came to Jesus, saying unto him, "Where wilt thou that we prepare for thee to eat the Passover?"

> *Matthew 26:17*

But Matthew still has it that Jesus ate the Passover with his disciples on the "first day of the feast", followed by his arrest and trial that night when all orthodox Jews should have been at home. In Luke, at least two different versions of events are found in the various Greek manuscripts, demonstrating the confusions that had arisen in the attempts to make sense of Mark's order of events. Most of the English translations have Luke following Mark's record of events.

John, incidentally, being more interested in the symbolism of the situation, has Jesus crucified at the very time the Passover victims were slain. Hence, John's expression, "Behold the Lamb of God, which taketh away the sin of the world!"[10] So he sets Jesus' last supper with his disciples on the evening before the Passover meal, which avoids any violation of the Passover, but entirely contradicts the synoptic account.

It appears, then, that Luke and Matthew, having no alternative account of the events, had no other recourse but to follow Mark, whatever their personal reservations may have been. So it is Mark – or whoever wrote this part of Mark's gospel – who is accountable for the muddle.

The story of the 'last supper' itself also has its difficulties. Prior to the meal, Jesus has told his disciples that he will be taken from them and crucified. It is also at this meal, according to the story, that Jesus states that one of them will betray him. Now surely such a comment would have come as a bombshell, disturbing the peace of their supper? Yet, in Mark, they go on eating as if nothing had happened, which seems unlikely. Matthew has them break off and discuss who it should be, which is more reasonable, but then Jesus identifies his betrayer as Judas and the other disciples simply let him leave in order to fetch the high priest and his party. Is it not improbable that knowing what Judas was about to do, they would have simply let him go?

In John, the writer tells a different story which avoids Judas being identified, yet subsequently permitted to leave, for Jesus' conversation with Judas is private. John also relates that none of the disciples realized what Jesus meant when he said to Judas, "That thou doest, do quickly." This seems more likely, but it also makes the two stories quite incompatible. And if no one overheard Jesus' conversation with Judas, how did it ever get recorded in John's gospel? Even after the betrayal, the differences between the stories do not cease, for while Mark and John say nothing on the matter, Matthew concludes his story with Judas hanging himself[11] and Luke – in *Acts* – records that Judas died from an accidental fall.[12]

These kind of discrepancies and incongruities – and there are many of them – are characteristic of the gospels, as we will note from time to time. In fact, when Luke and Matthew copy from Mark, the process of diversification can be observed in action.

Christianity was still only in its earliest days and such inconsistencies show that we are dealing with stories that spread in the manner of folklore, not as the oral or written history of an established tradition passed on with attention to accuracy and correct recall. When a story is related to others, it automatically undergoes modification and embellishment. The names of places and people may get changed and even the central character may vary. The same jokes told by the English about the Irish are related by the Americans of the 'Polacks', while the Irish tell them of the 'Kerrymen'. With stories of a religious nature, entirely different groups may claim the incident as being of their leader or Saviour. Everyone likes a good story and the best storytellers always recast their material, adding their own touches before passing it on, for no one is expected to take their stories as historical. Yet this is what has happened with many of the incidents related in the Christian gospels.

Many of the gospel stories are of a kind that was common in the literature and legends of the period. Miracle stories and signs from God are commonplace in the Old Testament, for example. It would also seem to have been a common facet of religious belief, then and even now, that a departed Saviour or holy man could go on helping others. Cult heroes and gods were routinely invoked for their powers of intervention in human affairs. Asclepius, the renowned physician of Greek and Roman mythology, was held to possess great healing powers long after his departure from this world (if indeed he ever existed). Similarly, a number of the mystery religions of Egypt, Greece and Rome put their faith in holy men of the past who, like Jesus, were said to have led miraculous lives, suffered tragic deaths and retained the ability to help their followers in the present life, as well as taking care of them after death.[13] In modern times, many departed Eastern mystics have similar miraculous stories related of them, while in the West, people make pilgrimages to the shrines of holy men and women of Christendom in the hope of healing or blessing, often relating tales of miraculous cures.

In all analyses and theories designed to account for the gospel content, there is always room for error, and no one really knows how Mark or any of the other gospels got into the condition in which we find them. A great many books have been written in the last two centuries, analyzing and theorizing about the New Testament documents. This alone demonstrates how unclear the picture is, and the more one studies it, the more unclear do its details become, for there are so many possibilities, and scholars are clever enough to have thought of many of them. But one thing on which almost all are agreed is that whoever put the gospel of Mark together was not an eyewitness of the events he reported. Nevertheless, however it came into existence, Mark unwittingly set a precedent which was followed by many others until almost every group had their own gospel.

Matthew – A Gospel for Jew and Gentile

Probably one of the main reasons why the compiler of Matthew's gospel used Mark as a source was that it constituted the only significant collection of such material available at the time. Yet it was evidently in need of expansion, to include more of Jesus' teachings. Contrasting sharply with that of Mark, Matthew is generally reckoned to have been compiled and edited by someone with a tolerably good command of Greek. Who he was is not known, but it was certainly not Matthew the tax collector disciple of Jesus, otherwise known as Levi. It has been commonly conjectured that this gospel originated somewhere in Asia Minor, possibly Antioch, one of the earliest centres of Christianity. Matthew's gospel is designed to appeal to both Jews and Gentiles, matching the population of Antioch at that time.

A strong Jewish element is observable throughout Matthew, leading some scholars to presume that the author had a Jewish background. Others, of course, suggest otherwise, some supposing that he may have once been a convert to Judaism. Its date is normally reckoned to be sometime between 80 and 95 AD, certainly after that of Mark, which is used as a source, often being copied over verbatim.

Providing evidence of his Judaic background is Matthew's continual use of quotations from the Old Testament. He resorts to them far more than the other gospel writers, structuring his entire work around them, a great many of his passages and stories being designed to lead up to variations on the formula:

> Now all this was done, that it might be fulfilled
> which was spoken of the Lord by the prophet, saying ...
>
> *Matthew 1:22*

Matthew fervently believed in Jesus as the promised Messiah, according to his interpretation of Biblical prophecies. The fact that many of these Biblical citations were taken out of context and actually meant something quite different did not deter him. In fact, he would have been only following a Jewish practice of the time if he had created stories to fit the prophecies, this having been an acceptable way of writing history. In all, Matthew uses around forty short Biblical quotations in order to 'prove' his various points.

All writers have reasons for writing: there is no action without motivation. And once it is recognized that Matthew's primary motive was the promotion of Jesus as the Jewish Messiah, according to that "which was spoken by the prophet", his compilation becomes more or less understandable. Of the three synoptic compilers, Matthew is also the best as a source of Jesus' sayings for while Mark uses very little teaching material, and Luke likes to paraphrase, Matthew is generally more faithful to his sources, though he is not averse to tinkering with a text if it does not quite say what he wants it to.

Matthew rearranged his material into general subject areas, creating five main sections, each containing a major portion of Jesus' teaching, the first being the Sermon on the Mount. The nativity story and the passion and resurrection events then supply a prologue and an epilogue. A source analysis reveals more of the distinct components making up these sections.

Firstly, there is Mark, whose rough style Matthew improves where he can. Matthew divides Mark's narrative into five major portions, frequently altering Mark's order of events, and slotting in five sections of Jesus' teachings, using various editorial seams and devices. Matthew's setting for the Sermon on the Mount, for instance, comes from Mark, who at this point has Jesus select his twelve disciples – an incident which Matthew reserves for later, using it to introduce another appropriate selection of Jesus' sayings.[14] Sometimes, Matthew also adjusts certain stories to fit some section of teaching he wishes to introduce. At others, the teachings are adjusted to fit the stories.

The teaching material itself comes in part from Q, the Greek source of Jesus' sayings and parables which Matthew shares with Luke. But there is also *M*, Matthew's special material, comprising both narrative and teaching. Part of *M* may have actually belonged to Q, but because it is not used by Luke it is difficult to determine its origin. At any rate, *M* itself is more than likely to have been comprised of two or more sources.

Finally, there are the nativity and infancy stories of Jesus, as well as Matthew's narration of the passion, crucifixion and resurrection. All these elements have come from separate sources, including anecdotal material passed orally from individual to individual.

Q is a document of continuing interest to our theme for it was a major source of Jesus' teachings, devoid of anecdote and miracle, and we will have more to say about it later. For the present, it is worth recording that the fourth-century Eusebius, who wrote the first 'history' of Christianity during the reign of the Emperor Constantine, comments that Papias, a mid-second-century Bishop of Hierapolis, wrote five volumes, entitled *The Sayings of the Lord Explained*. None of these volumes have come down to us, but Eusebius does record him as commenting:

Matthew compiled the *Sayings* in the Aramaic language, and everyone translated them as well as he could.

Papias, in Eusebius, History of the Church, HC p.152

It rings true that such an obviously educated and literate man as the tax collector Matthew should have written down and collected the sayings of his Master in their original language. Who would not wish to keep a record of his Master's words, so full of love, wisdom and inspiration? And naturally, Greek, Syriac and Coptic-speaking followers would have wanted their own translations. It is quite possible, therefore, that some or all of these sayings comprised the document called Q and that Matthew's gospel is credited to Matthew because it contains many of the sayings, parables and discourses which he collected.

Though there is no reason to doubt Eusebius in this instance, it should perhaps be pointed out that his work is sometimes suffused with a rose-tinted glow arising from Christianity's recent acceptance by the Emperor. Partially because of this, he is notoriously unreliable, mixing miracle, history and pure romance in his work. He is, however, the only witness to a number of earlier writings, especially of the Christian fathers, and he preserves some interesting and often tantalizingly incomplete material. In his defence, it must also be said that his sources must have been greatly limited, though far greater than our own today. Moreover, he was writing history according to the standards of his own times, not ours.

Matthew also demonstrates a tendency to heighten the miraculous, at least of those miracle stories he has found in Mark, where we have a control on his use of sources. Thus, Mark's single Gadarene demoniac and his one blind man at Jericho get doubled in Matthew's version.

Despite his Judaic background, Matthew also exhibits a marked antipathy to Pharisaic Judaism, a feature which has proved useful in setting an earliest date for the text. Prior to the sack of Jerusalem and the destruction of the Temple in 70 AD, the Pharisees played a background role to the Temple priests and Judaism was centred on the Temple. The aftermath of 70 AD, however, saw the rise of the Pharisees as the leaders of Judaism, though it would naturally have taken some time to come about. This, together with indications in Matthew of significant church organization, as well as current Roman persecution, has suggested a date during the first half of the AD 90s. The rule of Emperor Domitian (81-96 AD), notable for developing the Imperial cult of Emperor worship, was significant as the first major period of Christian persecution throughout the Empire, for the Christians refused to accept Domitian as a god. Many others probably declined to do so, too, but adopted a more pragmatic attitude towards it, in the interests of survival. Some scholars, however, put the date of Matthew as late as 135 AD, linking its references to persecution with the second Jewish revolt of 132-135 AD.

Unique to Matthew and helping to date this gospel is an interesting story and comment concerning the popular Jewish explanation of Jesus' disappearance from the tomb. Matthew relates that after the crucifixion, when Jesus' body had been placed in a sepulchre, the Roman guards first sit through an earthquake and then witness an angel of the Lord (whose "countenance was like lightning, and his raiment white as snow"[15]) roll back the stone from the tomb and sit on it. According to the story, "they did shake, and became as dead men".[16] As well they might!

Jesus' actual resurrection and exit from the tomb is not recounted, but at the conclusion of their watch the soldiers go into town and tell' the chief priests what had happened. At this, they are bribed with large sums of money to spread the story that Jesus' disciples had come during the night and removed his body from the tomb, while they (the soldiers) had slept. Matthew then adds, "And this saying (story) is commonly reported among the Jews until this day."[17]

Quite apart from the unlikelihood of anyone accepting a bribe if they had just witnessed such an obviously divine event, Matthew's story is clearly told to counter the prevalent belief that Jesus' body had disappeared from the tomb because some of the disciples had come and taken it. And his comment, that the story was related "until this day" presumes that a considerable period had elapsed between the supposed events and Matthew's writing of them.

It can also be asked, with justification, who actually recorded what had happened if the only eyewitnesses were bribed to say otherwise? And why did the Roman soldiers report to the Jewish chief priests rather than their own superior officers? There seems little doubt that the story is a later – as well as somewhat implausible – fabrication.

Matthew's characteristic use of Biblical citations is nowhere more evident than in his nativity story. True to his style and disposition, it is told "that it might be fulfilled". The details are all required by the 'prophecies' he is using. Thus, Jesus has to be born in Bethlehem because of the verse in *Micah* which he believes refers to Jesus:

> And thou Bethlehem, in the land of Juda,
> art not the least among the princes of Juda:
> For out of thee shall come a Governor,
> that shall rule my people Israel.
> *Matthew 2:6; cf. Micah 5:1*

Matthew has no problem with that for, in his version, Bethlehem is where Joseph and Mary live – in a house. However, he has three further 'prophetic' verses that he wants to fit in. After Jesus' birth, presumably taking place at their home, he therefore sends Joseph, Mary and Jesus into hiding in Egypt to escape from Herod the King who has heard through "wise men from the east" that the "King of the Jews"[18] has been born. This, says Matthew, is:

> That it might be fulfilled
> which was spoken of the Lord by the prophet,
> saying, "Out of Egypt have I called my son".
> *Matthew 2:15; cf. Hosea 11:1*

Herod then slaughters all the children of two years and under in Bethlehem and the surrounding area, "so that it might be fulfilled, according to the prophet Jeremiah":

> In Rama was there a voice heard, lamentation, and weeping, and great
> mourning, Rachel weeping for her children, and would not be comforted,
> because they are not.

Matthew 2:18; cf. Jeremiah 31:15

Leaving aside the fact that Matthew's quotations are taken out of context, the difficulty with this story is that however tyrannical Herod the
Great might have been, he would not have got away with mass infanticide. The Romans would hardly have turned a blind eye to it and the
people would certainly not have tolerated it. Moreover, there is absolutely no record of such an outrageous act anywhere in the history of
the period, neither in Josephus (who carefully compiled a list of all his
other crimes), nor anywhere else, not even in Luke. The general history of the period is quite well recounted and such a horrific deed
would not have gone unrecorded. Matthew's idea for such a slaughter
probably came from Pharaoh's killing of the first-born when he wished
to get rid of the infant Moses whom he had been informed would be
the cause of his downfall. In any case, can one really believe that God
would have permitted the birth of His Son to be heralded by such
cruelty?

Matthew then continues, weaving in his last prophetic quote as the
last line of his nativity story. When Herod has died, Joseph comes to
hear of it from an angel in a dream and returns to Palestine. And they
go and live in Nazareth. Why Nazareth? –

> That it might be fulfilled,
>   which was spoken by the prophets,
> "He shall be called a Nazarene."

Matthew 2:23

The major problem with this quote is not that it has been taken out of
context, but that no one can find any context for it at all! It does not
exist in any of the known Old Testament or allied apocryphal writings.

They have therefore concluded that the nativity story is one of the
elements introduced by Matthew to appeal to his Gentile readers. A
number of scholars have pointed out that to a Jew, the idea of God
fathering a child would have been repugnant,[19] for in the Hellenistic
world where the gods indulged in all manner of dubious activities involving both each other and human beings, such an idea would have
been quite acceptable.

Matthew's account is fundamentally different from that of Luke.

Luke also has Jesus born in Bethlehem. But since, according to him, Joseph and Mary actually lived in Nazareth *before* the birth of Jesus, Luke has to present a plausible reason for their journey to Bethlehem. So firstly, he relates how Jesus and John were born during the reign of Herod the Great. He then continues:

> And it came to pass in those days, that there went out a decree from Caesar Augustus, that all the world should be taxed. (And this taxing was first made when Quirinius was governor of Syria.) And all went to be taxed, every one into his own city. And Joseph also went up from Galilee, out of the city of Nazareth, into Judaea, unto the city of David, which is called Bethlehem; (because he was of the house and lineage of David:) to be taxed with Mary his espoused wife, being great with child.
>
> *Luke 2:1-5*

Everyone, of course, knows Luke's endearing story. When they get there, there is no room in any of the hotels and they have to make do with a stable. There, Jesus is born and laid in a makeshift crib – a manger. But the problem is this. While Herod the Great is known to have died in 4 BC, direct Roman rule did not come about until 6 AD. The first Roman census of the Judaea, conducted for the purpose of levying taxes, was indeed organized by Quirinius, the Roman governor of nearby Syria, but it could never have happened in the reign of Herod the Great nor even immediately afterwards. It could not have taken place before 6 AD, when Judaea was annexed by Rome. The census conducted by Quirinius is even recorded by the Jewish historian, Josephus, as being an unprecedented event of that year[20] arousing considerable feeling amongst the Jews, culminating in a local uprising. In fact, Quirinius held no office in Syria during Herod's reign. He did not take up the governorship of Syria until 6 AD. Nor is there any historical record of Augustus Caesar (63 BC-14 AD) ever ordering a census of the *entire* Roman Empire ("the whole world"). It would have been an unnecessary administrative nightmare. There may indeed have been local censuses in most of the Roman provinces, but not in Judaea until after its annexation. On several counts, therefore, Luke's story is simply an impossibility. His dates are adrift by at least ten years.[21]

Moreover, Luke – having less interest in fulfilling any passages from the scriptures – records no slaughter of the children and no trip to Egypt. He also has no wise men, but he does have some shepherds tending their flocks on the hill sides above Bethlehem. But does Luke's narrative read like reality or romance? At the birth of Jesus, they are first frightened by the appearance of an angel, followed by a "multitude of the heavenly host praising God". Recovering their composure, with one accord they leave their sheep to the mercies of the night and set off for Bethlehem, where – despite the large crowd and with no star to guide them – they immediately find the right stable.

Now, not only are the two stories of Matthew and Luke unlikely, reading more like legend, but some aspects of them are quite clearly incompatible as well as historically impossible. And the combination narratives told at Christmas and taught to children are yet a further development of the legends. The fact is that these two tales demonstrate that Matthew and Luke are unreliable, even if we excuse Luke's mistakes as those of an enthusiastic but amateur historian. How, then, can we be sure of anything else they may tell us in their gospels?

Luke-Acts – Christianity's First Defence

If Mark was written for Roman Christians undergoing hardship, and Matthew tried to reach out to both Jew and Gentile, Luke's primary, though not his only, purpose was to present Christianity to Roman officials as a harmless, natural and indeed the true extension of Judaism. He also tries to explain how it had come to be that there were so many Christians throughout the Empire. The point was that Judaism was tolerated within the Roman Empire, while Christianity was not. So if it could be shown that Christianity was actually the true expression of Judaism and that the Jews had actually gone astray in not recognizing Jesus as the Messiah, then Christians should be given the benefit of Roman tolerance.

Luke wrote a two-volume book that would have taken up two large papyrus rolls, but New Testament tradition has commonly divided them into the gospel and the *Acts of the Apostles* (not Luke's title), separating the two halves by placing John between. It has been pointed out many times, however, that this destroys the unity of the book and distracts the reader from understanding Luke's main purpose.[22]

Like Matthew, Luke's gospel is derived from a number of sources. He himself notes at the very outset, in a preface that encompasses both his books, that there were "many" of them:

> Forasmuch as many have taken in hand to set forth in order a declaration
> of those things which are most surely believed among us....
>
> *Luke 1:1*

Luke's account is addressed to "most excellent Theophilus", but who Theophilus was is pure conjecture. He could have been a literary device, a character of Luke's own invention, for the name means 'lover of God', but the scholarly consensus is that he was a well-placed Roman official, unlikely to have been a Christian, but one whom Luke identified, perhaps through personal acquaintance, as having the power to prevent the persecution which had broken out. Luke continues:

> It seemed good to me also, having had perfect understanding of all things from the very first, to write unto thee in order, most excellent Theophilus, that thou mightest know the certainty of those things, wherein thou hast been instructed.
>
> *Luke 1:3-4*

It has been suggested that wanting to tell Theophilus "the certainty of those things wherein thou hast been instructed" probably meant hearing Luke's version of Christianity, as opposed to the negative rumours and tales by which Theophilus had previously been informed. Luke's intention is to set the record straight, to tell Theophilus the truth of the matter, as he sees it. Hence his claims to have "had perfect understanding of all things from the very first" though other translations give the words a slightly different meaning. The *Revised Standard Version*, for example, has "having followed all things closely", while the *Authentic New Testament* translates "as I have carried out a thorough investigation of all circumstances from their beginnings".[23]

Pursuant to this task, Luke portrays all the Roman personalities in his stories, including Pilate, in a favourable light, demonstrating that the Romans had been fair-minded towards Jesus and the Christians. A Roman centurion is praised by Jesus for his faith. By using, in an exhortation to repentance, the example of some Galileans who had met their end at Pilate's hand, Jesus implies that Pilate had been in the right. And, in *Acts*, much is made of Paul's Roman citizenship, for he appeals to Caesar to escape certain death at the hands of Jerusalem's priestly hierarchy. By these and other pro-Roman angles, Luke seeks to please the ear of his Roman audience.

It is partly from an observation of the pro-Roman and apologetic angles that Luke is usually dated in the last decade of the first century, probably written around the same time as Matthew, this being the time of the Domitian persecutions. One of Luke's famous modifications to Mark helps us to date it after the long seige of Jerusalem and its ultimate fall in 70 AD. For in a passage commonly dubbed the 'mini-apocalypse', supposed to foretell the end of the world, Luke unashamedly puts into Jesus' mouth:

> And when ye shall see Jerusalem compassed with armies,
> then know that the desolation thereof is nigh.
>
> *Luke 21:20*

Writing 'prophecy' after the event was a common pastime in the ancient world, providing useful information to scholars seeking clues to date a document. How much of this apocalyptic prophecy, if any, is really attributable to Jesus is naturally a matter of debate, but this insertion – found only in Luke – most certainly is not.

Luke's gospel sources parallel those of Matthew. He has nativity and resurrection stories and he uses Mark and Q. He also has one or more unique sources, commonly designated L. Unlike Matthew, Luke does not generally go in for major rearrangement of his source material, but incorporates it in blocks. His insertions from Mark, for example, usually follow Mark's order. But having higher literary aspirations than Mark or Matthew, he takes more editorial liberty with his sources in the interests of both style and of the meaning which he wanted to convey, frequently paraphrasing, truncating and tailoring. All the same, his text is notoriously uneven in style, as he moves from source to source, though such features usually get lost in translation.

The way in which Luke handles his sources can be seen from the passage in Mark where Jesus advises his disciples to serve each other in a spirit of humility. Mark sets the passage shortly before the last supper, where it comes as Jesus' response to the sons of Zebedee who have asked for preferential treatment "in thy kingdom". Mark's version reads:

> But Jesus called them to him, and saith unto them,
> "Ye know that they which are accounted
>   to rule over the Gentiles exercise lordship over them;
>   and their great ones exercise authority upon them.
> But so shall it not be among you:
>   but whosoever will be great among you,
>   shall be your minister:
> And whosoever of you will be the chiefest,
>   shall be servant of all.
> For even the Son of man came not to be ministered unto,
>   but to minister, and to give his life a ransom for many."
>
> *Mark 10:42-45*

Matthew follows Mark in both wording and narrative sequence. Luke, however, cuts the story of the sons of Zebedee wishing to rule with Jesus in his kingdom, replacing it with a single and more general introductory sentence. He then edits Jesus' reply and relocates it during the last supper:

> And there was also a strife among them,
>> which of them should be accounted the greatest.
> And he said unto them, "The kings of the Gentiles
>> exercise lordship over them;
>> and they that exercise authority upon them are called benefactors.
> But ye shall not be so:
>> but he that is greatest among you, let him be as the younger;
>> and he that is chief, as he that doth serve.
> For whether is greater, he that sitteth at meat,
>> or he that serveth? Is not he that sitteth at meat?
> But I am among you as he that serveth."
>
> *Luke 22:24-27*

Luke has paraphrased and changed the meaning quite considerably. Perhaps he thought it unlikely that the sons of Zebedee would really have made such a request or perhaps he did not want to portray Jesus' close disciples in such a way to his Roman audience. Whatever his reasons, he changed the meaning of words attributed to Jesus, and since this is characteristic of him, and he does it again and again, it means that unless we have a means of checking on his source, we can never really be sure of what Luke writes.

This is particularly true when dealing with the sayings of Jesus taken from Q. As a result, from a comparative evaluation of their methods, it is generally said that the reconstruction of Q can proceed by following Luke's order, but Matthew's wording. Matthew is thus a better testimony than Luke to the actual words of Jesus, though Matthew, too, is not without his failings.

Luke, like all the gospel writers, also inserts brief incidents or has some individual or group ask a question, usually to introduce a selection of Jesus' sayings or to break up what was felt would otherwise have been too long a discourse. This technique is particularly apparent when Luke and Matthew are introducing the same sayings from Q. Following Mark's pattern, they were essentially writing a story, but since Q was almost completely lacking in narrative, it was necessary for them to create appropriate settings for Jesus' sayings, however briefly sketched. And since they were not copying from each other but from an independent manuscript, their settings and arrangement of material differ. Thus, while Matthew locates the beatitudes and the Lord's Prayer together with other long sections from *Q* in his 'Sermon on the Mount', the same sayings are found scattered throughout Luke's gospel in different places and in different settings. The beatitudes, for example, appear in a 'Sermon on the Plain' while the Lord's Prayer is found elsewhere, introduced with:

> And it came to pass, that as he was praying at a certain place, when he ceased, one of his disciples said unto him, "Lord, teach us to pray, as John also taught his disciples."
>
> And he said unto them, "When ye pray, say, ..."
>
> *Luke 11:1*

Such introductions, normally bearing a relationship to the sayings which follow, are amongst the commonest editorial devices of the gospel writers, especially Matthew and Luke. Usually, they are easily spotted and become even more apparent when Jesus' response seems inappropriate or unlikely. The interjection then sits awkwardly in its surrounding material.

In Matthew, for example, there is a long passage, probably originating in *Q*, comprised of 'woes' directed against the hypocrisy and spiritual ignorance of the "scribes and Pharisees". Matthew introduces it with a simple one-liner:

> Then spake Jesus to the multitude, and to his disciples.
>
> *Matthew 23:1*

And he goes on to reproduce the passage, which takes up the full thirty-nine verses of chapter 23, including:

> Woe unto you, scribes and Pharisees, hypocrites!
> For ye make clean the outside of the cup and of the platter,
>> but within they are full of extortion and excess.
> Thou blind Pharisee, cleanse first that
>> which is within the cup and platter,
>> that the outside of them may be clean also.

> Woe unto you, scribes and Pharisees, hypocrites!
> For ye are like unto whited sepulchres,

> which indeed appear beautiful outward,
> but are within full of dead men's bones,
> and of all uncleanness.
> Even so ye also outwardly appear righteous unto men,
> but within ye are full of hypocrisy and iniquity.
>
> *Matthew 23:25-28*

The meaning is clear: internal purity of mind is far preferable to external cleanliness, which may only serve to hide the dirt that lies within.

Luke's treatment of this passage contains a more significant narrative. He has Jesus sit down to eat with a Pharisee who observes that Jesus does not wash before eating, a custom followed by Jewish priests upon which we have already commented. In response, Jesus delivers his discourse against the Pharisees. The thirty-nine verses of Matthew, however, are truncated to fourteen and the language is also softened to some extent.

It would seem that Luke does not wish to spoil his portrayal of Jesus and the Christians as good citizens, of no harm to Rome, by the inclusion of material that would have Jesus branded as a local troublemaker. The Romans, it should be pointed out, had struggled with a century of revolt in Palestine, off and on, culminating in the sack of Jerusalem not long before. A number of political leaders had even proclaimed themselves as the Messiah, sent to liberate Palestine from Roman rule. The Roman authorities were therefore particularly allergic to Messianic claims, for all too frequently they meant trouble.

The parallel part of Luke's version reads:

> And as he spake, a certain Pharisee besought him to dine with him: and he went in, and sat down to meat. And when the Pharisee saw it, he marvelled that he had not first washed before dinner. And the Lord said unto him,

> "Now do ye Pharisees make clean
> the outside of the cup and the platter;
> but your inward part is full of ravening and wickedness.
> Ye fools, did not he that made that which is without
> make that which is within also?"
>
> *Luke 11:37-40*

One can imagine the response of a Pharisee who, having invited Jesus to dine with him, suddenly found himself under personal attack from his guest, and the story seems improbable. It is difficult to believe that Jesus would have done such a thing, and this feeling is correct for, as we have seen, Luke, like Matthew, has invented a setting for an otherwise independent selection of sayings attributed to Jesus.

It is possible, of course, that Luke used an alternate version of this tirade against the Pharisees, which must surely have been famous amongst the Christians of that time for its electric and plain-speaking content. It is also difficult to know, as with probably all of the sayings attributed to Jesus, whether these words came from Jesus, from one of his disciples or from someone else altogether. But the point is that Matthew and Luke have both invented their own settings for the sayings. The narratives are fictitious and the sayings have been modified.

The authorship of Luke and *Acts* has traditionally been assigned to Paul's companion of the same name. Paul mentions him affectionately in *Colossians* as "Luke, the beloved physician",[24] and there is a reference to him in *2 Timothy* ("only Luke is with me"[25]), though the authenticity of that letter is uncertain. But if this Luke really was the author, he would have been an old man by the time he decided to write his major work, for Paul's travels took place in the 50s, forty years or so before. Luke is said to have been a physician of Antioch in Syria and his two texts reveal the author to have been Greek-speaking with an excellent knowledge of Jewish customs and in close contact with Hellenistic Judaism. So the two are not incompatible.

Perhaps one of the sources of *Acts* was a diary written by Luke, from which the whole derived its name, much as Matthew's gospel may have acquired its name from the sayings of Jesus compiled by Matthew. *Acts* is certainly curious for its usage of 'we' in chapters 16, 20-21, and 27-28, where it relates events in the first person, the latter two chapters narrating the story of Paul's journey to Rome. But the general scholarly opinion is that the compiler was simply being faithful to his source, uncharacteristically copying it across as he found it. The sources of *Acts* and how Luke uses them are naturally more difficult to determine than those of his gospel, for there are no other versions of the same material, and – as always – there is doubt as to their authenticity.

Luke's gospel is also notable for including otherwise unrecorded information about John the Baptist, possibly derived from a lost book of the 'Nativity of John', a book produced by some of the later followers of John, claiming him to have been the Messiah.[26] Luke is the only source of information on John's birth and parentage, informing us that he had been Jesus' cousin, and relating the story of John's conception and consequent birth to a woman who was getting on in years and had not previously been able to conceive. Nowhere else in early Christian literature is a miraculous birth claimed for John the Baptist as well as Jesus. Luke certainly spread a wide net in his search for source materials.

Looking at these two books as a whole, it is clear that Luke's means of defending Christianity was to write its history, as it had so far unfolded. Starting with John the Baptist, he charts its progress through to Rome, the heart of the Empire, with the arrival there of Paul. But at that point his narrative ends, with Paul under house arrest, awaiting trial, but enjoying full liberty of speech and contact with his friends. Whether this was the high point on which Luke wished to leave his story or whether he wrote a third volume, long since lost, is unknown. It is noteworthy, however, that *Acts* is largely devoted to the travels of Paul and after the first few chapters remains exclusively with him. It is really, therefore, the exploits of Paul – its title, the *Acts of the Apostles,* is greatly misleading.

Perhaps it should also be added that there is a school of thought that believes *Acts* to be a fraudulent, second-century composition written to bolster the position of Pauline Christianity. The suggestion is not without supporting evidence, but – as usual – no certain conclusions can be drawn, one way or the other.

Luke's approach to history would naturally have been that of his own period. In the Hellenistic world, writing history was considered more of an art than a science. An extension of the ancient social art of storytelling, historical accounts were expected to be interesting and entertaining, so if the facts were dramatized and embellished, that was only to be expected. The speeches of key characters were a matter upon which the historian himself was judged, as much as the ones who were supposed to have delivered them. Even when the speech was a soliloquy, like Jesus' solitary converse with God in the Garden of Gethsemane, no one asked such awkward questions as to who had been there to make a verbatim record. Everyone knew that it was the historian's creation, based – perhaps – but not always, upon a modicum of fact.

Thucydides, for example, generally reckoned to be the most conscientious of Greek historians according to modern standards, explains in a well-known passage that while he has taken the greatest care to ascertain and record the historical facts as accurately as he could, whenever he relates a speech, he has himself put those words into the mouth of the character which he considered appropriate to the individual and the occasion.[27]

For this reason, there are instances where two historians have written of the same events, each quite knowingly creating their own entirely different speeches for the main protagonists. And the critics would have no doubt discussed, not which was the more accurate, but which the more powerful, emotive and dramatic speech. The historian would therefore invent speeches himself, especially when he had no other source of information.

Plato's dialogues of Socrates come into the same category. While Plato's earlier dialogues may have approximated to the content of Socrates' actual conversations, his later dialogues – written long after the death of his teacher – increasingly contain the thoughts and ideas of Plato himself, put into the mouth of Socrates. At best, Plato's dialogues are a recreation in Plato's style of Socrates' teachings.

Incident and dialogue alike, therefore, were liable to adaptation and invention. As Oxford University New Testament scholar Canon Streeter commented:

> History to all the ancients, except perhaps Thucydides and Polybius, was a branch, not of science, but of letters. Effective presentation was more valued than accuracy of detail. There is hardly a battle in Livy described in a way which would have worked out correctly on the ground – and yet war was the 'leading industry' of Rome. About minor details, no one in those days troubled; what was asked for was the broad facts graphically described.
>
> *B.H. Streeter, FGSO p.388*

Hellenized Jewish historians, like Josephus, adopted the same method, and so it seems did Luke, the approach thus explaining his paraphrasing and invention. According to the customs of the time, he was not being dishonest or unscientific. He was not writing a history for posterity. He was not to know that his writings would become part of the all-time, planetary best seller, one of the cornerstones of a religion in which millions upon millions of people would believe. In fact, many of the early Christians, Luke included, confidently expected an imminent end to the world and would have had no concern with posterity. They had a sense of urgency only to preach their gospel to as many people as they could in the time remaining.

It is more in *Acts* than in his gospel (where his sources acted as a constraint) that Luke uses the Hellenistic style of writing history. Peter, Stephen, Paul and others are all given extensive and eloquent, off-the-cuff speeches to deliver. But a brief study reveals that all these speeches bear the imprint of the writer's mind. They are all in very much the same style. And nowhere is any record ever made of the busy scribes who happened to be in these usually quite impromptu places, taking shorthand notes (though shorthand systems were extant at that time)!

The portions of *Acts* which seem to be the most accurately based upon actual events are those which relate to the travels of Paul. They have less of the miraculous about them and tie in tolerably well with the travel details we can glean from Paul's letters, though, interestingly, neither Luke's gospel nor *Acts* reflect any familiarity with these letters, written some thirty or forty years before. Chapters one to seven, as the *Acts* is presently organized, largely relate stories of the apostles' early ministry, chiefly Peter, ending with a long oration from Stephen in which he includes a synopsis of the entire traditional history of the Jews. Stephen is permitted by a very angry crowd to deliver this oration to them, terminating in his claim to "see the heavens opened, and the Son of Man standing upon the right hand of God". At this they throw him out of the city and stone him, the perpetrators of this violent act temporarily leaving their coats at "a young man's feet, whose name was Saul". Having been introduced, Saul, alias Paul, then occupies centre stage for the remainder of the book, Peter only figuring in a few more of the stories.

It is clear, therefore, that whoever 'Luke' was, his information was deficient as to the lives of Jesus and his apostles. In fact, Peter's main role in *Acts* is to give credence to Paul's ministry to the Gentiles. This, together with its main focus on Paul, is usually considered to reflect the fact that Luke originated from the Pauline branch of Christianity. The real history of Jesus' disciples in Palestine and elsewhere in the Roman Empire, together with the form of Christianity that later evolved from them, is largely unknown. In fact, when mentioned by the later fathers, all of whom seem to have been Pauline supporters, it is commonly in pejorative terms, and their various gospels have vanished leaving little more than a trace.

The Mystic Gospel of St John

John's gospel is of an altogether different character from the synoptics. Presumed even by the early fathers to have been the last of the four, the writer's purpose is primarily to convey the spiritual or mystic teachings of Jesus as he understood them. Even his portrayal of historical events is often subordinated to this purpose and his stories are told in such a way as to impart a spiritual meaning, a number of the familiar synoptic narratives becoming transformed in the process. The major part of this gospel also has a uniformity of style and teaching that is absent from the others.

There is considerable evidence from the gospel itself that the writer was familiar with Mark and probably Luke. In the case of Mark, John actually reproduces some of Mark's more unusual phraseology. Unlike Matthew and Luke, however, he is not copying Mark verbatim. The phrases are more likely to have come into his mind when thinking of particular incidents because of his familiarity with Mark. In the feeding of the multitude, Mark and John, for instance, both speak of "two hundred pennyworth of bread"[28] and the woman who anoints the feet of Jesus is said by both to use "spikenard, very costly" which could have been sold for "three hundred pence".[29]

Additionally, John assigns various names to places and persons left unidentified in Mark and Luke. The unnamed woman in Mark who anoints Jesus' feet is identified as Mary, the sister of Martha. He states that the "certain village" of Luke, where the sisters lived, was Bethany.[30] And at the time of Jesus' arrest, when the servant of the high priest has his ear removed, John furnishes the names of the parties as Peter and Malchus.[31] He also changes the order of events in a number of instances.

Such correspondences and seeming corrections, together with John's approach to the overall message and presentation of these earlier gospels, has led many scholars to conclude that a part of his purpose was to correct and augment these earlier records of Jesus' life and teachings, particularly from a spiritual point of view. Gone, for example, are the genealogies of Jesus, the nativity and virgin-birth stories, the temptation by Satan, the lists of the twelve apostles, the transfiguration and the passion soliloquy in the Garden of Gethsemane. The scribes and the Sadducees are replaced by the more generalized "Jews" or sometimes by the Pharisees alone, while the publicans, demoniacs and others are simply absent. There is no apocalyptic message either – the Jewish expectation of a Day of Judgment and an end of the world overseen by the Messiah is replaced by the quest for "eternal life" while surrounded by the condemnation of sin and death in this world.

Also missing are the familiar sayings and parables of Jesus found in Mark, Luke and Matthew. There is no Sermon on the Mount – or on the Plain. In their place are discourses and dialogues between Jesus and various other parties. And it requires only a brief study of these passages to realize that they have originated in an entirely different mind from the sayings attributed to Jesus in the synoptics. Their style and the thought processes they express are quite distinct. So although there is no doubt that they convey a deeply mystic message, the majority of scholars are agreed that they are the creation of John himself, based upon the teachings of Jesus. Jesus himself never spoke the words at all.

There is nothing unusual in this. John is clearly influenced by Hellenism and – as we saw in Luke – the creation of 'fictitious' speeches and dialogues was an accredited practice in Greek and Roman literature. As New Testament scholar Canon Streeter remarked several decades ago:

> Realizing this, we perceive that the original readers of the fourth gospel would never have supposed that the author intended the speeches put into the mouth of Christ to be taken as a verbatim report, or even as a précis, of the actual words spoken by him on the particular occasions on which they are represented as having been delivered.
>
> B.H. Streeter, FGSO pp.370-371

In John's gospel, the artificial construction of the dialogues make it seem even more improbable that such conversations actually took place. Jesus' various protagonists invariably say exactly the right – or the wrong – thing for Jesus to make the point he wants and for the dialogue to cover the ground its author intends. The "Jews" and Pharisees, for example, are commonly used as a butt. They repeatedly take the external, material and literal viewpoint, only so that Jesus may correct them. Similarly, the long and often beautiful discourses attributed to Jesus are the creation of the author designed to express particular spiritual truths.

This does not mean, of course, that John's gospel does not accurately convey the teachings of Jesus. If its author knew what he was talking about and had thoroughly assimilated Jesus' teachings, he may have conveyed things more accurately than some of the original sayings in Luke and Matthew that have been edited.

For the execution of his purpose, the author's characteristic device is metaphor, allegory and *double entendre*. Even the miracle stories and other events, when closely examined, are either more like parables with a mystical meaning or they are used to introduce a topic around which a spiritual discourse or dialogue is then constructed. In fact, the same is true of certain passages in the synoptic gospels which spring to life and meaning when seen as allegories or metaphors. Such writing was a literary style of the times and had been so for many generations. Many of the Old Testament writings, for instance, have been interpreted allegorically by the Rabbis of old and other commentators too, even the apparently historical portions. In this respect, John represents a fusion of Greek and Jewish cultural traits and this is generally evident throughout his gospel. As New Testament scholar George Milligan pointed out many years ago:

> The fourth evangelist deliberately sets himself to indicate the meaning and bearing of his facts, with the result that his gospel is a study, rather than in the strict sense of the word a history, of the life of Christ.
>
> So prominent indeed is this feature that it has led in certain quarters to the view that the gospel is nothing but a thorough-going allegory in which its writer deliberately invented situations and composed speeches in order to bring home to men's minds more fully the ideal conception of the Christ that had taken possession of him.
>
> *George Milligan, NTD pp.156-157*

John's frequent mystical allusions and double meanings are dealt with in our text as we encounter them, but a few illustrations may be of interest here. We have already noted, for example, that contrary to the narrative of the synoptic gospels, John has Jesus crucified on the day on which the Passover lambs were being sacrificed. This fits his earlier symbolism of Jesus as the "Lamb of God" who is sacrificed for the "sins of the world" and makes sense of his unique symbolic discourse on "eating the flesh and drinking the blood of the Son of God". This treatment of Mark's story suggests that John is indicating the external aspects of Jesus' life and death to be of little importance compared to their spiritual significance. Rather than directly criticize Mark's gospel for its literal interpretations, John's response is positive. He puts forward the spiritual side of things. In fact, his gospel is probably not so much a response to Mark as to the literalization and externalization which he saw spreading throughout Christianity and of which Mark's gospel was only a reflection. But in keeping with the necessities of his times, he rarely lays out his meaning in explicit terms. As Chicago New Testament scholar Donald Riddle once observed:

> He has hidden some of his meanings so successfully that they have been difficult for many of his readers to understand.
>
> *D.W. Riddle, GOG p.234*

Again, Jesus' conversation with the "Syro-Phoenician woman"[32] at Jacob's well is a construct around the metaphors of 'well' and 'water', enabling Jesus to make the distinction between the water of this world and the "Living Water" of the Word.

There are many examples of this kind of dialogue in John's gospel. For instance, when the "Jews" ask, "How knoweth this man letters, having never learned?", John is pointing out that mystics get their knowledge from within and need no outward tutoring. Consequently, Jesus' response of "My doctrine is not mine, but his that sent me"[33] is a continuation of the writer's thought. Jesus, he is saying, received his knowledge and teachings from God, not from what he had been taught in this world.

The use of *double entendre* is also evident throughout the fourth gospel, as in:

> While ye have light, believe in the Light,
>   that ye may be the children of light.
>
> John 12:36

Here, the writer is using multiple plays on the word "light". "While ye have light" means while you are alive in the human form. But it also means while you are with the "light" in the form of the Saviour. In both cases, advises the author through the medium of Jesus, believe in the mystic Light, in God within, seeking Him so that "ye may be the children of light", sons of the Father and true seekers of the inner Light of God.

In many respects, the majority of John's gospel is structured as a long homily or essay on its prologue, which sets out the mystic doctrine of the *Logos* who comes into this world as the "Word made flesh" for the salvation of souls. All the other themes are centred on this short introduction, as will become evident as we proceed. Consequently, John's gospel conveys a primarily mystical message. He pays little attention to the more human aspects of following the mystic path which are covered in Matthew and Luke. The Sermon on the Mount and many of the sayings and parables from Q are concerned with the human struggle of living a spiritual life. John's gospel relates the principles underlying the mystic path. In this way, he also amplifies – perhaps quite intentionally – the earlier gospels by providing the mystical foundation upon which the teachings of Jesus they present were based.

There are, of course, many variant opinions and theories among scholars attempting to account for the character of John's gospel. Some have attempted a source analysis of the type so successful with the synoptic gospels, particularly Matthew and Luke. Others have suggested a 'two author' scenario in which the dialogues and discourses of one party have been chopped up and inserted into the narrative of the other. But this does not readily explain the close integration of narrative and discourse, nor the sense of unity in the dialogues.

It is certainly true that there are ample signs of a later editorial hand at work in John's gospel and it is also possible that parts of the manuscript have become displaced. The last seven verses of chapter fourteen, for instance, leading up to the concluding, "Arise, let us go hence" are followed by a continuation of the discourse and would fit more appropriately as the conclusion to chapter sixteen, where this discourse actually comes to an end. And several other transpositions have been suggested in order to sort out some of the odd sequences in both events and discourses.

There are also a number of places where the same words are repeated as a part of another discourse. Writers tend to repeat certain phrases or ideas in roughly the same words and it may have been that the author of John's gospel composed his work using passages which he had previously written as independent pieces on the theme of the *Logos* and the Son of God. On five separate occasions, for instance, Jesus foretells his imminent departure beginning with the words, "Yet a little while" or "a little while" and, on each occasion, the ensuing sentences are very similar.[34] It is also possible that the writer intended to edit his work but never had the opportunity to do so. Perhaps he died, leaving his work on a collection of tablets or sheets of papyrus and a friend or pupil did his best to arrange them for publication, not wishing to make any major editorial changes but occasionally unsure of the author's intended sequence. But all these possibilities do not detract from the overall feeling that for the most part we are dealing with the work of one individual.

Certain passages in John's gospel, however, are commonly considered spurious, amongst them being the entire last chapter, chapter twenty-one. As long ago as 1641, Hugo Grotius put forward the view that this chapter was the addition of the church at Ephesus, where the gospel is generally presumed to have been written. The reasons are more complex than we can fully discuss here, but some of the more obvious pointers may be observed. To begin with, chapter twenty actually draws the gospel to a close:

> And many other signs truly did Jesus in the presence of his disciples, which
> are not written in this book. But these are written, that ye might believe
> that Jesus is the Christ, the Son of God; and that believing ye might have
> life through his name.
>
> *John 20:30-31*

Up to this point, most of the gospel, certainly of the more spiritual
portions, is demonstrably written in John's style. But the gospel, as we
presently have it, then continues:

> After these things Jesus shewed himself again to the disciples at the sea of
> Tiberias; and on this wise shewed he himself.
>
> *John 21:1*

The last chapter, which scholars have termed the 'appendix', then addresses itself to Christian issues of the time, which we discuss later. It
also presents a different understanding of the nature of the second
coming[35] from the remainder of the gospel. John's description is spiritual in character – that of the "Comforter" or Holy Ghost – while the
second coming in the appendix is material, as in Mark and the other
gospels. The material point of view also has apocalyptic overtones,
inferring an end of the world when Jesus will come again to judge the
world, another belief absent from the remainder of John's gospel. The
same dichotomy, however, is also observable between chapter twenty,
which relates the resurrection appearances, and the dialogues and
discourses where the author explains the rising from the dead in a
specifically spiritual manner.

It seems likely, therefore, that while the majority of the gospel is
attributable to one author of a mystic disposition, other parts have
been added, according to Christian beliefs as portrayed in Mark and
the synoptics, and with which the original author would not have been
in agreement. The major part of the gospel, beginning with the prologue and including the dialogues and discourses which continue up
to chapter seventeen, certainly seem to stem primarily from one author with only a few interpolations and editorial changes. The ensuing
material, mainly narrative in form, relating the arrest, trial and execution of Jesus, could also come from the same author, but the content is
so different that even this is uncertain. But it is unlikely that chapter
twenty and most improbable that chapter twenty-one were written by
the author of the main body of the gospel.

The matter is by no means simple, however, and given the wealth of scholarly theories and suggestions, it is not possible to do full justice to the subject in such a short introduction. What does seem certain is that the spiritual heart of John's gospel has been worked over by later hands and has also received a concluding narrative in keeping with such Christian beliefs as portrayed in the synoptics.

But the question still remains: who wrote the spiritual part of this enigmatic gospel, and who penned the additions? The answer is again unclear and has been the subject of considerable debate. John's gospel itself, as we have it now, is anonymous. It is true that the penultimate verse of the appendix does claim the gospel to be the reminiscences of the disciple "whom Jesus loved"[36] and whom tradition has always identified with John the son of Zebedee, but its last two verses are even more suspect than the appendix itself.

The indications are simple. Firstly, it is unlikely that John would have spoken of himself as the one that Jesus loved in preference to all the other disciples. Secondly, the verse in question is missing from one of the earliest manuscripts, the fourth-century *Codex Sinaiticus*. Thirdly, although the remainder of the gospel is written in the third person, the penultimate verse switches into the first person plural ("we"), while the last verse changes yet again into the first person singular ("I"). The penultimate verse is thus commonly considered to be an addition to the addition and many scholars maintain that last verse comes into the same category as well.

Further information is provided by the three New Testament letters, *1 John*, *2 John* and *3 John*, for they are traditionally attributed to the author of the gospel. *2 John* and *3 John* both identify their writer as "the Elder" or the "Presbyter". But these two letters are so short, containing little teaching material, that the only certain inference which can be drawn from them is that the Elder is a leader whose influence has spread further than his own local community. *1 John*, like the gospel, is anonymous and, unlike the other two letters, is more of an essay under the heading "On the Word of Life", containing many similarities of thought and phraseology to the discourses of fourth gospel. From this it may be presumed that it was written by the author of the fourth gospel or that its author had so immersed himself in the gospel that he expressed himself in the language and idiom of its discourses. But were *1 John* and the spiritual parts of John's gospel written by "the Elder" – and, if so, who was he?

The mid-second-century Papias is quoted by Eusebius as writing in the same extract of both John the son of Zebedee as well as "the Elder John", also describing the latter as a disciple of the Lord.[37] In another passage, Papias speaks simply of "the Elder"[38] as if the title alone were enough to identify him. Clearly, "the Elder" was not only another John, but had been a person of some standing in the early church of Asia Minor. Polycarp, Bishop of Smyrna in Asia Minor and martyred sometime after 155 AD at the age of eighty-six, also claimed to be a disciple of John, describing him as "one who had seen the Lord"[39] – but although he is probably referring to John the Elder, the reference is not definitive.

Now, the fourth gospel is commonly dated at around 90-95 AD, though the indications pointing to such a precise date are very few. Probably the most significant is that since the writer seems to be familiar with Mark and Luke, it must have been written after them. Secondly, for the writer to have spoken of the protagonists of Jesus as the "Jews" suggests a time when Christians and Jews had developed distinct identities. This – it is considered – would not have been until towards the end of the first century.

But presuming that John the Elder saw Jesus as a young man and became his disciple, he would have been in his late seventies, at least, when he wrote the gospel – and if John the Apostle had been the author, he would have been even older. But did John the Apostle live to such an age? According to Irenaeus, John lived at Ephesus, dying at a very advanced age during the reign of the Emperor Trajan (98-117 AD). There is also a late second-century letter preserved by Eusebius (c.260-340) that was sent by Polycrates, the Bishop of Ephesus, to Victor, Bishop of Rome (189-c.199), which states that John the beloved disciple, who had once been a high priest, was buried at Ephesus.[40] Polycrates also says that John was martyred, presumably at Ephesus. But another early document says that John and his brother James were killed by the Jews, which is unlikely to have taken place at Ephesus, and another claims that they were martyred in Jerusalem. If this were so, it must have been before the fall of Jerusalem in 70 AD. So once again, the traditions are confused and even the early Christians were unsure of the provenance of the fourth gospel. The ancient fathers were as liable to convey false information as the gospel compilers themselves.

The situation is further compounded by the need of the ancient churches to ascribe apostolic authority to their local gospels in order to impart an air of authority and authenticity to them, especially in the eyes of other communities. John's gospel was not immediately accepted by the church of Rome, for instance, probably because of its association with John the Elder, and it was necessary for the church of Asia Minor to promote their position. This was possibly the primary motivation underlying the addition of chapter twenty-one and possibly chapter twenty, as well. It also made the fourth gospel more in keeping with the teaching of Mark, the gospel commonly used in Rome. It helped to bring the fourth gospel into line with Christian belief, as depicted in the synoptics and derived from Paul, which was widespread in both the Eastern and Western churches.

There is plenty of evidence that John's gospel was not immediately acceptable to the orthodox church in other areas. Hippolytus, an early third-century Bishop of Rome, found it necessary to write a "Defence of the Gospel and Apocalypse (*Revelations*) of John" – but nobody defends what no one attacks, so his defence indicates controversy over the gospel's acceptability. Gaius, another notable orthodox father of Rome at that time, actually attributes both of these books to the gnostic, Cerinthus (a contemporary of John the Apostle), while the late fourth-century Epiphanius and Philaster speak of others who did so, too. And the attempt of Irenaeus to prove the existence of only four gospels, neither "more in number ... or fewer", presuppose that some people felt that at least one of the four was suspect.

Indeed, part of the purpose of the letter written by Bishop Polycrates of Ephesus to Bishop Victor of Rome was to point out the importance of the Asian church by mentioning John, Philip and other "great luminaries" of the early church in Asia Minor. For Victor, in a moment of arrogance, had excommunicated the churches in Asia Minor for not bowing to the will of Rome and accepting an alternative date for Easter.

One of the problems with the authorship, of course, is that there are too many Johns. There are some passages in the *Book of Revelation*, for example, also attributed to a John, and which bear some relationship to parts of the fourth gospel, but *Revelations* is such a complex and confused document that it is best considered later, on its own.

John's gospel, then, is by no means simple in its construction and even with the detailed analyses of many scholars, it has never been possible to draw any firm conclusions as to how its various elements have been put together. But whatever the truth of the matter, it can definitely be said that the fourth gospel, which we commonly call 'John's', contains some remarkable mystic texts of great beauty and clarity, to which we will have many occasions to refer.

NOTES AND REFERENCES

1. See *The Sources of the Second Gospel*, A.T. Cadoux and *The Gospel of Mark*, B.H. Branscomb.
2. *Mark* 6:30*ff* and 8:1*ff*.
3. *Mark* 15:16.
4. *Mark* 12:42.
5. *Mark* 15:39,44,45.
6. *Matthew* 27:54 and *Luke* 23:47.
7. *Mark* 5:1*ff*.
8. *Luke* 16:18.
9. *Exodus* 12:22, *KJV*.
10. *John* 1:29.
11. *Matthew* 27:5.
12. *Acts* 1:18.
13. See *GOG*, D.W. Riddle.
14. See *Mark 3:13, Matthew 5:1, Matthew 10:1*.
15. *Matthew* 28:3.
16. *Matthew* 28:4.
17. *Matthew* 28:15.
18. *Matthew* 2:1-2.
19. See, for example, D.W. Riddle, *GOG* pp.43-44.
20. See Josephus, *Antiquities* XVIII:26, where he dates it to the "37th year after Caesar's defeat of Anthony at Actium" (in 31 BC).
21. For a full discussion, see *HJPI* pp.399-427.
22. See, for example, H.J. Cadbury, *The Making of Luke-Acts* and D.W. Riddle, *GOG*.
23. *AuNT* p.119.
24. *Colossians* 4:14.
25. *2 Timothy* 4:11.
26. See the introduction to Luke in *AuNT* pp.117-118.
27. See Thucydides, *History of the Peloponnesian War* I:XXII, *TI* p.39.
28. *Mark* 6:37, *John* 6:7.
29. *Mark* 14:3,5; *John* 12:3,5.
30. *Luke* 10:38, *John* 11:1.
31. *John* 18:10, *Luke* 22:50, *Mark* 14:47.
32. *John* 4:5*ff*.
33. *John* 7:14-18.
34. *John* 7:33, 12:35, 13:33, 14:19, 16:16-19.
35. *John* 20:22.
36. *John* 21:20*ff*.
37. Eusebius, *History of the Church* 3:39, *HC* p.150.
38. Eusebius, *History of the Church* 3:39, *HC* p.152.
39. In Eusebius, *History of the Church* 4:14, *HC* p.167; from Irenaeus, *Against Heresies* III:III.4; *cf. AHI* pp.262-263.
40. Eusebius, *History of the Church* 5:24, *HC* p.231.

CHAPTER FOUR

Early Glimpses

How Well Did Jesus Speak Greek?

> And there were certain Greeks among them that came up to worship at
> the feast. The same came therefore to Philip, which was of Bethsaida of
> Galilee, and desired him, saying, "Sir, we would see Jesus." Philip cometh
> and telleth Andrew: and again Andrew and Philip tell Jesus.
>
> *John 12:20-22*

This rather intriguing little passage in John tells us that Philip must
have spoken Greek, for he was the one to whom the Greeks (or Greek
speakers) went when seeking an audience with Jesus. In *Acts*, Philip is
also sent to give discourses to the Samaritans;[1] he discusses Jesus' teachings with a well-placed Ethiopian Jew[2] and is said to live with his family,
including his four daughters, in Caesarea,[3] a Hellenistic city in northwest Palestine. All of these presuppose that Philip could speak Greek
and in John's gospel, by way of explanation, the writer (whoever he
was) asserts that Philip "was of Bethsaida of Galilee". To be compatible
with the statements in *Acts*, one presumes that although he lived in
Caesarea, he had been born and raised in Bethsaida.

Galilee was an area in northern Palestine about 60 miles long and
some 40-50 miles wide, of vague extent in more ancient times but with
borders defined by the Roman administration. The region had a long
history of a heterogeneous population. It was its cosmopolitan inhabitants who prompted the prophet Isaiah to call it "Galilee of the nations" or "Galilee of the Gentiles"[4] – a term which was probably in
common use at the time of Jesus. This meant that many of its citizens
would have spoken Greek, the international language of the times. In
fact, both Philip and Andrew are true Greek names. And since Jesus,
too, is said to have come from Galilee and his father ran a business there,
we are justified in asking how much Greek Jesus might have spoken.

The question can be asked, for instance, as to the language in which Jesus conversed with Pilate[5] or with the Roman centurion at Capernaum?[6] Further, the gospel writers do not speak about interpreters for Jesus, yet he is recorded as travelling in the country of the Gadarenes and the Decapolis.[7] The Decapolis (*lit.* 'ten cities') was a league of ten Hellenistic cities, including Damascus, situated in the northeast of ancient Palestine, established by Pompey in 63 BC and governed by Rome. And their language was Greek. How, then, did Jesus speak with them? It is also said that crowds from Galilee, the Decapolis and Transjordan[8] all followed him. These were all areas where Greek was commonly spoken. So how did he converse with them? And when he met the Syro-Phoenician woman "whose daughter had an unclean spirit",[9] and who is explicitly described as Greek (though this may have applied more to her religion than her language), what language would they have spoken?

A few of these people might possibly have spoken Aramaic, but it is far more likely that they would have conversed in Greek, a language that had been commonly used in that part of the world for the previous three hundred years and was the mother tongue of many.

The gospel compilers presume that there had been no problem in communication, for nothing is ever said about it, by way of explanation. Clearly, to those who lived at that time, the question must not have arisen for otherwise someone, at one time or other, would have added an explanatory gloss to one of these many passages in the gospels. The gospels were themselves written in Greek for the express purpose of communicating with the widest audience of people. From Asia Minor to Rome, Greek was the common language in which to communicate. It is highly likely therefore that not only would Jesus have spoken Greek, but would also have been taught it in the Sanhedrin schools.

After all, if he had a mission to teach so many people, it is likely that he would have equipped himself with the practical means by which to do so. Greek was used in all areas of the Roman Empire at that time.[10] When the Roman authorities wished to make something generally known to all their subjects, announcements were sent out in Greek. Only if it was an official decree would a Latin version be attached. Latin was only used within the higher echelons of the Roman administration; everyone else used Greek. The Emperor Claudius is recorded by Suetonius as having had such a love of Greek that not only had he studied all Greek literature and had even written twenty-eight volumes of history in that language, but he spoke of Greek and Latin as "both our tongues" and "often replied to Greek envoys in the Senate" in Greek.[11]

Jews outside Palestine were largely Hellenistic and would bring Greek with them, when coming to Jerusalem on pilgrimage or business. Palestine was surrounded by Greek-speaking countries and peoples, where Hellenistic culture dominated all aspects of society and life. In fact, the two dynasties of Jewish rulers in the two centuries before Jesus had themselves been greatly influenced by Hellenism and many Greek-speaking, Hellenistic cities existed within Palestine itself. The Herod of the nativity stories, Herod the Great (37-4 BC), modernised the ancient seaport town of Straton's Tower along Hellenistic lines, renaming it Caesarea. He also founded the Hellenistic cities of Antipatris and Phasaelis, to the north of Jericho. Indeed, there were a string of Hellenistic cities, running along the Mediterranean coast.

One of the ten cities of the Decapolis, Scythopolis, once the ancient Palestinian city of Beth-Shean and described by Josephus as "the biggest city of the Decapolis, not far from Tiberias",[12] lay not to the east but to the west of the Jordan, between the river and the Mediterranean, demonstrating how far Hellenistic culture had penetrated into Palestine from the east. Towns such as this naturally acted as social and organizational centres for the surrounding rural community, to which the use of Greek would naturally have spread.

Many of the Hellenistic cities around and within the heart of Palestine had been there for centuries and had always been Greek-speaking. And even though many of the inhabitants were Jews, Greek took precedence over Hebrew and Aramaic. There were a large number of such cities within 125 miles of Jerusalem. The seaport town of Jaffa was less than 50 miles from Jerusalem, while Nazareth was only 20 miles from Tiberias, a city founded by Herod Antipas (4 BC-39 AD) as the capital of Galilee and situated on the western shores of the Sea of Galilee. Tiberias had been built on the site of an ancient burial ground and since no orthodox Jew would live on the site of a desecrated graveyard, Herod had found it necessary to compel people to go and live there. Palestine was therefore so deeply infiltrated with Hellenism and Greek speakers that amongst the general population the Jewish and Hellenistic cultures must have been almost inextricably intertwined.

There is also considerable archaeological evidence that Greek was used throughout Palestine, at that time. It is found on first-century funerary inscriptions, which are often in both Greek and Hebrew or Aramaic, in some areas predominantly in Greek. These are not the tombs of only the rich, the influential and the educated. They are from all strata of society, frequently complete with spelling mistakes, and from their unskilled execution evidently made by the family members themselves rather than professional stonemasons. A marble plaque has also been unearthed, clearly from a burial ground and possibly from Galilee, warning all comers, on pain of capital punishment, not to disturb bodies lying in the tombs. And the warning is in Greek. This presumes that many people would have read it in that language as their mother tongue. There may have been a parallel plaque in Aramaic or Hebrew, too, but evidently Greek was in common use amongst the general public. The notice also presumes that a significant proportion of the general public could be expected to read and, as a consequence, to write.

Greek also appears in mosaics and inscriptions found in Palestinian synagogues of this era. There is a Greek inscription in a synagogue at Tiberias, so close to Nazareth, where the names of those who contributed to the building costs are preserved. Presumably, they were the names of prominent local Jewish citizens. Greek must have been the common language of the Jews who frequented the synagogue as well as that of its benefactors. Palestinian coins, too, from the first century BC, particularly those issued by the Hellenized Jewish rulers, were engraved in either Greek and Hebrew, or only Greek. Greek was also used by Jewish scribes and record keepers, and in correspondence. Papyri sent to Jewish leaders from Jewish centres within Palestine have been found in Greek, Hebrew and Aramaic. And the entire archives of one Jewish family have been uncovered containing numerous contracts, all in Greek. From this evidence, it is clear that many Palestinian Jews conducted their everyday business correspondence in Greek.

The writings of the Rabbis of this period also demonstrate a familiarity with Greek. This would have been more than helpful to them in their teaching, for many Jews outside Palestine were primarily Greek-speaking and the Bible, being the Jewish sacred writings, had been translated into Greek in Ptolemy's time, more than three hundred years before. In fact, it is this version of the Bible, the *Septuagint*, which is used by the New Testament writers in their quotations, rather than the Hebrew, demonstrating the widespread use of Greek amongst large sections of the population. The Biblical *Wisdom of Solomon*, probably dating from the first century BC, was actually written in Greek.

The great Jewish historian, Josephus, says that in his later life he took great pains to perfect his knowledge of the Greek language so as to be able to translate his own works. He knew that his writings would not have the circulation he desired in his own native Aramaic. But by his mid-twenties he must already have been well-versed in the language, for he visited Rome at the age of 26 (61 AD) where he defended a number of priests who had been sent there to face some insignificant charge. In his writings, Josephus makes it very clear that anyone who wished, even a slave, could gain a proficient knowledge of Greek.[13]

Many similar instances could be cited, but the above should be sufficient for present purposes. It is not being suggested that everyone was bilingual, but just as English has become the international language of our modern times, with even street children in English-speaking third-world countries picking up a few words here and there, so too was Greek familiar to everyone at that time, and even more so, since many areas used Greek as their primary tongue. After three hundred years of common use in the heart of their own homeland, many must have spoken it, even those who could neither read nor write.

To cast one's mind back into another time is not so easy, especially when certain incorrect preconceptions may have already taken root. The gospel compilers and other early Christians alike knew so little of Jesus' life history that they constantly resorted to anecdote and legend. This is why Luke and Matthew are so much at variance in their nativity stories, why Luke and Matthew recast the stories of Mark into their own framework, and why John is so fundamentally different from the synoptics. Nobody actually knew anything very much about either Jesus or John the Baptist and that situation still prevails today.

The impressions that we gain as children that Jesus and his disciples were unlettered comes from a blend of misconception and vague innuendo prompted by gospel compilers who were writing long after Jesus' death and knew practically nothing about him. How much do we know of the personal lives of those who lived fifty, sixty or seventy years ago – even past members of our own family – and of whom we possess only hearsay records? Even apparently informative statements can be inadvertently misunderstood.

When it is said, for example, that Jesus' father was a carpenter, this could be conveying quite the wrong impression for he could have been what we would call a builder. Perhaps, he was more of a contractor, taking on large assignments of various kinds using one of the commonest buildings materials of that time, wood. Perhaps he also built boats and ships – or parts for them – to put out on the Sea of Galilee, though Nazareth lies some 20 miles to the southwest. Businessmen, more than others, have a need to speak the language of their customers and in a cosmopolitan place like Galilee, whatever kind of carpenter he was, many of his local customers would have spoken Greek, let alone those that came from further afield. And naturally, if Jesus heard Greek spoken as a child, and if his father spoke it well, then he too would have picked it up, quite apart from what he might have learnt at school or from other children.

In fact, not only would Jesus have spoken Greek, but his brothers and sisters would have done so, too. His brother James is said to have been a well-placed priest in Judaism and was later a leader of the Christians at Jerusalem, after Jesus' death. Surely it would have been essential for someone holding such positions to have been not only literate but also conversant with the Greek language? The ability to communicate with all kinds of people would have been a key feature of his day-to-day running of affairs. Hellenized, Greek-speaking Jews and others were continuously visiting Jerusalem from all over the Roman Empire and the city itself would have had a strong cosmopolitan atmosphere. As the writer of *Acts* comments:

> There were (Jews), devout men living in Jerusalem from every nation under heaven.... Parthians, Medes and Elamites; people from Mesopotamia, Judaea and Cappadocia, Pontus and Asia, Phrygia and Pamphylia, Egypt, and the parts of Libya around Cyrene; as well as visitors from Rome – Jews and proselytes alike – Cretans and Arabs.
>
> *Acts 2:5,9-11, JB*

Greek would have been one of the main languages of interracial communication and, with such a diversity of followers, it is presumed that James must have spoken it. There is certainly a letter in the New Testament attributed to James which is written in the most impeccable Greek. So if Jesus' brother spoke Greek, then why not Jesus?

From the archaeological and historical information now available to us, we can conclude with a fair degree of certainty that Jesus would have been fluent in that language. He was probably able to read and write in both Greek and Aramaic and, with so many Greek-speaking followers, it is inconceivable that his sayings were not translated in his own lifetime, maybe even from Greek to Aramaic as much as from Aramaic into Greek. In a mixed audience, *ad hoc* translations would naturally have been made as soon as the meeting was over and people began to disperse, the one translating to the other whatever the great teacher had just said.

Parts of Q seem almost certainly to have originated in Aramaic, for when translated back into Aramaic, some of the passages in the Sermon on the Mount fall naturally into verse, much like translating

"On the bridge at Avignon" back into its original French.[14] Similarly, in a passage from Luke, previously quoted, commenting on the extensive ritual ablutions undertaken in Judaism in the hope of obtaining purity, Jesus points out that it is the inward part of man, his mind, which is more in need of cleansing:

> And the Lord said unto him,
> "Now do ye Pharisees make clean
> the outside of the cup and the platter;
> but your inward part is full of ravening and wickedness.
> Ye fools, did not He that made that which is without
> make that which is within also?
> But rather *give alms* of such things as ye have;
> and, behold, all things are clean unto you."
>
> *Luke 11:39-41*

The meaning of the last sentence, however, is odd. But all is revealed when the Greek is translated back into Aramaic. The Aramaic for "to give alms" is *zakkau*, while "to cleanse" is *dakkau*, two very similar words. Clearly, whoever did the translation into Greek had a defective Aramaic copy. 'To cleanse' gives us hope of providing a better meaning than 'to give alms' and, turning to Matthew, we find a reading which confirms it:

> Cleanse first that which is within the cup and platter,
> that the outside of them may be clean also.
>
> *Matthew 23:26*

Such linguistic clues demonstrate the Aramaic origin of these – and presumably other – verses, and we can conclude that Jesus certainly spoke Aramaic. This has never been in doubt. But there is no reason why he should not have been bilingual and why his sayings should not have circulated amongst his followers in both languages. And of course, not only would Jesus have spoken Greek, but so would many of his disciples.

Who Knew Jesus?

We have seen that there are question marks over the authenticity of almost everything in the New Testament. This is not a personal point of view, but one stemming from the research of the many scholars who have studied the matter over the last two hundred years, the majority of them committed Christians. Some have expressed far more radical opinions on the authenticity of the gospel contents than have been suggested here. Considering the results of this research, some accredited scholars have taken a further step and asked, "Is there really any evidence that Jesus ever existed?" This is not a ridiculous question and some space may be devoted to it.

The name of Jesus is known to almost every person on the planet. Throughout the world, there are many millions of people who reverence his name, professing to a belief in Christianity, from which they presume that they are followers of Jesus' teachings. We have assumed with them that Jesus did exist. Yet how do we know that the teachings ascribed to him in the gospels really originated with him? Translation errors such as *dakkau* and *zakkau* tell us that there was almost certainly some older, Aramaic stratum of teaching used by the gospel compilers. But is there any historical evidence that corroborates the gospel stories of his life and links them with Jesus' teaching? If Jesus generated so much interest during his own lifetime, surely some contemporary historian would have recorded something of him, as they did of other well-known personalities?

Such questions all arise from one common fact: the amount of available historical information concerning Jesus and the sum of his recorded sayings is astonishingly little. Indeed, so little is known of the one in whom billions of Christians have placed their faith that scholars and others have interpreted what there is to mean almost anything, according to their own beliefs and bent of mind. Jesus has been portrayed as a political agitator, a social reformer, a libertine, a Jew, a Pythagorean, an Essene, a Greek philosopher and more.

Even if his ministry did last for only three or four years, the words of such a great teacher would have filled a book in only a few days or even less. So even if everything that is written in Jesus' name did actually originate with him – which is most unlikely – we would still have only a fraction of his teachings and even less of his life story. In fact, New Testament scholar Canon Streeter once calculated that the stories told of Jesus in the four gospels could be compressed into no more than three weeks, if the forty days and nights said to have been spent in the wilderness were discounted. That is no life story. What exists in the gospels is hardly a biography in the sense that Plutarch, Suetonius and other historians of the day would have understood it. It is little more than a collection of unrelated anecdotes, many of which appear to have been invented or elaborated, for one reason or another, so that the same stories told in the different gospels differ from each other in numerous, often incompatible ways, as we have seen. The process of modifying and inventing stories or incidents can even be observed in action as Luke and Matthew copy Mark and Q. Yet the details of some of these stories have become fundamental to Christian belief, even though many of the inconsistencies are irreconcilable.

Outside the gospels, there are only four early historical references to Jesus. They are found in the works of the Jewish historian, Josephus, in the writings of the Roman historians, Tacitus and Suetonius, and in the letters of Pliny the Younger, a Roman governor of Bithynia. But together, they cover little more than half a page of a modern book.

Josephus was born the son of a Jewish priest in 37 or 38 AD, around the time of Jesus' crucifixion. Taking part in the Jewish uprising, culminating in the siege and eventual fall of Jerusalem and the destruction of the Temple in 70 AD, Josephus was appointed commander of Galilee. He was captured, however, and subsequently changed sides, spending some considerable effort in the attempt to convince his fellow countrymen that revolt against the might of the Roman Empire was foolhardy. From a practical point of view, he was probably right, but feeling ran strong against him in the steamy hot-house of Jewish politics and when the war was over he betook himself to Rome, where he lived a comfortable life under the protection of successive emperors. During this period, he wrote two monumental books of detailed Jewish life and history: *The Jewish War*, which he completed in 77 or 78 AD, and *Antiquities of the Jews*, which took him a further fifteen years.

These two invaluable books are the sole source of information on many aspects of Jewish life at this time and Josephus is of particular interest because he came from Galilee. Yet his reference to Jesus, found in the *Antiquities*, covers no more than a few lines for in his day the Christians were seen as just a minor sect, one amongst many in the wide-ranging Roman Empire. Yet even this short reference is considered by most scholars to have been tampered with by later Christian editors. Attempting to separate the original from later Christian editorial insertions, many scholars have tried to recover something approximating to the text of Josephus. Placing probable Christian interpolations in angle brackets, the passage reads:

> At about this time lived Jesus, a wise man, <if indeed one might call him a man>. He performed astonishing feats and was a teacher of such people as are eager for novelties. He attracted many Jews and many of the Greeks.

<He was the Messiah.> Upon an indictment brought by leading members of our society, Pilate condemned him to the cross, but those who had loved him from the very first did not cease to be attached to him. <On the third day he appeared to them, restored to life, for the holy prophets had foretold this and myriads of other marvels concerning him>. The brotherhood of the Christians, named after him, is still in existence to this day.

Josephus, Antiquities XVIII:63-64 (3.3), HJPI pp.432,437

Josephus was not a Christian, nor did he demonstrate much interest in or knowledge of them. He is unlikely, therefore, to have called Jesus the "Messiah", implied that he was something more than a man or endorsed the view that he had risen from the dead. These are all tenets of the Christian faith, and the "on the third day ..." is a tell-tale pointer to the editorial hand of a later Christian.[15]

Apart from this internal evidence from the passage itself, there is also external evidence of its adulteration by Christian editors. The early third-century Christian teacher, Origen, mentions this passage of Josephus in his writings,[16] also indicating the existence of a further passage in which Josephus expresses his disbelief in Jesus' Messiahship. But this latter passage has clearly been deleted by later Christian copyists, for it no longer exists in any of the extant manuscripts. Instead, it has been replaced by an affirmation of the point that Josephus once denied.

Those who support the view that Jesus never existed consider that this entire passage is a Christian interpolation, though it is difficult to explain away the comments of Origen, especially concerning the doubts cast upon Jesus as the Messiah. But in any event, the passage tells us nothing of the life of Jesus nor of his teachings.

The remaining historical references to Jesus are equally unsatisfying. The Roman historian, Tacitus (*c*.55-120 AD), writing towards the end of his life, mentions the Christians in his portrayal of the Roman Emperor Nero (54-68 AD) and his part in the great fire of Rome in 64 AD. He asserts that it had been a common belief at the time that the conflagration had been started under the express orders of Nero. Then, in order to divert public attention from this imputation, the Emperor had singled out the Christians to take the blame, seeing that there was already considerable prejudice against them. Under his orders, they were tortured and executed in a variety of excessively cruel ways. The Christians, says Tacitus, were named after a certain Christus who, in the reign of Tiberius, was put to death under Pontius Pilate:

They got their name from Christus, who received the death penalty in the reign of Tiberius, by sentence of the procurator Pontius Pilate. That checked the pernicious superstition for a short time, but it broke out afresh – not only in Judaea, where the plague first arose, but in the capital itself (Rome), where all things horrible and shameful in the world collect and find a home.

Tacitus, Annals XV:44, AT p.282, JCONT p.22

Modern historians, however, have questioned Tacitus' accuracy, pointing out that there may not have been sufficient Christians in Rome by the year 64 AD, only 30 years or so after the crucifixion. Others have suggested that the entire passage is a Christian interpolation, though it is hard to conceive of even a devious Christian editor using such strong language concerning their own faith.

Suetonius (75-150 AD), writing in his *Lives of the Caesars* at about the same time as Tacitus, also refers to Nero's persecution of the Christians, saying:

Punishment was inflicted on the Christians, a class of people given to a new and noxious superstition.

Suetonius, Lives of the Caesars (Nero) XVI:2, JCONT p.22, SII p.111

He also reports that in the reign of Claudius (41-54 AD), certain Jews were banished from Rome due to their persistent rioting:

Since the Jews were constantly causing disturbances at the instigation of Chrestus, he (Claudius) expelled them from Rome.

Suetonius, Lives of the Caesars (Claudius) XXV:4, JCONT p.22, SII p.53

The question naturally is, who was Chrestus? For not only was Chrestus a common slave name, but it was also a frequent Roman misspelling of Christus or Christ. Consequently, there is some disagreement as to whether or not this passage refers to the Christians. Presumably, the riots – if the Christians were indeed involved – arose from an anti-Christian feeling amongst the Jewish community. But once again there is the problem of the early date and whether there would have been sufficient Christians at that time to become a cause for Jewish concern. Scholars have also deliberated over whether Suetonius copied from Tacitus or Tacitus embellished a brief statement from Suetonius.

Pliny the Younger (c.62-113 AD), Roman governor of Bithynia during the reign of the Emperor Trajan (98-117), is the last source of contemporary information on the Christians. In his diligent though fastidious fashion, Pliny wrote to Trajan in 112, eighty years or so after the death of Jesus, asking for advice concerning the treatment of Christians. Basically, he says that he gives suspected Christians every opportunity to state and demonstrate their allegiance to the Emperor and the Roman gods, but if they still persist in their allegiance to Christ, he orders their execution since their "contumacy and inflexible obstinacy deserved chastisement". Some chastisement!

The method I have observed towards those who have been denounced to me as Christians is this: I interrogated them whether they were Christians; if they confessed it, I repeated the question twice again, adding the threat of capital punishment; if they still persevered, I ordered them to be executed. For whatever the nature of their creed might be, I could at least feel no doubt that contumacy and inflexible obstinacy deserved chastisement. There were others also possessed with the same infatuation, but being citizens of Rome, I directed them to be carried thither.

These accusations spread (as is usually the case) from the mere fact of the matter being investigated and several forms of the mischief came to light. A placard was put up, without any signature, accusing a large number of persons by name. Those who denied they were, or ever had been Christians, who repeated after me an invocation to the gods, and offered adoration, with wine and frankincense, to your image, which I had ordered to be brought for that purpose, together with those of the gods, and who finally cursed Christ – none of which acts, it is said, those who are really Christians can be forced into performing – these I thought it proper to discharge. Others who were named by that informer at first confessed themselves Christians, and then denied it; true, they had been of that persuasion but they had quitted it, some three years, others many years, and a few as much as twenty-five years ago. They all worshipped your statue and the images of the gods and cursed Christ.

They affirmed, however, the whole of their guilt, or their error, was that they were in the habit of meeting on a certain fixed day before it was light, when they sang in alternate verses a hymn to Christ, as to a god, and bound themselves by a solemn oath, not to any wicked deeds, but never to commit any fraud, theft or adultery, never to falsify their word, nor deny a trust when they should be called upon to deliver it up; after which it was their custom to separate, and then reassemble to partake of food – but food of an ordinary and innocent kind. Even this practice, however, they had abandoned after the publication of my edict, by which,

according to your orders, I had forbidden political associations. I judged
it so much the more necessary to extract the real truth, with the assistance of torture, from two female slaves, who were styled *deaconesses*: but
I could discover nothing more than depraved and excessive superstition.

Pliny the Younger, Letters of Pliny X:XCVI, PLII pp.403-405

Though the letter is not without human and historical interest, it tells
us only that there were Christians in the time of Pliny and Trajan, and
reveals something of their rituals. But it tells us nothing of Jesus –
neither of his life nor of his teachings.

The fact is, then, that early historical information outside the gospels is virtually non-existent and whatever history is recorded is more
likely to have actually originated from stories related by the early Christians themselves. But whatever they may have known, particularly in
the early days, is now lost, except the somewhat dubious portion re-
layed in the gospels. The gospels, however, as a source of history, immediately present us with enormous difficulties, as we have already
seen, and will encounter more as we proceed.

It is clear, then, that we cannot hope to verify any of the details of
the life of Jesus from the gospels or from any other source. From the
point of view of a Christian, this may be disconcerting. But from the
standpoint of this book, it matters little, for we will be concerned with
the teachings attributed to Jesus in relationship to the age-old mystic
teachings. And though the content of the gospels is fragmentary, dis-
jointed and has suffered at the hands of Christian editors, there is still
plenty there to help us understand his real teachings. Moreover, while
there is little or no history of Jesus to be gleaned from other sources,
there is a great wealth of extra-canonical literature – orthodox and
unorthodox – which supplements the gospels, helping us determine
what he actually taught.

Christmas, Christian Custom and the Aryan Deity Mithras

The year of Jesus' birth, largely based upon the dubious historical comments of Luke, is normally set at around 6 BC, towards the end of the
reign of Herod the Great. This would have put Jesus in his mid-thir-
ties at the time of his crucifixion. But there is a passing comment attributed to the "Jews" in John's gospel, who say to Jesus "thou art not
yet *fifty* years old"[17] and it has been pointed out many times that if
Jesus had been in his thirties, they would have said, "thou art not yet

forty years old". Consequently, there is considerable doubt over the year of Jesus' birth.

With the inaccurate and conflicting gospel information concerning the birth and early years of Jesus, it is by no means surprising to discover that no one has the vaguest idea of the actual day of the year on which he was born. The early fathers and the church in general have never made any secret of the fact. How then has December 25th come to be the date on which his birth is celebrated? The answer is: it was borrowed.

One of Christianity's early rivals in the Roman Empire was Mithraism, an ancient religion taking the ancient Aryan deity Mithras as its Lord and Saviour. The worship of Mithras is said to have been introduced to Rome by Pompey in the mid-first century BC, after his conquest of Pontus, an influential city on the Black Sea, at that time controlling all of Asia Minor under the rule of Mithradates VI. Retained from Aryan roots, Mithras appears as a minor deity in the Hindu *Vedas*, but in Persia Mithras grew in importance, becoming chief of the powers subordinate to *Ormuzd* (*Ahura Mazda*) in Zoroastrianism. It was as this powerful god that Mithraism flourished in the Roman Empire, enjoying a new lease of life in early Christian times, reaching its zenith during the second and third centuries AD. In 274 AD, the Emperor Aurelian (*c.*212-275) proclaimed Mithras to be the principal patron of the Roman Empire.

Mithraism spread rapidly, especially amongst the Roman military forces, for the same social and religious reasons as Christianity. Unifying many of the cults associated with the numerous gods of the Graeco-Roman world, for a time it became the most important single religion in the Mediterranean world. Temples and shrines to Mithras have also been found as far afield as Britain and Germany.

Mithras was also worshipped as the Sun God and an annual festival in honour of the "Birthday of the Invincible Sun" was held on the winter solstice, December 25th in the Julian calendar, the shortest day of the year after which the sun begins its journey back into northern skies. It was an event of great importance in the Roman world, marked by general festivities including the 'Great Games'. Naturally, the day was a public holiday and it seems that for practical reasons, this was the day chosen as the date on which Jesus' birthday should also be celebrated.

It appears likely, however, that the date was not fixed until the mid-fourth century, for it does not appear in the list of Christian feasts given by the late second and early third-century fathers, Tertullian (*c.*160-220) and Origen.[18] In fact, late in the second century, Clement of Alexandria, speaking of speculations concerning the birth date of Christ, condemns them as superstitions. And in 345, when the idea of fixing a day for celebrations must have been under review, Origen opposed the very idea of commemorating the birthday of Jesus.

Speaking of ancient holy men and prophets such as Jeremiah as the "saints", Origen pointed out that "not one from all the saints is found to have celebrated a festive day or a great feast on the day of his birth". In fact, he observes that Jeremiah said, "Cursed be the day in which I was born". And Origen comments that the prophet would not have said such things "unless he knew that there was something in this bodily birth that would seem worthy of such curses". For a mystic to leave the blissful realms and to enter a "bodily birth" with its multifarious vicissitudes is indeed a "curse", though mystics such as Jeremiah make such comments in order to awaken human beings to their predicament, not because they themselves are dissatisfied with God's will. Origen also says, "only sinners rejoice over this kind of birthday", adding that the celebration of birthdays is characteristic of rulers such as Pharaoh and Herod who celebrated their respective birthdays with festivities and by taking the lives of others.[19]

Both Clement and Origen must have felt that what was important in the life of a holy man was his teachings and the example of his life. To give importance to the external happenings of their lives is to demean the very purpose for which these mystics came into this world. But following the inevitable pathway of decline, the counsel of these early fathers was neglected. Accordingly, the first authentic mention of December 25th as the birth date of Jesus appears at the head of the *Depositio Martyrum* in a Roman chronography (a Christian almanac) dated 354[20] and written in 336. A list of Christian martyrs begins with an entry for December 25th, "Christ born in Bethlehem of Judaea". Christmas can thus be dated at least as far back as that, though only the date is listed, no festal celebrations being mentioned. This fits tolerably well with a comment of John Chrysostom (*c*.345-407) who mentions the day in a sermon preached at Antioch on December 20th 386 (or 388). And at about the same time, he also wrote that the day had only "lately" been fixed by the Church authorities:[21]

> On this day also the birthday of Christ was lately fixed at Rome in order that whilst the heathen were busied with their profane ceremonies, the Christians might perform their holy rites undisturbed.
>
> *John Chrysostom, Homily XXXI, GTR p.49*

Whether the festivities as practised in modern times, including the slaughter of millions of birds and animals, together with consumption of vast quantities of alcohol, are any less "profane" is debatable. Even the "Great Games" of the Romans are mirrored in the numerous worldwide sporting fixtures of Boxing Day.

The wise men or Magi in Matthew's nativity story also seem to owe their origin to Mithraism or Zoroastrianism, for their names, given by later tradition, are simply epithets for the Sun God. *Caspar* means the 'White One', *Melchior* is the 'King of Light', and *Balthazar,* the 'Lord of Treasures'. The magi, of course, were the Zoroastrian priests, though the Greek term, *magos,* had a spread of meaning which ranged from mystic or sage to soothsayer or magician. In fact, the story of the wise men seems to have been lifted from the Zoroastrian scriptures for, in the *Zend-Avesta,* Zarathushtra is credited with having prophesied that a Saviour was to be born of a virgin and his seed, adding:

> You, my children, shall be first honoured by the manifestation of that divine person who is to appear in this world: a Star shall go before you to conduct you to the place of his nativity; and when you shall find him, present to him your oblation and sacrifices; for he is indeed your lord and an everlasting king.
>
> *Zend-Avesta, MFC p.83*

Perhaps Matthew, or whoever originated the story, wished to demonstrate that Jesus was also the long-awaited saviour of the Zoroastrians.

Not only Christmas, but even the name and tradition of Sunday, is derived from Mithraic practice. It too was a Roman holiday and, before his conversion to Christianity, the Emperor Constantine made it compulsory to keep Sunday as a day of rest. Seven was the number assigned to Mithras, hence the seventh day of the week was consecrated to him and was known as the Lord's day long before the time of Jesus. No doubt on account of the public holiday, Sunday had long been used by the early Christians for their own religious meetings and gradually it became an established custom.

Christians have often referred to Sunday as the Sabbath, presuming that it is founded upon the Jewish day of rest. But the Jewish Sabbath, as is well known, runs from Friday evening to Saturday evening and has a number of traditional customs associated with it which have only very loosely been carried forward into Christianity.

The Christmas tree, too, may owe its origins to this ancient Persian god. More than a millennium before the Caesars, the mysteries of

Mithras were celebrated in Asia Minor in conjunction with those of the goddess Cybele. Here, Mithras appears bearing a ball in one hand and leaning on a fir tree, a tree into which he had been transformed for his infidelity to the goddess and which remained associated with his cult.

The Christmas tree was introduced into Britain from Germany where Mithraism had been more popular than in any other Western country in Roman times, and it has been conjectured the custom may in some way be connected.[22] Another theory suggests that the Christmas tree is derived from the Paradise Tree, which – in an ancient custom – was adorned with apples on December 24th in honour of Adam and Eve. The more likely theory, however, is that it owes its origins to the pagan Yule tree.

Yuletide was the Germano-Celtic festival associated with the winter solstice, an understandably important time in ancient European cultures, where the winters can be harsh, and a number of traditional Christmas social customs are derived from earlier 'pagan' practices. At the ancient Roman New Year festival, held on January 1st, houses were decorated with greenery and lights, while presents were given to children and to the poor. Likewise, Germanic Yuletide traditions included good fellowship, feasting, particular foods such as Yule cakes, lights, fires, the Yule log, greenery and fir trees, together with the exchange of gifts and greetings. In the eighth century, during Boniface's missionary activities amongst the Germanic tribes, he dedicated the fir tree to the 'Holy Child' to replace the sacred oak of Odin. It is from these customs, adapted to modern times, that most of the social traditions of Christmas are descended.

Because of these acknowledged pagan origins, in 1644, the English Puritans banned all such Christmas festivities by Act of Parliament, ordering that the day be kept as a fast. Charles II, however, restored the festivities after the Restoration of the monarchy (1660), though the Scots at that time continued to adhere to the Puritan view. In the United States, too, festal celebrations were suppressed because of their pagan origins and it is only since the nineteenth century that they have become increasingly popular and commercialized.

Jesus – of Nazareth?

Though Jesus' date of birth is a mystery, it might be thought that there is no doubt about the place in which he grew up – Nazareth. But this, too, is by no means certain. In the popular mind, it has always been tacitly understood that Jesus was called a Nazarene because he came from Nazareth. However, sects or religions were not usually named after a village or locality. Further, in addition to the historical incompatibilities between Matthew and Luke's nativity stories, casting doubt over the authenticity of either of them, some scholars have also pointed out that there is no reference to Nazareth as a village until the fourth century AD, even suggesting that some other village was later renamed to fit the legend.

No village of that name is ever mentioned in the Old Testament, for instance, and Josephus (*d.c.*100), who knew the area well, having once been the governor of Galilee, wrote a detailed account of the province, but never mentioned Nazareth. By the early fourth century, however, when Constantine, the first Christian Roman Emperor, ordered a listing of all places considered holy by the Christians, it seems that there was a village of Nazareth in Galilee, no doubt catering to the growing traffic of pilgrims.

Though the absence of a mention does not prove that Nazareth did not exist, there is further, more significant, evidence concerning the origins of the designation 'Nazarene'. In *Acts 24:5*, Paul is described as "a ringleader of the sect of the Nazarenes" and the term is also found in *Matthew 2:23* as a description of Jesus: "He shall be called a Nazarene." Moreover, the phrase "Jesus of Nazareth", encountered in *Acts 22:8* and again in *Mark 1:23*, is better translated as "Jesus the Nazarene", as it is in some well-respected translations of the New Testament.

The situation, however, is by no means simple, because in the gospels and *Acts*, two variants are encountered – Nazoraean (*Nazoraios*) and Nazarene (*Nazarenos*). In most standard translations, both of these are translated as 'Nazarene' or 'of Nazareth'. But the commonest of these is Nazoraean and while Nazarene might possibly be derived from Nazareth, Nazoraean could not. Attempting to derive Nazoraean from Nazareth would be like describing those who came from Northampton as Northomians rather than Northamptonians.

While there is no doubt that Jesus and his disciples were called Nazarenes or Nazoraeans, the origin of the term remains a matter of debate. The early Church fathers, many of whom were Greek-speaking, called themselves Christians (*Khristianoi*), a Greek term which arose at Antioch in the non-Jewish world. And the same fathers spoke of the Nazarenes, often disparagingly, as a Judaeo-Christian sect, adding further to the confusion by transliterating the word from Aramaic into Greek as Nazarenes, Nazoraeans, Nasoraeans and other variants.

Epiphanius even speaks of another sect, the Nasarenes (*Nasaraioi*) who were, he says, in existence before the time of Jesus. Consequently, he distinguishes between the Nasarenes and the Nazarenes (or Nazoraeans). But his motivation in making this distinction may be because he did not wish to acknowledge that there were Nazoraeans before the Nazoraeans – Christians before the Christians, so to speak. Moreover, Epiphanius does not enjoy a good reputation for accuracy, and scholarly opinion is divided as to whether there really were two sects or one. The use of dubious etymology to 'prove' a point was not uncommon amongst the early Christian fathers.

The situation is further compounded by the existence of the ancient and well-attested order of Jewish holy men known as the Nazirites (the *Nezirim*), mentioned in the Old Testament, and with whom both John the Baptist and James the brother of Jesus have often been linked. And scholars see no insuperable difficulty in deriving both Nasarene and Nazarene from the Hebrew *Nezirim*.

Those who have tackled the subject have suggested that the possible derivation of Nazarene is from the Hebrew *nazar,* meaning 'to keep watch', 'to heed', 'to guard' and so on.[23] In this sense, a true Nazarene would have been one who heeded the higher mystic Law or Word.

Another interesting possibility is opened up by two passages from the gnostic tractate, the *Gospel of Philip*, where the unknown author says:

'Jesus' is a private (personal) name. Christ is a public name (epithet). For this reason 'Jesus' is not particular to any language; rather he is always called by the name 'Jesus'. But the word for 'Christ' in Syriac is '*Messiah*', and in Greek it is '*Khristos*', and probably all the others have it according to the particular language of each. 'The Nazarene' is he who reveals what is hidden.

Gospel of Philip 56, GS p.332, NHS20 p.153

And:

The apostles before us used to employ the terms: 'Jesus the Nazoraean *Messiah*', which means 'Jesus, the Nazoraean, the Christ (anointed one). The last name is 'Christ', the first name is 'Jesus', the middle name is 'the Nazarene'.

'*Messiah*' has two meanings, 'Christ (anointed one)' and 'the measured'. 'Jesus' in Hebrew means 'the redemption'. '*Nazara*' means 'the truth', thus 'the Nazarene' means 'the truth' ('the Truthful One'?).

Gospel of Philip 62, GS p.337, NHS20 p.165

From these, it would seem that a Nazarene or Nazoraean was a follower of truth – presumably, in this context, gnostic or mystic truth. This would make a great deal of sense and would give the term a general meaning, quite likely to have been in use before the time of Jesus, as Epiphanius claims. In fact, even today, the Qur'an and Muslim religious writings refer to the Christians as the Nazara, an Arabic rendering of Nazarenes.

This suggestion is borne out by the earliest name used of themselves by the possibly pre-Christian Mandaeans of southern Iraq and Iran. The Mandaean language itself is Semitic in character, being a dialect of Aramaic, a further indication of their early roots. *Manda* means mystic knowledge or *gnosis* and the name they use for their laity is *Mandaiia*, meaning 'gnostics'. Their earliest designation, however, later used only for the priesthood, was *Nazoraiia* – or 'Nazoraeans'. The term is derived from *Nazirutha*, which covers a wide range of meaning including mystic enlightenment and the power (the Word) by which such a state of consciousness is achieved. It also refers to the associated mystic teachings. The closest word in English is probably 'Truth', in all its various connotations.

Whatever may be the facts of the matter, if Jesus was a mystic, a true man of God, a Nazoraean or Nazarene, in the Mandaean sense or in the sense suggested by the writer of the *Gospel of Philip*, then it is as probable a solution to the enigma as any other that Jesus taught the path to *Nazara* or *Nazirutha*, perfect understanding of mystic or gnostic truth. Hence, he and his disciples were called Nazoraeans or Nazarenes.

Did Jesus Travel East?

The absence of any definitive history and the evident gaps in Jesus' life about which absolutely nothing is known has led to an abundance of tales and theories. Twentieth-century apocryphal texts are almost as numerous as their counterparts of nearly two millennia ago. Bearing in mind the almost complete lack of genuine historical information, this kind of material needs to be approached with intelligence and discrimination.

The theory, for example, that Jesus spent some time in Tibet before his ministry is nineteenth century in origin, stemming from a book published in 1894 by a Russian journalist, Nicolas Notovitch. Notovitch claimed that the text of two ancient bound volumes inscribed as the *Life of Saint Issa* had been read to him while recovering from a broken leg in the Tibetan Buddhist monastery of Hemis, situated near the city of Leh, capital of the Ladakh district on the border of India and Tibet. Issa is the name given to Jesus in that part of the world.

According to Notovitch, the book was read by the abbot and translated by an interpreter. Then, working long hours into the night, Notovitch reworked the material by himself and wrote it down. Jesus, it was claimed, had travelled extensively in India during his early years, studying amongst the Buddhists, the Jains and the Brahmins, until he returned home to Palestine, preaching to the Zoroastrians in Persia, on his way. The tale then turns rapidly to the last days and crucifixion of Jesus, relating the events in terms clearly derived from the four gospels. In fact, the entire content of the book is pseudo-gospel in its style.

Notovitch claimed that the book was a Tibetan translation of an original Pali text, Pali being the sacred language of Theravada Buddhism. It was a neat idea, but he must have been unaware that Pali had never been used in Tibet, Buddhist texts usually being translated from Sanskrit or Chinese. The book also has a number of other errors which were soon pointed out by scholars of the time.[24] Hemis, for instance, was not such an unknown place as Notovitch had painted, but was quite commonly visited by western travellers. Moreover, the book did not appear in any of the great catalogues in which all Tibetan literature of any note had been listed.

Notovitch's book, however, was translated into a number of languages and became something of a sensation. Finally, therefore, after a period of seven or eight years, a Professor J. Archibald Douglas of Agra used a three-month vacation from his university to visit the monastery and investigate the story thoroughly, retracing Notovitch's journey. Aided by the retired postmaster of Leh as interpreter, he read Notovitch's entire book to the increasingly astonished ears of the abbot. The abbot then stated that he had been in his position for fifteen years and that during that time no European with a broken leg had been cared for in the monastery. He also pointed out that he had been a lama for forty-two years and was well acquainted with all Tibetan literature. He said that to his knowledge, the name Issa did not appear in any of this literature nor had he ever heard of any book in which it did. It was his firm opinion that no such book existed.

Notovitch had also claimed that, in his discussions, the abbot had made various statements concerning the ancient religions of the Egyptians, Assyrians and the Israelites. But in his interview with Douglas, the abbot pointed out that this would have been impossible since he knew absolutely nothing about these people or their religions. In short, Notovitch and the abbot had never met, nor did any of the very few possible interpreters at the monastery have any recollection of the events. Concluding, the abbot queried whether there was any means in the West by which such flagrant dishonesty could be punished. The interview was written down, witnessed, sealed with the abbot's official seal and later published.[25]

Faced with exposure, Notovitch changed his story, saying that there had indeed been no *Life of Saint Issa*, but he had gathered the story from the various monastery books. But this, too, was of no avail, for it was now known that he had never even visited the monastery. Douglas, however, did manage to verify one part of Notovitch's tale. He had been to Leh where he had been treated at the Moravian mission station, not for a broken leg, but for toothache. The story, however, lived on despite exposure, as good stories and old beliefs often do, and it has resurfaced in or been the 'inspiration' behind a number of other modern apocryphal writings.

The suggestion that Jesus did not die on the cross, but survived, fleeing to Kashmir where he lived to a great age, being buried at Srinagar, is also nineteeth century in origin. The story originated with Hazrat Mirza Ghulum Ahmad (*c.*1839-1908), a self-proclaimed Islamic Mahdi (the prophet who Muslims expect will come shortly before the Day of Judgment) and whose sect, the Ahmadiyya, still exists today. Jesus holds a unique place in Islamic thought, for not only is he credited with having been a true Messenger of God, but he is also supposed to come after the Mahdi, at the end of time, to defeat the Antichrist (who comes *after* the Mahdi and *before* Jesus) and usher in the Last Day.

There is an ambiguous verse in the *Qur'an* which can be interpreted to mean that Jesus did not die upon the cross ("They did not slay him, neither crucified him, only a likeness of that was shown to them"[26]). However, Sufi commentators and others have pointed out that the verse actually means that the real Jesus, his soul or real being, did not die upon the cross, in a physical sense, any more than the soul of anybody is extinguished when the physical body dies. However, it was important to Ahmad that Jesus did not die upon the cross, and his fortuitous finding of a tomb in Srinagar said to be of the prophet Yuz Asaf with its head directed to the east (as in Jewish rather than Islamic custom – Hindus cremate their dead), prompted him to announce that he had found the resting place of Jesus' physical remains.

Ahmad was aware of Notovitch's book, though it suited him not to pay attention to its fraudulent origins, and in the later Ahmadiyya literature, the *Life of Saint Issa* is quoted as an authentic text. It was also Ahmadiyya writers who combined the two stories, giving Jesus two visits to the East – one before and the other after his crucifixion. Other authors then followed in the same tradition, adding more material from here and there. The theories, however, would seem to be based upon conjecture, speculation and the stretching of data without adequate corroboration, though the local tourist industry in Kashmir has not been slow in exploitation of the story.

Paul

In addition to the gospel narratives, the passing remarks of historians and other sources of varying reliability, there is one further primary source of information that helps us understand the earliest Christian scene. That is, the remaining New Testament documents – the various epistles and the *Book of Revelation*. Of these, it is the letters of Paul that must first engage our attention, for their content is of considerable interest.

Paul's letters, probably written during the 50s and early 60s AD, are the earliest writings in the New Testament, and although they tell us remarkably little about the teachings of Jesus, they tell us quite a lot about the origins of Christianity. Paul is one of the most important, yet enigmatic characters of those early times and some of the few available facts about him help to highlight the part he played in the development of early Christianity.

On his own word, Paul was only a youth at the time of Jesus' death. He had never met Jesus and was never baptized by him. On the contrary, he claimed to have received his baptism directly from the Holy Spirit in a highly personalized way, for which we only have his word and his interpretation of what happened to him. Furthermore, he very rarely makes any reference to Jesus' teachings in his letters; he does not appear to believe in the virgin birth; and he is at odds with Peter and James the brother of Jesus, meeting them on only three occasions, on one of which, in Antioch, he upbraided Peter in public. Moreover, in the available literature – only *Acts* or Paul's letters – we never hear anything but Paul's side of the story.

From this literature, however, it is possible to glean something of his background. Paul came from a Jewish family of Tarsus. His father was a Pharisee, and so too, in his early, days, was he. To the Philippians,

Paul wrote that he was a Pharisee and in *Acts* he says that he was "a Pharisee, the son of a Pharisee",[27] also that he "lived in accordance with the strictest section of our Faith, as a Pharisee".[28] His father, however, had received Roman citizenship, making Paul a Roman citizen by birth.[29] A "sister's son" is also mentioned in *Acts*[30] – she informs the Roman tribune at Jerusalem of a plot against Paul's life. This tells us that he had at least one sister and that she lived in Jerusalem. One of Paul's modern biographers[31] also asserts that his mother died while he was still a child.

Neither *Acts* nor his letters give any indication of Paul's appearance, but there is a tradition, recorded in the apocryphal *Acts of Paul*, which provides an interesting description, though this document was written more than a hundred years after Paul's death:

> And a certain man named Onesiphorus, when he heard that Paul was come to Iconium, went out with his children Simmias and Zeno and his wife Lectra to meet him, that he might receive him into his house: for Titus[32] had told him what manner of man Paul was in appearance; for he had not seen him in the flesh, but only in the spirit.
>
> And he went by the king's highway that leadeth unto Lystra and stood expecting him, and looked upon them that came, according to the description of Titus. And he saw Paul coming, a man little of stature, thin-haired upon the head, crooked in the legs (bandy-legged), of good state of body, with eyebrows joining, and nose somewhat hooked, full of grace: for sometimes he appeared like a man, and sometimes he had the face of an angel.
>
> *Acts of Paul II:2-3, ANT pp.272-273*

Though meagre in their information on Paul's family and social background, Paul's letters and *Acts* help considerably in coming to understand his psychological make-up and the beliefs which motivated him. In his youth, Paul was a keen student of the deeper elements of Judaism. In *Galatians*, he writes:

> I progressed in Judaism far beyond many Jewish students of my time, for none was more keenly enthusiastic than I to master the traditional lore of my ancestors.
>
> *Galatians 1:14, AuNT p.277*

He was also of a mystic disposition, as we soon learn from his letters, and his studies of Pharisaism almost certainly included its more esoteric aspects. In *Ephesians* and elsewhere, for example, much in the manner of the gnostics of that time, he speaks of the "principalities and powers (*archons*) in heavenly places",[33] these being the realms and the rulers of the inner creation, the many mansions or heavens.

Paul not only accepted the existence of the heavens, but also the ability to enter them during human life. This is clearly indicated by the well-known passage in *2 Corinthians*, often considered to be auto-biographical, where he speaks of 'someone' who was "caught up to the third heaven":

> I will come to visions and revelations of the Lord.
> I knew a man in Christ above fourteen years ago,
>   (whether in the body, I cannot tell;
>   or whether out of the body, I cannot tell:
>   God knoweth;)
> Such an one was caught up to the third heaven.
>
> And I knew such a man,
>   (whether in the body, or out of the body,
>   I cannot tell: God knoweth),
> How that he was caught up into Paradise,
>   and heard unspeakable words (the Unspeakable Word?),
>   which it is not lawful (possible) for a man to utter.
>
>   *2 Corinthians 12:1-4*

"Fourteen years ago" would have been around the time of his miraculous 'conversion' or a little after and it is likely that his experience on the road to Damascus was something of this nature. Such experiences can be very powerful and life-changing, as Paul discovered, though his later interpretation of it – as his authority to go out and evangelize the Gentile world – may have been incorrect and the creation of his somewhat overheated mind.

Paul also knew that God, together with the heavens and all of His creation, lies within man himself. Hence, he says:

> Know ye not that ye are the temple of God,
>   and that the Spirit of God dwelleth in you?
>
>   *1 Corinthians 3:16*

His conception of the nature of the Son of God was also mystical. Whatever else the Son may have been to him in his understanding of

Jesus Christ, he also believed that the Son was the primary, mystic and creative Power by which everything is created. He says:

> For by him (the Son of the Father) were all things created,
>   that are in heaven, and that are in earth,
>   visible and invisible,
>   whether they be thrones, or dominions,
>   or principalities, or powers:
> All things were created by him.
>
> *Colossians 1:16*

This essentially mystic concept was well understood in both the Greek and Jewish world, where the same creative Power was known as the Wisdom of God (Greek, *Sophia* or Hebrew, *Hokhmah*). Elsewhere, Paul also equates this creative Power of God with the Wisdom of God, as we will later see, both terms being synonymous with the Word.

Paul also points out that the struggle of the devotee consists of countering the influence of the inner powers. His understanding of the "devil" is not that of a being made of "flesh and blood", but of a mystic power, of one who rules certain realms of the creation, with other powers under him. For Paul, the devil is akin to the higher "principalities" and "powers" and is responsible for the "darkness of this world":

> My brethren, be strong in the Lord, and in the Power of his might. Put on the whole armour of God, that ye may be able to stand against the wiles of the devil. For we wrestle not against flesh and blood, but against principalities, against powers, against the rulers of the darkness of this world.
>
> *Ephesians 6:10-12*

Many of Paul's ideas were therefore mystical and in line with the more universal teaching of all mystics, soon to be considered. But all in all, his thinking was a mixture, for he also taught what became the orthodox Christian beliefs of the risen Christ, redemption through the suffering of Jesus on the cross, the imminence of the Last Day, the resurrection of the dead and so on. His belief in the resurrection of the dead would not have been too difficult for him, for it was also a Pharisaic belief, a matter upon which they differed from the Sadducees.

By nature, Paul was a fanatic – or at least a man of extremes – possessing tremendous energy, enthusiasm and zeal. He excelled in his early studies, beyond all his peers, as we have seen, and he himself writes of his early persecution of the Christians:

You have heard, of course, of my behaviour when I practised Judaism, how
I ruthlessly hounded down God's Community (Church) and ravaged it.

Galatians 1:13, AuNT p.277

Paul fervently believed that he had been given a mission to convey the
teachings of Jesus to the Gentiles. In the execution of this mission, he
toured extensively throughout the Eastern Mediterranean regions. One
of the advantages of the Roman Empire was that the trade and communication routes by land and sea were kept open and more or less
free from brigands and pirates. As a consequence, Paul was able to
travel widely in Asia Minor, also visiting many areas of what we now
call Greece and what was formerly Yugoslavia, including Thessaly,
Macedonia and Rhodes. He also went to Cyprus and Phoenicia (the
coastal regions of what are now Lebanon, western Syria and northern
Israel).

During his years of freedom, wherever he went, Paul seems to have
gone out of his way to challenge the local priests and leaders by going
straight to the temples, synagogues and public places and speaking
out his beliefs in a manner guaranteed to give offence. As a result,
he was often the cause of disturbance and commonly the centre of a
minor or major riot. Speaking of his hardships, he wrote to the
Corinthians:

My labours have been harder, my terms of imprisonment longer, my
floggings beyond all bounds, my risks of death more frequent. Five times
I received from the Jews forty strokes less one, three times I have been
beaten with Roman rods, once I was stoned, three times shipwrecked, a
night and day consigned to the deep. Often I have taken to road, in peril
of rivers, in peril of brigands, in peril from my own nation, in peril from
Gentiles, in peril in town, in peril in the country, in peril at sea, in peril
from false brothers, in toil and hardship, often sleepless, in hunger and
thirst, often fasting, in cold and in nakedness.

2 Corinthians 11:23-27, AuNT p.314

On more than one occasion, he had to make a rapid exit from some
city because of the hatred and unrest he had stirred up. On other occasions he was turned out, sometimes being left for dead. In Damascus, he was let down from the walls in a basket (or a crate depending
upon the translation), to escape a group of Jews who were waiting
by the city gates to murder him. And during his first visit to Jerusalem
as a Christian, three years or so after his 'conversion', the disciples

ultimately had to take him to Caesarea and thence to Tarsus, because of plots against his life by local Jews whom he had antagonized.

Wherever he went, Paul seemed to stir up new trouble. The disciples living in Jerusalem had never previously encountered such extreme difficulties. Consequently, he must have been more than an embarrassment to them, probably endangering all their lives by his fanatical zeal, his argumentative nature and his desire to convert everybody. Moreover, he seems to have targeted those who were most likely to be hostile to him, particularly the Jewish priestly hierarchy, whom he only seems to have succeeded in angering and alienating.

According to *Acts*, Paul's last recorded journey was to Rome, as a prisoner of the Roman government. It began with a serious fracas which Paul himself provoked during his second visit to Jerusalem. He had, as was his custom, got himself into a serious dispute involving the high priest and others. The situation was already fraught when the high priest ordered him to be struck upon the mouth for his words of blasphemy. Realizing that the situation was taking a violent turn, Paul tried to create a diversion. By declaring that he was himself "a Pharisee, the son of a Pharisee", believing in the resurrection of the dead, as well as in angels and spirits – neither of which were countenanced by the Sadducees – he set the Pharisees and the Sadducees against each other. But the turmoil which ensued backfired on Paul, as all sides turned to vent their anger on him.

At this, the senior Roman officer at hand, coming to know that Paul was a Roman citizen, had to extract him by force and take him to the local castle for safekeeping. From there, hearing that a group of forty Jews had vowed neither to eat nor drink until they had assassinated him, he sent him with a heavily armed guard consisting of nearly five hundred men, to Felix, the Roman governor at Caesarea:

> And he called unto him two centurions, saying, "Make ready two hundred soldiers to go to Caesarea, and horsemen threescore and ten, and spearmen two hundred, at the third hour of the night. And provide them beasts, that they may set Paul on, and bring him safe unto Felix the governor."
>
> *Acts 23:23-24*

Unsure what to do, wishing to please the Jews and (according to Luke) hoping for a bribe, Felix kept Paul a prisoner for two years, after which Felix was succeeded by Porcius Festus. Almost immediately, Festus took a trip to Jerusalem where the head priests and leading Jews, still incensed with rage against Paul, asked that Paul be returned to Jerusalem, "intending to ambush and kill him on the way".[34]

Festus, the professional diplomat, replied by inviting them to come to Caesarea with him and make their charges there. A number of them did, but when the charges were made, many of them, says Luke, could not be substantiated. Festus, new to his office, wanted to please the Jewish leaders so that he could more effectively deal with them in other, no doubt far more important, matters. So he asked Paul if he would be willing to return to Jerusalem and be tried there, under Festus' jurisdiction.

But Paul knew that to be sent back to Jerusalem would have meant almost certain death. Forced into a corner, he exercised his right as a Roman citizen and appealed to Caesar, which meant having his case heard in the Imperial court. For this reason, he was sent to Rome, going by way of Crete, Malta (where they were shipwrecked) and Sicily. What happened to him there has never been fully ascertained, though according to tradition, he was executed in the time of Nero. But the irony is that, according to *Acts*, Herod Agrippa, who had been called in by Festus to help him deal with the case, had pointed out to Festus that since the charges really amounted to arguments over religious matters, "This man might have been set at liberty, if he had not appealed unto Caesar."[35]

By his own admission, Paul's teaching was from within his own self. He himself believed that he had received it all from "Jesus Christ", in a "revelation":

> But I certify you, brethren, that the gospel which was preached of me is not after man. For I neither received it of man, neither was I taught it, but by the revelation of Jesus Christ.
>
> *Galatians 1:11-12*

Despite his claim, his thinking was clearly influenced by the mystical concepts and manner of expression of his times.

One of the most remarkable features of Paul's teaching is that very rarely, if at all, in his extensive letters, does he ever seem to allude specifically to any of the sayings or discourses that we associate with Jesus through the gospels or even in any of the gnostic or other non-canonical sources.[36] It is as if Paul had never read any of it or if he had, was not interested. But unless the gospel teachings never actually originated with Jesus, they must have been extant at that time and the absence from his letters of almost anything that can be attributed to

Jesus can only be accounted for either by his lack of knowledge of it or his lack of interest.

Paul came into frequent contact with Christian groups which existed prior to his endeavours, almost certainly dating back to the time of Jesus, who had died only fifteen to twenty-five years before. He also met Peter on at least three occasions, twice in Jerusalem and once in Antioch. One cannot help but wonder, therefore, why Peter or any of the other disciples never gave him copies of material they had in writing concerning their Master's teachings. After all, Matthew is supposed to have recorded some of Jesus' sayings and surely others must have done so too, unless Jesus specifically requested otherwise.

Paul's lack of knowledge of Jesus' teachings raises the question of his relationship with Peter and the other Christians. With his record of Christian persecution, it would be more than understandable if they had not trusted him. According to *Acts,*[37] when Paul first arrived in Jerusalem, none of the brethren wanted to have anything to do with him, and it was only when Barnabas got to know him personally, taking him to the apostles, that any kind of bridge was formed. Yet even Barnabas, though he travelled with Paul for some while, finally parted company with him, after a serious disagreement concerning who they should take with them on a missionary trip.[38]

After his vision and conversion on the road to Damascus, Paul's first move was not to visit the apostles, but to go to Arabia, an enigmatic choice of places which has never been satisfactorily explained. What he did there has never been ascertained. Perhaps he spent some time in the solitude of the desert, in prayer and considering his next step. But it was not until three years after his return to Damascus that he went to Jerusalem to meet Peter. Of this period in his life, Paul was later to write:

> But when it pleased God, who ... called me by his grace, to reveal his Son in me, that I might preach him among the heathen; immediately I conferred not with flesh and blood. Neither went I up to Jerusalem to them which were apostles before me; but I went into Arabia, and returned again unto Damascus. Then after three years I went up to Jerusalem to see Peter, and abode with him fifteen days. But other of the apostles saw I none, save James the Lord's brother.[39]
>
> *Galatians 1:15-19*

Some years later, in Antioch, Paul records a second meeting with Peter, at which he upbraids Peter in public for being double-faced – for teaching the Jewish disciples to be circumcised and follow Jewish custom, on the one hand, yet eating with Gentiles (which a true Jew would never do), on the other. According to Paul, Peter withdraws from Gentile company when James arrives in Antioch, so as not to upset James and the disciples who accompany him. The uncompromising Paul considers this to be hypocritical, rather than diplomatic, and lets Peter know about his feelings – in public.

But it is impossible to know what was really going on because in his letters we only have Paul's side of the story, and *Acts* is of little help in building a balanced picture since it was written by a Pauline sympathizer. The dispute, at least in Paul's mind, seems to have been over whether Christian converts should be expected to follow Jewish religious laws, epitomized by circumcision, the Jews even being known as 'they of the circumcision'.

To the orthodox Jews, it was clearly such a heated issue that Peter may well have taken a pragmatic approach and told the disciples that provided they followed Jesus' teaching, there was no harm in following Jewish custom as well, wherever there was no conflict between the two. It may have been the best approach for the sake of peace and harmony within their families and communities.

Paul's only written record of his contact with Jesus' direct disciples is over the matter of external, Jewish observances. He does not relate any of the other things that Peter and the other disciples must have told him of their time with their Master or of the things that Jesus said. He is obsessed only with his own perceived mission to the Gentiles. And he is prepared to quarrel in public with Peter, the one whom Jesus himself appointed to stand in his place.

In his letters, Paul also exhibits another side of his complex personality. In response to criticism, he often devotes long passages to justifying himself and his behaviour. Sometimes, he is clearly disturbed by the treatment meted out to him or by the negative response he has received, and a torrent of emotion pours out of him. He had a deeply emotional, reactive and sensitive nature, and when challenged, he heads off in heated intellectuality to justify himself, his attitudes and actions (much of which is discretely toned down in the *King James Version*). At other times, he can be most tenderhearted, affectionate and – on occasion – amusing.

Even some of the miracles attributed to Paul fail to show him in a kindly light. On the island of Paphos, for example, according to *Acts*, rather than giving sight to the blind, he robs a man of his sight for disagreeing with him – or from Paul's point of view – for being a false prophet. At this, the Roman proconsul who employed the false prophet immediately believed – a pragmatic course of action! From Luke's point of view, of course, the incident provided another demonstration of high-placed Christian converts amongst the Romans and the accept-ability of Christian teachings.

It is noteworthy that nowhere in his letters does Paul speak of any such miraculous occurrences and, as one might expect, there are a number of discrepancies between what can be gleaned from Paul's let-ters and Luke's far later version of events. The accretion of miraculous legends is a common trait in the life stories of the holy, whatever their era, religion or cultural background.

Early Christian Communities

There is considerable evidence of the existence of sizable Christian communities soon after the death of Jesus. When Paul writes to the Roman Christians, for example, probably around 57 AD, it is to a com-munity which he has never previously visited, and it seems from what he writes that he is unsure whether any of them there will agree with his doctrinal point of view. Likewise, Peter, at the beginning of *Acts*, not long after the death of Jesus, is said to have addressed a group of about 120 disciples at Jerusalem:

> And in those days Peter stood up in the midst of the disciples, and said,
> (the number of names together were about an hundred and twenty,) ...
>
> *Acts 1:15*

Luke also mentions disciples in Damascus, Antioch, Joppa, Lydda, Caesarea, Ephesus and in many other places, who seem to have been there before Paul began his missionary activities. Paul himself speaks of places that he has visited where there were already disciples who were not of his calling. Moreover, from comments in his letters, it is clear that communities of his own converts existed alongside other Christian groups and that their relationship was not always harmonious. Paul himself castigates all others as following the wrong path, but one is left wanting to know more about these 'other' groups of Jesus' followers. Were they, in fact, Jesus' original disciples, dating from his lifetime?

The gospel writers themselves certainly speak of large crowds which gathered around both Jesus and John the Baptist, even following them from place to place, and one can only presume that many of these were baptized disciples. They were also drawn from many different localities, no doubt forming their own groups in their own home towns. Matthew, for instance, records that crowds from "Jerusalem, and all Judaea" went out to listen to John the Baptist, who seemed to have his headquarters in the desert:

> Then went out to him Jerusalem, and all Judaea, and all the region round about Jordan.
>
> *Matthew 3:5*

And John reports that

> Jesus made and baptized more disciples than John.
>
> *John 4:1*

So if "all Judaea" went out to listen to John the Baptist, then a greater number must have gone out to see Jesus. As John's gospel elsewhere records, "and a great multitude followed him".[40] There are also the well-known stories of the feeding of the five thousand and the four thousand, related by the gospel writers, while multitudes and great numbers of people who flocked to hear the great teacher are often mentioned. People obviously enjoyed being around their Master and must have gained great inspiration from it. As Mark records:

> And he began again to teach by the sea side: and there was gathered unto him a great multitude, so that he entered into a ship, and sat in the sea; and the whole multitude was by the sea on the land.
>
> *Mark 4:1*

And:

> When he came to his disciples, he saw a great multitude about them, and the scribes questioning with them. And straightway all the people, when they beheld him, were greatly amazed, and running to him saluted him.
>
> *Mark 9:14-15*

And again:

> And they came to Jericho: and as he went out of Jericho with his disciples and a great number of people....
>
> *Mark 10:46*

Similarly, Luke writes:

> But so much the more went there a fame abroad of him: and great multitudes came together to hear (him)....
>
> And it came to pass on a certain day, as he was teaching, that there were Pharisees and doctors of the law sitting by, which were come out of every town of Galilee, and Judaea, and Jerusalem.
>
> *Luke 5:15,17*

But crowds also came from much further afield, as Mark relates:

> A great multitude from Galilee followed him, and from Judaea, and from Jerusalem, and from Idumaea (south of Judaea), and from beyond Jordan; and they about Tyre and Sidon, a great multitude, when they had heard what great things he did, came unto him.
>
> *Mark 3:7-8*

And as Matthew recasts it:

> His fame went throughout all Syria.... And there followed him great multitudes of people from Galilee, and from Decapolis, and from Jerusalem, and from Judaea, and from beyond Jordan.
>
> *Matthew 4:24-25*

There are other similar instances, too. The conclusion that one reaches, therefore, is that by the time of Jesus' crucifixion, there were sizable communities of his disciples, spread throughout the Roman Empire. Places in Palestine, Asia Minor, Greece, various Mediterranean islands, Rome and Italy are all mentioned in this respect, and it is not improbable, considering the crowds that Jesus attracted when he spoke, that he had disciples in all these areas.

One thing is certain, whatever role the twelve apostles may have played, they were not the sole followers of Jesus. In fact, it is likely that the number twelve was an invention of the later gospel writers, possibly to fit in with the idea of the twelve disciples sitting upon twelve thrones judging the twelve tribes of Israel – an altogether odd sort of an idea to our modern mind, but consonant with Jewish thought of those times. Paul, writing in the 50s, never mentions anything in his letters concerning twelve disciples. He just speaks of the brethren, the elders and so on, amongst whom he includes James the brother of Jesus, though he is never mentioned in the gospels as a disciple.

There is also the evidence of the gnostic Mandaeans who give allegiance to John the Baptist. If his ministry was so short, how could his influence have reached Mesopotamia and Persia? Some passages found in the Slavonic edition of Josephus' *Jewish War*[41] are helpful here, for they indicate that John the Baptist could have had a far longer ministry than is commonly supposed, being active as a teacher during the time of the ethnarch Archelaus (4 BC-6 AD), successor to Herod the Great (*d*.4 BC), king of Judaea.

Both the synoptic gospels and Josephus agree that John the Baptist was beheaded during the ministry of Jesus in the early 30s AD and there is no reason to doubt them. So if the text of the Slavonic Josephus is authentic, it would mean that John had a public ministry lasting around thirty years. Such a chronology, of course, is inconsistent with Luke's account that John the Baptist was only six months older than Jesus and was consequently only a child during the reign of Archelaus. But then Luke's historical accuracy is known to be debatable. In fact, there are also historical inaccuracies in Mark's account of the death of John the Baptist. Herod Antipas had married the ambitious Herodias, wife of his half-brother, not of Philip the tetrarch, as Mark (followed by Matthew and Luke) states.[42]

It is certainly true that many of the communities giving allegiance to Jesus also contained disciples of John. Luke mentions Paul's meeting with some disciples of John at Ephesus[43] and in a tradition recorded in John's gospel,[44] Peter's brother Andrew (and possibly Peter too), though a disciple of John, was happy to accept Jesus as the Master in his place. Moreover, it seems unlikely that the teachings of John the Baptist and Jesus would have differed, whatever their later followers may have thought, and the two groups would have had a natural affinity to each other.

So once again, it appears that certain stereotyped pictures concerning the early Christian scene, the number of disciples and so on, are not supported by the evidence of the New Testament and other early literature.

Other New Testament Epistles

Luke and *Acts* take up a quarter of the New Testament, while the letters attributed to Paul occupy a further twenty percent. Between them, almost a half of the New Testament is thus overtly pro-Pauline in its sympathies. However, it cannot be assured that all of the letters attributed to Paul were written by him. Paul himself mentions in *2 Thessalonians* that letters forged in his name were already in circulation:

> Please do not get excited too soon or alarmed by any prediction or rumour or any letter claiming to come from us.
>
> *2 Thessalonians 2:2, JB*

Many scholars, noting the differences of tone, style and content between the main body of Paul's epistles and those to Timothy and Titus, have concluded that they were written by a later hand. And it is certain, for the same reasons, that the *Epistle to the Hebrews* was not written by Paul. But while *Hebrews* has no author's name built into it, *Timothy* and *Titus* do. So if they were not written by Paul, they were deliberate forgeries.

The authorship of the remaining four letters, *1 Peter, 2 Peter, James* and *Jude,* has always been a matter of debate, from the very earliest times. Writing in the first half of the fourth century, Eusebius, listing the New Testament texts, speaks of

> those that are disputed, yet familiar to most, include the epistles known as *James, Jude,* and *2 Peter,* and those called *2* and *3 John.*
>
> *Eusebius, History of the Church 25, HC p.134*

But even *1 Peter,* usually the most readily accepted, has a distinctly Pauline character, echoing Paul's sentiments, statements, beliefs and even wording, including that of an imminent second coming. As such, it seems most unlikely to have been written by Peter, probably originating with someone trying to gain support for Paul's teachings by putting them in the name of Peter.

Almost all scholars agree that *2 Peter* is a late forgery, written in the early second century to foster the idea that Peter and Paul ended their days in accord, with Peter acknowledging the doctrines of Paul. To begin within, the letter copies that of *Jude.* But more obviously, the author's manner of reference to Jesus, his description of Paul's letters as scripture, and his approach to those who have lost faith due to the late arrival of the second coming, all suggest a late date of writing. Contrary to their author's intentions, by demonstrating the rifts in early Christianity between Pauline groups and others, *1 Peter* and *2 Peter* actually inform us most convincingly of the divergence in teaching between Peter and Paul, for they could only have arisen because such differences existed.

The authenticity of the letter attributed to James, commonly assumed to be James the brother of Jesus, is also held in some doubt by many scholars due to the excellent Greek in which it is written (though the writer could have used a translator). But this is based upon the stereotype that Jesus and his followers were unlettered and spoke no Greek, a belief which is no longer tenable. The sincerity and spiritual depth of the letter is not in doubt and it is unlikely to be a forgery; the question is only over which James was the author, for he is not identified. Its message is simple, spiritual, with no signs of a developed Christology or theology, either of a Pauline or any other variety. Of the four letters, it conveys the most concerning the spiritual character of Jesus' teaching.

The very short letter from Jude, stated to be the "brother of James", could have been one of Jesus' brothers, and its tone and content are somewhat different from that of James, making reference to the various Jewish myths. Its subject is the behaviour of certainly "ungodly" people, "deceivers" who have come into the community, and it also suggests that the Last Day is imminent. It has little to recommend it as either associated with the letter of James or, indeed, with Jesus' real teaching. From these indications, it would also seem to be a forgery, perhaps from the same pen as *2 Peter*.

The Book of Revelation

The sole remaining New Testament document yet to be discussed is the obscure *Book of Revelation*. *Revelations* belongs to a category of Jewish literature which developed during the second and first centuries BC, having its antecedents in the earlier religious writings of Babylonian and Persian times. It was a literary form or style, a means of expression or an art form, which lasted for many centuries, predominating in certain Judaic, as well as Christian and gnostic circles.

In these revelations, imagery, metaphor, allegory, symbolism, cipher, numbers, colours and all such devices were used to convey the author's meaning, which often carried an eschatological message. At times, the revelationary writing could become like a literary version of a cryptic crossword, where nothing meant quite what it seemed.

The revelationary genre commonly consists of a fictitious ascent into the heavenly realms, usually in the company of an angel or some equivalent, spiritual being. Sometimes, the supposed recipient of the revelation is one of the patriarchs of old, thereby adding an air of authenticity to the events related. Once in the heavenly realms, the writer is shown certain things revealing either the structure and nature of the inner creation or concerning physical events about to take place. He or she may also be given instructions to do certain things or to convey certain messages.

A few of these revelations, like the *Ascension of Isaiah* and some of the gnostic tractates, contain interesting esoteric details concerning these inner regions. Others use the literary form to promote a prophecy of impending doom, disaster and the Day of Judgment, urging their readers to repent while time remains. Revelations with purported prophecies of the future were invariably written after the event – an easy way to write prophecy! Some were even used for political or propagandist purposes.

None of these revelational writers, however, were interested in the distant future. Their horizons were always circumscribed by their time and place. The attempt to read prophecies of the end of the world into such writings is therefore most unwise and certainly not what the original author or authors had in mind.

Writers and artists of all kinds, times and ages have been fond of symbols, but since no literary art form quite like this exists today, most people find the *Book of Revelation* to be quite impenetrable. Moreover, the difficulty that translators of the New Testament must have had in understanding the Greek text has added further to the confusion. But this is not all. Quite apart from problems introduced into earlier versions by Erasmus' retranslation from the Latin into Greek of the portions he could not find elsewhere, a source analysis of the text reveals that like the gospels and *Acts*, it too is a composite text. It is put together from at least two sources, with a number of additional interpolations. One of these texts may originally have been a Jewish revelation, overwritten by a later Christian editor.

There is an excellent illustration amongst the gnostic writings of the way in which 'revelations' such as this were written. In the important collection of gnostic texts known as the Nag Hammadi codices, there are two documents where it is clear that the one is a Christian overwriting of the other. The earlier document, *Eugnostos the Blessed*, begins as a discourse on mystical subjects, shifting emphasis to become more revelationary as it progresses. The second, the *Sophia of Jesus Christ*, is a Christian overwriting of *Eugnostos the Blessed* and is set entirely in the revelationary genre. And it is most intriguing to observe, almost at first hand, the Christianizing of a non-Christian writing, as well as the transformation of a discourse into a 'revelation', put into the mouth of Jesus and set as a post-resurrectional discourse.

According to his beliefs and bent of mind, the Christian writer makes a number of small omissions and one much larger one. But, most interestingly, as we have often suspected with the gospels, the disciples of Jesus are used to interpolate questions, breaking the original discourse into sections, as and how the later Christian editor thought fit. Clearly, this was an accepted practice in those times. Being able to watch the process in action, therefore, we can be assured that neither Jesus nor his disciples spoke any of the words attributed to them in this tractate. They all stem from the non-Christian writer of *Eugnostos the Blessed.*

The *Book of Revelation* is organized as a series of visions given variously by a voice or by several different angels, the first vision being the dictation of a letter containing seven messages for the seven churches in Asia Minor. But the text is altogether too complex to attempt a source analysis here. The book, however, is of value because, despite its oddities and confusions, it enshrines some most salient points of mystic teaching. These have clearly originated from an earlier stratum of Christian teaching or from the mystical milieu of the times, and it may be that one of the sources of this document was written in the apocalyptic style, but stemmed from one who understood the mystic teachings. Some of these more obviously mystical passages are quoted in the later chapters of this book.

Scholars are quite unclear who wrote its various parts. It has been pointed out that although written in very clumsy Greek, the writer thinks in Hebrew[45] and provides considerable further evidence of a Jewish background. But like all such writings, the author or authors are unknown. Even the third-century Dionysius commented on the marked differences in style and grasp of Greek between John's gospel and *Revelations.* The book is also missing from many early New Testament manuscripts and was never accepted by the Eastern churches as authentic. They were no doubt more familiar with the literary type than their more western counterparts. In fact, the early fourth-century father, Eusebius – having mentioned the four gospels, *Acts*, the letters of Paul, together with *1 John* and *1 Peter* as acceptable New Testament writings – testifies to this early dispute when he writes:

> To these may be added, if it is thought proper, the *Revelation of John.*
>
> *Eusebius, History of the Church 25, HC p.134*

Attributed to a 'John', who figures in the text as the one who claims the vision or rather the series of visions, no one is sure whether he has any connection with John the Elder or John the disciple, whether he was an altogether different John, otherwise unknown to history, or whether John was a pseudonym adopted by the last compiler-editor.

In its present form, the book probably originates from the end of the first century, during the period of Domitian persecution, for the writer speaks of his personal persecution. Indeed, he was probably lucky, for he had only been exiled to the island of Patmos, a Greek island in the Aegean, off the coast of Asia Minor, utilizing the time to write *Revelations*. That its date is after the first Jewish war and the fall of Jerusalem in 70 AD seems clear, for references are made, as if by way of prophecy, to events that took place during that war.

NOTES AND REFERENCES

1. *Acts* 8:5.
2. *Acts* 8:27*ff.*
3. *Acts* 21:8.
4. *Isaiah* 9:1, *KJV* and *Matthew* 4:15.
5. *Mark* 15:1*ff*, *Matthew* 27:1*ff*, *Luke* 23:1*ff*, *John* 18:29*ff.*
6. *Matthew* 8:5*ff* and *Luke* 7:1*ff.*
7. *Mark* 5:1 and 7:31.
8. *Mark* 3:8, *Matthew* 4:25.
9. *Mark* 7:26.
10. Much of the following information can be found in J.N. Sevenster, *DYKG*.
11. Suetonius, *Lives of the Caesars (Claudius)* V:XLII, *SII* pp.77-79.
12. Josephus, *Jewish War* III:446, *JW* p.225.
13. Josephus, *Antiquities* XX:262-265; see J.N. Sevenster, *DYKG* pp.61-76.
14. See Ian Wilson, *Jesus: the Evidence*, p.39.
15. For a full discussion of the passage from Josephus, see *HJPI* pp.428-441.
16. Origen, *Commentarium in Matthaeum* X:17; *Against Celsus* I:47.
17. *John* 8:57.
18. Tertullian, *De Baptismo* XIX, *WTI* p.254; Origen, *Against Celsus* 8:22, *OCC* p.468.
19. See Origen, *Commentary on Leviticus* 8:2*ff*, *OHL* pp.156-157; *cf. Jeremiah* 20:14-16, *Genesis* 40:20-22 (on Pharaoh) and *Mark* 6:21-27 (on Herod).
20. *Depositio Martyrum* 2:17, ed. Valentini-Zucchetti, Vatican City, 1942.
21. Though the secondary sources from which these two citations are taken are usually reliable, the unreferenced primary sources have remained elusive amongst John Chrysostom's voluminous writings!
22. E. Wynne-Tyson, *MFC* p.55.
23. For a discussion of these terms see *AAGA* pp.196-200, *NJL* pp.136-139, *SCO* pp.66-74.
24. *eg.* Max Müller, *The Alleged Sojourn of Christ in India*.
25. J.A. Douglas, *The Chief Lama of Hemis on the Alleged Unknown Life of Christ*.
26. *Qur'an* IV:157-159, *KI* p.95.
27. *Acts* 23:6.
28. *Acts* 26:5, *AuNT*.
29. *Acts* 22:28.

30. *Acts* 23:166*ff.*
31. Hugh Schonfield, *The Jew of Tarsus*, p.30, though the source of this information is not identified.
32. The *Acts of Paul* tell us that Paul sent Titus before him to announce his coming in every city which he was to visit.
33. *Ephesians* 3:10.
34. *Acts* 25:3, *AuNT* p.252.
35. *Acts* 26:32.
36. *1 Corinthians* 11:23-26 on the eucharistic meal is perhaps the only exception.
37. *Acts* 9:26-28.
38. *Acts* 15:36-41.
39. This account can be compared with Luke's much later record in *Acts* 9:19-30.
40. *John* 6:2.
41. Josephus, *Jewish War* (Slavonic), *JWF* p.404, *JIII* pp.645-648. For excerpt, see chapter 26, pp.920-921.
42. *Mark* 6:17*ff*, *Matthew* 14:3*ff*, *Luke* 3:19*ff*. See also *Luke* 3:1; Josephus, *Antiquities* XVIII:5 and *HJPI* pp.343-349.
43. *Acts* 19:1*ff.*
44. *John* 1:35.
45. See *AuNT* p.518.

CHAPTER FIVE

The Other Christians

Constantine and Christianity

In our survey of sources in search of the authentic teachings of Jesus, we have confined ourselves to the orthodox field of the New Testament. This is because the majority of people are only familiar with these texts and because they are the only ones accredited by orthodox Christianity. People have acquired faith in them through the habit of centuries. But since there was no canon of Christian 'scripture' until at least two hundred years after the departure of Jesus, we would be guilty of severe and partisan selection of material if we ignored the literature that so many early Christians considered to convey the teachings of their adopted Master. In this field, there is so much material to choose from, and such variety, that one is forced immediately to expand one's horizons as to what passed as Christianity in the first three centuries AD.

The canon itself arose out of the desire to restrict the diversity of Christian belief. For as long as there was no central body claiming the right to dictate to others what they should or should not believe, there could be no canon and no universally accepted creed of Christian belief. Local bishops might develop authority in their own community, but if they were not recognized as being anyone in particular elsewhere, then their circle of influence would naturally be circumscribed. As a consequence, while Christianity remained essentially unwelcome within the Roman Empire, largely tolerated but occasionally persecuted according to the whims of certain emperors, for just so long could there be no absolute canon, for there was no permanent power base to give it the necessary authority. But with the advent of Constantine in the early fourth century, Christianity at last gained what it had sought so long – Imperial favour.

Since the reforms of Diocletian (293-305), the Roman Empire had been ruled by a Tetrarchy, effectively a rule of four emperors. Ostensibly a good idea, the result, in fact, was devastating for the empire, for civil war broke out between them. And each one had a different attitude towards the Christians. Constantine's father, tolerant of the Christians, had been one of the original four, but was the first to die in 306 AD, after a period of just three years. The ensuing wars between the rival parties brought increasing power to Constantine until by 324 he was sole ruler of the empire.

The political history of the period is complex, but in 312 AD, Constantine completed his conquest of Italy, entering Rome in triumph. In that same year, he and his co-emperor Licinius, who ruled the Eastern provinces of the empire, met in Milan and the subsequent Edict of Milan granted unrestricted freedom of worship to all men. Significantly, it was the Christian religion which was named first and others, of which there were many, were simply identified as "any other cult". Licinius, however, was a Roman traditionalist, believing in the Roman gods, and it was not until Constantine defeated him in 324, becoming the sole ruler of the Roman Empire, East and West, that Constantine's reforms could really take in the whole of Christendom.

Dating from the time he came to power in Rome in 312, Constantine issued a series of decrees that gave increasing power and prominence to the Christians. Lavish Imperial gifts of land, property and finance to the Italian churches made them prosperous beyond their wildest dreams. It also made them loyal to Constantine and must have excited the interest of Christian groups throughout the empire, wondering if they too could share in the largesse. In 321, Constantine passed legislation encouraging bequests to the church, since "the church does not die", laying the foundation for the church's wealth in future centuries.

After Licinius' defeat in 324, with Byzantium (now Istanbul) falling under Constantine's command, the way was opened for Constantine to build a new capital in the East, to be renamed Constantinople. Constantine could hardly wait to move in and work was continued at a pace. By this time, he also seemed to have embraced Christianity with fervour and churches were being built, at Imperial expense, in all the major cities of the empire. Furthermore, starting with the Council of Nicaea in 325, though that initially caused more dissent than unity, he also tried, with some considerable success, to unite all the major warring factions of the church under one creed.

By the spring of 330, the rebuilding of Byzantium was sufficiently complete, with all the necessary paraphernalia of government, and

Constantine moved in. At the same time, he banned all idolatrous worship, pagan festivals and the offering of sacrifices from the capital. Christianity was to be its primary religion.

There is no doubt about Constantine's external support of Christianity. As a skilled organizer and administrator, he saw it as a way to bring some unity to his empire after the decades of civil war. He needed a bland religion, devoid of difficult beliefs and practices, yet capable of uniting people under one banner. Orthodox Christianity fitted the bill. But his personal relationship to Christianity is a matter of historical debate. Like all such generals and rulers, his prime concern was for himself. Religion and other matters were secondary to his personal ambitions and were to be used for the furtherance of good administration and harmony within his empire.

As to his conduct as a Christian, one has only to point to the oft-mentioned murder of his wife and son in 326, one year after the Council of Nicaea. Yet in that same year, Constantine, celebrating in Rome his twentieth anniversary as Augustus (one of the positions within the Tetrarchy), demonstrated in public his loathing for Roman religion and its sacrifices. Historians have pointed to this period as being one of transition in the Emperor's beliefs, but it has also to be remembered that he only asked for baptism when on his deathbed in 337. He kept open his personal options until his final hour.

Those who are interested in power and conformity are almost always the materialists and the conservatives, and Constantine was an exceptionally lucky break for those Christians who longed for recognition, power and status. He also came as a welcome reprieve from the sporadic outbreaks of violent persecution meted out by certain of the emperors, the last of which had been so recently, on the orders of Diocletian, in 303-304. By Imperial decree, books had been surrendered, Christian churches and buildings destroyed, Christians discriminated against, the clergy imprisoned and only freed if they would sacrifice to the Roman gods. The punishment for non-compliance was death in a variety of horrific ways. In the Eastern Empire, persecution was again renewed and continued by Maximin from 306 to 310.

But with Constantine's protection and support, the legalization of Christianity, followed later by its gaining of official status, gave the Christians a tremendous feeling of security. With simple survival no longer a problem, there began in earnest a jostling for political position and power within the Church and the promotion of one definitive Christian creed, theology and belief system over others. Constantine thus became the watershed that gave what became 'orthodox' Christianity the power it needed to eliminate all 'unorthodox' strains. This meant the 'purification' of all so-called heresies, involving an attack by the orthodox Christians on all their minor sects, many of whom were quite uninterested in power and material pursuits. But it also meant a further, deeply significant step in the materialization and crystallization of Jesus' teachings.

The measures that had been so recently meted out to them by the Imperial authorities were now used by the orthodox Christians against their own minority groups. On the orders of Constantine, with which many of the bishops were only too eager to comply, this involved the burning of 'heretical' books and frequently the burning or exiling of the 'heretics' too. Constantine wanted outward uniformity at all costs. Anything out of step threatened him. His idea of 'harmony' was entirely external, something to be enforced, and bishops were bullied and cajoled into compliance. There is no doubt that his approach also hastened the formation of a definitive canon of approved New Testament books, as the line was drawn with increasing rigidity between the 'orthodox' and 'unorthodox'. The existence of an approved canon also gave the orthodox an even greater justification for the destruction of those books deemed heretical. A further step had been taken in externalizing Jesus' teachings.

Yet much of value can be gleaned from these so-called heretical books. For many of them contained teachings and traditions that had originated with Jesus himself, just as much as the documents which ultimately found a place in the New Testament canon. After all, by this time, Christianity and what Jesus had taught had become only a matter of human interpretation and opinion, for no one could consult with Jesus, and the documents themselves, as we have seen, were in considerable disarray. To know what he really taught, all the available evidence must be studied, not just a few selected, edited works.

History is written by the winners – the material winners, one should add. But that does not mean that the one who wins is right. In fact, winning often requires the bending of principles, once held so dear. Historically, orthodox Christianity may have won the day, but they lost out spiritually. And despite the efforts of Constantine and the bishops, there is still more 'other' literature from early Christianity than there is orthodox material. And it is very interesting. Some of it, indeed, is also rather beautiful.

Apocryphal and Gnostic Literature

A great deal of unconsidered prejudice has traditionally encompassed apocryphal literature, though less now than in previous times, and it is useful to remind oneself that lack of knowledge is not a good basis upon which to form an opinion. The term 'apocrypha' is Latin, being derived from a Greek word meaning 'hidden' or 'secret' and – in the past – apocryphal literature was certainly hidden away from the general public, much of it being destroyed whenever discovered. Its content is characteristically 'deviant' from traditional or accepted beliefs and was frequently considered heretical. Canonical literature, on the other hand, is that which has been ratified by a high-level council of religious authorities to express accurately their religious beliefs.

Apocryphal literature has been subject to the same transmission and editorial processes as the New Testament. There is, however, much more of it, spanning a considerably wider range of languages, traditions and literary types. Old and New Testament apocrypha span a range of languages, including Greek, Coptic, Hebrew, Aramaic, Syriac, Ethiopic and others. In many ways, the classification 'apocryphal' is misleading, for the reality is that there is a wide spectrum of literature from ancient times, sometimes associated with the mainstream religions of Judaism and Christianity, and sometimes not. All of it, however, is reflective of the milieu whence it came and some of it is deeply mystical or gnostic in character.

As we noted earlier, *gnosis* is a Greek word meaning knowledge, specifically mystic or revelationary knowledge as opposed to that derived from the activities of thought and intellect. *Gnosis* of God meant direct knowledge and experience of Him, to see God and to know Him. It also meant knowledge of the worlds that lie within. Surveying what is known of Christianity's first three centuries, it is generally true that the wide spectrum of belief held by Christians at that time was generally polarized into two main camps – those who believed that Jesus had taught a primarily mystic, gnostic or esoteric path to God and those who formed what was later to become orthodox, exoteric Christianity. Generally speaking, these two streams reflect the spectrum of human nature present at all times, in all societies, cultures and religions. There are those whose primary interest is in externals and those who are seeking for a deeper and more inward reality. Such streams are consequently a characteristic feature of all religions.

Though there are many mystic and gnostic elements even in the earliest strata of 'orthodoxy', a number of the early orthodox Christian fathers developed an intense dislike of all gnostic teachers and their philosophy. Gnosticism seemed to challenge their beliefs more than any other intellectual system, theological outlook or difference of opinion within the church. It must have given them considerable feelings of insecurity, for a number of them devoted significant efforts to decrying the gnostics.

Irenaeus (120-202), Bishop of Lyons, Hippolytus (*fl.*210-236), Bishop of Rome, Tertullian (*fl.*190-220), Epiphanius (*c.*315-403) and Ephraim Syrus (*c.*308-373), in particular, all wrote long treatises condemning the gnostics and their teachings. And so successful were they and their fellow Christians in destroying these writings that until the late nineteenth century the treatises of the heresiologists remained the major source of information on these ancient groups.

The information they conveyed, however, is inadequate, for these fathers, some of them later canonized as saints, were interested in debunking rather than in understanding, and their writings are redolent with scorn, prejudice, misrepresentation and inaccuracy. In a modern world, there is little doubt that their writings could have landed them in court facing multiple charges of libel! Only occasionally, when they quote some passage in order to ridicule or refute it, are we able to gauge with any degree of certainty what the original writer had believed and taught, though even then we are unsure whether the excerpt has been accurately transmitted. All the same, we can glean much that is interesting, though often tantalizing in its obvious deficiencies, and it is through them that some knowledge of this side of Christian belief was preserved.

During the last one hundred and fifty years, our understanding of the gnostics has been greatly increased by a number of important manuscript discoveries. In the latter part of the nineteenth and in the early twentieth century, a few gnostic manuscripts, written in Coptic, turned up in the antiquarian bazaars of Cairo, found no doubt in the Egyptian sands. Then, in December 1945, on the east bank of the Nile, in the Naj' Hammadi region of Upper Egypt, not far from the ancient city of Chenoboskia, two brothers, digging out nitrogenous earth to fertilize their fields, found an earthenware pot, sealed with bitumen. Within it were twelve papyrus codices entirely devoted to gnostic teachings. Amongst these were many tractates that dealt specifically with Jesus' teachings, notably the *Gospel of Thomas* (being a collection of Jesus' sayings), the *Gospel of Philip* (a collection of interesting miscellanies giving a mystic interpretation of Jesus' teachings), and a number of other texts presenting Jesus' teachings in a mystic or gnostic light.

At the time of their burial, there must have been many more such writings in existence and many people have speculated as to why they were copied into these volumes and secreted. The most probable answer is that some far-sighted individual, realizing that the orthodoxy were closing in, wished to preserve something of universal spiritual value for posterity. Burying books in sealed jars was an accredited practice at such times (it is even mentioned in the Old Testament[1]) and the foresight and labour of whoever arranged the copying and the burying has been vindicated: for the first time in many centuries the 'heretics' have been enabled to speak for themselves.

These twelve codices, often called the Nag Hammadi library, contain a total of fifty-two gnostic tractates, of which six are duplicates and six were already extant at the time of the find, including a brief excerpt from Plato's *Republic*. Of the forty new tractates, about thirty are in a state of good or reasonable preservation, the remaining ten being more or less fragmentary. These gnostic texts, together with the few previous finds from Egypt, plus gleanings from the writings of the heresy-hunting fathers, represent the entire extant remains of such gnostic material, with the exception of Manichaean and Mandaean literature.

Fortunately, however, there are other apocryphal writings which help to increase our understanding of the mystic beliefs of the esoteric side of early Christianity. In particular, a series of 'Acts', written as fictional romances with one or other of the apostles as their central characters, provide further fascinating insights into the mystic and spiritual teachings attributed to Jesus.

Many of these are quite alien to Western literature and the Western mind of the present time, for the stories are often allegorical in character and the teachings are given by way of metaphor and parable. But like John's gospel, though the stories may be allegories, they have historical individuals as their main characters and the narratives read to some extent as if the events were real. The nearest equivalent in modern literature is probably historical fiction where the fictitious details of the story are fabricated around a historical framework. The difference is that the incidents narrated in these apocryphal writings are often allegories and the main intent of the author is to convey spiritual and mystic truth.

It was upon these books, of course, and others like them that the orthodox Christians, encouraged by Constantine, came down so hard. Yet, from the earliest times, the path of inner experience, whether it is called mysticism, gnosticism or any other name, was associated with the teachings of Jesus, and these writings, wherever we can find them, are a valuable resource in our search for what Jesus really taught. The *Acts of John* and the *Acts of Peter* are good examples of this genre, and material will be quoted from them in this book. But of all these apocryphal 'Acts', the richest source of mystical material is undoubtedly, the *Acts of Thomas*.

The *Acts of Thomas* is a second- or third-century Christian composition of unknown authorship, comprising tales and mystic discourses, written as if it were a brief history of the apostle Judas Thomas in India. Scholars are agreed that the majority of the extant manuscripts in Greek were translated out of the Syriac. Many also consider that the *Acts of Thomas* was originally written in Syriac. M.R. James and others, however, have suggested that the original language of composition was actually Greek, but was rendered into Syriac early on. The original Greek was then lost, except for a few fragments, and the existing Greek manuscripts stem from a retranslation of the Syriac back into Greek.

Whatever the truth of the matter, there are certainly differences between the Greek and Syriac versions, sometimes significant, and though the Syriac can be consulted for verification of the text, there are conclusive indications that the existing Syriac texts may stem from a line of manuscripts which has seen more editorial tampering from a Christian point of view than the Greek. Additionally, while the greater part of the text expresses a universal understanding of the mystic path, there are also passages which reflect early Christian practices and beliefs. Consequently, it is difficult to know what the original text might have been, and to what extent the existing text has been 'corrected' by later editors. Like so many ancient writings, the *Acts of Thomas* should be approached with an understanding of its uncertain provenance.

There is also a beautiful collection of forty-two devotional, mystic and often ecstatic poems, the *Odes of Solomon*, written in praise of the Lord, the Word and the Master. Their origin is again unknown but they are thought to have originated from the early Christian period, maybe stemming from the time of Jesus or perhaps before. Their expression of mystical truths employs literary images also found in the Jewish Wisdom literature and the Dead Sea Scrolls, as well as in Christian, Mandaean and Manichaean writings. The *Odes* are extant in both Syriac and Greek, and although exhibiting an undoubted semitic influence, scholars are divided as to which was the original language. They have been translated many times and help us considerably in our enquiry.

Also worthy of particular discussion is the pseudo-Clementine literature, previously mentioned, of which only the *Clementine Recognitions*, the *Clementine Homilies* and two *Epitomes* have come down to us. Of these the *Recognitions* and the *Homilies* are the most significant. The two books are actually variants of each other, though there is no scholarly consensus on which was written first and of the relationship between the two. In fact, it is probable that both of them are based upon earlier material, now lost. The authorship is attributed in the books themselves to Clement, Bishop of Rome during the closing years of the first century, who is said to have sent them to James the brother of Jesus in Jerusalem, but this is usually considered to be a part of the fiction. The *Homilies* are also prefaced with two letters to James from Clement and Peter.

The story consists of a spiritual romance, told by Clement in the first person, describing his travels in the East in the company of Peter. The plot provides a well-executed and entertaining framework while much of the text is taken up with the various discourses of Peter on spiritual matters. The date of composition is uncertain, scholarly opinion varying from the first to the fourth century and even later. But in their present form, the *Recognitions* were probably written between 211 and 231 AD, for they refer to the extension of the Roman franchise which took place throughout the Empire under the Emperor Caracalla (211-217 AD), and they are also quoted by Origen in his *Commentary on Genesis*, written in 231.

Both works were written in Greek, but the original text of the *Recognitions* has been lost and has consequently come down to us in a Latin translation made by Rufinus (*fl.*395-400). Rufinus claims to have made a fair translation, only omitting those portions which were difficult to understand. But he is notorious as an orthodox Christian and a ruthless editor-translator, and the extent to which he has tampered with the text cannot be ascertained.

At face value, the Clementine writings tell us something of the Judaeo-Christian side of early Christianity and, if this is genuinely their provenance, then they are the only works that do so. But whatever their origins, and despite interpolations and editorial modifications, they clearly stem from a mystic school of thought and contain some highly interesting material.

It should be observed that of the many sayings and discourses attributed to Jesus and the apostles in the apocryphal and gnostics texts, few may be considered indisputably authentic. They have been so credited for a number of reasons and from a variety of motivations.[2] Characteristically, the sayings validate, sanction or condemn particular beliefs or practices, according to the writer's point of view. Occasionally, they are polemical – like some of Jesus' New Testament strictures against the scribes and Pharisees. Often, sayings and stories from the canonical gospels are elaborated, condensed or altered in order to make a particular point or to make a meaning more explicit or more acceptable. Sometimes, two or more gospel sayings are combined into one. In other instances, new legends have come into being. There are a significant number of apocryphal resurrection stories, for instance, as well as a legendary correspondence between Jesus and King Abgar of Edessa, "monarch of the peoples of Mesopotamia".[3] And in addition to the nativity stories of Luke and Matthew, there are a number of other infancy legends amongst the apocryphal literature.

On occasion, sayings from other sources have also been mistakenly attributed to Jesus – though he may of course have used them. These include a number of local proverbs such as *Acts 20:35*, "It is more blessed to give than to receive". Sometimes, sayings from another source have deliberately been placed in Jesus' mouth. Thus, a number of passages from the Old Testament or the letters of Paul have been attributed to Jesus.

As in John's gospel, the 'orthodox' and 'unorthodox' alike adopted such practices, for it seems to have been quite acceptable at the time, and there is no doubt that there are many such instances throughout the New Testament as well as the extra-canonical literature, some of which have already been discussed. Given the paucity of the teaching material attributed to Jesus as well as the controversy over its meaning, together with the vagaries of human nature, none of this is surprising.

We have noted before that the wide range of Christian belief, past or present, cannot be constructed out of the four gospels alone, and many of the beliefs of the earliest Christians were handed down from person to person. In the process, Jesus' original teachings were altered, to a greater or lesser extent. But we have a window into the range of these beliefs through the apocryphal and allied literature.

The actual sayings, in or out of the New Testament, which can with certainty be attributed to Jesus is a matter of continuous scholarly debate and about which no firm conclusion will ever be reached. The only approach that remains, therefore, in the search for what he really taught is to study what the early Christians believed that he had taught. And to conduct a fair search, it is clearly of importance to survey *all* the early Christian literature, not just a small selection.

It is worth observing that whether or not Jesus said many of the things attributed to him does not rob these teachings of their power to affect people's lives, nor does it make them true or untrue. Inspiration, inner strength, spiritual understanding, good counsel and so on can certainly be obtained by reading the gospels and other literature, Christian or otherwise. But this inspiration comes from an appreciation of the truth inherent in these teachings, not from the supposed author who has long since passed away. A medicine may have been devised by a physician of the past, but its efficacy at the present time is due to the character of the medicine – not the intervention of the deceased doctor.

In addition to the apocryphal and canonical literature, Jesus' teachings are also to be found amongst the writings of the early Christian fathers. Those of a more mystical disposition, like Clement of Alexandria and Origen, found no difficulty in citing both the Old Testament prophets, together with the earlier Greek mystics and philosophers, in support of Jesus' teachings. In his *Miscellanies*, Clement wrote at great length on the spiritual and mystic life of the true gnostic, even describing Moses as a gnostic.[4] There are also the writings and sayings of the desert fathers, those solitaries, ascetics and monks who took to a life in the wilderness in their search for the inner realities of the soul. And there have been many other mystics, too, within the Christian fold, more notably in the past but also in the present. These all believed with certainty that the essence of Jesus' teachings had been mystical.

Again, searching amongst the liturgies of the early church, and even of the present time, passages are found that enshrine certain traditionally-preserved material from the past, often of a mystical nature not fully understood by those who chant or chanted them, yet holding meanings concerned with mystic truths. These, too, we will quote from time to time.

There were also certain individuals amongst the gnostics and mystics who gained prominence, becoming the target of personal castigation by the orthodox Christians. Simon Magus, said in the *Clementine Homilies* to have been the successor of John the Baptist, was one of the earliest recorded, but Valentinus, Basilides, Marcion, Bar Daisan and others have all been mentioned by the early fathers. In practically all instances, no clear body of writings or teachings can with certainty be ascribed to them and we know of them largely through the rantings of the early fathers. But, sometimes, interesting fragments are preserved which help us in our study.

Mani and Manichaean-Christian Writings

Of all these mystics, the most well-known to posterity was Màni, born around 216 AD, probably in Mesopotamia of Persian parents. Like so many mystics, only a fragmentary framework of Mani's life has survived, embellished by the legends that characteristically surround the memory of past holy men, many of the details being historically conflicting. According to the medieval Arabic scholar, al-Biruni (973-1048 AD), on Mani's own testimony, his place of birth was the village of Mardinu in what was then northern Babylonia.[5] It also seems that although his parents belonged to a royal family, they were of genuinely spiritual disposition.

Like Jesus, Mani showed early signs of a mystical disposition. Another medieval Arabic scholar, al-Nadim (*c*.935-990 AD), records the legend:

> Even when he was young, Mani spoke with words of wisdom and then, when he was twelve years old, there came to him a revelation. According to his statement, it was from the King of the Gardens of Light (the King of the heavens, God).
>
> *al-Nadim, Fihrist 9:1, FNII p.774*

Mani was commonly described as a 'Messenger' or a 'sent one', the Greek word being '*apostolos*' – an Apostle – one of Mani's commonest designations being the 'Apostle of Light'. Though used by Christianity in a particular sense, the term was used in the Middle East for prophets and mystics, indicating those who have a mandate from God, so to speak, to teach humanity. According to al-Biruni, Mani was the disciple of Fadarun,[6] of whom nothing else is known. Amongst Mani's first disciples were his parents and other influential members of his family.

During his lifetime, Mani travelled extensively and continuously, and his modern biographers have often observed that he must have been a man of exceptional charisma, also possessing an organizational flair akin to genius, for wherever he went centres sprang up. He had disciples stretching from northern India, through Persia, Mesopotamia and the Middle East into Egypt, and it seems likely that smaller centres were also founded further afield. Certainly, during the time of his legitimate successors, the community of disciples is known to have stretched from Rome to China.

Mani enjoyed the patronage of several kings, especially the great ruler of the Persian empire, King Shapur, by whom he was permitted to travel throughout the empire, teaching without hindrance. Two of Shapur's brothers also became his followers and it is likely that their example was followed by many other highly placed persons in the Persian empire. But the prevalent religion of this area of the Middle East was Zoroastrianism, the priestly classes being the magi, and there is no doubt that like the Jewish priests and Jesus, the magi were little enamoured of Mani's activities, for he put spiritual power directly into the hands of his followers, thereby undermining the role of the priests. Also like Jesus, he interpreted the received scriptures differently from the priests. He was, for example, universal in his outlook. In a book dedicated to King Shapur, he wrote:

> Wisdom and deeds (its practice?) have always from time to time been brought to mankind by the Messengers of God. So in one age they have been brought by the messenger called Buddha to India, in another by Zara-dusht (Zarathushtra) to Persia, in another by Jesus to the West. There-upon this revelation has come down, this prophecy in this last (present) age through me, Mani, the Messenger of God of Truth to Babylonia.
>
> *Mani, Shahburkan; in al-Biruni, Chronology of Ancient Nations 207, CAN p.190*

Mani taught that Jesus, Buddha and Zarathushtra had all been Saviours or perfect Masters of their time, but that the way to God lay through a living teacher. Mani also taught reincarnation, saying that until such time as a soul comes into contact with a perfect mystic, it remains within the labyrinth of birth and death, taking repeated births in this world under the influence of its past actions and desires. Al-Biruni also comments, "He maintained that he had explained *in extenso* what had only been hinted at by the Messiah (Jesus)".[7]

Though the magi were inimical to Mani, since he enjoyed the patronage of the king and other highly placed people, there was little they could do. But in 273 AD, after a reign of thirty years, Shapur died, being succeeded by his son, Hormizd, who held Mani in the same esteem as his father. But Hormizd was to rule for just one year, being succeeded on his death by his brother Bahram, who ruled from 274 to 277.

Bahram was hostile to Mani but did not act until three or four years after his succession to the throne, though he must have been keeping a close watch upon Mani through his 'intelligence network', a familiar practice then as now. Mani had been journeying down the lower Tigris, visiting his centres on either side of the great river, and was intending to travel on further eastwards through Persia and into the realm of the Kushanas, with his centres at Kabul and Gandhara (now Afghanistan and northwest Pakistan). The Kushanas were Buddhists and the chief tribe of the Yueh-Chi people of China, ruling over much of what is now northern India, Afghanistan and Central Asia during the first three centuries AD.

This was an area where Shapur's protection and support had been of great value to Mani in the past, but at this juncture a royal veto upon his further travels reached him from Bahram. Mani turned back, and he must have known what was awaiting him on his return, for according to a Coptic description of Mani's journey home, he counselled the disciples he met as he travelled, "Look on me and take your fill, my children. For bodily, I shall depart from you."[8]

Reaching his native Mesopotamia, Mani received orders from Bahram to present himself at the royal court. In the meantime, according to the Coptic text, the magi had prepared a *libellus*, a bill of impeachment which contained the accusation, "Mani has taught against our law"[9] – the Zoroastrian faith, like Judaism, being commonly known as the 'law'. On Mani's arrival, Bahram was about to leave on a hunting trip and an impromptu hearing was arranged. But the king had already made up his mind as to the outcome. On seeing Mani, according to the fragmentary remains of both a Coptic and Middle Persian text, he stormed:

"Thou are *not* welcome!"
  But the Lord answered, "Why? Have I done aught evil?"
  The king said, "I have sworn an oath not to leave thee in this land."
  And in an outburst of rage he thus addressed the Lord: "Ah, what need of thee, since thou neither goest to war nor followest the chase (go hunting)?"

                                        Manichaean Manuscript, MM pp.39-40

Mani was put into triple chains – three around his wrists, three around his ankles and one around his neck – a harsh shackling well known from records of the early Christian martyrs. A month later he died, the year being 277 AD. Al-Biruni writes that he "died in prison" and "his head was exposed before the entrance of the royal tent, and his body was thrown into the street, that he should be a warning example to others."[10] Al-Nadim repeats the story but also comments that some say he was executed and then his body cut in two, the two halves being gibbeted on separate gates of the king's capital of Jundi-Shapur. The far earlier Coptic manuscripts say that he died in prison, that his body was cut up and that his severed head was exhibited at one of city gates.[11] Such has been the end of many of the mystics who have taught nothing but love.

Mani taught from Jesus' teachings in a specifically mystic fashion and, although very little remains from his apparently prolific pen, there is enough amongst the writings of his followers to provide great insight into the mystical interpretation he gave of Jesus' teachings. And these are of great interest to us in this book.

A Coptic psalm book, for example, found by Professor Carl Schmidt in 1930 in the bazaars of Cairo, almost certainly unearthed in the desert, is most helpful here.[12] Dating most probably from the fourth century, it includes translations and versions of material that may have originated at a much earlier date. This priceless volume contains devotional writings of a mystic nature praising both Mani and Jesus as mystic Saviours, often in the same devotional song. Similar hymns and other writings, preserved in the ancient Persian dialect of Parthian and Turkish, were amongst the discoveries of a German expedition to Chinese Turkestan (in Central Asia, 500 miles or so north of Afghanistan) during the early years of the twentieth century. To these must be added a Chinese hymn scroll also found in Turkestan. Because of the difficulty in really knowing who first wrote this material – and there were certainly a number of psalmists and writers whose works are collected in these various texts – in this book, they have tentatively been called 'Manichaean-Christian' to indicate their association with both Jesus and Mani.

The religion which formed after the departure of Mani and his successors (about whom little is known), vibrant with the fresh influx of spirituality and unencumbered by the stultifying organization that had swamped and smothered the Christian church, spread rapidly throughout Persia, Mesopotamia and the Roman Empire. Centres had been established from China to Rome and as the direct disciples died, the religion no doubt formed around their heirs, just as it had earlier done around the descendants of Jesus and John the Baptist's disciples.

The timing, however, coincided with Christianity's rise to power, and the Christian authorities included the Manichaeans in their heresy-hunting efforts, for Mani had given a mystical interpretation of Jesus' sayings and parables which was contrary to their orthodox belief. At certain times and in some places, Manichaeism even threatened to replace Christianity as the major religion, so the response of the Christian authorities can be well imagined. The story is a long and violent one, far removed from the teachings of Jesus, and the last remnants of the Manichaeans (in southern France) were not wiped out until medieval times by the soldiers of the inquisition. It is because of this suppression that the writings of Mani and Manichaeans are now in short supply.

Allied to the Manichaeans were the Mandaeans, previously mentioned on several occasions, and it is certain that Mani had some association with them, and there is some indication that his parents were of this persuasion. The Mandaean writings, too, now enshrined in their own liturgical compositions, contain some highly interesting text.

The Mandaeans

> By the rivers of Iraq and especially in the alluvial land of al-Khaur where the Tigris and the Euphrates squander their waters in the marshes, meeting and mating at Qurnah before they flow into the Persian Gulf, and in the lowland of Persia along the Karun, which like its two sister rivers empties into the Gulf, there dwells the remnant of a handsome people who call themselves *Mandaiia*, Mandaeans (*lit.* gnostics), and speak a dialect of Aramaic. When the armies of Islam vanquished the Sassanids, they were already there and in such numbers that the Qur'an granted them protection as 'people of the book', calling them 'Sabaeans'.
>
> E.S. Drower, SA p.ix

Writing in 1960, Lady E.S. Drower was one of the last of only a handful of scholars who have studied the Mandaeans in detail, and of these there can have been none who developed such close personal associations as she, spanning a period of more than thirty years. The Mandaeans are – or were – a shy and secretive people, closely guarding their books, and although she was given her first Mandaean book in about 1920, she did not obtain a copy of their 'canonical prayer book', from whose translation we draw considerable material, until a return visit in 1954. These books were the personal and private property of the priests and were in constant use. At that time she also observed that, as a separate community, the Mandaeans were languishing. Education of their children in standard government schools had introduced twentieth-century attitudes. The numbers of the faithful were dwindling year by year and few of the younger generation were interested in entering the priesthood. The knowledge of their religion and its complex ceremonies was therefore dying out and must by now have almost entirely disappeared.[13]

Though the demise of an ancient people is always tinged with sadness, it is their literature which is of the greatest interest in the present context. Again quoting E.S. Drower:

That an ancient gnostic sect should have survived into our time is remarkable; that so many of their writings, their magical texts, their secret doctrine in the ritual scrolls and their liturgical literature has been preserved is little short of a miracle.

E.S. Drower, CPM p.viii

The antiquity of at least part of the Mandaean texts can be judged from Professor Torgny Säve-Söderbergh's discovery that a series of psalms (the *Psalms of Thomas*) in the Coptic Manichaean-Christian psalm book are adaptations, almost translations, of early Mandaean hymns.[14] Säve-Söderbergh dates them to the last quarter of the second century or earlier.

In addition to the richness of their imagery and the profusion of their texts, these writings are of particular interest for the parallels they present to the New Testament, especially the fourth gospel. They also reflect the content of other gnostic writings as well as some of the psalms ascribed to the Teacher of Righteousness, found amongst the Dead Sea Scrolls. The Mandaean acceptance (in two of their codices) of John the Baptist as one amongst a pantheon of Saviours, some of whom are undoubtedly mythical, is also intriguing, together with the fact that in the same books Jesus is represented as being a false prophet.[15]

Until the arrival of Islam in Mesopotamia seeking converts, Mandaean literature had been diffuse, scattered from place to place. But spurred into action by the influx of a competitive religion, a group of Mandaean reformers collected all the texts they could find and established a definitive body of Mandaean literature, much of which was only available to the priesthood. Existing writings were organized and probably edited in places, instructions for rituals were inserted into the canonical prayer book, and some new compositions also came into being. A period of strict observance for priesthood and laity then ensued.[16]

The Mandaeans themselves tell their story in semi-legendary form in one of the books written at this later date, preserving what had previously been passed down in the oral tradition. At the time of writing this account, there were two classes in existence. The laity were called the Mandaeans, while the priesthood were the Nazoraeans. In the story of their origins, however, the designation Mandaean is used only once, the name for the early members of this group being the Nazoraeans.[17]

The original Nazoraeans, it is related, were disciples of John the Baptist who fled from Jerusalem due to persecution, taking refuge in the Median hills and in the city of Harran in the north of Persia where there were fellow members of their faith. The persecutors, says the legend, were later punished by the destruction of Jerusalem, which places their exodus sometime before 70 AD, perhaps even in the pre-Christian era, but presumably in the time of John the Baptist. There is also a Mandaean tradition that they had once had fellow members in Egypt, and Epiphanius, as we have seen, states that their had been Nasarenes in Palestine before the time of Jesus.

Later, under the protection of a friendly Parthian king, some of them migrated south to Lower Mesopotamia. The Nazoraeans of the north were not of Judaic extraction but of the local population, which adds further to the speculation that John the Baptist had a following that had spread beyond the borders of Palestine. Indeed, many of the northern group – at least in later times – were amongst the intelligentsia, some gaining fame as scholars, physicians and so on in the early Islamic period. But as a less isolated community than their southern counterparts, their religion did not survive the passage of time.[18]

It seems likely, therefore, that the Nazoraeans – or Mandaeans – originated from the spiritual and gnostic milieu of Palestine which included the Essenes, the *Ebionim* (or Ebionites), the *Hasidim,* the Teacher of Righteousness, John the Baptist, Jesus and many others. The early date for John the Baptist's ministry indicated by the Slavonic translation of Josephus fits readily with the suggestion that they originated with a group of John the Baptist's disciples.

It is the same familiar story. Mystics come and give their teachings to their own personal disciples. But after their departure, splinter groups form, all more or less believing in the same principles but diverging in various ways as time goes by.

Pre-Christian Mystical Writings

In our search for insight into Jesus' teachings, we have been looking at the times immediately succeeding him, for it is there that we find those who interpreted his teachings. But there are prior sources, too, which would have been familiar to Jesus and his disciples and which tell us of the same perennial teachings. Indeed, for several millennia before Jesus and many centuries afterwards, the Mediterranean and Middle Eastern countries seem to have been the world's repository of mystic lore. Well-known amongst these were the mystic schools of Greece and Egypt.

The ancient Egyptians had long been noted for their occult and esoteric wisdom and in their number may well have been mystics of the
highest order. There is no doubt that the Greeks carried much that
had been learnt from ancient Egypt into their own literature and manner of expression. Hermes Trismegistus, for example, a mythological
Master in whose name many mystical treatises were written in Greek
during the first three centuries of Christianity, had his origins in earlier Egyptian tradition as the deity, Thoth, the father of all wisdom
and knowledge. In early Christian times, the esoteric 'religion of
Hermes' was widespread in Hellenistic circles throughout the Roman
Empire, and in gnostic writings there is convincing evidence of Hermetic influence. Indeed, there is a section from the Hermetic book,
Asclepius, amongst Nag Hammadi writings. And the northern Mandaeans or – more correctly, Nazoraeans – said in later times that their
faith was the same as that of Hermes and Agathodaemon,[19] another
mystic figurehead of Hermetic writings.

In the first few centuries AD, Egypt still retained something of its
mystical reputation and character, as demonstrated by the amount of
gnostic material translated into Coptic. The early Egyptian churches
were also notably more mystical than many of their counterparts elsewhere, and a number of beliefs and practices of the Christian Copts
were incorporated from their Egyptian milieu.

Amongst the Greeks, Pythagoras (*c.*580-507 BC) is the earliest of
the Greek mystics about whom anything is known, though his life and
teachings are hedged around by anecdote, legend and later accretion.
He was one of many Greek mystics and mystical philosophers whose
influence is still present in the world today. At the time of Jesus,
Pythagoreans were known an esoteric sect who wore a distinctive style
of dress, as have many monks and holy men throughout history.

As we have commented before, from well before the time of
Alexander, through trade and through Greek mastery of shipping in
the Mediterranean, Hellenistic culture had spread throughout the
Middle East and North Africa. Alexander's conquests in the fourth
century BC only established this influence more solidly, giving rise to
the extensive Hellenization in terms of language, philosophy and
culture present in the world that Jesus and his disciples would have
known.

It is not surprising, then, that Greek mystical thought was wide-
spread in Jesus' time and even later. The *Logos*, for example, is the
Greek term used in John's gospel for the Word as the creative Power of
God. And even though, in the centuries succeeding Constantine, the

Christian authorities closed down all the Greek schools of learning within their wide jurisdiction, the vitality of Greek thought was not obliterated, finding a refuge in Persia and elsewhere, and remaining hidden in those writings that survived.

Later, just as Greek philosophy and mystical thought had provided Christianity with a theology, so too was it called back into service in the great Islamic resurgence of interest in the classics from the tenth to the thirteenth centuries. Many of the Sufis such as ibn Massarah (*d.*931) and ibn 'Arabi (1165-1240 AD) quite intentionally set out to combine Greek mystical thought and expression with that of Sufism, and a number of Arabic words used by later Sufis have their derivation from the Greek.

Though a great deal of Greek philosophical writing has survived, mystical writings are in the minority, especially from pre-Christian times, many writers only being known from fragments of their works preserved as quotations in the works of others or simply as traditions. Orpheus, Pythagoras, Heraclitus (*c.*540-475 BC) and Empedocles (*c.*490-430 BC) come into this category, though we are fortunate that many of the works of Plato (*c.*427-347 BC) have come through, more or less intact, preserving for us something of the mystic philosophy of his teacher, Socrates (*c.*470-399 BC), as well as his own thoughts.

But of all the traditions to which Jesus and his Palestinian disciples would have been exposed, the most influential would naturally have been the Jewish. As a source of mystic teachings, the Jewish Bible – being a miscellaneous collection of material from a variety of sources including the Jewish prophets – has many gems, though some of its contents have a provenance even more hoary than the New Testament documents. Since both Jesus and his Jewish disciples would have been familiar with these scriptures, it is natural that he would have quoted from them, explaining their true spiritual meaning.

Many of these ancient scriptures, however – most of which were written several hundred years BC – are in as much of a muddle as the canonical gospels. *Genesis*, for instance, dating roughly from the ninth century BC, is generally reckoned to be comprised of at least two source documents, spliced together in not too expert a fashion. The evidence is various. One of these sources, for instance, seems to have used the term *Yahweh* for God while the other used *Elohim*. Consequently, in the *Genesis* we know, both terms are used – first a section using one followed by a section employing the other.

There are also two creation myths, the first up to *Genesis 2:4a*, covering the creation of the universe in six earthly days, followed by the second in *Genesis 2:4b-3:24* which tells the story of Adam and Eve. There are also two genealogies stemming from Adam and two inter-woven accounts of the Flood.

The same kind of composition is true of a number of other Biblical documents. Indeed, the first thing for which scholars search when making a critical analysis of any ancient book are the tell-tale seams, splices, varieties of style, lack of sequence in narrative, repetition and other signs that the document they are dealing with is an edited-together compilation of previously separate sources. As in the gospels, not all of these sources are of a mystical character and those that were are unlikely to have been incorporated unscathed or to have travelled the long journey to the present time untouched and devoid of edito-rial tampering. This is why Jesus advised his disciples to be "good money-changers", knowing how to select the true from the false.

Just as Jesus made extensive use of metaphor and parable, so too did his Jewish predecessors. It was the style of the times. In fact, their use of allegory was sometimes of seemingly so impenetrable a nature that hardly a word of it would appear to relate to spiritual or mystical matters, as in the *Song of Songs.* Yet in some instances, every word or phrase had a mystical meaning, even apparently historical narratives.

There is a language – almost a code – of mystical metaphors that is prevalent throughout this ancient Semitic literature, much of which was still in use in Jesus' time and which was carried forward into the later Sufi period, too. Without a detailed explanation of this method and its language, the texts can hardly be discussed, but it may be briefly noted that many of the Old Testament stories were not meant to be taken literally, even some of the seemingly 'historical' ones. In the com-mon literary style of those times, they were written in a symbolic lan-guage which expressed mystical truths and other matters in a codified form. Philo Judaeus, Jewish rabbis and teachers of all periods, the writ-ers of the pre-Christian Dead Sea Scrolls, as well as some of the early Christian fathers, have all interpreted Old Testament writings in this way. It is true that sometimes such interpretation may have owed much to the imagination, but it was generally appreciated that the key to understanding the original writer was to comprehend his imagery in a metaphorical fashion. Indeed, antecedents of the *Genesis* allegories can be found in the Mesopotamian, Babylonian and Sumerian myths of the Middle East, two thousand years or so BC.

Some Old Testament books, of course, contain more mystical teach-ings than others. Of these it is probably the Wisdom literature which has seen the least adulteration and is the most readily understandable to the modern mind. The Wisdom literature includes *Proverbs*, *Ecclesiastes*, *Job*, the *Psalms*, the *Song of Songs*, the *Wisdom of Solomon* and the *Wisdom of Jesus Ben Sirach*, also called *Ecclesiasticus*. Within these books there are some very interesting parallels to the gospel texts.

Reading through the Biblical Wisdom literature, it becomes clear that the term 'Wisdom' has two meanings. Firstly, it is the creative Power of God, identical with the *Logos* or Creative Word, the Power by which God has created the creation. This understanding has been borne out by the more detailed researches of many scholars, Christian and Jewish. Secondly, it refers to the spiritual wisdom or teachings, the esoteric description of the inner path and its practice, as well as the best advice on leading a spiritual life in this world while seeking God within oneself.

The Wisdom literature in the Old Testament was by no means the only such literature produced. As a literary style, it flourished in the Middle East and neighbouring countries from ancient times, and it can be confidently presumed that whatever has survived is only a fraction of what was written, for human beings have always needed and appreciated guidance on how to live. Egypt and Greece were especially prolific, at all times in their ancient history. In a like manner, from Palestine, Syria, Mesopotamia and Persia came proverbs, fables, wise sayings and epic poems all concerned with the same themes of human suffering dating, in some instances, as far back as the third millennium BC. Much of this style was later carried forward into the Sufi tradition, where we have such monumental literature as the *Mathnavi* of Jalal-ud-din Rumi, the *Conference of the Birds* by Farid-ud-din Attar, and many other writings comprised of fables and parables conveying mystic wisdom. Indeed, from the parables which have been left to us in the gospels, it seems that Jesus himself also taught in the same manner.

The Greek word 'philosopher' meant one who was a lover of wisdom (*philo-sophia*). Hence, the Greek mystics were considered philosophers in the true meaning of the term; what in modern times we call philosophers, the Greeks would have termed sophists or quibblers, a term often used in a pejorative sense. Likewise, when Socrates welcomed the company of philosophers at his death,[20] he meant the lovers of mystic wisdom, those who would remind him of God, not those akin to the intellectual professors and theologians of today!

In addition to the canonical Jewish literature, there are some remarkable texts with which Jesus and his disciples would have been familiar. Amongst these are the books of Enoch, *1 Enoch* and *2 Enoch*,

Enoch or Enos being the son of Seth and the grandson of Adam, according to the *Genesis*[21] story. F.C. Burkitt and R.H. Charles, two of the great Biblical scholars and pioneers of the past, have pointed out some remarkable similarities between certain parts of these books and the synoptics.[22] In the case of *1 Enoch*, this is particularly true of the apocalyptic discourse attributed to Jesus in Matthew and Mark. The similarity is so marked that Burkitt entertained no doubt that parts of these discourses have a direct literary dependence upon the prior text of *1 Enoch LXXII*. Using very similar phraseology, both speak of the "Son of Man" sitting on the "throne of his glory" and of a judgment of all nations when the "righteous" and the "elect" will receive the reward of salvation and the rest will be forever damned.[23]

This is entirely in keeping with the apocalyptic beliefs of the compilers of the synoptic gospels, Mark and Matthew in particular. And the Judaic character of both *1 Enoch* and Matthew further emphasizes Matthew's Judaic background. The same parallels are seen when the apocalyptic passages in the Biblical *Book of Daniel* are compared with those of Mark and Matthew. Matthew, following Mark, speaks of the "Son of Man coming with the clouds of heaven",[24] apocalyptic imagery borrowed from the *Book of Daniel* where Daniel says that in a 'dream' or 'vision' he saw that the "Son of man came with the clouds of heaven".[25] The context is likewise that of a 'revelation' describing the Day of Judgment and the separation of the righteous from the evil-doers.

Both *1 Enoch* and *Daniel* are undoubtedly pre-Christian, dating from the second century BC, and both are concerned with the coming of the Messiah, not with Jesus in particular. The later Christian writers have simply interpreted them as a prophecy concerning Jesus, while all the 'signs' concerning the end of the world are those which are common to *1 Enoch*, *Daniel* and other Jewish apocalypses of the period. *1 Enoch* is actually quoted and Enoch mentioned by name in the New Testament letter attributed to Jude.[26]

2 Enoch has an even greater number of similarities to the gospels, again indicating "a close connection if not a literary dependence".[27] Both Matthew and *2 Enoch* contain lists of comparable beatitudes. Matthew's "Blessed are the peacemakers", for instance, is paralleled by "Blessed is he who implants peace and love",[28] and there are other striking resemblances, too, to all four gospels as well as *Acts* and Paul's letters. Matthew's "be of good cheer, be not afraid",[29] for example, appears in a number of places in *2 Enoch*.[30]

From a study of its contents, which have many similarities to the Biblical Wisdom literature, it can be determined that most of *2 Enoch* was written in Greek, probably by a Hellenistic Jew living in Egypt. It can be dated early in the first century, certainly before 70 AD, and probably much earlier, because it is evident from the text that the Temple at Jerusalem is still standing. In addition to the New Testament parallels, *2 Enoch* is quoted by Origen[31] and occurs in a fragment of another writing quoted by Clement of Alexandria;[32] *2 Enoch* is also quoted in a number of Christian apocryphal writings. From all this information, it may be concluded that both books of Enoch were held in considerable esteem by the earliest Christians.

There are also many parallels of thought and expression between the gospels, the Wisdom literature and the Dead Sea Scrolls, the writings found at Qumran and commonly ascribed to the Essenes. It is to some of these magnificent psalms to which we briefly turn in the Epilogue. Perhaps it should also be noted that the wealth of modern 'Essene' texts can be largely discounted as apocrypha of twentieth-century origin.

There is, then, an abundance of ancient literature which helps us gain a deeper understanding of Jesus' teachings. All the same, we can never be completely sure of what he taught because of the uncertainties which have already been described concerning the history of ancient manuscripts and the diversification of belief which very rapidly surrounded his teachings. For this reason, we use one other source of information – the simple, universal teachings given by other mystics and Masters of the past which are preserved intact and which may still be learnt from Masters of the present time. These teachings have previously been outlined and it is now time to study all this material in depth to see what may emerge.

NOTES AND REFERENCES

1. *Jeremiah* 32:14-15.
2. See Joachim Jeremias, *Unknown Sayings of Jesus* pp.27-43, for an elaboration of the following.
3. See Eusebius, *History of the Church* 13, HC pp.65-70.
4. Clement of Alexandria, *Miscellanies* V:XI, WCAII p.265.
5. Al-Biruni, *Chronology of Ancient Nations* 208, CAN p.190.
6. Al-Biruni, *Chronology of Ancient Nations* 207, CAN p.189.
7. Al-Biruni, *Chronology of Ancient Nations* 208, CAN p.191.
8. *Manichaean Homilies* p.44, MM p.38.
9. *Manichaean Homilies* p.45, MM p.39.
10. Al-Biruni, *Chronology of Ancient Nations* 208, CAN p.191.
11. *Manichaean Homilies* pp.46-67; *Psalms* CCXXV, MPB p.17.
12. *A Manichaean Psalm-Book*, Part II, ed. and tr. by C.R.C. Allbery.

13. See E.S. Drower, *CPM* pp.vii-viii.
14. See Torgny Säve-Söderbergh, *Studies in the Coptic-Manichaean Psalm-Book.*
15. See E.S. Drower, *SA* pp.xi-xii.
16. See E.S. Drower, *SA* pp.xii-xiii.
17. See E.S. Drower, *SA* pp.xiii-xiv.
18. See E.S. Drower, *SA* pp.xiv-xvi,111-113.
19. See E.S. Drower, *SA* pp.111-113.
20. See Plato's *Phaedo.*
21. *Genesis* 4:26, 5:6.
22. See F.C. Burkitt, *JCA* pp.21-25; R.H. Charles, *APOTII* pp.426-429.
23. *Matthew* 24:1-51, 25:31-46; *Mark* 13:1-27, 14:62; *Enoch* LXII, *BE* pp.81-83.
24. *Matthew* 24:30 and 26:64; *Mark* 13:26 and 14:62.
25. *Daniel* 7:13, *KJV.*
26. *Jude* 1:14.
27. R.H. Charles, *APOTII* p.428.
28. *Matthew* 5:9; *2 Enoch* 52:11, *APOTII* p.461.
29. *Matthew* 14:27.
30. *2 Enoch* 1:8, 20:2, 21:3, *APOTII* pp.431,441,442.
31. Origen, *On First Principles* I:3.3, *WOI* p.35.
32. Clement of Alexandria, probably quoting the *Apocalypse of Zephaniah, Miscellanies* V:XI, *WCAII* p.267; *cf. APOTII* pp.427,439.

PART II

God, Man & the Creation

CHAPTER SIX

In Search of the Kingdom

Is There a Creator?

However much we may be absorbed in the affairs of living, at some stage in our lives, everybody, however fleetingly, wonders whether or not there is a God and if so – where is He? Even the adamant atheist – somewhere deep down in the recesses of his mind – is unsure if his assertions are correct or not. People have taken baptism or communion on their deathbed, for example, having previously rejected it all their lives. It demonstrates that they were still uncertain of their disbelief and they wanted to cover their options in the only way they knew how.

Logically, it is impossible to know for certain whether or not there is a God, for intellect and thought cannot perceive Him. Yet, through reason, it is possible to approach the subject. Mystics say that the amazing diversity, complexity, order and organization in the universe has not come into being by chance. There is a supreme Intelligence behind it all. Modern science may have discovered and described something of this incredible order, but cannot understand its origins. The existence of this order tells us something.

The story is related of a 'primitive' man who is walking in the wilderness when he comes across an old-fashioned pocket watch, lying on the ground. He picks it up, examines it, discovers how to wind it up and notices how intricately and beautifully all its parts fit together and interact with each other. It does not take him long to come to the conclusion that someone must have made it. He realizes that such a clever instrument could not have formed itself by chance. The pocket watch must have had a intelligent creator. The case is similar to the universe in which we live.

When we look up into a clear night sky, we can see thousands of stars. Yet with only a few exceptions, the stars are all members of our own local galaxy and represent far less than a billionth of the stars in the physical universe. Were we to look with a powerful telescope into the dark spaces between the stars, we would find myriads of tiny luminous points. But these tiny specks are not stars. They are entire galaxies. And only those that are close enough can be seen.

Our local galaxy, the Milky Way, is an average sort of a galaxy, possessing about 400 billion stars or suns. Some others contain even a thousand billion stars. And like over 90 percent of galaxies, the Milky Way is arranged in an orderly flat spiral disc, with arms as in a whirl or vortex. The stars circle around the centre of the this whirl; planets orbit around the stars; moons orbit around the planets. Yet, the moons, planets, stars and galaxies are ordered in such a way that they never collide with one another, though if they had happened to be much closer, then long ago they would have all fallen into each other by the force of gravity.

In the heart of matter itself, the same processes are at work. Intensely active points of matter – subatomic particles – circle and pirouette around each other following laws which man can hardly comprehend. Yet the same subatomic processes are at work in far off galaxies. Everything – at all places in the physical universe – bears witness to a repeating and universal order. Galaxies, billions of light years away, are built on the same fundamental patterns as we are ourselves. We even take it for granted that they should be.

In living creatures, the order is even more complex and fascinating. Each cell is teeming with highly organized activity. There are hundreds of thousands of interactions of various kinds every second. And not only are they all integrated with each other, but the entire living creature functions as a whole, with all its cells in harmony with each other. The ordered complexity even in the 'simplest' of creatures can hardly be envisaged.

Yet there is more. Scientists, intrigued by all the order and organization, have identified several thousand apparent coincidences in the natural world, without which neither life nor the physical universe could exist. They have called it the Anthropic Principle. Some of these are simple. There are, for instance, only three spatial dimensions. Why? Why not two or four – or more? Two dimensions would make it impossible to get about without constant collisions. Nothing could ever go *over* anything else, for there would be no 'over' or 'under'. On the other hand, the scientists calculate that four or more would create totally unstable planetary – and other – orbits. So three is just right.

Again, the light not only from our sun but also from billions upon billions of similar stars is at exactly the right frequency for life as we know it to exist. If it was of a higher frequency – as in x-rays and gamma rays – living systems would be blown apart. If it was of a lower frequency, as in radio waves, its energy would be insufficient to be absorbed and utilized.

The full extent of these apparent coincidences is illustrated by an example given by Canadian philosopher, John Leslie. Consider, he says, the case of a man who is brought before a firing squad. Dawn breaks and the condemned man is led out blindfold and stood against the wall. The firing squad is marched in – ten men with loaded rifles. The orders are given, they take aim and fire. But not one of the rifles functions. They *all* fail to go off. They had all been checked, oiled and cleaned immediately beforehand, yet not one shot is fired. So the blindfold is removed from the relieved prisoner and he walks away, a free man.

Now the odds against just one rifle misfiring are great. But the odds against ten rifles misfiring are beyond the bounds of coincidence. And not only that, but when each rifle is examined, it is discovered the *each of the ten misfired for a different reason.* It is not that there is just one common fault to which the misfiring can be ascribed, but a multiplicity of coincidences, all happening simultaneously.

This, observes the Anthropic Principle, is the nature of physical existence. The firing squad of nature contains a billion men with a billion rifles and they all simultaneously fail to go off. This is the degree of natural 'coincidence'. Clearly, it is not coincidence but design, though many people find this an extremely uncomfortable point of view, for it leads automatically to the question of a Designer. And a *hidden* Designer. That's the real problem – we cannot see Him!

The astronomer and writer George Greenstein has studied the nature of these coincidences in his book *The Symbiotic Universe.* At the very outset, he points out that the *cosmos is suited to life* but that scientists in general have taken this fact for granted and busied themselves with the study of its details. It is as if they had analyzed in great depth the patterns, rhythms and relationships to be found in an image on a screen, but – for the most part – had failed to address themselves to *how* that image got there. The origins of the truly remarkable wealth of coincidences, inexplicable by conventional scientific thought, that are found as fundamental building blocks in the construction of this image, have rarely been considered. Greenstein comments:

The habitability of the universe is an utterly astonishing thing.... In some strange and mysterious way, our universe is fundamentally a universe of life – a universe which takes life seriously, if you will. Only when enough people begin to take the idea seriously will further evidence leap forward as if spontaneously. And make no mistake about it: if that idea turns out to be correct, it is no exaggeration to say that a major revolution of thought is in the offing.

Whatever the explanation turns out to be for that massive series of coincidences whereby life arose in the universe, it is not going to be simple. Each and every one of them flows from the laws of nature and it is to these principles themselves that our thinking must turn.... What is new and incomprehensible here is that in some extraordinary way ... the laws of physics conform themselves to life.

George Greenstein, SU pp.12,27

Greenstein goes on to point out that the discoveries of science do not, in themselves, prove the existence of a God. Mystics would agree, for such evidence – however powerful – is only circumstantial, requiring human interpretation. All the same, such facts are proof of something bigger than chance as the overall controlling force in the material world. Before forming an opinion, therefore, of whether or not there is a God, it is wise to know something of the physical universe which He is supposed – or supposed not – to have created. Does it bear witness to a Designer? And the answer is: it does.

In the time of Jesus, of course, such scientific information was unknown. Indeed, such detail can blind us to what stands before our eyes. For from an observation of the order and rhythm in the seasons and the harmony inherent in the whole pageant of nature, many people have independently come to a realization of the same truth. Ancient, non-literate peoples, living close to nature and far from the taints of so-called civilization, have instinctively been aware that they live within the fold of a greater Being, while many of the philosophers of classical times have also arrived at the same conclusion. In fact, the Greek noun *kosmos*, from which the English 'cosmos' is derived, means 'order', stemming from a Greek verb 'to order', 'to arrange', 'to marshall'. Homer uses it for Greek generals marshalling their troops for battle. Moreover, *kosmos* also meant an adornment (hence our word 'cosmetic'), something which beautifies and gives pleasure to contemplate. The *kosmos*, therefore, implied the beautiful and well-arranged order of things.

Amongst the Greek philosophers and mystics, Anaxagoras of

Clazomenae (*c.*500-428 BC) and Diogenes of Apollonia (*fl.* late 5th century BC) both ascribed the order in all things to a divine Mind (*Nous*) or Intelligence. Similarly, Xenophon (*c.*431-355 BC) and Plato recorded dialogues in which Socrates used the same argument to support the existence of a divine Intelligence (*Logos* or *Nous*) behind all things. As Cleinias, one of Plato's characters in *The Laws*, says:

> Don't you think that the gods' existence is an easy truth to explain? ... Just look at the earth and the sun and the stars and the universe in general; look at the wonderful procession of the seasons and its articulation into years and months!

Plato, The Laws 885-886, TL p.412

More specifically, in Plato's *Philebus*, Socrates and Protarchus converse:

> SOCRATES: All the wise ... proclaim in unison that Intellect (*Nous*) is the king of heaven and earth....
>
> PROTARCHUS: ... To say that Intellect (*Nous*) regulates the universe does justice to the order we perceive in it, in the sun, moon, stars and the whole vault of heaven. For my part, I can never speak or think about it in any other terms.

Plato, Philebus 28c-e, P pp.80-81; cf. PISP pp.261-263

Again, in his *Memoirs of Socrates*, Xenophon records a conversation in which Socrates first notes the fittingness of bodily design:

> SOCRATES: Don't you think that it was for their use that He who originally created men provided them with the various means of perception, such as eyes to see what is visible and ears to hear what is audible? ... And apart from these, don't you feel that there are other things too that look like effects of providence (foresight, care). For example, because our eyes are delicate, they have been shuttered with eyelids which open when we have occasion to use them, and close in sleep; and to protect them from injury by the wind, eyelashes have been made to grow as a screen; and our foreheads have been fringed with eyebrows to prevent damage from the sweat of the head.... Are you in doubt whether such provident arrangements are the result of chance or of design?
>
> ARISTODEMUS: No indeed. Looked at this way, they seem very much like the contrivances of some wise and benevolent craftsman.

Xenophon, Memoirs of Socrates I.4.4ff, CS pp.90-91

Socrates then widens the perspective, going on to speak of mind and intelligence:

> SOCRATES: Do you believe you have some intelligence?
> ARISTODEMUS: Go on asking questions and you will get your answer!
> SOCRATES: Do you suppose that there is nothing intelligent anywhere else, knowing as you do that what you have in your body is only a small portion of all the earth there is, and only a little water out of a vast volume of it.... Do you really believe that by some lucky chance you have appropriated mind for yourself, and that it alone exists nowhere else, and that the orderliness of these vast masses of infinite multitude is due, as you say, to a kind of unintelligence?
>
> *Xenophon, Memoirs of Socrates I.4.4ff, CS p.91*

But Aristodemus protests that he is unable to observe the workings of this divine Intelligence in the same way that he can see the handicraft of artisans, to which Socrates responds:

> SOCRATES: You can't see your own mind either, although it controls your body. On that principle you can say that you do nothing by design and everything by chance.... My good friend, get it into your head that your own mind, which is inside you, controls your body as it wills; and in the same way you must believe that the intelligence which is in the universe disposes all things just as it pleases. If you accept that your vision has a range of several miles, you must not suppose that the eye of God lacks the power to see everything at once; and if you accept that your mind can take thought about affairs both here and in Egypt and in Sicily, you must not suppose that the wisdom of God is incapable of taking thought for all things at the same time.
>
> *Xenophon, Memoirs of Socrates I.4.4ff, CS p.91*

Aristotle, Cicero, Marcus Aurelius and many others of the classical period and throughout history have all invoked the same argument for the existence of a divine power or intelligence and the evidence cannot lightly be dismissed. The prime Mover in Aristotle's universe was God[1] and in *On the Cosmos*, a work attributed to Aristotle though commonly thought to be pseudonymous, the writer describes God's fundamental place in the universe:

> God, who is mightiest in Power, outstanding in beauty, immortal in life, and supreme in excellence ... though He is invisible to every mortal thing,

He is seen through His deeds. For it would be true to say that all the phenomena of the air, the land and the water are the works of God who rules the cosmos; from whom, according to Empedocles, the natural philosopher,

> "grows all that is and was and is yet to come,
> the trees and the whole race of men and women,
> beasts, birds and water-nurtured fish."

Pseudo-Aristotle, On the Cosmos 6:399, SRCPC pp.397-399

Similarly, Cicero (106-43 BC), the Roman consul, orator and writer who set himself the task of making Greek philosophy accessible to Romans, wrote in his *Tusculan Disputations*:

When we see the beauty and brightness of the sky, then the amazing speed,[2] which our thought cannot grasp, of its revolution; next the succession of day and night and changes of the seasons divided into four to suit the ripening of the fruits of the earth and the constitution of living bodies, and the sun their ruler and guide, and the moon marking as it were and indicating the days in the calendar by the waxing and waning of her light ...; (when we see) here ... where we live, (that) there cease not in due season:

> Skies to be shining and trees in leaf blossoming,
> Tendrils of joy-giving vines to be burgeoning,
> Foison of berries the boughs to be burdening,
> Fields to be rich with crops, flowers out everywhere,
> Fountains to bubble and grasses the meads cover:

... when then we behold all these things and countless others, can we doubt that some Being is over them, or some Author ... some Governor of so stupendous a work of construction?

Cicero, Tusculan Disputations I:XXVIII.68-71, TD pp.79-83

Cicero waxes poetic as he considers the matter and we have omitted much of his description. As Paul summarizes it in his letter to the Romans:

Ever since God created the world, His everlasting Power and deity – however invisible – have been there for the mind to see in the things He has created.

Romans 1:19-20

One Lord

While such discussions may be helpful and of interest, they are no substitute for experience. For what we accept today on logical considerations only, can be held in doubt tomorrow when we are confronted
with a different argument. Mystics, however, do not need reason or
intuition to help them understand the existence of God. They see
things for themselves, within their own selves, through their own personal experience. And all mystics, without exception, have taught the
existence of a Supreme Power. From the comments ascribed to him in
John's gospel, Jesus also saw things in this way. As he said:

> I and my Father are one.
> *John 10:30*

There is no doubt, then, that Jesus taught the existence of a God. Like
Moses and all the Jewish prophets, Jesus, most assuredly, taught that there
is *one* God. When asked what was the primary reality behind all things,
"which is the first commandment of all?", he immediately looked to the
mystics of the past to make his point. He quoted Moses in *Deuteronomy*:

> The first of all the commandments is,
>   "Hear, O Israel; The Lord our God is one Lord."
> *Mark 12:29, Deuteronomy 6:4*

By "one Lord" is meant that God is the supreme, eternal and self-existent
Power within whom everything else exists and has its being. If there is
something other than God, it means that He is not the Supreme Power,
that His Will does not prevail in all things and that He is not in complete
control of everything. He is the One from whom the multiplicity of creation has sprung and by whom it is continually sustained. It is He who
has created everything. Jesus, Paul and the writers of the gospels and other
Christian literature certainly considered this to be a fundamental truth
and in a number of places they speak of Him as the "Lord of heaven and
earth",[3] the creator of both the spiritual and the physical realms.

The Kingdom of God is Within You

Where then can He be found? As Jesus observes in John's gospel during
his discussion with Pilate, after his arrest:

> My kingdom is not of this world:
>> if my kingdom were of this world,
>> then would my servants fight,
>> that I should not be delivered to the Jews:
> But now is my kingdom not from hence.
>
> *John 18:36*

The "kingdom of God" is not to be found in this world nor does the Lord dwell in some far away place, beyond all comprehension and access. In Luke's gospel, Jesus is quite explicit as to where this one God is to be found:

> The kingdom of God cometh not with observation:
> Neither shall they say, "Lo here! or, lo there!"
> For, behold, the kingdom of God is within you.
>
> *Luke 17:20-21*

God is within. This primary, essential and fundamental truth has not only been taught by all mystics, but is understood intuitively by many people of all castes, races and religions. The understanding arises spontaneously in the minds of those who are drawn to an inner, spiritual life, for God is the essence of our being. If He is an ocean, then the soul is a drop. If He is a fire, the soul is a spark. If He is a sun, the soul is a ray of His light. If He is the supreme Reality, then the soul is our real self. The soul is in God and God is in the soul. He is the Supreme Being or Supreme Consciousness; the soul is an individual being or consciousness. Consequently, God is the essence of life and for this reason He has often been called the Living God.

A more expanded version of the saying in Luke is found in the *Gospel of Thomas*. Once known only from some Greek papyrus scraps discovered in the rubbish heaps of Oxyrhynchus, a version of the *Gospel of Thomas* was found in its entirety amongst the Coptic translations of the Nag Hammadi library. This gospel is very interesting, for not only does it contain none of the narrative material of the canonical gospels, but it is markedly mystic in its character. Further, while the gospel compilers, particularly the synoptic writers, have woven Jesus' sayings into an eschatological setting where the end of the world is imminently expected, the *Gospel of Thomas* provides virtually no setting for Jesus' sayings. And the continuous emphasis of these sayings is that the kingdom of God is within, it is there that God is to be found, and that to find Him is the purpose of human life. The passage reads:

Jesus said,
"If those who lead you say to you,
    'See, the kingdom is in the sky,'
        then the birds of the sky will precede you.
If they say to you, 'It is in the sea,'
        then the fish will precede you.
Rather, the kingdom is inside of you,
        and it is outside of you.

"When you come to know yourselves,
    then you will become known,
    and you will realize that it is you
    who are the sons of the Living Father.
But if you will not know yourselves,
    you dwell in (spiritual) poverty
    and it is you who are that poverty."

Gospel of Thomas 3, NHS20 pp.53-55

Using the pithy and direct style common to many Eastern mystics, Jesus points out that if – as some people evidently believed both then as well as now – God dwells somewhere up above in the physical sky, then the birds would already be in heaven. Or, if He dwelt in the depth of the sea, then all the fishes would already be with God. In fact, Jesus says that He is both within and without, for He pervades everywhere in His creation, being the essence within all things. Consequently, when the soul comes to know itself as it really is, as a particle of God, then God will also be known, for the two are one. For this reason, every soul can be called a "son of the Living Father", for all souls have sprung from Him. But this can only be realized when the soul comes to know itself. And if a person does not know themselves, then they dwell in a state of spiritual poverty and limitation, even considering themselves to be that impoverished state of being. Elsewhere in the *Gospel of Thomas*, the same idea is expanded:

Jesus said,
"It is I who am the Light which is above them all;
    it is I who am the All.
From me did the All come forth,
    and unto me did the All extend.
Raise the stone, and there you will find Me,
    cleave the wood and there I am."

Gospel of Thomas 77, NHS20 p.83; Oxyrhynchus Papyri 5:2, SOL p.12

Jesus says that he is one with the One Light of God from whom the "All", a gnostic expression meaning the entire creation, has been manifested. Consequently, Jesus, as the Creator, is present everywhere, in wood, stone and everything else. There is no place where He cannot be found. Hence, a similar saying from the same gospel reads:

> His disciples said to him,
> "When will the kingdom come?"
>
> Jesus said,
> "It will not come by waiting for it.
> It will not be a matter of saying
> 'here it is' or 'there it is'.
> Rather, the kingdom of the Father
> is spread out upon the earth (is everywhere),
> and men do not see it."
>
> *Gospel of Thomas 113, NHS20 p.93*

Jesus means that God and His eternal kingdom or reality are present everywhere, within and without, but people do not realize what they are seeing. And he also points out very clearly that there will be no special day on which the kingdom of God will come. God is already here, everywhere. In the *Teachings of Silvanus*, found along with the *Gospel of Thomas* in the Nag Hammadi library, a more metaphysical description of the same idea is given:

> Consider these things about God: He is in every place; on the other hand,
> He is in no place. With respect to His Power, to be sure, He is in every
> place; but with respect to divinity, He is in no place. So, then, it is possible
> to know God a little. With respect to His Power, it is true, He fills every
> place, but in the exaltation of His divinity nothing contains Him. Every-
> thing is in God, but God is not in anything.
>
> *Teachings of Silvanus 100-101, TS pp.45-47*

Let Us Make Man in Our Image

A well-known passage in *Genesis*, commonly quoted over the centuries by mystics and orthodox alike, reads:

And God said:
"Let us make man in our image, after our likeness:
    and let them have dominion over the fish of the sea,
    and over the fowl of the air, and over the cattle,
    and over all the earth, and over every creeping thing
    that creepeth upon the earth."
So God created man in His (own) image,
    in the image of God created He him;
    male and female created He them.

Genesis 1:26-27, KJV

As many mystics and philosophers of Jewish, Christian and Islamic origin have pointed out, *Genesis* and much of what Christians call the Old Testament, is written allegorically and is intended to be interpreted as such. God creating man in His own image, therefore, does not mean that God looks like the human form of a man. After all, if He were like a man, what nationality would He be? Would He be Eastern or Western, black, brown or white, or some other shade? And would He be bearded or clean-shaven? It means that, spiritually, man is made with the built-in potential to see or realize God within Himself. Man is built in God's spiritual image. This is a fundamental aspect of mystic teachings, for it means that not only is the soul a drop of the Ocean of God but that only when the soul comes into the human form can the ascent to God be commenced. For this, rather than for any biological reason, man is said to be the top of the creation, to "have dominion" over all other creatures. Though they too are souls, animals, birds and other creatures that "creepeth upon the earth" are not endowed in their present existence with the potential for finding God within. One never, for instance, saw a dog, a cat, a monkey or a bee engaged in interior prayer, seeking God within themselves.

The importance of the human form and the presence of God within has been emphasized in all mystic literature, that of the early Christians being no exception. In the *Acts of Thomas*, for example, there is a beautiful and intriguing piece of allegory and metaphor in which the soul is compared to a dancing girl, a "damsel", who sings and dances at a marriage party. And the unknown author uses her appearance, garments and different parts of her body as metaphors to depict the mystic nature of the human form:

> The damsel is the daughter of light, in whom consisteth and dwelleth the proud brightness of kings, and the sight of her is delightful, she shineth

with beauty and cheer. Her garments are like the flowers of spring, and from them a waft of fragrance is borne; and in the crown of her head the King is established, which with his Immortal Food (ambrosia) nourisheth them that are founded upon Him; and in her head is set Truth, and with her feet she showeth forth joy. And her mouth is opened, and it becometh her well: thirty and two are they that sing praises to her.

Acts of Thomas 2, ANT p.367

The poet says that the soul is, metaphorically, of royal blood. Her father is the divine King of Kings, the Lord Himself. She is a child of God; He is her King. Her natural estate is that of light, beauty and joy or divine bliss. Her "garments" are the natural light and purity of the soul which emanate from her when unencumbered by the body and the mind. She has her own light. And where is this to be found in a human being? "In the crown of her head the King is established." Within the head, within oneself, is God, the supreme Truth, to be found: "in her head is set Truth."

The "immortal food" of such a soul, "who is founded upon Him", is the spiritual current of God whose nourishment makes her dance with inner joy in the natural ecstatic worship of God – "with her feet she showeth forth joy". The "mouth" of the soul is like a "well", a deep cistern that is constantly filled from hidden, inner springs, from which she consumes the spiritual sustenance of the Living Water that flows from Him. And the reference to the "thirty-two" which "sing praises to her" would seem to be the thirty-two teeth in the mouth. It means that everything within her praises God, naturally, for she and God, her King, are of the same essence.

The above passage is translated from the Greek, and the process by which documents became tainted by religious doctrine is readily seen from an examination of the equivalent Syriac version where the "Damsel is the daughter of light" becomes "My Church is the daughter of light", while "her mouth is open and it becometh her well: thirty and two are they that sing praises to her" becomes "Her mouth is open, and it becometh her, wherewith she uttereth all songs of praise. The twelve Apostles of the Son, and the seventy-two (disciples) thunder forth (His praises) in her".[4]

The "damsel" has become the "Church". Her instinctive sense of worship and ecstatic inward dance has become the singing of hymns. And the "thirty-two" have altogether disappeared, being replaced by a heavily Christianized equivalent.

Amongst the mystical and devotional *Odes of Solomon*, similar metaphors are used in the description of God's presence within the head. There, He is described as a flowered wreath or garland upon the head of the devotee. But unlike the wreaths of this world, it does not wither and die, but buds, blossoms and bears fruit. For the Lord gives inner, spiritual life and an expansion of consciousness; His "fruits are full and perfect: they are full of Thy salvation":

> The Lord is upon my head like a wreath,
>   and I shall not leave Him.
> The wreath of Truth has been plaited for me,
>   and it has let thy branches bud within me;
>
> For it is not like a withered wreath that does not bud:
> But Thou art alive upon my head,
>   and Thou hast budded upon me.
> Thy fruits are full and perfect:
>   they are full of Thy salvation.
>
> *Odes of Solomon I:1-5, AOT p.691*

The soul, then, is the bright and pristine essence lying within the human form – a form which has a special purpose within the Lord's creation.

Treasure in Earthen Vessels

Probably one of the oldest human debates is whether man is his body or something other than that – his soul or spirit. Some people say that man's sense of being and self arise entirely from bodily activity; others that the body's activity and ordered function arise from the presence of the soul in the body. There is a saying preserved in the *Gospel of Thomas* in which Jesus, aware of such confusions, comments that a living body is truly something quite amazing and that it is indeed wonderful how the body derives its life and function from the spirit. But it would be still more wonderful, he says, if the eternal soul was a creation of bodily function. It is wonder enough that the sublime divine soul, the treasure house of all spiritual wealth, has come to dwell in the spiritually impoverished body:

> Jesus said,
> "If the flesh came into being because of spirit,
>   it is a wonder.

> But if spirit came into being because of the body,
>> it is a wonder of wonders.
> Indeed, I am amazed at how this great wealth
>> has made its home in this poverty."
>
> *Gospel of Thomas 29, NHS20 p.67*

It is the soul, "this great wealth" within the human form, which is to realize God. The body itself is only a temporary abode. As Paul comments when explaining his understanding of resurrection:

> Flesh and blood cannot inherit the kingdom of God;
> neither can the perishable inherit the imperishable.
>
> *1 Corinthians 15:50, AuNT*

Mystics have commonly described the body as a house, a clay pot and so on. Paul, for instance, calls it an "earthen vessel".[5] Such metaphors convey the idea that the body is a temporary dwelling for the soul, something which is easily damaged or broken, that the soul will not live in the corporeal form forever. And since the soul within is the source of a unending, incalculable spiritual wealth, the body has often been compared to an earthen vessel in which is secreted a precious treasure – the mystic treasure of God.

Jesus, too, pointed out the ephemeral, transitory character of this world and the physical body. His advice was to seek the "treasure in heaven", the treasures of God, within:

> Lay not up for yourselves treasures upon earth,
>> where moth and rust doth corrupt,
>> and where thieves break through and steal:
> But lay up for yourselves treasures in heaven,
>> where neither moth nor rust doth corrupt,
>> and where thieves do not break through nor steal:
> For where your treasure is, there will your heart be also.
>
> *Matthew 6:19-21*

He says that it is not worth collecting the things of the world which have no permanence. One's heart and mind should be directed towards the things of God which are eternal. And when the treasure is found, he says, it should be guarded well. It not something cheap to be exhibited before others for the sake of human pride:

> Again, the kingdom of heaven
>   is like unto treasure hid in a field;
> The which when a man hath found, he hideth,
>   and for joy thereof goeth
>   and selleth all that he hath,
>   and buyeth that field.
>
> *Matthew 13:44*

The body is likened to a field in which great wealth is hidden. When a man becomes aware of it, everything else should be set aside in the hidden or inner pursuit of that precious treasure. A similar example is found in the *Gospel of Thomas*, in a more elaborate variant of a saying found in Matthew:[6]

> Jesus said,
> "The kingdom of the Father is like a merchant
>   who had a consignment of merchandise
>   and who discovered a pearl.
> That merchant was shrewd.
> He sold the merchandise
>   and bought the pearl alone for himself.
> You too, seek his unfailing and enduring treasure
>   where no moth comes near to devour and no worm destroys."
>
> *Gospel of Thomas 76, NHS20 pp.81-83*

The body is like a miscellaneous "consignment of merchandise" in which there is only one thing of any value, the "pearl" or inner treasure of God and true spirituality. When it is realized that the "merchandise" of the body contains this pearl, it is worth discarding everything else in order to possess it.

Many other mystics have said the same thing. As Simon of Tai-butheh, a seventh-century, East Syrian Christian mystic wrote:

> A great and glorious treasure which has no likeness in the creation is hidden within you, O man! And if you had been conscious of it, even by accident only, you would have cried with the prophet: "I will not give sleep to mine eyes or slumber to my life, until I find out a place for this divine treasure that is hidden in me!"
>
> Glory be to Thee, glory be to Thee, glory be to Thee, O merciful God, who hast hidden in this earthy clay and in this dust of the earth (the

body) – a substance which constantly loosens and dissolves – an ineffable beauty and treasure that has no equal in heaven or in earth!

Had you known, O monk, what beauty is hidden in you ... you would have changed night for day in your pursuit of the treasure that is hidden in you!

Simon of Taibutheh, WSVII p.47

The Temple of God and the Sons of God

It is a universal practice amongst the followers of the various religions to construct buildings, later consecrated as sacred, in which it is supposed that God is present and where He is to be worshipped. There, elaborate rituals are performed and obeisance and worship are offered to man-made images in wood, stone and metal. Sometimes, food is even left out for the gods to consume, though the reality is that it is either taken by the priests or eaten by rodents. In Jesus' era, these religious buildings were the temples of the Roman and Greek religious cults, as well as the Jewish Temple at Jerusalem and the many synagogues.

Mystics of all times and places have spoken out against the futility of such practices. Just as they have called the body a house or a clay pot, they have also described it as the temple of God. For they say that the real place in which God is to be worshipped is within the temple of the human form.

Man, however, being more inclined to believe that God dwells within the buildings made by his own hands, neglects the temple made by God, the human form, in which the mystics say He does, in fact, reside. Indeed, so outward has man's attention become and so circumscribed his understanding that if someone desecrates or makes disparaging remarks about the man-made buildings that he thinks to be so sacred, he will go out and murder thousands of the natural temples made by God. Yet man can, with effort, rebuild any church or mosque or temple, but he is quite incapable of creating even the simplest life form, let alone a human being.

The body, then, is the temple of the Living God, the God who is the source of life and being, and He is to be found within this temple. This is the living temple designed by the Living God, expressly for the purpose of His living worship. God does not reside in the places *we* have created, He resides in the places *He* has created. Worship is not a matter of offering obeisance in any external manner in any particular place.

God is within and it is there that He is to be worshipped – spiritually, not physically. Hence Paul wrote:

> Know ye not that ye are the temple of God,
> and that the Spirit of God dwelleth in you?
>
> *1 Corinthians 3:16*

And again:

> And what agreement hath the temple of God with idols?
> For ye are the temple of the living God; as God hath said,
> "I will dwell in them, and walk in them;
> and I will be their God, and they shall be my people."
>
> *2 Corinthians 6:16, Leviticus 26:11-12, Ezekiel 37:27*

Here, Paul quotes from the mystics or prophets of the Old Testament to support his point. Similarly in *Acts*, in a speech no doubt written by Luke but put into the mouth of Paul, the apostle further expands upon the same theme. Speaking to the Athenians, he states expressly that God does not dwell in man-made buildings:

> God that made the world and all things therein,
> seeing that he is Lord of heaven and earth,
> dwelleth not in temples made with hands;
> Neither is worshipped with men's hands,
> as though He needed any thing,
> seeing He giveth to all life, and breath, and all things;
> And hath made of one blood all nations of men
> for to dwell on all the face of the earth,
> and hath determined the times before appointed,
> and the bounds of their habitation;
> That they should seek the Lord,
> if haply they might feel after Him,
> and find Him, though he be not far from every one of us:
> "For in Him we live, and move, and have our being;"
> as certain also of your own poets have said,
> "For we are also His offspring."
>
> *Acts 17:24-28*

Scholars of Greek literature have pointed out that Paul is probably quoting from the opening lines of *Phenomena* by Aratus of Cilicia or is referring to the *Hymn to Zeus* by Cleanthes, where this sentiment is expressed. God has made everything, Paul (or Luke) says, and does not dwell in buildings made with men's hands. He is the source of life and breath within all beings, and he gives existence to all things. All human beings are members of one family, "of one blood", all are made by Him. And all have the right both to seek as well as find Him, for "He be not far from every one of us" – "in Him we live and move and have our being; for we are His offspring".

The idea that we are the "offspring" or children of God was not a new one. In *2 Corinthians*, Paul paraphrases and amalgamates some of the Old Testament prophets where it is written that God 'said':

> "I ... will be a Father unto you,
>   and ye shall be my sons and daughters,"
>   saith the Lord Almighty.
>
> *2 Corinthians 6:18; cf. 2 Samuel 7:14, Isaiah 43:6, Jeremiah 31:9*

Such Biblical sayings are traditionally taken to mean that God is 'speaking' specifically to the children of Israel, but it is clear that Paul – who saw his mission as being to the Gentiles – interprets the meaning in the universal sense of God being the Father of all. As he reiterates in *Ephesians*, there is only:

> One God and Father of all, who is above all,
>   and through all, and in you all.
>
> *Ephesians 4:6*

We are all, therefore, the children of God. This is why Jesus called God the Father. He was not just the Father of Jesus, but the Father of everyone, at any time or place. As we read in John's gospel:

> As many as received him,
>   to them gave he power to become the sons of God.
>
> *John 1:12*

It was a traditional aspect of Judaism to consider God as the Father. The great Jewish prophet, Moses, had repeated it and Jesus was only using a manner of expression already familiar to his Jewish audience, at the same time explaining its real meaning to them. In *Deuteronomy*, for example, Moses says, "Ye are the children of your Lord God",[7] which in the Greek *Septuagint* translation reads "Ye are the sons of the Lord

your God". Again, in a later passage, Moses also asks, "Is not He thy
Father that hath bought thee? Hath He not made thee, and established
thee?"[8] And likewise, he challenges them, saying, "Of the Rock that
begat thee thou art unmindful, and hast forgotten God that formed
thee"[9] – an admonition which is applicable to practically everyone
in this world. All souls have the potential to become realized sons of
God, though most are not aware of that potential.

Even in later Christian understanding, the idea that God and His
heavenly creation are within, was not forgotten. One of the Coptic
apocryphal writings attributed to "our thrice blessed father, Abba
Theodosius, the Archbishop of Alexandria"[10] (a mid-sixth-century
patriarch of Alexandria), is a fictitious romance concerning the miraculous death of Jesus' mother. Mary, on the brink of death, is being
called to her eternal home by the "Holy Trinity", when – in the words
of the author – she responds:

> "Better is a day in Thy courts
>   than thousands (in this world).
> I had rather dwell in Thy courts, my Master."
>
> And again,
> "Thy Holy Ghost hath brought me to this holy mountain.
> Therefore I will go in unto Thy holy place,
>   and will worship at Thy temple,
>   O Thou whom my soul loveth."
>
> When she had said these things, she was in joy unspeakable, in the
> place whence grief has fled away.
>
> Theodosius, *Falling Asleep of Mary*, CAG pp.115-117

Here, as in many other places in the ancient mystic literature of the
Middle East, the "holy mountain" and "Thy temple" refer to the inner
realms and to the highest eternal abode of God Himself where the soul
worships naturally and blissfully. There, in the absence of all temporal
and material constraints all "grief has fled away". Note that the overriding factors in this worship are inner, spiritual love of God and "going in to Thy holy place". The soul's love and "joy unspeakable" can
only be experienced inside. There is nothing external about mystic love
and bliss.

In the *Acts of Thomas*, too, there are numerous references to the body
as the true temple of God. In one of his discourses, Judas Thomas says:

　　Blessed are the bodies of the holy,
　　　　for they have been made worthy to become temples of God.
　　　　　　　　　　　　　　　　Acts of Thomas 94, ANT p.406

And when offering a prayer on behalf of Jesus' followers, he ends with the request:

　　Make them holy shrines and temples of thee,
　　　　and let thy Holy Spirit dwell in them.
　　　　Acts of Thomas 156, ANT p.433, AAA p.289

Similarly, one of those who hear the apostle talk comes to him, saying:

　　I beg of thee, thou apostle of the new God
　　　　that thou wouldst turn unto me too, and pray for me,
　　　　that I also may obtain grace from this God whom thou preachest,
　　　　and that I may become a handmaiden of Him,
　　　　and that I too may be united with you in prayer
　　　　and in hope and in thanksgiving,
　　　　and that I too may become a holy temple
　　　　and He may dwell in me.
　　　　　　　　　　　　　　　Acts of Thomas, AAA p.222

And as one of the gnostic writers concludes:

　　Blessed are you, O soul,
　　　　if you find this One in your temple.
　　　　　　Teachings of Silvanus 109, TS p.63

Thieves in the Temple

It has been observed that there are many instances in the four canonical gospels where an incident is related that is only a fabrication in which to place some saying of Jesus. These stories, especially if they occur in Mark, then get reproduced, with various modifications, in Matthew, Luke and sometimes in John, demonstrating how stories get changed with the telling. A good example is Jesus' visit to the temple at Jerusalem where – according to the well-known story – he exhibits considerable displeasure that it has become a place of commerce.

　　In Mark, followed by Matthew and Luke, the incident takes place on Jesus' last visit to Jerusalem, where he meets his end. And although it is related in only a few sentences, it is given as a part of the reason why some of the Jewish priests became so angry with him that they wished to see him dead. In Mark, the passage reads:

> And they come to Jerusalem: and Jesus went into the temple, and began to cast out them that sold and bought in the temple, and overthrew the tables of the money-changers, and the seats of them that sold doves; and would not suffer that any man should carry any vessel through the temple.
>
> And he taught, saying unto them, "Is it not written, 'My house shall be called of all nations the house of prayer?' But ye have made it a den of thieves."
>
> *Mark 11:15-17*

Matthew truncates the already brief story to its essence, omitting the somewhat obscure sentence about carrying "any vessel" through the temple:

> And Jesus went into the temple of God, and cast out all them that sold and bought in the temple, and overthrew the tables of the money-changers, and the seats of them that sold doves, and said unto them, "It is written, 'My house shall be called the house of prayer; but ye have made it a den of thieves.'"
>
> *Matthew 21:12-13; cf. Isaiah 57:7, Jeremiah 7:11*

Luke, ever concerned about the size of his work, paraphrases both the story and Jesus' response, omitting the details of the various kinds of business being conducted:

> And he went into the temple, and began to cast out them that sold therein, and them that bought, saying unto them, "It is written, 'My house is the house of prayer: but ye have made it a den of thieves.'"
>
> *Luke 19:45-46; cf. Isaiah 57:7, Jeremiah 7:11*

In the synoptics, this story is a crucial part of the events leading up to Jesus' execution. John, on the other hand, sets the incident at the very beginning of his story in one of Jesus' early visits to Jerusalem. He also embellishes it with Jesus' making of a small knotted rope with which to lash the merchants, driving them, as well as their sheep and cattle, out of the temple and definitively pouring out the contents of the money-changers' cash boxes. Further, Jesus no longer quotes scripture and his concluding comment is changed to "take these things hence; make not my Father's house an house of merchandise":

And the Jews' passover was at hand, and Jesus went up to Jerusalem, and found in the temple those that sold oxen and sheep and doves, and the changers of money sitting. And when he had made a scourge of small cords, he drove them all out of the temple, and the sheep, and the oxen; and poured out the changers' money, and overthrew the tables, and said unto them that sold doves, "Take these things hence; make not my Father's house an house of merchandise."

John 2:13-16

Now although the two stories vary, the meaning of Jesus' comments is fundamentally the same and it is this to which attention should be directed. Understood mystically, he means that the real purpose of the temple of the human body is as a "house of prayer", the place in which real spiritual prayer and worship are to be conducted. The "den of thieves" refers to the passions and human weaknesses which rob the soul of its own innate treasure of bliss and divinity. Human imperfections were commonly described in Judaic and other Middle Eastern literature as enemies, thieves, wild beasts and so on. Jesus uses similar metaphors in a number of his parables and sayings.

One can readily imagine, therefore, how Mark, not understanding the mystical meaning of the saying on its own, set it in a story which seemed to make sense of it and was subsequently followed by Matthew and Luke, in their own ways. Or maybe Mark had encountered the saying already in its anecdotal setting and never questioned it. John, on the other hand, may have come across a version of the story either in the synoptics or elsewhere, deliberately altering it or using an already altered form. The details of his story also exhibit a greater familiarity with Temple practices than those of the synoptics.

The story probably had many variants and it is impossible to really know how it came into existence. But it would have been most incongruous for the Jesus who loved peace, gentleness and harmony to have created such a rumpus in the Temple, inciting anger and disharmony. Moreover, Mark's concluding comment, omitted by the other three, that he was allowed to walk away without being apprehended because the scribes and priests feared the people also seems improbable:

And the scribes and chief priests heard it, and sought how they might destroy him: for they feared him, because all the people were astonished at his doctrine.

Mark 11:18

This might have been true outside the temple, but the temple must have been sacred to most of those who went there, and surely neither the crowd nor the temple guards would have tolerated such unruly behaviour?

The narrative, therefore, is unsatisfying, but stripped of its anecdotal setting, the saying takes on a meaning that is completely at home with the remainder of Jesus' teachings: the human body is the temple of God, but we have permitted it to become infested with the thieves and dacoits of human desire and weakness.

Church and Temple

In early Christian days, a church was the community of Christians at any particular place. It was the association of the devotees and disciples called, in Greek, an *ecclesia*, which simply meant an assembly. The term was also commonly used for the assembly of citizens in any of the ancient Greek city states. From comments in *Acts*, Paul's letters and other early literature, it can be determined that the early Christians met simply in each other's homes, with a minimum of ritual and ceremony. Only in later times, when there were significant lulls between the sporadic outbursts of persecution and when the communities had grown too large to meet in individual homes, did they purchase or construct special buildings. Then, in the fourth century, as we have seen, in the time of Constantine, property and finance were given and bequeathed to the Christian organization and an extensive programme of building was commenced. Churches are thus the creation of later, formalized and materialized religion as a ceremonial elaboration of the otherwise simple need to have a place to meet.

Those buildings that were set aside for Christian ritual worship were also called churches. But neither Jesus, Peter, Paul nor any of the early Christians, whatever else they may have believed, had anything to do with church worship as it is known today. It seems far more likely that it would have appeared to them to be of the same character as the temple and synagogue worship for which they felt no need.

The outgoing nature of the human mind, however, with its innate tendency to materialize and crystallize everything, is very strong, and even disciples of a living Master may find themselves inclined to follow traditional patterns of thought and practice by giving importance to outward things. There is evidence of this trend in the early Christian literature, in particular in the *Epistle of Barnabas*.

This interesting letter, of unknown hand, possibly dates from the latter half of the first century and may even have been written by Paul's companion, Barnabas. That it was regarded as authentic teaching during the early development of Christianity is not in doubt, for it is present in a number of early manuscripts including the fourth-century *Codex Sinaiticus*. Eusebius, however, speaks of it as one of the "disputed writings"[11] such as *Jude, Hebrews*, the *Wisdom of Solomon* and others. In his gnostic *Miscellanies*, though, the more broad-minded Clement of Alexandria frequently quotes the writings of Barnabas in a gnostic context, including the one remaining extant epistle attributed to him.[12]

In the following extract, the writer condemns the construction of any external building and explains where the real temple of God is to be built. It seems that a group, probably of Christians, known both to the writer and his recipient, had built a temple – or a church – and consecrated it. The author, however, compares them to the "heathen", a reference to the followers of the Greek, Roman and allied religions who acknowledged many deities, to whom they built temples, much as the Hindus do today. Expressing attitudes such as this – common to mystics from all around the world – it is not surprising that the letter was finally dropped from the canon as the Christians built and consecrated more and more churches! It does, however, contain much good material from a spiritual point of view, the writer repeatedly drawing on the writings of past mystics to prove his point. He writes:

> I will also speak with you concerning the temple, and show how the wretched men erred by putting their hope on the building, and not on the God who made them, and is the true house of God. For they consecrated Him in the temple almost like the heathen.
>
> *Epistle of Barnabas XVI:1-2, AFI p.397*

He then quotes the prophet Isaiah who points out that if the Lord encompasses everything, then what building can man construct that can be expected to house Him? –

> But learn how the Lord speaks, in bringing it (what they did) to naught:

> "Who has measured the heaven with a span,
>   or the earth with his outstretched hand?
>   Have not I?" saith the Lord.

> "Heaven is my throne, and the earth is my footstool,
>   what house will ye build for me,
>   or what is the place of my rest?"

> You know that their hope was vain.
>
> *Epistle of Barnabas XVI:2, AFI p.397; cf. Isaiah 40:12,60:1*

If God is present within everything, says Isaiah, why try to confine Him to a temporal and material, man-made construction? The writer then continues by enquiring how and where the real temple of God can be built:

> But let us inquire if a (real) temple of God exists. Yes, it exists, where He himself said that He makes and perfects it. For it is written:

> "And it shall come to pass ...
>   that a temple of God shall be built
>   gloriously in the Name of the Lord."[13]

> I find then that a temple exists. Learn then how it will be built in the "Name of the Lord". Before we believed in God, the habitation of our heart was corrupt and weak, like a temple really built with hands, because it was full of idolatry, and was the house of demons through doing things which were contrary to God. But it "shall be built in the Name of the Lord."
>
> *Epistle of Barnabas XVI:6-8, AFI pp.397-399*

A worldly and material person is compared to a temple "full of idolatry", the worship or idolizing of material objects, and to a "house of demons", referring to the continuous and 'devilish' activity of human passions and weaknesses within a person's mind which make them behave incorrectly – "contrary to God" – in this world.

He then goes on to explain how the "temple of the Lord may be built gloriously" or spiritually. He says that it is through receiving the remission of sins and putting faith in the Name. In this way, a human being is rebuilt or reborn spiritually from within:

> Now give heed, in order that (you may understand how) the temple of the Lord may be built gloriously. Learn in what way (this can come about). When we received the remission of sins, and put our hope on the Name, we became new, being created again from the beginning; wherefore God truly dwells in us, in the habitation which we are.

How? His Word of faith, the calling of His promise, the Wisdom of the ordinances (the Law), the commands of the teaching ... Himself dwelling in us, by opening the door of the temple ... to us, giving repentance to us, and thus He leads us, who have been enslaved to death, into the incorruptible temple.... This is a spiritual temple being built for the Lord.

Epistle of Barnabas XVI:8-10, AFI p.399

He says that the beginnings of the "spiritual temple" are built at the time of mystic baptism, when the soul is mystically baptized into the "Name of the Lord", also called the "Word of faith" or the true "Wisdom" or Law of God. Then the soul is called as He had promised and follows the "commands of the teaching", follows the mystic path of the Word.

"He" also "opens the door of the temple" and comes to "dwell in us". This refers to the opening of the inner spiritual path when the soul is led from enslavement to the body of death, the physical body, into the "incorruptible temple". The soul leaves the body through an inner door, the single eye, and comes face to face with the One who has called her. This is real worship in the real temple of God – the human form – not any church or man-made building.

Ritual and Ceremony

When the monks of a certain monastery came together for evening prayers, the monastery cat would join the congregation, creating a disturbance. The abbot therefore requested that the cat be tied up during evening worship.

After the abbot died, the cat continued to be tied up every evening before vespers. Some while later, the cat died. The new abbot gave instructions that another cat should be obtained so that it could be tied up before evening prayers. Centuries later the practice still continued and some of the more learned monks even wrote theological treatises on the liturgical significance having a tied cat at evening prayers.[14]

Ritual sets in when clear thinking ceases and habit takes over. It is also something to fill the void in the absence of mystical, interior prayer. As such, it distracts the mind from inward contemplation, keeping it bound to this world. The writer of the *Epistle of Barnabas* must have understood this and that is why he came down so hard upon external observances.

The letter's encouragement of a non-ritualistic approach to worship and an internal attitude to spirituality suggests that it can be confidently credited with an early date of composition. Many Christian scholars, however, have designated such early Christianity as 'primitive', not realizing that the presumably 'sophisticated' Christianity of later times is actually many steps further away from the real teachings of Jesus. In a quotation in which the first part is taken from the *Psalms*[15] and the second part from a version of the *Apocalypse of Adam* which is no longer extant, the same writer also expresses his disapproval of temple sacrifice and the ritual burning of incense as a means of worshipping God:

> Sacrifice for the Lord is a broken heart,
>   a smell of sweet savour to the Lord is a heart
>   that glorifieth him that made it.
>
>   *Epistle of Barnabas II:10, AFI p.345*

The real sacrifice is not of any animal, nor is God impressed by the sweet fragrance of incense or by lighted candles or by any other such things. The real sacrifice is a "broken heart" – a humble and loving heart, where the ego has been broken down by the sweet scent of love and the inner longing to meet with God inside. This is what really pleases Him, what He finds to be a "smell of sweet savour".

The writer is equally disparaging of ascetic practices like ritual fasting or external renunciation of the world. Such practices were also common in those days, especially amongst the Jews. The real fast or abstinence, he says, is not for a man to humble himself externally and to make a show of it to others, but to abstain from or renounce all waywardness of mind and incorrect outward behaviour. To demonstrate his meaning, he once again turns to Isaiah for support:[16]

> To them he (Isaiah) says then again concerning these things,
> "Why do ye fast for me," saith the Lord,
>   "So that your voice is heard this day with a cry!
> This is not the fast which I chose," saith the Lord,
>   "not a man humbling his soul (abasing himself externally);
> Nor though ye bend your necks as a hoop,
>   and put on sackcloth, and make your bed of ashes,
>   not even so shall ye call it an acceptable fast."

But to us he says,

"Behold this is the fast which I chose," saith the Lord,
"loose every bond of wickedness,
set loose the fastenings of harsh agreements,
send away the bruised in forgiveness,
and tear up every unjust contract,
give to the hungry thy bread,
and if thou seest a naked man clothe him,
bring the homeless into thy house,
and if thou seest a humble man, despise him not,
neither thou nor any of the household of thy seed.

"Then shall thy light break forth as the dawn,
and thy robes shall rise quickly,
and thy righteousness shall go before thee,
and the glory of God shall surround thee."

"Then thou shalt cry and God shall hear thee;
while thou art still speaking He shall say,
'Lo I am here';
If thou puttest away from thee bondage, and violence,
and the word of murmuring (slander and calumny),
and dost give to the poor thy bread with a cheerful heart,
and dost pity the soul that is abased."

So then, brethren, the long-suffering one (Jesus) foresaw that the people whom he prepared in his Beloved (God) should believe in guilelessness, and made all things plain to us beforehand that we should not be shipwrecked by conversion to their law (to the practice of their religious observances).

Epistle of Barnabas III:1-6, AFI p.345; Isaiah 58:1-10

Generally, people think that they are worshipping and loving God by the performance of external ceremonies and through ascetic practices and penances of various kinds. But the author of the *Epistle of Barnabas* clearly disapproves of such practices, under whatever religious banner they may be performed. Jesus, too, spoke in a similar fashion and there is no reason to believe that the practices which he decried in Judaism would have been any the more acceptable to him under the name of Christianity. Echoing the words of Isaiah on fasting, he advises:

> Moreover when ye fast, be not, as the hypocrites,
>   of a sad countenance:
> For they disfigure their faces,
>   that they may appear unto men to fast.
> Verily I say unto you, they have their reward.
>
> But thou, when thou fastest, anoint thine head,
>   and wash thy face;
> That thou appear not unto men to fast,
>   but unto thy Father which is in secret:
>   and thy Father, which seeth in secret,
>   shall reward thee openly.
>
> *Matthew 6:16-18*

He points out that people often make a show of fasting and penance by pulling a long face or by otherwise advertising the fact. They want others to think them very holy and to give them respect and indeed they will get that "reward" or satisfaction, for people are easily fooled and impressed by external show.

But he advises his disciples that if they want to fast in order to feel light and give time to their spiritual exercises, they should make no outward show of it. They should look and behave normally, making no exhibition of themselves or their spirituality. The result will be that God, who sees and knows everything, will "reward them openly". He will inwardly and abundantly shower His grace upon them.

Jesus, here, seems to be talking specifically of fasting from food, but it is clear from a saying preserved in the *Gospel of Thomas* that the term was also understood in a more general sense to mean abstinence from the sensory pleasures and attachments of the world:

> Jesus said,
> "Except ye fast from the world,
>   ye shall in no wise find the kingdom of God."
> *Gospel of Thomas (Oxyrhynchus Papyri), ANT p.27, SOL p.10*

And the saying is echoed by Peter in one of the early Syriac apocryphal writings:

> No one who does not fast all his days shall see God.
> *Obsequies of the Holy Virgin, CALNT p.44*

Here, the meaning is even clearer, for no one can fast from food "all his days", else "his days" would be rapidly curtailed! The central idea, then, would seem to be that the world has to be renounced inwardly. External ascetic or religious practices help very little in controlling the mind. In fact, they may have the reverse effect by focusing attention on the material world and engendering pride in the practitioner. Jesus is therefore advising his disciples to keep their treasure hidden, not to cast it before swine, but to seek the Lord in secret, within.

Yet, in perhaps a perfect illustration of how the teachings of a mystic can be misunderstood through externalizing and literalizing, we read – almost with amazement – in the *Didache*, the earliest extant manual of Christian conduct, dating from the second century:

> Let not your fasts be with the hypocrites,
>   for they fast on Mondays and Thursdays;
> But do you fast on Wednesdays and Fridays.
>
> *Didache VIII:1, AFI p.321*

Jesus' observation on fasting in the *Gospel of Thomas* is extant in both Greek and Coptic, where it is followed by a saying whose meaning has been the cause of some considerable scholarly debate. Amongst the variant translations suggested have been:

> Unless ye keep the Sabbath as a Sabbath,
>   ye shall not see the Father.
>
> *Oxyrhynchus Papyri, SOL p.19*

And:

> Except ye make the Sabbath a real Sabbath,
>   ye shall not see the Father.
>
> *Oxyrhynchus Papyri, OLAG p.5*

And:

> If ye keep not the Sabbath for the whole week,
>   ye shall not see the Father.
>
> *Oxyrhynchus Papyri, ANT p.27*

The Sabbath day was, and still is amongst many Jews, a time when strict external rules apply as to what a person may or may not do.

Bearing in mind Jesus' relaxed approach to the Jewish Sabbath, as recorded in the gospels (epitomized in his famous saying, "the Sabbath was made for man, and not man for the Sabbath"[17]) and his attitude generally towards external observances, the meaning would seem to be that unless a person keeps every day as if it were a real Sabbath – a real holy day – they will be unable to find God within themselves.

Spirituality is not a one-day-a-week affair. It is a permanent and growing state of being. A truly spiritual person keeps their entire life holy – their thoughts, words and deeds always reflect the highest spiritual ideals. Their inner being is steeped in it at all times and every day is lived as if it were a real Sabbath or holy day, but without any external show or exhibition. Such a condition cannot be turned on for just one day a week and then neglected for the rest of the time.

Along the same lines, in one of the early codices of the New Testament, *Codex Bezae*, we find an addition to Luke's gospel:

> On the same day, seeing one working on the Sabbath,
>> he said unto him:
> "Man, if indeed thou knowest what thou doest,
>> thou art blessed:
> But if thou knowest not, thou art cursed,
>> and a transgressor of the law."
>
>> *Luke 6:4, Codex Bezae, ANT p.33*

The meaning is that if someone transgresses the external observances of the Sabbath through a deep understanding of true spirituality, then they are indeed blessed. But if they break the religious and social laws out of foolhardiness or a lack of sensibility to others' feelings, then they are simply behaving badly.

Jesus' emphasis is always on the spiritual as opposed to the ceremonial and ritualistic, for the latter cloud the mind and lead it outward. In Matthew, he makes it very clear that love and forgiveness amongst one's fellow human beings are far more important than any outward ceremony. Respect for the human temple is of much greater significance than respect for any man-made building. He says:

> If thou bring thy gift to the altar,
>> and there rememberest that thy brother
>> hath ought against thee;
> Leave there thy gift before the altar, and go thy way;

first be reconciled to thy brother,
and then come and offer thy gift.
Matthew 5:23-24

He says that even if somebody has got as far as the altar in the performance of some ritual, but having reached there it crosses his mind that he has upset a fellow human being, he should forget about his ritual and go and apologize and make things right with that other person. In other words, our dealings with the living temples of God are of far more importance than our dealings with the dead temples of stone and mortar.

Indeed, if we have hurt another person's feelings through our own misconduct or unkind words, the memory and realization of it will prey upon our mind and conscience, disturbing all efforts at true interior prayer until we have cleared the matter with the injured person.

Blind Leaders of the Blind

Many mystic teachers, Jesus included, have not been averse to making clear their opinions concerning the priests of their own times. Their reason has not been criticism for its own sake, nor even because they wanted to change things. Their interest is only that genuine spiritual seekers may understand that the path to God needs no intercession from any professional member of a religion, nor does it even lie within the confines of a particular religion. During some periods of history, and in some religions, the priestly class have acquired such influence over people that mystics have considered it productive to use strong language in order to get their point across. In a well-known passage from Matthew, for instance, probably originating in Q, Jesus says:

But woe unto you, scribes and Pharisees, hypocrites!
for ye shut up the kingdom of heaven against men:
For ye neither go in yourselves,
neither suffer ye them that are entering to go in.
Matthew 23:13

As commented earlier, Jesus means that real seekers of the inner, mystic truth may naively look to the priests to guide them. But since the majority of priests do not know how to enter the inner realms themselves or how to find the kingdom of God, they are unable to help. In fact, they are likely to unwittingly mislead people by promoting a variety of seemingly praiseworthy practices which, from a mystic point of view, are actually of no value.

Note, too, that Jesus again speaks of God as dwelling within man. He talks of entering the kingdom of heaven or the kingdom of God. Incidentally, although we have given only one example here, it is noticeable that Matthew changes almost all occurrences of the "kingdom of God" to the "kingdom of heaven", an expression not used by Luke and Mark. This is another example of an editorial hand at work, in this case demonstrating Matthew's Judaic scruples, substituting a metaphor rather than write the name of God. Luke provides an interesting variant of this saying:

> Woe unto you, lawyers!
>   for ye have taken away the key of knowledge:
> Ye entered not in yourselves,
>   and them that were entering in ye hindered.
>
> *Luke 11:52*

Here, the Pharisees have become "lawyers" and shutting up the kingdom of heaven has become taking away the "key of knowledge". The two passages, of course, mean the same thing when one understands that the "knowledge" in Luke's version is *gnosis* or mystic knowledge – inner experience. Mystics provide the key to understanding religious scriptures and entering the inner treasury. Those who misinterpret their teachings, whether they are priests, interpreters of Jewish religious law or anyone else, have effectively taken away the key from those who sincerely seek for inner understanding.

Although Luke presents a much truncated version of this section as compared to Matthew, he does preserve one interesting saying which Matthew omits:

> Woe unto you, scribes and Pharisees, hypocrites!
>   for ye are as graves which appear not,
>   and the men that walk over them are not aware of them.
>
> *Luke 11:44*

The meaning is similar. People put their faith in their religious leaders quite unaware that these teachers are – from a mystic point of view – spiritually dead inside. They are like graves, hidden in the earth, over which people walk without realizing where they are treading. In a number of the sayings preserved by Matthew in his much longer version of this section, Jesus calls them "ye blind guides", meaning that they are spiritually blind and unfit to guide others along the spiritual path. In another place he says of them:

> Let them alone: they be blind leaders of the blind.
> And if the blind lead the blind,
>   both shall fall into the ditch.
>
> *Matthew 15:14*

Only one who has travelled the inner path that leads to God and has reached that destination can guide others on the same road. As for the rest of us, we are blind and dead, and can only lead each other "into the ditch".

NOTES AND REFERENCES

1. *eg.* Aristotle, *Physics 7-8* and *Metaphysics* 12.
2. Cicero is thinking of a geocentric universe in which the heavenly bodies were presumed to travel at immense speeds. Strangely, he was correct: they do travel at tremendous speeds, but not around the earth.
3. *eg. Matthew* 11:25.
4. *Acts of Thomas, AAA* p.151.
5. *2 Corinthians* 4:7.
6. *Matthew* 13:46.
7. *Deuteronomy* 14:1, *KJV.*
8. *Deuteronomy* 32:6, *KJV.*
9. *Deuteronomy* 32:18, *KJV.*
10. *Falling Asleep of Mary, CAG* p.91.
11. Eusebius, *History of the Church* 6:13, *HC* p.253.
12. Clement of Alexandria, *Miscellanies* II:XX, *WCAII* p.66.
13. The writer's source is unknown.
14. Story freely adapted from Anthony de Mello, *The Song of the Bird*, p.63.
15. *Psalms* 51:17.
16. *Isaiah* 58:4-10.
17. *Mark* 2:27.

CHAPTER SEVEN

What is God?

The Nature of God

Mystics are acutely aware of the inability of human words and intellect to really convey anything of their experience of Him. Can words replace experience when it comes to conveying the magnificence and grandeur of some great mountain range or any of the wonders of nature? How much less, then, can God's splendour and power be caught in human language. As a consequence, the words of the mystics concerning Him, while full of praise and love, also express their failure to capture Him in words. As a Manichaean-Christian psalmist wrote:

> My God, Thou art a marvel to tell.
> Thou art within, Thou art without.
> Thou art above, Thou art below,
>   that art near and far,
>   that art hidden and revealed,
>   that art silent and speakest too;
> Thine is all the glory.
>
> *Psalms, MPB p.155*

Or as the writer of the *Teachings of Silvanus* cautions:

> My son, do not dare to say a word about this One,
>   and do not confine the God of all to mental images.
>
> *Teachings of Silvanus 102, TS p.49*

But here the writer is only pointing to the impossibility of capturing Him in human words and imagination, for he goes on to say a great deal about God. The early writer of the *Clementine Homilies* also suggests keeping speculation about the nature of God within simple bounds when he has Peter say:

220

Wherefore, Clement, my son, beware of thinking otherwise of God, than that He is the only God, and Lord, and Father, good and righteous, the Creator, long-suffering, merciful, the sustainer, the benefactor, ordaining love of men, counselling purity, immortal and making immortal, incomparable, dwelling in the souls of the good, that cannot be contained and yet is contained, who has fixed the great world as a centre in space, who has spread out the heavens and solidified the earth, who has stored up the water, who has disposed the stars in the sky, who has made the fountains flow in the earth, has produced fruits, has raised up mountains, hath set bounds to the sea, has ordered winds and blasts, who by the spirit of counsel has kept safely the body comprehended in a boundless sea.

Clementine Homilies II:XLV, CH pp.53-54

Apart from a few notable passages, very little is attributed to Jesus concerning the metaphysical nature of God, and it is to early Christian and allied writings, particularly those of a Hellenistic character, that we must turn. Hellenistic thought was generally far more inclined to speculate on the nature of God than Judaism. Amongst these texts, there seems to be general agreement on the subject and it may be presumed that these more or less accurately convey Jesus' teaching about God. They are also in accord with the descriptions of God found in practically all religious and mystical literature. In the prologue to the *History of Philip*, for instance, the unknown author says that he writes

in the name of the unbegotten nature of the immortal God.

History of Philip, AAA p.69

God, he says, is unbegotten and immortal. He is unborn and undying, existing beyond time and place, birth and death, past and future, for these are all His creations. He is, of course, beyond all human description and intellect, but in the attempt to understand something of what God is, many attributes have been ascribed to Him. Hence, the writer of the *Decease of Saint John* describes Him as:

The root of immortality,
　　and the fountain of incorruption,
　　and the foundation of the universe.

Decease of St John, AAA p.65

Expressing the same idea, but more expansively, the writer of the *Acts of Thomas* has Judas Thomas praise God by reference to His attributes:

To be glorified art Thou,
Lord of all, self-existent, unutterable,
who art hidden in the brightness of Thy glory
from all the worlds (all the realms of creation)....
To be glorified art Thou,
the Father serene (the source of peace)....
To be glorified art Thou, the feeder of all,
who art in all worlds, on high and in the deep,
and there is no place that is void of Thee....
To be glorified art Thou, the good Father,
who dwellest in the pure heart,
in the mind (soul?) of Thy worshippers....
To be glorified art Thou,
the Father omnipotent....
To be glorified art Thou,
the Father giving life to all.

Acts of Thomas, AAA pp.245-249

The gnostics, many of whom were influenced by Hellenistic culture, were more inclined towards metaphysical thought and explanation, and often had a great deal to say about God – and His incomprehensibility – as in the *Gospel of Truth* and the *Tripartite Tractate*, both treatises from the Nag Hammadi library:

As for the incomprehensible, inconceivable One,
the Father, the Perfect One,
the One who made the Totality (the Creation),
within Him is the Totality
and of Him the Totality has need.

Gospel of Truth 18, NHS22 p.85

And:

He is without beginning and without end. Not only is He without end – He is immortal for this reason, that He is unbegotten – but He is also invariable in His eternal existence.... He has not had anyone who initiated His own existence. Thus, He is Himself unchanged and no one else can remove Him from His existence ... and His greatness.... Nor is it possible for anyone else to change Him into a different form or to reduce Him, or alter Him or diminish Him ... who is the unalterable, immutable One, with immutability clothing Him.

Tripartite Tractate 52, NHS22 pp.193-195

The latter writer also points out that whatever names may be given to Him out of love, not one of them does Him justice, for He is far beyond all names and epithets:

> Not one of the names which are conceived, or spoken, seen or grasped, not one of them applies to Him, even though they are exceedingly glorious, magnifying and honoured. However, it is possible to utter these names for His glory and honour, in accordance with the capacity of each of those who give Him glory. Yet as for Him, in His own existence, being and form, it is impossible for mind to conceive Him, nor can any speech convey Him, nor can any eye see Him, nor can any body grasp Him, because of His inscrutable greatness and His incomprehensible depth, and His immeasurable height, and His illimitable will.
>
> This is the nature of the Unbegotten One, which does not touch anything else; nor is it joined (to anything) in the manner of something which is limited. Rather, He possesses this constitution, without having a face or a form, things which are understood through perception, whence also comes (the epithet) 'the incomprehensible'.
>
> If He is incomprehensible, then it follows that He is unknowable, that He is the One who is inconceivable by any thought, invisible by anything, ineffable by any word, untouchable by any hand. He alone is the One who knows himself as He is, along with His form and His greatness and His magnitude.... He transcends all wisdom, and is above all intellect, and is above all glory, and is above all beauty, and all sweetness, and all greatness, and any depth and any height.
>
> *Tripartite Tractate 54-55, NHS22 pp.197-199*

God, then, is not a human concept nor does He approximate to any human ideas about Him. He is not up above the clouds or far away in the depths of space, He lies within all and is the essence of all. The same writer then continues:

> If this One, who is unknowable in His nature, to whom pertain all the greatnesses which I already mentioned, if out of the abundance of His sweetness He wishes to grant knowledge so that He might be known, He has the ability to do so. He has his Power, which is His will.
>
> Now, however, in silence He Himself holds back, He who is the great One, who is the cause of bringing the Totalities (realms of creation) into ... being.
>
> *Tripartite Tractate 55, NHS22 p.199*

So despite all that can be said about His incomprehensibility, He can be known – but only when He so wills it. He is known through a special kind of knowing – *gnosis*, revelation or mystic experience – when the individual self evaporates and the soul merges into Him.

God is a Spirit

Jesus seems to have spoken of God in very simple language and mostly in terms of those attributes that relate to us as human beings. Only briefly, in John's gospel, does he speak of God's transcendent nature. "God is a Spirit"[1] are the words attributed to him, meaning that God is the essence of all spirituality. He is the Ocean of Spirit, the Supreme Spirit. He is that by which the entire creation exists and breathes.

Adding to this description, John also says that God is Light. In *1 John*, in a style very similar to John's gospel, he says, "God is Light and in him is no darkness at all",[2] meaning that the source of all Light is God. All mystics have spoken of the inner, divine light. This is no metaphor. The light of this world, as bright and as essential as it is, is like a shadow compared to the light within. In their attempt to convey some idea of the indescribable, some mystics have even said that God has the light of millions of our suns.

Paul, too, adds to this description of God's characteristics. He agrees that the "Lord is that Spirit",[3] probably referring to the Holy Spirit, adding that He is also the "Lord of peace".[4] But this is a peace which lies within ourselves, not outside in the world, for he writes, "Let the peace of God rule in your hearts"[5] and "God is not the author of confusion, but of peace".[6] While the author of *1 Timothy* also describes God as:

> The King eternal, immortal, invisible,
>   the only wise God.
>
> *1 Timothy 1:17*

To which the writer of *Revelations* adds:

> For the Lord God omnipotent reigneth.
>
> *Book of Revelation 19:6*

The Lord is the spiritual presence within everything and His will prevails throughout creation.

Man and God

Although in John's gospel there is extensive coverage of the relationship of the Son of God to the Father, it is man's relationship to God
which otherwise figures prominently in Jesus' teachings. All mystics
have described God as omniscient or all-knowing, since He dwells
within the deepest recess of our being and pervades His entire creation. In the beautiful Sermon on the Mount, Jesus brings this out in
human terms. He says that there is no need to pray to Him with a list
of needs and desires, for

> your Father knoweth what things ye have need of,
> before ye ask him.
>
> *Matthew 6:8*

Consequently, since God already knows everything about us and all
our needs, even before we think of them ourselves, Jesus advises surrendering ourselves entirely to Him:

> Therefore I say unto you,
> Take no thought for your life,
>   what ye shall eat, or what ye shall drink;
>   nor yet for your body, what ye shall put on.
> Is not the life more than meat,
>   and the body than raiment? ...
>
> Therefore take no thought, saying, "What shall we eat?"
>   or, "What shall we drink?"
>   or, "Wherewithal shall we be clothed?"
> For your heavenly Father knoweth
>   that ye have need of all these things.
>
> *Matthew 6:25, 31-32*

Since He is the doer within everything, He also knows everything. Jesus
says that life itself is far more than the body and its needs. If we have
faith in Him and utterly surrender ourselves to Him, then He will take
care of all our needs, leaving us free to attend to the things of God.
And he gives an example of the birds who are fed by divine providence
without their needing to sow or harvest:

> Behold the fowls of the air:
>> for they sow not, neither do they reap,
>> nor gather into barns;
> Yet your heavenly Father feedeth them.
> Are ye not much better than they?
>
>> *Matthew 6:26*

Birds are not greedy, he says, nor do they hoard supplies for the future. They only do what comes naturally to them and nature automatically provides for them. Man, however, though he is made in God's image, generally lacks the simple faith that he will be provided for. Forgetting that God lies both within and without himself, he tries to do it all out of his own ego and frequently makes a mess of things. Jesus then continues with a similar example, concerning the clothes we wear:

> And why take ye thought for raiment?
> Consider the lilies of the field, how they grow;
>> they toil not, neither do they spin:
> And yet I say unto you,
>> That even Solomon in all his glory
>> was not arrayed like one of these.
> Wherefore, if God so clothe the grass of the field,
>> which today is,
>> and tomorrow is cast into the oven,
>> shall he not much more clothe you,
>> O ye of little faith?
>
>> *Matthew 6:28-30*

He points out that we are generally quite worried about the clothes we wear. Yet look, he counsels, at the lilies, at the flowers of the field. They neither work for a living nor do they even last for very long. They are like grass which is grown today and made into oven fuel tomorrow. Yet they are still clothed by God in beauty. So if He looks after them while they live, will He not also look after us? "O ye of little faith?"

Likewise, Jesus also points out how little control we really have over our physical existence. By thought or desire alone, we cannot make things happen instantly according to our liking:

> Which of you by taking thought
>> can add one cubit unto his stature?
>
>> *Matthew 6:27*

It means that at best man has a greatly circumscribed or conditioned free will. In no sense is he a rival to the Lord. The Lord is the real and only doer, and man only thinks – because of his sense of separateness from God – that he has a will which is independent of Him. In fact, later on in Matthew, though it sounds very much like a part of the same original passage, Jesus points out that the Lord's will is involved in every event of creation, however apparently insignificant it may be. He says:

> Are not two sparrows sold for a farthing?
>   and one of them shall not fall on the ground
>   without your Father.
> But the very hairs of your head are all numbered.
> Fear ye not therefore, ye are of more value than many sparrows.
>
> *Matthew 10:30-31*

The Lord pervades His entire creation. He is present everywhere and within everything. He is present in every particle and in every event. Nothing happens without His order. His will prevails in all things, however apparently good or bad and however difficult it may be to understand. He concludes, therefore:

> But seek ye first the kingdom of God,
>   and His righteousness;
>   and all these things shall be added unto you.
> Take therefore no thought for the morrow:
>   for the morrow shall take thought
>   for the things of itself.
> Sufficient unto the day is the evil thereof.
>
> *Matthew 6:33-34*

The purpose for which God has created the human form is to seek Him within. Even man's intelligence is an aspect of this divine potential. Otherwise, there is no significant difference between man and other creatures, for all of them need food and protection, and all creatures are involved in reproduction. So bearing this in mind, Jesus advises that we should keep the spiritual goal in view and let the Lord take care of all our physical needs, in whatever way He thinks best. "Seek ye first the kingdom of God, and His righteousness; and all these things shall be added unto you."

Since God is omniscient and omnipresent, knowing better than we what we need, He also knows the innermost thoughts and desires of our hearts. Consequently, in the same collection of sayings, Jesus speaks of "thy Father which seeth in secret",[7] meaning that God knows what goes on within us, though it may be kept hidden and secret from everyone else.

Similarly, the gospel writers report in a number of places that Jesus, too, who was one with God and therefore had His knowledge, knew people's innermost thoughts. Indeed, as a prophet or mystic it was even expected of him. In Matthew, for example, when Jesus is being tried by the Sanhedrin, some of them abused him physically, adding tauntingly, "Prophesy unto us, thou Christ, who is he that smote thee?"[8] In John, Jesus tells the lady at the well, "Thou hast had five husbands; and he whom thou now hast is not thy husband."[9] To which she replies in the famous words, "Sir, I perceive that thou art a prophet."[10] And elsewhere we read, "and Jesus knowing their thoughts said ..." and "Jesus, perceiving the thought of their heart ..." and so on.[11] Such knowledge is a characteristic of all Masters, for they see things from a far higher level of consciousness, within, where all activities of the mind are an open book to them. It is a faculty far more extensive than any psychic or telepathic power of this world. In fact, as the soul rises within, through the inner regions, coming closer to God, His omniscience becomes manifest in the soul. Hence, the writer of *2 Timothy* says:

> The Lord give thee understanding in all things.
>
> *2 Timothy 2:7*

It was with this understanding of God's omniscience that Ignatius, Bishop of Antioch very early in the second century who was sent to Rome to die the death of a martyr, wrote in one of his letters:

> Nothing is hid from the Lord, but even our secret things are near Him. Let us therefore do all things as though He were dwelling in us, that we may be His temples, and that He may be our God in us. This indeed is so, and will appear clearly before our face by the love which we justly have to Him.
>
> *Ignatius, To the Ephesians XV:3, AFI p.189*

And similarly, the writer of the *Teachings of Silvanus* said:

God does not need to put any man to the test. He knows all things before they come to pass, and He knows the hidden things of the heart. They are all revealed and found wanting in His presence. Let no one ever say that God is ignorant. For it is not right to place the Creator of every creature in ignorance. For even things which are in darkness, before Him are as if in light.

Teachings of Silvanus 115-116, TS pp.75-77

God is Love

Mystics of all times and lands have said that God is unborn, self-existent, immortal, the Supreme Spirit, the Source of eternal life and so on. But perhaps most importantly of all from a human point of view, they have also said that the essential nature of God is love and from this love all His other qualities spring. Now, if God is love and the soul is created out of God's essence, the innermost nature of the soul must also be that of love. And since the relationship of a drop of love to an Ocean of Love can only be love, the soul's true relationship to God will again be of love and the path to God within will also be the path of love. Additionally, the highest relationship of one soul to any other will once more be one of love.

Hence, Jesus and all other mystics have advised that love is the best approach to everything and everybody in this world, whatever the circumstances may be, for God alone is real, everything else is a reflection. And since God is love and there is nothing else in existence save Him, the true nature of everything is also that of love. Whichever John it was who wrote the homily we now call *1 John* said all this most explicitly:

> Behold, what manner of love the Father
>   hath bestowed upon us,
>   that we should be called the sons of God....
> Beloved, now are we the sons of God.
>
> *1 John 3:1-2*

He says that just as a child comes from its parents, so does a soul originate with God. All souls are hence His children, his sons. And the relationship is one of love. Jesus also advised his disciples how to become the "children of God".[12] *1 John* continues:

Ye are of God, little children....
We are of God....
Beloved, let us love one another:
    for love is of God;
    and every one that loveth is born of God,
    and knoweth God.
He that loveth not knoweth not God;
    for God is love.

Beloved, if God so loved us,
    we ought also to love one another....
If we love one another, God dwelleth in us,
    and his love is perfected in us....

God is love;
    and he that dwelleth in love dwelleth in God,
    and God in him.

We love him, because he first loved us.
If a man say, "I love God", and hateth his brother,
    he is a liar:
For he that loveth not his brother
    whom he hath seen,
    how can he love God whom he hath not seen?
And this commandment have we from him,
    "That he who loveth God love his brother also."
                    1 John 4:4,6-8,11-12,16,19-20

The author points out that one who truly loves God will automatically love his fellow human beings. One who has hatred for his fellow man and yet professes to love God, "he is a liar". But it was Jesus, of course, who led the writer of this letter to his all-embracing understanding of love and it is clear that Jesus gave the greatest importance to love of God and man. Illustrating this is the famous passage concerning Jesus' first and second commandments. Mark's version reads:

And one of the scribes came, and having heard them reasoning together, and perceiving that he had answered them well, asked him, "Which is the first commandment of all?"

And Jesus answered him: "The first of all the commandments is, 'Hear, O Israel; The Lord our God is one Lord. And thou shalt love the Lord thy

God with all thy heart, and with all thy soul, and with all thy mind, and with all thy strength': this is the first commandment.

"And the second is like, namely this, 'Thou shalt love thy neighbour as thyself.' There is none other commandment greater than these."

And the scribe said unto him, "Well, Master, thou hast said the truth: for there is one God; and there is none other but he. And to love him with all the heart, and with all the understanding, and with all the soul, and with all the strength, and to love his neighbour as himself, is more than all whole burnt offerings and sacrifices."

And when Jesus saw that he answered discreetly, he said unto him, "Thou art not far from the kingdom of God". And no man after that durst ask him any question.

Mark 12:28-34

Love, said Jesus, is the beginning and the end of all the teachings of the mystics and prophets, and he draws his two commandments from the *Pentateuch,* in order to demonstrate that his teachings were not new. The first is to be found in *Deuteronomy* and the second in *Leviticus.*[13] Love is the essence of all religious and spiritual practices, he says. Love is the true religion of mankind. Hence, in Matthew's version, Jesus ends:

On these two commandments hang all the law and the prophets.

Matthew 22:40

He says that we should love God with every fibre of our being. The inclination of the soul is always towards the Lord, for love is constantly attracted by love. But the mind and emotions are generally full of thoughts, desires and feelings concerning the world and are hence not directed towards Him. They are so filled with pride, anger, greed, lust, attachment and all the other variants of human selfishness, worldliness and negative emotion that little or no place is left for the real love of God. Our attention – and as a consequence, our love – is distracted into the world and away from God. We are lovers of the world, not of God.

The first effort, therefore, must be to cleanse the mind and turn it towards the love of God. Only then does it become possible to follow the second commandment, that of loving one's neighbour as oneself. The true or real self is the soul, not the individual ego or personality. It is not possible to simultaneously love one's personal sense of ego and that of other people's, for the two are mutually at variance with each other.

Those who find God within, discover that their real self is God. They see that they are His children and that He is the essence of their being. They also come to see Him everywhere and in everyone. Then, wherever they look and wherever they go, they find nothing but God and His love. So naturally, being filled with His love, they love everything and everybody, treating all with respect, honesty, kindness, gentleness, understanding and all other good human qualities. This is truly loving "thy neighbour as thyself". A neighbour is not just one who lives next door, but everything and everybody with whom we come into contact. There can never be any restriction on love. An inner love for God who is omnipresent automatically reflects outwardly as a universal love in this creation.

This maxim of love for one's fellow man and for all creation was so well known to all of Jesus' disciples, as well as the followers of the early Christian religion, that Paul wrote:

> But as touching brotherly love ye need not that I write unto you:
> for ye yourselves are taught of God to love one another.
>
> *1 Thessalonians 4:9*

Many religious people speak more of the fear of God than of His love and they worship Him out of fear of punishment either in this world or in hell – or they hope for a reward in some heavenly realm after death or they are afraid that if they do not worship Him, some calamity or misfortune will befall them in this life. This kind of fear has commonly been induced and preached from the Christian pulpit. People even talk of 'putting the fear of God' into someone. But the author of *1 John* realized that this was a negative kind of love, possessing little value. He knew that genuine love of God gives a person such an understanding of everything and such a sense of confidence through living in God's presence that there is nothing left to fear, not even death. Hence, he wrote:

> There is no fear in love;
>> but (rather) perfect love casteth out fear:
>> because fear hath torment.
> He that feareth is not made perfect in love.
>
> *1 John 4:18*

The only beneficial fear of God is not really a fear at all, but arises out of love. It is a godly fear, a reverence and awe akin to worship. From this arises a fear of offending Him, just as we do not like to offend or hurt those in this world whom we love. It is also a fear of running counter to His will, not through fear of punishment but because the inner communion with God is interrupted by the discordant vibrations of the mind – by incorrect thought or behaviour and the wilfulness of the ego.

Love, then is ultimately the only true reality in the soul's relationship with God. The writer of a first-century letter traditionally attributed to Clement, Bishop of Rome towards the end of the first century, summarizes the matter most succinctly:

> Who is able to explain the bond of the love of God?
> Who is sufficient to tell the greatness of its beauty?
> The height to which love lifts us is not to be expressed.
> Love unites us to God.
>
> *1 Clement XLIX:2-5, AFI p.93*

"Love unites us to God." This is the beginning and the end of everything.

NOTES AND REFERENCES

1. *John* 4:24.
2. *1 John* 1:5.
3. *2 Corinthians* 3:17.
4. *2 Thessalonians* 3:16.
5. *Colossians* 3:15.
6. *1 Corinthians* 14:33.
7. *Matthew* 6:4.
8. *Matthew* 26:68.
9. *John* 4:18.
10. *John* 4:19.
11. See *Matthew* 9:4, 12:25 and *Luke* 5:22, 6:8, 9:47.
12. *Matthew* 5:9, 5:45; *John* 1:12, 11:52; *Luke* 6:35, 20:36.
13. *Deuteronomy* 6:4-5 and *Leviticus* 19:18.

CHAPTER EIGHT

The Word of God

In the Beginning Was the Word

There is considerable confusion in the minds of many modern Christians over the meaning of the Word of God. There was also the same confusion amongst many of the early Christians, as indeed there is in the gospels themselves. Many people – without giving the matter much thought – assume that the Word means the outer teachings or the message of Jesus and it is certainly true that, in many cases, the term is used in this sense. But in as many, if not more, instances, the Word of God means something far more fundamentally mystical.

The term is commonly translated from the Greek *Logos* and its most well-known usage comes at the beginning of John's gospel:

> In the beginning was the Word (the *Logos*),
>   and the Word was with God, and the Word was God.
> The same was in the beginning with God.
> All things were made by him (the *Logos*);
>   and without him (the *Logos*)
> was not any thing made that was made.
>
> *John 1:1-3*

John says that the Word has existed from the "beginning", from before time and before the creation came into being. This Word was a part of God – indeed it is and was God – and by means of this Word, this *Logos*, all things in creation were fashioned. The 'him', here, refers to the *Logos* and so as to make the distinction, Tyndale's original translation renders 'him' as 'it': "all things were made by it."

Now, a Word that was with God before the creation and by which all things were made is clearly no spoken word or verbal teachings. The Word that is being described is the creative Power of God, His

234

emanation by which the creation was brought into being and by which it is constantly maintained. This great truth is one of the most recurrent themes in the mystic writings of all ages and cultures.

Throughout history, God's creative Power has been called by a multitude of names and expressions. Amongst the Christian and allied literature alone, it has been called the Word of Life, the Word of God, the Creative Word, the *Logos*, the Image of God, the Wisdom of God, the Voice of God, the Cry, the Call, the Holy Name, the Holy Spirit, the Holy Ghost, the Power, the *Nous*, the Primal Thought, Idea or Mind of God, His Command, His Law, His Will and His Ordinances.

In the metaphorical language so beloved of the Middle East, it has also been described as the Living Water, the Bread of Life, Manna from Heaven, the Breath of Life, the Medicine of Life, the Herb of Life, the Tree of Life, the True Vine, the Root, the Seed, the Pearl, the Way, the Truth, the Letter and by many other figures of speech.

God, say the mystics, is One. The creation, however, is manifestly diverse and manifold, with everything in a state of constant flux. Nothing remains the same; everything constantly changes. Modern scientists, delving into the heart of matter, have determined that not only are the forces, molecules, atoms and subatomic particles comprising matter constantly in a state of highly energetic agitation, but that their very motion contributes to their existence. It is the motion or vibration within things which makes them appear to exist. If the motion stopped, then the universe would simply disappear like a mirage from the desert or like ripples from the surface of a pond. Motion and existence are virtually synonymous.

It is generally supposed that in any man-made system perpetual motion is unobtainable because there is always a loss of energy, in one way or another, sooner or later causing it to slow down and stop. The universe as a whole, however, appears to have no such built-in constraints. The activity of its tiniest particles, possessing spin speeds of thousands of revolutions and oscillations per second, shows no inclination to diminish. Yet no scientist can say where the primal energy comes from which keeps the universe in existence. They can measure it, describe it and also harness its energies, but they cannot say where it comes from or what it really is. At its most fundamental level, the physical universe remains a complete mystery.

Mystics say that this primal energy or vibration is the Word itself. It is this Power of God which drives things and sustains them in existence and creates the fundamental order and organization not only in the physical universe, but in the higher regions of creation, too.

The Word as the Creative Power

There is no doubt that the doctrine of the Word as the creative Power
of God and life-giver in creation was widespread at the time of Jesus. It
is mentioned in Judaic, Greek, Syriac and other literature both before
and after him. The early Christian writers also speak of it in this way.
The unknown author of *Hebrews* says:

> Through faith we understand that the worlds
>   were framed by the Word of God,
>   so that things which are seen
>   were not made of things which do appear.
>
> *Hebrews 11:3*

It is the unseen Word which has created all the worlds and regions
of creation. Material things do not owe their existence to any material agency. But until the Word has been experienced within, this
understanding, however logical it may seem, has an element of un-
tested faith in it. This faith is converted into knowledge only by experience. Expressing the same idea in the *Acts of Peter*, we find Paul
saying:

> O eternal God, God of the heavens,
>   God of unspeakable majesty (divinity),
>   who hast stablished all things by Thy Word.
>
> *Acts of Peter III:II, ANT p.305*

In the *Trimorphic Protennoia*, a gnostic tractate from the Nag Hammadi
library, written in the revelationary genre, the author – employing a
literary habit of the times – writes in the name of the Word:

> I alone am the Word, ineffable, unpolluted,
>   immeasurable, inconceivable.
> It (the Word) is a hidden Light,
>   bearing a Fruit of Life,
>   pouring forth a Living Water
>   from the invisible, unpolluted, immeasurable Spring....
>   being unreproducible, an immeasurable Light,
>   the source of the All (the Creation),
>   the Root of the entire Aeon (Creation).

It is the Foundation that supports
    every movement of the *Aeons* (realms of creation)
    that belong to the mighty Glory.
It is the Foundation of every foundation.
It is the [Life] Breath of the powers.

                Trimorphic Protennoia 46, NHS28 p.425

And the writer of the *Odes of Solomon* puts things in a more lyrical manner:

The mouth of the Lord is the True Word,
    and the gate of his Light....

The swiftness of the Word cannot be told,
    and like its telling,
        so too are its swiftness and its speed,
    and his course is without limit....

By him the worlds (of creation) spoke one to another,
    and those that were silent acquired speech;
And by him friendship and agreement came into being,
    and they spoke one to the other what they had to say;
And they were goaded on by the Word.

And they knew him who made them,
    because they were in agreement (harmony);
For the mouth of the Most High spoke to them,
    and through him His explanation had free course.

                Odes of Solomon XII:3,5,8-11, AOT p.703

Everything, says the poet, has been made by the Word whose ways are swifter than anything that can be humanly comprehended. Through the Word, all things are in harmony, for they are all the expression of God's Word, His Voice or His Speech. Metaphorically, everything has come out of the mouth of God. In another ode, the same idea is repeated:

There is nothing that is apart from the Lord,
    because He was before anything came into being.
And the worlds came into being by his Word.

                Odes of Solomon XVI:18-19, AOT p.706

The poet could hardly be more explicit.

The Logos of God

Although John's gospel contains many parallels to the Judaic Wisdom literature, it has also been called the Hellenistic gospel because of its use of Greek mystical terminology, in particular, the Word. The *Logos* is a term used extensively in Greek mystical literature dating back many centuries. It was quite familiar to Plato (*c.*427-347 BC), for example, four centuries before Jesus. In *Phaedrus*, Plato records the dialogue of Phaedrus with Socrates (*c.*470-399):

> SOCRATES: Now tell me, is there another sort of Word (*Logos*), that is brother to the written word (*logos*), but genuine? Can we see how it originates, and how much better and more powerful it is than the other?
>
> PHAEDRUS: What sort do you have in mind, and how is it generated?
>
> SOCRATES: The sort that exists together with Knowledge and is written in the soul of the student, that has the power to defend itself, and knows to whom it should speak and to whom it should remain silent.
>
> PHAEDRUS: You mean the Word of Knowing, alive and ensouled, of which the written word may correctly be called an image.
>
> SOCRATES: Precisely.
>
> Socrates (Plato), Phaedrus 276; cf. DP pp.185-186, PlEA pp.566-567

Perhaps with the idea of asserting the uniqueness of Christianity, Christian scholars have sometimes claimed that the *Logos* of Plato and the Greek mystics was different from the *Logos* of John's gospel. But this distinction is only intellectual or theological. Different writers and teachers may have emphasized different aspects at different times, but the fundamental Power itself is one and beyond all description. It has been referred to in many ways.

In the time of Jesus, the works of Plato and other Greek philosophers were well known in the Hellenistic world and since a great many of the Jews who lived outside Palestine spoke Greek, it is by no means surprising to find the Greek and Judaic cultures and modes of expression intertwined.

Possibly the most well-known of the Greek-speaking Jews, certainly in the field of mystic philosophy, was Philo Judaeus of Alexandria. His date of birth is not precisely known, but from some events of which he speaks that can be dated, it is clear that he was a contemporary of Jesus. And though there is no evidence of contact between the two of them, many of Philo's writings undoubtedly stem from the same mystical milieu. It is this that makes his writings of interest in our search for the real teachings of Jesus.

Philo is acknowledged to be one of the greatest compilers, synthesizers and commentators of his age. As such, though his interpretations of Jewish scriptures are often personal, he is not fundamentally inventing any theories of his own but is simply presenting the mystical understanding of his time. Consequently, his comments regarding what he variously calls the *Logos*, the divine *Logos*, the Word of God or the holy Word are most revealing. Describing the *Logos* as the Power by which God orders and organizes His creation, Philo says:

> The discernible order in all things is nothing else than the *Logos* of God, perpetually engaged in the action of creation.
>
> *Philo, On the World's Creation 6, PhI pp.20-21, TGHI p.235*

And again:

> We shall find that the cause of it (the universe) is God, by whom it came into existence. The matter of it is the four elements, out of which it has been composed. The instrument by means of which it has been built is the *Logos* of God. And the object of its building is the Goodness of the Creator.
>
> *Philo, On the Cherubim 35, PhII pp.82-83, TGHI p.235*

Speaking within the context of his times, Philo describes the matter of the physical universe in terms of the Greek understanding of its four perceivable states or conditions. Its purpose he asserts to be good, despite external appearances, while the means or instrument by which creation comes about is the *Logos*, elsewhere pointing out that the *Logos* is second only to God:

> But the most universal (of all things) is God, and next to Him, the *Logos* of God.
>
> *Philo, Allegorical Interpretation II:21, PhI pp.278-279, TGHI p.230*

To Philo, then, as to so many others of his period, the Word or *Logos* was commonly understood as God's creative Power, a term for which there were many synonyms.

The Word as Wisdom

One of the commonest terms for the Word, encountered particularly
in Greek and Hebrew literature, is Wisdom, called in Greek, *Sophia*,
and in Hebrew, *Hokhmah*. Like the Word, Wisdom has an exoteric
meaning, referring simply to human understanding and knowledge.
But in many places it very clearly refers to the creative Power of God.
In a commonly encountered literary style of the times, writers would
also 'assume' the identity of the Word or Wisdom, writing in the first
person, as in the earlier excerpt from the *Trimorphic Protennoia*. We
see this in an expansive passage from *Proverbs* which begins with lines
that are reminiscent of the opening to St John:

> Yahweh created me when His purpose first unfolded,
>> before the oldest of His works.
> From everlasting I was firmly set,
>> from the beginning, before the earth came into being.
>
> The deep was not, when I was born,
>> there were no springs to gush with water.
> Before the mountains were settled,
>> before the hills, I came to birth;
>> before He made the earth, the countryside,
>> or the first grains of the world's dust.
> When He fixed the heavens firm, I was there,
>> when He drew a ring on the surface of the deep,
>> when He thickened the clouds above,
>> when He fixed fast the springs of the deep,
>> when He assigned the sea its boundaries, ...
>> when He laid down the foundations of the earth,
> I was by His side, a master craftsman,
>> delighting Him day after day,
>> ever at play in His presence,
>> at play everywhere in His world,
>> delighting to be with the sons of men.
>
> *Proverbs 8:22-31, JB*

Wisdom, then, is God's creative Power "ever at play in His presence".
Expanding upon the same theme, in the *Wisdom of Solomon*, a Greek
composition probably dating from the first century BC, there are

some beautiful passages concerning the nature of Wisdom, who, being a feminine noun in both Greek and Hebrew, is referred to here as "she":

> For she is within herself a spirit intelligent, holy,
>> unique, manifold, subtle,
>> active, incisive, unsullied,
>> lucid, invulnerable, benevolent, sharp,
>> irresistible, beneficent, loving to man,
>> steadfast, dependable, unperturbed,
>> almighty, all-surveying,
>> penetrating all, intelligent,
>> pure and most subtle spirits;
> For Wisdom is quicker to move than any motion;
> She is so pure she pervades and permeates all things.
>
> She is a Breath of the Power of God,
>> pure emanation of the glory of the Almighty;
>> hence nothing impure can find a way into her.
> She is a reflection of the eternal Light,
>> untarnished mirror of God's active Power,
>> Image of His goodness.
>
> Although alone, she can do all;
>> herself unchanging, she makes all things new....
>
> She is indeed more splendid than the sun,
>> she outshines all the constellations;
>> compared with light she takes first place,
>> for light must yield to night,
>> but over Wisdom,
>> evil (and darkness of the soul) can never triumph.
> She deploys her strength from one end of the earth to the other,
>> ordering all things for good.

Wisdom of Solomon 7:22-30, 8:1, JB

Again echoing the opening lines of St John, as well as those of *Proverbs*, in the *Wisdom of Jesus Ben Sirach*, written in Hebrew during the early second century BC (*c.*190 BC) and later translated into Greek by the author's grandson (*c.*130 BC), we find:

> Before all other things Wisdom was created,
>   shrewd understanding (mystic insight) is everlasting.
> For whom has the root of Wisdom ever been uncovered?
> Her resourceful ways, who knows them?
> One only is wise, terrible indeed,
>   seated on His throne, the Lord.
>
> He himself has created her, looked on her and assessed her,
>   and poured her out on all His works
>   to be with all mankind as His gift,
>   and He conveyed her to those who love Him.
>
> *Wisdom of Jesus Ben Sirach 1:4-10, JB*

Again, Wisdom is portrayed as both God's creative Power, created by Him for this purpose – He has "poured her out on all His works" – and she is also present with "*all* mankind", though the poet says that she comes only to those who love Him.

Paul – writing perhaps twenty years after the death of Jesus and having been trained in the Jewish schools of mystical thought – was, naturally enough, familiar with all the writings concerning the Wisdom of God. And he writes unequivocally that the "Wisdom of God" was a part of the Christian "mysteries" – the secret teachings imparted to novitiates:

> The hidden Wisdom of God which we teach in our mysteries
>   is the Wisdom that God predestined to be for our glory
>   before the ages began.
>
> *1 Corinthians 2:7, JB*

While in the letter attributed to James the brother of Jesus, the writer is echoing the *Wisdom of Solomon* when he says:

> The Wisdom that is from above is first pure,
>   then peaceable, gentle, and easy to be entreated,
>   full of mercy and good fruits,
>   without partiality, and without hypocrisy.
>
> *James 3:17-18*

Wisdom, then, was another synonym for the Word, a Power well known to the mystics long before the time of Jesus.

The Word as the Son of God

Amongst the writings of the earliest Christian fathers, not only is Wisdom definitively identified with the Word or *Logos*, but also with the Son of God, and though the subject is discussed later in considerable detail, it is convenient to say something of the matter here. Justin Martyr (*c.*114-165) writing in the middle of the second century equated Wisdom, the Word and the Son with other terms used to describe the same Power:

> I am now going to give you, my friends, another testimony from the Scriptures that God before all His other creatures begat as the Beginning, a certain spiritual Power proceeding from Himself, which is called by the Holy Spirit, sometimes the Glory of the Lord, and sometimes Son, and sometimes Wisdom, and sometimes Angel, and sometimes God, and sometimes Lord and *Logos*, and on another occasion he calls himself Captain, when he appeared in human form to Joshua the son of Nun....
>
> The Word of Wisdom, who is himself this God begotten of the Father of all things, and Word, and Wisdom, and Power, and the Glory of the Begetter, will bear evidence to me, when he speaks by Solomon, the following....
>
> *Justin Martyr, Dialogue with Trypho LXI, OPJG pp.20-21, WJMA p.170*

He then quotes the passage from *Proverbs* previously cited. Irenaeus, too, Bishop of Lyons later in the same century, well-known for his castigation of the gnostics, quotes from *Proverbs* in the attempt to demonstrate the eternal nature of the Son of God and his identity with Wisdom. Here, as with Justin Martyr, the Son is identified primarily with the creative Power of God:

> We have abundantly shown that the *Logos*, that is the Son, was always with the Father, and he says through Solomon (in *Proverbs*) that *Sophia* (Wisdom) also, who is the Spirit, was with Him before any created thing. For "By Wisdom Yahweh set the earth on its foundation."
>
> *Irenaeus, Against Heresies IV:XX.3, OPJG p.23; cf. Proverbs 3:19-20*

Irenaeus, like Justin, then goes on to quote the famous passage from *Proverbs*, concluding:

> So there is one God, who by His Word and His Wisdom has made all things.
>
> *Irenaeus, Against Heresies IV:XX.4, OPJG p.23*

God, then, is the Father and His first emanation is – metaphorically – His First-born Son. And when He wishes to bring souls back to Himself, He sends this Son to take on a human form. Hence, it says at the beginning of John's gospel:

> And the Word was made flesh, and dwelt among us, ...
> full of grace and truth.
>
> *John 1:14*

A Master is the "Word made flesh", the Word in human form. And naturally, one who has the consciousness of God within himself will be "full of grace and truth". This is the least that can be said of such beautiful, graceful and divine beings.

Christians generally believe, of course, that Jesus was the only incarnation of the Word to come into this world. The subject is considered thoroughly in the appropriate chapter, but it may be pointed out here that this is not what the mystics themselves have taught. As the author of the *Wisdom of Solomon* says:

> In each generation she (Wisdom) passes into holy souls,
> she makes them friends of God and prophets;
> For God loves only the man who lives with Wisdom.
>
> *Wisdom of Solomon 7:27, JB*

Wisdom is always present in the world in the form of a mystic – the "friends of God and prophets", the "friend of God" being a term commonly used in the Middle East for true holy men. The same idea is attributed to Jesus in a saying recorded in Luke's gospel:

> Therefore also said the Wisdom of God,
> I will send them prophets and apostles,
> and some of them they shall slay and persecute.
>
> *Luke 11:49*

"Prophets" and "apostles" – mystics or Messengers – are sent by this Power, though some of them – like Jesus, John the Baptist and others mentioned in the Old Testament – are persecuted and killed.

There are many other places in the ancient literature of this period which speak of the incarnation of the Word in this world. In the gnostic, *Trimorphic Protennoia*, for example, the writer says:

> It is a Word by virtue of Speech;
>> it was sent to illumine those who dwell in the darkness.
>>>> *Trimorphic Protennoia 46, NHS28 p.425*

The Word is sent to the people of this world – the realm of darkness – in order to bring "illumination" to those who are genuinely interested. Likewise, the poet of the *Odes of Solomon* writes:

> The dwelling place of the Word is a Man,
>> and his truth (reality) is love.
> Blessed are those who have understood everything
>> through him (that Man or the Word),
>> and have known the Lord in his truth.
>>>> *Odes of Solomon XII:12-13, AOT p.703, OPS p.107*

He says that the Word takes up special abode in a particular Man – a Master or Son of God. And the reality of both the mystic Word and its manifestation in a Master is that of divine love. Such a Master shows his disciples everything. Hence the poet concludes, "Blessed are those who have understood everything through him" – they truly come to know the Lord.

There is no doubt that Jesus was understood to have been an incarnation of the Word or Wisdom of God. Paul, for instance, speaks of Jesus as:

> Christ the Power of God and the Wisdom of God.
>>>> *1 Corinthians 1:24*

And amongst the apocryphal and gnostic writings, Jesus – as the Saviour – is commonly identified with the Word and with Wisdom. In the *Acts of Thomas*, for example, Judas Thomas says:

> What I shall think concerning thy beauty, O Jesu,
>> and what I shall tell of thee, I know not,
>> or rather I am not able, for I have no power to declare it, ...
> Glory to thee, Wise Word!
> Glory to thee, thou Hidden One who hast many forms!
> Glory to thee, who for us put on manhood!
>>>> *Acts of Thomas 80, ANT p.401, AAA p.216*

Similarly, in the *Acts of John*, the writer clearly demonstrates his assurance of the identity and unity of the Word of Wisdom, the Word, the Holy Ghost, the Father and Jesus, when Jesus says:

> I would keep tune with holy souls.
> In me know thou the Word of Wisdom.
> Again with me say thou:
> Glory be to thee, Father;
> Glory to thee, Word;
> Glory to thee, Holy Ghost.
>
> *Acts of John 96, ANT p.254*

As a result of contact with the Son of God, as both the creative Power and as a Master, souls are enabled to realize their own true heritage as "sons of God". Thus, John's gospel says:

> He was in the world, and the world was made by him,
> and the world knew him not.
> He came unto his own, and his own received him not.
> But as many as received him,
> to them gave he power to become the sons of God,
> even to them that believe on his Name.
>
> *John 1:10-12*

The world is made by God through His Word, and this Word comes into the world in the form of a perfect Master. Yet the majority of people fail to recognize him for who he is. God comes to His own progeny, the souls who owe their origin and essence entirely to Him, yet He remains incognito. Only to those who recognize Him and follow His teachings are given the power to return to God, to realize that they are all His sons.

The Word as the Bread of Life

One of the many images used by Jesus for the Word was the Bread of Life, a term drawn from the earlier teachings of Moses. Matthew and Luke, for example, record that Jesus was tempted in the desert to turn stones into bread:

> Then was Jesus led up of the Spirit into the wilderness to be tempted of
> the devil. And when he had fasted forty days and forty nights, he was

afterward an hungered. And when the tempter came to him, he said, "If thou be the Son of God, command that these stones be made bread." But he answered and said, "It is written, 'Man shall not live by bread alone, but by every Word that proceedeth out of the mouth of God.'"

Matthew 4:1-4; cf. Deuteronomy 8:3

The story is possibly an anecdote told so that the passage attributed to Moses could then be quoted, but whatever its origins, it indicates that while the sustenance of the body is physical food, the true nourishment of the soul is the Word. For this reason, the Word has also been called the Bread of Life. Interpreting the *Exodus* story allegorically, it is also the "manna" fed to the children of Israel wandering in the desert of this world in search of the Promised Land or eternal realm of God. In this quest, they are led by their Saviour Moses, after their escape from Egypt, a symbol of the physical universe. Philo Judaeus explicitly interprets this passage mystically and metaphorically, when he writes:

> For He nourisheth us with His *Logos* – the most universal (of all things)....
> And the *Logos* of God is above the whole cosmos; it is the most ancient and most universal of all created things....
>
> Therefore let God announce His (good) tidings to the soul in an image (a metaphor): "Man shall not live by bread alone, but by every Word that proceedeth out of the mouth of God",[1] – that is, he shall be nourished by the whole of the *Logos* and by (every) part of it. For 'mouth' is a symbol of the (whole) *Logos*, and 'Word' is its part."
>
> *Philo, Allegorical Interpretation III:61, PhI pp.418-419, TGHI p.248*

In St John's gospel, Jesus himself interprets *Exodus* in this way, the dialogue almost certainly being one of John's constructs enabling him to bring out the mystic meaning in the story of Moses. According to John's narrative, some people comment to Jesus that God gave the children of Israel manna to eat as a sign of His care for them. They want to know what sign or proof Jesus will give them of himself:

> They said therefore unto him,
> "What sign shewest thou then, that we may see,
>   and believe thee? What dost thou work?"
> Our fathers did eat manna in the desert;
>   as it is written, 'He gave them bread from heaven to eat'.
>
> *John 6:30-31*

But Jesus replies that it was not Moses who produced the manna, but God, and in any case, the manna was not a physical food but was symbolic of the spiritual nourishment of the Word "which cometh down from heaven and giveth life unto the world (the creation)". The Word or "Bread of God" emanates from the "kingdom of heaven" and is the source of life and existence throughout the creation. He says:

> Then Jesus said unto them,
> "Verily, verily, I say unto you,
>> Moses gave you not that Bread from heaven;
>> but my Father giveth you the true Bread from heaven.
> For the Bread of God is he which cometh down from heaven,
>> and giveth life unto the world (the creation)."
>
> Then said they unto him,
> "Lord, evermore give us this Bread."
>
> And Jesus said unto them,
> "I am the Bread of Life:
>> he that cometh to me shall never hunger;
>> and he that believeth on me shall never thirst."
>
> *John 6:32-35*

Jesus says that one who comes into contact with the "Bread of Life", the Word within, is fully satisfied. All the hungers, thirsts and desires of this world fade away in the eternal satisfaction and bliss produced by contact with the Word of God. Jesus also speaks of himself as the Bread of Life, the Word of God. While he lived in this world, he was the Word personified, the "Word made flesh" and the "Bread of Life". Later in this same chapter, he continues:

> "Verily, verily, I say unto you,
>> He that believeth on me hath everlasting life.
> I am that Bread of Life.
> Your fathers did eat manna in the wilderness, and are dead.
> This is the Bread which cometh down from heaven,
>> that a man may eat thereof, and not die.
> I am the Living Bread which came down from heaven:
>> if any man eat of this Bread, he shall live for ever."
>
> *John 6:47-51*

No bread of this world can permit someone to live for ever. Taking the *Exodus* story at face value, Jesus points out that the children of Israel who ate the manna from heaven have all died. Everyone lives out their normal span of life and dies, according to the laws of nature, just as the disciples of Jesus have died. "He shall live for ever" means that through inner experience of the Word of God, the "Living Bread", the soul will reach the eternal realm of God Himself, will realize its innate indestructibility and immortality, and will dwell there for all eternity.

Philo Judaeus again confirms this interpretation. He points out that the soul and body, being formed from different sources, require different kinds of sustenance. For the soul, he says, is "a particle of God" and the body is formed of the earth:

> The body, then, has been formed out of earth, but the soul is of the upper aether, a particle detached from God: "for God breathed into his face a Breath of Life, and man became a living soul."[2]
>
> *Philo, Allegorical Interpretation III:55, PhI pp.408-409, TGHI p.246*

And a little further on, he continues:

> You will see that the soul is not nourished with earthly things that decay, but with such rays of grace as God shall pour like rain out of that lofty and pure region of life which the prophet (Moses) has called heaven....
>
> *Philo, Allegorical Interpretation III:56, PhI pp.408-409, TGHI p.246*

> Does thou not see the food of the soul, what it is? It is the *Logos* of God, (raining) continuously, like dew, embracing all the soul, suffering no portion to be without part of itself.
>
> But this *Logos* is not apparent everywhere, but (only) in the man who is destitute of passions and vices; and it is subtle and delicate both to conceive and be conceived, surpassingly translucent and pure to behold.
>
> It is, as it were, a coriander[3] (mustard) seed. For tillers of the soil say that if you cut the seed of the coriander into countless pieces, each of the portions into which you cut it, if sown, grows exactly as the whole seed would have done.
>
> Such, too, is the *Logos* of God, able to confer benefits both as a whole and by means of every part, yes any part you light upon.
>
> *Philo, Allegorical Interpretation III:59 PhV pp.414-415, TGHI p.247*

Again, he says:

This is the teaching of the hierophant and prophet, Moses, who will say: "This is the bread, the food which God hath given to the soul,"[4] for it to feed on, His own Word, His own *Logos*; for this Bread which He hath given us to eat is this Word.

Philo, Allegorical Interpretation III:60, PhI pp.416-419, TGHI p.247

The Word as Living Water

Perhaps an even more common metaphor for the Word was the Water of Life or the Living Water. The expression dates at least from the earliest Mesopotamian times, two thousand years or more before the time of Jesus, and it is found in many writings both within and outside the Bible. Practically all the mystics of the East have used the expression, including the Sufis of Islam.

The term is readily understood. To begin with, bread and water are the basic essentials for maintaining life in this world. Moreover, in a desert climate, nothing is more important to life than water. Without water, there can be no life, a fact that is readily forgotten in temperate zones. Therefore, just as water brings life to a physical desert, so too does the Word bring life a heart that is parched and dry for want of true spiritual inspiration. In the spiritual desert of this world, the Living Water brings life, for it is the current of God's life force bringing everything into being. We encounter the term in John's gospel, where Jesus uses the expression much like he uses its parallel, the Bread of Life:

> If any man thirst, let him come unto me;
>   let him that believeth in me, drink.
> As the scripture hath said,
>   'Out of his breast (from within himself)
>   shall flow rivers of Living Water.'
> *John 7:37-38; cf. JB, KJV, RSV*

The scriptural quotation is not found anywhere in this precise form, though there are a number of Biblical passages which refer to fountains or rivers of Living Water. The meaning, however, is clear enough. Jesus says that if anyone is truly seeking God, is athirst with a true longing to really understand the mystic reality, he should go to one who is the "Word made flesh", one from whose "breast" flows an abundance of the Living Water that nourishes the soul. One who believes in and follows the Word personified will be put into contact with the mystic river of Living Water deep within himself. Jesus is talking here to the people of his own time and place, not to those who would come in future times.

Living Water is also found in the story of Jesus' meeting at Jacob's well with the Syro-Phoenician woman. But, as we have seen before, the narrative is almost certainly a fabrication to suit the discourse, the two being created together as an integral part of the way in which John presents Jesus' teachings. After all, there was no one else there to record their conversation. According to the story, Jesus asks the woman to draw some water for him and she responds:

> How is it that thou, being a Jew,
> askest drink of me, which am a woman of Samaria?
> For the Jews have no dealings with the Samaritans.
>
> *John 4:9*

Upon which, forgetting his own need for water, Jesus suggests that in reality the woman should be requesting water from him. He says:

> If thou knewest the gift of God,
> and who it is that saith to thee, 'Give me to drink;'
> thou wouldst have asked of him,
> and he would have given thee Living Water.
>
> *John 4:10*

The "gift of God" is a common expression for mystic baptism with the Living Water of the Word, a gift obtainable only from a perfect Master. But the woman does not recognize Jesus for who he really is, nor does she catch his real meaning. So, taking him literally, she points out that Jesus has no bucket or container with which to draw any water, so how could he give it to her? This opens the way for Jesus to reply:

> Whosoever drinketh of this water shall thirst again:
> but whosoever drinketh of the Water
> that I shall give him shall never thirst;
> But the Water that I shall give him shall be(come) in him
> a well of water springing up into everlasting Life.
>
> *John 4:10,13-14*

He says that those who drink physical water will naturally "thirst again" since the satisfaction of material needs and desires is only temporary.

But the Living Water quenches all lower thirsts or desires by filling the soul with the intoxication of divine love and the essence of all life, and is therefore fully and completely satisfying. All yearnings of the world are then swept aside.

Though Jesus spoke of the Word as the Living Water, we might not have grasped the meaning of these two isolated passages in St John were it not for a multitude of references to the term in other literature. In the *Book of Revelation*, for instance, this inner wellspring of life is described as the Water of Life. In one passage, God reputedly says to the visionary author:

> I am Alpha and Omega, the Beginning and the End.
> I will give unto him that is athirst
>   of the fountain of the Water of Life freely.
> He that overcometh shall inherit all things;
>   and I will be his God, and he shall be my son.
>
> *Book of Revelation 21:6-7*

And in the epilogue of the same book, according to the writer, Jesus reiterates the same message in words clearly echoing St John's gospel:

> Let him that is athirst come.
> And whosoever will,
>   let him take the Water of Life freely.
>
> *Book of Revelation 22:17*

In fact, there are so many uses of this metaphor in a specifically mystical context – with which Jesus and his disciples would have been familiar – that only a few may be given here. The Judaic use of the term can be traced back to its occurrence in *Genesis* where it is described as a river that flows out of Eden. Philo Judaeus points out that this is to be interpreted allegorically. Eden, he says, is a metaphor for the eternal realm of God, and the river is the *Logos*, the current of God's Creative Word or Wisdom, which flows out from Him, bringing spiritual nourishment to the souls of those who seek her:

> And the divine *Logos* flows down from Wisdom like a river from a source, that it may irrigate and water – as though they were a garden (*lit.* paradise) – the heavenly shoots and plants of virtue-loving souls that grow upon the sacred Mountain of the gods.
>
> *Philo, On Dreams II:36, PhV pp.550-551, TGHI p.243*

The "sacred Mountain of the gods" is a reference to the inner regions, the holy mountains of the spirit through which the souls who follow the path of the *Logos* must pass through on their ascent to the Source.

Similarly, speaking of the psalmist as "one of the companions of Moses" – that is, a spiritual brother, one who shared the same spiritual understanding – Philo writes:

> Accordingly, one of the companions of Moses, likening this Word to a river, says in the *Hymns*: "The river of God was filled with water".[5]
>
> Now it is absurd that any of the rivers flowing on earth should be so called; but, as it seems, he (the psalmist) clearly signifies the divine *Logos*, full of the flood of Wisdom, having no part of itself bereft or empty thereof, but rather, as has been said, being entirely diffused throughout the universe and raised up on high by reason of the perpetual and continuous course of that eternally flowing fountain.
>
> *Philo, On Dreams II:37, PhV pp.552-553, TGHI p.243*

In another passage, Philo again uses the same imagery of the *Logos* running out from God like a stream, flowing through all things. Commenting on a line from the *Psalms* which reads, "the strong current of the river makes glad the City of God",[6] he points out that the "City" cannot be Jerusalem, for there are neither rivers nor sea nearby. The "City of God", he says, has two meanings. Firstly, it is the universe or creation:

> The stream of the divine *Logos* continually flowing on with its swift and ordered current, does overflow and gladden the whole universe through and through.
>
> *Philo, On Dreams II:37, PhV pp.552-555, TGHI p.245*

And secondly, says Philo, the psalmist

> uses this name (the City of God) for the soul of the Sage, in whom God is said to walk as in a city. For "I will walk in you," he says, "and will be your God."[7]
>
> *Philo, On Dreams II:37, PhV pp.554-555, TGHI p.245*

Furthermore, he adds, the soul of a spiritual seeker, like the Sage, holds itself out like a "most holy drinking vessel" awaiting the "Cup-bearer of God" – the divine *Logos* – who is not only Master of this spiritual feast but is one with the draught he pours:

And when the happy soul that stretches forth its own inner being as a
most holy drinking vessel – who is it that poureth forth the sacred measures of true joy but the *Logos*, the Cup-bearer of God and Master of the
feast – he who differs not from the draught he pours – his own self free
from all dilution, who is the delight, the sweetness, the forthpouring, the
good-cheer, the ambrosial drug (to take for our own use the poet's terms)
whose medicine gives joy and contentment.

Philo, On Dreams II:37, PhV pp.554-555, TGHI p.245

There are plenty of other references, too, amongst the Old Testament
writings. The Jewish prophet Jeremiah, for example, says:

My people have committed a double crime:
> they have abandoned me,
> the fountain of Living Water,
> only to dig cisterns for themselves,
> leaky cisterns that hold no water.

Jeremiah 2:13, JB

To the Lord and to a Master, all souls are "my people". Whoever they
may be, from whatever caste, creed or social background they may
come, all people are the children of God. So Jeremiah says that the
souls in this world have largely abandoned God, they have turned away
from Him who lies within, turning their attention away from the creative Power within which gives life. We have "dug leaky cisterns" – we
have sought for Life in the outward affairs of the physical creation
where everything passes away or dies. Or we have sought fruitlessly
for God in man-made churches, temples or mosques and in the rituals and ceremonies of outward religion, when in reality He lies within
our own selves. The precious inner water of spirituality has thus leaked
away into the world by our trying to find happiness, satisfaction and
spirituality in places where it cannot be found.

Traditionally, such sayings of the Biblical prophets have been interpreted to refer only to the people of Israel. That God should have been
claimed to support just one nation alone has been called the 'scandal
of particularization'. But although understood in this manner by Jews
and Christians alike, it is unlikely that any mystic would have been so
narrow-minded. Mystics are the epitome of universality, transcending
all barriers of nation, religion and culture. Moreover, Philo and other
mystically-minded commentators have consistently provided a universal

and allegorical interpretation. Our interpretation, therefore, also follows in an old tradition.

The same metaphorical language is employed by the prophet Joel who is describing something of the bliss of mystic contact with this sweet water when he speaks of the 'day of the Lord', meaning the soul's ascent to the inner realms. This is the land that truly flows with sweet nourishment for the soul, 'milk and honey' or "sweet wine" coming from the "mountains" (the inner regions) of the Lord:

> And it shall come to pass in that day,
> that the mountains shall drop down sweet wine,
> and the hills shall flow with milk,
> and all the brooks of Judah shall flow with waters;
> And a fountain shall come forth of the house of the Lord,
> and shall water the valley of Shittim.
>
> *Joel 4:18, JPS*

The "valley of Shittim" is this world, often referred to as a valley. The Lord keeps His creation nourished and sustained at all times by means of "brooks" or rivers of the Living Water of the Word, the "fountain" that comes from the "house of the Lord", watering the "valley of Shittim".

The prophet Isaiah also uses similar imagery. Speaking in the name of Yahweh, he describes the creation as the "delightful vineyard" which requires continuous watering:

> Sing of the delightful vineyard!
> I, Yahweh, am its keeper;
> Every moment I water it
> for fear its leaves should fall;
> night and day I watch over it.
>
> *Isaiah 27:2-3, JB*

The creation is a constant manifestation of the Lord in which He is forever present in dynamic action. If the Living Water of God's creative Power were withdrawn from the creation, it would immediately be dissolved. Hence, there is no second when this Power is not active – "for fear its leaves should fall". In another passage, he speaks of the "wells of salvation" which bring "joy" or bliss to thirsty souls in this world:

> Behold, God is my salvation;
>   I will trust, and not be afraid:
> For the Lord Yahweh is my strength and my song;
> He also is become my salvation.
> Therefore with joy shall ye draw water
>   out of the wells of salvation.
>
> *Isaiah 12:2-3, KJV*

The same metaphor is found in the *Psalms*, where it is described as God's "River of Pleasure" and the "Fountain of Life":

> Yahweh, protector of man and beast,
>   how precious God, Your love!
> Hence the sons of men
>   take shelter in the shadow of Your wings.
>
> They feast on the bounty of Your house,
>   You give them drink from Your River of Pleasure;
>   yes, with You is the Fountain of Life,
>   by Your Light, we see the light.
>
> *Psalms 36:6-9, JB*

And in the well-known twenty-third psalm, where the psalmist writes almost entirely in metaphors, each of which has a particular meaning, the "still waters" that restore the soul are the Living Waters of the Word, while the "green pastures" are the inner realms or mansions of the soul:

> The Lord (Yahweh) is my shepherd; I shall not want.
> He maketh me to lie down in green pastures:
> He leadeth me beside the still waters.
> He restoreth my soul.
>
> *Psalms 23:1-3, KJV*

In the *Wisdom of Jesus Ben Sirach*, the "Law" or *Torah* of Judaism is also given a mystical interpretation. It, too, is used as a synonym for the Word, and we will encounter the term in even more explicitly mystical contexts in a few places throughout this book. In this extract, Ben Sirach links the Law, Wisdom, the "Bread of understanding" and the Living Water. Speaking of the search for Wisdom and the discipline required to follow that mystic path, he writes:

Whoever fears the Lord will act like this,
    and whoever grasps the Law will obtain Wisdom.
She will come to meet him like a mother,
    and receive him like a virgin bride.
She will give him the Bread of understanding to eat,
    and the Water of Wisdom to drink.

Wisdom of Jesus Ben Sirach 15:3, JB

Similarly, the devotional writer of the *Odes of Solomon* speaks of the "Living Spring of the Lord":

Draw for yourselves water from the Living Spring of the Lord,
    because it has been opened to you.
And come, all you who thirst, and take a draught,
    and rest by the Spring of the Lord,
    for fair it is and pure,
    and gives rest to the soul.

For its waters are far pleasanter than honey,
    and the honeycomb of bees is not to be compared with it;
Because it flows forth from the lips of the Lord,
    and from the heart of the Lord is its Name.
And it came unhindered and unseen,
    and until it was placed within them, men did not know it.
Blessed are they who have drunk from it,
    and have found rest thereby.

Odes of Solomon XXX:1-7, AOT p.720, OPS p.130

Likewise, in the *Acts of Thomas*, Judas Thomas, speaking of this world as "this thirsty land" and "this place of them that hunger", describes Jesus as the one who brings water, food and rest.

And he shall be to you a fountain
    springing up in this thirsty land;
And a chamber full of food
    in this place of them that hunger,
    and a rest unto your souls.

Acts of Thomas 37, ANT p.383

He also says that he has substituted the damp spring that was once within him for the free-flowing, Living Spring of his Master:

> The moist spring that was in me have I dried up,
>> that I may live and rest beside thy Living Spring.
>>>> *Acts of Thomas 147, ANT p.429*

The gnostic writers explicitly identify the Word with the Living Water and the wellspring of the creation, the Source of all life:

> It (the Word) is a hidden Light,
>> bearing the Fruit of Life,
>> pouring forth Living Water
>> from the invisible, unpolluted, immeasurable Spring.
>>>> *Trimorphic Protennoia 46, NHS28 p.425*

And:

> He (the Father) is a Spring,
>> which is not diminished by the Water
>> which abundantly flows from it.
>>>> *Tripartite Tractate 60, NHS22 p.207*

And addressing the souls of this world as dreamers, the writer of the *Concept of Our Great Power* says:

> You are sleeping, dreaming dreams.
> Wake up and return (to God),
>> taste and eat the true food!
> Hand out the Word and the Water of Life!
> Cease from the evil lusts and desires.
>> *Concept of Our Great Power 39-40, NHS11 pp.303-305*

The later Manichaean-Christian writers, in the third or fourth century, acknowledged Jesus, as well as their own Master, Mani, as a great mystic and Saviour. In one of their psalms, Jesus is described in elaborate imagery which links together a number of metaphors for the Word:

> Jesus dug a river in the world;
>> he dug a river, even he of the Sweet Name.
> He dug it with the spade of Truth,
>> he dredged it with the basket of Wisdom,

the stones (souls) which he dredged from it
are like drops of incense (Fragrance);
All the waters that are in it are roots of Light.
Psalms of Thomas XII, MPB p.217

Among the most persistent users of the expression were the Mandaeans. Intriguingly, despite the fact that they lived in what is now southern Iraq, one of their terms for the Living Water was the "Jordan", indicating their distant Palestinian origins. In fact, the term still persists in their language as a word for *any* river or stream, though in the earlier years of the twentieth century, many amongst them did not even know that elsewhere in the Middle East was a river called the Jordan. They speak of the creative outpouring of the Word as:

Biriawis (the Heavenly Jordan), source of Living Waters,
    first upsurging that sprang forth (from God),
    great outburst of the Radiance of all-abundant Life!
CPM 44 p.40

And, interestingly, like the story told in John's gospel, they commonly use the metaphor of a well or a wellspring:

This is a Wellspring of Life
    which sprang forth from the Place of Life:
    we drink thereof, of this Fount of Life and Light
    which Life (God) transmitted ...
    which crossed worlds, came,
    cleft the heavens and was revealed.
CPM 45 p.41

The Wellspring of Life, the Word, says the writer, passes through all the heavens, the higher realms of creation, and is manifest or "revealed" in this world as a Master.

The Word as Life, Light and the Breath of God

From a practical human viewpoint, the relationship between God and the Word is very simple: in the creation, God is known only through His Word. The source of life and spiritual light in the creation is the Word and the source of the Word is God, the supreme Ocean of Life and Light. As Jesus says in John's gospel:

> For as the Father hath life in himself;
>> so hath he given to the Son to have life in himself.
>>>>>>>> *John 5:26*

The Father is the source of life, but He has passed it on to the Son to bring into the creation. This is true of the Son as both the creative Power and as a Master. So not only does the Word provide the creative dynamism behind everything in creation, it is also the essence of life and consciousness itself, present within every soul. God has given birth to all souls by means of the Word. It is the creative Life Force within all.

In mystical writings, as in the Mandaean extracts, life and light are commonly associated with God and His creative Power. In St John, having spoken of God and the Word, the opening continues:

> In him (the *Logos*) was life;
>> and the life was the light of men.
>>>>>> *John 1:4*

God, as the Word, is the source of life. This Power is also the spiritual light at the heart of everything. It lies within all of us, and yet, as John observes:

> And the light shineth in darkness;
>> and the darkness comprehended it not.
>>>>>> *John 1:5*

The inner light is within everyone, but we do not see it because the mind is directed towards the world of the physical senses. Consequently, the mind and soul remain in darkness – both metaphorically and literally – for when we close our eyes we see nothing but darkness. Hence, echoing the words of John's gospel, Jesus says in St Matthew:

> If therefore the light that is in thee be darkness,
>> how great is that darkness!
>>>>>> *Matthew 6:23*

To have that treasury of light within and yet be unable to enjoy it is indeed a great darkness.

Many of the metaphors used by Jesus, which appear only in St John, are also found extensively in Mandaean writings. The relationship between John's gospel and the Mandaeans have thus intrigued many scholars, for the Mandaeans traditionally give allegiance to John the Baptist but not to Jesus. Clearly, Jesus, the writer of John's gospel and the Mandaeans all drew from a common source, and one cannot help but wonder what the history of John the Baptist and Jesus really was.

Conveying the same meaning as John's gospel, the Mandaeans speak of the Supreme Lord as "First Life", "Great Life" or simply "Life", as in:

> Thou wast established, First Life;
>> thou wast in existence before all things.
> Before Thee no being existed.
>
> *CPM 24 p.20*

And:

> Well is it for him whom the Great Life knoweth
>> but woe to him whom the Great Life knoweth not!
> Well is it for him whom the Great Life knoweth,
>> who keepeth himself alien from the world,
>> from the world of imperfection.
>
> *CPM 165 p.145*

The one who is drawn by God, says the writer, keeps himself detached or "alien" from this world of imperfection. In another passage, the eternal realm of God is called "Great Life", the "Place of Life", the "House of Life", the "everlasting abode" and the "Place of Light":

> Bow thyself! and worship!
>> prostrate thyself and praise the Great Life.
> Praise the Place of Life to which thy fathers go....
>
> Good one! Rise to the House of Life
>> and go to the everlasting abode!
> They will hang thy lamp amongst lamps of Light
>> and they will shine in thy time, and at thy moment.
> Arise! Behold the Place of Light!
>
> *CPM 92 pp.96-97*

The unknown mystic poet of antiquity exhorts the soul to seek God now. He advises, "hang thy lamp", the lamp or light of the soul, in the realm of divine Light. Then, in your own lifetime, "in thy time, and in thy moment", you will be able to see God, to "behold the Place of Light", to rise to the "House of Life".

The Word, then, springs from God, the Ocean of Life and Light and brings life and light into the creation. This is why Philo, Jesus and others also described the Word as the Bread of Life, the immortal food and so on, for without continuous sustenance, there is no life, physically or spiritually. Hence, another term for the Word was the Breath of Life.

The expression is found in *Genesis* (which is attributed to Moses) and Philo Judaeus, describing the *Logos* as the "most life-giving thing" in the creation, says that Moses called it the "Breath of God":

> (Moses) called (it) the Breath of God, because it is the most life-giving thing (in the creation), and God is the cause (source) of life.
>
> *Philo, On the World's Creation VIII, PhI pp.22-23, TGHI p.232*

Just as physical life cannot exist without breath, similarly the essence of life, consciousness and existence cannot exist without the *Logos*. As in a previous excerpt,[8] Philo is referring to the allegory of Adam and Eve in *Genesis* which says:

> And the Lord God formed man of the dust of the ground,
>   and breathed into his nostrils the Breath of Life;
>   and man became a living soul.
>
> *Genesis 2:7, KJV*

The expression is also found in the story of Noah's Ark, where it is used in three very similar instances, the first of which reads:

> And, behold, I (God), even I, do bring a flood of waters upon the earth, to destroy all flesh, wherein is the Breath of Life, from under heaven; and every thing that is in the earth shall die.
>
> *Genesis 6:17, KJV*

The term is actually found throughout the Bible. In one of the *Psalms*, for instance, the Word is described as the means by which God has created and gives continuous life and sustenance to His creation – "by the Breath of His mouth":

> By the Word of the Lord were the heavens made;
>   and all the host of them by the Breath of His mouth.
>
> *Psalms 33:6, JPS*

Terms like 'wind', 'air' and 'breath' as images for the Spirit or Word are common in the mystical writings of Jesus' era. The reasons for this are not hard to understand. The Spirit is the subtlest aspect of creation, pervading all, yet invisible to the physical senses. So, too, is air the most refined of the physically observable states of material substance. Further, the Spirit cools the mind and comforts the soul held captive in the burning furnace of the sensual world, just as a light wind brings welcome coolness from the heat of the sun.

But perhaps the greatest reason for this imagery is that the Spirit brings life to a human form. The soul is a drop of the Spirit. In its essence, the soul is pure Spirit, a particle of God. When the soul takes up residence in a body, we say there is life. When the same soul departs, then death immediately ensues. Similarly, it is the breath which determines the presence of physical life. When somebody stops breathing for anything but the briefest of periods, they are dead. It is the simplest means for determining whether or not a person is alive.

It is the powerful life energy of the Spirit which holds a body together. The difference in activity between inert matter and living tissues is almost unbelievable. Living tissues are highly organized, ultra-dynamic systems in which complex molecular structures are built up and broken down all the time. There are hundreds of thousands of integrated and highly organized interactions per cell per second. In inert matter, this kind of activity is absent; and when a body dies, such activity ceases very rapidly. It is the presence of the soul within, acting through the mind, which provides this energy and organization to otherwise inert matter, creating what we observe as a physical body. Without this, the complexity, order, integration and activity very rapidly cease.

Breath, then, means life and it is not surprising that the mystics of old, losing no opportunity in the employment of a good metaphor, commonly used these terms for the Spirit. In fact, in both Greek and Hebrew the same word is used for both 'spirit' and 'wind' (*pneuma* and *ruach*). Additionally, the Greek word *pneuma* literally means 'that which blows' or 'that which is blown', being derived from the verb *pnein*, meaning 'to blow'. The Greek is also at the root of the English word 'pneumatic' which means 'spiritual' as well as 'inflatable'. This potential for word play was not overlooked by the author of John's gospel, when he has Jesus say:

> The wind (*pneuma*) bloweth (*pnei*) where it listeth,
>   and thou hearest the sound thereof, ...
> So is every one that is born of the Spirit (*pneuma*).

John 3:8

Jesus is speaking of the sound of the Word, a discussion of which is reserved for the next chapter. But it may be remarked that since this word play works well in Hebrew, Aramaic and Greek, it cannot be used as a guide to the language in which this part of John's gospel was originally written.

Elsewhere in the ancient literature, we have already seen in the *Wisdom of Solomon* how Wisdom is described as a "Breath of the Power of God".[9] There is a more metaphorical example in the *Wisdom of Jesus Ben Sirach*, where Wisdom is described as "breathing out a scent":

> I (Wisdom) have exhaled a perfume
>   like cinnamon and acacia,
> I have breathed out a scent like choice myrrh.
>
> *Wisdom of Jesus Ben Sirach 24:15, JB*

In fact, the 'breathing of the Spirit' into the soul is a commonly encountered image. It is found, for example, in the *Acts of Thomas*, where – in a prayer for spiritual help and support – Judas Thomas speaks of Jesus as:

> (Thou) who breathest thine own Power into us
>   and encouragest us and givest confidence
> in love unto thine own servants.
>
> *Acts of Thomas 81, ANT p.401*

Certainly, one who has been even lightly touched by divine love understands the feeling of confidence and contentment that it brings. The mind and soul are comforted and warmed, held secure; the mind and its scattering tendencies are restrained and the lower self or ego is increasingly forgotten as the attention becomes focused upon that which is higher. God's "Power" is indeed "breathed" into a soul from within. The same metaphor is used in John's gospel in one of the traditional stories of the resurrection, where Jesus says:

> "Peace be unto you: as my Father hath sent me,
>   even so send I you."
> And when he had said this, he breathed on them,
>   and saith unto them,
> "Receive ye the Holy Ghost."
>
> *John 20:21-23*

But this breath is no physical breathing. It is an infusion of the Spirit from within. Similarly, the author of the *Odes of Solomon* is speaking of the Masters who have true knowledge of God when he writes:

> They spoke the Truth from the inspiration
> which the Most High breathed into them.
>
> *Odes of Solomon XVIII:15, AOT p.709*

Amongst the gnostic texts, writing of the creative Power which brings life to the creation, the author of the *Tripartite Tractate* says:

> This is what the prophet called the "Living Spirit" and the "Breath of the exalted *Aeons* (inner realms)" and "the Invisible".
>
> *Tripartite Tractate 105, NHS22 p.283*

He gives no indication, however, of the prophet to whom he is refer-ring. Alluding to the *Genesis* allegory, the writer of the *Gospel of Philip* says that the soul of man, typified as Adam, came into being through this Breath, which is the spiritual partner or essence of man:

> The soul of Adam (man) came into being
> by means of a Breath.
> The partner of his soul is the Spirit.
>
> *Gospel of Philip 70, NHS20 p.183*

And the same idea is expressed in the *Apocalypse of Adam*, when 'God' says:

> Do you not know that I am the God who created you?
> And I breathed into you a Spirit of life as a living soul.
>
> *Apocalypse of Adam 66, NHS11 pp.159-161*

In a slightly different use of the metaphor, contrasting the spiritual winter brought about by the cold blast of worldliness with the warmth and life occasioned by the breathing of the Holy Spirit, the author of the *Gospel of Philip* again writes:

> When that spirit (*or* wind) (of the world) blows,
> it brings the winter.
> When the Holy Spirit breathes,
> the summer comes.
>
> *Gospel of Philip 77, NHS20 p.197*

"That spirit" of the world also refers to the Evil or Unholy Spirit, Satan, the power which engenders a love for this world, as opposed to the Holy Spirit, which is the Word of God. This epithet of Satan as the spirit, wind or "air" of the world is also found in a few other places. In his letter to the Ephesians, for example, Paul refers to him as:

> The Prince of the power of the air,
>   the spirit that now worketh
>   in the children of disobedience.
>
> *Ephesians 2:1-5*

Likewise, the realms of the spirit were sometimes referred to as the "air", as in the revelationary *Ascension of Isaiah*:

> And he took me up into the air of the sixth heaven and I beheld a glory I had not seen in the five heavens while I was being taken up, and angels resplendent in great glory.
>
> *Ascension of Isaiah VIII:1-2, AOT p.800*

From this and many other such examples which could be given, it becomes quite clear that when it is said that Jesus or any of the Jewish prophets of old were taken up "into the air" or ascended into heaven, it did not mean that they ascended into the physical atmosphere of planet earth (an ascent which would have become increasingly chilly). It means that they ascended spiritually through the spiritual regions, within themselves.

In fact, the Word was also called the "Living Air" or just the "Air" or the "Wind", as it is in John's gospel, the term being encountered in the Manichaean psalms:

> How is the Living Air,
>   the Breath of Life that surrounds the Father?
> The Great Spirit of the Land of Light,
>   the (source) of all the *aeons* (inner realms)?
>
> *Psalms of Heracleides, MPB p.197*

Life, Water, Fire, Breath, Air, Wind – all these, then, were used in a variety of lyrical metaphors for the Spirit or Word of God. Just as water brings life to the desert, fire brings essential heat and light to physical existence, bread maintains life in the body, and breath and air are required for the continuation of life, so the creative current of the

Word became known as the Living Water, the Living Fire, the Bread of Life, the Breath of Life, the Living Air and the Word of God. God, too, being the Source of life and consciousness, was called the Living God.

Once more we find the same reality being described. It is so important and fundamental to the highest mystic understanding of things that the mystics never tire of repeating the same perennial truth in every conceivable manner. And once again we see that sayings attributed to Jesus in the gospels are greatly illumined when considered within the greater context of his times. His sayings were not unique but were drawn from a fertile background of rich language used by all the mystics of his time and place.

The Logos as God's Image

Philo also suggests an interesting interpretation of Moses' phrase "God's Image", found in *Genesis*. God's Image, he says, is actually the *Logos*, and from this Image arises the inner spiritual light. That is to say, the light that can be seen inside is derived from the *Logos*:

> And he (Moses) calls the invisible and spiritual divine *Logos*, the Image of God. And of this, the image (in its turn) is that spiritual light, which has been created as the image of the divine *Logos*.
>
> *Philo, On the World's Creation VIII, PhI p.25, TGHI p.232*

Man being made in the Image of God therefore means, according to Philo's interpretation, that he is created out of this Image, out of the *Logos* – something upon which all the mystics who have taught the path of the Word have agreed. And like them, Philo asserts that the creation, too, has been fashioned out of this Image or *Logos*:

> The *Logos* is the Image of God by which the whole cosmos was made.
>
> *Philo, On Monarchy II:V, WPJIII p.194, TGHI p.234*

But this interpretation is not Philo's alone for, interestingly, Paul also speaks of God's "dear Son" and "First-born" in the same way. God, he says,

> hath translated us into the kingdom of his dear Son
> ... who is the Image of the invisible God,
> (and) the First-born of every creature:

> For by him were all things created,
>> that are in heaven, and that are in earth,
>> visible and invisible,
>> whether they be thrones, or dominions,
>> or principalities, or powers:
> All things were created by him, and for him.
>> *Colossians 1:13,15-16*

The "principalities and powers" are a reference to the inner realms and their rulers, part of the higher hierarchy of creation, the "invisible" "things ... that are in heaven".

Using a similar analogy, Philo also describes the *Logos* as God's "Shadow", a shadow being something to which the original is inextricably bound and whose nature it reflects, like an image or reflection. He also points out that the *Logos* is like a blueprint or "archetypal model" from which everything else in creation comes into being, including man:

> But God's Shadow is His *Logos*, by using which, as if it were an instrument, He made the cosmos. And this Shadow is as it were the archetypal model of all else. For just as God is the Original of the Image, to which the title shadow has just been ascribed, so, (in its turn) is that Image the model of all else, as the prophet (Moses) made clear at the beginning of the law-giving, when he said: "And God made man according to the Image of God"[10] – implying that the Image had been made as representative of God, and man being made according to this Image.
>> *Philo, Allegorical Interpretation III:31, PhI pp.364-367, TGHI p.236*

These, then, are yet further metaphors for this primal Power. It is God's Image or Likeness, and it is also His Shadow. And this Image is in its turn the image or "archetypal model" of all else in creation.

The Word as the Holy Name

Another of the many terms for the Word which has been used by mystics of all times and cultures is the Name, the True Name or the Holy Name. The expression, the 'name of God', like the Word and Wisdom, has two meanings, inner and outer.

Outwardly, man has given many names to God, in different languages, by different peoples and at different times. All of them last for some time and then, falling into disuse, are gradually forgotten. At best, these names are descriptive of some attribute or quality of God, as in the 'Supreme One', the 'Ocean of Love' and so on. But no name or word can be holy or sacred in itself, nor can any one name be more applicable to God than any other, for God Himself is far beyond all humanly-invented names.

Further, in everyday language, it is commonly said that things may be done in someone's 'name', and the term is also used in a similar manner for doing things in the 'name of God'. This means the performance of some act as if the one named – God – were the doer and is consequently the one who is ultimately responsible for the deed. But this is another outer meaning and there are many instances in mystic literature where the term clearly means something else. When Judas Thomas, for example, is asked for the name of his Master Jesus, he replies:

> Thou art not able to hear his True Name now at this time,
>> but the name that is given to him is Jesus the Messiah.
>>> *Acts of Thomas, AAA p.294*

Or as the Coptic, *Martyrdom of St Thomas*, a document derived from the *Acts of Thomas*, has it, "thou canst not hear his Hidden Name".[11] Or as Jesus says in the mythological *Preaching of Andrew*:

> Let your hearts be strengthened by my Name,
>> and you shall learn that I am with you,
>> and dwell within you.
>>> *Preaching of Andrew, MAA p.10*

Clearly, there is a Name which cannot be heard with the physical ears, which dwells within and which purifies an individual from human weakness, for no external name can possess such qualities. This Name is the Word or *Logos* and there are many instances in the ancient literature where this becomes clear. In a prayer offered by John in the *Acts of John*, the Name is that which gives salvation from "ruthless Deceit":

> We glorify thy Name,
>> which converteth us from Error
>> and ruthless Deceit (Satan):
> We glorify thee who hast shown
>> before our eyes that which we have seen:

> We bear witness to thy loving-kindness
>> which appeareth in divers ways:
> We praise thy merciful Name, O Lord.
>> *Acts of John 85, ANT p.250*

And similarly in an extract from the prophet Joel:

> And it shall come to pass,
>> that whosoever shall call on the Name of the Lord
>> shall be delivered.
>> *Joel 3:5, JPS*

To a Manichaean-Christian psalmist, it is a power which saves the soul from the turbulence of this world:

> In the midst of the sea (of this world), Jesus, guide me,
>> do not abandon us that the waves may not seize us.
> When I utter thy Name
>> over the (stormy) sea (of the mind)
>> it stills its waves.
>> *Psalms, MPB p.151*

And the writer of *Proverbs* adds that the "Name of Yahweh" is like a "tower" which lifts the soul "on high":

> The Name of Yahweh is a strong tower;
>> the righteous man runneth into it
>> and is set up on high.
>> *Proverbs 18:10, JPS*

All this is characteristic of the Word and this is what is meant by the Name of God. But why is God's creative Power called His Name?

It can be readily understood that in the oneness of God, there is no place for names, for when only He exists who is to name whom? But when the primal Emanation or outpouring of His creative Power is projected or manifested, there is – in a sense – a second. There is God and there is His creative Power. The road leading to the multiplicity of creation has begun and with this first Power comes the potential for names, for there is now one who can know the other. This first Power is called God's Name. And since the real Master is this mystic Word or Name, this is what Judas Thomas means when he says that Jesus has a "True Name" or a "Hidden Name" which cannot be physically expressed.

In the New Testament itself, mention of the Name is always either ambiguous or relates to the outer meaning of the term. But with an understanding of its mystic import, together with an awareness that the early Christians and other mystical schools of this period used the term to mean the mystic Word, one begins to wonder about the original sense intended by certain of these ambiguous passages. For example:

> Our Father which art in heaven,
> hallowed be Thy Name.
>
> *Matthew 6:9*

"Hallowed be Thy Name" could be simple praise of God – or a specific reference to the Holy Name or Word. Likewise, "ye shall be hated of all men for my Name's sake"[12] is again ambiguous, though either way the general meaning is that the people of the world will often sense that there is something different about those who give their allegiance to a Master, and by an unconscious reaction they will exhibit prejudice or hatred. Similarly, in one of John's *double entendres*, Jesus says of his disciples:

> While I was with them in the world,
> I kept them in thy Name.
>
> *John 17:12*

He means that he shepherded them spiritually and kept them following the mystic path of the Word. Similarly, John observes:

> But as many as received him,
> to them gave he power to become the sons of God,
> even to them that believe on his Name.
>
> *John 1:12*

This passage is particularly clear, for it takes only a little consideration to realize that belief alone cannot take a soul back to God and make the soul a realized "son of God". But the Name or the Word most certainly can.

Pointing to Moses' use of the same expression, Philo Judaeus also describes those who have experienced the mystic Wisdom as the "sons of God", adding that those who have not attained this state should strive to do so by taking the help of God's "First-born *Logos*", which he says is also called the "Beginning" or Source and the "Name of God":

> But they who have attained unto (divine) Knowledge are rightly called sons of the One God, as Moses also acknowledges when he says: "Ye are the sons of the Lord God"[13] and "God who begat thee"[14] and "Is not He Himself thy Father?"[15]....
>
> And if a man should not as yet have the good fortune to be worthy to be called a son of God, let him strive manfully to set himself in order, according to God's First-born, the *Logos*, who holds the eldership among the angels, their ruler as it were. And many names are his, for he is called the 'Beginning' (Source) and the Name of God, and His *Logos* and the Man-after-the-Image.
>
> *Philo, On the Confusion of Tongues XVIII, PhIV pp.88-91, TGHI p.233*

The *Logos*, Philo points out, is called by many names. It is Wisdom. It is also the "Angel-chief", the highest Power of all powers and rulers in the creation. It is also the "Beginning" or Source, the Greek term used by Philo being the same as that found in the opening lines of John's gospel, where it means the Source which is before or beyond time, rather than in the beginning of time. Clearly, the writer of John's gospel was familiar with the same forms of mystical expression as Philo. The English expression, "Man-after-the-Image" is a valiant effort to translate the untranslatable, referring to the *Logos* as the essence of man, and therefore the Primal Man, the Heavenly Man or the Archetypal Man, made in the 'Likeness' or "Image" of God. Perhaps, too, it refers to the Master whose real form is the *Logos*, the Image or Likeness of God.

The Name, then, is another term for the Word, just as it is in so many other languages of the East. The various groups of gnostic Christians, some of whose writings were found in the Nag Hammadi library, understood it in this way too. For example:

> I invoke You, the One who is
> and who pre-existed in the Name
> (which is) exalted above every name.
>
> *Prayer of the Apostle Paul, NHS22 p.9*

And:

> This Great Name of Thine is upon me,
>   O Self-begotten Perfect One,
>   who art not outside me.
>
> *Gospel of the Egyptians 66, NHL p.218*

Taking the matter further, in the Valentinian *Gospel of Truth*, the Son is identified with the Word as the First-born emanation of God, and also with the Name. This is explained in a somewhat tortuous passage:

> Now the Name of the Father is the Son. It is He who first gave a name to the one (the Son) who came forth from Him.... His is the Name; His is the Son. It is possible for him (the Son) to be seen (in human form). The Name, however, is invisible because it alone is the mystery of the invisible which comes to ears that are completely filled with it by him (the Son). For indeed, the Father's Name is not spoken, but it is apparent (manifested) through a Son.
>
> *Gospel of Truth 38, NHS22 p.111*

The unspoken, invisible Name, says the writer, can only be known through the Son in manifested, human form. In fact, the Name can be *heard*: it "comes to ears that are completely filled with it by him (the Son)". The accessibility of the Name or Word only through a Son and the faculty of the soul to *hear* the Name within are key aspects of the mystic path, to be discussed at length in future chapters.

The Word as the True Vine and the Tree of Life

One of the oldest and most frequently encountered Middle Eastern metaphors for the Word of God or His Wisdom is the Tree of Life. The expression has been used by Jewish mystics and many others throughout the ages, but we are touching here upon an extensive subject, for, like Living Water, the term can be traced back to the earliest Mesopotamian cultures, two or three thousand years before the birth of Jesus.

In Judaism, the Tree of Life is first found in the *Genesis* allegory where it stands in Eden as the Tree whose fruit bestows eternal life. And out of Eden, symbolic of the eternal realm, runs the river of

Living Water which nourishes the whole creation. But in ancient Mesopotamia, the motif of the Tree of Life with the river of Living Water flowing from its roots was so common that it is even found upon their pottery and other artifacts.

No particular species is ascribed to the Tree of Life in *Genesis*, but the Middle Eastern writers of antiquity, always appreciative of a good image, have used many species as metaphors for this eternal Tree, drawing on the characteristics of each to enhance the meaning. It has been the cypress tree and the cedar of Lebanon, both much prized for a variety of reasons, giving shade from the heat of the sun, symbolic of the burning fire of human passions in this world. It has been called a palm tree whose fruit is found at the top, to be obtained only after much effort and a steep ascent. It has also been an apple tree, the provider of a sweet and nourishing fruit.

In the *Wisdom of Jesus Ben Sirach*, in a passage where Wisdom is 'talking', she likens herself to a cinnamon tree, an acacia and to other sources of precious and delicate fragrance. She also describes herself as spreading her "branches like a terebinth" and as a vine "putting out graceful shoots" bearing the "fruit of glory and wealth":

> I have exhaled a perfume like cinnamon and acacia,
> I have breathed out a scent like choice myrrh,
>   like galbanum, onycha and stacte,
>   like the smoke of incense in the tabernacle.
> I have spread my branches like a terebinth,
>   and my branches are glorious and graceful.
> I am like a vine putting out graceful shoots,
>   my blossoms bear the fruit of glory and wealth.
>
> *Wisdom of Jesus Ben Sirach 24:15-17, JB*

Perfume and fragrance were also common expressions for the Word, being allusions to its intoxicating power. Hence, Wisdom is the "smoke of incense in the tabernacle" – the sweet intoxication experienced within the tabernacle of the human form upon contact with the Word. She is also like the "branches" of a "terebinth", since she supports and sustains the entire creation with its multitude of higher realms and its amazing diversity. Or she is like a vine with its fragrant blossom and profuse, nutritious harvest, a reference to the abundance of the mystic treasure.

These and many other species, then, have been ascribed to the Tree of Life by different mystics and the one which Jesus uses in St John's gospel is the vine. In a well-known passage, he describes himself as the True Vine and his disciples as the "branches" which receive life and bear fruit through attachment to its trunk. Like so many others, this passage echoes the style of the Wisdom literature, being written in the first person:

> I am the True Vine, and my Father is the husbandman.
> Every branch in me that beareth not fruit he taketh away:
> > and every branch that beareth fruit,
> > he purgeth (purifieth) it,
> > that it may bring forth more fruit.
>
> Now ye are clean through the Word
> > which I have spoken unto you.
> Abide in me, and I in you.
> As the branch cannot bear fruit of itself,
> > except it abide in the vine;
> > no more can ye, except ye abide in me.
>
> I am the Vine, ye are the branches:
> > he that abideth in me, and I in him,
> > the same bringeth forth much fruit:
> > for without me ye can do nothing.
>
> If a man abide not in me,
> > he is cast forth as a branch, and is withered;
> > and men gather them, and cast them into the fire,
> > and they are burned.
>
> If ye abide in me, and my words (Word) abide(s) in you,
> > ye shall ask what ye will, and it shall be done unto you.
> Herein is my Father glorified, that ye bear much fruit;
> > so shall ye be my disciples.
>
> *John 15:1-8*

Jesus' meaning is very clear. Those who follow his teachings and live within the Word will bear the fruit of salvation and union with God. But those who are not attached to this True Vine of the Word are 'burned' (metaphorically) in fires of the creation. They have to remain in this world and suffer a multitude of vicissitudes and troubles.

Although this is the only passage in the gospels which speaks of the True Vine, the term is used extensively elsewhere. It is also, naturally enough, related to the metaphor of wine, for mystic communion and contact with the Word within bring about a state of spiritual bliss and intoxication. As the author of the twenty-third psalm says, "Thou preparest a table (a banquet) before me in the presence of my enemies (the human weaknesses) ... my cup runneth over". The term wine is one of the commonest metaphors of all mystic literature, used even by Christian mystics such as St John of the Cross and others, where it invariably refers to spiritual intoxication and never to the wine of this world.

In the Nag Hammadi *Teachings of Silvanus*, the terms "True Vine" and "wine" are used explicitly in this same mystic context:

> Give yourself gladness from the True Vine of Christ. Satisfy yourself with the true wine in which there is no drunkenness nor error. For it (the true wine) marks the end of drinking since there is usually in it (the power) to give joy to the soul and the mind through the Spirit of God.
>
> *Teachings of Silvanus 107, TS p.59*

The same terms of wine and Vine are also found amongst the Manichaean-Christian writings in Coptic, though whether the original dates back to the time of Jesus is unknown. One of the psalmists prays:

> Jesus, my true guard, mayest thou guard me:
>   First-born of the Father of the Lights, mayest thou guard me.
> Thou art the Living Wine, the child of the True Vine,
>   give us to drink a Living Wine from thy Vine....
>
> Who will not rejoice when the sun is about to rise on him?
> Thou art a perfect day, being like unto thy Father in heaven.
> Thou invitest us: thou hast broached for us a new wine.
> They that drink thy wine, their heart rejoices in it.
> They are drunk with thy love
>   and gladness is spread over their [hearts].
> They think of them that are on high (the Masters)
>   and arm themselves to fight against the Dragon (Satan).
>
> The Word of God is sweet when it finds (inner) ears to hear it.
> It lodges not in a mind that is shut,
>   it makes not its way to a shrine (temple, body) that is polluted.
> It lodges with the maidens (the pure ones, the initiates)
>   and dwells in the heart of the continent.
> They with whom it lodges – its grace spreads over them.

> They gird up their loins and arm themselves
>> to fight with the Dragon (the Serpent, Satan).
>>> *Psalms, MPB p.151*

Here, Jesus is explicitly called the "True Vine", the "Living Wine" and the "First-born of the Father". It is through the sweetness of contact with this Power that human weakness and Satan himself are overcome. The "True Vine" is also identified with the "Word of God". But – says the devotee – this Power can only be contacted by a mind that is open to it and by a heart that is pure.

Among the most frequent users of the metaphor of the True Vine as the Tree of Life and the Word of God were the Mandaeans, with their roots dating back to John the Baptist. From a study of the Mandaean writings one is tempted to conclude that many of Jesus' examples and parables stemmed from John the Baptist's teachings. There are so many illustrations of this expression in Mandaean writings that we are spoilt for choice. They speak, for example, of:

> The Vine which is All-Life
>> and the great Tree which is All-Healings....
>> the Stem of splendour, radiance, light and honour
> whose branches are a thousand
> and its tendrils a myriad.
> Well is it for him who hath looked on that Tree!
>> *CPM 9 p.7*

And in their *John-Book* (the 'John' being John the Baptist), we find:

> How beautiful is the Living Tree (Tree of Life),
>> and beautiful the birds (souls) that are on it!
>>> *John-Book, JM p.131, MEM p.148*

Another Mandaean hymn speaks of the Word as *Yawar* (*lit.* radiance), the "Radiance of Life" which shines forth from God. This, too, is called the "First Vine", the Power from whom all further cuttings, shoots and branches grow:

> *Yawar*, the great Radiance of Life, the First Vine
>> who is planted in the ground (being)
>> of the mighty First Life.
>>> *SA p.84*

The metaphor is also found amongst the Christian apocryphal writings. In the *Acts of Thomas*, Judas Thomas speaks of "the drink of the True Vine" and the "immortal food":

> But we speak of the world which is above,
>> of God and angels, of watchers and Holy Ones,
>> of the Immortal Food (ambrosia)
>> and the draught of the True Vine,
>> of raiment that endureth and groweth not old,
>> of things which eye hath not seen nor ear heard,
>> neither have they entered into the heart of sinful men,
>> the things which God hath prepared for them that love him.
> Of these things do we converse
>> and of these do we bring good tidings.
>
> *Acts of Thomas 36, ANT p.382, MEM p.140*

Interestingly, the identification of the True Vine with the Tree of Life is endorsed by the Syriac version. For while the Greek which we have quoted speaks of "the immortal food and the draught of the True Vine",[16] the Syriac version talks of "the incorruptible food of the Tree of Life and of the Draught of Life".[17]

The writer of the *Book of Revelation* uses the metaphor of the Tree of Life in conjunction with that of the Living Water when he says:

> Blessed are they that do his commandments (do what he says),
>> that they may have right to the Tree of Life,
>> and may enter in through the gates (the single eye)
>> into the City (of God).
>
> *Book of Revelation 22:14*

And:

> And he shewed me a pure river of the Water of Life,
>> clear as crystal,
>> proceeding out of the throne of God and of the Lamb.
> In the midst of the street of it,
>> and on either side of the river,
>> was there the Tree of Life,
>> which bare twelve manner of fruits,
>> and yielded her fruit every month:
> And the leaves of the Tree were for the healing of the nations.
>
> *Book of Revelation 22:1-2*

Which means, symbolically, that this Tree gives sustenance to the peoples of all nations, at all times, all the twelve months of the year. Its bounty never ceases. The expression was also used extensively by some of the early Christian fathers. Mixing his metaphors, in Middle Eastern fashion, the fourth-century Ephraim Syrus, for example, identifies the Tree of Life with the Bread of Life:

> Come, let us cling to the Tree,
> who gave us the Bread of Life.
> *Ephraim Syrus, ESR p.354, MEM p.139*

While another Syrian, the fifth- or possibly sixth-century, Isaac of Antioch, speaks of the "Tree" as one which needs no sustenance, but from which hangs a "Fruit of Light", the Light of God:

> Come, marvel at the Tree,
> that groweth without watering,
> and on which the Fruit of Light hangeth.
> *Isaac of Antioch, IADSI p.256, MEM p.140*

These, then, are all metaphors and terms for the same Power of God, and the extent to which they were used by the earliest Christians and allied writers indicates the central place which the Word occupied in the teachings of Jesus. And though we are only given glimpses of these expressions in the four canonical gospels, a search amongst the other literature of the period highlights and illuminates Jesus' real meaning.

Wisdom Summons You

There are a number of interesting parallels between the language of the gospels and that of the Old Testament. There is the prologue to St John, for example, concerning the creation of everything by the Word, and its similarities to passages in *Proverbs* and the *Wisdom of Jesus Ben Sirach*. We have also shown that the Bread of Life and Living Water as metaphors for the Word were not the invention of Jesus or John but were used extensively in the literature of the period, dating many centuries if not millennia before. Similarly, the famous "I" passages attributed to Jesus in St John and St Matthew, clearly reflect the passages in the Wisdom literature where Wisdom speaks. Again, Jesus' discourses and dialogues in St John, in the first person, seem to be a synthesis of Hellenistic and Judaic literary styles. All this becomes understandable when seen in the context of the times.

There are other instances, too. In a well-known passage from St Matthew, Jesus invites all those who recognize their human situation to come to him and find spiritual rest:

> Come unto me, all ye that labour and are heavy laden,
>   and I will give you rest.
> Take my yoke upon you, and learn of me;
>   for I am meek and lowly in heart:
>   and ye shall find rest unto your souls.
> For my yoke is easy, and my burden is light.
>
> *Matthew 11:28-30*

In both *Proverbs* and the *Wisdom of Jesus Ben Sirach*, Wisdom makes the same invitation, using the metaphors of food and drink for the spiritual sustenance of which she is the source:

> Come and eat my bread,
>   drink the wine I have prepared!
> Leave your folly and you will live,
>   walk in the ways of perception (consciousness).
>
> *Proverbs 9:5-6, JB*

And:

> Come unto me all ye that desire me,
>   fill yourselves with my fruits;
> For my memory is sweeter than honey,
>   my inheritance than honeycomb.
>
> *Wisdom of Jesus Ben Sirach 24:19, JPS*

And again:

> She (Wisdom) will give him
>   the Bread of Understanding to eat,
>   and the Water of Wisdom to drink.
> He will lean on her and will not fall,
>   he will rely on her and not be put to shame....
> He will find happiness and a crown of joy,
>   he will inherit an everlasting name.
>
> *Wisdom of Jesus Ben Sirach 15:3-4,6, JB*

Also in St John, Jesus speaks of a person who is attached to the world as he who "hateth the light" and a person who is detached from worldly affairs as he who "hateth his life in this world":

> Every one that doeth evil hateth the light,
>> neither cometh to the light,
>>> lest his deeds should be reproved.
>>>> *John 3:20*

And:

> He that loveth his life shall lose it;
>> and he that hateth his life in this world
>>> shall keep it unto life eternal.
>>>> *John 12:25*

In *Proverbs*, the same idea is expressed in very similar language:

> For the man who finds me finds life,
>> he will win favour from Yahweh;
> But he who does injury to me does hurt to his own soul,
>> all who hate me are in love with death.
>>> *Proverbs 8:32-36, JB*

In another passage, Jesus points out that he came from God, "from heaven", not for his own ego and glory, but under instructions from the Supreme, to do God's work on earth – while he was here:

> For I came down from heaven, not to do mine own will,
>> but the will of Him that sent me.
>>> *John 6:38*

Likewise, Jesus Ben Sirach points out that his motivations are not selfish. Rather, he is writing for all real seekers of the Lord:

> Observe that I have not toiled for myself alone,
>> but for all who are seeking Wisdom.
>>> *Wisdom of Jesus Ben Sirach 24:34, JB*

Jesus and his disciples would naturally have been familiar with this literature. So when Jesus quotes, paraphrases or echoes the teachings of Moses, Isaiah, the Wisdom literature or any other writings extant at that time, it is his way of explaining their real mystic meaning. He is showing that the Jewish prophets and sages who wrote the Biblical literature said the same things and spoke of the same higher reality.

The writer of the *Odes of Solomon* employs the same technique, weaving together metaphors from both Jesus' teachings as well as the earlier Biblical literature. Consider the poem on page 257, for example, which – in only a few lines – echoes passages from *Proverbs*, the *Wisdom of Jesus Ben Sirach*, the *Psalms* and the gospels of John and Matthew.

The writer of the *Teachings of Silvanus*, one of the Nag Hammadi library tractates, does the same thing, tying together many strands of teaching from Jesus, the Wisdom literature and other mystical writings in a long discourse on Christ as Wisdom. And in this extract, it is also apparent that the writer speaks of Christ as the Word or Wisdom:

> My son, listen to my teaching which is good and useful, and end the sleep (of physical existence) which weighs heavy upon you. Depart from the forgetfulness (of God) which fills you with darkness. If you had been unable to do anything, I would not have said these things to you, but Christ has come in order to give you this gift. Why (then) do you pursue the darkness when the light is at your disposal? Why do you drink stale water though sweet is available for you? Wisdom summons you, yet you desire folly. Not by your own desire do you do these things, but it is the animal nature (the lower tendencies of the mind) within you that does them.
>
> Wisdom summons you in her goodness, saying, "Come to me, all of you, O foolish ones, that you may receive a gift, the understanding which is good and excellent. I am giving to you a high-priestly garment which is woven entirely out of Wisdom...."
>
> For the Tree of Life is Christ. He is Wisdom. For he is Wisdom; he is also the Word, He is the Life, the Power, and the Door. He is the Light, the Angel, and the Good Shepherd. Entrust yourself to this one who became all for your sake.
>
> Knock on (within) yourself as upon a door, and walk upon (within) yourself as on a straight road. For if you walk on the road, it is impossible for you to go astray. And if you knock with Wisdom, you knock on hidden treasures.
>
> For since he (Christ) is Wisdom, he makes the foolish man wise. Wisdom is a holy kingdom and a shining robe. It (Wisdom) is like much gold which gives you great honour. The Wisdom of God became a type of fool (became man) for you so that it might take you up, O foolish one, and make you a wise man....

O Lord Almighty, how much glory shall I give Thee?
No one has been able to glorify God adequately.
It is Thou who hast given glory to Thy Word
    in order to save everyone, O Merciful God.
It is he (the Word, the Christ, the Master)
    who has come from Thy mouth
    and has risen from Thy heart:
    the First-born, the Wisdom,
    the Prototype, the First Light.

For he is a light from the Power of God,
    and he is an emanation of the pure glory of the Almighty.
He is the spotless mirror (reflection) of the working of God,
    and he is the image of His goodness.
For he is also the Light of the eternal Light.
He is the eye which looks at the invisible Father,
    always serving and acting by the Father's will.
He alone was begotten by the Father's good pleasure.
For he is an incomprehensible Word,
    and he is Wisdom and Life.
He gives life to and nourishes all living things and powers.
Just as the soul gives life
    to all the members (of the body),
    he rules all with (His) Power and gives life to them.
For he is the beginning and the end of everyone,
    watching over all and encompassing them.
He is troubled on behalf of everyone,
    and he rejoices and also mourns.
On the one hand, he mourns for those who have received
    as their portion the place of punishment (this world);
    on the other, he is concerned about every one
    whom he arduously brings to instruction (initiates into his fold).
But he rejoices over everyone who is in purity.

    Teachings of Silvanus 88-89, 106-107, 112-113, TS pp.21-23, 57-59, 69-71

The writer makes it clear that Christ, as the power that brings salvation, is the same as Wisdom, the Word, the Tree of Life, the First-born Son and the Power of God. Like Jesus, he echoes the sacred writings of the times in which people had faith and with which they were familiar – in order to demonstrate that he was not giving any new teachings but simply repeating the same truths which previous mystics had reiterated.

The point is that the teaching concerning the Word or Wisdom is not new. Since the Word has existed since the dawn of creation, so too has the teaching concerning it. As the author of *1 John* points out, the teaching of the Word is "no new commandment", but is as old as creation itself:

> Brethren, I write no new commandment unto you,
>   but an old commandment
>   which ye had from the beginning.
> The old commandment is the Word
>   which ye have heard from the beginning.
>
> *1 John 2:7*

And Jesus also commented:

> Heaven and earth shall pass away:
>   but my words shall not pass away.
>
> *Luke 21:33*

Since words belong to the earth and will pass away with the earth, this means that Jesus' real teaching or path is a perennial and eternal truth which comes from beyond the creation. If the Word has always existed, then the path of the Word must have existed at all times, too. And presuming a double meaning and play on "my words", the excerpt would also mean:

> Heaven and earth shall pass away:
>   but my Word shall not pass away.

A statement which is also true.

Many Names for the Word

In fact, throughout recorded history, mystics have spoken of this primary, creative Power, calling it by a multitude of names, and we end this chapter with some further passages from the early Christian writings which demonstrate yet again how all these terms referred to the same Power. In the *Acts of John*, for instance, Jesus is said to have sung:

> Glory be to thee, Father.
> Glory be to thee, Word:
> Glory be to thee, Grace.

Glory be to thee, Spirit:
Glory be to thee, Holy One:
Glory be to thy Glory, Amen.

We praise thee, O Father;
We give thanks to thee, O Light,
    wherein darkness dwelleth not.
                Acts of John 94, ANT p.258

This list also brings the doxology ending the Lord's Prayer into sharper focus:

For thine is the kingdom,
    and the Power, and the Glory, for ever.
                Matthew 6:13

For the "Power" and the "Glory" are both terms for the Word. Also from the *Acts of John* is an even more definitive list which alludes to a number of Jesus' parables, analogies and sayings which we have yet to discuss, but which the writer clearly took as references to the Word:

We glorify Thy Name
    that was spoken through the Son ...

We glorify Thy Way; we glorify Thy Seed,
    the *Logos*, Grace, Faith, Salt, True Pearl Ineffable,
    the Treasure, the Plough, the Net,
    the Greatness, the Diadem.
Him that for us was called (became) the Son of Man,
    that gave us Truth, Rest, Knowledge, Power,
    the Commandment, the Confidence, Hope, Love,
    Liberty, Refuge in Thee.

For Thou Lord, art alone the Root of immortality,
    and the Fount of incorruption,
    and the Seat of the ages:

Called by all these names for us now,
    that calling on Thee by them
    we may make known (come to know) Thy greatness
    which at the present is invisible to us,

but visible only to the pure,
being manifested in thy manhood only.

Acts of John 109, ANT p.268

Similarly, in the *Acts of Peter*, also referring to the parables and metaphors of Jesus, Peter says:

This Jesus ye have, brethren, the Door, the Light,
the Way, the Bread, the Water, the Life,
the Resurrection, the Refreshment, the Pearl,
the Treasure, the Seed, the Abundance (harvest),
the Mustard Seed, the Vine, the Plough,
the Grace, the Faith, the Word:
He is all things and there is none other greater than he.

Acts of Peter III:XX, ANT p.322

And lastly, in the *Death of St John*, clearly echoing the *Acts of John* but
with some interesting variations, John speaks of Jesus as:

Thou who alone art Jesus the Christ, the saving Name.
Thou art the life-giving Bread
which came down from heaven for the salvation of the world.
We bless thee who hast made us meet for the path of Life.

We thank thee; thou art the Creative Word;
Thou art the Guide and the Door into grace;
the abundant Salt, the Rich in Jewels;
the Ear of Corn; the Life, Righteousness,
Strength, Wisdom, the Refuge, the Repose,
the Rest, the Vinestock, the Root, the Fountain of Life;

Who permitteth himself to be called by that name because of man,
that he might be saved and renewed
from the former open wickedness of his deeds
into which he had fallen through sin.
For to thee belongeth glory for ever and ever."

Death of St John, MAA p.57

There can be no doubt, then, that Jesus, Paul, the gospel writers,
especially John, many of the early Christians, Moses and many of the
Hebrew prophets, the writers of the Biblical Wisdom literature, Philo

Judaeus, Mani, the Mandaeans and many, many others, all agreed as to the supreme importance of the Word in any mystic teaching or path that purports to lead the soul to salvation and to an understanding of the Lord's creation.

So the question naturally presents itself, how? How does the Word or *Logos* help man? Here, Jesus' teachings are in accord with those of other mystics. Firstly, through contact with a living Master, a "Word made flesh" – an incarnation of the Word – a person receives mystic baptism into the Word. Then, by following his instructions, the soul experiences mystic communion with the real form of the Master, the Word of God within. The soul then sees the Light and hears the Sound of the divine Word and is carried by this great Column of Life, Sound and Radiance, back to God. This is the true call of God, calling the soul back to her eternal Home. For this reason, the Word has often been called the divine Music or the Voice of God.

NOTES AND REFERENCES

1. *Deuteronomy* 8:3.
2. *Genesis* 2:7.
3. The grain of mustard seed of the gospels and of the gnostics.
4. *cf. Exodus* 14:15.
5. *Psalms* 65:9. Philo follows the *Septuagint*. The *King James Version* has "Thou greatly enrichest it with the river of God, which is full of water."
6. *Psalms* 46:4.
7. *Leviticus* 26:12.
8. See p.249: Philo, *Allegorical Interpretation* III:55, *PhI* pp.408-409, *TGHI* p.246.
9. *Wisdom of Solomon* 7:25.
10. *Genesis* 1:27.
11. *Martyrdom of St Thomas, MAA* p.96.
12. *Matthew* 10:22.
13. *Deuteronomy* 14:1, *KJV* – "Ye are the children of the Lord your God." The *Septuagint*, the Greek translation used by Philo, has "Ye are the sons of the Lord your God."
14. *Deuteronomy* 32:18, *KJV* – "God that formed thee." The *Septuagint* has "God who begat thee."
15. *Deuteronomy* 32:6.
16. *Acts of Thomas* 36, *ANT* p.382, *MEM* p.140.
17. *Acts of Thomas, AAA* p.177.

CHAPTER NINE

Divine Music & the Voice of God

Hearing the Word

From our limited human viewpoint, one of the most significant characteristics of the Word of God must surely be that it can be heard within when a person practises the correct spiritual exercises or sometimes even spontaneously for brief periods when the mind is quiet and deeply concentrated. The Word is heard in the form of the most beautiful music. It is the primal and pristine music of creation's dawn, of the beginning of everything. It resounds unceasingly within every particle of creation and within every soul. It is awe-inspiring, breathtaking and blissful. And it automatically instills in its listeners a sense of true worship, something quite different and a million times deeper and more real than the feelings any ritual or ceremony can generate. This is the Voice of God, the divine Sound, the divine Music, the real Music of the Spheres which keeps the universe and all souls in existence. It is the Holy Ghost or Holy Spirit. As Jesus said:

> The hour cometh, and now is,
>> when the true worshippers shall worship the Father
>> in spirit and in truth:
> For the Father seeketh such to worship Him.
> God is a Spirit:
>> and they that worship Him
>> must worship Him in spirit and in truth.
>
> *John 4:23-24*

Ceremonial worship is of the mind and is an invention of man. Often, in such worship, a person sings hymns, repeats set prayers or kneels down, while the mind roams the universe, thinking of all the affairs which occupy the daily life of the individual. Family affairs, business

288

affairs, social affairs and love affairs, worries, concerns and interests, activities and pastimes – in fact everything except the worship of God come to the mind at such times. Indeed, if we are honest, the majority of us have not the slightest idea of the real nature of worship. People generally go to church – or to a synagogue or mosque or any other 'holy' building – more out of habit or for various human or ritualistic purposes than for a burning desire to truly know and worship God.

But in this passage from St John, Jesus says that since God is Spirit, worship of Him must also be of a spiritual nature – and the highest form of Spirit that man may contact is the Holy Spirit of the Word. "The hour cometh, and now is", he says – the time is always right – for the "true worshippers" to worship the Father, for God is always in search of sincere seekers. Nevertheless, He must be worshipped inwardly, in the spirit, not in any external fashion.

In life, our highest or most inspired moments are often those of complete absorption in something. Depending on the person, it may be beautiful music, the pageants and wonders of the natural world or some other experience of the five senses. These experiences all have a number of features in common. Firstly, there is the mental concentration of the individual: if the mind is thinking about other things or wanders off, the enjoyment is impaired or lost. Secondly, there is a forgetfulness of the individual self and some degree of merging with the object of concentration. Thirdly, since the panorama presented to the senses is constantly changing, the experience does not last for ever. In fact, though its general effect may sometimes last for a while afterwards, the limited power of an individual to concentrate usually means that such feelings persist – at the most – for only an hour or two. Often, they last for only a few minutes. All the same, feelings such as these must be distantly akin to those of real worship.

The sights, sounds and phenomena of this world are of a limited duration. The Music of the Word, the divine Music, however, goes on and on, for as long as creation lasts. The music of this world is created by making sound vibrations in the air. The divine Music is created by God as His Primal Vibration by means of which He fashions and sustains His creation. External music is heard with the outer ears. The divine Music is heard with the 'ear' of the soul, the hearing faculty of the soul.

The soul has two primary internal faculties – the power to hear and the power to see – inner hearing and inner vision. From the vibration of the Word also issues divine light, self-luminous, soft, nourishing, sustaining, beautiful and bright beyond all comparison with the light of this world. Like sound, the light of this world is also a vibration –

oscillating electromagnetic energy. Similarly, within, the soul is able
not only to hear the vibration of the Word but also to see it. In this
world, most objects are seen by means of reflected light. Inside, light
emanates from everything as an expression of its internal vibration
and movement, of the creative Power maintaining its existence.

Listening, then, to the sound and seeing the light of the Word, the
soul becomes entranced and unites with the Word, being taken to the
place from which the Word arises – God. This is the path of the Word – an
entirely mystic journey within oneself. And the secret of how to follow
that path is the greatest 'mystery' of all time. As Jesus said to his disciples:

> It is given unto you to know
> the mysteries of the kingdom of heaven.
>
> *Matthew 13:11*

He is also speaking of these two internal spiritual faculties when he
says to his disciples:

> Blessed are your eyes, for they see:
> and your ears, for they hear.
> For verily I say unto you,
> that many prophets and righteous men
> have desired to see those things which ye see,
> and have not seen them;
> And to hear those things which ye hear,
> and have not heard them.
>
> *Matthew 13:16-17*

"Prophets and righteous men" refers to the many mystically-attuned
souls in this world who have longed to traverse the inner regions and
return to God – to "know the mysteries of the kingdom of heaven".
But they have not heard them. "Yet," Jesus tells his disciples, "you have
heard and seen these things". The same idea is conveyed in the *Gospel
of Thomas*:

> Jesus said,
> "I shall give you what no eye has seen
> and what no ear has heard
> and what no hand has touched
> and what has never occurred to the human mind."
>
> *Gospel of Thomas 17, NHS20 p.61*

And in a reconstruction of one of the Oxyrhynchus gospel fragments, which – though the style is similar – is not found in the version of the *Gospel of Thomas* found at Nag Hammadi, Jesus says:

> Thou hearest with one ear
>> [but the other ear thou hast closed].
> *Oxyrhynchus Papyri, Logion VIII, OLAG p.6*

Which means that we hear with our outer ears but the inner ear is closed or deaf. The author of the *Testimony of Truth* clearly had this saying of Jesus' in mind when he wrote:

> I will speak to those who know to hear not with the ears of the body but with the ears of the mind. For many have sought after the truth and have not been able to find it; because there has taken hold of them [the] old leaven of the Pharisees and the scribes [of] the (Judaic) Law.
>> *Testimony of Truth 29, NHS15 p.123*

He is writing, he says, to those who have awakened their inner ears, the "ears of the mind". And echoing Jesus' words, he says that many of those who have sought the Truth have been unable to find it because they have looked in the wrong place. They have searched for truth amongst the traditional religious interpretations of the priests and learned men of the time, the "Pharisees and the scribes". In like vein is a passage quoted frequently by many of the early Christians, orthodox and unorthodox alike. Its most famous usage is by Paul:

> But as it is written,
> "Eye hath not seen, nor ear heard,
>> neither have entered into the heart of man,
>> the things which God hath prepared for them that love him."
>
> But God hath revealed them unto us by his Spirit:
>> for the Spirit searcheth all things,
>> yea, the deep things of God.
>
> For what man knoweth the things of a man,
>> save the spirit of man which is in him?
> Even so the things of God knoweth no man,
>> but the Spirit of God.

> Now we have received, not the spirit of the world,
> but the Spirit which is of God;
> that we might know the things
> that are freely given to us of God.
>
> *1 Corinthians 2:10-12*

Paul is speaking of the things which are seen and heard in the Spirit – spiritually. The "eye" and "ear" of this world cannot perceive the things of the spiritual realms. Man cannot even conceive of the way things are in those higher regions and the sights and sounds to be experienced there. They are known through faculties of the mind and soul, not of the body. But through the Spirit or Word, all the secrets of the creation, inner and outer, can be "revealed", even the "deep things of God" Himself. They have been "prepared" for the soul by God to be experienced through the Spirit. Paul explains that just as self-knowledge can only be experienced by the individual self, so can the spiritual things of God only be known through His Spirit. And, incidentally, he also points out that such spiritual gifts are "freely given". No true Master ever takes any money from another person for teaching these secrets.

The writer of John's gospel is in his element when speaking of the sound of the Word for it lends itself so naturally to *double entendre*. The Word of Jesus, of the Son of God, is both the inner Music and the outer teachings, and in the *King James Version*, at least, the translation is such that this double meaning is readily conveyed. Jesus says, for instance:

> The word (Word) which ye hear is not mine
> but the Father which sent me.
>
> *John 14:24*

The word or teachings of a Master as well as the Word itself both come from God. The Master has not invented either of them. Again, he says:

> It is the Spirit that quickeneth;
> the flesh profiteth nothing:
> The words (Word) that I speak unto you,
> they are Spirit, and they are Life.
>
> *John 6:63*

It is the Creative Word which is "Spirit" and "Life", for no human words can truly be described as "Spirit" and "Life". "It is the Spirit that quickeneth" – not the "flesh" or physical words. But the words or teachings of a Master do convey the message of the Spirit and Life and without that outer word, the inner Word cannot be contacted. Hence, both are required for a person to receive "Spirit" and "Life". Along the same lines, in another passage, Jesus says:

> Why do ye not understand my speech?
> Even because ye cannot hear my word (Word).
>
> *John 8:43*

And later in this same discourse, he adds:

> He that is of God, heareth God's words:
> Ye therefore hear them not,
>   because ye are not of God.
>
> *John 8:47*

The meaning is the same in both cases. Only one who is a real seeker of God will both understand a Master's words and hear his Word. One who cannot hear the Word, cannot really understand a Master's teachings.

Whoever wrote the Manichaean-Christian psalms, which relate to both Jesus and Mani, also understood that the Word could be heard within. There are innumerable examples to choose from:

> Christ is the Word of Truth:
>   he that hears it shall live.
>
> *Psalms, MPB p.158*

And:

> Lo, Wisdom is flourishing:
>   where is there an ear to hear it?
>
> *Psalms, MPB p.153*

And as the psalmist asks in a psalm employing a double meaning in reference to the response of those who are unreceptive to both the inner and the outer call of the Masters:

> [He who covers] his eyes with his fingers,
>   who shall [come] to him?
> Into whose ears shall they call, if he hears not? ...

He shall suffer what the corpses suffer,
    for they called into his ears, he did not hear.
                        Psalms of Thomas XIV, MPB p.221

One who makes himself blind by blocking out the light – how can a Master manifest himself to such a one? One who cannot hear, even when the call is ringing in his ears, within himself – how can such a one accept a Master? Such people, says the psalmist, whose attention is directed entirely towards the world, are like corpses. They are spiritually dead. They neither understand a Master's teachings, nor do they respond to the inner call, nor do they hear the music of the Word. Similarly, in an excerpt we have seen before:

> The Word of God is sweet
>   when it finds (inner) ears to hear it.
> It lodges not in a mind that is shut,
>   it makes not its way to a shrine (temple, body)
>   that is polluted.
> It lodges with the maidens (the pure ones, the initiates)
>   and dwells in the heart of the continent.
> They with whom it lodges – its grace spreads over them.
> They gird up their loins and arm themselves
>   to fight with the Dragon (the Serpent, Satan).
>   *Psalms, MPB p.151*

The Word of God, says the poet, cannot be heard by everyone. It requires a special ear – one that is pure. But whoever does hear it is filled with the Lord's grace and is enabled to fight the spiritual battle and overcome the forces of Satan.

The Sound of Divine Music

In their attempts to describe the divine Music, mystics have often likened it to the sound of various musical instruments. Christian, Judaic and allied writings often mention lyres, trumpets, lutes, flutes and harps, in particular. In the *Book of Revelation*, the divine Music is called the "Voice from heaven", the "Voice of harpers" and by other similar expressions:

> And I heard a Voice from heaven,
>   as the Voice of many waters,
>   and as the Voice of a great thunder:

> And I heard the Voice of harpers
> harping with their harps.
>> *Book of Revelation 14:1-2*

The author of the *Odes of Solomon* also speaks of the Spirit of the Lord resounding like a harp within:

> As the wind (*or* spirit) moves over the harp,
> and the strings speak,
> So does the Spirit of the Lord
> speak in my members,
> and I speak by his love.
>> *Odes of Solomon VI:1-2, AOT p.694*

Using the same wordplay as John's gospel, the poet says that just as the wind makes music when blowing over the strings of the harp, so too is the Sound of the Spirit heard in "my members" – in all parts of his being. It is from this inspiration of love that the poet writes.

In the *Acts of John*, according to the story, John raises a young man from the dead, who then upbraids John's disciples for wasting their opportunity of being in the human form. The writer, of course, is speaking to his readers. "You have lost the places of music," he says "and have gotten ... places wherein roaring and howling and mourning ceaseth not, day nor night." You have lost your inner treasure and kingdom and have descended into the hell of this world. You have exchanged the Music of the Word for the cries of pain and suffering of this world:

> For now in a little time ye have lost
> the kingdom that was prepared for you,
> and the dwelling-places builded of shining stones,
> full of joy, of feasting and delights,
> full of everlasting life and eternal light:
>
> And have gotten yourselves places of darkness,
> full of dragons, of roaring flames,
> of torments, and punishments unsurpassable,
> of pains and anguish, fear and horrible trembling.
>
> Ye have lost the places of music (*lit.* organs),
> and have gotten on the other hand

places wherein roaring and howling and mourning
ceaseth not, day nor night (birth in this world).

Nothing else remaineth for you
 save to ask the Apostle of the Lord
 that like as he hath raised me to life,
 he would raise you also from death
 unto salvation and bring back your souls
 which now are blotted out of the Book of Life.

Acts of John XVII, ANT p.261

Here, as elsewhere, the raising from the dead is not physical, but spiritual. The anecdote is a means of conveying spiritual truth and is not meant to be taken literally.

Apocalyptic revelations of the period also speak of music, particularly the sound of a trumpet which awakens the dead from their graves at the end of the world. But the dead in their graves are the souls entombed in physical bodies and the only sound that will awaken us is the music of the mystic Word. This perhaps is the esoteric meaning lying behind the words attributed to Jesus in St Matthew's apocalypse:

And he (the Son) shall send his angels with a great sound of a trumpet,
 and they shall gather together his elect (the chosen ones, the initiates)
 from the four winds, from one end of heaven to the other.

Matthew 24:31

It is the Masters who call their allotted souls, by means of the divine Music, from wherever they are in the world. There are certainly places in other writings where the Master is described as an angel.

In mystic literature, listening to the divine Music is often described by veiled allusion as 'singing the praises of the Lord', 'singing songs to Him' or 'playing musical instruments to Him'. In churches, temples and man-made religious buildings, the commonest aspects of ritual and liturgy are the lighting of candles and the playing and singing of religious music. They are found in nearly every religion of the world. But it is likely that both of these practices have arisen as an externalization of mystic teachings, for the true Light and the true Music are to be found and worshipped inside, in the true sanctuary, temple or holy place of the human form, at the inner, mystic altar of God.

In one of the Nag Hammadi tractates, the *Second Apocalypse of James*, James the brother of Jesus, speaking as Redeemer, encourages the soul to listen to the divine Music by saying:

> Play your trumpets, your flutes
>   and your harps of this (heavenly) house.
> The Lord has taken you captive from the Lord,
>   having closed your ears,
>   that they may not hear the sound of my Word.
>
> Yet you [will be able to pay] heed in your hearts....
> (For) behold, I gave you your (heavenly) house ...
>   in which He promised to give you an inheritance.
>
> *Second Apocalypse of James 60, NHS11 p.141*

He points out that it is by the Lord's design that the soul is held captive in this world, prevented from hearing the "sound of my Word". Yet, he says, you can still hear this Music "in your hearts", within yourself, because the Redeemer is able to give the soul a place in the eternal realm, the heavenly house, a place promised as the soul's true inheritance.

References to the divine Music as the singing of hymns and the playing of musical instruments are found even more explicitly in a number of the Manichaean-Christian hymns, psalms and poems. In the following, it is uncertain from the context whether the psalm is addressed to the Master, to the Lord or to the soul. However, the references to the lute and to the inner music are very clearly allusions to the inner Music, not to the songs and instruments of this world:

> Thou art a lover of hymns,
>   thou art a lover of music ... playing the lute.
> Thou makest music unto the Father
>   and playest the lute to the beloved Son.
> Thou makest music to the ambrosia
>   and playest the lute to the King of Life.
> Thou makest music to the Land of Light
>   and playest the lute to the Living Air.
> Thou makest music to the *aeons* (inner realms)
>   and playest the lute to the *Aeon of the Aeons* (the Word).
> Thou makest music to the Tree of Life....

> Thou art a lover of hymns, thou art a lover of music....
>   they make music before thee.
>
> *Psalms, MPB pp.168-169*

Similarly:

> The chariots of Light are (at) the gate
>   to the realm of God,
>   glad is the Song that sounds from them.
> *MMIII p.888; cf. JRAS (1966) p.120, ML p.140*

In Manichaean imagery, the "chariots of Light" were the conveyance of the soul to the "realm of God". They were no physical means of transport, but vehicles of both Light and Sound, for "glad is the Song that sounds from them". The allusion, of course, is to the divine Word, the 'vehicle' of mystic transport, which draws the soul to its true, eternal home. In another psalm, the soul is drawn up out of the body into the inner realms through the sound of the "trumpet", calling her to the realms of immortality:

> Save me, O blessed Christ,
>   the Saviour of the holy souls.
> I will pass up into the skies (inner realms)
>   and leave this body upon the earth.
> The trumpet sounds, I hear,
>   they are calling me up to the immortals.
> I will cast away my body upon the earth
>   from which it was assembled.
> *Psalm CCLXI, MPB p.75*

Another psalm describes the divine Music as "thy ... holy trumpet sounding summer and winter". This again carries the soul "far from the world" and its family attachments, signified as "my parents". The soul ascends to God, beyond both the earth and all the inner heavens:

> Jesus Christ, in whom I have believed,
>   stand with me in the hour of my need.
> I also am one in the number of thy hundred sheep
>   which thy Father gave into thy hands
>   that thou mightest feed them....

When I hear the Cry of thy ... holy trumpet
   sounding summer and winter ... I follow thee.
I betook myself far from the world,
   I left my parents, I passed unto the Lord
who is greater than heaven and earth.

Psalm CCLXXIII, MPB p.93

In another, the liberated souls are described as playing the harp and the lute and "singing unto the hidden Father". But, again, no material meaning is intended:

The victorious ones (liberated souls)
   that are laden with garlands, ...
   that pay tribute to their king,
   their harps in their hands,
   the lutes with them,
   their harps in their hands,
   singing unto the hidden Father –
Their lutes are with them
   as they make music unto him.

Psalms, MPB p.133

In the Parthian hymns, speaking of the Sound of these realms, the devotee writes simply:

[All is filled] with happiness
   and sweet delightful song.

Huwidagman I:60, MHCP p.75

The Wind Bloweth

The Word of God, then, the divine Music, can be heard within. Or at least we can say that Jesus and many other mystics have taught this to be so. Certainly, there are an abundance of expressions in early Christian writings, the New Testament included, that allude explicitly or implicitly to hearing the inner Music and which are clearly a part of a mystic tradition which originated with Jesus.

The meaning of these passages is sometimes perfectly clear, at others, one reads of a "great sound from heaven" or a "voice from heaven" where it is uncertain whether the writer is speaking in guarded language, with *double entendre*, or whether he is actually unaware of the true nature of the mystic Sound. Nor, of course, can we always rely upon the English translators to accurately convey the meaning, especially when they are dealing with the more esoteric texts.

In the New Testament, another of the passages that springs to mind is found – like so many of the deeply mystical passages – in St John's gospel. According to the story, during a discussion with a certain Pharisee called Nicodemus concerning the meaning of being born of the Spirit, Jesus comments enigmatically:

> The wind (*pneuma*) bloweth (*pnei*) where it listeth,
>   and thou hearest the sound thereof,
>   but canst not tell whence it cometh,
>   and whither it goeth:
> So is every one that is born of the Spirit (*pneuma*).
>
> *John 3:8*

As we will later be discussing in greater detail, when a soul is "born of the Spirit" – is mystically baptized – and commences the spiritual practice, the first goal is concentration of the attention at the single eye or eye centre. When the attention is active below this point, scattered into the senses, it cannot hear the Sound of the Spirit, the divine Music, which resounds ceaselessly within. Only when some degree of concentration is attained at this centre do the first distant echoes of the Sound become audible.

As long as the attention is below the eye centre, the soul cannot tell from which direction the Sound is coming. Just as the wind makes a whooshing sound, yet no one can see it, nor can it be known from its sound alone where or when the wind arises or where it will go, so too with the soul's hearing of the Spirit. No one can determine, to begin with, when this sweetest of Sounds will come to him or where it comes from. However, by listening intently to it, deeper concentration is achieved and the soul is gradually drawn up and out of the body, automatically finding its way to the source of the Sound. This, says Jesus, is what happens to everyone who "is born of the Spirit" – who is reborn or baptized in the Spirit and who hears the Sound within.

As we saw earlier, the writer of John's gospel is actually using a play on the word *pneuma* which has a double meaning. In fact, the first line is equally well translated as, "the Spirit breathes where it chooses, and you hear its Voice". But because the wordplay does not work in English, the translation fails to convey the *double entendre* of the original.

Whatever its origin, an understanding of this wordplay makes us wonder about the famous story in *Acts* where the apostles are said to have received the 'gift of tongues', enabling them to go and preach to the rest of the world. According to Luke, they are all attending the Jewish festival of Pentecost:

> And when the day of Pentecost was fully come,
> they were all with one accord in one place.
> And suddenly there came a sound from heaven
> as of a rushing mighty wind
> and it filled all the house where they were sitting.
> And there appeared unto them cloven tongues like as of fire,
> and it sat upon each of them.
> And they were all filled with the Holy Ghost,
> and began to speak with other tongues,
> as the Spirit gave them utterance.
>
> *Acts 2:1-4*

The authenticity of the tale is doubtful and there is no corroboration of it from any other source, but the traditional element of a "sound from heaven as of a rushing mighty wind" is surely a significant feature, even if the writer of *Acts* has misunderstood it. It is also likely that this anecdote is derived from an earlier, lost stratum of mystical teaching in which the "house where they were sitting" was the bodily house or temple within which the Sound is genuinely heard, while the "tongues like as of fire" associated with it were a reference to the inner flame or light spoken of by mystics of all ages and cultures. Certainly, it is true that the mystic Sound and fire would have "filled (them) with the Holy Ghost", and they would certainly have heard a "sound from heaven". But it would have been an inner heaven, not the physical sky. The turning of the mystical and the esoteric into the mythological and exoteric is quite in accord with the externalization of mystic teachings observed in all religions of the world.

The Voice of God

Familiarity with a term can readily obscure its meaning and it is easily overlooked that the audibility of the Creative Word is actually implied in the term 'Word'. Metaphorically, God's speech is His Word, His Breath, His creative Force which streams out of His 'mouth', which emanates from Him. For this reason, the Word has commonly been called the Voice of God, and sometimes His Discourse, His Speech or His Conversation. Additionally, since words are used in this world to call people or even to awaken them, the Word of God has also been called His Cry or His Call, for by means of it He calls souls back to Himself.

We have already noted some passages in the New Testament which seem to refer to the audibility of the mystic Word. There are also some passages which allude to this mystic Word as the Voice. In John's gospel, for instance, there is the Baptist's comment concerning Jesus:

> He that hath the Bride is the Bridegroom:
>   but the friend of the Bridegroom,
>   which standeth and heareth him,
>   rejoiceth greatly because of the Bridegroom's Voice:
> This my joy therefore is fulfilled.
> He must increase, but I must decrease.
>
> *John 3:28-30*

Using a common metaphor of the times, John the Baptist refers to the Master as the Bridegroom. Jesus, he says, is always happy and full of inner bliss because he is constantly with his divine Beloved or Bride, within. He is always with God, even though he is incarnate in a human form. But the "friend(s) of the Bridegroom" – the disciples of a Master – they also become happy when they are with their Master because they can hear their Master's "Voice", his "Word", within themselves.

The Voice is also an essential aspect of Jesus' discourse on the good Shepherd,[1] where – quite intentionally – the expression has a double meaning. Outwardly, the "Voice" refers to the call of a Master: recognition of who he is by his disciples-to-be and their acceptance of his teachings. But it is also an allusion to the mystic Word:

> He that entereth in by the door
>   is the shepherd of the sheep.
> To him the porter (doorkeeper) openeth;
>   and the sheep hear his Voice:
>   and he calleth his own sheep by name,
>   and leadeth them out.
> And when he putteth (leadeth) forth his own sheep,
>   he goeth before them,
>   and the sheep follow him: for they know his Voice.
>
> *John 10:2-4*

And later, he says:

> My sheep hear my Voice, and I know them,
>   and they follow me:
> And I give unto them eternal Life;
>   and they shall never perish,
>   neither shall any man pluck them out of my hand.
>
> *John 10:27-28*

Again, when Jesus was brought before Pilate, Jesus says – with the same double meaning:

> To this end was I born,
>   and for this cause came I into the world,
>   that I should bear witness unto the Truth.
> Every one that is of the Truth heareth my Voice.
>
> *John 18:37*

This passage only makes sense from a mystic point of view with the 'I' that speaks referring as much to the Word as to Jesus. It means that only those who are baptized into the mystic Truth of the Word will hear its Voice and only those who are predisposed to do so will really understand what the Master is talking about. If "Voice" had been meant in an entirely physical sense, then the comment would have been bizarre, for Jesus' ministry only lasted for a very short time and very few people, comparatively speaking, could ever have heard his voice.

In another place in St John, Jesus – according to the story – is explaining a Voice which has come from heaven, glorifying him. He says:

> This Voice came not because of me,
>   but for your sakes.
> Now is the judgment of this world:
>   now shall the prince of this world (Satan) be cast out.
> And I, if I be lifted up from the earth,
>   will draw all men unto me.
>
> *John 12:30-32*

Taken physically, the story is miraculous and incredible, but remembering that this is John's gospel makes it likely that there is an allegorical interpretation. For it is true that the mystic "Voice" from heaven does come to this world for the sake of the souls here, not for the glory or "sake" of the Master. And coming, not to "all men", but to "every one that is of the Truth" – to those souls that a Master draws to himself – Satan is "cast out" or vanquished. This, says Jesus, is the "judgment of this world".

Mystics do not teach that there is a universal Day of Judgment, as was the Jewish and Christian expectation at that time. For each individual, there is certainly a day of reckoning when the soul leaves the body at the time of death. Then, according to its deeds, desires and attachments during life, the soul is 'judged' and its onward course determined.

So even taken metaphorically, this passage is a curious mixture of universal mystic teachings and later Christian belief. For, if it were taken literally, history would have proved Jesus to be wrong, since "all men" have not been drawn to Christianity. And there also seems little likelihood of any Day of Judgment waiting just around the corner.

Biblical and allied literature abounds, of course, with human voices resounding from heaven and God speaking in human words, but such passages should not be taken literally. Mystics have never suggested that God communicates in these ways. "God is a Spirit" and His communication is always spiritual. When He wants to communicate in human terms, He comes to the human level and takes on a human body in the form of a perfect Master. He does not scare the wits out of people by speaking in a huge and sonorous voice from behind a cloud!

Amongst the writings of the early Christian period, there are many references to the Voice of God, where it is explicitly equated with the Word. In the *Acts of Peter*, it is unequivocally stated to be something quite different from the physically uttered word "which cometh forth by means of art whose nature is material". It is a Voice which "is perceived in silence", is "not heard openly" and "goeth not into the ears of flesh". For the mystic Voice of God is only heard within when the mind becomes still and silent, bringing with it further peace and stillness to the mind and soul. Again, it is emphasized that when the soul gives thanks to God, it is "not with these lips ... nor with this (physical) tongue by which truth and falsehood issue forth".

These statements appear as part of a discursive prayer by Peter to Jesus, delivered while Peter is hanging upside down on the cross. But, like the *Acts of Thomas*, the *Acts of Peter* is not meant to be taken historically. It is a spiritual romance, a framework or device used by the writer to express spiritual truths.

In this extract, the cross is also given a symbolic meaning. To the people of those times, being crucified was commonly called, 'being hung upon the tree', an idiom which mystical writers were quick to use as an allusion to the Word as the Tree of Life. As a result, there are many references in the ancient literature to spiritual crucifixion – the denial of self by becoming 'nailed to' or absorbed into the Tree of Life. Such 'nailing' consists of the "conversion" or "repentance" of man – of his turning towards God, away from the world and the body. According to this particular tale, Peter, from his extremely painful upside-down position, delivers a dissertation upon the symbolic meaning of the cross. He says:

> What else is Christ,
>   but the Word, the Sound of God?
>
> So that the Word is the upright beam
>   whereon I am crucified.
> And the Sound is that which crosseth it,
>   the nature of man.
>
> And the nail which holdeth the cross-tree
>   unto the upright, in the midst thereof,
>   is the conversion and repentance of man.
>
> Now whereas thou hast made known
>   and revealed these things unto me, O Word,
>   called now by me the Tree of Life,
> I give thee thanks, not with these lips
>   that are nailed unto the cross,
> Nor with this (physical) tongue
>   by which truth and falsehood issue forth,
> Nor with this word which cometh forth
>   by means of art whose nature is material;
>
> But with that Voice do I give thee thanks, O King,
>   which is perceived in silence,
>   which is not heard openly,
>   which proceedeth not forth from organs of the body,
>   which goeth not into ears of flesh,
>   which is not heard of corruptible substance,
>   which existeth not in the world,
>   neither is sent forth upon earth, nor written in books,
>   nor is owned by one and not by another:

But with this, O Jesu Christ, do I give thee thanks,
with the silence of a Voice,
wherewith the spirit that is in me loveth thee,
speaketh unto thee, seeth thee, and beseecheth thee.

Thou art perceived by the Spirit only.
Thou art unto me father, thou my mother,
thou my brother, thou my friend,
thou my bondsman, thou my steward:
thou art the All and the All is in thee:
And thou ART, and there is nought else that IS save thee only.

Unto him therefore do ye also, brethren, flee,
and if ye learn that in him alone ye exist,
ye shall obtain those things whereof he saith unto you:
"which neither eye hath seen nor ear heard,
neither have they entered into the heart of man."

Acts of Peter III:XXXVIII-XXXIX, ANT p.335

This passage leaves no doubt that neither the Voice nor the Word are of this world. The Word is even called the "Sound of God" and is identified with the true "nature of man". Moreover, as in Jesus' assertion, "they that worship Him, must worship Him in spirit", Peter specifically states that his worship is not through any material organ of the body, but through a "Voice ... which existeth not in the world, neither is sent forth upon earth, nor written in books, nor is owned by one and not by another ... wherewith the spirit that is in me loveth thee".

Incidentally, "the nail which holdeth the cross-tree unto the upright, in the midst thereof, is the conversion and repentance of man" is almost certainly a reference to the single eye, the point of access to higher realms of consciousness. From this point, the mind and soul can repent or turn again towards God by following the sound of the mystic Voice, or they can flow out into the world, becoming absorbed there and deaf to the Voice of the Silence, within.

In the *Acts of Thomas*, we find the term being used in the same way. Here, the Voice is equated with the Comforter, the "port and harbour" or safe haven of those who travel through the inner realms. In a song of praise and gratitude to his Master Jesus, Thomas describes him as:

O Companion and ally of the feeble;
Hope and confidence of the poor (in spirit);

Refuge and lodging of the weary;
Voice that came forth from the Height,
  Comforter dwelling within the hearts of thy believers
  port and harbour of them
  that pass through the regions of the rulers.

Acts of Thomas 156, AAA p.288, ANT p.432

In another passage, the Voice is explicitly stated not to belong "to the nature of this bodily organ", that the Voice is in no way similar to a physical voice. In this excerpt, a young man is talking about Jesus to the apostle Thomas:

But I beseech thee, O man of God,
  cause me to behold him again,
  and to see him that is now hidden from me,
That I may also hear his Voice
  whereof I am not able to express the wonder,
  for it belongeth not to the nature
  of this bodily organ.

Acts of Thomas 34, ANT p.381

The expression is very common amongst the gnostic writings. There is a passage, for instance, in the Nag Hammadi tractate, *Thunder: Perfect Mind*, which is quite explicit as to the audibility of the Word issuing forth from the Silence of God. Here, it is the Word or Voice who is speaking:

I am the Silence that is incomprehensible
  and the Idea (Thought) whose remembrance is frequent.
I am the Voice whose Sound is manifold
  and the Word whose appearance is multiple.
I am the utterance of my Name....
I am the Wisdom of the Greeks
  and the Knowledge of the barbarians....

I am the hearing which can be attained by everyone
  and the Speech which cannot be grasped.
I am a mute who does not speak,
  and great is my multitude of words (emanations, realms)....

I am the name of the Sound
  and the Sound of the Name....

> For I am the One who alone exists,
>> and I have no one who will judge me.
>> *Thunder: Perfect Mind 14, 16, 19, 20, NHS11 pp. 237, 241, 249, 253*

Here, too, we encounter another term commonly used for the Word – the "Idea" or Thought (*Ennoia*) of God. Just as all human action arises from thought, so too have the mystics said that the creation – being God's 'activity' – arises from His Thought. It is just a way of expression, of course – it is not suggested that God thinks like human beings. The term is actually drawn from Greek mystical expression, as is *Nous*, a term used by philosophers such as Plato, to refer to God's creative Power as His 'Mind' or 'Intelligence', something of a higher order altogether from our own mind and intelligence.

The terms *Nous* and *Ennoia* were commonly utilized by the gnostics and mystics of early Christian times. Irenaeus writes that gnostic teachers such as Simon Magus, Menander, Valentinus, Basilides and "a multitude of gnostics" including "Ophites and Sethians", all spoke of the *Ennoia* or *Nous* as the source of all creation,[2] though his descriptions are somewhat confused.

In the gnostic tractate, the *Thought of Norea*, the *Ennoia*, the *Nous*, the *Logos* and the "Voice of Truth" are all clearly identified with each other:

> Father of All, *Ennoia* (Thought) of the Light
>> *Nous* dwelling in the Heights,
>> above the regions below, Light dwelling in the Heights,
>> Voice of Truth, upright *Nous*, untouchable *Logos*,
>> and ineffable Voice, incomprehensible Father!
>> *Thought of Norea 27, NHS15 p. 95*

Similarly, in the *Trimorphic Protennoia*, the Word, the Thought, the Voice, and the Son are identified as the creator of all things, the essence within all and the Saviour of souls from the darkness of the physical universe:

> I am the Invisible One within the All....
> I am immeasurable, ineffable, yet whenever I wish,
>> I shall reveal myself of my own accord.
>> I am the head of the All.
> I exist before the All, and I am the All,
>> since I exist in everyone.

I am a Voice speaking softly.
I exist from the first.
I dwell within the Silence....
And it is the hidden Voice that dwells within me,
    within the incomprehensible, immeasurable Thought,
    within the immeasurable Silence.

I descended to the midst of the underworld (this world)
    and I shone down upon the darkness.
It is I who poured forth the water.
It is I who am hidden within Radiant Waters.
I am the one who gradually put forth (manifested,
    emanated) the All by my Thought.
It is I who am laden with the Voice.
It is through me that *Gnosis* comes forth....
I am perception (enlightenment) and knowledge,
    uttering a Voice by means of Thought.

I am the real Voice.
I cry out in everyone,
    and they recognize it (the Voice),
    since a seed (of me) dwells in (each of) them.
I am the Thought of the Father
    and through me proceeded the Voice,
    that is, the knowledge of everlasting things....

I revealed myself ... among those who recognize me.
For it is I who am joined (who am within) everyone
    by virtue of the ... exalted Voice,
    even a Voice from the Invisible Thought.

And it is Immeasurable,
    since it dwells in the Immeasurable One....
It is a Light dwelling in Light....

It is we, alone [and separated in the] visible [world],
    [who] are saved by the hidden [Wisdom,
    by means of the] ineffable, immeasurable [Voice].
And that which is hidden within us (the soul)
    pays the tributes of his fruit to the Water of Life.

> Then the Son who is perfect in every respect –
>   that is, the Word who originated through that Voice,
>   who proceeded from the Height;
>   who has within him the Name; who is a Light –
> He (the Son) revealed the everlasting things
>   and all the unknowns were known.
>
> *Trimorphic Protennoia 35-37, NHS28 pp.403-407*

Similarly, in an untitled gnostic text from the *Bruce Codex*, the Father and Source of all is described:

> He is the First Father of the All (the creation).
> He is the First Being....
> He is the First Source.
>
> He it is whose Voice has penetrated everywhere.
> He is the First Sound
>   whereby the All perceived and understood.
>
> *Untitled Text 1, BC p.226, FFF p.547*

The Mandaean writings, too, are replete with references to the Voice, the Word or the Command of God:

> By means of his Voice and his Word,
>   vines (souls and the creation)
>   grew and came into being.
>
> *CPM 1 p.1*

And:

> Praised be that Voice, Strength, Word and Command
>   which comes from the House of Abathur (God).
>
> *CPM 25 pp.21-22*

In a passage reminiscent of similar passages in the Wisdom literature, the "Voice of Living Waters" proclaims its pre-existence over the creation, poetically described as the "awakening without", and the transmutation or diversification of the "Wellsprings" of Living Water into the multiplicity of creation:

Before the Wellsprings were transmuted,
    before the awakening without,
    before ye were in existence,
I was in the world:

The Voice of Living Waters,
    waters which transmute the turbid waters,
    they become clear and shining;
They gush forth and cast out impurities....

Voices cry aloud proclamations
    planning schemes, all of them talk!
But one Voice cometh and teacheth about this and that.

                    CPM 121 pp.116-117

In this world, says the unknown poet, teachings, paths, philosophies and religions abound – "all of them talk!" But when the "one Voice" comes, the "Word made flesh", the perfect Saviour, he teaches about the essence of all things, for he is all-wise. Only through mystic communion with this "one Voice" can the solution to all questions be truly found. In another hymn, the same theme is continued:

Voices have been voiced,
    opinions have been given,
    all kinds of pronouncements;
Yet there cometh one Voice
    and teacheth all voices.
There cometh one Saying
    and teacheth all sayings.
There cometh one Being,
    who explaineth them one by one.

                    CPM 153 p.133

And again:

For this mystery, this explanation,
    is a Voice which explaineth voices,
    a Word which interpreteth all words:
It is a Good Man who teacheth,
    addressing each individually.

                    SA p.22

The Voice or Word, then, answers all the questions and solves all the conundrums of life. And it is to be contacted through its personification, "a Good Man", a perfect Man, who takes individual responsibility for the spiritual progress, liberation and eventual God-realization of each soul.

Amongst the Manichaean-Christian writings, also, there are similar teachings concerning the Voice and the inner music. One of the Parthian hymns reads:

> Blessed and praised be this mighty Power,
>   the light and beneficent God,
>   the perfect Man (*Sraoshabray*)....
> May he protect us for wonderful joy
>   and accept from all of us this pure prayer,
>   Living Voice and divine Song.
> So be it for ever and ever!
>
> *BBB, ML p.64*

Here, the "perfect Man" refers to the *Sraoshabray* which literally means the 'Column of Glory' or the 'Column of Sound', being derived from *Sraosha*, a far earlier term for the mystic Sound, used by the ancient Persian mystic Zarathushtra around 1500 BC. Mani, it will be remembered, taught that Zarathushtra and Jesus had both been perfect Saviours in their own day. Interestingly, Zarathushtra's language was similar to the most ancient forms of Sanskrit, where the root *shru* means to 'hear' and a derived form of *Sraosha*, *Sraoshav*, was also used in later Persian as a term for the Tree of Life.

Wherever we turn, therefore, amongst the highest mystic teachings, this Power receives the place of prime importance. Indeed, there is no perfect Master who has ever failed to teach the path of the Sound, for this Power is the essence of a true Master.

Speaking Waters

Although there are a great many passages which speak of the audibility of the Word, relatively few descriptions are of a personal nature, for in most cases, mystic experiences are kept secret by those individuals who are fortunate enough to have them. They are a personal treasure whose effect is not to be dissipated by talking of them. All the same, just as there are many recorded cases of individuals being inundated with light within or even spending time in heavenly places, so too are there many cases where people have heard the heavenly Music within themselves. Few such records come from as far back as our present context. Nevertheless, there are some instances amongst the writings of the early Christian mystics where the inner sound is described in a more personal way. In the *Odes of Solomon*, for instance, there is a beautiful and poetic description of this high estate:

> And Speaking Waters touched my lips
> from the Lord's Spring, plenteously;
> And I drank, and was intoxicated
> by the Living Water that does not die;
> And my intoxication was not without knowledge,
> but I abandoned ego,
> and turned towards the Most High, my God,
> and became rich through his gift;
>
> And I abandoned folly (Illusion, Error),
> which is cast over the earth,
> and I stripped it off and cast it from me;
> and the Lord renewed me with his garment,
> and possessed me by his Light,
> and gave me the immortal rest from above,
> and I became like the land which blossoms
> and rejoices in its fruits.
>
> *Odes of Solomon XI:6-12, AOT p.701, OPS pp.105-106, OSC p.52*

"Speaking Waters" is, of course, a reference to the audibility of the Word, the Life Stream, within. In fact, the expression contains a word-play and one translator renders it, "the waters of the *Logos*".[3] The soul drinks of this "Living Water", is intoxicated with spiritual bliss and gains real mystic "knowledge". Her consciousness expands and she increasingly perceives through mystic vision how the creation is put together. She gives up ego, adherence to the small and limited self, and expands into the consciousness of the Lord. She becomes spiritually "rich" through His "gift" of baptism or initiation into the "Speaking Waters".

The soul is lifted out of the spiritual ignorance or "folly" which besets almost all mankind, "which is cast over the earth". She becomes clothed in a "garment" of light and is refreshed with the eternal, undying, unending music of this Audible Life Stream. She becomes like fertile earth which supports burgeoning vegetation and yields a rich harvest of life-sustaining fruit and crops. The devotee then continues:

> The Lord is like the sun
>   upon the face of the ground:
> He enlightened my eyes,
>   and my face received the dew;
> And my breath (spirit) took pleasure
>   in the pleasant fragrance of the Lord;
> And he brought me to His Paradise,
>   where are the riches of the pleasure of the Lord.
> And I worshipped the Lord because of his glory.
>
> *Odes of Solomon XI:13-17, AOT pp.701-702*

The soul sees the inner light, is spiritually enlightened and illumined. She enjoys the "fragrance" of the Lord – yet another metaphor for the Word of God. She is transported into the higher regions and finally to the abode of God Himself, "His Paradise". There, the soul, entranced in ecstasy, automatically and instinctively worships the glory of the Lord. This is real worship; worship *of* the Spirit, *in* the Spirit. It is here, too, that the soul truly comes to know herself as pure spirit. Hence, in an extract from the revelationary, gnostic tractate, *Allogenes*, the Sound is poignantly described as the "Blessedness" by which the soul comes to know its real nature:

> There was within me a stillness of silence
>   and I heard the Blessedness
>   whereby I knew my real self.
>
> *Allogenes 60, NHS28 p.223*

In a more discursive vein, amongst the writings of 'Abdisho' Hazzaya, a seventh-century Syrian Christian mystic, there are some interesting references to both the sound and the light inside, experienced with the "eyes of his mind" and the "ears of his heart":

> We say that we see light in the sphere of spirituality (the inner realms), but this light is not like our material light. We say also that we have there a spiritual food, but that food is not like the one we have here; we say further that our mind will perceive there the sound of the glorification of the spiritual hosts, and that it will there have speech and conversation, but that speech does not resemble the one which we hold one with one another (in this world).

The sound that is heard there by our mind is so fine (subtle) that our senses are not able to receive it, and a corporeal tongue is not able to utter and describe that which is made manifest there to the mind, whether it be made through our sense of vision or through that of hearing....

Blessed is the man who has been found worthy of this gift and of this confidence and has seen this glorious vision with the eyes of his mind, and heard with the ears of his heart the fine (subtle) sound which, from the state of serenity, is revealed to a spiritual man.

Believe me truly, O brethren, when I say unto you that whenever the mind hears the sound of the spiritual beings with its intelligible (mental or spiritual) ears, all its work (focus of attention) is performed high above the senses of the body and ... its ... faculties, which become silent and restful, as in sleep, through the happiness it receives....

From this glorious and holy vision you will fall into ecstasy over that broad world, the benefits of which are ineffable. From this ecstasy you will derive a flow of spiritual speech and knowledge of both worlds: of the one that has passed and the one that shall pass, and also a consciousness of the mysteries of future things, together with a holy smell and taste; the fine (subtle) sounds of the spiritual intelligences; joy, jubilation, exultation, glorification, songs, hymns and odes of magnification; communion with the spiritual hierarchies; vision of the souls of the saints (devotees); sight of Paradise; eating from its Tree of Life, and intercourse with the saints who dwell in it, together with other ineffable things.

The above are the signs, which if you find in yourself, you will know that the Holy Spirit, which you received from the holy baptism, is working in you....

In it (a particular spiritual condition) a man hears the Voice of a fine (subtle) sound of glorification, which the faculties of the body and of the soul are unable to bring to the utterance of the material tongue. This condition and this glorification are of the sphere of the next world and the earnest (foretaste) of the future benefits.

'Abdisho' Hazzaya, WSVII pp.160,162,167,171

Amongst the more well-known Christian mystics, there are a fair number of references to experiences of this divine Music. St Augustine (354-430), for example, speaks of it in a commentary on *Psalm 41*, telling the story of this psalm as if he were describing the experience of the psalmist as he makes his way to God. He too speaks of the "ears of the heart":

It was going up to the tabernacle (of God within) that he (the psalmist) arrived at the house of God.... By following the leadings of a certain delight, an inward mysterious and hidden pleasure, as if from the house of God there sounded sweetly some instrument; and he whilst walking in the tabernacle, hearing a certain inward sound of spiritual music, led on by its sweetness and following the guidance of the sound, abstracting his attention from all noise of flesh and blood, made his way on, even to the house of God....

In the house of God there is a never-ending festival.... The angelic choir makes an eternal holiday: the presence of Gods's face, joy that never fails.... From that everlasting, perpetual festivity there sounds on the ears of the heart a certain strain, melodious and sweet, provided only the world does not drown the sounds....

But seeing that "the corruptible body presseth down the soul and the earthly tabernacle weigheth down the mind that museth on many things",[4] even if we have in some way dispersed the clouds by walking as longing leads us on, and for a brief while have come within reach of that sound, so that by an effort we may catch something from that house of God, yet through the burden, so to speak, of our infirmity, we sink back to our usual level and relapse to our ordinary state.... For (he that was) ... led on by delight of that inward, spiritual sound to feel contempt for outward things and be ravished by things interior, is but mortal man still, is still groaning here, still bearing about the frailty of the flesh, still in peril in the midst of the offences of this world.

St Augustine, on Psalm 41:4, APII pp.188-190, WM pp.29-30

Augustine, who would almost certainly have known about the inner sound through an earlier, nine-year association with the Manichaeans, describes its captivating quality as if he himself had had experience of it. He also notes how the "corruptible body presseth down the soul", how readily "all noise of flesh and blood" and the distractions of the world can "drown the sounds" and how easy it is, even for one who has made some inner progress – to "be ravished by things interior" – to be pulled down again into the body.

Later Christian mystics also spoke of this same sweet, enrapturing divine Melody. The German mystic, Henry Suso (*c.*1295-1365), who was influenced by his association with Meister Eckhart (*c.*1260-1327), speaks of it in his autobiography, *The Life of the Servant*. He describes (in the third person) how he would take time for himself in the chapel during the early morning and how his devotions were often accompanied by a sweet melody in his soul. Once at this time, while he sat thus at rest, he heard within himself a gracious melody by which his heart was greatly moved.

Henry Suso, Life of the Servant VI, LS p.10; cf. LBHS pp.19-20, MS p.277

The English mystic and hermit, Richard Rolle (*c.*1300-1349) of north Yorkshire, while still a young man, similarly describes his

receiving of this heavenly and ghostly sound, the which belongs to the songs of everlasting praise and the sweetness of unseen melody; because it may not be known or heard but of him that receives it, whom it behoves to be clean and departed from the earth.

Richard Rolle, Fire of Love I:15, LRR p.92

Like St Augustine, he too observes that in order to hear this sound, a person must have no thought of the world in his mind, but must be "clean and departed from the earth". He then continues:

Whiles also I took heed praying to heaven with my whole desire, suddenly, I wot not in what manner, I felt in me the noise of song, and received the most liking heavenly melody which dwelt with me in my mind.... And henceforth, for plenteousness of inward sweetness, I burst out singing what before I said, but forsooth, privily, because alone before my Maker. I was not known by them that saw me as, peradventure, if they had known me (what I was experiencing), they would have honoured me above measure and so I should have lost part of the most fair flower and should have fallen into desolation.

In the meanwhile, wonder caught me that I should be taken up to so great mirth whiles I was in exile (in this world); and because God gave gifts to me that I knew not to ask, nor trowed I that any man, not the holiest, could have received any such thing in this life.

Richard Rolle, Fire of Love I:15, LRR p.92

Again, expressing himself poetically, Luis de Leon (1527-1591), a Spanish monk of the Augustinian order and a brilliant professor of theology at the University of Salamanca, wrote:

> At whose blest Sound divine, my soul –
>   that in forgetfulness hath lain –
>   with a new light doth shine.
> And unto memory plain,
>   of its first splendid origin, attain.

Up through the fields of air (spiritual realms) it wings,
 till in the highest sphere it dwells.
And a new music there, it hears,
 music that wells undying,
 and all other kinds excels.

Luis de Leon, A Fransico de Salinas, SSMI p.264

And likewise, Mechthild of Magdeburg (*c.*1210-1297), a German nun and probably abbess of the Dominican Convent of St Agnes, writes:

When my Lord comes
 I am beside myself.
For there cometh with Him such sweet Melody
 that all carnal desire dieth within me:
And His sweet Music puts far from me
 all sorrow of heart.

Mechthild of Magdeburg, Flowing Light of the Godhead II:3, RMM pp.29-30

These passages all speak of the same experience of inner sound, and though it is true that they do not equate it with the Word of God, this is because such experiences are only the very beginning of what is attainable. As the soul advances further, it perceives for itself that the real source of sound, light and, indeed, the entire creation is the Word.

NOTES AND REFERENCES

1. *John* 10:1-5, 27-30.
2. Irenaeus, *Against Heresies* I:I.1, I:XXIII.2,5, I:XXIV.3-4, I:XXIX.1, I:XXX.1, *AHI* pp.4,87,89,90,101,104.
3. *MEM* p.143.
4. *Wisdom of Solomon* 9:15.

CHAPTER TEN

Many Mansions

Earthly and Heavenly Things

We have spoken on a number of occasions about the extent of the creation and, in particular, of the spiritual realms or heavens. They have also been mentioned in a number of the quotations we have used. An understanding or – some might say – a belief in the existence of a hierarchy of higher realms of creation has been common to practically all schools of mysticism and it is time now to consider the evidence that Jesus, too, taught the existence of higher spiritual worlds lying within man.

To the materially-oriented mind it is difficult enough to conceive of God being within oneself. Even if a person comes to grips with that idea, in a general sort of way, they are then confronted with the suggestion that God's creative Power is both visible and audible within oneself. The idea that light and sound are to be found within one's own head is past credibility for many people whose entire range of experience lies within the realm of their five senses. The suggestion, therefore, that vast spiritual regions also lie within seems almost beyond belief.

Mystics speak only of what they have experienced inside, but people have difficulty in believing them because they have not had that experience themselves. Jesus was acknowledging this when he said:

> Verily, verily, I say unto thee,
> > we speak that we do know,
> > and testify that we have seen;
> > and ye receive not our witness.
> If I have told you earthly things,
> > and ye believe not, how shall ye believe,
> > if I tell you of heavenly things?

> *John 3:11-12*

319

And Paul, too, speaks of that which lies behind the veil of the temporal and transitory:

> We look not at the things which are seen,
>   but at the things which are not seen:
> For the things which are seen are temporal;
>   but the things which are not seen are eternal.
>   *Romans 4:17-18*

No one denies that the votaries of all religions believe not only in both heaven and hell, but also in a God. So the question has to be asked, "Where are they?"

In simple terms, there would appear to be only two alternatives: either they are inside of man – in a spiritual dimension, so to speak – or they are outside him. But God, being spiritual, is unlikely to be up in the material sky, hiding behind the clouds or secreted in the vast distances of space. Certainly, modern science has found no indications of any likely place where God could hide, far out in the depths of space! Nor is there any evidence that He and the heavens lie in some hidden, external and super-physical dimension. In fact, those who have described genuine mystic experiences of the heavens have all said that the heavens lie within.

The spiritual regions are – by definition – spiritual and non-material. They, like God, can be presumed to exist wherever the spirit dwells and it would seem that there is only one 'place' where they could be. As Jesus himself taught, God and His creation are inside – attainable not through an ascent into matter, but through an ascent in being or consciousness, the two terms being used synonymously for our purposes. For this reason, access to the spiritual realms has often been termed an expansion of consciousness, leading to a state of super-consciousness. God, too, has also been described as an Ocean of Consciousness or an Ocean of Being. Entry into the inner realms requires, therefore, a non-physical technique, a being-oriented technique, if you like, a means of exploring the depths of one's own consciousness. Nowadays, such a practice is called meditation or spiritual practice, though previously, it was simply called prayer – or interior prayer, the prayer of silence, contemplation, devotion and other similar names.

In ancient times, there were a number of aspects of the mystic teachings which were kept secret, for a variety of reasons. Firstly, it can be seen from the deaths of Jesus, John the Baptist and many other mystics that teaching the mystic path was not a safe occupation. The

Masters, who taught only love, were liable to lose their lives because of it. And their disciples, too, were open to persecution and possibly execution if their beliefs were fully known.

More than their beliefs, however, their spiritual practices, though quite simple and harmless, were likely to be misunderstood, especially by an intolerant, fearful and often superstitious public. It can readily be imagined how accusations of witchcraft, magic and the black arts followed, if it were heard – most likely in a garbled form – that some particular mystic and his disciples attempted to leave their bodies and reach the heavenly regions and beyond during their own lifetimes. Or if it were said that they listened to heavenly music inside their own heads that no one else could hear. It is certainly recorded in the gospels that Jesus and his disciples were themselves accused of being magicians of a lower order,[1] as were some of the gnostics. Moreover, the suggestion that man can attain union with God, can see God and can actually become God Himself, has always made the orthodox uneasy, despite the fact that all mystics have stated this to be a fundamental truth and the primary goal of the highest spiritual endeavour.

Anything that challenges the mind, its beliefs and its habits, will cause a reaction in the one challenged. Anything that challenges people to control themselves or to look within themselves will usually induce a negative response, as they seek to shrug off the challenge. And if such people have political or other power to wield, they are likely to use it against the perceived source of their discomfort. As a result, it has only been in the last century or so that democratic and legal measures have been passed in certain parts of the world protecting minority groups and supporting toleration. For this reason, only in recent times have the Masters been able to speak out without the danger of their lives or freedom being curtailed before they had fairly begun their intended ministry.

It was not only the likelihood of persecution that occasioned secrecy. It was also because only a person with adequate guidance should attempt spiritual practice. To go exploring into unknown territory without a guide is foolhardy. The inner being of man is a vast domain for which suitable guidance is required to avoid the many dangers and pitfalls. Moreover, the secrets of spiritual exercises are only of real value to those who wish to practise them. To others, they are only of academic interest and such people will be unlikely to really appreciate their true nature. Spiritual practice is something to be engaged in and experienced. It is not a suitable subject for scholarly dissertation.

Furthermore, in those days, anything written down was hardly likely to survive one round of copying before it was changed, edited, borrowed or completely garbled. There were no multiple print-runs where every copy could be guaranteed to be the same as the original. Writers have always found inspiration in the works of others and, in the case of mysticism, the material of others has commonly been reworked in a variety of ways and for a variety of motives. The desire to shine as a spiritual teacher, for example, or simply to act the wise one, is an especially common manifestation of spiritual ego. Usually, the result of such free borrowing is ever-increasing confusion as writers copy from each other, none of whom have really experienced what they are talking about or possess adequate guidance on the matter.

The teachings of the Masters, in particular, because they are so universal and so powerful in their message, get borrowed by everyone and rarely end up reflecting with any accuracy what the Masters actually taught. We have found this to be the case with the New Testament and it is true in so many other instances, ancient and modern.

So rather than put the details of spiritual practice and the teachings associated with it into public circulation, providing fuel for the dilution and garbling process, mystics must have thought it far safer to keep them secret. After all, written instructions and details alone cannot really help others. Ultimately, contact with a Master is also required, providing the opportunity to impart teachings of a confidential nature.

We have an explicit statement of this approach in the *Clementine Homilies*, where James the brother of Jesus explains Peter's request that his books of teachings should not be handed out indiscriminately to all and sundry:

> If we should give the books to all indiscriminately, and they should be corrupted by any daring men, or be perverted by interpretations as you have heard that some have already done, it will remain even for those who really seek the truth, always to wander in error. Wherefore it is better that they should be with us, and that we should communicate them with all the fore-mentioned care to those who wish to live piously, and to save others. But if any one, after taking this adjuration, shall act otherwise, he shall with good reason incur eternal punishment.
>
> *Epistle of Peter to James V, Clementine Homilies, CH p.5*

As with so many of these ancient documents, there is a threat of dire consequences should anyone tamper with the writer's words or meaning. All the same, the practice of keeping books out of public circulation is clearly indicated in this extract, for all the reasons we have been describing.

In any case, pure spiritual teachings are not meant for everyone and there is no point in parading that which is sublime and beautiful before those who have no capacity for appreciation. It is only a waste of time and the end result can often be negative. As Jesus said:

> Give not that which is holy unto the dogs,
>> neither cast ye your pearls before swine,
>> lest they trample them under their feet,
>> and turn again and rend you.
>>> *Matthew 7:6*

As a consequence, the more esoteric aspects of mystic teachings have characteristically been kept either as closely-guarded secrets or have been described in such circumspect language that only those who were meant to understand would understand. The same is still true, today, though to a lesser extent.

The Mysteries

In the ancient Middle East, these secret teachings and practices were commonly known as the 'mysteries'. The term was used particularly of the Egyptian and Greek 'mystery schools' from where it spread throughout the ancient Middle East. Indeed, almost every esoteric sect had its own secret initiation ceremonies and esoteric practices, commonly called the 'mysteries' of that particular group.

There is considerable evidence that part of Jesus' teaching, too, was secret, given only to the disciples. This is why he told them that they alone could understand what he taught and others not:

> It is given unto you to know
>> the mysteries of the kingdom of heaven,
>> but to them it is not given.
>>> *Matthew 13:11*

That is to say that his disciples had been taught the "mysteries", the techniques of entering the "kingdom of heaven" while still living in the human body. They could therefore understand his teachings and parables in that light, but others could not really understand what he had to say. Supporting this suggestion, the second-century Clement of Alexandria quotes an unnamed, "certain gospel" where Jesus says:

> (Keep) my secret (mystery) for me
> and for the sons of mine house.
>
> *Clement of Alexandria, Miscellanies V:X, ANT p.36*

And the writer of the *Clementine Homilies* seems to be referring to the same source when he quotes Jesus as saying:

> Ye shall keep my secrets (mysteries) for me
> and for the sons of mine house.
>
> *Clementine Homilies XIX:XX, ANT p.36*

Again, confirming this tradition of secret teachings, in the *Acts of John*, Jesus instructs his disciples:

> Keep silence about my mysteries.
>
> *Acts of John, AA p.15*

And also in the gnostic *Second Book of Jeu*:

> These mysteries which I shall give to you, preserve, and give them to no man except he be worthy of them. Give them not to father nor to mother, to brother or to sister or to kinsman, neither for food nor drink, nor for woman-kind, neither for gold nor for silver, nor for anything at all of this world. Preserve them, and give them to no one whatsoever for the sake of the good of this whole world.
>
> *Second Book of Jeu 43, NTA1 p.263*

However, although many things may never have been divulged beyond the circle of Jesus and those he baptized, the real mysteries were not so much secret teachings as indescribable, inner experiences gained through spiritual practice. This is made clear in the Nag Hammadi *Apocalypse of Peter*:

> And he (Jesus) said to me, "Be strong, for you are the one to whom these mysteries have been given, to know them through revelation."
>
> *Apocalypse of Peter 82, NHL p.377*

Here, revelation means mystic experience. Peter knows the "mysteries" through direct, personal experience of higher realities. But such revelation comes about not only by diligent spiritual practice, but, as Jesus says to Peter, it is "given" through the grace and spiritual blessings of a Master. The same idea is expressed in the *Acts of Thomas* where Judas Thomas – or the author of the *Acts of Thomas*, rather – describes Jesus as:

> Revealer of the mysteries of the Exalted (One), ...
> utterer of hidden things,
> and shewer of the works of our God, ...
> giver of life in secret.
>
> *Acts of Thomas, AAA p.189*

In the same book, he also says that Jesus was not the first to have revealed these "mysteries". Addressing God, he says that the "mystery of the First-born" has been revealed to the "prophets" – to all the mystics of this higher path. As always, the "First-born" is the Word, the first emanation or "Son" of the Father, which incarnates in all Masters:

> To be glorified art Thou, the good Father,
> who didst reveal the mystery of Thy First-born
> to the prophets by the Spirit of Holiness (Holy Spirit)....
>
> To be glorified art Thou, the Father giving life to all,
> who hast revealed the mysteries of Thy Son
> by the Spirit to His saints (devotees),
> in tranquillity and rest.
>
> *Acts of Thomas, AAA pp.246,247*

And similarly:

> To be glorified art Thou, the Father benign,
> who hast given us peace by the hand of our Life-giver,
> and hast revealed unto us
> Thy glorious and holy mysteries
> by the hearing of Thy doctrine (Word?).
>
> *Acts of Thomas, AAA p.250*

In another passage, Jesus himself is described as a "hidden mystery" who reveals "many mysteries":

> Jesu, the hidden mystery that hath been revealed unto us,
>> thou art he that hast shown unto us many mysteries.
> Thou that didst call me apart from my fellows
>> and spakest unto me one Word wherewith I am inflamed,
>> and am not able to speak it unto others.
>
> *Acts of Thomas 47, ANT p.387*

A Master is indeed a mystery, for his reality, like all other souls, is not the body or any of the external appearances. His "mystery" is that of the "Word made flesh". This Judas Thomas makes clear. It is the "one Word" which constitutes the "hidden mystery" of Jesus and which shows his disciples the "many mysteries".

Likewise in the Nag Hammadi tractate, the *Trimorphic Protennoia*, the mystic Son is portrayed both as the Word and the teacher of "ineffable mysteries". He is also the revealer of "everlasting things" to the denizens of this world – "those who dwell in darkness" or "those who dwell in the abyss":

> Then the Son who is perfect in every respect,
>> that is, the Word who originated through that Voice; ...
> He revealed the everlasting things
>> and all the unknowns were known.
> And those things difficult to interpret and secret,
>> he revealed....
> And he revealed himself to those who dwell in darkness,
>> and he showed himself to those who dwell in the abyss;
> And to those who dwell in the hidden treasuries (realms)
>> he told ineffable mysteries.
> And he taught unrepeatable doctrines to all those
>> who became sons of the Light.
>
> *Trimorphic Protennoia 37, NHS28 p.407*

The "unrepeatable doctrines" must once more be an allusion to the mystic Word, since all human and verbal doctrines are naturally repeatable. But the Word is "unrepeatable" and secret because it is non-physical, revealing knowledge of God and the creation which cannot by its very nature be conveyed in any human language. This knowledge is obtained only by transcendent transport into the higher spiritual regions.

The "mysteries", then, was a general expression covering many aspects of secret teaching, practical instruction and mystic experience of the inner regions. And it is very clear that the disciples of Jesus were taught his "mysteries". This is mentioned consistently in the gospels and elsewhere, though what they comprised was not recorded for posterity.

Many Mansions

Amongst the secret teachings related to instruction in spiritual practice would have been a description of the inner regions. It is probably for this reason that we do not find much mention of them in the New Testament. All the same, there are some very obvious pointers, the most well-known and most commonly quoted being in John's gospel. Towards the time of his departure, when Jesus is reassuring his disciples that he will always be with them spiritually, he says:

> In my Father's house are many mansions:
>   if it were not so, I would have told you.
> I go to prepare a place for you.
>
> And if I go and prepare a place for you,
>   I will come again, and receive you unto myself;
>   that where I am, there ye may be also.
>
> And whither I go ye know, and the way ye know.
>
> *John 14:2-4*

Jesus is telling his disciples that he will be soon be leaving them, but that they should not worry because he will be preparing a place for them in his "Father's house" – in the inner mansions of creation. He will manifest himself within them in a spiritual form and according to their individual spiritual advancement, he will take each one to a place which befits them, either during their lifetime or at the time of their death. Ultimately, he says, he will take them all where he is going, back to the Father. "That where I am, there ye may be also." And he points out that they know where he is going and that they also know the way or the path they have to tread. For he has already taught all this to them and answered all their questions on the matter. This was a part of his "mysteries" or secret teaching. He is returning to God and he has taught them the path to the inner mansions, the heavenly regions, and to God Himself. This, *per se*, is the road travelled by those who develop mystic contact with the Word of God. The Word itself is the mystic highway upon which the soul travels.

That these "many mansions in my Father's house" do indeed refer
to the inner, heavenly regions is demonstrated by a passage found in
the writings of the late second-century Irenaeus, attributed to the early
second-century, Papias. In this excerpt, the mansions are linked to the
"thirty-fold", "sixty-fold" and "hundred-fold" harvest yielded by the
seeds sown by the divine Sower in Jesus' famous parable. The plants
that grow from his sowing are, of course, the souls in whom the Master
has sown the Word of God. In this extract, the three results or harvests
are equated with the "heavens", "Paradise" and the "City (of God)",
these being increasingly higher gradations of the inner hierarchy.
Papias – if indeed it was he – wrote:

> As the presbyters say, then (in the higher state) those who are deemed
> worthy of an abode in heaven shall go there, others shall enjoy the delights
> of Paradise, and others shall possess the splendour of the City (of God).
> For everywhere the Saviour will be seen, according to the worthiness of
> those who see Him.
>
> But that there is this distinction between the habitation of those who
> produce an hundred-fold, and that of those who produce sixty-fold, and
> that of those who produce thirty-fold. For the first will be taken up into
> the heavens, the second class will dwell in Paradise, and the last will
> inhabit the City (of God).
>
> On this account the Lord said, "In my Father's house are many
> mansions": for all things belong to God, who supplies all with a suitable
> dwelling-place, even as His word says, that a share is given to all by the
> Father, according as each one is or shall be worthy....
>
> The presbyters, the disciples of the apostles, say that this is the
> gradation and arrangement of those who are saved and that they advance
> through steps of this nature; and that, moreover, they ascend through
> (in?) the Spirit to the Son, and through the Son to the Father.
>
> *Papias (?) in Irenaeus, Against Heresies V:36.1-2, WAF p.444*

In other words, souls are taken up and find a place, according to their
spiritual advancement, after which they continue to ascend "through
steps of this nature" until, in the company of the Son, they finally reach
the Father.

The same term is also used for the inner realms in the *Doctrine of
Addai*, where the unknown Addai, supposedly one of Jesus' disciples,
while lying on his deathbed, advises those around him that they should
only consider themselves to be travellers in this world, waiting to go
into the "blessed mansions":

Wherefore, as wayfarers and sojourners, who tarry for a night and return early to their homes, so may you yourselves consider concerning this world, that from here ye go forth to the places where the Son went to prepare for every one worthy of them. As with kings of countries, their armies go forth before them, and prepare for them a dwelling-house for their honour. So this King of ours, behold, he is gone to prepare for his worshippers blessed mansions in which they may dwell.

For it was not in vain God created the children of men; but that they might worship and glorify Him here and there for ever. As He passeth not away, so those glorifying Him cease not.

Doctrine of Addai the Apostle, DAA pp.42-43

Worship of the Lord, concludes Addai, is why God has created man, and those who do so find the innate immortality of the soul. In another passage from the same document, there is an affirmation of this immortality of the soul and its transition to higher realms upon death. "The souls of men" do not die with the body, asserts the writer, but "live and rise, and have mansions". The consciousness and life of the soul do not cease, for the "Image of God" dwells within it:

All the souls of men, which depart from this body, die not; but they live and rise, and have mansions, and a dwelling-place of rest, for the understanding and the intelligence (consciousness) of the soul do not cease, because the Image of God (the *Logos*) is represented (reflected) in it, which dieth not.

Doctrine of Addai the Apostle, DAA pp.44-45

Similarly, in the second of the two books of Enoch so favoured by the early Christians, Enoch exhorts his followers to follow a good life, for

in the great time (to come)
are many mansions prepared for men,
good for the good, and bad for the bad,
without number many.

2 Enoch 61:2, APOTII p.466

Again, it is clear that the mansions refer to the heavenly regions. Likewise, the fourth-century Christian generally known as Aphrahat the Persian Sage, whose writings were well known in the Syriac language of Eastern Christianity, writes inspiringly of the "mansions of the saints":

In that place they shall forget this world.
There they have no want;
    and they shall love one another with an abundant love.
In their bodies there shall be no heaviness,
    and lightly shall they fly "as doves to their windows".[2]
In their thoughts they shall not remember wickedness at all,
    nor shall anything of uncleanness arise in their heart.
In that place there shall be no natural desire,
    for there they shall be weaned from all appetites.
There shall not arise in their heart anger or lasciviousness;
    also they shall remove from them all things that engender sins.
Fervent in their heart will be the love of each other;
    and hatred will not be fixed within them at all.
They shall have no need there to build houses,
    for they shall abide in light, in the mansions of the saints.
They shall have no need of woven raiment,
    for they shall be clothed in eternal light.
They shall have no need of food,
    for they shall recline at His table and be nurtured for ever.
The air of that region is pleasant and glorious,
    and its light shines out, and is goodly and gladsome.
Planted there are beautiful trees,
    whose fruits fail not, and whose leaves fall not.
Their boughs are glorious, their perfume delightful,
    and of their taste no soul shall grow weary for ever.
Spacious is the region, nor is it limited;
    yet its inhabitants shall see its distance
    even as that which is near.
There the inheritance shall not be divided,
    and no man shall say to his fellow:
"This is mine and that is thine."
They shall not be bound there in the desire of covetousness,
    nor shall they go astray there concerning recollection [of God].
There a man shall not love his neighbour with special reverence,
    but abundantly shall they all love one another after one fashion.
They shall not marry wives there, nor shall they beget children;
    nor shall there the male be distinguished from the female;
But all shall be sons of their Father who is in heaven;
    as the Prophet said:
"Is there not one Father of us all;
    is there not one God who created us?"[3]

Aphrahat the Persian Sage, Demonstrations XXII:12, HEDA pp.405-406

The City and the Mountain

It will be noted that Papias described the eternal realm of God as the "City". This is a frequently encountered expression in ancient Judaic and Christian literature where it is a shorthand for the "heavenly Jerusalem", "Mount Zion" or the "holy Mountain", all being references to the dwelling place of God Himself. The unknown writer of *Hebrews* uses it:

> Ye are come unto Mount Zion,
>   and unto the City of the Living God,
>   the heavenly Jerusalem.
>
> *Hebrews 12:22*

Externally, Zion is the hill upon which the city of Jerusalem is built and the term has also come to mean the Jewish nation. Consequently, Jews and Christians alike have sometimes taken these kind of expressions to mean the external Jerusalem. But Jewish and Christian mystics throughout the ages have all pointed out that the real meaning is the eternal realm within.

In the guarded, metaphorical language of the times, the inner regions were therefore known as the mountains or the holy mountains. They were also called the gardens, the pastures, the meadows and so on. Hence, we find in the *Book of Revelation*:

> And he (an angel) carried me away in the spirit
>   to a great and high mountain,
>   and shewed me that great City, the holy Jerusalem,
>   descending out of heaven from God,
>   having the glory of God:
> And her light was like unto a stone most precious,
>   even like a jasper stone, clear as crystal.
>
> *Book of Revelation 21:10-11*

Being "carried ... away in the spirit" demonstrates that the "great and high mountain" referred to an inner realm, for the writer does not claim to have been carried away physically. Similarly, the early third-century Christian writer, Origen, quotes from the lost *Gospel of the Hebrews* which expresses more or less the same idea when Jesus says:

> Even so did my Mother, the Holy Spirit,
>> take me by one of my hairs
>> and carry me away on to the great mountain Tabor.
>
>> *Gospel of the Hebrews, Origen,*
>> *Commentary on John 2:12.87 (on John 1:3), OG p.85*

Again, the writer – putting words into the mouth of Jesus – is talking of being carried spiritually, not physically, on the current of the Word or Spirit, to the "great mountain Tabor", an allusion to the inner realms, the name presumably being drawn from Mount Tabor lying southwest of the Sea of Galilee. There are a great many examples of the use of such expressions in Judaic, Mandaean, Manichaean, Christian and other writings, the Biblical *Psalms* being particularly rich in such images. The twenty-fourth psalm, for example, says that only he has a right "to climb the Mountain of Yahweh" – to ascend to God – who is pure in heart and whose deeds ("whose hands") are pure, who is utterly honest and imbued with truth, and who worships only God, not the "worthless things" of this world:

> Who has the right to climb the Mountain of Yahweh,
>> who the right to stand in his Holy Place?
> He whose hands are clean, whose heart is pure,
>> whose soul does not pay homage to worthless things
>> and who never swears to a lie.
>
> The blessing of Yahweh is his,
>> and vindication from God his saviour.
> Such are the people who seek him,
>> who seek your presence, God of Jacob!
>
>> *Psalms 24:3-6, JB*

Similarly, there is the well-known passage from psalm one hundred and twenty-one:

> I will lift up mine eyes unto the hills (mountains)
>> from whence cometh my help.
> My help cometh from the Lord (Yahweh)
>> who made heaven and earth.
>
>> *Psalms 121:1-2, KJV*

Though external hills or mountains may be a beautiful and inspiring sight, nothing physical is intended here, for the "hills" and the "Lord" are explicitly equated, the second two lines serving to underline and explain the first two.

The same imagery is found in the Mandaean literature, where the inner realms are referred to as the "mountains" or as the "mountains of radiance, light and glory"[4] and so on. In the following excerpt, the writer addresses these mystic mountains in lyrical language:

> To the mountains I say
>   "How fragrant are your odours,
>   how delightful your perfume!
> Within you, all is full of brightness!"
>
> *CPM 157 p.135*

And back comes the response:

> They reply, "The Being who passed through our midst
>   hath no tangibility or substance,
>   no substance or tangibility hath he,
>   nor is there any kind of desire in him.
> The Being who passed amongst us,
>   released some of his Life-giving Power amongst us."
>
> *CPM 157 p.135*

The Being, of course, that gives life to the inner realms, is the Word and its personification in the Master. This is the Life-giving Being.

Allusions to the higher realms as "mountains" are common in mystic literature and it is clear that later Christians and others, like their earlier counterparts, understood such Biblical references in this way. The medieval Spanish mystic, Marina de Escobar, writing of her heavenly experiences, uses the expression to describe her ascent to increasingly higher realms or "mountains":

> The Lord one day said to me: "Thou art greatly afflicted, come with Me; I will bring thee to My holy Mountain and I will recreate thee in the house of My prayer." And suddenly I was led in the spirit to a high mountain whence the whole world was visible to me. A heavenly light shone for an instant like a flash of lightning and, with a majesty that impelled my admiration, I saw thereby the immensity of the Divine Essence.
>
> And the Lord said to me: "Take courage, for thou shalt mount up still higher. That which thou hast seen is but little in comparison with that

which still remains". And I was brought up to another higher mountain. And there, a light, much stronger that the first, shone forth again like a flash of lightning, and revealed to me, still more clearly, the same Divine Essence. I saw more things than I had seen before.

Again the Lord said: "Courage, for thou must mount still higher." And instantly I was taken up to a third and yet higher mountain which seemed to reach to the highest summit of heaven. And a light like a flash of lightning shone out with a brilliancy greater than that with which the others had shone before and it showed me the Essence of God, His perfections and His hidden judgments.

I was astounded at the spectacle of this immensity! ... And I said to myself interiorly: "Lord how incomprehensible are Thy judgments! Who shall understand them?" And God answered: "The little and the humble of heart, those who have left all for Me and who seek only to please Me".

Marina de Escobar, VMEI III:II, GIP pp.276-277

Marina de Escobar also speaks of the "heavenly Jerusalem", clearly understanding it as a metaphor for a mystical reality to be experienced within:

The angels approached my soul and detached her from the sensible faculties (withdrew her from the body). I found myself before the heavenly Jerusalem which was encircled by an exceedingly vast river, of great beauty and brightness.

Marina de Escobar, VMEI III:I, GIP p.274

He Leadeth Them Up Into a High Mountain

Searching through the ancient literature one finds a great many such examples. An understanding that the inner realms were known as mountains makes one look again at some of the gospel narratives, wondering if, behind the stories we have today, lies an earlier stratum of allegorical writing. Could the remarkable story of the transfiguration of Jesus, for instance, as written down in Mark's gospel and reproduced by the compilers of Matthew and Luke, actually be a misinterpretation of descriptions of inner experiences? Mark's narrative reads:

And after six days Jesus taketh with him
    Peter, and James, and John,
    and leadeth them up into an high mountain
    apart by themselves:
And he was transfigured before them.

And his raiment became shining,
  exceeding white as snow;
So as no fuller on earth can white them.

Mark 9:2-3

At this point in the narrative, two of the old Jewish mystics appear –
Elias (Elisha) and Moses – talking with Jesus, following which

  there was a cloud that overshadowed them:
  and a voice came out of the cloud, saying,
  "This is my Beloved Son: hear him."
And suddenly, when they had looked round about,
  they saw no man any more,
  save Jesus only with themselves.

And as they came down from the mountain,
  he charged them that they should tell no man
  what things they had seen,
  till the Son of man were risen from the dead.
And they kept that saying with themselves,
  questioning one with another
  what the rising from the dead should mean.

Mark 9:2-3,7-10

The story has many features that indicate a mystical origin. Jesus'
"shining raiment" is a reference to the appearance of the soul in the
spiritual regions, full of light and radiance. One of the commonest
metaphors in the ancient literature is to the soul's 'robe of glory' or
'shining garment'. Jesus' "transfigured" form is the inner spiritual form
of the Master, met by disciples of a Master on the threshold of the
inner journey. Going "up into an high mountain" refers to the ascent
of the soul into the heavenly regions. The disciples are taken up in the
company of their Master and remain with him. Being alone with the
Master, away from the affairs of the world and the crowding of other
disciples, is also a characteristic of the inner realms.

  Their meeting with mystics who have already died indicates the
spiritual nature of the encounter. Disciples who – due to their religious background – have a particularly strong attachment to particular mystics of the past are sometimes satisfied by being able to meet
those mystics inside. The Word takes on the form of the mystic
whom they wish to meet. Hence, Jesus' Jewish disciples meet with

Elias and Moses. But this is all spiritual, internal; there is nothing physical about it.

The "voice" is the divine Music heard by the soul in these realms and the "Beloved Son", who the disciples are instructed to "hear", is the Word and its manifestation in the Master. Being requested not to divulge their experiences is also suggestive of an inner experience.

The disciples "questioning ... what the rising from the dead should mean" is more indicative of the questioning that the early Christians, *after* Jesus' time, would have had. "Rising from the dead" refers to the ascent of the soul from the physical body into the inner regions – passing from the deathly existence of this world into the life of the Spirit within. During his own lifetime, Jesus would have explained all this to his disciples and there would have been no need for them to question its meaning. After his departure, however, the subject may have remained as a part of the tradition, but its meaning would have become obscure. Hence, the later Christians would have questioned its meaning.

The comment about telling "no man ... till the Son of Man were risen from the dead" is probably present to explain how the story became known after Jesus had expressly told his disciples not to tell anyone. It is also a part of the later legends concerning Jesus' post-resurrection appearances and helps to support that belief. Such a comment, together with the way the entire story appears in Mark and hence in Matthew and Luke is understandable, since it was written down long after Jesus had died and not by one of his direct disciples. As a consequence, the mystical elements of the story are all present, but have become garbled and externalized. Though many of the Christians at that time were still of a mystical disposition, they would no longer have understood the teachings as Jesus had given them. And by that time, a physical resurrection was a part of Christian belief in some circles.

Though some may have taken the story literally, others did not. It is certain that many of the early Christians continued to understand it in a mystical way, for variants of the 'incident' are related in an explicitly mystical manner. Thus, in the *Acts of Peter*, Peter says:

> Our Lord, willing that I should behold
>   his majesty in the Holy Mount, ...
>   I ... saw the brightness of his light,
>   fell as one dead and shut mine eyes,

And heard such a Voice from him
 as I am not able to describe,
 and thought myself to be blinded
 by his brightness....

 And he gave me his hand and raised me up;
 And when I arose I saw him again
  in such a form as I was able to take in.
     Acts of Peter III:XX, ANT p.321

The "Holy Mount" indicates that Peter's experience took place on the inner planes. There, Peter sees the spiritual or light form of his Master, Jesus. Peter was dead to the world and the body, his eyes and senses closed, his attention withdrawn from them. And he hears the sweet Voice of the Word emanating from the spiritual form of Jesus and is overwhelmed by "his brightness". But Jesus holds him, figuratively, by the hand: he raises him up out of the body, appearing to Peter in a subtle form, a form suited to Peter's inner advancement. And note, too, that this was all "Our Lord, *willing* that I should behold his majesty" – the inner Master is only met by *his* will, not by the will of the disciple.

Another version of the same story is also encountered in the *Acts of John*, once again with clearly mystical elements:

 And at another time he taketh with him
  me and James and Peter unto the mountain
  where he was wont to pray,
 And we saw in him a light
  such as it is not possible for a man
  that useth mortal speech to describe what it was like.

 Again in like manner he bringeth us three up
  into the mountain, saying: "Come ye with me...."

 And I ... drew nigh unto him softly,
  as though he could not see me,
  and ... saw that he was not in any wise
  clad with garments (of this world),
  but was seen of us naked (as a pure soul),
  and not in any wise as a man,
  and that his feet were whiter than any snow,

> so that the earth there was lighted up by his feet,
> and that his head touched the heaven.
>
> *Acts of John 90, ANT pp.251-252*

Like all good tales – especially those with a kernel of truth in them –
the transfiguration story clearly got around, appearing in a variety of
guises, according to the beliefs and intentions of those relating it. And
in the process, it too became transfigured and the original meaning
lost and obscured by legend. Nevertheless, the mystical aspects are
clearly discernible.

Elsewhere in the gospels, there are incidents involving mountains,
upper rooms and so on, where it is possible that the story is based
upon a misunderstanding of an earlier stratum of mystic teaching. In
Matthew, for example, after the crucifixion, the "eleven disciples" meet
with Jesus in a "mountain". Again, this would have been a meeting
with the spiritual, light form of their Master, though according to
Matthew's narrative, some of them still have doubts:

> Then the eleven disciples went away into Galilee,
>   into a mountain where Jesus had appointed them.
> And when they saw him, they worshipped him:
>   but some doubted.
> And Jesus came and spake unto them, saying,
>   "All power is given unto me in heaven and in earth."
>
> *Matthew 28:16-18*

The "power" over all things "in heaven and in earth" is the Word. It
means that when the disciples met the light form of Jesus inside, on
the spiritual planes, they came to understand that he really was one
with the Word and did indeed have "all power". Up to this point it
had only been an intellectual belief and therefore open to doubt,
for it was not based upon personal experience. And naturally enough,
when they did experience things for themselves, their souls were
filled with awe, love, reverence and the natural worship of the soul for
its Lord.

In another place, Matthew relates that Jesus goes "up into a mountain apart to pray". Possibly, Jesus did seek the solitude of nature
when he wanted to find a quiet place for mystic prayer, but one
wonders if perhaps it could also refer to his ascent into the inner
'mountains':

> And when he had sent the multitudes away,
> he went up into a mountain apart to pray:
> and when the evening was come, he was there alone.
>
> *Matthew 14:23*

There are other mountain stories, too, in the gospels. In the accounts given by Matthew and Luke concerning the temptation of Jesus, Jesus is taken up "into an exceeding high mountain" where he is shown "all the kingdoms of the world, and the glory of them".[5] No mountains of this world can afford such a view, of course, nor are the "kingdoms of the world" particularly glorious, but what is true is that from the inner realms, the working of all the creation below is open to view – not so much in sight as in consciousness – and a soul who has reached there also has power over all that lies beneath. The incident would therefore seem to indicate that Jesus, like all Masters, had the power to dominate the world but declined to use it. Perhaps, in an earlier version, now lost, the story was actually an allegory or parable designed to explain the power and humility of a Master. Either way, the narrative indicates that Jesus was understood to have access to those inner 'mountains' from where the entire creation below can be viewed.

Principalities and Powers, Gods and Angels

Just as we are all 'rulers' – in a very limited sense – over all that comes within the scope of our mind and sphere of action, and just as the Lord is the ruler of all, permeating every part of His creation, His will prevailing in every detail, so too, acting as the central powerhouses of the inner realms, there are beings who control all creation within the span of their vastly expanded consciousness. The subject is not readily amenable to human intellectual understanding, but all Masters have taught the existence of a multitude of such powers, all of them being the creation, projection or emanation of the Supreme Lord, through His mystic Word. The inner realms and their rulers or administrators are projected together as part of the way in which the creation functions. These rulers are like sub-powers or sub-stations of the Lord's primary creative Power.

In an earlier look at Paul's teachings, we noted that he believed in the existence of higher realms and even seems to have had experience of them. In fact, from the way in which he speaks of them, it is clear that he expects his audience to automatically accept their existence, too, for he never tries to prove his point. But not only does he speak of heavenly realms, but also of their rulers. One presumes, therefore, that on such a fundamental issue, Jesus must also have taught the same.

In translation, Paul calls the inner realms, "principalities", a term used for a domain or state which is ruled over by a prince. The very term itself, therefore, presupposes the existence of rulers of the inner realms.

Though we might be at variance with certain key aspects of Paul's version of Jesus' teachings, he certainly understood many of the salient points common to all mystic teachings and he is in accord with them on this issue. He speaks of the "principalities and powers in heavenly places"[6] and of Christ as the "head of all principality and power".[7] He also describes Jesus as "having spoiled (conquered) principalities and powers ... triumphing over them".[8] And in *Colossians*, speaking of the Son as God's creative Power, he says:

> By him (the Son) were all things created, that are in heaven,
>   and that are in earth, visible and invisible,
>   whether they be thrones, or dominions,
>   or principalities, or powers:
> All things were created by him, and for him:
> And he is before all things,
>   and by him all things consist.
>
> *Colossians 1:16-17*

On occasion, he spoke of these rulers as lesser gods, but he never hesitated to point out that above them all, as the Supreme Creator, was the one God:

> There is none other God but one.
> For though there be that are called gods,
>   whether in heaven or in earth,
>   (as there be gods many, and lords many,)
> But to us there is but one God,
>   the Father, of whom are all things.
>
> *1 Corinthians 8:4-6*

Paul believed in the physical resurrection of Jesus, though in a spiritualized physical form. It is this of which he speaks when he says that Jesus has been taken up to be with God. But he also points out that God is "far above all principality and power". With this latter statement we can agree. God, says Paul,

> set him (Jesus) at his own right hand in the heavenly places,
>   far above all principality, and power,
>   and might, and dominion, and every name that is named,
>   not only in this world,
>   but also in that which is to come (*i.e.* the higher worlds).
>
> *Ephesians 1:20-21*

Many of the early Christians had the same beliefs. In the *Acts of John*, Jesus, identified with the mystic Son of God, is described as superior to all powers and principalities of creation. In fact, John invokes Jesus as God Himself:

> Upon Thee that art the only God do I call ...
>   unto whom every power of principalities is subjected:
>   unto whom all authority boweth.
>
> *Acts of John 79, ANT p.248*

And even when speaking of the human Jesus, he says:

> It is not a man whom I preach unto you to worship,
>   but God unchangeable, God invincible,
>   God higher than all authority and all power,
>   and elder and mightier than all angels
>   and creatures that are named, and all *aeons* (inner realms).
> If then ye abide in him, and are builded up in him,
>   ye shall possess your soul indestructible.
>
> *Acts of John 104, ANT p.256*

John is speaking of Jesus as both God and His creative Power, the One who is higher than all else in the creation. "If then ye abide in him", he says, if the attention is kept firmly upon him and the soul is elevated to his level through transcendent contact with the Word, then "ye shall possess your soul indestructible". Then, the soul will regain all its lost power and knowledge of its own true nature. It will realize its own essential indestructibility, immortality and oneness with God.

So it was not only Jesus who came from a level far higher than these inner realms, with their rulers and angelic inhabitants. His disciples also passed through these regions during their spiritual practice. We see this in the *Acts of Thomas*, where Jesus, identified as the Son of God and the Voice of God, is described as the "port and harbour of them that pass through the regions of the rulers". He is the

> Voice that came forth from the Height,
> Comforter dwelling within the hearts of thy believers
> port and harbour of them
> that pass through the regions of the rulers.
>
> *Acts of Thomas 156, AAA p.288, ANT p.432*

In many places in the ancient literature, these rulers are called gods, angels and archangels, as in one of the Nag Hammadi tractates, the *Sophia of Jesus Christ*, being the Christian overwriting of the non-Christian *Eugnostos the Blessed*. Both these two tractates describe the hierarchy of creation. There, on the subject of the rulers and their regions, we read:

> He (the Father) was given great authority
> and He ruled over all creation.
> He created gods and angels and archangels,
> myriads without number for retinue from that Light.
>
> *Eugnostos the Blessed 77, NHL p.229*

And correspondingly:

> Now First-begotten is called 'Christ.'
> Since he has authority from his Father,
> he created a multitude of angels without number
> for retinue, from Spirit and Light.
>
> *Sophia of Jesus Christ 104-105, NHL p.231*

Aeons, Totalities, the Pleroma and the All

There are innumerable references to these realms and rulers in the gnostic and other literature of Egypt and the ancient Middle East, where – although many complex systems and descriptions of the hierarchies were put forward by the various authors and teachers – the same fundamental truths are encountered again and again. All and everything, higher and lower, repeat these writers, is the creation of the Supreme Lord, many of them automatically presuming that Jesus had taught the same. Simon Magus, for example – according to Irenaeus – taught that all powers originate from the *Ennoia* or Word of God:

For this *Ennoia,* leaping forth from Him (God), and comprehending the
will of her Father, descended to the lower regions and generated angels
and powers by whom he (Simon) also declared this world was formed.

Irenaeus, Against Heresies I:XXIII.2, AHI p.87

Many names were also given to these powers, rulers and higher regions. They are the *aeons,* the sovereignties and the totalities, the airs,
the spaces and the waters, the angels, the powers and the *archons.* The
seats of power are also called the 'thrones', just as God Himself was
said to occupy the highest 'throne'. And the entire creation is known as
the All, the Totality or the *Pleroma,* also translated as the Fullness, while
the Source of them all, the Word and the Father, is known as the Root,
the *Aeon of Aeons* and by many other names. Thus, in the *Trimorphic
Protennoia,* where the Word is speaking, we read:

> I dwell within all the sovereignties and powers
>> and within the angels
>> and in every movement that exists in all matter.
>> *Trimorphic Protennoia 47, NHS28 p.427*

And in the *Gospel of Truth:*

> All the emanations of the Father are *pleromas,*
>> and the Root of all His emanations
>> is in the One who made them all grow up in Himself.
> He assigned them their destinies.
> Each one then is manifest.
>> *Gospel of Truth 41, NHS22 p.115*

Again, in the *Apocryphon of John,* another revelationary tractate, the
resurrected Jesus tells his disciples:

> He (God) is pure (and) immeasurable....
> He is an *aeon*-giving *Aeon....*
> He is life-giving Life....
> He gives the immeasurable, incomprehensible Light.

> How am I to speak with you about Him?
> His *Aeon* is indestructible,
>> at rest and existing in [silence, reposing]
>> (and) being prior [to everything.

For He] is the head of [all] the *aeons*,
[and] it is He who gives them power in His goodness.

Apocryphon of John 4, NHL pp.106-107

Looking back across history at a manner of expression so different from our own, we may be surprised at the licence these writers permitted themselves in putting words into Jesus' mouth. Yet they all demonstrate again and again that their understanding of Jesus was as the greatest of all mystics: as a gnostic Saviour who came from God, who was the Word personified both in this world and in the higher realms, and who had full and free access to all parts of the Lord's creation. So it is with all perfect Masters.

The Heavenly Hierarchy

Descriptions of the divisions of creation, as given by the mystics, have varied from time to time, from place to place and from people to people. This may cause confusion; but it need not. Firstly, it must be understood that we are dealing with something which is utterly non-material. Human language is material and designed to cope with the things of this world, though even when used within this limited sphere, language and words can soon lead to misunderstandings. But the higher regions are of an altogether more subtle and transcendent nature and though there may be many reflections in this world of things that pertain to the higher realms, physical language is really quite incapable of portraying them.

Thus, when mystics speak of regions that are 'higher' and 'lower' or 'outer' and 'inner', or when they describe the soul as 'going up' and 'coming down', they are speaking metaphorically. They are not referring to physical space. The heavenly realms are higher or lower in their degree of spirituality, not spatially. From the soul's point of view they also relate to the expansion in consciousness experienced as the soul 'ascends' or 'rises up'.

God is the 'realm' of Supreme Spirit or Universal Consciousness and everything is emanated or projected from that pure Source. The hierarchy of creation is manifested by God's creative Power which 'moves downward' or 'outward' from the divine Source forming the creation. As it 'moves', the purity pertaining to each successive realm decreases. Finally, the creative current or Power reaches the region of greatest impurity – the physical universe. Between God and the physical universe

– say the mystics – lies a gradation of realms of decreasing purity. It can also be said, therefore, that those of greater purity are 'closest' to God, that they are 'higher up' in the hierarchy or that they are 'deeper within'. All such expressions are attempts to use the inadequate medium of words to convey something of this mystic reality.

It is because the hierarchy of creation is not amenable to verbal portrayal that various, apparently conflicting descriptions have been given of the total number of regions in the creation. Some mystics have spoken of three major divisions, others five, some seven, others eight or twelve and amongst some of the gnostics, the numbers multiply into the hundreds – three hundred and sixty-five, the number of days in a year, being a standard of one school. This confusing situation is not improved by the fact that the higher regions are reflected in the lower regions. In the gnostic tractate, *Zostrianos*, for instance, these reflections are called the "*aeon* copies".[9]

Just as the light from the sun may be reflected in a bucket of water and thence onto a wall, so too is everything a reflection of what lies above. This means that those who have never seen either the sun or its reflection in water, but only heard descriptions of it, will be likely to confuse their experience of the hazy light upon the wall for the bright and fiery sun that shines high up in the sky. That is, those who have attained only to lower realms may confuse them for the higher realms, for the character of these regions is the same – only their degree of purity is different. In fact, in modern times, there are those who equate these higher regions with particular psychological and intellectual states of mind, bringing everything down to the level of our own greatly limited human experience, feeling that nothing can exist beyond that.

The situation is further compounded by the fact that, as the soul ascends, it is so entranced with the beauty and glory of each stage that it may mistakenly understand a lower stage to be the ultimate. While this may seem strange at first sight, it is in fact no more peculiar than the fact that many souls in this world consider that the physical universe is the beginning and end of everything, and that nothing lies beyond it. In fact, many souls in this world are deluded into thinking that they are controlling everything around them. This is the nature of the ego through which we all function. Even if we can understand rationally that God must be the Supreme Doer of everything, we still tend to think that we are doing it ourselves.

It is all a part of the divine design. If God wants the creation to continue, He has to hide behind – or within – veils of his own devising. And they need to be of an increasingly subtle character as the soul ascends. These veils remain in place for every soul until the time comes for Him to call that soul back to Himself. And for that, too, He has a system. He permits souls to pass through all reflections and obstructions by allowing them to travel on the primal current of His Word.

Masters have said that the source of everything is the eternal realm of God Himself, which may hardly be termed a region. Here, it is all-Light, all-Sound, all-bliss, all-Love. Next to God, as the first emanations in the hierarchy of creation, are spiritual regions in which there is no admixture of any mind or matter. In these realms, the soul knows itself as pure or naked soul, a drop of the Creator, separated from Him only by His will. This area of creation is a vast reservoir of power, light and Word force, pregnant with potential and possibility for creation and manifestation in the realms beneath.

Below these realms of pure spirit, the soul enters the regions of mind and matter, known in western terminology as the causal, astral and physical universes. As the soul descends from the purely spiritual realms, it first encounters the mind in the causal realm, a region of the subtlest mental essences and energies. This realm has been called the Universal Mind. Within it are the seed forms or blueprints of what is manifested below. Just as a thought or idea of something in our human mind can be manifested outwardly as a material object, so too do the subtle 'ideas' of the Universal Mind take on expression in the astral world, becoming fully externalized in the material universe. The astral and causal regions are blissful and full of a scintillating light. Their sights and sounds are beguiling, entrancing the mind and soul of the observer. In fact, the astral and causal realms constitute the heavens to which most religious people aspire to go after death.

Also in these subtle realms of the mind are the hells described by all religions. They may be considered as coarse areas within the sub-astral zones where the devilish and hellish thoughts and mental impressions of a human life are lived out in a realm of subtle, mental torture. While the Supreme Lord rules out of mercy, the law prevailing in these three realms of the mind is that of pure justice, of cause and effect. We reap what we sow.

We may reap a reward in heaven if we have lived a genuinely good and pure life or a punishment in some hellish zone if our mind has been inclined to wickedness in our lifetime. The law of cause and effect, however, has other even more significant and far-reaching consequences. But the remainder of this discussion we will defer until the next chapter, while we briefly look at some of the descriptive systems mentioned by the Christian and other allied writers of antiquity.

Seven Heavens

The simple description given above distinguishes the physical universe and two higher regions – the astral and the causal – all three being realms of mind and matter, though of an increasingly subtle nature as the soul ascends. Proceeding higher, there is a vast spiritual area situated above the realm of mind and matter, sometimes divided into two main regions. Above that lies the eternal realm. That gives us five super-physical regions, plus the material universe. Some mystics have further subdivided the eternal realm into three 'regions', together with the Supreme Lord and Nameless Source of all, making four in all. This would bring our grand total to eight super-physical regions – four eternal and four created. Mystics also say that all the realms below the eternal, being created, are liable to periodic reabsorption into God or dissolution.

In the gnostic and mystic literature of two thousand years ago, we can discern traces of a considerable number of such descriptive systems. But the particular regions to which they actually refer are difficult to determine and the "*aeon* copies", the reflection of the higher regions in the lower, makes matters doubly difficult. The sun gives off light and heat, but so does a candle, and from a description that spoke only of light and fire it would be difficult to determine whether it was the candle or the sun which was being described. Especially if a person presumed, due to lack of experience, that nothing could really be as bright as the description given of the sun.

The literary style which was commonly used for descriptions of the inner regions was a 'revelation', and there are many of them, relating to numerous schools of thought. But one never knows how much is pure fabrication and imagination based upon the author's reading of other texts and discussions with others, and how much is based upon his own experience or the teaching of one who was conversant with the higher realms. All the same, the revelation genre can only have stemmed from a belief that it was possible to enter the heavenly realms during one's own lifetime, for they all speak of these experiences being given to normal human beings.

Probably the commonest descriptive system was that of the seven heavens – a pre-Judaic system that originated in Mesopotamia or Persia many, many centuries before Jesus. It is the origin of our popular expression for great happiness, "in the seventh heaven". A number of Jewish and Christian 'revelations' chart the ascent of some individual through these regions and all of them bear the same general characteristics.

348 *Many Mansions*

Firstly, the soul is taken through the regions by a guide. Access is not permitted without one. Secondly, each succeeding region is superior in brightness, purity and spirituality to the one below. Thirdly, God Himself is situated either in the seventh heaven or above the heavens altogether, according to the predilection and system of the author. Some descriptions even speak of twelve heavens.

That the writers of the synoptic gospels credited Jesus with the power to ascend through these heavens seems fairly clear. They relate that the "heavens were opened" to Jesus as soon as he received baptism:

> And Jesus, when he was baptized, went up straightway out of the water. And, lo, the heavens were opened unto him, and he saw the Spirit of God descending like a dove, and lighting upon him.
>
> *Matthew 3:16; cf. Mark 1:10, Luke 3:21*

The story cannot be accepted literally, for it would be too bizarre, and some metaphorical meaning is clearly bound up in it. But whatever its origins, the general meaning would seem to be that after his baptism, Jesus immediately came into contact with the Holy Spirit and was able to travel through the inner heavens. After all, Jesus himself pointed out that the "kingdom of heaven is within you", and regarding the existence of the "many mansions", he said, "if it were not so, I would have told you".[10] So since he also asserted "we speak that we do know",[11] it must be presumed that he had access to the inner mansions during his own lifetime, as well as going there after his death to "prepare a place" for his disciples.

Concerning Jesus' particular teaching on these regions, only fragments have come down to us from here and there. Indicating the transitory nature of all the heavens below the eternal realm, is a saying from the *Gospel of Thomas*, though it is a shame we no longer have the full context:

> Jesus said,
> "This heaven will pass away,
> and the one above it will pass away."
>
> *Gospel of Thomas 11, NHS20 p.57*

From this it may be presumed that Jesus was not intending to leave his disciples in any heaven that was liable to dissolution. This is why he speaks so many times of the "kingdom of heaven" and the "kingdom of God", referring to the eternal region, the highest of them all.

Paul also refers implicitly to the seven heavens in the famous passage from *2 Corinthians* where he describes "a man in Christ" who was "caught up to the third heaven".[12] Describing such mystic experiences as "visions and revelations" given by the Lord, Paul writes definitively of the "third heaven" and "Paradise", much as Papias did in his description of the harvest yielded by the first two types of "seed". He also speaks of the "unspeakable words" heard in those heavens, which must surely be an allusion to the "Unspeakable Word", for there are no words of any kind in the utterly non-physical, higher realms.

In the *Acts of Thomas*, too, the writer refers to the seven heavens when describing the Holy Spirit, the "compassionate Mother" as "she that revealeth the hidden mysteries" and the "Mother of the seven houses" or mansions, an allusion to the seven heavens:

> Come, compassionate Mother....
> Come, she that revealeth the hidden mysteries.
> Come, Mother of the seven houses (mansions),
>   that thy rest may be in the eighth house.
>
> *Acts of Thomas 27, ANT p.376*

Note here that "rest", an ancient term commonly used for the eternal peace of union with God is said to be in the "eighth house", that is – beyond the seven heavens.

It seems, then, that the heavens, their rulers and entry to them during the present lifetime as well as after death were a key aspect of Jesus' mysteries, his secret teachings.

Through the Seven Heavens

From a mystical point of view, one of the most interesting amongst the many revelationary writings is the *Ascension of Isaiah*, another composite document, parts of it stemming from the early Christian period. Here, according to the narrative, the prophet Isaiah becomes so uplifted while giving a spiritual discourse that he is taken up on an ecstatic trip through the seven heavens. The story itself, of course, is only intended as a framework upon which to hang spiritual truths. The writers of these ancient mystic romances such as the *Acts of Thomas* and others, often took their central personality from history or mythology rather than inventing totally new and unknown personalities as in modern fiction. By choosing archetypal characters such as

Isaiah, they were also able to convey something concerning the nature of their central character. In this case, Isaiah was revered in Judaism as a great prophet and mystic, and this is the way we are intended to understand the Isaiah of the story.

The ascent begins when Isaiah is giving a spiritual discourse to a gathering of people, including a number of other prophets, which here refer to other mystics and mystically-minded souls:

> And while he was speaking in the Holy Spirit in the hearing of all, he suddenly became silent, and his spirit was caught up into heaven, and he no longer saw the men who were standing in front of him. But his eyes were open although his lips were silent, and the spirit of his body (his soul) was taken up from him. And only his breath remained in him, for he was in a vision.
>
> And the angel that was sent to explain things to him in the vision was not of this world, nor was he one of the angels of glory of this world, but had come from the seventh heaven.
>
> *Ascension of Isaiah VI:10-13, AOT pp.795-796, OTP2 p.165*

While Isaiah was speaking to the people who were gathered there, his attention was drawn inside and he went up into the inner, heavenly realms. Since his attention was not functioning at the physical level, through the physical senses, he no longer saw those who were sitting around him. His soul went inside and only "his breath" or his life energy remained in the body, maintaining its operation. Isaiah had left his body while still alive in this world and had gone into the higher realms. And the writer indicates the height of Isaiah's ascent by pointing out that the angel or being that he met inside as his guide was neither from this world, nor was he from one of the lower heavens, but came from the highest heaven, the seventh heaven. The narrative continues:

> And, apart from the circle of the prophets, the people who were there did not believe that the holy Isaiah had been caught up into heaven. For the vision that the holy Isaiah saw was not a vision of this world, but of the world that is hidden from man. After Isaiah had seen this vision he gave an account of it to Hezekiah and to his son Josab and to the other prophets who had come.
>
> But the officials and the eunuchs and the people did not hear it, but only Samnas the scribe, and Joachim, and Asaph the recorder, for they were doers of righteousness and the fragrance of the Spirit was in them. But the people did not hear it, for Micah and his son Josab had sent them

away when the wisdom (perception, consciousness) of this world had been taken from him (Isaiah), and he had been left looking like a corpse.

Ascension of Isaiah VI:14-17, AOT pp.796, OTP2 p.165

But "apart from the circle of the prophets" – those who were conversant to one degree or another with the mystic teachings – nobody believed in or realized what had happened to Isaiah. Most people do not believe in things imperceptible to their five physical senses. They are even largely unaware of the non-physical nature of their emotions and thoughts, let alone of the higher realms which lie within them. In the story, therefore, two of those who did understand these things sent the general populace away when Isaiah went inside "and was left looking like a corpse", for they would not have understood what was happening and might have created an unwanted disturbance.

The story then progresses and, during Isaiah's vision, he is taken up by his angel guide to each of the seven heavens. Amongst other things, the story seems to be a way for the author to provide inspiration to his readers by describing some aspects of these inner realms. As in other 'revelational' descriptions, each heaven is described as more glorious, beautiful and full of light than the one below, something with which all mystics have agreed.

The actual identity of the angel may or may not be significant, but no soul can travel through the inner realms without a guide – an angel or being who has access and understands the way. For the disciples of a Master, this guide is the spiritual form of their Master, and very few other human beings ever gain access to these realms during their lifetime, certainly not on any permanent or repeatable basis. However, the writer does not make the identity of the angel any more explicit than to say that he came from the seventh and highest heaven.

Angels, of course, have become an integral part of religious thought over the centuries. It is necessary, therefore, to divest the mind of a multitude of images gleaned unconsciously from one's cultural background which may have little or no relevance to the being that the writer of this and other similar 'revelations' had in mind.

The angel then takes the soul up through the various heavens and we rejoin the story at the sixth heaven:

And he (the angel) took me up into the air (spiritual space) of the sixth heaven and I beheld a glory I had not seen in the five heavens while I was being taken up, and angels resplendent in great glory. And the praises there were sublime and wonderful....

And ... I asked him and said to him, "Why are there no companions
for the angels on the right?" And he said, "From the sixth heaven and
above it there are no more angels on the left, nor is there a throne set in
the middle, but they have their direction from the power of the seventh
heaven, where He dwells that cannot be named; from the Chosen One,
whose name has not been revealed, and whose Name none of the heavens
can learn."

Ascension of Isaiah VIII:1-7, AOT p.800, OTP2 p.168

References to the left and the right hand paths and to regions on the
left and the right hand side are very common in the mystic literature
of all ages and cultures. They represent the duality or separateness of
all regions which lie outside the realm of God. There is that which
leads upwards towards God and that which leads downwards into the
creation – these are designated as being of the right and left hand. This
duality, however, ceases in the eternal realms.

As we have said, for the purposes of description, mystics have categorized the creation in a variety of ways. Here, the five regions, in
which there is still separation from God are represented as the five
heavens comprising the creation. In these realms, the rulers or "angels"
all have counterparts – there are those on the right and those on the
left. But in the sixth, there is no division, for it is part of the eternal
realm of God Himself, who dwells in the seventh heaven. And it is
from this seventh heaven that all other powers, rulers, "thrones" or
"angels" "have their direction" or derive their power. Further, this
Supreme Lord is the Nameless One "whose name has not been revealed". In the story, the angel continues to describe this Supreme and
Nameless Lord:

"For it is to His Voice alone that all the heavens and the thrones respond;
and I have been empowered and sent to bring you up here so that you
may behold this glory."

Ascension of Isaiah VIII:8, AOT pp.800-801, OTP2 p.168

It is from "His Voice" that the "heavens and the thrones" – the regions
and their rulers – have come into being. It is to the Lord's tune that
they dance and "respond".

And I glorified and praised my Lord, because through sharing in his lot I
was to go up there. And he said to me, "Hear then this again from your
companion. When by the angel of the Spirit you have been taken up there

from that alien body of yours, then will you receive the garment that you will see, and you will also see other garments numbered and stored up there. And then will you become equal to the angels of the seventh heaven."

Ascension of Isaiah VIII:13-15, AOT p.801, OTP2 p.168

The "garment" or the robe of glory is a metaphor for the soul's own true spiritual nature of divinity and light. At this stage, the soul will become the same as all other souls who live and bask in the ocean of the Supreme Being in the seventh heaven.

And he took me up into the sixth heaven, and there were no angels on the left nor was there a throne in the middle, but all the angels looked the same and their praises were equal. And strength was given to me, and I also sang praises with them, and the angel who was accompanying me also, and our praises were like theirs. And they glorified the Father of all, and his Beloved, the Christ, and the Holy Spirit, all with one voice. But it was not like the voice of the angels who were in the five heavens, nor was it like their speech; but the voices were different there, and there was much light there.

Ascension of Isaiah VIII:16-20, AOT p.801, OTP2 p.169

The Voice or Sound, which emanates from and pervades all souls who dwell here, is different from the Sound heard in the lower heavens; and this realm is full of a light even brighter than that of the lower realms. All the souls here are full of the natural worship, glory and intense love of the Supreme Father, of His Beloved Son, the Master – the "Christ" – and the Holy Spirit, the Word.

And then, when I was in the sixth heaven, I thought that the light which I had seen in the five heavens was darkness. And I rejoiced and gave praise to him who had bestowed such light upon those who await his promise. And I entreated the angel who was accompanying me that I might not have to return from there to the world of the flesh. For truth to tell, Hezekiah and Josab, my son, and Micah, there is great darkness here (in the physical world).

Ascension of Isaiah VIII:21-24, AOT pp.801-802, OTP2 p.169

From the sixth heaven, the beginnings of the eternal realm, even the great light of the lower heavens seems like such darkness that Isaiah is full of a blissful gratitude and wonderment that such an incredible treasure of light and eternal beatitude should be "bestowed ... on those who await his promise", upon His chosen souls, His initiates. Indeed, so great is his bliss and utter contentment that he begs that he may not have to return to his physical body, for by comparison this world is full of darkness and misery.

> And the angel who was accompanying me realized what I was thinking and said, "If you rejoice in this light, how much more will you rejoice in the seventh heaven when you see the light where the Lord is and his Beloved, and also the garments and the thrones and the crowns stored up for the righteous, for those, that is, who believe in that Lord who will descend in your human form. For great and marvellous is the light that is there. But as for your not returning to your body – the time has not come for your coming here."
> And when I heard this I was sad; but he said to me, "Be not sad."
>
> *Ascension of Isaiah VIII:25-28, AOT p.802, OTP2 p.169*

As we commented earlier, many mystics have pointed out that the eternal realm of God, the Godhead, has aspects, often being described as fourfold in character. But here, the writer is using the ancient belief in seven heavens as his system of description and, having ascribed five of these to the created domains, he is left with only two for the eternal regions of God. The sixth heaven, therefore, he describes as supremely bright, making even the lower heavens seem dark by comparison. It is also beyond all division and is eternal. And the seventh heaven he designates as the utterly Supreme Abode of the "Glorious One". He also emphasizes that the "righteous", the chosen ones, are those who believe in the "Lord who will descend in your human form", that is – as a Son of God. In fact, the angel had previously said that one of the reasons why Isaiah was being taken up was:

> "So that you may see the Lord of all these heavens and of these thrones, transforming himself until He becomes like you in form and in appearance."
>
> *Ascension of Isaiah VIII:10, AOT p.801, OTP2 p.168*

The angel then adds that a soul cannot leave the body permanently until the "time has ... come", until a person's designated lifespan has been completed. And Isaiah is sad at the thought of having to return to his physical body, for existence there is so blissful. He is then taken up into the seventh heaven where he says:

> I saw ... a glorious One ... and the righteous came near him and wor-
> shipped.... And I asked the angel who led me and I said to him, "Who is
> this one?" And he said to me, "Worship him, for this is the angel of the
> Holy Spirit who speaks in you and also in the other righteous ones." And
> the eyes of my spirit were opened and I beheld the Great Glory.
> *Ascension of Isaiah IX:35-37, AOT p.805, OTP2 p.172*

The Voice of the Word, the Holy Spirit, "speaks" in the soul of everyone, though only the initiated – "you and the other righteous ones" –
come to hear it in all its full glory and power; and then, only when
the "eyes of the spirit" – the spiritual eye or single eye – is opened.
It is this power which transforms an individual, making him pure,
subtle, bright, holy and "righteous", in the truly spiritual rather than
the religious sense.

> And I heard then the voices and the praise that I had heard in each of the
> six heavens – that I had heard as I ascended. And all the voices and the
> praise were addressed to that Glorious One, whose glory I could see.
> *Ascension of Isaiah X:1-2, AOT p.806, OTP2 p.172*

The highest, eternal realm of God is the source of all that lies below.
Everything emanates from here. All the sounds or "Voices" of the lower
heavens are contained within the Sound or Voice of this realm. And
with the Voice comes natural praise and worship. In that high estate,
the soul automatically knows and understands the nature of true worship, for the drop and the Ocean are of the same essence. The soul is
entranced in the love, bliss and wonder of the divine Voice, and all
such worship is automatically directed towards the Lord. This is true
worship "in Spirit", as Jesus called it.

> And I heard and saw the praise which was being directed to him. And the
> Lord and the angel of the Spirit heard everything and saw everything.
> And all the praise which comes up from the six heavens is not only heard
> but seen.
> *Ascension of Isaiah X:3-5, AOT p.806, OTP2 pp.172-173*

And most significantly, this worship is both visible and audible, "is
not only heard but seen" – these being the two primary faculties of the
soul and the two characteristics of the Word or Voice.

> And I heard the angel, who was accompanying me, speaking to me; and

he said, "This is the One Eternal Being who dwells in the high world and
rests within his Holy Ones."

Ascension of Isaiah X:6, AOT pp.806, OTP2 p.173

The "Holy Ones" – notably in the plural – are the Masters, and the
remainder of the revelation describes the appointment of the Master
by the "Voice" and his descent through the lower heavens until he incarnates in a human form.

Altogether, the *Ascension of Isaiah*, especially its origins, is intriguing, leaving many questions unanswered. Only extracts have been
given here, but it is clear that the original writer, whoever he or she
was, has a deep understanding of the inwardness of God and His creation, and of the existence of a hierarchy of inner worlds. He also mentions the uniqueness of the human form as the only vehicle in which
God can be realized. He speaks of the inner door, of the soul leaving
the body as if it were dead, of this world as one of great darkness, of
the appointment of a Master by the Voice of God and of the Lord's
coming to this world as a Master in the disguise of a human being. All
these are characteristics of the highest mystic teaching.

All the same, the document contains a fair degree of Christian
dogma, especially in those portions that have been omitted from the
above extracts. How then did such a writing come into existence? All
the scholarly translators speak of obvious interpolations, and there are
also a substantial number of variations between the extant versions of
the text. It is possible therefore, that the *Ascension of Isaiah* was written by an early Christian who was still very much in touch with the
mystical side of the tradition, but who had not fully understood it.
Consequently, he had woven various strands of Christian dogma into
the universal mystic teaching. Alternatively, there could once have been
an original revelational writing which an early Christian editor with
some degree of mystical understanding wove into the present story,
adding, deleting and amending the material as he went along.

Either way, the existence of the mystical tradition within early Christianity, stemming directly from the teachings of Jesus, is once more in
evidence, and the same familiar mystic truths are once again encountered.

The Five Greatnesses

There were, as we have said, a number of systems used at the time of
Jesus to describe the inner hierarchy of creation and it is difficult to

determine which he used, especially since his teachings on the matter were essentially secret. He may even have described the creation in a number of ways, according to the various existing systems, showing how the different descriptions were all saying essentially the same thing.

Due to the secrecy, whatever information we have on the subject must have leaked out in various ways and has probably been blended with the guesswork and imagination of later Christians. Knowing that Jesus had taught something on the matter, but being in possession of only limited information, they could only combine it with their own previous religious and mystical background.

Together with the 'seven heavens' system, the other most probable contender for Jesus' descriptive system is that of the five heavens. Gnostic descriptions, attributed to Jesus by their authors, and which enumerate multiple heavens into the hundreds are less likely to have originated with him, most of all because Masters like to keep things simple and practical. After all, complex intellectual descriptions of these heavens help very little, being more for the satisfaction of people's curiosity and more likely to distract the mind from the simple love of God and the practical pursuit of the spiritual path.

The Masters' purpose in coming to this world is to take their chosen and allotted souls through and beyond all the heavens of creation, bringing them to the "kingdom of heaven", to God Himself. They do not want their disciples to get lost in these regions, either actually or even through thinking about them to excess. As a result, they describe the bare minimum, so that their disciples may recognize the landmarks and pass through. Any other essential guidance can be given inside when they meet with their disciples on the inner planes, where it will be better understood and utilized. An experienced and competent guide who travels with you is of far greater value than a map provided in advance, however detailed.

Descriptions of the creation as comprised of five main realms are found in a number of places in ancient Christian and Middle Eastern literature. In particular, it was taught by the third-century Iranian mystic, Mani, who spoke of them as the Five Greatnesses. The relevance of his teachings to those of Jesus, it will be remembered, is that Mani insisted that he had not brought any new teachings, and that his teachings were the same as those of Jesus. He also believed – like many others, both before and since – that the gospels did not accurately convey Jesus' teachings, but contained significant omissions and additions.

The Five Greatnesses are mentioned in a number of Manichaean writings, but in only one is there anything like a step by step description of them, though sadly, the descriptions of the first two are lost. In this system, it is the fifth region which is the "self-existent" eternal realm. Picking up the description from the third realm, we read:

... the third, the blessed places without count and number,
   wherein dwell the light gods, angels, elements,
   the powers in great bliss and joy.

The fourth, the Unborn Air
   in the Light Paradise,
   wondrous, beautiful to behold,
   immeasurable its goodness for them.
By supernatural power it shall, by itself,
   bring into being the gods' marvellous dress and garment,
   throne, diadem, and fragrant wreath,
   ornaments, and finery of all kinds.

The fifth, the Light Earth (Land of Light),
   self-existent, eternal, miraculous;
In height it is beyond reach,
   its depth cannot be perceived.
No enemy and no injurer walk this Land.
Its divine pavement is of the substance of diamond
   that does not shake in all eternity.
All good things are born from it:
   adorned, graceful hills wholly covered with flowers,
   grown in much excellence;
   green fruit-bearing trees
   whose fruits never drop, never rot,
   and never become wormed;
Springs flowing with ambrosia
   that fill the whole Paradise, its groves and plains;
Countless mansions and palaces,
   thrones and benches that exist in perpetuity
   for ever and ever.

Thus arranged is the Paradise (of creation),
   in these Five Greatnesses.
They are calm in quietude and know no fear.
They live in the light, where they have no darkness;

in permanent life, where they have no death;
in health without sickness;
in joy, where they have no sorrow;
in charity without hatred;
in the form of friends, where they have no separation;
in a form that is not brought to naught;
in a divine body where there is no destruction;
on ambrosial food without restriction,
wherefore they bear no toil and hardship.

In appearance they are ornate, in strength powerful,
and in wealth exceeding rich;
of poverty they know not even the name.
Nay, they are equipped, beautiful and embellished;
no damage occurs to their bodies.
Their garment of joy is finery that never gets soiled,
of seventy myriad kinds, set with jewels.
Their places are never destroyed.

SFMC, BSOAS XII p.308

Mystics are at a loss when it comes to describing the inner mansions of the soul. Words describe only the things of this world, and even that, quite inadequately. No experience, even of physical things, can truly be transmitted or conveyed by words. Experience and words are fundamentally different.

Mystics have therefore consistently described the inner realms in terms of the most beautiful, fabulous and enduring things of this world. But to know what those worlds are really like, the individual must go there and find out for himself. One can note, however, that only the fifth realm is described as self-existent and eternal, and this is certainly consistent with the teachings of later mystics of the East.

Five Trees in Heaven

The Manichaeans have often been linked with the *Gospel of Thomas*, the *Acts of Thomas* and other 'Thomas' literature, and in our search for Jesus' description of the inner heavens, there is an intriguing passage in the *Gospel of Thomas* which deserves attention. But first we need to backtrack, momentarily.

In the *Ascension of Isaiah*, the writer describes how he has heard the "voices" of all the heavens during his ascent. This is precisely in accord with the teachings of the higher mystics. They say that as the soul ascends, the Music of the Word is heard differently, often being likened to different musical instruments. Within the great mansions of creation, the Sound of the Word can be heard resounding, and though the Word is one, in each realm its sound is different. Just as a river is one, yet makes a different sound when it bubbles over the rocks, descends over a waterfall or flows through the plains, so too is the divine Sound heard differently at different points in its journey into creation.

Looking at creation as consisting of five main regions, the sounds of the inner realms have sometimes – naturally enough – been called the Five Sounds and there is an interesting section in the *Gospel of Thomas* which seems to refer to them in this manner. Jesus said:

> If you become my disciples
>   and listen to my words (my Word?),
>   these stones will minister to you.
> For there are Five Trees for you in Paradise
>   which remain undisturbed summer and winter
>   and whose leaves do not fall.
> Whoever becomes acquainted with them
>   will not experience death.
>
> *Gospel of Thomas 19, NHS20 p.61*

Jesus says that a true disciple who follows the path of the Word and implicitly obeys the instructions of his Master, becomes so much at one with God and all of His creation, through attunement to the Word, that all of nature comes to help him in his path through life. Hence, he says, "these stones will minister to you".

Explaining the matter further, Jesus goes on to refer to "Five Trees for you in Paradise". The use of the term 'Trees' would seem to be a reference to the Tree of Life, a common metaphor for the Word, as we have seen. Consequently, the "Five Trees" refers to the Sound as it is heard in each of the five main regions of creation. The fact that their leaves do not fall either in winter or in summer alludes to the continuous, life-giving presence of the Word in these realms. Naturally, therefore, when a person is in contact with these Five Trees or Five Sounds, he is in touch with the essence of everything and his life becomes of a fundamentally different character to what it previously was.

Jesus then concludes by saying that a soul who comes into inner, mystic contact with these Five Trees will not experience death. Now this is a strange saying, echoing a number of similar statements in the canonical gospels about the avoidance of death, for Jesus and his disciples lived no more than a normal span of human life, perhaps less. What then, did he mean by such statements?

For an answer, we have to seek the help of other mystics, many of whom have referred to this world as the world of death, because all that is born here must die. And that is the crux of the matter. Before there can be a death, there has to be a birth. Conversely, once there has been a birth, there is bound to be a death. So to avoid death, it is necessary to avoid birth.

Many mystics, however, have pointed out that in the normal run of things the two go on and on, one following the other, in a cycle of repeated deaths and rebirths. So when Jesus says that "whoever becomes acquainted with" or gains mystic knowledge or experience of these Five Trees or Five Sounds, "will not experience death", it seems that he is speaking in a veiled way about reincarnation, probably another facet of the mysteries taught only to his initiates. But this is a topic associated with the realm and rule of Satan, a subject we must now address.

NOTES AND REFERENCES

1. *eg. Mark* 3:22; also Morton Smith, *Jesus the Magician.*
2. *Isaiah* 60:8.
3. *Malachi* 2:10.
4. *CPM* 58 p.51.
5. *Matthew* 4:8.
6. *Ephesians* 3:10.
7. *Colossians* 2:9-10.
8. *Colossians* 2:15.
9. *Zostrianos* 129, *NHL* p.430.
10. *John* 14:2.
11. *John* 3:11.
12. *2 Corinthians* 12:1ff.

CHAPTER ELEVEN

Sin and Satan

God, Evil and Satan

One of the greatest puzzles and paradoxes presented to thinking and observant people is that a God who is said to be all love, all peace and all bliss should have designed a creation in which there is so much hatred, discord and suffering. No one can deny the presence of good and bad in this world. There is love and hatred, joy and misery, honesty and deception, violence and harmony, tolerance and prejudice, contentment and dissatisfaction, kindness and malevolence, healing and killing, living and dying, and a great deal more of the same ilk in the spectrum of human life. Even the other species which inhabit the planet, great or small, live in a state of continual tension. Their moments of happiness – if such there be – are tempered at all times by the vicissitudes of life. One creature takes another for its food in a continual round of eat and be eaten. Life is precious to all, yet death is so easily and rapidly encountered.

Even people who seem to be living in a state of comfort and ease harbour their secret agonies. The wealthy man fears the loss of his money and assets. He is afraid of fire, flood, thieves, the tax man and worse. He is worried that ill health and lawsuits will eat up his resources. The beautiful and the handsome are distressed by the discovery of a wrinkle or a receding hairline. The famous are concerned about their status in the public eye, so notably fickle. The powerful and influential know in their hearts that no one stays in power for ever and the man in power today may be the man dismissed, the man in gaol or the man assassinated tomorrow. Acclaim can so easily turn into disgrace and they live in fear that one day their turn will also come.

The poor man fares no better. He is worried about the source of his next meal. He has no resources to spend should he fall sick. He is constantly concerned about how he is going to support his family and find the bare necessities of life. And the lives of the rich or poor alike can be made a misery by an angry, vindictive or unfaithful spouse. Ill health, old age and senile dementia are no respecters of social status or wealth. The apparently affluent man finds himself in poverty when his debts outstrip his income or his investments fail.

No one has ever lived a life of total happiness or of unmitigated misery and suffering. Some have more of one and less of another, and the balance can change as life goes by. Moreover, happiness is usually short-lived, for the human mind tires of everything in time, often quite rapidly. Even long-cherished goals, achieved after prolonged and concerted effort, fail to bring the happiness anticipated.

The problem is that man seeks happiness in the pleasure of material things which have no permanency, but change constantly. Consequently, they are unable to provide any durable happiness, for the source of happiness is constantly shifting and altering. Furthermore, the mind itself moves constantly and what satisfies it today fails to do so tomorrow. In fact, all pleasure and happiness can be satiated, giving place to boredom or aversion.

A person has only to read the newspapers, watch television or make an honest appraisal of their own life to know that existence in this world is a mixture of pleasure and pain, with little if any real inner happiness or bliss. The question remains, therefore, why has God who is all love made such a maelstrom of a creation in which neither the happiness nor the misery bear any relationship to the utter love and bliss which are said to be His own inherent nature? Why is it that He seems to have utterly failed to share His best qualities with the souls inhabiting this world? It even seems as if the very fabric of life here precludes the possibility of divine love, supreme bliss and eternal beatitude.

If God is the Supreme Lord, it means that He is ultimately responsible for everything that happens in His creation. If He is within everything and is the primal doer within all things, then He must also be the creator of misery, suffering, hatred and all the rest. If He is not, then He is not supreme. How then has this state of affairs transpired?

Mystics and gnostics have described the creation as being arranged in a vast hierarchy with all substations drawing their power from the Supreme Lord, yet acting autonomously, so to speak, within their own realms. Just as each individual person in this world functions as if they had free will and a separate identity of their own, but yet are all bound together in one whole by universal forces and laws of nature, so too do the rulers and administrators of the higher realms act within the will of the Supreme, yet with seeming independence.

In this hierarchy of creation, there is one ruler who affects our human lives more than all the rest. Mystics have depicted him (or 'it') as the architect of all the problems which beset the souls inhabiting this world. We have already spoken of this power as the Negative Power or the Universal Mind, but over the ages, this ruler has been called by almost as many names as God Himself. It is our suggestion that it is to this power that Jesus is referring when he speaks of Satan or the Devil.

In the gospels, the negative force in human life is called Satan, Beelzebub, the Devil, the Prince of the World, the Prince of Devils, the Strong Man, the Enemy, the Adversary and the Wicked One. Other common terms were Belial, Beliar, the Evil One, the Prince of Darkness, the Wolf, the Serpent and many more. Mostly, these were not names of Jesus' invention but had been used by many mystics and others of the past. In fact, the gospel writers use the various names according to their own particular fancy. Thus, for example, in the parable of the sower, where Mark has Jesus refer to Satan, Matthew has him talk of the Wicked One, while Luke speaks of the Devil.

Although there is no doubt that Jesus taught the existence of Satan, very little is recorded in the gospels of his teachings concerning the Devil's nature, origins and how he functions in this world, making it the way it is. He is simply mentioned by Jesus, here and there. It is not surprising, therefore, that the early fathers had no fixed teaching on the subject and opinions varied, while later Christian teaching is somewhat confused and people's ideas concerning Satan are much at variance. Satan is often described as a 'fallen angel' who disobeyed God, for example. Yet there is no support for this concept amongst the sayings of Jesus nor does it explain the processes by which Satan influences human thought and behaviour or why God is seemingly so unable or unwilling to control him. The matter therefore remains pretty much of a mystery and many theologians, ancient and modern, have altogether avoided discussion of the Devil's actual nature as too much of an embarrassment to rationality.

A study of the early Christian and allied literature, however, together with a knowledge of the teachings given by many other mystics on this subject, helps to clarify our understanding. They have pointed out that it is this Negative Power and a multitude of lesser powers within his domain who are responsible for the administration of this world. Indeed, this power is the governor of more than just this world; he is the administrator and ruler of three worlds or realms – the physical, astral and causal regions. The Negative Power – or Satan, if we consider him to be the same – is thus the ruler of the heavenly realms which the advocates of most religions aspire to enter after death.

It must be understood that we are dealing here with cosmic processes of vast proportions and all tendencies to anthropomorphize both God and Satan are purely figures of speech. We are speaking of powers and forces that lie way beyond our ken as human beings and the only means of really comprehending them is direct, personal, mystic experience. Satan is no more a red-faced devil with pointed ears and a forked tail, living amongst sulphurous fires, than God is a kindly old man with a long beard inhabiting a damp cloud.

Now, the Christian concept of the Devil or Satan is essentially that of a being who is entirely dark and evil. Even traditional Jewish thought at the time of Jesus saw Satan in this way. He is envisaged primarily as the ever-present tempter of humanity in this world and as the ruler of hell where souls are punished and burnt for their sins. But the Negative Power of which mystics speak is of an altogether different nature. For them, the Negative Power is the source of all diversity within the realms of mind and matter. He is the originator – in a sense, the creator – of *everything* in this world. He is responsible for the veil of duality and separation which has been thrown over the pristine oneness and purity of God. Duality implies both good and bad, light as well as darkness. The one cannot exist without the other, for they are two sides of the one coin. The good and the light of Satan's realm are hence relative and not to be mistaken for the incomparable and pure love, light and bliss of God.

The Negative Power only moulds and projects the primal energy of God. He has no reality independent of God. As a consequence, for as long as Satan or the Devil is perceived as entirely negative and separate from God, his role in creation will remain a paradox. But as soon as he is seen as an expression or a stepping down of the Lord's power, then his function and existence become more intelligible.

The early Christian gnostics clearly spoke of this power as the chief *archon* or ruler of this and other worlds and they called him by such names as the Demiurge, Samael and Ialdabaoth. Perhaps in deference to Jewish and early Christian belief, some gnostics of the Valentinian school did differentiate between the Demiurge and the Devil, teaching that the Devil was created by the Demiurge as one of his subordinate angels or *archons* and was the ruler of this material world only. The second-century Marcion, and probably other gnostic Christians, also taught the same. But either way, the Devil or Satan, as the ruler of this world, was seen as the creator of *all* its characteristics – its apparent good as well as its more obvious imperfections. In fact, the gnostics considered the entire material world to be inherently negative or 'evil' in the sense that it is a prison for the soul, keeping it separate from God.

Jesus and Paul also speak of Satan as the prince or ruler of this world, which would include both its good and bad, and there are plenty of places where the gospels as well as the gnostic and other literature support the view that Jesus taught a far wider understanding of Satan than Christians now hold or that the Jews held at that time.

Generally speaking, scholars have classified gnostic teachings as fundamentally dualistic, since they sometimes appear to promote the idea of two eternally separate gods or powers who vie for the control of this world. Some gnostic schools may indeed have come to believe in this, as did later Zoroastrianism, but this is not what the mystics themselves have taught. In many cases, scholars and others have been too hasty in judging all references to such a power as rigorously dualistic. When correctly understood, the idea is actually less dualistic than the traditional concept of Satan, for in the mystic scheme of things the Negative Power or Demiurge has a definite role to play, given to him by the Supreme Lord.

It may be argued that this view of the Negative Power is so different from Christian and Jewish concepts of Satan that it is confusing to use the name Satan. This is readily agreed, but the problem then remains as to which name should be used? Ideally, since we are in search of Jesus' teachings, the term used should be the one most frequently employed by him. But the gospels are not so obliging as to make it clear what name or names Jesus actually favoured and whether he differentiated between the Devil and the Demiurge. We have therefore used the more general 'Negative Power', the more specific 'Universal Mind' and, in relating the subject to Jesus' teachings, we have used the terms 'Satan' and the 'Devil'. To utilize gnostic terms such as the 'Demiurge' would only cause further confusion, since they are too unfamiliar to people of the present time.

Part of the misunderstanding has arisen from the concept of Satan as pure evil, a belief which has traditionally permeated much of Christian thought. It has given rise, for example, to the conventional Christian concept of sin as something entirely negative and evil. Mystics, on the other hand, have viewed sin from a far wider and less emotive perspective. To them, the good and bad of this world are inextricably bound together as dual aspects of 'sin', the one existing by virtue of the other. The pure goodness or perfection of God is beyond both and there is plenty of evidence in the gospels that Jesus saw things in this way, too.

A further extension of this thought has also given rise to the Christian attitude which sees the individual as all bad. We are to consider ourselves as entirely 'sinful', having no good within ourselves. We are "miserable offenders" and "there is no health in us"[1] as the liturgy has it. Not even God is thought to be within – He is somewhere without. Mystics see this as an essentially negative, deeply stultifying and even self-indulgent or self-pitying attitude of mind. They see the soul as the real self and as being of the same essence of God. Man is separated from God because of his mind, the false self and agent of the Negative Power. *This* self or mind, it is true, is of the Negative Power, of Satan, but the life force of the soul within is beyond the play of duality and is a drop of the pure love of God. If we repeat to ourselves that we are comprised of nothing but sin and evil, we only emphasize and give reality to the illusion of the mind. It is actually a trick of the mind and plays directly into the hands of Satan, giving reality to the false sense of self at the expense of what is real. Moreover, when the mind becomes genuinely interested in spiritual evolution, it becomes a friend to the soul and no longer an enemy.

We have equated Satan with the Universal Mind and though the latter is not a term used by Jesus or any of the early Christians, it is useful to us in our modern age as a means of understanding how the Negative Power influences everything within his domain. All souls living within the physical, astral and causal regions function through what they consider to be individual minds and individual bodies. There is a causal body and a causal mind corresponding to the causal realm; an astral body and an astral mind corresponding to the astral realm; a physical body and physical mind corresponding to the physical realm. These bodies and minds, like the realms themselves, are all aspects of the greater or Universal Mind – that is, of Satan. Consequently, the mind and the body can be considered as agents or aspects of Satan.

At the human level, the mind includes memory, intellect, emotion, thought, foresight, discrimination, intuition and all other mental faculties, energies and tendencies. This encompasses human weaknesses, strengths and everything else that we recognize as human, all these being expressed through the body and its various sensory and motor functions. In fact, the body itself is really an outward expression or manifestation of mental tendencies and characteristics, all very much a part of Satan's system.

Explained through a mixture of myth, metaphor and metaphysics, Satan's role of keeping souls away from God has always been a fundamental aspect of gnostic teachings and has been described by many other mystics, too, throughout the ages. They have all said that Satan's 'brief' or 'instructions' from the Lord is to preserve the overall balance of creation, keeping souls imprisoned within his domain, preventing their escape and return to God.

It is understandably difficult to comprehend how the Devil could be acting within the overall will of God. The problem is an ancient one and the paradox was the source of a question put to Peter in the *Clementine Homilies* during a discussion on the origins of evil and of Satan:

> When Peter said this, Lazarus, who also was one of his followers, said: "Explain to us the harmony, how it can be reasonable that the Wicked One should be appointed by the righteous God to be the punisher of the impious...?"
>
> And Peter said: "I indeed allow that the Evil One does no evil, inasmuch as he is accomplishing the law given to him. And although he has an evil disposition, yet through fear of God he does nothing unjustly; but, accusing the teachers of truth so as to entrap the unwary, he is himself named the accuser (the Devil)."
>
> *Clementine Homilies XX:IX, CH p.320*

Peter simply states the matter to be so, for there is no fully satisfying intellectual answer to a question which is essentially that of why God has made such a creation. The problem is intellectually intractable, for if God is the Supreme Power and Creator, He must have created Satan too. Or, taking the situation as it is now, if God is entirely opposed to the activities of Satan, why should He permit his continued existence? Satan's very existence seems to presume that God actually needs him in order to manifest His creation. Considered logically, this would mean that God is the ultimate author of sin, something which is difficult to comprehend. It would also mean that God does not want all souls to be with Him, at least at the present time. These considerations may seem paradoxical enough but actually the problem is even more complex for the question of individual free will, real or apparent, is also involved, as well as the need to determine what it is which is held to be free – the soul, the mind or the body?

It is no surprise that there are no completely satisfying answers to all these conundrums, and mystics have summarized the matter by pointing out that the human mind cannot comprehend God's purpose and design. But as long as God wishes the show to go on, Satan must continue with his allotted task, for were all souls to return to God, then the creation would come to an end.

Satan's role of keeping souls captive is accomplished very simply by occupying their attention with the varied phenomena and activities of his creation. Through the senses, the attention of the mind is held inexorably upon the play of life in this world. So effective is this process that many souls become so absorbed in the sensory world that they refuse to believe that anything else exists, even coming to consider their own minds as nothing more than an expression of the material forces which they perceive through their senses. Souls thus remain in prison because of their absorption with the activities and 'amenities' provided here. This is why the gnostics have described the material world as entirely evil, for whether good or bad, like a man struggling in quicksand, actions of any kind only serve to hold the soul here more securely.

The soul, the drop of the divine ocean of God, on its descent from Him, enters Satan's realm, the region of the Universal Mind, and is equipped with an individual mind and causal body, losing its pristine consciousness of God. One of the gnostic terms for the mind was thus the "counterfeit spirit", for it leads the pure soul astray. The mind itself, however, is not independent. Descending to the physical universe, it is drawn out into the world of matter, through attraction to the bodily senses and motor functions, and dwells here. Though the soul should control the mind and the mind should control the senses, in practice, the soul is actually dominated by the mind and the mind is dominated by the senses. But how does the mind – the Negative Power or Satan – maintain such punitive command?

Sin and the Law of Cause and Effect

Satan or the Universal Mind is the most super-powerful, ultra-logical, mega-computer in existence and there is one supreme principle operating throughout 'his' realms: causality – a multi-dimensional, multi-faceted, super-dynamic 'law' of cause and effect. Just as the film in a movie projector splits the white light of the lamp into a multiplicity of coloured images upon a screen, so does the Universal Mind split the oneness of God's creative Power into myriads of dancing, causally interconnected 'parts'. Thus, whatever happens within the domain of the Universal Mind takes place for some 'reason'. There is an immediate cause behind it. And in their turn, all events and actions have their corresponding effects. This is the primal law of the Universal Mind and is clearly reflected in this world of matter where all the laws of nature understood by man are observed to conform to this principle. At the back of everything that happens here, there is a cause, indeed a fabric of causes, themselves being a part of an endless, complex network or labyrinth of causes and effects.

In the world of matter, everyone acknowledges the existence of this law, consciously or unconsciously. What is not so readily observable or known is that it functions at the level of the mind as well as at the material level. Whatever somebody does, it originates in their mind, however fleeting their thought or mental intention may have been. Whatever happens to a person from without similarly affects their mind, to a greater or lesser extent. Now, all mental activity leaves its impressions upon the mind and these impressions bear fruit. They too become the cause of further thought and action. The mental impressions of childhood, for example, play a major part in determining the character and behaviour of the later adult. The mind is therefore an integral part of the tangled skein of cause and effect.

Now, this law admits of no exception. Nothing is forgotten or forgiven. Whatever goes into the mind must find outward expression in one way or another. Whatever actions a person performs must find corresponding reactions at a subsequent stage of the drama. Yet, during the course of an individual's life, the opportunity for such expression may hardly be given. Suppose a person develops a strong association with someone who then dies, so that there has been no opportunity for the impressions – positive or negative – in both their minds to bear fruit. Or suppose someone has desires which are never fulfilled. As a result, they die with these unfulfilled desires still active within their minds. There is then 'unfinished business' remaining in the mind. In fact, in the course of one lifetime, there is often very little opportunity for all of a person's thoughts and actions to bear fruit in an appropriate manner. The individual therefore dies with all this accumulated mental debris still awaiting expression. There are thus a multitude of potential causes all awaiting their accumulative effects.

This is Satan's trump card for holding souls at the physical level, for there is no other way for these impressions to bear fruit than for the soul and mind to reincarnate, to take birth in another body, to return to the stage where the play was set in motion. After death, the immortal and eternal soul is accompanied by its mind. Only the body dies, returning to the matter whence it came. But usually, in no time at all, the soul takes another body, drawn to it inexorably by the attachments and inclinations of the mind, driven by the overwhelming law of cause and effect. All actions and all desires thus bear fruit in future lives. Eastern mystics have called this the law of *karma* and they have described its processes in great detail.

Now the maintenance of his sphere, keeping all souls within his realm, is the role given to Satan by the Lord and he is most assiduous in his duty, so to speak. And we can see now, how he does it. Satan is the power or ruler who keeps souls in the labyrinth of birth and death. He is the mind accompanying all souls who dwell within his realm. Under the influence of their past, souls take birth. And while living out their lives, they create new impressions – according to the way they live – which have their effects in future lives.

In Christianity, bad actions and bad thoughts are called 'sin'. The term, however, also needs discussion for, according to the mystics, both good and bad actions bear fruit. The law of cause and effect is not designed purely for the punishment of the wicked. Good actions and good desires result in better lives in the future, while bad actions result in worse lives, but the law of cause and effect is always satisfied. It is a law of strict justice and judgment, functioning automatically just as surely as a rubber ball thrown against a wall will rebound.

Sin is generally considered to consist of only bad actions and thoughts. But this is just one side of the coin. People talk of 'sinful deeds' and 'sinful thoughts', though actually all actions and thoughts – good or bad – leave their mark upon the mind. Like Satan, the term 'sin' has accumulated such religious overtones around it, as something entirely bad and associated in the minds of many with feelings of guilt, shame and remorse, that it becomes difficult to think clearly about it. The general understanding of sin includes only a fraction of the whole affair and needs to be considerably expanded.

It can be said that sin and its consequences are of three kinds. There is 'destiny', comprising both the framework and a great deal of the details of the present life, moulded from the reactions and expressions of past actions and desires. Then there are 'new' actions and desires incurred in the present life, out of which future lives are created. But perhaps the most significant of all are the 'stored' sins.

The wealth of impressions formed on the mind during the course of one life is usually so great that only a small fraction are required to make up the destiny of the next. The remainder are stored deep within the mind, an ever-increasing burden of past sins which weigh down the soul. From this storehouse of sin some elements of future lives may be drawn, but for the most part the mountain only goes on increasing as life succeeds life. And it is this burden of the past which contributes the major barrier to the soul in its attempt to free itself from the mind. If these sins were removed, the soul would fly up to God like a skyrocket. The pure soul has thus become like a precious jewel encased in mud. As the writer of the Nag Hammadi *Gospel of Philip* puts it:

> When the pearl is cast down into the mud
>   it does not lose its value,
> Or if it is anointed with balsam oil
>   will it become more precious.
> But it always has value in the eyes of its owner.
> Compare the sons of God: wherever they may be,
>   they retain their value in the eyes of their Father.
>
> *Gospel of Philip 62, NHS20 p.165, GS p.337*

The only escape from this burden of sin and the otherwise endless round of birth and death is the salvation offered by an enlightened Saviour, a mystic teacher who is one with the Word and who has been appointed by God to come to this world and liberate those souls who are ready to go. Salvation, therefore – from a mystic point of view – means being saved from the realm of birth and death, from the domain of Satan, the Universal Mind, and being taken back to God, the original home of the soul.

Hints and suggestions of many aspects of this universal and perennial mystic teaching are to be found throughout Jesus' sayings and parables in the gospels, as well as elsewhere in the Old and New Testaments. And amongst the early Christian and allied literature, particularly in the writings stemming from the gnostic stream of Christian thought, it is the prevalent teaching. Consequently, in the absence of any definitive and well-presented exposition of Jesus' teachings on the subject, one is tempted to presume that since so much else in his teachings conforms to the universal teachings of all other mystics, that Jesus taught this principle, too. The evidence, as we will see, is considerable.

The Enemy Within

Despite the lack of anything clear-cut, a great deal can be determined of Jesus' teaching on the matter. Where, for example, did he consider Satan to be? The answer is readily determined from a perusal of his sayings and parables. In his parable of the sower, for instance, the Sower or Saviour sows the seed of the Word in the disciple. That is to say, he initiates or baptizes the soul. But some seed, says Jesus, falls by the wayside and before it can even begin to germinate, it is eaten up by the birds. In Matthew, Jesus' explanation reads:

> When any one heareth the word of the kingdom,
>   and understandeth it not,
>   then cometh the Wicked One,
>   and catcheth away that which was sown in his heart.
> This is he which received seed by the wayside.
>
> *Matthew 13:18-19*

He means that there are those souls who are initiated by the Saviour and hear what he has to say. At the time, they are more or less convinced about his teachings, but they still have such strong desires for worldly living that they are almost immediately swept away into the affairs of the world and entirely forget about him. These desires, says Jesus, originate with the "Wicked One", with Satan.

Similarly, Jesus tells another parable about a farmer who sows "good seed" in his field, unmixed with any weed seeds. He says:

> The kingdom of heaven is likened unto a man
>   which sowed good seed in his field:
> But while men slept, his enemy came
>   and sowed tares among the wheat, and went his way.
> But when the blade was sprung up, and brought forth fruit,
>   then appeared the tares also.
>
> So the servants of the householder came and said unto him,
>   "Sir, didst not thou sow good seed in thy field?
>   From whence then hath it tares?"
> He said unto them, "An enemy hath done this."
>
> *Matthew 13:24-28*

And the explanation Jesus gives is this:

> He that soweth the good seed is the Son of man;
>   the field is the world;
>   the good seed are the children of the kingdom;
> But the tares are the children of the Wicked One;
>   the enemy that sowed them is the Devil.
>
> *Matthew 13:37-39*

The Master initiates a soul: he "sowed good seed in his field". But the disciple still harbours worldly desires in his mind and does not give full attention to the spiritual path. These desires and bad actions therefore grow together along with his spirituality, which is consequently choked to some extent. And these desires and bad actions, which hinder spiritual progress, Jesus says, originate with the Devil; they are the "children of the Wicked One". This is the meaning understood in the *Acts of Thomas*, when Judas Thomas prays:

> Let not my seed of wheat be changed for tares out of thy land;
>> let not the Enemy carry it away
>> and mingle his own tares therewith;
> For thy land verily receiveth not his tares,
>> neither indeed can they be laid up in thine houses.
>
> *Acts of Thomas 145, ANT p.428*

From these examples alone it can be seen that Jesus did not consider the Devil to be an external power, any more than he taught that God is outside. Satan, like God, dwells within man and is responsible for his misconduct and his wayward mind. For the mind itself is an agent of the Universal Mind and the fabric of the entire world is within its grasp. Man's everyday thought, conduct and course of life is largely determined by the mind. It is therefore from within the mind of man that sin proceeds. It can be seen that Jesus taught this principle, too, for in St Matthew, he says:

> Not that which goeth into the mouth defileth a man;
>> but that which cometh out of the mouth,
>> this defileth a man.
>
> *Matthew 15:11*

And:

> Do not ye yet understand, that whatsoever entereth
>> in at the mouth goeth into the belly,
>> and is cast out into the draught?
> But those things which proceed out of the mouth
>> come forth from the heart; and they defile the man.
> For out of the heart proceed evil thoughts, murders, adulteries,
>> fornications, thefts, false witness, blasphemies:
> These are the things which defile a man:
>> but to eat with unwashen hands defileth not a man.
>
> *Matthew 15:17-20*

Jesus is referring to the complex Jewish food rituals and various ablutions that were considered essential for spiritual cleanliness. He points out that everything sinful comes from within and has nothing to do with external rituals.

Again in Matthew, Jesus uses the examples of a fruit tree and of a viper to explain that whatever is the nature of something within itself, the same will be expressed outwardly:

> Either make the tree good, and his fruit good;
> or else make the tree corrupt, and his fruit corrupt:
> For the tree is known by his fruit.
> O generation of vipers, how can ye, being evil,
> speak good things?

> For out of the abundance of the heart the mouth speaketh.
> A good man out of the good treasure of the heart
> bringeth forth good things:
> And an evil man out of the evil treasure
> bringeth forth evil things.
>
> *Matthew 12:33-35*

He then adds that there is nothing so small that it is not taken into account upon the "Day of Judgment":

> But I say unto you, that every idle word that men shall speak,
> they shall give account thereof in the Day of Judgment.
> For by thy words thou shalt be justified,
> and by thy words thou shalt be condemned.
>
> *Matthew 12:36-37*

The "Day of Judgment" is the time of death, when each soul is automatically judged according to the sum total of its deeds, good or bad, small or large. If a person has wasted their life in frivolous pursuits and idle gossip then they will be judged accordingly and will take another birth that befits their deeds and desires. If a person has performed good deeds, then they can say that they have justified being in the human body. But for a mystic, good deeds means spiritual practice, worshipping the Father in Spirit and in Truth, attaching the mind and soul to the Word of God within. Otherwise good deeds are as binding to this world as bad ones. The one results in golden chains, the other in iron chains. But in both cases, the soul remains fettered to the body.

Echoing these words from St Matthew, in one of the Coptic apocryphal texts, Jesus tells his disciples to teach people that they will be called to give account of *all* their deeds, "good or evil":

> A just balance and a just measure are those
> 　　wherewith my Father will take account with you....
> A single word of jest that ye shall speak
> 　　shall be required of you.
> Even as no one can escape death,
> 　　so no one can escape those things which he hath done,
> 　　whether it be good or evil.
>
> *Death of Joseph I, CAG p.131*

A story in the *Acts of John* further emphasizes the point that everything comes from within. Here, a young man has killed his father and taken as a lover the wife of another man. The youth, realizing his excess, in his remorse then mutilates himself. But later on, John points out to him that it is Satan who has put it into his mind both to kill his father and become a victim to lust as well as to physically attack his "unruly members". And he adds that it is not the bodily organs in themselves which are sinful, but the thought and desire that lies behind them:

> But John said to him, "He that put it into thine heart, young man, to kill thy father and become the adulterer of another man's wife, the same made thee think it a right deed to take away also the unruly members. But thou shouldst have done away, not with the place of sin, but the thought which through those members showed itself harmful: for it is not the instruments that are injurious, but the unseen springs by which every shameful emotion is stirred and cometh to light.
>
> "Repent therefore, my child, of this fault, and having learnt the wiles of Satan thou shalt have God to help thee in all the necessities of thy soul."
>
> *Acts of John 54, ANT p.240*

Satan is thus equated with the power of the mind. Satan, like God, dwells within and operates from there, and the spiritual battle is to be fought within.

Incidentally, castration and mutilation, even self-mutilation, were not uncommon in those days. Eunuchs were a common part of royal households and often occupied positions of trust and authority. The great Christian teacher, Origen, in an excess of youthful zeal and in an attempt to curb his desires, also mutilated himself, an act which

he later regretted. But Jesus points out the truth of the matter, when
he says:

> There are some eunuchs,
>> which were so born from their mother's womb:
> And there are some eunuchs,
>> which were made eunuchs of men:
> And there be eunuchs,
>> which have made themselves eunuchs
>> for the kingdom of heaven's sake.
> He that is able to receive it,
>> let him receive it.
>
> *Matthew 19:12*

Some people are born in this way, he says. Others are made so by others. But the highest eunuchs are those who become celibate for the
sake of God-realization. This is the highest "eunuch" of all, for it is far
easier to change outward appearances than to control the mind and
the desires which lie within it.

A Servant of Sin

Satan, conceived as the Universal Mind, is a prevailing power in this
world and everyone is under its influence through the promptings of
their own mind. That is why Jesus called him the ruler or prince of
this world. This may be hard to swallow, but mystics have repeated it
over and over again, in many different ways. All souls in this world are
thus the slaves of Satan, the slaves of the mind, and the slaves of sin.
Only a truly enlightened soul is free from the power of the mind and
free from sin, and only those who come under the protection of an
enlightened teacher and are mystically baptized by him, can be made free.
Jesus makes this very clear in a number of places. There is a long section
in St John, for instance, where – according to the story – he is in conversation with some Jews, some of whom believe in him and others not:

> Then said Jesus to those Jews which believed on him,
> "If ye continue in my Word,
>> then are ye my disciples indeed;
> And ye shall know the Truth,
>> and the Truth shall make you free."

They answered him,
"We be Abraham's seed,
    and were never in bondage to any man:
    how sayest thou, 'Ye shall be made free?'"

Jesus answered them,
"Verily, verily, I say unto you,
    whosoever committeth sin is the servant of sin.
And the servant abideth not in the house for ever:
    but the Son abideth ever.
If the Son therefore shall make you free,
    ye shall be free indeed."

John 8:31-36

He says that only those who continue to follow his teachings ("my word") and who persist with their spiritual practice ("who continue in my Word"), are his true disciples. Because only through that practice can they experience the mystic "Truth", another synonym for the Word. Only that Word can take them beyond the realm of Satan, freeing or liberating them from his grasp.

But – in John's dialogue – the disciples respond that they are Jews, having Abraham as their ancestral father. They are not slaves and never have been. How then do they have need of being set free? Jesus observes that those who commit sin, who commit actions in this world, are automatically bound by the consequences of those actions. They are bound by the law of cause and effect, by the law of *karma*. They are therefore the servants or slaves of sin.

He then adds that such a servant "abideth not in the house for ever". The "house" is the body and souls are forced to move from house to house, from body to body, under the influence of their sins. Only the Son, only the Master, "abideth ever". The Master, the Son, lives eternally, not in a physical form, of course, but spiritually. He is free from the dictates of sin and does not have to move from house to house, from body to body.

"If the Son therefore shall make you free, ye shall be free indeed." If a soul comes under the protection of a Master who is free, then that soul can also be made free, can be liberated from sin, from birth and death, from Satan, and can be taken back to the Father. This is what Jesus meant when he said:

Come unto me, all ye that labour and are heavy laden,
    and I will give you rest.

> Take my yoke upon you, and learn of me;
>> for I am meek and lowly in heart:
>> and ye shall find rest unto your souls.
> For my yoke is easy, and my burden is light.
>> *Matthew 11:28-30*

Since a Master has no sins of his own, he is genuinely free and is in a position to help others.

Your Father the Devil

Jesus then continues, speaking presumably to other Jews who were not his disciples:

> "I know that ye are Abraham's seed; but ye seek to kill me,
>> because my Word hath no place in you.
> I speak that which I have seen with my Father:
>> and ye do that which ye have seen with your father."

> They answered and said unto him,
> "Abraham is our father."

> Jesus saith unto them,
> "If ye were Abraham's children,
>> ye would do the works of Abraham.
> But now ye seek to kill me,
>> a man that hath told you the Truth,
>> which I have heard of God: this did not Abraham.
> Ye do the deeds of your father."
>> *John 8:37-41*

Jesus says that he realizes that they have Abraham as their ancestor, but Abraham was also a great prophet or mystic and if they were truly Abraham's children, spiritually speaking, then they would act as Abraham had taught. Yet, he says, you are plotting to kill me, something which Abraham would never have done. They do not recognize who Jesus really is because "my Word hath no place in you", because they are neither initiated by him into the Word nor are they destined to become his initiates. Although Jesus has come from the Father, is speaking only of his own personal, inner experience when teaching them, and is relating only what is true, they do not believe him, because "ye do the deeds of your father". And he goes on to explain who their father is:

> Then said they to him,
> "We be not born of fornication;
> 　we have one father, even God."
>
> Jesus said unto them,
> "If God were your father, ye would love me:
> 　for I proceeded forth and came from God;
> 　neither came I of myself, but He sent me.
> Why do ye not understand my speech?
> Even because ye cannot hear my Word.
>
> "Ye are of your father the Devil,
> 　and the lusts of your father ye will do.
> He was a murderer from the beginning,
> 　and abode not in the Truth,
> 　because there is no Truth in him.
> When he speaketh a lie, he speaketh of his own:
> 　for he is a liar, and the father of it."
>
> John 8:42-45

Jesus says that he has come to this world, not of his own will, but because he has been sent by God – "I proceeded forth and came from God." Consequently, he is truly doing God's will and those who are really seeking God will recognize and believe in him – "ye would love me". The fact that they did not recognize him means that they were in the grip of Satan, for it is either Satan or the Supreme Lord who oversees the progress of a soul through life. This is the point that Jesus is making – there are only two possible 'fathers' – God or the Devil.

Jesus therefore points out to them that although they think that they are following God's will, in fact they are entirely in the grip of their own mind, in the grip of Satan. So their father may be more accurately described as Satan, not the Supreme Lord, for they are doing Satan's will, not God's will.

This is the case with everyone in this world. We are all deceived by our own minds, by Satan. In fact, the entire world is a deception practised upon the soul by this Negative Power. Hence, Jesus calls him a "liar" and the father of all lies. He is a "murderer" because he murders the mystic Truth, obscuring Reality under the veil of illusion, impermanence and reflection. He is also a "murderer" because he has brought all souls into the realm where death is a certain reality. He "murders" or takes the life of all creatures, then sends them back into rebirth and takes their life over again. Nobody could be a greater murderer than that! Jesus then continues:

> "And because I tell you the Truth, ye believe me not.
> Which of you convinceth (convicteth) me of sin?
> And if I say the truth, why do ye not believe me?
> He that is of God heareth God's words (Word):
> > ye therefore hear them (it) not,
> > because ye are not of God."
>
> *John 8:45-47*

No one, Jesus says, can show him to be a victim of sin, yet they still do not believe him. This is because they are completely under the control of Satan and when they are told the truth, they automatically reject it. Only those who are destined for a particular mystic teacher will really understand and accept him. Others will always have a multitude of reasons why they think him to be wrong. This is the way the Negative Power – the mind – functions.

> Then answered the Jews, and said unto him,
> "Say we not well that thou art a Samaritan,
> > and hast a devil?"
>
> Jesus answered, "I have not a devil;
> > but I honour my Father, and ye do dishonour me.
> And I seek not mine own glory:
> > there is one that seeketh and judgeth."
>
> *John 8:48-50*

The people then accuse Jesus of having a devil inside him, a common belief of those times, used to explain a wide variety of diseases, conditions and attitudes of mind. Interestingly, the belief is not so far from the truth in an odd kind of a way, for all diseases, mental conditions and so on arise from the sins of the past by the law of cause and effect, mediated through normal physical processes. And since these are all under the ultimate jurisdiction of the Negative Power, the Devil, they can be described as his 'devils'. But this is a subject we will be discussing later, in somewhat greater detail.

Jesus replies in the language of the times, looking at their comment from a higher point of view. He is not of the Devil, he reaffirms, but is of the Supreme Father. "I seek not mine own glory", he says, for the Lord "seeketh and judgeth" – He will take care of and be a judge of that.

Die in Your Sins

Jesus now adds a seemingly obscure comment:

> "Verily, verily, I say unto you,
> If a man keep my saying, he shall never see death."
>
> *John 8:51*

"Keep my saying" means 'keep my Word' or 'keep my word' – the meaning is the same either way. Those who follow the practice in which they are instructed by a true mystic, those who follow his words and listen to the music of the Word within, will never die. It means that they will escape from this material realm, governed by Satan, where death is a certain reality. Earlier in this same conversation, Jesus makes the same point even more clearly when he tells them:

> "I go my way, and ye shall seek me,
>   and shall die in your sins:
>   whither I go, ye cannot come."
>
> Then said the Jews,
> "Will he kill himself? Because he saith,
>   'Whither I go, ye cannot come.'"
>
> And he said unto them,
> "Ye are from beneath; I am from above:
>   ye are of this world; I am not of this world.
> I said therefore unto you,
>   that ye shall die in your sins:
> For if ye believe not that I am he,
>   ye shall die in your sins."
>
> *John 8:21-24*

Jesus says that they cannot follow him to the Father, because they have not attained that degree of grace and spiritual progress. In fact, while he is free and returns to God, they will die encompassed and enslaved by their own sins. "Ye are from beneath", he says, "I am from above. Ye are of this world, but I am not of this world." I am free of all sins and bondage to this world, but you are not. "Ye shall die in your sins", he says, repeating himself three times for emphasis. You will live and die in this world and take birth here again and again. Only if a person believes in him, only if they are initiated by him and follow his instructions, can they be saved from this fate. Jesus similarly said, in a passage we have previously discussed:

> This is the bread which cometh down from heaven,
>> that a man may eat thereof, and not die.
> I am the Living Bread which came down from heaven:
>> if any man eat of this Bread, he shall live for ever.
>
> *John 6:50-51*

And:

> And whosoever liveth and believeth in me
>> shall never die.
>
> *John 11:26*

But – according to John's dialogue – the Jews do not understand him. Taking Jesus literally, they immediately point out that everyone has to die, so how can he say that one who follows him "shall never see death"?

> Then said the Jews unto him,
> "Now we know that thou hast a devil.
> Abraham is dead, and the prophets; and thou sayest,
> 'If a man keep my saying, he shall never taste of death.'
> Art thou greater than our father Abraham,
>> which is dead? and the prophets are dead:
> whom makest thou thyself?"
>
> *John 8:51-53*

Even Abraham and the great prophets of old had to die. So they ask, are you making yourself out to be better than them?

> Jesus answered,
> "If I honour myself, my honour is nothing:

it is my Father that honoureth me;
      of whom ye say, that He is your God:
"Yet ye have not known Him; but I know Him:
      and if I should say, I know Him not,
      I shall be a liar like unto you:
But I know Him, and keep His saying (Word).

"Your father Abraham rejoiced to see my day:
      and he saw it, and was glad."

Then said the Jews unto him,
"Thou art not yet fifty years old,
      and hast thou seen Abraham?"

Jesus said unto them,
"Verily, verily, I say unto you,
      before Abraham was, I am."

John 8:54-58

Jesus points out that the praise or honour someone accords himself is
unreal and of no meaning. It is only pride and egotism. But there is a
real honour which comes from God. It is His grace and presence within
a soul. Jesus says that he "knows Him" and God's will is expressed
through him. He would be telling a lie if he said otherwise. In fact, he
adds, even Abraham is pleased with him. This provokes the Jews still
more and Jesus responds enigmatically that he was in existence before
Abraham. The reality of all Masters is the Word, and Jesus is meaning
that the Word has been present since the very beginning of creation,
that there has always been a Master – the Word personified – in this
world.

   This dialogue, therefore, as recorded in St John, reveals some interesting details of Jesus' teaching concerning God, Satan, sin and death.
Whether such a conversation really took place is open to question, of
course, for it is so characteristic of John's way of expressing certain
aspects of Jesus' teachings, full of double meanings. The "Jews" are
simply used as a foil and a literary device in order to put across various
points, much as the scribes and Pharisees are used in all four canonical gospels. Its meaning, however, is in keeping with that of so many
other mystics throughout the ages.

Already Condemned

Dying in sin, never tasting death, inheriting eternal life – these are common themes in the gospels and from further passages we can learn more of Jesus' teaching on the matter. Again in John, we read:

> Verily, verily, I say unto you, he that heareth my Word,
>   and believeth on Him that sent me,
>   hath everlasting life,
>   and shall not come into condemnation;
> But is passed from death unto life.
>
> *John 5:24*

Jesus is again referring to this world as the realm of "death" and also of "condemnation". It is the realm of condemnation because the soul is condemned to take birth and die here according to its own past sins. But the soul who is fortunate enough to be baptized into the Word and to hear the music of the Word within, is rescued from death and condemnation and is taken to the Source of eternal life, God Himself. There is little else that this extract could mean. As Jesus says elsewhere in John:

> For God sent not his Son into the world
>   to condemn the world;
> But that the world through him might be saved.
>
> He that believeth on him is not condemned:
>   but he that believeth not is condemned already,
>   because he hath not believed
>   in the Name of the Only-Begotten Son of God.
>
> *John 3:17-18*

No Master comes to condemn or judge the world. The people of this world have enough problems of their own creation without having the direct condemnation of God added to their burden. In fact, we are "condemned already" by virtue of our being here. Living in this world is a just reward or recompense for sins of the past. Jesus further elaborates:

> And this is the condemnation,
>   that light is come into the world,
>   and men loved darkness rather than light,
>   because their deeds were evil.

> For every one that doeth evil hateth the light,
>   neither cometh to the light,
>   lest his deeds should be reproved.
> But he that doeth truth cometh to the light,
>   that his deeds may be made manifest,
>   that they are wrought in God.
>
> *John 3:19-21*

In such a state of "condemnation" are they that when "light is come into the world", when a Master comes to this world, people do not recognize him for who he really is. They generally prefer the darkness of their own minds to the inner light that a Master can give. And Jesus explains that the reason for this is "because their deeds were evil" and because "everyone that doeth evil hateth the light, lest his deeds should be reproved". It is evil deeds, sins or *karmas* that keep a person away from God. Moreover, everyone has a conscience, a higher mind, and in his or her heart of hearts, they know what they are doing and thinking. Therefore, they are fearful of coming to a Master because they know that their way of being will be exposed, not to the world at large, but to themselves. They also know that change will be required. So they are apprehensive, for usually people would rather live in illusion and ignorance than face the truth about themselves.

But the real seekers of the mystic Truth, says Jesus, "cometh to the light". These are the initiated ones who are doing the deeds of God, following the path that leads back to Him. As Jesus also said:

> I am the light of the world:
>   he that followeth me shall not walk in darkness,
>   but shall have the light of life.
>
> *John 8:12*

Those that follow a Master will not be left in darkness, but will be led up to the Source of all Light and Life.

The Region and the Shadow of Death

'Walking in darkness' was a common mystic expression in ancient times for living in this world. Matthew quotes the prophet Isaiah, who says:

> The people which sat in darkness saw a great light;
>> and to them which sat in the region and shadow of death
>> light is sprung up.
>
> *Isaiah 9:2, KJV; Matthew 4:16*

But there is no reason from the context to suppose that Isaiah was referring only to Jesus as the "great light", as the compiler of St Matthew would have us believe. All perfect Masters are great lights in this world, the "region and shadow of death". A similar expression is found in the twenty-third psalm:

> Yea, though I walk through the valley
>> of the shadow of death, I will fear no evil.
>
> *Psalms 23:4, KJV*

The "valley of the shadow of death" is this world and the psalmist says that even though he is living in this world, in the realm of the Evil One, he has no fear, for the Lord is with him.

Jesus also spoke of this world's inhabitants as "the dead" when he advised one of his more vacillating followers to "let the dead bury their dead".[2] A comment which means that although somebody may have to perform his various family duties, he should not let them distract him from following the mystic path. The people of this world are very happy to deal with the world, so "let the dead bury their dead". A disciple's focus of attention should be elsewhere.

Outer Darkness, Hellfire, Sheol

Many expressions and metaphors were used for this world by the mystical writers of Jesus' era. Terms alluding to darkness, misery, death, captivity and slavery were commonplace. Hence, the darkness, the region of death, the valley of death and the many terms for hell, including the outer darkness, Hades, Amente, Sheol, Gehenna, hellfire and the Pit, were all used for this world, as well as for the hellish zones themselves. Just as Satan, in his restricted meaning, was considered to be the lord of hell, so in his expanded sense was he lord of the hell that includes this world.

A number of Jesus' parables end with the unfortunate ones of his story being consigned to "hellfire" or "outer darkness". The compilers of the gospels probably understood these to mean hell itself, but it is by no means certain that this is what Jesus intended, for the usage is more meaningful within the whole context if Jesus was actually referring to this world.

There is, for example, the parable of the wedding feast. A king invites the rich and influential people of the world to his son's wedding, but they are too busy to attend. He therefore extends his invitation to the common people off the street. Grateful for the invitation, they all come, but one arrives improperly attired:

> And when the king came in to see the guests,
>> he saw there a man which had not on a wedding garment:
> And he saith unto him,
> "Friend, how camest thou in hither
>> not having a wedding garment?"
> And he was speechless.
>
> Then said the king to the servants,
> "Bind him hand and foot, and take him away,
>> and cast him into outer darkness;
>> there shall be weeping and gnashing of teeth."
>
> *Matthew 22:11-13*

One might have thought the king to be somewhat harsh, for it is most unlikely that any of the common people taken from the streets would have had their wedding garments with them. But we are in the realm of allegory. Briefly, the parable means that the Lord (the king) sends his Son to this world in order to consummate the mystic marriage with his chosen souls. He comes to unite the soul to God. But he does not come for the self-important people of the world, whoever they may be, because they are too involved in the world. He comes for the real people – the street people – so to speak, the ordinary, honest, sincere and unassuming folk who struggle along as best they can. Everyone is invited to the wedding feast, to the mystic marriage, but the one who comes without his 'robe of glory', without the divine garment of the soul, procured by means of interior prayer, is not allowed to enter. He is "bound hand and foot" and "cast ... into outer darkness", where "there shall be weeping and gnashing of teeth". It means that the soul is returned as a captive to this world, where it undergoes much suffering – "weeping and gnashing of teeth" – a human, rather than hellish, description.

Jesus uses the expression once again in the parable of the three servants. Their master gives each of them a small capital sum and then leaves them to their own devices. Two of them invest the money wisely and double their money. But the third one does nothing useful with it all. In fact, he digs a hole in the ground and buries it. Interpreted allegorically, the capital given for investment is human life. When the master returns – that is, at the time of death – each soul is asked what they have done with their life. The ones who have used their life wisely in seeking God are rewarded by being taken back to Him:

> His lord said unto him,
> "Well done, good and faithful servant;
>   thou hast been faithful over a few things,
>   I will make thee ruler over many things:
> Enter thou into the joy of thy Lord."
>
> *Matthew 25:23*

But the one who has wasted his life, after making various ineffectual excuses, is condemned by his master. Says he:

> "Cast ye the unprofitable servant into outer darkness:
>   there shall be weeping and gnashing of teeth."
>
> *Matthew 25:30*

As in the parable of the wedding feast, Jesus means that the soul who wastes his life as a human being is returned to this world once again.

We find corroboration of this interpretation of "outer darkness" in a number of places in the allied literature of the period. Origen, for example, suggests that it refers to life in "this coarse and earthly body" beyond the "reach of any light of understanding":

> The 'outer darkness', too, is in my judgment, not to be understood as a place with a murky atmosphere and no light at all, but rather as a description of those who through their immersion in the darkness of deep ignorance have become separated from the reach of any light of understanding....
> Perhaps, the 'gloom and darkness' should be taken to mean this coarse and earthly body.
>
> *Origen, On First Principles II:X.8, OFP p.145, WOI p.144*

Just as explicitly, there is a passage in the Nag Hammadi, *Gospel of Philip*, where the author speaks of the inner and the outer man, the inner man being the soul, the outer man, the physical body. He is referring to the soul incarnate in this world when he speaks of

> the inner and the outer
> and what is outside the outer.
> *Gospel of Philip 68, NHS20 p.177*

What lies "outside the outer" is the physical universe itself, which lies "outside" the physical body. He then adds:

> Because of this the lord (Jesus) called corruption "the outer darkness": there is not another outside of it.
> *Gospel of Philip 68, NHS20 p.177*

The physical universe is the lowest or outermost region of creation: "there is nothing outside of it". Corruption is another term commonly used for this world in the sense that all here is impermanent and changing, tending towards destruction, decay and death. It is also the world where nothing is what it seems to be. Everything is fraudulent and illusory. Hence, Paul wrote to the Christian community at Corinth, quoting the mystics Isaiah and Hosea:

> So when this corruptible shall have put on incorruption,
> and this mortal shall have put on immortality,
> then shall be brought to pass the saying that is written,
> "Death is swallowed up in victory."[3]
> "(Then) O death, where is thy sting?
> O grave, where is thy victory?"[4]
> (But) the sting of death is sin;
> and the strength of sin is the law.
> *1 Corinthians 15:54-56*

Only when man has realized the true immortality of the soul (though to Paul this meant in a resurrected and spiritualized physical body) is he able to swallow up death in victory, removing the ever-present fear and pain of death and rebirth. And in keeping with all mystic teachings, Paul points out that it is sin which feeds death and gives it the power to sting. And sin is governed or given strength by a universal law, the law of cause and effect, of judgment and equivalent retribution.

Again from the Nag Hammadi library, the writer of the *Tripartite Tractate* is even more explicit when he describes the world as the pit of ignorance which is called the 'outer darkness', and 'Chaos' and 'Hades' and the 'Abyss'.

Tripartite Tractate 89, NHS22 p.255

And the writer of the *Odes of Solomon*, speaking of his salvation and ascent from this world, says that he has been "raised" up from the "depths of Sheol" and drawn from the "mouth of death", both being references to this world:

> The Lord is my hope:
>> I shall not be ashamed in Him.
> For according to his glory, He made me....
>> and according to his compassion he raised me up....
> And He brought me up from the depths of Sheol,
>> and from the mouth of death He drew me....
>
> And the Lord cast down my Enemy by his Word,
>> and he became like the chaff which the wind carries away.
> And I gave praise to the Most High,
>> because He made great His servant
>> and the son of his handmaid.

Odes of Solomon XXIX:1-4,10-11, AOT pp.719-720

From excerpts such as these, it also seems that terms such as hell and Sheol were a means of speaking covertly to "those who have ears to hear" of rebirth in this world. Amongst the communion liturgies of the Nestorian Christians of the Middle East, still in use in the nineteenth century but clearly harking back to a far earlier mystical tradition not yet completely extinguished, we read of the Bread or Medicine of Life, the Word, which permits one who partakes of it to "escape hell":

> Behold, the Medicine of Life,
>> which descended from on high....
> Put forth now your hands, O ye who are dying,
>> and have taken up your abode in Sheol
>> on account of your sins.
>
> Take and be forgiven, and attain unto life,
>> and reign with Christ,
>> and sing and say:

"Alleluia, this is the Bread of which
if any man shall eat he shall escape hell."
Nestorian Liturgies, NRII p.167

It is clear that those who are to "put forth now their hands" are the people of the world, who "have taken up their abode in Sheol on account of their sins". The fourth-century Christian, Ephraim Syrus uses the same metaphor in his poetry when he speaks of being in the "Abyss of the dead" and in "Hades":

> From the height of Eden the Adversary cast me down,
>> and in the Abyss of the dead
> he threw me down that he might deride me.
> My beautiful garments (of pure spirituality)
>> were swallowed up and do not exist.
> I was confused and overthrown,
>> and hurled down into Hades.
>
> And behold I am made a nest of worms,
>> and moth and tape-worms gnaw at me.
> My Saviour, thy resurrection shall renew me.
>> *Ephraim Syrus, SESHS IV:629.2, MEM p.59*

Note, in this excerpt, how Adam, the one who dwelt in "Eden", is automatically taken to be symbolic of the individual soul, not as a historical figure. Ephraim says, "from the height of Eden, the Adversary cast *me* down", not Adam. He is speaking of the soul's descent from the eternal realm into the hell of this world.

There are a great many such examples, then, that could be quoted from a wide range of literature and there is absolutely no doubt that although terms such as Hades, Sheol, outer darkness and others were used in reference to the hellish zones of creation, they were also commonly employed to mean this world. Indeed, it is one of the strangest of all human characteristics that although we live in a world of misery, often intense, even bemoaning our plight, few of us realize that we are already in a hellish place, living under a sentence of death.

The Serpent More Subtle Than Any Beast

In the *Genesis* allegory of Adam and Eve, Satan as the Negative Power is cast as a serpent, "more subtle than any beast of the field",[5] through whose agency and deception man is cast out of Eden, symbolic of the eternal abode of God. Adam and Eve are tempted by the serpent to eat of the tree of knowledge of good *and* evil, symbolizing the essential duality and division which characterizes Satan's realm. This is another indication that the original mystic understanding of Satan was as the cosmic ruler of a realm which encompasses the relative good of this world, as well as its evil. God had instructed Adam and Eve:

> But of the tree of the knowledge of good and evil,
> thou shalt not eat of it:
> For in the day that thou eatest thereof,
> thou shalt surely die.
>
> *Genesis 2:17, KJV*

But although they are disobedient, they do not die in a literal sense. Eating from the tree, they become aware of their nakedness, clothing themselves in fig leaves and in skins made by God Himself:

> Unto Adam also and to his wife did the Lord God
> make coats of skins, and clothed them.
>
> *Genesis 3:21, KJV*

This apt metaphor depicts the naked soul which, on its journey outwards from God, takes on various coverings of body and mind as it descends into the domain of Satan, the "coats of skins" being the physical body of flesh and blood which surround the soul in the physical arena of good and evil. This is where, as God said, "Thou shalt surely die". Entering the realm of Satan, they are condemned to spiritual death, as well as physical birth and death. And man is destined to eat more and more of this "tree of knowledge of good and evil". He is to become closely acquainted with the realm of duality and death. According to the allegory, God says:

> Because thou hast ... eaten of the tree,
> of which I commanded thee, saying,
> "Thou shalt not eat of it":
> cursed is the ground for thy sake;
> In sorrow shalt thou eat of it all the days of thy life;
> Thorns also and thistles shall it bring forth to thee;
> and thou shalt eat the herb of the field;
> In the sweat of thy face shalt thou eat bread,

> till thou return unto the ground;
> For out of it wast thou taken:
> for dust thou art, and unto dust shalt thou return.
>
> *Genesis 3:17-18, KJV*

Because of his association with the Serpent, man suffers. The fruit of the tree of good and evil is no longer sweet. What seemed interesting and enticing because of its scintillating diversity turns out to be a source of constant trouble and headache. "Thorns also and thistles shall it bring forth to thee." Man has to labour hard in the ground of the physical universe to eke out a living which is ultimately terminated by a death which he cannot avoid. Moreover, his association with the Serpent has only just begun:

> And the Lord God said unto the serpent,
> "... I will put enmity between thee and the woman,
>   and between thy seed and her seed;
> It shall bruise thy head, and thou shalt bruise his heel."
>
> *Genesis 3:14-15, KJV*

Man is destined to fight with the Serpent for as long as he lives in this world of death. When it says, therefore, that man will die if he eats the fruit of the tree of knowledge of good and evil, it does not mean that his soul is forever extinguished. This is not what happens in the *Genesis* allegory. If the soul had been extinguished, that would have been the end of the story. What happens is that the soul comes to live in the realm of death where the fruit of eating from the tree of knowledge of good and evil becomes "thorns and thistles" and the "sweat of thy face".

This is also, perhaps, the mystic meaning behind the Christian concept of 'original sin'. The primal 'sin' or *karma* allocated by God is not that with which a soul enters this world at birth. It is the soul's original and first desire, experienced at creation's dawn, to enter the realm of good and evil, the domain of Satan. Ultimately, it is this primal desire or 'original sin' which has led the soul into bondage. But it must be said, too, that it was by the Lord's design that the soul entered the realm of Satan and the arena of birth and death. The entire show is happening by His will. The 'original sin' or urge to experience His creation was put into souls by Him so that He could have a creation.

One has to remember that to the Jewish people, this story was an ingrained part of their culture and belief, and the mystically-minded amongst them understood it allegorically. Philo Judaeus, for instance, and many others have written extensively on the allegorical interpretation of *Genesis* and other Biblical books, and the terms and metaphors encountered there had become a part of common mystic parlance. As we can see from his parables, Jesus, too, was a lover of allegory and must have explained the Jewish scriptures to his disciples, for they would naturally have been interested in the real meaning of their holy books. Hence, speaking of this world as the realm of death, as Jesus did in John's gospel, had a long heritage behind it. It was the fate of Adam and Eve: "in the day that thou eatest thereof, thou shalt surely die."

Also alluding to this ancient allegory, Satan was often referred to as the Serpent, the Dragon and by similar terms. In *Revelations*, for example, he is described as the "great dragon" and the "Serpent ... which deceiveth the whole world":

> And the great Dragon was cast out,
> that old Serpent, called the Devil, and Satan,
> which deceiveth the whole world.
>
> *Book of Revelation 12:9*

It is Satan, then, who is responsible for the soul's separation from Eden, the eternal realm. It is owing to the activities of Satan that the soul is condemned to death in the physical universe. The soul dies in its sins due to the machinations of the Devil and the whole world is said to be deceived by him. But man – and the world – is full of good as well as bad. So this, once again, helps to make it clear that Satan was originally understood to be the author of both, making Jesus' teaching on the subject more understandable. And there is further evidence that Jesus taught an expanded understanding of the true nature of Satan.

In Danger of the Judgment: Cast Into Prison

Origen, after commenting that the 'outer darkness' is a metaphor for this world, adds:

> The expression 'prison' must be thought of in a similar way.
>
> *Origen, On First Principles II:X.8, OFP p.145*

The simile is common throughout the mystic literature of the world. Since the mind and soul are held captive in the body through their enslavement to past sins, mystics have often described this world as a dungeon or a prison, and Jesus was no exception. Turning to St Matthew, we find the term used in association with a short discourse on "judgment":

> Ye have heard that it was said by them of old time,
> "Thou shalt not kill;"
>   and whosoever shall kill shall be in danger of the judgment:
> But I say unto you,
>   that whosoever is angry with his brother without a cause
>   shall be in danger of the judgment:
> And whosoever shall say to his brother, "Raca,"
>   shall be in danger of the council:
> But whosoever shall say, "Thou fool,"
>   shall be in danger of hellfire.
>
> *Matthew 5:21-22*

Raca is an Aramaic word implying that a person is empty-headed or a nitwit, but the Greek term translated as "thou fool", to the Jew, meant something considerably more abusive. It referred to the worldly fool in the sense of one who is ignorant of God, one who turns himself from God towards the world, a rebel against God, this being the inward state of most of us.

Jesus is saying that all actions, from the apparently insignificant to the taking of life, must be accounted for. Whoever takes life will have to answer for it. If an individual has to answer for every "idle word", he will certainly be answerable for every killing, idle or otherwise. Jesus is pointing out the universal extent of the principle of accountability. Everything has its reaction. Everything has to be paid for. Even an outburst of anger or the smouldering of resentment and hatred bring a person into danger of judgment. Even one who calls someone else a nitwit will have to pay for it, while the fool of this world, the out-and-out worldly man, and his accuser, will both be in danger of "hellfire".

As we have said, all actions, thoughts, desires, intentions, ambitions and motivations originate in the mind and leave their impressions there, like grooves or marks in soft clay. At the time of death, all these must be accounted for. The soul faces judgment and according to the record of its life, deeply etched into the fabric of its own mind, the soul is judged. The good soul, one who has lived a good, loving, spiritual and selfless life, may spend some time in a heavenly realm. But a mind that is full of innumerable negative tendencies of rancour, hatred, anger, violence, ill will, unbridled sexual appetite, greed, attachment to the material and sensual things of the world, egotism and all forms of self-centredness, will either be drawn into some hellish zone or be immediately reincarnated into the hell of this world.

Many people may find it easier – or at least more comfortable – to believe in the existence of a heaven rather than a hell, but the belief is unwarranted in the face of experience, for a little observation readily reveals that an evil-minded person in this world is in a such a state of agitation and suffering that they are already in hell – a hellish state of mind. They are burning in the fire of their own passions. After death, therefore, when deprived of a physical body through which to give vent to all these hellish traits, their mind becomes their only reality on some sub-astral realm. Like a foul dream formed out of the worst contents of the mind, they find themselves in hell, in a place of intense suffering unalloyed by any physical outlet or means of expression.

But for souls who leave this world, neither heaven nor hell are permanent dwelling places. Sooner or later, the immediate effect of the good or bad impressions within the mind are worked off and the desires and tendencies towards living in the world draw the soul back into another body to repay other debts and fulfil other desires which can only be paid off by a return visit. Hence, Jesus adds:

> Agree with thine adversary quickly,
>> whiles thou art in the way with him;
> Lest at any time the adversary deliver thee to the judge,
>> and the judge deliver thee to the officer,
>> and thou be cast into prison.
> Verily I say unto thee,
>> thou shalt by no means come out thence,
>> till thou hast paid the uttermost farthing.
>
> *Matthew 5:25-26*

He points out that there is a very good reason why it is always best to keep relationships harmonious in this world. While people are still here, living in this world, it is best to keep the account clear. Do not let anger, rancour, resentment and so on, build up. Clear things with people as much as possible, while going along in life. Otherwise, all these apparently minor or major things will add up. Then, at death, the soul will have to face the "judge" – the exacting law of Satan – and the soul will be "cast into prison" – the prison of this world and the prison of the body. And there the soul will have to stay until all accounts have been settled – "until thou hast paid the uttermost farthing".

It means that every detail is recorded and accounted for in one way or another. Jesus then makes the same point concerning sexual desire. He says:

> Ye have heard that it was said by them of old time,
> "Thou shalt not commit adultery:"
> But I say unto you, that whosoever
>   looketh on a woman to lust after her
>   hath committed adultery with her already in his heart.
>
> *Matthew 5:27-28*

He points out that not only is the act binding but also the thought or desire is equivalent to the act because it can bring a soul back into the world in a another life for the fulfilment of that desire or craving. Strong desire for sensual, physical and bodily sensations can only be satisfied through living in a body. Hence, Jesus continues:

> And if thy right eye offend thee, pluck it out,
>   and cast it from thee:
> For it is profitable for thee
>   that one of thy members should perish,
>   and not that thy whole body should be cast into hell.
> And if thy right hand offend thee, cut it off,
>   and cast it from thee:
> For it is profitable for thee
>   that one of thy members should perish,
>   and not that thy whole body should be cast into hell.
>
> *Matthew 5:29-30*

The meaning is similar. Seemingly small impressions upon the mind can bring a soul back into the "hell" of this world. It is better therefore to clear these out of the mind now, to "cut them off", rather than to pay for them later. A literal interpretation cannot be intended here, for one cannot imagine Jesus recommending that we dismember ourselves. In a similar passage, he says:

> Woe unto the world because of offences!
> For it must needs be that offences come;
>   but woe to that man by whom the offence cometh!
> Wherefore if thy hand or thy foot offend thee,
>   cut them off, and cast them from thee:

> It is better for thee to enter into life halt or maimed,
>> rather than having two hands or two feet
>> to be cast into everlasting fire.
> And if thine eye offend thee, pluck it out,
>> and cast it from thee:
> It is better for thee to enter into life with one eye,
>> rather than having two eyes to be cast into hellfire.
>
> *Matthew 18:7-9*

"Woe unto the world because of offences": the world is in travail and trouble on account of its sins and offences. Yet "it must needs be that offences come": no person can escape such sins because the very fabric of the world is sin. Souls take birth here because of sin. Everything, good or bad, great or small, bears fruit in one way or another. Therefore, it is best to do whatever is humanly possible to avoid increasing one's load of sins.

Payment for Sin

This theme of recompense and retribution – an essential aspect of the wider understanding of the nature of Satan – is present throughout Jesus' teachings. There is an incident related by Luke, for instance, where Jesus seems to have been sitting chatting with a group of disciples when someone raises the subject of Pontius Pilate's recent slaughter of some Galileans. Perhaps they had been involved in a terrorist plot and had been caught, the nationalists – the zealots, as they were called – being very active at that time:

> There were present at that season some that told him of the Galileans, whose blood Pilate had mingled with their sacrifices. And Jesus answering said unto them, "Suppose ye that these Galileans were sinners above all the Galileans, because they suffered such things? I tell you, nay: but, except ye repent, ye shall all likewise perish."
>
> *Luke 13:1-3*

Jesus listens, but then he turns the subject around and says that although they may have seemed to be more guilty than anyone else, that was not in fact the case. He agrees implicitly that their fate was indeed the result of their past sins, but he points out that everyone is the victim of their sins, and all who do not "repent" will have to face the consequences. He then reminds them of another incident, where eighteen people had been killed accidentally when a building collapsed:

> "Or those eighteen, upon whom the tower in Siloam fell, and slew them, think ye that they were sinners above all men that dwelt in Jerusalem? I tell you, nay: but, except ye repent, ye shall all likewise perish."
>
> *Luke 13:4-5*

Again, by presuming that their accidental death was due to past sins, he acknowledges the principle of payment for sin in this life. But he adds that everybody is in the same boat. "Except ye repent", he says, unless you turn towards God, you will have to suffer the consequences of your past sins.

Jesus also points out that this same principle applies in spiritual life. And, here, he also observes that the motivation behind the deed goes a long way towards determining its effect in the future. He says:

> He that receiveth a prophet in the name of a prophet
>   shall receive a prophet's reward;
> And he that receiveth a righteous man
>   in the name of a righteous man
>   shall receive a righteous man's reward.
> And whosoever shall give to drink
>   unto one of these little ones a cup of cold water
>   only in the name of a disciple,
>   verily I say unto you,
>   he shall in no wise lose his reward.
>
> *Matthew 10:41-42*

Someone who comes to a prophet or a mystic, knowing him to be such and seeking spirituality, receives "a prophet's reward". He receives true mystic realization and spirituality in return. Others, who see such a mystic only as a good or "righteous man", receive benefits at that level. They become better human beings and in future lives are rewarded with more comfortable circumstances in life. And one who only does some small service for "one of these little ones" – one of the Lord's pure and humble Sons – adopting the attitude of a true disciple, he too will gain an appropriate reward. No one returns empty-handed from a perfect mystic. Everyone is benefited to some extent – but the degree of benefit depends upon the inner motivation and attitude of mind.

Whatsoever a Man Soweth

Paul, too, recognized this same principle, though the contents of his letters are insufficient to fully ascertain how far he went along with it, particularly in regard to reincarnation. All the same, it indicates that this concept was familiar to the early Christians, many of whom, in the time of Paul, would have been the direct disciples of Jesus. In *Galatians*, he says:

> Be not deceived; God is not mocked:
> > for whatsoever a man soweth,
> > that shall he also reap.
> For he that soweth to his flesh
> > shall of the flesh reap corruption;
> But he that soweth to the Spirit
> > shall of the Spirit reap life everlasting.
> And let us not be weary in well doing:
> > for in due season we shall reap, if we faint not.
> As we have therefore opportunity,
> > let us do good unto all men,
> > especially unto them
> > who are of the household of faith.
>
> *Galatians 6:7-10*

His meaning is that whatever a person does will come back to them in like manner, just as Jesus said. This is the law of cause and effect, of *karma*. Paul says that if someone seeks the Spirit, he will reap true spirituality and will find immortality, "life everlasting". If he seeks after the things of the world and of the body, then that is what he will reap. One is rather uncertain, however, about Paul's understanding of higher spirituality and what he means by "he that soweth to the spirit", for he seems to equate spirituality with "well doing", seeking spiritual rewards from good human behaviour. But, as Jesus said, true spirituality is worship of the Father "in Spirit and in Truth". It is spiritual practice which has its reward in the Spirit. The deeds of this world, good or bad, can only be fully repaid in this world. At best, they will prepare a person for receiving true spirituality by making them humble, but they can never supplant spiritual practice.

Paul's meaning is clearer in another instance where there is no doubt that he is speaking specifically of giving in charity. He is writing to a group of his disciples, urging and cajoling them into giving bountifully to the common purse – particularly for the benefit of the poor, the widows and the orphans amongst them – when he adds as an incentive:

> But this I say, he which soweth sparingly
>> shall reap also sparingly;
> And he which soweth bountifully
>> shall reap also bountifully.
> Every man according as he purposeth in his heart,
>> so let him give;
>> not grudgingly, or of necessity:
> For God loveth a cheerful giver.
> And God is able to make all grace abound toward you;
>> that ye, always having all sufficiency in all things,
>> may abound to every good work.
>
> *2 Corinthians 9:6-8*

Such unstinted generosity and loving open-heartedness are the hallmark of a spiritual person, but such qualities do not of themselves take a soul out of the body, through the higher realms and back to God. For that, some other practice is required.

There are many other places in Paul's letters where he speaks of sin and its relationship to spirituality. In *Romans*, for instance, he writes of the "law of sin and death", coming very close to speaking explicitly of reincarnation:

> There is therefore now no condemnation to them
>> which are in Christ Jesus,
>> who walk not after the flesh, but after the Spirit.
> For the law of the Spirit of Life in Christ Jesus
>> hath made me free from the law of sin and death.
>
> *Romans 8:1-2*

Jesus has used the term translated as "condemnation" in the same way. Those who followed Jesus were no longer "condemned" in the sense that they would be freed from the condemnation of birth and death. And Paul's meaning seems quite clear when he asserts that through the "law of the Spirit of Life" he has been made "free from the law of sin and death". By means of the Holy Spirit, a soul is freed from condemnation, from the law which governs "sin and death". Actually, there is a great deal more in this letter concerning sin and death which is very much in line with an understanding of *karma* and reincarnation, and which anyone interested in Paul's teaching may study for themselves.

Those Who Sow in Winter, Reap in Summer

The metaphor of sowing seeds for a future harvest – which epitomizes the principle of cause and effect – is used in many places in the mystic literature of the period. The gnostic writer of the *Gospel of Philip* uses it to point out that whatever is to be achieved in the higher realms has to be begun here, while in the human form:

> Those who sow in winter reap in summer.
> The winter is the world,
>   the summer the other eternal realm (*aeon*).
> Let us sow in the world
>   that we may reap in the summer.
> Gospel of Philip 52, NHS20 p.145

The same point is made in the *Doctrine of Addai*. After asserting that the soul does not die when the body dies, but goes into the inner mansions, the writer adds that the soul is not able to receive its "reward and recompense" without its association with the body:

> For it (the soul) is not as the body, without feeling, which perceives not the odious corruption which has come upon it. Reward and recompense, it (the soul) is not able to receive without it (the body); because that labour was not of it alone, but also of the body in which it dwelt.
> Doctrine of Addai the Apostle, DAA p.45

Binding the Strong Man

The problem, then, faced by all human beings is how to escape from the grip of Satan and his law of justice and recompense. We need to 'cast out' the Devil from within ourselves. However, one of the commonest accusations against mystics of those days was that they themselves were the children of the Devil or that they derived their power from the Devil. Jesus, Simon Magus, the disciples and others were all, by their turn, accused of a liaison with Satan. Jesus had a neat response to this. "Is it not unlikely," he reasoned, "that I should cast out devils by the power of the Prince of devils? Why would Satan help to cast out his own agents? If he did that he would no longer be able to administer his realm."

In Matthew, the saying is set after an introductory anecdote in which Jesus heals a man who was both blind and dumb by 'casting out a devil'. But in Mark, from whom Matthew is copying, there is no such introductory story and we have the saying devoid of anything but the most rudimentary surrounding narrative:

> And the scribes which came down from Jerusalem said (of Jesus),
>   "He hath Beelzebub, and by the Prince of the devils
>   casteth he out devils."

> And he called them unto him, and said unto them in parables,
> "How can Satan cast out Satan?
> And if a kingdom be divided against itself,
>   that kingdom cannot stand.
> And if a house be divided against itself,
>   that house cannot stand.
> And if Satan rise up against himself,
>   and be divided, he cannot stand, but hath an end.
> No man can enter into a strong man's house,
>   and spoil his goods, except he will first bind the strong man;
>   and then he will spoil his house."

> *Mark 3:22-32*

Or as the same saying appears in the *Gospel of Thomas*:

> Jesus said,
> "It is not possible for anyone
>   to enter the house of a strong man
>   and take it by force unless he binds his hands;
> Then he will be able to ransack his house."

> *Gospel of Thomas 35, NHS20 p.67*

Jesus' graphic example neatly summarizes the human predicament. Our body is a house in which a "strong man" has taken up his abode, in which Satan has come to live. Satan's agent is the mind itself and the spiritual treasure lying within our house can only be obtained by binding the "strong man", by completely controlling the mind. This is no small task for most of us do not even realize that there is a treasure hidden in our house or that our house has been taken over by a "strong man". But as to Jesus' teaching on how the "strong man" can be bound, the answer must be left open and addressed in future chapters.

NOTES AND REFERENCES

1. *General Confession, Book of Common Prayer.*
2. *Matthew 8:22.*
3. *Isaiah 25:28.*
4. *Hosea 13:4.*
5. *Genesis 3:1, KJV.*

CHAPTER TWELVE

Did Jesus Really Teach Reincarnation?

What Makes Us All So Different?

Reincarnation means that when a body dies, the soul goes on in the company of the mind. And the mind, in which desires and the impressions of past events are etched in seed form, brings the soul back into another body for the fulfilment or expression of those seeds. An understanding of reincarnation is therefore quite incomplete without an appreciation of its great corollary, the law of cause and effect. Conversely, the law of cause and effect, when considered as a recompense for deeds and desires, good or bad, seems deficient and full of inconsistencies if it is not considered along with reincarnation. Once reincarnation and the law of cause and effect are understood as parts of one picture, then so much else falls into place.

No child is born without being hemmed in on all sides by the constraints of circumstance. Our minds are largely conditioned by these circumstances and by our upbringing. Deep habits of mind have already been set before we become adult and have had a chance to develop the capacity to think for ourselves. To some extent, some individuals may be able to break the mould of their childhood years, but why do some surmount this conditioning more than others? Again, some children are born with infirmities or diseases of various kinds. Some are born with unusual talents or skills not possessed by either of their parents. And everyone is born with recognizable and innate characteristics and personality. What is it that determines these circumstances, infirmities, talents and personality? Why do we all receive such different starts in life? And why is the course of life so different for everyone? How does all this come about?

Jesus, Paul and so many others certainly taught that man has to reap the fruit of his actions. Yet experience and observation tell us that, in the course of one lifetime, just recompense is not meted out. The good do not get the best of everything while the bad suffer. Often it is the reverse. Good people may have to undergo the severest sufferings and misery, while the selfish, the greedy and the proud may go through life more or less unscathed. And how are the circumstances of birth to be understood in the context of recompense for sin? If souls are coming into birth for the first time, from where do they acquire their circumstances? Why are some born poor, some rich, some crippled, some diseased? Why is everybody so different?

There is no doubt that Jesus recognized the law of cause and effect as regards the consequence of actions. Remember Luke's story of those executed by Pilate and the accidental deaths at the tower of Siloam. He also used terms like prison, judgment, freedom from sin, outer darkness and so on, that were employed by others of his era who did most certainly teach reincarnation. But did he actually teach that souls returned in life after life? And if so, why is it not clearly stated in the gospels?

Well, many of the reasons have already been covered. The gospels, as we have seen, are a very poor record of what Jesus actually taught. They are not and never were designed as a definitive statement of his teachings. With the possible exception of the dialogues and discourses of John, they were compiled by those who were not his direct initiates and who had their own ideas about things. And they underwent three or four hundred years of copying and editing before we have our first copies of them. Anything could – and probably did – happen.

All the same, in addition to the many places in the canonical gospels where Jesus speaks of sin and justice in a way which fits precisely with an understanding of reincarnation, there are also a few instances which seem to point more specifically to a belief in reincarnation.

Elias is Come Already

Perhaps the most frequently quoted of these passages concern the association of the prophet Elias (Elijah) with Jesus and John the Baptist. We pick up the trail in Mark's gospel where the gospel compiler indicates that some of the people thought that John was a reincarnation of Elias or another of the past Jewish mystics, demonstrating that such notions were not unfamiliar to the people of those times:

> And king Herod heard of him (Jesus); (for his name was spread abroad:) and he said, that "John the Baptist was risen from the dead, and therefore mighty works do shew forth themselves in him."

Others said, that "it is Elias". And others said, that "it is a prophet, or as one of the prophets". But when Herod heard thereof, he said, "it is John, whom I beheaded: he is risen from the dead."

Mark 6:14-16

Again in Mark, we find that some people thought that maybe Jesus was a reincarnation of Elias or even John the Baptist:

And Jesus ... asked his disciples, saying unto them, "Whom do men say that I am?" And they answered, "John the Baptist: but some say, Elias; and others, one of the prophets."

And he saith unto them, "But whom say ye that I am?" And Peter answereth and saith unto him, "Thou art the Christ".

Mark 8:27-29

In another passage from Mark, Jesus himself is reported to have said that Elias had already come:

And they (the disciples) asked him (Jesus), saying, "Why say the scribes that Elias must first come?"

And he answered and told them, "Elias verily cometh first, and restoreth all things; and how it is written of the Son of man, that he must suffer many things, and be set at nought. But I say unto you, that Elias is indeed come, and they have done unto him whatsoever they listed, as it is written of him."

Mark 9:11-13

Luke more or less follows Mark in both these passages, though with his familiar paraphrasing, but Matthew, also copying Mark, changes Mark's meaning around, adding quite pointedly that Jesus meant them to understand that John the Baptist was the reincarnation of Elias:

And his disciples asked him, saying, "Why then say the scribes that Elias must first come?"

And Jesus answered and said unto them, "Elias truly shall first come, and restore all things. But I say unto you, that Elias is come already, and they knew him not, but have done unto him whatsoever they listed. Likewise shall also the Son of man suffer of them." Then the disciples understood that he spake unto them of John the Baptist.

Matthew 17:10-13

And elsewhere, Matthew promotes the same point of view in a passage unique to his gospel, when he has Jesus say of John the Baptist:

> For all the prophets and the law prophesied until John. And if ye will receive it (if you are willing to accept it – *RSV*), this is Elias, which was for to come. He that hath ears to hear, let him hear.
>
> *Matthew 11:13-15*

So Matthew very clearly indicates his belief that John the Baptist was a reincarnation of the prophet Elias, and this fits in very well with Matthew's use and interpretation of Jewish scripture to 'prove' his message concerning Jesus.

The compiler of John's gospel on the other hand, no doubt familiar with the synoptic gospels as well as the many wild stories that were going around, seems to want to put the record straight for he has John flatly deny that he is a reincarnation of Elias:

> And this is the record of John, when the Jews sent priests and Levites from Jerusalem to ask him, "Who art thou?" And he confessed, and denied not; but confessed, "I am not the Christ."
>
> And they asked him, "What then? Art thou Elias?" And he saith, "I am not." "Art thou that prophet?" And he answered, "No."
>
> *John 1:19-21*

The general meaning, then, that can be drawn from these various passages – assuming their authenticity – is twofold. Firstly, that the concept of reincarnation, at least amongst prophets, was not unfamiliar or unusual to the Jewish people of those times. Indeed, Elias and many of their mystics were expected to come again, as was later believed of Jesus. Secondly, and something with which all mystics have concurred, all mystics are one. They are one with God, one with the Word and one with each other. They are all waves from the same ocean. Hence, when Jesus says, "Elias has come already", he was probably referring in a general way to the many mystics who have come to this world. And when he adds, "they have done to him whatsoever they listed", he is pointing out that mystics have characteristically been badly treated by the rulers and priests of the organized religions of their times.

But there is a difference between mystics coming to this world and the manner in which the rest of us take birth. As Jesus said, we are enslaved by sin. We die in our sins. We continually come to the realm of death because of our sins. Mystics of the highest order, on the other hand, come because they are sent by the Father. They are free to come and go as they please and are not the servants of sin. As the prophet Jeremiah wrote in the opening lines of his book:

> Then the word of the Lord came unto me (Jeremiah) saying, "Before I formed thee in the belly I knew thee; and before thou camest forth out of the womb, I sanctified thee, and I ordained thee a prophet unto the nations."

> *Jeremiah 1:4-5, KJV*

So it is with all perfect mystics. They come by the will of God, not through the compulsion and constraints of their own past sins.

Who Did Sin?

Another passage which is commonly quoted by those seeking evidence that Jesus taught reincarnation is the story in St John of Jesus and the man born blind:

> And as Jesus passed by,
>   he saw a man which was blind from his birth.
> And his disciples asked him, saying,
> "Master, who did sin, this man, or his parents,
>   that he was born blind?"
>
> Jesus answered,
> "Neither hath this man sinned, nor his parents:
>   but that the works of God should be made manifest in him."

> *John 9:1-3*

Taking the story at face value, the disciples clearly presume that the suffering of the blind man and his parents is due to sin. And since the man was born blind, it seems that they are thinking of some past existence, for how else could an embryo or a newborn baby have committed any sin?

The reply, however, is incongruous, for Jesus says that neither the parents nor the man have sinned but that the situation has been divinely arranged so that he can perform the miracle of restoring sight to the blind man. That God would have created such suffering simply so that Jesus could perform a miracle seems an untenable idea. With so many sick people already in need of help, surely there would have been no need for a baby to be born blind simply for the sake of a miracle later in his life. Moreover, many other similar miracle stories in the synoptic gospels are clearly associated with the forgiveness of sins – again pointing to the direct relationship between sin and physical infirmity. And they end happily with Jesus curing the sick person of his or her particular condition, telling them that their sins are forgiven. "Go and sin no more",[1] he says on several occasions and in one instance he even adds, "lest a worse thing come unto you"[2] – the "worse thing" being rebirth in this world due to 'more sin'.

But in this example in St John, Jesus says that neither the man nor his parents have sinned. Perhaps, then, the dialogue was originally one of John's metaphorical passages with a double meaning, implying both the physical and the spiritual blindness into which all souls are born – both being the result of sin. A later editor then changed Jesus' reply, thus creating the confusion. Maybe the edited response was an attempt to deal with the observation, "What about people whom Jesus forgave of their sins, curing them of infirmities which they had had since birth?" For if it were agreed that sickness was the result of sin, then naturally those who are born with infirmities must have committed sins before their birth – in a previous life. So all in all, the question raised by the disciples is a good one, indicating a belief in the sins of past lives. But the reply as we now have it is definitely odd.

A Secret Teaching

With all the evidence of editorial tampering, it is not surprising to find that specific mention of reincarnation is missing from the gospels. This is not so, however, amongst the beliefs of the early Christians. Many of them, especially the gnostically-inclined, believed in reincarnation, presumably thinking that Jesus had taught it, too. The teaching may, of course, have been a part of the secret 'mysteries'. In a letter from Jerome (c.347-420) to the ascetic, Demetrias (c.398-460) – though from his other writings it is clear that Jerome (at least in his later years) did not personally entertain the belief – we read:

> The doctrine of transmigration has been secretly taught from ancient times to small numbers of people, as a traditional truth which was not to be divulged.
>
> Jerome, Epistola ad Demetriadem, REWA p.38

Likewise, the Christian writer Arnobius, writing around 300 AD, says:

> (It) is said in the more hidden mysteries, that the souls of the wicked go into
> cattle and other beasts after they have been removed from human bodies.
>
> *Arnobius, Against the Pagans 2:16, ASCPI p.130*

Although it cannot now be ascertained with certainty whether reincarnation was a part of Jesus' 'mysteries', the early Christian teacher,
Clement of Alexandria (*fl.*180-200), does comment that there were
many things which Jesus did not entrust to all and sundry:

> He (Jesus) did not certainly disclose to the many what did not belong to
> the many; but to the few to whom he knew that they belonged, who were
> capable of receiving and being moulded according to them. But secret
> things are entrusted to speech, not to writing.
>
> *Clement of Alexandria, Miscellanies I:I, WCAI p.356*

Teachings such as these, then, were conveyed by word of mouth, not
in writing. For, as he adds later:

> There is great danger in divulging the secret of the true philosophy to
> those whose delight it is unsparingly to speak against everything, not
> justly; and who shout forth all kinds of names and words indecorously,
> deceiving themselves and beguiling those who adhere to them.
>
> *Clement of Alexandria, Miscellanies I:II, WCAI p.361*

People only want to argue and debate, he says, "deceiving themselves"
and others. Likewise, speaking of his own teaching, he says quite clearly
that he does not write down everything he thinks:

> It is requisite, therefore, to hide in a mystery the wisdom spoken, which
> the Son of God taught.... Such were the impediments in the way of my
> writing. And even now I fear, as it is said, "to cast the pearls before swine,
> lest they tread them under foot, and turn and rend us."[3] For it is difficult to
> exhibit the really pure and transparent words respecting the true light, to
> swine-ish and untrained hearers. For scarcely could anything which they
> could hear be more ludicrous than these to the multitude; nor any subjects on
> the other hand more admirable or more inspiring to those of noble nature.
>   "But the natural (worldly) man receiveth not the things of the Spirit
> of God; for they are foolishness to him."[4]
>
> *Clement of Alexandria, Miscellanies I:XII, WCAI p.388*

The worldly man, he says, rejects spiritual teachings instinctively, since they appear to him to be "ludicrous", though the same things are full of inspiration to "those of noble nature". Hence, he quotes Jesus' advice on the subject: "cast not your pearls before swine". The same idea is conveyed by Clement's pupil, Origen, who comments:

> This word (mystery) is usually applied to the deeper and more mystical doctrines which are rightly concealed from the multitude.
>
> *Origen, Against Celsus V:19, OCC p.278*

The Old Testament prophets also seem to have followed this principle and it is one of the reasons why allegory and parable were so commonly used in ancient times. Certainly, the Old and New Testaments, while clearly expressing a belief in a retribution for sin, give only veiled references or asides concerning reincarnation. In *Genesis*, as we have seen, Adam and Eve are cast out of Eden, sentenced to die and given a "coat of skins" for use in this world. There is, however, one clear Old Testament reference to reincarnation in the *Wisdom of Solomon*:

> I was a boy of happy disposition,
> I had received a good soul as my lot,
>   or rather, being good, I had entered an undefiled body.
>
> *Wisdom of Solomon 8:19-20, JB*

A statement which would appear to mean precisely what it says.

In *Revelations*, in a long discourse said to have been made to the author by the spiritual form of Jesus, there are a number of assertions which seem to indicate liberation from reincarnation through contact with the Word of God, called the "Tree of Life", the "hidden Manna", the "new Name" and "my Voice". And, as in John's gospel, rebirth is called the "second death":

> He that hath an ear,
> let him hear what the Spirit saith unto the churches:

> "To him that overcometh
>   will I give to eat of the Tree of Life,
>   which is in the midst of the paradise of God....

> "He that overcometh
>   shall not be hurt of the second death....

"To him that overcometh
   will I give to eat of the hidden Manna,
   and will give him a white stone,
   and in the stone a new Name written,
   which no man knoweth saving he that receiveth it....

"He that overcometh,
   the same shall be clothed in white raiment;
   and I will not blot out his name out of the Book of Life,
   but I will confess his name before my Father,
   and before His angels....

"Him that overcometh
   will I make a pillar in the temple of my God,
   and he shall go no more out:
And I will write upon him the Name of my God,
   and the Name of the City of my God ...
   and I will write upon him my new Name....

"Behold, I stand at the door, and knock:
   if any man hear my Voice, and open the door,
   I will come in to him,
   and will sup with him, and he with me.

"To him that overcometh
   will I grant to sit with me in my throne,
   even as I also overcame,
   and am set down with my Father in His throne....

"He that overcometh
   shall inherit all things;
   and I will be his God, and he shall be my son."
                               Book of Revelation, 2:7,11,17; 3:5,12,20,21; 21:7

"Overcoming" means overcoming the power of Satan, gaining mastery over the many facets of the mind, becoming free from sin and from the realms of mind and matter. And the result, says Jesus, is that "he shall no more go out" and "shall not be hurt of the second death" – he will no more go out into the physical creation and face death in this world. "I will come unto him", and he will "sup with me", will "sit with me in my throne", will become a permanent "pillar in the temple of my God", "shall inherit all things" and will become the "son" of God – all these are allusions to the soul's attainment of union with God. After which, there is no returning to this world.

"Being clothed in a white raiment" is a reference to the 'robe of glory', the true garment or nature of a pure soul, unencumbered by mind and body, which the soul experiences after rising above the realm of Satan. Being named in the "Book of Life" is another expression commonly found in the ancient literature and refers to those who are destined or chosen to receive initiation from a true Saviour. Later Christians, of course, took it to mean anyone who was a Christian, according to their concept of Christianity.

Intriguingly, these verses, although appearing at regular intervals throughout chapters two and three, with the last one located in chapter twenty-one, fit so well together that one wonders if they once constituted a complete and independent poem, split up and used by the compiler of this strange book.

Immortality, Pre-existence & Reincarnation

It is not surprising that so many of the early Christians believed in reincarnation. It was a widespread philosophy at that time and it would not have been unusual if Jesus had taught it. Many other mystics of the time did so, where it was an integral and natural extension of the belief in an immortal soul as the essence and real nature of man. The innate immortality of the soul is a belief that is common amongst spiritually-minded people and has been endorsed by many mystics. And naturally, if the soul is immortal and of the same essence as God, a drop of the divine Ocean, and as a consequence does not live and die with the physical body, then it must have come from somewhere before this life and go on somewhere else afterwards. The question is, where does it come from and where does it go to and what determines its passage? Reincarnation, together with an understanding of the higher realms and the possibility of the soul's sojourn there, provides the obvious answer.

The Greeks had an ancient mystical tradition of which the indestructibility, immortality and reincarnation of the soul were an essential aspect. Pythagoras (*c.*580-507 BC), Heraclitus (*c.*540-475 BC), Empedocles (*c.*490-430 BC), Socrates (*c.*470-399 BC), Plato (*c.*427-

347 BC), Aristotle (384-322 BC), teacher to Alexander the Great, and many others all believed in and taught reincarnation. Greek influence in the Middle East was considerable. Even before the time of Alexander (*c.*356-323 BC), Hellenistic philosophy and culture had spread throughout the Middle East and North Africa, maintaining an influence until well into the Christian era.

But there were many besides the Greek mystics who taught reincarnation. The ancient Egyptians were convinced of it; Zarathushtra probably taught it; the Druids believed in it; and the philosophy was prevalent in Judaism, too. It is likely that the Essenes accepted it, for they taught the immortality of the soul and its escape from the bodily prison, while Josephus reports that rewards in an afterlife followed by a new life on earth, at least of the virtuous, was also an accepted doctrine in Pharisaism, though there is some scholarly dispute over whether Josephus is referring to reincarnation or resurrection:[5]

> (The Pharisees) believe that souls have an immortal vigour in them and that, under the earth (in the afterlife), there will be rewards and punishments, according as they have lived virtuously or viciously in this life; and that the latter are to be detained in an everlasting prison, but that the former shall have the power to revive and live again (on earth): on account of which doctrines, they are greatly able to persuade the body of the people.
>
> *Josephus, Antiquities XVIII:14 (1.3), JCW p.376*

And more explicitly:

> They (the Pharisees) say that all the souls are imperishable, but that the souls of good men only pass into other bodies, but the souls of bad men are subject to eternal punishment.
>
> *Josephus, Jewish War II:163 (8.14); cf. JCW p.478, JII pp.385-387*

Given the prevalence of the belief in the ancient world, therefore, there is no doubt that Paul the Pharisee would have been familiar with reincarnation and there are passages in his letters which certainly indicate at least his partial acceptance of the doctrine.

The Alexandrian Jew, Philo Judaeus, whose comments we have already quoted in connection with the *Logos*, was also a proponent of this philosophy and clearly saw no incompatibility between his allegorical and mystical interpretation of the Jewish scriptures and Greek mystical thought. He wrote:

The air is the abode of incorporeal souls, since it seemed good to their Maker to fill all parts of the universe with living beings.... Some souls, such as have earthward tendencies and material tastes, descend to be fast bound in mortal bodies, while others ascend.... Of these last, some, longing for the familiar and accustomed ways of mortal life, again retrace their steps, while others pronouncing that life great foolery call the body a prison and a tomb, and escaping as though from a dungeon or a grave, are lifted up on light wings to the upper air and range the heights for ever.

Others there are of perfect purity and excellence, gifted with a higher and diviner temper, that have never felt any craving after the things of earth, but are Viceroys of the Ruler of the universe.... The sacred record (the scriptures) is wont to call them "angels" or messengers.

Philo, On Dreams I:22, PhV pp.369-373

Note how, like Jesus, he calls the body a "prison", and a "grave". And he mentions, too, the existence of higher souls, "of perfect purity and excellence" who operate within the will of God, though from the full context it is clear that he is not speaking here of those souls who incarnate as Saviours. In another book, he says:

Some of the souls have descended into bodies, but others have never deigned to be brought into union with any of the parts of earth.... But the others, descending into the body as though into a stream, have sometimes been caught in the swirl of its rushing torrent and swallowed up thereby, at other times have been able to stem the current, have risen to the surface and then soared upwards back to the place from whence they came.

These last, then, are the souls of those who have given themselves to genuine philosophy (*lit.* love of Wisdom), who from first to last study to die to the life of the body, that a higher existence immortal and incorporeal in the presence of Him who is Himself immortal and uncreated, may be their portion.

But the souls which have sunk beneath the stream, are the souls of the others who have held no count of Wisdom. They have abandoned themselves to the unstable things of chance, none of which has aught to do with our noblest part, the soul or mind, but all are related to the dead thing which was our birth-fellow, the body, or to objects more lifeless still, glory, wealth, and offices, and honours, and all other illusions which like images or pictures are created through the deceit of false opinion by those who have never gazed upon true beauty.

Philo, On the Giants III, PhII pp.451-452

The immortality of the soul was certainly taught by the early Christians. We find the belief amongst a number of the early fathers and also in the *Doctrine of Addai,* as we already have seen. Orthodox Christian dogma, however, denies the existence of the soul prior to birth. This has been the doctrinal position since at least the sixth century. Souls are said to be created along with the body. After death, they go to heaven or hell, perhaps via an interim stay in purgatory. There they await the 'last day' when all of them will be reunited with their bodies and be judged according to the deeds of their one and only chance at human life.

But the idea is odd, as well as unfair. For – since the dogma also says that only Christians go to heaven – what of those people who came before Jesus? What of all those who have never had an opportunity to know of Christianity, before or since? Some parts of the planet have only been discovered by Christians in the last few hundred years and other places are still almost inaccessible to outsiders. Are these poor souls condemned to hell because of the exigencies of geography and delayed exploration on the part of evangelical Christians? Is not hell getting rather crowded? And heaven, too?

Moreover, since all bodies decay in a very short time, once the soul has departed, with all of its material being naturally recycled into other forms and even other humans, who will claim the atoms when the final trumpet sounds? Will it not be an awful mess when they all get up? And what of those whose bodies were cremated?

Again, would God really give some souls a head start over others, condemning others to hell owing to the very circumstances of their birth? – which He had arranged for them? And if all souls were the same prior to their taking birth, why are their circumstances arranged so differently? How is the allotment made? Due to the natural workings of human psychology and childhood conditioning, most people adopt the religion of their birth. So this would mean that those who are born into good Christian families stand a better chance than all the rest of reaching heaven, while those born outside Christendom, perhaps with no opportunity to ever know of Christianity, are destined for eternal punishment before they start, even if they have led the most pure and holy lives.

But does Christianity really have a monopoly on goodness and holiness? Or on heaven? Does God love only Christians? Would God, the universal Father and Creator of all, said to be all love, really be so partisan as to surround himself with the members of just one religion? Is not the whole idea more akin to our restricted and close-hearted, human thought processes than the love and universality of God?

And what of all the other creatures who inhabit this world? What part has God assigned to them in His grand design? Are they just incidentals, of no account or purpose? Is their suffering of no significance? And does it also mean that God has created such a vast physical universe purely for the sake of tiny, insignificant planet earth and its human inhabitants? Is God so parochial and narrow-minded? Are all the other planets, stars and galaxies purely to keep man company by night?

Such ideas and theories all bear the hallmark of man's limitations and there is no doubt that many of the early Christians presumed the pre-existence of the soul and its immortal nature. Logic, as well as a sense of the eternal within themselves, automatically led them to this conclusion. Many, however, remained undecided as to whether the soul returned or not in further incarnations. But this left the question open as to where the souls were, prior to human incarnation. Did they rest in some vast 'soul-pool' awaiting their turn to be a human being?

The early Christian fathers who struggled with these problems were divided in opinion. But their uncertainty only emphasizes the fact that the four gospels, as in so many other instances, give no clear direction. The great St Augustine (354-430), for instance, Bishop of Hippo (396-430) in North Africa, became one of the most influential of all the early church fathers. Raised in Catholicism, for nine years he became a Manichaean – and Manichaeans believed in reincarnation, as we will see. But after his return to Christianity, he remained in doubt upon this issue. In his *Confessions*, speaking of his childhood and musing over the problems of a baby being born in sin and guilt, he wrote:

> Say, Lord to me ... say, did my infancy succeed another age of mine that died before it? Was it that which I spent within my mother's womb? ... And what before that life again, O God my joy, was I anywhere or in any body? For this I have none to tell me, neither father nor mother, nor experience of others, nor mine own memory.
>
> Augustine, *Confessions* I:VII.9, CSA p.7

His honesty is appealing. "For I have none to tell me ... nor experience of others, nor mine own memory". Clearly, he did not feel that the gospels were an adequate guide upon the subject, and belief alone he could not trust.

After relinquishing both Christianity and Manichaeism, Augustine languished in doubt and scepticism. But moving to Rome, he came into contact with the Neo-Platonists, particularly the writings of Plotinus (205-270 AD), which brought new life to his spiritual seeking. Of Plato and Plotinus, he writes:

> The message of Plato, the purest and most luminous in all philosophy,
> has at last scattered the darkness of error, and now shines forth mainly in
> Plotinus, a Platonist so like his master that one would think they lived
> together, or rather – since so long a period of time separates them – that
> Plato is reborn again in Plotinus.
>
> *Augustine, Against the Academics III:18, RR p.80*

But Augustine was not the only one to have received inspiration from
the Greek philosophers. Plotinus was a disciple of Ammonius Saccas
who in 193 AD founded the famous Alexandrian School of Neo-
Platonism. The school was also called the Eclectic Theosophical School
or the Philalethians, the 'lovers of truth'. Ammonius left no written record
of his teaching, but he generated a revival of interest in the philosophy
of Plato which lasted many centuries. And amongst those who attended
his discourses was the Christian philosopher and theologian, Origen.[6]

Also deeply influenced by the ancient teachings of the Greek mystics was Clement of Alexandria who became head of a private school
opened by his teacher Pantaenus (*d.c.*190 AD) for Christian catechu-
mens, those undergoing pre-baptismal instruction. Thoroughly
steeped in Greek mystical philosophy, Clement would have been quite
familiar with the idea of reincarnation and the immortality of the soul.
Not all his writings have survived, however, and those that have are
unlikely to have escaped editorial tampering on sensitive issues. All
the same, he seems to have believed in the pre-existence of the soul
and its immortality. In his *Exhortation to the Heathen*, he writes:

> Before the foundation of the world were we, who, because destined to be
> in Him, pre-existed in the eye of God before – we the rational creatures
> of the Word of God, on whose account we date from the beginning; for
> "in the beginning was the Word".
>
> *Clement of Alexandria, Exhortation to the Heathen I, WCAI p.22*

Clement and his student Origen, who took over the school after Clement, both coming from the heady intellectual and cosmopolitan atmosphere of Alexandria, were amongst the first to bring Greek philosophy
to 'orthodox' Christianity. Recognizing in Jesus' teachings the same
truths that the ancient Greek mystics had taught, Clement, Origen,
Augustine and others like them helped create a means by which the
intelligentsia could approach Christianity. But they also demonstrated
the truth that people take the teachings of the mystics and fit them
into their own background and way of thinking. This is how religious

doctrine slowly forms around a mystic's teachings, the result being something similar, yet subtly different, slowly moving further and further away from the centre.

Origen, too, believed and taught the pre-existence of the soul. But passages can be found amongst his writings which – in different places – express both a belief and disbelief in reincarnation. Part of the problem is that a large proportion of his writings have been lost and those that survive exist mostly in a Latin translation provided by the notorious late fourth-century Rufinus (*c.*340-410).

Rufinus took it upon himself, not only to translate Origen, but also to 'correct' him, and where we have both the original Greek and Rufinus' Latin version, it can be observed that he indulges in considerable paraphrasing, deletion, addition and general rewriting of Origen's original, correcting whatever he sees as Origen's 'heresies'. In an extant letter to a certain Macarius, he admits to this method, justifying it by saying that he had only removed what he deemed to be the 'heretical interpolations' of others or that he had clarified the meaning by adding passages from Origen's other works.[7] But scholars have not normally considered his explanation to be plausible. Other early Christians, including Jerome, also made Latin translations of Origen, but only those of Rufinus have survived and there is little doubt that many of the confusions and contradictions in Origen's writings are due to his 'translations'.

Jerome and Rufinus lived during the first century after Christianity had received Imperial approval. Christianity was busy formalizing its beliefs and theology and, at the same time, Latin was gradually replacing Greek as the *lingua franca* of the Roman Empire and of Christianity. It was therefore necessary for translations to be made so that the Latin-speaking Christian fathers could read the writings of their predecessors.

Though praising him in his younger days, Jerome later became greatly antagonistic to Origen's views and together with others, including Archbishop Theophilus of Alexandria (infamous for instigating the burning of the ancient and world-famous library at Alexandria in 391 AD), he conducted a crusade against Origen's teachings and his followers.

For his part, Origen had regularly attended the lectures of Ammonius Saccas and made a thorough study of the works of Plato, Pythagoras, the Stoics and others. With this training in Greek philosophy, it would have been by no means odd if he had taught reincarnation as a part of Christian doctrine and both Jerome and Theophilus[8] attribute this belief to him. Jerome – who had the advantage of a Greek text in front of him, untouched by Rufinus – writes, quoting Origen:

> The following passage is a convincing proof that he (Origen) holds the transmigration of souls and annihilation of bodies. "If it can be shown that an incorporeal and reasonable being (a soul) has life in itself independently of the body and that it is worse off in the body than out of it; then beyond a doubt bodies are only of secondary importance and arise from time to time to meet the varying conditions of reasonable creatures. Those who require bodies are clothed with them, and contrariwise, when fallen souls have lifted themselves up to better things, their bodies are once more annihilated. They are thus ever vanquishing and ever reappearing."
>
> *Jerome (quoting Origen), Letter (CXXIV) to Avitus 15, PWJ p.244*

As Origen's writings now stand, mostly in the Latin translation of Rufinus, Origen is often ambivalent or contrary in the way he speaks of reincarnation. In his reply to Celsus, however, the author of a treatise refuting Christianity, he does seem to be endorsing the view:

> Is it not more in conformity with reason (and I say this now following Pythagoras, Plato and Empedocles, whom Celsus often mentions) that there are certain secret (hidden) principles by which each soul that enters a body does so in accordance with its merits and former character?
>
> *Origen, Against Celsus I:XXXII, OCC p.32, WOI p.432*

And:

> The soul, which is immaterial and invisible in its nature, exists in no material place without having a body suited to the nature of that place. Accordingly, it at one time puts off one body which was necessary before, but which is no longer adequate in its changed state, and it exchanges it for a second.
>
> *Origen, Against Celsus VII:XXXII, WOII p.454*

And in *On First Principles*, he says:

> The soul has neither beginning nor end.... Every soul ... comes into this world strengthened by the victories or weakened by the defeats of its previous life. Its place in the world, as a vessel appointed to honour or dishonour, is determined by its previous merits or demerits. Its work

(actions) in this world determines its place in the world which is to follow this.

Origen, On First Principles, REWA p.36[9]

Origen himself, though controversial in his day, gained wide respect, and influenced the development of Christian doctrine for at least three centuries. Jerome at one time considered him to be the "greatest teacher of the Church after the apostles";[10] the late fourth-century Gregory, Bishop of Nyssa (374-395), called him the "prince of Christian learning in the third century";[11] and Origen's pupil and friend, Gregory Thaumaturgus, mid-third-century Bishop of Neo-Caesarea, spoke warmly in his *Panegyric on Origen*[12] of Origen's charm of manner, his generous friendship, his wide sympathy, and his consummate wisdom.[13] It was through him, said Gregory, that he had come to appreciate the Greek philosophers and their great relevance to the teachings of Jesus. But in the end, Origen's teachings fell from favour and, in 543 AD, the Byzantine Emperor Justinian convened a local synod at Constantinople whose purpose was to condemn the teachings of Origen. This was the official beginning of a process which ended in the discrediting of Origen's theology, so far as orthodox Christianity was concerned.

From the earliest times, matters of Christian belief and creed were decided by councils of bishops and the higher clergy. But dating from the era of Constantine, the course of such councils and their decisions were frequently under the authority of the emperor whose interests were invariably political rather than spiritual. Some emperors interfered more than others and early in the sixth century, Justinian, who had been at odds with Pope Vigilius for several years, assumed authority over the entire Church, issuing Imperial edicts that regulated public worship, dictated ecclesiastical discipline and even determined doctrine. By this time, only one centre of Greek philosophy remained, the University of Athens. And in 529 AD, Justinian, jealous of his reputation for strict orthodoxy, decreed that no one should henceforth teach the ancient philosophy and this last centre was closed, many of the scholars fleeing to Persia where they found sympathy for their doctrines. Throughout the Empire, only Christian schools of learning were now permitted and all philosophy was to be conducted within the strict walls of an ever-tightening, orthodox Christian dogma. The Dark Ages of ignorance had begun.

In 553 AD, Justinian convened the Fifth Ecumenical Council at Constantinople, ostensibly to bring peace between the Eastern and

Western arms of the Church. The result, however, was a schism between the East and the West which lasted seventy years. The Council was held very much on Justinian's terms and Pope Vigilius, although in Constantinople, refused to attend, for with the exception of six bishops from Africa, all those present were from the East.

Among the items on the agenda were the anathemas (curses) derived from Justinian's depositions against Origen and his teachings. The first was aimed directly at a belief in pre-existence and reincarnation:

> If anyone assert the fabulous pre-existence of souls, and shall assert the monstrous restoration which follows from it: let him be anathema.
>
> *Anathemas Against Origen I, SECUC p.318*

Justinian's original draft was even more explicit:

> Whoever thinks that human souls pre-existed ... but that satiated with the vision of God, they had turned to evil, and in this way the divine love in them had died out and they had therefore ... been condemned to punishment in bodies, shall be anathema.
>
> *Anathematisms of the Emperor Justinian Against Origen I, SECUC p.320*

From these it may presumed that Origen did indeed teach reincarnation as a part of Christian doctrine. Strangely, however, there is no evidence that the anathemas were ever ratified and on technical grounds, at least, there is still no objection to a Christian belief in the pre-existence of the soul and in reincarnation, particularly since the Pope did not attend the meeting. It must be obvious, however, that by the time Jesus' teachings had become the subject of Imperial edicts, warring bishops and exasperated Popes, the real understanding and interest in the spirituality and path of love Jesus taught had long since been submerged and forgotten.

Reincarnation Amongst the Early Christians

History is written by the 'winners' who see only the chain of events involved in their own development. Modern Christianity traces its history from the ancient, so-called 'orthodox' stream of early Christianity and it is not a history of which they can be proud. Orthodoxy in religion, philosophy, science or in any other human affair is often synonymous with rigidity of mental outlook and an emphasis on material considerations. This leads to hatred, violence, destruction, murder, power struggles, desire for property and wealth, jealousy, pride, greed, theft, extreme prejudice, usurping the rights of others and much more. In Christianity, so much of its history has so clearly been so far, far away from the teachings of Jesus upon which it professes to be founded. As Jesus told the Jews who sincerely thought that they were worshipping God, "ye are of your father the Devil". So much of it has been the product of the human mind, not of God.

In the early years, long before Constantine, there were many schools of thought amongst those who called themselves Christian, many of them far more deeply spiritual and mystic than the conservative and orthodox stream. Unconcerned about ecclesiastical or political power and motivated more by a sincere desire for truth, they were little interested in forming strong organizations, dictating dogma or increasing their numbers. Their ambitions were personal and spiritual, not material and evangelical, and such schools of thought have faded with time, for their strength was inner and it departed with the individuals concerned.

Within this gnostic or esoteric stream of Christianity were many who believed in reincarnation, for it was more or less a standard part of the 'gnostic myth', birth in successive bodies being the lot of the individual soul when imprisoned in matter. And they believed that Jesus had given the same teachings, too. Scholars have classed them all as gnostics, and sadly our main source of information on these teachers are the heresy-hunting Church fathers like Irenaeus, Hippolytus and Epiphanius, each one of whom speaks of 'heretics' who believed in reincarnation.

Although gnosticism by no means began in Christian times, the earliest gnostic named by these fathers is Simon Magus, a contemporary of Jesus, mentioned in *Acts* and said, it may be recalled, in the *Clementine Homilies* and *Recognitions* to be a successor of John the Baptist. A Samaritan by birth, Simon Magus taught of the *Logos*, its emanations as creation, the descent of the soul into the realm of birth and death and its salvation through a qualified Saviour. This is the age-old mystic doctrine and, in his summary of Simon's teachings, Irenaeus writes of the captive soul and its salvation:

> And Thought (the *Ennoia* or *Logos*) was made prisoner by the powers and angels (rulers) that had been emanated by her. And she suffered every kind of indignity at their hands to prevent her reascending to her Father, even to being imprisoned in the human body and transmigrating into other ... bodies, as from one vessel into another.... So she, transmigrating

from body to body, and thereby also continually undergoing indignity, at last became a common prostitute; and she was the 'lost sheep'.

"Wherefore also," (says the Saviour), "am I come to take her away for the first time and free her from her bonds; to make sure salvation to men by my *Gnosis*."

Irenaeus, Against Heresies I:XXIII.2-3, AHI pp.87-88, FFF p.169

None of Simon's works have survived, even as fragments quoted by others, but his association with John the Baptist is of recurring interest. We know little of what John actually taught, but since a disciple will normally teach the same path as his Master, did John, too, like his disciple Simon, also teach reincarnation?

Basilides was another of the well-known gnostic teachers. Active in Alexandria around 125-135 AD, his later followers claimed that he had received his doctrine through a line of apostolic succession. His influence must have been considerable, because followers were still active in fourth-century Egypt.

Eusebius reports that Basilides published twenty-four volumes of *Interpretations of the Gospels*. He also wrote his own poetry or songs and compiled his own edition of a gospel. All these have been lost, many copies being burnt, no doubt, as heretical, for only reports and brief quotations have come down to us – seven by Clement of Alexandria and one by Origen. Irenaeus and others also give an account that probably originated with Justin Martyr around 150 AD. From the little that remains, it seems that Basilides' teachings were centred around the conventional gnostic or mystic path, which inevitably included reincarnation. Clement of Alexandria reports:

> The hypothesis of Basilides says that the soul, having sinned before in another life, endures punishment in this.
>
> *Clement of Alexandria, Miscellanies IV:XII, WCAII p.176*

Clement also noted that the mid-third-century gnostic, Theodotus, had recorded Basilides' teaching of reincarnation. In this extract, Theodotus is speaking of an interpretation given by the followers of Basilides to a passage from *Deuteronomy*:[14]

> The followers of Basilides refer "God visiting the disobedient unto the third and fourth generation" to reincarnation.
>
> *Theodotus, Excerpta ex Theodoto 28, ETCA p.63*

The interpretation is enlightening, for the Jewish belief that punishment for sins is exacted from future generations seems bizarre. Here, it is suggested that the idea is a misunderstanding of reincarnation, the "third and fourth generation" referring to future births.

In Origen's sole quotation, he comments that Basilides even credited the apostle Paul with a belief in transmigration into forms lower than that of man, basing this assertion upon an interpretation of a passage from *Romans*:

> The apostle (Paul) has said, "I was once alive apart from the law," at some time or other. That is (Paul means), before I came into this body, I lived in the kind of body that is not subject to the law: the body of a domestic animal or bird.
>
> *Basilides, in Origen's Commentary on the Epistle to the Romans (Romans 7:7),*
> *GS pp.438-439*

Amongst the many other gnostic Christians who taught or believed in reincarnation was the well-known Valentinus (*fl.*140-160 AD) from whom many later gnostic schools were descended, some still extant in the seventh century. He and his contemporary Marcion (*fl.*140-160 AD) were both respected members of the church at Rome for many years, Valentinus even being considered to fill the post of bishop. The fourth-century Epiphanius indicated that Valentinus taught reincarnation, together with the little known Colarbasus, though whether his comment included Marcion as well is ambiguous:

> (Marcion) believes that the same soul is in men and animals. This futile conjecture is made by many misguided sects. Valentinus and Colarbasus, and all gnostics and Manichaeans, claim that there is a reincarnation of souls, and that there are transmigrations of the soul of (spiritually) ignorant persons – as they themselves call them.... They say that the soul returns and is reembodied in each of the animals until it recognizes (the truth), and is thus cleansed and set free, and departs to the heavens.
>
> *Epiphanius, Panarion I:III:24, PES p.298*

Epiphanius and others may have derided the gnostics leaders, but other early Christians, though they disagreed with them on many points, afforded them considerable respect. Clement of Alexandria, for example, highlights Basilides, Valentinus and Marcion as outstanding personalities of the previous generation.[15] As regards reincarnation, he also records that Theodotus, a later follower of Valentinus, speaking of the liberating power of mystic baptism, observed:

> But it is not only the (spiritual) washing (of baptism) that is liberating,
> but the knowledge of who we were, and what we have become; where we
> were, into what we have been thrown; whither we hasten, from what we
> are redeemed; what birth is, and what rebirth.
>
> *Theodotus, Excerpta ex Theodoto 78, ETCA p.89, GR p.45*

Irenaeus also mentions the Carpocratians, who – according to a document that he has before him – state that in Jesus' saying which begins
"Agree with thine adversary quickly", the "adversary" is the Devil; the
"judge" is the chief of the world-building powers, that is, an agent of
the Negative Power concerned with the administration of the physical
universe; the "officer" is the power who oversees the formation of a
new body; and the "prison" is the body itself. The Devil or Satan is
thus perceived as the ruler of the lesser *archons* and the teaching is
credited to Jesus. Irenaeus then continues:

> Again, they interpret these expressions, "Thou shalt not go out thence
> until thou pay the very last farthing," as meaning that no one can escape
> the power of those angels who made the world, but that he must pass
> from body to body, until he has experience of every kind of action which
> can be practised in this world, and when nothing is longer wanting to
> him, then his liberated soul should soar upwards to God who is above
> the angels, the makers of the world.
>
> *Irenaeus, Against Heresies I:XXV.4, AHI pp.95-96*

The "experience of every kind of action which can be practised in this
world" is probably a misunderstanding by Irenaeus or perhaps by the
Carpocratians themselves. It means – as mystics have always taught –
that a soul must clear all the effects of its past *karmas* or actions before
it can attain liberation from reincarnation and the powers which rule
this world. Only then can it return to God. Like so many others, therefore, the Carpocratians also saw mystical meaning in the words of
Jesus. But, as we have seen before, such teachings were not given to the
world at large. Irenaeus thus concludes:

> And in their writings we read, as follows, the interpretation which they
> give (of their views), declaring that Jesus spoke in a mystery to his disciples
> and apostles privately, and that they requested and obtained permission
> to hand down the things thus taught them, to others who should be
> worthy and believing.
>
> *Irenaeus, Against Heresies I:XXV.5, AHI p.96*

The early third-century father, Hippolytus, also writes of the Naassenes, a group of gnostic Christians who appear to have been his contemporaries. They, too, believed in the gnostic path and seem to have taught reincarnation as the means by which the soul is trapped in matter. Hippolytus has a Naassene text in front of him as he writes, the author of which is evidently pointing out the mystic truths to be found in all the ancient religious traditions of his time and place. But Hippolytus castigates him for this, accusing him of creating his 'system' out of the philosophies and mythologies of the past. Clearly, he does not understand the universal nature of the mystics and their teachings.

Though Hippolytus' account is garbled, enough remains to establish that the Naassene writer is referring to the ancient myths of Mesopotamia, the Old Testament, the Greeks and the Romans, interpreting them allegorically and indicating their universal mystical meaning. He says, for instance, that the Greek god, Hermes, equivalent of the Roman Mercury, symbolizes the *Logos*, because the *Logos* carries God's 'message' or creative Power into creation, even appearing in this world as the "originator of souls", a "conjuror of the dead" and a "guide" – a divine Messenger or Master by whom souls are "awakened, and brought to recollection of themselves".[16]

At the same time, the writer also points out the mystic meaning of Jesus' sayings in the gospels, relating them to previous mystic teachings. Tantalizingly, Hippolytus only cites snatches of this Naassene text, except at the end of his short dissertation where he quotes a Naassene hymn. The hymn begins by speaking of God's First-born, creative Power (His *Nous*). From *Nous* then emanates "bitter *Chaos*", the labyrinth of the mind created by the Negative Power through whose dominion the individual soul is incarnated in this world, held captive by the "law of toil". Subsequently, the soul wanders in the maze of pain and pleasure, birth and death until the Saviour, Jesus, is sent on a mission of redemption with the "secrets of the holy path called *Gnosis*":

> Mind (*Nous*) was the first, the generative Law of all;
> Next was this First-born's *Chaos* then outpoured;
> Thirdly, the soul received its law of toil.

> Wherefore, surrounded with a nimble (variable) form,
>   with care o'erpowered, it succumbs to death.
> Now holding sway, it sees the light,
>   anon, cast into piteous plight, it weeps.

Now it weeps,
    now thrills with joy;
And as it wails, it hears its doom (judgment)
    now hears its doom, now dies....
Wandering haplessly,
    it treads the labyrinth of ills (rebirth).

But Jesus said, "Father behold,
    a strife of ills across the earth
    makes (man) to wander from thy Breath (Spirit).
He seeks to shun the bitter *Chaos*,
    but knows not how to flee.

"For this reason, O Father, send me.
Bearing seals (of release), I will descend,
    though all the *aeons* I will travel;
All mysteries I will reveal
    and show the forms of gods (to those I save).
The secrets of the holy Path
    called *Gnosis* will I impart."

    Naassene Hymn, in Refutation of All Heresies V:V, FFF pp.205-206, RAH p.153

It seems evident that were these ancient writings available to us in their entirety or even in larger fragments than we have, they would almost certainly provide us with much material to support our thesis. For very commonly, amongst the Nag Hammadi library and other extant gnostic tractates, as well as amongst the apocryphal literature, we find references to the soul being held captive in the prison of the body, being rescued by a Saviour from the darkness of this world, ascending from the realm of death and so on. Many of these are of a Christian character and presume that Jesus gave these teachings.

The *Apocalypse of Paul*, for instance, tells the familiar revelational story of an ascent through the heavens, this time, the central character being Paul. In the fourth heaven, he witnesses the judgment of a soul who leaves this world, the "land of the dead". And the soul is quite unaware of the sins it had been committing:

In the fourth heaven ...
    I saw the angels resembling gods,
        the angels bringing a soul out of the land of the dead.
    They placed it at the gate of the fourth heaven.

And the angels were whipping it.
The soul spoke, saying,
"What sin was it that I committed in the world?"

The toll-collector who dwells
   in the fourth heaven replied, saying,
"It was not right to commit all those lawless deeds
   that are in the world of the dead."

The soul replied, saying,
"Bring witnesses! Let them show you
   in what body I committed lawless deeds.
Do you wish to bring a book to read from?"

Apocalypse of Paul 20, NHS11 p.55

Three witnesses are then brought forward who testify against the soul, who realizes the truth of what they say. The story then continues:

When the soul heard these things,
   it gazed downward in sorrow.
And then it gazed upward.
It was cast down.
The soul that had been cast down went
   to a body which had been prepared for it.
And behold its witnesses were finished.

Apocalypse of Paul 21, NHS11 p.57

In the *Dialogue of the Saviour*, Jesus points out that a person suffers from whatever he does not understand. Thus, he who does not understand birth will not understand death, and "he is no stranger to this world" – he will suffer for his lack of understanding by returning to this world again and again:

If one does not understand how fire came into existence, he will burn in it, because he does not know the root of it.... If one does not understand how the body, which he bears, came into existence, he will perish with it.... Someone who will not know the root (source) of wickedness is no stranger to it. Whoever will not understand how he came (into birth) will not understand how he will go (at death), and he is no stranger to this world.

Dialogue of the Saviour 134, NHS26 p.69

Again, according to the revelational story related in the *Apocryphon of John*, speaking of what we call the mind as the "counterfeit spirit", the spiritual form of Jesus is answering questions put to him by the disciple John. We pick up the dialogue where Jesus is telling John that while incarnate in the body, the soul upon whom the Spirit of Life "descends" will definitely "attain salvation". It is John who is relating the story:

> He (the Saviour) answered and said to me, "If the Spirit descends upon them, it is quite sure that they will attain salvation.... Indeed, the Power (Holy Spirit) will descend unto everyone – for without it no one can stand up (live in the body). And after they are born, if the Spirit of Life increases – if the Power comes to them – it strengthens that soul, and nothing can lead it into the works of wickedness. But those upon whom the counterfeit spirit descends will be beguiled by it and go astray."
>
> *Apocryphon of John 26, GS p.48, NHL pp.119-120*

The "Power" or the "Spirit" is present within everybody, else they could not "stand up" or exist in this world. The Spirit is the essence of life. But if the "Power comes to them", if they are baptized or initiated, then the "Spirit of Life increases", the soul will become increasingly conscious of the Spirit within itself and be greatly strengthened by it. Nothing can now lead that soul away from the mystic path. But those who become victims of the "counterfeit spirit", of the mind, are "beguiled and go astray".

> But for my part I said, "Sir, so when the souls of these people have come forth from their flesh, where will they go?"
>
> And he smiled and said to me, "The soul in which the Power will become stronger than the counterfeit spirit, is strong and will flee from wickedness. And by the intervention (grace) of the Incorruptible One, it will attain salvation and be taken into the repose of the *aeons* (higher realms and ultimately, God)."
>
> *Apocryphon of John 26, GS p.48, NHL p.120*

The soul in which the Spirit has taken root will, by His grace, be taken back to God.

> But for my part I said, "Sir, then where will the souls of these others, who have not known to whom they belong, reside?"
>
> And he said to me, "In the case of those others, the counterfeit spirit has increased within them while they were going astray. And it weighs down the soul, and beguiles it into the works of wickedness, and casts it

into forgetfulness (or deep sleep). And after it has come forth (from the body at death) it is given into the charge of the authorities (rulers), who exist because of the (great) *Archon* (Ruler, *i.e.* Satan). And they bind it with bonds and cast it into the prison (of the body). And they go around with it until it awakens out of forgetfulness and takes *gnosis* unto itself. And in this way, if thus it becomes perfect, it attains salvation."

Apocryphon of John 26-27, GS p.48, NHL p.120

But the others, who have followed the inclinations and promptings of their own mind, the "counterfeit spirit", fall into forgetfulness of God. They fall asleep so far as He is concerned. And after death they are taken by the "authorities", the lesser powers who operate within the rule of the great *Archon*, the Negative Power. They "bind it with the bonds" of its own sins and "cast it into the prison" of the body, staying with it and keeping it bound until such time as the soul awakens, gains true knowledge and attains salvation.

The graphic term "counterfeit spirit" is found in a number of the gnostic tractates. In the *Pistis Sophia*, for example, Mary Magdalene asks Jesus, "Who compels men until they commit sin?" It is a good question and Jesus explains that a human being is comprised of the "Power", the "soul", and the "counterfeit spirit", all three being bound together in a physical body. The Power is the Creative Word, and the "soul" is the drop of that Power which is either dragged down by the "counterfeit spirit" or upwards by the Word. The "counterfeit spirit" is the mind with its material desires and tendencies. Of these three elements in human constitution, Jesus says:

Each one of them perceives according to its nature. The Power perceives in order to seek the Light of the Height. The soul, on the other hand, perceives in order to seek the region of righteousness which is mixed, which is the region of commixture. The counterfeit spirit however seeks all evil and desires and all sins. The body does not itself perceive anything unless its material substance receives power (from the soul and mind).

Pistis Sophia 111, PS p.282, PSGG p.235

The "region of righteousness which is mixed" is a technical gnostic term referring to the astral and causal realms which are subtle and spiritual compared to the physical universe, but where the pure soul is still mixed with the mind, with the elements of Satan's domain. The term could also be translated as the 'region of mixed spirituality'. In the *Pistis Sophia* and other gnostic tractates, these realms are also known as the "regions of the Midst". To begin with, says Jesus, the soul, associated with the mind, yearns only for the more spiritual atmosphere of the "region of righteousness which is mixed" even though they are still within the domain of Satan. But the "counterfeit spirit ... seeks all evil and desires and all sins". It is only interested in the body and the things of this world. Jesus then explains:

> And the Power within moves the soul to seek after the Place of the Light (the eternal realm) and the whole Godhead. And the counterfeit spirit inclines the soul and compels it to commit all its iniquities, with all its passions and all its sins continually. And it remains allotted to the soul, and it is hostile to it and causes it to commit all these wicked things and all these sins....
>
> Moreover, if it comes to rest by night or by day, it moves it with dreams or with desires of the world, and it causes it to desire everything of the world. In a word, it incites it to all things which the *archons* have commanded for it. And it becomes hostile to the soul, causing it to do what it does not wish. Now at this time, Maria, this is the enemy of the soul, and it is this which compels it until it commits all sins.
>
> *Pistis Sophia 111, PS pp.283-284, PSGG p.236*

The soul is pulled towards the world by the mind and is drawn towards God by the "Power within", the Spirit. Even when a person is resting or dreaming, the "counterfeit spirit" continues to project desires of the world before them.

Jesus' reply continues at length, but in essence, he says that the soul goes on in this way until the time of death, all its sins being witnessed by the "retributive ministers", the administrators of the mind, the lesser powers within Satan's realm. Or one can say that all the deeds of the soul are witnessed by the mind itself which receives corresponding impressions. Then, at the time of death, the soul is taken by "retributive receivers", the angels of death, is judged, and is allotted a place accordingly, the sinful soul being punished in hell. Jesus then points out that at this stage the "counterfeit spirit" itself becomes the guide of the soul and the soul is forced to go where the mind leads it:

> And the counterfeit spirit becomes the receiver of the soul, being assigned to it and transferring it (the soul) according to the chastisement (due to it) on account of the sins which it has caused it to commit. And it has great hostility towards the soul.
>
> *Pistis Sophia 111, PS p.284, PSGG p.237*

Subsequently, after its punishment in hell is over, the soul is brought before the ruler in charge of rebirth (a 'she'). The soul is then handed over to her "receivers" or helpers and is

cast ... into a body which is worthy of the sins which it has committed. And verily I say to you that she does not release that soul from the changes of the body before it has completed its last cycle, according to its due.

Pistis Sophia 111, PS pp.285-286, PSGG p.238

Jesus concludes this description by echoing the words from St Matthew, "Verily I say unto thee, thou shalt by no means come out thence, till thou hast paid the uttermost farthing." A quote which demonstrates once more the meaning these early Christians gave to this saying of Jesus.

The inner journey of a soul who has "received the mysteries of light" and has not fallen a prey to the "counterfeit spirit" during its physical lifetime is then described. In this extract, the accumulated sins or *karmas* of the soul, those which have been stored up from innumerable past lives within the mind but have so far received no opportunity for expression as the destiny of a physical lifetime, are referred to collectively as the "destiny". Jesus says:

Moreover, if there is a soul which has not listened to the counterfeit spirit in all his works, and becomes good and receives the mysteries of the light (initiation) ... when the time of the coming forth of that soul from the body is completed, the counterfeit spirit follows after that soul.

It, with the destiny (here, stored sins or *karmas*), follows after it on the path on which it is to go to the Height. And before it can betake itself into the Height, it (the soul) says the mystery of the releasing of the seals and all the bonds of the counterfeit spirit with which the *archons* bound it (the counterfeit spirit) to the soul. And when they are said, the bonds of the counterfeit spirit are released, it ceases to come into that soul, and it releases the soul....

Now when it happens that the soul says the mystery of the releasing of its seals and all the bonds of the counterfeit spirit, it (the counterfeit spirit) ceases entering into the soul and ceases being bound to it. And at the (same) time it (the soul) says a mystery and releases the destiny to its place in the presence of the *archons* which are on the way of the Midst. And it says the mystery and releases the counterfeit spirit ... to the place in which it was bound to it.

Pistis Sophia 112, PS pp.286-287, PSGG pp.238-239

When the time comes for an initiated soul who has not been led astray by the "counterfeit spirit" to leave the body, the mind goes along with the soul as it ascends towards God, the "Height", the eternal realm. And on the journey, there comes a point where the mind or "counterfeit spirit" and its encrusted "destiny" or store of past sins, are "released" or left behind. They return to their place of origin, the *archons* from whence they came. "Saying the mystery" means that the soul has the divine password of the Word, which opens all the doorways to the Height which lies above the realm of the mind, above the realm of Satan. This is the 'open sesame' which carries a soul through all barriers and gateways on the inner ascent. The soul then becomes free and naked, glowing with its own great radiance:

> And in that moment it (the soul) becomes a great outpouring of light, shining exceedingly. And the retributive receivers which have brought it forth from the body are afraid at the light of that soul, and they fall upon their faces. And in that moment, that soul becomes a great outpouring of light and becomes entirely winged with light, and penetrates all the regions of the *archons* and all their orders of light, until it goes to the region of its Kingdom.
>
> *Pistis Sophia 112, PS p.287, PSGG p.239*

The "retributive receivers" who had at one time caused the soul such great distress, casting it into hell and into body after body, are now in awe of the pure soul's splendour and its innate robe of glory. Now the soul is so powerful that its consciousness "penetrates every place of the *archons* and all their ranks of light". The soul has a greater power than Satan and all his *archons* or rulers and administrators. The soul's enlightenment gives it all knowledge of all the domains of Satan.

> And that soul dismisses their destiny to them, saying: "Receive back your destiny; I do not come to your regions from this time (onwards): I have become a stranger unto you for ever, being about to go to the region of my inheritance...."
>   And it says to them: "There, take ye your counterfeit spirit; I do not come to your regions from this time onwards; I have become a stranger to you for ever."
>
> *Pistis Sophia 112, PS pp.289-290, PSGG p.241*

And the soul dismisses the "counterfeit spirit" and its associated "destiny" or store of sins, saying that it will now no longer be returning to their realms, that it is going onwards to the eternal realm to claim its rightful "inheritance". In this narrative, then, Jesus is telling the story of the liberation of the soul from the clutches of the mind, the realm of Satan, and from the accumulated effect of sins from countless past lives. This is the beginning of true salvation, culminating in union with God.

The expression "counterfeit spirit" is particularly apposite, for by projecting itself as the ego or individual sense of self, the mind usurps the place of the soul, the real or higher self. And by this masquerade, the individual is deceived into acting according to what he thinks to be his own advantage when, in fact, the situation is exactly the reverse. Ego or the false self, the "counterfeit spirit" or mind that causes separation from God, is the primary weapon of the Negative Power in his deceit of souls, for the very 'I' that acts in this world is the agent of Satan. No wonder Jesus said "Ye are of your father the Devil". This is our human situation.

Drunken, Mad and Forgetful

Mystics from all lands and times have said that the souls trapped in the round of birth and death have fallen asleep or that they have entered the realm of forgetfulness or that they have become drunk or mad in their frantic pursuit of material things which continually elude their grasp. They have become spiritually ignorant of their own true heritage and live a life of death. In the *Gospel of Thomas*, for example, Jesus says:

> I stood in the midst of the world
>   and in the flesh was I seen of them,
> And I found all men drunken,
>   and none found I athirst (for God) among them,
> And my soul grieveth over the sons of men,
>   because they are blind in their heart, and see not.
>
> For empty they came into the world,
>   and empty too they seek to leave the world.
> But for the moment they are intoxicated.
> When they shake off their wine, then they will repent.
>
> *Gospel of Thomas 28, NHS20 p.65, OLAG p.50*

The Masters come to this world and observe that everyone is madly and drunkenly chasing after evanescent phantoms which have no permanent substance. Empty-handed they enter and empty-handed they leave, but in the interim they are intoxicated by the mind and the senses. Only when the effect of this "wine" is dispelled will a person repent and seek the spiritual path. The same idea is expressed in one of the Manichaean-Christian psalms where Jesus is called the "Saviour" and "Paraclete" (meaning mediator):

> Come, my Lord Jesus, the Saviour of souls,
>> who hast saved me from the drunkenness
>> and Error (Illusion) of the world.
> Thou art the Paraclete whom I have loved since my youth:
>> thy Light shines forth in me like the lamp of light:
> Thou hast driven away from me the oblivion of Error:
>> thou hast taught me to bless God and his Lights.
>
> I have distinguished this pair of trees
>> of this pair of kingdoms ...
>> the bitter fountain and the holy essence of God.
> The Light I have distinguished from the Darkness,
> life from death,
> Christ and the church I have distinguished
>> from the deceit of the world.
> I have known my soul and this body that lies upon it,
>> that they are enemies to each other before the creations....
> The body of death indeed and the soul are never in accord.
>
> The god of this *Aeon* (Satan)
>> has shut the heart of the unbelieving
> And has sunk them in his Error
>> and the deceit of drunkenness.
> He has made them blaspheme against the God of Truth,
> His Power and His Wisdom.
>
> *Psalm CCXLVIII, MPB pp.56-57*

Note, here, that to "blaspheme against the God of Truth, His Power and Wisdom" means to turn the mind away from Him and towards the world. In another of these psalms, this "drunkenness" and 'blasphemy' is called a "madness":

Come, my Saviour Jesus, do not forsake me.
I wandered throughout the whole world,
 I witnessed all the things that are in it.
I saw that all men run vainly to and fro.

O how long is the evil genius
 and madness of the darkness
  wherein they have been bound?
For they have forgotten God,
 who came and gave himself up to death for them.

Psalm CCXLIV, MPB p.51

And again:

Since I was bound in the flesh I forgot my divinity.
I was made to drink the cup of madness,
 I was made to rebel against my own self.
The powers and principalities came within,
 they armed themselves against me.
My Lord Jesus, do not abandon me.

Psalms, MPB p.116

All these passages repeat the same thing. The souls are bound by Satan and his "powers and principalities" in the labyrinth of death and rebirth. Here, they become drunk and mad, forgetting who they really are, blaspheming through their material tendencies, against the Supreme Lord. The only escape lies in the protection offered by one who is a Master of these powers.

The Cup of Forgetfulness

The literary tradition of discourses or question and answer sessions with the risen or spiritual form of Jesus that we have seen in *Revelations*, the *Apocryphon of John*, the *Pistis Sophia*, the *Dialogue of the Saviour* and so on, gained considerable support amongst the Christian gnostics. Perhaps they reflected real sessions held with the living Jesus, incorporating some of his discourses and answers recorded while he lived. Of these, it is probably the *Pistis Sophia* which has the most abundant and explicit references to reincarnation, some of which we have already encountered.

Strictly speaking, *Pistis Sophia* (*lit.* faith-wisdom) is a misnomer, for it only relates to the first two tractates in this codex. The other tractates are entitled the *Books of the Saviour* and amongst other things, they relate the content of question and answer sessions between the risen Jesus and his disciples. Whether there is any historical accuracy to these accounts is most uncertain. But as with so many of these ancient documents, including the canonical gospels, they tell us what people considered Jesus to have taught.

In the *Books of the Saviour*, a number of Jesus' answers concerning reincarnation are given in response to one or other of the disciples asking him the fate of people who behave in particular ways. The questions and their answers are clearly stylized, following a repeated formula and need not be taken literally. All the same, they demonstrate the principle of rebirth according to an individual's actions. Jesus is asked, for example, about the fate of the slanderer, the murderer, the thief, the arrogant man and so on. The reply to each is a description of various unpleasant experiences that the soul will meet in some hellish realm, after which it is given birth in a human body with a variety of defects. Some are born lame, some deformed, some constantly afflicted with various troubles and so on. The rebirth, for example, of one who curses others is said to be:

> And there comes Jalouham, ... he who gives the cup of forgetfulness to the souls, and he brings a cup full of the water of forgetfulness and he gives it to the soul, and it drinks it and forgets every region and all regions to which it has gone (since death). And it is cast into a body in which it will spend its time continually troubled in heart. This is the punishment of the man who curses.
>
> *Pistis Sophia 144, PS p.374, PSGG p.315*

The "cup of forgetfulness" is an image derived from Greek mythology. According to the myth, Lethe, the river of forgetfulness, runs through Hades and all who drink of it forget their past. The myth is probably a metaphor for the forgetfulness of the soul upon taking birth in this world. The soul forgets not only its past lives and sins, but also its divine origin with God.

After a number of similar descriptions, John then questions Jesus about the fate of someone who has done only good deeds, but has not received the initiation that will enable him to pass by the *archons* of Satan's realm. He asks:

> A man who has not committed sin, but has continually done good, but
> he has not found thy mysteries in order to pass the *archons*: when he
> comes forth from the body, what will be done with him?
>
> *Pistis Sophia 147, PS p.381, PSGG p.322*

Jesus replies that when he dies, he will first spend some time in the
inner realms. Then, like the others he will be given the cup of forgetfulness, followed however by a cup of soberness:

> Afterwards a receiver ... also brings a cup which is filled with under-
> standing and wisdom, and there is soberness in it. And he gives it to the
> soul, and it is cast into a body which is not able to sleep nor is it able to
> forget, because of the cup of soberness which was given to it. But it will
> be a goad to its heart continually, to seek for the mysteries of the light
> until it finds them ... and inherits the eternal Light.
>
> *Pistis Sophia 147, PS p.383, PSGG p.323*

The reward of a pure life is that the soul is given the great nostalgia, a
longing to find the spiritual truth which continually goads it onwards
to seek and question everything until it finds the "mysteries of the
Light", the initiation that can take it back to God, through which it
will "inherit the eternal Light". It is never able to completely fall asleep,
to become drunken or to forget its divine origin. Something is always
stirring in it to make it seek the divine Reality.

Concluding this series of replies, John then asks what becomes of
the person who has committed all manner of sins, but does at last
come to a Saviour and receive the "mysteries of the Light":

> John said: "A man who has committed every sin and every iniquity, but at
> last has found the mysteries of the Light: is it possible for him to be saved?"
>
> Jesus said: "Such a one who has committed every sin and every iniquity,
> and finds the mysteries of the Light, and performs them and completes
> them, and does not cease from them nor does he commit sins: he will
> inherit the Treasury of the Light."
>
> *Pistis Sophia 148, PS p.383, PSGG p.324*

Jesus replies that if such a soul fulfils everything that is expected of
him after receiving initiation, if he lives his life purely and correctly,
and attends diligently to his spiritual practice, then "he will inherit the
Treasury of the Light" – then he will be taken back to God.

Similarly, in another reply from an earlier part of these 'dialogues',

Jesus tells Andrew that he and his fellow disciples, because they have
undergone such suffering through reincarnation, from their "trans-
ference into different kinds of bodies", and because they have detached
themselves from the world and been initiated, and "received the mysteries of purification" – they "will go to the Height":

> Now at this time, thou Andrew and all thy brethren, thy fellow-disciples,
> because of your renunciations and all your sufferings which you have
> received in every place, and your changes in every place, and your
> transferences into different kinds of bodies, and because of all your
> afflictions; and that after all these things you have received the mysteries
> of purification, you have become refined light, exceedingly purified. For
> this cause, therefore, you will go to the Height; you will enter into all the
> regions of all the great emanations of the Light, and become rulers (kings)
> in the eternal kingdom of the Light.
>
>   But when you come forth from the body and go to the Height and
> reach the place of the *archons*, then all the *archons* will be put to shame
> before you, because you are (have come from) the dregs of their matter
> and you have (now) become light more pure than all of them.
>
> *Pistis Sophia* 100, PS p.252, PSGG p.209

And not only will they go to the Light, becoming "rulers" in the eternal kingdom of God, but in the process they will also pass far beyond
all the lesser rulers or "*archons*" in the creation. These *archons* will "be
put to shame", so to speak, because the souls from the pits of matter
have become so purified that they can now pass beyond all such lower
rulers.

Transmigration of the Soul

Though talking in a general way about reincarnation, we have only
touched in passing on a topic which is usually more difficult for people
to accept. Mystics of this higher path of the Word have characteristically taught that the soul descends into lower forms, that is to say,
transmigration of the soul or, as the Greek philosophers called it,
metempsychosis. Not only does the soul return to this world, but it can
also go down the scale and take birth in one of the lower species. No
wonder that physical bodies have been called graves, tombs, prisons,
dungeons and pits.

It requires little grasp of arithmetic to realize that the human population of the world is constantly changing. At the present time and for the past several thousand years, so far as we can tell, the population has been generally increasing. If we accept reincarnation as a principle in life, a very obvious question is raised: "Where are all these souls coming from?" Some people might suggest that they are incarnating from the heavenly regions, but a brief survey of the world tells us that the new influx of population does not exhibit heavenly tendencies. In fact, the reverse would appear to the case. The world is becoming increasingly selfish, materially-minde en violent and criminal.

But while the human population has been rising, the numbers of the lower species have been declining, especially of the larger animals. Since the early years of the twentieth century, motorized transport alone has replaced millions of horses and everybody nowadays is aware of the environmental impact of human 'progress' in the last one hundred years. Can the increase in human population be explained simply by the transmigration of souls from lower forms?

Mystics point out that the law of cause and effect is strict. "Thou shalt by no means come out thence, till thou hast paid the uttermost farthing."[17] All deeds and desires must be accounted for. Nothing is ever wasted in nature. We have all encountered people whose minds are bestial and low, whose thoughts run constantly on tracks of anger, hatred, bitterness, greed, lust, selfishness and more. And we have all known animals – dogs, cats, horses and others – whose nature has been unselfish, affectionate, attentive and caring. After the death of one physical form, the mind has no physical structure about it at all and it is drawn automatically into a form most suited to its inner tendencies. A vicious person may thus take birth in some carnivorous animal where it can work out its desires. And so on. Even the destiny of the form in which the mind and soul incarnate is determined by the impressions on the mind.

Mystics also say that the human form is a very special opportunity, for in no other form can the soul begin the journey back to God. The human form is blessed with the faculty of discrimination. Metaphorically, man has eaten from the tree of knowledge of good and evil and in that sense has the capacity to make a choice in all his actions. Essentially, this choice, hemmed in on all sides by circumstance and destiny, is that within himself he can move towards God or towards the world, towards God or mammon. As Jesus said:

No man can serve two masters:
For either he will hate the one, and love the other;
   or else he will hold to the one,
     and despise the other.
Ye cannot serve God and mammon.

Matthew 6:24

Man has this much free will: to search for God or to deny Him. The free will is deeply conditioned by the past, determining the present, but however submerged it may be, man has been created with this dispensation and blessing. And from God's point of view, this is His purpose in creating the human form.

The other species do not have this privilege. They are creatures of instinct and the lower in the order they are, the less is their degree of consciousness and the more are they hemmed in by pre-programmed instincts. One can say that their mental apparatus is different from that of man. As the Greek and other mystics have said, the soul is the same, but the overcoat and other garments that surround it are constituted differently.

Finding oneself in the human form, therefore, is a precious opportunity, not to be wasted. This is the meaning of the parable of the three servants, where each is given a lump sum for investment and why the lord says of the one who wastes the opportunity:

Take therefore the talent from him, and give it unto him which hath ten talents. For unto every one that hath shall be given, and he shall have abundance: but from him that hath not shall be taken away even that which he hath. And cast ye the unprofitable servant into outer darkness: there shall be weeping and gnashing of teeth.

Matthew 25:28-30

What a human being, a potential servant of the Lord "hath", is the human form. But if he does not use it profitably in the search for God – the purpose for which it has been uniquely designed by God – then it is taken away from him and he loses the opportunity. This is what Jesus means in Matthew when he says to his disciples, concerning those who do not understand and accept his teachings:

It is given unto you to know
   the mysteries of the kingdom of heaven,
     but to them it is not given.

> For whosoever hath, to him shall be given,
>   and he shall have more abundance:
> but whosoever hath not,
>   from him shall be taken away even that he hath.
>
> Matthew 13:11-12

Knowing Jesus' teaching of love and compassion, this seems harsh. Yet he is making the distinction between the mercy of the Master and the justice of the Negative Power. Those who are "given ... to know the mysteries of heaven" are the personal disciples of the Master. They are "whosoever hath" – and they will be given more and more from the Master's treasury. Ultimately, they will receive everything and be taken back to God. But "whosoever hath not", he will lose "even that he hath": he will lose the opportunity of having taken human form and may even have to go down the scale of evolution into lower species.

As the writer of the *Gospel of Philip* points out, every soul automatically gravitates towards its own kind, and an individual can only receive help and love from another who is at the same level. So if you become an animal, then spiritually speaking, there is no one who can help you:

> Human beings associate (*lit.* 'breed') with human beings. Horses associate with horses, donkeys associate with donkeys. Members of a species usually associate with those of the same species. Just so, spirit unites with spirit ... and light merges with light. If you are born a human being, it is human beings who will love you. If you become spirit, you will unite with the spirit. If you become light, you will merge in the light. If you become one of those who belong above, it is those who belong above who will be with (*lit.* rest upon) you. If you become a horse or ass or bull or dog or sheep or another of the animals which are outside or below, then neither human being nor spirit ... nor light will be able to love you. Neither those who belong above nor those who belong within will be able to rest in you, and you have no part with them.
>
> Gospel of Philip 78-79, GS p.349, NHS20 pp.199-201

The uniqueness of the human form is brought out clearly by the mid-second-century Christian philosopher, Justin Martyr, in his *Dialogue with Trypho, a Jew*. The book consists of a dialogue, presented in the classical Greek style, between Justin and Trypho, a Jew, concerning the doctrines of Christianity, though how much – if any – of the conversation is historical is unknown. It is the content which is of interest and importance.

Before reading this excerpt, it needs to be noted that terms for mind, soul, intellect, personality, being, ego and the like are commonly interchanged by scholars, philosophers and translators, ancient and modern. This can often be confusing when reading ancient writings, whether in translation or in the original language. Even in modern times, the terms 'mind', 'soul' and 'spirit' have a wide spread of meaning, depending upon their context and who is using them. In the case of Justin Martyr, he was a philosopher-theologian, not a mystic, and although he describes the soul as the divine, immortal essence in man, it is not entirely clear how he thinks of the human mind, for he speaks of the mind as being able to see God. The general meaning of the passage is not impaired, however, and we join the dialogue where Trypho and Justin are discussing whether it is soul or the bodily senses which can see God:

"Is there then," says he (Trypho), "such and so great power in our mind? Or can a man not perceive by sense sooner? Will the mind of man see God at any time, if it is uninstructed by the Holy Spirit?"

"Plato indeed says," replied I, "that the eye of the mind is of such a nature, and has been given for this end, that we may see that very Being when the mind is pure itself, who is the Cause of all discerned by the mind, having no colour, no form, no greatness – nothing, indeed, which the bodily eye looks upon; but it is something of this sort, he goes on to say, that is beyond all essence, unutterable and inexplicable, but alone honourable and good, coming suddenly into souls well-dispositioned, on account of their affinity to and desire of seeing Him."

"What affinity, then," replied he, "is there between us and God? Is the soul also divine and immortal, and a part of that very regal Mind (*Nous*, of God)? And even as that sees God, so also is it attainable by us to conceive of the Deity in our mind, and thence to become happy?"

"Assuredly," I said.

"And do all the souls of all living beings comprehend Him?" he asked; "or are the souls of men of one kind, and the souls of horses and of asses of another kind?"

"No; but the souls which are in all are similar," I answered.

"Then," says he, "shall both horses and asses see, or have they seen at some time or other, God?"

"No," I said; "for the majority of men will not, saving (those) as shall live justly, purified by righteousness, and by every other virtue."

"Is it not, therefore," said he, "on account of his affinity, that a man sees God, nor because he has a (rational) mind, but because he is temperate and righteous?"

"Yes," said I; "and because he has that whereby he perceives God."

"What then? Do goats or sheep injure any one?"

"No one in any respect," I said.

"Therefore these animals will see (God) according to your account," says he.

"No; for their body being of such a nature, is an obstacle to them."

He rejoined, "If these animals could assume speech, be well assured that they would with greater reason ridicule our body; but let us now discuss this subject, and let it be conceded to you as you say. Tell me, however, this: Does the soul see (God) so long as it is in the body, or after it has been removed from it?"

"So long as it is in the form of a man, it is possible for it," I continued, "to attain to this by means of the mind; but especially when it has been set free from the body, and being apart by itself, it gets possession of that which it was wont continually and wholly to love." ...

"And what do those suffer who are judged to be unworthy of this spectacle?" said he.

"They are imprisoned in the bodies of certain wild beasts, and this is their punishment."

"Do they know, then, that it is for this reason they are in such forms, and that they have committed some sin?"

"I do not think so."

"Then these reap no advantage from their punishment, as it seems, moreover, I would say that they are not punished unless they are conscious of the punishment."

"No indeed."

"Therefore souls neither see God nor transmigrate into other bodies; for they would know that so they are punished, and they would be afraid to commit even the most trivial sin afterwards. But that they can perceive that God exists, and that righteousness and piety are honourable, I also quite agree with you," said he.

"You are right," I replied.

Justin Martyr, Dialogue with Trypho IV, WJMA pp.91-93

From this excerpt, it is clear that Justin accepts the divinity, immortality and hence the pre-existence of the soul, and that he believes souls encased in the bodies of lower species to be the same as those within human beings. But like Augustine, he seems undecided as to whether souls transmigrate or not. All the same, the fact that he raises the issue demonstrates that the question was a valid one at that very early period in the development of Christian thought.

The question concerning the lack of memory of previous lifetimes is an interesting one, too, often raised as a refutation of reincarnation. Regarding this, it may be observed that we are quite unable to remember the events even of the present lifetime. We usually recall (and that imperfectly) only the highlights or things which have impinged upon us forcibly, for one reason or another. Even the details of events in the morning are forgotten by the evening, and most of our yesterdays are soon lost in oblivion. If we were to carry an entire and complete memory of all events in our conscious minds we would be tortured by mental and emotional overload. This would be even more so, if we remembered all the events of previous lifetimes. Just as sleep is required for sorting out the day's impressions, relegating many to the subconscious, so too is the period between births a necessary time of sorting and forgetting.

It might be maintained that a memory of past lives would enable us to live better lives in the present. This point is raised by Justin and Trypho who decide – on the principle that punishment only works if a person knows why they are being punished – that transmigration would only be reasonable as a hypothesis if the soul knew why it had descended into lower forms. But if, owing to the power of habit, we do not learn from our mistakes in *this* life, continuing to live in the same old way, how can we expect to learn from our mistakes in *past* lives? Even in this life, we often fail to accept that it is our own attitudes and reactions which have got us into a mess. The evidence should make things very obvious to us, but human perception is clouded and our human ego is such that despite the clearest of signs that something is our own fault, we deny it to ourselves and others. The human mind is not usually a clear mirror in which wisdom dwells, undistorted! We may see the process in others, how they are responsible for the events which overtake them, but often we cannot see it in ourselves!

In any case, if the Lord wants this creation to continue, He has to keep it going according to certain rules. He has to keep the souls unaware, to some extent, of what is going on. Otherwise, they would all want to return to Him immediately and that would be the end of the creation. This is part of the role assigned to Satan and "if Satan rise up against himself, and be divided, he cannot stand, but hath an end". Forgetfulness of the past and unconsciousness of its influence is essential if separation from God and the wheel of birth and death is to continue.

Moreover, though the soul may not learn the individual lessons, it can be seen that those souls who return to God have learnt the underlying lesson – that separation from God, being enmeshed in mind and matter and moving from one body to another, is painful. The fundamental lesson to be learned from existence in this world is that this pain can be alleviated only by returning to Him. Maybe this is the divine purpose in suffering and separation?

Mani and Jesus

Amongst the most intriguing mystic literature of the early Christian period is the Manichaean, some of it clearly stemming from the time of Mani (216-277 AD) himself. As we have previously noted, Manichaean psalms or hymns often refer to Jesus and we have commonly called these Manichaean-Christian. One cannot help but wonder, therefore, whether some of them might not have dated back to the time of Jesus himself and have simply been adopted by the followers of Mani and his successors because they recognized in them the same teachings that their own Master had taught.

Without further finds of ancient Christian manuscripts, we will probably never know, but one thing is certain. Mani taught that the soul goes around in the cycle of birth and death, including transmigration into lower forms, until such time as it meets a perfect Saviour who brings about its liberation and return to God. And he taught that Jesus had given the same teachings. That is to say, a near contemporary of Jesus and a fellow mystic, asserted that Jesus, too, had taught the reality of both reincarnation and transmigration. This is a very powerful testimony, brought out abundantly in the Manichaean writings found in Parthian, Coptic and Chinese.

With a knowledge of the metaphors used by the mystics of those times, these Manichaean-Christian psalms or hymns are almost self-explanatory, the following being only a selection. One psalmist writes, for instance:

> Protect me in my corporeal existence, Jesus.
> Oh Lord, save my soul from this birth-death
>   full of love is your throne, bright....
>
> *HRII p.67, ML p.107*

And expressing the distress of a soul trapped incarnate in this world, another poet pleads:

Who will release me from all the pits and prisons,
    in which are gathered lusts that are not pleasing?
Who will take me over the flood of the tossing sea –
    the zone of conflict in which there is no rest?
Who will save me from the jaws of all the beasts
    who destroy and terrify one another without pity? ...
Who will lead me beyond rebirths, and free me from them all –
    and from all the waves, in which there is no rest?
I weep for my soul, saying: may I be saved from this,
    and from the terror of the beasts
    who devour one another!

The bodies of men, and of birds of the air,
    of fish of the sea, and four-footed creatures
    and of all insects –
Who will take me beyond these and save me from them all,
    so that I shall not turn
    and fall into the perdition of those hells?
So that I shall not pass through defilement in them,
    nor return in rebirth.

Huwidagman IVa:1-9, MHCP pp.81-83

Here there is no doubt that the poet is describing reincarnation into the bodies of animals, birds and other species as falling into "pits", "prisons" and "hells" where creatures hunt, kill and devour others. Similarly, describing this world, the psalmist writes:

Wretchedness will overtake all its inhabitants
    and perdition of hell in which there is no mercy.

Who will save me from these and take me beyond them all,
    so that I shall not be devoured
    in the distress of those hell-deeps?

Huwidagman IVb:2, MHCP p.85

And again, where the world is also called the "pit of destruction" and the "dark valley":

Who will willingly save from the pit of destruction,
    and from the dark valley where all is harshness?
Where all is anguish and the stab of death.

Helper and friend is there none therein,
　　never to eternity is there safety there.
It is all full of darkness and fume-filled fog;
　　it is all full of wrath and there is no pity there;
　　all who enter are pierced by wounds.
It is waterless through drought,
　　and hardened by hot winds.
No golden drop of water is ever found therein.
Who will save me from this, and from all stabs,
　　and take me afar from all distress of hell? ...

[Those who dwell there]
　　are struck by merciless blows in the deep;
　　there is no health for all their sicknesses.
Not all the lusts and the comfort of wealth
　　will help them in that hellish place....
Not all their idols, altars and images
　　can save them from that hell.
They are oppressed by anguish and by merciless....

Who will take me far from [it,
　　that] I may not plunge [into] them,
　　and that I may not tumble
　　and fall into every bitter hell.
[All who enter] there find no way out.
　　　　Huwidagman V:1-6,9-10,19-20, MHCP pp.87-91

Souls in this world are "full of darkness" within themselves and nothing glows with its own innate light, as it does in the higher realms.
"There is no pity" or mercy; everything happens according to the law
of justice. "All who enter are pierced by wounds", everyone is the victim of sin or *karma*, no soul who comes here can escape their destiny.
No pleasures or comforts, nor any religious practice can save a soul
from the troubles of physical existence. No one can find their own way
out of such a labyrinth.

Some people may think that this is an overstatement and the poet is
certainly trying to attract the attention of the reader by use of explicit
language. But many other mystics have also spoken in similar terms of
the state of souls in this world. Out of compassion, they are trying to
awaken us from a deep slumber. But such is the state of madness,
drunkenness, forgetfulness or spiritual ignorance that the majority of

souls here are quite unaware of their plight. Moreover, the poet is writing with a purpose and later on in this same cycle of hymns, the other side of the coin is presented, when the Saviour – the Helmsman – comes to bring release to the captive soul:

> When I had repeated these words, with soul a-tremble,
>> I beheld the Saviour as he shone before me.
> I beheld the sight of all the Helmsmen,
>> who had descended with him to array my soul.
> I lifted up my eyes toward that direction,
>> and saw all deaths were hidden by the Envoy.
>
> All ravages had become remote from me,
>> and grievous sickness,
>> and the anguish of their distress.
> The sight of them was hidden,
>> their darkness had fled away.
> All was divine nature, without peer.
> [There shone forth] Light, elating and lovely
>> [and full] of gladness, pervading all my mind.
> In joy unbounded he spoke with me,
>> raising up my soul from deep affliction.
>
> To me he sayeth,
> "Come, spirit! fear not.
> I am thy Mind (*cf. Nous*),
>> thy glad tidings of hope." ...
> I am thy Light, radiant, primeval,
>> thy Great Mind (*cf. Vahman*) and complete hope."
>> *Angad Roshnan VI:1-10, MHCP pp.139-141*

The Saviour appears both outside as a human being and inside in his radiant form of light. He is the *Nous* or *Logos* and the essence of everything. *Vahman* is derived from *Vohu Mana* (*lit.* Great Mind, Primal Mind), a term used by Zarathushtra for the Word or *Logos*, Zoroastrianism having been a prevalent religion of the Middle East, especially Persia, at that time. Continuing the hymn, the Saviour then reiterates the promise of all Masters:

> "From each dungeon shall I release thee,
>> bearing thee afar from all wounds [and afflictions].

I shall lead thee forth from this torture.
Thou shalt no [more] feel fear at each encounter....

"Beloved! beauty of my bright nature!
From these shall I lead thee forth, and from all prisons.
I shall save thee from all perdition,
    and free thee forever from all wounds.
Through perfect Light [I shall cleanse] from thee
    all the filth and corrosion that thou hast passed through....
I shall not wish to leave thee longer
    in the hands of the Sinner (Satan);
    for thou art my own, in truth, for ever.

"Thou art the buried treasure,
    the chief of my wealth,
    the pearl which is the beauty of all the gods.
And I am the righteousness sown in thy limbs,
    and in the stature of thy soul –
    the gladness of thy Mind (*cf. Nous*).
Thou art my Beloved, the love in my limbs (parts);
    and the heroic Mind,
    the essence of my limbs (parts, members).
And I am the Light of thy whole structure,
    thy soul above and base of life.
From the holiness of my limbs didst thou descend
    in the beginning into the dark places,
    and didst become their light."

Angad Roshnan VI:32-33,42-45,49-55, MHCP pp.143-149

The Master promises to release the soul from the tortures of birth and death, expressing his undying love for the soul. The real Master is the Light, the "heroic Mind" or *Nous*, and the soul is a "limb" or part of that Power. The Master has come to bring salvation to his own "limbs". From the beginning, even when it descended into the "dark places" of this world, the soul has been a part of him and he has come to redeem his own. The Master continues with great affection and compassion, saying:

"Through thee a Diadem was bound on all foes;
    it became manifest and held sway
    during the hours of tyranny.

> For thy sake was there battle and tremor
>   in all the heavens and the bridges of the earths.
> For thy sake ran [and sped] all the powers (*cf. archons*) over...
> For thy sake were bound
>   [the princes] and all the powers....

> "For thy sake shone forth the Apostles (Messengers, Masters)
>   and became manifest, who reveal the Light above,
>   and uncover the root of darkness.
> For thy sake the gods went forth and became apparent.
> They struck down death, and darkness they slew."
>
>   *Angad Roshnan VI:56-59,61-62, MHCP pp.149-151*

The Master joins the 'holy war' on behalf of the soul. The "foes" of the mind and all the "dark powers" of Satan are overcome with the help of the Apostles, the Messengers or Masters who come to this world entirely for the sake of rescuing souls.

> "Thou art the exalted Trophy,
>   the Sign of Light that puts darkness to flight.

> "And I am come forth to save thee from the Sinner (Satan),
>   to make thee whole from pain,
>   and to bring gladness to thy heart.
> All thou hast desired of me I shall bestow upon thee.
> I shall make new thy place within the lofty Kingdom.
> I shall set open before thee the gates in all the heavens,
>   and shall make smooth thy path,
>   free from terror and vexation.

> "I shall take thee with might, and enfold thee with love,
>   and lead thee to thy Home, the Blessed Abode.
> For ever shall I show to thee the noble Father;
>   I shall lead thee in, into his presence, in pure raiment.

> "I shall show to thee the Mother of the Beings of Light;
>   for ever shalt thou rejoice in lauded happiness.
> I shall reveal to thee the holy Brethren,
>   the noble [ones] ... who are filled with happiness.
> For ever shalt thou [dwell] joyful among them all,
>   beside all the Jewels and the venerable gods.

"Fear and death shall never overtake thee more,
  nor ravage, distress and wretchedness.
Rest shall be thine in the Place of Salvation,
  in the company of all the Gods
  and those who dwell in quietness (peace)."

  Angad Roshnan VI:63-73, MHCP pp.151-153

The Master will carry the soul with his own power through all the realms of the "Sinner", of Satan, the Prince of Sin. He will take the soul to God, the "Mother of the Beings of Light". He will introduce the soul to the "holy Brethren", the Masters and other pure beings who inhabit those bright realms. The soul will never have to leave their company nor return to this world. This is the promise of all Masters.

In another similar though fragmentary hymn, the Master pledges to release the soul from "every one of the rebellious powers", the agents of the mind, the Negative Power, and from all the forces which prevail in Satan's realm:

"I shall save thee from every one
  of the rebellious powers
  who have frightened thee with fear.
[I shall release] thee from all deceit and turbulence ...
  and the torment of death....
  and ... every watch-post ... of every enemy....
[I will make an end] of the activity
  of all forces of destruction,
  and all sickness which has dismayed thee with death.
I will overthrow before thee all....
  and from every prison which eternally....
I shall make thee free from all the powers....
  all the princes ... will fall before thee....

"Thou shalt not fall within ...
  where all is full of fire, distress, and stabs.
I shall free thee from the hands of the guardians of hell,
  [who show no] mercy to spirit and soul."

  Huwidagman VIa:3-4,8-9, VIb:11-12,14,21-22, MHCP pp.95-101

Again, in another hymn, the Master encourages the soul to step out of the body – the "house of affliction" and the "dwelling of death" – and return to its "native abode", its original home with God:

"Come, spirit, fear no more!
Death has fallen, and sickness fled away.
The term of troubled days is ended,
     its terror departed amid clouds of fire.

"Come, spirit, step forth!
Let there be no desire for the house of affliction,
     which is wholly destruction and the anguish of death.
Truly thou wast cast out from thy native abode.

"And all the pangs thou hast suffered in hell
     thou hast undergone for this,
     in the outset and beginning.
Come yet nearer, in gladness without regret;
     lie not content in the dwelling of death.
Turn not back, nor regard the shapes of the bodies,
     which lie there in wretchedness,
     they and their fellows.
See, they return through every rebirth,
     through every agony and every choking prison.
See, they are reborn among all kinds of creatures,
     and their voice is heard in burning sighs."
                    Angad Roshnan VII:1-9, MHCP pp.155-157

The Master points out the sufferings of birth and rebirth in the various "kinds of creatures". Come away, he urges, from the alluring beauty
which vanishes like a mirage, leaving only distress in its wake:

"Come yet nearer, and be not fond of this beauty
     that perishes in all its varieties.

"It falls and melts as snow in sunshine,
     there is no abiding for any fair form.
It withers and fades as a broken rose,
     that wilts in the sun, whose grace is destroyed.

"Yet come, thou spirit, and be not fond
     of the sum of hours and the fleeting days.
Turn not back [to all this] outward show;
     desire is death, and leads to destruction."
                    Angad Roshnan VII:10-14, MHCP pp.157-159

Come away, he then continues, to the "Height" and to your "native abode", your real and natural home. Your "pledge", your spiritual inheritance awaits you. Forget this world and all its anguish:

> "Hence, spirit, come! ...
> I shall lead thee to the Height,
>   [to thy native abode].
> I shall show thee the pledge (?) ...
>   the hope thou hast yearned for....
> Remember, O spirit!
> Look on the anguish that thou hast borne
>   through the fury of all thy ravagers."
> *Angad Roshnan VII:15-17, MHCP p.159*

Finally, again in a sadly fragmentary poem, the majority of which is lost, the devotee concludes:

> The Saviour of my soul revealed these things to me....
> [Upon that day of] departing he came with mercy to me,
>   and [saved me] from every anguish and prison.
> *Huwidagman VII:10-11, MHCP pp.105-107*

And after considerable *lacunae* in the manuscript, we again find the Master talking to the soul, promising release:

> All who affright thee will fall down in thy presence;
>   agony in overwhelming might will hold their statures prone.
> Truly thou shalt pass their border,
>   and shalt not be held at their watchposts.
> Thou shalt be saved from anguish, ...
>   thou shalt not fall into hell, nor into....
>
> [Thou shalt lie] no longer within the foul body, ...
>   [thou shalt no more endure] that [heaviness]
>   amid all sicknesses....
>
> But thou shalt pass in safety by every ...
>   thou shalt reign in gladness
>   and in freedom [for evermore].
> Thou shalt enter into that land....
>   and shalt rejoice in the gladness of that....

Thou shalt abide in tranquillity....
and anguish [shall never overtake thee] more.
    Huwidagman VII:19-22, VIIIa:1-3, MHCP pp.107,111

Despite the missing passages, the meaning is clear: the Master will bring the soul past every ruler and obstruction to the land of eternal rest. There is no doubt that these writings stem from the heart of a devotee. They are no religious litany or ceremonial words, but a *cri de coeur* from one who has found a Master. In this case, it was probably Mani.

Soon after the departure of Mani and his appointed successors, his teachings, like those of Jesus, became the focus of a new religion, and the Christians treated the Manichaeans with great enmity and hostility. The Manichaeans, for their part, acknowledged both Mani and Jesus as their Saviours, tending towards a Christian bias, and despite the burning of their books and the killing and prejudicial treatment of their people, they survived until late into the Middle Ages, only being finally dispersed during the thirteenth century: persecution sometimes has a way of concentrating and refining a people's spirit. By that time, there were over seventy gnostic groups, under different names and in every part of Europe, many considering themselves to be the true heirs of Christianity, following Jesus' real teachings. And for the most part, they believed in the transmigration of the soul and that Jesus' earthly mission had been the liberation of earth-bound, captive souls. Despite the efforts of the orthodox, the early Christian belief in reincarnation had not been entirely suppressed.

The collective name given to these medieval gnostics was the Cathars, meaning the 'pure ones', from the same root as the word '*catharsis*' meaning purification. There were the Paterins of Italy, the German Cathars, the Paulicians of Armenia, the Bogomils of Bulgaria and the Albigensians of southern France. Keeping company with them were other esoteric groups including the Knights Templars, the Troubadours of southern Europe, the Rosicrucians, the Hermetic philosophers and the Alchemists. These too, together with the Jewish Kabbalists, Islamic gnostic groups such as the Ishmaelis and some of the Sufi mystics, all openly taught reincarnation.

So widespread did the Cathars become in the twelfth and early thirteenth centuries that Henry Lea wrote in his classic and definitive study of the Inquisition (*The History of the Inquisition in the Middle Ages*) that the movement spread so rapidly and resisted so stubbornly the sternest efforts of suppression that at one time it may be fairly said to have threatened the permanent existence of Christianity itself.

Henry Lea, HIMAI p.89

Indeed, few people realize that what was later formalized as the Inquisition was begun by Pope Innocent III (1160-1216) with the express purpose of eradicating them – by force. So well-respected were the Albigensians of the Languedoc area of France and so beloved and trusted were they for their industry, morality and general sweetness, that they were dubbed *"les bonnes hommes"*, the good men. Their intention was to restore the original purity of Jesus' teachings of love and spirituality in their own lives, and they actually tried to practise Jesus' precepts as preserved in the gospels. Large numbers of people in Toulouse, Beziers and other cities were of this faith, where they had the protection of the powerful Count Raymond of Toulouse. The character and quality of their education, local government and social structure were also far in advance of their age and they had for so long enjoyed the freedom to worship in their own way that the local orthodox clergy feared to discipline them.

Pope Innocent, realizing that they posed a threat to the Catholic Church, summoned the nobles of Europe to a crusade, the first ever waged by Christians against Christians. The Albigensians' rich lands and property were to be the prize, and for all those who took part the Pope generously proclaimed complete remission of all sins, not only of the past but of any future time as well. Moreover, as a bonus, all debts owed by the crusaders to Jewish moneylenders were to be cancelled.

First blood was drawn at the massacre of Beziers on July 22nd 1209. When Abbot Arnaud-Amaury, the commander of the crusade, was asked how they should distinguish the heretics from the faithful, he replied, "Slay all, God will know his own."[18] And six or seven thousand people were massacred in the church of St Madeleine alone, probably one of the greatest slaughters of innocent people Europe had seen for centuries.

Surely someone at that time must have recalled the words of Jesus as he spoke to his disciples towards the end of his days, warning them of the difficult times ahead and the extremes of conduct that would be shown by religious zealots and prejudiced rulers:

> Yea, the time cometh, that whosoever killeth you
> will think that he doeth God service.

> And these things will they do unto you,
> because they have not known the Father, nor me.
>
> *John 16:2-3*

At that time, Jesus was referring to the Jews and Romans. In later centuries, it was Christians themselves who behaved that way.

The wars against the Albigensians, with their inquisitional courts and intermittent periods of peace, continued for a further forty-six years until the surrender of Queribus in 1255. But the 'success' of this means of discovering, suppressing and extirpating 'heresy' proved so appealing to the Popes and catholic clergy that the Inquisition was formally founded in 1232 to carry on the work. This malevolent organization continued for six centuries until its formal dissolution in 1820.

Reincarnation, as a Christian belief, was forced underground. Only the most daring of philosophers, writers and theologians ever voiced it in public. Not until the second half of the nineteenth century did it begin to surface once again. Indeed, this 'lost chord' of Jesus' teachings is still only slowly being rediscovered.

NOTES AND REFERENCES

1. *John* 5:14, 8:11. See also *Matthew* 9:2.
2. *John* 5:14.
3. *Matthew* 7:6.
4. *1 Corinthians* 2:14.
5. See also *Jewish War* III:374 and *Against Apion* II:218, where Josephus, himself a Pharisee, reiterates the same belief.
6. Some scholars suggest that it was another Origen who attended the discourses of Ammonius Saccas. Either way, there is no doubt that Origen the Christian philosopher was deeply immersed in Greek thought.
7. Rufinus, *Letter (LXXX) of Rufinus to Macarius* 2, *PWJ* p.169.
8. See Jerome, *Letters* XCVIII:10*ff.*
9. The book and chapter number of this quote from Origen have proved elusive!
10. Jerome (adopted from Didymus, blind theologian of Alexandria), *Homilies on Ezekiel, OFP* p.i.
11. Gregory of Nyssa, *REWA* p.35.
12. Gregory Thaumaturgus, *Panegyric on Origen, WGTDA.*
13. *OFP* p.i.
14. *Deuteronomy* 5:9.
15. Clement of Alexandria, *Miscellanies* VII:XVII, *WCAII* pp.485-488.
16. Hippolytus, *Refutation of All Heresies* V:II, *RAH* pp.135-136.
17. *Matthew* 5:26.
18. *Encyclopaedia Britannica*, 9th edition, *Albigenses.*

CHAPTER THIRTEEN

Repentance and Forgiveness

We All Have Sin

One of the greatest deceptions played upon us by the Negative Power, through our mind, is the thought that everything is just fine. This is why mystics have described the people of this world as dreamers! Man is born naked and ignorant and usually dies in the same condition, generally making his exit with an even heavier burden than he brought with him on entry. He is born because of sins; his life is woven out of his sins; he creates more sins; and he dies because of sins. Yet, sublimely unaware of the hidden and controlling processes, and despite the suffering and unhappiness which come to everyone in life, man commonly thinks and behaves as if he had no fundamental problems. One might have thought that a little honest introspection would disillusion us, but often, it does not.

Even amongst those who try to follow a spiritual path, there is a tendency to think that they are all right, it is others who are in need of spiritual help. Some folk even get to thinking that they are spiritually enlightened when, in fact, they have yet to reach the very first staging post upon the true spiritual journey. Everything in this physical creation is a reflection and one thing is readily mistaken for another. Thus, an understanding of spiritual matters, at a human level, is quite different from mystic transport even into the astral realms, let alone the union of the soul with God, far above the entire domain of Satan. Such human understanding should not be mistaken for the highest reality.

Mystics are deeply aware of man's ignorance and self-delusion. With great compassion, tinged perhaps with affectionate humour as well as tolerance, they observe the human race, like a crowd of dirty schoolchildren who have been playing in the mud, each claiming to be perfectly clean and in no need of a bath. Like muddy children, we look at others, pointing out how dirty *they* are, never noticing how filthy we are ourselves. The very fact that we are in this world means that we are carrying a heavy burden of sins. Our lives are fabricated from our sins. But until a soul comes to realize this fact, it will never feel the necessity of spiritual cleansing.

Jesus was deeply aware of this side to human nature and to exemplify the point he tells the story of a "publican" and a self-righteous priest, in this case a Pharisee. Publicans were tax collectors in the Roman Empire and somehow, in the synoptic gospels, they came to epitomize the sinful man. Perhaps they were noted for extortion and corruption, or at the very least were notorious for collecting every penny due. It is Luke who relates the parable:

> And he (Jesus) spake this parable unto certain which trusted in themselves that they were righteous, and despised others. Two men went up into the temple to pray; the one a Pharisee, and the other a publican.
> The Pharisee stood and prayed thus with himself, "God, I thank thee, that I am not as other men are, extortioners, unjust, adulterers, or even as this publican. I fast twice in the week, I give tithes of all that I possess."
> And the publican, standing afar off, would not lift up so much as his eyes unto heaven, but smote upon his breast, saying, "God be merciful to me a sinner."
> I tell you, this man went down to his house justified rather than the other: for every one that exalteth himself shall be abased; and he that humbleth himself shall be exalted.
>
> *Luke 18:9-14*

The priest thinks that he is on the right track and has no need of forgiveness. He follows the outer conventions of his religion, leads a good moral life and thinks that to be sufficient. The publican, on the other hand, asks only for mercy. The one is proud before God, the other humble. And it is the humble sinner, aware of his shortcomings, says Jesus, whom God will hear.

The same point is brought out in one of Jesus' sayings, set by Mark when Jesus sits down to eat with the publican, Levi. According to the story, Jesus sees Levi sitting and collecting taxes and says, "Follow me". Levi immediately gets up and invites Jesus and many others to a meal at his house:

> And as he passed by, he saw Levi the son of Alphaeus sitting at the receipt of custom, and said unto him, "Follow me". And he arose and followed him. And it came to pass, that, as Jesus sat at meat in his house, many

publicans and sinners sat also together with Jesus and his disciples: for there were many, and they followed him.

And when the scribes and Pharisees saw him eat with publicans and sinners, said unto his disciples, "How is it that he eateth and drinketh with publicans and sinners?"

When Jesus heard it, he saith unto them, "They that are whole have no need of the physician, but they that are sick: I came not to call the righteous, but sinners to repentance."

Mark 2:14-17

Jesus points out that he has not come for the self-righteous who think that they are already pure. He has come for those who are sincerely seeking true spirituality and know they need help.

Incidentally, in St Matthew's gospel, the same story is copied across almost verbatim, except that Levi becomes Matthew and elsewhere in this gospel, the writer speaks pointedly of "Matthew the publican".[1] Luke follows Mark as regards the name, and one wonders whether one of the contributors to or editors of Matthew was trying to correct Mark according to his own information or to change the name for some other reason. Most people have assumed that Levi was another name for Matthew and this may have been the case, but there is no evidence for it, although Luke and Mark, like Matthew, both list Matthew as being one of the twelve disciples. It is another one of those incongruities which point to the gospels' human origins and will probably remain unresolved. From the point of view of the spiritual meaning, of course, such variants matter little, but they do alert us to be discriminating in our reading of these ancient texts. As Jesus advised his disciples, concerning the scriptures of his own day: "Be ye good money-changers", learning to sift the true from the counterfeit.

The same meaning is conveyed in another parable found in Matthew. Jesus is speaking to the "chief priests and the elders of the people" concerning John the Baptist, when he says:

"But what think ye? A certain man had two sons; and he came to the first, and said, 'Son, go work to day in my vineyard.' He answered and said, 'I will not': but afterward he repented, and went.

"And he came to the second, and said likewise. And he answered and said, 'I go, sir': and went not.'

"Whether of them twain did the will of his father?" They say unto him, "The first."

Jesus saith unto them, "Verily I say unto you, that the publicans and the harlots go into the kingdom of God before you. For John came unto you in the way of righteousness, and ye believed him not: but the publicans and the harlots believed him: and ye, when ye had seen it, repented not afterward, that ye might believe him."

Matthew 21:28-32

Jesus likens the priests to the second son who only paid lip service to his father, but never actually went to work for him. The "publicans and the harlots", on the other hand, are like the first son. At first, they refuse to listen to the mystics. But later, realizing and accepting that they are sinners, they come to believe in the mystics and relinquishing their previous way of life, they start to follow the spiritual path. It is far easier for a mystic to reach a sincere 'sinner' than an insincere, self-righteous person. Though misled, such a 'sinner' is more in contact with him or herself and can recognize illusion more readily than the one who has created an illusory self-image of religious superiority and imitation sanctity.

There is a beautiful story in John which brings home the same point. Interestingly, since the incident is not present in the oldest manuscripts of St John and its origin is uncertain, it is omitted from many modern Bibles. But its meaning is so much in keeping with the remainder of Jesus' teaching that it is worth relating here. It concerns the woman caught in adultery and the story is of the same character as other material in John's gospel. Either it was intended more as a parable than 'history' or it was woven around Jesus' saying, "He that is without sin among you, let him first cast a stone", a saying that could have been a common aphorism in those times, much as we say, "Those who live in glass houses should not throw stones." The story goes:

And early in the morning he (Jesus) came again into the temple, and all the people came unto him; and he sat down, and taught them. And the scribes and Pharisees brought unto him a woman taken in adultery; and when they had set her in the midst, they say unto him, "Master, this woman was taken in adultery, in the very act. Now Moses in the law commanded us, that such should be stoned: but what sayest thou?"

This they said, tempting him, that they might have (cause) to accuse him. But Jesus stooped down, and with his finger wrote on the ground, as though he heard them not. So when they continued asking him, he lifted up himself, and said unto them, "He that is without sin among you, let him first cast a stone at her." And again he stooped down, and wrote on the ground.

And they which heard it, being convicted by their own conscience, went out one by one, beginning at the eldest, even unto the last: and Jesus was left alone, and the woman standing in the midst. When Jesus had lifted up himself, and saw none but the woman, he said unto her, "Woman, where are those thine accusers? Hath no man condemned thee?"

She said, "No man, Lord." And Jesus said unto her, "Neither do I condemn thee: go, and sin no more."

John 8:2-11

The meaning, of course, is self-evident. No one is in a position to judge others, for we are all the victims of our sins. This point is made explicitly by the author of *1 John*:

> This then is the message
> which we have heard of him,
> and declare unto you,
> that God is Light,
> And in Him is no darkness at all.
>
> If we say that we have fellowship with Him,
> and walk in darkness,
> we lie, and do not the truth....
> If we say that we have no sin,
> we deceive ourselves,
> and the truth is not in us.

1 John 1:5-8

"God is Light", says the writer. Therefore, unless we are experiencing that Light within ourselves, we are in a state of sinfulness, for it is only sin which stands between us and the Lord. The inner darkness is caused by the sins of the past and the impure nature of the mind. Consequently, if we experience darkness within, as almost everybody does, and yet maintain that "we have no sin", "we deceive ourselves".

Human ignorance of sin is the theme of a passage in the Nag Hammadi *Book of Thomas the Contender*. The style is probably more of a sermonizing than modern tastes enjoy, but the meaning is nonetheless clear:

> Woe to you, captives, for you are bound in caverns!
> You laugh! In mad laughter you rejoice!

You neither realize your perdition,
>   nor do you reflect on your circumstances,
>   nor have you understood
>   that you dwell in darkness and death!

On the contrary, you are drunk with the fire
>   and full of bitterness.
Your mind is deranged on account
>   of the burning that is in you,
>   and sweet to you are the poison
>   and the blows of your enemies!

And the darkness rose for you like the light,
>   for you surrendered your freedom for servitude!
You darkened your hearts
>   and surrendered your thoughts to folly,
>   and you filled your thoughts
>   with the smoke of the fire that is in you! ...

Woe to you who hope in the flesh
>   and in the prison that will perish!
How long will you be oblivious?
And how long will you suppose
>   that the imperishables will perish too?
Your hope is set upon the world,
>   and your god is this life!
You are corrupting your souls! ...

Woe to you in the fire that burns within you,
>   for it is insatiable! ...
Woe to you because of the wheel
>   that turns in your minds!

Book of Thomas the Contender 143, GS pp.407-408, NHS21 pp.197-199

The root of all sin lies in the mind and the root of the mind is separation, the illusory sense of a separate identity from God. At the human level, this is expressed as the ego, the sense of personal self that underlies all human weaknesses. So strong is this power of ego that we even take pride in our weaknesses. The mind feels proud of its conquests over others, of deceiving them and getting the better of them. It is proud of its acquisitions and possessions. It is proud of sexual prowess, of its animal urges. It is proud of the eloquence of its angry outbursts, its clever conniving and its witty criticisms which slice and hurt others quite unnecessarily. It is proud of anything and everything, good, bad or insignificant. Even a thief feels proud of a robbery, especially if he is not apprehended. The mind and its ego are self-perpetuating. As one of the characters in the *Acts of Thomas* puts it:

> Thou hast not heard the tidings of the new life,
>> and the Voice (Word) of the Preacher of Life (the Master)
>> hath not fallen on thine (inner) ears.
> For not yet hast thou tasted the Medicine of Life (Word)
>> nor art thou freed from longings for the perishable.
>
> Thou standest in the temporal life,
>> and the everlasting life thou knowest not.
> Thou standest clad in robes that grow old
>> and long not for those that are eternal.
>
> Thou art proud of this beauty which vanisheth,
>> and carest not of the unbecoming state of thy (eternal) soul.
> Thou art proud of a number of slaves,
>> and thine own soul from slavery thou hast not set free.
> Thou art proud of the pomp of many attendants,
>> and thou art not delivered from the judgment of death.
>
>> *Acts of Thomas 135, AAA p.269, ANT p.423, MAA p.232*

Unless a soul comes into contact with a mystic who can teach it to hear the sweet music of the Word of God within, it will remain attached to this world, to one degree or another. Only the "Voice" can take a soul back to God, eliminating the sense of self that binds it to this world. Therefore, as the author of the *History of Philip* has Philip say to the people of Carthage:

> Renounce Satan, my brethren, and believe in the Messiah.
> Flee from the darkness, and come to the celestial Light.
> Quit the destroying left hand,
>> and the unconquered right hand shall receive you.
> Be delivered from the fiery Gehenna,
>> and ye shall rejoice and be glad in the Paradise of Eden.
> Strip off the old man,
>> who is corrupted by the lusts of error,

and put on the new man, Jesus the Messiah,
who is renewed by knowledge in the likeness of His Creator.
Avoid and flee from the desire of women, which burns like fire,
and destroys those who are inflamed with it;
and trust in God and be glad.

History of Philip, AAA p.80

The human condition, then, is one of sinfulness and the only way
the problem can be effectively addressed is by turning towards God.
It may be observed however that self-pity, remorse, bemoaning one's
fate and thinking of oneself as entirely sinful and unworthy are negative, self-indulgent attitudes which are of no help, for we remain
obsessed with ourselves – the root of the problem. From a human
point of view, what is required is a practical approach to the situation,
to light a candle rather than to curse the darkness. Jesus called this
repentance.

Repentance

Metanoia, the Greek word translated as 'repentance', implies a change
of heart, a change or reversal of direction, mentally, within oneself.
Mystically, it signifies redirection of the attention from the world towards God. Presently, we are obsessed with the sensory panorama of
the world and with worldly activity: the soul is a slave to the mind
and the mind is held captive by the senses. Repentance, in the real
sense of the term, means that the soul begins to dominate the mind
and the mind to control the senses. When the direction of the attention has become entirely inward, then the soul travels towards God,
ultimately reuniting with Him. Changing from one way of life to
the other is repentance. Attaining union with Him is the fruit of
repentance.

According to Matthew, both Jesus and John the Baptist began their
teaching with an exhortation to repentance:

In those days came John the Baptist,
preaching in the wilderness of Judaea,
And saying, "Repent ye:
for the kingdom of heaven is at hand."

Matthew 3:1-2

And:

> From that time Jesus began to preach, and to say,
> "Repent: for the kingdom of heaven is at hand."
>
> *Matthew 4:17*

Like all mystics, they both point out that our attention is running in entirely the wrong direction. Mystics come to help us reverse this process. This, in a nutshell, is their purpose in coming to this world. Without their help, it is impossible to reverse the trend of the mind, for it has been going outward into the world for millions of lifetimes. Consequently, both Jesus and John the Baptist advise, "repent": turn the attention away from the world, towards God. "For the kingdom of heaven is at hand": for God is not far away. He is very close; in fact, He is within you.

Jesus relates a number of parables to illustrate what he means by true repentance and also – being the other side of the coin – the Father's desire for His children to return to Him. There is the well-known parable of the one lost sheep. This parable is not found in Mark, and both Matthew and Luke have variants, possibly from different sources. Luke's version reads:

> What man of you, having an hundred sheep, if he lose one of them, doth not leave the ninety and nine in the wilderness, and go after that which is lost, until he find it? And when he hath found it, he layeth it on his shoulders, rejoicing. And when he cometh home, he calleth together his friends and neighbours, saying unto them, "Rejoice with me; for I have found my sheep which was lost."
>
> I say unto you, that likewise joy shall be in heaven over one sinner that repenteth.
>
> *Luke 15:4-7*

Here the "lost sheep" is the one who repents. In Matthew, the lost sheep is one of the "little ones" – the 'allotted sheep' or 'chosen sheep' that the Master searches out and does not rest until he has taken home:

> For the Son of man is come to save that which was lost. How think ye? If a man have an hundred sheep, and one of them be gone astray, doth he not leave the ninety and nine, and goeth into the mountains, and seeketh that which is gone astray? And if so be that he find it, verily I say unto you, he rejoiceth more of that sheep, than of the ninety and nine which went not astray.

> Even so it is not the will of your Father which is in heaven, that one of
> these little ones should perish.
>
> *Matthew 18:11-14*

The meaning of both versions is ultimately the same, however, for it is only the chosen sheep who will truly repent and be carried back to the Father's home. The "Son of man" comes for his allotted souls. They are the only ones who truly "repent", who turn their attention homewards, towards their divine Home. But they only do so because their Saviour seeks them out, inspiring them with his grace and initiating them with the mystic Word. He is more desirous that they should return than they are to go home with him. He is the Good Shepherd who never wearies of caring and seeking for his sheep. If we take one step toward him, he takes a hundred steps towards us.

Echoes of this parable are found throughout the early Christian literature. In the Manichaean-Christian psalms, for example, the Son of God is described as:

> The Shepherd of the sheep that wanders
> in the desert (wilderness) of this world.
>
> *Psalms of Heracleides, MPB p.193*

And in another, the psalmist is speaking of the Master when writing:

> There is a Shepherd giving pasture:
> he came seeking his sheep.
>
> *Psalms, MPB p.171*

And in others, the devotee writes:

> I am thy sheep: thou art my good Shepherd.
> Thou camest after me and didst save me
> from the destructive wolves.
>
> *Psalm CCLI, MPB p.60*

> I am like a sheep seeking for its pastor;
> Lo, my true Shepherd I have found,
> he has brought me to my fold again.
>
> *Psalm CCLIII, MPB p.63*

And:

> O wandering sheep,
>> thy Shepherd seeks thee.
> O noble one despised (the soul).
>> thy King searches for thee.
>
> *Psalms, MPB p.146*

Jesus also tells a similar story of a woman who loses one piece of silver out of ten, subsequently devoting all her time and energy to finding it:

> Either what woman having ten pieces of silver, if she lose one piece, doth not light a candle, and sweep the house, and seek diligently till she find it? And when she hath found it, she calleth her friends and her neighbours together, saying, "Rejoice with me; for I have found the piece which I had lost."
>
> Likewise, I say unto you, there is joy in the presence of the angels of God over one sinner that repenteth.
>
> *Luke 15:8-10*

The meaning is the same; the Lord is very happy, so to speak, when souls repent and return to Him. But probably the most well-known and perhaps the least understood of Jesus' parables concerning repentance is that of the prodigal son. Found only in Luke, it tells the perennial story of the soul's departure from the 'house' of the Father, its stay in this world, its repentance, and its eventual return home:

> A certain man had two sons. And the younger of them said to his father, "Father, give me the portion of goods that falleth to me." And he divided unto them his living. And not many days after the younger son gathered all together, and took his journey into a far country, and there wasted his substance with riotous living.
>
> And when he had spent all, there arose a mighty famine in that land; and he began to be in want. And he went and joined himself to a citizen of that country; and he sent him into his fields to feed swine. And he would fain have filled his belly with the husks that the swine did eat: and no man gave unto him.
>
> And when he came to himself, he said, "How many hired servants of my father's have bread enough and to spare, and I perish with hunger! I will arise and go to my father, and will say unto him, 'Father, I have sinned against heaven, and before thee, and am no more worthy to be called thy son: make me as one of thy hired servants.'"

And he arose, and came to his father. But when he was yet a great way off, his father saw him, and had compassion, and ran, and fell on his neck, and kissed him. And the son said unto him, "Father, I have sinned against heaven, and in thy sight, and am no more worthy to be called thy son."

But the father said to his servants, "Bring forth the best robe, and put it on him; and put a ring on his hand, and shoes on his feet. And bring hither the fatted calf, and kill it; and let us eat, and be merry. For this my son was dead, and is alive again; he was lost, and is found." And they began to be merry.

Now his elder son was in the field: and as he came and drew nigh to the house, he heard music and dancing. And he called one of the servants, and asked what these things meant. And he said unto him, "Thy brother is come; and thy father hath killed the fatted calf, because he hath received him safe and sound."

And he was angry, and would not go in. Therefore came his father out, and entreated him. And he answering said to his father, "Lo, these many years do I serve thee, neither transgressed I at any time thy commandment: and yet thou never gavest me a kid, that I might make merry with my friends. But as soon as this thy son was come, which hath devoured thy living with harlots, thou hast killed for him the fatted calf."

And he said unto him, "Son, thou art ever with me, and all that I have is thine. It was meet that we should make merry, and be glad: for this thy brother was dead, and is alive again; and was lost, and is found."

Luke 15:11-32

All souls are equal sons in the eyes of their rich Father. In the parable, one soul stays with the Father and the other takes his inheritance, his spiritual treasure, his divine soul, and goes out into the creation. There, he "wastes his substance" – he wastes his innate divinity – "in riotous living" – in the enjoyment of sensual pleasures and worldly pursuits. He squanders his precious attention on the world. As a result, he suffers extreme hunger of the spirit, because nothing in this world is ever able to give lasting satisfaction. He is like the son of a rich man who ends up looking after pigs, so hungry that he would even eat their food were it offered to him. The pig, of course, is an unclean animal in Jewish thought, symbolizing the pits of uncleanliness, and pigs do indeed spend a great deal of time with their noses in any rubbish which they can find. This epitomizes the soul's condition in the world. Although the son of a munificent father, by following his own will, the son – or soul – has ended up in the company of pigs.

But the son is honest enough to realize his condition. He remembers his father's wealth and determines to make his way homewards. Out of remorse, however, he feels that he should only be taken back as a servant, since his sense of unworthiness and guilt weigh heavily upon his conscience. His father sees him while he is still far away from home and comes out to greet him, for the father is happier about his son's return than the son himself. The father only has feelings of love for his son, but the son is still distracted by remorse and guilt.

The son then says his piece concerning his unworthiness, but his father does not listen to him. He arranges great festivities; he dresses his son in the "best robe", in the robe of glory, the soul's true garment of light. "For this my son was dead, and is alive again; he was lost, and is found." The soul has returned from the land of the dead, the physical universe. He was lost in the lower creation, tempted and deceived by the Negative Power, but he has returned to his spiritual home with the Father.

Meanwhile, the young man's brother is envious, but their father points out that he has no cause for jealousy, because "thou art ever with me and all that I have is thine". The souls who dwell with the Father and who have never been sent out into the creation are one with Him and all that He is, and they always have been. But the younger son, concludes Jesus, "was dead, and is alive again; and was lost, and is found".

The parable means that the Father is very happy to welcome his errant children home again. It also means that there is no cause for feelings of unworthiness and guilt. The Father is all love. We only need to forget ourselves and all our past, to look ahead to Him and to seek only Him, to repent completely, turning the entire attention towards Him. Guilt and unworthiness are forms of self-absorption and are further tricks of the mind to keep us from devoting all our energy and attention to the mystic path and seeking the Father within. Though we may sometimes entertain such feelings, they do not constitute the real repentance. True repentance is to follow the example of the prodigal son: to turn around and return home.

The mystic nature of this change of direction is clearly voiced in the early Christian and allied literature. As Judas Thomas says in the *Acts of Thomas*:

> Repent ye, therefore, and believe the promise
> and receive the yoke of meekness and the light burden,
> that ye may live and not die.
> These things get, these keep.

> Come forth of the darkness
>   that the Light may receive you!
> Come unto him that is indeed good,
>   that ye may receive grace of him
>   and implant his Sign (his Word) in your souls.
>
>   *Acts of Thomas 28, ANT p.377*

Or as the writer of *Zostrianos*, a Nag Hammadi revelationary tractate, says:

> Do not be led astray.
> The *Aeon of the Aeons* (the Word)
>   of the Living Ones (the Masters) is great;
> Yet so also is the punishment
>   of those who are unconvinced....
>
> Many bonds and chastisers surround you:
>   flee quickly before death reaches you.
> Look at the Light; flee the darkness:
>   do not be led astray to your destruction.
>
>   *Zostrianos 131-132, NHL p.430*

It is, as these writers point out, through the grace and mercy of the Father, through the Saviour, that the son can repent and return home.

Mercy and Justice

The second-century Marcion, and probably most of the other gnostics too, taught that the essential characteristic of the Demiurge or Negative Power is justice, while that of God is pure love. So significant are the differences between Devil's law of justice and the Lord's rule of love and mercy, that some of the gnostics went so far as to say that the God of the Old Testament was actually the Demiurge, for he is often portrayed as a judgmental God rather than a God of mercy and love. And though the observation may have been too sweeping, since the Old Testament writings are a very mixed collection, depicting God in many different ways according to the conceptions of the various writers, it does illustrate the deep divide between justice and mercy.

The Lord, being so full of love, mercy and forgiveness, would find it impossible to run a creation in which souls are separated from Him were He not to enlist the aid of the Negative Power. For the Lord is so loving that He would automatically forgive all and anything that kept souls separated from Himself. Whatever the son may have done, his father will always give him a warm welcome home. God's unconditional mercy is the message of the parable of the prodigal son.

Satan's primary law, on the other hand – the law of the mind – is the law of cause and effect, the law of justice, the law of *karma*. Everything in his realm is a recompense, a response or a reaction to what has gone before, while at the same time new seeds are being sown for the future. In this way, no soul can ever escape unaided, for by the very nature of things in the domain of the Universal Mind, all souls are required to act – and they are then bound by the results of those actions. Once they have stepped into the quicksand, every move only serves to further entrap them.

It would appear to our limited understanding that the Lord – having created this arrangement – wishes it to continue. He has made just one great exception. He can come, whenever and wherever He wants, in the guise of a human being, a realized Son of God, to rescue those souls whom He so desires and who desire Him. In fact, this is an essential part of His great plan of creation. For these blessed souls, though they still have to go through their lives in this world, He operates a law of forgiveness, mercy and love. And since the Son and God are one, the same love and mercy which are found in God are also found in a Master. It is for this reason that Jesus and all mystics have been described as merciful, compassionate, forgiving, loving and kind, for this is what they truly are. In the *Acts of Thomas*, for example, Judas Thomas refers to his Master as:

> O Jesu Christ,
> Son that understandest the perfect mercy!
>
> *Acts of Thomas 39, ANT p.384*

And:

> Jesu most high, Voice arising from perfect mercy,
> Saviour of all, the right hand of the Light,
> overthrowing the Evil One in his own nature,
> and gathering all His nature (his own kind)
> into one place.
>
> *Acts of Thomas 48, ANT p.387*

The "perfect mercy" is the mercy of God. In another passage, he praises Jesus as:

> Glory to Thee, Thou Gracious One!
> Glory to Thee, Living Word!
> Glory to Thee, Thou Hidden One, who hast many forms!
> Glory to Thy mercy, which hath abounded unto us.
> Glory to Thy grace, which hath been upon us! ...
>
> Thou art the Word of Heaven.
> Thou art the hidden light of the understanding,
> 　and the shewer of the way of Truth,
> 　　the dispeller of darkness and the destroyer of Error.
>
> *Acts of Thomas 80, AAA p.216-217, ANT p.401*

In the *History of John*, John also speaks of this sublime quality, referring to Jesus' words of forgiveness from the cross when he was made to die such a horrific death for teaching nothing but love. Who is there, amongst normal human beings, who would not have felt at least some degree of resentment and bitterness? Yet Jesus asks the Father to "forgive them, for they know not what they do".[2] Hence, John repeats the story in a prayer of praise to God:

> Thy dear Son, our Lord Jesus the Messiah,
> 　when the Jews took him to slay him, prayed and said,
> "Forgive them, for they know not what they do."
> This mercy, then, which is eternally in Thee,
> 　is also found in Thy Son, for ye are one.
>
> *History of John, AAA p.11*

Mercy and forgiveness are essential. After millions upon millions of lifetimes in the millions of years in which the soul has been in this creation, it has accumulated such a vast storehouse of old sins or *karmas* that without forgiveness of these sins, it can never escape. And though contact with the divine Music of the Word is the purifier, *par excellence*, of souls, a soul can only come into contact with that divine cleansing agent when the Word in human form, a Son of God, takes the soul under his protection and guidance, overseeing its entire future. Everything happens by the mercy of the divine will, not by the will of the individual.

Hence, in the Nag Hammadi *Second Apocalypse of James*, Jesus' brother James, speaking as the Redeemer or Saviour, counsels:

> Renounce this difficult way (of the world),
>> which is so changeable,
>> and walk in accordance with Him who desires
>> that you become free men with me,
>> after you have passed above every [realm].
>
> *Second Apocalypse of James 59, NHS11 p.139*

He then adds that this is possible by the mercy of the Lord, for He is not a "wrathful" but a "kind Father":

> For He (the Lord) will not judge you
>> for those things that you did,
>> but will have mercy on you.
> For it is not you who did them,
>> but it is your Lord (who did them).
> [He was not] a wrathful one, but He was a kind Father.
>
> *Second Apocalypse of James 59, NHS11 p.139*

Paradoxical as it may seem, it is by the Lord's will that souls have been sent out into the creation and have become the slaves of their actions. Consequently, it is only by His will that they can return. The Lord is the only one who has created such a creation, has set it in motion and who constantly sustains it by His will, according to laws which He Himself has designed. So since it is the Lord who has involved the soul in sin, it is up to Him to show His mercy and kindness by forgiving all its misdemeanours.

The devotees have many ways of recounting and remembering God's mercy. In the *Acts of John*, John points out that, despite the fact that man has completely ignored the God who lives within him, God has shown only mercy and compassion in return. In the world, if someone ignores us, we very soon become grudging, resentful, even revengeful. It is fortunate, therefore, that the Lord who provides everything and is ignored by almost everyone, never adopts such an attitude. John says:

> We have not learned ... to render evil for evil;
> For God, though we have done much ill
>> and no good toward Him,
>> hath not given retribution unto us, but repentance.

And though we were ignorant of his Name
   He did not neglect us but had mercy on us;
And when we blasphemed Him,
   He did not punish but pitied us;
And when we disbelieved Him
   He bore us no grudge;
And when we persecuted His Brethren (the Masters)
   He did not recompense us evil
   but put into our minds repentance
   and abstinence from evil,
   and exhorted us to come unto Him.

               Acts of John 81, ANT pp.248-249

In this context, 'blaspheming' the Lord is the opposite of repentance. It means to turn the mind away from Him, towards His creation. But, says John, despite our misdeeds, ignorance, 'blasphemy', disbelief and even persecution of His Messengers, He does nothing "but put into our minds repentance". He only encourages His dirty children to return into His loving arms. This same mercy is portrayed by Jesus when he said:

He that is not with me is against me;
   and he that gathereth not with me scattereth abroad.

Wherefore I say unto you,
   all manner of sin and blasphemy
   shall be forgiven unto men:
But the blasphemy against the Holy Ghost
   shall not be forgiven unto men.

And whosoever speaketh a word against the Son of man,
   it shall be forgiven him:
But whosoever speaketh against the Holy Ghost,
   it shall not be forgiven him,
   neither in this world, neither in the world to come.

               Matthew 12:30-32

If we permit our attention to be "scattered abroad" in the world, forgetting all about God and the "Holy Ghost", how can we ever be forgiven, whatever beliefs we may profess? For we are walking away from the one who is offering forgiveness: we are "against" him. But even if a disciple has doubts about the "Son of man", the Master, provided he turns towards God in his spiritual practice, he can be forgiven, since doubts, weaknesses, difficulties and struggle are a natural, understandable part of being in the human form and can be surmounted.

It is only through the Holy Ghost or the Word that sins are forgiven. If someone turns his back on the spiritual practice that brings him into contact with the Word, then neither forgiveness nor repentance can come. Forgiveness comes with repentance, when a person turns inwardly towards the Lord. Blasphemy, here, does not mean the use of bad language in regard to God for, though coarse and unmannerly, it is hardly a heinous sin incapable of being forgiven.

Again emphasizing the Lord's willingness to forgive, Philip says in the *History of Philip*:

> Who has believed in Him, and He has forsaken him?
> Or who has trusted in Him, and He has cast him off?
> Or who has called upon Him, and He has not answered him:
> Because the Lord is gracious and merciful,
>   and forgiving of sins,
>   harkening to the voice of those that do His will.
> Believe, my dear friends,
>   for He will forgive you your sins
>   when ye turn to Him with all your heart,
>   with a pure mind free from doubt.
>
> *History of Philip, AAA pp.80-81*

The Lord is all mercy and forgiveness, never turning His back on any souls that turns to Him. As Judas Thomas concludes in the *Acts of Thomas*:

> Thou, Lord, art He that in all things
>   showest compassion and sparest men.
> For men by reason of the Error that is in them
>   have overlooked Thee,
> But Thou hast not overlooked them.
>
> *Acts of Thomas 25, ANT p.375*

The Lord's love and mercy are unconditional. Man may ignore God, but God never ignores man.

Five Men on a Roof

The belief is present in the gospels and in the early Christian literature, and has remained a tenet of Christianity throughout the ages, that Jesus came to this world to forgive sins. Christians have come to assert that this covers everybody who applies, so to speak, whatever their degree of sincerity. They also believe that forgiveness of sins can only be performed by Jesus. Mystics themselves, however, point out that each soul must come into contact with its own living Saviour, one who is alive in the body, for this forgiveness to come about.

There is no doubt that Jesus was credited with the power to forgive sins. There are a number of miracle stories in the gospels, for instance, where Jesus heals sick persons, concluding with comments like, "Thy sins be forgiven thee". Fact or fiction, these stories reiterate the belief that the circumstances of life are related to the sins of the past.

In one story, narrated in the synoptic gospels, when Jesus is questioned by the scribes, he adds that the "Son of man hath power on earth to forgive sins". That is, he speaks specifically of the Son of man's ability and authority to forgive those sins that make up the fabric of our life in this world. The incident, too, is not without its humorous side, if we may be permitted a light-hearted digression at this point, the original version being found in Mark:

> And again he entered into Capernaum, after some days;
>> and it was noised that he was in the house.
> And straightway many were gathered together,
>> insomuch that there was no room to receive them,
>> no, not so much as about the door:
> And he preached the word (Word?) unto them.
>
> And they come unto him,
>> bringing one sick of the palsy,
>> which was borne of four.
> And when they could not come nigh unto him for the press,
>> they uncovered the roof where he was:
>> and when they had broken it up,
>> they let down the bed wherein the sick of the palsy lay.
>
> When Jesus saw their faith,
>> he said unto the sick of the palsy,
> "Son, thy sins be forgiven thee."

> But there were certain of the scribes sitting there,
> and reasoning in their hearts,
> "Why doth this man thus speak blasphemies?
> Who can forgive sins but God only?"
>
> And immediately when Jesus perceived in his spirit
> that they so reasoned within themselves,
> he said unto them,
> "Why reason ye these things in your hearts?
> Whether is it easier to say to the sick of the palsy,
> 'Thy sins be forgiven thee'; or to say,
> 'Arise, and take up thy bed, and walk?'
> But that ye may know that the Son of man
> hath power on earth to forgive sins."
>
> *Mark 2:1-10*

Now, many people must have wondered about the details of this story. What kind of a roof was it that the people had "broken up"? Was is mud or thatch or something similar? Was it flat or sloped? Could it really have borne the weight of the four bearers and the sick man, plus his "couch"? And how is it that the people inside did not come out or send word to someone, requesting the assiduous four to desist from damaging the house? Surely someone would have stopped them and, even despite the crush, have arranged access? And in any event, was it really such a neighbourly thing to have done?

Matthew certainly did not like the idea for he omits the destruction of the roof and simply has the man brought in to Jesus on his bed. Luke, too, clearly feels uncomfortable about the details, but being of a more creative bent and not averse to changing things, his version, at this point, reads:

> And when they could not find by what way they might bring him in because of the multitude, they went upon the housetop, and let him down through the tiling with his couch into the midst before Jesus.
>
> *Luke 5:19*

Luke specifies a tiled roof, presumably sloped (or the rain would have got in). This would solve the problem of large quantities of dirt and debris falling upon the surprised heads of Jesus and his audience while the determined four resolutely broke in through a mud or thatched roof. But Luke also has the paralysed man lowered accurately, right in front of Jesus. How five people, one of them paralysed and lying on a "couch", could have accomplished this while scrambling around on a sloped roof is difficult to imagine. Tiled roofs usually require closely spaced vertical rafters and horizontal tile battens from which to hang the tiles. So the difficulties of letting down a paralysed man in his bed between the rafters and the battens must have been considerable. The unfortunate man is more likely to have ended up unceremoniously decanted into a heap on the floor with several broken bones to add to his already considerable problems! Perhaps the sins that Jesus forgave him also included those of breaking and entering!

But whatever its authenticity, the story does indicate the degree of resolve required to follow a Master, as well as the intensity of feeling that is generated around him. As in one of Luke's stories where a certain Zacchaeus climbs a tree to get a better look, many disciples have figured out various ruses for catching just a glimpse of their Master.

God's Forgiveness of Man

Mercy and compassion lead to forgiveness and mystics have observed, perhaps light-heartedly, that if the Lord had nothing to forgive, His qualities would be wasted. In the gnostic *Gospel of Truth*, the author comments that the eternal One, "Incorruptibility", "breathed forth" in order to provide forgiveness for the sinner. Just as it is the nature of a physician to seek out the one who is sick, so too, he says, is it the nature of the Spirit to seek out those in need of forgiveness:

> It is for this reason that Incorruptibility breathed forth; it pursued the one who had sinned in order that he (the sinner) might (find) rest. For nothing else but forgiveness remains for the Light when it comes to the deficiency (the creation) as the Word of the All. Just as the physician runs to the place where sickness is, because that is his nature.
>
> *Gospel of Truth* 35:25-34; cf. NHS22 p.107

It is, of course, just a way of saying things, but other mystics have similarly observed that a doctor is only concerned about those who are sick or that a laundry man is only interested in dirty clothes. By this they mean that a Master comes to this world for no other purpose than to forgive sins. Consequently, he is never grudging in his mercy and compassion. Without sickness, there would be no doctor; without dirty clothes, there would be no laundry man; and without sinful human beings there would be no Master. Hence, in the *Pistis Sophia*,

> the Saviour answered and said:
> "I forgive and I will forgive.
> For this reason has the First Mystery sent me".
>
> *Pistis Sophia 100, PS p.253, PSGG p.210*

Likewise, in an ancient Arabic, Christian apocryphal writing, the *Acts of Andrew and Bartholomew*, Jesus says:

> I forgive the sins of those who return unto Me;
> and I will accept their repentance.
>
> *Acts of Andrew and Bartholomew, MAA p.11*

It is, however, necessary to first recognize that we are in need of forgiveness. As John the Elder says in *1 John*:

> If we confess our sins,
> he is faithful and just to forgive us our sins,
> and to cleanse us from all unrighteousness.
> If we say that we have not sinned,
> we make him a liar,
> and his word (Word) is not in us.
>
> *1 John 1:9-10*

The forgiveness of sins that God, through His Son, is able to bestow upon human beings, is a constant theme in Christian writings, early or late, and in every school of Christian thought. It is, one supposes, a reflection of man's awareness – even if he is only half honest with himself – that his thoughts and conduct leave much to be desired and that it is these which lead him away from God. In *Acts*, for example, in one of Peter's speeches, we find:

> Repent ye therefore, and be converted,
> that your sins may be blotted out,
> when the times of refreshing shall come
> from the presence of the Lord.
>
> *Acts 3:19*

And:

> To him (Jesus) give all the prophets witness,
>> that through his Name whosoever believeth in him
>> shall receive remission of sins.
>
> *Acts 10:43*

And in the *Acts of Thomas*, a group to whom Judas Thomas has been talking, say:

> O man of God, the God whom thou preachest,
>> we dare not say that we are his,
>> for the works which we have done are alien unto him
>> and not pleasing to him;
> But if he will have compassion on us and pity us and save us,
>> overlooking our former deeds,
>> and will set us free from the evils
>> which we committed being in error,
>> and not impute them unto us
>> nor make remembrance of our former sins:
> We will become his servants
>> and will accomplish his will unto the end.
>
> *Acts of Thomas 38, ANT p.383*

To which Thomas replies:

> He reckoneth not against you,
>> neither taketh account of the sins
>> which ye committed being in error,
>> but overlooketh your transgressions
>> which ye have done in ignorance.
>
> *Acts of Thomas 38, ANT p.383*

Without forgiveness of past sins, the soul cannot rise above the realm of sin and escape from the domain of Satan, the Negative Power. In the gnostic tractate, the *Second Book of Jeu*, Jesus has just finished initiating or baptizing a group of disciples, described as "giving to them all these mysteries", when he explains:

> It is necessary that you should receive the mystery of the forgiveness of sins, so that you may become sons of the Light, and completed in all the mysteries.
>
> *Second Book of Jeu 51, BC p.126*

And in the same book, he also says:

> Now because of this, every man who will believe in the Son of the Light
> (the Saviour) must receive the mystery of the forgiveness of sins, so that
> he will be completely perfected and completed in all mysteries, because
> this is the mystery of the forgiveness of sins....
>
> Now because of this I say to you that when you receive the mystery of
> the forgiveness of sins, every sin which you have committed knowingly
> and those which you have committed unknowingly, those which you have
> committed from your childhood until today and until the releasing of
> the bonds of the flesh of *Heimarmene* (the ruler of *metempsychosis*,[3] *i.e.*
> the Negative Power), will all be erased, because you have received the
> mystery of the forgiveness of sins.
>
> *Second Book of Jeu 49, BC p.117*

He says that all sins committed right up until the soul is released from
the grip of the body are forgiven. In fact, in another extract, it is also
made clear that not only are the sins of this life cleared or erased, but
also the sins of past lives, "which he has committed since the foundation of the world until today":

> For it is necessary that every man who will believe in the kingdom of the
> Light should perform the mystery of the forgiveness of sins only once.
> For to every man who will perform the mystery of forgiveness of sins, all
> the sins which he has committed knowingly or unknowingly, from his
> childhood until today, and which he has committed since the foundation
> of the world until today, will all be erased, and he will be made to be a
> pure light and taken to the Light of these Lights.
>
> *Second Book of Jeu 44, BC p.104*

Only in this way can a soul become a "pure light" and be taken to the
"light of these Lights", to God. Naturally, such forgiveness is mystical
in character and not a matter of human sentiment.

Forgiveness of sins was by no means a new concept. It is as old as
creation and as old as religion. The Old Testament writers all pray for
such forgiveness and no doubt many of them understood what it en-
tailed, too. Certainly, the early gnostic Christians understood the Old
Testament in a mystic way. In the *Pistis Sophia*, for example, the twenty-
fourth psalm is provided with a mystic interpretation, verse by verse,
one of twenty *Psalms* and five *Odes of Solomon* which are treated in

this manner. Four of its verses are arranged below with the explanation following each verse:

    (7)   Remember not the sins of my youth and those of my ignorance.
    Remember me rather according to the greatness of Thy mercy,
       for the sake of Thy beneficence, O Lord.

    (7)   Concerning my transgression which I have committed
       from the beginning in my ignorance,
        do not count it against me, O Light;
    But rather save me
       through Thy great mystery of forgiveness of sins,
       because of Thy goodness, O Light.

                      Pistis Sophia 46, PS pp.82,79, PSGG pp.67,65

The "sins of my youth" is taken as a veiled reference to reincarnation, the writer of the *Pistis Sophia* interpreting it as "my transgressions which I have committed from the beginning". "Ignorance" is understood as nescience, spiritual ignorance of man's true nature and the condition to which he has fallen. Likewise, "remember me according to the greatness of Thy mercy" means salvation through the "forgiveness of sins" because of the Lord's "goodness".

    (11) For Thy Name's sake, O Lord, forgive me my sin,
       for it is very great.

    (11) For the sake of the mystery of Thy Name, O Light,
       forgive my transgression, for it is great.
            Pistis Sophia 46, PS pp.82,80, PSGG pp.68,65

For "Thy Name's sake" is seen as a reference to the Holy Name, the "mystery of Thy Name", the mystic Word. It is only this Power which can forgive such a heavy burden of sin.

    (15) My eyes are directed to the Lord at all times;
       for it is He who will draw my feet out of the snare.

    (15) Moreover I have ever believed in the Light,
       that it is this which will save my feet
       from the bonds of the darkness (this world).
           Pistis Sophia 46, PS pp.83,80, PSGG pp.66,68

The "snare" is identified with the darkness and bondage of this world. Only complete attention directed to the "Light" – to the Lord – at all times will bring salvation to the captive soul.

(18) Look upon my humbleness and my distress,
        and forgive me all my sins.

(18) And look upon the distress of my oppression
        and forgive my transgression.

Pistis Sophia 46, PS pp.83,81, PSGG pp.68,66

Have compassion upon me in this wretched condition of worldliness and forgive my sins, says the writer. This is the only hope for a soul. But those who are too proud to beg at His door will not be admitted to the grace of His forgiveness.

The same understanding of forgiveness is found in the *Acts of Thomas*. Judas Thomas speaks of his Master "blotting out" all "former actions" and "earthly desires" that hold a soul to this world, and he also describes these actions as those which "accompany you", "depart with you" and proceed "before you":

He (Jesus) will blot out your former actions,
        and will cleanse you from all your earthly desires
        that abide (hold you) on the earth,
        and will heal you of all your trespasses which accompany you
        and depart with you and are found before you.

Acts of Thomas 58, AAA p.197, ANT p.392

Like a herald walking before a procession, announcing someone's coming, our sins go before us, determining and heralding our future. There are many such veiled references in the *Acts of Thomas* to reincarnation and the law of *karma*, a book that was adopted by the Manichaeans as worthy of careful study.

Without the clearance of these sins, the soul can never go beyond the domain of Satan. The extremely subtle region at the height of the Universal Mind or Negative Power is described by Jesus in the *Second Book of Jeu* as the realm of the "six *aeons*", beyond which the soul cannot proceed without the erasure of sins that lie upon the mind:

But when you reach the six *aeons*, they will restrain you until you receive the mystery of the forgiveness of sins, because it is the great mystery which is in the Treasury of the Innermost of the Innermost. And it is the whole salvation of the soul. And all those who will receive that mystery will surpass all gods and all rulerships of all these *aeons* ... for this is the great mystery of the Unapproachable One which is in the Treasury of the Innermost of the Innermost.

Second Book of Jeu 49, BC p.117

He says that it is this mystic forgiveness of sins which leads to salvation. "It is the whole salvation of the soul." Those who receive this blessing will ascend beyond all the rulers and powers of the creation. This indeed is the meaning of the line in the Lord's Prayer which, in the *Acts of Thomas* and elsewhere, reads:

And lead us not into temptation;
but deliver us from the Evil One.
Acts of Thomas 144, ANT p.427

The one small change makes the meaning more explicit. It is hardly necessary to remind the reader that in both Matthew and Luke, the corresponding line reads:

And lead us not into temptation,
but deliver us from evil.
Matthew 6:13

Salvation is thus clearly equated with deliverance or liberation from the realm and power of the "Evil One", the Negative Power or Satan, as we also find in one of the *Odes of Solomon* where the devotee writes of deliverance from the "Evil One" through the Lord's "compassion", "kindness", guidance and His "Name", a reference to the Word:

Like the eyes of a son on his father,
    so are my eyes, O Lord, continually towards Thee; ...
Turn not Thy compassion away from me, O Lord,
    and take not Thy kindness from me.
Stretch out Thy right hand to me continually, O my Lord,
    and be a guide to me until the end
    because of Thy good pleasure.
I shall be pleasing before Thee because of Thy glory,
    and because of thy Name
    I shall be delivered from the Evil One;

And Thy gentleness, O Lord, will abide with me,
  and the fruits of Thy love.

Odes of Solomon XIV:1-6, AOT p.704

Similarly, in *Acts*, according to the speech related by Luke, Paul claims
that Jesus instructed him in a vision to preach to the Gentiles:

To open their eyes and to turn them from darkness to light,
  and from the power of Satan unto God,
  that they may receive forgiveness of sins,
  and inheritance among them which are sanctified
  by faith that is in me.

Acts 26:18

And in his letters, speaking of the same deliverance, he advises:

Giving thanks unto the Father,
  which hath made us meet to be partakers
  of the inheritance of the saints in Light:
Who hath delivered us from the power of darkness,
  and hath translated us into the kingdom of his dear Son:
In whom we have redemption through his blood,
  even the forgiveness of sins.

Colossians 1:12-13

Salvation entails repentance or the turning of the mind and soul to
God, the forgiveness of sins and the release from Satan.

Ransom, Tax and Head Money

It is the Master or Saviour in his real form as the Creative Word who
takes on the administration of the sins or *karmas* of his disciples. This
is how the process of salvation or emancipation comes about. All the
souls in Satan's domain have a debt which they owe to Satan. This
must be paid before escape can be effected. And the Master – not his
physical form, but his higher, mystic Word form – schedules the repayment of that debt for his disciples.

The payment is made in a variety of ways. The disciple clears the
karma of his destiny by going through it, with the help and guidance
of his Master. Other *karmas* or sins, stored up from the past, are cleared

by spiritual communion with the music of the Word. And – most importantly – the Master himself clears a great deal of the old debris. No soul can ever hope to repay the debts of countless past lives by his or her own efforts. Unless a Master himself accepts responsibility for these obligations, the soul's indebtedness to Satan will continue and the soul will remain in his domain.

A Master does this either by paying the debt through his own wealth of the Word or by taking the *karmas* upon his own body. Because he has either come directly from God or has already cleared all his own debts through contact with the Word and the blessings of his own Master, a Master has no *karmas* or sins of his own. Therefore, when he takes birth, he is truly free and is able to assume the *karmas* of his disciples. All of a Master's apparent sufferings or ill-health arise from his accepting the sins of his disciples. He pays part of the debt to Satan through his own body – by payment in flesh and blood. This is what is really meant by "redemption through his blood". And this is the meaning of Jesus' crucifixion. His physical suffering on the cross was simply a means of assuming some of the sins or *karmas* of his disciples. All Masters have to leave this world and, just as they did in life, they make it an opportunity to pay off more of their disciples' *karmas*.

We will return to these important topics, but this process by which a Master pays for the sins of his disciples is also described in the gospels and the early Christian literature. The Son of God is said to be a "ransom" for the sins of his disciples. In Mark, copied by Matthew, Jesus says:

> Whosoever will be great among you,
>> shall be your minister:
> And whosoever of you will be the chiefest,
>> shall be servant of all.
> For even the Son of man came not to be ministered unto,
>> but to minister, and to give his life a ransom for many.
>>
>> *Mark 10:43-45*

Jesus is teaching his disciples to serve one another rather than exercise authority over each other. For he says that the "Son of man", meaning the Master, does not come to be served, but only to serve. Not only is his entire life spent in the service of his disciples – for he is sent by God and comes for no other purpose than to perform this service – but his life is a "ransom for many". The Master pays the debt of *karma* on behalf of his disciples, thereby freeing them from captivity. Both in his life and by his death, in a variety of ways, a Master pays the "ransom" to Satan that ensures the freedom of his disciples. But it is a "ransom for *many*" – not all.

The idea of the Master taking on the sins of others is expressed by John the Baptist, as recorded in John's gospel:

> The next day John seeth Jesus coming unto him,
>> and saith, "Behold the Lamb of God,
>> which taketh away the sin of the world."
>
> *John 1:29*

The lamb being a sacrificial animal in Judaism and other religious cults of the time, Jesus is described as a sacrifice to atone for the "sin of the world" – the sin or *karma* collected by souls while being in this world. It cannot mean that Jesus took away the sins of the inhabitants of the entire planet earth, past and future. If he had done that, then the world would have ceased to exist, right there and then, for without *karma* or sin this world cannot continue. No soul comes here without a debt of past sin to repay.

There are many places in early Christian writings where Jesus is described as one who pays the "ransom" on behalf of his disciples. In the *Acts of Thomas*, for example, Judas Thomas describes Jesus as:

> My Lord and my God, that travellest with thy servants,
>> that guidest and correctest them that believe in thee,
>> the refuge and rest of the oppressed,
>> the hope of the poor and ransomer of captives.
>
> *Acts of Thomas 10, ANT p.368*

And he continues, making his meaning even more explicit:

> Jesus Christ, Son of compassion and perfect Saviour,
>> Christ, Son of the living God,
>> the undaunted Power that hast overthrown the Enemy,
> And the Voice that was heard of the rulers,
>> and made all their powers to quake,
> The Ambassador that wast sent from the Height
>> and camest down even unto hell,
> Who didst open the doors and bring up thence
>> them that for many ages were shut up
>> in the treasury of darkness,

> And showedst them the way
> that leadeth up unto the Height.
>
> *Acts of Thomas 10, ANT p.369*

Jesus ransomed the "captives" – souls who have "for many ages been shut up" or imprisoned in body after body – from the "hell" of this world, the "treasury of darkness"; and he took them back to God. This, incidentally, is another passage in the early Christian literature that speaks almost specifically of reincarnation.

Jesus is also hinting at the same idea when he speaks of paying tax to "Caesar", the incident being recorded by Mark and copied over by Matthew and Luke:

> Then went the Pharisees, and took counsel how they might entangle him in his talk. And they sent out unto him their disciples with the Herodians, saying, "Master, we know that thou art true, and teachest the way of God in truth, neither carest thou for any man: for thou regardest not the person of men. Tell us therefore, what thinkest thou? Is it lawful to give tribute unto Caesar, or not?"
>
> But Jesus perceived their wickedness, and said, "Why tempt ye me, ye hypocrites? Shew me the tribute money." And they brought unto him a penny.
>
> And he saith unto them, "Whose is this image and superscription?" They say unto him, "Caesar's".
>
> Then saith he unto them, "Render therefore unto Caesar the things which are Caesar's; and unto God the things that are God's." When they had heard these words, they marvelled, and left him, and went their way.
>
> *Matthew 22:15-22*

Jesus means that whatever debt of sins a person has in this world must be paid to the ruler of this world, that is, to the Negative Power, here symbolized as Caesar, the ruler of the Roman Empire. And what belongs to God is what remains – the soul. The soul should be rendered unto God or returned to God.

Early Christian writings indicate that this is the way in which the saying was commonly interpreted. In the *Pistis Sophia*, for instance, Mary makes a number of comments concerning Jesus' discourse on the association of the soul with the "counterfeit spirit", and its surrendering of the "destiny" to the rulers of Satan's realm before it can leave. This passage was discussed in the last chapter. Mary then continues:

The second thought, moreover, thou hast now just finished saying to us concerning the soul which received the mysteries: "When it comes to the region of the *archons* of the way of the Midst, they come forth before it in exceeding fearfulness.... And it gives the destiny to its (appropriate) region, and it gives the counterfeit spirit to its own region. And it gives the apology and the seals of every one of the *archons* which are upon the ways of the Midst. And it gives the honour and the glory and the eulogy of the seals and the songs of praise to all those of the region of the Light."

Concerning this word, my Lord, thou hast spoken once through the mouth of our brother Paul, saying: "Give tax to whom tax is due, fear to whom fear, give custom to whom custom is due, give honour to whom honour is due, and give eulogy to whom eulogy is due; and do not owe anything to another."

Pistis Sophia 113, PS pp.293-294, PSGG p.244

"Tax", "tribute" and "custom" are all terms used for payments levied by a higher authority, and which are unavoidable, however much one may wish to be free of them. Similarly with the debt of sin owed to Satan. It must be paid to the higher authority.

This passage in the *Pistis Sophia* relates both to Jesus' saying and also to its echoes in Paul's epistle to the *Romans*, a letter in which Paul talks at great length concerning judgment, condemnation, retribution, recompense, sin, mercy and so on. In this letter, he is saying that all souls in this world are subject to the higher rulers or powers of creation. All have been given power by God and are simply carrying out their task as directed by Him. But, as in this world, only the criminal need fear the police; only the one who does evil need fear the *archons* or rulers. He says:

> Let every soul be subject unto the higher powers.
> For there is no power but of God:
> the powers that be are ordained of God.
> Whosoever therefore resisteth the power,
> resisteth the ordinance of God:
> And they that resist shall receive to themselves damnation.
> For rulers are not a terror to good works,
> but to the evil.

> Wilt thou then not be afraid of the power?
> Do that which is good,
> and thou shalt have praise of the same:
> For he is the minister of God to thee for good....

Render therefore to all their dues:
    tribute to whom tribute is due;
    custom to whom custom;
    fear to whom fear;
    honour to whom honour.

Owe no man any thing, but to love one another:
    for he that loveth another hath fulfilled the law.
For this, thou shalt not commit adultery,
    thou shalt not kill, thou shalt not steal,
    thou shalt not bear false witness,
    thou shalt not covet;
And if there be any other commandment,
    it is briefly comprehended in this saying, namely,
    thou shalt love thy neighbour as thyself.

Romans 13:1-9

As far as possible, he says, create no debts to others. But the debts to which he refers are not financial, for in order to avoid creating such debts, Paul advises following the commandments of Moses concerning good conduct in this world.

It is not entirely clear in this letter whether Paul is referring to worldly authorities or the higher powers in creation. But he probably means both, for earlier in the same letter, he quite explicitly states that despite the power of such rulers and the subjection of the soul, there is ultimately nothing that can keep a soul separate from God, so long as the longing for God is present. Here, the "angels", "principalities" and "rulers" clearly refer to the inner hierarchy of creation:

I am persuaded, that neither death,
    nor life, nor angels,
    nor principalities, nor powers,
    nor things present, nor things to come,
Nor height, nor depth, nor any other creature,
    shall be able to separate us from the love of God.

Romans 8:38-39

Although all debts of sin or *karma* have to be paid, ultimately, when the longing and love of the soul become sufficient, nothing can keep it away from God. It is only the layers of past sin upon the mind that obscure the natural love and affinity of the soul for God, and when true love of God is present, none of the "principalities" and "powers", the realms and *archons* of Satan's domain, nor anything else in creation, can stand between the soul and God. Hence, in *Ephesians*, he writes unequivocally that the spiritual struggle is essentially against these rulers or higher powers, they being the source of human sin and wrong-doing.

> My brethren, be strong in the Lord,
> and in the Power of His might.
> Put on the whole armour of God,
> that ye may be able to stand
> against the wiles of the Devil.
>
> For we wrestle not against flesh and blood,
> but against principalities, against powers,
> against the rulers of the darkness of this world,
> against spiritual wickedness in high places.
>
> *Ephesians 6:10-12*

The "Power of His might" is the creative Power, the one force which comes from beyond or above these rulers, including Satan, and is therefore the only force by which a soul can overcome them. And alluding to the extent of the Devil's domain, he speaks of "spiritual wickedness in high places". Quoting Paul and endorsing his point of view, one of the gnostic authors of the Nag Hammadi library also writes:

> For our struggle is not against flesh and blood ...
> but against the world rulers of this darkness
> and the spirits of wickedness.
>
> *Expository Treatise on the Soul 131, NHS21 p.153*

In a passage from the *Acts of Thomas*, Judas Thomas specifically equates the "powers" with the "tax-gatherers" and the collectors of tribute. Speaking in metaphors of overcoming these powers, he says of Jesus:

> The bound, whom thou didst deliver to me, I have slain;
> The unbound, who is in me, do thou set free,
> and let not my soul be kept back from its trust....
>
> The powers shall not perceive me,
> nor the rulers take counsel against me;

> The tax-gatherers shall not see me,
>   nor the collectors of tribute oppress me.
>
> *Acts of Thomas, AAA p.282*

The mind, bound down with all its debts, is the "bound" one. This, the Master enables the disciple to conquer or "slay". He delivers the mind, bound hand and foot, so to speak, to the disciple, for it is the Master, ultimately, who enables the disciple to control his mind. The "unbound", the pure soul, the essence of life within, is set free to soar above the realms of Satan and return to God. Then, neither the "powers", the "rulers", the "tax-gatherers" or the "collectors of tribute" – all synonyms for the administrative powers within the realm of Satan – can have any hold over the soul. And this, says Judas Thomas is because the Master himself arranges payment of the debt. Hence, he describes Jesus as:

> This, who was called an impostor,
>   and who is the True, that deceiveth not,
>   and the payer of the tax
>   and the head-money for his disciples and for himself;
> This, of whom the Enemy, when he saw him,
>   was silent and afraid,
>   and asked him who he was and what was said of him.
>   And he (Jesus) did not make known to him (Satan) the Truth,
>   because there is no Truth in him (Satan).
>
> *Acts of Thomas, AAA p.278*

Or, as another translation has it:

> And he payeth the toll and the poll tax for himself
>   and for his disciples.
>
> *Acts of Thomas 143, FAJT p.30, MEM p.89*

The debt of sin has to be paid to Satan, tax has to be paid to Caesar, but through his mercy and forgiveness, a Master makes this payment on behalf of his disciples.

Man's Forgiveness of Man

The counterpart to God's unstinted forgiveness of man is man's forgiveness of man. Like all mystics, Jesus taught that if we want the Lord to forgive us for the sins of innumerable lifetimes, we must first learn

to forgive others their (by comparison) few and inconsequential trespasses against us. If we want the Lord to come and dwell in our hearts,
we must begin by developing some of His characteristics of love and
mercy. We must, so to speak, make our hearts a place where He can
feel at home. As Jesus said:

> Blessed are the merciful:
> for they shall obtain mercy.
> *Matthew 5:7*

And, as he pointed out elsewhere, we are not only in need of forgiveness ourselves, but must also forgive others:

> And forgive us our debts,
> as we forgive our debtors....
> For if ye forgive men their trespasses,
> your heavenly Father will also forgive you:
> But if ye forgive not men their trespasses,
> neither will your Father forgive your trespasses.
> *Matthew 6:12-15*

Or as we find it in Mark:

> And when ye stand praying, forgive,
> if ye have ought against any:
> That your Father also which is in heaven
> may forgive you your trespasses.
> But if ye do not forgive,
> neither will your Father which is in heaven
> forgive your trespasses.
> *Mark 11:25-26*

Our burden of sin is vast. We are "heavy laden" and desperately in need
of help and forgiveness, so there is no merit in trying to carry our
burden on our own. But we do need to develop a soft and loving heart,
tolerant and forgiving by nature. It is only then that the Lord's love
and final forgiveness can find its way into our hearts. He is always forgiving and draws us towards Himself, but we have to become receptive to His love by opening our hearts to His qualities and by permitting Him to enter our inner beings. But then, He is also the one who
will soften our hearts and make us receptive to Himself.

If our heart is closed, if we have grievances in our mind against others, when we sit for spiritual practice or prayer, instead of concentrating within, our mind will immediately bring all its disturbances and upsets to the fore. Hence, as Paul wisely remarked:

> Let not the sun go down upon your wrath:
> neither give place to the Devil.
> *Ephesians 4:26-27*

His well-known maxim means that we should try to clear upsets with other people as soon as possible and carry no burdens and grudges in our mind. This is to our own advantage. There is no need to emulate the man who, upon boarding a train, insists upon continuing to carry his luggage.

Jesus, as always, has a parable to relate to bring home his meaning. According to the story told in St Matthew, it begins when Peter asks him about forgiveness of others:

> Then came Peter to him, and said,
> "Lord, how oft shall my brother sin against me,
>   and I forgive him? Till seven times?"
> Jesus saith unto him,
> "I say not unto thee, until seven times:
>   but, until seventy times seven."
> *Matthew 18:21-22*

He means that we should go on forgiving others for as long as it takes. There should be no limits or conditions. Our forgiveness, like the Lord's, should be unreserved. Jesus then continues:

> "Therefore is the kingdom of heaven
>   likened unto a certain king,
>   which would take account of his servants.
> And when he had begun to reckon,
>   one was brought unto him,
>   which owed him ten thousand talents.
> But forasmuch as he had not to pay,
>   his lord commanded him to be sold,
>   and his wife, and children, and all that he had,
>   and payment to be made.
> The servant therefore fell down, and worshipped him, saying,

'Lord, have patience with me, and I will pay thee all.'
Then the lord of that servant was moved with compassion,
    and loosed him, and forgave him the debt.

"But the same servant went out,
    and found one of his fellow servants,
    which owed him an hundred pence:
And he laid hands on him,
    and took him by the throat, saying,
    'Pay me that thou owest.'
And his fellow servant fell down at his feet,
    and besought him, saying,
    'Have patience with me, and I will pay thee all.'
And he would not: but went and cast him into prison,
    till he should pay the debt.

"So when his fellow servants saw what was done,
    they were very sorry,
    and came and told unto their lord all that was done.
Then his lord, after that he had called him, said unto him,
    'O thou wicked servant, I forgave thee all that debt,
    because thou desiredst me:
Shouldst not thou also have had compassion on thy fellow servant,
    even as I had pity on thee?'
And his lord was wroth, and delivered him to the tormentors,
    till he should pay all that was due unto him.

"So likewise shall my heavenly Father do also unto you,
    if ye from your hearts
    forgive not every one his brother their trespasses."

Matthew 18:23-35

The meaning, of course, is very clear. There is another incident which comes from Luke's storehouse of stories, where the same point is made, with the addition that the greater the love a soul has for the Lord, the more are sins forgiven. Conversely, the more sins that are forgiven and the more a soul realizes this, the more grateful and loving does it become. It is, after all, only ego and pride which prevent a soul from realizing its sad condition and from being filled with love and forgiveness. Luke writes:

And one of the Pharisees desired him that he would eat with him. And he went into the Pharisee's house and sat down to meat. And, behold, a woman in the city, which was a sinner, when she knew that Jesus sat at meat in the Pharisee's house, brought an alabaster box of ointment, and stood at his feet behind him weeping, and began to wash his feet with tears, and did wipe them with the hairs of her head, and kissed his feet, and anointed them with the ointment.

Now when the Pharisee which had bidden him saw it, he spake within himself, saying, "This man, if he were a prophet, would have known who and what manner of woman this is that toucheth him: for she is a sinner."

And Jesus answering said unto him, "Simon, I have somewhat to say unto thee." And he saith, "Master, say on."

"There was a certain creditor which had two debtors: the one owed five hundred pence, and the other fifty. And when they had nothing to pay, he frankly forgave them both. Tell me therefore, which of them will love him most?"

Simon answered and said, "I suppose that he, to whom he forgave most." And he said unto him, "Thou hast rightly judged."

And he turned to the woman, and said unto Simon, "Seest thou this woman? I entered into thine house, thou gavest me no water for my feet: but she hath washed my feet with tears, and wiped them with the hairs of her head.

"Thou gavest me no kiss: but this woman since the time I came in hath not ceased to kiss my feet. My head with oil thou didst not anoint: but this woman hath anointed my feet with ointment. Wherefore I say unto thee, her sins, which are many, are forgiven; for she loved much: but to whom little is forgiven, the same loveth little."

And he said unto her, "Thy sins are forgiven."

And they that sat at meat with him began to say within themselves, "Who is this that forgiveth sins also?" And he said to the woman, "Thy faith hath saved thee; go in peace."

Luke 7:36-50

It is the faith and love that matter most, not external appearances. It is these that lead to the Lord's forgiveness. And we are talking here of reality, not theory or theology.

Judgment and Criticism

An old man and his young grandson were riding along on a donkey, one hot day. Bystanders commented, "Look at those two, forcing that poor donkey to carry both their weights." So the man got down, leaving the young boy to ride the donkey alone.

Then the people said, "Look at that young man. He is riding while his grandfather has to walk in the heat of the sun. There is no respect for old age these days." So the boy got down and the old man rode on the donkey.

But then the young boy had to run to keep pace with the donkey and the people remarked, "Just look! That little boy has to run along in the hot sun while the older man takes it easy." So the man got down and the two of them picked up the donkey and carried it along....

Generally, people are supercritical of everything others do, but never look within their own selves to see how they would stand up to the criticism they mete out to others. But Jesus points out that even at a human level, whatever we put out comes back to us:

> Judge not, that ye be not judged.
> For with what judgment ye judge,
>   ye shall be judged:
> And with what measure ye mete,
>   it shall be measured to you again.
>
> And why beholdest thou the mote
>   that is in thy brother's eye,
>   but considerest not the beam
>   that is in thine own eye?
> Or how wilt thou say to thy brother,
> "Let me pull out the mote out of thine eye;"
>   and, behold, a beam is in thine own eye?
> Thou hypocrite, first cast out the beam
>   out of thine own eye;
>   and then shalt thou see clearly
>   to cast out the mote out of thy brother's eye.
>
> *Matthew 7:1-5*

If we think angry, jealous or critical thoughts about others, this is what we will receive back from them. It does not matter what kind of a face we may try to put on things externally or what we may say hypocritically, deceiving both ourselves and others; for what is really within us will automatically express itself and receive an automatic and equivalent response. The mind is very powerful and puts out messages in many different ways, some subtle, some gross, and these are all communicated to others, often at an unconscious level, determining the way others respond to us. The best solution to solving any discord, therefore, is always to change our own attitude. When we change our attitude, the other person automatically changes.

But mostly, says Jesus, we see all the tiny defects that others have and never realize our own gross imperfections. Often, the imperfections we seem to see in others are only reflections of the imperfections we have within ourselves. If we were full only of love and genuine understanding, we would never feel critical of anyone at all, but would have only kindness, tolerance and contentment within ourselves. So first, Jesus advises, we must eliminate our own imperfections and then our mind will be able to see whether or not other people are really imperfect and what our attitude should be towards them.

Interestingly, Luke, perhaps from one of his special sources, has an addition to the passage found in Matthew. According to him, the words of Jesus were:

> Judge not, and ye shall not be judged:
>   condemn not, and ye shall not be condemned:
>   forgive, and ye shall be forgiven:
> Give, and it shall be given unto you;
> Good measure, pressed down, and shaken together,
>   and running over, shall men give into your bosom.
> For with the same measure that ye mete
>   withal it shall be measured to you again.
>
> *Luke 6:37-38*

He gives the example of the shopkeeper who can either be mean or generous. He can either fill a jar loosely and far below the brim, or he can pack in as much as he can, even letting it overflow the top. This is the way others will respond to us, Jesus says. They will give to us in whatever way we give to them. But such giving is more by way of heart, than it is of goods. It is a question of inner attitude and a generous heart. As Paul said, "The Lord loves a cheerful giver." And so does everybody else!

Incidentally, "with what measure ye mete it shall be measured to you again" is a precise exposition of the law of *karma*, of cause and effect. This law is prevalent at every level of human existence, hidden or obvious.

Lastly, on this subject area which has occupied us for the last three chapters, there is a passage found in Luke and Matthew, probably originating in Q, where Jesus says that, like the old man and his grandson, whatever Masters do in this world, they will also be criticized, because worldly and even spiritual people do not really understand them.

We tend to look at a Master and judge his actions according to the way our own minds work. If we have ego in our minds, we will think we see it in him because that is the way our minds function and because we tend to see in others what we have in ourselves. But Masters are not motivated like other human beings. Their actions stem from the purest and highest point of all. Moreover, they see into our minds and perceive our thoughts as we see pickles in a glass jar. And although Masters are not disturbed by human thoughts concerning them, they do feel for those who throw away a priceless opportunity through misjudgment.

Both Jesus and John the Baptist appear to have experienced such criticism. John, it seems, at least according to the very limited material available about him, led a more austere life than Jesus, but whatever either of them did, people found a cause for criticism. Hence, Jesus remarked:

> Whereunto shall I liken this generation?
> It is like unto children sitting in the markets,
>   and calling unto their fellows, and saying,
> "We have piped unto you, and ye have not danced;
>   we have mourned unto you, and ye have not lamented."
>
> For John came neither eating nor drinking, and they say,
> "He hath a devil."
> The Son of man came eating and drinking, and they say,
> "Behold a man gluttonous, and a winebibber,
>   a friend of publicans and sinners."
> But Wisdom is justified of her children.
>
> *Matthew 11:16-19*

We are, he says, like street children in the marketplace, who are never satisfied whatever other people may do. Like sceptics, we stand on the sidelines casting aspersions and criticisms. Whatever others do is wrong, in our view. We make clever comments and pass all manner of uninformed judgment on the Masters and their teachings, but never really get involved enough to understand things for ourselves. And thereby we miss a golden opportunity. For these Sons of God are

motivated only by the highest love and only come to this world for
our benefit.

Tying Some Strands Together

So far, in our study of Jesus' teachings, we have seen that the sayings
attributed to him are actually in keeping with the language of mystic
expression in vogue at that time. By setting his words in their true
context rather than considering them in isolation or in the light of
traditional, but later, interpretations and beliefs, his meaning comes
into sharper focus. Examining matters with an open mind, therefore,
we find considerable evidence that Jesus was a wise and loving teacher
of the universal and perennial mystic philosophy.

All the same, whichever way we look at the gospel teachings, there
are frequent oddities, surprising *non sequiturs*, obvious evidence of
copying and irreconcilable contradictions. Consequently, all scholars
who have no contrary beliefs to support have admitted that Jesus'
teachings have undergone editing, selection, compilation, and rearrangement. Observing the human tendency to externalize, literalize and
crystallize what is subtle, mystical and sublime, the direction of this
editorial process can only have led away from his original meaning.

It must be remembered that there is absolutely no evidence of Jesus
having made any attempt to ensure that his life and teachings were
adequately recorded for posterity. Rather, there is much to suggest that
a large part of what he taught was given in secret, in guarded language,
and was never intended for extended public consumption. If Jesus had
really wanted to start a new religion, surely he would have made better
provision for the clear presentation and preservation of his teachings?
The works of Philo Judaeus, Josephus and so many others have survived, so it would not have been particularly difficult. But the fact is
that he left nothing definitive. And what little has survived is fragmentary and has been worked over by those who never met him and
who had their own ideas about what he had taught. The only reasonable conclusion that can be drawn is that Jesus (unlike Paul) had no
intention of starting a religion and that the teachings of Christianity
are not an exact match with those of Jesus.

Jesus must have understood so well what happens to the teachings
of the mystics when they fall into the hands of those who only partially understand them or who do not understand them at all. He
would have known that those spiritual seekers who were to be pulled

out of the maelstrom of human interpretations would find their own Master to guide them, in their own time, whenever they were ready. It was simply unnecessary for him to compile any work for posterity which – without the guidance of a living Master – would still be misunderstood and misinterpreted. And, in any event, the atmosphere of the times was such that it was unwise to give out the full mystic teachings.

All mystics have pointed out that the mystic path is a path of practice and inner experience. Spirituality is not something that can be understood simply by reading a book on the subject. Books can point to the reality, but to be really understood, that reality must be experienced. And that experience does not come without great effort at specific, spiritual practice – and who can be sure that they know what that practice is unless there is a fully qualified practitioner to teach them? Consequently, however much or however little the Masters of the past may have written, a living Master will always be required for a living disciple. That way, there is far less likelihood of misunderstandings due to human misinterpretation.

We have considered Jesus' teachings on God, the Word, the Devil, and man's situation in this world, together with the need for repentance and forgiveness. To escape from this human plight, the role of the Master, the Saviour or the Son of God is of cardinal importance. A Master who is the "Word made flesh" retunes his disciples to the mystic Word; he instructs them in the art of interior prayer and teaches them how to live in this world. These, primarily, are the themes of the remaining two parts of this book.

NOTES AND REFERENCES

1. *Matthew* 10:3.
2. *Luke* 23:34.
3. *Heimarmene* was a name given to the ruler of the processes of *metempsychosis* by Empedocles, a Greek Pythagorean philosopher of the fifth century BC. He also called this divinity *Physis* ('Nature'). The relevant citation of Empedocles is given by Stobaeus who is quoting Porphyry: Stobaeus, *Eclogae* I:49.60, *SDMG* p.54.

PART III

The Son of God

CHAPTER FOURTEEN

The Son of God: The Living One

The Only-Begotten Son

The role of the Master is central to the path of the Word and no aspect of this ancient philosophy can be adequately discussed without mentioning the Masters. As a result, it has been more or less inevitable that we should reach this point in our discussion with some of the ground already covered. In all the topics so far discussed, we have had occasion to speak of the Masters and, in this chapter, we will attempt to tie these various strands together and further elucidate the nature and duties of the Masters in the economy of the Lord's creation. Interestingly, it is St John's gospel which provides us with most of Jesus' teachings concerning the Masters. Matthew, Luke and Mark contribute comparatively little.

It is generally thought in Christianity that Jesus was the only Son of God. Jesus is said to be His Son because it is claimed that Joseph was not physically involved in Jesus' conception. Mary, it is believed, was a virgin. We will return to the subject of the virgin birth later, but the question we need to ask here is: who or what is the Son of God? Is it the physical body of Jesus? Is it the soul which lived in that body? Or is it the Spirit or Holy Ghost?

Specific answers to this question are few and far between in the New Testament. All the same, unless one studied the other mystical literature of the period, one might be led to believe that the term, the 'Son of God' had been coined by Jesus. But nothing could be further from the truth, for the term is one of the commonest in every branch of that ancient literature, where its meaning is fully explained.

In the metaphorical language of those times, God was known as the Father and His first emanation, His Creative Word or Power, was described as His First-born and only 'offspring', His "Only-Begotten Son". The Son of God is therefore God's primal creative outpouring.

Naturally, there is only one such primal Power and all else in the creation is derived from it. Hence, this mystic 'Son' is His 'only' son.

This is so important and habits of thought are so deeply ingrained that we may repeat it. Although Jesus and other Masters have been called the Sons of God, God's creative Power – the Creative Word – was *also* called His Son. Moreover, since He has only one such Power, this Son was also known as His Only-Begotten Son. 'Only-Begotten' did not refer to Jesus – it referred to the Word.

The Greek term translated as "only-begotten" and used in St John's gospel and many other places, is *monogenes*, which is more accurately rendered as 'begotten of one' or 'alone-begotten'. In the Nag Hammadi, *Apocryphon of John*, for instance, Jesus explains that the Father

> begot a spark of light with a light resembling blessedness.... This was an
> Only-Begotten child ... which had come forth. It is the only offspring, the
> Only-Begotten one of the Father, the pure Light.
>
> *Apocryphon of John 6, NHL p.108*

This "spark of light" emanating from the Father is the Word. In an untitled gnostic treatise from the *Bruce Codex*, the Son is described as the "Only-Begotten *Logos*" and speaking of the many powers and realms in creation, the same text says that they emanate from the "Only-Begotten One":

> Now all these powers surround the Only-Begotten One
> like a crown.
>
> *Untitled Text 7, BC p.236*

Adding:

> It is he (the Only-Begotten One) who came forth
> from the endless, characterless, formless
> and Self-Begotten One (God) who has begotten Himself.
> (It is he) who came forth
> from the Ineffable and Immeasurable One,
> who exists verily and truly.
> It is he within whom exists the truly existent One.
> That is to say, the incomprehensible Father
> exists in His Only-Begotten Son....

This is he of whom John spoke:
   "In the beginning was the Word,
   and the Word was with God
   and the Word was God.
This one without whom nothing exists,
   and that which has come into being in him is life."...

This is the Creative Word which commands the All
   (the realms of creation) that they should operate....
This is he to whom the creation prays as God,
   and as Lord, and as Saviour,
   and as the one to whom they are submitted.
This is he at whom the All marvels
   because of his beauty and comeliness....

Thou art existent, thou art the Only-Begotten One,
   the light and the life and the grace.

Untitled Text 7, BC pp.237-238

The Son of God, the Only-Begotten One and the Only-Begotten Son are therefore further synonyms for the Creative Word, the *Logos*, Wisdom and so on. Pursuing the metaphor, the mystic writers of antiquity also described this Power as God's "First-born Son". Hence, speaking of God as the shepherd of the various parts of His creation who follow His command like a flock of sheep, Philo Judaeus says:

This hallowed flock, he leads with right and law, setting over it His own true Logos, His First-born Son, who shall succeed unto the care of this sacred flock, as though he were some viceroy of a great king.

Philo, On Husbandry 12, PhIII p.135, TGHI p.238

The same idea is echoed by the third-century father, Eusebius. Writing of the "divine Word, the First-Begotten", he describes God's creative Power as

(the) essential Wisdom that was before time itself, the living Word that in the beginning was with the Father and was God.... Before anything was created and fashioned, visible or invisible, he was the First-(born) and Only-Begotten of God; the commander-in-chief of the spiritual and immortal host of heaven; the angel of mighty counsel; the agent of the ineffable purpose of the Father; the fashioner, with the Father, of all things; the second cause, after the Father, of the universe; the Child of God, true and Only-Begotten.

Eusebius, History of the Church I:2, HC pp.33-34

Similarly, in the Nag Hammadi *Tripartite Tractate*, the writer says, in somewhat metaphysical language:

> Just as the Father exists in the real sense, the One before whom there was no one else and the One apart from whom there is no other unbegotten one, so too the Son exists in the real sense, the one before whom there was no other, and after whom no other son exists.
>
> Therefore, he is a First-born and an only Son, 'first-born' because no one exists before him and 'only Son' because no one is after him.

Tripartite Tractate 57, NHS22 pp.199-201

There is no doubt, therefore, that the "Only-Begotten Son" does not refer to the man, Jesus, nor does it imply that he was born of a virgin through the intermediary of the Holy Ghost. Indeed, John's gospel and *1 John*, the only places where this term is encountered in the New Testament, never mention anything about a virgin birth. The "Only-Begotten Son" refers to the creative Power of God.

All the same, since the Masters are a personification of this Power, Jesus and other mystics, too, were also described as the "Only-Begotten Son" and the "First-born Son". Such appellations are found throughout the ancient Christian literature. In the *Acts of Peter*, for example, Paul describes Jesus as the "First-Begotten". Speaking to a group of new believers, he counsels them to imbibe all the good human virtues, following which:

> Then shall ye have for your guide everlastingly
> the First-Begotten of all creation,
> and shall have strength in peace with our Lord.

Acts of Peter III:II, ANT p.305

And in the *Acts of Thomas*, Judas Thomas praises Jesus, saying:

> Glory be to the Only-Begotten of the Father!
> Glory be to the First-born of many brethren!
> Glory be to thee, the Defender and Helper
> of them that come unto thy refuge!

Acts of Thomas 60, ANT p.393

While in one of the Manichaean-Christian psalms, we find:

> Thou art a mighty light: Jesus, enlighten me:
> First-born of the Father.
> lamp of all the *Aeons*.
> flower of the Mother of the Lights.
> snare of the Snarer (Satan)....
>
> Glory due to thee,
> O First-born of the Father.
>
> *Psalms, MPB pp.166-167*

And in another, the Master is described as:

> The first Emanation....
> the First-born of his Father.
>
> *Psalms, MPB p.137*

The reason why both the Word and the man, Jesus, are described as the Only-Begotten Son is very simple. The Word and the Master are one. The real essence of a Master, indeed of all souls, is the Living Word, the Life Force within all things. And a Master is the Word incarnate. Hence, in St John, we read:

> And the Word was made flesh, and dwelt among us,
> (and we beheld his glory,
> the glory as of the Only-Begotten of the Father,)
> full of grace and truth.
>
> *John 1:14*

The Word Was Made Flesh

The mystery of Jesus, then, and the mystery of all perfect Masters is that they are the "Word made flesh". They are realized incarnations of the creative Power of God. And since a "son" is essentially a metaphor relating to human life and to human beings, the Master is also referred to as the "Son of God" or the "Son of man".

It is from this reality that the Christian concept of the Trinity has come into being. There is God the Father, the Word as the Holy Ghost, and the Master as the human Son of God, a manifestation of the Word at the human level. Over the centuries, this Trinity has been the subject of a great deal of theological discussion and the nature of Jesus and his relationship to God and the Word has been the focus of numerous Church councils, anathemas, and even serious schisms within the Christian community. But this only serves to demonstrate that no amount of intellectual thought will ever be able to figure out how God, in the form of His Word, takes birth in a human form and appears as a human being. How can the mind of man be expected to understand God and His incarnation? It can barely understand the mysteries of this world.

Jesus, however, and all other mystics who have taught this path, have made it very clear that man can only hope to reach God through the intermediary or intercession of a perfect Son of God, at the human level. Hence, John the Baptist says of Jesus:

> Of his fullness have all we received, and grace for grace.
> For the law was given by Moses,
> > but grace and truth came by Jesus Christ.
>
> No man hath seen God at any time;
> > the Only-Begotten Son,
> > which is in the bosom of the Father,
> > he hath declared him.
>
> > > *John 1:16-18*

He means that the "law" or the teaching concerning this path was also given by the mystic Moses, a prophet in whom all the Jews had faith, but since Moses was dead, it was essential to go to a living Son of God, in this case, Jesus. For no one can see God unless the "Only-Begotten Son" "declares" or reveals Him to a soul. Similarly, Jesus says:

> No man hath ascended up to heaven,
> > but he that came down from heaven,
> > even the Son of man which is in heaven....
>
> For God so loved the world,
> > that he gave his Only-Begotten Son,
> > that whosoever believeth in him should not perish,
> > but have everlasting life.
> For God sent not his Son into the world to condemn the world;
> > but that the world through him might be saved.

He that believeth on him is not condemned:
> but he that believeth not is condemned already,
> because he hath not believed
> in the Name of the Only-Begotten Son of God.
>> *John 3:13,15-18*

Jesus says that God is so loving that He has sent His only Son, the Word, into the world to save human beings from the condemnation and judgment – not of 'hellfire' – but of birth and death.

But this was no new concept. Philo Judaeus, the Alexandrian contemporary of Jesus who shows no indication of knowing about Jesus, says (while speaking of the mystic symbolism inherent in Biblical descriptions of the garments of the high priest):

> For it was necessary that he who was consecrated to the Father of the creation, should have His Son, the most perfect in virtue, as intercessor, both for the forgiveness (*lit.* an amnesty or forgetfulness) of sins and for the abundant supply of the most unstinted blessings.
>> *Philo, On the Life of Moses II:26, PhVI p.515, TGHI pp.250-251*

The Son of God is required as the mediator between God and man and this includes both the primal Power of the Word and its manifestation as a physically incarnate, living Master.

I and My Father

John's gospel is a rich source of Jesus' teachings concerning himself, his mission and his relationship to God. And though these have to be understood within the context of what is known about John's gospel, they remain of the greatest value in determining Jesus' teachings. According to John, Jesus makes the incredibly definitive statement:

> I and my Father are one.
>> *John 10:30*

There is no difference, he says, between himself and God, between the Master and God. And emphasizing the point that he is God in human form, with all the power of God, he says (to Philip):

> He that hath seen me hath seen the Father; ...
> Believest thou not that I am in the Father,
>   and the Father in me?
> The words that I speak unto you I speak not of myself:
>   but the Father that dwelleth in me, He doeth the works.
> Believe me that I am in the Father, and the Father in me:
>   or else believe me for the very works' sake.
>
> *John 14:9-11*

A Master is entirely absorbed in God, he has no ego or separate identity of his own at all. Consequently, all his words and deeds come from God. If you cannot believe that, he says, then consider the way a Master lives and works. No normal human being could keep up that level of perfection and the way of life of a Master. In all his dealings with people, he is always in complete control of himself. He never loses his temper, demonstrates pride, irritability, impatience or displays any other human imperfection. His understanding of human nature and his wisdom are never at fault. He is never at a loss for an answer – sometimes a surprising and thought-provoking response – as we find with many of Jesus' replies. His energy and capacity for work is also incredible and his need for sleep is very little.

But to "believe ... for the very works' sake", it is necessary to have contact with a living Master, someone who can be met as one human being to another. Nobody is or should be expected to believe in a Master of the past on the basis of other people's experience and their stories. Another person's experience has no power at all compared to one's own personal experience. Jesus is talking to his contemporaries, not to us. He then adds that his followers will also be enabled to live in the same way:

> Verily, verily, I say unto you,
>   He that believeth on me,
>   the works that I do shall he do also;
>   and greater works than these shall he do;
>   because I go unto my Father.
>
> *John 14:11*

They will be able to become like him, "because I go unto my Father": because he has access to God, and through the power of God he can mould his disciples until they too become God.

My Doctrine is Not Mine

True Masters do not make things up according to philosophical speculation or their own way of thinking. Jesus also makes this very clear.
Again in St John, he says that he has been sent from God and that he
only teaches what is true and which he has "heard" or experienced
with God:

> He that sent me is true;
>> and I speak to the world those things
>> which I have heard of Him.
>>> *John 8:26-27*

Such knowledge comes from within, needing no external study.
Whether Jesus was educated or not, we do not really know, but following a story given in St John, Jesus is in conversation with some antagonistic Jews who – on hearing him speak so eloquently and profoundly
– wonder how anyone could teach in such a way without the kind of
scholarly education which they had received:

> And the Jews marvelled, saying,
>> "How knoweth this man letters, having never learned?"
>>> *John 7:15*

But Jesus points out that his teachings are not his own invention. They
are those of God Himself. And since he is one with God, he has never
had to learn anything. He teaches from his own personal, direct experience of God and the mystic reality, needing no one to teach him
Jewish theology or religious studies. This is a most important point,
for the teachers of this world teach from their own ideas or beliefs
about things. Jesus therefore continues:

> My doctrine is not mine, but His that sent me.
> If any man will do His will,
>> he shall know of the doctrine,
>>> whether it be of God, or whether I speak of myself.
>>> *John 7:16-17*

Because a Master teaches from his own experience, not only does he
always get it right or true, but he does not invent things that sound

good according to his own bent of mind or simply to elicit praise from other people. He, above all else, *knows* what he is talking about. He is teaching a path which is as old as God and which stems from Him, which is a built-in part of the creation, like a law of nature. But for somebody to really appreciate this, Jesus says, it is necessary to "do His will", to follow the mystic path that leads back to Him. Then only can they be really sure. For the mystic path is not a path of philosophy, information or belief, but of transformation, being and personal experience. Jesus then adds, perceptively:

> He that speaketh of himself seeketh his own glory:
>> but he that seeketh His glory that sent him,
>> the same is true, and no unrighteousness is in him.
> Did not Moses give you the law,
>> and yet none of you keepeth the law?
> Why go ye about to kill me?
>
> *John 7:18-19*

Jesus is well aware that other teachers have their own personal motivations determined by egotism and pride, in however subtle a form, and he repeats that only a person who truly seeks God's "glory" rather than his own is the "true" teacher. "And no unrighteousness is in him": the motivations of a perfect Master are entirely pure and devoid of ego.

Then, since his questioners are Jews, Jesus points out that Moses taught the same mystic path or "law" to them and that he also taught them not to kill. Yet they, who profess to follow Moses and to be educated in his teachings, are planning to break one of Moses' most fundamental commandments. "Why go ye about to kill me?" Jesus asks. He is only teaching the love of God and yet they are so alarmed and disconcerted that they want to get rid of him as fast as possible. Jesus then concludes this dialogue by repeating the same point:

> I am not come of myself,
>> but He that sent me is true, whom ye know not.
> But I know Him:
>> for I am from Him, and He hath sent me.
>
> *John 7:28-29*

And elsewhere he reiterates:

> He that sent me is with me:
>> the Father hath not left me alone;
> For I do always those things that please Him.
>> *John 8:29*

And again:

> I have not spoken of myself;
>> but the Father which sent me,
>> He gave me a Commandment, what I should say,
>> and what I should speak.
> And I know that His Commandment is life everlasting:
>> whatsoever I speak therefore,
>> even as the Father said unto me, so I speak.
>> *John 12:49-50*

Here, John again employs one of his favourite *double entendres*, for another term used for the Word in the ancient literature was God's "Commandment" – the order or Will of God by which the creation came into existence. Hence, "His Commandment is life everlasting" refers to the Word by which the soul returns to God, as well as to the outer teachings which lead the soul to contact with this mystic "Commandment".

Jesus therefore says that he obeys this higher "Commandment" which God has "spoken" to him. Consequently, whatever he teaches is direct from God for he is one with the Father and is the "Word made flesh". This is true of all Masters who are one with God and are the personification of His "Commandment".

brings back to life

The Son Quickeneth whom He Will

A Master's will is entirely merged with God's Will and there are a number of places, especially in St John, where Jesus emphasizes this, pointing out that the Son only does what the Father wishes. For example:

> Verily, verily, I say unto you,
>> the Son can do nothing of himself,
>> but what he seeth the Father do:
> For what things soever He doeth,
>> these also doeth the Son likewise.

> For the Father loveth the Son,
>   and sheweth him all things that Himself doeth:
>   and He will shew him greater works than these,
>   that ye may marvel.

John 5:19-20

Jesus again says that he does nothing to boost his own personal fame or glory. He is entirely merged in the Will of the Father and has no ego of his own. As a result, there is great love between Father and Son, for it is only the illusory sense of individual self, the "counterfeit spirit", that stands between a soul and God. And just as a father will do anything for a loving and obedient son, so anything that seems to be done by the Son is actually being done by God. Masters may do many things which make their disciples "marvel", but all such things happen because of the love between God and Son which makes them one. Jesus then continues:

> For as the Father raiseth up the dead,
>   and quickeneth them;
> Even so the Son quickeneth whom he will.

John 5:21

The "dead" who are "raised up" are the souls in this world who never think of God, even in their dreams. Spiritually, they are dead. Yet, when they come into contact with a Master, their whole life is turned around, they "repent", and eagerly begin the inner journey back to Him. But it is through the "Son", through the Master, that souls are "quickened" or brought back to life. He continues:

> For the Father judgeth no man,
>   but hath committed all judgment unto the Son:
> That all men should honour the Son,
>   even as they honour the Father.
> He that honoureth not the Son
>   honoureth not the Father which hath sent him.

John 5:22-23

The Father has so arranged things that the salvation of man is entirely committed to the care of the Master. Those who wish to worship the Father have to do so through the Son. Those who "honoureth not the Son honoureth not the Father which hath sent him": they do not really worship the Father at all, to whatever religion they may belong. They only worship a God of their own mental or intellectual conception. God can only be approached through the Son, through a Master.

For This Cause Came I into the World

Generally, souls take birth in this world because of their sins. Their 'purpose' in coming is to fulfil their debt of sin. Masters, on the other hand, are free from all such constraints and come with a different purpose altogether. Jesus, too, is very clear about his intention in coming to the world and his role in relationship to the real seekers of the mystic truth. In St John's gospel, he says:

> To this end was I born,
>   and for this cause came I into the world,
>   that I should bear witness unto the Truth.
> Every one that is of the Truth heareth my voice.
> *John 18:37*

He has no other purpose than to teach the path back to God and to lead those who are so destined – "everyone that is of the Truth" – back to Him. Only they "heareth my Voice". This has a double meaning, inner and outer. Only they will be attracted to the teachings of a Master, outwardly, and will come to hear the mystic Voice of the Word within themselves. As he also said:

> I am the Way, the Truth, and the Life:
>   no man cometh unto the Father, but by me.
> If ye had known me, ye should have known my Father also:
>   and from henceforth ye know Him, and have seen Him.
> *John 14:6-7*

Only through the Son of God can a soul be led back to the Father, the Source of life and being. The real Son of God or Master is the Word; that is the Way or the path that leads back to Him. One who really knows such a Master comes to know the Father also, for he ascends with the Son on the current of the Word, back to God, within. In fact, Jesus says that the disciple who believes in him actually believes in God:

> He that believeth on me, believeth not on me,
>   but on Him that sent me.
> And he that seeth me seeth Him that sent me.
>
> *John 12:44-45*

"He that seeth me, seeth Him that sent me". A disciple is actually seeing God when he sees his Master. His vision is veiled only by his own mind and body and by the coverings of mind and body that God has to take on in order to function in this world as a Master. He goes on:

> I am come a light into the world,
>   that whosoever believeth on me
>   should not abide in darkness.
>
> *John 12:46*

Those who believe in him will be lifted out of the realm of darkness. As he repeats at another place:

> I am the light of the world:
>   he that followeth me shall not walk in darkness,
>   but shall have the light of life.
>
> *John 8:12*

Masters, however, are never vindictive or judgmental. Regarding the great mass of humanity who do not believe in a Master's teachings, Jesus says:

> And if any man hear my words, and believe not,
>   I judge him not:
> For I came not to judge the world,
>   but to save the world.
> He that rejecteth me, and receiveth not my words,
>   hath one that judgeth him:
> The Word that I have spoken,
>   the same shall judge him in the last day.
>
> *John 12:47-48*

No Master comes into the world to judge its people and Jesus points out that there is no need, for we are already judged and condemned by our own actions. According to the law of cause and effect, we will reap the fruit of our actions and desires. On our day of death, on our "last day", we will be judged accordingly and will go wherever the contents of our minds take us. The "Word" is the Power behind all powers. Hence, the automatic judgment meted out in the realm of the Negative Power is by God's will. This is the meaning of the "Word that I have spoken, the same shall judge him in the last day". It is John's familiar wordplay.

As Long as I am In the World

A Master comes to this world only for a brief period, and although Jesus said that he came into the world to be the light of the world, he nevertheless pointed out that this was only true for as long as he was in the world:

> I must work the works of Him that sent me,
>   while it is day:
> The night cometh, when no man can work.
> As long as I am in the world,
> I am the light of the world.
>
> *John 9:4-5*

"While it is day" means, while he is alive in this world. After his death, when "the night cometh" – "no man can work". After that, it is necessary for a living being to find a living Master of their own time. Likewise, Jesus explains:

> Yet a little while is the light with you.
> Walk while ye have the light,
>   lest darkness come upon you:
> For he that walketh in darkness
>   knoweth not whither he goeth.
> While ye have light, believe in the Light,
>   that ye may be the children of light.
>
> *John 12:35-36*

There is a double meaning, here, revolving around the word 'light'. While a person is alive in the human form, "while ye have light", he should seek the Light and should follow the mystic path, for when "darkness" or death comes, no one knows where they will go. They may not even take birth again as a human being, but go down into the lower species.

It also means that while the "light is with you", while a disciple is with his Master, he should take advantage of his Master's presence and guidance and work on the spiritual path. For the time will come when even a Master will have to leave this world. No physical body can live here for ever, nor indeed would a Master ever wish to do so, when he can soar through the inner realms and return to God unencumbered by any fleshly overcoat. When his term of duty in the dark dungeon of this world is over and after helping his allotted prisoners to escape, a Master is happy to return to God. This is what Jesus meant when he said to a group of Jews who were not his disciples:

> Yet a little while am I with you,
> and then I go unto Him that sent me.
> Ye shall seek me, and shall not find me:
> and where I am, thither ye cannot come.
>
> *John 7:33-34*

Only his initiates can follow a Master back to God, after his departure. Others remain in the world, according to the dictates of their own *karma*.

False Prophets

A true Master is appointed or authorized by God to do his work in this world. He is sent here for that purpose alone. Whatever else he may do out of compassion, his primary function is to effect the salvation of souls. Hence, Jesus advises his disciples:

> Labour not for the meat which perisheth,
> but for that meat which endureth unto everlasting life,
> which the Son of man shall give unto you:
> for him hath God the Father sealed.
>
> *John 6:27*

The Master is able to give "everlasting life" to his disciples for only one reason: "for him hath God the Father sealed". He has the Lord's stamp of approval and authority. But if there are those who have this highest authority, who do only what the Father wants them to do, it presumes there must be others who are not "sealed" by God, who teach from their own personal motivations.

Everything in creation is reflected or copied from something higher. Ultimately, everything is emanated from God in a complex process of projection and reflection, of splitting and division. The purpose of the Negative Power is to keep souls in this creation and he does so, not by creating his own reality, but by reflecting the Lord's Reality. He has no power of his own separate from that of God. All he has is given by the Lord and he can only weave mirages, obscurities and illusions. And the soul is taken in because a reflection always contains something of the original, it has an air of reality about it; yet it is not the real thing.

The same is true of the many spiritual teachers of this world. While it is up to the individual to discern as best as he can who is the highest teacher and who is not, it remains true that not all those paths which speak of spirituality and mysticism are the same. All roads do not lead to Rome. In fact, the majority of roads were built to lead to other places altogether. There are mystics and spiritual teachers who come from the higher regions with particular tasks to perform in the material creation. They come to keep the world a tolerable place, so to say, to keep the balance of good and evil. They are like philanthropists who visit a gaol to offer solace to the inmates, teaching them how to live there and how to become contented with their lot, giving them comfort in one way or another.

No doubt, their work is necessary, but actually it lulls souls to sleep, giving them a false sense of security. The perfect Masters, however, the true Sons of God, come with the sword of the Word to cut the chains of sin or *karma* that bind souls to this world and to set them free. They are the ones who really teach about the highest Reality. They speak plainly, even outspokenly, and do not fudge the issue. Full of love, they are uncompromising when it comes to teaching their allotted souls how to escape from this world. There is no point, neither is there anything loving or caring, in letting a child stray from the road into the wilderness in order to avoid upsetting that child. There is always a way of lovingly, but determinedly, keeping the child on track. This is the way of the Masters.

The highest Masters, therefore, are a breed apart and of a different calibre altogether and though they say very little about other teachers, since it would be in poor taste and because their teachings are independent of the weaknesses of other systems, they do, from time to time, point out that people should be wary. There are a number of places where Jesus says just this.

There is, for instance, the 'mini-apocalypse' of Mark, variants of which are found in Luke and Matthew. Now although this 'mini-

apocalypse' is set as a prophecy spoken by Jesus concerning the end of
the world, scholars are generally agreed that it was probably compiled
later than 65 AD, at least thirty or forty years after the death of Jesus,
when some Christian groups were expecting an imminent end to the
world. So although some of the sayings contained in it may be authentic, the setting is not, and amongst these sayings are a few concerning "false prophets". For example:

> Many false prophets shall rise, and shall deceive many.
>
> *Matthew 24:11*

And, more substantially:

> Then if any man shall say unto you,
> "Lo, here is Christ, or there"; believe it not.
> For there shall arise false Christs, and false prophets,
>   and shall shew great signs and wonders;
> Insomuch that, if it were possible,
>   they shall deceive the very elect.
>
> Behold, I have told you before.
> Wherefore if they shall say unto you,
> "Behold, he is in the desert"; go not forth:
> "Behold, he is in the secret chambers"; believe it not.
>
> For as the lightning cometh out of the east,
>   and shineth even unto the west;
> So shall also the coming of the Son of man be.
> For wheresoever the carcase is,
>   there will the eagles (vultures) be gathered together.
>
> *Matthew 24:23-28*

Every good thing gets copied. It is practically a law of nature and the
Masters' teachings are no exception. For there are people who appropriate these teachings, promoting themselves as real Masters. As a result, even the "very elect" – a term used in those times for the initiates
– can be deceived for some time. But there is no need for concern. A
Master is like the sun that rises in the east and travels to the west. He
cannot be overlooked. Those who are meant to recognize him will
automatically do so. "For wheresoever the carcase is, there will the
eagles be gathered together": just as vultures automatically gather

around a carcase in the desert, so too will those who are destined to receive initiation from a Master be automatically drawn to him by one road or another. Though a somewhat gruesome example, the sight of vultures gathering to a dead body from all quarters of the sky has always been a common sight in hot climates and one that would have been readily understood by Jesus' audience.

In another passage, quite independent of the mini-apocalypse, Jesus suggests a way of determining who a real Master is:

> Beware of false prophets,
>> which come to you in sheep's clothing,
>> but inwardly they are ravening wolves.
> Ye shall know them by their fruits.
> Do men gather grapes of thorns, or figs of thistles?
> Even so every good tree bringeth forth good fruit;
>> but a corrupt tree bringeth forth evil fruit.
> A good tree cannot bring forth evil fruit,
>> neither can a corrupt tree bring forth good fruit.
> Every tree that bringeth not forth good fruit is hewn down,
>> and cast into the fire.
> Wherefore by their fruits ye shall know them.
>
> *Matthew 7:15-20*

By "false prophets" Jesus means the many pseudo-saints who appear in this world, often gaining a large following, but ultimately leading people nowhere in particular. He is also referring to the priests of organized religions who teach people to perform various rites and rituals, give incorrect interpretations of the scriptures and generally lead their congregations up blind alleys.

The "fruits" of a true prophet by which they may be known are the results achieved by their disciples: the way they live, and the love and devotion they develop for God and for the whole creation. A person can only teach and share with others what they already have within themselves. Following a true Master should lead, at first, to an increase in understanding at all levels, human as well as spiritual. Within the context and constraints of an individual's destiny, *karma* and character, one who follows the path laid out by a Master and attends to spiritual practice, should slowly become a better human being – a better husband, wife, son, daughter, brother, sister, friend, citizen and so on. Spiritually, their love and devotion should also increase. It may take time, but as the years pass, those who work sincerely on the path can look back and see that they are getting somewhere. Then, by degrees, sooner or later, the inner doors will open and they will begin the inner ascent to God, achieving liberation from birth and death in the process. This is the ultimate fruit of following a perfect Master.

But a fruitless tree, one who gets nowhere spiritually for whatever reason, is "hewn down and cast into the fire" – such a soul will have to undergo rebirth in the fires of this world.

To recognize a real Master is by no means easy, since ignorance of the inner estate of others is the normal human condition. For this reason, the author of *1 John*, speaking of "false prophets" who are "already ... in the world", advises:

> Beloved, believe not every spirit (every soul),
>> but try the spirits whether they are of God:
> Because many false prophets are gone out into the world.
>
> Hereby (by this means) know ye the Spirit of God:
> Every spirit that confesseth that Jesus Christ
>> is come in the flesh is of God:
> And every spirit that confesseth not that Jesus Christ
>> is come in the flesh is not of God:
> And this is that spirit of antichrist,
>> whereof ye have heard that it should come;
>> and even now already is it in the world.
>
> *1 John 4:1-3*

John says that not all souls can be trusted, even those who give spiritual teachings, for "many false prophets are gone out into the world". This is the case wherever and whenever perfect Masters are particularly active. But, says John, an easy test can be applied. Those who accept that Jesus has come from God are of God. Otherwise, they are of the "spirit of antichrist", of the Negative Power, which "even now already is it in the world", and has always been in the world, since it is that which makes the world the way it is.

John is talking to the people of his own time and to those who have already found Jesus. He says that those who are really teaching the path to God will automatically know within themselves that Jesus, too, is from God. If they do not know that, then they are not of God. And if they are not of God, then there is only one other alternative: they are of the Devil. Hence, he continues:

> Ye are of God, little children,
>> and have overcome them (false prophets):
>> because greater is he that is in you (Jesus),
>> than he that is in the world (Satan).
>>> *1 John 4:4*

The "little children", the disciples of Jesus, have "overcome" all hurdles, whether they are "false prophets" or anything else of this world, "because greater is he that is in you than he that is in the world" – because their Master Jesus is more powerful than Satan. Describing such false teachers, John continues:

> They are of the world:
>> therefore speak they of the world,
>> and the world heareth them.
>>> *1 John 4:5*

Their focus of interest lies in how people live in this world. Their apparently spiritual teachings are actually confined to making the world and its people more comfortable. Consequently, people who are interested in the world "heareth them". Their spirituality is really a subtle form of materiality, because it is associated far more with living in this world than escaping from this place altogether and returning to God. This is another way by which they may be recognized.

Saints describe this world as a dungeon, a prison, a place of death and so on. For the most part, even many seemingly spiritually-minded people find this too hard to take. They are still in love with the world and have all sorts of reasons why they should go on thinking and caring about the world. It still holds great interest for them. Hence, they will remain here and take further births here. By good deeds and through spiritual yearning, they may earn better circumstances for themselves but, all the same, they will have to return here to reap that reward. The purpose of perfect Masters is different. They come to this world to release their disciples altogether. Therefore, John concludes:

> We are of God: he that knoweth God heareth us;
>> he that is not of God heareth not us.
> Hereby know we the Spirit of Truth,
>> and the Spirit of Error.
>>> *1 John 4:4-6*

"They are of the world" but "we are of God", says John. The power of God and the power of Satan can be readily distinguished. Those that follow a Master are of God, they know the "Spirit of Truth". Those that do not are of Satan, the "Spirit of Error".

The Living Master

It is a strange fact that although it seems easy enough for people to accept a departed Master as their Saviour with very little knowledge of who he really was and what he really taught, the thought of taking a Master who is presently alive in the body as a guide to God is often disturbing. Somehow, a Son of God is far easier to believe in if he is relegated to a safe distance in history and has become a habitual part of one's culture.

The problem, of course, is the mind. Acceptance of a true and living Master into one's life sounds the death knell of the ego and the multifarious weaknesses of the mind which does not like to change its habitual patterns or to receive advice from others. Further, no one is without a conscience and it can be disturbing to recognize – perhaps almost subconsciously – that here is someone who will see into one's heart as fish can be observed in an aquarium. Moreover, since the primary function of the Negative Power is to prevent souls from leaving his domain, the greatest risk that he encounters is that a soul may come into contact with a true and perfect living Master. The mind, therefore, the agent of the Negative Power, immediately tries to reject a Master under one pretext or another and in most cases it is completely successful. This is why Jesus said:

> No man can come to me,
> except the Father which hath sent me draw him.
>
> *John 6:44*

Unless there is direct intervention and inspiration from a power from beyond the mind, the soul is forever beguiled by the mind and keeps on revolving within its sphere.

All the higher mystics have taught the necessity of a spiritual director or living Master. The reasons are totally practical. As Jesus emphasizes in so many places, the essential relationship between God, the Son of God and the soul is that of love, and the mystic path is primarily one of divine love. But how does a person set that ball of love rolling? Mere sentimentality, infatuation, human emotion and affection are something quite different from the bliss and intoxication of the divine love spoken of by all the mystics. So how does a person approach such a love or even begin to get a glimmering of what it might be like?

A human being has only the normal range of human emotions. We are capable of intense feeling of one kind or another, and most people, at some time in their life, have felt the intensity of being in love with another human being. At least, we have felt a deep sense of attachment to parents, to husband or wife, to children, to friends or even to a pet. This is all a very faint and distant echo of the intensity of divine love, and it is always for some other *living* being, human or otherwise – or it is love for someone we have known when they were alive.

So when the mystics advise us to love God with all our heart and mind and soul, one wonders where to begin, for we cannot love a God whom we have never met and of whom we have had no experience. We may have an idea or an intellectual concept of Him, but we cannot really love an intellectual concept or an ideal. And even if we did manage to generate some degree of devotion to such a concept, it would still be in our minds. We would have only fallen in love with an idea inside our own heads, not with God Himself. It would only be another reflection or deception of the mind, of Satan. How then can a human being love God?

To get around this difficulty, people say that Jesus is their intermediary. They recognize that it is very difficult to love God directly because of the apparent chasm between man and God. But the same problems still arise. Loving Jesus can only mean loving one's mental concept of him – a combination of dogma and religious belief, together with some personal colouring, pictorial imagination and childhood conditioning. It is like falling in love with someone we have never met. We fall in love, not with the person, but with our ideas about them. And if we actually meet them, we are tongue-tied, for we have developed no real association with them. Everything has gone on entirely in our own head, not in real experience. Similarly, if we say we love Jesus, if we happened to meet him, we might be very surprised indeed, for everyone has their own idea of what he would have been like. What is required is reality, not imagination.

God, who has created this creation, is not unaware of our difficulties. After all, He is the one who has made us the way we are. He also knows our capacity for self-deception and delusion, for He is the one who has created the Negative Power and put the mind within each one of us. Therefore, when He wants to draw a soul back to Himself,

He sends His Son, the Word, to take birth as a human being, as a perfect Master, the Son of God in human form.

Now, a human being we can love. We can talk and communicate with him; we can ask him questions relating to our own personal difficulties on the spiritual path; we can hear him laugh and joke, see him smile, perhaps even shed a tear. John records, for instance, that Jesus was wearied from a journey, wept for a friend and while on the cross said, "I thirst".[1] A Master is in the world with us, living like us, and we can observe the way he deals with the normal problems of human life which beset us all and can cause us so much grief. He becomes a perfect exemplar, something far more meaningful than a code of ethics and moral formulae by which to live. He is a perfect human being for, within himself, he is divine.

Moreover, a Master is so beautiful and captivating to look at, his manner of speech is so charming and full of deep wisdom, the look in his eyes is so alluring and the atmosphere around him is so powerful and sustaining, that anyone having even the slightest degree of love within them feels attracted towards him like a magnet. A Master is divine love incarnate and since the essence of our own souls is love, there is an instant bond between the Master and the soul. In fact, his means of drawing his souls to himself is primarily that of love. He awakens love in the hearts of his chosen souls and when they hear about him or meet him, something inside them is irresistibly attracted.

Indeed, one of the ways in which a perfect Master can be recognized is to try and resist him. If he can be resisted, either we are not meant for that Master or he is not a real Master at all. If he is a real Master, sooner or later his pull will become more than we can counter and we will go to him and follow his instructions as best we can. Look at the stories of Jesus and some of his disciples. He simply had to say, "Follow me", and they did. Whether or not the stories are exactly true is difficult to know, but the essential meaning is that the Master beckoned with his call of love and his disciples-to-be came running.

But it is only because the Master is alive as a human being that so much love, faith and trust can be engendered. To some extent, a person can see what they are getting into. It seems unreasonable that blind belief in humanly formulated religious dogmas and in a Master of the past about whom so little is known and so much has been invented should be a part of the Lord's plan for taking souls back to Himself. There is far too much scope for the human mind to cloud the issue. When He comes, He does the job properly, as one might suspect. And He does the job Himself. He does not leave it to the vagaries of the human mind to transmit His message. After all, the mind is the agent of the Negative Power, designed by the Lord to keep souls separated from Himself. How then can the human mind, riddled with imperfections and weighed down by sins of the past, be expected to lead the soul to God? Its job is quite the reverse.

A living, physically incarnate Master is a part of the Lord's grand design and the world is never without at least one perfect, living Son of God. There can be more, though a disciple is only concerned with his own Master and, for him, his Master is the source of all inspiration, guidance and instruction. To begin with, a Master initiates or baptizes a soul by connecting or retuning the soul to the Word within. The Word is present within everybody, but to be in conscious contact with it, to hear its endless divine melodies, the soul needs tuning in. This is a task which only a perfect mystic, who knows how to reconnect the inner wiring, can perform.

From the time of initiation onwards, a Master takes up his abode within his disciple in a spiritual, light or radiant form. In fact, the real form of the Master is the Word and whatever spiritual level the disciple reaches, the Master takes on an appropriate form to help and guide him. The personal contact is never lost, indeed it grows stronger and greater. Outside, in the world, for purely practical reasons, the disciple cannot always be with his Master. But inside, he can always be with him. At the physical level, the Master is there in his physical form. At the astral level, his spiritual form is a scintillating, shining astral form. At higher levels, he takes on forms suited to those levels. He never leaves any one of his disciples, at any time, for he is the Life Force itself, the essence within everything. Hence, Jesus said:

> Lo, I am with you alway, even unto the end of the world.
> *Matthew 28:20*

The "end of the world" is an idiom which means forever. Once initiated, a Master is always with his disciples. In fact, as we have previously discussed, he takes over the administration of the *karma* of his disciples. Henceforth, everything that happens in the life of a disciple takes place by the Master's will. Though the events of life are a part of the disciple's *karma*, part of the load of past sins which he has to clear, the hand of his Master is always present to guide him through. Furthermore, many sins of the past are dealt with by the Master himself. He has the power to forgive past sins and he does just that. His rule is one of love and mercy, never justice.

In this world, a Master is also required to instruct his disciples in the techniques of spiritual practice. He is there to oversee their spiritual progress and to answer any questions they may have on spiritual matters. If the mind invents its own form of spiritual practice, then it can be assured that that practice will not take the soul out of birth and death. As in any other branch of human study, a suitably qualified teacher is required if success is to be attained.

To begin with, a disciple may take the Master as a friend, a brother or a father. But later, if he sincerely attends to his spiritual practice, he will realize that his Master is vastly more than that. A Master, however, does not look for glory or praise from human beings. As Jesus pointed out so many times, he does his Father's will, not his own will. A Master knows that belief is a poor substitute for experience and he is intent on empowering his disciples with their own experience, so that they can see the reality for themselves through direct perception and not rely on what others say or suggest they should believe. But all this takes time and sceptic, timorous mortals who sit upon the shore of the sea, fearing to launch out in any direction, usually get nowhere. What is required is action, not philosophy. To help us, then, we need someone at our own level.

He Became Like Me

The son of a king, it is said, once became insane, thinking himself to be a turkey. Consequently, he removed all his clothes and took to living underneath a table, eating only grains, seeds and pieces of bone. Naturally, the king was distressed and called his best physicians to see if they could help. But to no avail. The king's son was convinced he was a turkey and went on behaving as he thought a turkey should.

At last, a wise man arrived at the palace, assuring the king that he could cure his son. The king was delighted and asked him to proceed, posthaste. At this, the wise man immediately removed all his clothes, joined the young man beneath the table and began to eat only grains, seeds and pieces of bone.

Looking at the newcomer with surprise, the king's son asked the wise man, "Who are you and what are you doing here?" At which the wise man responded, "And who are *you* and what are *you* doing here?" The young man insisted, "I am a turkey," to which the wise man replied, "I am also a turkey, like you."

After this, the two turkeys sat together and talked until they became good friends. The wise man then signalled the king's courtiers to bring him a shirt which he put on, saying to the king's son, "Do you think that a turkey is not allowed to wear a shirt? By wearing a shirt, he does not cease to be a turkey." The young man agreed and consented to wear a shirt.

Some while later, the wise man indicated that a pair of trousers should be brought to him. Putting them on, he commented to the king's son, "One does not cease to be a turkey simply by wearing trousers." The young man saw the sense in that and agreed to wear some trousers. By degrees, the wise man got himself and the young man properly dressed.

The wise man then requested that normal food be brought to them. Beginning his meal, he said to the king's son, "Being a turkey surely does not mean that one cannot eat good food? One can still eat good food and remain a turkey." The young man agreed once again and began to eat food appropriate to a king's son.

Reflecting on the changes brought about thus far, the wise man then said to the king's son, "Do you really think that a turkey must remain confined beneath a table? Surely a turkey should be permitted to roam around as he chooses? No one should have a right to tell him where to go." The young man consented and the two of them came out from underneath the table. And since he was now dressed like a human being, eating like a human being, and standing upright like a human being, he also started to behave like a human being and was soon restored to his proper place as the king's son.

"Similarly," summarizes the Jewish story-teller, "the *Zaddik* (*lit.* righteous one) robes himself in worldly garments and behaves like ordinary people in order to draw them to God's service."[2]

This story, taken from the Jewish Hasidic mystical tradition which flourished in late eighteenth-century Poland, expresses precisely the role of the Master – or the *Zaddik* as he was called by the *Hasidim* (*lit.* the pious ones). He comes to the world, becomes like us, gains our confidence and then lovingly guides us back to our true estate.

We find this same theme expressed throughout early Christian writings and, indeed, all mystical literature associated with the Masters. In the *Odes of Solomon*, for example, the devotee expresses his gratitude to the Master who "became like me, in order that I might accept him":

My joy is the Lord, and my course is towards Him:
    this my path is beautiful;
For I have a Helper to the Lord.
He made himself known to me,

without grudging, in his generosity;
For in his kindness he set aside his majesty.
He became like me, in order that I might accept him:
in appearance he seemed like me,
in order that I might put him on.
And I did not tremble when I saw him,
because he had compassion for me.
He became like my nature,
in order that I might learn to know him,
And like my form,
in order that I might not turn away from him.

Odes of Solomon VII:2-6, AOT p.696

A Master becomes like us, so that we may become like him. This is the essence of the matter. The same idea is expressed in the *Acts of John*, when John gives praise to his Master, who willingly "came down into bondage" and "slavery" for the sake of human beings:

O what a greatness that came down into bondage!
O unspeakable liberty brought into slavery by us!
O incomprehensible glory that is come unto us! ...

Father that hast had pity and compassion on the man
that cared not for Thee.
We glorify thee, and praise and bless
and thank thy great goodness and long-suffering,
O holy Jesu, for thou only art God, and none else:
Whose is the might that cannot be conspired against.

Acts of John 77, ANT p.247

The same thought is found in the Manichaean-Christian writings. Speaking of the "Son of the Living God, the Physician of souls", the psalmist says:

God became man, He went about in all the world.
He received a man's likeness, a slave's vesture.

Psalms of Heracleides, MPB p.193

Similarly, in the *Acts of Thomas*, one of the characters gives thanks that the Master has come down to the human level so that the soul may come to appreciate his greatness:

I give Thee thanks, O Lord, ...
Who hast shown me Thyself
  and revealed unto me all my state wherein I am; ...

That hast made thyself lowly
  even down to me and my littleness,
  that thou mayest present me unto Thy greatness
  and unite me unto Thyself.

Who hast not withheld thine own bowels (self) from me
  that was ready to perish;
But hast shown me how to seek myself
  and know who I was,
  and who and in what manner I now am,
  that I may again become that which I was:

Whom I knew not, but Thyself didst seek me out:
Of whom I was not aware,
  but Thyself hast taken me to Thee:
Whom I have perceived
  and now am not able to be unmindful of him:
Whose love burneth within me,
  and I cannot speak it as is fit,
  but that which I am able to say of it is little and scanty,
  and not fitly to say unto him even that which I know not:
For it is because of his love that I say even this much.

Acts of Thomas 15, ANT pp.370-371

The devotee says that it is only because the Master came to the human level and himself "didst seek me out" that he was made to realize the state he was in, who he really was, and how he might return to his former state. It is only because the Master came in human form that the soul saw him and cannot now forget him at all, having developed a deep and burning love and longing for him – though this is still only "little and scanty" compared to the heights of love, yet to be attained. Indeed, says the disciple, "it is only because of his love that I say even this much".

More specifically, in the revelationary *Ascension of Isaiah*, the devotee explains how he heard the Master Jesus being appointed or commanded to come down into this world and at every level to take on a form appropriate to that level. We are not to take the 'revelation' literally, of course. It is only the writer's way of expressing a particular mystic truth:

> And I heard the Voice of the Most High, the Father of my Lord, saying to my Lord the Christ, who will be called Jesus, "Go forth and descend through all the heavens: descend to the firmament and through that world as far as the angel who is in Sheol (this world); but to Haguel (perdition, hell) you shall not go. And you must transform yourself so as to be like all those who are in the five heavens. And you must take care to transform yourself so as to be like the angels of the firmament as well, and also like that of the angels who are in Sheol. And none of the angels of that world will know that you are Lord with me of the seven heavens and of their angels."
>
> *Ascension of Isaiah X:3-9, AOT pp.806-807, OTP2 p.173*

At every level, the Master is in disguise. He wears the 'local dress' and appears just like everyone else at that level. No one realizes that he is the Lord, come to visit His creation. And what should be so surprising about such a visit? Many kings of this world have put on common garb and gone about amongst their subjects.

The Christ, the Messiah and the Living One

Understanding of the role played by the living Master is found throughout the early Christian and allied literature. There, he is called the Living One, the Standing One, the Redeemer, the Saviour, the Liberator, the Deliverer, the Helper, the Messenger, the Apostle, the Envoy, the Intercessor, the Paraclete, the Messiah, the Christ, the Sage, the Man of Understanding, the True Prophet, the True Teacher, the Holy One, the Righteous One, the Teacher of Righteousness and other similar names. And alluding to the many parables and allegories in which the Master plays a central role, he is called the Sower, the Helmsman, the Fisherman, the Shepherd, the King, the Physician, the Gardener, the Lamb, the Brother, the Bridegroom, the Beloved One and so on.

The concept of the Messiah was central to Jewish belief. In Hebrew, Messiah means the 'anointed one', the one who is anointed and appointed by God to act as an intermediary for human beings. Many of the Old Testament prophets speak of the Messiah, for this is the essence of their own teaching. All perfect Masters are Messiahs, appointed by God to perform their task, and the highest prophets and mystics have all spoken of the Masters, in one way or another. Often, they have done so in oblique and guarded language because the nature of their times has dictated it, in order to avoid persecution and conflict.

The Latin word *Christus* and the Greek *Khristos*, from which our word 'Christ' is derived, mean the same thing, stemming from the Greek root *kriein*, meaning 'to anoint'. They are direct translations of 'Messiah'. 'Christ' means the 'anointed one' of God, an appointed living Master of his time. Hence, 'Jesus Christ' simply means 'Jesus the anointed one'. Interestingly, in the Manichaean-Christian writings, the term 'Christ' refers to both Jesus and Mani, depending on the context. And even in some of the gnostic treatises, it is by no means certain that the one who is referred to as Christ was actually Jesus. Often, there is no indication who the Master was. Christ, like Messiah, was a general term for a Master though the term has generally been appropriated by Christianity.

The term originates in early Semitic and pre-Semitic custom where the coronation of a king was marked by his being anointed with a little oil. In the language of mysticism at that time, both God and the Master were also known as the King. Hence, as we commonly find in the *Psalms*, the mystics and devotees would pray to the Messiah or King to deliver them from their enemies. The 'enemies', however, refer to the mind and its host of imperfections and passions. But by taking the writings of the mystics literally, the belief developed that a Messiah would come who would release them from their temporal enemies. He would be sent from God to be both their spiritual and temporal head, eliminating all the enemies of Israel. However, since God is the loving Father of all souls, such violent and partisan behaviour on His part is most unlikely and no mystic would ever teach such a thing. The belief, like so many others in religion, is almost certainly due to human literalization and a misunderstanding of a spiritual truth.

The Jewish people are still awaiting the coming of their Messiah, while the Christians say that he came in the form of Jesus – and are now awaiting his second coming. Man seems to have an innate capacity to delay his final salvation until some date in the future. Procrastination is the thief of salvation, for whatever we have to do, we have to do it now, while we have the opportunity of a human birth, for "the night cometh when no man can work". Taking the help of a spiritual King, man has to battle within himself to overcome the enemies of the mind. The holy war is to be waged in secret, entirely in the inner arena, and that battle must be engaged right now. As we find in the *Gospel of Thomas*:

Jesus said,
"Take heed of the Living One while you are alive,
    lest you die and seek to see him
    and be unable to do so."

Gospel of Thomas 59, NHS20 p.75

The Living One, as an expression for a living Master, is common in Christian and Manichaean-Christian writings. The Master is "Living" because he is physically incarnate in this world. He is alive in a human sense. And he is "Living" because he is one with the source of Life, God Himself. In the *Acts of Thomas*, for example, Judas Thomas encourages some disciples, saying:

Jesus the holy, the Living One,
    shall quickly send help unto you.

Acts of Thomas 169, ANT p.437

The One Lord is also called the Living One, since He is the one Source. Hence Judas Thomas says to Jesus:

To thee be glory, Living One who art from the Living One;
    to thee be glory, Life-Giver of many;
    to thee be glory, Help and Aider
    of those who come to thy place of refuge;
    to thee be glory, thou that art wakeful from all eternity,
    and the Awakener of men, living and making alive.
Thou art God, the Son of God, the Saviour and Helper,
    and Refuge, and Rest of all those who are weary in thy work;
    the Giver of Rest to those who, for thy Name's sake,
    have borne the burden of the whole day at mid-day.

Acts of Thomas, AAA p.199

He is the "Life-Giver of many" because of his gift of baptism, which bestows new life, spiritually. As God, he gives life to all as the life essence within every soul. He is the Helper of all who are baptized into his fold. He is the one who never sleeps, for the Creative Word is ever active and about its business. He gives eternal bliss and beatitude to "those who are weary in thy work", to those who have striven on the mystic path. They "have borne the burden of the whole day at mid-day" means that they have laboured throughout their lives in the burning heat of the physical world. It is an allusion to Jesus' parable of the labourers.

Again, in the gnostic *Books of Jeu,* Jesus is continuously called the Living One. In this example, the apostles, Matthew, John, Philip, Bartholomew and James, all praise Jesus simultaneously, saying:

> O Lord Jesus, thou who livest,
>> whose goodness extends over those
>> who have found thy Wisdom
>> and thy form in which thou gavest light;
> O light-giving Light that enlightened our hearts
>> until we received the Light of Life;
> O True Word, that through *gnosis* teaches us
>> the hidden knowledge of the Lord Jesus, the Living One.
>
> *First Book of Jeu 3, BC p.41*

Similarly, in one of the Manichaean-Christian *Psalms of Thomas,* the Master is described as the "Living One" who releases the captive souls from the "Enemy" and his "rulers" – from Satan and the powers of the mind. Souls are like "fish" caught in a net, "birds" imprisoned in a cage or "sheep" lost in the wilderness. They are the "wealth" of the Living One whom he returns to their original home, the "Land of Rest":

> He broke their snares that were set,
>> he burst also their nets that were spread,
>> he let the fish out to their sea;
> He let the birds fly in the air,
>> he let the birds fly out in the air;
> He let the sheep into their fold;
> He rolled up his wealth,
>> he took it, he took it up to the Land of Rest.
> That which the Living Ones took was saved:
>> they will return again to that which is theirs.
>
> *Psalms of Thomas I, MPB p.205*

In another of these psalms, the soul is described as:

> O the treasure of the Great Ones of Life,
>> the jewel of the living Mighty Ones.
> O the great treasure of the Living Ones....
>
> I am a [flame] of the Living Ones,
>> a lamp of Light entire....

> The Living Ones send after thee....
> They took an Envoy, they sent him after me,
>   he grasped the [palm] of my hand,
>   he [carried] me up to the Land of Peace.
>
> *Psalms of Thomas V, MPB pp.210-211*

And likewise, the soul lost in this world expresses its hope of salvation through the "Living Ones":

> I am expecting the Living Ones to send aid after me:
>   the Living Ones shall send me power,
>   my Brethren shall bring the Light.
>
> *Psalms of Thomas XIII, MPB p.218*

Saints, Prophets and the Law

A great many mystics have been born in this world and many more will come here. In fact, there is always at least one "Living One" in the world at any time, sometimes more. When they come, they explain the teachings of those past mystics in whom people have put their faith, but whose real meaning has been misconstrued. Scholars have often described such mystics as syncretists, those who combine religious doctrines into one system; but this is a misunderstanding.

 Mystics teach the truth. Being universal in their outlook, they will draw on any sources with which people are familiar so long as they contain an element of truth. To scholars with an academic interest in the varieties of doctrine rather than in reality, this may appear as syncretism, but actually it is something far more than that.

There is a good example of this seeming syncretization in the third century AD. At that time, the mystic Mani and his successors travelled extensively, amongst their disciples being those with Christian, Zoroastrian, Jewish, Greek and other backgrounds. They therefore taught these communities from the writings the people held sacred, also speaking of other Masters of the past who had lived in other parts of the world in order to demonstrate that all mystics, from all nations, had given the same teachings.

The result, in Manichaean-Christian writings, is some interesting cross-cultural combinations of terminology and expression. In the manuscripts from Turkestan, for instance, in a passage headed "*In Praise of Jesus*", the writer weaves together metaphors from Christian,

Greek, Judaic and other sources, petitioning and praising the Master as the "King of *Nous*", the "precious Tree" of Life, the "compassionate Father", the "merciful Mother" and the "great Saint":

> The King of *Nous* is clean and pure,
>   and always wide awake:
> For the believing and comprehending,
>   he [guides them on the way].
> Whoever there is, progressing and developing surely,
>   he conducts him into safety on the even road....
>
> O ever-flourishing precious Tree,
>   the ocean of Nature and Life,
>   listen mercifully to my true petition:
> Thy Name belongs to the boundless fame of the Holy Land,
>   and thy skill belongs
>   to the boundless skill of the Holy Soil.
>
> Compassionate Father of all the natures of light (souls),
>   merciful Mother of all the robbed!
> Now save me from the jackals and wolves
>   as was promised by Jesus of Light.
>
> The great Saint is naturally an infinite treasure,
>   containing in full every kind of precious rarity,
>   for distribution among all the poor and the needy:
>   each of whom will be satisfied according to his wish.
>
> The great Saint is truly the second venerable Lord....
> For the voluntary, clean, and pure retainers (disciples),
>   he propagates the Holy Edict (Law, Word)
>   and gives them understanding.
>
>   *LSMH 9,12-15, BSOAS XI pp.176-177*

And he continues:

> Pray give me the fragrant Water of Emancipation....
>   cleanse my wonderful nature from dust and dirt....
> Send down the springtime of the Great Law
>   to prosper the ground of my (true) nature (my soul):
>   and cause the flowers and fruits

of the tree of my (true) nature (soul) to thrive.
Pray pacify the great billows and waves of the fiery sea,
    the surrounding canopies of the dark cloud and mist.
Compel the sun of the Great Law to shine universally,
    and make my heart and nature (soul) always bright and pure.

Pray dispel my morbidity and dullness of many ages....
    grant the Medicine of the Great Law
    to heal and restore me quickly,
    and silence them with the Holy Spell
    and drive them from me.
I am burdened with many obstacles, such as these,
    and also with other countless sufferings.

LSMH 30-34, BSOAS XI p.178

He portrays the Master as the embodiment of the "*Nous*", the "Tree" of Life, the "Holy Edict", the "fragrant Water of Emancipation", the "Great Law", the "Medicine of the Great Law" and the "Holy Spell". These are all terms for the Word, the Power of God that – through the intermediary of a living Master – can forgive sins and release souls from transmigration where they have been trapped for many ages. The devotee goes on to say that the "great Saint", whom he identifies with Jesus, is the storehouse of spiritual treasures and the source of liberation, peace and spiritual healing:

The great Saint will see, know, and naturally pity me:
    I pray I may have calamities and afflictions no more.
I petition only that Jesus will have mercy,
    and liberate me from the bondage
    of all devils and spirits.
I am now living in the pit of fire:
    quickly guide me into the peace
    of the clean and pure Land!

O great King of healing for all manner of ills,
O great Radiance for all that dwell in the dark,
    diligently reassemble all those who are scattered,
    all who have lost their hearts! ...

I have already perished now: pray reanimate me;
I am already in the darkness: pray enlighten me....

Ignorance, delusion, and desire have for long ensnared me.
Bestow the Medicine of the Great Law
    and let me be healed!

LSMH 35-38, BSOAS XI p.179

His plea is always the same: to be released from the bondage of sin and reincarnation, and to return to his original home, the eternal realm, the "clean and pure Land". For this, he petitions the "great Saint" whom he calls by a variety of epithets.

In early Christian times, it was the devotees who were called saints and the term simply referred to those of pure heart and intention. Paul, for example, often speaks of his fellow Christians as the "saints" or he sends his regards to the "saints which are at Ephesus" or at "Philippi" and so on. But later, only certain Christians were deemed worthy of the title, which was – and still is – awarded posthumously.

In the earliest centuries, the faithful believed that anyone who had suffered a martyr's death had demonstrated by giving their lives for Jesus that they were perfect Christians. According to the belief, they had attained eternal life through their sufferings and were then and forever united to Christ. Consequently, the Christians of those times, still suffering oppression, venerated the martyrs, begging them to intercede on their behalf before God. Towards the end of the Roman persecutions, this veneration was extended to any who had suffered for their faith, and soon after was further augmented to include all those who were considered to have led exemplary Christian lives. In particular, this meant those who had led lives of great austerity and penance or who had been great theologians according to the Catholic creed or who had excelled in evangelical zeal or in deeds of charity.

As time passed, the number of deceased who were so elevated increased markedly, especially between the sixth and tenth centuries. New feasts were added to the ecclesiastical calendars and a number of legendary and mythological lives were also written. All that was required for canonization was the popular reputation of a holy or charitable life and – most of all – that miracles be associated with their veneration. The theory was simple. If invoking the help of a deceased holy person resulted in what was deemed a miracle, then it could be assumed that the deceased had the ear of God and was able to intercede on behalf of petitioners.

The system, however, was open to abuse and, gradually, the general consensus of opinion concerning a person's elevation to 'sainthood' was augmented by referring the matter to the local bishop. He was expected to make a thorough investigation of the individual's life and the authenticity of the miracles attributed to the invoking of the prospective saint's name. The bishops, however, commonly sought the advice of the Pope and the matter gradually became a papal decision. Finally, in 1234, under Gregory IX, during the excessively authoritarian days of the Inquisition, this became the only legal means of canonization and a strict legislative procedure was laid down by which a person might be canonized. Miracles and a supposedly holy life, however, remained the primary rationale for canonization.

It is evident from their writings, however, that many of these 'saints', especially from the earliest times, were far from perfect human beings. St Irenaeus, St Epiphanius and St Ephraim, for example, all wrote long treatises against those they perceived as heretics, slanging, slandering and misrepresenting them in as many ways as one can imagine. Hardly loving one's neighbour!

The term 'prophet' has similarly changed its meaning as time has passed. Nowadays, the term is reserved for holy men or mystics, particularly Jewish patriarchal holy men of Biblical times. Its meaning has also become centred on the ability to foretell the future, stemming partially perhaps from the Jewish and Christian assertion that the Jewish prophets foretold the coming of the Messiah.

But, again, in Jesus' day, the term had a wider meaning. It was a name given to those who had a talent for expressing spiritual truths and could give a coherent discourse on spiritual matters. This was called the 'gift of prophecy' and in early Christian times, at least, it implied 'speaking in the Spirit'. As Jesus recommended to his disciples when brought before religious or secular authorities:

> Take no thought how or what ye shall speak:
>   for it shall be given you in that same hour
>   what ye shall speak.
> For it is not ye that speak,
>   but the Spirit of your Father which speaketh in you.
>
> *Matthew 10:19-20*

It is true, however, that a considerable degree of purity and control of the mind is required before a person can know that he is genuinely inspired by the Spirit. Otherwise, it may be just his own mind talking.

In the gospels, when Jesus uses the terms "prophets" or the "Law and the prophets", he was generally referring to the Jewish mystics and their teachings, as in:

> Think not that I am come
>> to destroy the Law, or the prophets:
>> I am not come to destroy, but to fulfil.
>
> *Matthew 5:17*

By which he meant that he had not come to "destroy" everything that the prophets had taught. Rather, he had come to "fulfil" their teachings, to impart the same teachings which they had given and to teach the same truths. To orthodox Judaism, the "Law" or *Torah* particularly applied to the Jewish concept of Moses' teachings as recorded in the *Pentateuch*. But Jesus' frequent use of such expressions once again demonstrates that he did not consider himself to be the only Master sent by God, but one amongst many.

Nor did the early Christians necessarily promote the idea that Jesus was the only Saviour who had ever come to this world. In the *Acts of John*, John says very clearly that this process of salvation has been going on "from the foundation of the world":

> O God that sentest us into the world:
>> that didst reveal Thyself by the Law and the prophets:
>> that didst never rest,
>> but always from the foundation of the world
>> savedst them that were able to be saved:
>
> That madest Thyself known through all nature:
>> that proclaimedst Thyself even among beasts:
>> that didst make the desolate and savage soul tame and quiet:
>
> That gavest Thyself to it
>> when it was athirst for thy words (Word):
>> that didst appear to it in haste when it was dying:
>
> That didst show thyself to it as a Law
>> when it was sinking into lawlessness:
>
> That didst manifest thyself to it
>> when it had been vanquished by Satan:
>
> That didst overcome its Adversary when it fled unto thee:
>> that gavest it thine hand
>> and didst raise it up from the things of Hades:

> That didst not leave it to walk after
>> a bodily sort (in the body);
>> that didst show to it its own Enemy:
> That hast made for it
>> a clear (pathway of) knowledge toward Thee.
>
> *Acts of John 112, ANT pp.268-269*

Here, as we have seen before, the "Law" is yet another term used for the Word by the mystics of old. It is the primal Law or Command by which the creation is created and maintained. God, he says, is revealed by this Law and by His "prophets", His mystics. The salvation of souls has been going on since the beginning of time. The prophets or mystics are a manifestation of this Law. That the "Law" came to refer to the body of teachings and external observances whose origins are attributed to Moses is yet another example of the externalization of a mystic's teachings.

The use of "Law" and the "Commandment" as terms for the Word are especially common amongst the *Manichaean-Christian* writings, as we have seen in those from Turkestan. There, the writer mixes his metaphors, calling it the "Medicine of the Great Law", the "Holy Edict" and other similar epithets.

In the *Clementine Recognitions*, two terms are particularly used for the Living One and the true Master – the "Standing One" and the "True Prophet". In an interesting, though brief, dissertation on the history of Simon Magus, the writer says that Simon:

> Wishes himself ... to be thought to be the Christ, and to be called the Standing One.
>
> *Clementine Recognitions II:VII, CR p.196*

The "Standing One" means the 'Existing One', for only one who stands can exist or live. Those who are dead do not stand up. But the term also carries overtones of eternity, of standing for ever, in the sense that the position of Mastership will last for as long as the creation continues. Moreover, the term is also equated with the Christ or the Messiah. As we mentioned earlier, according to this book, Simon is involved in a dispute with a certain Dositheus, both of whom were disciples of John the Baptist, over who was the Baptist's rightful successor and hence the "Standing One". The facts of the matter, of course, are impossible to determine, especially since the writer is expressly anti-Simon in his sympathies, writing derogatively of him at all times. Nevertheless, the argument is clearly over who was the true living Master.

The *Clementine Recognitions* is an intriguing book, written in the style of a spiritual romance, probably stemming from the Judaic side of early Christianity. Its central character is Peter who, far from being the uneducated fisherman of popular conception, is portrayed as well-versed in Greek literature and an erudite speaker. It is in one of his discourses that he speaks of the living Master as the "True Prophet", pointing out that seeking and finding such a teacher by no means robs a person of their power of discrimination and ability to make decisions for themselves:

> But I would not have you think that ... I take away the power of judging concerning things; but I give counsel that no one walk through devious places and rush into errors without end. And therefore I advise not only wise men, but indeed all men who have a desire of knowing what is advantageous to them, that they seek after the True Prophet; for it is he alone who knoweth all things, and who knoweth what and how every man is seeking.
>
> For he is within the mind of every one of us, but in those who have no desire of the knowledge of God and His righteousness, he is inoperative; but he works in those who seek after that which is profitable to their souls, and kindles in them the light of knowledge. Wherefore seek him first of all; and if you do not find him, expect not that you shall learn anything from any other.
>
> But he is soon found by those who diligently seek him through love of the truth, and whose souls are not taken possession of by wickedness. For he is present with those who desire him in the innocency of their spirits, who bear patiently and draw sighs from the bottom of their hearts through love of the truth; but he deserts malevolent minds, because as a Prophet he knows the thoughts of every one.
>
> *Clementine Recognitions VIII:LIX, CR pp.397-398*

The True Prophet, says Peter, is within everyone and from there he can see who is ready for him, who really desires and longs for him. Consequently, he adds, that whenever someone is ready, the Prophet appears and makes himself known:

> And therefore let no one think that he can find him by his own wisdom, unless, as we have said, he empty his mind of all wickedness, and conceive a pure and faithful desire to know him. For when any one has so prepared

himself, he himself as a Prophet, seeing a mind prepared for him, of his own accord offers himself to his knowledge (makes himself known to the individual).

Clementine Recognitions VIII:LIX, CR p.398

In another passage, having discussed the approach of philosophers and noted that they are always in disagreement with each other and uncertain about the nature of reality, he comments:

And, therefore, since amongst these (philosophers) are things uncertain, we must come to the True Prophet. Him, God the Father wished to be loved by all, and accordingly He has been pleased wholly to disregard those opinions which have originated with men, and in regard to which there is nothing like certainty – in order that he (the True Prophet) might be the more sought after, and that he whom they had obscured should show to men the Way of Truth. For on this account also God made the world.

Clementine Recognitions VIII:LXII, CR p.399

In other words, it is on account of the inherent uncertainty of intellectual philosophizing and the incorrect interpretations of the teachings of past mystics that the True Prophet should be sought after, for he has the certainty and knowledge that stem from inner experience and his words carry weight and authority. Indeed, "on this account also God made the world": this world has been created by God so that souls may have the opportunity to return to Him through the agency of the True Prophet. The same idea is expressed in the early Christian, *Epistula Apostolorum*, where Jesus says:

On account of those who pervert my words
    I have come down from heaven.
I am the *Logos*;
I became flesh, labouring and teaching
    that those who are called will be saved.

Epistula Apostolorum 39 (Coptic), NTA1 p.219

This section in the *Clementine Recognitions* then concludes with Peter pointing out that God is present within everyone, wherever he may be on earth. But for those who seek Him "not purely, nor holily, nor faithfully" – for those who do not seek or worship Him in the right way – it is as if He were dormant, for He does not respond to them.

And for those who do not believe in His existence at all, it is as if He were completely absent:

> "He is everywhere near to them who seek Him, though He be sought in the remotest ends of the earth. But if any one seek Him not purely, nor holily, nor faithfully – He is indeed within him, because He is everywhere, and is found within the minds of all men – but, as we have said before, He is (as if) dormant to the unbelieving, and is held to be absent from those by whom His existence is not believed."
>
> And when Peter had said this, and more to the same effect, concerning the True Prophet, he dismissed the crowds.... And after this, we also, with Peter, went to our lodging, and enjoyed our accustomed food and rest.
>
> *Clementine Recognitions VIII:LXII, CR pp.399-400*

It is clear, then, that the writer of this early Christian book understood a great deal concerning the nature of the perfect Master, the way to God, and how a Master finds the seeker rather than the reverse. And there are many other examples from a great many sources that could be quoted if space permitted, where the same universal truths are voiced again and again. After the death of Jesus, the fast-developing Christian religion may have split very rapidly into a multitude of groups promoting differing points of view. But the root from which they grew would seem to have been the age-old mystic teachings of the Masters.

The Physical Presence of the Master

Luke, despite his frequent paraphrasing and altering of Jesus' words, had access to a source of unique stories and sayings that somehow possess an air of simplicity and authenticity, rather than fabrication, even though he sometimes weaves them in with the miraculous. They are the kind of uncontrived, seemingly unimportant, incidents that a disciple will treasure in his heart for the sweet feelings of happiness, love and joy he has received from being in the presence of his Master. Perhaps one of Luke's special sources was some notes written down by one of Jesus' close disciples, dating from the time of Jesus, or perhaps the incidents were passed on by word of mouth. Masters have a way of coming out with memorable comments in response to the mundane or of making highly humorous remarks when least expected, and naturally, a disciple always likes to recall these special moments.

There is the occasion when Jesus is warned by some friendly Pharisees to leave town in case Herod should kill him, since he had already executed John the Baptist. But Jesus responds without trace of fear or concern that he will continue about his business. "Go ye, and tell that fox ..."[3] he says. How his disciples must have smiled to hear their local tyrant being addressed as a "fox"! And how the people must have warmed to him, gaining confidence from him, when they saw that he remained unafraid in the face of danger.

On another occasion, after Jesus had been out across the Sea of Galilee, apparently on a day trip with some of his disciples, Luke reports:

> And it came to pass, that, when Jesus was returned,
>   the people gladly received him:
> For they were all waiting for him.
>
> *Luke 8:40*

Quite apart from demonstrating once again that Jesus' following extended far beyond the well-known twelve disciples, the incident is quite plausible. For such is the bond of love that disciples will happily wait far longer than a day in the hope of catching just a glimpse of their Master, even if they have only recently been with him.

The reason is very simple. The Masters radiate a unique air of love, bliss, light and happiness around them. The atmosphere seems to be surcharged, wherever they may be, filling their disciples and others who are receptive to it with feelings of great joy and vitality. Naturally, therefore, disciples will wait contentedly all day if they think they will see their Master again. Such feelings are not unique to the followers of Jesus.

Luke tells a similar story concerning a certain Zacchaeus, a man "little of stature". Jesus was passing through Jericho and a large number of people having come to know of his presence had turned out to see their Master. The crowd was great and Zacchaeus was small, so he climbs into a tree in order to get a better view. But Jesus, seeing him, calls him down and invites himself to lunch with his devoted disciple. Zacchaeus, of course, is overjoyed:

> And Jesus entered and passed through Jericho. And, behold, there was a man named Zacchaeus, which was the chief among the publicans, and he was rich. And he sought to see Jesus who he was; and could not for the press, because he was little of stature. And he ran before, and climbed up into a sycamore tree to see him: for he was to pass that way.
> And when Jesus came to the place, he looked up, and saw him, and

said unto him, "Zacchaeus, make haste, and come down; for today I must abide at thy house." And he made haste, and came down, and received him joyfully.

Luke 19:1-6

There is little reason to suppose that the colourful elements of this story have been invented, for they bear scant relationship to Jesus' subsequent sayings, providing no obvious motive for their invention. Luke simply had both the story and the sayings and put them together in his gospel. And anyway, there is something humorous about a little man climbing a tree in order to get a better view and Jesus calling him down by name and so aptly responding to his disciple's desire to be close to him by inviting himself to lunch. It is the kind of tale that gets told and retold.

He Taught Them as One Having Authority

True Masters create an impression on almost everyone they meet. Even the most worldly are forced to admit that there is something unique in their bearing and deportment. They speak without haranguing or shouting, yet their words penetrate the hearts and minds of their listeners. They may be educated or they may not, but it matters little so far as their ability to give the mystic teachings is concerned. As Jesus said of himself, they teach from personal experience, not from education or study.

Because he is different from others in ways that people sense but find hard to pin down, a Master is also likely to generate differences of opinion. We find this in a short comment in St John:

Then the Jews sought him at the feast, and said, "Where is he?" And there was much murmuring among the people concerning him. For some said, "He is a good man". Others said, "Nay; but he deceiveth the people." Howbeit no man spake openly of him for fear of the Jews.

John 7:11-13

There are many instances of Jesus' unique personality recorded in the gospels and elsewhere. From his childhood, he seems to have shown signs of great spirituality and of an understanding far in advance of his years. In this respect, Luke relates another of the personal incidents that could so easily have come from a disciple's notebook. It is the kind of story that disciples relate about their Master:

And the child grew, and waxed strong in spirit, filled with wisdom: and the grace of God was upon him. Now his parents went to Jerusalem every year at the feast of the passover. And when he was twelve years old, they went up to Jerusalem after the custom of the feast. And when they had fulfilled the days, as they returned, the child Jesus tarried behind in Jerusalem; and Joseph and his mother knew not of it. But they, supposing him to have been in the company, went a day's journey; and they sought him among their kinsfolk and acquaintance. And when they found him not, they turned back again to Jerusalem, seeking him.

And it came to pass, that after three days they found him in the temple, sitting in the midst of the doctors, both hearing them, and asking them questions. And all that heard him were astonished at his understanding and answers. And when they saw him, they were amazed: and his mother said unto him, "Son, why hast thou thus dealt with us? Behold, thy father and I have sought thee sorrowing." And he said unto them, "How is it that ye sought me? Wist ye not that I must be about my Father's business?"

Luke 2:40-49

The story indicates that Jesus had a divine purpose to fulfil. Masters are born to their destiny as divine teachers. Right from their childhood, especially with the benefit of hindsight, people who knew them recall their particular spiritual quality.

In later years, Jesus developed a style of teaching that left people speechless for its clarity, character and the nature of his explanations, especially concerning the real meaning of the Jewish scriptures and other writings. Even in the time of the gospel compilers, several decades after Jesus' death, the memory of his impact was not forgotten. As Matthew relates:

And it came to pass, when Jesus had ended these sayings, the people were astonished at his doctrine. For he taught them as one having authority, and not as the scribes.

Matthew 7:28-29

His teachings and interpretations were those of one who *knew* what he was talking about, not those of an intellectual theologian.

According to another story found in Luke, during a visit to the region of Galilee in which "he taught in their synagogues", Jesus includes his home village of Nazareth[4] on his itinerary. Luke continues:

And, as his custom was, he went into the synagogue on the Sabbath day, and stood up for to read. And there was delivered unto him the book of the prophet Esaias. And when he had opened the book, he found the place where it was written, "The Spirit of the Lord is upon me, because he hath anointed me to preach the gospel to the poor; he hath sent me to heal the brokenhearted, to preach deliverance to the captives, and recovering of sight to the blind, to set at liberty them that are bruised, to preach the acceptable year of the Lord."

And he closed the book, and he gave it again to the minister, and sat down. And the eyes of all them that were in the synagogue were fastened on him.

And he began to say unto them, "This day is this scripture fulfilled in your ears." And all bare him witness, and wondered at the gracious words which proceeded out of his mouth.

And they said, "Is not this Joseph's son?" ...

And they were astonished at his doctrine: for his word was with power.

Luke 4:16-22,32

Jesus' "word was with power" and "he taught as one having authority". This is true of all who really know what they are talking about and when the one who speaks is talking of a God with whom he is one, the impression he creates can be imagined, though it may be said in passing that not one of the twentieth-century attempts to portray Jesus on the screen or in print comes anywhere near the real thing. Masters do not function through the human emotions which drive the rest of us, and they are inevitably portrayed with human characteristics that are somewhat less than perfect. Their holiness and purity is of an innocent character. They are personable and charismatic with a sense of spontaneity about them. They make genuine contact with others. Truly, one has to meet a Master to get any inkling of what they are like.

Masters also have a way of moving in this world that gives them almost an air of magic. Most of us cut a course through life that bears all the hallmarks of our own mind and temperament. But Masters make another kind of impression. They are not constrained by subconscious fears and motivations, nor are their actions controlled and destined by sins and *karmas* of the past. Neither have they any past sins to clear, nor do they commit sins. They are truly free and can do entirely as they please. This is a state that can hardly be imagined. They have the power and the freedom of God within themselves, and it is something of this inner character which is manifested in the manner in which they pass through this world. As the writer of *1 John* puts it, in a style and language remarkably similar to that of Jesus' discourses in John's gospel, "whosoever is born of God" – "sinneth not":

> We know that whosoever is born of God sinneth not;
>   but he that is begotten of God keepeth himself,
>   and that Wicked One toucheth him not.
>
>   *1 John 5:18*

A Master is able to keep himself pure and untainted. Even while living in the midst of Satan's realm, "that Wicked One toucheth him not". Similarly, the writer says in the same letter:

> Little children, let no man deceive you:
>   he that doeth righteousness is righteous,
>   even as he (Jesus) is righteous.
> He that committeth sin is of the Devil;
>   for the Devil sinneth from the beginning.
> For this purpose the Son of God was manifested,
>   that he might destroy the works of the Devil.
>
> Whosoever is born of God doth not commit sin;
>   for His Seed (His Word) remaineth in him:
>   and he cannot sin, because he is born of God.
>
>   *1 John 3:7-9*

One who commits sin is in thrall to the Devil. That is why, says John, the Son of God has come as Jesus, to undo the entanglement of the Devil. And the Son who "is born of God doth not commit sin" because the Word of God, His Seed or essence, is always with him. He is therefore quite unable to do anything which will in any way bind him to this world. But this is so different from the way the majority of us go through life that it is almost impossible to imagine what it would be like to witness it in action. Even to somebody who has only an inkling of such matters, it is awe-inspiring.

Some hint of this is to be found in a number of the gospel narratives. It seems that no one could lay a hand on Jesus without his full agreement. Consider Luke's narrative concerning Jesus' visit to Nazareth where the people were so angry that they took Jesus to the top of a hill, wanting to "cast him down headlong". Luke relates that Jesus, "passing through their midst, went his way".[5] When he had decided that enough was enough, he simply walked away from them and they could not touch him.

John relates a similar incident when some of the Jews were so incensed at Jesus' teaching in the Temple that they wished to cause him physical harm:

> Then took they up stones to cast at him: but Jesus hid himself, and went out of the temple, going through the midst of them, and so passed by.
>
> *John 8:59*

"Jesus hid himself" can hardly mean that he found a quiet corner to hide away, for all eyes would have been upon him. Moreover, he passed "through the midst of them". John is almost suggesting that Jesus made himself invisible, but he must be referring to the peculiar quality that surrounds a Master. They could not touch Jesus or cause him harm because he did not wish them to. The way he moved and everything else about him prevented them from hurting or restraining him. As John concludes his narration of another incident in the temple:

> These words spake Jesus in the treasury, as he taught in the temple: and no man laid hands on him; for his hour was not yet come.
>
> *John 8:20*

No one can even enter a Master's company, let alone harm him, if he does not wish it. Masters are supremely powerful and in full control of everything, even though they live within the will of God and are seen to obey the laws of nature.

Another incident of some significance which indicates Jesus' natural presence and authority is to be found in Matthew, copied over from Mark. Jesus is asked, "By what authority doest thou these things? And who gave thee this authority?"

> And when he was come into the temple, the chief priests and the elders of the people came unto him as he was teaching, and said, "By what authority doest thou these things? And who gave thee this authority?"
>
> And Jesus answered and said unto them, "I also will ask you one thing, which if ye tell me, I in like wise will tell you by what authority I do these things. The baptism of John, whence was it? From heaven, or of men?"
>
> And they reasoned with themselves, saying, "If we shall say, 'From heaven'; he will say unto us, 'Why did ye not then believe him?' But if we shall say, 'Of men'; we fear the people; for all hold John as a prophet."

And they answered Jesus, and said, "We cannot tell." And he said unto them, "Neither tell I you by what authority I do these things."

Matthew 21:23-27

What he means is that his authority is the same as that of John the Baptist and that if they did not believe John then they are not going to believe him either. As in so many instances, Jesus demonstrates remarkable diplomacy, self-possession and the ability to handle people, a characteristic of all true mystics. And this passage not only indicates that people believed the baptism of John to be of a heavenly nature – whatever that may mean – but it also raises the question of Jesus' relationship to the mysterious figure of John the Baptist.

NOTES AND REFERENCES

1. *John* 4:6, 11:35, 19:28.
2. Quoted in Ben Zion Bokser, *Jewish Mystical Tradition*, p.244.
3. *Luke* 13:32.
4. *Luke* 4:15*ff.*
5. *Luke* 4:29*ff.*

CHAPTER FIFTEEN

The Son of God:
A Burning and a Shining Light

Jesus and John the Baptist

A man once took his son on a journey to visit an elder of their community who was noted for his wisdom and sound advice. The man's son ate too much sugar and too many sweetmeats and he wanted the elder to convince the boy to relinquish the habit. When they reached the elder's home, the man explained the problem concerning his son. Without any hesitation the wise man responded: "Please return tomorrow at the same time."

The man and his son travelled home and the next day, they once again set out to visit the elder. When they reached his home, the elder said to the boy, "Young man, it is very unhealthy to eat so much sugar and sweets, you should try to give them up." Then he was silent.

The father was perplexed and also irritated. "But you could have told him that yesterday," he said, "instead of which we had to go all the way home and return again today."

The wise man replied, "Yes, but you see, I myself used to take a lot of sugar. So I thought that if I was going to advise someone else to give it up, I should at least be free of the habit for a day."

If we advise others to do something which we do not do ourselves, then it is unlikely to have much effect. As the saying is, example is better than precept. Masters are always perfect examples of everything they teach. Hence, if a Master is to teach the necessity of a Master, it is necessary for him to have a Master, too. Later followers characteristically like to portray their Master as if he had no Master, for they do not like to think that their Saviour was ever in need of help himself. But in order for a Master to convince others that in order to find the kingdom of God it is necessary to have a Master, he himself must have a Master. Otherwise, his own life would contradict his teaching and few discriminating people would believe him. As the gnostic writer of the *Tripartite Tractate* says:

> So that we might not be in doubt ... even the Son himself, who has the position of Redeemer of the Totality (creation), [received] redemption as well – he who had become man....
>
> Then, after he had first received redemption from the Word which had descended upon him, all the rest received redemption from him, namely those who had taken him to themselves. For those who received the one who had received redemption also received what was within him.
>
> *Tripartite Tractate 124-125, cf. NHS22 p.317*

Jesus, then, like all other Masters, would most certainly have had a Master and the individual most likely to have been his teacher was one who flits mysteriously in and out of the pages of the gospels – John the Baptist.

Sadly, little can be gleaned from the gospels of the life and teachings of John the Baptist and, apart from a passing comment in Josephus and his mention in the Mandaean writings, nothing else is known of him. Paul and the writers of the other New Testament documents never mention him at all. It does seem, however, that he had a close association with Jesus from his earliest years. According to an account found only in Luke, John also had a miraculous birth, to a pious and elderly couple who had never previously had a child, despite their desire for one. As Luke puts it:

> And they had no child, because that Elizabeth was barren, and they both were now well stricken in years.
>
> *Luke 1:7*

Moreover, again on the authority of Luke alone, Elizabeth and Jesus' mother Mary were cousins. In Luke's narrative, the angel Gabriel, who according to Jewish mythology acts as a messenger of God, tells Mary:

> And, behold, thy cousin Elizabeth, she hath also conceived a son in her old age: and this is the sixth month with her, who was called barren.
>
> *Luke 1:36*

Mary then goes to visit Elizabeth and stays with her for three months:

> And Mary abode with her about three months, and returned to her own house.
>
> *Luke 1:56*

If Jesus and John were related, as Luke claims, and John was only six months older than Jesus, it is highly likely that they played together as children. Certainly, one can presume that Mary and Elizabeth would have kept in touch and that the two boys would at least have known each other.

The other gospels tell us almost nothing of John, and the popular images of a wild man derived from the few sentences concerning him are almost certainly inaccurate. Where he lived, what he taught, how long his ministry was and so on are all matters of conjecture. However, the observation in the synoptic gospels that "all hold John as a prophet"[1] indicates that his teachings were of a mystical character, a supposition which is further supported by stories concerning Simon Magus and Dositheus, in the *Clementine Recognitions*, as well as by some of the sayings attributed to him in St John.

From John's gospel we also learn that at least one of Jesus' close disciples, Andrew, the brother of Peter, was a disciple of John the Baptist before meeting Jesus – or at least before knowing who Jesus was destined to become:

> Again the next day after John stood, and two of his disciples (with him), and looking upon Jesus as he walked, he saith, "Behold the Lamb of God!"
>
> And the two disciples heard him speak, and they followed Jesus. Then Jesus turned, and saw them following, and saith unto them, "What seek ye?" They said unto him, "Rabbi (which is to say, being interpreted, Master), where dwellest thou?"
>
> He saith unto them, "Come and see." They came and saw where he dwelt, and abode with him that day: for it was about the tenth hour. One of the two which heard John speak, and followed him, was Andrew, Simon Peter's brother.
>
> *John 1:29-40*

Jesus himself is full of praise for John the Baptist, as would any perfect disciple of a perfect Master. He says:

> He was a burning and a shining light:
>   and ye were willing for a season
>   to rejoice in his light.
>
> *John 5:35*

Jesus says that he was a perfect guide on the mystic path, "a burning and a shining light", but like all Masters, he only came for a season, for a "little while". Similarly, in Matthew, Jesus describes John as "a prophet and more than a prophet" and as a Messenger of God, a Middle Eastern term commonly used for the mystics:

> Jesus began to say unto the multitudes concerning John, "What went ye out into the wilderness to see? A reed shaken with the wind? But what went ye out for to see? A man clothed in soft raiment? Behold, they that wear soft clothing are in kings' houses. But what went ye out for to see? A prophet? Yea, I say unto you, and more than a prophet. For this is he, of whom it is written, 'Behold, I send my Messenger before thy face, which shall prepare thy way before thee.'"
>
> *Matthew 11:7-10*

John was neither a man of luxurious living, nor was he a "reed shaken by the wind". "John is no reed shaken by men's opinions like a reed swayed at the behest of every wind",[2] as the fourth-century Epiphanius explains it. A true mystic or prophet does not base his teachings on opinions or intellectual speculation, but on repeatable, verifiable, inner experience. Jesus' metaphor is thus aptly chosen. He then adds:

> "Verily I say unto you, among them that are born of women there hath not risen a greater than John the Baptist: notwithstanding he that is least in the kingdom of heaven is greater than he. And from the days of John the Baptist until now the kingdom of heaven suffereth violence, and the violent take it by force. For all the prophets and the law prophesied until John."
>
> *Matthew 11:11-13*

No one, he says, is greater than John the Baptist. Such is his power and grace that "from the days of John" people have been going back to God in great numbers – a comment supported by the many reports concerning the multitudes that came to listen to both John and Jesus. "For all the prophets and the law prophesied until John." All the prophets and mystics of the past have said that there will be Masters or Messengers in the future. This is what Isaiah, Jeremiah and the other Judaic prophets are talking about in those passages which have been taken to refer directly to Jesus. Isaiah and the others all had disciples of their own. What would have been the practical advantage in teaching their disciples about one particular Master who was going to come several hundred years in the future? How would it have helped? If one reads these passages in their context, it can be seen that they do not refer to any particular mystic of the future, but to all Masters, to all Messiahs.

"Notwithstanding, he that is least in the kingdom of heaven is greater than he" is an odd statement, since it contradicts Jesus' assertion of the sentence before. Nor does it mean anything in a mystical sense for all souls are equal before God. It seems likely, then, that this sentence is what scholars call a gloss, the addition of a later editor.

Just as Jesus praised his Master, so too did John praise his successor. There is a good reason for this. Unless a Master prepares his disciples for his successor, they will never accept the successor in his place. The love they bear for their own Master is personal, and however much they may know intellectually that the successor is also a perfect Master, they will still find it difficult to go to him and take the considerable advantage to be gained from his presence and guidance. Therefore, a Master will always praise his successor-to-be and may even hint to his disciples in advance who he will be. Consequently, we read in John's gospel:

> John bare witness of him (Jesus), and cried, saying, "This was he of whom I spake, He that cometh after me is preferred before me: for he was before me. And of his fullness have all we received, and grace for grace."
>
> *John 1:15-16*

And:

> The next day John seeth Jesus coming unto him, and saith, "Behold the Lamb of God, which taketh away the sin of the world. This is he of whom I said, After me cometh a man which is preferred before me: for he was before me."
>
> *John 1:29-30*

And again:

> John answered them, saying, "I baptize with water: but there standeth one among you, whom ye know not. He it is, who coming after me is preferred before me, whose shoe's latchet I am not worthy to unloose."
>
> *John 1:26-27*

And in Matthew, where his saying becomes:

> "I indeed baptize you with water unto repentance: but he that cometh after me is mightier than I, whose shoes I am not worthy to bear: he shall baptize you with the Holy Ghost, and with fire."
>
> *Matthew 3:11*

It must be recalled that John the Baptist is not speaking to us. He is speaking to his disciples. They already have faith in him and believe him to be the highest. They were, no doubt, correct, but John knew that he was to be beheaded and that they would still need further guidance and inspiration in this world. He did not want them to be deprived of the benefit of his successor's company through the influence of their own feelings and emotions. He therefore uses the strongest possible language to tell them about his successor and to persuade them to go to him. For his part, Jesus is acknowledging this responsibility to John the Baptist's disciples when he says:

> And other sheep I have, which are not of this fold: them also I must bring, and they shall hear my voice; and there shall be one fold, and one shepherd.
>
> *John 10:16*

Traditionally interpreted as the Gentiles, the "other sheep" would actually have been the Baptist's initiates, like Andrew and probably many others. Ultimately, all Masters are one, for they are all waves from the same Ocean. The disciples, too, will all return to that Ocean. Inside, they all become absorbed in the music and intoxication of the divine Word. All initiates, from whatever time and place, comprise one fold, for they are all being taken back to God by the one Shepherd of the Word. The closer the soul gets to God, the less divisions there are. All becomes one. From the highest point of view, there is one fold and one shepherd.

But at the human level, a Master, being supremely humble, will always praise his successor and request that everybody gives the same love to him which they did to himself. And, for his part, the successor will always praise his Master. We find this interplay going on when Jesus comes for his initiation:

> Then cometh Jesus from Galilee to Jordan unto John, to be baptized of him. But John forbad him, saying, "I have need to be baptized of thee, and comest thou to me?"
>
> And Jesus answering said unto him, "Suffer it to be so now: for thus it becometh us to fulfil all righteousness. Then he suffered him."
>
> *Matthew 3:13-15*

In his humility, John protests that he should be accepting Jesus as *his* Master, not the reverse. But Jesus persuades him, saying, "Thus it becometh us to fulfil all righteousness." He means that all Masters, even if they have come direct from God, must still take a Master and receive initiation. This is the way things are done in this world and this is what they have to do. But there is a difference between the baptism of a regular human being and that of a perfect soul who has descended from God. The one has a great burden of sins from many past lives weighing them down, while the other has no sins of their own and is free to go back to God, even while still living in the human form. Hence, in the stories of Jesus' baptism we read:

> And Jesus, when he was baptized, went up straightway out of the water. And, lo, the heavens were opened unto him, and he saw the Spirit of God descending like a dove, and lighting upon him. And lo a voice from heaven, saying, "This is my beloved Son, in whom I am well pleased."
>
> *Matthew 3:16-17*

Because he had come from God, with no sins of his own, as soon as Jesus received initiation, he had access to the inner heavens and to the Voice of God. Likewise, the other features of the baptism stories – the water and the "Spirit of God descending like a dove" and the "voice from heaven" – are mystic symbols which through the retelling have become externalized and literalized. The water is the Living Water of the Word, the peaceful and gentle dove is a symbol of spirituality that has been used in the Middle East for centuries, while the "voice from heaven" is the divine Music.

People see the Master according to their own cultural background and many of the Jews, especially at that turbulent time in their history, were living in expectation that the Messiah would come to solve all their problems. As Luke reports:

> The people were in expectation, and all men mused in their hearts of John, whether he were the Christ, or not.
>
> *Luke 3:15*

Human nature being as it is, there were many claimants to this title. The majority of people would have been quite unaware of what a real Messiah was, as indeed they are now. John and Jesus, on the other hand, would have understood. Hence, in a passage from John's gospel where the Baptist denies that he is the Christ, the expected Messiah or a perfect Master, it is only out of humility that he does so – unless he meant that he was not the Messiah according to Jewish expectations. It is only rarely that a Master will say who he really is and then usually only in a roundabout way. For it is not by words proclaiming themselves that their disciples become convinced of who and what their Master is. It is by an altogether deeper means. The passage reads:

> And this is the record of John, when the Jews sent priests and Levites from Jerusalem to ask him, "Who art thou?" And he confessed, and denied not; but confessed, "I am not the Christ." And they asked him, "What then? Art thou Elias?" And he saith, "I am not." "Art thou that prophet?" And he answered, "No."
>
> Then said they unto him, "Who art thou? That we may give an answer to them that sent us. What sayest thou of thyself?"
>
> He said, "I am the voice of one crying in the wilderness, make straight the way of the Lord," as said the prophet Esaias.
>
> *John 1:19-23*

John knows that the "priests and Levites" are not real seekers of God but are only checking him out for other reasons. He therefore replies diplomatically by quoting a saying of the prophet Isaiah. He says that he is a "voice ... crying in the wilderness" – that he is a mystic teacher of the Voice of God to souls lost in the wilderness of this world. He has come here to teach the straight path or way to God. So in a veiled way, like Jesus when asked the source of his authority, John does tell them who he is, but the priests do not understand what he means. On another occasion, when asked a similar question, he replies:

> "Ye yourselves bear me witness, that I said, 'I am not the Christ, but that I am sent before him.' He that hath the bride is the bridegroom: but the friend of the bridegroom, which standeth and heareth him, rejoiceth greatly because of the bridegroom's voice: this my joy therefore is fulfilled. He must increase, but I must decrease."
>
> *John 3:28-30*

Once again, it is out of humility that John says he is "not the Christ", for in the end he concurs that he is equal with Jesus when he says, "He must increase, but I must decrease". He means that his ministry as a Master is nearly over, for he knew that he would soon be beheaded. But Jesus' ministry has only just begun. He will therefore "increase". And he also says that Jesus is the "bridegroom" now: he has the bride, that is, he is now the one with God's mandate. But John, as the bridegroom's friend is very happy to see this, for this is the divine will and Masters are far above all human jealousy and power struggles.

The metaphor of the Master as the bridegroom is also used in connection with John when Jesus is asked why his disciples never fast, as
was the Jewish custom:

> Then came to him the disciples of John, saying, "Why do we and the
> Pharisees fast oft, but thy disciples fast not?"
>
> And Jesus said unto them, "Can the children of the bride-chamber
> mourn, as long as the bridegroom is with them? But the days will
> come, when the bridegroom shall be taken from them, and then shall
> they fast.
>
> "No man putteth a piece of new cloth unto an old garment, for that
> which is put in to fill it up taketh from the garment, and the rent is made
> worse. Neither do men put new wine into old bottles: else the bottles
> break, and the wine runneth out, and the bottles perish: but they put new
> wine into new bottles, and both are preserved."
>
> *Matthew 9:14-17*

Jesus says that when the children of the bride-chamber – the disciples
– are with the Master, the "bridegroom", they are very happy and feel
no need to give themselves to unnecessary rituals and ceremonies. But
when their Master leaves, then they are tempted to return to the rituals and ceremonies that they once practised. And he compares the
Master to a new piece of cloth or to new wine. New cloth and new
wine are treated as new and utilized for new garments or put into new
bottles. Likewise, the disciples and their Master are like something new.
They are fresh and vital with real inner life. They do not want to put
themselves into the old rituals and ceremonies from which they have
so recently escaped. If anyone tries to force them into such things, they
cannot tolerate it and they again break away from them. The old bottles
or the old garment break, for the disciples can no longer be contained
in them.

The problem, of course, with all these stories is that we have such
meagre information to go on – quite insufficient to reconstruct history – and, with the little that we have, we are unsure how much of it
is accurate and how much has been altered as it passed from one person to another. After all, these gospels were written down many decades after Jesus and John the Baptist lived, as we have remarked so
many times. Nevertheless, something of the truth can still be glimpsed
in the tradition that has been preserved.

Jesus' Successor

Just as John the Baptist paved the way for Jesus, so Jesus, too, when it came his turn to depart, made a point of preparing a way for his successor. Speaking of his impending death, he said:

> Now I tell you before it come, that, when it is come to pass, ye may believe that I am he. Verily, verily, I say unto you, he that receiveth whomsoever I send receiveth me; and he that receiveth me receiveth Him that sent me.
>
> *John 13:19-20*

He says that whoever he appoints to take his place after his death is just the same as himself and whoever receives this successor with love, actually receives his own Master.

Who Jesus' successor was also seems reasonably clear. From the very beginning of the gospel accounts, Jesus hinted that Peter would be the one to follow him. Contrary to popular conceptions, Peter was not without an exposure to spiritual matters prior to his meeting with Jesus, for his own brother was a disciple of John the Baptist.

In St John, we read that after John the Baptist had told Andrew that Jesus was the Christ or future Master, Andrew's immediate response was to go home and get his brother Peter. One imagines that he would only have done this if Peter had an interest in such things and it is possible, if not likely, that Peter, too, was a disciple of John. The narrative in St John reads:

> He (Andrew) first findeth his own brother Simon, and saith unto him, "We have found the Messias, which is, being interpreted, the Christ." And he brought him to Jesus. And when Jesus beheld him, he said, "Thou art Simon the son of Jona: thou shalt be called Cephas, which is by interpretation, 'a stone.'"
>
> *John 1:41-42*

Jesus gives him a nickname. Cephas is the Hebrew for a rock or a stone and Peter is the equivalent in Greek, the source of a wordplay which we find in an incident related in St Matthew which again reinforces the idea that Peter was his successor:

> When Jesus came into the coasts of Caesarea Philippi, he asked his disciples, saying, "Whom do men say that I the Son of man am?"

And they said, "Some say that thou art John the Baptist: some, Elias; and others, Jeremias, or one of the prophets."

He saith unto them, "But whom say ye that I am?" And Simon Peter answered and said, "Thou art the Christ, the Son of the Living God." And Jesus answered and said unto him, "Blessed art thou, Simon Barjona: for flesh and blood hath not revealed it unto thee, but my Father which is in heaven."

Matthew 16:13-16

Jesus asks his disciples who people think he is. They reply that some say he is the image of John the Baptist. This is what the disciples of John would have said, for they would have seen their own Master in Jesus. Others think he is the incarnation of one of the Jewish prophets in whom they had faith. But Peter says that he realizes Jesus to be the Son of God, to which Jesus responds:

And I say also unto thee, that thou art Peter,
  and upon this rock I will build my church;
And the gates of hell shall not prevail against it.

And I will give unto thee
  the keys of the kingdom of heaven:
And whatsoever thou shalt bind on earth
  shall be bound in heaven:
And whatsoever thou shalt loose on earth
  shall be loosed in heaven.

Matthew 16:17-20

Jesus says that he will build his "church", his "flock", the community of his disciples upon Peter, meaning that Peter is to be his successor. He makes this clear when he says that he will give the "keys to the kingdom of heaven" to Peter. The "keys" refer to the initiation into the "mysteries" of the "kingdom of heaven". Those who Peter will "bind on earth" will be "bound in heaven": those who are bound to the Word while in a human form will be taken back to God. And those who Peter will "loose on earth", those who he does not initiate, will not be "bound in heaven". They will not return to God, but will take another birth in this world. They will have nothing to bind them to God and will return here.

There is another interesting gospel passage which suggests that Peter was appointed by Jesus as his successor. It appears, however, in the last chapter of St John, chapter twenty-one, commonly considered by scholars to be a fraudulent addition. All the same, it can provide us with some valuable information. The chapter relates two post-resurrectional incidents, the first where Peter and the disciples go fishing and subsequently eat some fish, while the other follows on from this and concerns Jesus' appointment of Peter as his successor:

> So when they had dined, Jesus saith to Simon Peter, "Simon, son of Jonas, lovest thou me more than these?" He saith unto him, "Yea, Lord; thou knowest that I love thee." He saith unto him, "Feed my lambs."
>
> He saith to him again the second time, "Simon, son of Jonas, lovest thou me?" He saith unto him, "Yea, Lord; thou knowest that I love thee." He saith unto him, "Feed my sheep."
>
> He saith unto him the third time, "Simon, son of Jonas, lovest thou me?" Peter was grieved because he said unto him the third time, "Lovest thou me?" And he said unto him, "Lord, thou knowest all things; thou knowest that I love thee." Jesus saith unto him, "Feed my sheep."
>
> *John 21:15-17*

The interest centres around why such an insertion should have been made. Help in understanding this can be had from the immediately prior incident of the fish which relates to early Christian controversy over whether Jesus was vegetarian and is probably an insertion from the anti-vegetarian camp. We will take up this discussion later, but presuming similar reasons for inclusion of the story of Peter's appointment leads us to the interesting conclusion that there was also controversy over the true successor to Jesus, the incident being related to assert that it had been Peter. If so, who else claimed the position? There could, of course, have been claimants who were never recorded in any history or legend, but the most obvious possibility would seem to be James the brother of Jesus, for he is stated to have been the "Redeemer" after Jesus in some of the gnostic writings, such as the *Second Apocalypse of James*.

It is clear from Paul's letters that James was not always in accord with Peter, particularly over the practice of Jewish customs.[3] Moreover, James is never mentioned as one of Jesus' close disciples during his lifetime. In fact, John's gospel reports that none of Jesus' brothers believed in him:

> For neither did his brethren believe in him.
>
> *John 7:5*

One wonders, therefore, how James came to be known as the head of the church in Jerusalem after Jesus' departure? The records are once again contradictory and no certain conclusions can be drawn, but the principle of Mastership or Messiahship is certainly demonstrated, as well as the importance of genuine appointment by the predecessor.

It is at least possible, then, that John the Baptist, Jesus and Peter – all three of whom were executed – constituted a line of mystics. The historical data is admittedly scant, but otherwise it is hard to understand what the various sayings and traditions could mean.

If I Bear Witness of Myself

The problem is, of course, that it is not easy to recognize a real Master. It is difficult enough to enter into the being – and determine the motivations and degree of consciousness – of any other person, let alone one who is perfect, especially, when we ourselves are imperfect. So even if a Master were to claim to be so, that would not help us, for how could we be sure he was telling the truth? And peering across the gulf of centuries, provided only with sparse and unreliable information, the problem is almost intractable.

We are confronted, then, with our basic human condition – that of ignorance. Despite all our assertions, material or spiritual, we very rarely know for sure that we are right. In science, what seems right and proven beyond a doubt today, is discovered to be incorrect or at least inaccurate and incomplete tomorrow. In human affairs, we do not know the future nor even what will happen to us in the next two minutes. In relationships, we are usually unsure of what other people are thinking or what their motivations are or why they think and act the way they do. We know nothing, yet we may think we know a lot. Because our horizons are so limited as to what *can* be known, we are even ignorant of our own ignorance.

In mysticism, we only really know the truth of things through personal, direct, inner experience. But that experience cannot be conveyed to others by word of mouth or by other normal human means of communication. Consequently, the fact that a Master has experience of God does not automatically convince others. If a Master were to say that he had become one with God, rather than believe in him, most people of the world would be more likely to think that he had gone mad or had developed megalomaniac tendencies. How, then, can Masters convince others of their attainment and their duties in this world?

The answer is that they cannot, nor do they wish to. They have only come for their own allotted sheep and they have their own ways of providing those particular souls with enough conviction to enable them to start out upon the mystic path and in time to prove things for themselves through inner experience. In fact, only rarely will a Master even claim to be a Master, as we saw with John the Baptist, who denied being the Christ. Mostly, if asked, they are more likely to say that they are humble servants simply doing the task requested of them by their own Master.

They, more than anyone else, know that the world is full of people proclaiming themselves to be all sorts of things, which they may or may not be, but which people are quite unable to verify. Masters are not in the business of convincing others through force of character, by charisma or by whipping up peoples' emotions into a state of religious frenzy. They want people to discriminate for themselves and to do things from a sense of personal conviction and understanding. No Master is interested simply in collecting large numbers of disciples. Numbers are of no importance to them at all; rather, they are more likely to constitute a problem, and Masters sometimes do things that drive away all but the sincere and the discerning.

In the gospels, for example, Jesus is reported as saying and doing so many things which – if they are true – cannot have endeared him to the general run of people. Indeed, after Jesus had spoken about himself as the "Living Bread which came down from heaven", and had said that it was necessary to 'eat his flesh' and 'drink his blood'[4] in order to attain eternal life – a subject which we discuss more fully in a later chapter – the gospel writer relates:

> Many therefore of his disciples, when they had heard this, said, "This is a hard saying; who can hear it?"
>
> When Jesus knew in himself that his disciples murmured at it, he said unto them, "Doth this offend you? What and if ye shall see the Son of man ascend up where he was before? It is the Spirit that quickeneth; the flesh profiteth nothing: the words (Word) that I speak unto you, they are Spirit, and they are Life. But there are some of you that believe not."
>
> For Jesus knew from the beginning who they were that believed not, and who should betray him. And he said, "Therefore said I unto you, that no man can come unto me, except it were given unto him of my Father."
>
> From that time many of his disciples went back, and walked no more with him. Then said Jesus unto the twelve, "Will ye also go away?"
>
> Then Simon Peter answered him, "Lord, to whom shall we go? Thou

hast the words (Word) of eternal life. And we believe and are sure that thou art that Christ, the Son of the Living God."

John 6:60-69

Jesus knows that not everyone who listens to him is a sincere seeker, believing what he says. He knows who is meant for him and who is not. So he gives occasion to those who are doubtful, to leave him, feeling satisfied that they have done the right thing. They may come back later or even in another life, but for the time being it is better that they leave so that they do not disturb his sincere followers. And, according to the narrative, Jesus then asks his close disciples whether or not they are going to leave as well. But Peter is too wise. He knows that no one else has ever displayed such wisdom and given him so much inwardly, for no one else in the world has anything to compare with what a Master gives. So he realizes that he has nowhere else to go, even if sometimes he does not understand what his Master says or does. Hence, he says, "Lord, to whom else shall we go?" Whatever his feelings, even his doubts or misgivings, he has cast a shrewd eye over the world and all it has on offer, and can find no better path to follow and no individual more trustworthy.

Masters, of course, are deeply aware of our human situation and, bearing this in mind, they do give some indications of who they are and by what means a person can humanly satisfy himself concerning both the truth of their teachings as well as their personal authenticity. There are a few passages in St John where Jesus addresses this issue:

> If I bear witness of myself, my witness is not true.
> There is another that beareth witness of me;
> > and I know that the witness
> > which he witnesseth of me is true.
> Ye sent unto John, and he bare witness unto the truth....
> He was a burning and a shining light:
> > and ye were willing for a season to rejoice in his light.
>
> *John 5:31-33,35*

First of all, he acknowledges that those who bear witness of themselves, who claim themselves to be something or another, are usually unreliable. They should not be believed on their own account. So he cites as a witness his own Master, John the Baptist, in whom many people had faith. You have already asked John the Baptist, he says, and he has testified on my behalf, that I am his rightful successor. But John came only for a certain period, a certain "season", and now if you want what John had to offer, you have to come to me. Then he adds:

> But I receive not testimony from man:
>> but these things I say, that ye might be saved.
>>
>>> *John 5:34*

He says that he neither seeks nor needs man's approval or testimony in order to carry out his mission, even though his work is on behalf of man. He is simply offering salvation, if anyone should be interested. He continues:

> But I have greater witness than that of John:
>> for the works which the Father hath given me to finish,
>> the same works that I do, bear witness of me,
>> that the Father hath sent me.
> And the Father Himself, which hath sent me,
>> hath borne witness of me.
>>
>>> *John 5:36-37*

Jesus adds that the "works which the Father hath given me to finish", of taking souls back to God, are an even better witness than John the Baptist. For people can still disbelieve in John since they are at the human level and cannot tell from external appearances who he really is. But those who experience his "works", who are initiated and have been set upon the mystic path and have had their own experiences inside, they have the greatest witness of all. And the witness or proof that they receive is that God has sent him and is with him. But to the non-initiates, he says:

> Ye have neither heard His Voice at any time,
>> nor seen His shape.
> And ye have not His Word abiding in you:
>> for whom He hath sent, him ye believe not.
>>
>>> *John 5:37-38*

They have neither heard the Voice of God within themselves, nor have they seen God or seen the light within, because they have not been initiated into the Word. And the reason they have not received initiation is because they have not believed in the Master that God has sent. He continues:

> Search the scriptures;
> For in them ye think ye have eternal life:
>   and they are they which testify of me.
>
>   *John 5:39*

Then he cites another witness. If they really want to know about a Master, Jesus recommends that they "search the scriptures" in which they put their faith. He suggests that they read their own holy books very thoroughly and with understanding, for the writings of the mystics of the past always speak of future Masters and the path back to God through such Saviours or Messiahs. So the scriptures always "testify" of the Masters.

> And ye will not come to me, that ye might have life.
> I receive not honour from men.
> But I know you, that ye have not the love of God in you.
> I am come in my Father's name, and ye receive me not:
>   if another shall come in his own name, him ye will receive.
> How can ye believe, which receive honour one of another,
>   and seek not the honour that cometh from God only?
>
>   *John 5:40-44*

Jesus knows that they will not come to him, for they are not destined to do so and they have no real love for God within themselves, however well-placed within their religious organization they may be. He is not interested, he says, in receiving the short-lived acclaim of the people of this world. And he points out that when someone comes "in my Father's name" and teaches the straight and simple path to God, few people care to listen to him. But when someone comes and promotes himself and his own ideas, then there are always a great many who will gather around him.

People like to praise each other and receive commendation in return, to indulge in mutual back-slapping and ego-boosting. But they are only strengthening and promoting the cloud of illusion in which they live, removing themselves further and further from Reality. "How can ye believe, which receive honour one of another." When ego and self-importance are uppermost in a person's mind, then they can never find God. Only those who "seek ... the honour that cometh from God only" – those who seek the current of His grace and love – can ever hope to find the path that leads to Him.

Do not think that I will accuse you to the Father:
  there is one that accuseth you, even Moses, in whom ye trust.
For had ye believed Moses, ye would have believed me:
  for he wrote of me.
But if ye believe not his writings,
  how shall ye believe my words?

John 5:45-47

He repeats here, as elsewhere, that whatever people may do or think, he has not come to accuse, to judge or to condemn. For Moses himself, whom they claim to be their guide and prophet, is already accusing them in the sense that he has taught the same teaching that Jesus is giving and they are not understanding or following what he says. "If ye believe not *his* writings," he says, "How shall ye believe *my* words?" If you really understood what Moses said, then you would follow me, for – as he also said concerning Abraham – "he wrote of me", in the sense that he gave the same teaching that all Masters have given.

Since all Masters give their teachings from the mystics in whom people already have faith, so Jesus, who is talking to the Jews, draws upon the writings of Moses, Abraham, Isaiah and the other Jewish prophets of old. But naturally, people have developed their own ideas and dogmas around these teachings and formed them into a religion to which they have become tightly bound, however bizarre those dogmas may be. As a result, they cannot tolerate anyone who tries to tell them anything different.

This has been the fundamental cause of the persecution which mystics and their followers have had to face throughout recorded history. People get very edgy when their beliefs are challenged or even when they are asked to view their beliefs with a discriminating mind, for dogma rarely stands the test of reason. Mystic teachings on the other hand, when correctly taught and properly understood, are both logical and open to personal experimentation. No one is asked to take anything on blind faith. Mystic teaching is actually a pointer to a technique whereby the claims and tenets can be put to the test right now – not after death, when it is too late to choose another path.

In another dialogue from St John, Jesus again speaks of himself and his authority to teach. According to John's narrative:

Then spake Jesus again unto them, saying,
  "I am the light of the world:

he that followeth me shall not walk in darkness,
but shall have the light of life."

John 8:12

And Jesus is challenged:

> The Pharisees therefore said unto him,
> "Thou bearest record of thyself;
> thy record is not true."

John 8:13

But back comes the response:

> Jesus answered and said unto them,
> "Though I bear record of myself, yet my record is true:
> for I know whence I came, and whither I go;
> but ye cannot tell whence I come, and whither I go."

John 8:14

Jesus says here that if he does bear witness of himself, he knows what he is talking about and his "record is true". He knows that he has come from God and he knows how to return to Him. He knows Truth from beginning to end and is in a position to talk about himself. As he continues:

> Ye judge after the flesh; I judge no man.
> And yet if I judge, my judgment is true:
> for I am not alone,
> but I and the Father that sent me.

John 8:15-16

He judges nobody, yet if he does make any assessment of a person or situation, he does know what he is talking about, for he is one with the Creator of all. They, on the other hand, judge only by external appearances and according to their own preconceptions, knowing nothing about his inner life. They are therefore in no position to judge him. He then adds:

> "It is also written in your law,
> that the testimony of two men is true.

> I am one that bear witness of myself,
>   and the Father that sent me beareth witness of me."
>
> Then said they unto him, "Where is thy Father?"
> Jesus answered, "Ye neither know me, nor my Father:
>   if ye had known me, ye should have known my Father also."
>
> *John 8:17-19*

He says that according to Jewish law, two witnesses are required in order to establish the truth of a matter. To satisfy that requirement, he cites himself and God, for they both know who he really is. But again he points out that since they do not have access to God, they cannot really know who he is. Therefore, they cannot verify either the witness that he bears of himself, or that of God.

No Man Receiveth His Testimony

Everything that a Master says or does is a "testimony" or a witness to what he has experienced inside. He is not spinning out an intellectual philosophy but is describing what he himself has seen and heard with his inner sight and his inner hearing. Most people, however, do not receive this testimony from a Master. They treat it as just one of the many religious and intellectual systems that are always present in the world. This point is again made very clear in John's gospel where it is John the Baptist, this time (though the style and language remains that of John's gospel), who says:

> He that cometh from above is above all:
>   he that is of the earth is earthly,
>   and speaketh of the earth:
> He that cometh from heaven is above all.
> And what he hath seen and heard,
>   that he testifieth;
>   and no man receiveth his testimony.
>
> *John 3:31-32*

The Son of God, who "cometh from above", speaks only of his own personal inner experience, "what he hath seen and heard", but few people believe him.

He that hath received his testimony
    hath set to his seal that God is true.
For he whom God hath sent speaketh the words of God:
    for God giveth not the Spirit by measure unto him.
The Father loveth the Son,
    and hath given all things into his hand.

John 3:33-35

But the one who does receive the testimony of a Master comes to know for certain that God is the supreme Truth, for the Master "whom God hath sent" receives everything that the Father has. The Father does not give the grace of his Spirit "by measure" to the Son. There is no counting or measuring where the Lord is concerned. His love is infinite and is given without stint. And whatever is given to the Son is also given to his disciples, through him. As Jesus says, the Father "hath given all things into his hand".

He that believeth on the Son hath everlasting life:
    and he that believeth not the Son shall not see life;
    but the wrath of God abideth on him.

John 3:36

Souls are either turned towards God or towards the creation. There are only two possible directions. They are either moving away from Him, further into separation, or they are on the road to union with Him. In the Old Testament, separation from God is often called God's 'anger' or 'wrath', for there is no greater rebuttal than for God to seem to take His love away from a soul. Therefore, John the Baptist concludes, he that "believeth not the Son", will not find God, "but the wrath of God abideth on him" – he will remain in the creation, specifically in the realm of birth and death where all is misery and suffering. But the one who follows the Son of God "hath everlasting life": he will find the eternal source of Life within himself.

Notes and References

1. *Matthew* 21:26.
2. Epiphanius, *Panarion* I:II,26.7.4, *PES* p.88.
3. *Galatians* 2:11ff.
4. *John* 6:32ff.

CHAPTER SIXTEEN

A Man of Miracles?

Miracles

It is commonly believed that the lives of holy men and women are associated with miraculous events. This may be true, but the greatest miracle of all must surely be that God comes into the physical creation in the form of a man, a human personification of His creative Power. The Ocean encloses itself in a teapot and enters the sphere of humanity as a Master, bringing with him the supreme love of God and the grace to share it with all who are drawn to him. From being fully engrossed in the world, these souls are then turned around and become eager to find God. Man – born spiritually blind – is given spiritual vision by a Son of God and enabled to see clearly the illusion of this world and the path to God. This is most surely the greatest and most significant of all miracles that can come upon any soul.

Yet, being human, we have come to marvel at the miraculous only when it is reduced to material things. If someone receives the grace of God, such that their soul flies up into the higher realms – if anyone cares to believe them – we say they are blessed or fortunate and then we probably forget about it. Some intellectuals even try to explain away such experiences as distortions of the human psyche. But if some physical event takes place that seems to defy the laws of nature in the sensory world, then there is an immediate surge of curiosity and interest. True, many wish only to discredit the account, but the point is that the degree of our materiality is exposed by that in which we have the greater interest. However much we may claim to be spiritual seekers, the majority of us have far more interest in sensory phenomena than we do in the divine.

Miracles stories are a characteristic feature of the cults and religions that form around the teachings of past mystics. In many instances, the stories told are common to these different cults or religions, often very obviously borrowed from each other. The miracle story remains the same – only the name of the central character changes. Being fathered by God or by gods, virgin births, healing of sickness and infirmity of various kinds, miraculous provision of food and drink, control of the weather and the elements – these are not at all unusual in the folklore and legends that surround the mystics of the past. Professor Morton Smith once calculated that one hundred and twenty four miracles or claims to miraculous powers were attributed to Moses in the *Pentateuch*, thirty-eight to Elisha in *II Kings*, one hundred and seven to the Greek mystic and contemporary of Jesus, Apollonius of Tyana, in Philostratus' *Life of Apollonius of Tyana*, and more than two hundred to Jesus in the canonical gospels alone.[1] But, by absorbing it in glamour and in non-essentials, such legends only distract the mind from what is really important in a mystic's teachings.

Mystics, of course, are able to perform miracles of a physical and material nature. If they are one with God and one with His creative Power, then the 'secrets' of creation are an open book to them. If they can take birth in this world by their own will and organize their life according to the work they have to do, then it is true enough to say that there is nothing about such mystics which is not miraculous. Their consciousness is one with the supreme consciousness or being of God. Everything lies within themselves and within their power. They have the Power of God within them.

In fact, even an individual who can concentrate his mind to some extent, withdrawing it from the senses through ascetic or spiritual practices, develops the power to perform miracles. As Jesus said:

> If ye have faith as a grain of mustard seed,
>> ye shall say unto this mountain,
> "Remove hence to yonder place";
>> and it shall remove;
> And nothing shall be impossible unto you.
>> *Luke 17:20*

And also:

> If ye had faith as a grain of mustard seed,
>> ye might say unto this sycamine (mulberry) tree,
> "Be thou plucked up by the root,

and be thou planted in the sea;
And it should obey you."

Luke 17:6

This world, through the operations of *karma*, is spun out by the mind. Even sensory phenomena are really aspects or experiences of the mind, as is the body itself, and when the mind is sufficiently controlled and concentrated, the sensory world can be increasingly manipulated at will. But control of the mind and an increase in faith and surrender to God develop naturally together. Mystics have often pointed out that the performance of miracles is a path of egotism, of setting up one's own will in opposition to God's will, and mystics of a higher order do not indulge in such displays. They look on them as party tricks, distractions or seductions to way-lay seekers on their inner journey, catching them by their curiosity and pulling them from the narrow path that leads to God. The Negative Power, Satan or the Universal Mind, has a trap for every kind of individual, whether they be materially- or spiritually-minded.

Jesus' Miracles According to Mark, Matthew and Luke

Nevertheless, the gospels record that Jesus performed not just one or two miracles, but hundreds if not thousands of them. Mark, Matthew and Luke, in particular, record in a number of separate places that he healed *all* those who were brought to him, from all the surrounding areas and countries. The gathering must have been multinational as well as multilingual:

And Jesus went about all Galilee, teaching in their synagogues, and preaching the gospel of the kingdom, and healing all manner of sickness and all manner of disease among the people. And his fame went throughout all Syria: and they brought unto him all sick people that were taken with divers diseases and torments, and those which were possessed with devils, and those which were lunatic, and those that had the palsy; and he healed them. And there followed him great multitudes of people from Galilee, and from Decapolis, and from Jerusalem, and from Judaea, and from beyond Jordan.

Matthew 4:23-25

And again:

And when they had passed over, they came into the land of Gennesaret, and drew to the shore. And when they were come out of the ship, straightway they knew him, and ran through that whole region round about, and began to carry about in beds those that were sick, where they heard he was.

And whithersoever he entered, into villages, or cities, or country, they laid the sick in the streets, and besought him that they might touch if it were but the border of his garment: and as many as touched him were made whole.

Mark 6:53-56

Matthew, of course, does not fail to comment that all these miracles were being performed "that it might be fulfilled which was spoken by Esaias the prophet":

When the even was come, they brought unto him many that were possessed with devils: and he cast out the spirits with his word (Word), and healed all that were sick: that it might be fulfilled which was spoken by Esaias the prophet, saying, "Himself took our infirmities, and bare our sicknesses."

Matthew 8:16-17; cf. Isaiah 53:4

The gospels contain a number of other similar assertions concerning the many miracles of Jesus. It is noteworthy, however, that a high proportion of the specific miracles related by the three synoptic writers are to be found in Mark's gospel, which is almost certainly the primary written source of these particular tales. The healing of "Simon's wife's mother" who "lay sick of a fever",[2] of a "leper ... beseeching him",[3] of "one sick of the palsy",[4] of a man "which had a withered hand",[5] Jesus asleep in the boat and awakening to calm a "great storm of wind",[6] the healing of the Gadarene demoniac,[7] the raising from the dead of the daughter of Jairus, one of the "rulers of the synagogue" (*i.e.* a synagogue official), into which is inserted the healing of a "woman with an issue of blood twelve years",[8] of an epileptic "who foameth, and gnasheth with his teeth",[9] and of a blind man at Jericho[10] – all these occur in Mark, Matthew and Luke.

The major variations are Matthew's change to the healing of the paralytic man (Mark and Luke have him let down through the roof, but Matthew has him brought in through the door), while the one blind man and the single demoniac of Mark and Luke become two apiece in Matthew. Additionally, Mark, followed by Matthew, tells the story of the cursing of the barren fig-tree,[11] introduces a second "loaves and fishes" story in the feeding of the four thousand[12] and relates that Jesus cast out a devil from the "young daughter" of "a Greek, a Syro-Phoenician" woman.[13] But Luke does not follow them. Perhaps he felt that the spurious cursing and killing of a fig-tree because it failed to provide out-of-season fruit for Jesus was too far-fetched. He must have thought that Jesus would never have been so petulant or so ignorant of the seasons. His omission of the second and almost identical feeding of the multitude was probably on grounds of space, which his constant paraphrasing and shortening show that he was anxious to conserve. And as regards the story of the Syro-Phoenician woman's daughter, where Jesus at first refuses to heal the girl because the woman is not a Jew, Luke, with his gospel for the gentiles, must have felt the story not only to be inappropriate for his purposes but also uncharacteristic of the all-loving Jesus.

Blindness, deafness, dumbness, paralysis, leprosy and so on require no medical skill to diagnose and name, and the synoptic writers seem eager to include stories of healing from all such easily recognizable conditions. Mark has the healing of a deaf man[14] and a blind man at Bethsaida.[15] Matthew and Luke relate stories concerning the healing of a dumb man[16] and the healing of the paralysed servant of a Roman centurion.[17] Luke tells the tale of how Jesus healed ten lepers[18] simultaneously and raised from death the only son of a widow,[19] while Matthew adds a second story concerning the healing of two more blind men.[20]

Mark, then, is the foremost recorder of miracle stories in the synoptic gospels. Nine out of his fourteen miracle stories are related almost verbatim by Matthew and Luke and a further three are copied across by Matthew. Matthew and Luke between them only supply five further stories, all of which are repeats to one extent or another of Mark's prior pattern.

Who, then, was Mark? How much reliance can be placed upon his narration? And where did he get his stories from? The honest answer, as we have seen, is that nobody really knows. All we can say is that the compiler of Mark's gospel seems to have been far more interested in miracle stories than in Jesus' actual teachings. The rationale he presents for believing in his version of Jesus' life and teachings is, "Look at all the miracles he performed." After relating these stories, briefly interspersed with fragments of Jesus' teachings and apocalyptic messages, he moves on to the passion, the crucifixion and the resurrection. His terse message is that the Messiah came, proved who he was by his miracles and by rising from the dead, and that he will soon be coming again at an imminent ending of the world. Everyone should therefore repent, be baptized and get ready for his coming.

Whoever Mark was, the last thing he expected was that his gospel would become the focus of belief for the next two thousand years. As far as he was concerned, the last times were already at hand and he did not expect there to be another two thousand years. One can only surmise what his reaction would have been if he had known that future scholars and others would pore over his words, trying to extract from them the last ounce of meaning and information.

Jesus' Miracles According to John

The compiler of John's gospel has a different approach to Jesus' miracles. To begin with, he relates only seven miracles, each one having been very carefully selected. Like Mark they are also depicted as signs that Jesus is the Son of God. Further, although he does suggest at one place that Jesus performed "many miracles"[21] (unless this is a later interpolation), at no point does he say that Jesus went about healing everybody of all and every kind of disease. On the contrary, Jesus comes to the pool of Bethesda and sees a "great multitude of impotent folk, of blind, halt, withered". But while there is little doubt that Mark would have had them all *cry out* to Jesus for help, followed by his healing them all, in John's story, Jesus singles out one man only and *asks* him if he would like to "be made whole":

> Now there is at Jerusalem by the sheep market a pool, which is called in the Hebrew tongue Bethesda, having five porches. In these lay a great multitude of impotent folk, of blind, halt, withered, waiting for the moving of the water. For an angel went down at a certain season into the pool, and troubled the water: whosoever then first after the troubling of the water stepped in was made whole of whatsoever disease he had.
>
> And a certain man was there, which had an infirmity thirty and eight years. When Jesus saw him lie, and knew that he had been now a long time in that case, he saith unto him, "Wilt thou be made whole?"
>
> *John 5:2-5*

The man is subsequently healed and one is left to presume that the others were left just as they were. John, aware that one good story beats by far a multitude of loose ones, also makes each of his seven carefully chosen stories into a cameo, thereby heightening the 'wonder' element of each miracle. The man at the pool of Bethesda had been sick for *thirty-eight years* without improvement, and had never been able to get down to the water in time.

Similarly, John's 'raising from the dead' story outdoes all the others. Lazarus has not just died, he has been dead *four days* and as his sister Martha points out, "Lord, by this time he stinketh".[22] John is nothing if not graphic, for at Jesus' command Lazarus then "came forth, bound hand and foot with grave clothes: and his face was bound about with a napkin".[23] The scene is worthy of the grizzliest horror story. Again, when John has Jesus heal a blind man, it is not just someone who has recently suffered a deterioration of sight. It is the most difficult of all cases, a man "which was blind from his birth".[24]

But perhaps the most significant of all the differences in John's approach to Jesus' miracles is that he uses three out of his seven as a platform to give Jesus' teachings. While in the synoptic gospels, Jesus only upbraids the people for their lack of faith or praises them for the faith which has resulted in their being healed, John makes the story of the feeding of the five thousand into the starting point for the discourse on the true "Bread from heaven".[25] Similarly, the man who was blind from birth becomes the focus of a discourse on spiritual blindness, while the raising of Lazarus is at the centre of a discussion on death and resurrection. Additionally, a comment from a certain Nicodemus concerning Jesus' ability to perform miracles being proof that he is a "teacher come from God", leads into a short discourse on being spiritually "born again".[26]

Furthermore, it cannot be without significance that John's remaining miracle stories all seem to possess a symbolic meaning, as with many of the incidents related in his gospel, just as the story of the woman at the well is an integral part of the discourse on Living Water. The man at the pool of Bethesda, for example, is *chosen* by Jesus for healing out of a multitude of sick people, symbolic of the few souls that are drawn to a Master out of the many spiritually sick people of this world who have been here for so long a time. Even the place of his healing, "having five porches" may be symbolic of the "five trees" or mansions of the Word where true healing takes place. Likewise, the miracle of turning water into wine at a marriage feast has a symbolic meaning, the discussion of which is deferred until the next chapter.

Only three of John's seven miracles appear in the synoptic gospels and, of these, two are modified. The paralysed servant of a Roman centurion of Capernaum in Matthew and Luke becomes the fevered son of a nobleman in John,[27] though other elements of the story are identifiably the same. In John's version of the feeding of the five thousand, the "loaves" gain a touch of character, becoming "barley loaves".[28] Only his story of Jesus' walking on the water remains essentially the same.[29]

But altogether, the compiler of John's gospel brings in his miracles with great circumspection. He does not spread them around liberally and gratuitously like Mark, Matthew and Luke. In the total structure and message of his gospel, each miracle is made to play a definitive part. In fact, according to John, Jesus himself decries the importance of miracles. In Matthew and Luke, for instance, the centurion of Capernaum is praised for his faith:

> When Jesus heard it, he marvelled, and said to them that followed, "Verily I say unto you, I have not found so great faith, no, not in Israel."
>
> *Matthew 8:10*

But in John, the nobleman receives a rebuke for wanting a sign:

> Then said Jesus unto him,
> "Except ye see signs and wonders,
>   ye will not believe."
>
> *John 4:48*

Elsewhere in Mark, however, Jesus comments adversely upon those who want to gain faith through witnessing miracles, as in his response to the man with an epileptic son:

> "O faithless generation, how long shall I be with you?
> How long shall I suffer you? Bring him unto me."
>
> *Mark 9:19*

And to the Pharisees:

> And the Pharisees came forth, and began to question with him, seeking of him a sign from heaven, tempting him. And he sighed deeply in his spirit, and saith, "Why doth this generation seek after a sign? Verily I say unto you, there shall no sign be given unto this generation."
>
> *Mark 8:11-12*

In fact, despite all the miracles which Mark attributes to him, Jesus seems to have had an aversion to performing miracles and to knowledge of them being made public. In many places, he specifically instructs the fortunate recipients of his miracles to tell no one about it, though the reverse is usually the result:

> And he charged them that they should tell no man: but the more he charged them, so much the more a great deal they published it.
>
> *Mark 7:36*

As fascinating as it may be to witness physical miracles, the simple fact is that miracles in themselves do not confer spirituality. Spirituality comes through spiritual practice, through purification of the mind and the cleansing of its myriad impure tendencies, freeing it from the force of many ingrained habits. How can simply witnessing a miracle do that? Nor do miracles confer true faith in and reliance on God. Faith in God develops naturally as the ego is worn down. How can this happen by seeing a miracle?

What helps a person is personal experience within themselves. Sometimes, it is true, a Master does perform what we might call a miracle on behalf of a disciple, but that miracle is personal and is tailored exactly to that individual's need. It matches their stage of development and trend of mind so precisely that the personal message of that miracle is driven firmly home. That can help to generate faith in that individual. But it is a special and personal grace from Master to disciple and is meant to be kept private. As soon as a person begins to talk about it, then their ego comes into play and they start to lose whatever they have been given. This is why we hear that Jesus never wanted people to broadcast what he had done for them. It was not only his humility and desire to avoid notoriety, but also his desire that those he had helped should reap the maximum benefit.

Moreover, in a world where there will never be any lack of illness and suffering, physical cures are, by nature, temporal. Jesus made no claim to solve the perennial problem of sickness and in any case those whom Jesus is said to have cured of physical ailments would all have died within a few decades at the most. The help given by a perfect Master is always both spiritual and lasting, and his real impact upon such souls would have been spiritual and permanent.

As for second-hand miracle stories – a narration of other people's experiences – passed from one person to another, changing as time goes by, little benefit is to be gained from them. They are more likely to attract attention to the physical world, turning the mind away from God. For in all such circumstances, it is the impact upon the individual concerned at that particular point in his spiritual evolution which constitutes the reason why the Master performed the miracle. And that personal impact, not even the recipient himself can convey to others, should he even want to.

It seems most likely, therefore, that the miracles stories told of Jesus are greatly exaggerated. He may have performed some miracles, but not as many as are attributed to him and not in such a public manner. Even from an analysis of the stories themselves, one becomes dubious of their authenticity, as we have already seen. Additionally, Masters are great artists of subtlety and never make an exhibition of themselves, nor do they try to generate faith by such displays. But miracle stories do get told and passed on, becoming amplified and externalized in the process. This is in the nature of the human mind.

Apostolic Miracles

Mark, followed by Matthew and Luke, reports that not only did Jesus himself perform miracles, but so did his disciples. When Jesus sends his apostles to go and give spiritual discourses, Mark claims that he also gave them the power to effect cures, cast out devils and so on. John, however, makes no such comment. In fact, he indicates that even John the Baptist "did no miracle".[30]

No specific apostolic miracles are described in the gospels, but in *Acts*, as well as in practically all the apocryphal writings concerning the apostles, they continue in the synoptic tradition, healing all and everybody. Likewise, their miracles and those of Jesus become one of the key factors in proving that their preaching was correct and that Jesus was the Son of God. The compiler-writer of *Acts* claims, for example:

> By the hands of the apostles were many signs and wonders wrought among the people.... And believers were the more added to the Lord, multitudes both of men and women. Insomuch that they brought forth the sick into the streets, and laid them on beds and couches, that at the least the shadow of Peter passing by might overshadow some of them.
>
> There came also a multitude out of the cities round about unto Jerusalem, bringing sick folks, and them which were vexed with unclean spirits: and they were healed every one.
>
> *Acts 5:12,14-16*

Many apostolic miracles are also related in the apocryphal writings, where perhaps one of the most entertaining is Peter's raising of a sardine from the dead which he had seen hanging in a shop window. Such stories exemplify the extent to which imagination can take over!

> And Peter turned and saw a herring (sardine) hung in a window, and took it and said to the people: "If ye now see this swimming in the water like a fish, will ye be able to believe in him whom I preach?" And they said with one voice: "Verily we will believe thee."
> Then he said – now there was a bath for swimming at hand: "In thy name, O Jesu Christ, forasmuch as hitherto it is not believed in, in the sight of all these, live and swim like a fish." And he cast the herring into the bath, and it lived and began to swim. And all the people saw the fish swimming, and it did not so at that hour only, lest it should be said that it was a delusion (phantasm), but he made it to swim for a long time, so that they brought much people from all quarters and showed them the herring that was made a living fish, so that certain of the people even cast bread to it: and they saw that it was whole.
> And seeing this, many followed Peter and believed in the Lord.
>
> *Acts of Peter III:XIII, ANT p.316*

Paul, too, who is really the central character of *Acts* and the reason for the writer's compilation of it, is credited with many miracles. In fact, the writer declares that Paul had special gifts of healing:

> God wrought special miracles by the hands of Paul: so that from his body were brought unto the sick, handkerchiefs or aprons, and the diseases departed from them, and the evil spirits went out of them.
>
> *Acts 19:11-12*

Paul also heals a man who had been a cripple since birth,[31] cures the son of a chief of his fever,[32] remains unaffected by the bite of a viper[33] and raises a young man from the dead who, having fallen asleep during one of Paul's discourses, had fallen out of a third-storey window and been killed.[34]

This all makes for entertaining and romantic reading but one cannot help but wonder at its authenticity for when we turn to Paul's letters for some verification of these miracles, we can find absolutely none. He does speak, it is true, of those amongst his groups of converts who have the power to perform miracles, but he mentions it as one of a number of psychic 'gifts', such as talking with tongues, prophecy and so on. He certainly makes no claim to possessing such a faculty himself and the gift of miracles as he describes it seems to be more in the line of what people these days call a laying on of hands. It is certainly not in the same class as the miracles described in the gospels and in *Acts*.

In fact, the contrast between the style of Paul's letters and that of *Acts* is considerable. His letters come across as the writings of a real person, writing to real people about real problems, trying to convince them of things he most fervently believed in. They ring true as genuine letters. The events he describes sound real, while much of *Acts* has a rather romantic air about it.

Moreover, although Paul describes many things in his letters which he has said and done, he never mentions having performed any miracles. Indeed, quite apart from healing everybody he meets (with or without a handkerchief), he speaks quite candidly of his own serious illness and even that of his companions. If Paul had the power to perform miracles, he certainly did not use it on himself or his friends. In *2 Corinthians*, he speaks of a particular chronic complaint, a "thorn in the flesh", of which he cannot rid himself, despite his prayer before God:

> And lest I should be exalted above measure through the abundance of
> the revelations, there was given to me a thorn in the flesh, the messenger
> of Satan to buffet me, lest I should be exalted above measure. For this
> thing I besought the Lord thrice, that it might depart from me.
>
> *2 Corinthians 12:7-8*

He takes his illness in a positive spirit as part of the Lord's means of keeping him humble because of all his "revelations", but he is clearly unable to shift the problem. Whether it was sciatica, rheumatism, or something more dramatic such as epilepsy, is never made clear. He also seems to have extended his stay amongst the Galatians due to illness, probably this same complaint, taking the opportunity to preach to them, though at the time of writing his letter, he seems to have fallen out of their favour:

> You have never treated me in an unfriendly way before; even at the
> beginning, when that illness gave me the opportunity to preach the Good
> News (gospel) to you, you never showed the least sign of being revolted
> or disgusted at my disease that was such a trial to you; instead you
> welcomed me as an angel of God, as if I were Jesus Christ himself. What
> has become of this enthusiasm you had?
>
> *Galatians 4:12-15, JB*

In another letter, he speaks of a friend "who almost died":

> It is essential, I think, to send brother Epaphroditus back to you. He was
> sent as your representative to help me when I needed someone to be my
> companion in working and battling, but he misses you all and is worried
> because you heard about his illness. It is true that he has been ill, and
> almost died, but God took pity on him, and on me as well as him, and
> spared me what would have been one grief on top of another.
>
> So I shall send him back as promptly as I can; you will be happy to see
> him again and that will make me less sorry. Give him a most hearty
> welcome, in the Lord; people like him are to be honoured. It was for
> Christ's work that he came so near to dying, and he risked his life to give
> me the help that you were not able to give me yourselves.
>
> *Philippians 2:25-30, JB*

How different, then, are these real missives from the hyperbole of *Acts*
and certain parts of the gospels. Again, we are led to the conclusion
that – at best – the miracle stories are the result of some fact plus a
great deal of imagination and later elaboration.

Blind in Their Hearts

Perhaps the point of greatest significance in a study of these miracles
is that practically all of them, whether in St John or the synoptics, are
also used by the mystical writers of the time – and often by Jesus, too –
as metaphors for spiritual truths. We are all spiritually blind, deaf and
dumb. We are crippled and have forgotten how to walk straight in this
world. We are carrying a heavy burden of weaknesses and sins from
which we need to be healed. Our will power is paralysed and withered
by our attraction to the world of the senses. In fact, we have become
spiritually dead and full of darkness – we need to be raised from the
dead, to come out of the tomb of the body, not after four days but after
many ages. Spiritually, we "stinketh" with the accumulated sins of
many lifetimes!

To accomplish this, we need a spiritual physician to help us to overcome the feverish activities of the mind, to learn how to walk upon
the stormy waters of this world, to cast out the devils and demons of
human weakness from within ourselves and to overcome the Devil
himself. With the help of a Son of God, we must bathe in the pool of
Living Water and come up healed after many years of infirmity without

anyone having previously helped us to take that dip. We need to eat the true Bread of Life and to drink the wine of divine love at the marriage of the soul with God.

As we have observed so many times before, the Masters come and give their pure and spiritual teachings, but soon after their departure and even during their lifetime, the human mind takes over, externalizing and literalizing the mystic truths they teach. It would come as no surprise, then, were we to discover the real history of the New Testament writings, if the stories concerning many of Jesus' supposed miracles turned out to be externalizations of spiritual realites.

There are many hints of this amongst his extant sayings. For example, like many other mystics, he describes the people of this world as blind. He referred to the Pharisees as "ye blind guides",[35] "ye fools and blind",[36] and "blind leaders of the blind",[37] adding that "if the blind shall lead the blind, both shall fall into the ditch".[38] And in the *Gospel of Thomas*, he speaks of the whole world as blind:

> My soul grieveth over the sons of men,
>> because they are blind in their heart and see not.
>> *Gospel of Thomas 28, OLAG p.5; cf. NHS20 p.65*

More enigmatically, in St John, he says:

> For judgment I am come into this world,
>> that they which see not might see;
>> and that they which see might be made blind.
>> *John 9:39*

"They which see not" are those who, having eyes for the world, see and understand nothing of spiritual realities. They only see the world. Jesus says that he has come to make them blind to the world and open their inner eyes to God. Similarly, in Matthew, when asked why he uses parables so much as a means of giving spiritual teachings, he observes:

> Therefore speak I to them in parables:
>> because they seeing see not;
>> and hearing they hear not,
>> neither do they understand.
>> *Matthew 13:13*

He speaks in metaphors because the majority of people would not understand him even if he spoke the truth plainly, and he goes on to paraphrase the mystic Isaiah (Esaias) who said the same thing:

> And in them is fulfilled the prophecy of Esaias,
>   which saith,
> "By hearing ye shall hear,
>   and shall not understand;
>   and seeing ye shall see, and shall not perceive:
>
> "For this people's heart is waxed gross,
>   and their ears are dull of hearing,
>   and their eyes they have closed;
>   Lest at any time they should see with their eyes,
>   and hear with their ears,
>   and should understand with their heart,
>   and should be converted, and I should heal them."
>
>   *Matthew 13:14-15, Isaiah 6:9-10*

Jesus is speaking of spiritual blindness and spiritual deafness. People see and hear a mystic or come into contact with his teachings even in their own sacred writings, but they do not understand – "hearing ye shall hear, and shall not understand; seeing ye shall see, and shall not perceive". And the reason for this is that the mind or heart has "waxed gross and their ears are dull of hearing" – the mind has become obsessed with the gross things of the world of the material senses. It is this alone that prevents the otherwise pure soul from automatically understanding the spiritual reality, from turning the attention towards God – from being "converted" – and from being healed, not of physical infirmities, but of the spiritual disease which covers the soul in blemishes, the 'disease' of sin.

Because Jesus knows that he has given spiritual eyes and ears to his disciples so that they may see and hear within themselves, he adds, as we have noted before:

> But blessed are your eyes, for they see:
>   and your ears, for they hear.
> For verily I say unto you,
>   that many prophets and righteous men
>   have desired to see those things which ye see,

and have not seen them;
and to hear those things which ye hear,
and have not heard them.

Matthew 13:16-17

The writer of John's gospel also quotes the same passage from Isaiah. But he presents it as a prophecy concerning Jesus, though in its original context it is evident that Isaiah is speaking generally of the condition of man and man's response to himself and to all mystics:

He (God) hath blinded their eyes,
and hardened their heart;
that they should not see with their eyes,
nor understand with their heart,
and be converted, and I should heal them.

John 12:40, Isaiah 6:9-10

Again, this time according to Luke, Jesus quotes another passage from Isaiah where he says:

The Spirit of the Lord is upon me,
because he hath anointed me
to preach the gospel to the poor;
He hath sent me to heal the brokenhearted,
to preach deliverance to the captives,
and recovering of sight to the blind,
to set at liberty them that are bruised,
to preach the acceptable year of the Lord.

Luke 4:18-19, Isaiah 61:1-2

Isaiah is an "anointed" one, a true Messiah of his time, appointed by God to teach the real seekers of spirituality. The "poor" are the "poor in Spirit", the humble. The "brokenhearted" are those who long for the Lord but are heavily oppressed by the darkness of this world within themselves. They are "captives" in this world to whom Isaiah, Jesus and all such mystics bring "deliverance". They restore spiritual "sight to the blind", "set at liberty them that are bruised" and buffeted from being a slave of their sins. And they teach that the "acceptable year of the Lord", the best time to find and worship Him, is right now.

The Physician of Souls

Outside the New Testament, there is no doubt that in many instances the miracles of Jesus are taken, not as physical miracles, but as symbols for the spiritual healing of the soul. One of the commonest expressions for the Master, for example, is the "Physician of souls" and it is made apparent that, unlike the transitory healing of the temporal body, the healing given by this Physician is of an entirely spiritual and eternal nature. Hence, in the *Acts of Thomas*, Judas Thomas says:

> Why marvellest thou at his cures of the body
> which are ended by dissolution (death)?
> Especially when thou knowest that healing of his
> which passeth not away....
> And why lookest thou unto this temporal life,
> and hast no thought of that which is eternal?
>
>   *Acts of Thomas 78, AAA p.215, ANT p.400*

And Mygdonia, a devotee of Judas Thomas, is describing him when she says:

> He is a Physician of souls,
> and is different from all other physicians:
> For all other physicians do heal bodies that are dissolved,
> but he – souls that are not destroyed.
>
>   *Acts of Thomas 95, AAA p.228, ANT p.406*

Similarly, in the *Doctrine of Addai the Apostle*, Addai refers to Jesus as:

> The Physician of troubled souls,
> and the Saviour of future life,
> the Son of God, who came down from heaven,
> and was clothed with a body and became man.
>
>   *Doctrine of Addai the Apostle, DAA p.18*

While a Manichaean-Christian psalmist speaks of him as:

> Jesus, the Physician of the wounded,
> the Redeemer of the living souls,
> the Path which the wanderers seek,
> the Door of the Treasure of Life.
>
>   *Psalm CCXIX, MPB p.2*

And in a similar psalm which alludes specifically to Jesus' miracles, but gives them a spiritual meaning:

> The Son of the Living God,
>> the Physician of souls....
>
> The Father who is in the Son,
>> the Son who is in the Father....
>
> He revived the dead
>> from the death of their sins.
>
> He opened the eyes that were closed
>> at the time of the man born blind.
>
> He caused the ears of the unhearing soul to hear.
>
>> *Psalms of Heracleides, MPB pp.193-194*

Spiritually, almost all souls are born blind. They are also spiritually dead due to their burden of sins. It is the "Physician of souls", says the writer, who raises them from this death, opens their eyes and makes the "unhearing soul" hear the music of the Word.

This spiritual Physician also charges no fee. He is the "Physician who healest freely". In the *Acts of John*, John says:

> Now is the time of refreshment
>> and of confidence toward thee, O Christ;
>
> Now is the time for us who are sick
>> to have the help that is of thee,
>> O Physician who healest freely;
>
> Keep thou mine entering in hither safe from derision.
>
>> *Acts of John 22, ANT p.231*

Help, healing and "entering in hither" – entering the higher realms – are all held to be in the hands of this "Physician". Judas Thomas also describes Jesus in a similar vein:

> O Companion and ally of the feeble;
>
> Hope and confidence of the poor (in spirit)....
>
> Physician that healest without payment....
>
> Thou didst descend into Sheol (this world) ✗ *netherworld?*
>> with mighty power,
>> and the dead saw thee and became alive....

Be unto them a Guide in the land of Error:
Be unto them a Physician in the land of sickness:
Be unto them a rest in the land of the weary:
    make them pure in a polluted land,
Be their Physician both of bodies and souls:
    make them holy shrines and temples of thee,
    and let thy Holy Spirit dwell in them.

Acts of Thomas 156, AAA pp.288-289, ANT pp.432-433

Heal Us from Our Sins

It is, of course, human weakness and the sins or debts of countless past lives which constitute the disease of the soul, as many of these ancient writers have indicated. The writer of the gnostic, *Tripartite Tractate*, for instance, says just this when he states unequivocally that "passion is sickness",[39] while a Manichaean-Christian psalmist writes that souls die "from the wounds and lesions of greed and lust". Then it is Jesus, he says, the life-giving Master, who raises them from this death:

Blessed and praised be Jesus, the vivifier,
    the New *Aeon*, the true raiser of the dead;
Who indeed is the mother giving life
    to those who have died from the wounds
    and lesions of greed and lust;
And the healer of those who have become unconscious
    through the illness of the body of death.

BBB, ML p.65

Souls "become unconscious" through being reborn into the "body of death", says the writer. Then they forget who they are and from where they have come. This is the "illness" of the soul. Rebirth in this world takes place because of the sins and debts of the past and, as we find in early Christian poetry from Syria, healing comes about when the "Physician of the Height" makes atonement for them:

Blessed be the Son of the Good
    who atoned our debts!
Blessed is the Physician of the Height
    who healed our disease.

BDB p.37 V, MEM p.160

Likewise, in the Christian revelational writing, the *Shepherd of Hermas*, an angel says:

> You who are suffering for the Name,
>> ought to glorify God,
>> that God deemed you worthy to bear this Name
>> and that all your sins should be healed.
>
>> *Shepherd of Hermas IX:XXVIII.5, AFII p.287*

And again:

> But you I bid to keep these commandments,
> and you shall have healing for your sins.
>> *Shepherd of Hermas X:II.4, AFII p.301*

The Mandaean writers, too, spoke of being healed of sins by the "Physician":

> Physician, the healer of his friends!
>> Heal us from our sins and do not condemn us!
> Physician, the healer of souls!
>> Heal us and do not condemn us!
>
>> *GSBM p.55, MEM p.161*

And one of the gnostic writers explains the matter precisely:

> Our soul indeed is ill because she dwells in a house of poverty, while matter strikes blows at her eyes, wishing to make her blind. For this reason she pursues the Word and applies it to her eyes as a medicine, opening them....
>
> Thus the soul [must look upward to the] Word at all times, to apply it to her eyes as a medicine in order that she may see, and her light may conceal (cover, overcome) the hostile forces that fight with her, and she may make them blind with her light, and enclose them in her presence, and make them fall down in sleeplessness, and she may act boldly with her strength and with her sceptre.
>
>> *Authoritative Teaching 27-28, NHS11 pp.271-273*

The soul's illness, he says, is derived from association with matter and only the Word can restore sight and light, helping in the fight against the "hostile forces" of the mind and its weaknesses. This, then, is the true spiritual healing, and it can only be given by the Word and its personification in a Master. This is why a Manichaean-Christian psalmist addresses the people of this world:

> The Light has shone forth for you,
>   O you that sleep in hell....
> Drink of the Water of memory, cast away oblivion.
> He that is wounded and desires healing,
>   let him come to the Physician.
>
> *Psalm CCXLVIII, MPB p.57*

Likewise, in another psalm, of which little remains but a patchwork of lines, the devotee asks to be made "whole", that is to return to the original home of the soul, becoming one with God, being clothed with a "new body" – the soul's innate garment of light:

> Who shall lead me to that land without tremors? ...
> Who shall answer me with pity? ...
> Who shall make me whole? ...
> Who shall take off from me this ... body,
>   and clothe me in a new body?
>
> *Angad Roshnan IIIc:3,11,137, MHCP pp.135-136*

The Master, then, is the Physician who brings healing through atonement and forgiveness of past sins. He is the Physician of "sick souls", and there are many other instances where Jesus is described in this fashion. In a long paean of praise in the *Acts of Thomas*, for example, Judas Thomas describes Jesus as:

> Healer of sick souls,
>   life-giver of the universe,
> and Saviour of (His) creatures.
>
> *Acts of Thomas, AAA pp.153-154*

He also prays to Jesus as:

> My Lord and my God, that travellest with thy servants,
>   that guidest and correctest them that believe in thee,
>   the refuge and rest of the oppressed,
>   the hope of the poor and ransomer of captives,
>   the Physician of the souls that lie sick

and Saviour of all creation,
that givest life unto the world and strengthenest souls.

Acts of Thomas 10, ANT p.368

And:

To be praised art thou, the Son, the Peacemaker,
who hast healed our wounds,
and persuaded our hardness of heart,
and collected our wandering,
and made us walk in thy Truth:
Through thee we have known thy Father.

Acts of Thomas, AAA p.248

Here, the "wounds" are clearly equated with "hardness of heart", "wandering" in this creation and walking straight on the path of mystic Truth. They are spiritual "wounds" and the healing, once again, is spiritual, not physical, as we again find when one of the characters in this book thanks God

who hast rid me of this disease
that is hard to be healed and cured
and was abiding in me for ever,
and hast implanted sober health in me.

Acts of Thomas 15, AAA pp.157-158, ANT p.370

The "disease" that "abides forever" is the disease of rebirth in this world. This is a long-term, chronic condition.

More specifically, in the *Acts of John*, John – who must have been a natural and lifelong bachelor – gives thanks to his Master for having been protected from both marriage and from falling prey to sexual desire, describing it as the "secret disease of my soul". Jesus, he says, is the one:

Who didst rid me of the foul madness
that is in the flesh:
Who didst take me from the bitter death
and establish me on thee alone:
Who didst muzzle the secret disease of my soul
and cut off the open deed.

Acts of John 113, ANT p.269

The "secret disease" is the desire that lies hidden within. The "open deed" is the act itself. Through the strength given by his Master Jesus, John says that he has been able to overcome this "foul madness" and "bitter death" of sexual desire. He has been healed of this ancient disease. Similarly, in a Manichaean-Christian psalm, the soul begs for the healing of the great Physician:

> I heard the Cry of a Physician,
>> the Cry of an Exorcist coming to me;
> I heard the Cry of a Physician
>> healing his poor ones;
> He stands (lives), he heals his beloved ones,
>> perfecting all his believers....
>
> O Physician, heal me, loose my bonds!
> Heal me, O Charm-looser,
>> for thy healing is not of the earth!
> Thy cures are not of this world,
>> thy healing is of the land of the Living Ones.
>
> *Psalms of Thomas XIV, MPB pp.220-221*

Again, the precise nature of this healing is clearly described: "thy healing is not of this world" but "is of the land of the Living Ones". The demons, curses and "bonds" from which this "Exorcist" and "Charm-looser" releases the soul are of another nature altogether. For "he stands" – he lives, he exists. He is the Standing or Existing One. This divine Physician is one who not only lives within the soul, but also lives on earth as a human being, as a Living One, a living Master. More specifically, in the *Acts of John* – who must have natural and lifelong bachelor – gives thanks to his Master for having been protected from both marriage and from falling prey to sexual desire, describing it as their secret disease of my the one:

The Medicine of Life

It is evident that the Physician and his healing lie at the heart of a family of metaphors centred on the imagery of disease and cure. Naturally, the "medicine" of this divine Physician is the Word, for this is the only Power which is able to forgive sins and to heal the mind of all its imperfections. It is at this that John is hinting (in the *Acts of John*) when he observes – while in conversation with the philosopher Craton:

For as that is a vain medicine whereby the disease is not extirpated, so is it a vain teaching (path) by which the faults of souls and of conduct are not cured.

Acts of John XIV, ANT p.257

In the poems attributed to the fifth-century Narsai, a Nestorian Christian of Syria, the Word is explicitly stated to be the means of healing. In this extract, "our race" refers to the world of human beings, while sickness and "sores", of course, are spiritual imperfections:

The skilful Physician in his mercy wanted
    to heal our race which was sick,
    and to close our sores which were bad,
    and to heal by means of his Word.

Narsai, SWN p.43, MEM p.160

The same idea appears in many other places, too, as in the Mandaean texts:

Thou art the Physician who healest the souls
    by means of the Word.

IMK p.44, MEM p.162

And:

Let healing be theirs
    by virtue of the Word of Truth.

CPM 20 p.15

Often, the Word is referred to explicitly as the "Medicine of Life". This is the mystic truth which lies behind the ancient legend of a miraculous cure-all, a panacea for all ills, that surfaces in the mythology of practically all cultures. Hence, the fourth-century Christian father, Ephraim Syrus, wrote:

Glory to the Medicine of Life,
    that he was sufficient
    and cured the sickness of the souls
    through His doctrine (Word?).

Ephraim Syrus, ESCN p.55, MEM p.130

Similarly from the Nestorian, Narsai, where the Word is called the "Medicine of the Spirit":

(He is) a Physician who heals the diseases
    that are in the midst of the soul;
And it behoves him that is sick in his mind
    to run to him continually.
He knows how to lay the Medicine of the Spirit
    upon the thoughts;
And he cuts off iniquity with the iron
    of the divine mercy.

Ye sick of soul, come, draw near to them
    that have knowledge,
    and shew the spots of your mind to the hidden glance.
Ye that travel in the Way, come,
    and join the company of the wise,
    and make a prosperous journey
    to the appointed place of life everlasting.

                    Narsai, LHN XXXII pp.73-74

And the same idea is expressed by a Manichaean-Christian psalmist:

Many are the labours that I suffered
    while I was in this dark house.
Thou therefore, my true Light, enlighten me within.
Set me up, for I have tumbled down,
    and help me with thee to the Height.
Be not far from me,
    O Physician that hast the Medicines of Life.
Do thou heal me of the grievous wound of lawlessness.

                    Psalms, MPB p.152

"Lawlessness" means living outside the divine Law or Word, living in one's own will, the will of the mind, the agent of Satan. This condition is healed by the dynamic Power that manifests God's will – His Word, the "Medicines of Life". It is the working of this Power to which the psalmist is referring when, in the same psalm, we read "my diseases passed far from me":

In a moment, my God, Thy mercy became one with me.
Because of Thy strong protection,
    lo, my diseases passed far from me.

Lo, joy has overtaken me
    through Thy right hand that came to me.

Psalms, MPB p.153

Taking the metaphor further, in another one of these Manichaean-Christian psalms, the writer draws an analogy from ancient medical practice, saying that the divine Physician has two kinds of medicine, the "burning medicines" and the "cool medicines":

The Physician of souls, he is the Light-*Nous*;
    this is the New Man;
The burning medicines are the Commandments.
But the cool medicines,
    they are the forgiveness of sins:
He that would be healed,
    lo, of two kinds are the Medicines of Life.

Psalm CCXXXIX, MPB p.40

The "burning medicines" are the Master's instructions and his Law or Commandment – another term for the Word. These eradicate sins and cleanse the soul by spiritual scrubbing. Here, the soul feels that it is actively participating in the process. And the "cool medicines" are the "forgiveness of sins". This is the gift of the Master to a soul, when the soul does nothing but enjoy the cooling bounty of the Master. Both medicines are required. Again, in an even more elaborate use of the metaphor, the psalmist writes:

Lo, the great Physician has come:
    he knows how to heal all men.
He has spread his medicine-chest,
    he has called out: "He that wishes, be cured."

Look at the multitude of his cures:
    there is no cure save in him.
He does not recoil from him that is sick,
    he does not mock him that has a wound in him.
A skilful one is he in his work:
    his mouth also is sweet in its words.

He knows how to cut a wound,
    to put a cool medicament upon it.

He cuts and he cleanses;
 he cauterises and soothes in a single day.

Look, his loving kindness
 has made each one of us reveal his sickness.
Let us not hide our sickness from him
 and leave the cancer in our members....

He has the antidote that is good
 for every affection (for the world)....

May he give us a cure that heals our [sickness]:
 the forgiveness of our sins,
 that he may bestow it upon us all.
May he wipe away our iniquities,
 the scars that are branded on our souls.

Psalm CCXLI, MPB pp.46-47

Once more, it is clear that all these medicines and their healings are spiritual, not physical. Moreover, the healing comes about through the mediation of a Master, the "great Physician". Hence, a Mandaean text addressed to "my Lord, *Manda-d-Hiia*, Lord of all healings",[40] praises him as:

the Medicine that cureth pains,
the Healer who cureth all who love his Name.

CPM 179 p.162

Ministers of That Drink

In another of these Mandaean poems or prayers, the "Medicine" is identified as "Water". As in Christianity, the later Mandaeans took this to be physical water and used the poem as a part of their rituals, but the meaning is evidently the Living Water of the Word which figures so prominently in their writings:

Healer, whose Medicine is Water, come!
Be thou a healer to thy devotees,
 to thy devotees be thou a healer....

On him whom thou hast healed, do thou,
my Lord, bestow soundness.

CPM 71 pp.59-60

"Soundness", health and wholeness are all terms that refer to both physical as well as spiritual well-being and it is the spiritual meaning which is intended here. Similarly, speaking of the Masters as the "Ministers of that Drink", those who administer the Living Waters of the Word, the devotional writer of the *Odes of Solomon* uses metaphors that are clearly derived from physical ailments, but whose meaning is spiritual:

Blessed, therefore, are the Ministers of that Drink,
those who have been entrusted with his Water:
They have refreshed the dry lips,
and have raised up the will that was paralysed;
And souls that were near to expiring
they have held back from death;
And limbs that were fallen
they have straightened and raised up:
They have given strength to their coming,
and light to their eyes;
For everyone has known them in the Lord,
and by means of the Waters they lived eternal life.

Odes of Solomon VI:13-18, AOT p.695

The thirsty, the paralysed, those close to death, those with "fallen" or drooping limbs and weakness of the eyes – by bathing in the true Living Waters are restored to spiritual health – "they lived eternal life".

The Tree Which is All-Healings

Since the Word was also called the Tree of Life or the "True Vine" as it appears in John's gospel, so – amongst the Mandaean writings – this Vine was also called

the Vine which is All-Life
and the great Tree which is All-Healings.

CPM 77 p.84

And, more elaborately:

> This is a tree which is a Tree of Life,
>   and a Vine, a Vine of Life!
> Satisfying fare that is superior to all means of healing
>   is that which thou hast brought, revealed
>   and given to these souls!
> Blessed is this pure oblation
>   which goeth before its Giver....
>
> It is a deliverer of the bound,
>   it cheereth those who are in affliction,
>   causeth sucklings to flourish,
>   is the sight of the blind
>   and the hearing and pleasure of the deaf.
>
> It establisheth speech in the mouths of the stammering,
>   and the deaf and the dumb.
> Its presence is praised,
>   for thereby souls are held together.
> And it provideth means of ascent
>   to the great Place of Light
>   and to the everlasting abode.
>
>   *CPM 375 pp.269-270*

This "Tree" brings sight to the blind, speech to the dumb, "satisfying fare" to all who are hungry, and the "means of ascent to the great Place of Light and to the everlasting abode". The deaf hear and take "pleasure" in it. There can be no doubt as to its mystical meaning.

Casting Out Devils

One of the more difficult ideas to comprehend from Jesus' time is that of devils, demons or unclean spirits. Modern thought has little place for them, especially as the personified imps with red, hairy faces and forked tails of popular imagination, and as they appear in the icons of the Eastern Churches, pulling the saints from the ladder of ascent to heaven. But nowhere in the ancient literature of Jesus' era are they described in this manner. Again, we observe a Western literalization of a more fluid Eastern concept.

Devils and demons have been a part of Eastern and Middle-Eastern thought for as long as religious and cultural history can be traced, and from the variety of writings that abound concerning them, there is no doubt that ideas about them varied greatly. What Jesus taught on the subject we do not know, for nowhere are there any sayings where he speaks about devils in any clear-cut way. Besides, mystics do not come to rearrange social and cultural beliefs. They work within whatever social and religious climate they find themselves, and where required for the furtherance of their spiritual teaching, they give the mystic meaning behind those religious and cultural beliefs in which people have put their faith.

There are, after all, many ways of describing the same thing, and if the people of the past spoke of devils while we describe the same things by means of more abstruse, intellectual and scientific concepts, there may not be so much difference after all. Realities are one thing; descriptions and idioms are another. The one remains constant, the other changes with the passage of time. But each era has a tendency to think that they have a better idea about things than their predecessors, though even the descriptions of science, seemingly so concrete, get changed, sometimes radically, as time goes by.

In the popular mind of Jesus' day, practically everything unknown seems to have been attributed to devils. As someone says to Jesus in Mark's gospel:

> Master, I have brought unto thee my own son,
> which hath a dumb spirit.
>
> *Mark 9:18*

However, the description of this particular devil's activities – "he foameth and gnasheth with his teeth, and pineth away"[41] – is generally considered symptomatic of epilepsy. Similarly, any mental aberration – even that of 'deviant' belief – was thought to be due to the workings of a devil and, if we examine it, the root of the idea may not be so fantastical after all.

Jesus and other mystics, too, have certainly taught the existence of a Devil. As we have described it, the Devil or Universal Mind is the power by which the one stream of the Word is broken up and reflected into an infinity of parts, forming the causal, astral and physical universes, in their turn. Each of these sub-streams of power can be called a devil – or an angel – depending upon whether the working of that force is considered to be for good or evil, that being the fundamental duality or balance of opposites within the realm of the Devil.

Consequently, even the faculties of a human being can be regarded as 'devils' or 'angels', for they are all derived or reflected from higher powers or energies. For one who has been unconsciously habituated to think only in the idioms of modern science, the idea that all physical energies are only reflections of something higher is difficult at first to grasp. But many mystics have said that this world and everything in it is a reflection or a projection of what lies within, coming into being by this means.

Many of the mystic writers of Jesus' time certainly thought of devils and angels as derived powers within the realm of the Devil. The gnostic texts, for instance, are full of complex descriptions of the many emanations that comprise creation. One belief that is encountered, not too infrequently, is that the human form with its organs, limbs, systems and faculties is the result of the interactions of three hundred and sixty-five angels, presumably one for each day of the year!

Spiritual ascent, therefore, requires that man overcome the Devil, the Universal Mind, by overcoming all the minor 'devils' – and angels, too. He has to cast out the 'devils' of human weakness from within himself, to rise up from the 'devils' that support the human form and pass through the higher realms of higher 'devils' until the soul escapes from the domain of the Devil altogether.

However we may care to think of it, we are certainly opposed by no mean array of forces in our struggle to make spiritual progress. Lust, anger, greed, pride, jealousy and other unworthy passions are not will-o'-the-wisps. They exist within us as strong urges that cannot be ignored and it makes little difference from a day-to-day, practical point of view how we view them, for the struggle remains the same. When we have risen above the human sphere in mystic transport, we will be in a position to examine the situation and see how it came about. Then we can decide whether it really makes much difference whether we speak in terms of faculties, weaknesses or devils.

Casting out devils, therefore, is another of Jesus' miracles which has a basis in spiritual truth, making us wonder once more whether Jesus really healed so many people of their temporal and physical ailments or whether such stories arose as a later externalization of his teachings. Looking through the writings of that period, we find considerable evidence which leads us to adopt the spiritual interpretation.

There is no doubt that Satan or the Negative Power was called the Devil and that this Devil was seen as our main human problem. In the *Acts of Thomas*, Judas Thomas prays:

Let the gall of the Devil be removed from us.

Acts of Thomas 158, ANT p.438

And similarly, a Manichaean-Christian psalm contrasts the "Holy Spirit" with the "Unclean Spirit". Alluding to the *Genesis* story, where the Devil – the "Unclean Spirit" – is allegorized as a "snake" and to other Judaic writings where the pure spirituality and the love of God are symbolized as a "white dove", the psalmist writes:

> The living kingdom shall be revealed again,
>> the love of God, the white dove.
> For the Holy Spirit was likened to a dove,
>> but the Unclean Spirit was likened to a snake.
> The dove and the snake are enemies to each other;
>> the dove does not dwell in a pool unclean.
> For the Holy Spirit does not take gold and silver,
>> but the Unclean Spirit is a lover of gold and silver.
>
> *Psalms, MPB p.156*

The battle of life, says the psalmist, is between these two. But this battle is won only through the help of an intermediary. Thus, referring again to the *Genesis* allegory, the Coptic *Book of the Resurrection of Jesus Christ* describes Jesus' advent in this world and his bringing of salvation to the "sheep that had gone astray":

> So Jesus went down into Amente (this world),
>> and scattered the fiends,
>> and cast chains on the Devil,
>> and redeemed Adam and all his sons (*i.e.* man).
> He delivered man,
>> and he shewed compassion upon his own image.
> He set free all creation, and all the world,
>> and he treated with healing Medicine
>> the wound which the Enemy had inflicted on His son.
> He brought back into his fold
>> the sheep which had gone astray –
>> he the holy and faithful Shepherd.
> And he brought back Adam again to the state
>> wherein he was at first,
>> and forgave them (men, Adam's 'sons') their sins.
>
> *Book of the Resurrection of Jesus Christ, CADUE p.184*

The idea of one fundamental Devil was not confined to Semitic and other Middle Eastern religions. It is also encountered, for instance, in the Graeco-Egyptian literature ascribed to Hermes Trismegistus. In a Hermetic tractate found amongst the Nag Hammadi codices, Hermes says:

> Listen, Asclepius! There is a great Demon. The great God has appointed him to be overseer or judge over the souls of men.... Now, when the soul comes forth from the body, it is necessary that it meet this Demon. Immediately he – the Demon – will surround this one (the soul), and he will examine him in regard to the character that he has developed in his life.
>
> *Asclepius 76, NHS11 p.443*

This is a way of pointing out that, at the time of death, man has to face judgment for all his actions and desires. How this happens is beyond verbal portrayal and this description is probably as good as any other. But however it may be described, man is accountable for his actions to the "great Demon" – the Devil or Satan.

Under the dominion of this Devil are all the 'sub-devils' who administer the creation within the Devil's realm. A fifth-century manuscript of Mark, discovered in Egypt early in the twentieth century, has an interesting addition to chapter fourteen which presents this point of view, where the lesser devils are called "unclean spirits":

> This age of wickedness and unbelief is under Satan
> who, by means of unclean spirits,
> permitteth not men to apprehend the true power of God:
> Therefore do thou now reveal thy righteousness.
>
> *Mark 16:14 addition (Freer logion), ANT p.34*

The authenticity of this passage is unknown, of course, although there is other evidence that points to our version of Mark being a less than all-inclusive version of a text that in its full form was distributed only to those "who had ears to hear". However, the insertion is mentioned by Jerome,[42] writing in the early fifth century, as appearing in some manuscripts, especially Greek copies, so it does at least date back to a relatively early period.

All souls in this world, then, are held in thrall by these "devils". As Judas Thomas prays in the *Acts of Thomas*:

> Let these souls be healed and rise up
> and become such as they were

before they were smitten of the devils.
Acts of Thomas 81, ANT p.401

And in the *Acts of John*, we find man's uncontrollable predilection for the things of this world described as a devil. "Mammon," says John, "is the name of a devil":

> For he that loveth money is the servant of Mammon:
> And Mammon is the name of a devil
>> who is set (rules) over carnal gains,
>> and is the master of them that love the world.
>> *Acts of John XVI, ANT p.259*

Likewise, in the early Christian revelation, the *Shepherd of Hermas*, an 'angel' – who has been discoursing previously on quarrelling, evil-speaking, malice and rage – describes these weaknesses collectively as a "demon":

> The Lord will heal your former sins,
>> if you cleanse yourselves from this demon.
>> *Shepherd of Hermas IX:XXIII.5, AFII p.277*

Human imperfections – physical or mental – were thus ascribed to devils or demons. In fact, in the *Apocryphon of John*, there is a passage where the writer has Jesus describe the constitution of matter according to the philosophical concepts of the day. From these states of matter, he says, arise the "demons which are in the body":

> The origin of the demons which are in the whole body is determined to be four: heat, cold, wetness, and dryness. And the mother of all of them is matter. And he who reigns over the heat is *Phloxopha*; and he who reigns over the cold is *Oroorrothos*; and he who reigns over what is dry is *Erimacho*; and he who reigns over the wetness is *Athuro*. And the mother of all of these, *Onorthochrasaei*, stands in their midst since she is illimitable, and she mixes with all of them. And she is truly matter, for they are nourished by her.
> *Apocryphon of John 18, NHL p.115*

And from these "demons", he continues, the "passions come forth":

The four chief demons are: Ephememphi who belongs to pleasure, Yoko who belongs to desire, Nenentophni who belongs to grief, Blaomen who belongs to fear. And the mother of them all is Aestesis-Ouch-Epi-Ptoe. And from the four demons passions came forth. And from grief came envy, jealousy, distress, trouble, pain, callousness, anxiety, mourning, etc. And from pleasure much wickedness arises, and empty pride, and similar things. And from desire comes anger, wrath, and bitterness, and bitter passion, and unsatedness, and similar things. And from fear comes dread, fawning, agony, and shame.

Apocryphon of John 18, NHL p.115

It is these passions and demons which keep man's attention bound to this world and away from the inner reality. Hence, a Manichaean-Christian psalmist writes:

Who will lead me beyond the walls
and take me over the moats,
which are full of fear and trembling
from ravaging demons?
Who will lead me beyond rebirths,
and free me from ... all the waves,
in which there is no rest?

Huwidagman IVa:4-5, MHCP p.83

Man's problems, then, lie with his "demons", but – as many mystics have remarked – no soul can be induced to fall unless he has something within him that already wants to be tempted and to fall. Put into 'demon' terminology, we find Peter saying the same thing in the *Clementine Recognitions*, where he goes on to point out that since Jesus had no such negative qualities within him, there was never any chance of him falling to the Devil's temptations, as related in the gospels:

This we would have you know assuredly, that a demon has no power against a man, unless one voluntarily submit himself to his desires. Whence even that one who is the Prince of Wickedness, approached him who, as we have said, is appointed of God, King of Peace, tempting him, and began to promise him all the glory of the world; because he knew that when he had offered this to others, for the sake of deceiving them, they had worshipped him. Therefore, impious as he was, and unmindful of himself, which indeed is the special peculiarity of wickedness, he presumed that he should be worshipped by him by whom he knew that he was to be destroyed.

Clementine Recognitions IV:XXXIV, CR p.301

And in the *Clementine Homilies*, Peter also says that the soul itself would never consent to the impurity suggested by the "demons":

> Whence many, not knowing how they are influenced, consent to the evil thoughts suggested by the demons, as if they were the reasoning of their own souls.

Clementine Homilies IX:XII, CH p.154

This really is the root of the matter. The soul – the real self – like a diamond encased in mud, is innately pure and has only one inclination – to return to God. It is the work of the mind to distract the soul from this primal longing. The mind is not the real self. It is a counterfeit self. It is something other than the soul. It is an agent of the Devil or we can say that it is a devil and that all its faculties and imperfections are devils, too. They are all something other than the real self, acting from within as if they were the real self. Truly, we are possessed by devils who are legion – but not of the red-faced, pointy-eared variety! These devils are far more subtle, for we willingly follow in their footsteps and never fear them. We even take them for our own real self. This is some devil!

The essential problem, therefore, is how to replace the counterfeit with the real, how to replace the Devil with God. In another passage from the same book, Peter is speaking to a group of people in Tripolis, a Mediterranean trading port now in northern Lebanon. Describing himself, by analogy, as a "good merchantman" and his teachings as "wares", he says that it is by accepting his wares that a soul is enabled to escape the effect of the "demons":

> Many forms of worship, then, having passed away in the world, we come, bringing to you, as good merchantmen, the worship that has been handed down to us from our fathers, and preserved; showing you, as it were, the seeds of plants, and placing them under your judgment and in your power. Choose that which seems good unto you.
>
> If, therefore, ye choose our wares, not only shall ye be able to escape demons, and the sufferings which are inflicted by demons, but yourselves

also putting them to flight, and having them reduced to make supplication to you, shall for ever enjoy future blessings.

Clementine Homilies IX:VIII, CH p.152

It is by putting our demons to flight, by casting out our devils, that the soul regains its original purity and is enabled to "enjoy future blessings". And this, says the writer, comes about by accepting the wares of one such as Peter or Jesus.

Once again, then, we see that the supposed, external miracles of Jesus have an inner, mystical origin. Whatever else the people of these times may have supposed devils or demons to have been, giving rise to the many gospel and apocryphal stories, another side of the tradition represented these miracles as specifically spiritual and mystical. It seems likely that this was Jesus' teaching on the matter, too.

Stormy Weather

Amongst the most graphic of the gospel miracle stories are those where Jesus either walks upon the water to reach the disciples' boat and still the stormy sea or is awakened from slumber in the rear of their small boat to perform the same feat. Both tales appear in Mark and both are copied across by Matthew. Luke, however, omits the walking on the water and John, the other story. It is in Matthew, incidentally, where we have the further episode of Peter asking if he may also try walking on the water. But, in the event, his faith wavers – when "he saw the wind boisterous, he was afraid"[43] – and he begins to sink. A pointed reminder that the performance of miracles is a mental activity, depending upon uninterrupted inner concentration.

It is quite possible, of course – since the whole of nature must consciously or unconsciously rejoice at the presence of a Master – that the weather around Jesus seemed on occasion to have a charmed quality, providing ample fuel for miracle stories. Perhaps some disciples were indeed saved from shipwreck by their Master's omnipresent hand or by his physical presence, or maybe he brought cool breezes with him in the heat of the summer or showers to settle the dust. There is no reason to presume that there is no substance to the comment:

> What manner of man is this,
>> that even the winds and the sea obey him!
>
> *Matthew 8:27*

But like all the other miracle stories, when referred to by later mystic writers, this family of miracles is given a spiritual interpretation, suggesting that they, too, were derived from a misunderstanding of Jesus' many analogies drawn from nature. Surveying the early references to the images encountered in these miracle stories, we find such a comment in the letter attributed to James the brother of Jesus. He writes that if we sincerely seek understanding or guidance from within, then we will certainly receive it. But the mind must be calm and receptive, not wavering "like a wave of the sea driven with the wind and tossed", for then the mind's own ideas and suggestions overwhelm the Lord's promptings and direction:

> If any of you lack wisdom, let him ask of God that giveth to all men liberally, and upbraideth not; and it shall be given him. But let him ask in faith, nothing wavering. For he that wavereth is like a wave of the sea driven with the wind and tossed.
>
> *James 1:5-6*

Now, if this letter was really written by Jesus' brother, then it is not unlikely that James used one of his brother's examples. And Matthew, too, would have had such an analogy in mind when he penned the addition to Jesus' marine promenade. From the New Testament documents themselves, then, we have some confirmation that Jesus and his followers did indeed use aquatic metaphors to convey spiritual meaning.

It is, however, amongst the Manichaean-Christian psalms, more than any other literature, that we find the commonest use of such imagery. In one long passage, where a psalmist is speaking generally of life in this world and more specifically of the human passions, he likens the state of the soul to that of a ship tossed helplessly in a storm, slowly being broken apart by the force of the wind and waves. These storms, he says, are caused by the fury of the "demons, the banished princes", the powers or rulers within the realm of the banished Prince or Devil:

> All the demons, the banished princes,
>> transfixed me with fear,
>> and dismayed me with anguish.
> Their fury gathered, like a sea of fire.
> The seething waves rose up that they might engulf me.
>
> I am like [ships] which course
>> over the heart of the ocean....

In every region gathered stormy winds and rain
    and the fume of all fogs, lightning and thunder
    and banked clouds of hail,
    the crash and roar of all the waves of the sea.

The skiff rises up,
    lifted on the crest of the wave,
    and glides down into the trough, to be hidden within.
With all the beams [splintered]
    and on every side water [pouring] in.
All the clamps become loosened by [the buffeting],
    the iron rivets are plucked out by [the pounding].
Each wale [gets submerged] by these drownings,
    the masts are flung together in the turmoil.
The rudders have dropped off into the sea,
    [fear grips] those on board.
The helmsmen and all the pilots weep bitterly
    and lament aloud.
There was terror and wreck [before] the break of day.

          Angad Roshnan I:18-20,22-30, MHCP pp.117-119

Here, we get an insight into ancient shipbuilding techniques and the helplessness of small wooden sailing boats in a tempest at sea. This, says the psalmist, is the state of the soul, tossed about in this world. Nothing can be relied upon; everything slowly breaks apart under the pressure of life's buffeting. The same idea is found earlier in the same hymn:

My soul weeps within,
    and cries out at each distress and stab.
This carrion form (the body) is ended for me,
    and the hour of life, with its turbulent days.
It was tossed and troubled as a sea with waves,
    pain was heaped on pain, whereby they ravage my soul.

          Angad Roshnan I:11-13, MHCP p.115

Who, then, is to save the soul from the wind and storms? It is, of course, the divine Saviour and in one of these psalms he appears, saying:

I shall deliver thee from all the waves of the sea,
    and from its deep

wherein thou hast gone through these drownings....
I shall set thee free from every sickness,
    and from every distress at which thou hast wept.
I shall not wish to leave thee longer
    in the hands of the Sinner (Satan);
For thou art my own, in truth, for ever.

Angad Roshnan VI:45-50, MHCP p.147

One of the commonest and favourite expressions of the Manichaean-Christian psalmists was that the souls are taken in ships of light across the stormy ocean of this world and up through all the heavens, back to their original home. Hence, the psalmist also writes that the "ships" have come into the "harbour" to take the soul "to thy habitations", to the soul's true home:

O soul, forget not thyself,
    nor faint, nor eat out thy heart.
Lo, the ships are moored for thee,
    the barks are in the harbour.
Take thy merchandise aboard
    and sail to thy habitations.

Psalms, MPB p.147

The "merchandise", here, is the spiritual treasures or riches. The 'merchant' soul, far from home in a foreign land, is to collect her treasure of spirituality and sail to her true and promised land. Again, speaking of the soul as sailing in a ship that is crossing the ocean of the creation, the devotee writes:

Lo, my ship I have brought to the shore;
    no storm has overwhelmed it, no wave has seized it....
I was heading for shipwreck before I found the ship of Truth;
    a divine tacking was Jesus who helped me....
An unspeakable grace overtook me.

Psalm CCLIII, MPB p.63

But naturally, the soul cannot be expected to pilot her own ship independently. An experienced helmsman is required. Hence, the Masters were commonly referred to as the Helmsmen, the "Helmsmen of Light"[44] or as:

> The First Man, our Helmsman, ... our First Guide,
>   thou art our Shepherd that feeds us.
>   *Psalm CCXXIV, MPB p.13*

And:

> Father whose sons are many.
> Watcher that guards his tower.
> Shepherd unsleeping.
> Helmsman that is not drunken.
> King, the God of Truth.
> Wearer of the unfading crown.
>   *Psalms, MPB p.136*

This epithet, however, did not start with the third-century Mani. Such a simile must have been an obvious one in a world when seafaring was a common but hazardous occupation and there is no reason to believe that Jesus did not use it also. In fact, we find the same family of metaphors in the gnostic *Teachings of Silvanus*, penned almost certainly before the time of Mani, perhaps far earlier. Speaking of the worldly man, he writes:

> He swims in the desires of life and he has sunk. To be sure, he thinks he
> finds profit when he doing all those things which are without profit. The
> wretched man who goes through all these things will die because he does
> not have the *Nous*, the Helmsman. But he is like a ship which the wind
> tosses to and fro, and like a loose horse which has no rider.
>   *Teachings of Silvanus 90, TS p.25*

The devotee soon realizes this and consequently many have written, begging the Lord or their Master to "ferry" them across the ocean of phenomena:

> I see a great dread from the earth up to the skies;
>   woe is me therefore:
> Where can I escape unless thou ferry me across, my Lord?
>   *Psalm CCLII, MPB p.61*

The sincere disciple understands that nothing can be accomplished without his Master's help and guidance:

Guide for me my Spirit
in the midst of the stormy sea.

Psalms, MPB p.150

And:

In the midst of the sea, Jesus, guide me.
Do not abandon us that the waves may not seize us.
When I utter thy Name over the sea it stills its waves.

Psalms, MPB p.151

This, then, is the heart of the matter. The Master – with his Word, his *Nous* or his Name – is the one who brings the mind under control, stilling its turbulent waves. Therefore, the psalmist writes:

Jesus is a ship:
blessed are we if we sail upon it.

Psalms, MPB p.166

Here, the Master is not only the pilot, but also the ship. It is the ship of the Master, of the Word, in which the soul can sail. Similarly:

A north (fair) wind blowing upon us is our Lord Mani,
that we may put out with him and sail to the Land of Light.

Psalms of Heracleides, MPB p.193

And more extensively:

The ship of Jesus has come to port,
laden with garlands and gay palms.
It is Jesus who steers it,
he will put in for us until we embark.
The holy ones are they whom he takes,
the maidens are they whom he [carries with him].

Let us also make ourselves pure
that we may make our voyage....
The ship of Jesus will make its way up to the Height.
It will bring its cargo to the shore
and return for them that are left behind....

He will bring them [safely]
    to the Harbour of the Immortals.
It is laden with garlands
    and gay palms for ever and ever.

Psalms, MPB pp.151-152

The Master takes those of his disciples who have become pure. They are the "holy ones" and the "maidens". "Let us also make ourselves pure," says the psalmist, so that the Master may take us to the "Harbour of the Immortals", the eternal realm.

But to achieve this purity, all that the soul, the "daughter of Wisdom" can do is to hold on with endurance and fortitude, ever watchful that the mind does not lead her astray. Then she will be taken across and ascend up to the Light:

How great is thy fortitude, O daughter of Wisdom:
    for thou hast not yet wearied, watching over the Enemy.
For thee the ships are waiting on high
    that they may draw thee up and take thee to the Light.
Lo, the Perfect Man is stretched out
    in the middle of the world,
    that thou mayest walk in him
    and receive thy unfading garlands.

Psalms, MPB p.163

All that is required is to go aboard and set sail for the promised land. As a consequence, the psalmist writes:

On those ships of light ...
    shall your souls go aboard.
Psalms of Thomas VII, MPB p.213

And:

Now go aboard the Ships of Light
    and receive thy garland of glory
    and return to thine own Kingdom
    and rejoice with all the *Aeons*.
Psalm CCXLVI, MPB p.55

Then the soul enters the ship – comes into contact with the divine Music within – and really sets out upon the inner journey. She leaves the "garment" of the body here on earth and putting on the "immortal robe" of the soul's own innate splendour is ferried across the creation in the ship of the Word, "the ferryboat of Light":

> I have left the garment upon the earth,
> the senility of diseases that was with me;
> The immortal robe I have put upon me.
>
> Ferry me across to the sun and the moon,
> O ferryboat of Light that is at peace.
>
> *Psalm CCLXIV, MPB p.81*

Then, all is peaceful and still, like springtime after a hard winter or like the calm after a storm at sea:

> Lo, all trees ... have become new again.
> Lo, the roses have spread their beauty abroad,
> for the bond has been severed
> that does harm to their leaves.
> Do thou also sever the chains and the bond of our sins.
>
> The whole Air is luminous ... today,
> the earth too puts forth blossom also,
> the waves of the sea are still:
> For the gloomy winter has passed
> that is full of trouble.
>
> Let us too escape from the iniquity of evil.
> Forgive the sins of them that know thy mystery,
> to whom there has been revealed
> the knowledge of the secret of the Most High
> through the holy Wisdom, wherein there is no Error.
>
> *Psalm CCXXII, MPB p.8*

The Manichaean-Christian psalms, then, using metaphors associated with the sea, tell the story of the soul's plight in this world and its return home. As we have already seen in *James* and the *Teachings of Silvanus*, other early writers also used the same family of expressions. The fourth-century Christian, Ephraim Syrus, for instance, mixing his metaphors in characteristically Middle Eastern fashion, speaks of Jesus as both the "Shipmaster" and the "glorious Tree":

> O skilful Shipmaster,
>   thou who hast conquered the raging sea,
> Thy glorious Tree hath come to the Harbour of Life....
> Blessed be he who hath been a shipmaster for his soul,
>   who hath preserved and brought out his treasure.
>
> *Ephraim Syrus, SESHS IV:601.15, MEM p.98*

The soul, too, is its own "shipmaster" bringing its treasure safely to port in the "Harbour of Life".

But the nearest of all these ancient writings to the time of Jesus are the *Odes of Solomon*, possibly written by a devotee of Jesus himself. Here, the writer not only alludes unquestionably to Jesus' so-called walking on the water, he also interprets the story metaphorically. The "Lord bridged them by his Word", he says. And, in a shift of the analogy, the waters are not a stormy sea, but the torrent and "mighty rivers" of the world:

> Mighty rivers are the power of the Lord,
>   which carry headlong those who despise them,
>   and twist their steps,
>   and ruin their fords,
>   and seize their bodies,
>   and destroy their souls;
> For they are swifter than lightning
>   and faster.
>
> But those who cross them in faith
>   will not be shaken.
> And those who walk on them without blemish
>   will not be perturbed;
> Because the Lord is a Sign in them,
>   and the Sign becomes the path
>   of those who cross in the Name of the Lord.
>
> Put on, therefore, the Name of the Most High,
>   and know Him,
>   and you will cross without danger,
>   because the rivers will be obedient to you.
>
> The Lord bridged them by his Word,
>   and walked, and crossed them on foot;

And his footprints remain on the waters,
    and have not been obliterated,
        but are like a piece of wood which is firmly fixed:
On this side and that, the waves are lifted up,
    but the footprints of our Lord Christ remain,
        and are not effaced, or obliterated;

And a path has been established for those
    who cross after him,
        and for those who follow in the steps of his faith,
    and worship his Name.

Odes of Solomon XXXIX:1-13, AOT pp.727-728

The torrents of the world, says the poet, are powerful enough to carry away all those who do not treat them with respect, trying to cross them without faith in God. But those who have that faith "cannot be shaken". Those who are pure in mind, "who walk on them without blemish will not be perturbed" by the world and all its craziness. For there is nothing within "those who follow in the steps of his faith" that can be attracted or "carried headlong" by the "mighty rivers ... of the Lord".

Moreover, the Lord is also a "Sign in them" – a term used for true, mystic baptism, as we will later see. They have a "path" to follow, the path of the "Name of the Lord". One who has "put on" this "Name" can "cross without danger" of falling in, because the "rivers will be obedient to you" – the mind will have been brought under control.

And the source of the strength to walk on the waters of the world without being affected comes from the "Lord Christ", the Lord's anointed one. He has "bridged them by his Word". He has also "crossed them on foot" – he has come to the foot of the creation and shown by his own example that it can be done. Moreover, the path he lays out is firm, secure and easy to see even in the midst of turbulent waters. It is like planks of wood laid down in the rushing stream but which remain where they are, unaffected by the current. It is, in other words, an eternal path. It is never "effaced or obliterated". It is a "path ... established for those who cross after him", for those who follow the path of the Word, for those who "worship his Name".

This poem is rather extraordinary, for it alone tells us all we need to know about the spiritual manner in which the miracles of Jesus were understood by the people of his own time.

Fishers of Men

Since everything in this world is a reflection or projection of what exists in the higher realms, life here provides many analogies and symbols for mystic truths. Similes have always been the favoured device of the poet – mystic or otherwise. Considering all this aquatic imagery, therefore, one begins to wonder about the stories of those disciples who are cast in the gospels as fishermen. Is this, too, a later misunderstanding of a mystic truth?

It is Mark, followed by Matthew, who relates the calling of Peter, his brother Andrew and the sons of Zebedee, James and John. Matthew's version reads:

> And Jesus, walking by the sea of Galilee, saw two brethren, Simon called Peter, and Andrew his brother, casting a net into the sea: for they were fishers. And he saith unto them, "Follow me, and I will make you fishers of men". And they straightway left their nets, and followed him. And going on from thence, he saw other two brethren, James the son of Zebedee, and John his brother, in a ship with Zebedee their father, mending their nets; and he called them. And they immediately left the ship and their father, and followed him.
>
> *Matthew 4:18-22*

Luke, however, replaces this incident with a more elaborate miracle story in which Peter, who seems from the narrative to have met Jesus just recently, has been fishing all night without any success. Jesus, who has come with him in the boat, then tells him to go further out into deeper water, before letting down the net. The result is that they catch so many fish that the net breaks and they have to take the assistance of their partners, James and John, who are close at hand. Understandably, all of them are greatly astonished, Peter even telling Jesus, "Depart from me; for I am a sinful man, O Lord." Following which, according to Luke:

> Jesus said unto Simon, "Fear not; from henceforth thou shalt catch men." And when they had brought their ships to land, they forsook all, and followed him.
>
> *Luke 5:11*

These two stories make their appearance in the synoptic gospels at the beginning of Jesus' ministry and since the consequence of them both is that Simon, Andrew, James and John become the followers of Jesus and – observing the similarity of wording in the closing lines – there seems little doubt that Luke substituted his version for Mark's at this juncture in the narrative. Perhaps the intelligent Luke thought it improbable that four people busy about their work would have suddenly dropped everything and gone to Jesus without ever having previously met him, simply because he said, "Follow me".

In fact, bearing in mind the spiritual basis of practically all the other miracle stories, one wonders if indeed both versions of the tale were concocted in reverse from the saying concerning "fishers of men", together with the tradition that those who came to Jesus lost interest in everything of the world and followed him one-pointedly. Following Jesus, however, is unlikely to have been meant in a purely physical fashion. It would have implied that his disciples followed his teachings and instructions implicitly. Wherever they went and whatever they were doing, their Master was the focus of their inner lives.

Historically, the two stories are incompatible unless one takes the charitable view that Mark and Matthew were unaware of the real details of what happened, which were later supplied by Luke. But even this is unlikely, for when we turn to St John, we find – as we have already noted – that an entirely different story is related. John tells us that Andrew was already a disciple of John the Baptist and when, one day, John the Baptist tells Andrew that Jesus is to be the Messiah, Andrew immediately goes home, gets Peter and they go to Jesus together.

Now, there is no way that this story is compatible with those of either Mark or Luke. Moreover, nowhere does John's gospel mention anything about any of Jesus' disciples being fishermen, except in the last chapter. But this chapter, containing the story of Jesus' third and last resurrection appearance to his disciples, is generally reckoned by scholars to be a later and quite intentionally fraudulent addition. So the fact that it makes a point of depicting Peter as a fisherman and of Jesus cooking and eating fish, only serves to demonstrate that the discrepancies in the gospel narratives were noted by the early Christians and that the writer of this chapter was trying unsuccessfully to smooth away the differences. It is probable that this chapter was also motivated by other allied considerations, as we will later be discussing.

But the common feature in all the gospel stories – whether they are spurious or otherwise – is the imagery and it is here that the truth may be sought. For all Masters are "fishers of men". The souls who are drawn to them are like fish, attracted by the bait of his love, manifesting initially as an interest in his teachings. And once caught in his net, they are taken by him to the eternal abode. In fact, one of the terms listed in the *Acts of John* for the Word is the "Net", the divine snare that catches the fish and takes them back to God. The passage also alludes to a number of other parables and sayings of Jesus:

> We glorify Thy Way; we glorify Thy Seed,
>> the *Logos*, Grace, Faith, Salt, True Pearl Ineffable,
>> the Treasure, the Plough, the Net,
>> the Greatness, the Diadem.
> Him that for us was called (became) the Son of man,
>> that gave us Truth, Rest, Knowledge, Power,
>> the Commandment, the Confidence, Hope, Love,
>> Liberty, Refuge in Thee.
>
> *Acts of John 109, ANT p.268*

Like so many of the parables, metaphors and sayings of Jesus, the idea of a Master as a fisherman catching souls in his net has antecedents in earlier Judaic literature with which Jesus would naturally have been familiar. It is, after all, only an extension of the metaphor of Living Water. Just as fish swim in the water of the world, so do all souls – consciously or unconsciously – swim in the Living Waters of the Word. It is not surprising, therefore, to find that the expression is extant amongst the writings of the earlier Jewish mystics.

In *Ezekiel*, for example, the prophet relates an allegory or parable, told as a revelation or a vision, in which a river flows out from under the threshold of the Temple at Jerusalem, increasing in volume as it flows along. All manner of fish live and thrive in this river. Says the prophet:

> Wherever the river flows,
>> all living creatures teeming in it will live.
> Fish will be very plentiful,
>> for wherever the water goes it brings health,
>> and life teems wherever the river flows.
>
> There will be fishermen on its banks;
>> fishing nets will be spread from En-gedi to En-eglaim.
> The fish will be as varied and as plentiful
>> as the fish of the great sea (the Mediterranean).
>
> *Ezekiel 47:9-10, JB*

The narrative, of course, is an allegory for there is no river at Jerusalem. The "river" is the Life Stream of the Word flowing out from the heavenly Jerusalem, from the real "Temple" of God, the source of life and being, the spiritual centre to which all worship is addressed. In this river swim all the souls in creation, of many different kinds, whether they know the origin of their life force or not. And all along its banks are "fishermen", probably an allusion to the prophets or mystics.

Similarly, the prophet Jeremiah, writing in what seems to be an allegory depicting the return of souls to God from their dispersion in the creation, speaks of the "many fishermen" who will be sent to collect the "sons of Israel" from their dispersion through "all the countries":

> People will ... say, ... "As Yahweh lives who brought the sons of Israel out of the land of the North and back from all the countries to which he had dispersed them". I will bring them back to the very soil I gave their ancestors. I will now send many fishermen – it is Yahweh who speaks – and these will fish them up.
>
> *Jeremiah 16:14-16, JB*

They will be brought back "to the very soil I gave their ancestors": they will be returned to their ancestral and original home. And those who find them and bring them home he calls "fishermen" – seemingly a metaphor for the Masters. But the Old Testament is in as much of a muddle as the New, maybe more, and the literature of that period being so allegorical, it is not always easy to determine the meaning with any certainty.

The Fisher of Souls

One of the most extensive uses of this metaphor, where there is no doubt as to the meaning, is amongst the discourses, sayings, stories and allegories attributed to John the Baptist in the Mandaean *John-Book*. There, a significant proportion of the imagery echoes that of the gospels, but yet is different enough to make it fairly sure that the parables are not simply later derivatives of New Testament material put in the Baptist's name. In fact, the tempting conclusion is that we are actually looking at echoes of the earlier teachings given by John the Baptist, and one cannot help but wonder whether Jesus' expression, "fishers of men" was actually derived from the teachings of his own Master, John the Baptist. Allowing for the passage of time and a certain degree of dilution of the mystic message, the teachings in this book are found once again to be the simple teachings of all the great mystics. And here, too, we find extended stories of the "loving Shepherd", the "Sower", the "heavenly plough", and the "Fisher of Souls" – all these being epithets of the Master in those times.

The allegory of the "Fisher of Souls" tells the tale of the "Chief Fisher", the "Fisher who eats no fish". His duty is to catch the "good fish", the "fish who do not eat filth". These, he carries away in a "ship whose wings are of glory, that sails along as in flight ... in the heart of the heaven", steered by a "rudder of Truth". He scares away the great fish-eating bird with the music of his fisherman's flute. His chosen fish are attracted by his "Call" and the sound of "Voice sublime". They listen to his "wondrous discourses", the divine Music, and are taken back to the "regions of light".

The other fish, "who eat foul-smelling water-fennel" and are easily tempted by a bait of "bad dates", are left to a host of evil fishers who obstruct the work of the Chief Fisher and have no interest in the welfare of the fish they catch. They are always quarrelling with each other, deceiving one another in a variety of ways and eating bad fish.[45]

The interpretation seems fairly straightforward. The Master (the "Chief Fisher") comes to the world to collect those souls (the "fish") who have lost interest in its foul nature. The remainder stay here to be caught and eaten up by the forces who administer this world. The story is a long one, however, and we must leave it at this point, with only a brief excerpt from the initial declaration of the divine Fisher:

> A Fisher am I, a Fisher elect among fishers.
> A Fisher am I who among the fishers is chosen,
>   the Head of all catchers of fish.
> I know the shallows of the waters; ...
> I come to the net-grounds (this world),
>   to the shallows and all the fishing-spots,
>   and search the marsh in the dark all over....
>
> The fisher-trident which I have in my hand,
>   is instead a *margna* select, a staff of Pure Water,
>   at whose sight tremble the (other) fishers.
> I sit in a boat of glory
>   and come into this world of the fleeting.
>
> *John-Book, GJB pp.71-72*

The allegory, then, is intriguing, for one cannot help wondering whether Jesus also used a parable not too dissimilar from it in his description of the Master's work in this world – a parable which became the origin of the various gospel stories associated with fish.

In almost every instance, then, we have seen that there is reason to believe that the stories concerning Jesus' miracles have arisen from a modicum of fact mingled with a literalization of spiritual truths and mystical imagery. Historically, it is impossible to know precisely what took place, but we are left once again with an arrow pointing us in the direction of Jesus as a teacher of the highest mystical reality.

NOTES AND REFERENCES

1. See Morton Smith, *Jesus the Magician*, p.109.
2. *Mark 1:29-31, Matthew 8:14-15, Luke 4:38-39.*
3. *Mark 1:40-45, Matthew 8:2-4, Luke 5:12-16.*
4. *Mark 2:1-12, Matthew 9:1-8, Luke 5:17-26.*
5. *Mark 3:1-6, Matthew 12:9-14, Luke 6:6-11.*
6. *Mark 4:35-41; Matthew 8:18, 23-27; Luke 8:22-25.*
7. *Mark 5:1-20, Matthew 8:28-34, Luke 8:26-39.*
8. *Mark 5:21-43, Matthew 9:18-26, Luke 8:40-56.*
9. *Mark 9:14-29, Matthew 17:14-21, Luke 9:37-42.*
10. *Mark 10:46-52, Matthew 20:29-34, Luke 18:35-43.*
11. *Mark 11:12-14, 20-25; Matthew 21:18-19, 20-22.*
12. *Mark 8:1-10, Matthew 15:32-39.*
13. *Mark 7:24-30, Matthew 15:21-28.*
14. *Mark 7:31-37.*
15. *Mark 8:22-26.*
16. *Matthew 12:43-45, Luke 11:24-26.*
17. *Matthew 8:5-13, Luke 7:1-10.*
18. *Luke 7:11-17.*
19. *Luke 7:11-16.*
20. *Matthew 9:27-31.*
21. *John 11:47.*
22. *John 11:39.*
23. *John 11:44.*
24. *John 9:1.*
25. *John 6:31-58.*
26. *John 3:1ff.*
27. *John 4:43-54, Matthew 8:5-13, Luke 7:1-10.*
28. *John 6:1-15.*
29. *John 6:16-21.*
30. *John 10:41.*
31. *Acts 14:8-11.*
32. *Acts 28:7-8.*
33. *Acts 28:3-6.*
34. *Acts 20:9-10.*

35. *Matthew* 23:24.
36. *Matthew* 23:16,17,19.
37. *Matthew* 15:14.
38. *Matthew* 15:14.
39. *Tripartite Tractate* 95, *NHS22* p.265.
40. *CPM* 72 p.61.
41. *Mark* 9:18.
42. Jerome, *Dialogue against Pelagius* II:15, *eg. JDPW* pp.317-318.
43. *Matthew* 14:30.
44. *Psalms, MPB* p.139.
45. The various citations: *John-Book, GBJ* pp.71-80.

CHAPTER SEVENTEEN

Holy Food, Holy Mother

Flesh and Blood

We have seen that a comprehension of how the human mind external-
izes and literalizes spiritual truths and mystic experience proves invaluable in helping to understand how Jesus' teachings have formed
into a religion. These observations of decline apply as much to the
discussion of his miracles and teachings as they do to the sacred rites
and unique beliefs of the Christian religion. Probably all of these can
be traced to some aspect of the mystic teachings found in the gospels
and the other mystic literature of that period or of earlier times.

In this book, we are attempting primarily to study Jesus' teachings
rather than Christianity, but some beliefs are so deeply rooted in the
Christian mind and are so much a part of Christianity that it is worth
trying to gain some idea of how they came into existence. In this chapter, therefore, we consider in particular the Christian rite of the
eucharist and the belief in Jesus' Immaculate Conception.

The eucharist is partially founded upon Mark's story of Jesus' last
supper with his disciples. His version reads:

> And as they did eat, Jesus took bread, and blessed, and brake it, and gave
> to them, and said, "Take, eat: this is my body." And he took the cup, and
> when he had given thanks, he gave it to them: and they all drank of it.
> And he said unto them, "This is my blood of the new testament, which is
> shed for many. Verily I say unto you, I will drink no more of the fruit of
> the vine, until that day that I drink it new in the kingdom of God." And
> when they had sung an hymn, they went out into the Mount of Olives.
>
> *Mark 14:22-26*

Matthew's version[1] is essentially a direct copy of Mark, while Luke,
with his penchant for paraphrase, has Jesus bless the "cup" and have it

passed around *before* the meal. This is followed by Jesus' blessing of
the bread, to which he adds the words which have come into the Christian sacrament, "do this in remembrance of me". Then after supper,
Jesus again passes around the cup, telling them, "this cup is the new
testament in my blood, which is shed for you".[2]

The authenticity of this story and the accuracy with which Jesus'
words were recorded rests entirely with Mark who was not an eye-witness, but was writing some thirty to forty-five years later. In fact, at
face value, it is not at all clear what is meant by Jesus' words, if indeed
he actually said them.

Turning to John's gospel for elucidation, we are surprised to find
that John records absolutely nothing concerning any conversation
which Jesus may have had at his last supper with the disciples. His
narrative reads:

> Now before the feast of the passover, when Jesus knew that his hour was
> come that he should depart out of this world unto the Father, having
> loved his own which were in the world, he loved them unto the end. And
> supper being ended, the devil having now put into the heart of Judas
> Iscariot, Simon's son, to betray him....
>
> *John 13:1-2*

Jesus then takes a basin of water and begins to wash his disciples' feet.
As in so many instances, the compiler of John's gospel – who must
have been aware of the contents of the other gospels – relates a different story. It is from an earlier part of John's gospel, however, that we
get more than a hint of the origins and meaning of the last supper
'conversation', as recorded in the synoptic gospels. As discussed in the
chapter on the Word of God, Jesus says:

> I am the Bread of Life:
>   he that cometh to me shall never hunger;
>   and he that believeth on me shall never thirst.
>
> *John 6:35*

And again:

> I am the Living Bread which came down from heaven:
>   if any man eat of this Bread,
>   he shall live for ever.
>
> *John 6:51*

The "Living Bread" or the "Bread of Life" are metaphors for the Creative Word which sustains and nourishes all life. It is the source of all being and existence in the creation. This is clear enough, but Jesus then continues:

> The Bread that I will give is my flesh,
> which I will give for the life of the world....
> Verily, verily, I say unto you,
> except ye eat the flesh of the Son of man,
> and drink his blood, ye have no life in you.
> Whoso eateth my flesh, and drinketh my blood,
> hath eternal life;
> and I will raise him up at the last day.
>
> For my flesh is meat indeed,
> and my blood is drink indeed.
> He that eateth my flesh, and drinketh my blood,
> dwelleth in me, and I in him.
> As the living Father hath sent me,
> and I live by the Father:
> so he that eateth me, even he shall live by me.
> This is that Bread which came down from heaven: ...
> he that eateth of this Bread shall live for ever.
>
> *John 6:51,53-58*

Though the metaphor is a very strange one – eating the flesh and drinking the blood of another – the meaning again seems clear. What gives substance and life – flesh and blood – to a Master, the "Son of man", is the Word. A Master, therefore, is the "Bread which came down from heaven"; he is the "Word made flesh". And one who drinks that blood and eats that flesh is one who comes into contact with such a Master and through him is enabled to experience inner communion with the real essence of a Master – the Word, the "Living Bread".

But why did Jesus choose such a grisly metaphor? Few suggestions have been proffered on this point, perhaps because its later use in Christian ritual has been so crucial to Christian practice and belief. But the most probable answer would seem to be that it is associated with John's metaphor of the Lamb of God being given as a sacrifice for sins.

Judaic and pagan custom in the time of Jesus involved the ritual slaughter of lambs, sheep, oxen and other animals for the supposed purpose of appeasing God or some deity, for invoking forgiveness of sin or for seeking blessings upon some undertaking. The flesh of these animals was then eaten and, in some rituals, the blood was even drunk by the priests. Though to a modern mind, the practice may seem abhorrent, such sacrifices were an essential aspect of many religions of those times. During special festivities, the precincts of the Jewish Temple and other 'holy' temples must have run with the blood of slaughtered animals. It must have also been a considerable source of revenue.

Naturally, mystics are against such practices, for how can God be worshipped and His forgiveness obtained by the killing of His creatures – causing them untold fear and suffering – and then feasting upon their dead remains? Rather, such things coarsen the mind, turning it far away from God, generating a heavy burden of sin and *karma*. Hence Jesus, Paul and many others spoke out against the sacrificial killing of animals. And as a part of his exhortation to abandon ritual slaughtering and feasting, Jesus observed that the only sacrifice which genuinely resulted in the atonement of sin was the sacrifice of the Son of man, the Lamb of God, the Master, by his coming to this world and taking on the sins of his disciples. Similarly, the only consumption of flesh and blood which appeased or pleased the Lord, leading to His true love and worship was to eat the "flesh" and drink the "blood" of this "Son of man", the "Word made flesh" – not that of innocent animals.

Jesus Blesses Bread

This, then, gives us an understanding of the words in St John. But what of the origins of the last supper as narrated in St Mark? Is that an entirely fictitious fabrication, designed and written at a later date to justify the eucharistic meal which so very rapidly became a ritual amongst the early Christians – or is there an element of truth in it?

Tradition has to arise from something. Consequently, it often includes an indication of its origin, however muddled and confused it may have become. In this case, it is possible that the scene of the last supper – and the resulting celebration of the eucharist – draws together two strands of tradition. Firstly, there is the "flesh and blood" metaphor relating to communion of the soul with the Creative Word and secondly, there is Jesus' blessing of bread and water.

The blessing or consecration of food and drink by the priests is a common ritual in practically all religions. The practice is very similar to that of a general grace or blessing at the start of a meal. Though usually performed in a perfunctory manner, such a blessing – if it comes from a sincere heart – is not without its effect. Everything a person does is coloured in a subtle way by the mind, mood and motivation they bring to bear. The mood of a cook, for instance, affects the character as well as the flavour of a meal. Putting one's love and attention into some thing or some person has an effect, according to the content of one's own mind. Moreover, such associations also exert an influence on us. A gift from someone we love is cherished, however simple it may be, because of the association, while more costly items from other sources may have very little value to us.

Mystics of the East and Middle East have made use of these mental strings of association by blessing food for the benefit of their disciples. But this is not a matter of ritual. It is a question of love and association, faith also being involved on the part of the recipient for the full benefit of such a blessing to take effect.

Given the universal prevalence of such a practice, there is no reason to doubt that Jesus, too, would have followed the same custom. Simply by his breaking bread and giving it to his disciples they would have felt that his blessing had been imparted, whether he said anything or not, and likewise with the cup.

The synoptic version of the last supper, then, seems to combine this blessing of food by Jesus – which he probably did whenever he sat down to eat with his disciples – with metaphors concerning the Word as the Living Bread, the Living Water and the divine wine of love.

There is also another source from which the external aspects of the eucharist could have been derived. Cult meals were common to a number of sects and religions in early and pre-Christian times. The Roman religion of Mithraism was one of these, taking the ancient Persian-Aryan god Mithras as their deity, and a number of modern scholars, as well as early Christian fathers, have observed that their rituals had a great many similarities to those of Christianity, including baptism for the forgiveness of sins through a rite very similar to the eucharist.

So close in character were these rituals – which predated Christianity – that the early Christian father, Tertullian, was even moved to write that the Devil had plagiarized (by anticipation) the later Christian rite:

It is his (the Devil's) character to pervert the truth, mimicking the exact circumstances of the divine sacraments (*i.e.* the eucharist) in the mysteries of idols.

Tertullian, On the 'Prescription' of Heretics XL; cf. TTSPH p.89, WTII p.49

Likewise, in the mid-second century, Justin Martyr wrote of the eucharistic sacrament of the body and the cup

> which the wicked devils have imitated in the mysteries of Mithras, commanding the same things to be done.
>
> *Justin Martyr, First Apology LXVI, WJMA p.65*

The more historical assumption is that the ritualistic details of the Christian eucharist were at least partially introduced by Roman converts familiar with the older Mithraic ritual. This is in keeping with the way in which religious customs come into existence. Beliefs and practices of extant religions are incorporated, with or without modification, into the new, though they too may have a lost or hidden esoteric meaning.

Water or Wine?

It is significant that although Mark's gospel, followed by Matthew and Luke, has Jesus speak of the "fruit of the vine", it is not stated whether this was wine or grape juice, while the discourse in St John identifies no particular drink as symbolic of the 'blood of the Son of man'. Even in Paul's mention of the eucharist, only the "cup" is mentioned – not wine.[3] The significance lies in the alcoholic content of wine and the fact that John the Baptist and many early Christian and other spiritual groups abstained from alcohol. Abstention from intoxicants has always been a part of mystic teachings, as we will later be discussing. So if Jesus was the mystic that the teachings attributed to him suggest he was, then it is certain that he would have abstained, too.

Later custom presumed that the drink was wine, which has come down to the present time, traditionally mixed with water. But in many early Christian writings, the eucharistic drink is very firmly stated to be that of water alone. In the *Acts of John*, the *Acts of Paul*, the *Acts of Peter* and other apocryphal literature, it is almost always bread and water that is offered by the apostles as blessed food and drink. For example:

> Now they brought unto Paul bread and water for the (eucharistic) sacrifice, that he might make prayer and distribute it to every one.
>
> *Acts of Peter III:II, ANT p.304*

And again:

> (And Paul) brake bread and brought water also and gave her to drink
> with a word.
>
> *Acts of Paul (Hamburg papyrus), ANT p.573*

And sometimes, it is only bread:

> He (John) brake the bread and gave unto all of us, praying over each of
> the brethren that he might be worthy of the grace of the Lord and of the
> most holy eucharist.
>
> *Acts of John 110, ANT p.268*

In the *Acts of Thomas*, the taking of blessed bread and water almost
invariably follows baptism:

> And when she was baptized and clad, he (Judas Thomas) brake bread
> and took a cup of water and made her a partaker in the body of Christ
> and the cup of the Son of God.
>
> *Acts of Thomas 121, ANT p.418*

In fact, while the Greek text of the *Acts of Thomas* never speaks of wine
as a part of the eucharist, wine has been added to a *later* Syriac text in
some places. The Greek, for example, reads:

> And when they were baptized ... he set bread on the table and blessed it.
>
> *Acts of Thomas 133, ANT p.422*

While the corresponding Syriac has:

> And when they were baptized ... he brought bread and wine, and placed
> it on the table, and began to bless it.
>
> *Acts of Thomas, AAA p.268*

Yet, significantly, a fragment from a much *earlier* Syriac text has the
same wording *omitting* the words "and wine".[4]

The same editorial process can be observed in the later Ethiopic
version of the *Acts of Thomas* where wine has again been slipped into
the translation when only water is present in the Greek and Syriac texts.
So while the Greek reads:

> He laid his hands on them and blessed them, and brake the bread of the eucharist and gave it them.
>
> *Acts of Thomas 29, ANT p.377*

The Ethiopic, demonstrating a characteristically verbose and loose translation throughout, has:

> And he took pure bread and a cup full of wine, he gave thanks, and brake the bread, and gave to the people that had been baptized of the body of our Lord and of his precious blood.
>
> *Acts of Thomas 28, AA p.52*

This tendency can be observed in other ancient documents, too, as between the Greek text of the *Acts of John* and the Syriac. The Greek contains no mention of wine, while the Syriac does. Once again, we see how easy it was to alter texts to fit later beliefs and practices. And again, it is noticeable that the changes are almost invariably in the direction of descent and decline, away from the self-control, natural discipline and spirituality of the true mystic teachings. This trend is almost a principle which can be used to determine which is the older and more reliable reading when faced with variant texts.

There is no doubt that some of the early Christian groups used only bread and water in their eucharist. Groups such as the Ebionites (Judaic Christians) who lasted into the fifth century and represent the descendants of some of Jesus' direct disciples in Palestine, are well known to have abstained from 'strong drink'. The fourth-century Epiphanius writes:

> And they (the Judaic Christians) ... perform the mysteries annually in imitation of the holy rites (eucharist) in the church by using unleavened bread and for the other part of the mystery, by using water only.
>
> *Epiphanius, Panarion II:16.1, CIEKE pp.142-143, VJC p.158*

Similarly, concerning the mid-second-century gnostic teacher, Marcion, Epiphanius complains, "he uses water in the mysteries (the eucharist)".[5] In fact, it would be no surprise if many of the mystically inclined had not practised the external eucharistic ritual. The early second-century father, Ignatius, certainly writes of another such group in his *Epistle to the Smyrnaeans*:

They abstain from eucharist and prayer, because they do not confess that the eucharist is the flesh of our Saviour Jesus Christ who suffered for our sins.

Ignatius, To the Smyrnaeans VII:1, AFI p.259

The first half of his letter is largely taken up with a warning against 'heretical' teachers who do not hold the same doctrines as himself. These he castigates as "unbelievers" and "beasts in the form of men whom you must not only not receive but, if it is possible, not even meet".[6] But it is clear from the context that he speaking of the more mystically-oriented groups of early Christians.

Living Bread, Living Water, Living Wine

As we have seen before, the apocryphal acts, especially the *Acts of Thomas*, are remarkable for their use of symbolism, metaphor and allegory. Even the stories of seemingly ritualistic baptism and eucharist only seem to be a structure upon which to hang spiritual truths, for they are usually accompanied by short discourses where the external rites are given an inner mystic meaning. There is, for instance, Judas Thomas' blessing of bread:

> Living Bread, which came down from heaven,
>   the eaters of which die not!
> Bread, that fillest hungry souls with thy blessing!
>
> *Acts of Thomas, AAA p.268*

Judas is ostensibly blessing ordinary bread, but the words he utters refer to the mystic reality. Such words, of course, echo those of John's gospel and there are many such references in the ancient literature. In *Joseph and Aseneth*, for example, an allegorical romance from early Christian times, in a symbolic reference to baptism, Aseneth is told:

> From today you will be made new,
>   and refashioned, and given new life;
> And you shall eat the Bread of Life
>   and drink the Cup of Immortality,
>   and be anointed with the Unction of Incorruption.
>
> *Joseph and Aseneth XV, AOT p.488*

There is no hint in this story of any external rite. The "Bread of Life", the "Cup of Immortality" and the "Unction of Incorruption" are all metaphors for the Word through which a disciple is "made new" or "born again" when they receive initiation. Then they are given an impulse of "new life"; they are "refashioned" and enabled to repent, to change their way of being, inwardly, and begin the journey homewards. The meaning is entirely mystic and inward, as it is in John's gospel.

In the Manichaean literature, too, the same metaphors are used devoid of any eucharistic setting:

> He gave the Bread of Life to the hungry;
> the clothing he brought to the naked.
>
> *Psalm CCXXVIII, MPB p.23*

Here, the hungry are the people of this world – since we are all spiritually hungry. We are also naked of the true garment of radiance that is the soul's natural inheritance.

In fact, bread, water and wine were all used as mystic metaphors for the Word. Water meant the Living Water of the Word, while wine referred to the sweet intoxication of divine love and bliss experienced through mystic communion with the divine Music. The use of Living Water and the True Vine have previously been discussed and wine is also a universally encountered mystic simile, frequently found amongst the early Christian liturgies, as well as the gnostic and Manichaean-Christian writings. All of these lead us further to the opinion that the eucharist as a ritual is an externalization of a mystic reality.

In the *Acts of Thomas*, for example, the Living Bread or "Immortal Food", the "Wine that giveth ... neither thirst nor desire", the "Living Spirit", the "Truth" and "Wisdom" are all equated when Judas Thomas speaks of the "Father of all" as:

> (He) whose proud light they have received,
>   and are enlightened by the sight of their Lord;
> (He) whose Immortal Food they have received,
>   that hath no failing,
>   and have drunk of the Wine
>   that giveth them neither thirst nor desire.
> And they have glorified and praised,
>   with the Living Spirit,
>   the Father of Truth and the Mother of Wisdom.
>
> *Acts of Thomas 7, ANT pp.367-368*

In an early Christian hymn of the late fourth-century Syrian, Cyril-lonas, a pointedly mystical interpretation is given of Jesus' last supper:

> This is the Vine that giveth to drink
> to mankind so that they obtain their lives.
> This is the Vine that through its drink
> comforteth the souls of the mourners.
> This is the Vine that through its Wine
> purifieth creation from iniquity.
>
> It is the cluster that pressed itself out
> at eventide in the upper chamber,
> and gave itself in the cup to his disciples
> as the testament of Truth.
> O Vine, how strong thou art,
> thou whose riches are never lacking.
>
> *Cyrillonas, GC p.580, MEM p.134*

The "Vine" is the Word, being the same as Jesus' "True Vine". The "Wine" from this "Vine" "purifieth creation from iniquity" – undoubt-edly a reference to the Word, for no worldly wine, even in the hands of a priest, could be expected to perform such a function.

It is also that which was drunk "at eventide in the upper chamber" and "gave itself in the cup to his disciples". This is an interesting allu-sion to the last supper, for the "upper chamber" in which Jesus is sup-posed to have eaten the last supper with his disciples is here given a mystical meaning, too. It refers to the upper regions where this "cup" is to be truly found and drunk.

It is also the "testament of Truth" – the covenant of Truth and the means of knowing the Truth. Again, this is a reference to the Word and it explains Jesus' otherwise mysterious words in St Mark:

> This is my blood of the new testament,
> which is shed for many.
>
> *Mark 14:24*

The Word is the ever-new "testament" or covenant, the eternal 'agree-ment' or bond between God and man. It is "shed for many" in the sense that a Master's life, as a personification of the Word, is given as a sacrifice for his disciples.

In a Nestorian eucharistic liturgy, it is clear that although the ritual was practised externally, the hope was that the bread and the wine would take on the character of their higher mystic counterpart:

> Behold, the Medicine of Life,
>   which descended from on high,
>   is dispensed in the church,
>   and is hidden in the sacraments,
>   in the bread and wine.
>
> Put forth now your hands, O ye who are dying,
>   and have taken up your abode in Sheol
>   on account of our sins;
> Take and be forgiven, and attain unto life,
>   and reign with Christ, and sing and say:
> "Alleluia, this is the Bread of which
>   if any man shall eat he shall escape hell."
>
> *NRII XXXII:2 pp.167-168*

Those "who are dying" are the souls of this world, those who "have taken up their abode in Sheol on account of their sins". It is evident that the writer of this liturgy understands that it is the mystic Bread and Wine which will forgive the sins of the "dying", permitting the soul to escape from the "hell" of this world. But it is a vain hope that such power can be transferred into earthly food, as is commonly believed in Christianity even to the present day.

In another extract from early Christian writings, this time from the fifth- or perhaps sixth-century Syrian poet, Isaac of Antioch, the eucharist is described as the "Medicine" which heals the sick and raises the dead. But, as we have seen, these are spiritual healings, not physical miracles. Here, the "eucharist" refers to the inner, mystic communion of the soul with the Word:

> She gave therefore the Medicine at last,
>   the eucharist, which healeth the sick
>   and vivifieth the dead
>   and closeth the wounds.
>
> *Isaac of Antioch, IADSII p.30, MEM p.146*

The writers of the Manichaean-Christian psalms were also fond of these metaphors and we encounter them in a number of places.

Jesus, for example, is described as the "Living Wine, the child of the True Vine":

> Thou art the Living Wine,
>> the child of the True Vine.
>
> Give us to drink a Living Wine from thy Vine.
>
> *Psalms, MPB p.151*

In another, there is an allusion to the eucharist, when the psalmist says that the Holy Spirit has "brought the cup of Water":

> The Holy Spirit has come unto us....
> He has brought the cup of Water,
>> he has given it to his church also.
>
> *Psalms, MPB p.184*

Again, the "Son of the Living God, the Physician of souls" is likened to the "sweet spring of Water" and the "True Vine" that springs from the "Living Wine":

> The Son of the Living God,
>> the Physician of souls,
>> come, sing to him, the Saviour of spirits....
>
> The holy Bread of Life
>> that is come from the skies (inner realms).
> The sweet spring of Water that leaps unto life.
> The True Vine, that of the Living Wine.
>
> *Psalms of Heracleides, MPB p.193*

And in a reference to Jesus' saying concerning new wine in new bottles, we read:

> Lo, Wisdom is flourishing:
>> where is there an ear to hear it?
> Lo, the New Wine we have found:
>> we would have new bottles for it.
>
> *Psalms, MPB p.153*

The ever-new and eternally fresh wine of the Word or Wisdom can only find a place in a freshly-cleaned and renewed human heart. It can never come to dwell in old "bottles", full with the sins of innumerable past lives and the engrained habits of ritualistic and ceremonial worship. This saying of Jesus, then, is another instance in which he uses the metaphor of wine with a mystic meaning. Similarly, in a passage which echoes lines from both *Proverbs* and the *Song of Songs*:

> Wisdom invites you,
>   that you may eat with your spirit.
> Lo, the New Wine has been broached:
> Lo, the cups have been brought in.
> Drink what you shall drink,
>   gladness surrounding you.
> Eat that you may eat,
>   being glad in your spirit.
>
> *Psalms, MPB p.158*

In all these contexts, the eating and drinking refer to the spiritual nature of man, the soul taking its nourishment and sustenance from its intoxicating contact with the Word within.

The True Pihta Bread

In the Mandaean literature, we find the same story. Here, the 'holy Bread' is known as *Pihta*, which means 'the opened' or 'the revealed', used in the sense of God's 'opening' or 'revealing' himself in the act of creation. *Pihta*, then, is God's opening or emanation – His creative Power or Word. Thus, speaking of the "Father of Radiance", a Mandaean poet writes:

> He arose and broke Bread (*Pihta*) in secret
>   and gave thereof to the sons of men
>   and established his Abode in secret.
>
> *CPM 38 p.38*

The Bread of the Word is given to the "sons of men" "in secret", that is, mystically, inside. And as a result they can enjoy the true communion with Him in His eternal "Abode". Hence, the devotee says:

> He who partaketh of this Bread (*Pihta*),
>   put out for him,

will be sinless in the Place of Light,
the everlasting abode.

CPM 43 p.40

As before, this mystic "Bread" also cleanses the soul of all past sins. But most significant of all amongst the Mandaean writings on this subject is an allegory 'told' by the pure "white *Pihta*" itself, clearly symbolic of the Word. The pure *Pihta* tells of its degradation (in the minds of human beings) from pure mystic essence to the bread of this world, where it is taken as physical food, "fodder for beasts" and eaten in religious ceremony.

In the story, the Word comes to this world "as food for Adam and his sons", that is, as spiritual sustenance for man. This represents the coming of a Master to this world. The first few generations understand and follow his teachings, without externalizing and perverting them. But after that, misunderstandings creep in and things are "omitted" and "subtracted" from the original teachings. In general, it is a simple and explicit tale of the degeneration of a mystic's teachings concerning the Word, the Living Bread, into a religion. The "Seven", incidentally, refer to the five planets as they were known at the time, plus the sun and moon. They are an astrological allusion commonly used metaphorically in Mandaean writings for the powers of destiny or *karma* – to the powers of Satan:

The white *Pihta* am I!
The creature of light, I came into existence.
Pihta am I, the white,
    for *Yawar* (*lit.* radiance) was my Transplanter.
My Creator was *Yawar*,
    from his treasury he brought me....
He took me, brought me down;
    set me down in the earthly world,
    as food for Adam and all his sons.

Whilst the first generation existed,
    they ate me in good faith,
    in good faith did they eat me;
No trickery did they perform with me,
    they performed with me no misuse.
Nor did they omit or subtract from me
    they committed no omission or subtraction

and the creatures of the Seven
had no dominion over me.

When a second generation came into being
   they too ate me aright,
   sincerely they ate me:
No trickery did they perform with me,
   they performed with me no crooked dealing.
They did not omit or subtract from me,
   from me they neither omitted nor subtracted
   and the creatures of the Seven had no power over me.

When a third generation arose,
   Adonai (*lit.* 'my Lord') built a House,
   a house did Adonai build,
   and the Seven obtained a hold in it.
Then it was dispersed
   amongst the three hundred and sixty-two nations.
And then I was taken from their midst and they cast me
   amongst the three hundred and sixty-two nations.

Then they ate me with falsehood,
   with falsehood did they eat me.
Wrongly did they use me,
   they used me falsely.
And did with me that which was deficient and lacking,
   that which was deficient and lacking they did with me
   and creatures of the Seven gained dominion over me.

Then strength was taken from me,
   and radiance, order, taste and glory,
   and they made me the fodder of beasts.
Souls departed from their bodies without their measure.

                                                CPM 353 pp.244-245

So the Living Bread of which mystics speak, the creative Power of the
Supreme Word, is ultimately replaced by physical bread, eaten by the
mouth, "fodder of beasts" – food for human beings so lacking in true
spirituality that they have become like beasts. The fact that this eating
is performed in a symbolic ritual conducted in the name of a departed
mystic makes not the slightest bit of difference to its lack of efficacy.

Physical bread remains physical bread and the vast creative Power of God is not to be found therein. There is no record of anyone ever having attained union with God by eating a piece of bread, whatever that bread was supposed to represent.

When the mystic teachings are misunderstood, as by human nature they are bound to be, they become debased, ending up as food for "beasts" – the source of all manner of justification for human weakness and external religious practice. Then, all the "strength ... radiance, order, taste and glory" is "taken from" the teachings. As a result, souls who have come to this world and put their faith in the religions that have formed around those teachings, die without taking with them the true spiritual inheritance that is their human birthright.

Such is the case of those who mistake outward ritual for inward truth. And, as we have seen, there are ample instances which demonstrate that the eucharist, the last supper and the discourse in St John all have a mystical meaning and were never intended to be interpreted literally or externally.

Water into Wine

Just as Christianity condones many practices that run counter to Jesus' teachings, so too do the Mandaeans, despite such poems in their literature, practise a form of eucharistic sacrament. In this ritual, though in modern times the priest does mix water into the wine, water alone has traditionally been used. But most intriguingly, during the course of some of their rituals, this water which is added is itself considered to be miraculously converted into wine, while the priest chants:

> Truth maketh you whole!
> Water into wine!
> *Alma Rishaia Rba 260, PNC p.18*

Now, in our previous discussion of miracles, we deferred discussion of the first miracle recorded by John's gospel at Cana in Galilee, where Jesus turns water into wine at a wedding feast. But maybe this Mandaean refrain, together with our study of the eucharist, can give us an insight into its real meaning.

As a story alone, the miracle is difficult to comprehend. Why would Jesus turn water into wine and help to make everybody drunk at a party? But a knowledge of John's predilection for symbolic anecdotes, miraculous or otherwise, makes us wonder if it was meant more as a parable than a miracle story, its key feature being Jesus' conversion of water into wine.

Looking at the Mandaean refrain, the turning of water into wine is equated with "Truth maketh you whole!" That is, the tasteless water of an imperfect and worldly human being is turned into the sweet wine of perfection through the intermediary of the Truth, the Word of God. Or, expressed in another way, the Master turns the insipid water of worldly or intellectual knowledge into the full and rich wine of divine knowledge or mystic experience. Or, again, the bland water of religion is turned into the intoxicating wine of spirituality. In fact, there is another Mandaean verse where this meaning is explicitly stated:

> Like the mingling of wine with water,
>   so may thy Truth, Thy righteousness and Thy faith
>   be added to those who love Thy Name of Truth.
>
> *CPM 45 p.41*

Is this the real meaning of John's first miracle story? It is by no means an original suggestion. The fourteenth-century English mystic, Walter Hilton, for example, in his *Ladder of Perfection*, contrasting the intellectual grasp or knowledge of spiritual matters with divine or mystic knowledge, points out:

> Knowledge by itself stirs the heart to pride, but united to love it turns to edification. By itself, this knowledge is like water, tasteless and cold. But if those who have it will offer it humbly to our Lord and ask for his grace, he will turn the water into wine with his blessing as he did at the request of his Mother at the marriage-feast.
>
> In other words, he will turn this savourless knowledge into wisdom, and cold naked reason into spiritual light and burning love by the gift of the Holy Spirit.
>
> *Walter Hilton, LP pp.4-5*

The conversion of the water of ordinary man into the wine of divinity is a Master's primary task. Hence John concludes this miracle story:

> This beginning of miracles did Jesus in Cana of Galilee, and manifested forth his glory; and his disciples believed on him.
>
> *John 2:11*

It does seem, then, as if John is again speaking symbolically. He makes this 'miracle' the very first which Jesus performs, since this is the primary purpose of a mystic's life. Bringing spirituality to human hearts is what manifests forth the glory of a Master – not helping people to get drunk at a marriage party! And it is this transformation within themselves which makes his disciples believe in him, bringing real faith into their hearts – something which a miracle with worldly water and human wine could never do.

But there is another significant aspect to this story. As Walter Hilton pointed out, the conversion is made by Jesus at a marriage party at the request of his mother. Now, marriage is a very common symbol for the mystic union of the soul with the Lord, and has been used by mystics of all ages and cultures. Additionally, a Master manifests in this world at the 'request' or 'command' of the Holy Spirit or Wisdom, often known in ancient times as the Mother. Jesus, then, goes to the marriage and at the request of his mother he converts water into wine. The Master comes to this world at the request of the Holy Spirit or Wisdom, the divine Mother, and converts the water of man into the wine of God. The story symbolizes the mystic marriage of the soul with God.

The Virgin Mother

Evidence that the miracles stories, the eucharist and the last supper are literalizations of mystic truth, together with a possible symbolic meaning of Jesus' 'mother' in the story of the marriage at Cana, makes one wonder if the same is also true for another of Christianity's sacred beliefs – that Jesus' mother was a virgin.

Taking the matter from the beginning, we have previously observed that neither John's gospel nor that of Mark make any mention of a virgin birth. It is probable, therefore, that the writers of these two gospels did not hold the belief, for surely they would otherwise have mentioned it? By the time that John's gospel was compiled, the belief was certainly in existence, for it was recorded in the gospels of Matthew and Luke. Moreover, if the writer of the major part of John's gospel was indeed John the Apostle, then he would have been a close companion of Jesus, the one to whom Jesus had entrusted his mother after his death. Having been so close to them, it is hardly likely that he would have failed to mention such a momentous and significant fact, had it been true.

In the case of Mark, not only does he make no mention of it, despite his love of the miraculous, he also relates that Jesus ignores his mother and brothers when told that they were standing outside, wanting to talk to him. In fact, according to Mark, Jesus responds that his real mother and brothers are those sitting around him and those who live in the will of God.[7] Although the anecdote is probably only a setting for Jesus' observation, Mark would hardly have invented or related such a story if he had held Jesus' mother in esteem as having given birth to Jesus by divine intervention. It also seems unlikely that Jesus would have spoken of his mother in such a fashion, whether or not she had given birth to him by miraculous means.

Matthew and Luke both copy over Mark's story of Jesus' response to his mother and brothers,[8] but while the more literal Matthew copies Mark almost verbatim, despite its incongruity alongside his story of the virgin birth, Luke truncates and softens Jesus' response to make it more acceptable and probable. All the same, the use of Mark's anecdote by Matthew and Luke is surprising and is only understandable when it is appreciated that the actual cult and worship of the Virgin Mary were not prevalent when they were writing. This was a later introduction stemming from second-century embellishments to her life story, though even less is known of her than of Jesus.

Apart from the two short narratives at the beginning of Matthew and Luke, there are no further references to the subject anywhere else in the gospels. Not one of the sayings or parables of Jesus ever refer to it. Jesus never speaks about his early life and he clearly gave equally little importance to the history of his birth. In fact, in the entire New Testament, the virgin birth is *only* mentioned in Matthew and Luke. Neither Paul – whose letters date from the 50s and 60s AD – nor *Acts*, nor the *Book of Revelation*, nor the writers of any of the other epistles, even hint at it. Given his loquacious character, one would have expected Paul to speak of it had he considered it a part of Christian belief, just as he constantly reiterates his belief in Jesus' physical resurrection. Indeed, one wonders whether the idea was even extant during Paul's lifetime, for surely he would have encountered it and given his opinion on the matter, even if he had not believed in it? Indeed, Paul actually speaks of the physical birth of Jesus using explicitly physical terms:

Concerning his Son Jesus Christ our Lord,
which was made of the seed of David
according to the flesh;

> And declared to be the Son of God with power,
>   according to the Spirit of Holiness.
>
> *Romans 1:3-4*

As we have discussed earlier, the infancy stories provided by Matthew and Luke are historically incompatible. But not only that – the two virgin-birth stories also have their differences. Matthew relates:

> Now the birth of Jesus Christ was on this wise. When as his mother Mary was espoused to Joseph, before they came together, she was found with child of the Holy Ghost. Then Joseph her husband, being a just man, and not willing to make her a public example, was minded to put her away privily.
>
> But while he thought on these things, behold, the angel of the Lord appeared unto him in a dream, saying, Joseph, thou son of David, fear not to take unto thee Mary thy wife: for that which is conceived in her is of the Holy Ghost. And she shall bring forth a son, and thou shalt call his name Jesus: for he shall save his people from their sins.
>
> Now all this was done, that it might be fulfilled which was spoken of the Lord by the prophet, saying, "Behold, a virgin shall be with child, and shall bring forth a son, and they shall call his name Emmanuel," which being interpreted is, God with us.
>
> Then Joseph being raised from sleep did as the angel of the Lord had bidden him, and took unto him his wife. And knew her not till she had brought forth her first-born son: and he called his name Jesus.
>
> *Matthew 1:18-25*

Luke, on the other hand, records that:

> The angel Gabriel was sent from God unto a city of Galilee, named Nazareth, to a virgin espoused to a man whose name was Joseph, of the house of David; and the virgin's name was Mary. And the angel came in unto her, and said, "Hail, thou that art highly favoured, the Lord is with thee: blessed art thou among women."
>
> And when she saw him, she was troubled at his saying, and cast in her mind what manner of salutation this should be. And the angel said unto her, "Fear not, Mary: for thou hast found favour with God. And, behold, thou shalt conceive in thy womb, and bring forth a son, and shalt call his name Jesus. He shall be great, and shall be called the Son of the Highest: and the Lord God shall give unto him the throne of his father David. And he shall reign over the house of Jacob for ever; and of his kingdom there shall be no end."

> Then said Mary unto the angel, "How shall this be, seeing I know not a man?"
>
> And the angel answered and said unto her, "The Holy Ghost shall come upon thee, and the power of the Highest shall overshadow thee: therefore also that holy thing which shall be born of thee shall be called the Son of God. And, behold, thy cousin Elizabeth, she hath also conceived a son in her old age: and this is the sixth month with her, who was called barren. For with God nothing shall be impossible."
>
> And Mary said, "Behold the handmaid of the Lord; be it unto me according to thy word." And the angel departed from her.
>
> *Luke 1:26-38*

In Matthew, it is Joseph who meets the angel. In Luke, it is Mary. And the meeting constitutes the bulk of the story. The two stories are not essentially incompatible, of course, but the variants seem more like the ramifications of legend, rather than of history. Matthew, characteristically, also has a quote from scripture prefaced with his familiar introduction, "all this was done, that it might be fulfilled". It has been pointed out many times, however, that Matthew's quote from Isaiah[9] refers to a maiden or young woman, not necessarily a virgin. In any case, when seen in its context, whatever the whole passage from *Isaiah* may mean, it requires more than a fair stretch of the imagination to conclude that it is a prophecy concerning Jesus. This has been an entirely Christian claim, something which Judaism has never accepted.

Jesus' Brothers and Sisters

There is also the knotty problem of Jesus' brothers and sisters. Four brothers and two sisters is the total usually given. It is Mark who introduces them, to whom they cause no embarrassment, as he does not subscribe to the belief in a virgin birth. They appear in the narrative when Jesus returns to Galilee, where the people knew him from his childhood. Surprised at his wisdom and his teachings, they say:

> "Is not this the carpenter, the son of Mary, the brother of James, and Joses, and of Juda, and Simon? And are not his sisters here with us?" And they were offended at him.
>
> But Jesus, said unto them, "A prophet is not without honour, but in his own country, and among his own kin, and in his own house." And he

could there do no mighty work, save that he laid his hands upon a few sick folk, and healed them.

Mark 6:3-5

In characteristically Marcan style, although Jesus can do "no mighty work" in Galilee, he still manages to heal a "few sick folk" – throwaway miracles one might call them.

The more literal and conservative Matthew copies Mark almost verbatim[10] and one presumes that he intended his readers to assume that Jesus was the eldest of Mary's large family, for his last word on the subject reads:

And he (Joseph) knew her not till she had brought forth her first-born son.

Matthew 1:25

The observation, it may be noted, is contrary to the belief in Mary as a perpetual virgin, a doctrine that prevailed after the middle of the second-century and which has always been a matter of debate within the Church, though in modern times it finds general acceptance only in Catholicism. Luke also adds to his story of Jesus' birth that Mary "brought forth her first-born son",[11] leading the reader to presume that, later, she had more children. But he is evidently uncomfortable about naming Jesus' brothers and sisters, for he modifies the tale of Jesus' visit to Galilee, omitting all mention of them:

And they said, "Is not this Joseph's son?" And he said unto them, "Ye will surely say unto me this proverb, 'physician, heal thyself': whatsoever we have heard done in Capernaum, do also here in thy country."

And he said, "Verily I say unto you, no prophet is accepted in his own country."

Luke 4:22-24

But omitting Jesus' brothers and sisters leaves the saying concerning the acceptability of a prophet in his own country without a lead-in, especially since Luke is forced to delete Mark's reference to "his own kin" since it has no relevance in the absence of Jesus' brothers and sisters. To compensate, he introduces a unique contribution: "Physician, heal thyself". If Luke was really the "Doctor Luke" of Paul's letters, then the saying would have struck him professionally, but in the context it fits awkwardly, leaving the narrative and Jesus' words without continuity, exhibiting the signs of an editorial hand. Luke, then, felt uncomfortable with Mark's naming of Jesus' brothers and sisters and one wonders why, especially since Luke later mentions Jesus' mother and brothers in the incident where they ask to see him, while in *Acts*, he depicts them as a part of the circle of apostles.[12]

John also speaks of Jesus' brothers, stating unequivocally, "neither did his brethren believe in him"[13] and since there is no good reason why such a comment should have been invented, it is likely to be founded upon some truth.

Historically, there is no doubt that Jesus did have at least one brother, James, because Paul and other writers speak of him and there is even a letter attributed to him in the New Testament. Paul had actually met James and would probably have known the exact relationship which he bore to Jesus, and the part he played in the early Christian community at Jerusalem. Even the first-century historian, Josephus, mentions him. But the matter of Jesus' brothers and sisters is clearly an embarrassment to those Christians who believed in the virgin birth, particularly since – according to tradition – they all seem to have been *older* than Jesus. Is this the source of Luke's discomfort?

The existence of older brothers and sisters was clearly at variance with any stories of a virgin birth and a number of myths grew up which attempted to explain away the difficulty. Perhaps the most ingenious of these was the tale that Joseph had been a widower. His previous wife, ran the story, had borne him six children, but had died while James was still very young. Joseph was then betrothed to Mary and subsequently married her, Jesus being the one and only child of their union. Subsequently, Mary helped to raise James and the other children.

The story's first appearance in an extant document is in the second- or third-century infancy gospel, the *Protoevangelium of James*,[14] but it had probably been around in the oral tradition for some time previously. This writing was of considerable popularity well into medieval times and a large number of manuscripts of it are to be found, many containing significant variations. The story is also encountered in some of the Coptic apocryphal writings, most probably relying on the *Protoevangelium* as their source, where it is also stated that the names of Jesus' half-sisters were Lydia and Lysia,[15] though elsewhere, other names are given.

But there remain a number of difficulties even with this version of events. Why, for example, are these brothers and sisters not mentioned by Luke and Matthew in their infancy stories? James would certainly have been too young to have been left at home while his parents travelled to Bethlehem or Egypt, depending on whose version of the story you read. Moreover, if Luke's story of the census was correct, then the entire family would have been required to travel to Bethlehem. Yet the gospel stories never portray Joseph, Mary and Jesus as travelling with six variously-aged children in tow.

It is unlikely that we will ever know the true history of Jesus and his family, nor does it make any difference to his teachings. These discrepancies are mentioned simply to highlight the incompatibilities between the various virgin-birth and associated stories. Like chickens in a farmyard invaded by a hungry dog or like naughty children trying to explain themselves when caught red-handed, the variants of the story scatter once reality is left behind. The most likely explanation is that Jesus was simply a child from a large family. But that, of course, does not satisfy the advocates of a virgin birth.

The House of His Servant David

Luke and Matthew also make the curious attempt to trace Jesus' family tree. But they present two entirely different genealogies in which practically all the names differ. Even the name of Joseph's father differs, appearing as Jacob in Matthew and as Heli in Luke. Luke is also more ambitious. Starting with Joseph, he traces Jesus' ancestry back through David, all the way to Adam, while Matthew starts with Abraham and works forward. These genealogies have almost certainly been inserted by Luke and Matthew from independent written sources, their purpose being to prove that Jesus was born in the 'house of David', also having Abraham for an ancestor. There were probably many such genealogies in existence at that time, for there were always many claimants to the Messiahship and names could very easily be changed as necessary.

Now since these family lineages both lead to Joseph as the father of Jesus, they probably came from the pens of those who did not give credence to a virgin birth. For the whole point of the virgin-birth story was that Joseph was *not* the father of Jesus. In fact, Joseph was not even married to Mary at the time of her conception – they were only "betrothed". This was a feature required by the virgin-birth stories, for no one would have accepted that Mary had still been a virgin, had they already been married.

Although the genealogies sit awkwardly alongside stories of the virgin birth, the tracing of Jesus' ancestry to David was too important for Luke and Matthew to omit. Caught between necessity and contradiction,

Luke found it necessary to add the parenthetical "as was supposed", qualifying Joseph as the father of Jesus:

> And Jesus ... being (as was supposed) the son of Joseph, which was the son of Heli ... etc.
>
> *Luke 3:23*

The more literal Matthew, on the other hand, as in the instance of Jesus' brothers and sisters, lets them remain in contradiction, standing unqualified alongside each other.

The importance of Jesus' ancestry stems from the Jewish belief that the Messiah would come in the 'house of David'. All four of the gospel writers mention the fact – John once and the synoptics on many occasions, Jesus often being referred to as the "Son of David".[16] Additionally, Luke's angel says to Mary:

> He shall be great, and shall be called the Son of the Highest: and the Lord God shall give unto him the throne of his father David.
>
> *Luke 1:32*

While Matthew's angel pointedly calls Joseph, "thou son of David".[17] Likewise, again in Luke has Zacharias, the father of John the Baptist, say:

> Blessed be the Lord God of Israel;
>   for he hath visited and redeemed his people,
> And hath raised up an horn of salvation for us
>   in the house of his servant David;
> As he spake by the mouth of his holy prophets,
>   which have been since the world began.
>
> *Luke 1:68-70*

It was of great importance to the early Christians to prove that Jesus was the promised Messiah, from the 'house of David'. It would seem, however, that the true meaning of this belief is not physical, but spiritual. David's son Solomon, the first in the 'house of David', is described in *1 Kings*, as the greatest amongst wise men:

> Yahweh gave Solomon immense wisdom and understanding,
>   and a heart as vast as the sand on the seashore.
> The wisdom of Solomon surpassed the wisdom
>   of the sons of the East, and all the wisdom of Egypt.

He was wiser than any other, ...

> he composed three thousand proverbs,
> and his songs numbered a thousand and five....

Men from all nations came to hear Solomon's wisdom.

1 Kings 4:29-32, JB

Solomon's understanding is compared to the wisdom of Egypt and the East, traditionally the ancient repositories of mystic lore. That is, his wisdom was that of a mystic and being born in the 'house of David' or Solomon actually refers to the spiritual successorship or lineage of the Masters. The Messiah or Christ was the 'anointed one', the one who *messiah* was sealed or appointed by God to act as Saviour. It was, as we have seen, a term that was synonymous with 'Saviour' or 'perfect Master'. And the lineage of a perfect Master is spiritual, from Master to successor. In this sense, all Masters, all Messiahs or Christs, come from the same 'family' – but spiritually, not physically. Matthew and Luke were thus mistaken in thinking that they had to trace Jesus' real parentage to David.

After all, if you do the mathematics, within only 15 or 20 generations everyone can trace their ancestry to practically anyone they choose. If each father had three children, then after 15 generations the original ancestor would have a little more than 43 million descendants. The subsequent generation would produce 130 million descendants, the one after that 390 million – and so on. So much for royal ancestry! No wonder the author of *1 Timothy*, even if the letter was a fraud, counselled:

> Neither give heed to fables and endless genealogies.
>
> *1 Timothy 1:4*

Amongst these "fables" may well have been stories of a virgin birth.

Who Believed in the Virgin Birth?

Not only is the doctrine of the virgin birth absent from the New Testament, except for the two stories in Luke and Matthew, but many early Christians also rejected the idea. The Ebionites, the earliest Judaic Christians living in Palestine and closest to the scene of the original events, certainly repudiated it. Epiphanius reports of them:

> They say that Jesus was begotten of the seed of a man, and was chosen; and so by the choice of God he was called the Son of God from the Christ

that came into him from above in the likeness of a dove. And they deny that he was begotten of God the Father.

Epiphanius, Panarion 30:13.7-8, ANT p.10

Likewise, the unknown author of the *Constitutions of the Holy Apostles* wrote of the

Ebionites who will have the Son of God to be a mere man, begotten by human pleasure and the conjunction of Joseph and Mary.

Constitutions of the Holy Apostles VI:VI, CHA p.149

To a Jew, the idea of God fathering a child on a human mother would have been abhorrent and it is not surprising that it failed to catch on amongst the Judaic Christians. The belief in such divine intervention was primarily one that would have appealed to non-Jews, especially those influenced by Greek culture, where Zeus and the other gods were famed for their sexual exploits with human women, frequently fathering children. In fact, some of the bucolic scenes in the *Protoevangelium of James* are clearly Christian propaganda aimed at giving Jesus a prominent place amongst the heroes and gods of Greek tradition.

Many of the Syrian Christians, as well as the writer of the *Acts of Thomas*, must also have rejected the idea, especially in the early centuries, for it is implicit in their belief that Judas Thomas was not only Jesus' brother, but his *twin* brother, too! For them, 'Didymos Judas Thomas' was the one who founded the churches in the East, especially in Edessa, and later tradition – as we find in the *Acts of Thomas* – even has him travelling to India. In fact, the Greek *didymos* and the Aramaic *Thomas* both mean 'twin'. He was hence 'Judas the Twin' corresponding to the Juda of Mark's list of Jesus' brothers.

A great many of the more gnostically inclined gave no credence to the story either. The author of the Nag Hammadi, *Gospel of Philip* is unequivocal:

Some said, "Mary conceived by the Holy Spirit."
They are in error. They do not know what they are saying.

Gospel of Philip 55, NHS20 p.151

Irenaeus speaks of the gnostic teacher, Cerinthus, as having taught an ordinary birth for Jesus. In his *Against Heresies*, he writes:

> Cerinthus, again, a man who was educated in the wisdom of the Egyptians ... He represented Jesus as having not been born of a virgin, but as being the son of Joseph and Mary according to the ordinary course of human generation, while he nevertheless was more righteous, prudent, and wise than other men.
>
> *Irenaeus, Against Heresies I:XXVI, AHI p.97*

Hippolytus likewise says that the gnostic Elchasai, from whom a number of sects came into being, lasting until the fifth century and mostly associated with the Judaic side of Christianity, taught the same. According to Hippolytus, Elchasai also said that Jesus was a soul who had come to this world in the past (presumably as a Saviour) and would go on incarnating here in the future – another indication of a belief in reincarnation in early Christianity:

> He (Elchasai) asserts that Christ was born a man in the same manner common to all and that he was not for the first time (on earth) ... but that both previously and frequently again, he had been born and would be born: would thus appear and exist undergoing alterations of birth and having his soul transferred from body to body.
>
> *Hippolytus, Refutation of All Heresies, RAH IX:IX p.347*

Hippolytus also writes of the gnostics Carpocrates[18] and Apelles[19] as being dissidents on the matter of the virgin birth. In fact, it is to be expected that many of the gnostically oriented would have repudiated the belief since they represented the esoteric stream of Christianity and as such were more interested in the inward aspects of Jesus' teachings than externals. Certainly, the evidence is that there were more than a few who rejected the idea, for Irenaeus, Hippolytus and the other heresiologists devote a considerable amount of effort to refuting the 'heretics' and their followers, and arguing the validity of their own point of view.

The mystic Mani also rejected the virgin birth, though ironically, in the manner of the legends that gather around a mystic after their death, the later Manichaeans of China said that Mani's mother had given birth to him out of her chest. In fact, Jesus was not alone in being credited with a virgin birth. The gnostic Simon Magus was so acclaimed, as was Zarathushtra, while Apollonius of Tyana, a Greek mystic and contemporary of Jesus who became well known in the Roman world, was said to have been the son of the Greek sea god, Proteus, who was credited with the ability to change his shape at will. Proteus, says the legend, appeared to the mother of Apollonius in the form of an Egyptian demon, just before the sage was born.[20] And unlike Mary, so the story goes, she was not in the least afraid of the apparition.

Throughout history, legends of a miraculous birth have consistently been woven around the lives of the great and it was commonly claimed in the ancient Middle Eastern world that many of their warriors and heroes – mythical or historical – had been the offspring of a deity. According to legend, the mythical Dionysus, Perseus, Ra and Atys had all been born of the union of a god and a virgin. And it was said of the deity Mithras that at the beginning of time before the earth was populated, some shepherds observed the young and naked Mithras emerging from a rock as the sun arose, carrying a flaming torch in one hand and a knife in the other, and wearing a Phrygian cap. Understandably, the shepherds worshipped him, testifying that on account of the cold, he climbed into a tree and made himself a garment of fig leaves.

Emperors such as the powerful Julius Caesar (100-44 BC) and Augustus (63 BC-14 AD) were also reported to have been the sons of a deity who became their champions during life, thus accounting for their power and conquests. Augustus was claimed to have been the son of Apollo, for his mother, while sleeping in the Temple of Apollo, had yielded to the embrace of a serpent which had left permanent marks upon her body. Ten months later, Augustus had been born.

The Chinese myth of Mani's birth gives us an insight into why such legends come into existence. They stem from the fact that human beings are often utterly confused, embarrassed and obsessed by sex. Otherwise, what is so wrong about a Master taking birth in the normal human way? Their bodily existence is natural in every other respect and there is nothing wrong with sex other than what we make of it in our own thoughts and actions. Jesus himself frequently speaks of being the "Son of man" as well as the "Son of God". So if he claimed to be the "Son of man", then surely it means that a man had been involved? Indeed, if he could avoid the father – why need he have selected a mother? If he was going to do things in a miraculous way, then why should he not have simply descended from the skies as an adult, ready to begin his ministry, complete with any knowledge of this world he might have needed? Why choose the one means of miraculous entry that would have been the most difficult to prove?

Again, one of the reasons why a Master takes human birth and lives like us is to be a living example of all he teaches. But if at the very outset he arrives by way of a miracle, how could he then be a living example of perfect humanity? He would have already demonstrated that he was not genuinely human at all and hence not a valid exemplar for mankind.

The Mystic Mother and the Virginal Spirit

From a mystic point of view, this is really the heart of the matter and it is probable that most of those of a gnostic or mystic disposition discounted all stories of the virgin birth. Those who are truly of a spiritual bent of mind possess a different set of values from those whose minds are locked onto physical phenomena as the only reality. They are realists and pragmatists in a way that the materially-minded may find hard to understand. Moreover, there is a mystical element enfolded in the myth of the virgin birth which may once again prove to be the origin of what later became misinterpreted and externalized. We have already encountered it in the discussion of Jesus' miracle of turning water into wine. The real, spiritual and mystic 'mother' of Jesus or any perfect mystic is the pure and unsullied Holy Spirit.

In Semitic languages, all objects and things – all nouns – have a gender. This may be a difficult concept to grasp for those who speak only English, yet it is a common feature of many languages. In such languages, the gender is significant and it seems very odd when mistakes are made. Now, the Hebrew and Aramaic words for the Holy Spirit and the creative Wisdom of God are feminine. God, on the other hand, is masculine. For this reason, God is known as the Father while His creative Power, that which gives birth to the entire creation, is called the Mother of all things. She is also, metaphorically speaking, pure and virginal, for she gives birth without any intermediary. She has the innate purity of God.

A Master is the personified form of this great Power. A Son of God – as the "Word made flesh" – is hence born of the pure and virginal Mother or Holy Spirit, through the will of the Father. So Jesus, truly, was born of a virgin – but not a virgin of this world. Is this where the story of Jesus' birth originated?

Many of the gnostics and others of Jesus' time used such expressions in their descriptions of creation. According to both Jerome and Origen, for instance, Jesus refers to "my Mother the Holy Spirit"[21] in the *Gospel of the Hebrews.*

Similarly, we learn from a story related in a Coptic text that the late fourth-century archbishop, Cyril of Jerusalem (*d.*387), once sent for a monk of Maioma of Gaza who was teaching that the Virgin Mary was actually a "power". Called to give an account of his heretical belief, the monk replied:

> "It is written in the *Gospel to the Hebrews* that when Christ wished to come upon the earth to men, the good Father called a mighty Power in

the heavens which was called Michael, and committed Christ to the care thereof. And the Power came down in to the world and it was called Mary, and was in her womb seven months...."

The archbishop (Cyril) answered and said: "Where in the four gospels is it said that the holy Virgin Mary, the mother of God, is a 'force'?"

And the monk answered and said: "In the *Gospel to the Hebrews*".

And Apa Cyril answered and said, "Then according to thy words, there are five gospels? ... Whose is the fifth gospel?"

And that monk said unto him: "It is the gospel that was written to the Hebrews."

Discourse on Mary Theotokos, MCT pp.637-638

According to the story, Cyril then convinced him of his error, the monk repented, and Cyril burned the books. Whether the incident is fictitious or not and whether the *Gospel to the Hebrews* mentioned is the same as that from which Jerome and Origen quote is less than sure. All the same, it demonstrates the understanding that some early Christians had of the nature of the virgin mother, this account, of course, being set in a mythological form.

Like the Holy Spirit, Wisdom was also commonly called the Mother, as in the *Clementine Recognitions* where the creative Power is described as "Wisdom, the Mother of all things".[22] In fact, the term 'Mother' was used in a number of mystic and gnostic contexts as an epithet of both the Supreme Lord and His creative Power, as well as lesser powers, too. Just as a child 'emanates' from a human mother, so do the realms and powers of creation emanate from that which is higher. In the *Teachings of Silvanus*, the "Mother" is "Wisdom", the creative Power:

> Return, my son, to your first Father, God, and Wisdom your Mother, from whom you came into being from the very first.
>
> *Teachings of Silvanus 91, TS p.27*

The same writer also speaks of the creative Power as the "Hand of the Father" which "forms all" and is also called the "Christ" and the "Mother of all":

> Only the Hand of the Lord has created all these things. For this Hand of the Father is Christ and it forms all. Through it, all has come into being since it became the Mother of all.
>
> *Teachings of Silvanus 115, TS p.75*

In the *Untitled Text* of the *Bruce Codex*, the "Mother" is the supreme, unknowable One who dwells in the "twelfth deep", the highest 'region' of this descriptive system. And demonstrating how gender was completely flexible in the hands of the poet and bore no actual relationship to the mystic reality, *she* is also the "eternal" and "ineffable" *Father* ! –

> The twelfth deep ... is the Truth
> > from which has come all truth.
> This is the Truth which covers (contains) them all.
> This is the Image of the Father.
> This is the mirror of the All (the creation).
> This is the Mother of all the *aeons*.
> It is this which surrounds all the deeps.
> This is the *Monad* (the One)
> > which is unknowable or is unknown.
> This Characterless One in which are all characters,
> > which is blessed for ever.
> This is the eternal Father.
> This is the ineffable Father;
> > not understood, unthinkable, inaccessible.
> > > *Untitled Text 2:12, BC p.229*

But in the same tractate, the "Mother" is also the "Creative Word" who is the "Lord and Saviour and Christ":

> This Creative Word became a Power of God,
> > and Lord and Saviour and Christ
> > and King and Good and Father and Mother.
> > > *Untitled Text 12, BC p.248*

In another passage, it is said that from this "Mother" arises "her First-born Son" – the Master – who is given the means to travel throughout the entire creation, taking on forms appropriate to whatever region he happens to be in:

> Afterwards the Mother established her First-born Son.
> She gave to him the authority of the sonship.
> And she gave to him hosts of angels and archangels.
> And she gave to him twelve powers to serve him.
> And she gave to him a garment
> > in which to accomplish all things.

> And in it were all bodies:
>> the body of fire (astral) and the body of air (causal)
>> and the body of earth (human), and the body of wind,
>> and the body of angels, and the body of archangels,
>> and the body of powers, and the body of mighty ones,
>> and the body of gods, and the body of lords.
> In a word, within it were all bodies
>> so that none should hinder him
>> from going to the Height or from going down to the abyss.
>
> *Untitled Text 16, BC pp.256-257*

The bodies of "fire", "air" and "earth" are probably the astral, causal and physical bodies, while the rest are an attempt to express in human words the power of the "Son" to manifest in any part of the creation. In this world, the Son is the "Word made flesh" because flesh is what bodies are made of in this world. In the higher worlds, he takes on a form appropriate to wherever he happens to be. In truth, he can manifest in all places at once, as does the Creative Word or Mother who is the essence and real form of the Son.

A common appellation of the Mother was also the Virgin. And amongst the gnostic writings in particular both the Creator and the creative Power as well as other powers in the creative hierarchy were known by epithets like the "Virginal Spirit", the "Virgin of the Light" and so on. *Zostrianos*, for example, speaks of the "Virgin Light".[23] The *Second Book of Jeu* describes the "baptism of fire" that is given by the "Virgin of the Light".[24] *On the Origin of the World* speaks of the "Virgin of the Holy Spirit".[25] In the *Pistis Sophia*, the "Virgin of the Light"[26] is the power responsible for overseeing the rebirth of souls according to their deeds. In the *Gospel of the Egyptians*, the Creator is described by such expressions as the "great, invisible, incomprehensible Virginal Spirit"[27] and the "great, invisible, uncallable, unnameable Virginal Spirit"[28] And the *Apocryphon of John* describes the Supreme Lord as the "invisible, Virginal Spirit who is perfect"[29] from whom the *"Pronoia"*, the "thinking" or Primal Thought, proceeds as the creative Power.

Such terms are also very common in the Manichaean-Christian texts, where scholars have tended to use the term 'Maiden' rather than 'Virgin' in their translations, though it comes to the same thing. Like the gnostics, these writings characteristically speak of the Holy Spirit as the "glorious Maiden of Light",[30] the "Mother, the Maiden of all that lives",[31] the "Mother of the beings of Light"[32] and by other similar expressions. We read, for instance:

The Maiden of Light is the Holy Spirit.

> *Psalms, MPB p.116*

And, like the *Logos*, she is also the "Likeness" or Image of God:

> Lo, the Light of the Maiden has shone forth on me,
> the glorious Likeness.
>
> *Psalm CCLXIV, MPB p.81*

In the Mandaean writings, the term "Mother" is again used with a variety of meanings, including the source of all things earthly that draw souls to this world. But she is also the creative Power of the Supreme "Father of Greatness", the "Wellspring of the mysteries",[33] the "Wellspring, my Mother from whom I derive (my) being"[34] and

> the Treasure-of-Life, Mother of all worlds,
> she from whom the upper, middle
> and lower worlds emanated....
> Her name is *Nazirutha* (mystic Truth).
>
> *Thousand and Twelve Questions 5, TTQ p.111*

There is no doubt, therefore, that terms such as "Virgin" and "Mother" were used in specifically mystical contexts, though the meaning of the terms could vary to some extent depending upon the writer and the context. It is also certain that Jesus and his disciples would have been quite familiar with this kind of terminology and that some of them, if not Jesus himself, must have used it in their explanation of the mystic teachings. So, following the well-trodden pathway of descent, one can readily imagine how – somewhere along the line – the description of a mystic truth became literalized as a physical virgin-birth story.

NOTES AND REFERENCES

1. *Matthew 26:26ff.*
2. *Luke 22:17-20.*
3. *1 Corinthians 11:23ff.*
4. *Acts of Thomas, MAA p.231.*
5. Epiphanius, *Panarion I:III.42.3, PES p.274.*
6. Ignatius, *To the Smyrnaeans II,IV, API pp.253-255.*
7. Mark 3:31-35.
8. *Matthew 12:46, Luke 8:19.*
9. *Isaiah 7:14.*

10. *Matthew 13:55-56.*
11. *Luke 2:7.*
12. *Acts 1:14.*
13. *John 7:5.*
14. *Protoevangelium of James, NTA1 pp.370-388.*
15. *Death of Joseph II, CAG p.131.*
16. *Mark 10:47,48, 11:10; 12:35ff; Matthew 9:27, 12:23, 15:22, 20:30,31, 21:9,15, 22:42ff; Luke 18:38,39, 20:41ff; John 7:42.*
17. *Matthew 1:20.*
18. Hippolytus, *Refutation of All Heresies VII:XX, RAH* p.300.
19. Hippolytus, *Refutation of All Heresies VII:XXVI, RAH* p.306.
20. Philostratus, *LATI* pp.11-13.
21. *Gospel of the Hebrews*, in Origen, *Commentary on John* 2.12.87 (on *John* 1:3), *PEJCS* p.127.
22. *Clementine Recognitions II:XII, CH* p.199.
23. *Zostrianos 129, NHL* p.429.
24. *Second Book of Jeu 46, BC* p.110.
25. *On the Origin of the World 105, NHL* p.176.
26. *Pistis Sophia, PS* and *PSGG* – many places, throughout.
27. *Gospel of the Egyptians 49, NHL* p.212.
28. *Gospel of the Egyptians 55 & 65, NHL* pp.214 & 217.
29. *Apocryphon of John 4, NHL* p.107.
30. *Psalm CCXXXVII, MPB* p.37.
31. *Psalms, MPB* p.145.
32. *Angad Roshnan VI:69, MHCP* p.153.
33. *Alma Rishala Rba 415, PNC* p.31.
34. *Thousand and Twelve Questions 21, TTQ* p.118.

PART IV

The Return of the Soul

CHAPTER EIGHTEEN

Baptism: Chosen and Born Again

What Is Baptism?

The majority of Christians have believed since the very earliest times
that all those who profess faith in the tenets of Christianity will be
'saved' and 'go to heaven', whatever may be understood by such expressions, just as long as they have been baptized. We find assertions
to this effect throughout all Christian literature. The long ending to
Mark, for example, though appended at some unknown later date,
demonstrates the traditional importance of baptism:

> He that believeth and is baptized shall be saved;
>   but he that believeth not shall be damned.
>
>   *Mark 16:16*

Likewise, in the apocryphal *Acts*, when someone asks "Command me
what I should do, that I may live", the apostle John replies:

> Believe in the Name of the Father, the Son,
>   and the Holy Ghost, the one God, and be baptized,
>   and thou shalt receive eternal life.
>
>   *Travels of John, MAA p.46*

But what is the nature of this baptism? Is it simply a human ritual
or is it something more? In Mark, followed by Matthew and Luke,
when Jesus' authority to teach is challenged, he responds with the
question:

> The baptism of John, was it from heaven? Or of men?
>
>   *Mark 11:30*

671

Not only does he imply that the authority to teach such things is the same as the authority to baptize, he also indicates that there is a difference between baptism "from heaven" and the baptism "of men". It is also presumed in this same incident that baptism from heaven can only be given by a prophet. For the "chief priests and elders," relates Mark, were afraid to reply "of men", "for all hold John as a prophet".[1] Evidently, man can be expected to give a human baptism and a true prophet or mystic to give baptism "from heaven". What, then, is baptism "from heaven"?

When we turn elsewhere in the gospels for elucidation, we find that the subject is mentioned in only a few places and that most unsatisfyingly and unclearly. To begin with, John the Baptist is said to baptize with "water unto repentance" and Jesus with the "Holy Ghost and with fire". According to St Matthew, John the Baptist says:

> I indeed baptize you with water unto repentance:
>> but he that cometh after me is mightier than I,
>> whose shoes I am not worthy to bear:
> He shall baptize you with the Holy Ghost, and with fire.
>
> *Matthew 3:11*

But what does this mean? As we have previously pointed out, it would be unwise to take the images literally. The Holy Ghost is of course the Holy Spirit or Word and "fire" must be a metaphor for the inner light, for no one ever suggested that Jesus set fire to his disciples!

The compiler of John's gospel – or a later editor – however, is adamant that John the Baptist baptized in real, physical water and the point is made in several places. John the Baptist speaks of "he that sent me to baptize with water"[2] and we also read:

> And John also was baptizing in Aenon near to Salim, because there was much water there: and they came, and were baptized.
>
> *John 3:23*

This would seem to be a human baptism, yet, in Matthew, Jesus has indicated that John's baptism was that of a prophet and was hence, "from heaven"! It seems likely, therefore, that somewhere along the line, baptism in the Living Water of the Word, the real "water unto repentance" which is genuinely capable of washing away sins, became literalized into this kind of anecdote concerning John the Baptist.

Baptismal sects had long flourished in the ancient Middle East and it would have been so easy for later followers, in the absence of inner understanding and a Master who could effect the correct kind of baptism, to replace the higher, mystic baptism with an external ritual with which they were already familiar. Moreover, after the departure of a Master, in order to enhance the status of their adopted Master, subsequent adherents commonly assert that their Master had no Master. Consequently, these and other gospel passages were probably designed to portray John the Baptist as being less than Jesus, despite Jesus' considerable praises of John, as previously discussed. It must be remembered that despite its avowedly mystical contents, John's gospel was the last to be compiled, perhaps as much as two or three generations after the death of Jesus. One presumes that parts of its teaching do indeed date back to the time of Jesus, but other parts definitely stem from a time when the new religion of Christianity was well under way. The same is true, of course, of all the gospels.

But there is another angle which helps shed light upon the mystery. The Mandaeans, that intriguing gnostic sect whose followers acknowledge John the Baptist as a Saviour and who have existed into the twentieth century in the southern marshlands on the borders of Iran and Iraq, also practise baptism in water. But their sacred writings very clearly reveal that the water they talk about is the Living Water of the Word. As mentioned earlier, one of their terms for *any* stream or river is a 'jordan', a term used frequently in their scriptures for the divine 'stream' of Living Water. So being baptized in the 'Jordan' did not mean a dip in the muddy waters of a Palestinian river, but a mystic immersion, a washing of the soul and mind in the Living Water. There are many examples from their writings that could be given to demonstrate this point. For instance:

> Blessed art thou, Road of the Teachers,
>> Path of the Perfect
>> and Track that riseth up to the Place of Light....
> Praised art thou, Jordan of Living Water,
>> for from thee we obtain purity....
> Blessed be the Voice of Life
>> and praised be the great Beam which is all Light!
>> *CPM 71 pp.58-60*

Similarly, in a passage where the Word is referred to as the "First Vine", equivalent to the "True Vine" of Jesus or the Tree of Life, one of their mythical Saviours, *Hibil* (the Biblical Abel, son of Adam) baptizes or "raiseth up living souls in the Jordan":

> By it (the power of the First Vine),
>   Hibil raiseth up living souls in the Jordan,
>   those worthy of the great Place of Light
>   and of the everlasting abode.
>
> By it they will be established
>   and raised up in the House of the Mighty Life.
> It will raise those souls
>   who go to the Jordan and are baptized:
> They will behold the great Place of Light
>   and the everlasting abode.
>
> *CPM 14 p.10*

And again, speaking of the spiritual development of souls, portrayed here as "vines", branches on the Tree of Life, the poet writes:

> The vines shone in the Water
>   and in the Jordan they grew mighty.
>
> *CPM 177 p.159*

Similarly, a Mandaean poet writes of two mythical Saviours, *Silmai* and *Nidbai* as:

> The two delegates of *Manda-d-Hiia* (*lit.* Knowledge of Life),
>   who rule over the great Jordan of Life,
>   for they baptize with the great baptism of Light.
>
> *CPM 9 p.8*

The imagery is intriguing, for their use of the term 'jordan', the Aramaic character of their language, their references to both Jewish mythical characters as well as John the Baptist and Jesus, together with their own account of themselves, all point to their origins in Palestine around the time of Jesus and John the Baptist. It seems likely, therefore, bearing in mind how little we really know of the lives of these two great spiritual teachers, that the gospel stories concerning baptism in water have arisen from a misunderstanding of something far more deeply mystical. For no perfect Master would ever waste time baptizing people in water. How can physical water, sprinkled on the physical body, be expected to wash the soul of the impurities and sins of count-less past lives or even of the present life?

The Mandaeans were not the only ones who regarded the highest baptism as something spiritual, rather than physical. Many of the early Christians did so, too, especially amongst the gnostic groups. The pithy writer of the sayings recorded in the *Gospel of Philip*, for example, com-ments almost scathingly of the baptism which comprises nothing more than immersion in water:

> If one go down into the water and come up without having received any-thing and says, "I am a Christian," he has borrowed the name at interest. But if he receive the Holy Spirit, he has the Name as a gift. He who has received a gift does not have to give it back, but of him who has borrowed it at interest, payment is demanded.
>
> *Gospel of Philip 64, NHS20 p.169*

True baptism is a gift of the Holy Spirit, the Holy Ghost or the Word, something which naturally only a perfect prophet or mystic can be-stow, and it must be presumed that this was "baptism from heaven" given by both Jesus and John the Baptist.

Important as such baptism may be, the actual giving of baptism by Jesus is hardly mentioned in the gospels. In fact, there are only two comments on the subject, both in St John:

> After these things came Jesus and his disciples into the land of Judaea; and there he tarried with them, and baptized.
>
> *John 3:22*

And:

> When therefore the Lord knew how the Pharisees had heard that Jesus made and baptized more disciples than John, (though Jesus himself baptized not, but his disciples,) he left Judaea, and departed again into Galilee.
>
> *John 4:1-3*

The parenthetical "though Jesus himself baptized not, but his disciples" is an interesting aside and may perhaps point to a practice in which people are accepted for baptism by a Master, while the instructions are actually given to them by disciples designated to do so by the Master. Baptism, it must be recalled, was a part of the 'mysteries', involving

instructions concerning spiritual practice and including various esoteric teachings not normally divulged to the general public. Consequently, what was imparted at that time would have been a closely-
kept secret. It is also likely that there were language problems which
particular disciples who spoke the relevant languages were appointed
to overcome. Perhaps this was the origin of the 'twelve disciples', for it
is clear that Jesus had many more than twelve. As we read in the above,
"Jesus made and baptized more disciples than John".

Whatever the facts may have been, Jesus does give some indications
in the gospels that the baptism he gave was more than just a dunking
in the water. Luke records Jesus as saying:

> But I have a baptism to be baptized with!
>
> *Luke 12:50*

And on another occasion, in a story found in Mark and copied across
almost verbatim into Matthew and Luke, Jesus is asked by James and
John for seats on either side of him "in thy glory". Mark relates:

> Jesus said unto them,
> "Ye know not what ye ask:
>   can ye drink of the cup that I drink of?
> And be baptized with the baptism
>   that I am baptized with?"
> And they said unto him, "We can."
>
> And Jesus said unto them,
> "Ye shall indeed drink of the cup that I drink of;
>   and with the baptism that I am baptized
>   withal shall ye be baptized."
>
> *Mark 10:38-39*

Though these passages are traditionally interpreted as references to
Jesus' forthcoming crucifixion, taken at face value, it would seem that
Jesus is actually talking of a very special kind of baptism. Not only
that, but he is indicating that it is the same as that with which he was
baptized by John the Baptist, upon which, as Mark and the synoptic
gospels report, the "heavens were opened unto him".[3] He and his disciples have both received the same form of baptism and his disciples
obviously expect to reap the same fruits as Jesus: "Ye shall indeed drink
of the cup that I drink of."

Except a Man Be Born Again

Perhaps Jesus' most well-known reference to spiritual baptism is the passage in St John concerning being "born again". Omitting the narrative in which it is set, Jesus says:

> Verily, verily, I say unto thee,
>> except a man be born again,
>> he cannot see the kingdom of God....
>
> Verily, verily, I say unto thee,
>> except a man be born of water and of the Spirit,
>> he cannot enter into the kingdom of God.
>
> *John 3:3,5*

Without this kind of baptism, says Jesus, it is not possible to "enter into" or to "see the kingdom of God", the eternal realm. Being "born of water and of the Spirit" again refers to the Living Water, not to physical water, for how could physical water enable someone to enter the higher regions, let alone to "see the kingdom of God"? It is also possible that "of water" is a later interpolation to Jesus' saying, for in the ensuing verses he goes on to explain what he means, making a clear distinction between physical birth and spiritual birth. But he speaks only about being "born of the Spirit":

> That which is born of the flesh is flesh;
>> and that which is born of the Spirit is spirit.
>
> *John 3:6*

Physical birth involves the physical body, he says, and spiritual birth involves the spirit or soul. The two are quite distinct. Baptism is called a new birth because it represents a new beginning. The baptism given by a Master enables a person to truly repent, to change the inner direction of their mind and soul and to turn again towards God. Jesus then gives a hint of what being baptized in this way actually means to a soul:

> Marvel not that I said unto thee,
>> ye must be born again.
> The wind bloweth where it listeth,
>> and thou hearest the sound thereof,

> but canst not tell whence it cometh,
>   and whither it goeth:
>   So is every one that is born of the Spirit.
>   *John 3:7-8*

He makes a veiled reference to the Sound of the Spirit, the divine Music of the Word which only those baptized into this Word can fully appreciate, "so is every one that is born of the Spirit". Mystic baptism is for this very purpose. It is an inner, mystic touch of soul to soul, from the soul of the Master to the soul of the disciple. It is a retuning of the soul to the Creative Word, present within all, yet heard by very few. It is the acceptance of a soul by the Master into his fold. The only proviso is, as we have previously pointed out, that both the disciple and the Master who does the baptism or initiation must be living in the body at the same time.

Except it be Given Him from Heaven

Christian baptism is to be had for the asking or – in the case of babies – even without the asking, a practice associated with the desire for numbers that has nothing to do with Jesus and dates back at least to the second century, for both Irenaeus and Origen speak of it. Almost any baptism is considered effective. Those who receive baptism on their deathbed, while barely conscious and hardly aware of what is going on, together with those who are baptized as infants and who have not the slightest idea what is happening to them, are all considered to be securely in the fold. Indeed, those who have led completely dissolute lives, but have yet professed a faith in Jesus, will be saved and their sins forgiven as long as they have been baptized; while those who have led good lives, yet have not subscribed to a belief in Christianity are condemned to hell.

The point is that man thinks that salvation and forgiveness of all sins are his for the asking, as long as he happens to believe in the right religion and the right Saviour – and is baptized. But – one has to question – does this sound reasonable? What do the vagaries of *belief* – more the happenstance of birth in a particular country than anything else – have to do with salvation? Would God be so partisan as to reward only those who happen to back the right belief system, often replete with bizarre, unreasonable and unverifiable assertions? Does this not sound more like the ideas and narrow-mindedness of man than the beneficence, mercy and love of God? And what do Jesus and the other Masters have to say about those who profess to be their followers long after they are safely dead and cannot upbraid them, nor tell them how to conduct themselves, nor give them the correct instructions for interior prayer and mystically baptize them in the Holy Spirit?

Jesus, at least, is very clear that it is not man's prerogative to put himself on anybody's short list for salvation and the forgiveness of sins. He says that it is God's privilege:

> No man can come to me, except the Father
>   which hath sent me draw him:
> And I will raise him up at the last day.
> It is written in the prophets,
> "And they shall be all taught of God."
>
> Every man therefore that hath heard,
>   and hath learned of the Father, cometh unto me.
> Not that any man hath seen the Father,
>   save he which is of God, he hath seen the Father....
>
> Therefore said I unto you,
>   no man can come unto me,
>   except it were given unto him of my Father.
>
>   *John 6:44-46,65; Isaiah 54:13*

No one can come to God, he says, unless he is drawn by God. Jesus is quite explicit and even repeats himself. Only one who is drawn by God will be "raised up" or taken back to God after his departure from this world. And he quotes one of the past mystics, Isaiah, to support his point. "Being taught of God" refers to those who are drawn by God to a mystic who himself knows God through inner experience. They are the ones who genuinely hear and learn about God, not just those who read the scriptures or have only intellectual knowledge of God or who profess faith in one religion or another. Nevertheless, he says, even a soul who is drawn by God to a Master can only see God by becoming completely "of God". This requires tremendous effort and application to spiritual practice and does not just happen automatically. In fact, in this instance, Jesus – alias John – is probably referring to the Master, to himself. The Master is the one who is truly "of God" and "hath seen the Father". Reinforcing the point that spirituality is a gift from God, John the Baptist also says:

A man can receive nothing,
>   except it be given him from heaven.
>
>   *John 3:27*

And in St Matthew, Jesus repeats the same thing in another way:

I thank thee, O Father, Lord of heaven and earth,
>   because Thou hast hid these things
>   from the wise and prudent,
>   and hast revealed them unto babes.
>   Even so, Father: for so it seemed good in Thy sight.
>
>   All things are delivered unto me of my Father:
>   and no man knoweth the Son, but the Father;
>   neither knoweth any man the Father, save the Son,
>   and he to whomsoever the Son will reveal him.
>
>   *Matthew 11:25-27*

Jesus indicates that the "mysteries of the kingdom of heaven" are not given to the "wise and prudent" – the worldly-wise and self-righteous people who think that salvation is theirs by right, simply by their professing certain beliefs, without making any spiritual effort. In fact, he says, the Father puts all such affairs into the hands of His Son. And only the Son "and he to whomsoever the Son will reveal him" will ever have the experience of God and see Him face to face. Though as Jesus also pointed out, the Son is one with God and only lives in the Father's will – so the Son's will is the Father's will.

Again, in St John, Jesus underlines the fact that a human being cannot choose his Master. It may seem that way from the outside, but the strings have to be pulled from within in a particular manner. All his disciples, he says, have been personally "chosen" by himself:

Ye have not chosen me, but I have chosen you,
>   and ordained you,
>   that ye should go and bring forth fruit,
>   and that your fruit should remain:
>   That whatsoever ye shall ask of the Father in my name,
>   He may give it you.
>
>   *John 15:16*

All disciples are "chosen" by their Master and "ordained" to "bring forth fruit": they are destined to make spiritual progress. And so close do they become to the Master that whatever they ask will be given to them. A little later in this same discourse, where Jesus is explaining to his disciples that they cannot expect the world to love them, he again indicates that he has "chosen" them "out of the world", suggesting that they are very much in a minority:

> If ye were of the world, the world would love his own:
> But because ye are not of the world,
>> but I have chosen you out of the world,
>> therefore the world hateth you.
>
> *John 15:19*

In another passage, Jesus says that it is by the will of God that he has come from Him to collect certain souls and take them back to Him:

> All that the Father giveth me shall come to me;
>> and him that cometh to me I will in no wise cast out.
> For I came down from heaven, not to do mine own will,
>> but the will of Him that sent me.
> And this is the Father's will which hath sent me,
>> that of all which He hath given me I should lose nothing,
>> but should raise it up again at the last day.
>
> *John 6:37-39*

"All that the Father giveth me shall come to me": the souls for whom a Master comes are allotted or destined by God. And they will all come to their Master, by one route or another, depending upon the individual. Even the Master has no choice in the matter, for he comes to do God's will, not his own will. Therefore, not one of them will be "cast out". No one will be neglected; "of all which he hath given me, I should lose nothing". Not one sheep will be lost. But, he adds, there are two conditions:

> And this is the will of Him that sent me,
>> that every one which seeth the Son,
>> and believeth on him, may have everlasting life:
> And I will raise him up at the last day.
>
> *John 6:40*

The soul must *see* the Son and *believe* in him. *Seeing* the Son implies that both the individual and the Master are alive in the body at the same time. A past Master, one who has died, cannot be seen by anyone now. His physical form, like that of all those who die, has returned to the matter whence it came and no longer exists.

Believing in the Son means that the soul has sufficient faith in the Master to ask for and receive initiation or mystic baptism. Such souls will be "raised up at the last day": a Master comes in his radiant, spiritual form and meets all his disciples inside, on their day of death. They are raised up from the body and their onward course determined according to their spiritual advancement.

Those who have cleared all their sins or *karmas* are taken back to God. Those who are detached from the world and have no sins or *karmas* which can draw them back to this world are placed in one of the "many mansions" where they continue with their spiritual practice and make further progress. Those who have drifted away from the teachings of their Master or have only paid lip service to him or have neglected their spiritual practice may be given another human birth with better circumstances and atmosphere for following the mystic path.

But once a soul has been initiated, the Master – in the form of the Word – remains with that soul forever and those who have to take another birth will once again be drawn to a Master, receive the mystic baptism, pick up where they left off in their previous births and continue on the path. All initiated souls will ultimately be taken back to God, but some may have to take a limited number of further births before they get release from birth and death and return to God.

So a Master "loses nothing" of the souls which the Father has "given" him. All will be "raised up on the last day" – a Master meets all his disciples at their time of death and takes care of them. What happens after that depends upon each individual's burden of sins, together with the grace and blessings of the Master.

I Pray for Them – I Pray Not for the World

There is a series of discourses, once again in John's gospel, stretching from the end of chapter thirteen up to the end of chapter seventeen, where Jesus, knowing that his work in this world is coming to an end and that he will soon be crucified, speaks directly to his disciples concerning his departure. Amongst these farewell discourses, there is a prayer addressed by Jesus to God, on behalf of his disciples, which is of interest in the present context. For he reiterates very clearly that he is interested only in his own disciples, not in the entire world.

This prayer, incidentally, highlights another facet of the writings of the mystics. Jesus does not need to pray outwardly to God to take care of his disciples. He is already one with God and knows full well that he will not be leaving his disciples orphaned. He will always be with them, taking care of them from within. They are destined to return to God and nothing can stop them, not even themselves. So he is only praying for his disciples' benefit, so that they may have greater faith that he is with them and is guiding them. Or, indeed, if these discourses were actually written by John in the name of his Master, then they are simply a very beautiful means of conveying Jesus' teachings and giving confidence to the disciples. Either way, according to John's gospel, Jesus says:

> Father, the hour is come;
> glorify Thy Son, that Thy Son also may glorify Thee:
> As Thou hast given him power over all flesh,
>   that he should give eternal life
>   to as many as Thou hast given him.
>
> *John 17:1-2*

He says that the time has come for him to return to God. That is his glorification. And because of this union of Father and Son, the Son has "power over all flesh": he has complete power in this world to "give eternal life". But he only gives it "to as many as Thou hast given him", to those who have been chosen and drawn to him.

> And this is life eternal,
>   that they might know Thee the only true God,
>   and Jesus Christ, whom Thou hast sent.
>
> *John 17:3*

He points out that the meaning of "life eternal" is to "know Thee the only true God" through the Master, Jesus the anointed one of God, who has been sent by God.

> I have glorified Thee on the earth:
>   I have finished the work which Thou gavest me to do.
>
> *John 17:4*

He has "glorified" God on earth by giving the teachings regarding the return to God and by collecting together and initiating as many as God has given him. This was the work allotted to him by God and he has "finished" that work. He is not responsible for those who will live in this world after him or those who lived before him. So although it is Christian belief that Jesus can take care of everybody, it is not a belief supported by Jesus' sayings. In fact, this saying, as well as others, indicate entirely the opposite.

> And now, O Father, glorify Thou me with Thine own self
> with the glory which I had with Thee before the world was.
>
> *John 17:5*

So now, he says, take me back to You, where I have been since before the creation. That is, Jesus existed before the creation, before he came to this world, and will continue to exist for ever. This is true of all souls, whether they are Masters or not. But the difference is that a Master returns to God when he leaves this world. Other souls do not, unless they have made sufficient spiritual progress.

> I have manifested Thy Name unto the men
> which Thou gavest me out of the world:
> Thine they were, and Thou gavest them me;
> and they have kept Thy Word.
>
> *John 17:6*

Jesus says that he has given the gift of the Name, the Word, to those "which Thou gavest me out of the world". He has initiated those who were marked by God to receive initiation from him. "Thine they were and Thou gavest them to me" and "they have kept Thy Word": they have been initiated, have followed the teachings and have practised the Word – they have kept themselves in contact with the music of the mystic Word, within themselves.

> Now they have known that all things
> whatsoever Thou hast given me are of Thee.
> For I have given unto them the words (Word) which Thou gavest me;
> and they have received them (It),
> and have known surely that I came out from Thee,
> and they have believed that Thou didst send me.
>
> *John 17:7-8*

Through association with Jesus, his disciples had come to realize the extraordinary fact that everything about their Master was of God and reflected God Himself, because he had been sent by God. And they had come to know this because they had followed his "words" or his teachings and had been connected to the mystic Word within themselves. This knowledge, therefore, was not of an intellectual nature, nor was it blind belief, but was based on direct personal experience.

> I pray for them: I pray not for the world,
>> but for them which Thou hast given me;
>> for they are Thine.
> And all mine are Thine, and Thine are mine;
>> and I am glorified in them.
>
> *John 17:9-10*

Jesus again repeats that he is only interested in "them which Thou hast given me". "I pray for *them*," he says, "not for the world". " I am glorified in them": they have come to know who I really am and they worship me accordingly.

> And now I am no more in the world,
>> but these are in the world, and I come to Thee.
> Holy Father, keep through Thine own Name
>> those whom Thou hast given me,
>> that they may be one, as we are.
>
> *John 17:11*

And now, since I am leaving the world to "come to Thee", I pray that You should take care of them through "Thine own Name", the Word, which is the real form of the Master. Jesus is leaving his disciples only in the sense that the beautiful physical form and all its divinely human attributes which they have grown to love so much is going to die. But the real Master, the inner, spiritual Name or Word, will remain with them and they will be able to contact this spiritual form of their Master within themselves. In this way, they will become one with the Master, one with the Word and one with God, just as the Master and God are one.

> While I was with them in the world,
>> I kept them in Thy Name:
>> those that Thou gavest me I have kept,
>> and none of them is lost....

> And now come I to Thee;
>   and these things I speak in the world,
>   that they might have my joy fulfilled in themselves.
>
> *John 17:12-13*

A Master takes care of all his disciples, without any exceptions. "None of them is lost." And now that Jesus is returning to God, he is saying all these things "that they might have my joy fulfilled in themselves": so that they may feel comforted and consoled that they are not being orphaned.

> I have given them Thy Word; and the world hath hated them,
>   because they are not of the world,
>   even as I am not of the world.
>
> *John 17:14*

Now that they are attached to the sweet music of the Word inside, "they are not of the world": they have no real interest left in the world. As a result, the people of the world start to hate them – especially in those days of religious prejudice. For people do not understand those who see things so differently and have no concern for the things of the world. Feeling threatened, they react violently, not realizing the stupidity and ignorance of their response.

> I pray not that thou shouldst take them out of the world,
>   but that thou shouldst keep them from the evil (the Evil One)
> They are not of the world, even as I am not of the world.
> Sanctify them through Thy Truth: Thy Word is Truth.
>
> *John 17:15-17*

Jesus does not ask that they should immediately die and be taken "out of the world", much as his disciples might have preferred that course. They still had to stay here and go through the remainder of their destiny, while growing in inner prayer. But he prays that they should be protected from "the evil", from the Evil One,[4] from Satan. Neither he, nor they, are of the world and Jesus only prays that the Lord will "sanctify them through" His Word of Truth, for it is only the Word which can make a soul truly pure and holy.

Jesus is again saying this on behalf of his disciples, for both he and they know that it is the Master who will continue to bless them and shower his grace on them from inside, slowly pulling them up to himself and to God.

> As thou hast sent me into the world,
>> even so have I also sent them into the world.
> And for their sakes I sanctify myself,
>> that they also might be sanctified through the Truth.
>
> *John 17:18-19*

Just as Jesus came into this world and was a living example for his disciples, so he taught his disciples to be living examples of his teachings to others. Though the history is confused and impossible to trace with any accuracy, it seems that Jesus sent twelve close disciples into the world to give discourses to the people and possibly to give initiation instructions on his behalf. As John comments at one place, "Jesus himself baptized not, but his disciples".⁵ Those initiated under Jesus' instructions, while he was still living, would have been as much his disciples as those who were given the instructions directly by Jesus himself. The inner mystic baptism would have been the same, as well as the instructions, even though disciples initiated in this manner may not necessarily have had the opportunity to have seen Jesus. But such instruction could only have been given to those who had been accepted for initiation while Jesus was alive in the body. Therefore he says:

> Neither pray I for these alone, but for them also
>> which shall believe on me through their word;
> That they all may be one; as Thou, Father, art in me,
>> and I in Thee, that they also may be one in us:
> That the world may believe that thou hast sent me.
>
> *John 17:20-21*

Not only did he pray for those disciples who were physically present with him at that time, but also for those who, though far away, had become his disciples – during his lifetime – through contact with his 'twelve'. Perhaps some of these discourses in John's gospel circulated amongst Jesus' disciples, in whatever form they may have been at that time. They would have been a great source of inspiration and comfort in the time to come, especially for those in distant places or those who were unable to be present with Jesus in his last days.

It is also possible that these lines were edited to fit in with later Christian concepts regarding the salvation of the whole world. But Jesus is quite clear about that. He says in so many other places that he did not come for the whole world. He came only for his own disciples, whoever they may have been. It is concerning these that he continues:

And the glory which Thou gavest me I have given them;
    that they may be one, even as we are one:
I in them, and Thou in me,
    that they may be made perfect in one;
And that the world may know that Thou hast sent me,
    and hast loved them, as Thou hast loved me.

                                                    John 17:22-23

A Master gives to his disciples the divine Light and power which is within himself. Everything that happens to a disciple is a gift from the Master. And ultimately the disciple, the Master and the Lord all become one. Then the disciples become shining and "perfect" examples of their Master, such that everyone with whom they come into contact, especially those who are also meant for the Master, can see that they have been given something very special by their Master, because of his great love for them and the love of God for his Son.

Father, I will that they also,
    whom Thou hast given me, be with me where I am;
That they may behold my glory, which thou hast given me:
    for thou lovedst me before the foundation of the world.

                                                    John 17:24

Whatever a Master pleases or desires will come to pass, for his will is one with God's will. How pleased and reassured Jesus' disciples must have felt, therefore, when they heard or read these words of their Master. He wants them to come to him at his level. He wants them to join him with God so that they can be full of the bliss and love that comes from being with the Master inside. And again, he reiterates, this has all taken place because of the love of God which existed before the creation came into being.

O righteous Father, the world hath not known Thee:
    but I have known Thee,
    and these have known that Thou hast sent me.
And I have declared unto them Thy Name,
    and will declare it:
That the love wherewith Thou hast loved me may be in them,
    and I in them.

                                                    John 17:25-26

He therefore concludes this short and inspiring discourse by pointing out once more that the people of the world at large know nothing of God. Only the Son of God and those "that Thou hast sent me" ever come to really know Him – through "Thy Name" which is "declared" or given by the Son. And the reason for it all is so that the game of divine love might be played: "that the love wherewith Thou hast loved me may be in them, and I in them".

It can be seen that in this discourse Jesus is talking to his direct disciples, not to all Christians for all time to come. Only those souls that he has baptized will he be taking back to God. No wonder Jesus spoke so forcefully of the baptism he imparted to those souls who were given to him. As he said in St Luke:

> But I have a baptism to be baptized with;
> and how am I straitened till it be accomplished!
>
> *Luke 12:50*

The meaning of the Greek is ambiguous and this passage is variously rendered in different translations. So although any interpretation can only be tentative and the saying has traditionally been taken as a foretelling of Jesus' crucifixion, its meaning, as it stands, coincides perfectly with Jesus' teaching concerning baptism. Jesus had a certain baptism to give to certain souls, a mystic baptism in the Holy Spirit, and there was no rest for him until he had "accomplished" that God-given responsibility and taken those souls back to God. Only then could he himself return to his beloved heavenly Father. This is true of all perfect Masters. A task that can be "accomplished" has a definite end. Naturally, after his death, he could no longer baptize anybody. So once again, Jesus is speaking of a particular task, spanning a particular period of time – his own lifetime – in which that task must be "accomplished" or fulfilled.

The Good Shepherd

Whatever Christianity may have come to believe, then, when we study Jesus' gospel teachings, there seems little doubt that he was specifically interested only in those who would be drawn to him by God during his own lifetime. He was not concerned about the future. That would be taken care of by Masters who were sent for those times. He came into the world to give salvation only to those who were destined or chosen for it during his period on earth. None of those would be left behind. As he said in his parable of the lost sheep:

> The Son of man is come to save that which was lost.
>
> *Matthew 18:11*

And again:

> It is not the will of your Father which is in heaven,
> that one of these little ones should perish.
>
> *Matthew 18:14*

Jesus' parable of the Good Shepherd, although it also covers other aspects of the mystic path, also underlines the same point, that Jesus came for his own allotted sheep:

> Verily, verily, I say unto you,
> He that entereth not by the door into the sheepfold,
>   but climbeth up some other way,
>   the same is a thief and a robber.
> But he that entereth in by the door
>   is the shepherd of the sheep.
> To him the porter (doorkeeper) openeth;
>   and the sheep hear his voice:
>   and he calleth his own sheep by name,
>   and leadeth them out.
> And when he putteth (leadeth) forth his own sheep,
>   he goeth before them,
>   and the sheep follow him: for they know his Voice.
> And a stranger will they not follow,
>   but will flee from him:
> For they know not the voice of strangers.
>
> *John 10:1-5*

Jesus is speaking of other spiritual teachers, the "false prophets" who are unable to lead their disciples back to God. Those who are destined for a particular Master recognize him, "they know his Voice" – a reference both to the Master himself as well as to the Voice of God, the divine Word. Ultimately, such souls will not follow anyone else, for the shepherd "calleth his *own* sheep by name" – each individual sheep is known to him. They will be drawn irresistibly to the Master for whom they are destined. Again, he reiterates:

My sheep hear my Voice, and I know them, and they follow me:
And I give unto them eternal life; and they shall never perish,
 neither shall any man pluck them out of my hand.
My Father, which gave them me, is greater than all;
 and no man is able to pluck them out of my Father's hand.

John 10:27-30

He specifically speaks of "my sheep". They are the ones to whom he will give "eternal life". No one can deprive them of this destiny, for "my father, which gave them to me, is greater than all". And again:

I am the good Shepherd,
 and know my sheep, and am known of mine.
As the Father knoweth me, even so I know the Father:
 and I lay down my life for the sheep.

John 10:14-15

The Master knows his sheep and they recognize him. And a Master gives up his entire life to the service of his disciples. He "lays down his life" for them. In the end, he even dies for them in the sense that he takes some of their sins or *karmas* onto his own body both during life and at the time of death. This is no problem or hardship to one who is the master of life and death, one with the Supreme Creator.

Those That Are Mine

As in every instance and with every topic we discuss, it can be demonstrated again and again that many of the early Christians and indeed all those who have followed this ancient path have understood and taught the same principles. The same is true of the expression, the 'chosen ones of God', also called the 'elect'. The theme is prevalent throughout the Old Testament writings, where Judaism commonly presumes that it refers literally to the 'children of Israel' in a nationalistic sense. But a close examination of the context reveals that often this is not the case. The same idea is found in orthodox Christian, gnostic, Mandaean and Manichaean writings. Indeed, the mystics of Persia, the East and elsewhere – ancient and modern – have also said the same thing: Masters do not come to this world for everybody. They come for certain particular or chosen souls.

The followers of all sects and religions, however, believe and state in one way or another that they are the ones who have got it right, that they are the 'chosen ones'. So the observation that this is also taught by the mystics might make them, too, seem to be sectarians. But this is not actually so. It is simply that in the economy of life, not everybody is meant to do the same thing. It would be a strange and impossible world if they did.

In fact, while the majority of those who profess to be the 'chosen ones' become more narrow in their outlook, the true disciples of a true Master become increasingly broad-minded and universal, until ultimately they share the love of God for His entire creation. After all, God is one. There is no one who belongs to His club but Himself. But that does not make Him a sectarian! It makes Him universal. So it is with those who truly seek and love Him.

The existence of the counterfeit proves the existence of the real. There can be no counterfeit coin unless there is a real one. So if there are so many 'wrong' paths, then surely there must be a right path to follow? In that case, *someone* must have got the answer. Others, however, may neither accept nor understand this and the writer of the *Wisdom of Solomon* puts it most succinctly:

> People look on, uncomprehending;
>   it does not enter their heads
>   that grace and mercy await the chosen of the Lord,
>   and protection, his holy ones.
>
> *Wisdom of Solomon 4:14-15*

For this reason, Jesus indicates in the *Gospel of Thomas* that only a very few are chosen:

> Jesus said, "I shall choose you, one out of a thousand,
>   and two out of ten thousand,
>   and they shall stand (exist) as a single one
>   (and they will all become one)."
>
> *Gospel of Thomas 23, NHS20 p.65*

It may seem unfair, but an understanding of reincarnation takes much of the sting out of the idea. With the passage of time and with rebirth after rebirth, many souls will be taken back. Seen in this context, all those who are seeking God, whatever way they may have chosen, are on the right path as long as they feel sincere and comfortable that it is the correct path for them. Nobody can say that only the path which he is following will lead to God, for that is the beginning of religion, sectarianism and division. As long as we are sincere, then that sincerity will ultimately lead us to our goal.

As regards the Masters, theirs is a path that will exist for as long as the creation continues. They say that it is the true and natural 'religion' upon which practically all other religions are based, directly or indirectly. And the opportunity they present is always available for those who wish to take advantage of it. In mystic literature, it is these who have been called the 'chosen ones'.

This is clearly expressed in the early Christian *Odes of Solomon*, one of the purest of all the mystic writings from that period, where the devotee writes in the name of a Master who is almost certainly Jesus:

> Keep my secret, you who are kept by it:
>> keep my faith, you who are kept by it;
> And know my knowledge, you who know me in truth;
>> love me with affection, you who love.
> For I do not turn my face from those that are mine,
>> because I know them;
> And before they came into being I perceived them;
>> and on their faces I set my Seal.
>
> *Odes of Solomon VIII:10-15, AOT p.698*

In the Nag Hammadi *Second Apocalypse of James*, where we encounter the tradition that James the brother of Jesus was appointed to be his successor, James is instructed by Jesus only to attend to "those who are mine and now ... those who are yours" – not to "strangers":

> For you are not the Redeemer
>> nor a helper of strangers.
> You are an illuminator and a Redeemer
>> of those who are mine,
>> and now of those who are yours.
> You shall reveal to them;
>> you shall bring good among them all.
>
> *Second Apocalypse of James 55, NHS11 p.131*

Similarly, in the *Trimorphic Protennoia*, the descended Saviour states:

> I revealed myself among my members
>> which are mine.
>
> *Trimorphic Protennoia 49, NHS28 p.431*

Amongst the Mandaean writings, the theme is also a common one, as when the Saviour says:

> I call to my chosen ones so that
>   ye may not turn your thought away from me.
> *CPM 89 p.92*

In another hymn, the Master requests his "chosen" ones not to distort or misinterpret his teachings:

> Rightly do I say to you, my chosen, ...
>   pervert and change me not, alter me not by hand,
>   pervert not nor alienate me:
> O men who have heard the Voice of Life!
> *CPM 88 pp.91-92*

And:

> The Voice of Life calleth
>   and the ears of the chosen hearken.
> *CPM 155 p.134*

There is no doubt, in all these extracts, of the meaning.

Written in Heaven – the Book of Life

The mystics and their devotees of that period, with their characteristically eastern love of metaphor, used a number of images to express this reality. They said, for example, that the names of the "chosen" were "written in heaven" or in the "Book of Life". As Jesus said to those he had baptized:

> Rejoice, because your names are written in heaven.
> *Luke 10:20*

In Christian apocryphal writings, the term is clearly used in reference to those who are marked for initiation. In the *Robe of Glory*, for instance, an allegorical Syriac poem found in the *Acts of Thomas*, the soul who has fallen fast asleep in "Egypt" (the physical universe) is sent a 'letter', symbolic of the Word. The 'letter' comes from the Father by the hand of the "Brother" (the Master) conveying much inspiration to the languishing soul. And amongst other things, it says:

> Up and arise from thy sleep,
>   and listen to the words of our letter!
> Call to mind that thou art a son of kings!
> See the slavery – (and) whom thou servest!
> Remember the pearl
>   for which thou didst speed to Egypt!
> Think of thy bright robe,
>   and remember thy glorious toga,
>   which thou shalt put on as thine adornment.
> Thy name is named in the Book of Life,
>   and with thy Brother whom thou hast received,
>   thou shalt [return to] our Kingdom.
>   *Acts of Thomas 108:43-48, AAA p.241, ANT p.412, HS p.19, RG p.15*

Likewise in the allegorical romance of *Joseph and Aseneth*, Aseneth is to be married to Joseph, who (in the story) symbolizes the Master. Marriage is an ancient symbol for divine union and in this instance it signifies the initiation of Aseneth. Hence, she is told:

> Take heart, Aseneth:
>   your name is written in the Book of Life,
>   and it will never be blotted out.
> From today you will be made new,
>   and refashioned, and given new life.
>   *Joseph and Aseneth XV, AOT p.488*

She is to receive baptism into the Word of Life and her name will never be erased or "blotted out" from the "Book of Life" – another common usage of the term. This variant of the expression is encountered in the *Acts of John* where a young man who – according to the story – has just been 'raised from the dead' (lifted up from the death of this world) through mystic baptism, recommends to others standing by:

> Nothing else remaineth for you save to ask the apostle of the Lord that like as he hath raised me to life, he would raise you also from death unto salvation and bring back your souls which now are blotted out of the Book of Life.
>   *Acts of John XVII, ANT p.261*

The author of the Nag Hammadi *Gospel of Truth*, writing in metaphors, not only speaks of the chosen ones, the "little ones", as being "inscribed in the Book of the Living", but he also equates this Book with the Word of Life itself, words being the essence of a book. Talking specifically about Jesus, he says that when Jesus came to this world, at first the clever and self-righteous ones came to him; but they only wished to test him. Then came the chosen ones, the "little children" who "manifested the living Book of the Living" "in their hearts", within themselves, meaning that they had personal, inner experience of this mystic "Book":

> He (Jesus) became a quiet and peaceful guide (*lit.* a pedagogue, a trained slave who supervises the education of children). In a school, he appeared, where he spoke the Word in the capacity of a Teacher. And there came to him those who – in their own estimation – were wise, testing him, but he confounded them because they were not truly wise men.
>
> After all these, there came the little children also, those to whom belongs the knowledge (*gnosis*) of the Father. Having been strengthened (initiated) they learned about the nature of the Father. They gained knowledge (*gnosis*) and they were known; they were glorified and they glorified. In their hearts was manifested the living Book of the Living (the Word) – that (Book) which is written in the Thought and the Mind of the Father, which from before the foundation of the Totality (the creation) was within His Incomprehensibility – that (Book) which no one can take up without being put to death (without coming to this world).
>
> Had that Book not been manifested (as a Master), none of those who believe in salvation could have attained it. For this reason the merciful and faithful Jesus was patient in accepting suffering by taking up that Book; since he knew that his death would mean life for many.
>
> *Gospel of Truth 19-20, GS pp.254-255, GT pp.56-62, NHS22 p.87*

The Book "which is written in the Thought and the Mind of the Father", which existed "from before the foundation of the Totality (the creation)" is the Word. It is the source of creative activity, the "Thought and Mind" of God, so to speak. To human beings, it is a teaching, a practice, a way and something to be experienced. But a soul can only "take it up" by "being put to death" – by taking birth as a human being, for only in the human form can a soul receive initiation into the Book of Life.

Similarly, a Master can only teach this "Book" by coming to this world of death. His taking birth here is a "death": leaving the realms of life and light, he enters the choking sphere of darkness and death, for he knows that "his death would mean life for many". By his coming here, he can release many souls from entanglement in birth and death, taking them back to eternal life with God. Without such a Master, even those who understand the true nature of salvation cannot attain it.

The passage is full of the same double meanings and wordplays around the theme of 'life' and 'death' that are found in John's gospel. Continuing in the same vein, speaking specifically of Jesus but actually of all Masters in general, the author adds:

> He draws himself down to death though clothed in life eternal. (Then) having divested himself of the perishable rags (of the body), he put on imperishability, something which no one can take from him. Having entered the empty ways of fear (this world), he escaped the clutches of those who had been stripped naked by forgetfulness – for he was knowledge (*gnosis*) and perfection (personified) – and read out the contents (of the Book of the Living)....
>
> And those who are to receive the teaching are the living ones who are inscribed in the Book of the Living. It is about themselves that they are given instruction, receiving it from the Father, turning again to Him.... He has brought many back from Error.
>
> *Gospel of Truth 20,22, GS pp.255,256, GT pp.66-70,78, NHS22 pp.87-91*

The Master, though at one with the eternal, takes on the "perishable rags" of the body and comes to this world: "he draws himself down to death". He "enters the empty ways of fear": he is not troubled by its spiritually dead, ignorant and forgetful inhabitants, stripped "naked" of all their innate spirituality, for he is *gnosis* personified. And he "reads out the contents" of the Book of the Living: he teaches them about the Word.

But not everyone is destined to hear it. Only "those who are to receive the teaching" are "inscribed in the Book of the Living": only they are tuned to the Word of God. And this "teaching" is "about themselves", it concerns the real nature of the soul or self. It comes from the Father and entails their repentance, their "turning again to Him". And further on, the author adds that the Master has "brought many back from Error": over the millions of years in which the creation has existed, many have been returned to God from the Illusion and "Error" of this world.

Children of Light and Children of Darkness

Those whose attention has been turned around and are facing God are of a different character from those whose attention is continuing to run out into the world. The lives of initiates have been brought under the jurisdiction of a Saviour who tempers everything with mercy, love and forgiveness. They are on the path back to God. The lives of others are determined by Satan, the Negative Power, and his rule of justice. They are on the path that meanders through the realm of birth and death.

Masters, therefore, make a distinction between those who are following the path to God and those who are following the mind, using various names to designate these two basic kinds of people and these two attitudes to life. In Jesus' time, his followers were called the "children of light", the "children of God", the "little ones" or the "little children", contrasted with the "children of darkness", the "children of the Wicked One", the "children of disobedience" and so on.

It should be said, of course, that a true "child of the light" – a true disciple – is very rare and since most disciples are still struggling with the outgoing tendencies of their minds, perhaps only a Master himself would really qualify for the name. The majority of disciples have yet to overcome the power of Satan, and dark traits will still lurk within them. They are no different from other human beings. But they are on the road to God and in that sense may be termed the "children of light".

We have just seen that the writer of the *Gospel of Truth* describes those who are destined for a Master, whose names are written in the Book of the Living, as the "little ones". Such expressions are found throughout the early Christian literature, including the New Testament. In St Matthew, we read:

> At the same time came the disciples unto Jesus, saying,
> "Who is the greatest in the kingdom of heaven?"
> And Jesus called a little child unto him,
>   and set him in the midst of them, and said:
>
> "Verily I say unto you, except ye be converted,
>   and become as little children,
>   ye shall not enter into the kingdom of heaven.
> Whosoever therefore shall humble himself
>   as this (as a) little child,
>   the same is greatest in the kingdom of heaven.

And whoso shall receive one such little child
   in my name receiveth me.
But whoso shall offend one of these little ones
   which believe in me,
     it were better for him that a millstone
   were hanged about his neck,
     and that he were drowned in the depth of the sea."

Matthew 18:1-6

The setting, here, would seem to be anecdotal since the "little child" and the "little ones which believe in me" are more likely to mean initiates, not small children as the narrative implies. As in so many instances, the saying does not really match the story. "Except ye be converted" means the same as repentance – a person has to be converted from one way of living to another. The mind has to be turned away from the world and towards God. But to achieve this, they must be flexible, humble and innocent, like little children. They must relinquish all sense of individual self and ego. Such a disciple, says Jesus, "is greatest in the kingdom of heaven": he is the one who best pleases the Father and who attains the highest level of spirituality.

So much love does a Master bear towards his "little ones", says Jesus, that if anyone renders any service to one of his disciples, in the name of their Master, it is as if he had served the Master directly. But if anyone abuses or hurts one of his chosen, "little ones", then it were better if he had not been born – "that he were drowned in the depth of the sea" – in the sense that such a person is unaware of the real spiritual purpose of human life and who a Master really is. For all the use they have made of being in a human form, they might just as well have not been born or have been born into one of the lower species. Jesus is also using this purposefully forceful example to impress upon his disciples that they must live harmoniously and lovingly together, serving each other whenever and wherever they can.

This distinction between those who are following the path leading back to God and those pursuing the road that leads to rebirth in Satan's realm is brought out quite uncompromisingly in *1 John*, where John writes:

We know that we are of God,
   and the whole world lieth in wickedness.

1 John 5:19

And:

> In this the children of God are manifest,
>> and the children of the Devil:
> Whosoever doeth not righteousness is not of God,
>> neither he that loveth not his brother.
> For this is the message that ye heard from the beginning,
>> that we should love one another.
>
> *1 John 3:10-11*

And again:

> We are of God: he that knoweth God heareth us;
>> he that is not of God heareth not us.
> Hereby know we the Spirit of Truth,
>> and the Spirit of Error.
>
> *1 John 4:6*

Jesus, too makes the same distinction in the explanation of his parable where tares are sown by the "Enemy" (the Devil) into a field of "good seed". He says:

> He that soweth the good seed is the Son of man;
>> the field is the world;
> The good seed are the children of the kingdom;
>> but the tares are the children of the Wicked One;
> The Enemy that sowed them is the Devil.
>
> *Matthew 13:37-39*

Paul, too, makes the same distinction. In *Romans*, he writes:

> They that are after the flesh
>> do mind the things of the flesh;
> But they that are after the Spirit,
>> the things of the Spirit.
> For to be carnally minded is death;
>> but to be spiritually minded is life and peace.
> Because the carnal mind is enmity against God:
>> for it is not subject to the Law of God,
>>> neither indeed can be.
> So then they that are in the flesh cannot please God.

But ye are not in the flesh, but in the Spirit,
    if so be that the Spirit of God dwell in you.
Now if any man have not the Spirit of Christ,
    he is none of his.

Romans 8:5-9

In *Ephesians*, he speaks of the change of heart that comes to those who
have been baptized by the Spirit, calling those who are motivated by
the "Prince of the power of the air" (Satan), the "children of disobedience". The term is an apt one, for one who has an individual sense of
self will automatically obey the promptings of that lower self. Consequently, they will be out of tune with the divine will and will hence be
disobedient to God. They will be obedient to their master, Satan, but
disobedient to God and to the Master. They will be subject to the law
of recompense and be heedless of the true Law or Word of God. Paul
writes:

And you hath he quickened,
    who were dead in trespasses and sins;
Wherein in time past ye walked
    according to the course of this world,
    according to the Prince of the power of the air –
    the spirit that now worketh
    in the children of disobedience:
Among whom also we all had our conversation
    in times past in the lusts of our flesh,
    fulfilling the desires of the flesh and of the mind;
And were by nature the children of wrath, even as others.

But God, who is rich in mercy,
    for His great love wherewith He loved us,
    even when we were dead in sins,
    hath quickened us together with Christ,
    (by grace ye are saved;)
    and hath raised us up together,
    and made us sit together in heavenly places in Christ Jesus:
That in the ages (*aeons*) to come
    he might shew the exceeding riches of his grace
    in his kindness toward us through Christ Jesus.
For by grace are ye saved through faith;
    and that not of yourselves:

it is the gift of God:
Not of (our own) works, lest any man should boast.
For we are His workmanship.

Ephesians 2:1-10

Those who live "according to the cause of this world", says Paul, are the "children of disobedience", "fulfilling the desires of the flesh and of the mind" – continually running after sensual pleasures and following the promptings and desires of their minds. They are "dead in trespasses and sins". Paul also calls them the "children of wrath" – those who are suffering the "wrath" of God by being separated from Him in the creation.

But, says Paul, God has brought spiritual life to those who had been "dead in trespasses and sins", raising them up from the body so that they may "sit together in heavenly places in Christ", may traverse the heavenly realms together, in the company of the Lord's anointed one, the Christ, the Master. And lest anyone should start thinking themselves to be exclusive and superior to others, he adds that this is His grace, the "gift of God" – "for we are all His workmanship".

NOTES AND REFERENCES

1. *Matthew* 21:26; cf. *Mark* 11:32, *Luke* 20:6.
2. *John* 1:33.
3. *Matthew* 3:16; cf. *Mark* 1:10, *Luke* 3:21.
4. See the *Jerusalem Bible* and the *Revised Standard Version*, etc.
5. *John* 4:2.

CHAPTER NINETEEN

Baptism:
The Gift, The Seal, The Sign and The Seed

The Gift of God

As Paul observes, it is by grace, by the "gift of God", that a soul is
chosen to receive the supreme blessing of the Lord. It is by no means
surprising, therefore, to discover that amongst a number of other expressions, initiation or baptism in the Holy Spirit was also known as
the "gift of God".

While everything else in this world has strings of one kind or another attached to it, often financial, the gift of initiation is *always* given
without *any* charge whatsoever. This has always been the case and will
remain so. Masters are free from all those *karmic* constraints that otherwise force souls to give and take in this world. They alone, therefore,
are in a position to set up their lives in such a way that they can always
be the givers. They never sully the spiritual with material concerns.
Their love, like that of God, is given ungrudgingly, without stint and
without any conditions attached. This is the only utterly pure and selfless love to be found in this world and is itself a gift. Most human love
comes with an abundance of personal need and many other characteristically human provisos attached, but not so the love and spiritual
generosity of the Masters. No one can be as open-hearted and open-
handed as a Master.

There are many places in the ancient literature where this expression is used. Speaking of baptism in the *Acts of Peter*, Peter relates that:

> He (Jesus) did them good and gave them the gift of God.
>
> *Acts of Peter I, ANT p.302*

In the *Acts of John*, John, giving baptism to a young man, prays to
Jesus:

703

Now also let thy gift be accomplished in this young man.

Acts of John 75, ANT p.246

In the *Acts of Thomas,* Judas Thomas speaks of the "gift of the Holy Ghost" and of "thy heavenly gift". Expressing his gratitude to Jesus, he says:

Our souls give praise and thanks unto thee, O Lord,
    for they are thine:
Our bodies give thanks unto thee,
    which thou hast accounted worthy to become
    the dwelling-place of thy heavenly gift.

Acts of Thomas 94, ANT p.405

And, in the *Story of St James,* a crowd of people beg the apostles to give them the "gift of Christ":

"We entreat you, O good servants of God, to give us the gift of God, which ye have given to our friend.... We entreat you, O disciples of the Christ, that ye would make us meet for the gift of the Christ."

Story of St James, MAA p.33

Amongst the New Testament writings, in the letter attributed to James the brother of Jesus, the writer says that such a gift comes from God, which he equates with being born of the "Word of Truth":

Every good gift and every perfect gift is from above,
    and cometh down from the Father of Lights,
    with whom is no variableness, neither shadow of turning.
Of His own will begat He us with the Word of Truth,
    that we should be a kind of firstfruits of His creatures.

James 1:17-18

In the *Gospel of the Twelve Apostles,* this "gift that is from Thyself" is equated with the grace, mercy and compassion of God, the *gnosis,* knowledge or mystic experience that comes from Him and the indwelling of the Holy Spirit:

We beseech thee, our Lord and God
    not to deprive us of Thy grace,
    but establish us in that grace

and enrich us in (that) knowledge that comes from Thee,
and cause Thy Holy Spirit to dwell in us,
and give us the mercies and compassion that come from Thyself:
And perfect with us the gift that is from Thyself;

And with those that call truly on Thy Name,
let no error come nigh us,
and let not the Devil smite us with his destroying arrows:
And let us not taste of the poison of the cruel Serpent;
for this was the cause of the fall of our father Adam.

Gospel of the Twelve Apostles, G12A p.28

Those that receive this gift are also "those that call truly on Thy Name", the true and mystic Name or Word. It is this Power alone which can keep away the power of the Devil, the Negative Power, the power that weaves the web of "error" or illusion.

The devotional writer of the *Odes of Solomon* attributes everything he has attained to this "gift", including the "ascent of my soul" and the return to God:

And I grew up according to His gift,
and I rested in His perfection;
And I spread out my hands in the ascent of my soul,
and stood erect towards the Most High,
and was delivered with (unto) Him.

Odes of Solomon XXXV:6-7, AOT p.724

It is, says the devotee, the source of all spiritual riches:

I abandoned ego,
and turned towards the Most High, my God,
and became rich through His gift.

Odes of Solomon XI:8-9, AOT p.701, OPS p.105, OSC p.52

Thy Glorious Mysteries

Following a common expression of the times for initiation into any esoteric sect, being given initiation or baptism into the mystic Word was also described as the "mysteries" or receiving the gift of the "mysteries". In the *Acts of Thomas*, for example, Judas Thomas is described as the "receiver of the secret mysteries of the Son of God"[2] and "sharer in the holy mysteries of God"[3] He also prays that certain souls "be confirmed by thy glorious mysteries", calling this confirmation or baptism, the "gift of gifts":

> Let them therefore have boldness in thee,
>> and be confirmed by thy glorious mysteries,
>> and receive the gifts of thy gifts.
>> *Acts of Thomas, AAA p.165*

Similarly, to one who had recently been baptized, he says:

> May our Lord make thee worthy of his divine mysteries.
>> *Acts of Thomas, AAA p.223*

The same expression is used in the *History of John* when a group of people ask for initiation, saying:

> We beg of thee, servant of the Living God,
>> do what thou pleasest,
>> and let us participate in the living mystery,
>> that we may live and not die; and this in haste.
>> *History of John, AAA p.38*

Likewise, in the *Books of the Saviour*, generally called the *Pistis Sophia*, Jesus is said to speak of

> the gift of the great mystery
> and its exceedingly great glory.
> *Pistis Sophia 117, PS p.302, PSGG p.251*

The "mysteries", then, a term used with a wide spread of meaning, also referred to the mystic baptism given by a Master.

Baptism for the Forgiveness of Sins

In the *Books of the Saviour*, Jesus also says that he has brought these "mysteries" to the world because everyone is dominated by sin:

> I have brought the mysteries into the world
>> because all are under sin.
> And they all are in need of the gift of the mysteries.
>> *Pistis Sophia 134, PS p.350, PSGG p.293*

And there are many places throughout these writings where he says that the only escape from the domain of Satan and the grip of sin is through this "gift of the mysteries", for it brings with it the complete forgiveness of God, through the Saviour:

> The Saviour answered and said to Mary: "Amen, Amen, I say to you, every man who will receive the mysteries of the Ineffable, not only if he transgresses once and again turns and repents will he be forgiven, but every time he transgresses, while he is still living, if he turns again and repents, without hypocrisy ... he will be forgiven every time, because he has received the gift of the mysteries of the Ineffable, and also because those mysteries are merciful and forgiving at all times."
>> *Pistis Sophia 119, PS p.304, PSGG p.254*

According to the narrative, Jesus says that even if an initiate continues to act sinfully after "receiving the mysteries", as long as he sincerely continues struggling towards the light, he will be forgiven again and again, because he has "received the gift of the mysteries".

Baptism for the remission of sins is the universal dogma of Christianity, of course. Few people, however, really stop to consider what it actually means and whether the ritual baptism received at the hands of a priest is the same as the baptism that Jesus "was baptized with" and whether it actually works. But although the real meaning may have long been misunderstood, the traditional purpose of baptism has always been for the forgiveness or "remission of sins". Jesus himself says in Mark's gospel:

> Unto you it is given to know
>> the mystery of the kingdom of God:
> But unto them that are without,
>> all these things are done in parables:
> That seeing they may see, and not perceive;
>> and hearing they may hear, and not understand;
> Lest at any time they should be converted,
>> and their sins should be forgiven them.
>> *Mark 4:11-12*

The "mystery of the kingdom of God" was made known to Jesus' disciples, but not to others, for it was not intended that everyone "should be converted", that they should be turned around and should start seeking God – or that "their sins should be forgiven them". Such forgiveness only comes to those who are given the mystic baptism. As Judas Thomas says in the *Acts of Thomas*:

> This baptism is of the remission of sins:
>> this is the bringer forth of new men;
>> this is the restorer of understandings; ...
>> and the establisher of the new man in the Trinity,
>> making him a partaker in the remission of sins.
>
>> *Acts of Thomas 132, AAA p.267, ANT p.422*

And again, when giving baptism to a group:

> In thy name, O Jesu Christ,
>> let it be unto these souls for remission of sins
>> and for turning back of the Adversary
>> and for salvation of their souls.
>
>> *Acts of Thomas 157, ANT p.433*

Or likewise, in the *History of John*, where it is said that John

> baptized them in the Name of the Father
>> and the Son and the Spirit of Holiness,
>> for the forgiveness of debts and the pardon of sins.
>
>> *History of John, AAA p.54*

Or as the writer of the *Gospel of Philip* summarizes it, when speaking of the crop harvested by those who receive this baptism:

> Then the slaves will be free and the captives ransomed.
>
>> *Gospel of Philip 85, NHS20 p.213*

It is once again quite evident that such a baptism is more than any ritual immersion. A baptism that can forgive sins and results in the liberation of captive souls is clearly of a rather special nature.

The Sign and the Seal

In ancient times, the mark of personal endorsement and authority was the seal. Using a metallic finger ring or an arm bracelet, engraved with an individual design, a person could seal a letter, a container or any other document with wax and stamp it with their own personal mark or sign.

Derived from this practice, amongst the many metaphors used by the ancient Middle Eastern mystics, those souls who were destined for their particular fold were also called the 'marked souls', those who were 'sealed with the Sign of Life' and by other similar expressions. In fact, the 'seal' was also used as a term for initiation or baptism. It is encountered in *Isaiah*:

> I bind up this testimony,
> I seal this revelation
> in the heart of my disciples.
>
> *Isaiah 8:16, JB*

Paul also uses the expression in reference to the baptism of Jesus when he speaks of being "sealed with the Holy Spirit":

> After that ye believed,
> ye were sealed with that Holy Spirit of promise,
> which is the earnest (pledge) of our inheritance.
>
> *Ephesians 1:13-14*

To 'seal', here as elsewhere in these writings, is meant in the sense of a personal mark or seal, not of something which is tightly closed, and there are a great many such examples of its use that can be quoted. In the *Acts of Paul*, for instance, an eager devotee asks to be given the "seal in Christ":

> And Thecla said: "Only give me the seal in Christ
> and temptation shall not touch me."
>
> *Acts of Paul 25, ANT p.277*

While at another place, the same writer describes a baptism:

> And in that hour, he (Hermocrates) was (made) whole, and received the grace of the seal in the Lord, he and his wife.
>
> *Acts of Paul III, ANT p.282*

Likewise, in the *Acts of Peter*, there is a story which depicts the eagerness of one of the characters for baptism when he takes advantage of being becalmed at sea to seek the "seal of the Lord":

> Now when there was a calm upon the ship in Hadria (the Adriatic), Theon showed it (pointed it out) to Peter, saying unto him: "If thou wilt account me worthy, (as one) whom thou mayest baptize with the seal of the Lord, thou hast an opportunity (now)."
>
> *Acts of Peter III:V, ANT p.308*

Similarly, in the *Acts of Thomas*, a woman begs Judas Thomas for baptism:

> And·the woman besought him, saying: "O apostle of the Most High, give me the seal, that that Enemy (the Negative Power) return not again unto me." Then he caused her to come near unto him and laid his hands upon her and sealed her in the name of the Father and the Son and the Holy Ghost: and many others also were sealed with her.
>
> *Acts of Thomas 49, ANT p.388*

And Judas Thomas observes that having received baptism, such souls are then in a position to realize "eternal life":

> Thou hast received thy seal, get for thyself eternal life.
>
> *Acts of Thomas 121, ANT p.418*

The expression is also used frequently in the Mandaean writings, where the "Jordan", as we have seen before, is the river of Living Water. "*Bihram* the Great" is one of the Mandaeans' many acknowledged Saviours, probably mythological:

> Bound and sealed are these souls
>> who went down to the Jordan
>> and were baptized in the name of the Great Life.
> They have been baptized
>> with the baptism of *Bihram* the Great.
> Their souls have been secured
>> with bonds of righteousness (Truth)
>> and with the bonds of *Zhir*, the great Light of Life.
>
> *CPM 26 pp.22-23*

Note, too, how baptism is also called being "secured with the bonds of righteousness and with the bonds of *Zhir*, the great Light of Life". The expression is the same as Jesus' comment to Peter, "whatsoever thou shalt bind on earth, shall be bound in heaven" — binding being yet another metaphor used for initiation. Amongst the Mandaean writings, baptism is also called 'receiving the pure Sign', where the "Sign" is a synonym for the Word, as in:

> Let every man whose strength enableth him
> and who loveth his soul,
> come and enter the Jordan (of Living Water)
> and be baptized and receive the pure Sign,
> put on robes of radiant light
> and set a fresh wreath upon his head.
>
> *CPM 18 p.13*

It is, of course, the Master, the "Forgiver of sins, trespasses and follies", who gives this "pure Sign":

> On the day that Light ariseth,
> Darkness returns to its place.
> The Forgiver of sins, trespasses, follies,
> stumblings and mistakes will remit them
> for those who love his Name of Truth,
> and for those souls who went down to the Jordan,
> were baptized and received the pure Sign.
>
> *CPM 31 p.28*

The writer of the *Acts of Thomas* uses a similar expression, too, when one of the characters asks Judas Thomas for initiation, saying:

> Give me the Sign of Jesus the Messiah,
> and let me receive his gift from thy hands.
>
> *Acts of Thomas, AAA p.257*

In another Mandaean poem, the Master speaks directly to the initiated souls as "men who have received the Sign" and "my chosen ones", exhorting them, for their own benefit, to continue on the path he has shown to them:

To you do I call and you do I teach,
   men who have received the Sign.

Hearken not to the talk of all peoples and generations;
Let not their stumblings cause you to stumble,
   stumble not because of their stumblings! ...

Certainly have ye held to established Truth,
   ye have held to the certainty
   about which I have instructed you.
I call to my chosen ones so that
   ye may not turn your thought away from me.

Because any man who is not steadfast in thought,
   whose mind is turned against me,
   whose mind is turned from me,
   great and not small will be his hurt.

                           CPM 89 p.92

What brings a soul to perfection is becoming truly free of sin, going beyond the realm of the Universal Mind, the Negative Power, and reaching the eternal abode. But that only happens when your number is counted – counted in the number of the chosen ones of a Master, the "sons of my Sign". For this purpose, then, says the poet, writing in the name of the Master:

Betimes I will come and will fly
   and will reach the sons of my Name,
   the sons of my Sign,
   and the sons of the great Family of Life.
I will bind you together into the bundle of Life
   and I will build you into a great building of Truth
   and will bring you forth to the great Place of Light
   and to the everlasting abode.

                           CPM 76 p.80

"Betimes" – in good time – a Master will come, he will "fly" like a bird from the highest realm, and will contact the "sons of my Name, the sons of my Sign". Gathering together his allotted family, he will return them to their true home, the everlasting abode.

Similarly, amongst the Manichaean-Christian psalms, it is the Master, the "Righteous One" who comes to this world, "is stretched out in the midst of the world", so that souls may be "sealed with thy Seal", can be "illumined" by him, can be healed of their sins, can walk in joy and gladness and can be drawn by him to the "Land of Light":

> Lo, the perfect Man is stretched
>   out in the midst of the world
>   that thou mayest walk in him
>   and receive thy unfading garlands.
> Lo, the Righteous One will illumine thee.
> Lo, Knowledge and Wisdom will put thy clothes upon thee.
> Lo, the medicine-chest of the Physician
>   will heal thy wounds....
>
> Walk, therefore, in joy, drawn to the Land of Light,
>   sealed with thy Seal and with thy unfading garlands.
> Walk also in gladness: thy sufferings have passed today;
> Lo, the harbour of peace – thou hast moored in it.
>
> *Psalms, MPB p.163*

The Five Seals

It was discussed in an earlier chapter on the "many mansions" that mystics have spoken of five primary regions in the Lord's creation. In gnostic writings, these were called the "five Trees" with their five rulers or *archons*. Corresponding to these are the five Sounds, the varying music of the Word as it manifests and sustains the five regions of creation.

The baptism or initiation given to souls in this world takes many forms. It ranges from the entirely ritualistic, performed only with a sprinkling of water and possessing no spiritual value whatever it may symbolize, to the highest initiation which can take a soul all the way back to God. But a person can only give what they have attained within themselves, whatever their intellectual understanding may be, and a mystic can only take a soul to the region that he himself has reached. Consequently, different mystics may initiate souls to the first, second or third regions, and so on, but only a perfect Master, by definition, can initiate and take a soul to the fifth region, that of God Himself, the true region or kingdom of God.

In a significant number of the gnostic tractates associated with Jesus' teachings, mention is made of receiving, or being baptized, with the "five Seals", where the "five Seals" correspond to the "five Trees" or the "five Sounds", all being ways of describing the same essentially indescribable reality. And though in some instances the full context is confused, it would seem that some teacher or teachers, around Jesus' era, baptized souls with the "five seals". This was considered to be the highest form of baptism and in the minds of these writers, Jesus was one of those who gave this kind of baptism.

One such text is the *Apocryphon of John*, where Jesus describes how he came from the Light of God, down into the darkness of this world, taking his abode in the "prison of the body". Here, he gives the mystic Call, and those who hear the sound of his Call are awakened, given hope that they can escape from this hell, and are "sealed ... in the Light of the Water with five Seals, in order that death might not have power over him from this time on":

> I am the light which exists in the Light,
>   I am the remembrance of the *Pronoia* (Primal Thought) –
> I went that I might enter into the midst of darkness
>   and the inside of Hades....
>
> And I entered into the midst of their prison
>   which is the prison of the body.
> And I said, "He who hears, let him get up from the deep sleep."
>
> And he (man) wept and shed tears.
> Bitter tears he wiped from himself and he said,
> "Who is it that calls my name,
>   and from where has this hope come to me,
>   while I am in the chains of the prison?" ...
>
> And I raised him up and sealed him
>   in the Light of the Water with five Seals,
>   in order that death might not have power over him
>   from this time on.
>
> *Apocryphon of John 30-31, NHL p.122*

The "Light of the Water with five Seals" is clearly the Living Water with its five principal stations and Sounds which are encountered on the inner ascent.

Similarly, in the *Trimorphic Protennoia*, a 'revelationary' description is given of how the Christ, the anointed one, receives his divine appointment to act as Saviour in this world. In this passage, it is the Christ or Master who is 'speaking':

> I hid myself within them all
>   (all the powers and beings in creation)
>   until I revealed myself among my members
>   which are mine (*i.e.* to my chosen ones).
> And I taught them about the ineffable Ordinances,
>   and about the (chosen) brethren;
> That they (these Ordinances) cannot be invoked
>   by any of the realms and ruling powers,
>   but only by the sons of Light.
> (For) they are the Ordinances of the Father:
>   they are the glories that are higher than every glory;
> They are the [five] Seals that are perfect
>   through the Intellect (*Nous*). (*Word*)
>
> *Trimorphic Protennoia 49, GS p.100, NHS28 p.431*

The "Ordinance" belongs to the same family of terms for the Word as the "Commandment", the "Order" or the "Law" – the Word being the expression of God's will or law in creation. The "ineffable Ordinances" are thus the expressions of this primary Ordinance – the Word as it appears in each of the five regions. And these Ordinances "are the five Seals that are perfect through the *Nous*" – they are the expressions of the perfect *Nous* or Word. And they can only be invoked by the "sons of Light" – the Masters and their disciples – not by any other power or ruler within the Lord's creation. The Master then continues, saying that he will not leave this world:

> Until I have revealed myself [to all my brethren]
>   and until I have gathered together all my brethren
>   within my [eternal kingdom].
>
> And I proclaimed to them the [five] ineffable [Seals
>   in order that I might] dwell in them
>   and they also might dwell in me.
>
> *Trimorphic Protennoia 50, GS p.100, NHS28 p.433*

As the Master gathers each soul to himself, he gives them the "five ineffable Seals" so that he may take up his place within each of his chosen "brethren" and that they may live with him, spiritually and inwardly.

Hence, he describes the salvation of a particular soul:

> And he (the soul) received the five Seals
>   from [the Light] of the Mother, *Protennoia*,
>   and it was [granted] him
>   to partake of [the mystery] of knowledge,
>   and [he became a light] in Light.
>
> *Trimorphic Protennoia 48, NHS28 p.429*

So close an association does the soul develop with these "five Seals" or five Sounds that it merges into them as it ascends. Hence, one of the Manichaean-Christian writers says that they are "thy kin", they are close 'relatives', part of one's own self. They are:

> These sure Seals that are upon thee are thy kin, O soul,
>   by reason of which no demon can touch thee;
> For thou hast worshipped aright
>   him who has broken the goad of Error:
> Thou hast laid thy treasures in the heavens.
>
> *Psalm CCXLV, MPB p.52*

And because of them, the soul is enabled to overcome all the forces of the Negative Power and, as Jesus said, "to lay up for yourselves treasures in heaven".[5]

A number of other gnostic writings also speak of these "five Seals", including the *Pistis Sophia*. The *Gospel of the Egyptians* also mentions them in a few places, saying that:

> The five Seals ... and they (the Masters) who rule over the *aeons* (the Masters) ... were given the command to reveal to those who are worthy.
>
> *Gospel of the Egyptians 55, NHL p.204*

In the *Second Book of Jeu*, the "living Jesus" associates the "five Trees" with the "great Seal" and the "great Name" – both epithets of the Word. From them will be received the "mystery" or divine knowledge which they possess, "which is the great mystery" – the greatest knowledge and initiation of all:

> Again you will go in to their interior to the rank of the five Trees of the Treasury of the Light, which are the unmoved (eternal) Trees. They will give to you their mystery which is the great mystery, and their great Seal

and the great Name of the Treasury of the Light, which is king over the
Treasury of the Light.

Second Book of Jeu 50, BC p.119

The soul will receive the "great Seal" of the "great Name", the Word
"which is king over the Treasury of the Light", the eternal realm of God.

Sealed on the Forehead

Pointing once again to the mystic nature of this seal, there are a number of instances where it is specifically stated to be located in or on the
forehead. Even in undoubtedly mythological texts, the tradition is continued. The *Acts of Andrew and Matthias*, for example, relates a story
in which some of the apostles are attacked by devils:

> And (one of) the devil(s) said: "Now we will kill you like your Master,
> whom Herod slew." ... But they saw the seal on his forehead and were
> afraid.

Acts of Andrew and Matthias 26-27, ANT p.457

There is a mystical reason why the forehead should be so designated.
As we will discuss more fully in the next chapter, the soul and mind
have their headquarters in the human form at a place in the forehead
behind the two eyes. From here, the currents of the mind and soul
spread throughout the body, enlivening it. It is also from this centre
that they spread out into the world.

Now since initiation is a touch of soul to soul, the soul of the
Master to the soul of the disciple, from a human point of view it can
be said to take place in the head – specifically, the forehead. Moreover,
because the mind also has its human focus at the same location,
with the destiny for that life written into it, so it is also said that a
person's destiny is 'written on their forehead' – not physically, but
mentally. And since initiation or baptism – like everything else – is
written into a person's destiny, so it, too, can be said to be 'written on
the forehead'.

This is the meaning behind such metaphors, as we saw earlier in an
excerpt from the *Odes of Solomon*:

> For I do not turn my face from those that are mine,
>   because I know them;

And before they came into being I perceived them;
    and on their faces I set my seal.
              Odes of Solomon VIII:14-15, AOT p.698

There are a number of places where the early Christians speak of baptism in this way, echoing the earlier mystical teaching before it became mixed with other elements. In the *Book of Revelation,* for example, in a passage purporting to foretell the end of the world, we read:

I saw four angels standing on the four corners of the earth,
    holding the four winds of the earth,
    that the wind should not blow on the earth,
    nor on the sea, nor on any tree.
And I saw another angel ascending from the east,
    having the seal of the Living God:
And he cried with a loud voice to the four angels,
    to whom it was given to hurt the earth and the sea,
Saying, "Hurt not the earth, neither the sea, nor the trees,
    till we have sealed the servants of our God in their foreheads."
And I heard the number of them which were sealed:
    and there were sealed an hundred and forty and four thousand
    of all the tribes of the children of Israel.
Of the tribe of Juda were sealed twelve thousand.
              Book of Revelation 7:1-5

The writer then continues in a similar vein to list the "sealing" of twelve thousand souls from each of the twelve tribes of Israel, making a total of "an hundred and forty and four thousand". This must have been a prevalent belief amongst some of the early Judaeo-Christians. Later on, the same author describes with evident relish the horrors to be meted out on the expected 'Day of Judgment', to the unbaptized – to "those men which have not the seal of God in their foreheads":

And the sun and the air were darkened
    by reason of the smoke of the pit.
And there came out of the smoke locusts upon the earth:
    and unto them was given power,
    as the scorpions of the earth have power.
And it was commanded them that they should not hurt
    the grass of the earth, neither any green thing,
    neither any tree;

But only those men which have not
   the seal of God in their foreheads.

Book of Revelation 9:2-4

Such vividly painted apocalypses are fairly commonplace in the ancient literature, especially of Judaism, and were carried forward for some time into early Christianity. The recipes of torture, fire, plagues and destruction all follow a similar pattern, repeating and copying each other in apocalyptic zeal. It need hardly be added that perfect Masters do not teach such things. The torture they speak of is apparent enough in the ever-present suffering of the souls living in this world.

The expression, having the "seal of God in their foreheads" is a favourite of this ancient writer. Elsewhere, he speaks of the "hundred and forty and four thousand, having his Father's name written in their foreheads"[6] and conversely, of those who have the "mark upon their foreheads"[7] of the "Beast" – possibly another epithet of Satan, also called the Wolf, the Enemy and so on, as we have seen.

A similar expression is also used in the Syriac *History of John*, when John, about to perform a baptism in Jesus' name, says: "I will place a seal upon (what is) between your eyes",[8] while the *Second Book of Jeu* relates:

> Jesus ... baptized all his disciples with the baptism of the Holy Spirit. And he gave to them the gift. He sealed their foreheads with the seal ... which made them to be numbered within the inheritance of the kingdom of the Light.
>
> And the disciples rejoiced with very great joy because they had received the baptism of the Holy Spirit, and the seal which forgave sins and which purified iniquities and made them to be numbered among the inheritance of the kingdom of the Light.

Second Book of Jeu 47, BC pp.113-114

Jesus "sealed their foreheads with the seal", a process equated with "baptism of the Holy Spirit", the "gift", the "seal which forgave sins and which purified" and being "numbered among the inheritance of the kingdom of the Light". These, then, were all terms employed in reference to the true spiritual baptism, the mystic touch of soul to soul. They were not, however, the only expressions by which Jesus and his disciples spoke of baptism.

The Sower and His Seed

One of Jesus' most well-loved parables is the sower of the seed, where, as he himself explains, the "seed" is the Word of God and the "sower" is the Master. The sowing of the seed, then, meant baptism in the Holy Spirit, as later gnostic users of Jesus' metaphor make clear. This may be readily appreciated, but the remainder of the story may not be so well understood, for again, it is specifically mystical and relates to the different kinds of disciples to whom Masters give their mystic gift. The parable is found in all three of the synoptic gospels. In Matthew's version, Jesus says:

> Behold, a sower went forth to sow;
> And when he sowed, some seeds fell by the way side,
>   and the fowls came and devoured them up:
>
> Some fell upon stony places, where they had not much earth:
>   and forthwith they sprung up,
>   because they had no deepness of earth:
> And when the sun was up, they were scorched;
>   and because they had no root, they withered away.
>
> And some fell among thorns;
>   and the thorns sprung up, and choked them:
>
> But other fell into good ground, and brought forth fruit,
>   some an hundredfold, some sixtyfold, some thirtyfold.
> Who hath ears to hear, let him hear.
>
> *Matthew 13:3-9*

Jesus relates a simple agricultural story to people who lived close to the land and the scene he depicts would have been the common experience of any farmer at that time, perhaps even nowadays. When a farmer goes to sow, his main intention is to sow his seed in fertile soil. All the same, by the very nature of things, he has so much seed in his bundle that some of it falls by the roadside while he is on his way to the field. Other seed falls onto stony parts of his field, where it is unable to thrive. And some falls amongst weeds which choke its growth. But the majority falls into fertile ground where, according to the degree of fertility, it gives a higher or lower yield. Jesus then explains his parable:

Hear ye therefore the parable of the sower.
When any one heareth the word of the kingdom,
　　and understandeth it not, then cometh the Wicked One,
　　and catcheth away that which was sown in his heart.
This is he which received seed by the way side.

But he that received the seed into stony places,
　　the same is he that heareth the word,
　　and anon with joy receiveth it;
Yet hath he not root in himself, but dureth for a while:
　　for when tribulation or persecution ariseth because of the word,
　　by and by he is offended.

He also that received seed among the thorns
　　is he that heareth the word;
And the care of this world, and the deceitfulness of riches,
　　choke the word, and he becometh unfruitful.

But he that received seed into the good ground
　　is he that heareth the word, and understandeth it;
Which also beareth fruit, and bringeth forth,
　　some an hundredfold, some sixty, some thirty.

Matthew 13:18-23

As in John's gospel, hearing the "word" of the kingdom carries a double meaning. It implies contact with the mystic teachings, as well as baptism in the Holy Spirit, the sowing of the Word by the Master within the soul of a disciple. Jesus points out that many kinds of people come to a Master and receive initiation. Some hear the teachings but "understandeth it not" – they receive initiation through the influence of relatives or friends, perhaps, but do not really understand what has been given to them or what they have to do to make that seed bear fruit. And hardly have they been initiated than the "Wicked One", the Negative Power, tempts them in various ways and they are unable to resist. They go on living their lives as they always have done and, like other people of the world, they are swept away by the activities of physical existence and the pleasures of the senses.

The disciple who receives his "seed" into "stony places", continues Jesus, "forthwith ... sprung up" – "anon with joy receiveth it". He understands the mystic teachings to some extent and immediately asks for initiation. But his sincerity is only superficial – he "hath not root in himself" – and he remains on the path, attending to his spiritual practice, only for so long as he is not put to the test. And as soon as troubles come his way, particularly those things that make it difficult for him to follow the path, such as ridicule or antagonism from his family or community, "he is offended" and gives up the struggle. His sense of spiritual direction is easily deflected and he falls away.

The one who "received seed among thorns" is he that "heareth the word" – he does understand the mystic path and may even be in touch, to some extent, with the music of the Word within himself. Yet, he also has many material tendencies, perhaps lying dormant in his sub-conscious mind. Consequently, he is still deluded by the lure of wealth and by other concerns of this world and even if he continues with his spiritual practice, his progress is hampered at every step by his worldly and sensual desires. He therefore "becometh unfruitful": he does not make significant spiritual progress in this life.

But, naturally, the main purpose of the sower is to sow his seed in fertile ground where it will bear fruit. These are the disciples who "heareth the word and understandeth it": they understand the mystic path; they know what is required of them; and they are not overly dis-tracted by their duties in the world but learn to keep everything in balance. They are the ones who get some results in their spiritual practice.

Even amongst these, however, they do not all bear the same fruit: they bring forth, "some an hundredfold, some sixty, some thirty". Dis-ciples respond differently to baptism, for each one is carrying a differ-ent burden of sins or *karmas* from past lives and it is the clearing of this load which determines individual progress. Some have a lighter load, some a heavier load. Moreover, some have been initiated in past lives and are only picking up the threads from previous incarnations as disciples. Others are just starting out upon the path and may thus have more to clear.

As a result of these differences in their background, some will progress all the way back to God: they achieve a "hundredfold" result. Some gain access to the higher regions, but still have a further way to go before they reach home. This they will slowly accomplish after death. And others may have been able to meet the spiritual form of the Master and after death will progress onwards from there. So al-though the majority of them are not required to take another birth in this world, there is still a difference in their spiritual progress, due to the difference in their load of past sins or *karmas*.

This is the meaning of Jesus' famous saying which he uses to sum-marize both this and other parables with a similar meaning:

> But many that are first shall be last;
>   and the last shall be first.
>
> *Matthew 19:30*

And:

> So the last shall be first, and the first last:
>   for many be called, but few chosen.
>
> *Matthew 20:16*

His meaning is that there is no seniority amongst disciples. Those who come to the mystic path early in life may not make such good progress as those who come during their latter years. Those who are initiated first may be the last to return to God. "Many (may) be called" to follow the path, "but few are chosen" to return to Him in this life.

Some may have to take two or three more lives before sufficient *karmas* have been cleared for them to have no further inclination to return here, and no *karmas* that are strong enough to bring them back. All will ultimately be taken back to God, but not all will go at the same speed, nor will they be all taken at once.

Hearing a parable such as this, each disciple begins to look within himself and wonder which kind of seed he is. Therefore, as Luke records, Jesus consoled them, saying:

> Fear not, little flock;
>   for it is your Father's good pleasure
>   to give you the kingdom.
>
> *Luke 12:32*

A Master loves every one of his sheep. No one will be forgotten. Every disciple will ultimately receive the same spiritual treasure, but there is likely to be a difference in the time it takes each individual to reach home.

Incidentally, this parable is a further indication that Jesus had more than just a few disciples. He relates it because, in a large group of disciples, there is likely to be a significant spread of enthusiasm for the mystic path, as well as apparent spiritual progress. And since, in the initial stages, disciples can be just as human as everyone else, they are likely to feel jealous of others whom they think – rightly or wrongly – are making better progress than themselves. Jesus is therefore telling them why these apparent differences exist and that their progress has nothing to do with when they were initiated. Everyone simply has to do his best and leave everything else to their Master, for "it is your Father's good pleasure to give you the kingdom" – as and when He thinks fit.

Like to a Grain of Mustard Seed

The real mystic baptism given by a true Master may seem at first sight to be something of little significance. This is because, apart from the instruction in spiritual practice and the conveyance of certain esoteric information, there is very little to it, externally. Whatever it may become in a later religion, the true baptism does not entail dressing up in any special way, nor does it involve any kind of ritual. The real initiation is the acceptance of a soul by a Master and the retuning of that soul to the Word or Holy Spirit, something which takes place beyond the field of normal human perception.

While it is true that some souls do have inner experiences at the time of initiation, as did Jesus himself according to the gospel stories ("the heavens were opened unto him"[29]), for most individuals it is the beginning of a long and laborious struggle. As many mystics have said, the soul's stay in this world has continued through millions of lifetimes and the downward, material tendencies have become deeply ingrained. That this trend can be reversed in just a few lifetimes indicates the degree of grace that is extended by the Masters to their disciples.

However, if a disciple gives the required time and effort to the spiritual exercises and moulds his life according to the principles taught by his Master, then, by degrees, he will begin to realize just what it is that the Master has done for him. Jesus illustrates this by a number of other analogies associated with the parable of the sower. He says, for instance:

> The kingdom of heaven is like to a grain of mustard seed,
>   which a man took, and sowed in his field:
> Which indeed is the least of all seeds:
>   but when it is grown, it is the greatest among herbs,
>   and becometh a tree, so that the birds of the air
>   come and lodge in the branches thereof.
>
> *Matthew 13:31-32*

Baptism, he says, is like a mustard seed, which starts off tiny, emerges as a very small seedling, and yet grows into a tall plant, almost like a shrub, so that birds can even come and sit amongst its foliage. In the

Middle East, given favourable conditions, 'mustard' (actually, coriander) can grow up to ten feet in height.

What he means is that, to begin with, a disciple may take his initiation very lightly. But if he practises according to instructions, his spiritual awareness steadily grows and he becomes aware of the changes that are taking place in his inner life. He becomes a better human being; he gains increasing control over his mind and emotions; and while still living in the body, he slowly learns to go through the gateway of death, to meet the radiant form of the Master within and to traverse the inner regions. Ultimately, he is taken back to God and the sins or *karmas*, not only of this life, but of millions of past lives are burnt up or forgiven. All this results from the sowing of the seed of the Word. Something apparently small and insignificant grows into something very big indeed.

In an identical analogy, again taken from the everyday life, Jesus says that baptism is like the leaven or yeast that is used to raise bread. Only a very small quantity is required to raise a large amount of bread dough:

> The kingdom of heaven is like unto leaven,
>> which a woman took, and hid in three measures of meal,
>> till the whole was leavened.
>
> *Matthew 13:33*

Baptism into the divine Word may seem like something small but in the end it makes a heavily earthbound soul rise up and become one with God, just as a little leaven raises heavy dough. Incidentally, the term used for a "measure" is a *seah*, three of which make something in the order of ten gallons, by volume.

In order for a disciple to make good use of the gift of initiation, he must develop an appreciation of what has been given to him. Illustrating the best attitude to adopt, Jesus says:

> The kingdom of heaven is like unto treasure hid in a field;
>> the which when a man hath found, he hideth,
>> and for joy thereof goeth and selleth all that he hath,
>> and buyeth that field.
>
> *Matthew 13:44*

When someone hears that there is a treasure hidden in a particular field, he may keep silent, but he is prepared to sell everything he has in order to possess that field for he knows that nothing is too great a price to pay in exchange for such a treasure. Similarly, when an individual has come to know that the greatest of all treasures is hidden within his own self and that he has been given the means of finding it, nothing should be too much trouble in the effort to uncover it. The sincere disciple should be ready to sacrifice anything to obtain the inner treasure. Again, Jesus says:

> The kingdom of heaven is like unto a merchant man,
>   seeking goodly pearls:
> Who, when he had found one pearl of great price,
>   went and sold all that he had, and bought it.
>
> *Matthew 13:46*

A seeker is like a merchant in search of valuable pearls. But when he finds one of a value and quality surpassing everything else he has, he relinquishes everything in his efforts to obtain it. Just so, when the seeker finds that the spiritual pearl can be obtained within himself as long as he lives the right kind of life and diligently attends to his spiritual practice, he relinquishes all other desires of the world and devotes all his attention to finding it and making correct use of the human form he has been given.

Sow in Me Thy Word of Life

Metaphors concerning the sower and the seed are commonplace in early Christian writings, where they are almost invariably associated with baptism. In the Arabic *Death of Saint John*, John addresses Jesus as:

> O thou Lord Jesus the Christ,
>   who hast bound this perishing garland (of the body)
>   together with the everlasting one (the soul)
>   and all these coloured flowers (individual souls)
>   unto the Flower of Sweetness (the Word);
> Who has sown his life-giving Word in our hearts,
>   he who alone maketh beautiful
>   the sweetness of the souls and the bodies.
>
> *Death of St John, MAA p.56*

The writer of the *Acts of Thomas*, never one to overlook a good image, is also fond of it, as we might have expected. Having received baptism through Judas Thomas, one devotee says, "I have received the Living Seed of the Word";[10] another says that he has "sown life in me";[11] while one who is anxious for initiation praises God, saying "Thou didst show me my remissness and didst sow in me thy heavenly love",[12] imploring Judas Thomas:

> I beg of thee, apostle of God, sow in me thy Word of Life, so that I may again hear perfectly the Voice of Him who delivered me unto thee and said to thee, "This is one of those who shall live through thee, and henceforth let him be with thee."
>
> *Acts of Thomas, AAA p.176*

Additionally, speaking of his own initiation and the protection afforded by his Master, Judas Thomas himself thanks Jesus, saying, "Thou art he that from childhood hast sown life in me and kept me from corruption".[13]

In the *Odes of Solomon*, writing in the name of the Master, the poet links release from captivity with baptism, which he calls the sowing of "my fruits":

> I was crowned by my God,
>   and my crown is the Living One;
> And I was justified (authorized) by my Lord,
>   and my deliverance is incorruptible (unchangeable)....
>
> He gave me the way of His steps (the path to Him),
>   and I opened the gates that were shut....
> And nothing seemed to me to be shut,
>   because I was the opening of everything.
>
> And I went to all my prisoners to release them,
>   that I might leave no man bound and binding.
> And I gave my knowledge without grudging,
>   and my prayer was in my love.
>
> And I sowed my fruits in hearts,
>   and I transformed them in myself.
> And they received my blessing and lived,
>   and were gathered to me and delivered,

> because they became my members,
>   and I am their head.
> Glory be to thee, our head, O Lord Christ.
>
> *Odes of Solomon XVII:1-2,8,10-16, AOT pp.707-708*

In the gnostic *Tripartite Tractate*, the Master is said to sow the Word "in an invisible way", pointing to the hidden, mystic nature of true baptism:

> And he sowed in him in an invisible way
>   a Word which is destined to be knowledge.
>
> *Tripartite Tractate 88, NHS22 p.253*

And in *Marsanes*, bearing fruit from the "imperishable Seed" is linked with self-control and detachment from the world, as it is in Jesus' parable of the sower:

> [Control] yourselves, receive the imperishable Seed,
>   bear fruit, and do not become attached to your possessions.
>
> *Marsanes 26, NHS15 p.295*

Amongst the Manichaean writings, in a discourse on the nature of the real or "Living Self" – the soul – the "pure Word" is described as both the "Seed" or essence of the soul, as well as the "Pilot" or Helmsman "for the soul in the body". That is, the real Master for a soul incarnate in the body is the Word, the "Seed", the soul's own essence:

> Understand your Seed:
>   the pure Word that in itself is the Pilot
>   for the soul in the body.
> And through it (the pure Word),
>   fully know that the false word, (مینا)
>   which leads to the hell of darkness,
>   is a pilot of hell.
>
> *MMIII pp.870-875, ML p.48*

Only through the "pure Word" can the counterfeit or "false word" – the mind – be known for what it is, as that which leads the soul into the hell of this world in birth after birth.

Wherever we look, then, amongst these mystical writings, we find echoes of Jesus' teachings that provide us with an insight into what his sayings and parables really meant.

Planted in Heaven

Associated with the sowing of the seed is the metaphor of planting, another image commonly used in the mystical literature of this period, the gospels included. According to a story related in St Matthew, for example, Jesus is commenting upon the uselessness of the rituals performed by the Jewish priests and Pharisees. When someone says that the Pharisees are offended at his remarks, Jesus responds:

> Every plant, which my heavenly Father hath not planted,
> shall be rooted up.
>
> *Matthew 15:13*

Assuming that the anecdotal setting of this saying is relevant, Jesus is saying that their feelings will not alter the reality. What people may *think* to be the value of rituals and ceremonies does not effect their actual efficacy at all. Simply following the external observances of a particular religion entitles no one to return to God. Only those who are "planted" by the "heavenly Father" *from heaven* are truly on the path that leads back to Him. Others "shall be rooted up" – they will bear no fruit and will be thrown back into the labyrinth of birth and death. As John the Baptist also said, when speaking of baptism:

> And now also the axe is laid unto the root of the trees:
> therefore every tree which bringeth not forth good fruit
> is hewn down, and cast into the fire.
>
> *Matthew 3:10*

The meaning is the same. Those trees or plants – those souls – "which bringeth not forth good fruit" are "hewn down, and cast into the fire". They will bear no fruit, but will once again be cast into the fire of this world. And, as Jesus clarified, unless they are planted in heaven or properly initiated, they will be unable to bear the fruit of God-realization, however sincere they may be. If they are really genuine, it will entitle them to initiation at some future date but, until that time comes, they will remain within the round of birth and death.

As always, there is ample material in the literature of the period to demonstrate that this metaphor was used with the meaning indicated. In the Manichaean-Christian psalms, alluding to Jesus' parable of the Sower and speaking of the chosen ones as "his elect" and "his men of knowledge", the psalmist writes:

> He planted his shoots in the field of his elect.
> He sowed the Seed in the soil of his men of knowledge.
>
> *Psalms of Heracleides, MPB p.194*

In the Nag Hammadi tractate, the *Gospel of Truth*, the writer speaks of the initiates as the "plantings" of Christ, the Lord's anointed one, "planted ... in his paradise":

> He (Christ) is good. He knows his plantings,
> because it is he who planted them in his paradise.
>
> *Gospel of Truth 36, NHS22 p.109*

In the Mandaean writings, in a passage comprised almost entirely of the metaphors and lyrical images so beloved of the Middle Eastern writers, the initiates are called the "plants which the Jordan hath planted and raised up":

> How lovely are the plants which the Jordan
>   hath planted and raised up!
> Pure fruit have they borne
>   and on their heads they set living wreaths.
> *Yawar-Ziwa* rejoiceth in the good plants
>   which the Jordan planted and raised.
> The plants rejoice and flourish
>   in the Perfume of *Manda-d-Hiia*
>   which breatheth upon them.
>
> *CPM 83 pp.90-91*

Yawar-Ziwa (*lit.* dazzling radiance) is a name for God the Father, while *Manda-d-Hiia* (*lit.* knowledge of life) is both a mythological Saviour and the Word itself. Hence, the "Perfume of *Manda-d-Hiia*" is the sweet emanation of God – an allusion to the Word, often termed the Fragrance or Perfume. It is "breathed upon" the "plants", which "rejoice and flourish", the breathing once again being a further reference to the Word as the Breath of Life, as we have seen before. In another Mandaean passage, this time from their *John-Book*, the Saviour speaks of *Miryai*, a mythical devotee symbolizing the soul:

> I am come to heal *Miryai*
>   and bring Water to the good, precious plants,
>   the grape-vines standing at the mouth of Frash.

In a white (pure) bucket I draw
    and bring Water to my plants.
I carry and take
    by my arms of splendour and bring Water.
I carry and take and bring Water.
Blessed be he who hath drunk from my Water!
He drinketh and is healed and made firm (whole).

John-Book, JM p.132, MEM p.153

The "Water" which heals the soul is, of course, the Living Water which the Master brings to his plants. "Blessed be he who has drunk from my Water!"

In one of the poems amongst the Manichaean-Christian writings found in Turkestan, allusions to Jesus' parables of the Sower and the Tares are encountered, touched with images we have seen in Mandaean and Manichaean writings. In a long poem, where the "Law" and the "Commandments" are synonyms for the Word, the devotee expresses his humility before the Master, saying:

I am ... the bright
    and sweet-scented seed of the great Saint,
    thrown into the dense forest
    and thorny shrubs (of this world).
Bestow great mercy: pray take and adopt me,
    convey me to the vault of Light
    in the garden of the Law.

I am also the vine branch of the great Saint,
    once planted in the garden of the Law,
    the clean and pure park,
    suddenly strangled by creepers
    and entwined by climbers,
    extracting my wonderful strength
    and leaving me to languish and wither.

I am also the fertile soil of the great Saint,
    on which have been grown
    the five poisonous trees by the devils;
I only hope that the great hoe of the Law,
    the sharp knife and sickle,

will hew down and cut, burn them out,
and make me clean and pure.

All the rest of the evil weeds and the thorny shrubs,
    pray, destroy all of them
    with the fire of (thy) Commandment.

LSMH 67-70, BSOAS XI p.182

The devotee is the "seed", the "vine branch" and the "fertile soil" who has been overtaken by the entanglements of physical life and the strength of the human passions – the "dense forest", the "thorny shrubs", the "creepers", the "climbers", the "five poisonous trees" and the "evil weeds". He is, however, one of the Master's initiates and consequently, despite his condition, he has the hope and the Master's personal assurance that he will be able to surmount all his problems, by means of "(thy) Commandment".

This hope and faith is reciprocated by the Master; indeed, it is he who has begun the process. He is the one who plants and cares for his "plantings"; the "plants" only respond to his love and care. In the Manichaean-Christian *Psalms of Thomas*, which scholars have demonstrated are actually translations into Coptic from earlier Mandaean psalms perhaps via the Syriac, the Master is called the "Chooser of the righteous". He plants his "beloved ones" "beyond the confines of this world" and "attends" to them so that they "sleep not nor slumber":

Where hast thou gone, O Chooser of the righteous?
Thou Chooser of the righteous,
    all thy sons seeking after thee,
all thy sons are seeking after thee,
    thy beloved ones expect thee....
Thy sons seek after thee,
    thy beloved ones expect thee daily,
thy disciples seek after thee,
    looking for thy Form within themselves.

I went forth to plant a garden
    beyond the confines of this world,
choosing and planting in it the plants
    that grew in the Living Ones (the Masters).

I will give orders to the Gardener:

"Attend to my trees, my new plants;
    attend to my new plants
    that they sleep not nor slumber,
they sleep not nor slumber,
    that they forget not the order
    that has been given them."

Psalms of Thomas XIII, MPB p.218, SCMP p.120

This is the duty of the Masters – to initiate or plant their chosen souls and then to guard over them and guide them on the spiritual path so that they should "sleep not nor slumber".

Similar expressions are found in the Judaic *Apocalypse of Baruch*, a revelationary text probably dating from the second half of the first century AD, where initiates are described as being "justified in My Law" or having the "root of Wisdom" "planted in their heart":

Also (as for) the glory of those who have now been justified in My Law, who have had understanding in their life, and who have planted in their heart the root of Wisdom, then their splendour shall be glorified in changes (will undergo transformation), and the form of their face shall be turned into the light of their beauty, that they may be able to acquire and receive the world which doth not die, which is then promised to them.

Apocalypse of Baruch LI:3, AB p.68

Such souls, says the writer, will undergo "changes" or transformation. They will be able to leave their bodies and experience the "light of their beauty" in the higher regions. They will "acquire and receive the world which doth not die" – they will return to the eternal realm, the kingdom of God, which has been "promised to them" by virtue of their initiation.

The same metaphor is again found in the *Odes of Solomon* when the poet says:

And I said, Blessed, O Lord,
    are those who have been planted in Thy ground.
And those who have a place in Thy paradise,
    and grow up in the growth of Thy Trees
    and have moved from darkness to light.

Behold, all thy labourers are excellent,
    who perform good works (spiritual practice?),

and turn from wickedness to thy pleasantness,
And have turned the bitterness of the trees away from them,
    when they were planted in Thy ground.

And everything has become like a relic (reminder) of thee,
    and an eternal remembrance of thy faithful servants.
For there is much room in thy paradise,
    and there is nothing that is unprofitable;
        but everything is full of fruits.
Praise be to thee, O God,
    the pleasure that is in the eternal paradise.

Odes of Solomon XI:18-24, AOT p.702

And referring to the Word as the Good Tree, the Tree of Life, the author of the *Acts of Thomas* has Judas Thomas say:

Thou Lord art he that revealeth hidden mysteries
    and maketh manifest words that are secret:
Thou Lord art the planter of the Good Tree,
    and of thine hands are all good works engendered.

Acts of Thomas 10, ANT p.369

There is a common and crucial thread running through these last few extracts. The disciples are *daily* seeking for the Master *within themselves*: "Thy sons seek after thee, thy beloved ones expect thee *daily*. Thy disciples seek after thee, looking for thy Form within themselves." The Master is there to ensure that "they sleep not nor slumber, that *they forget not the order that has been given them*." As a result of being planted with the "root of Wisdom" and being "justified in My Law", they are transformed into beings of light and are enabled to "receive the world which does not die" within themselves. They are described as excellent "labourers ... who perform good works", "good works" which are "engendered" entirely by the Master's "hands".

All these are allusions to the practice taught to disciples at the time of "planting", at the time of initiation or baptism. They are references to the practice of interior prayer, of spiritual meditation. Having access to the radiant form of the Master within oneself, being transformed into a being of light and returning to the eternal realm do not take place without great effort. Much "labour" has to be exerted. It is probable, therefore, that "good works" or "good deeds" are euphemisms or maybe only poor translations for what would be better rendered as 'spiritual practice'. The Master watches over his disciples, inspiring them from within and without to attend to their spiritual exercises – their "good works" – preventing them from falling back into the long sleep of worldliness and forgetfulness of the "order" to meditate "that has been given them". The point is that baptism is only a prelude to the greatest adventure of all – true spiritual meditation.

NOTES AND REFERENCES

1. *Acts of Thomas* 52, ANT p.389.
2. *Acts of Thomas*, AAA p.180.
3. *Acts of Thomas*, AAA p.185.
4. *Matthew* 16:19.
5. *Matthew* 6:20.
6. *Book of Revelation* 14:1.
7. *Book of Revelation* 20:4.
8. *History of John*, AAA p.37.
9. *Matthew* 3:16; cf. *Mark* 1:10, *Luke* 3:21.
10. *Acts of Thomas*, AAA p.226.
11. *Acts of Thomas* 15, ANT p.370.
12. *Acts of Thomas*, AAA p.174.
13. *Acts of Thomas* 144, ANT p.428.

CHAPTER TWENTY

Knocking at His Door:
The Strait Gate and The Single Eye

Few There Be that Find It

Mysticism or true spirituality is a path of action, of spiritual practice. It is something you live and do, something you experience. Essentially, it is something that happens to you, not something you believe in. It is an experience, not an intellectual philosophy. There may be certain principles which at the outset can be considered as beliefs or guides, but the intention is to turn all such belief into experience and direct, personal knowledge while still living in the world as a normal human being. This is the nature of *gnosis* as it was understood by those we call the gnostics and this is what all true mystics have taught.

Religious belief and intellectual philosophy, on the other hand, are largely theoretical. At best, they – and the sacred writings from which religion is derived – are descriptions of mystic experience and a guide to attaining it. At worst, they are little more than clever words that serve only to lead us round in mental circles. Spiritual practice or meditation is the means of turning the unknown into the known, of turning belief into experience and of automatically testing the correctness of that belief in the process.

Inner experience is one thing; to the one who has it, it is more real than any other experience. Interpretation and intellectual analysis, belief and dogma, ritual and ceremony, on the other hand, are all outgoing activities of mind and body, adopted as the primary means of approaching God by those who follow no path of inner spiritual practice. It is these which are usually considered to constitute the basis of religion.

Religion binds, spirituality frees. Religion binds the mind into the straitjacket of dogma and material observances. Spirituality frees the soul from the constraints of the world, the body and the mind. Religion suppresses individual thought, often runs counter to logic and normal human perceptions, and is suspicious of personal experience.

Spirituality encourages individuals to think clearly and to understand, to perceive and to experience things for themselves. Religion insists that the relationship to God must be through a host of external intermediaries, whether they be people, beliefs or ceremonies. Spirituality leads the individual to a personal relationship with the divine.

Mystic experience, spiritual practice, true spirituality and following the mystic path are like the eating of a cake. Religious teachings are only a recipe for that cake – or they are travel brochures designed to entice the reader to undertake the journey to another land. But nothing can supplant the experience of travel and of arrival at the chosen destination. And no amount of reading a recipe can assuage one's hunger.

But while no one would ever care to substitute the reading of recipes for a meal or the study of maps for travel, the most important thing in life – the discovery of what life actually *is* within oneself – is commonly relegated to the status of a recipe or a map. People think about it, discuss it and talk learnedly about it, but do not act upon it. This is a part of the veil of illusion and ignorance which has been cast upon mankind. Man is fooled into thinking that his ideas constitute reality and he therefore fails to seek experience of that reality. That God, the source of all life and creation, can actually be known within oneself in a level of consciousness that far exceeds that of this world, is scarcely recognized.

To modernize the metaphors, man has become contented with musing upon the contents of a handbook on car maintenance, remaining sublimely unaware that motor cars actually exist and are intended for use in travel. We are talking here of the majority of mankind. Though many are aware of the existence of a higher reality, very few know what to do and are willing to take the necessary steps to find it. As Jesus said:

> Narrow is the way which leadeth unto Life,
> and few there be that find it.
>
> *Matthew 7:14*

Treasures in Heaven

Mystics never tire of encouraging their disciples to find this higher reality. Their argument is very simple. No one is going to live in this world forever. Consequently, everything collected here is only of temporal value. Moreover, once acquired, things are likely to become a burden and a source of worry, rather than an asset, for everything changes constantly. They require maintenance and safeguarding from the many forces of destruction and dissipation. Hence, Jesus advised:

> Labour not for the meat which perisheth,
>> but for that meat which endureth unto everlasting life,
>> which the Son of man shall give unto you.
>
> *John 6:27*

The labouring of which Jesus speaks is the effort of interior prayer, of meditation, of spiritual practice. It is this kind of labour which enables a soul to know "everlasting life", to realize its own immortality. Such realization cannot be expected to come upon somebody without any effort or practice on their part. Those who think that the labour consists in performing good deeds in this world are mistaken. The reward for good deeds is reaped in the sphere of deeds, in this world, in future lives. Good deeds ennoble a person, no doubt, but they do not lead to a meeting with God. They may prepare a person to begin the spiritual journey, but they are no substitute for it. Hence, Jesus also said:

> If any man will come after me, let him deny himself,
>> and take up his cross, and follow me.
> For whosoever will save his life shall lose it:
>> and whosoever will lose his life for my sake shall find it.
>
> *Matthew 16:24-25*

He says that if anyone really wishes to follow him, to "come after me", he must detach himself from the world and devote himself to spiritual practice. To "take up his cross" is a reference to the practice of meditation, as we will shortly see. And he points out that "any man" who is only concerned about his life in this world, who only wishes to "save his life", living entirely for himself and his own pleasure, will ultimately "lose it". He will die like everybody else and nothing he has achieved will be of any value to him. Not only will he lose all his worldly gain but he will also have lost or wasted his opportunity of being in the human form, and there is no guarantee that he will return again as a human being.

But "whosoever loses his life for my sake", whoever dedicates himself to the Master, practises meditation according to the Master's instructions and lives the way of life that the Master teaches, putting this as his first priority in life, "will find it". He will find his own immortality;

he will find God; he will find the mystic and eternal Source of his own life. And he adds:

> For what is a man profited, if he shall gain the whole world,
> and lose his own soul?
> Or what shall a man give in exchange for his soul?
>
> *Matthew 16:26*

Even if someone becomes the ruler and owner of the entire world, it is of no real value. Not only will he have to relinquish it one day, but in the process of gaining worldly things, a person forgets the eternal reality of their own soul. The opportunity of finding this is lost as the soul once again plunges into rebirth. Nothing, Jesus says, is too high a price to pay in exchange for realizing the immortality of the soul and escape from birth and death. There is nothing of comparable value that can be given in exchange. Hence, he also says:

> Lay not up for yourselves treasures upon earth,
> where moth and rust doth corrupt,
> and where thieves break through and steal:
> But lay up for yourselves treasures in heaven,
> where neither moth nor rust doth corrupt,
> and where thieves do not break through nor steal:
> For where your treasure is, there will your heart be also.
>
> *Matthew 6:19-21*

He advises that we devote our time to that practice which will build a treasure in heaven, that we put all our heart and desire into that practice and give only secondary importance to worldly affairs. We should perform our worldly duties diligently and lovingly, but with no expectation or desire to gain any permanent benefit from them. This would be unrealistic and only create a framework for frustration and unhappiness. The first priority should be meditation.

The Single Eye

In times past, there were good reasons why mystics were unwilling to divulge the secrets of spiritual practice to any but their initiates. In modern times, they are not so reluctant. All the same, it is inadvisable to begin meditation without adequate guidance. There are several reasons for this.

Firstly, before commencing meditation a person should gain as full an understanding as they can of what they are getting themselves into. No one should be in a hurry to start any form of spiritual practice without laying an adequate foundation. True mystics are not looking to collect numbers; they want their disciples to be sincere and dedicated seekers of the mystic reality. If a person is unconvinced that this is what they are really looking for, then – like the seed that falls by the wayside, on shallow ground or amongst thorns – they will fail to bear fruit. And human nature being as it is, they will be more likely to blame the path or the teacher than themselves. Consequently, the net result of their endeavour may not be positive. It is therefore better to take all the time required in the search for the right path, even if it takes a lifetime. This is not time wasted, but time gained.

Secondly, meditation under the guidance of a perfect Master has the efficacy it does only because of the Master's grace and blessings on the disciple. Even if somebody managed to discover all the essential details of the spiritual practice but had not been accepted as a disciple, they would be acting on their own. They would have no one to oversee the repayment of their *karmic* debt, no one to meet them on the inside, no one to guide them externally or internally if they got into difficulties, no one to shower blessings and inspiration upon them in so many ways. They would be trying to climb to the top of an unknown mountain on their own, without real knowledge of the way or how to climb, and they would be likely to get lost or worse. To go adventuring into the realms of one's own being without the guidance of one who knows the way is simply foolhardy.

But what form of spiritual practice or mystic prayer do the Masters teach? Mystics say that the headquarters of the mind and soul in the human body is in the forehead, immediately behind and above the two eyes. This focus of attention has hence been called the eye centre, the centre of consciousness or the thinking centre. This is why the hand automatically goes to the forehead when we wish to concentrate upon some problem. We do not strike our knees or other parts of our anatomy. But there is nothing physical about this 'location'. It could not be discovered by a surgeon, any more than thoughts and feelings can be observed by physical observation or dissection. It is a mental or subtle centre.

From this point, the attention drops down into the body, spreading out and scattering into the world through the sense organs and the organs of activity. And the more a person's attention strays away from this centre of consciousness, the less is their awareness and consciousness of what is happening to them. Consequently, the more a person is scattered into the world, the less do they realize it. This is a dangerous situation.

The mind is never still, not even for a moment. Even when exhausted from the activities of the day, the mind remains active during sleep, generating dreams associated with a person's worldly and mental life, both conscious and subconscious. In this way, a person passes their entire life, completely obsessed with the world.

The first task, therefore, faced by any spiritual aspirant is to still this constant worldly activity of the mind. Since the mind is in the habit of thinking, the Masters suggest that the habit be utilized in meditation. So that the mind can develop the habit of inward concentration, they give their disciples certain words which are to be repeated mentally, with the attention fixed at the centre between the two eyes.

The practitioner is to sit down in a comfortable position, close the eyes, forget the outside world and repeat these words. It sounds very simple, but to begin with, the mind runs out again almost immediately, the person remaining quite unaware of it. As soon as the individual does realize that their mind has started thinking about the world once again or has become distracted by input from the senses, they are to restart the repetition of the words. Then again, the mind will run out – and again it is to be brought back to repetition of the words. This is the start of the "labour" of meditation, and "labour" it is, for the mind which has been running freely in the creation for millions of years is more difficult to control and imprison than any wild animal.

When somebody first takes to spiritual practice, most of the time is spent with the mind roaming freely while they are sublimely unaware of it. This, however, is not time wasted for, by degrees, the mind is slowly reined in, trained to the new habit and learns to repeat the words. Like a child who is unwilling to go to school but is reluctant as an adult to leave his higher education, the mind rebels at first, but when it has developed a taste for it, is most unwilling to give it up.

No time limit can be given as to how long it will take any individual to accomplish this task of mental concentration. It depends upon the influences and tendencies of past lives which differ from person to person. Some may even have begun the practice in past lives, while others are coming to it afresh. As a result of these tendencies, some individuals are devoted and dedicated to the practice while others are half-hearted and go through the exercise more as a matter of routine.

But as soon as any degree of concentration and stillness, even of the body, is achieved, the consciousness begins to withdraw towards the eye centre. The result is that the extremities of the body – the hands, feet, arms and legs – start to become numb due to the withdrawal of consciousness. As concentration increases, the attention collects still further at the eye centre and the lower part of the trunk becomes numb. This numbness extends first up to the navel, then up to the heart and upper abdomen, then up to the neck and finally the practitioner is so concentrated at the eye centre that their entire sense of being and existence is focused there.

To begin with, the individual experiences nothing but darkness and silence inside. The only 'noise' is the continuous chuntering of their own mind. But as the attention withdraws and the mind begins to quieten down and concentrate, they begin to experience flashes of light which slowly stabilize into a bright and even light. At the same time, the disciple begins to hear echoes of the divine Music of the Word. Then, by degrees, the soul and mind leave the body and enter the astral realms. Together with these experiences, the mind continually repeating the words or listening to the Sound, a great sense of peace and bliss begins to fill the individual, often continuing throughout the whole day.

The process is similar to that of death, the difference being that, firstly, the practice is under the control of the practitioner and, secondly, the connection with the body is not broken. When death comes, the attention is first withdrawn from the extremities and those who are dying will sometimes say that their feet and legs have gone cold or numb. Attention then withdraws further, sometimes with a gurgle or 'death rattle', as the soul leaves the chest and throat, and the soul and mind exit through the eye centre. When the soul departs, the eyes sometimes turn upward involuntarily and death rapidly ensues. As we find in one of the Coptic apocryphal writings, a fictional account of the death of Joseph, ostensibly narrated by Jesus himself:

> And I put my hand in under his heart,
> and I found his soul brought to his throat,
> for it was about to be brought up from his body.
>
> *Death of Joseph XIX, CAG p.139*

The same process of withdrawal takes place when the soul leaves the body in meditation, the difference being that life functions are maintained for as long as the individual has not completed their destiny in this world. After the meditation is over, they return to the body and continue with their daily life, the point of departure and re-entry being at the eye centre.

The first part of the practice of meditation, then, as taught by the Masters, entails withdrawal of the attention from the world and from the body, focusing it at the eye centre. It must be understood that this process has nothing in common with the inducement of a trance-like or hypnotic state. The practitioner gains increasing self-control and self-mastery. His awareness and consciousness expands, coming more and more under his own direction. Self-control and self-possession are not diminished, but enhanced.

Now, there are a number of places in the gospels where Jesus alludes to this practice, but since instructions concerning such techniques would have been a part of his 'mysteries', taught in private to his disciples, he uses metaphors in his public teachings. The import of these metaphors, however, becomes clear when we find that they have been used by other mystics, not only of his period, but of all times and countries. Jesus speaks, for example, of the 'single eye':

> The light of the body is the eye:
>   if therefore thine eye be single,
>   thy whole body shall be full of light.
> But if thine eye be evil,
>   thy whole body shall be full of darkness.
> If therefore the light that is in thee be darkness,
>   how great is that darkness!
>
> *Matthew 6:19-23*

The inner light is to be seen at the level of the eyes, he says, but only when "thine eye be single" – only when the attention is single-mindedly and entirely focused at this point, this 'single optic'. If the mind is full of bad thoughts and worldly tendencies, then all that we see inside is darkness. And if we, as beings of light, are full of darkness – "how great is that darkness!"

The Strait Gate

The eye centre or single eye lies on the threshold of the inner realms. After fully concentrating at this point, the next step is for the soul to enter the astral worlds. For this reason, Jesus and many other mystics have referred to the single eye as a narrow "gate". Jesus said:

> Enter ye in at the strait gate:
>   for wide is the gate, and broad is the way,

> that leadeth to destruction,
> and many there be which go in thereat:
> Because strait is the gate, and narrow is the way,
> which leadeth unto life, and few there be that find it.
>
> *Matthew 7:13-14*

The single eye is a narrow gateway – so narrow that only a deeply humble, loving, devoted and concentrated mind can pass through it. It is a "strait gate", a narrow passage, 'strait' being an archaic word meaning 'narrow'. A mind that is still interested in the world cannot enter this passage, even if that interest is for the apparent welfare of mankind. Nor can a mind that wants to demonstrate its spirituality to others and play the teacher or the wise man. The vehicle of transport at this point is the mind itself and there can be no deception. As Paul commented, "Be not deceived; God is not mocked."[1] Utter sincerity and absence of ego is required. Or as Jesus said, "Where your treasure is, there will your heart be also." We go where our mind takes us, according to its *actual* inclinations and habits rather than those which we would like it to exhibit or that we would like others to think that we possess.

Consequently, the "gate" or "way, that leadeth to destruction" – to rebirth in this world, the realm of death and destruction – is "broad" and easy, and most of us follow this path. Very few are really sincere enough to narrow down the mind sufficiently for it to enter through this "strait gate". Very few can tread the "narrow way", the difficult path along a razor's edge, that leads up behind the waterfall of life and into the secret passage.

Jesus is not talking here to those who would come after his time and call themselves Christians, however well-meaning their intentions may be. He never spoke to the world at large. He is speaking to the very select few that were prepared to make the necessary sacrifices in order to tread the path he taught. As he said: "I pray not for the world, but for them which Thou hast given me."

Through the Eye of a Needle

Jesus' famous saying in St Matthew concerning a camel and the eye of a needle is almost certainly another reference to this narrow passage-way that leads out of the body into the higher realms:

"And again I say unto you, it is easier
> for a camel to go through the eye of a needle,
>> than for a rich man to enter into the kingdom of God."

When his disciples heard it, they were exceedingly amazed,
> saying, "Who then can be saved?"
But Jesus beheld them, and said unto them,
"With men this is impossible;
> but with God all things are possible."

Matthew 19:24-26

To "enter the kingdom of God" entails passing through this narrow gateway. The body is like an upright needle and so fine and subtle is this mental passage that it is like the eye of a needle, like a tiny opening in the head of the body. No one who is attached to the riches of this world can possibly pass through for their thoughts are too wild and scattered, and their ego is too big.

That a "rich man" means one who desires the things and sensations of the world, is brought out by the disciples' response. Very few people are rich, yet they ask, "Who then can be saved?" – Because they know that everybody, rich or poor, is attached to this world. Jesus replies that with his own efforts alone, man can never achieve such a high spiritual estate as to "enter the kingdom of God". "But with God all things are possible." With God's help, through the Son or Master, as Jesus continually reiterates in John's gospel, it is possible for souls to be taken inside.

Incidentally, many people have speculated about the origins of this saying. Some have suggested that there was a narrow gateway in Jerusalem called the eye of a needle, through which a man could barely pass, let alone a camel. Others have wondered whether in the Greek of those days one of the words for a rope was a 'camel' (*kamelos*). Certainly, one of the traditional materials used to make ropes was camel hair and even in modern times, the Greek word for a particular kind of thick hairy rope is *trichia*, derived from *tricha* which means a 'hair'. So there is no reason why in those days the word for a thick camel-hair rope could not have been *kamelos* – a camel. But whatever the origin of the expression, the spiritual meaning remains the same.

Knock and It Shall Be Opened

Like the "strait gate", the single eye was also known as a 'door', a door being a passage from one place to another, in this case, from the body to the inner regions. It is also an entrance which is usually closed and on which it is necessary to knock before admittance can be gained. As an analogy for spiritual practice, the example is precise, for the devotee knocks most determinedly and repeatedly upon this inner door. Each repetition of the words is like a knocking. It is a repetition of the same action, again and again, until the one within the house comes and opens the door. Jesus therefore says:

> Ask, and it shall be given you;
> seek, and ye shall find;
> knock, and it shall be opened unto you.
>
> *Matthew 7:7*

"Ask, and it shall be given you" implies that the individual must want to meet the Lord. His desire and his spiritual longing constitute his asking which, ultimately, will lead him to meditation itself. And if he asks he will definitely be given the object of his desire for he only asks because he is being pulled inwardly by the Lord. And if the Lord is pulling a soul, it means that He intends to give that soul the entire spiritual wealth.

"Seek, and ye shall find" conveys a similar meaning. If someone is sincerely seeking the Lord, he is bound to find Him, because He is actually the one who is seeking us. And again, in the end, all the longing and seeking has to find practical expression in meditation. No one ever found God without it.

"Knock, and it shall be opened unto you." "Knocking" is the culmination of asking and seeking. That is, meditation. The devotee must become like a persistent beggar at the door of a rich man. Sooner or later, if he persists with sincerity and humility, refusing to go away, knowing that there is no other door at which to knock, he will be permitted entrance and allowed to share in the rich man's treasure. In the meantime, the continuous knocking is required to refine the sincerity of desire and spiritual longing in the mind of the disciple. Only when all traces of I-ness have been removed from the mind will the soul be allowed to enter in. Hence, Jesus repeats:

> For every one that asketh receiveth;
>   and he that seeketh findeth;
>   and to him that knocketh it shall be opened.
>
> *Matthew 7:8*

He then expands on the theme:

> Or what man is there of you, whom if his son ask bread,
>   will he give him a stone?
> Or if he ask a fish, will he give him a serpent?
> If ye then, being evil,
>   know how to give good gifts unto your children,
>   how much more shall your Father which is in heaven
>   give good things to them that ask him?
>
> *Matthew 7:9-11*

He says that if, as normal human beings, if "being evil", we always re-spond generously to the children whom we love, how much more will the Father respond to us, who are all His children, if in all humility and sincerity, we knock upon his door, asking and seeking just for Him. And if we feel that He is neglecting us and not giving us what we de-serve, then we are only demonstrating the very reasons why He does not seem to give to us: we are thinking of ourselves and not of Him for His is a house where there is only room for one – Himself. Only when we cease to exist as separate individuals will entry to His house be possible.

A Door Was Opened in Heaven

Sometimes, the metaphor was used the other way around with the Master standing on the inside of the door, knocking to see if there is anyone awake on the other side. If the soul is asleep in the pleasures and activities of the world, he goes away. Or even if the soul is sitting in meditation but is constantly distracted, mentally, and is rarely present before the door, then too he knows that the soul is not yet completely sincere in the desire to come inside. But if the soul is fully awake and quietly awaiting the coming of the owner of the house with full alert-ness and no distraction of the mind – that is, if the soul is fully con-centrated at the single eye, only awaiting the coming of the Master – then, sooner or later, the Master will open the door and welcome the soul.

In *Revelations*, for example, one finds the "Spirit" speaking in a letter addressed to the church in Laodicea, supposedly dictated to the writer by an angel:

> Behold, I stand at the door, and knock:
>> if any man hear my Voice, and open the door,
>> I will come in to him,
>> and will sup with him, and he with me.
>
> *Book of Revelation 3:20*

The Spirit, the Master, waits at the inner door, the single eye. He knocks and calls with his "Voice", and if any soul hears it, he goes within, partaking of the nourishment of the Living Water or Bread of Life. Later, the same writer says:

> After this I looked,
>> and, behold, a door was opened in heaven:
> And the first Voice which I heard
>> was as it were of a trumpet talking with me;
>> which said, "Come up hither,
>> and I will shew thee things which must be hereafter."
> And immediately I was in the Spirit.
>
> *Book of Revelation 4:1-2*

After the door is opened, the soul hears the sound of the Voice of God like that of a "trumpet". But the "trumpet" is no trumpet of this world; it is the divine Music, so beautiful and captivating that it draws the soul into the higher regions. "Come up hither," it 'says' and "I will shew thee things" – all knowledge of creation will in time be revealed to the soul. As the writer says, "immediately I was in the Spirit." This is the effect of hearing the Voice of God and passing through the inner door. Again in *Revelations*, the "Spirit" says:

> Behold, I have set before thee an open door,
>> and no man can shut it:
> For thou hast a little strength,
>> and hast kept my Word, and hast not denied my Name.
>
> *Book of Revelation 3:8*

It is the Master who brings the disciple to the point where he can sit in front of the inner door. He has given the disciple the "little strength" that is required for this, a strength derived from keeping the "Word" and not denying the "Name" of the Master – it implies following his teachings and keeping in contact with the Word of God, inside.

I am the Door of the Sheep

According to St John's gospel, Jesus also describes himself as the "door of the sheep" – a further use of the same metaphor. It is through the Master that a soul is enabled to find the inner door where the Master waits in his astral form. Hence, in Jesus' parable of the good Shepherd, Jesus says:

> Verily, verily, I say unto you,
> I am the door of the sheep....

> I am the door:
> by me if any man enter in, he shall be saved,
> and shall go in and out, and find pasture.
> > *John 10:7,9*

Through the Master, the soul is enabled to "go in and out", to travel at will in the inner realms and to return to the body. And there, the soul "finds pasture", the food of the soul being the sweet, life-giving music of the Word.

Knock on Yourself as Upon a Door

Glancing through the early Christian and other mystic literature of the period, one encounters ample evidence that this door was perceived as an inner mystic door, within oneself, upon which the individual should knock. In one of the Nag Hammadi tractates, for example, James says:

> Once when I was sitting deliberating (meditating),
> he (Jesus) opened the door.
> > *Second Apocalypse of James 50, NHS11 p.121*

As a consequence of which, a revelation or mystic experience follows. In the Mandaean writings, this door is specifically described as the "door" through which the soul leaves the body:

> The soul ... when she desireth to depart from the body, openeth a door
> for herself to escape from the body and goeth forth like a dove.
>
> *Thousand and Twelve Questions 282, TTQ p.189*

And, echoing Jesus' words from the gospels, the Saviour is portrayed
as the one who opens this inner door, revealing the inner pathway
back to God:

> Lo thou camest and didst open a door,
>> thou didst level a road and tread out a path,
>> didst set up a boundary-stone
>> and didst knit together a community.
> Thou wast Helper, Saviour and Guide
>> to the Father of the great Family of Life,
>> and didst knit it together in a communion of Life,
>> didst build it into a great building of sound construction
>> and didst bring it forth to the great Place of Light
>> and the everlasting abode....
>
> And those who seek from him shall find,
>> and to those who ask of him, it will be given.
> Day by day, hour by hour, behold us
>> who exist in thy Name
>> and are sustained by calling on thy Name.
>
> *CPM 76 pp.79,82*

The "family of Life" are the chosen initiates of a Master who are
taken back to the "great Place of Life and the everlasting abode". By
seeking, they find. By asking, they are given. And "day by day, hour
by hour" – at all times – the Saviour watches over all those who
"exist in thy Name", who are inwardly sustained by contact with the
divine Name.

Similarly, in the Manichaean-Christian psalms, again echoing the
canonical gospels, the psalmist writes explicitly that the means of
seeking and knocking is that of prayer. "They prayed" and "it was
given them":

> We are thy peoples, the sheep of thy fold:
>> let us come in to thy gates and appear unto thee.
> They that sought found;
>> they prayed, it was given them;

> They knocked at the door,
> 　the door was opened to them.
> 　　　　　　　*Psalms, MPB p.156*

But the prayer that opens the inner door is no verbal or set prayer, but the mystic prayer of spiritual practice which only the "sheep of thy fold", the disciples of a Master, can practise. Hence, the psalmist continues:

> Come inside, my brethren, by the narrow door,
> 　and let us comfort one another with the Word of Truth.
> For the world has gone astray,
> 　men looking for the door.
> The door was shut against them,
> 　the door was not opened to them.
> Looking for God they found not what God is;
> 　their god is their belly, their glory is their shame.
> 　　　　　　　*Psalms, MPB p.156*

Those that enter by the "narrow door" are comforted with the "Word of Truth". The entire world is seeking peace and ease, they are looking for the doorway to happiness. But the "door was shut against them" for they are more interested in their "belly", in the pleasures of the world than in the spiritual treasure.

Some of the most revealing passages concerning this inner door are found in the Nag Hammadi *Teachings of Silvanus*, where Jesus' sayings are evidently being taken in a mystical way that relates to spiritual practice:

> Knock on (within) yourself as upon a door, and walk upon (within) your-self as on a straight road. For if you walk on the road, it is impossible for you to go astray. And if you knock with Wisdom, you knock on hidden treasuries....
>
> 　Do not tire of knocking on the door of Reason (the *Logos*), and do not cease walking in the way of Christ. Walk on it so that you may receive rest from your labours. If you walk on another way, there will be no profit in it. For also those who walk on the broad way will go down at their end to the perdition of the mire. For the underworld is open wide for the soul, and the place of perdition is broad. Accept for yourself Christ, the nar-row way. For he ... bears affliction for your sin....
>
> 　Open the door for yourself that you may know the One who is. Knock on (within) yourself that the Word may open for you. For he is the king of faith and the sharp sword, having become all for everyone, because he wishes to have mercy on everyone.

> My son, prepare yourself to escape from the world-rulers of darkness (the *archons*) and of this kind of air (region) which is full of powers. But if you have Christ, you will conquer this entire world. That which you will open for yourself, you will open. That which you will knock upon for yourself, you will knock upon, benefiting yourself.
>
> *Teachings of Silvanus 106-107,103,117, TS pp.57-59,51,117*

The writer's meaning is unmistakable. The door is within oneself. This is where the spiritual seeker must knock. It is the door through which Wisdom, the *Logos* or the Word may be contacted. "Knock on yourself that the Word may open for you," he says, unequivocally.

The "straight road" which leads to "hidden treasuries" and "rest from your labours" is the "narrow way" of "Christ", the anointed one, the Master, as opposed to the "broad way" that leads back into this "underworld", the "place of perdition". Walking in this way and knocking on this door lead to escape from all the *archons* of the Negative Power.

Entry through a closed door is commonly effected by means of a key. Jesus uses this metaphor in St. Matthew, where he seems to be appointing Peter as his successor. He says that he will give him the "keys of the kingdom of heaven" which implied that Peter was to be the one after him who would open the inner door for future disciples. Evidence that Jesus' meaning was indeed taken as mystical is to be found in the *Clementine Homilies* where, echoing Jesus' words in the gospel, Peter is said to have spoken of the

> key of the kingdom, which is knowledge (*gnosis*), which alone can open the gate of life, through which alone is the entrance to eternal life.
>
> *Clementine Homilies III:XVIII, CH p.64*

Similarly in the *Books of the Saviour*, where Jesus says:

> I have brought the key of the mysteries of the kingdom of heaven, otherwise no flesh in the world would be saved. For without the mysteries no one enter into the kingdom of the Light, be he righteous or a sinner. For this cause, therefore, have I brought the keys of the mysteries into the world, so that I may release the sinners who will believe in me and hearken unto me.
>
> *Pistis Sophia 133, PS p.346, PSGG p.289*

A gate or a door convey the same idea, of course, and both terms were used by the mystics of antiquity. Again in the *Books of the Saviour*, Jesus says to Mary:

And now, therefore, as I have come, I have opened the gates of the Light.
And I have opened the ways which lead into the Light. And now, therefore, he who will do what is worthy of the mysteries, let him receive the
mysteries and enter into the Light.

Pistis Sophia 135, PS p.350, PSGG p.293

To do what is 'worthy' of a key is to open a door or a gate. To "do
what is worthy of the mysteries" is meditation. One who uses this
key will open the "gates of the Light" and "enter into the Light". This is
the desire of every spiritual aspirant and the same refrain is repeated
continually in the ancient literature. It is present in the Manichaean-
Christian psalms:

> Open to us the passage of the vaults of the heavens
>   and walk before us to the joy of thy kingdom,
>   O Glorious One.
>
> *Psalm CCXL, MPB p.41*

It is found in the liturgical writings of the Nestorian church:

> Open unto me the gates of righteousness –
>   the gates of heaven have been opened.
> The gates of the spiritual Bride-chamber
>   are opened for the forgiveness of the sins of men,
>   and through the gift of the Spirit on high,
>   mercy and peace are now vouchsafed to all mankind.
> Enter in, therefore, O ye who are called,
>   enter into the joy which is prepared for you! ...
> O thou true Door, open to the lost,
>   and call us to enter thy Treasury on high.
>
> *NRII XLI p.196*

And in the Coptic *Life of the Virgin*, as she is dying, Mary says:

> Open to me the gates of righteousness,
>   and I will enter into them,
>   and be manifested to the face of my God.
>
> *Life of the Virgin, CAG p.39*

In fact, this is the fundamental prayer of the soul to God. All these
passages convey the same meaning: it is the Master who opens the way

for the soul to leave the body through the inner door, meet the light form of the Master within and traverse the inner regions back to God.

Seek When You Are Sought

As with almost every other saying of Jesus, there is ample proof from other mystic literature that what Jesus meant by "seek and ye shall find" was the quest for God. The saying is echoed so frequently in gnostic and similar writings that it became an idiom of the times, where it invariably refers to spiritual seeking. That it is God who must be sought is made very clear in the *Untitled Tractate* of the Bruce Codex:

> Thou alone are the Infinite One,
>   Thou alone art the Deep,
>   and Thou alone art the Unknowable One.
> And thou art He for whom everyone seeks,
>   and they do not find Thee;
> For none can know Thee without Thy will,
>   and none can bless Thee without Thy will.
>   *Untitled Text 17, BC p.258*

In the Mandaean sacred poetry, the term is very commonly found, clearly echoing Jesus' saying, though how the door, seeking and asking should have found their way into the Mandaean literature is a mystery, unless the saying was one previously used by John the Baptist or was commonly used in mystical literature prior to Jesus' time. The one to whom the following poem is addressed is the Mandaean mythical Saviour, *Manda-d-Hiia*:

> Those who seek of Him find,
>   and to those who ask of Him it will be given.
> For to him that standeth at a closed door
>   thou wilt open the closed door.
> In the Realm of Light thou wilt wipe away
>   and remove from us our sins, trespasses, follies,
>   stumblings and mistakes....
> Thou wilt raise us up as sinless and not as guilty,
>   as virtuous and not as vicious before thee, *Manda-d-Hiia*.
>   *CPM 35 p.35*

In the *Books of the Saviour*, Jesus speaks of "seeking ... the mysteries of the kingdom of the Light". The meaning, again, could not be clearer:

> You have not left off seeking until you found all the mysteries of the kingdom of the Light which have purified you and made you into refined light, exceedingly purified, and you have become purified light.... Cease not to seek day and night until you find the purifying mysteries.
>
> *Pistis Sophia 100, PS pp.249-251, PSGG pp.207-208*

And in the *Gospel of Thomas*, Jesus says:

> Let not him that seeketh cease seeking till he find,
> and when he findeth, he shall marvel,
> and having marvelled he shall reign,
> and having reigned he shall rest.
>
> *Gospel of Thomas 2, ANT p.26, NHS20 p.53*

Jesus means that when the seeker really begins to travel the inner path, he "marvels" and is lost in awe and wonder at the things that are revealed to him within. Then, progressing further, he regains his birthright as the son of the divine King and "reigns", becoming one with God. And becoming one with Him, he attains "rest" – a term commonly used by the mystics of that time to mean the eternal beatitude, bliss and peace of being one with God.

Looked at from another angle, the quest for God is the search for the real nature of one's own self, the soul. Hence, in the *Acts of Thomas*, Judas Thomas praises God, saying, He "showed me how to seek my own soul":

> Glory to Thee, O God –
> who did not withhold His mercy from me who was lost,
> but showed me how to seek my own soul.
>
> *Acts of Thomas, AAA p.175*

It is the Master who directs the attention of the soul so that it may rediscover its real nature. In fact, such seeking only comes about because the Master seeks the soul. As Judas Thomas says of Jesus:

> (Thou) hast shown me how to seek myself
> and know who I was,
> and who and in what manner I now am:

That I may again become that which I was:)
   whom I knew not, but thyself didst seek me out.

Acts of Thomas 15, ANT pp.370-371

This is what is meant in the Mandaean texts, where the poet, writing in the name of the Master, reiterates that the "chosen ones" are sought out and "raised up" by the Word itself:

Ye are set up and raised up, my chosen ones,
   by the Word and Certitude that came to you.
The Word and the Certitude that came to the good,
   the True Word which came to believers.
My chosen, ye sought and ye found,
   moreover ye shall seek and ye shall find.

CPM 99 pp.100-101

Since it is the Master who initiates the seeking, the writer of the gnostic *Zostrianos* remonstrates with the soul to release itself unhesitatingly from this world when the Saviour has come for it, counselling, "seek when you are sought":

Release yourselves,
   and that which has bound you will be dissolved.
Save yourselves so that your soul may be saved.
The kind Father has sent you the Saviour
   and given you strength.
Why are you hesitating?
Seek when you are sought; when you are invited,
   listen, for time is short.

Zostrianos 131, NHL p.430

This is the essence of the entire affair. When the soul is pulled, its correct response or duty is to ask, to seek and to knock upon the inner door until it opens.

A City Called Nine Gates

Many Eastern mystics have described the body as a house or a city of nine gates, for there are nine portals through which the attention can spread out into the world. These are the two eyes, two ears, two nostrils, the mouth and the two lower apertures. The inner door has consequently been called the tenth door. Nine doors lead out while one leads within.

It is intriguing, therefore, to find this metaphor in a couple of places in the early Christian texts. The most definite mention comes in a charming allegory concerning a certain Lithargoel, symbolic of the Master, who invites Peter, the apostles and all the poor people of a certain place called "Habitation" to his own city. His purpose is to give them a priceless pearl, the "pearl of great price", the treasure of spirituality. Everything in this story is symbolic, much as it is in other spiritual romances, like the *Acts of Thomas*, and when Peter asks Lithargoel for the name of his city, the reply is metaphorical. Peter asks:

> "What is the name of the place to which you go, your city?" He said to me, "This is the name of my city, 'Nine gates'. And let us praise God that we are mindful that the tenth is (in) the head."
>
> *Acts of Peter and the Twelve Apostles 6, NHS11 p.217*

The matter could hardly be stated more succinctly. "Habitation" means this world, which souls inhabit but where they do not permanently dwell. However, it is the realm where the Master, Lithargoel, finds his souls. The place where he is taking them is within the city of nine gates, within the body, and the gateway to this city lies in the head, at the single eye. The story continues and the meaning is further clarified when the companions find themselves seated outside this gateway to Lithargoel's city:

> A great joy came upon us and a peaceful carefreeness like that of our Lord. We rested ourselves in front of the gate, and we talked with each other about that which is not a distraction of this world. Rather we continued in contemplation of the faith.
>
> *Acts of Peter and the Twelve Apostles 8, NHS11 p.221*

The writer is alluding to concentration of the attention at this inner gateway. "Great joy" and "peaceful carefreeness like that of our Lord" comes over them and they keep their minds focused upon the inner reality, avoiding all distractions of this world.

The other reference to this metaphor is to be found in the *Acts of Thomas* in an episode where the soul in human form is likened to a beautiful dancing girl at a marriage party. Each part of her body is given a symbolic interpretation, amongst them being the observation that her ten "fingers point out the gates of the city" of the human form:

The damsel is the daughter of light, in whom consisteth and dwelleth the proud brightness of kings, and the sight of her is delightful, she shineth with beauty and cheer... her fingers point out the gates of the city.

Acts of Thomas 6, ANT p.367

Whether references to the ten portals of the body was a common but secret part of Jesus' esoteric teachings or where the metaphor came from is difficult to say. Nevertheless, its presence amongst the early Christian literature is intriguing. Perhaps it came from the Buddhist missionaries sent by Ashoka to Alexandria and the Middle East who had been active in Alexandria for generations. Or maybe it came with those who travelled the trade routes to India, China and the Far East. Or it could have spontaneously arisen as a self-evident observation of our human constitution.

The Five Names

We have spoken generally about the repetition of words during spiritual practice but have omitted mention of their precise nature. It is with considerable wisdom, however, that mystics have chosen the words which their disciples should repeat. Every word in this world has a meaning and with that meaning comes an association and a tendency to lead the mind into thinking of that thing. This is the nature of language. If we hear the word 'house', we start thinking about houses – probably our own house or some other house we know. If the name of a friend or relative is mentioned, our thoughts gravitate towards them and our relationship with them. All words have associations and were a Master to give his disciples words that are related to the activities, things and people of the world, the mind would automatically be led into thinking about the world. As a result, it would not focus at the single eye, as intended.

The Masters, therefore, need to give their disciples words or names that have no association with the things of this world. This narrows down the field considerably, and the words that they have chosen are names given to the rulers of the five main spiritual realms. The idea is not for an individual to start thinking about those rulers at the time of meditation, but so that any association which their mind does have with these names should be of an inward nature. As we have previously observed, the mind goes towards whatever it dwells upon.

Different Masters have given different names to these five rulers in their various languages and at various times, but the power possessed by these names lies not so much in the names themselves as in the Master who has given them. For example, if one boy calls another boy by his name, the one may choose to ignore the other. But if his school headmaster calls out his name, the boy automatically responds. The name spoken is the same in both instances: the difference lies in the power or authority of the one who utters it.

Similarly, with the five names. They are given by a Master. A disciple keeps them secret to avoid confusing others and to keep his personal association with them pure and associated entirely with the Master and with the inner regions through which he will have to pass on his return to God. Were a disciple to tell the names to others, then the names would develop an association in his mind with those people, drawing his mind towards them whenever he repeated them. In any case, if someone were to discover what these names were, and were to begin the spiritual practice, he would be most unlikely to get very far unless the names came with the permission, blessing and initiation of a living Master.

Practically all occult or esoteric paths, especially of the past, have spoken of 'names of power', which are guarded by their holders as great secrets. Whether such names really possess any power or not is a moot point, but the underlying idea is correct. Details of the five names given by a Master and the precise method of their practice have also been kept secret from non-initiates in all ages and even their existence is rarely mentioned in the mystic literature of the past. All the same, there are a few places in the early Christian literature where there is no doubt that this is what is being discussed.

The Nag Hammadi *Teachings of Silvanus*, for instance, a tractate which is worth careful study, has a number of specific references to meditation, as we have already noted. Comparing the soul to a city, the author likens the "words" to the "gates", shedding light and preventing the entry of "robbers" and "savage wild beasts":

> My son, throw every robber out of your gates. Guard all your gates with torches which are the words, and you will acquire by all these means a quiet life (inner peace). But he who will not guard (against) these things will become like a city which is desolate through being captured. All kinds of wild beasts have trampled on it, for thoughts which are not good are evil wild beasts. And your city will be filled with robbers, and you will not be able to acquire peace for yourself, but only all kinds of savage wild beasts. The Wicked One, who is a tyrant, is lord over these. While direct-

ing this, he (the Wicked One) is (hidden) beneath the great mire. The whole city which is your soul will perish.

Teachings of Silvanus 85, TS p.15

This neatly summarizes the battle or labour of repetition of the words. They are used to cast out of the mind all the thoughts that come from the Wicked One, the Negative Power, who remains unseen behind the turmoil of the mind. He is hidden "beneath the great mire".

In the *Pistis Sophia*, the author actually gives the five names of the five rulers purported to have been the five names used in those days and in that country, though how authentic they are is open to question. But the passage does demonstrate that even the details of this teaching are ancient and universal, just as the Masters have always said. In this excerpt, it is Jesus who is speaking:

> "I have told you, for the first time, the names of these five great rulers with which the men of the world are wont to call them. Hearken now then that I may tell you also their incorruptible names, which are:
>
>
> *Orimouth* correspondeth to *Kronos*
> *Mounichounaphor* correspondeth to *Ares*
> *Tarpetanouph* correspondeth to *Hermes*
> *Chosi* correspondeth to *Aphrodite*
> *Chonbal* correspondeth to *Zeus.*
>
> These are their incorruptible names."

> And when the disciples had heard this, they fell down, adored Jesus and said: "Blessed are we beyond all men, because thou hast revealed unto us these great wonders."

Pistis Sophia, PSGG p.299

One should note that despite the writer's assertion that these five names are "incorruptible", this is actually not the case. All names that are written or uttered – as these are – are the creation of man and have a history in time. They are therefore 'corruptible'. It is the five Seals or Sounds which are "incorruptible" in the sense that they are unwritten and unspoken, having the same permanency as the Word itself.

The passage is nevertheless of great interest for the names "with which the men of the world are wont to call them" are, of course, the names of Greek gods. One wonders, therefore, whether these gods were once described by mystics as the rulers of the various inner realms, like the majority of the Hindu pantheon, becoming externalized and woven into mythology over the course of time. From this passage and others like it in this ancient literature, we can certainly be sure that some of the mystically-minded in Jesus' time interpreted the Greek gods in this way, with *Zeus*, the Father of the gods, being seen as the Supreme Being and Source. And it also indicates that the path of the "five Seals" and the "five names" was taught as much then as it is now, though whether the writer of the *Pistis Sophia* was one who fully understood the mystic path is another matter.

We have already discussed the significance of the "five Seals". That these "Seals" also had important names given to them that were used by the initiates is made very clear from a passage in the gnostic *Trimorphic Protennoia*:

> He who possesses the five Seals with their particular names,
>   has stripped off the garments of ignorance (body and mind)
>   and put on a shining light.
> And nothing will come before him (inside)
>   that belongs to the powers of the *archons*.
> Within people of this sort darkness will dissolve
>   and ignorance will die.
>
> *Trimorphic Protennoia 49, GS p.100, NHS28 p.431*

He who has been given the initiation of the "five Seals", together with their five "particular names" is enabled to leave the body and mind behind. For them, all darkness and ignorance will be dissolved and no inner power can stand in the way of such a soul.

This extract highlights another purpose of the five names. "Nothing will come before him (inside) that belongs to the powers of the *archons*." A disciple uses the five names in the inner realms to test any spirits or beings that come before him, for no negative power can stand in their presence. Remember, we are dealing here with realms of the mind, and the repetition of these names in the mind, backed by the power of the Master, creates a powerful energy or vibration which has an immediate effect on higher planes. Even in this world, repetition alone has the power to calm the mind not only of the initiate but also of those around him, to a greater or lesser extent. The names are a powerful protective force and a significant help under all circumstances. They calm and control the surging waves of thought and emotion, thus empowering the one who repeats them.

Indications of this purpose are also to be found in other gnostic writings. In the *Second Book of Jeu*, for instance, in an extract where the rulers, administrators and 'guardians' of the inner regions are called the "watchers", Jesus says:

> Then the watchers of the gates of the Treasury of the Light see the mystery
> of the forgiveness of sins which you have performed.... And they see the
> seal on your foreheads, and they see the cipher in your hands. Then the
> nine watchers open to you the gates of the Treasury of the Light, and you
> go into the Treasury of the Light. The watchers will not speak with you,
> but they will give you their seals and their mystery.
>
> *Second Book of Jeu 49, BC pp.118-119*

The "seal on your foreheads" is initiation into the mystic Word and the "cipher in your hands" refers to the names. Equipped with these, a soul is enabled to pass through all the regions. The soul may have no communication with these rulers, but they give their permission, so to speak, for the soul to pass through their realms because the soul has the sign of the highest authority – that of the Master, the Son of God.

Take Up His Cross Daily

As we commented earlier, Jesus describes the withdrawal of the attention to the single eye as 'taking up the cross', an expression which is perhaps a little more difficult to understand than his other analogies. It must be remembered that when he said this, Jesus had not yet been crucified. Consequently, any relationship of this expression to Jesus' future death on the cross would have been lost on his disciples and is unlikely to have anything to do with his meaning. Luke's variant of this saying is the most interesting. According to him, Jesus said:

> If any man will come after me, let him deny himself,
> and take up his cross daily, and follow me.
>
> *Luke 9:23*

Taking up the "cross *daily*" refers to the *daily* practice of meditation, without which no one can claim to be a real disciple or follower of their Master. Hence, in Matthew, Jesus also says:

He that taketh not his cross, and followeth after me,
is not worthy of me.

Matthew 10:38

If a disciple does not meditate, he is not worthy of his Master, for spiritual practice is the essence of a Master's teachings. But how does 'taking up the cross' refer to meditation?

In those days, crucifixion was a common form of execution used by the Romans. Even mass executions were performed by this means. Crucifixion therefore referred to dying a slow and lingering death, something which must have preyed on the minds of many in those violent times. Now, the practice of meditation is that of going through the process of death while still alive. The cross thus represented the slow and difficult death of withdrawal from the body during meditation.

But the cross had an even more detailed metaphorical significance, a further clue to which comes from a long passage in the *Acts of Peter* where it is depicted as a symbol of the spiritual life. According to the story, Peter is talking from the cross and the part of his discourse which interests us, here, is this:

> For what else is Christ, but the Word, the Sound of God?
> So that the Word is the upright beam whereon I am crucified.
> And the Sound is that which crosseth it, the nature of man.
> And the nail which holdeth the cross-tree unto the upright
> in the midst thereof is the conversion and repentance of man.
>
> *Acts of Peter XXXVIII, ANT p.335*

He says, first of all that the real Christ is the "Word, the Sound of God." One cannot be more explicit than that. Being crucified was also known colloquially as being 'hung on the tree', an idiom that lent itself to those conversant with the mystic path, for the Word was also known as the Tree of Life. Peter – or the writer – therefore says that the Word is the main trunk of the cross. It is the Tree of Life. The devoted disciple is "crucified" or loses his sense of individuality by dying while living and merging with the divine Music. His ego is crucified on the Tree of Life.

The branch "which crosseth it" represents the true "nature of man" – his soul. He is a branch of the Tree of Life: his reality is that of the divine Sound. And the "nail which holdeth the cross-tree unto the upright in the midst thereof is the conversion and repentance of man."

The nail represents the single eye, the point from which man can either descend into the world or can "repent", can be "converted" and can turn again towards God.

The cross and its different parts, therefore, had a number of inter-related and symbolic meanings. It was the Tree of Life, the soul of man, the point of 'intersection' where man is able to repent or turn to God – and it also represented the process of dying while living. In Jesus' use of the metaphor, the vertical axis of the human body is the main up-right of the cross; it is man's essential life force, the Living Word. The horizontal branch crosses this main axis at the eye centre, the focus of the soul and mind in the human form. And to "take up his cross" means to repent, to withdraw all consciousness to this point and to die while living. Generally, "taking up the cross" is taken to mean self-denial, enduring persecution or labouring to be a good Christian, but the true 'self'-denial *is* spiritual practice. Nothing crucifies the sense of self or ego as effectively.

There are other references in the early literature to the cross and to crucifixion as a mystic metaphor. In his hymns, the fourth-century Christian, Ephraim Syrus makes frequent use of the Tree of Life as a symbol for both the Word and for Jesus. In a few instances, he also equates it with the Cross:

> The Tree of Life is the Cross
>   which gave a radiant life to our race.
> *Ephraim Syrus, SESHS IV:769.2, MEM p.126*

From the context, it is clear that Ephraim's meaning is specifically Christian. All the same, he is using the traditional mystic imagery of his place and time which he must have encountered in his reading. Ignatius does the same when he speaks of the "branches of the Cross" and its "fruit ... incorruptible".[2] And the metaphor is again used in the Manichaean-Christian psalms, where the psalmist speaks of the Word as the "Cross":

> The Cross of Light that gives life to the universe,
>   I have known it and believed in it;
> For it is my dear soul, which nourishes every man,
>   at which the blind are offended because they know it not.
> *Psalm CCLXVIII, MPB p.86*

The psalmist says that he or she has "known it" – experienced it. It is within the soul itself, and "nourishes every man" – it is the Power which gives life to all. But the "blind" people of the world are "offended" or disturbed whenever they hear about it, because it is beyond their comprehension and challenges their material tendencies and dogmatic religious beliefs.

With this understanding, then, of the symbolism of the cross as used in the mystical literature of the period, it is not being over-imaginative to interpret Jesus' comments about taking up the cross daily as being references to spiritual practice. He could not, remember, talk openly of meditation techniques.

Eyes and Ears of the Mind and Soul

It has been noted on a number of occasions that the mind and soul have the ability to see light and have other visions of the higher worlds. The divine Music of the Word can also be heard, as we have described in a previous chapter. These two primary mystic faculties are awakened when the consciousness withdraws from the body, focuses at the eye centre and goes within. Jesus spoke of both faculties:

> The dead shall hear the Voice of the Son of God:
>   and they that hear shall live.
>
> *John 5:25*

And:

> He that followeth me shall not walk in darkness,
>   but shall have the light of life.
>
> *John 8:12*

Jesus means that the followers of a Son of God come to hear the inner Voice of the mystic Son – the Word – and to see the inner light that comes from the Source of all life. Once again, there are ample references to these spiritual faculties in the ancient mystic writings associated with Jesus' teachings, and later Christian mystics used the same expressions, too. The inner eye, in particular, was called the "eye of the mind", the "eye of the soul", the "eye of the heart", the "eye of understanding" and various other names. St Augustine speaks of his glimpses of the inner worlds, for instance, seen with the "eye of the mind":

Lo, we have just now been gladdened by certain inward delights; with the eye of the mind, we have been able to behold, though but with a momentary glance, something not susceptible of change.

St Augustine, on Psalm 41:4, APII p.190

Writing poetically, the medieval German mystic, Mechthild of Magdeburg, calls it the "eyes of my soul":

> A light of utmost splendour
>   glows on the eyes of my soul.
> Therein have I seen the inexpressible ordering of all things,
>   and recognized God's unspeakable glory –
>   that incomprehensible wonder –
>   the tender caress between God and the soul, ...
>   the unmingled joy of union,
>   the living love of Eternity
>   as it now is and evermore shall be.

Mechthild of Magdeburg, Flowing Light of the Godhead II:3, RMM p.30

Similarly, the medieval English mystic, Richard Rolle, speaks of both the "eyes of the heart" as well as the "heavenly door" in a specifically mystical context:

> In process of time, great profit in ghostly (spiritual) joy was given me. Forsooth three years, except three or four months, were run from the beginning of the change of my life and of my mind, to the opening of the heavenly door; so that, the Face being shown, the eyes of the heart might behold and see in what way they might seek my Love and unto Him continually desire. The door forsooth yet biding open, nearly a year passed until the time in which the heat of everlasting love was verily felt in my heart.

Richard Rolle, Fire of Love I:15, LRR p.91

In the earlier literature, there are also a great many such references. In the *Acts of John*, for example, John thanks Jesus who

> didst open the eyes of my mind.

Acts of John 113, ANT p.269

To open the inner eye and to hear with the inner ear, all attention must be withdrawn from the bodily senses. Hence, in the *Acts of Peter*, Peter says:

Separate your souls from every thing that is of the senses, from every thing that appeareth, and does not exist in truth. Blind these (outer) eyes of yours, close these (outer) ears of yours, put away your doings that are seen; and ye shall perceive that which concerneth Christ, and the whole mystery of your salvation.

Acts of Peter III:XXXVII, ANT p.334

Peter also says that when a person has firm faith in Christ, the faculties of inner seeing and hearing will both be opened:

If there be in you the faith that is in Christ, if it be firm in you, then perceive in your mind that which ye see not with your eyes, and though your ears are closed, yet let them be open in your mind within you.

Acts of Peter III:XXI, ANT p.322

Likewise, in the *Doctrine of Addai*, Addai says that:

By his true faith (in the Son) a man is able to acquire
the eye of the true mind.

Doctrine of Addai the Apostle, DAA p.28

Such firm faith, however, that can enable a man "to acquire the eye of the true mind" is not a matter of emotion or intellect but of understanding and can only be obtained by controlling the mind by spiritual practice. Otherwise, an uncontrolled mind that is attracted to the world and tries to understand things through reasoning alone will always remain sceptical and in doubt. Expanding upon this theme, Addai continues:

Let not the secret eye of your mind from the Height above be closed....

Be ye not judges concerning the words of the Prophets. Remember and consider that by the Spirit of God they are said; and he who accuses the Prophets, accuses and judges the Spirit of God. May this be far from you! Because the ways of the Lord are straight, and the righteous walk in them without stumbling; but the infidels stumble in them, because that they have not the secret eye of the secret mind, which has no need of questions in which there is no profit, but loss.

Doctrine of Addai the Apostle, DAA pp.40,42

Those whose "secret eye of the mind" is open will never question what the Masters, the "Prophets" say, for they have come to realize just who a Master is. But "infidels", those who follow the ways of the mind, have no real understanding; they pass judgment and ask questions which are meaningless and even injurious to themselves. To this, the writer of the *Clementine Homilies* adds that the perfect Master, the "faultless Prophet", in this case Jesus, sees and knows all things through this "boundless eye of his soul":

> For, being a faultless Prophet, and looking upon all things with the boundless eye of his soul, he knows hidden things.
>
> *Clementine Homilies III:XIII, CH p.62*

The expression is also found in the *Ascension of Isaiah*. Speaking of his inner ascent, Isaiah says:

> The eyes of my spirit were open
> and I saw the Great Glory.
> *Ascension of Isaiah IX:37, AOT p.805*

Similarly, the writer of the *Apocryphon of James* speaks of the inner ascent as "sending our mind(s) farther upwards" where angelic sights are seen and heard:

> And when we had passed beyond that place, we sent our mind(s) farther upwards and saw with our eyes and heard with our ears hymns and angelic benedictions and angelic rejoicing. And heavenly majesties were singing praise, and we too rejoiced.
>
> *Apocryphon of James 15, NHS22 p.51*

And the same reality is described in the Mandaean writings:

> The eyes of the heart shine secretly.
> *Alma Rishaia Zuta 335, PNC p.79*

"Secretly" means that such inner vision is hidden from outer eyes. No one else need ever know what a disciple sees within himself. It is a secret gift of the Master, bestowed when the disciple is sufficiently prepared for it by spiritual practice. This is why it is said of Jesus in the mythological *Story of St James*:

> And he enlightened the eyes of their hearts;
> and shewed them all the just men

who have gone to their rest from Adam to John,
and they were shining in glittering raiment.

Story of St James, MAA p.30

It is the Master who "enlightens the eyes of the heart", while the "glittering raiment" they acquire refers to the astral and higher garments of the soul, including the pure light of the soul itself when freed from the mind. Naturally, after the opening of such vision, the disciples thank their Master:

> And when the disciples had seen this spiritual vision their hearts were strengthened, and they were glad, and fell to the earth and worshipped, saying: "We thank Thee, O our Lord and our Master, Jesus the Christ, for the beauty of thy work to us poor men."

Story of St James, MAA p.30

The Master's part in the opening of the inner eye is affirmed in all mystic writings. In the Manichaean-Christian psalms, the devotee says:

> O Jesus, the true hope,
>   whom I got for myself in knowledge,
>   aid me, my Lord, and save me....
> Thou hast opened the eyes of my heart,
>   thou hast shut the eyes (of the body).

Psalm CCLXX, MPB pp.88-89

Similarly, in an allegorical Mandaean poem in which the Master is a merchant selling his goods in this world, those who buy them have their eyes "filled with light":

> Many a one who bought my goods,
>   his eyes were filled with light.
> His eyes were filled with light,
>   and he seeth the Great One
> in the House of Perfection.

MaL pp.154-155, MEM p.91; cf. CPM 90 p.94

His inner eye is opened and he sees God, the "Great One", in the eternal realm, the "House of Perfection". The only precondition for the receipt of such a gift is that of love, devotion and surrender of the individual self into the Master's powerful and loving hands. In return for this, the Masters give everything that they have: God Him-self. In another Mandaean poem, the Master describes himself as the "Vine of Life", a "Tree of Glory from whose Fragrance" or emanation everyone draws life. Those who come into contact with this Tree of the Word, says the poet, hear its "Discourse" and are filled with the inner light:

> A Vine am I, the Vine of Life,
>> a Tree whereupon there is no lie
>> (no untruth or illusion).
> A Tree of Glory,
>> from whose Fragrance everyone is living.
> Everyone who listeneth to its Discourse (Sound)
>> his eyes fill with light.
>>> *GSBM p.59, MEM p.149*

The inner vision of one who hears the mystic Sound is automatically awakened, for the Light comes from the Sound. Demonstrating the close integration of these two faculties, after hearing a description of the inner realms, Matthew says, in the *Acts of Matthew*:

> And when I had heard this from them, I longed to dwell in their country;
> and my eyes were dazzled from hearing the sweetness of their speech.
>> *Acts of Matthew, MAA p.101*

And even more pointedly, in a passage from the *History of John* to which the translator has deemed it necessary to add an apologetic footnote saying that although the wording may appear odd, the lines appears as such in both his versions of the manuscript, the disciples say:

> Let us bestow our labour,
>> and let light shine in the ear
>> which the Evil One has blinded,
>> and let the father of lying (the Evil One)
>> be crushed beneath the feet of us all.
>>> *History of John, AAA p.4*

And again, in the Nag Hammadi, *Dialogue of the Saviour*, Jesus says to his disciples:

Have I not told you that by a visible Voice
  and flash of lightning
  will the good be taken up to the Light?

Dialogue of the Saviour 136, NHS26 p.73

While the devotee who wrote the *Odes of Solomon* says:

As the sun is a joy to those who seek its day,
  so my joy is the Lord;
Because he is my sun, and his rays roused me,
  and his light dispelled all the darkness from my face.
I obtained eyes by him, and saw his holy day:
  ears became mine, and I heard his Truth.

Odes of Solomon XV:1-4, AOT p.705

All of these writers and a great many more from all times and all peoples have borne witness to the reality of the inner creation and the soul's ability to experience it through mystic sight and hearing while still living in the body. Yet, as Jesus said:

If I have told you earthly things,
  and ye believe not, how shall ye believe,
  if I tell you of heavenly things?

John 3:12

Man hardly believes in the spiritual wealth that lies within him.

Heavenly Reasoning

In addition to the reluctance of ancient writers to speak openly about meditation, the difficulty in finding references to this ancient practice is compounded by the disinclination of scholars to acknowledge its existence and make appropriate translations. This problem is made particularly acute by the fact that there are very few terms which are used exclusively for spiritual practice. Some idea of the difficulty can be gained by consideration of our own words 'meditation', 'contemplation' and 'spiritual practice'. Meditation and contemplation also mean the quiet consideration of something by means of thought, the exact opposite of the control, concentration and stilling of the mind for which we have used the term. And while spiritual practice could also be taken to mean various ascetic practices, attempts to translate equivalent terms from other languages can readily end up as 'pious deeds' or 'good deeds' – again, something quite different from true meditation.

A perusal of the literature of this period, however, gives us many examples where the writer would seem to be speaking of meditation, some of these being more evident than others. Beginning with the gnostic *Teachings of Silvanus*, we encounter a word derived from the Greek term *Logos* and translated as "reasoning". A study of the context and the rest of this tractate, however, reveal that the word almost certainly refers to meditation. Speaking of the human passions as "savage beasts" and "barbarians", the writer says:

> Do not pierce yourself with the sword of sin. Do not burn yourself, O wretched one, with the fire of lust. Do not surrender yourself to barbarians like a prisoner, nor to savage beasts which want to trample on you. For they are lions which roar very loudly. Be not dead lest they trample on you. You shall be a man! It is possible for you through 'reasoning' (meditation, contact with the *Logos*) to conquer them.
>
> *Teachings of Silvanus 108, TS p.61*

Normal human reasoning, of course, is incapable of controlling human weaknesses to any great extent, as the writer must have been well aware. He must, therefore, be speaking of something else, as we see in another excerpt where he continues with the military metaphors:

> O wretched man, what will you do if you fall into their hands? Protect yourself lest you be delivered into the hands of your enemies. Surrender yourself to this pair of friends, Reason (*Logos*) and Mind (*Nous*), and no one will be victorious over you. May God dwell in your camp, may his Spirit protect your gates, and may the divine Mind (*Nous*) protect the walls. Let holy Reason (*Logos*) become a torch in your mind, burning the wood which is the entirety of sin.
>
> *Teachings of Silvanus 86, TS p.17*

Mystically, the *Logos* and the *Nous* are synonymous, both being commonly encountered terms for the Word of God – *Nous*, generally translated as Mind, being quite different from the Universal Mind or Satan. It is through this *Logos* or *Nous*, says the writer, that all negative tendencies can be overcome and by means of which the "whole of sin" can be burnt up or destroyed. This is the teaching of all perfect Masters.

There is little else that this passage can mean. The writer is not referring to human reasoning and the human mind as powers which can burn up sin. In fact, he speaks specifically of the "*Nous* of *divinity*" and the "*holy Logos*" to emphasize his meaning. There is little that is divine or holy about ordinary human reason!

In another extract from this tractate, the Word is called the "True Vine of Christ" from which the soul may drink the "true wine", the divine ambrosia, the intoxicating bliss of conscious contact with God's own creative Power. But to do this, says the writer, you must first nurture your "reasoning powers":

> Give yourself gladness from the True Vine of Christ. Satisfy yourself with the true wine in which there is no drunkenness nor error. For it (the true wine) marks the end of drinking since there is usually in it (the power) to give joy to the soul and the mind through the Spirit of God. But first, nurture your 'reasoning powers' before you drink of it (the true wine).
>
> *Teachings of Silvanus 107-108, TS pp.59-61*

This "true wine" brings an end to the "drunkenness" of materiality, for it brings great "joy to the soul and mind", since it stems from the "Spirit of God". "But first", a person must "nurture their 'reasoning powers'", their ability to meditate on the *Logos*. This is the only way by which the drunkenness of materiality can be ended and contact with the *Logos* established. And this practice is not one of merely thinking about the *Logos*, but of concentrating the mind by specific spiritual exercises and coming into contact with the divine Music or Sound of the "*holy Logos*". So again, the scholarly translation does not adequately convey the writer's intended meaning, though the recipient of this letter or homily, struggling daily with his spiritual practice, would have immediately understood it. The writer was using a term commonly employed in their community for spiritual practice.

The use of such Greek terms is not without its antecedents, as well as modern parallels. In modern Greece, the word used for meditation is *dialogismos* (*lit.* by means of *logos*), a term having no other meaning or use at the present time. The corresponding verb is *dialogizomai*, meaning 'to meditate'. In ancient times, the verb was similar, *logizomai*, and the noun was *logismos*.[3]

Like *Logos*, *logizomai* also has several meanings including to count, to calculate, to reckon, to reason, to infer and so on. But in certain crucial passages – as we have seen – none of these are adequate. The meaning, of course, hinges on the meaning of *Logos*. If *Logos* is understood as 'reason', then *logizomai* can be translated as 'to reason' and *logismos* as 'reasoning'. But if *Logos* is taken in its esoteric, mystic sense as the divine, omnipresent, sustaining Power, then the verb *logizomai* can be translated as giving attention to the *Logos* or listening to the divine Word within, while *logismos* will mean meditation in the sense of spiritual practice.

In the *Teachings of Silvanus*, the term translated as "reasoning" is *logismos* and, from this tractate as well as earlier Greek literature, it is clear that its intended meaning is indeed meditation or spiritual practice. In *Phaedo*, for instance, one of the most mystical of Plato's dialogues, *Socrates* says:

> She (the soul) will calm passion by listening to the *Logos* within (by *logisomos*, by 'reasoning' or meditation) and by always being in it and by beholding what is true and divine and not the object of opinion. And being nurtured by it, the soul will seek to live in this way for as long as she lives so that, when she dies, she will enter That which is kindred and similar to her own nature, and be freed from human ills.
>
> Socrates (Plato), Phaedo 84a-b; cf. DPI p.439, PACII p.63, PIEA pp.290-293

Most scholarly translators, themselves predisposed to intellect and rationalism, take *logismos* to mean 'reasoning', consequently rendering the first line as, "by following reason..." or "by reasoning...". Thus, the mistranslation of a single word converts the meaning from a mystic to an intellectual sense.

Philo Judaeus also uses the term in the same way. In *On Monarchy*, for instance, he is speaking of the quest for God as the most worthwhile "employment", however difficult it may be, for it brings in its train a state of bliss – of "indescribable pleasures and delights":

> Even if it is very difficult to ascertain and very hard properly to comprehend, we must still, as far as it is possible, investigate the nature of His essence; for there is no employment more excellent than that of searching out the nature of the true God, even though the discovery may transcend all human ability, since the very desire and endeavour to comprehend it is able by itself to furnish indescribable pleasures and delights.
>
> Philo, On Monarchy I:V, WPJIII p.183

He then goes on to speak of those who have gone beyond mere discussion of this quest and through "reasoning" (meditation) have ascended into the realms of the spirit, becoming drenched in "unalloyed light", such that the "eye of his soul becomes dazzled and confused (awe-struck) by the splendour":

> And the witness of this fact are those who have not merely tasted philosophy with their outermost lips, but who have abundantly feasted on its reasonings and its doctrines; for the reasoning (meditation, *logismos*) of these men, being raised on high far above the earth, roams in the air (spirit), and soaring aloft with the sun, and moon, and all the firmament of heaven, being eager to behold all the things that exist therein, finds its power of vision somewhat indistinct from a vast quantity of unalloyed light being poured over it, so that the eye of his soul becomes dazzled and confused (awe-struck) by the splendour.
>
> *Philo, On Monarchy I:V, WPJIII p.183*

Clearly, no normal reasoning processes could induce such an expansion of consciousness, even in a person of superlative imagination. But meditation or spiritual practice certainly does. That is a part of its purpose.

In the ancient literature of this period, there are many other direct references, as well as veiled allusions, to spiritual practice. Writing to a certain Rheginus, the gnostic author of the *Treatise on the Resurrection* concludes with an exhortation to practise meditation as the means of experiencing the true nature of resurrection and of escaping from re-incarnation in another body:

> It is fitting for each one to practise in many ways (to meditate a great deal), to gain release from this element (the body) so that he may not wander aimlessly but rather might recover his former state of being.
>
> *Treatise on the Resurrection 49, GS p.324, NHS22 p.157*

One of the scholars who has translated this passage does point out that the word translated here as "practise" also means to lead an ascetic life, which we might interpret loosely as meaning a spiritual life. "Practise" thus refers to spiritual practice. Similarly, says this translator, the Greek verb rendered as "wander aimlessly" is sometimes used in other contexts to refer specifically to reincarnation. This reinforces our interpretation, for the only "practice" which can lead to release from repeated rebirth, "to recover" one's "former state of being", the true nature of the pure soul, is spiritual communion with the mystic Word of God.

The same confusion is found in translations of the Manichaean literature. Here, there is no doubt that the mystic Mani taught meditation, for the references are more than a few. Moreover, it must be remembered that since Mani taught that his teachings were the same as those of Jesus, Zarathushtra and other mystics, he must also have presumed that Jesus had also taught the same practice of meditation as he did. The first excerpt from the Manichaean literature illustrates the use of such expressions as "pious meditation" and "pious deeds" in scholarly translations. It comes from the fragments of a letter purporting to have been written by Mani to his devoted disciple Mar Ammo:

> In this time of sin (*i.e.* while being in this world), the pure devout one must sit down in pious meditation, and he should turn away from sin and increase what is pious, so that....
>
> And therefore I have spoken these words, in order that everyone may himself pay attention to them and carefully listen to them. For everyone who hears and believes them and keeps them in his head and is active in pious deeds (spiritual practice) shall find salvation from this birth-death and be saved from all sins.
>
> Because I, Mar Mani, and you Mar Ammo, and all those people of old and also those fortunate ones that are born in this time, and likewise also those that will be born in the future, shall be saved from this birth-death through this pure Commandment and through this perfect Wisdom (*i.e.* the Word), through this activity (the practice of meditation) and this humility (*i.e.* loss of the ego through merging into the Word). Because in this birth-death there is nothing good except only the merit of the pious deeds (spiritual practice) that men of knowledge (*i.e. gnosis*) perform.
>
> Those who follow me, Mar Mani, and hope in God *Ormuzd* and want the pure and just Elect (the Masters) as leaders, they are the ones that are saved and find salvation from this birth-death and reach eternal redemption.
>
> *MMIII pp.854-857, ML p.58*

As with 'reasoning', no "pious deeds" of this world can lead to "eternal redemption" from "this birth-death". The only truly "pious deeds" or "pious meditation" which can have this result is contact with the "pure Commandment" and "perfect Wisdom". This is something which all Masters have taught. It is meditation on the Word or Wisdom that leads to release from birth and death. Thus, one of the Manichaean-Christian psalmists writes:

Jesus my Light, whom I have loved, take me in unto thee....
I have constantly practised in thy holy Wisdom,
   which has opened the eyes of my soul
   unto the light of thy glory and made me see
   the things that are hidden and that are visible,
   the things of the abyss (this world)
   and the things of the Height.

Psalm CCLXVIII, MPB pp.85-86

This is no intellectual or philosophical expression, but a statement of experience. The practice of the Word of Wisdom has "opened the eyes of my soul". The inner eye has been opened and the soul has seen both God and the whole of creation, inside and out. *This* is the fruit of meditation. This is precisely what is supposed to happen in meditation.

Again, in a devotional song praising the Perfect Man (the Master) as the *Sraoshabray* (the Column of Sound and Glory, the divine Light and Music of the Word, the refuge, the "house and covering for all souls"), meditation is called the "pure prayer, living Voice and divine Song" – clear allusions to meditation upon the divine Music or the Voice of God:

Blessed and praised be this mighty Power,
   the light and beneficent God, the Perfect Man.
House and covering for all souls,
   Road and Path for all lights and redeemed souls
   may he be blessed so that his Radiance of Life
   may shine upon the elect Path
   and bring forth peace, health and confidence for us in all lands.
And may he protect us for wonderful joy
   and accept from all of us this pure prayer,
   living Voice and divine Song.
So be it for ever and ever!

BBB, ML pp.64-65

Similarly, amongst the Manichaean-Christian writings from Turkestan, though the translation is somewhat stilted, spiritual practice is referred to as the admonition to "think and consider the real and right Law, day and night":

Stop all sorts of evil doings,
   and be sent back to your own Originator! ...

> Control your thoughts, and rectify
> and regulate them constantly;
> Think and consider (meditate upon)
> the real and right Law (the Word), day and night,
> and persistently select and clarify the five wonderful Bodies.
> If there are those who suffer in the transmigration of hell, ...
> it is really because
> they do not recognize the five Light-Bodies,
> and are therefore severed
> from the Country of Peace and Happiness.
> *LSMH 245-247, BSOAS XI p.197*

No one can think about a matter "day and night". But meditation on the Word, the "real and right Law", does most certainly lead to the constant experience of its music at all times. For the "Law" and the divine Music are the essence of life and consciousness itself. Incidentally, the advice to "persistently select and clarify the five wonderful Bodies" and the references to the "five Light-Bodies" are presumably references to meditation upon the "five Greatnesses", the five forms of the Sound as it descends through the five realms of creation. The translation could perhaps be better but the general meaning seems clear enough.

The same exhortation to "meditate in His love, by night and by day" is also found amongst the *Odes of Solomon*, devotional poetry so obviously written by one who understood the mystic path and the ecstatic transport of spiritual practice:

> Let us all, therefore,
> become one in the Name of the Lord,
> and let us honour Him in His goodness;
> And let our faces shine in His Light,
> and let our hearts meditate in His love,
> by night and by day....
>
> And His Word is with us all along our way,
> the Saviour who gives new life to us
> does not reject our souls.
> The man (Jesus) who humbled himself (came to this world),
> but was exalted by his own righteousness.
> The Son of the Most High appeared
> in the perfection of his Father;
> And the light dawned from the Word,

> that was beforetime in Him....
> that He might give life to souls for ever
> by the Truth of His Name.
>   Let there arise a new song
>   from those who love Him.
>
> *Odes of Solomon XLI:5-6,11-14,16, AOT pp.729-730,*
> *OPS p.138, OSB pp.128-129, OSC p.141*

Now, none of this is religious sentimentality or hyperbole but a description in poor words of the mystic experience of the writer. Such divine love "by night and by day" is *only* to be experienced through mystic prayer. One who has such love is in a state of meditative bliss all the time. This is the fruit of spiritual practice.

The *Clementine Recognitions* and the *Clementine Homilies* are also replete with allusions to meditation. In one passage, it has been translated as "heavenly reasoning", where it is portrayed as something which relates to man's purification before God and is necessary in order to worship Him. It is also something which man alone can practice and which animals cannot. In the story, it is Peter who says:

> However, it is necessary to add something to these things which has not community (normal concourse) with man, but is peculiar to the worship of God. I mean purification.... But (of) what (kind)? If purity be not added to the service of God, you would roll pleasantly like the dung-flies.
>
> Wherefore as man, having something more than the irrational animals, namely rationality, purify your hearts from evil by heavenly reasoning.... For our Teacher also, [dealing with] certain of the Pharisees and Scribes among us ... – and as Scribes know the matters of the law more than others – still he reproved them as hypocrites, because they cleansed only the things that appear to men, but omitted purity of heart and the things seen by God alone.
>
> *Clementine Homilies XI:XXVIII, CH p.187*

Animals, like man, keep their bodies clean by washing. Neither ritual ablutions nor normal daily bathing make us any different from them. The true purity and cleanliness, therefore, which makes a person fit to come before God, requires a great deal more than physical cleansing. And the question which every genuine seeker after God must answer is how that inner purity is to be obtained. Peter says that this purity is to be achieved by "heavenly reasoning" – by meditation or contact with the holy *Logos*.

There are many other allusions to spiritual practice in the Clementine literature. One of the central characters, for example, is praised (to his previously long-lost mother) as being a "man of consideration",[4] another scholarly translation that only makes sense in the context if it means a "man of meditation" – a wise and spiritual man. But the commonest expression used for meditation is the highly ambiguous "good works" or "good deeds". It occurs in a great many places, some more clearly being references to meditation than others. It is almost invariably Peter who is speaking, as for instance:

> We do not neglect to proclaim to you what we know to be necessary for your salvation, and to show you what is the true worship of God, that, believing in God, you may be able, by means of good works, to be heirs with us of the world to come.
>
> *Clementine Recognitions V:XXXV, CR p.325*

And:

> We are sent for this end, that we may betray his (Satan's) disguises to you; and melting your enmities, may reconcile you to God, that you may be converted to Him, and may please Him by good works.
>
> *Clementine Recognitions V:XXVIII, CR p.321*

And:

> I counsel every learner willingly to lend his ear to the word of God, and to hear with love of the truth what we say, that his mind, receiving the best Seed, may bring forth joyful fruits by good deeds.
>
> *Clementine Recognitions V:VIII, CR p.307*

It is through "good works" or "good deeds", Peter says, that souls can "be heirs ... of the world to come", can "please God" and can "bring forth joyful fruits". But it is only meditation which fulfils these conditions, for good deeds in this world may ennoble a person, but they do not lead to mystical experience, to the true worship of God. In fact, the popular Christian conception that "good works" will lead a person to salvation is not even supported by orthodox Christian doctrine. Something more is required.

In the latter extract, Peter also says that it is necessary to first receive the "best Seed" – to be initiated into the Word – before a person "may bring forth joyful fruits by good deeds". And he reiterates this theme in a number of places where he speaks of baptism as being "born anew by means of Waters which were first created" – an allusion to the Creative Word:

> When you have come to the Father, you will learn that this is His will, that you be born anew by means of the Waters which were first created (*i.e.* Living Water, the Word). For he who is regenerated by Water (spiritually baptized), having filled up the measure of good works, is made heir of Him by whom he has been regenerated in incorruption....
>
> Merit accrues to men from good works, but only if they be done as God commands. Now God has ordered every one who worships Him to be sealed by baptism; but if you refuse, and obey your will rather than God's, you are doubtless contrary and hostile to His will.... But when you have been regenerated by Water, show by good works the likeness in you of that Father who hath begotten you....
>
> For He has given a law, thereby aiding the minds of men, that they may the more easily perceive how they ought to act with respect to everything, in what way they may escape evil, and in what way tend to future blessings; and how, being regenerate in Water, they may by good works extinguish the fire of their old birth.
>
> *Clementine Recognitions VI:VIII,X, IX:VII, CR pp.332-333,405*

The writer is saying that baptism in "Water" is required before "good deeds" are acceptable to God. Moreover, "merit accrues to men from good works, but only if they be done as God commands": only meditation performed under the guidance of God's Messenger or Master bears fruit, for all other meditation is practised according to the promptings of the mind and leaves the soul within the realms of the mind. By "good works" of this nature man can realize himself as built in the "likeness" of God the Father "who hath begotten" him. Only by spiritual practice – not by any worldly action – can a soul realize that it is truly made in the image or "likeness" of God. And this is God's "law". Only by this means and by being spiritually immersed in the Living Water of the Word can souls escape from the "fire of their old birth", the fire of sensuality.

It is, says Peter, through ignorance and illusion that the soul has become the slave of the mind:

> By reason of your erroneous judgments, you have become subject to demons (*i.e.* the mind). However by acknowledgement of God Himself,

by good deeds you can again become masters, and command the demons as slaves, and as sons of God be constituted heirs of the eternal kingdom.

Clementine Homilies X:XXV, CH p.172

However, "by good deeds", he says, the soul can again become the master of the mind and return to God as His son and heir. But again, experience itself tells us that simply behaving well in this world cannot take a soul back to God. Indeed, without the spiritual strength and awareness given by meditation, a person cannot withstand the tendencies of their mind and will be unable to continuously perform good deeds, certainly not without some thought of egotism entering the mind, thereby annulling all their efforts. Hence, we may conclude, with Peter:

> Therefore do not refuse, when invited, to return to your first nobility; for it is possible, if ye be conformed to God by good works. And being accounted to be sons by reason of your likeness to Him, you shall be reinstated as lords of all.

Clementine Homilies X:VI, CH p.163

When invited to return to Him, the invitation should be accepted, for "by good works" – by spiritual practice – it is possible to be reconciled to God and to regain one's rightful sonship. Man has only to make the sincere effort to meditate, seeking God within, for His grace and blessings to descend.

NOTES AND REFERENCES

1. *Galatians* 6:7.
2. Ignatius, *To the Trallians* XI:2, *AFI* p.223.
3. For further discussion, see *PACI* p.55*ff*.
4. *Clementine Homilies* XII:XXXIII, *CH* p.203.

CHAPTER TWENTY-ONE

Knocking at His Door:
Labourers into His Harvest

Procrastination

Say Not Ye, There are Yet Four Months

Mystic teachings are nothing if they are not lived and experienced. Man, however, with his deeply ingrained worldly tendencies, is easily distracted and readily postpones the time when he will settle down to long, protracted meditation and effort on the spiritual path. The mind generates multiple excuses for procrastination. This is one of its simplest and most effective tricks. In the morning, it says, "I have so much to do today, I will do it this evening." In the evening, it says, "I am now too tired. I must not damage my health. I will do it in the morning." In youth, it says, "Let me wait until I am married and have settled down." When married, it says, "Let me wait until my children have grown up. I have such a big mortgage and have to earn a living for my family; they also need my time." When the children have left home, the mind says, "Now, I have to save enough for a comfortable retirement. Then I can attend to spiritual practice." And when retirement comes, then the habits of a lifetime are so deeply set and the body has started to deteriorate in such a variety of ways that the mind cannot take to meditation.

It is all the spinning of illusion on illusion. All mystics have said that the time for spiritual practice is right now. Whatever the circumstances, whatever the apparent difficulties, they can all be surmounted by one who makes the effort and attends to meditation. Mystics have constantly advised man not to waste his brief time in this world. Life, they say, is for seeking the eternal. Hence, in the *Acts of Thomas*, when Judas Thomas is threatened with death by King Misdaeus, he only expresses his unconcern, saying:

> This life hath been given as a loan,
> and this time is one that changeth;
> But that life whereof I teach is incorruptible;

> And beauty and youth that are seen
>> shall in a little cease to be.
>> *Acts of Thomas 127, ANT p.420*

And in the Manichaean-Christian psalms, there is a similar most poignant passage:

> The years pass like months,
>> the months fly away like moments.
> These (bodies) are houses which are given on lease;
>> years they are, taken on loan.
> I am not sick at heart for the bodies,
>> but for the treasure of the Living Ones (the Masters)
>> that is lodged in them.
>> *Psalms of Thomas XIII, MPB p.218, SCMP p.120*

It is not so much the body which suffers, he says, but the souls who are "lodged" in them. In another, the psalmist first describes the people of the world, saying:

> They pass their whole life,
>> given over to eating and drinking and lust....
> They quarrel with one another
>> for a possession that passes away:
> Because of a fatal treasure
>> they come to fight with one another.
>> *Psalm CCLXV, MPB pp.81-82*

And he then continues:

> Why, O my soul, dost thou fritter thy life away now? ...
>> lest they take thee before the judge (Satan)
>> by reason of (...?) and lusts?
> The days of thy life are running from thee:
>> why dost thou vainly waste thy zeal
>> on the things of the earth and puttest behind thee
>> all the things of heaven?
> Thou hast spent thy life sunk in the worries
>> and cares of the world,
>> working thyself into a decline
>> through the pains and the sorrows.

Thou art a stranger, housed in a body of the earth defiled:
How long therefore hast thou been heedless
    of what thou ignorantly doest?
Thou toilest all thy time to nourish thy bodies:
    yet hast thou not worried, poor thing,
    in what way thou canst be saved.
Thou weepest and sheddest tears for a son or a friend dying:
    yet thy own departing,
    the thought of it enters not into thy heart.

Look therefore at that which is hidden from thee
    and see from today henceforth:
Lo, the way to travel is before thee, forget not thy departing.
Choose not the life of this body before eternal life:
    put the fear of God in thy heart
    and thou shalt live without toil.

Psalm CCLXV, MPB p.82

His meaning requires no elucidation. Life passes by so fast and, before we know what has happened, it has come to an end without anything of spiritual value having been accomplished. This is why Jesus said:

Say not ye,
"There are yet four months, and then cometh harvest?"
Behold, I say unto you,
    lift up your eyes, and look on the fields;
    for they are white already to harvest.

John 4:35

Taking an agricultural example, so favoured by Jesus, he says that the harvest of spirituality is ready to be reaped and gathered in. There is no point in procrastination. "Lift up your eyes", he says, almost certainly another allusion to spiritual practice. Lift up your consciousness to the level of the eyes, to the single eye. Go within and reap the pure white harvest of the spirit. Similarly, Matthew records:

Then saith he unto his disciples,
"The harvest truly is plenteous, but the labourers are few;
Pray ye therefore the lord of the harvest,
    that he will send forth labourers into his harvest."

Matthew 9:37-38

He says that there is no lack of "harvest", the spiritual treasure is infinite, enough to provide for the entire creation. "But the labourers are few": very few people are really prepared to dedicate themselves completely to the task of reaping this harvest. Everyone has excuses and distractions of one kind or another – physical, emotional, mental, psychological or any other kind. And since it is only a Master, the "lord of the harvest", who can inspire the right attitude of devotion and dedication in the minds of his disciples, Jesus recommends them to beg for his grace and blessings to enable them to become true labourers.

The author of the *Acts of Thomas* seems to have been fond of this parable, making a number of allusions to it. Judas Thomas speaks of Jesus as the one:

> That givest wages unto them that have laboured.
>
> *Acts of Thomas 141, ANT p.426*

He requests his reward for making his "fields" pure white and fit for harvesting:

> My fields are white and are already fit for reaping;
> may I receive my reward.
>
> *Acts of Thomas, AAA p.281*

And he says that he has

> laboured for his grace that is come upon me,
> which departeth not from me.
>
> *Acts of Thomas 160, ANT p.434*

As to the real nature of this grace and the fruit of the devotee's labours, the writer of the *Odes of Solomon* is unequivocal. It is the Word of God which comes to a soul:

> His Word came to me,
> that gave me the fruits of my labours,
> and gave me rest in the grace of the Lord.
>
> *Odes of Solomon XXXVII:3-4, AOT p.725*

This is the fruit of labouring at spiritual practice.

Be Ye Doers of the Word

Exhortation to live and practise the mystic teachings is to be found
throughout all mystic writings, for practice is the essence of all mysticism and faltering man needs encouragement. Hence, James the
brother of Jesus writes to the disciples:

> Be ye doers of the Word,
>   and not hearers only,
>   deceiving your own selves.
>
> *James 1:22-25*

Those who only pay lip service to the teachings, talking learnedly and
wisely but never really putting them into practice, are only deceiving
themselves. "Be ye doers of the Word", he says. Follow the teachings
and become attached to the music of the Word within. Similarly, in
the *Book of Revelation*, an 'angel', said to be speaking on behalf of Jesus,
says:

> Behold, I come quickly; and my reward is with me,
>   to give every man according as his work shall be....
> Blessed are they that do his commandments,
>   that they may have right to the Tree of Life,
>   and may enter in through the gates into the City.
>
> *Book of Revelation 22:12,14*

Everyone is rewarded according to his actions. If they follow "his commandments" and live the path that has been laid out for them, then
will they have a right to the Tree of Life, the Word, and can enter
"through the gates" – the single eye or inner door – "into the City", the
"heavenly Jerusalem", the "City of God", all these being Judaic terms
for the eternal realm or the kingdom of God.

The emphasis on action rather than words is again underlined in
Jesus' parable of the two men, one who built his house on sand and
the other on rock. Jesus prefaces the parable with some comments on
lip service:

> Not every one that saith unto me, "Lord, Lord,"
>   shall enter into the kingdom of heaven;
> But he that doeth the will of my Father which is in heaven.

Many will say to me in that day, "Lord, Lord,"
　　have we not prophesied in thy name?
　　and in thy name have cast out devils?
　　and in thy name done many wonderful works?
And then will I profess unto them, "I never knew you":
　　depart from me, ye that work iniquity.

Matthew 7:21-23

Simply saying that "so-and-so is my Master and I believe that he is the Lord" does not entitle a person to "enter into the kingdom of heaven". Action is required: only "he that doeth the will of my Father" can enter in. And elsewhere, as we have seen, Jesus is very clear about what is meant by doing the will of the Father. He then narrates the parable:

Therefore whosoever heareth these sayings of mine,
　　and doeth them, I will liken him unto a wise man,
　　which built his house upon a rock:
And the rain descended, and the floods came,
　　and the winds blew, and beat upon that house;
　　and it fell not: for it was founded upon a rock.

And every one that heareth these sayings of mine,
　　and doeth them not, shall be likened unto a foolish man,
　　which built his house upon the sand:
And the rain descended, and the floods came,
　　and the winds blew, and beat upon that house;
　　and it fell: and great was the fall of it.

Matthew 7:24-27

The disciple who hears the Master's teachings and "doeth them", who gives full time to spiritual practice as instructed by his Master, Jesus likens to a man whose house is built upon a rock. When waves of difficulty arise in the life of such a disciple, he passes through them without too much discomfort and without losing the thread of his meditation. The peace of mind, the understanding and the stability of character which he has been able to build by meditation see him through all the hard times. He is a "wise man".

But the disciple who never really bothers to follow the teachings and is lax in attending to his spiritual practice is like a man who built his house on sand, without any sure foundation. For when difficulties arise in his life, his mind is overwhelmed and carried away. He becomes submerged in his difficulties and wallows in them, becoming so obsessed by the physical events of life that whatever little meditation he was doing gets completely swept away and forgotten. He, says Jesus, is a "foolish man".

At Night My Soul Longs for You

One of the most difficult aspects of attending to meditation while leading a normal life in the world is to find a suitable time for it. Mystics recommend, at least in modern times, that a person devote one-tenth of their time to the practice. That means two and a half hours, a not insignificant period. Yet even with that, with twenty-one and a half hours still devoted to the world and to resting the body in sleep, the emphasis is still likely to lie heavily on the worldly side. For this reason, mystics advise that even during the day a disciple should repeat the names whenever mentally free, thus keeping the mind oriented towards God. It is held on a leash and is in a more receptive mood when the time for meditation comes.

But what is the most appropriate time for spiritual practice? Mystics throughout the ages have been quite unequivocal about this. They say that the best time is in the early morning, before everyone else arises. During the day, a person is busy with various commitments and duties, and the mind and body get tired. Consequently, if he sits in the evening, he is liable either to replay in his mind the events of the day or simply to fall asleep. The best time, therefore, is in the latter half of the night, before the dawn. This has been called God's own time.

All times are good for meditation, but the hours before the dawn have a number of distinct advantages. The atmosphere is quiet, the body and mind are relaxed and rested after sleep, one does not expect any disturbances or interruptions, and concentration comes more easily. Ultimately, the body and mind get such rest and energy from contact with the divine Music that the devotee only rarely slips into the unconsciousness of sleep. While the body rests, the soul flies up above the eyes and spends the entire night listening to the inner Music and traversing the inner realms. This is real meditation and is the fruit of assiduous and devoted repetition of the names, together with the grace and blessings of the Master.

There are numerous references in mystic writings to nightly meditation, often combined with the expression of deep spiritual yearning for union with God. In the words of Isaiah:

> At night my soul longs for you
>   and my spirit in me seeks for you.
>
>   *Isaiah 26:9, JB*

In the *Psalms*, the psalmists speak of communion with the mystic Name and the divine Law at all times – "all night", "all day", "before dawn" and "throughout the night":

> Where I live in exile (on earth),
>   Your statutes are psalms for me.
> All night, Yahweh, I remember Your Name
>   and observe Your Law....
> Meditating all day on Your Law,
>   how I have come to love it! ...
> I am up before dawn to call for help,
>   I put my hope in your Word.
> I lie awake throughout the night,
>   that I might meditate on Thy Word.
>
>   *Psalms 119:54-55,97,147 (JB), 148 (JPS)*

Here, "Your statutes" probably refer to both the mystic teachings as well as to the divine Law or Word which support a soul in "exile" in this world. In fact, in an earlier line of this psalm, the devotee speaks of himself as "exile though I am on earth".[1] The same refrain of longing at night and in the early hours is repeated in another psalm:

> It is good to give thanks to Yahweh,
>   to play in honour of Your Name, Most High,
>   to proclaim Your love at daybreak
>   and Your faithfulness all through the night
>   to the music of the zither and lyre,
>   to the rippling of the harp.
>
>   *Psalms 92:1-3, JB*

As we have seen before, the references to musical instruments are veiled allusions to meditation upon the divine Music. The psalmist is not recommending an all-night 'jam session'! In another, we read of instruction "in the night":

> I bless Yahweh, who is my counsellor,
>   and in the night my inmost self instructs me;

> I keep Yahweh before me always,
>   for with him at my right hand nothing can shake me.
>
>   *Psalms 16:7-8, JB*

The "inmost self" is the soul, the Word and ultimately God Himself. Hence, the 'counsel' of Yahweh and instruction from the "inmost self" come to the same thing. But that which unites the self with God is long listening to the Word.

As time passes, a divine yearning and nostalgia takes hold of all devotees who sincerely seek for Him. It is this that draws them nightly to their meditation. It is this longing for God of which the psalmist is writing, when he says:

> My soul thirsts for God,
>   the God of Life;
> When shall I go to see
>   the face of God?
> I have no food but tears,
>   day and night....
>
> In the daytime may Yahweh
>   command His love to come,
> And by night may His song be on my lips,
>   a prayer to the God of my life! ...
>
> Send out Your Light and Your Truth,
>   let these be my guide,
> To lead me to Your holy Mountain
>   and to the place where You live.
>
>   *Psalms 42:2-3,8, 43:3, JB*

"By night may His song be on my lips" is an allusion to listening to the divine Music in nightly meditation, for otherwise people are asleep at night. "Your Light and Your Truth" are the Word that is sent out from God. This is the only true "guide" that can lead a soul to the eternal region, "Your holy Mountain". Similarly:

> God, you are my God, I am seeking You,
>   my soul is thirsting for You,
>   my flesh is longing for You,
>   a land parched, weary and waterless;

> I long to gaze on You in the sanctuary (within),
>> and to see Your power and glory.
>
> Your love is better than life itself,
>> my lips will recite Your praise;
>> all my life I will bless You,
>> in your Name lift up my hands;
> My soul will feast most richly,
>> on my lips a song of joy and, in my mouth, praise.
>
> On my bed I think of You,
>> I meditate on You all night long,
>> for You have always helped me.
> I sing for joy in the shadow of Your wings;
>> my soul clings close to You,
>> Your right hand supports me.
>
> *Psalms 63:1-8, JB*

This psalm is a simple expression of the soul's yearning and the joy of contact with His presence and with His "Name". "On my bed I think of You" carries a double meaning. It alludes to nightly meditation, but also to the eye centre, the point in the body at which the soul withdraws from the world, falling asleep as far as the world is concerned. The Lord always helps such devotees who take shelter in the "shadow of Your wings" and whose souls cling to Him.

Echoing these words, in the mystic allegory of the *Song of Songs*, the lover, symbolic of the soul, speaks of her love for the divine Beloved:

> On my bed, at night, I sought him
>> whom my heart loves.
> I sought but did not find him.
>
> *Song of Songs 3:1, JB*

And:

> Before the dawn-wind rises,
>> before the shadows flee,
>> I will go to the mountain of myrrh
>> to the hill of frankincense.
>
> *Song of Songs 4:6-7, JB*

The fragrant "mountain of myrrh" and the "hill of frankincense" are allusions to the holy City, the Mountain of God, the eternal realm. This longing reaches its zenith at night and in the early morning hours before the dawn. Hence, the lover speaks to the Beloved:

> Before the dawn-wind rises,
>   before the shadows flee,
> Return! Be, my Beloved,
>   like a gazelle,
>   a young stag,
>   on the mountains of the Covenant.
>
> *Song of Songs 2:17, JB*

The beloved Master travels freely through all the inner realms. He has the skill of a "gazelle" or a "young stag" on the "mountains of the Covenant", the mountains of the divine Law, the inner regions. He is the Master and Lord of all domains within the Lord's creation.

These mystic sentiments are universal and are not associated with any particular religion or culture. Psalms of divine longing are to be found in many languages, an expression of the soul's individual relationship with God. One of the Manichaean-Christian psalmists, for example, expresses the same powerful feeling:

> Rabbi, my Master, I will serve thy Commandment
>   in the joy of my whole heart.
> I will not give rest to my heart,
>   I will not give sleep to my eyes,
>   I will not give rest to my feet
>   until I have brought the sheep to the fold.
>
> *Psalms of Heracleides, MPB p.187*

The "sheep" is the soul and the "fold" is the eternal abode. Nothing is too much trouble; the soul that truly longs for union with God permits nothing to stand in its way. The devotee yearns continually for that meeting. Echoing the same words, yet making a clear allusion to concentration at the centre between the two eyebrows, an ancient Mandaean poet also writes:

> No sleep cometh to mine eyes,
>   to mine eyes no sleep cometh
>   and my brow keepeth vigil.
>
> *CPM 149 p.130*

And the poet of the *Psalms of Solomon* describes the devotee as the one who is "saved" and "guided" by contact with the "Name of the Lord":

> Happy the man whose heart is set
>> to call upon the Name of the Lord;
> When he makes mention of the Name of the Lord,
>> he will be saved.
> His ways are guided by the Lord....
>
> He arose from his sleep
>> and blessed the Name of the Lord:
> In peacefulness of heart
>> he sang to the Name of his God.
>
> *Psalms of Solomon VI:1-2,4, AOT p.663*

"He sang to the Name of his God" and to "mention" or to "call upon the Name of the Lord" are veiled allusions to meditation upon the mystic and holy Name, for it must be self-evident that repeating any verbal name of God, however assiduously, can never result in salvation. And the devotee performs this 'mentioning' by "arising from his sleep" – a double meaning alluding to arising from the sleep of this world as well as nightly rest.

Morning Prayer

Considering the matter of early rising from a practical standpoint, there is an interesting passage in the *Clementine Recognitions*, concerning Peter's morning 'prayer':

> As soon as day began to advance the dawn upon the retiring darkness, Peter having gone into the garden to pray, and returning thence and coming to us, by way of excuse for awaking and coming to us a little later than usual, said this: "Now that the spring-time has lengthened the day, of course the night is shorter; if, therefore, one desires to occupy some portion of the night in study (meditation), he must not keep the same hours for waking at all seasons, but should spend the same length of time in sleeping, whether the night be longer or shorter, and be exceedingly careful that he do not cut off from the period which he is wont to have for study (meditation), and so add to his sleep and lessen his time of keeping awake. And this also is to be observed, lest haply if sleep be

interrupted while the food is still undigested, the undigested mass load the mind, and by the exhalation of crude spirits render the inner sense confused and disturbed.

It is right, therefore, that that part also be cherished with sufficient rest, so that, those things being sufficiently accomplished which are due to it, the body may be able in other things to render due service to the mind.

Clementine Recognitions VI:I, CR p.327

Peter goes "into the garden to pray". He seeks out a quiet place and on returning advises the disciples that because the lengthening days of spring and summer will mean less hours of darkness, they will need to adjust their daily schedules. This includes the timing of sleep, as well as their evening meal so that the food is digested by the morning and does not draw the attention down nor disturb the mind. Peter is not specific, but he does point out that care should always be taken that the time given to meditation is not curtailed, nor even the amount of time required for sleep. Sufficient rest is required to permit the mind to be alert and avoid falling back to sleep again soon after sitting in meditation.

It is clear from this passage that Peter's "prayer" is to be equated with what the scholars have translated as "study" and that both these terms refer to spiritual practice. It is another instance of scholarly ambiguity. Quite apart from the fact that simple and illiterate people, as many of Jesus' disciples most probably were, could hardly be expected to rise at night and study, there is absolutely no indication in any early Christian literature whatever that Jesus advocated pre-dawn, scholarly study as the means of reaching God! Rather the reverse, in fact.

The problem of falling asleep in meditation is a common one, for in sleep the attention withdraws from the world but slips down below the single eye, and unconsciousness ensues. In meditation, the attention is to be kept at the single eye in full consciousness. But if the practitioner is at all bored or has had insufficient sleep or has an "undigested mass" of food in the stomach, drawing the body energies downward, it is very easy to be overcome by drowsiness and sleep. Hence, in the *Doctrine of Addai*, Addai counsels against falling prey to tiredness during "prayer at the stated times":

Let not weariness in prayer at the stated times draw near to you. Take heed to the truth, which ye hold, and to the teaching of the truth, which ye have received, and to the inheritance of salvation, which I commend to you.

Doctrine of Addai the Apostle, DAA p.40

Or as the writer of the *Teachings of Silvanus* advises when speaking of knocking at the inner door:

> Do not admit sleep to your eyes nor drowsiness to your eyelids.
>
> *Teachings of Silvanus 113, TS p.71*

Fundamental human problems, spiritual or mundane, change very little.

Spiritual practice, then, is probably the origin of what became ritual morning prayers, both in Judaism and Christianity. It is, of course, an understandable feeling that it is good to start and end a day in the name of the Lord. But the real question is "what kind of prayer?" In the Mandaean writings, the mystic nature of morning prayer is made very clear. Here, the Word is described as the "great Jordan of the First Life" and the "sublime Vine". Every day, the soul offers her "prayer and praise" – her meditation – before it:

> By the bank of the great Jordan of the First Life,
>   a sublime Vine standeth erect.
> Each and every day my prayer and praise
>   riseth before it.
>
> *CPM 156 p.134*

And in another, prayer is identified as "uttering words of radiance" and being "absorbed in thoughts of light". It is a prayer arising from the "everlasting abode", resulting in the "forgiveness of sins" and which is offered "when we have arisen from our sleep":

> We have purified our hands in Truth
>   and our lips in faith.
> We have uttered words of radiance
>   and were absorbed in thoughts of light....
> Honour resteth upon the *'uthras* (pure souls) who sit in glory.
> This is the prayer and praise which came to them from
>   the great place of Light and the everlasting abode.
> We praise Him with it when we have risen from our sleep,
>   before any have spoken falsehood.
> For any man who prayeth this prayer
>   there will be forgiving of sins and transgressions
>   in the great place of Light and in the everlasting abode.
>
> *CPM 115 pp.111-112*

The only "prayer" which accurately fits this description is meditation upon the Word of God and the return to God.

Prayer in Secret

Prayer is actually one of the commonest terms used for spiritual practice, but since the term has always applied to the verbal and ritual prayers of religion as well, when reading through these ancient documents, it is sometimes difficult to sort out one meaning from the other.

Just as Jesus said that real worship of the Father is to worship Him in the Spirit, so the highest prayer to God is meditation upon His own mystic Son, His Word. This is why Jesus said:

> When thou prayest, thou shalt not be as the hypocrites are:
> for they love to pray standing in the synagogues
> and in the corners of the streets, that they may be seen of men.
> Verily I say unto you, they have their reward.
>
> *Matthew 6:5*

There is always an element of show in set prayers, performed in public places, whether in a synagogue, a church, a temple, a mosque or even on the street corner. The one who prays is conscious of those around him and he is never able to forget himself and to concentrate entirely on the Lord. Jesus says that such people are only interested in receiving the praise of men, wanting to be seen as holy and spiritual people. This is the reward they will get and this is the reach of their prayers.

The real prayer of meditation is to be practised "in secret". No one else need ever know that a person practises mystic prayer. It is a private affair between the soul and the Lord and is best performed in solitude. If anyone else enters a person's thoughts at the time of such prayer, the attention is distracted from the single eye and the individual will be unable to reach even the very first staging post on the inner journey. Hence, Jesus continues:

> But thou, when thou prayest, enter into thy closet,
> and when thou hast shut thy door,
> pray to thy Father which is in secret;
> and thy Father which seeth in secret shall reward thee openly.
>
> *Matthew 6:6*

The open reward of the Father is that He will shower His grace in great abundance upon the soul. If someone keeps their love for God a secret, saying nothing about it to others, then God realizes their spiritual maturity and fills them with His love. He does not keep His love a secret from them. And emphasizing the point that real prayer is silent communion with God in meditation rather than set prayers or "vain repetitions", he adds:

> But when ye pray, use not vain repetitions,
>> as the heathen do: for they think
>> that they shall be heard for their much speaking.
> Be not ye therefore like unto them:
>> for your Father knoweth what things ye have need of,
>> before ye ask Him.
>
> *Matthew 6:7-8*

Nor, he adds, is there any point in putting a daily demand list before the Lord either for personal needs or for the perceived needs of others or even for the world at large. This is the Lord's creation and He knows best how to run it. He needs no input from us. He knows the individual needs of every soul and within the constraints of their *karma*, He makes provision for every soul, human or otherwise, whatever their religion or country.

Verbal prayers, mental or spoken, make no difference to a person's destiny. If something appears to happen as a result of prayer it only means that it was in the destiny of the individual for it to happen in that way. Desires or prayers certainly seem to make things happen, but that is only a part of the outworking of the law of *karma*. Moreover, verbal prayers actually reveal that a person has no faith in God's omniscience and dispensation. They imply that He must be reminded of His duties and of each individual's needs or that perhaps He is about to make a mistake and requires correction. But God does not have a human mind. He is omnipresent and everything lies within the ocean of His Being. The highest prayer, therefore, is surrender of the self: to lose the sense of I-ness, to eliminate the 'I' which wants to promote itself before God, and to submit entirely to His will. "Thy will be done," as Jesus said.

When mystics do give us verbal prayers, they are not given as words to be repeated parrot-fashion and *ad nauseam*. They are only meant to reflect the attitude we should adopt in life. But the mind always goes for the easy option. It would rather repeat the Lord's Prayer several times a day, even continuously, hardly giving its meaning a moment's consideration, than sit down in silent, solitary meditation and really grapple with the mind. This is the same with the people of every religion, for it is an aspect of the human mind, not of any particular religious belief or practice.

The writer of the pithy sayings found in the *Gospel of Philip* summarizes the extent to which external prayers and rituals are useful when he observes:

> An ass which turns a millstone did a hundred miles walking. When it was loosed it found that it was still at the same place. There are men who make many journeys, but make no progress towards any destination. When evening came upon them, they saw neither city not village, neither human artifact nor natural phenomenon, power nor angel. In vain have the wretches laboured.
>
> *Gospel of Philip 63, NHS20 p.167*

Like a donkey that goes round and round, thinking that it has travelled far and accomplished much, such rituals are a waste of time, leaving the person precisely where they started – walking round in circles.

Jesus, too, in the *Gospel of Thomas*, comments on the futility of external observances, ascetic practices or even good deeds:

> If you fast, you will give rise to sin for yourselves;
> and if you pray, you will be condemned;
> and if you give alms, you will do harm to your spirits.
>
> *Gospel of Thomas 14, NHS20 p.59*

Such practices do not take a person nearer to God. Rather, by engendering ego and pride, and creating an illusion of going somewhere spiritually, they can prevent a person from selecting the right path. The author of one of the Nag Hammadi tractates summarizes it neatly:

> It is therefore fitting to pray to the Father and to call on Him with all our soul – not externally with the lips but with the spirit, which is inward.
>
> *Expository Treatise on the Soul 135, NHS21 pp.161-163*

Similarly, in the *Books of the Saviour*, Mary must be referring to meditation upon the Word when she speaks of the soul

who has become negligent and has not prayed in the prayer which takes
away the evil of the souls and purifies them.

Pistis Sophia 130, PS p.327, PSGG p.273

For no verbal or ritual prayer can remove the impressions of past sins
even of this life, let alone those of so many previous incarnations. This
is the province of the Creative Word alone.

Similarly, when Paul advises "pray without ceasing",[2] he cannot be
referring to any external verbal prayer for that would simply be impractical. A person could not talk, walk, eat, sleep and continue with
the normal activities of life if continuously engrossed in external
prayer. He must be referring, therefore, to an inward practice that
maintains continuous contact with God. To begin with, this entails
the practice of repetition of the names during the day, whenever the
mind is mentally free. But as the practitioner progresses, the soul
comes into contact with the Word, which becomes his constant companion and to which all feelings of worship and prayer are automatically directed. Hence, Paul advises in another letter, speaking of the
spiritual path as taking on the "whole armour of God":

Take the helmet of salvation, and the sword of the Spirit, which is the
Word of God: praying always with all prayer and supplication in the
Spirit, and watching thereunto with all perseverance.

Ephesians 6:17-18

"Praying always", he says, entails being "in the Spirit" – it is a spiritual
state of being, not an external mode of worship. As we find in the New
Testament letter attributed to Jude, another brother of Jesus, possibly
the same Judas Thomas made famous in the *Acts of Thomas*:

But ye, beloved, building up yourselves on your most holy faith, praying
in the Holy Ghost, keep yourselves in the love of God.

Jude 1:20-21

The highest prayer, then, is loving meditation on and communion with
the Word of God. There is no other practice as efficacious.

NOTES AND REFERENCES

1. *Psalms* 119:19, *JB*.
2. *1 Thessalonians* 5:17.

CHAPTER TWENTY-TWO

Death, Resurrection and Ascension

Father Forgive Them

Almost everyone in the world is afraid of death, to a greater or lesser extent. Whether or not they care to admit it, there is always some sense of apprehension regarding the unknown. In fact, since only mystics have positive knowledge of what death is and of what will happen to them at that time and afterwards, they alone are unafraid of it. Far from dreading death, they see it as a release from the bondage of the body and the suffocating atmosphere of the physical universe, whose fabric is woven of sin and *karma*. And when the time comes for a perfect Master or any of his advanced disciples to die, they simply leave their body behind, going into the higher worlds in full consciousness. The process is entirely under their control and they have absolutely no fear.

This absence of fear is evident in the gospel accounts of Jesus' death, even hemmed about as they almost certainly are by unreliable anecdotes. As the time of his departure draws near, Jesus continues about his business, finding the time to give consolation to his disciples rather than accepting it from them. He makes his last journey to Jerusalem knowing full well the fate that awaits him, yet he does not flinch. He even makes arrangements to have a last meal with his disciples, telling them:

> Go into the city to such a man, and say unto him, "The Master saith, 'My time is at hand; I will keep the passover at thy house with my disciples.'"
>
> *Matthew 26:18*

And although he knows that it is Judas Iscariot who will betray his whereabouts to the Jewish authorities who were after him, Jesus takes no steps to stop him. In fact, according to St John's gospel, he even encourages him with the words:

"That thou doest, do quickly."

John 13:27

Again, later on, when he is in the Garden of Gethsemane, although according to the story he asks for "this cup"[1] to be taken away from him, he makes no attempt to escape, despite the knowledge that he is soon to be arrested. Here, incidentally, we have Jesus' very short and well-known soliloquy faithfully recorded by Mark and followed by Matthew and Luke, who all inform us that not only was Jesus apart by himself, but that his disciples were fast asleep at the time. As Matthew relates, after Jesus had been by himself for some while,

> he came and found them asleep again: for their eyes were heavy. And he left them, and went away again, and prayed the third time, saying the same words. Then cometh he to his disciples, and saith unto them, "Sleep on now, and take your rest: behold, the hour is at hand, and the Son of man is betrayed into the hands of sinners. Rise, let us be going: behold, he is at hand that doth betray me."
>
> *Matthew 26:43-46*

Subsequently, in the synoptics, although Judas greets Jesus with a kiss in order to identify him to the Jewish authorities so that they can arrest him, Jesus still welcomes him as a friend:

> And Jesus said unto him, "Friend, wherefore art thou come?" Then came they, and laid hands on Jesus, and took him.
>
> *Matthew 26:50*

And when one of Jesus' companions, left unnamed in the synoptics but identified in John's gospel as Peter, draws his sword and starts a fight, Jesus tells him to put it away again, saying that if he had wanted it, God could have sent him ample help:

> And, behold, one of them which were with Jesus stretched out his hand, and drew his sword, and struck a servant of the high priest's, and smote off his ear. Then said Jesus unto him, "Put up again thy sword into his place: for all they that take the sword shall perish with the sword. Thinkest thou that I cannot now pray to my Father, and he shall presently give me more than twelve legions of angels?"
>
> *Matthew 26:51-53*

Or, according to the variant account in St John:

> Then said Jesus unto Peter, "Put up thy sword into the sheath: the cup
> which my Father hath given me, shall I not drink it?"
>
> *John 18:11*

Or with a colourful miraculous touch from Luke:

> And Jesus answered and said, "Suffer ye thus far." And he touched his ear,
> and healed him.
>
> *Luke 22:51*

Incidentally, the intelligent Luke, probably thinking that it was unlikely for Jesus' followers to have been carrying arms, makes a rather
dubious provision for it in an earlier part of the narrative:

> And he (Jesus) said unto them, "When I sent you without purse, and
> scrip, and shoes, lacked ye any thing?" And they said, "Nothing".
>
> Then said he unto them, "But now, he that hath a purse, let him take
> it, and likewise his scrip: and he that hath no sword, let him sell his
> garment, and buy one. For I say unto you, that this that is written must
> yet be accomplished in me, 'And he was reckoned among the trans-
> gressors': for the things concerning me have an end."
>
> And they said, "Lord, behold, here are two swords." And he said unto
> them, "It is enough."
>
> *Luke 22:35-38*

In the face of death, then, Jesus is never portrayed as being disturbed,
angry, resentful or vindictive – the common human reactions to such
circumstances. In fact, according to Luke (though the line is missing
from a number of ancient manuscripts), even when nailed to the cross,
Jesus is said to have expressed his forgiveness of those who were so
cruelly treating him:

> Then said Jesus, "Father, forgive them; for they know not what they do."
>
> *Luke 23:24*

Later, again according to Luke, when he died, he did so by a voluntary
act (quoting *Psalm 31*):

> And when Jesus had cried with a loud voice, he said, "Father, into thy hands I commend my spirit": and having said thus, he gave up the ghost.
>
> *Luke 23:46; cf. Psalms 31:5*

And the Roman soldiers were surprised that anyone should have died so rapidly on the cross, in a matter of only six hours.

In Matthew, following Mark, Jesus' last words are a recitation of the twenty-second psalm – a psalm of longing to be with God, that starts, "My God, my God why hast Thou forsaken me". It sounds surprising, but the full context shows it to be more a devotee's longing 'complaint' about his separation from God than a reproach for being really forsaken. John's gospel, it might be added, keeps matters at a mundane level at this point, giving Jesus no dramatic last words but only instructing his 'beloved disciple' to take care of his mother, Mary. A practical and caring human touch, so characteristic of a Master, that somehow rings true.

How authentic all this is, of course, we have no way of knowing, for none of the gospel compilers were eyewitnesses, except perhaps John, but were only writing from hearsay – hence all the variations and accretions to the story. Moreover, would the Romans really have allowed people to go near their execution grounds? If not, then how could anybody have been close enough to hear what Jesus was saying? Indeed, Luke himself records:

> And all his acquaintance, and the women that followed him from Galilee, stood afar off, beholding these things.
>
> *Luke 23:49*

Such difficulties, however, never bothered the compiler of Matthew's gospel for, throughout his narration of the events, he is as intent as ever on one of his primary aims: demonstrating that Jesus was the Jewish Messiah, according to his interpretations of their sacred writings. As he asserts after relating the story of Jesus' arrest:

> But all this was done, that the scriptures of the prophets might be fulfilled.
>
> *Matthew 26:56*

Yet, whatever the actual events of Jesus' last days, one common thread runs through all the variant narratives: Jesus was fully aware of his impending death and it did not trouble him. In their own different ways, all the stories demonstrate that he remained loving and forgiving to the last, never losing his cool, the epitome of non-violence in all his words and deeds. This is the attitude of a mystic and of a deeply spiritual man. No one else could have adopted such an attitude, for his mind would simply not have permitted him.

A Setting Free from the Body

This enlightened attitude to death is brought out very clearly in the apocryphal literature. In the *Acts of Thomas*, for example, when Judas Thomas is about to meet his end, like Jesus, he also speaks of death as something which he could avoid if he so desired, but to which he is actually looking forward. For not only will he be set free from the body, but he will also meet the radiant, spiritual form of his Master, inside, and reap the harvest of his labours:

> For if I had willed not to die,
>   ye know that I am able to do so.
> But this which is called death, is not death,
>   but a setting free from the body;
> Wherefore I receive gladly
>   this setting free from the body,
>   that I may depart and see him
>   that is beautiful and full of mercy,
>   him that I love, him who is my Beloved:
> For I have toiled much in his service,
>   and have laboured for his grace that hath supported me,
>   and which departeth not from me.
>
> *Acts of Thomas* 160, AAA pp.291-292, ANT p.434

And he advises those around him to seek the inner form of Jesus:

> Look for the coming of Christ,
>   for he shall come and receive you,
>   and this is he whom ye shall see when he cometh.
>
> *Acts of Thomas* 160, ANT p.434

So it is with all those disciples who have devotedly attended to their spiritual practice throughout their life. In many instances, the inner Master will have informed them some time in advance of their impending departure and they look forward to it with joyful anticipation.

Raised from the Dead

Jesus must have been so happy to have left his maimed body and returned to his heavenly Father. Yet orthodox Christian belief has it that
he rose from the dead in his physical body on the third day after his
crucifixion. But why should a soul who had just escaped from the
prison of the body want to re-enter it once again? What would have
been the practical advantage in it? What then do mystics mean when
they talk of 'rising from the dead'?

It has been described how repetition of the words given by a Master
leads a soul through the gates of death while still living in the body.
Now since mystics have characteristically spoken of this world as the
realm of the dead and have described its inhabitants as being dead, it
is understandable that being taken up from here into the land of the
living and going through the experience of dying while living was commonly called being raised from the dead. It is a resurrection – not *of* –
but *from* the body. This is the real and mystic meaning of resurrection
and rising from the dead.

Resurrection of physical bodies on some distant Day of Judgment is
a religious idea originating in the ancient Middle East. The belief existed long before Christianity, being a tenet of Zoroastrianism.
Mithraism, too, one of the most prevalent of the many Roman religions or cults which spread throughout the empire from the Middle
East to Britain, also taught the resurrection of the dead on some far-
off Day of Judgment. It was also held by the Pharisaic side of Judaism,
and Paul, having been raised as a Pharisee, firmly believed in it, making it a part of early Christianity in the non-Jewish world. He brings it
into his letters on many occasions and it is almost certainly he who is
largely responsible for its presence in Christianity today.

 But it was a concept introduced when the real meaning of being
raised from the dead had been forgotten. It is, once again, an
externalization of an inward spiritual truth, and many early Christians did not accept it, especially the more truly mystical amongst
them. Indeed, even Paul's teaching on the subject is that the resurrection body will be of an etherealized or spiritualized nature that turns
the "corruptible" physical form into an immortal one. The resurrection body will not, he wrote, be made of the same physical substance
as the present body:

> Behold, I shew you a mystery;
> We shall not all sleep,

but we shall all be changed, in a moment,
   in the twinkling of an eye, at the last trump:
For the trumpet shall sound,
   and the dead shall be raised incorruptible,
   and we shall be changed.
For this corruptible (body) must put on incorruption,
   and this mortal (body) must put on immortality.

                   1 Corinthians 15:51-53

This, of course, has a mystical air about it, but it is still essentially physical, and many Christians, then and now, being at the material level, have understood the resurrection to be entirely physical in character. Yet significant numbers amongst the early Christians understood the real meaning of dying while living, of being raised from the dead, and of spiritual ascension and resurrection, to be entirely mystical. And this is the way they interpreted Jesus' teachings on the subject. It will be remembered that Jesus said:

Marvel not at this: for the hour is coming,
   in the which all that are in the graves
   shall hear his Voice, and shall come forth;
They that have done good,
   unto the resurrection of life;
And they that have done evil,
   unto the resurrection of damnation.

                   John 5:28-29

Everybody will die. Those who have "done good" – those who have heard the Voice of God within will go back to God. This is the "resurrection of life". They will be raised up from the "grave" of the body. And those who have "done evil", who have simply increased their load of sins, will experience the "resurrection of damnation" – they will be condemned to rebirth in this world. They will be resurrected or returned to physical life in another body. Likewise, Jesus says:

Verily, verily, I say unto you,
   he that heareth my Word,
   and believeth on Him that sent me, hath everlasting life,
   and shall not come into condemnation;
But is passed from death unto life.

> Verily, verily, I say unto you,
>> the hour is coming, and now is,
>> when the dead shall hear the Voice of the Son of God:
> And they that hear shall live.
>
> *John 5:24-25*

And:

> Verily, verily, I say unto you,
>> if a man keep my saying, he shall never see death.
>
> *John 8:51*

But these and a number of other similar extracts have already been discussed in an earlier context and we will confine ourselves in this chapter to further passages which demonstrate the mystical meaning of resurrection from the dead.

To begin with, it is clear that the mystics have described life in the body as living in a tomb or a grave. That the body "temple" has become a "tomb" for the soul is made evident in the *Teachings of Silvanus*. He counsels a reversal of the process:

> You were a temple, but you have made yourself a tomb. Cease being a tomb, and become again a temple, so that uprightness and divinity may be restored to you.
>
> *Teachings of Silvanus 106, TS p.57*

Similarly, in the *Second Apocalypse of James*, James begs to be brought out "alive" from the "tomb" of the body, the domain of "sin", the "Enemy" or the "Judge":

> Save me from an evil death!
> Bring me from a tomb alive....
> Save me from sinful flesh,
>> because I trusted in you with all my strength!
> Because you are the life of the life,
>> save me from a humiliating Enemy!
> Do not give me into the hand of a Judge
>> who is severe with sin!
>
> *Second Apocalypse of James 63, NHS11 p.147*

This petition is addressed to Jesus, for it is always the Master to whom the devotee looks for help in being raised from such a grave. Hence, in the *Books of the Saviour*, Matthew interprets a line from one of the *Odes of Solomon* to mean:

> Thou hast freed them from the graves
> and hast removed them from the midst of the corpses.
>
> *Pistis Sophia 71, PS p.158, PSGG p.131*

The soul who is so raised is "removed" from the company of "corpses", the spiritually dead people of this worldly graveyard.

Mystics, then, see the people of this world as the dead. In order to find true spiritual life, they advise us to learn how to pass through the process of actual physical death while still living. Their language is consequently full of double meanings and many people are confused by it. It is not surprising, therefore, that in the *Apocryphon of James*, a passage which has been taken by some scholars as an exhortation to physical martyrdom, would actually appear to be nothing of the sort. When Jesus advises that we "become seekers of death" his meaning is mystical, not physical. We are the "dead who seek for life", he says, by endeavouring to go through the process of dying while living:

> Become seekers of death, like the dead who seek for life; for that which they seek is revealed to them. And what is there to trouble them? As for you, when you examine death, it will teach you election. Verily I say unto you, none of those who fear death will be saved; for the kingdom of God belongs to those who put themselves to death. Become better than I; make yourselves like the Son of the Holy Spirit!
>
> *Apocryphon of James 6, NHS22 p.37*

He says that if you "examine death", if you confront death and through mystic experience come to know what it is, then it will teach you "election" – how to rise up from the body and go back to God. The people of the world, "those who fear death", he says, will never be saved. Only those who "put themselves to death", who learn after great effort in meditation to withdraw the mind and soul from the body and pass into the higher worlds, will be able to find the "kingdom of God". Only in this way can they become "like the Son of the Holy Spirit".

The meaning is the same when a Manichaean-Christian psalmist writes:

> He that dies lives,
>> he that labours (in meditation) has his rest.
>>> *Psalms, MPB p.159*

And likewise, in a protracted allegorical tale in the *Acts of John*, a young man who has been turned back from his degenerate way of life by a vision and by the intervention of John, says to him:

> I would become one of them that hope on Christ,
>> that the Voice may prove true which said to me,
>> "Die that thou mayest live":
>
> And that Voice hath also fulfilled its effect,
>> for he is dead – that faithless, disorderly,
>> godless one (that I was) –
> And I have been raised by thee,
>> I who will be faithful, God-fearing,
>> knowing the Truth,
>> which I entreat thee may be shown me by thee.
>>> *Acts of John 76, ANT p.247*

The "Voice", the divine Music, by drawing a soul out of the body while the individual is still living in this world, is the Power which permits the person to die while living, to "die that thou mayest live". The "Voice" also purifies the soul of all lower tendencies. Thus, dying while living also means dying to the old self and being raised up by a mystic through the process of meditation.

As we have seen before, the 'dead' of this world have also been commonly called those who 'sleep'. Hence, Judas Thomas says, enigmatically, in the *Acts of Thomas*:

> Lo, I sleep and awake,
>> and I shall no more go to sleep;
> Lo, I die and live again,
>> and I shall no more taste of death.
>>> *Acts of Thomas 142, ANT p.427*

He means that death, euphemistically called sleep, will bring an awakening to a higher Reality, after which he will no longer have to return to this world and undergo the sleep of materiality nor ever again experience death. More plainly, in the *Acts of John*, the soul is exhorted:

Awake, thou also, and open thy soul.
Cast off the heavy sleep from thee.

Acts of John 21, ANT p.230

Paul, too, uses the same metaphor, contrasting the sleep, darkness and drunkenness of the world with the wakefulness, light and sobriety of spirituality:

Ye are all the children of light,
  and the children of the day:
  we are not of the night, nor of darkness.
Therefore let us not sleep, as do others;
  but let us watch and be sober.
For they that sleep, sleep in the night;
  and they that be drunken are drunken in the night.
But let us, who are of the day, be sober.

1 Thessalonians 5:5-8

And quoting a text that has never been identified, he also writes:

Wherefore he saith, "Awake thou that sleepest,
  and arise from the dead,
  and Christ shall give thee light."

Ephesians 5:14

Using the same metaphor, the author of the *Psalms of Solomon* makes the question personal, addressing himself:

Why do you sleep, my soul,
  and why do you not bless the Lord?

Psalms of Solomon III:1, AOT p.658

And again, making it evident that the sleep of the soul is to be equated with being "far from God":

When my soul slumbered, away from the Lord,
  I almost slipped in the lethargy
  of the sleep of those far from God –
My soul was almost poured out to death,
  close to the gates of Sheol, alongside the sinner,

> with my soul separated from the Lord God....
> had not the Lord succoured me in his everlasting mercy.
>
> He goaded me, as a horse is spurred,
>   to awaken me to Him,
>   my Saviour and Helper at all times saved me.
>
> *Psalms of Solomon XVI:1-4, AOT p.675*

A devotee will always give credit to his Master, his "Saviour and Helper at all times", for his release from "sleep" and "death". Judas Thomas does the same:

> Glory be to thee, the Defender and Helper
>   of them that come unto thy refuge!
> That sleepest not, and awakest them that are asleep,
>   that livest and givest life to them that lie in death!
>
> *Acts of Thomas 60, ANT p.393*

A Master is awake to God. He is truly alive. He also has the power to awaken "them that sleep" and to give "life to them that lie in death". This is the true, mystic resurrection.

Expecting a Resurrection that is Empty

There is no doubt that many of the earliest Christians did not believe in a physical resurrection of any kind. In a number of Paul's letters, for example, he speaks of other Christian teachers who disagreed with his interpretations. And though we never hear their side of the story and cannot always determine the exact nature of the controversy, some kind of answer is found in the *Acts of Paul*. Speaking of Paul's letters to the Corinthians, we read:

> There were certain men come to Corinth, Simon and Cleobius, saying:
> "There is no resurrection of the flesh, but that of the spirit only."
>
> *Acts of Paul III:VII, ANT p.288*

It must be remembered that such differences of opinion were present from the earliest times. Paul was active in the 50s and 60s AD when many of Jesus' direct disciples were still alive, both in Palestine and elsewhere, and they would never have believed Paul in preference to their own Master. Amongst the disciples of Jesus, Paul's position always seems to have been that of an outsider.

Similarly, the New Testament letter, *2 Timothy*, written as if from Paul but probably an early second-century composition, even names two of those who rejected the doctrine of physical resurrection:

> Avoid empty and worldly chatter (*i.e.* intellectual speculation); those who indulge in it will stray further and further into godless courses, and the infection of their teaching will spread like gangrene. Such are Hymenaeus and Philetus; they have shot wide of the truth in saying that our resurrection has already taken place, and are upsetting people's faith.
>
> *2 Timothy 2:16-18, NHL p.4*

The exact nature of the resurrection has remained a subject of recurrent debate in Christianity. Origen, for example, did not take the belief in a crudely material sense. He considered that resurrection was a subject,

> deep and hard to explain, and needs a wise man of advanced skill more than any other doctrine in order to show that it is worthy of God and that the doctrine is a noble conception.
>
> *Origen, Against Celsus VII:32, OCC p.420*

Upon which he expanded:

> Anyone interested should realize that we require a body (here) for various purposes because we are in a material place, and so it needs to be of the same character as that of the nature of the material place.... But in order to know God we need no body at all. The knowledge of God is not derived from the eye of the body, but from the mind (soul) which sees that which is in the image of the Creator and by divine providence has received the power to know God.
>
> *Origen, Against Celsus VII:33, OCC p.421*

Again, indicating that the more subtle forms within still bear a resemblance to the physical form in some respects though of an altogether more spiritual nature, Origen writes:

> It is necessary for the soul that is existing in corporeal places to use bodies appropriate to those places. Just as if we became aquatic beings, and had to live in the sea, it would be no doubt necessary for us to adopt a different

state similar to that of the fish, so if we are to inherit the kingdom of
heaven and to exist in superior (higher, heavenly) places, it is essential for
us to use spiritual bodies. This does not mean that the form of the earlier
body disappears, though it may change to a more glorious condition.

Origen, On Resurrection I:22.4-5, OCC p.420

Origen is clearly speaking of the ascent of the soul through what in
modern times are termed the astral and causal bodies, and the soul's
own innate 'garment' of light, and this is fundamentally in accord with
the teachings of the mystics. As might be expected, it was the gnostic
or esoteric side of Christianity which characteristically rejected the idea
of the resurrection as something crudely physical. The early Christian
father, Tertullian (*fl.*190-220 AD), seems to have believed in an entirely physical form of resurrection and in *On the 'Prescription' of Heretics,* he speaks reproachfully of the second-century gnostics, "Marcion
... and Apelles and Valentinus who all impugn the resurrection of the
flesh".[2] In another treatise attributed to him, *Against All Heresies,*
though this text is normally held to be pseudonymous, the writer says
of Basilides, "the resurrection of the flesh he strenuously impugns, af-
firming that salvation has not been promised to bodies";[3] and of Cerdo,
"a resurrection of the soul merely does he approve, denying that of the
body".[4] The same writer also lists a certain Marcus and Colarbasus[5] as
rejecting the doctrine of a physical resurrection, though little else is
known of them except that they also held gnostic views disapproved
of by the heresy-hunting fathers.

To this inventory, Irenaeus also adds Simon Magus and Carpocrates.[6] And the mid-second-century father, Justin Martyr, castigates
"some who are called Christians, but are godless, impious heretics,
teach(ing) doctrines that are in every way blasphemous, atheistical and
foolish"[7] and "who say there is no resurrection of the dead, and that
their souls, when they die, are taken to heaven".[8]

The list of names, of course, is but the tip of the iceberg and is only
an indication of how widespread was the stream of Christian belief
that ran counter to the strictures of those who considered themselves
'orthodox'. The general consensus of these groups was that the resurrection was to be understood as an ascent of the soul, not the body.

One of the more explicit gnostic references to the spiritual under-
standing of resurrection is quoted and paraphrased in the works of
Hippolytus. According to Hippolytus, the gnostic writer of a
Naassene text quotes from St Matthew when describing the resurrec-

tion as the ascent of the soul from the grave of the body through the "gate of heaven":

> Again, he exclaims, "the dead shall start forth from the graves",[9] that is, from the earthly bodies, being born again spiritual, not carnal. For this, he says, is the resurrection that takes place through the gate of heaven, through which, he says, all those that do not enter remain dead. ... For he says, (man) becomes a god when, having risen from the dead, he will enter into heaven through a gate of this kind.
>
> Paul, the apostle, he says, knew of this gate, partially opening (revealing) it in a mystery (an allusion), and stating "that he was caught up by an angel, and ascended as far as the second and third heaven into paradise itself; and that he beheld sights and heard unspeakable words which it would not be possible for man to declare."[10]
>
> These are, he says, what are called by all the secret mysteries, "which (also we speak), not in words taught of human wisdom, but in those taught of the Spirit."[11]
>
> *Hippolytus, Refutation of All Heresies V:III, RAH pp.143-144*

This is precisely as we have presented matters. A little later, says Hippolytus, the Naassene writer adds that only the inwardly pure can enter this gate of spiritual resurrection:

> And into this (gate), he says, no unclean person shall enter, nor one that is natural and carnal; but it is reserved for the spiritual only.
>
> *Hippolytus, Refutation of All Heresies V:III, RAH pp.147-148*

With such enticing fragments, the story might have been concluded were it not for the discovery of the texts comprising the Nag Hammadi library, which has fortuitously furnished us with some direct examples of the gnostic beliefs concerning resurrection. The writer of the *Gospel of Philip*, for instance, is explicit:

> Those who say that the Lord died first and then rose up are in error, for he rose up first and then died.
>
> *Gospel of Philip 56, NHS20 p.153*

He says that Jesus did not die and then arise in his physical body. He ascended inwardly to the higher regions during his lifetime – and then died. Therefore, he adds:

> Those who say they will die first and then rise are in error. If they do not first receive the resurrection while they live, when they die they will receive nothing.
>
> *Gospel of Philip 73, NHS20 p.189*

And also:

> While we are in this world it is fitting for us to acquire the resurrection, so that when we strip off the flesh we may be found in rest.
>
> *Gospel of Philip 66, NHS20 p.173*

Whatever has to be achieved has to be achieved now. If somebody does not learn how to rise into the higher realms during life, how can they expect to suddenly acquire the ability after death? The author of the *Testimony of Truth* repeats the same thing:

> Some say, "On the last day we will certainly arise in the resurrection." But they do not know what they are saying.... Do not expect, therefore, the carnal resurrection....
>
> They err in expecting a resurrection that is empty.... [They do] not [know] the Power [of God], nor do they [understand how to interpret] the scriptures [on account of their] double-mindedness (confusion of thought).... [Those who do not have] the life-giving [Word] in their [heart will die].... [We have been born] again by [the Word].
>
> *Testimony of Truth 34-35,36-37,40, NHS15 pp.135-145*

He implies that only those who "know the Power of God", the "life-giving Word" and have been "born again" can come to know what is really meant by "resurrection". Other gnostic writers are specific as to the actual nature of the true spiritual resurrection:

> It is fitting that the soul regenerate herself and become again as she formerly was. The soul then moves of her own accord (becomes a free soul), and – for her rejuvenation – she has received the divine nature from the Father, so that she might be restored to the place where originally she had been. This is the resurrection from the dead. This is the ransom from captivity. This is the upward journey of ascent to heaven. This is the way of ascent to the Father.
>
> *Expository Treatise on the Soul 134, NHS21 pp.159-161*

The soul, he says, must regain knowledge of her divine nature, of who she really is and must return to her original home, the "place where originally she had been". "*This* is the resurrection from the dead." It is also being ransomed from the captivity of this world and the true spiritual ascent through the inner heavens back to God. As another writer says:

> But the resurrection ... is the revelation of what is, and the transformation of things, and a transition into newness.
>
> *Treatise on the Resurrection 48, NHS22 p.155*

And again:

> We are drawn to heaven by him (our Saviour, the Lord Christ),
>   like beams by the sun, not being restrained by anything.
> This is the spiritual resurrection.
>
> *Treatise on the Resurrection 45, NHS22 p.151*

Resurrection, then, is the spiritual or mystic ascent of the soul from the body – not a raising of dead bodies whose atoms have long since been recycled by natural processes.

In the *Acts of Paul*, the term is given an interesting slant: resurrection in a new body is equated with reincarnation, souls being resurrected in the children of future generations:

> And we will teach thee of that resurrection which he asserteth, that it is already come to pass in the children which we have, and we rise again when we have come to the knowledge of the true God.
>
> *Acts of Paul II:14, ANT p.275*

But the writer also adds that coming to mystic knowledge or *gnosis* of God is the true rising from the dead. In the *Apocryphon of James*, it is reiterated that the Spirit raises the soul, bringing life to it, while its encounters with the body only serve to entrap it in the realm of death:

> It is the Spirit that raises the soul,
>   but the body that kills it.
> *Apocryphon of James 12, NHS22 p.47*

And amongst the Mandaean writings, the terminology of 'rising up' is used again and again for the rising up of the soul to the eternal realm:

> Rise up, rise up, soul,
>   ascend to thy First Homeland!

> Rise, rise to thy First Homeland,
> > the place from which thou wast transplanted,
> > to the place from which thou wast transplanted,
> > to thy good dwelling, the dwelling of 'uthras (pure souls),
>
> Bestir thyself! Don thy garment of glory
> > and set on thy living wreath.
> Rise! inhabit the skintas (inner realms)
> > amongst the 'uthras thy brethren.
>
> *CPM 94 pp.97-98*

And likewise:

> Good one! Rise to the House of Life!
> And go to the everlasting abode!
> They will hang thy lamp amongst lamps of light.
>
> *CPM 92 pp.96-97*

Jesus, then, neither rose from the dead in his physical body, nor did that physical form later ascend to the skies in a physical manner, nor are the dead awaiting a day on which they will all rise from their graves. The disciples did, no doubt, see their Master within themselves after he had departed, and he may even have appeared to them outside. But that would have been his spiritual, light form, a form so beautiful and pure, emanating so much love, that no soul who sees it can resist its attraction.

NOTES AND REFERENCES

1. *Mark* 14:36.
2. Tertullian, *On the 'Prescription' of Heretics* XXXIII, *TTSPH* p.80.
3. Pseudo-Tertullian, *Against All Heresies* I, *WTIII* p.261.
4. Pseudo-Tertullian, *Against All Heresies* VI, *WTIII* p.269.
5. Pseudo-Tertullian, *Against All Heresies* V, *WTIII* p.269.
6. Irenaeus, *Against Heresies* II:XXXI, *AHI* p.241.
7. Justin Martyr, *Dialogue with Trypho* LXXX, *WJMA* p.199.
8. Justin Martyr, *Dialogue with Trypho* LXXX, *WJMA* pp.199-200.
9. *Matthew* 27:52-53.
10. *2 Corinthians* 12:2.
11. *1 Corinthians* 2:13.

CHAPTER TWENTY-THREE

The Second Coming and The Comforter

Till They See the Son of Man Coming

For nearly two thousand years, Christians have awaited the second coming of Jesus. Many of the earliest Christians, including Paul and the compilers of the synoptic gospels, expected him to return during their own lifetimes. Clearly intending it to mean the end of the world according to apocalyptic expectations, Matthew presents Jesus as saying:

> Verily I say unto you, there be some standing here,
>> which shall not taste of death,
>> till they see the Son of man coming in his kingdom.
>
> *Matthew 16:28*

And Luke places a similar saying in his version of the mini-apocalypse:

> Verily I say unto you,
>> this generation shall not pass away,
>> till all be fulfilled.
>
> *Luke 21:32*

But Jesus did not come in the way they expected, nor is there any evidence that he ever will. Evidently, either their beliefs were wrong, or Jesus himself was mistaken, or these sayings were never actually uttered by him, or he meant something entirely different. Many Christians admit that a convincing explanation is hard to find. Our suggestion is that in sayings such as these, Jesus was referring to the disciples' inner meeting, during their own lifetime, with the spiritual form of their Master. But not all disciples will achieve this during their lifetime, before they "taste of death". "There be *some* standing here," said Jesus, not *all*.

That the 'second coming' of Jesus is in a spiritual form is reiterated throughout the early Christian texts. In the *Epistula Apostolorum*, for example, which contains a post-resurrection dialogue between Jesus and his disciples, they ask him how he will appear at his second coming. He replies:

> Truly I say to you, I will come as does the sun that shines, and shining seven times brighter than it in my brightness; with the wings of the clouds carrying me in splendour and the sign of the cross before me, I will come down to the earth to judge the living and the dead.
>
> *Epistula Apostolorum (Coptic) 17, OG p.141*

Though this early document promotes the orthodox Christian belief regarding the second coming, it nevertheless demonstrates the understanding that the form in which Jesus would 'come again' was bright and spiritual beyond all comparison.

The Inner or Light Form

The real second coming is a practical and personal affair. When the attention of the mind and soul are fully withdrawn from the world and from the body, when they have focused completely at the single eye, then the attention need travel only a little further inward before, on the threshold of the astral worlds, the disciple meets the radiant form of the Master. Like the physical form, the astral form is a projection of the Word. At whatever level the disciple is, so the Master takes a form appropriate to that level.

If the disciple has found the physical form to be beautiful beyond all other human forms, that is nothing compared to the light, the beauty, the radiance and the love that surround and emanate from the Master as he is seen on the inner planes. From this point onwards, the disciple knows from experience that he is never alone. He gazes at his Master with utterly rapt attention. He can seek and receive any guidance he desires. He can ask any question, communicating mind to mind and soul to soul. He is utterly content and enfolded in love and bliss. There is nothing that can compare with this experience; and it is the longing for this meeting which ultimately drives and draws a disciple to attend assiduously to meditation. As he rises up through the body towards this point, he realizes increasingly that his Master is always with him. Yet the veil of his own mind still lies between. But when he meets that radiant form of light, then he sees face to face.

The 'first coming', then, is the meeting with the physical Master.
The 'second coming' is the encounter with the inner Master. And although the references in the synoptic gospels may be ambiguous, this
meaning is made abundantly clear in St John when Jesus bids farewell
to his disciples.

Jesus' Farewell Discourses

Like so many parts of St John, these farewell discourses seem to be in a
muddle, particularly chapters fourteen and sixteen. The meaning is
clear enough, but a number of the sayings are repeated, the sequence
often seeming to backtrack unnecessarily, and many scholars have suggested that they are not in their original form or order. It is also possible that the gospel compiler tried rather unsuccessfully to combine
two versions of the same discourse into one. Whatever happened, taking great care not to alter the meaning, we have attempted here to
bring some sequence to these two chapters by a gentle reordering of
the sayings into one continuous discourse. This rearrangement can be
followed by those who are interested by examining the references to
each quotation.

Jesus begins by letting his disciples know that he will soon be leaving them, as far as his physical form is concerned:

> Little children, yet a little while I am with you.
> Ye shall seek me: ...
> (but) whither I go, thou canst not follow me now;
> But thou shalt follow me afterwards.
>
> *John 13:33,36*

As Jesus has previously said, he is returning to his Father, to God. And
although the disciples cannot follow him immediately because they
have not yet made sufficient spiritual progress, they will be able to
follow and meet with him again, later on. He then consoles them and
indicates where he will be meeting with them:

> Let not your heart be troubled:
> ye believe in God, believe also in me.
> In my Father's house are many mansions:
> if it were not so, I would have told you.
> I go to prepare a place for you.
> And if I go and prepare a place for you,

> I will come again, and receive you unto myself;
> that where I am, there ye may be also.
>
> *John 14:1-3*

He is going to prepare a place for them in the inner "mansions", in the heavenly regions. And naturally, if he is going to prepare a place for them inside, he is the one who will "come again, and receive you unto myself". He will come and take them there – and the form in which he comes will, of course, be a form that is suited to those regions. The physical form he has left here – the form in which he will come to them will be of a more subtle and radiant character altogether. He then adds:

> And whither I go ye know, and the way ye know.
>
> *John 14:4*

They know that he has the power to return to God and he has also taught them the path and techniques of spiritual practice, the "way" in which they can follow after him – by knocking at his door, by passing through the "strait gate" and so on. He then reiterates:

> Yet a little while, and the world seeth me no more;
> but ye see me: because I live, ye shall live also.
> At that day ye shall know that I am in my Father,
> and ye in me, and I in you.
>
> *John 14:19-20*

Soon, he says, he will have departed from the world, and the people of the world will not be able to see him again. As far as they are concerned, he will be dead and gone. But his disciples will be able to see him. Because Jesus has attained realization of the immortal life with God, so will his disciples also be able to achieve this spiritual estate. And when they attain this, then "ye shall know that I am in my Father, and ye in me, and I in you." Then they will know from their own experience rather than by faith and intuition that he is really one with God, that he is within them and that they will eventually attain union with him, that they will all become one.

But how are they to really reach this level of spiritual attainment? It is, he says, by love and obedience to his "commandments":

> If ye love me, keep my commandments.
> He that hath my commandments, and keepeth them,

he it is that loveth me:
And he that loveth me shall be loved of my Father,
    and I will love him, and will manifest myself to him.
If a man love me, he will keep my words:
    and my Father will love him, and we will come unto him,
    and make our ábode with him.
He that loveth me not keepeth not my sayings:
    (and the word which ye hear is not mine,
    but the Father's which sent me).

John 14:15,21,23,24

One who loves his Master will implicitly follow his instructions, for he realizes that they are given for his own spiritual benefit. And if he follows those instructions out of love for his Master, he will draw down upon himself the love of God. And when the disciple's love is sufficiently pure, then, says Jesus, "I will love him, and will manifest myself to him" and also, "we will come unto him and make our abode with him". He will appear within that disciple, manifesting himself in his radiant, spiritual form.

But one who does not love the Master will not obey him, for the only obedience he asks is one that springs from love. He will not fine a disciple or punish him in any way if he does not follow what he says. There is absolutely no coercion or compulsion of any kind, neither material, nor emotional, nor psychological. The only 'compulsion' is that of the disciple wanting to please the one he loves and of the longing to see the Master in his radiant form. In fact, Jesus adds that it is not him they are obeying, but the "Father which sent me". As he said before, his "sayings" or his teachings were not his own, but were of God.

Jesus then speaks again of the disciples' meeting with his radiant form, this time calling it the "Comforter":

And I will pray the Father,
    and he shall give you another Comforter,
    that he may abide with you for ever;
Even the Spirit of Truth; whom the world cannot receive,
    because it seeth him not, neither knoweth him:
    but ye know him;
For he dwelleth with you, and shall be in you.
I will not leave you comfortless: I will come to you.

John 14:16-18

The "Comforter" is translated from the Greek, *Parakletos*, the Paraclete, other words used to translate this term being Advocate, Intercessor, Intermediary, Counsellor, Protector, Helper and Support. They all convey something of the nature and function of the Word and its manifestation in the spiritual form of the Master. The physical Master will die one day, but the inner form will "abide with you for ever". It is manifested out of the Word, the "Spirit of Truth". But this form cannot come to the people of the world, because they are not acquainted with the true Word of God. "But ye know him," says Jesus, speaking of this mystic Comforter, "for he dwelleth with you, and shall be in you."

Then he again assures his disciples – not the whole world – that although the Master may die and leave his disciples, physically, "I will not leave you comfortless: I will come to you." He will be with them and manifest himself to them in a higher form. There can be no other reasonable interpretation of these sayings. Jesus is identifying his light form with the Spirit, making it personal when he says, "I will come to you". Then, once more, he repeats himself:

> These things have I spoken unto you,
>   being yet present with you.
> But the Comforter, which is the Holy Ghost,
>   whom the Father will send in my name,
>   he shall teach you all things,
>   and bring all things to your remembrance,
>   whatsoever I have said unto you.
>
> *John 14:25-26*

The radiant form of the Master, the "Comforter" – manifested out of the "Holy Ghost" – will "teach all things to you". There are many things concerning the inner spiritual journey which cannot be conveyed in human words. Nor is it even necessary for disciples to know about them until they reach that point. One thing at a time, then move on to the next. The inner Master and the Word will teach the secrets of creation and the road back to God, when and where it is required. The Master could tell his disciples so much concerning the beauties of the inner regions and so many other wonderful things but, being below the level of the single eye centre, they are still insufficiently advanced along the path to be able to understand. So he only gives them the broad outline and waits until the appropriate moment before other things can be revealed.

Jesus also says that the constant ringing of the heavenly Music at all times of the day or night will "bring all things to your remembrance". It will be a constant inner reminder of the path that the Master has taught, and will keep the mind on a tight rein, ready at all times to go within, whenever the opportunity comes. As he also said:

> I have yet many things to say unto you,
>> but ye cannot bear them now.
>
> *John 16:12*

The Master has many things to show a disciple that he could never dream of, that are beyond the comprehension of the human mind. All these, he will show to the disciple when they travel together through the inner regions and return to God. He continues:

> Howbeit when he, the Spirit of Truth, is come,
>> he will guide you into all truth:
> For he shall not speak of himself;
>> but whatsoever he shall hear, that shall he speak:
>> and he will shew you things to come.
>
> *John 16:13*

As he has said before, whatever the spiritual form of the Master, the Spirit of Truth, teaches or shows to the disciple, either inside or outside, all comes directly from God. He does not invent it out of his own thinking or imagination. Then he says:

> He shall glorify me: for he shall receive of mine,
>> and shall shew it unto you.
> All things that the Father hath are mine:
>> therefore said I, that he shall take of mine,
>> and shall shew it unto you.
>
> *John 16:14-15*

"Of mine" are the chosen souls of the Master. The Spirit will take these souls and show all these marvels to them. And the Spirit "shall glorify" the Master – the disciples will become aware of who the Master really is, in all his true glory. For these chosen souls are in reality the Father's chosen ones, and it is He – through the Master or the Spirit – who reveals everything to them.

And in that day ye shall ask me nothing.
Verily, verily, I say unto you,
    whatsoever ye shall ask the Father in my name,
    he will give it you.
Hitherto have ye asked nothing in my name:
    ask, and ye shall receive, that your joy may be full.
And whatsoever ye shall ask in my name, that will I do,
    that the Father may be glorified in the Son.
If ye shall ask any thing in my name, I will do it.

John 16:23-24, 14:13-14

On the day when the disciple meets the radiant form of his Master inside, he will have nothing to ask. When still outside in the world, a disciple may have many doubts and questions. Sometimes he may even wonder if the Master and his teachings are just another fraud, like so much else. But when he experiences the inner meeting, then all his doubts disappear and he has nothing to ask, because everything becomes clear. All his deepest desires and longings are fulfilled in that meeting. Whatever a soul could ever dream of asking for is already fulfilled and even more than that.

Nevertheless, he says that whatever a disciple asks for will be granted, because he knows that by the time a disciple reaches this level he is only concerned with the things of the Spirit. The Master has the power to grant any request, but the advanced disciple only wants more and more of the spiritual reality to be revealed to him. It is this that he asks for and this that he receives. He then adds:

These things have I spoken unto you in proverbs:
    but the time cometh,
    when I shall no more speak unto you in proverbs,
    but I shall shew you plainly of the Father.
At that day ye shall ask in my name:
    and I say not unto you,
    that I will pray the Father for you.

John 16:25-26

In this world, he says, everything has to be described "in proverbs", by metaphor and example, because words are inadequate to convey the nature of the inner reality. But in the inner realms, everything can be seen "plainly" – by direct experience and perception. Moreover, in this world, a Master avoids many of the questions that his disciples ask, because they are unanswerable. So he says that they will have to ask the Father about it when they reach Him, or he sidesteps the question in some other way. But in that world, answers can be given, for the spiritual consciousness is advanced enough for the answer to be contained and comprehended. And that 'answer' is given by way of direct mystic revelation, not in human words.

> For the Father himself loveth you,
>> because ye have loved me,
>> and have believed that I came out from God.
> I came forth from the Father, and am come into the world:
>> again, I leave the world, and go to the Father.
> I am not alone, because the Father is with me.
>
> *John 16:26-27,32*

All this happens, he says, because God loves each and every individual soul. Through their love for the Master, the disciples have entered the sphere of divine love. They now experience the love of God within themselves. And that experience has grown out of the faith and realization that their Master has come from God and is always with them. It is faith and love which has led them to this mystic understanding. He says:

> These things I have spoken unto you,
>> that in me ye might have peace.
> In the world ye shall have tribulation:
>> but be of good cheer; I have overcome the world.
>
> *John 16:33*

Jesus points out that he is only saying all of this for their benefit and peace of mind. Although they may have to undergo various forms of suffering in this world, they should not be too perturbed, for he has "overcome the world" – he has overcome the Negative Power and will bestow the fruits of that conquest upon them, too. He continues:

> Peace I leave with you, my peace I give unto you:
>> not as the world giveth, give I unto you.
> Let not your heart be troubled,
>> neither let it be afraid.
>
> *John 14:27*

He is again comforting them, saying that although he is leaving them,
he has something to give them which is far beyond anything the world
has to offer. The joy and peace which will come from their meeting
with the inner Master has no comparison in this world. So they have
absolutely nothing to fear. He then says:

> Ye have heard how I said unto you,
>> I go away, and come again unto you.
> If ye loved me, ye would rejoice,
>> because I said, "I go unto the Father":
>> for my Father is greater than I.
> But now I go my way to Him that sent me;
>> and none of you asketh me,
> "Whither goest thou?"
>> *John 14:28, 16:5*

He says that although they may feel unhappy at the thought of his
impending departure, yet if they really thought about what he had
told them, then they would "rejoice". They would be happy that he is
able to leave the world forever and return to his Father. He is returning to God and requests that no one should ask him to remain here.
And he adds that he has told them of his departure, and of his return
to them in his radiant form, so that when it actually happens to them,
they may not think that they are just imagining things:

> And now I have told you before it come to pass,
>> that, when it is come to pass, ye might believe.
>> *John 14:29*

Until an individual has experienced something, there will always be an
element of doubt about its reality or at least a lack of full understanding concerning its real nature. Therefore, Jesus says that the "Comforter" will be the "witness", the proof that everything he has said is true:

> But when the Comforter is come,
>> whom I will send unto you from the Father,
>> even the Spirit of Truth,
>> which proceedeth from the Father,
>> he shall testify of me:
> And ye also shall bear witness,
>> because ye have been with me from the beginning.
>> *John 15:26-27*

"From the beginning" means from the time of their initiation. When a disciple has been initiated for some time, his experiences with the Master, even outside in this world, give him a great deal of faith. So the inner and the outer experiences combine together to make a disciple absolutely unshakable in his conviction about the path he is following, about who the Master is and what the Master is doing for him.

Jesus then explains that his leaving them is actually necessary for their spiritual advancement. This is the bitterest of all pills that a Master asks his disciples to swallow:

> A little while, and ye shall not see me:
>> and again, a little while, and ye shall see me,
>> because I go to the Father.
> Verily, verily, I say unto you,
>> that ye shall weep and lament,
>> but the world shall rejoice:
>> and ye shall be sorrowful,
>> but your sorrow shall be turned into joy.
> A woman when she is in travail hath sorrow,
>> because her hour is come:
>> but as soon as she is delivered of the child,
>> she remembereth no more the anguish,
>> for joy that a man is born into the world.
> And ye now therefore have sorrow:
>> but I will see you again,
>> and your heart shall rejoice,
>> and your joy no man taketh from you.
>
> *John 16:16,20–22*

Jesus again repeats that he is leaving them, but that he will come to them within, after a "little while". He says that they will naturally be devastated when he leaves his physical form, for they have become so attached to him and so deeply in love with him. But – just as a woman in labour suffers great pain in childbirth which is translated into joy as soon as the child is born – so too will this pain of separation be transformed into joy when the disciples see him inside. "I will see you again," he says, and the bliss of this meeting will be permanent and eternal, not being dependent upon anything of the senses or the changeable world. It will be a "joy no man taketh from you".

> But because I have said these things unto you,
>   sorrow hath filled your heart.
> Nevertheless I tell you the truth;
>   it is expedient for you that I go away:
> For if I go not away,
>   the Comforter will not come unto you;
> But if I depart, I will send him unto you.

John 16:6-7

In fact, he says that "it is expedient for you that I go away". Just as a child is not born without the pain of childbirth, so too will a disciple be unable to meet the radiant form of the Master unless he is first struck by the anguish of separation. While the Master is with his disciples physically, they may attend to their meditation, but the focus of their lives tends towards being with the outer form of the Master. Being with the radiant form sounds good, but it does not have the immediate appeal that arises from the thought of being with the physical Master. The love for the outer form is no doubt essential, for without it the burning desire to meet the Master inside can never develop. "Nevertheless", in order for this love to be directed inwardly, so that the radiant form can be met, "it is expedient" for the Master to leave them physically. It is by leaving his disciples that the Master creates the conditions in which their love can mature and deepen, culminating in their seeing him within.

This entire discourse, then, or collection of sayings, circles around the single topic of Jesus' leaving his disciples physically, but subsequently returning in his radiant, spiritual form, within them. He never refers to any supposed last day on which he will be coming. He is not talking to the world at large, but to his own disciples.

The Son of Man is Within You

Meeting with the inner, light form of the Master is the first major milestone in the life of a disciple, and there are a great many references and allusions to it in the literature associated with early Christianity. In the canonical gospels, there are the stories of Jesus' 'transfiguration', already discussed in the chapter concerning the inner mansions. These almost certainly refer to the vision of the radiant form on the inner 'mountains'. The incident is also mentioned in the *Acts of Thomas*, where Judas Thomas underlines the fact that this form cannot be seen either with physical vision or without the help of the Master. He speaks of Jesus,

> whose divine form on the mount
> we were not able to see by ourselves alone.
>
> *Acts of Thomas, AAA p.278*

He means that it is by the Master's grace and blessings that a disciple is enabled to meet the "divine form". In the Nag Hammadi *Gospel of Mary*, enlarging on the words of Luke's gospel, it is made very clear that this form is to be found within. Jesus says:

> Beware that no one lead you astray, saying,
> "Lo here!" or "Lo there!"
> For the Son of man is within you.
> Follow after him!
>
> *Gospel of Mary 8, NHS21 p.459*

And likewise in the *Preaching of Andrew*, Jesus says:

> Let your hearts be strengthened by my Name,
> and you shall learn that I am with you,
> and dwell within you.
>
> *Preaching of Andrew, MAA p.10*

The form that dwells within is the Word which manifests as the radiant form. But this is only known when the "heart" is "strengthened by my Name" – when the soul is made spiritually strong by listening to the divine Music. The same idea is repeated in the *Acts of Peter*.

> Let us therefore bow our knees unto Christ,
> which heareth us, though we cry not;
> It is he that seeth us,
> though he be not seen with these eyes,
> yet is he in us:
> If we will, he will not forsake us.
> Let us therefore purify our souls of every evil temptation,
> and God will not depart from us.
> Yea, if we but wink with our eyes, he is present with us.
>
> *Acts of Peter XVIII, ANT p.320*

From his place within, the Master watches his disciple, seeing every-thing. "Though he be not seen with these eyes, yet he is in us." Once initiated, he does not leave a soul, but will see him through to the end, purifying him of all past sins. He is so close that to a pure and loving soul, he can be contacted behind the eyes – in the twinkling of an eye. As Judas Thomas says in the *Acts of Thomas*:

> Jesu, who alway showest thyself unto us –
> > thyself hast given us this power,
> > to ask and to receive;
> And hast not only permitted this,
> > but hast taught us to pray:
> Who art not seen of our bodily eyes,
> > but art never hidden from the eyes of our soul.
>
> *Acts of Thomas 53, ANT pp.389-390*

Jesus is the one who has taught his disciples how to pray correctly so that he may be seen, not with the "bodily eyes" but with the "eyes of the soul". Again, in this same book, Judas Thomas says to one who wishes to see Jesus:

> He appeareth not unto these bodily eyes,
> > but is found by the eyes of the mind.
>
> *Acts of Thomas 65, ANT p.395*

Incidentally, the only complete Syriac versions that we now have of the *Acts of Thomas* are probably translated out of the Greek and in places contain some very obvious insertions that lose the mystical meaning. Here, for example, the Greek "but is found by the eyes of the mind" is replaced in the Syriac by "but by faith is recognized in his works and glorified in his healings" – which conforms more to ortho-dox Christian doctrine but is altogether woolly in its meaning. The direction of loss is always a movement from the spiritual towards the religious, from reality towards doctrine:

> As far as thou art able, stretch thy mind upward,
> > because He is not visible now to these bodily eyes,
> > but by faith is recognized in His works
> > and glorified in His healings.
>
> *Acts of Thomas, AAA p.203*

Both here and elsewhere in the Syriac version, however, the translator or later copyists were apparently content that Judas Thomas should recommend that one who longed to see Jesus within should "stretch thy mind upward" or:

> Stretch thy mind towards our Lord.
>
> *Acts of Thomas, AAA p.194*

There seems little doubt, then, that Jesus taught of a spiritual form which could only be contacted within oneself. Both the canonical and apocryphal literature speak of it.

Reveal to Me Thy Beautiful Image

There is no greater longing that can strike a soul than the longing to find God within. This indeed is the only true longing or desire in creation; all others are poor copies. It is a homesickness to overshadow all yearnings, a divine nostalgia that grips the soul and will not let it rest until the goal is reached.

For a soul held captive in this world, who has only a vague idea of what God is like, such a longing begins as a longing to be with their Master. The longing starts in this world. However much one has ever longed to be with another person, it is only a dim and distant reflection of the longing of a loving disciple to be with their Master. But as the love for the physical Master matures and the devotee's spirituality awakens and develops, so too does the longing grow to see the Master on the inner planes. And since such divine longing is inspired by the Master, then, naturally, it is intended that he will answer it. As Jesus said:

> Blessed are they that mourn:
> for they shall be comforted.
>
> *Matthew 5:4*

And:

> Blessed are they
> which do hunger and thirst after righteousness:
> for they shall be filled.
>
> *Matthew 5:6*

Mystically, "righteousness" infers true spirituality, inner holiness and devotion to God, though it is a word whose meaning has been restricted by religion, losing much of its higher import. Jesus means that those who "hunger and thirst" after true spirituality, those who genuinely long for God, will certainly find Him. And those who long to see their Master inside will definitely meet him. This we have already discussed and it is in the Manichaean-Christian psalms that some of the most beautiful and poignant writings are found concerning the longing for and the meeting with the light form of the Master.

Sometimes, no specific term is used for this inner form, yet the meaning is evident from the context. Thus, the devotee, knowing that it is the Master who will reveal himself whenever he so desires, begs that "Jesus Christ" should "show thyself to me quickly and save me":

> Jesus Christ in whom I have believed,
>> show thyself to me quickly and save me.
> O merciful and good, full of mercy ....
> O First-born, Jesus, whom I have loved,
>> do not forsake me in my tribulations.
>>> *Psalm CCLXXII, MPB p.91*

In another extract, following an allusion to the Voice of God, the psalmist prays to be granted the vision of the "angelic form of Christ", another expression for the radiant form:

> Every voice I have heard,
>> but no other Voice pleased me save thine....
>
> I thirst for Life.
> Be not long in opening to me,
>> for my heart has thirsted....
> O angelic form of Christ,
>> open to me, crown me.
>>> *Psalms, MPB pp.154-155*

And in the *Acts of Thomas*, a devotee prays that her death may come soon, so that she may then be assured of meeting with that "Beautiful One of whom I have heard tell":

> Would that the days pass swiftly from me, O my mother,
>> and that all the hours were one,
>> that I might go forth from this world,
>> and go the sooner to behold that Beautiful One,

of whom I have heard tell,
even that Living One and Giver of life.
Acts of Thomas 129, AAA p.265, ANT p.421

Amongst the Coptic psalms, one of the commonest terms for the Master's spiritual form is the Greek word, *Eikon*, as found in the word 'icon' or 'ikon'. Its literal meaning is a 'representation', an 'image' or a 'likeness', which is precisely how the light form manifests. In Christianity, an icon has come to mean any pictorial representation of Jesus or any of the Christian saints, demonstrating that the real *Eikon* has always had its place in Christianity, but following the common pattern, the inner has been replaced by the outer. In one of these psalms, the devotee speaks of the purity of the spiritual form – "thy unsullied brightness" – begging to be released from the powers and distractions of the mind and asking Jesus to reveal "thy beautiful Image":

> Jesus, the light of the faithful, I beseech thee,
>> do not forsake me.
>
> Thy beautiful Image, my Father,
>> reveal it to me and thy unsullied brightness....
> Let it arise and come unto me quickly....
>
> Do not forsake me, even me thy slave,
>> in the presence of the sons of matter
>> (the powers of the mind, human weaknesses):
>> do not allow any of the demons
>> (also the powers of the mind)
>> to prevail over me, as I come unto thee.
> I see a merciless crowd (of them) like vultures surrounding me:
> Jesus, reveal thyself to me in the day of my need.
>
> Sever the nets of fear
>> (the worries and dreads of this world,
>> and timidity at going inside) ...
>> and do thou guard thy sheep of Light
>> from the wild destructive wolves.
> Reveal thy face to me, O holy and unsullied brightness;
>> for thou art my good Shepherd, my true merciful Physician.
>> *Psalm CCLII, MPB p.61*

In another psalm, the "Image" is counted as one of three gifts given by the Master to a disciple:

> Hail Perfect Man, holy path that draws to the Height,
>   clear air, mooring-harbour of all that believe in him:
>   open to me thy secrets
>   and take me to thee from affliction.
>
> As I come unto you today,
>   ye Kings of Light, ye Helmsmen,
>   open to me your doors and take me in unto you.
> Let me be counted worthy of my three gifts:
>   the Image, Love, and the Holy Spirit.
>
>   *Psalm CCLXVI, MPB p.83*

Likewise, in one of the Parthian psalms, an equivalent term is used and the same petition is made:

> We will stretch out our hand in prayer
>   and direct our (inner) eye
>   towards that Image of yours....
> You we praise, Jesus, the Splendour, New *Aeon*.
> You are, you are the Righteous (God),
>   the (noble) Healer, the most beloved Son,
>   the most loved Self....
>
> Come in peace, Awakener of the sleeping
>   and Arouser of the sleepy!
> You who make the dead arise!
>
>   *MMII p.312, ML p.107*

And again, from the Coptic, the devotee in ebullient mood challenges the Beloved:

> I have long been calling thee, my Saviour,
>   until thou shouldst answer me....
>
> Where is the boiling of thy mercies,
>   that thou hast suffered me to be so long in my prayer?
> If my voice has reached thee,
>   then how has thy mercy tarried?

If I have turned to thee a little,
> thou oughtest to turn to me much....

I have wearied of calling thee:
> O doorkeeper, open the door to me.

I will not stem my tears, O Powerful One,
> unless thou wipe away my sin.

> *Psalms of Heracleides, MPB p.188*

The disciple has been spending long hours in "prayer", in spiritual practice, longing to see the inner form. You are said to be the merciful one, says the devotee, so please demonstrate your mercy. I have done the little that was in my power, now you should do all that lies within your power. "O doorkeeper, open the door to me" – open the inner door. I will not cease calling on you until all my sins are forgiven.

These psalms, then, are all pleas for the inner door to open and for the inner, radiant form of the divine Beloved to be revealed. In other psalms, we find that this request has been granted:

O First-born (Son), take me in unto thee.
Lo, the path of Light has stretched before me
> unto my First City (First or Primal Home)....

The Image of the Saviour has come unto me....

O First-born (Son), the gates of the skies (heavens)
> have opened before me through the rays of my Saviour
> and his glorious Likeness of Light.

I have left the garment upon the earth,
> the senility of diseases that was with me;

The immortal robe I have put upon me....

O excellent toil wherewith I have toiled.
O my end that has had a happy issue.
O my eternal possession.
Glory and victory to our lord Mani and his holy elect.

> *Psalm CCLXIV, MPB p.81*

The inner "gates of the heavens" have opened by the grace of the "Saviour and his glorious Likeness of Light" – his light form. Now the body has been left behind, "I have left the garment upon the earth" with all its age-old sins and troubles, its "senility of diseases". The soul has rediscovered its natural "immortal robe", its robe of glory. And the

psalmist remembers the "toil" – the labour in spiritual practice, the
true eternal treasure and the happy outcome of all endeavours, in the
end giving praise this time to the mystic Mani, as the Master.

In yet another psalm, the "Image" is described as the "bringer of
gladness", which the "eye of the soul" has seen:

> The Image ... the bringer of gladness....
>> the joyous eye of my soul looks at them.
>>> *Psalm CCLXXX, MPB p.101*

And in another, the Masters are described as "them of the dear Image":

> Lift up thy face, O Loved one,
>> look into my face, see how I gaze at thee,
>> with no evil glance in my eyes....
>
> I have lived since I heard thy sweet Voice ...
>> O glorious one;
> For I have seen them of the dear Image.
>>> *Psalm CCLXXXIII, MPB p.104*

In another, the liberated soul is addressed by the psalmist. The soul
has been released from all bondage so that the "joyous Image of Christ
– thou shalt have thy fill of it now":

> Thou hast been released
>> from the grievous bonds of the flesh:
> Thou hast been garlanded in justification
>> over all thy enemies (powers of the mind).
> The joyous Image of Christ –
>> thou shalt have thy fill of it now:
> Go thy way therefore victoriously to thy City of Light.
>
> Thou art glad because thou hast mixed with the holy angels:
>> upon thee is set the seal of thy glorious purity.
> Thou art joyful because thou hast seen
>> thy divine Brethren (the Masters) with whom
>> thou shalt dwell in the Light for ever.
>
> The authority of the flesh –
>> thou hast passed quickly beyond it:

thou hast ascended like a swift bird
    into the air of the gods (the inner realms)....

Thou hast quickly escaped from the fearful [realm of darkness];
    [thou hast] found rest in the Paradise of Life.
Thou hast reached the place
    wherein there is neither heat nor cold,
    where there is neither hunger nor thirst....

Thou hast been victorious,
    O Mani, thou hast given the victory to them
    that have shown zeal for God.

Psalm CCLIV, MPB pp.64-65

And credit is given to the mystic Mani who is the Christ or Master in this psalm.

There is another term for the radiant form of the Master, found especially in the Manichaean-Christian writings, which scholars have translated in a number of ways, variants being the "Familiar", the "Pair-Companion" and the "Twin". Indeed, in the allegorical romance of the *Acts of Thomas*, where Judas Thomas is said to be the twin brother of Jesus, the connection is frequently used in a metaphorical manner suggestive of the radiant form. The term suggests the Likeness or the Image, since twins are doubles of each other. Hence, the radiant form has sometimes been called the 'astral double' of the Master, because it resembles his physical form in appearance.

Once again, illustrating the inward and spiritual nature of this form, in one of the Coptic psalms, the devotee speaks of "gazing at my Familiar with my eyes of light":

I was gazing at my Familiar with my eyes of light,
    beholding my glorious Father,
    him who waits for me ever,
    opening before me the gate unto the Height.

I spread out my hands, praying unto him;
I bent my knees, worshipping him also,
    that I might divest myself
    of the image of the flesh
    and put off the vesture of manhood.

Psalm CCXXVI, MPB p.19

The devotee worships "my Familiar ... my glorious Father" and humbles his mind – metaphorically, he says, "I bent my knees" – so that he may be able to "divest (himself) of the image of the flesh": so that he could leave his body, the "vesture of manhood", and be completely united with him.

The Mandaeans, too, had similar terms for the radiant form of the Master. In an allegorical poem, for example, the Master is "commissioned" by God, the "Great Life", and told to manifest his "divine Image" to the chosen souls, the "elect righteous":

> Go, go thou Dazzling One,
> > show thy divine Image to the elect righteous
> > that they may see thee and shine.
>
> > > > *CPM 366 p.258*

The disciple, for his part, hearing the mystic call of the "Dazzling One" is caught up in the longing to see the Master within. This is the intense longing that drives sleep from the mind, even keeping the devotee awake all night, seated blissfully and lovingly in meditation. Hence, the disciple says:

> Early I arose from my sleep: I stood,
> > into radiance that was great I looked;
> I gazed into radiance that was great,
> > into the Light which is boundless.
> When clothed in robes of radiance
> > and light was thrown on my shoulders,
> > a wreath of ether he set on my head
> > and set in on the head of all his race.
> He (the Master) hymned,
> > and the *'uthras* (beings) with him hymn,
> > and the light-rays (souls) answer his Voice.
> And it rouseth sleepers and maketh them rise up
> > from their sleep.
> He said to them "Arise, ye sleepers who lie there,
> > rise up, ye stumblers who have stumbled.
> Arise, worship and praise the Great Life
> > and praise his Counterpart,
> > that is the Image of the Life,
> > which shineth forth and is expressed in sublime Light."
>
> > > > *CPM 114 pp.110-111*

Here, the disciple arises from his sleep to practise meditation. With all attention withdrawn from the world, he experiences great light and radiance within himself. The Master's "Voice" awakens those who sleep, not only in their beds, but in the slumber land of this world. And they are to arise not only from their nightly slumbers but to rise up to and pass through the inner door where, "in sublime Light", they can meet "his Counterpart", the radiant form of their Master, the "Image of the Life". Such writings do not represent religious hopes or theological precepts. They are experiences of devoted disciples, though as time passes, they become the liturgies and psalms of religion, often repeated parrot-fashion with little or no understanding of their real meaning.

People who have no inkling of such inner experiences cannot begin to comprehend such yearning, though there are many descriptions of it in the mystic literature of the world. In the *Acts of Thomas*, echoing a number of Jesus' parables, Judas Thomas also speaks of his spiritual endeavours and of his meeting with the radiant form within:

> Mine eyes, O Christ (O anointed one),
>> look upon thee (within myself),
>> and mine heart exulteth with joy (bliss)
>> because I have fulfilled thy will
>> and perfected thy commandments;
> That I may be likened unto that watchful
>> and careful servant (disciple)
>> who in his eagerness neglecteth not to keep vigil.
>
> For I have not slumbered idly in keeping thy commandments:
> In the first sleep and at midnight and at cockcrow,
>> that mine eyes may behold thee,
>> all the night have I laboured,
>> to keep mine house from robbers,
>> lest it be broken through.
>
> My loins have I girt close with truth
>> and bound my shoes on my feet,
>> that I may never see them gaping:
>
> Mine hands have I put unto the yoked plough
>> and have not turned away backward,
>> lest my furrows go crooked.

The plough-land is become white and the harvest is come,
    that I may receive my wages.

My garment that groweth old (the body) I have worn out,
    and the labour (meditation) that hath brought me unto rest
    have I accomplished.
I have kept the first watch and the second and the third,
    that I may behold thy Face and adore thine holy brightness
    (meet thy light and radiant form)
    and rest beside thy Living Spring....

All thy fullness hath been fulfilled in me....
The dead man (the 'deadened' soul) have I quickened,
    and the living one (the mind and ego) have I overcome,
    and that which was lacking (true spirituality) have I filled up.

Do thou, then, grant me, Lord,
    that I may pass by in quietness and joy and peace,
    and pass over and stand before thy glory.
And let not the Devil look upon me,
    but let his eyes be blinded by thy Light
    which thou hast made to dwell in me.

    Acts of Thomas 146-148, ANT pp.429-430; cf. AAA p.283, MAA p.238

The metaphors largely allude to the parables of Jesus. The "house" is
the human form, particularly the inner being of the disciple. The "robbers" are the thieves of human weaknesses – distractions of the mind
and senses. The remainder of the allusions are self-explanatory.

    In a similar vein, the writer of the *Odes of Solomon* also speaks of
the meeting with this radiant form of light:

My Helper raised me up to his pity
    and his deliverance,
    and I put off darkness, and put on light....

And I was raised up in his light,
    and I passed before his face;
And I came near to him,
    praising and thanking him.

    Odes of Solomon XXI:2-3,6-7, AOT p.711

This is what happens when the radiant and spiritual form is encountered. The soul is "raised up in his light" and comes before "his face", his shining form. And the soul is filled with a wordless love, worship, praise and sense of gratitude.

Behold, the Bridegroom Cometh!

Returning to the canonical gospels, there is a reference to this inner form in one of Jesus' parables: the parable of the ten virgins, five of whom were wise and five, foolish. The story is only found in St Matthew:

> Then shall the kingdom of heaven be likened unto ten virgins,
>> which took their lamps, and went forth to meet the Bridegroom.
> And five of them were wise, and five were foolish.
> They that were foolish took their lamps, and took no oil with them:
>> but the wise took oil in their vessels with their lamps.
> While the Bridegroom tarried, they all slumbered and slept.
> And at midnight there was a cry made,
>> "Behold, the Bridegroom cometh; go ye out to meet him."
>
> Then all those virgins arose and trimmed their lamps.
> And the foolish said unto the wise,
>> "Give us of your oil; for our lamps are gone out."
> But the wise answered, saying,
>> "Not so; lest there be not enough for us and you:
>> but go ye rather to them that sell,
>> and buy for yourselves."
>
> And while they went to buy, the Bridegroom came;
>> and they that were ready went in with him to the marriage:
>> and the door was shut.
> Afterward came also the other virgins, saying,
>> "Lord, Lord, open to us."
> But he answered and said,
> "Verily I say unto you, I know you not."
>
> Watch therefore, for ye know neither the day nor the hour
>> wherein the Son of man cometh.
>
> *Matthew 25:1-13*

The Bridegroom is another very common and ancient image used for the Master, particularly his inner form. Often, the disciple is symbolized as the bride and the spiritual union as the mystic marriage. In this case, however, the disciples are represented by the ten virgins, half of whom are wise and half foolish. The lamp signifies the soul which has the potential to shine brightly, shedding light all around, as long as it is filled with oil to make it burn. The oil is therefore the meditation which makes the soul shine brightly and burn in the fires of longing and separation from the Beloved.

All the souls are expecting the Bridegroom, the Master, to come. But only half of them make the necessary arrangements and put oil in their lamps. Only half the disciples ever meditate in the way and to the degree that their Master has requested them. The others procrastinate, failing to make adequate preparation for his coming. They are lax in their spiritual practice.

While they await the Bridegroom, "they all slumbered and slept" – they all slumber in this world, outside the door, the single eye within which the Bridegroom is to be met. Then, at midnight, when the night is darkest, the Bridegroom comes and the ten virgins are called out to meet him. Midnight, when most people are fast asleep, signifies that a disciple must be inwardly vigilant at all times, always holding himself in readiness for the coming of his Master. And perhaps it also refers to the night-time when the disciples are expected to be awake in their meditation, awaiting their Master's appearance.

The five wise ones are ready. They have kept oil in their lamps and the flames of their souls are burning brightly. With great joy, they "went in with him to the marriage" – they are taken in through the inner door and merge into the Bridegroom on the inner planes.

But the five foolish ones are not at all ready. Despite the fact that they knew that sooner or later he was going to come, they had still permitted themselves to be distracted by the world – its pleasures, its pains and its activities. So they turn to their wiser sisters and ask for some of their oil. But in what may seem like a mean gesture, the wise ones refuse, saying, "Not so; lest there be not enough oil for us and you". It means that spiritual wealth and spiritual practice is personal and cannot and should not be transferred, even if a person wants to do so. Each one must go out and "buy for yourselves": everyone has to do their own spiritual practice. No one else can do it for them.

So while the foolish ones are frantically trying to remedy their mistake at the last minute, the Bridegroom goes in with the wise virgins and closes the door behind him. And when the foolish ones come and knock upon the door, the Bridegroom refuses to let them in, declining even to know them. It means that they have wasted their opportunity of being in the human form and of being the disciples of a Master. Since they are initiated, they will be given another opportunity in another birth; but in this birth, the door is shut to them.

Summarizing the parable, Jesus then concludes: "Watch therefore, for you know neither the day nor the hour wherein the Son of man cometh." There is a double meaning, here. Firstly, a disciple – being in darkness – cannot know how close he is to the opening of the inner door when the Master will take him inside and meet him in his radiant form. Consequently, he must always endeavour to keep himself in readiness by concentrating fully at the inner door and remaining there in an attitude of genuine humility and love until the door is opened. If somebody is boring through a wall of unknown thickness, light only appears from the other side when the last millimetre has been broken through. Similarly, an individual cannot know until the goal is reached how close he or she has been to attaining it. Therefore, the effort must be maintained, whatever the apparent progress or lack of it.

Secondly, human life is fragile and death can come at any moment. And since a Master in his radiant form will always meet his devoted disciples at the time of their death, this is also a time when such disciples can look forward to a meeting with him. But generally, no one knows when death will come. A person cannot presume that there is still plenty of time in which to meditate, for one may expire very suddenly. 'There is many a slip between the cup and the lip.' Hence, Jesus says to his disciples, "Watch therefore" – stay alert and do not fall into the deep sleep of worldliness. Always continue with your spiritual practice.

As a part of this family of marriage metaphors, the inner realms were also called the "Bride-chambers", the "Bride-chambers of light" and other similar expressions. It is here that the Bridegroom is met and spiritual union is experienced. And there are many references in the early literature both to this parable of Jesus, as well as to the inner meeting with the Bridegroom. In the Manichaean-Christian psalms, there are some very obvious allusions:

> Let us also, my brethren, put oil in our lamps
> (attend to our meditation) until our Lord passes in.
> Let us not slumber and sleep until our Lord takes us across,

> his garland upon his head, his palm in his hand,
> wearing the robe of his glory,
> and we go within the Bride-chamber and reign with him,
> all of us together.
>
> *Psalms of Heracleides, MPB p.193*

As in the excerpts concerning the Image, there are many places where the devotee expresses a longing to be with the inner Master. The first of these alludes to the parable of the ten virgins, as well as equating the vision of "thy Image" with the meeting in "thy Bride-chambers":

> Let me be worthy of thy Bride-chambers
>   that are full of light.
> Jesus Christ, receive me
>   into thy Bride-chambers, thou my Saviour....
> I am a maiden (devotee) unspotted and holy.
>
> Let me see thy Image, my holy Father,
>   which I saw before the world was created,
>   before the darkness (the Negative Power) presumed
>   to stir up envy against thy *Aeons*.
> Because of it (darkness) I became a stranger
>   to my (divine) kingdom.
> (But now) I have severed its root,
>   I have risen victoriously on high.
>
> Purify me, my Bridegroom, O Saviour,
>   with thy Waters ... that are full of grace....
>
> [My lamp] shines like the sun,
>   I have lighted it, O Bridegroom,
>   with the excellent oil of purity.
> [I am] a maiden [unspotted and holy],
>   making music unto thee, my Saviour
>   (listening to the divine Music)....
>
> Christ, take me into thy Bride-chambers....
> Let me rejoice in all the Bride-chambers,
>   and do thou give me the crown of the Holy Ones.
>
> *Psalm CCLXIII, MPB pp.79-80*

And similarly:

> Take me into thy Bride-chambers
>> that I may chant with them that sing to thee
>> (them that listen to the divine Music).
>
> *Psalms, MPB p.117*

And:

> Have mercy on my poverty, have compassion upon my sins.
> Teach me the way to Life that I may come to thee rejoicing.
> I will dwell in thy *aeons*, thy Bride-chambers of Light.
> Hearken to my cry, hear my prayer.
> Glory to thee, my God, and thy Father on high.
>
> *Psalms of Heracleides, MPB p.197*

In another, the psalmist exhorts his fellow disciples, the "sons of Light", to exert themselves on the spiritual path in order that they may be taken up into the "Bride-chamber":

> Take me up to thy habitations, Jesus, my Bridegroom....
>> I have set myself to please thee to the end....
>
> Fight, O sons of Light:
>> yet a little while and you will be victorious.
> He that shirks his burden will forfeit his Bride-chamber....
>> I have become divine again even as I was.
>
> *Psalm CCXLIX, MPB p.58*

In other psalms, the soul describes being taken up out of this world of "death" into the "Bride-chambers", being cleansed of all sins and filled with Living Water from the "fountain that is full of life":

> My Saviour has not deserted me,
>> he has sated me from his fountain
>> that is full of life....
> I have cast away from my eyes
>> this sleep of death which is full of Error....
>
> The cleansing of immortality,
>> I have been cleansed therein

by the hands of the Holy Ones (the Masters).
They summon me to the Bride-chambers of the Height:
I will go up clothed in the robe.

Psalm CCLXI, MPB pp.75-76

And in a similar vein, also alluding to Jesus' parable of the lost sheep
and other sayings:

Christ, my Bridegroom, has taken me to his Bride-chamber,
I have rested with him in the land of the immortal.
My brethren, I have received my garland.
My own land I have beheld, my Father I have found,
the godly have rejoiced over me,
my *aeons* have welcomed me.
My brethren, I have received my garland.
There is a gain, my brethren,
none shall be able to take it from me:
an imperishable treasure,
to which thieves find not the way.

I am like a sheep seeking for its pastor;
Lo, my True Shepherd I have found,
he has brought me to my fold again.
Lo, the fight I have finished....

Since I found my Saviour I have walked in his steps.
I have not hung back at all
in respect of this garland to receive it.
O how great is the joy that is prepared for the perfect.
all of you, my brethren, we [shall] inherit it....

Glory and honour to Jesus,
the king of the Holy Ones and his holy elect.

Psalm CCLIII, MPB pp.63-64

And again:

O First-born (Son), I have become a holy Bride
in the Bride-chambers of Light that are at rest,
I have received the gifts of the victory.

Psalm CCLXIV, MPB p.81

And praising the "true Bridegroom" who has taken the soul into the light:

> Glory to thee, my true Bridegroom,
>> Christ of the Bride-chambers of Light,
>> and all his holy elect.
>
> *Psalm CCLXXXI, MPB p.102*

In the early Christian liturgies, especially those of the Eastern branches of the church, the same expressions are commonly found. The origins of these liturgies and songs of praise are uncertain, but it is more than likely that they are derived from earlier devotional writings, either being copied in toto or being based upon the same ideas and imagery, thereby preserving the mystic meaning even if the writer did not fully comprehend it. In the ancient Syrian *Chaldaean Breviary*, for example, we read of the "Bride-chamber – a spiritual one" that has been inextricably "knotted" to the "church", to all disciples in the community of a Master's followers:

> A Bride-chamber, our Lord hath knotted to his church,
>> a spiritual one.
>
> *Chaldaean Breviary, BCB 1:407, MEM p.116*

More specifically, the soul is addressed as the "Bride" for which the Master, the "Son of the King", has built a "glorified Bride-chamber" – the secret trysting place within, where the Master meets with the disciple:

> In the Holy of Holies, which cannot be described,
>> the Son of the King hath built to his Bride,
>> a glorified Bride-chamber.
>
> *Chaldaean Breviary, BCB 3:425, MEM p.116*

Ephraim Syrus also uses the same imagery in his hymns:

> The Bride-chamber that fails not,
>> my brethren, ye have received....
> Your vesture is shining, and goodly your crowns....
> Crowns that fade not away are set on your heads....
> Who would not rejoice in your Bride-chamber,
>> my brethren.
>
> *Ephraim Syrus, Hymn of the Baptized XIII:3,5,11,13, HEDA p.283*

And finally in a beautiful Nestorian hymn, the "Bridegroom in his chamber" is himself described:

> The Bridegroom in his chamber is like
>> the sun that riseth out of the East,
>> whose rays pervade the firmament,
>> and whose light giveth joy to the creation.
>
> The Bridegroom in his chamber is like
>> the Tree of Life in the church,
>> whose fruits are good for food
>> and whose leaves for medicine.
>
> The Bridegroom in his chamber is like
>> the spring which runs through Eden,
>> of which the wise have drunk,
>> and by which the foolish have obtained knowledge.
>
> The Bridegroom in his chamber is like
>> an unblemished pearl,
>> which the chief merchants bought,
>> and through which they were enriched and ennobled.
>>   *NRII XLIII p.275; SPŻ p.732, MEM p.118*

Here, as we have seen before, the sun, the light, the fruit, the food, the leaves, the medicine, the river and the pearl are all metaphors for the Creative Word and the treasure of spirituality which all men seek.

The *rendezvous* with this beautiful, radiant and spiritual form of their Master is the first goal to which the devotees of the universal mystic path aspire. It is without doubt that in such passages these early writers were referring to this meeting. This, indeed, is the real 'second coming'. The only obstacles to experiencing it are those that lie within the mind. For only a pure and perfect soul can come before the radiance of one who is purity and perfection personified.

CHAPTER TWENTY-FOUR

Be Ye Therefore Perfect:
Perfection and Imperfection

Perfection – Human and Divine

It is an interesting fact that most religions are in agreement on the subject of what is right and wrong in human thought and conduct. Indeed, though there may be some deviations due to culture, most human beings, regardless of religious or other beliefs, are generally agreed upon the subject. Good thought and behaviour are not, as some modern scientists would have us believe, simply a matter of biological expediency and the survival of the species. Clouded, confused and deeply buried as it may be by personal, social, cultural and religious conditioning, man has a conscience. He has something inside himself which tells him when he is overstepping the mark. This is a universal characteristic, present within everyone, regardless of religion or belief.

True, man also has a remarkable aptitude for creating a dense barrier between his actions, his thoughts and his innermost conscience. But if a person develops the capacity of introspection and self-awareness even to a small degree, he will discover that he has an inner guide which tells him what is right and what is wrong. This conscience arises from the higher qualities of the mind. It is a reflection of the life, energy and sense of spiritual direction which the mind receives from the soul.

Now since the primal desire of the soul is to return to God, this innate understanding of right and wrong is directly related to the human aspects of the life that must be led in order that He may be realized. Jesus summarizes the matter in his characteristically succinct style:

> Be ye therefore perfect,
> even as your Father which is in heaven is perfect.
>
> *Matthew 5:48*

God is perfection and man must acquire the virtues constituting human perfection as a part of his spiritual journey towards union with the divine. There is, therefore, human perfection and divine perfection, the one being a reflection of the other.

From God's point of view, His perfection is His oneness, His purity and His love. In Himself, there is only purity and oneness; there is nothing other than Him. He is Himself alone. Consequently, He is perfectly pure, unmixed with anything else. In His creation, He is the author of all, the intelligence within all, the order within all. If it seems to us that the creation has imperfection, then that is only from our point of view. If the creation is to continue, it has to be the way it is or all the souls would immediately return to Him. There has to be something to keep souls here – and that something is what we call imperfection. Just as a shadow only exists because of the light, so too does imperfection only exist because of perfection. From His point of view, the creation is entirely as He wants it: it is perfectly imperfect.

Mystics and gnostics, more than others, understand the divine qualities. In the writings of Jesus' era the Lord is called the "complete, perfect One",[1] the "holy and perfect Mother-Father",[2] the "perfect *Aeon*",[3] the "self-begotten perfect One",[4] the "perfect Light"[5] and so on. He is also described as "good, faultless, perfect, complete",[6] "perfect, having no defect"[7], the "perfect Blessed One of the eternal and incomprehensible Father and the infinite Light"[8] and by other similar epithets.

Moreover, since He is beyond all the duality of His creation, it can also be said that He is beyond perfection and imperfection. Hence, the writer of the gnostic revelation, *Allogenes* says:

> He is perfect, and He is greater than perfect....
> He is prior to perfection....
> He entered into Himself and manifested,
>   being all-encompassing,
>   the universal One that is higher than perfect....
> (He is) the God who is beyond perfection.
>
> *Allogenes* 47,53,61, NHS28 pp.197,209,225

From this great Ocean of perfection and purity emanates the Word, the Son of God, and its manifestation in the Masters. A Master is thus perfection personified. He is "perfect, because of the Word",[9] "Christ ... the perfect man",[10] the "perfect Saviour",[11] the "perfect Son, the Christ, the Only-Begotten God"[12] and

the Son who is perfect in every respect,
that is, the Word who originated through that Voice;
who proceeded from the Height;
who has within him the Name;
who is a Light.

Trimorphic Protennoia 37, NHS28 p.407

The divine perfection of a Master is expressed in the physical world as human perfection. Hence, the Manichaean-Christian writer of the manuscripts found in Turkestan says:

Those Saints are pure, humble, and always happy in body:
  their frames of diamond require no sleep;
Since they have neither dream and whim,
  nor nightmare,
How can it be said they have fear and dread? ...

The minds and thoughts of the Saints
  are entirely honest and true:
Pretension and deceit, vanity and affectation
  are by nature never theirs.
From their bodies, mouths, and minds,
  the deeds (that come forth) are always clean and pure;
How can it be said they ever uttered a false saying?

LSMH 285,287, BSOAS XI pp.201-202

And in an extract from a poignant song of longing at the death of Mar Zako, one of Mani's successors, an unknown disciple describes his Master's qualities with the evident affection and love of a devotee:

O Mar Zako, Shepherd, blessed Teacher,
  without reason separation from you now has come to us.
We shall no longer look unto your shining eyes
  and no longer listen to your sweet words.
O God *Sraoshav* (Sound)[13] with the sweet Name,
  brilliant Lord, there is no one like you among all gods.

We are depressed, sorrowfully we sigh, weep,
  we will always remember your love.
You were the throne-keeper in all realms,
  sovereigns and magnates reverenced you.

Lovely and kind was your nature,
   mild your talk that never showed bitter anger.

Great Giant, strong in patience,
   you tolerated everybody, you were renowned for it.
Righteous, innocent, merciful, giftful,
   generous, compassionate, kind father,
   who made happy the oppressed;
You who saved numberless souls from distress
   and guided them to their Home.
Strong, good, powerful one, who like all apostles,
   Buddhas and gods, have now gone to your throne:

To you first I pay homage,
I, the smallest of your sons who has been left an orphan
   and an exile by you, dear father.

Come hither, let us write a letter
   to the beneficent King of Light.
From him we will beg: Forgive our sins!

                              MMIII pp.866-867, ML pp.31-32

It is from a divine and perfect Saviour that human beings receive the grace to become perfect, too. Then, as Jesus said, the disciple will become like his Master:

The disciple is not above his Master:
   but every one that is perfect shall be as his Master.

                              Luke 6:40

A disciple can never become spiritually greater than his Master, but he can certainly reach the same spiritual level. This great refrain and promise is echoed in all the early Christian literature. Paul, for instance, encourages his group in Corinth to strive for perfection:

Having therefore these promises, dearly beloved, let us cleanse ourselves
   from   all filthiness of the flesh and spirit, perfecting holiness in the fear
   of God.

                              2 Corinthians 7:1

In the *Apocryphon of John,* Jesus says that perfection comes to "those on whom the Spirit of the Lord will descend":

> Those on whom the Spirit of Life will descend
> and with whom he will be with the Power,
> they will be saved and become perfect
> and be worthy of the Greatness
> and be purified ... from all wickedness
> and the involvements in evil.
> Then they (will) have no other care than the incorruption alone,
> to which they direct their attention from here on,
> without anger or envy or jealousy or
> desire and greed of anything.
>
> *Apocryphon of John 25, NHL p.119*

Another gnostic writer expresses his gratitude for being enabled to attain perfection:

> We bless thee eternally.
> We bless thee, once we have been saved,
> as the perfect individuals,
> perfect on account of thee,
> those who became perfect with thee who is complete.
>
> *Three Steles of Seth 121, NHL p.398*

While a Manichaean-Christian psalmist writes of the joy of such perfection:

> O how great is the joy
> that is prepared for the perfect: ...
> all of you, my brethren, we [shall] inherit it....
> Glory and honour to Jesus,
> the king of the Holy Ones (the Masters),
> and his holy elect.
>
> *Psalm CCLIII, MPB p.64*

Blessed Are the Pure in Heart

From a human point of view, the striving for virtue and the conquest of negative tendencies is generally seen as a laudable *goal*. Mystically, however, this human struggle in which everyone is automatically involved whether they like it or not, is perceived only as a *means* to an end. The first staging post on the mystic path is the withdrawal of the attention from the world and from the body to the single eye. What prevents this withdrawal is the constant play of innumerable human imperfections. All of them, in their own individual ways, distract the mind from its centre and draw it downward and outward. They keep the mind and soul concerned with this world so that they cannot travel into the higher realms.

To clean a cup is a useful exercise only if it is then filled. Striving for human excellence is like cleaning a cup. Passing through the "strait gate" or the single eye and coming into contact with the music of the Word of God is filling the cup with the essence of spirituality. It is contact with the Word which brings the highest perfection or purity to a soul. As Jesus said, speaking unequivocally of *seeing* God and relating the ability to do so to the state of a person's inner purity:

> Blessed are the pure in heart:
>   for they shall see God.
>
> *Matthew 5:8*

Similarly, in the letter attributed to James:

> Draw nigh to God, and he will draw nigh to you.
> Cleanse your hands, ye sinners;
>   and purify your hearts, ye double minded.
>
> *James 4:8*

But this purity must be of a far higher order than that normally achieved by the votaries of religion. Hence, Jesus said:

> For I say unto you,
>   that except your righteousness shall exceed
>   the righteousness of the scribes and Pharisees,
>   ye shall in no case enter into the kingdom of heaven.
>
> *Matthew 5:20*

And in the *Acts of Thomas*, Judas Thomas intimates the high spiritual character of such purity:

> Blessed are the holy,
>   whose souls have never condemned them,
>   for they have gained them
>   and are not divided against themselves:

> Blessed are the spirits of the pure,
>> and they that have received the heavenly crown....
> Blessed are the bodies of the holy,
>> for they have been made worthy to become temples of God,
>> that Christ may dwell in them.
>
> *Acts of Thomas 94, ANT pp.405-406*

Purity is the same as perfection and entails turning away from the multifarious entanglements of the world towards God, and ultimately 'seeing God', attaining union with Him.

Many Obstacles Fall into the Way

God, then, is the essence of perfection and purity, and at a human level man must develop the qualities of human perfection as a means of reaching up to Him and partaking of His divine nature. The reason why human perfection is required is very simple. All bad or negative qualities arise in a mind that has become besotted with the creation and has forgotten the Lord. They stem from the desire of the individual to gain something for himself, either by way of physical goods, personal kudos, sensual pleasure or in some other way.

The common factor is always the enhancement of the individual self, usually at the expense of others. In reality, however, this self does not exist. It is only an illusion of the mind, a counterfeit self, a reflection of the real self or soul. Thus, when the attention is attracted and entrapped by the unreal, it moves away from reality. Or, put more simply, when somebody becomes obsessed with anything other than God, he moves away from God.

In the preparation for mystic union with God or even for entry to the inner realms, correct thought and conduct is required at the human level. A general guide would seem to be that whatever takes a person towards God is good and whatever takes them away from Him is bad. It is noticeable, therefore, that all the universally acknowledged human virtues are associated with selflessness, quietness of mind and carefreeness concerning the goods and pleasures of the world, while the negative qualities are characterized by selfishness and attachment, leading to restlessness of mind and constant worry over physical things.

Even a cursory glance at the inventories of negative qualities found in the writings of early Christians groups – however divergent their interpretations of Jesus' teachings may otherwise have been – reveals the same fundamental traits of selfishness, self-indulgence and worldly gain for self-oriented motives. Paul, for instance, was fond of belabouring his communities with lists of various evils. In *Romans*, he speaks of those who are

> filled with all unrighteousness, fornication, wickedness, covetousness, maliciousness; full of envy, murder, debate, deceit, malignity; whisperers, backbiters, haters of God, despiteful, proud, boasters, inventors of evil things, disobedient to parents, without understanding, covenant-breakers, without natural affection, implacable, unmerciful: who knowing the judgment of God, that they which commit such things are worthy of death, not only do the same, but have pleasure in them that do them.
>
> *Romans 1:29-32*

In *1 Corinthians*, he writes in a similar vein:

> Know ye not that the unrighteous shall not inherit the kingdom of God? Be not deceived: neither fornicators, nor idolaters, nor adulterers, nor effeminate, nor abusers of themselves with mankind, nor thieves, nor covetous, nor drunkards, nor revilers, nor extortioners, shall inherit the kingdom of God.
>
> *1 Corinthians 6:9-10*

And in *Galatians*:

> Now the works of the flesh are manifest, which are these: adultery, fornication, uncleanness, lasciviousness, idolatry, witchcraft, hatred, variance, emulations, wrath, strife, seditions, heresies, envyings, murders, drunkenness, revellings, and such like: of the which I tell you before, as I have also told you in time past, that they which do such things shall not inherit the kingdom of God.
>
> *Galatians 5:19-21*

Paul, of course, is speaking as an impassioned human being, not – on his own admission – without his own human imperfections, and it is noteworthy that his personal prejudices also creep into such lists. One wonders what he meant by "heresies", for example. For one man's heresy can be another's path to God! In general, however, the principle remains. All such tendencies are generally recognized as wrong by all those who try to live a decent, godly life.

There are many other such inventories amongst the writings we have been quoting and they make for salutary rather than inspirational reading. Three more will suffice – firstly, from the *Acts of John*, where John enumerates both the sins themselves and some of the factors which prepare the way for them:

> Many obstacles fall into the way and prepare disturbance for the minds of men: care, children, parents, glory, poverty, flattery, prime of life, beauty, conceit, lust, wealth, anger, uplifting, slackness, envy, jealousy, neglect, fear, insolence, love, deceit, money, pretence, and other such obstacles, as many as there are in this life: as also the pilot sailing a prosperous course is opposed by the onset of contrary winds and a great storm and might, waves out of calm, and the husbandman by untimely winter and blight and creeping things rising out of the earth.
>
> *Acts of John 68, ANT p.244*

Secondly, the *Didache*, a book that is reckoned to be the earliest church manual on conduct and other matters, describes such action and thought as the "way of Death":

> The way of Death is this: first of all, it is wicked and full of cursing, murders, adulteries, lusts, fornications, thefts, idolatries, witchcrafts, charms, robberies, false witness, hypocrisies, a double heart, fraud, pride, malice, stubbornness, covetousness, foul speech, jealousy, impudence, haughtiness, boastfulness, persecutors of the good, haters of truth, lovers of lies, knowing not the reward of righteousness, not cleaving to the good nor to righteous judgement, spending wakeful nights not for good but for wickedness, from whom meekness and patience is far, lovers of vanity, following after reward, unmerciful to the poor, not working for him who is oppressed with toil, without knowledge of Him who made them, murderers of children, corrupters of God's creatures, turning away the needy, oppressing the distressed, advocates of the rich, unjust judges of the poor, altogether sinful. May ye be delivered, my children from all these.
>
> *Didache V:1-2, AFI pp.317-319*

And thirdly, the *Epistle of Barnabas*, which likewise enumerates the characteristics of the "way of Death" or the "way of the "Black One", by which he presumably means Satan. Both these documents stem from the earliest years of Christianity and the two lists bear sufficient resemblances to each other to assure us that either the one copied from the other or that they both referred to a third document, earlier than both of these. It is yet another example of the way these ancient documents got about, appearing in a variety of places with no acknowledgement of sources! The writer says:

> The Way of the Black One is crooked and full of cursing, for it is the way of death, ... and in it are the things that destroy their soul: idolatry, frowardness, arrogance of power, hypocrisy, double-heartedness, adultery, murder, robbery, pride, transgression, fraud, malice, self-sufficiency, enchantments, magic, covetousness, the lack of the fear of God; persecutors of the good, haters of the truth, lovers of lies, knowing not the reward of righteousness, who "cleave not to the good", nor to righteous judgement, who attend not to the cause of the widow and orphan, spending wakeful nights not in fear of God, but in the pursuit of vice, from whom meekness and patience are far and distant, "loving vanity, seeking rewards", without pity for the poor, working not for him who is oppressed with toil, prone to evil speaking, without knowledge of their Maker, murderers of children, corrupters of God's creation, turning away the needy, oppressing the afflicted, advocates of the rich, unjust judges of the poor, altogether sinful.
>
> *Epistle of Barnabas XX:1-2, AFI p.407*

The Colours Wherewith I Bid Thee Paint

It is a sad fact that while human nature enjoys retailing the tally of another's sins, it finds far less pleasure in contemplating the converse virtues. This is reflected in the early Christian writings, for lists of sins outweigh lists of the corresponding virtues by about three to one! There are, however, more than sufficient for our needs, one of them, in the *Acts of John*, being introduced by means of an entertaining anecdote.

Lycomedes, one of John's devotees, commissions the painting of a picture of the apostle which he hangs in his private room, bedecked with garlands, and with lamps and altars placed before it as if it were an idol. Then, whenever he comes and goes from his house, he enters this room and practises a form of idol worship, even though the living John is actually staying with him in his own home. John starts to tease him about these clandestine disappearances and Lycomedes' secret is discovered. Thereupon, with great good humour, but without equivocation, John remonstrates with Lycomedes that he is still a victim of his old forms of religious worship. Just as we worship in dead buildings while the living God is within the temple of our body, so too is Lycomedes worshipping a dead painting when the living apostle is with him. The point that the author is wishing to make is that we worship the dead and neglect (or even persecute) the living.

John therefore concludes that, at best, a painting can only capture his physical features, but not the inner qualities of the soul, and in a delightful passage, he tells Lycomedes that he should learn to paint in another kind of colouring material altogether. We pick up the story where the painter commissioned by Lycomedes has made a start:

> The painter, then, on the first day made an outline of him (John) and went away. And on the next he painted him in with his colours, and so delivered the portrait to Lycomedes to his great joy. And he took it and set it up in his own bedchamber and hung it with garlands: so that later John, when he perceived it, said to him: "My beloved child, what is it that thou always doest when thou comest in from the bath into thy bedchamber alone? Do not I pray with thee and the rest of the brethren? Or is there something thou art hiding from us?"
>
> And as he said this and talked jestingly with him, he sent into the bedchamber, and saw the portrait of an old man crowned with garlands, and lamps and altars set before it. And he called him and said: "Lycomedes, what meanest thou by this matter of the portrait? Can it be one of thy gods that is painted here? For I see that thou art still living in heathen fashion."
>
> And Lycomedes answered him: "My only God is he who raised me up from death with my wife: but if, next to that God, it be right that the men who have benefited us should be called gods – it is thou, father, whom I have had painted in that portrait, whom I crown and love and reverence as having become my good guide."
>
> And John who had never at any time seen his own face said to him: "Thou mockest me, child: am I like that in form, excelling thy Lord? How canst thou persuade me that the portrait is like me?" And Lycomedes brought him a mirror. and when he had seen himself in the mirror and looked earnestly at the portrait, he said: "As the Lord Jesus Christ liveth, the portrait is like me: yet not like me, child, but like my fleshly image. For if this painter, who hath imitated this my face, desireth to draw me in a portrait, he will be at a loss, needing more than the colours that are now given to thee...."

"But do thou become for me a good painter, Lycomedes. Thou hast colours which he giveth thee through me, who painteth all of us for himself, even Jesus, who knoweth the shapes and appearances and postures and dispositions and types of our souls. And the colours wherewith I bid thee paint are these: faith in God, knowledge, godly fear, friendship, communion, meekness, kindness, brotherly love, purity, simplicity, tranquillity, fearlessness, grieflessness, sobriety, and the whole band of colours that painteth the likeness of thy soul, and even now raiseth up thy members that were cast down, and levelleth them that were lifted up, and tendeth thy bruises, and healeth thy wounds, and ordereth thine hair that was disarranged, and washeth thy face, and chasteneth thine eyes, and purgeth thy bowels, and emptieth thy belly, and cutteth off (remove attention from) that which is beneath it. And in a word, when the whole company and mingling of such colours is come together, into thy soul, it shall present it to our Lord Jesus Christ undaunted, whole and firm of shape.

"But this that thou hast now done is childish and imperfect: thou hast drawn a dead likeness of the dead."

Acts of John 27-29, ANT pp.233-234

These then, presented in a story form, are some of the human virtues, and similar breakdowns of human good qualities are to be found in a number of other places. In the *Acts of Peter*, for example, Paul says:

Wherefore, ye servants of God, arm yourselves every one in your inner man with peace, patience, gentleness, faith, charity, knowledge, wisdom, love of the brethren, hospitality, mercy, abstinence, chastity, kindness, justice: then shall ye have for your guide everlastingly the First-begotten of all creation, and shall have strength in peace with our Lord.

Acts of Peter III:II, ANT p.305

And in the revelational *Shepherd of Hermas,* an angel gives the 'names' of certain maidens who appear in an allegorical vision as personifications of human virtues:

The first is Faith, the second Temperance, the third is Power, the fourth is Long-suffering, and the others who stand between them have these names: Simplicity, Guilelessness, Holiness, Joyfulness, Truth, Understanding, Concord, Love. He who bears these names and the Name of the Son of God, "shall be able to enter into the kingdom of God."

Shepherd of Hermas IX:XV, AFII p.259

Many of these early Christian documents originated with those who were no longer in contact with the mystic teachings in their purest form. As a result, it is likely that their authors were unfamiliar with the kind of spiritual practice taught by Jesus to his disciples. In the absence of such interior prayer, the spiritual struggle becomes essentially earthbound, its arena becoming entirely that of contending with human imperfections and the effort to acquire 'virtue' and 'holiness'. Such a struggle is always limited in its success, for the power of the Word and its emissary, the perfect Master, cannot be invoked. Consequently, there have only been a very few people who by this effort, together with some form of contemplative prayer, have been able to withdraw all consciousness from the body and enter even the lower reaches of the heavenly realms.

Difficult though it may be, the struggle for human purity is only a means to contacting the inner Music, and it is this Music which ultimately brings perfection to a human being. The best and most effective approach, therefore, in the quest for human perfection is to seek divine perfection through meditation on the Word of God. Then, all the good human qualities rise to the surface automatically, like cream on milk. As Jesus said:

> But seek ye first the kingdom of God,
>   and His righteousness;
>   and all these things shall be added unto you.
>   *Matthew 6:33*

One who seeks God also acquires all the virtues comprising human perfection, for He is the one from whom all perfection comes. But one who seeks human perfection alone, possessing only the inadequate means of personal struggle, may fail to achieve even that.

In the four gospels, Jesus speaks at some length on human weakness and virtue, and in the next chapter his teachings on this subject are considered in greater detail. First, however, it will be useful to lay out a framework within which the matter may be discussed.

Faculty, Weakness and Virtue

All human imperfections or weaknesses arise from an imbalance in normal human instincts, which then operate without control, rather than with understanding. Conversely, human virtues – in their highest expression, found only in a perfect mystic – are normal human characteristics functioning in one who has a divine and complete understanding not only of human life but of all creation.

For example, the nature of life in this world requires that man has the inclination and the potential both to acquire and possess things. Man needs clothing, shelter and food for the continuation of his individual existence, and he is built with the instinct or faculty to figure out ways of acquiring things and retaining them in his personal possession for as long as he needs them. This is a matter of practicality. It would be intolerable to begin every day with the search for a home, clothing and a source of food, though it is the lot of some. The ability to acquire and possess helps to make possible the living of human life for its highest purpose – the quest for God within oneself.

Man, however, forgets that possessions and acquiring them are only a means of sustaining life and he makes of them an end in themselves. The faculty of acquisition thus becomes an obsessive greed to acquire more and more, way beyond the bounds of need. Likewise, the instinct of possession becomes an intense attachment to and love for the objects thus acquired. Man then dwells in the illusion that they are *his*, not realizing that they can never belong to him in any permanent way and are only there for his use while living in this world. They are not his, they never were his, and they never can be his. Everything, whether soul or substance, is a part of and belongs to God.

The balanced approach to these two faculties or instincts may therefore be described as *unattachment* to possessions and *contentment* with the basic necessities of life. The term 'unattachment' is used advisedly, rather than the alternative 'detachment', which could suppose an uncaring and aloof manner, quite the reverse of the truly spiritual person.

Similarly, with other human faculties. Man is made with a procreative instinct. In the majority of instances, however, the purpose of this faculty is forgotten in the desire for sensual pleasure and self-gratification. Procreation thus degenerates into lust. Its balanced use, on the other hand, requires its employment only within prescribed limits for the purposes of starting a family and for human closeness. Though it may be hard to contemplate for most human beings, especially in the present age, celibacy is a great virtue, an ideal to be considered, even in married life after the desired number of children have been born. After all, despite modern attitudes to sex, adultery is still grounds for divorce and public scandal. Whatever his actions may be, man knows that there is something not quite right about it.

The same is true in the utilization of the senses. Man can employ them for balanced observation, appreciation and appropriate action in the Lord's creation, or, like a bee falling into honey, he can dive in too deep, indulging himself and his appetites. Thus arise the wider aspects of lust as indulgence in any of the senses. This includes such weaknesses as gluttony – overindulgence in the otherwise natural need for food and drink. On consideration, then, most people would agree that self-control is both desirable and essential for a balanced and successful life.

Again, man has a drive and an executive ability – an ability to get up and go and accomplish things, together with a mind that can direct and manipulate that drive. But it has to be kept within bounds and held under control, otherwise – running in an unconscious manner – whenever it meets with the unavoidable obstructions of life, the individual will feel frustration and impatience, turning into anger. The corresponding virtue, then, is to accept unreservedly the circumstances of life which obstruct one's way – that is, patience, forbearance, tolerance and forgiveness.

All of these four faculties have one feature in common. They are all designed for the benefit of the individual, for one's *self*. As a human being, even a Master will have a human identity that places him in balanced juxtaposition to the rest of the world, just like everybody else. But the difference is that his inner being is not identified with his human identity, but with God. His human identity is simply a faculty for use at the human level, just as knees or any other part of the body have a function in a physical way. It is an aspect of being at the human level and a Master uses it in this way, under full and perfectly enlightened control.

In most people, however, this sense of human identity, an aspect of the mind, has taken over the position of the self. This is an illusion. It is what was described by some of the gnostics as the "counterfeit spirit". It is the counterfeit or false self, not the real self. In its imbalanced form, human identity becomes the ever-present human ego, asserting itself as selfishness and I-ness in every aspect of life. It is the source of pride and vanity, and it gives force to all human weaknesses. Attachment, greed, lust and anger all exist because of ego. Take away the illusory sense of self from these and they become their balanced counterparts – unattachment, contentment, chastity and forbearance.

These five faculties, together with their corresponding weaknesses and virtues, can be considered as the primary colours in the spectrum of human character. From their cross-multiplication, joined together with other human talents and natural faculties, arise an infinite variety and combination of human characteristics, imperfections and virtues. Let us consider these five faculties in this light.

Firstly, without due consideration and control, the need for acquisition develops into greed giving rise to miserliness, misrepresentation, jealousy, dissatisfaction, ingratitude, deceit, bribery, robbery and selfish manipulation of all kinds. Conversely, the balanced understanding of this faculty leads to contentment, satisfaction, gratitude, generosity, munificence, a charitable disposition and preference for giving rather than taking, honesty, sincerity, integrity and straightness in all one's dealings.

Secondly, the necessity for certain fundamental possessions becomes attachment to the things of life, leading to worry, anxiety, narrow-mindedness, prejudice, partisanship, exclusivity, fear and procrastination. On the other hand, a balanced perception of the true nature of possessions engenders unattachment, discrimination, broad-mindedness, sharing, fearlessness and promptness in disposing of the affairs of life.

Thirdly, frustration to our sense of drive breeds anger with its associated colours of resentment, criticism, scolding, abuse of others, slander, impatience, impetuousness, being readily discouraged and giving up easily, intolerance, taking offence easily, fighting, cursing and habitually blaming others for all misfortune. Understanding that the nature and structure of life is such that obstructions will always be presenting themselves gives a person the strength and wit to find ways around all difficulties. Hence arise tolerance, forbearance, patience, endurance, steadfastness, consideration, forgiveness, kindness, thinking and speaking well of others and supporting them in many ways, a love of peace and harmony together with sweet and graceful speech and action.

Fourthly, indulgence in the procreative faculty or any of the senses for purely personal pleasure becomes lust – the father of lewdness, pornography, rape, adultery, obscenity, vulgarity, gluttony and sensual indulgence of any kind, including the craving for drugs, alcohol, tobacco or anything else. A balanced approach to the senses leads to chastity, self-control and a subtle appreciation of correct limits and boundaries in physical life.

Lastly, without some degree of spiritual insight, the natural human sense of self becomes a massively enlarged ego engendering pride, vanity, ostentation, feelings of both superiority and inferiority, selfishness, self-assertion, constantly interrupting others, bigotry, bullying, a domineering character, the desire for power, disrespect of others and usurping of their rights. Conversely, a true appreciation of human identity and one's relationship to all else in the Lord's creation lead to humility, meekness, selflessness, a desire to serve, a perception of the inherent equality of all souls, the ability to truly listen to others, and a respect for all people and their rights and position within the fabric of human relationships.

Naturally, most of these and other sins and virtues contain elements of other tendencies within them and this exposition is by no means intended as a watertight analysis of human psychology. Jealousy, for instance, may involve thwarted sexual desire or arise from attachment to people or to material possessions or ideas, while every vice reveals an inordinate enlargement of the self or ego. Similarly, a truly humble person will automatically be kind, generous, patient and self-controlled. Nevertheless, this framework does give us a useful handle by which to approach Jesus' teaching on the subject.

NOTES AND REFERENCES

1. *Tripartite Tractate* 53, NHS22 p.195.
2. *Apocryphon of John* 14, NHL p.113.
3. *Apocryphon of John* 31, NHL p.122.
4. *Gospel of the Egyptians* 67, NHL p.218.
5. *Trimorphic Protennoia* 45, NHS28 p.423.
6. *Tripartite Tractate* 53-54, NHS22 p.197.
7. *Eugnostos the Blessed* 72, NHL p.225.
8. *Second Treatise of the Great Seth* 59, NHL p.366.
9. *Second Treatise of the Great Seth* 49, NHL p.363.
10. *Gospel of Philip* 55, NHS20 p.151.
11. *Sophia of Jesus* 96,98,100,106,107,114, NHL pp.225,226,228,232,239.
12. *Trimorphic Protennoia* 38, NHS28 p.409.
13. *Sraoshav* is derived from *Sraosha*, a term used by Zarathushtra for the mystic Sound. Here, the Master is identified with the Sound and with God.

CHAPTER TWENTY-FIVE

Be Ye Therefore Perfect:
Fight the Great Fight

Take Heed and Beware of Covetousness

Jesus speaks unequivocally on the uselessness of the obsessive involvement in this world which leads a person to neglect or ignore the spiritual purpose of human life. We have discussed in earlier chapters Jesus' sound advice:

> Lay not up for yourselves treasures upon earth,
>> where moth and rust doth corrupt,
>> and where thieves break through and steal:
> But lay up for yourselves treasures in heaven,
>> where neither moth nor rust doth corrupt,
>> and where thieves do not break through nor steal:
> For where your treasure is, there will your heart be also.
>
> *Matthew 6:19-21*

Likewise, the beautiful discourse concerning the "lilies of the field" and so on, located in Matthew's Sermon on the Mount, can hardly be bettered as an expression of divine unconcern for the things of the world. Luke also has two parables to relate which further emphasize the point that whatever man may collect in this world will be of no use in the place where he is bound to go when death catches up with him, usually before he is ready to depart. The first is of a rich man and a beggar man named Lazarus:

> There was a certain rich man, which was clothed in purple and fine linen, and fared sumptuously every day. And there was a certain beggar named Lazarus, which was laid at his gate, full of sores, and desiring to be fed with the crumbs which fell from the rich man's table: moreover the dogs came and licked his sores.

And it came to pass, that the beggar died, and was carried by the angels into Abraham's bosom: the rich man also died, and was buried; and in hell he lift up his eyes, being in torments, and seeth Abraham afar off, and Lazarus in his bosom. And he cried and said, "Father Abraham, have mercy on me, and send Lazarus, that he may dip the tip of his finger in water, and cool my tongue; for I am tormented in this flame."

But Abraham said, "Son, remember that thou in thy lifetime receivedst thy good things, and likewise Lazarus evil things: but now he is comforted, and thou art tormented. And beside all this, between us and you there is a great gulf fixed: so that they which would pass from hence to you cannot; neither can they pass to us, that would come from thence."

Then he said, "I pray thee therefore, father, that thou wouldst send him to my father's house. For I have five brethren; that he may testify unto them, lest they also come into this place of torment."

Abraham saith unto him, "They have Moses and the prophets; let them hear them."

And he said, "Nay, father Abraham: but if one went unto them from the dead, they will repent."

And he said unto him, "If they hear not Moses and the prophets, neither will they be persuaded, though one rose from the dead."

Luke 16:19-31

The moral of the story is self-evident. Not only is the collection of wealth in this world a short-sighted policy, but it leads a person into all manner of deception and other vices, landing him in a ticklish situation after death, to say the least. The gathering of such wealth is thus a very poor investment of one's time as a human being. Yet strangely, as Jesus points out, though there is no lack of spiritual teaching to this effect in the sacred literature of the world, people are not only unwilling or unable to hear the message which is so universally and so frequently given to them, but even when a living Master comes and personally explains these matters face-to-face, they are unable to understand what he is telling them.

This is the effect of greed and attachment to the material possessions and affairs of physical existence. The mind runs like a steamroller out of control, functioning entirely as a creature of habit, locked into an unconscious race to acquire as much as it can in the shortest possible time – or simply to exist from day to day, scratching together a living in whatever way is opportune. If somebody ever thinks of God and the spiritual dimension to life, the thought is fleeting as more pressures and distractions pile in, and the result is a fatal procrastination.

A wise man, therefore, will never forget that he has to leave this world one day, and will prepare himself, living his life accordingly. This is what is meant in the *Acts of John*, when John says:

> Before all things it is needful that the believer should look before at his ending and understand in what manner it will come upon him, whether it will be vigorous and sober and without any obstacle, or disturbed and clinging to the things that are here, and bound down by desires.
>
> *Acts of John 69, ANT p.244*

Luke's second parable explains the same point:

> The ground of a certain rich man brought forth plentifully. And he thought within himself, saying, "What shall I do, because I have no room where to bestow my fruits?" And he said, "This will I do: I will pull down my barns, and build greater; and there will I bestow all my fruits and my goods. And I will say to my soul, 'Soul, thou hast much goods laid up for many years; take thine ease, eat, drink, and be merry.'"
>
> But God said unto him, "Thou fool, this night thy soul shall be required of thee: then whose shall those things be, which thou hast provided?" So is he that layeth up treasure for himself, and is not rich toward God.
>
> *Luke 12:16-21*

Luke uses this parable as an introduction to the material which is found in Matthew's Sermon on the Mount and again the meaning is clear. The avaricious man makes plans for this world, putting off all thoughts of spiritual endeavour. He builds a treasure in this world which he must leave here for the taxman and for his heirs who often cannot restrain their impatience for his departure, subsequently squabbling over his estate after he has gone. But he collects none of the spiritual wealth which will be of value to him, not only during life, but also after death. As Luke again records:

> One of the company said unto him, "Master, speak to my brother, that he divide the inheritance with me."
>
> And he said unto him, "Man, who made me a judge or a divider over you?" And he said unto them, "Take heed, and beware of covetousness: for a man's life consisteth not in the abundance of the things which he possesseth."
>
> *Luke 12:13-15*

Masters do not come to this world to sort out our endless, self-created problems. They come to remind us of the deep slumber into which we have fallen, to encourage us to think of our long-term spiritual welfare and to take us out of this world for all time. Man, however, finds it difficult to turn his mind away from the world. Initiates and non-initiates alike are tempted by the allurements of physical life. As Jesus says in his parable of the sower, there are some disciples whose seed has fallen amongst thorns:

> And that which fell among thorns are they, which,
> when they have heard, go forth, and are choked
> with (the) cares and riches and pleasures of this life,
> and bring no fruit to perfection.
>
> *Luke 8:14*

And in an excerpt where the "enemies" are the weaknesses and temptations of the mind, a Manichaean-Christian psalmist observes:

> The enemy of my soul is the world,
> its riches and its deceit.
> All life (here) hates godliness:
> what am I doing in the place of my enemies?
>
> *Psalm CCLXI, MPB p.75*

More specifically, the author of the Nag Hammadi *Authoritative Teaching* describes how a desire first enters somebody's mind as a small concern, but soon begins to grow and dominate the person:

> Now these are the foods with which the Devil lies in wait for us. First he injects a pain into your heart until you have heartache on account of a small thing of this life, and he seizes you with his poisons. And afterwards he injects the desire of a tunic so that you will pride yourself in it, and love of money, pride, vanity, envy that rivals another envy, beauty of body, fraudulence. The greatest of all these are (spiritual) ignorance and ease (idleness).
>
> *Authoritative Teaching 30-31, NHS11 p.279*

It is better therefore to reject a desire when it first enters the mind, or else it grows in stature, very soon enveloping itself with an aura of necessity. As the same writer says:

In this very way we exist in this world, like fish. The Adversary spies on us, lying in wait for us like a fisherman, wishing to seize us, rejoicing that he might swallow us. For he places many foods before our eyes, things which belong to this world. He wishes to make us desire one of them and to taste only a little, so that he may seize us with his hidden poison and bring us out of freedom and take us into slavery. For whenever he catches us with a single food, it is indeed necessary for us to desire the rest. Finally, then, such things become the food of death.

Authoritative Teaching 30, NHS11 pp.277-279

Nothing brings lasting satisfaction. So once the habit of succumbing to desire is established, the mind will move on from one desire to another. Giving space to one desire therefore leads to being trapped by many desires and the "freedom" of the spirit is replaced by the "slavery" and "death" of this world. Then, as John points out in the *Acts of John*, people "do not possess riches but are possessed of them":

Even the lovers of the world do not possess riches,
　　but are possessed of them.
For it is out of reason that for one belly
　　there should be laid up so much food as would suffice a thousand,
　　and for one body so many garments
　　as would furnish clothing for a thousand men.
In vain, therefore, is that stored up
　　which cometh not into use,
　　and for whom it is kept, no man knoweth,

As the Holy Ghost saith by the prophet:
"In vain is every man troubled who heapeth up riches
　　and knoweth not for whom he gathereth them."
Naked did our birth from women bring us into this light,
　　destitute of food and drink:
Naked will the earth receive us which brought us forth.

We possess in common the riches of the heaven;
　　the brightness of the sun is equal for the rich and the poor,
　　and likewise the light of the moon and the stars,
　　the softness of the air and the drops of rain,
　　and the gate of the church and the fount of sanctification,
　　and the forgiveness of sins, and the sharing in the altar,
　　and the eating of the body and drinking of the blood of Christ,

and the anointing of the chrism, and the grace of the Giver,
and the visitation of the Lord, and the pardon of sin:

In all these the dispensing of the Creator is equal,
without respect of persons.
Neither doth the rich man use these gifts after one manner
and the poor after another.

Acts of John XVI, ANT pp.259-260

In God's eyes, says John, everyone has the same spiritual heritage
and is freely provided by God with the same blessings and the same
gifts of nature. Why then spend life striving for that which is beyond
our needs?

What Shall We Do Then?

Given consideration and honest introspection, such truths are self-
evident, yet in practice it is hard to overcome even the most fundamental and obvious of human weaknesses. How are greed and the tendency to over-accumulate to be overcome? The question is an old one
and was asked of Jesus:

And the people asked him, saying,
"What shall we do then?"
He answereth and saith unto them,
"He that hath two coats,
let him impart to him that hath none;
and he that hath meat, let him do likewise."

Then came also publicans to be baptized, and said unto him,
"Master, what shall we do?"
And he said unto them,
"Exact no more than that which is appointed you."

And the soldiers likewise demanded of him, saying,
"And what shall we do?"
And he said unto them,
"Do violence to no man, neither accuse any falsely;
and be content with your wages."

Luke 3:10-14

Jesus' answer was that new habits of sharing and generosity should be established in the mind, replacing the old ones. Man should learn to give to others of his surplus wealth and possessions. "Publicans" – the tax collectors – who were no doubt open to bribery and corruption, should be straight in all their dealings. Or, more generally, those who are involved with money or business should be scrupulously honest and never take advantage of their position by overcharging or gaining an excess profit, with one excuse or another. And wage earners and professional people, such as soldiers, should not abuse their positions of power over others. Furthermore, they should be content with their remuneration, rather than always demanding more and more.

The advice is hard, for it requires a great deal of faith in the protection of God even to give away surplus possessions. All the same, it seems that many of Jesus' disciples put his advice into practice, for there are a number of anecdotes to this effect. Clement of Alexandria relates:

> It is said that Zacchaeus (or, as some say, Matthias), the chief publican, when he had heard the Lord, who condescended to come to him, said: "Behold, the half of my goods I give in alms, Lord: and if I have defrauded any man of ought, I restore it fourfold." Whereupon also the Saviour said: "The Son of man is come today and hath found that which was lost."
>
> *Gospel of Matthias, in Clement of Alexandria, Miscellanies IV:6.35, ANT p.13*

By using excess wealth for the benefit of others, a person is saved from indulging in the weaknesses to which rich living is heir. Moreover, they begin to realize that there is far greater pleasure in giving than in receiving and they gradually develop a taste for serving others. This all helps to detach them from the things of the world and to humble the mind. It narrows down the mind's outward tendencies, leading it towards its mental focus at the single eye. Spiritual practice, accumulation of the spiritual treasure, is thus helped by acts of true service. Hence, Jesus again advises:

> Sell that ye have, and give alms;
>> provide yourselves bags which wax not old,
>> a treasure in the heavens that faileth not,
>> where no thief approacheth, neither moth corrupteth.
> For where your treasure is, there will your heart be also.
>
> *Luke 12:33-34*

And in *Acts*, Paul is credited with quoting an otherwise unrecorded saying of Jesus:

> It is more blessed to give than to receive.
>
> *Acts 20:35*

The mind, however, finds an opportunity for pride and self-interest even in good deeds. Egocentric thoughts die hard and many of those who give in charity like the world to know that they are being so generous. Jesus has an answer to this, too:

> Take heed that ye do not your alms before men,
> to be seen of them: otherwise ye have no reward
> of your Father which is in heaven.
> Therefore when thou doest thine alms,
> do not sound a trumpet before thee,
> as the hypocrites do in the synagogues
> and in the streets, that they may have glory of men.
> Verily I say unto you, they have their reward.
>
> But when thou doest alms,
> let not thy left hand know what thy right hand doeth:
> That thine alms may be in secret:
> and thy Father which seeth in secret
> Himself shall reward thee openly.
>
> *Matthew 6:1-4*

Jesus says, do not take pride in charitable acts of any kind. Keep the matter secret between yourself and the Lord, so that egotism may not enter your mind. "Let not thy left hand know what thy right hand doeth": do not even let yourself know what you are doing – do not congratulate yourself on your generosity. Those who seek recognition for their giving will receive it. People will say how good and generous they are and they will feel proud. But they will receive no spiritual benefit – in fact, they will become trapped deeper still in egotism. Moreover, they will have to receive a reward for their charity in another life, reincarnating once again in the prison house of this world. So he says, keep the mind humble. Only then will the Father "reward thee openly" – only then will He shower the abundant blessings that follow true humility and the spirit of service.

But greed is a powerful force and as Judas Thomas says:

> Scantly are rich men found in almsgiving.
>
> *Acts of Thomas 66, ANT p.395*

The richer the man, the more difficult he finds it to give. Or if he does give, he gives only that which hardly touches his pocket. Yet, the true giver will give without counting the cost and out of a deep desire to serve and to give back to the Lord, in however seemingly insignificant a way, something of the treasures which He so willingly bestows. This is brought out so clearly in the well-known story of the widow's mite. It is another of Luke's stories:

> And he (Jesus) looked up,
>   and saw the rich men casting
>   their gifts into the treasury.
> And he saw also a certain poor widow
>   casting in thither two mites.
>
> And he said, "Of a truth I say unto you,
>   that this poor widow hath cast in more than they all:
> For all these have of their abundance
>   cast in unto the offerings of God:
> But she of her penury hath cast in
>   all the living that she had."
>
> *Luke 21:1-4*

Godliness with Contentment is Great Gain

It is clear that Jesus taught generosity and a spirit of real service to others as a part of the spiritual path. From this is derived great satisfaction and contentment with one's lot. Those who give to others come to realize that the Lord provides all their needs and necessities of life, without their ever asking. Faith is a great power by which a person's understanding grows that God is with them at all times. As the unknown writer of the letter to the *Hebrews* says:

> **Let your conversation be without covetousness;**
> **and be content with such things as ye have:**

For he hath said,
"I will never leave thee, nor forsake thee."

Hebrews 13:5

And in a famous extract from the letter to Timothy which holds true, whoever wrote it:

Godliness with contentment is great gain.
For we brought nothing into this world,
    and it is certain we can carry nothing out.
And having food and raiment let us be therewith content.

But they that will be rich fall into temptation and a snare,
    and into many foolish and hurtful lusts,
    which drown men in destruction and perdition.
For the love of money is the root of all evil:
    which while some coveted after,
    they have erred from the faith,
    and pierced themselves through with many sorrows.

But thou, O man of God, flee these things;
    and follow after righteousness, godliness,
    faith, love, patience, meekness.
Fight the good fight of faith, lay hold on eternal life,
    whereunto thou art also called,
    and hast professed a good profession
    before many witnesses.

1 Timothy 6:6-12

I Came Not to Send Peace, But a Sword

We discussed in an earlier chapter (see page 214), how Jesus spoke of "fasting from the world", meaning that a person should endeavour to remain unattached to the world as they go through life. There are other places, too, where he speaks of such detachment. He says, for instance:

Think not that I am come to send peace on earth:
    I came not to send peace, but a sword.

Matthew 10:34

Bearing in mind the remainder of Jesus' teachings, this comment may at first sight seem remarkable. The full context, however, makes his meaning clear. He continues:

> For I am come to set a man at variance against his father,
>   and the daughter against her mother,
>   and the daughter in law against her mother in law.
> And a man's foes shall be they of his own household.
> He that loveth father or mother more than me
>   is not worthy of me:
> And he that loveth son or daughter more than me
>   is not worthy of me.
>
> *Matthew 10:35-37*

Jesus is talking of the deep attachments that we develop for our family members and loved ones. He says that he has come with a "sword", the sword of the Word, to separate people from each other, not physically, but mentally. The point is that we become so involved with each other that we forget the real purpose of human life. If we permit our family members and others to consume our time and attention to the extent that we have no time for our own selves, then our thoughts will never refocus at their headquarters in the single eye and we will never even begin to travel the inner path that leads to God.

If a king invited us to his palace, but while eating his food and enjoying his hospitality, we ignored him altogether, giving our attention entirely to our fellow guests, we would rightly be considered impolite. Similarly, to neglect the One who is the Source of life and has given us the human form for the primary purpose of God-realization, paying more attention to His creation than to Him, makes us "unworthy" of Him. "Unworthy" in the sense that we will remain in our attachments, in the realm of birth and death, and will not return to Him, nor even be able to find the spiritual form of the Master inside ourselves. This is why Jesus says that he who loves his family members "more than me is not worthy of me". The same point is made elsewhere in Matthew. According to the story:

> Then answered Peter and said unto him,
> "Behold, we have forsaken all, and followed thee;
>   what shall we have therefore?" ...

And Jesus said unto them: ...

"Every one that hath forsaken houses, or brethren,
    or sisters, or father, or mother, or wife,
    or children, or lands, for my name's sake,
    shall receive an hundredfold,
    and shall inherit everlasting life."

                              Matthew 19:27,29

Those who have "forsaken" – have detached themselves from – all their possessions and family members "shall inherit everlasting life": they will receive their spiritual inheritance and will return to God. Indeed, if we can only develop the same attachment to God that we have for our fellow human beings, then we will come under His protection and begin the journey back to Him. This, at least, is what Judas Thomas comments to a king who had been speaking of his deep love and attachment for his wife:

And Judas went with him laughing, and said to him:
"Believe me, my child,
    if men loved God as much as they love one another,
    they would ask of Him all things and receive them,
    and none would do them violence."

         Acts of Thomas 128, AAA p.265, ANT p.421

Jesus even goes so far as to say that his real family members are those who "do the will of my Father which is in heaven". The saying comes as the conclusion of an incident where he is told that his mother and brothers are standing outside, wanting to see him:

While he yet talked to the people,
    behold, his mother and his brethren stood without,
    desiring to speak with him. Then one said unto him,
"Behold, thy mother and thy brethren stand without,
    desiring to speak with thee."

But he answered and said unto him that told him,
"Who is my mother? And who are my brethren?"
And he stretched forth his hand
    toward his disciples, and said,
"Behold my mother and my brethren!
For whosoever shall do the will

of my Father which is in heaven,
the same is my brother, and sister, and mother."
Matthew 12:46-50

Whether or not the story itself is authentic is, as always, open to question, especially since it seems unlikely that the loving Jesus would really have snubbed the members of his own family. The incident – which Matthew has taken from Mark's original – was probably fabricated around the saying, "whosoever shall do the will of my Father which is in heaven, the same is my brother, and sister, and mother". The meaning, however, remains the same.

We consider our family members to be the ones who are really closest to us, but Jesus says that those who are closest to him are those who live in the "will of my Father" – those who follow his teachings and put into practice what he says. All our relationships in this world arise from associations in past births. People come and go in our lives according to a pre-set path and no human being can guarantee that they will always be with us or be close to us. Even if they are, physical proximity does not necessarily mean a closeness of heart. But, once initiated, a Master is always with his disciples. He will never leave them until he has taken them back to God. He and they and God will all become one. And the closeness of this mystic union is real and lasting, of a different order altogether from even the closest of human relationships.

Honour Thy Father and Thy Mother

Taking these anecdotes at face value, together with Jesus' other sayings concerning family attachments, one might be led to believe that he was advocating the break-up of family unity and normal social interaction. But this cannot have been his intention, for elsewhere, he says:

> Blessed are the peacemakers:
> for they shall be called the children of God.
> *Matthew 5:9*

Clearly, he advocates harmony, as indeed he does when advising that we turn the other cheek to would-be aggressors. Severing family relationships only leads to disharmony and to great disturbance of mind, taking a person even further away from God and making spiritual practice very difficult. Jesus is hardly likely to have encouraged such a course of action.

So on the one hand Jesus is advocating the "forsaking" of everybody for his sake, also saying that he has come with a sword to separate family members from each other. Yet on the other, he is recommending family harmony. There is no contradiction in this. We have already noted that Jesus spoke out strongly against divorce:

> And the Pharisees came to him and asked him, "Is it lawful for a man to put away his wife?" – tempting him.
>
> And he answered and said unto them, "What did Moses command you?"
>
> And they said, "Moses suffered to write a bill of divorcement, and to put her away."
>
> And Jesus answered and said unto them, "For the hardness of your heart he wrote you this precept. But from the beginning of the creation God made them male and female. For this cause shall a man leave his father and mother, and cleave to his wife; and they twain shall be one flesh: so then they are no more twain, but one flesh. What therefore God hath joined together, let not man put asunder."
>
> And in the house, his disciples asked him again of the same matter. And he saith unto them, "Whosoever shall put away his wife, and marry another, committeth adultery against her. And if a woman shall put away her husband, and be married to another, she committeth adultery."
>
> *Mark 10:2-12*

He says that Moses only provided a dispensation for divorce because people are so hardhearted that they cannot get along together and would break apart anyway. So being ever practical, as mystics are, Moses provided a legal framework for such separations so that an even greater mess would not ensue, causing further human suffering. But later, when alone with his disciples, Jesus goes on to describe all those who divorce their spouse and remarry as adulterers. In our modern society, this may be hard to swallow. But without entering into the rights and wrongs of divorce, it is quite evident that Jesus did not advocate physically "forsaking" one's family.

In fact, the reverse would seem to have been the case. When dying on the cross, according to John's version, Jesus even arranges for the welfare and safeguarding of his mother, the gesture of a caring and loving son. And elsewhere, he repeats Moses' ten commandments, amongst which are injunctions to give due respect to one's parents:

And, behold, one came and said unto him, "Good Master, what good thing shall I do, that I may have eternal life?"

And he said unto him, "Why callest thou me good? There is none good but one, that is, God: but if thou wilt enter into life, keep the commandments."

He saith unto him, "Which?" Jesus said, "Thou shalt do no murder; thou shalt not commit adultery; thou shalt not steal; thou shalt not bear false witness; honour thy father and thy mother: and, thou shalt love thy neighbour as thyself."

The young man saith unto him, "All these things have I kept from my youth up: what lack I yet?"

Jesus said unto him, "If thou wilt be perfect, go and sell that thou hast, and give to the poor, and thou shalt have treasure in heaven: and come and follow me." But when the young man heard that saying, he went away sorrowful: for he had great possessions.

Matthew 19:16-22

This is the heart of the matter. Outer life must go on, all family and other duties being lovingly performed. It is the inner obsession with the "possessions" and "riches" of the world that constitute the problem, not the external circumstances. In fact, mystics advise that there is no need for a disciple to alter his or her external circumstances unless they are absolutely contrary to following the mystic path. More than anything else, it is a person's inner attitude that must change. The only adjustments needed to a disciple's outer life are those which bring it into line with the requirements of the spiritual path. In this way, a person will become a better husband, a better wife, son, daughter, friend, employee, employer and so on.

In short, an attitude of love and selflessness should pervade a person's inner and outer life. As Jesus said, quoting Moses, "Love thy neighbour as thyself" and also:

> Therefore all things whatsoever ye would
> that men should do to you, do ye even so to them:
> For this is the law and the prophets.
>
> *Matthew 7:12*

It is all a matter of love and harmony. Someone who has the love of God in their heart becomes soft and warm-hearted, and will always be kind and considerate to others. They will go to great lengths even to avoid hurting the feelings of others. This is the "law and the prophets"; this is what all the mystics have taught.

The inculcation of harmony in every sphere of life is frequently emphasized in early Christian writings, as in *1 Peter*:

> Likewise, ye younger, submit yourselves unto the elder. Yea, all of you be subject one to another, and be clothed with humility: for God resisteth the proud, and giveth grace to the humble. Humble yourselves therefore under the mighty hand of God, that he may exalt you in due time.
>
> *1 Peter 5:5-6*

And the same idea – according to the social customs of the times – is behind Paul's advice to the Colossians and the Ephesians:

> Wives, submit yourselves unto your own husbands, as it is fit in the Lord. Husbands, love your wives, and be not bitter against them.
>
> *Colossians 3:18-19*

> Children, obey your parents in the Lord: for this is right. Honour thy father and mother ... that it may be well with thee, and thou mayest live long on the earth. And, ye fathers, provoke not your children to wrath: but bring them up in the nurture and admonition of the Lord.
>
> Servants (*lit.* slaves), be obedient to them that are your masters according to the flesh, with fear and trembling, in singleness of your heart, as unto Christ; not with eye-service, as men-pleasers; but as the servants (*lit.* slaves) of Christ, doing the will of God from the heart; with good will doing service, as to the Lord, and not to men: knowing that whatsoever good thing any man doeth, the same shall he receive of the Lord, whether he be bond or free.
>
> And, ye masters, do the same things unto them, forbearing threatening: knowing that your Master also is in heaven; neither is there respect of persons with him.
>
> *Ephesians 6:1-9*

Everything is to be done well in this world; all obligations are to be fulfilled. But the motivation should be to please God, to be in harmony with Him, to see Him in everything, living in His presence, to please "your Master ... in heaven" – not to be in inner subservience to other men, whatever the outward form may be. The same principle is repeated in the letters known as *1 Timothy* and *Titus*:

> Let as many servants (*lit.* slaves) as are under the yoke count their own masters worthy of all honour, that the name of God and his doctrine be not blasphemed. And they that have believing masters, let them not despise them, because they are brethren; but rather do them service, because they are faithful and beloved, partakers of the benefit.
>
> *1 Timothy 6:1-2*

And:

> Exhort servants (*lit.* slaves) to be obedient unto their own masters, and to please them well in all things; not answering again; not purloining, but shewing all good fidelity; that they may adorn the doctrine of God our Saviour in all things.
>
> *Titus 2:9-10*

Likewise, the early second-century father, Ignatius, writes to Bishop Polycarp:

> Do not be haughty to slaves, either men or women.
>
> *Ignatius, To Polycarp IV:3, AFI p.273*

It is worth observing that most modern translations of the New Testament letters correctly speak of "slaves", not "servants", showing the wide social spectrum from which early Christians were drawn, a hallmark of any group of true spiritual seekers. The realization, however, that early Christianity accepted slavery might raise a few eyebrows. It is not that Jesus or Paul condoned or did not condone slavery. It is simply that mystics do not come to change the social order. That is a job for others to perform. No social conditions are externally ideal, nor can they ever be so, for their imperfections will always reflect the imperfections within the minds of the people who comprise them. Only if everyone sought God within themselves as their first priority in life, would the world really alter for the better. Moreover, the attempt to change the world can become deeply emotive and political, consuming vast amounts of time and energy, focusing a great deal of attention upon the world, and making meditation very difficult.

Happiness, peace, freedom and equality are to be found within and, though no doubt there were atrocities, many slaves must also have been treated as valued members of a household and have led contented lives. Certainly, many rich men have been bound far more securely to this world than their slaves or those who work for them. By virtue of their past sins and *karmas*, everyone in this world is a slave. The only escape is to open the inner trap door in the roof of our body, effecting an exit by silently and secretly taking the attention into the realms of the Spirit.

Mystics, therefore, advise that we remain where we are and work our way up within ourselves, maintaining peace and harmony in all our human relationships, fulfilling our family and other genuine obligations with love and affection. If we live with certain people for long periods of our lives, then we are naturally bound to form some kind of attachment to them. This is normal and human, and we could hardly exist without it. But with spiritual development, often without changing our outer circumstances very much, the reality of our situation and the impermanence of this world become so strongly borne in upon us that in attachment we remain unattached, feeling free to depart without regrets when the time comes.

Turn to Him the Other Also

We have considered Jesus' teachings on greed and contentment, as well as attachment and unattachment. The third of our five broad categories of weakness and virtue is that of anger or wrath and its opposites of forbearance, tolerance, forgiveness and patience.

There are few who would deny the destructive power of anger. Homes and families have been torn apart by it. Businesses have failed because of it. Communities have been ravaged by it. People pass their lives locked into the misery of resentment and the desire for revenge, refusing to have contact or speak with those they feel have crossed their will and done them wrong, or shouting, arguing and fighting with them when they meet. Nations have gone to war because of irreconcilable anger and hatred between their leaders or their peoples. Thousands upon thousands of innocent and previously uninvolved people have died; wives have been left as widows; children have been left fatherless or orphaned; families have been shattered.

Though the original perpetrators suffer whether or not they realize it, anger often embroils many innocent people in the fracas. Bystanders take sides and join the fight. Anger can erupt like fire in dry brushwood, bringing death to vast areas before it is brought under control or burns itself out. Sometimes, the underlying embers have been smouldering as resentment for a long time, blazing into fire when some seemingly insignificant trigger sets it off. One match can burn down an entire forest.

Anger comes about whenever the 'I' is challenged or frustrated in its desire for something or upon encountering an obstacle while travelling unthinkingly down some pre-set, habitual path. Almost everyone experiences anger to a greater or lesser extent, even if only in its less apparent forms as impatience, frustration, intolerance, mental criticism of others and so on. Anger is the destroyer of peace and harmony. The mind is shattered and scattered to the four winds, and attempts to meditate are utterly disturbed by the churning of thought and emotion. Under the influence of anger, the mind spreads out into the world, readily becoming a prey to greed, lust and other weaknesses. When Jesus speaks of this tendency of the mind, which he does in a number of places, he invariably suggests a countermeasure. Forgive people "seventy times seven"[1] he advises Peter, and if, he also says – taking a Jewish example – while going to the temple, you recall some unpleasant incident with a fellow human being: first go and be reconciled with them before offering any gift.[2] Harmony in all one's relationships is a prerequisite for the calm mind required for true prayer and the spiritual worship of God. As Paul so wisely commented, "Let not the sun go down upon thy wrath",[3] and as we find in the letter attributed to James the brother of Jesus:

> Wherefore, my beloved brethren,
>   let every man be swift to hear,
>   slow to speak, slow to wrath:
> For the wrath of man worketh not the righteousness of God.
> Wherefore lay apart all filthiness
>   and superfluity of naughtiness,
>   and receive with meekness the engrafted Word,
>   which is able to save your souls.
>
> *James 1:19-21*

This is the ultimate point. By a pure life, man cleanses himself such that the "engrafted Word" can make its home within him, forgiving all his sins. But Jesus has some further, deeply perceptive comments to make upon this subject.

In modern times, the philosophy of non-violence has been promoted by a number of eminent people. As they have demonstrated, there is a great power in this approach – more power than in fighting. But the idea is not a new one. It has always been a part of good human behaviour, by whatever name it is called, and Jesus taught the same. Beginning by quoting the Jewish scriptures (*Exodus*), he says:

Ye have heard that it hath been said,
"An eye for an eye, and a tooth for a tooth"[4]
But I say unto you, that ye resist not evil:
> but whosoever shall smite thee on thy right cheek,
> turn to him the other also.
And if any man will sue thee at the law,
> and take away thy coat, let him have thy cloak also.
And whosoever shall compel thee to go a mile,
> go with him twain.
Give to him that asketh thee,
> and from him that would borrow of thee turn not thou away.

Matthew 5:38–42

This is the way he suggests dealing with angry or insistent people. Rather than losing one's temper, resulting in two foolish people instead of one, Jesus suggests giving in to them. Even if it means putting oneself out to some extent, find a way of removing or diverting any obstruction before it becomes a source of contention.

This is easy to say, of course, but when confronted, the ego comes into play, making it difficult to defuse the situation or to apologize, especially if one feels that the other person is in the wrong. It is not easy to detach the mind from a situation sufficiently to be able to say, "I'm sorry. It's my fault. I probably approached you in the wrong way" – or simply to keep silent or walk away without giving rise to further offence by the way one does so. But this is the approach that Jesus always recommends. The attitude he suggests is always that of love, never of anger, pride and confrontation. As he continues:

Ye have heard that it hath been said,
"Thou shalt love thy neighbour, and hate thine enemy."[5]
But I say unto you, love your enemies,
> bless them that curse you,
> do good to them that hate you,
> and pray for them which despitefully use you,
> and persecute you;
That ye may be the children of your Father which is in heaven:
> for He maketh His sun to rise on the evil and on the good,
> and sendeth rain on the just and on the unjust.

For if ye love them which love you, what reward have ye?
> Do not even the publicans the same?

> And if ye salute your brethren only,
>   what do ye more than others?
> Do not even the publicans so?
>
> *Matthew 5:43-47*

Most people, he points out, repay feeling for feeling and action for action. They like those who like them and hate those who hate them. This is the way of the mind. But there is little credit to us if we love somebody who loves us. It happens automatically in human relationships. What Jesus suggests is something far more difficult. When faced with hostility or dislike, he recommends refusing to let the mind go in a negative, reactive direction. Rather than repaying them in like kind, he says, turn the mind around and send back love in response. In the majority of instances, if someone is sincere and finds the right way of doing it, the other person automatically changes their attitude and approach. Real and sincere love can work wonders in an instant, while anger and retaliation will only make the situation worse.

People only get angry out of insecurity and that can only be countered and healed by means of love. Nothing else works so effectively. Whatever we put out, comes back to us. This is a law of nature. So if we put out love, good will and understanding, that is what will automatically be returned to us.

Hence, Jesus also adds that if we only greet our "brethren", then that is nothing unusual. Even the most hard-hearted and sinful people behave in that way. He advises us to be loving to everybody, to greet even those people who turn their heads away when they see us. Not only to greet our bosses and superiors, but to give respect to everyone who comes in our path, whoever they are.

Just as the sun gives light to everyone whoever they may be and just as the clouds drop rain upon all without discrimination, just so does the Lord give love and life to every soul, and just so does Jesus recommend that we develop love in our hearts for the entire creation. In this way, we can become universal like the Lord Himself and imbibe His qualities. As this same passage appears in Luke:

> For if ye love them which love you,
>   what thank have ye?
> For sinners also love those that love them.
> And if ye do good to them which do good to you,
>   what thank have ye?
> For sinners also do even the same.

And if ye lend to them of whom ye hope to receive,
  what thank have ye?
For sinners also lend to sinners,
  to receive as much again.

But love ye your enemies, and do good,
  and lend, hoping for nothing again;
And your reward shall be great,
  and ye shall be the children of the Highest:
for He is kind unto the unthankful and to the evil.
Be ye therefore merciful, as your Father also is merciful.

Luke 6:32-36

Just like the sun and the clouds, the Lord gives to all without asking anything in return, seeking no reward. Hence, Jesus urges us to give love ungrudgingly, without holding back, looking for no reward of any kind, neither physical, verbal nor psychological. Then we will receive the mercy and grace of God, a love and bliss that far outweigh any reward this world can offer.

Jealousy and Strife Have Overthrown Great Cities

Possibly standing second only to anger in its destructive potential is jealousy. A mixed emotion, arising from various combinations of all the primary weaknesses, jealousy behaves like a cancer, eating up a person from inside. Often it cloaks itself in self-righteousness, like a concealed disease in an apparently healthy person, or it sits sniping and carping from the sidelines, or it bursts out in wild and uncontrollable rage. To counter it, we need open-heartedness of the highest degree and sincere well-wishing for all souls in the Lord's creation, whoever they may be. He is the only one with the power to give, so it is His decision whom to give to and what to give and how much. Gratitude for our many blessings, seeing what *we* have rather than what *others* have, is another antidote. As the saying goes, "count your blessings".

This does not mean, of course, that if another person has stepped beyond the bounds of propriety as regards our personal life, that we do not have the right to take effective measures to remedy the situation. Marital infidelity is the obvious example here, giving rise to understandable jealousy in the other partner. We have the right as well as the duty to hold our relationships together. Nevertheless, the innocent party should be genuinely innocent and should maintain that attitude and strengthen it, though usually, even in such situations, all parties are at fault to some degree, in various different ways. It does, as they say, take two to tango – or in this case – three. But there are many causes of jealousy. The feeling that someone else has what we would like is its starting point – and that can apply to almost anything.

Jealousy is as old an emotion as human beings. As we read in a letter written nearly two thousand years ago, and attributed to the late first-century bishop, Clement of Rome:

> Jealousy has estranged wives from husbands, and made of no effect the saying of our father Adam, "This is now bone of my bone and flesh of my flesh."
>
> Jealousy and strife have overthrown great cities, and rooted up mighty nations....
>
> Through jealousy and envy the greatest and most righteous pillars of the Church were persecuted and contended unto death.
>
> *1 Clement VI:3, V:2, AFI pp.19,17*

Whosoever Looketh on a Woman to Lust after Her

The Negative Power has many ways of reflecting the Lord's reality and projecting illusion at the physical level. Of these, there is perhaps none more powerful and compelling than the sex drive, which expresses in physical terms a human being's intense desire for union. Even deeply spiritual people can still be troubled by sexual desire, and many tales are told of ascetics and holy men who have gained seeming mastery over human passions only to be bitten by the serpent of lust, often when it was least expected. The moral tenets of all major religions are in unanimity on this point: sex and God do not mix. As Paul wrote:

> The body is not for fornication,
>   but for the Lord;
> And the Lord for the body.
>   *1 Corinthians 6:13*

Human beings are not to live for sex. From God's viewpoint, the purpose of this body is to seek Him, for He can only be found if the search is begun while humanly incarnated.

Yet sex, in its better aspects, is associated with warmth and companionship, and the expression of deep affection between a man and a woman. People call it love and there is no doubt that even normally selfish people will rise above self-interest for the sake of one they love, though the relationship need not be sexual. Sex, too, is essential from the point of view of procreation and there is no denying that it is a strong, instinctive and involuntary biological urge. Without it, there might be no incentive to propagate the species and physical life would come to an end. In fact, all species have sex. Even plants have male and female aspects. It is an absolutely universal system. Why, then, do mystics come down so hard upon it? Jesus goes so far as to say:

> Ye have heard that it was said by them of old time,
>> thou shalt not commit adultery:
> But I say unto you,
>> that whosoever looketh on a woman to lust after her
>> hath committed adultery with her already in his heart.
>> *Matthew 5:27-28*

Though Jesus is talking specifically of sex outside of marriage, not only does he condemn adultery, he also indicates that even the thought or desire for sex is undesirable.

Given modern attitudes, people often find this aspect of spirituality harder to comprehend than any other. The reasons can be considered as twofold, though the two are intimately associated. Firstly, the desire for anything or anybody of this world will bring a soul back into this world in a future life. The stronger the desire, the deeper the binding to physicality. No one would deny the intense physical nature of sex and, according to the universal law of cause and effect, what is sown must be reaped. And desire for physical sensations can only be fulfilled by reincarnating in a physical body. Sex – even the thought or desire for sex – is one of the strongest chains binding the soul to this world. Moreover, its fulfilment does not necessarily require a human birth – all species have a sex urge where this desire from past lives can be fulfilled. Souls can thus regress from the human form under the influence of this very powerful force.

Secondly, for one who wishes to focus their attention at the single eye during spiritual practice and to maintain that point as their mental headquarters throughout the waking hours, permitting the attention to play with great force and attraction at practically the lowest level in the human body is entirely counterproductive. Furthermore, tremendous energy, both subtle and gross, is expended during sex. Even athletes and sportsmen keep away from their wives and girlfriends before the big events so as to conserve their energies. All of this energy, if sublimated and utilized, is of great help in spiritual endeavour and is a great hindrance if allowed to flow outwards. Besides, any act that makes the mind stick tenaciously to matter reverses the upward trend that the practitioner is trying so hard to establish by means of meditation.

The energy utilized in sex also detracts from energies that are normally utilized by the body for the maintenance of health. Thus, those who waste their energies in sexual indulgence are prone to various complaints including poor complexion, weakened eyesight, lack of physical and mental stamina, listlessness, inability to concentrate, liability to common infections and so on, depending on the individual.

Part of the problem in clearly understanding the matter is that sex is surrounded by a host of social taboos, inhibitions, guilt complexes, and religious rules and prohibitions. On the other hand, it is presented in our modern media as something to be sought after and indulged in as much as possible, as a vital and predominant part of normal life. The reality, of course, in most folk's lives, is very different and most of the media hype is actually a ruthless exploitation of people's biological urge for sex, used subliminally and incessantly to advertise practically anything on earth. Everything is linked to sex in order to sell it, young people being particularly targeted. Social attitudes have reached such proportions that in many parts of the westernized world, people are considered abnormal if they wish to turn their minds away from the subject and, when they do, they are often ridiculed as prudes and killjoys.

The mystic approach is very simple, straightforward and practical. It is not a matter of condemnation, subconscious complexes, labelling others as sinners or of any other emotional or subliminal response. It is simply that a person cannot go up and down at the same time. A person only has one mind and that cannot be focused simultaneously at two very different places. Concentration of the attention at the single eye, learning to enter the spiritual realms while living, coming into contact with the divine Music and treading the inner path to God are simply incompatible with indulgence in sex or anything which draws the attention so powerfully into the body and the physical realm. As Judas Thomas says in the *Acts of Thomas*:

> Fornication blindeth the mind
> and darkeneth the eyes of the soul,
> and is an impediment
> to the life (*lit.* conversation) of the body,

> turning the whole man unto weakness
> and casting the whole body into sickness.
>
> *Acts of Thomas 28, ANT p.376*

The "eyes of the soul" will not open; they remain blind for as long as a person is a victim to this desire, while bodily health and vigour – so useful in meditation – are undermined. Expanding on the subject, when asked by king Misdaeus why he should teach such a doctrine, Judas Thomas explains that the Lord requires His devotees to be clean of all material tendencies:

> And Misdaeus said unto Judas: "Wherefore teachest thou this new doctrine, which both gods and men hate, and which hath nought of profit?"
>
> And Judas said: "What evil do I teach?"
>
> And Misdaeus said: "Thou teachest, saying that men cannot live well except they live chastely with the God whom thou preachest."
>
> Judas saith, "Thou sayest true, O king: thus do I teach. For tell me, art thou not wroth with thy soldiers if they wait on thee in filthy garments? ... Indeed, thou wouldst have thy subjects follow thy conversation and thy manners, and thou punishest them if they despise thy commandments: how much more must they that believe on Him serve my God with much reverence and cleanness and security, and be quit of all pleasures of the body, adultery and prodigality and theft and drunkenness and belly-service and foul deeds?"
>
> *Acts of Thomas 126, ANT p.420*

Many other early Christians held a similar view. Paul is unequivocal:

> Flee fornication. Every (other) sin that a man doeth is without the body; but he that committeth fornication sinneth against his own body.
>
> *1 Corinthians 6:18*

Similarly, the author of the Nag Hammadi, *Teachings of Silvanus*, wrote:

> It is a great and good thing not to love fornication and not even to think of the wretched matter at all, for to think of it is death. It is not good for anyone to fall into death. For a soul which has been found in death will be without reason. For it is better not to live than to acquire an animal's life. Protect yourself lest you are burned by the fires of fornication. For many who are submerged in (that) fire are (unknowingly) its servants....

O my son, strip off the old garment of fornication, and put on the garment which is clean and shining, that you may be beautiful in it. But when you have this garment, protect it well. Release yourself from every bond so that you may acquire freedom. When you cast out from yourself the desire whose devices are many, you will release yourself from the sins of lust....

Do not pierce yourself with the sword of sin. Do not burn yourself, O wretched one, with the fire of lust. Do not surrender yourself to barbarians like a prisoner, nor to savage beasts which want to trample on you. For they are like lions which roar very loudly. Be not dead lest they trample on you. You shall be a man! It is possible for you through 'reasoning' (meditation) to conquer them.

Teachings of Silvanus 104-105,108, TS pp.53-55,61

And in the *Book of Thomas the Contender,* Jesus ostensibly says:

Therefore it is said that everyone who seeks the truth from true Wisdom will make himself wings so as to fly, fleeing the lust that scorches the spirits of men.

Book of Thomas the Contender 140-141, NHS21 p.187

It is Better to Marry Than to Burn

Mystics, however, are very practical and they know that a person cannot leave sexual desire or, indeed, any other worldly attachment, all at once. The process has to be gradual. If someone tries to give up certain things through force of will, but is still struggling with desire for them within him or herself, then there is a very real danger that suppression will build up to such an extent that the lid gets blown off and the person becomes even more dominated by the desire than might otherwise have been the case.

The mind cannot exist in a vacuum. Only attachment to something higher can create real and lasting detachment from what is lower. That which is higher is the beautiful music of the Word, the enchantment of the inner light and contact with the spiritual form of the Master. When a person becomes absorbed in these, then the desire for physical things fades out naturally, of its own accord. If you try to take a penny from a beggar, he will resist. But if you give him a diamond, he will immediately forget the penny.

It seems that although some of the early Christians taught a rigid asceticism, even (as in the *Acts of Thomas*) the complete withdrawal of one marriage partner from another, Jesus himself taught the middle way, for some of his disciples were undoubtedly married and remained so. In fact, although tradition has it that the disciple John always remained unmarried, the synoptic gospels all mention "Simon's wife's mother"[6] – which leads us to presume that Simon Peter was married. Paul confirms this supposition when he speaks of "other apostles, ... the brethren of the Lord (Jesus), and Cephas (Peter)"[7] as all being married. In fact, it is highly likely that the majority of Jesus' disciples were married by the time they came to him. Jesus certainly mentions attachment to wife and family in a number of places and he himself could have been married, for the gospels say nothing explicit on the matter, though Paul might have been expected to mention it.

Marriage, as opposed to enforced celibacy, is the way of love and harmony, both with oneself and with one's spouse. Then, within the walls of marriage and its other commitments, husband and wife can lead a controlled and balanced sex life, according to mutual co-operation. Paul – though he himself remained celibate and unmarried – seems to have taught the same. In *1 Corinthians*, he summarizes his understanding of the matter with "it is better to marry that to burn":

> Now concerning the things whereof ye wrote unto me: it is good for a man not to touch a woman. Nevertheless, to avoid fornication, let every man have his own wife, and let every woman have her own husband. Let the husband render unto the wife due benevolence: and likewise also the wife unto the husband. The wife hath not power of her own body, but the husband: and likewise also the husband hath not power of his own body, but the wife.
>
> Defraud ye (withhold yourselves) not one the other, except it be with consent for a time, that ye may give yourselves to fasting and prayer; and come together again, that Satan tempt you not for your incontinency (through lack of self-control – *RSV*).
>
> But I speak this by permission, and not of commandment. For I would that all men were even as I myself. But every man hath his proper gift of God, one after this manner, and another after that.
>
> I say therefore to the unmarried and widows, it is good for them if they abide even as I. But if they cannot contain, let them marry: for it is better to marry than to burn.
>
> *1 Corinthians 7:1-9*

Celibacy, as Paul suggested to those who were unmarried, is the ideal, but it depends upon the nature of the individual. As the writer of the gnostic *Authoritative Teaching* says, supporting Jesus' comment regarding a lustful glance:

> If a thought of lust enters into a virgin man,
> he has already become contaminated.
>
> *Authoritative Teaching 25, NHS11 p.267*

So some people can manage celibacy and others not. Marriage also evens out many other tendencies towards imbalance that can otherwise develop in a solitary person. But outside marriage, 'fornication' has almost always received universal condemnation, as we have seen. In our modern world, this may seem to be going against the grain, but two further points may be considered here. Firstly, sex generates a powerful attachment to another person. People do not generally forget their lovers, however long ago it may have been. And these attachments will all bear fruit in some future life, in one way or another. They can bring a soul back into this world.

Secondly, the psychological walls of a legally binding marriage provide some hedge against the mind's tendencies to go on roaming. If an individual is afraid of commitment, it means that whatever they may say, they are actually holding on to mental reservations permitting them to ditch their situation and their partner, if they feel like it. The mind, being slippery by nature, finds it very easy to justify things and a marriage contract according to prevailing social customs makes the relationship more secure. This is why all cultures have developed formalized marriage bonds.

With commitment on both sides, partners will then try to work out the difficulties that are bound to arise. Without it, there will always be an escape clause in the back their minds, perhaps creating a fear of honest expression in the relationship. Endurance and finding ways to make things work, adjusting to the other, learning to be adaptable and so on, all build character and determination, qualities essential for success in meditation. He who runs away at the first hint of problems will run away from meditation too, before he has barely started the practice. Determination and commitment are required for success in both.

Within marriage, if there is full consent from both partners and both can manage it without overdue suppression, celibacy is very helpful. Love and affection can be expressed in many other ways than the physicality of sex and there is much to be said for a pure and holy relationship of man and wife. As we saw earlier, Jesus commended it:

> For there are some eunuchs,
>> which were so born from their mother's womb:
> And there are some eunuchs,
>> which were made eunuchs of men:
> And there be eunuchs,
>> which have made themselves eunuchs
>> for the kingdom of heaven's sake.
> He that is able to receive it,
>> let him receive it.
>
> *Matthew 19:12*

Jesus is not talking of self-mutilation, but of abstinence, within or outside marriage. This is something which he is evidently advocating, but, as he concludes, "he that is able to receive it, let him receive it". There is no point in attempting celibacy or remaining unmarried if a person has

> eyes full of adultery,
>> and that cannot cease from sin –
>
> *2 Peter 2:14*

though there are many, even in the married state, to whom this description still applies.

Many mystics have remained unmarried so that they can devote themselves uninterruptedly to their spiritual practice without the demands of wife and family. In an anecdote told in the Mandaean *John-Book*, when asked why he remained unmarried, John the Baptist explains that desire for a woman would dull his mind, causing him to neglect his "night-prayer":

> When Yahya (John the Baptist) heard this, a tear gathered in his eye; a tear in his eye gathered, and he spake: "It would be pleasant to take a wife, and delightful for me to have children. But only if I take no woman – and then comes sleep, desire for her seizes me and I neglect my night-prayer. If only desire does not wake in me, and I forget my Lord out of my mind. If only desire does not wake in me, and I neglect my prayer every time."
>
> *John-Book, GJB p.53*

Sex pulls the attention down, making it unable to enjoy the bliss of meditation. Moreover, as Jesus points out, when making a brief appearance in the *Acts of Thomas*, sex also leads to all the complications of family which can serve as constant distractions from prolonged periods of spiritual practice:

> Know this, that if ye abstain from this foul intercourse, ye become holy temples, pure, and are saved from afflictions, manifest and hidden, and from the heavy cares of life and children, whose end is bitter sorrow. For if indeed ye get many children, for their sakes ye become grasping and covetous, stripping orphans and over-reaching widows, and ye will be grievously tortured for their injuries (an allusion to rebirth?).
>
> For the greatest part of children are the cause of many pains. For either the king falls upon them, or a demon lays hold of them, or paralysis befalls them, or they become either lunatic or blind or deaf or dumb or foolish. And if they be healthy they come to ill either by adultery, or theft, or fornication, or covetousness, or vain-glory; and through these wickednesses ye will be afflicted by them.
>
> *Acts of Thomas 12, AAA pp.155-156, ANT p.369*

As Jesus also said, "a man's foes shall be they of his own household".[8] It can be members of our own family, more than anyone else, who hinder us in our spiritual pursuit.

In the *Clementine Homilies*, Peter gives an instructive discourse on chastity, both physical and also spiritual. He points out that sex is a natural faculty designed for the purposes of bearing children, and that by its means humanity continues, from amongst whom are drawn a "multitude of superior beings who are fit for eternal life". Used within these bounds, man does not "act impiously". It is only when "he rushes to adultery" that he has to pay for it, for "he makes a bad use of a good ordinance":

> For lust has, by the will of Him who created all things well, been made to arise within the living being, that, led by it to intercourse, he may increase humanity, from a selection of which a multitude of superior beings arise who are fit for eternal life. But if it were not for lust, no one would trouble himself with intercourse with his wife; but now, for the sake of pleasure, and, as it were, gratifying himself, man carries out His will. Now, if a man uses lust for lawful marriage, he does not act impiously; but if he rushes to adultery, he acts impiously, and he is punished because he makes a bad use of a good ordinance.
>
> *Clementine Homilies XIX:XXI, CH p.307*

But speaking of the loving and co-operative relationship of a chaste couple, he also says, not without some element of humour:

> He who wishes to have a chaste wife is also himself chaste, gives her what is due to a wife, takes his meals with her, keeps company with her, goes with her to the Word that makes chaste, does not grieve her, does not rashly quarrel with her, does not make himself hateful to her, furnishes her with all the good things he can, and when he has them not, makes up the deficiency by caresses.
>
> The chaste wife does not expect to be caressed, recognizes her husband as her lord, bears his poverty when he is poor, is hungry with him when he is hungry, travels with him when he travels, consoles him when he is grieved, and if she have a dowry larger than is usual, is subject to him as if she had nothing at all. But if the husband have a poor wife, let him reckon her chastity a great dowry.
>
> The chaste wife is temperate in her eating and drinking, in order that the weariness of the body, thus pampered, may not drag the soul down to unlawful desires. Moreover, she never assuredly remains alone with young men, and she reveres the old; she turns away from disorderly laughter, gives herself up to God alone; she is not led astray; she delights in listening to holy words, but turns away from those which are not spoken to produce chastity.
>
> *Clementine Homilies XIII:XVIII, CH pp.221-222*

And he also adds that so great is this virtue that if it had not been a natural law or requirement for even the best of people to receive spiritual baptism before they could "enter into the kingdom of God", then salvation might have been obtained "solely on account of chastity alone":

> Above all, I wish you to know how much chastity is pleasing to God. The chaste woman is God's choice, God's good pleasure, God's glory, God's child. So great a blessing is chastity, that if there had not been a law that not even a righteous person should enter into the kingdom of God unbaptized, perhaps even the erring Gentiles might have been saved solely on account of chastity.
>
> *Clementine Homilies XIII:XXI, CH pp.223-224*

Knowing man's obsession with sex, mystics have done their best to bring us to a correct understanding of it by painting not only the down-side, but also the up-side of the picture. Again, in the *Clementine Homilies* and as a part of the same discourse, there is a beautiful example of the latter where Peter speaks at length on the virtue of *spiritual* chastity. For here it is clear that he is speaking by analogy and that the "chaste woman" is the devoted and one-pointed soul who remains free from all taints and impurities of the world. Her love is directed solely towards the "Bridegroom", the "Son of God", and she takes no other 'lovers' of this world in the sense of letting the thought of anyone or anything else enter her mind. Her "ornaments" are the love and "fear of God", her fear being born of love – the fear to displease her divine Beloved by turning her mind to anything or anyone else:

> The chaste woman is adorned with the Son of God as with a Bridegroom. She is clothed with holy light. Her beauty lies in a well-regulated soul; and she is fragrant with ointment, even with a good reputation. She is arrayed in beautiful vesture, even in modesty. She wears about her precious pearls, even chaste words. And she is radiant, for her mind has been brilliantly lighted up. Into a beautiful mirror does she look, for she looks into God. Beautiful ornaments does she use, namely, the fear of God, with which she admonishes her soul. Beautiful is the woman, not because she had chains of gold on her, but because she has been set free from transient lusts.
>
> The chaste woman is greatly desired by the great King (God); she has been wooed, watched and loved by Him. The chaste woman loves her husband from the heart, embraces, soothes, and pleases him, acts the slave to him, and is obedient to him in all things, except when she would be disobedient to God. For she who obeys God is without the aid of watchmen, chaste in soul and pure in body.
>
> *Clementine Homilies XIII:XVI, CH pp.220-221*

She is "clothed with holy light"; her perfume is "a good reputation"; her "vesture" is "modesty"; her "precious pearls" and jewellery are "chaste words"; her radiance is that of her inner being and so on. The "chaste woman", here, is clearly the soul devoted to God. Such is real spiritual chastity or purity of mind, of which the physical counterpart is only a reflection. Not even the mind, let alone the body, is permitted to entertain anything else but God.

Chastity, then, is of great help spiritually. But even when somebody lives that way, there still lies one more, ever-present weakness, hiding in the recesses of the mind, ready to bite the soul. Clement of Rome chastens the chaste man:

> Let not him who is pure in the flesh be boastful,
>> knowing that it is Another
>> who bestows on him his continence.
>>> *1 Clement XXXVIII:2, AFI p.75*

Man readily forgets by Whose strength it is that he has been enabled to live a pure life: spiritual pride thus feeds on the dying embers of old and weary human passions.

Whosoever Shall Exalt Himself

No weakness is more ubiquitous than that of pride and egotism. The ego is an all-pervasive part of the fabric of human existence. Everyone has a sense of self with which he or she is fully identified. Yet this sense of self constantly changes, as external circumstances change. We speak of my wife, my husband, my children, my house, my work, my ideas, my this and my that. Everything is accompanied by the same refrain of 'me'.

Yet it is clear, even to a moment's reflection, that nothing can really belong to anyone. As we can readily observe when accompanying a coffin to the graveyard or the cemetery, even our body is not ours. "We brought nothing into this world, and it is certain we can carry nothing out." We assert our rights and our presence in every sphere of life without ever asking the question as to who this 'I' really is and whether or not it has any permanent existence or even if it really exists at all. As the Manichaean-Christian psalmist puts it:

> Men are thinking that they are at rest;
>> yet they know not that trouble is preparing for them.
> They run and burst forth until the hour overtakes them:
>> they have been called, they have not understood;
> They have gone to and fro in vanity (ego).
>> *Psalm CCLIII, MPB p.63*

Everyone is born in ego and dies in ego. Whatever we do is hedged about by ego. So strong and powerful is this ego that it is responsible for drawing us down and crystallizing us into a body which isolates us not only from God and our true spiritual selves, but also from every other living being in this world. It is on account of ego and our sense of separateness that we have so little understanding of what goes on in the minds of other people, even those with whom we may have lived for many decades.

Pride, vanity, boasting, selfishness and self-assertion of every kind are the more obvious phases of our ego, but the primary problem is the sense of 'I' itself. There is, it is true, a balanced use and understanding of this human faculty of 'I', but unless a soul has risen above the human level and gained access to the inner worlds, an enlarged and imbalanced 'I' will colour all a person's thoughts and actions. Indeed, more subtle forms of this 'I' still exist until the soul gains freedom from the Universal Mind, the highest reaches of the Negative Power, and steps out into the purely spiritual worlds as a free and naked soul.

Any mystic who traverses these higher realms is aware of the ubiquitous nature of this human malady, and there are many places where Jesus counsels watchfulness against pride. "Whosoever shall exalt himself shall be abased; and he that shall humble himself shall be exalted,"[9] he says, meaning that ego is sufficient to bring a soul back into this world – where they "will be abased". But one who is truly humble, the converse of I-ness, surrendering all sense of self before God, is one who has gone beyond the realms of the Universal Mind. Such a one is truly "exalted" spiritually.

The saying comes in a passage where Jesus is talking about the priests of his time. They give the teachings of Moses, he says, which should be followed. But since the priests do not follow these teachings, they themselves should not be emulated, for their primary motivation is only that of pride and the desire for prominence:

> Then spake Jesus to the multitude,
>   and to his disciples, saying,
> "The scribes and the Pharisees sit in Moses' seat:
> All therefore whatsoever they bid you observe,
>   that observe and do; but do not ye after their works:
>   for they say, and do not.
> For they bind heavy burdens and grievous to be borne,
>   and lay them on men's shoulders;
>   but they themselves will not move them
>   with one of their fingers.
>
> "But all their works they do for to be seen of men:
>   they make broad their phylacteries,[10]
>   and enlarge the borders of their garments,

and love the uppermost rooms at feasts,
and the chief seats in the synagogues,
and greetings in the markets,
and to be called of men, 'Rabbi, Rabbi'.

"But be not ye called Rabbi:
for one is your Master, even Christ;
and all ye are brethren.
And call no man your father upon the earth:
for one is your Father, which is in heaven.
Neither be ye called masters:
for one is your Master, even Christ.
But he that is greatest among you shall be your servant.
And whosoever shall exalt himself shall be abased;
and he that shall humble himself shall be exalted."

Matthew 23:1-12

Jesus advises his disciples not even to permit themselves to be called "Rabbi" or "master", for this might only increase their egos. They should not let other people give them praise or put them on a pedestal for their presumed spirituality. For it can be very easy for a disciple to get on to a spiritual ego-trip, as the saying goes, when the reality is that there is only the Master and his disciples, all disciples being the same. "All ye are brethren", says Jesus. No disciple is better or worse than another. In fact, as we have seen elsewhere, Jesus recommends that those who have apparently prominent positions within the community of disciples should consider themselves to be the servants of their brothers and sisters. This is the attitude that a Master himself adopts.

The opposite of egotism is humility, engendered and reinforced by serving others. That Jesus taught this attitude by example as well as by precept is evident from a story related in St John, when Jesus – knowing that "he was come from God and went to God" and that he was all-powerful – washes his disciples' feet in order to demonstrate to them the degree of humility and service which they should develop in themselves:

Jesus knowing that the Father had given all things into his hands, and that he was come from God, and went to God; He riseth from supper, and laid aside his garments; and took a towel, and girded himself. After that he poureth water into a basin, and began to wash the disciples' feet, and to wipe them with the towel wherewith he was girded.

Then cometh he to Simon Peter: and Peter saith unto him, "Lord, dost thou wash my feet?" Jesus answered and said unto him, "What I do, thou knowest not now; but thou shalt know hereafter."

Peter saith unto him, "Thou shalt never wash my feet." Jesus answered him, "If I wash thee not, thou hast no part with me."

Simon Peter saith unto him, "Lord, not my feet only, but also my hands and my head." Jesus saith to him, "He that is washed needeth not (to wash) save to wash his feet, but is clean every whit: and ye are clean, but not all." ...

So after he had washed their feet, and had taken his garments, and was set down again, he said unto them, "Know ye what I have done to you? Ye call me Master and Lord: and ye say well; for so I am. If I then, your Lord and Master, have washed your feet; ye also ought to wash one another's feet. For I have given you an example, that ye should do as I have done to you. Verily, verily, I say unto you, The servant is not greater than his lord; neither he that is sent greater than he that sent him. If ye know these things, happy are ye if ye do them."

John 13:3-10,12-17

The story is characteristic of John's gospel where the events themselves are often more like those in a parable and are intended as metaphors for mystic truth. Jesus starts to wash his disciples' feet, but when he comes to Peter, Peter understandably declines to let his Master perform such a lowly task. Jesus counters this by saying that Peter does not know what he is really doing for him. Peter is still reluctant, but Jesus continues, "If I wash thee not, thou hast no part with me". At which Peter immediately catches his drift and asks that every part of him should be washed.

The meaning being conveyed at this point is entirely mystical. The disciple, at the physical level, is unable to appreciate what his Master is doing for him inside. Only "hereafter" – after he has died or when he has gone within – will he be able to see with his own inner eyes how much the Master has helped him by washing away or forgiving his mountain of ancient sins. Without this cleansing, no soul can meet and unite with their Master inside – "if I wash thee not, thou hast no part with me". When Peter realizes Jesus' meaning, he asks to be washed all over – since every sincere disciple realizes how much spiritual purification he needs.

Jesus then speaks of himself. "He that is washed needeth not (to wash) save to wash his feet". The Master is the one who "is washed" and "is clean every whit". He has no sins of his own and is completely pure. There is a play on words, here, for the same Greek word means both spiritually 'pure' as well as physically 'clean'. The phrase, "save (for) ... his feet" is lacking in some ancient manuscripts and makes better sense of the passage if omitted.

If the phrase did indeed belong to John's original text, then "he ... needeth not, save to wash his feet" probably means that the Master only needs to pay off the sins which he has taken onto his own body, something which he can do whenever and however he sees fit. The "feet", here, would represent the 'foot' of creation[11] – the physical universe, where a Master takes birth and takes onto his own body the sins of his disciples. The Master himself is totally pure and free from sin. He only has to wash his "feet" – to wash away the sins of his disciples at the physical level. But this is an elaboration of a kind which John normally avoids and it seems more likely that the phrase is a later editorial insertion, like the explanation concerning the angel who stirred the water at the pool of Bethesda.

Jesus then adds, "ye are clean, but not all", an observation which is followed by the comment that this is a reference to Judas Iscariot. But the comment is quite unlike John's normal allegorical style, for his meaning is rarely so external and or made so literally. It is not unlikely, therefore, that this line is also a later editorial gloss, inserted to give recognizable meaning to an otherwise obscure comment. This is the way that it is commonly understood in Christianity, but there is also a simple mystical interpretation. "Ye are clean" would mean that the disciples, having come into contact with the Word, are in the process of being purified. "But not all" – they are not yet fully cleansed of sins, more washing still being required.

This, then, is John's characteristic style of story, with the import of the incident now reverting to the physical act of service. Jesus has set them an example that they would never forget, more powerful than any words or discourse, and he reminds them that they should adopt this attitude of humility and service towards each other. They all know this, of course, because there must have been many other things along the same lines which he had similarly taught them. So he adds that since they understand the point he is making, they should put it into practice. "If ye know these things," he says, "happy are ye if ye do them."

Blessed Are the Meek

There are many places in the gospels where Jesus emphasizes, directly or indirectly, the importance of humility on the spiritual path. It is impossible, for example, for anyone with an overactive ego to pass through the "strait gate", the "narrow way" or the "eye of a needle". No one can go inside and carry all their human baggage with them. The two are mutually incompatible. A person has to become small and humble, empty of self, before they can gain admittance at the hidden door. This is what Jesus meant when he said:

> Blessed are the poor in spirit:
>> for theirs is the kingdom of heaven.
>>
>>   *Matthew 5:3*

The "poor in spirit" are those who are humble, destitute of pride, who have eliminated ego from within themselves. They will be able to enter into the "kingdom of heaven" – they will be able to reach the eternal abode of God Himself. Again, also from the beatitudes, Jesus says:

> Blessed are the meek:
>> for they shall inherit the earth.
>>
>>   *Matthew 5:5*

The "meek" means those who have the strength of humility within themselves, such that they do not react to other people by wanting to fight back verbally or physically in the attempt to justify themselves and prove that they are in the right. They always retain their inner calm and composure. As such, they are contented on this earth and can be said to have "inherited" it. Other people, in the attempt to make parts of the world their own, are constantly frustrated in their efforts.

Jesus also compares the humble person to a little child, in the sense that a child is always simple and innocent, bearing no ill will towards anybody. He is pure and unsullied by the evils of the world. Unless we become like that, he says, we cannot "receive the kingdom of God":

> And they brought young children to him,
>> that he should touch them:
>> and his disciples rebuked those that brought them.
> But when Jesus saw it, he was much displeased,
>> and said unto them,

"Suffer the little children to come unto me,
and forbid them not: for of such is the kingdom of God.
Verily I say unto you, whosoever shall not receive
the kingdom of God as a little child,
he shall not enter therein."
And he took them up in his arms,
put his hands upon them, and blessed them.

Mark 10:13-16

Though, as always, the setting is questionable, the meaning remains the same. Humility, meekness, innocence, purity and love – these are the virtues Jesus is advocating here.

Overcoming the Enemy

Elsewhere in the ancient literature, there are, of course, many references to pride and humility, for it is one of the more obvious human blemishes. Even non-spiritual people recognize the various expressions of pride and arrogance as distasteful aspects of the human psyche. Amongst the gnostics, the author of the *Teachings of Silvanus* advises relinquishing the kind of mental process that counters every good suggestion or piece of advice:

Listen, my son, to my advice. Do not be arrogant in opposition to every good opinion, but take for yourself the side of the divine *Logos*.

Teachings of Silvanus 91, TS p.27

In the *Pistis Sophia*, Jesus recommends the relinquishing of pride so that the "mysteries of the light" may be experienced and a person may be saved from the "pits of fire" – either rebirth in this world or a sojourn in some hellish region:

Say to them: renounce pride and boasting,
that you may be worthy of the mysteries of the Light,
and be saved from the pits of fire.

Pistis Sophia 102, PS p.257, PSGG p.214

In the *Acts of John*, John points out that someone may be vain because of their beautiful or handsome body, but if they want to know the final truth of the matter, then they should take a look at a dead body.

Youth gives way to old age and wrinkles, and sooner or later everybody dies. Why then, the pride? –

> Thou also that art puffed up
>> because of the shapeliness of thy body,
>> and art of an high look,
>> shalt see the end of the promise thereof in the grave.
>
> *Acts of John 35, ANT p.235*

On the subject of meekness, Judas Thomas echoes the words of Jesus, pointing out that by this virtue, the "Enemy" of Satan is overcome:

> Blessed are ye meek,
>> for you hath God counted worthy
>> to become heirs of the heavenly kingdom.
> Blessed are ye meek,
>> for ye are they that have overcome the Enemy:
> Blessed are ye meek,
>> for ye shall see the face of the Lord.
>
> *Acts of Thomas 94, ANT p.406*

And:

> Meekness hath overcome death
>> and brought him under authority;
> Meekness hath enslaved the Enemy,
>> meekness is the good yoke;
> Meekness feareth not and opposeth not the many,
>> meekness is peace and joy and exaltation of rest.
>
> *Acts of Thomas 86, ANT p.403*

Similarly, the early second-century Christian father, Ignatius, advises turning a situation around and returning positive virtues in exchange for the negativity of others:

 Be yourselves gentle in answer to their wrath; be humble-minded in answer to their proud speaking; offer prayer for their blasphemy; be steadfast in the faith for their error; be gentle for their cruelty, and do not think to retaliate.

Let us be proved their brothers by our gentleness and let us be imitators of the Lord, and seek who may suffer the more wrong, be the more destitute, the more despised; that no plant of the Devil be found in you but that you may remain in all purity and sobriety in Jesus Christ, both in the flesh and in the Spirit.

Ignatius, To the Ephesians X:2-3, AFI p.185

For by this means, he says, Satan – the "Prince of this world" – is vanquished:

I have need therefore of meekness, by which the Prince of this world is brought to nothing.

Ignatius, To the Trallians IV:2, AFI p.217

Keeping souls separate from God is the primary purpose of the Negative Power. Such separation, within Satan's domain, automatically means the presence of ego, in however subtle a form it may be. Therefore, complete conquest of the ego also involves the complete conquest of the "Prince of this world". Hence, the late first-century writer of *1 Clement*, says:

Let them exhibit the lovely habit of purity; let them show forth the innocent will of meekness; let them make the gentleness of their tongue manifest by their silence; let them not give their affection by fractious preference, but in holiness to all equally who fear God.

1 Clement XXI:7, AFI p.47

And:

Frowardness and arrogance and boldness belong to those that are accursed by God, gentleness and humility and meekness are with those who are blessed by God.

1 Clement XXX:8, AFI p.61

Being "accursed by God" means being separated from Him. Self-assertion and egotism or "frowardness and arrogance" are the means of such separation at the human level. The humility comes as a result of God's blessing. Hence, advises Clement, let no one become proud of "his own humility":

Let him who is humble-minded not testify to his own humility, but let him leave it to others to bear him witness.

1 Clement XXXVIII, AFI p.75

Divers Temptations

As we have seen, for every weakness, Jesus presents the positive virtue or antidote, for not only are mystics full of compassion, they are also very practical. They only come to help us, never to pass judgment or to condemn us. As Jesus said, we are already condemned: we are already in enough of a mess. Moreover, no mystic ever said that the spiritual path was easy. They know that we will find it difficult because we are born with our sins, we live with sins and we die with sins. Like it or not, we are born to struggle with ourselves whether or not we realize it.

Though we may speculate as to why the Lord has set things up in such a manner, it is self-evident that He has, and since human answers hold out no hope of real comprehension, it is actually the day-to-day practical approach to our situation which is of most significance to us. In this respect, the writer of the letter attributed to James the brother of Jesus suggests adopting a positive attitude towards the human struggle:

> My brethren, count it all joy
> when ye fall into divers temptations;
> Knowing this,
> that the trying of your faith worketh patience.
> But let patience have her perfect work,
> that ye may be perfect and entire, wanting nothing.
>
> *James 1:2–4*

Take it, he advises, as a challenge, knowing that the overcoming of temptation strengthens our faith and determination, leading us towards perfection. Temptation is what puts character and stamina into our being, making us fit and able to apply ourselves to spiritual practice and to scale the mystic heights. He continues:

> Blessed is the man that endureth temptation:
> for when he is tried,
> he shall receive the crown of life,
> which the Lord hath promised to them that love Him.
> Let no man say when he is tempted, "I am tempted of God":
> for God cannot be tempted with evil,
> neither tempteth He any man:
> But every man is tempted,
> when he is drawn away of his own lust, and enticed.

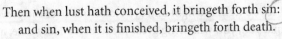

Then when lust hath conceived, it bringeth forth sin:
and sin, when it is finished, bringeth forth death.

James 1:12-15

We are only tempted by things when we already have the seeds of such desires or tendencies within us. It is our "own lust" by which we are "drawn away". We cannot blame our temptation upon God or on someone or something else. Everything is within ourselves and it is there that the battle is to be joined. Hence, in the *Acts of Peter*, Paul counsels some new disciples to give up their former pattern of life and adopt a new and virtuous way of living:

> Men and brethren which now have begun to believe on Christ,
>> if ye continue not in your former works
>> of the tradition (religious practices) of your fathers,
>> and keep yourselves from all guile and wrath
>> and fierceness and adultery and defilement,
>> and from pride and envy and contempt and enmity,
> Jesus the living God will forgive you
>> that ye did in ignorance.
>
> Wherefore, ye servants of God,
>> arm yourselves every one in your inner man
>> with peace, patience, gentleness, faith, charity,
>> knowledge, wisdom, love of the brethren, hospitality,
>> mercy, abstinence, chastity, kindness, justice.
>
> Then shall ye have for your guide everlastingly
>> the First-begotten of all creation,
>> and shall have strength in peace with our Lord.

Acts of Peter II, ANT p.305

When this battle is truly joined, then the "First-begotten of all creation", the Son of God, the Word and its personification in a Master, will be there to give his strength and blessings and ensure success. As the author of the *Teachings of Silvanus* says, seeming to take an analogy from the gladiatorial arena:

> Fight the great fight as long as the fight lasts, while all the powers (*archons*) are staring after (watching) you – not only the Holy Ones, but also all the powers of the Adversary. Woe to you if you are overcome while everyone

is watching you! If you fight the fight and are victorious over the powers which fight against you, you will bring great joy to every Holy One, and yet great grief to your enemies. Your Judge helps you completely since he wants you to be victorious.

Teachings of Silvanus 114, TS p.73

In this context, the "Holy Ones" and the "Judge" are the Masters. In the amphitheatre, there are those who want a particular gladiator to win and those who wish him to lose. The "powers of the Adversary" and the Master are both observing the fight of the soul, so to speak. But success for one who has a Master is assured, since the Master never forsakes a soul. He "helps you completely since he wants you to be victorious". And since the Master's will is the same as God's will, there is no doubt about the final outcome. The contest can and will be won.

NOTES AND REFERENCES

1. *Matthew* 18:22.
2. *Matthew* 5:23-24.
3. *Ephesians* 4:26.
4. *Exodus* 21:24.
5. Although "Love thy neighbour" is found in *Leviticus* 19:18, the second part is not. The saying is probably a popular idiom of the times.
6. *Mark* 1:30, *Matthew* 8:14, *Luke* 4:38.
7. *1 Corinthians* 9:5.
8. *Matthew* 10:36.
9. *Matthew* 23:12.
10. A small case containing Biblical passages, worn on the head or arm by Jewish men during weekday morning prayer.
11. A metaphor encountered elsewhere in the early literature, *eg.* "the head came down to the feet", which speaks of the Saviour's descent from God to this world (*Odes of Solomon* XXIII:16, *AOT* p.714).

CHAPTER TWENTY-SIX

Thou Shalt Not Kill

Spiritual Reasons for Being Vegetarian

Mystics have generally had a predisposition towards vegetarianism and abstinence from alcohol and those of the highest order have always taught it as a prerequisite for following the mystic path. It is natural to ask, therefore, whether Jesus also followed the same practice.

Like reincarnation, vegetarianism and abstinence from alcohol were common in early Christianity though they were later eradicated, as far as possible, by the orthodoxy. But like both spiritual practice and reincarnation, there is plenty of indirect evidence to demonstrate that Jesus was indeed vegetarian and drank no alcohol, though no direct, unequivocal statement from him on the subject has survived.

Spiritual practice, reincarnation and dietary restrictions are amongst the first casualties in the steady decline of a mystic's teachings into a religion and the reason is not hard to find. It is the character of the human mind. The mind is involved in the world. It does not want to meditate and without the personal guidance of a mystic, there is soon no knowledge of *how* to meditate, at least in the way the mystic taught. As a result, the correct form of spiritual practice is rapidly forgotten, giving way to doctrine as the essence of the nascent religion or sect.

But doctrine is always open to interpretation, especially where there is limited primary source material available in writing. Even otherwise, the first tenets to go are always those that restrict the mind's activities and its desire for sensual pleasures. The mind does not want to exercise self-control and finds ways to justify proceeding in the way in which it has always done. After sex, man's greatest sensual pleasures probably come from eating, and his imagination has enabled him to develop a range of menus and recipes that entail taking the life of practically every other living species on the planet. Even snakes, snails, insects, rats, frogs, dogs and other creatures are not exempt. Man eats and drinks everything and is reluctant to sacrifice these pleasures. Therefore, he finds ways of convincing himself that his dietary appetites will do him no harm. Mystics, however, point out that they very definitely do.

The primary rationale which all mystics give for instructing their disciples to be vegetarian is that of reincarnation and the law of *karma*. This gives us part of the reason why reincarnation is one of the early casualties of mystic teachings. For wherever reincarnation has been retained as a general belief, there too you will find a traditional belief in vegetarianism. This has been true of the ancient Greek mystics and the Pythagoreans, the gnostics, the Manichaeans, the Hindus, the Sikhs, the Buddhists and the Jains. All these are or were traditional believers in both reincarnation and vegetarianism. Once somebody accepts the possibility of reincarnation, then the forces that drive rebirth are also brought into sharp focus and it becomes very easy to understand that whatever suffering is caused in this world must be paid for in this world. Get rid of reincarnation from your religion and it becomes very easy to eliminate vegetarianism, too. An understanding of *karma* and reincarnation impresses on the mind the fact that everything has to be paid for in the future.

Every thought and action leaves its impression upon the mind. All suffering caused to other creatures, whether directly or indirectly, has its effect. Everything gets recorded in the deep recesses of the mind and automatically bears fruit in future lives. If someone is partially or totally responsible, during the course of their life, for the deaths of a thousand fish or a thousand chickens or a thousand cows, then they will have to pay for it in the future. They may not need to be killed by each of those animals, individually and in separate births, but they will certainly have to undergo the equivalent suffering, in one way or another.

So the question then becomes, what creatures should we eat? -- since all have life, even plants. The answer is: those forms whose killing causes the least suffering -- and that means plants and other species from the vegetable kingdom. Mystics have tried to explain the gradation of creatures in this world in a variety of ways. But it does seem clear, even to casual observation, that some orders of life have a higher level of consciousness than others. Even this point can be argued, of course, and people do, but it would be generally fair to accept -- all facetiousness apart -- that a human being has a greater degree of intelligence and consciousness than a cabbage or a mushroom. Between the two, there is a wide spectrum of creatures of descending consciousness. Dogs and dolphins are usually considered more intelligent than parrots and canaries. Birds are higher than frogs and snakes. And reptiles would seem to be at a higher level than grass and dandelions.

Members of the vegetable kingdom are characterized by their inability to move about of their own accord. Unlike all other species, they have no legs, wings, fins, tails, *cilia* or other organs of mobility. For the distribution of their species, they have to hitch a ride with another species or travel by wind or wave. One can presume, then, that plants do not have the intelligence to 'want' to go somewhere or to even 'consider' the matter at all. A dog, on the other hand, clearly knows (more or less!) where he is going and why, as anyone who has a pet will readily concur. A creature who knows how to get about, must have both means and motive – to have the ability to get there and to know what it wants to do when it arrives. Mobility thus implies greater intelligence and a higher kind of mental activity than that of plants.

Even in our legal system, we tacitly acknowledge this gradation between the species. If I pluck a flower or a vegetable from my neighbour's garden, he will – at the most – be angry with me. If I steal his chickens, the result may be a fine. If I kill his horse, I may go to jail. If I kill or kidnap my neighbour, then I am in very serious trouble. It is the same with the killing of living creatures for our food. The higher the animal in the spectrum of consciousness, the greater its awareness and the greater its suffering – and the greater is the *karmic* penalty incurred.

This, then, is the essential reason why mystics insist that their disciples be vegetarian, eating only produce from the vegetable kingdom. But there are other allied reasons, too. Firstly, killing other creatures or having them killed for us hardens the mind and heart. It is simply a lack of sensitivity to the suffering of other creatures that permits us to eat a dead animal without considering the fear and pain it has undergone. Even if its death was instantaneous, life is precious to all and no creature willingly surrenders its life. It wanted to go on living. We took the law into our own hands and killed it – or by our desire for its meat were responsible for its death by reason of supply and demand.

Such an act is not a loving act and turns our mind away from love and compassion. If we want to expand our own heart towards the Source of all light, life and love, then we must act in accordance with those cosmic principles. How can we face God, expecting Him to shower His love and grace upon us, if every day we are killing, eating and causing suffering to the other forms in His creation? We are asking Him to forgive us for our sins and yet we are continually responsible for hurting others, hardly giving it a moment's thought. Under such circumstances, how can we expect His compassion and His mercy?

Secondly, those who have studied the matter say that a balanced vegetarian diet is more healthy and less full of toxins than meat. They also say that it makes better economic sense to be vegetarian than to eat meat. These and other considerations may all be true, but the primary reason why mystics advise abstention from meat is to avoid adding to our already heavy burden of sins. If we are practising meditation with the intention of clearing this load, it makes little sense to be struggling so hard to clear it and at the same time to be constantly adding to it.

In practice, many people who find themselves seeking spirituality slowly come to a realization that they no longer wish to eat the flesh of dead animals. It no longer agrees with them, in one way or another. As their own awareness, love, compassion and sensitivity increases, they automatically find themselves drawing away from the consumption of meat. Then, as they do so, they experience the benefit in terms of a greater lightness of heart and inner peacefulness, and sooner or later they are naturally inclined to take a clear decision to become strictly vegetarian. If they are lucky enough to meet a perfect Master, he will certainly insist that they become so if they wish to receive initiation into his fold.

Was Jesus Vegetarian?

From our study of Jesus' teachings, it is quite evident that he taught the law of recompense for sins. And if he also taught reincarnation as so many of the more mystically-minded, early Christians believed, he would certainly have been vegetarian and have taught vegetarianism to his disciples. What is also clear is that he was of such a kind, loving, forgiving, merciful and compassionate disposition that it is difficult to imagine him even hurting another creature, let alone placing it upon his plate and eating it.

Jesus' philosophy of non-violence was as far advanced as that of any other teacher of this subject, probably all of whom have also been vegetarian. How can one who advises turning the other cheek, giving your cloak to one who has already taken your coat and walking two miles with one who has already coerced you into going one mile with them, be thought to have happily eaten up the bodies of slaughtered animals? How can one who is so far removed from thoughts of violence and revenge that he recommends extending unlimited forgiveness to others, advises loving your enemies and doing good to those who treat you badly, have been expected to have condoned the killing of other creatures for his food?

Jesus also reiterated the commandment attributed to Moses, "thou shalt not kill",[1] as we find it in the *King James Version* of Mark and Luke.[2] In many modern translations, however, the key word has been changed to "murder" in both the Old and New Testaments, though the meaning in *Deuteronomy* is ambiguous and could mean either or both. 'Murder' implies only human beings, 'killing' refers to all life, and the translators must have been aware of the implications of their change.

But there is another passage amongst the books attributed to Moses, this time in *Genesis,* where the meaning is stated clearly:

> And God said,
> "Behold, I have given you every herb bearing seed,
>   which is upon the face of all the earth,
>   and every tree,
>   in the which is the fruit of a tree yielding seed;
> To you it shall be for meat."
>
> *Genesis 1:29, KJV*

There is no doubt about the vegetarianism inherent in this piece of advice. So although the provenance of these Biblical writings is largely a mystery and their meaning often obscure and allegorical, this passage at least is clear enough and applicable to all human beings in all ages and cultures. This is one of the reasons why Jesus said:

> Did not Moses give you the law,
>   and yet none of you keepeth the law?
>
> *John 7:20*

Jesus, who spoke so definitively about the hypocrisy of the Pharisees and Jewish priests, is hardly likely to have behaved hypocritically himself. How, then, can he be expected to have killed for his food? Can one imagine Jesus with a gun, a knife or a sword, or going out as a hunter or a butcher? The picture is quite inconsistent with everything else he taught.

So although there is no explicit quotation from Jesus recorded in the gospels on the subject, the evidence of the remainder of his teachings alone is more than suggestive. It would have been most inconsistent of him if he had not abstained from killing animals and eating meat.

After all, bearing in mind the approach of the orthodox Christian authorities as well as the attitude of the Roman emperors who adopted Christianity, would one really expect any references to vegetarianism to be present in the canonical gospels? They had three or four hundred years and ample opportunity to adjust any 'difficult' passages to their own liking. And since everyone in those days changed texts willy-nilly to fit their own beliefs, they could so easily have justified their editorial excursions in the name of 'correcting earlier errors'.

Those of rigid, hardhearted, angry and aggressive – even violent – character, as many of the orthodox authorities seem to have been, are hardly likely to have entertained vegetarian leanings. Such people like their food and drink and will go to all lengths to substantiate their position in order to continue in the way they always have done. This is the nature of the human mind. The response and reaction come from a deeply subconscious place to preserve and enforce one's own personal beliefs. So if – in the face of Jesus' teachings to the contrary – they could condone causing misery and hardship, even exile, torture and death, to their fellow human beings, they are hardly likely to notice a discrepancy between their killing of animals for food and Jesus' teachings of love and compassion. Nor would they feel any twinges of conscience in adjusting Jesus' teachings to suit themselves. Like the Pharisees and Jewish priests before them, they were already too far away from the teachings they professed to follow.

Locusts and Wild Honey

Definitive records of Jesus as a vegetarian may be absent, but with his predecessor, John the Baptist, the case is somewhat different. As we have them now, the gospel texts vary. John's gospel makes no mention of the matter at all. Matthew follows Mark, speaking of "locusts and wild honey":

> John had his raiment of camel's hair, and a leathern girdle about his loins; and his meat was locusts and wild honey.
>
> *Matthew 3:4*

And:

> John was clothed with camel's hair, and with a girdle of a skin about his loins; and he did eat locusts and wild honey.
>
> *Mark 1:6*

While Luke makes no mention of John the Baptist's food, but does introduce an angel who declares that John will abstain from all alcoholic drinks:

> He shall be great in the sight of the Lord, and shall drink neither wine nor strong drink; and he shall be filled with the Holy Ghost, even from his mother's womb.
>
> *Luke 1:15*

It is generally reckoned that Luke is referring to the Nazirite vow, an ancient Jewish rule of asceticism, described in the book of *Numbers*,[3] which specifically mentions abstention from "wine and strong drink" and who Epiphanius tells us also "forbid all flesh-eating and do not eat living things at all".[4] Luke, however, in seeming to designate John the Baptist as a Nazirite, may only have been jumping to conclusions based upon the popular stories that had grown up regarding John's dietary habits.

Locusts, one might observe, are not vegetarian food and advocates of vegetarianism have tried to explain the term away by various means. Some say that it referred to the evergreen locust tree or carob (*Ceratonia siliqua*), so called because its pods, often curved, resemble locusts. The tree is widely distributed from Spain to the eastern Mediterranean regions where its flat, leathery pods, three to twelve inches long, with their sweet pulpy interior (they contain about 50% sugar) are eaten by animals and also by man, in times of scarcity. Traditionally, the tree has also been called 'St John's Bread', indicating how widespread was the belief that John the Baptist's diet did indeed include the pods of the locust tree rather than insects. In all probability, it is also the pods of this tree which are referred to in Luke's parable of the prodigal son as the "husks that the swine did eat".[5]

Incidentally, in North America, the locust tree is the common name given to any tree of about twenty native American species belonging to the genus *Robinia*, such as the well-known black locust (*Robinia pseudoacacia*), introduced into Europe in 1636. The carob and the North American species are different, but related, both being leguminous.

One group of early Christians in Palestine, the Ebionites, who were undoubtedly vegetarian, claimed that the correct Greek word was not locust (*akris*) at all, but *enkris* (cake) and it would certainly have been easy enough for such a mistake to have occurred during the transmission of early manuscripts. But whether or not the "locusts" were carob pods or cakes, some explanation along these lines must be correct, for otherwise it is difficult to comprehend how such a strange diet should have been imputed to John the Baptist.

The Ebionites and another closely allied group, the Nazoraeans, had their own gospels, neither of which have survived in anything other than brief quotes and citations amongst the writings of the Church fathers. The *Gospel of the Ebionites* was probably a 'harmony' or a synthesis, in Greek, of the canonical gospels, but we are solely dependent upon Epiphanius for the few extant references. The *Gospel of the Nazoraeans* is usually said to have been a translation into Aramaic or Hebrew from the Greek of Matthew, with considerable expansion, but again very little remains and that only in citations by Jerome, Eusebius and Origen. The position is further confused by Irenaeus (120-202, *fl*.178-185) who speaks of the *Gospel of the Ebionites* as a version of Matthew.

Their interest to us in the present context is that, according to Epiphanius, the Ebionites believed that both John the Baptist and Jesus[6] had been vegetarian, and their *Gospel of the Ebionites* reflects this. Regarding John, Epiphanius quotes:

> It came to pass that John was baptizing; and there went out to him Pharisees and were baptized, and all Jerusalem. And John had a garment of camel's hair and a leathern girdle about his loins, and his food was wild honey, the taste of which was that of manna, as a cake dipped in oil.
>
> *Gospel of the Ebionites, in Epiphanius, Panarion 30:13.4, NTA1 p.157*

And the reference to Jesus comes where Jesus declines to eat the Passover meal with his disciples, though this, as well as the excerpt concerning John the Baptist, probably only reflect the fact that the Ebionites were vegetarian and had modified or written their version of the gospel according to their own beliefs, as did all the other groups at that time. What is of more interest is how this group of early Christians came to be traditionally vegetarian and why they thought that Jesus and John the Baptist had been so, too.

Outside the gospels, information on John the Baptist is scarce, but in the Slavonic edition of the *Jewish War*, evidently writing from popular hearsay and legend, Josephus relates:

> At that time there was a man going about Judaea remarkably dressed: he wore an animal hair (garment) upon those parts of his body not covered by his own. His face was like a savage's. He called on the Jews to claim

their freedom, crying, "God sent me to show you the way of the Law, so that you can shake off any human yoke: no man shall rule you, but only the Most High who sent me."

His message was eagerly welcomed and was followed by all Judaea and the district around Jerusalem. All he did was to baptize them in the Jordan and dismiss them with an earnest exhortation to abandon their evil ways: if they did so they would be given a king who would liberate them and master the unruly, while he himself acknowledging no master. This promise was derided by some but believed by others.

The man was brought before Archelaus and an assemblage of lawyers, who asked who he was and where he had been. He replied: "I am a man called by the Spirit of God, and I live on stems, roots and fruit."

Josephus, Jewish War (Slavonic), JWF p.404

And:

He was a strange creature, not like a man at all. He lived like a disembodied spirit. He never touched bread.... Wine and other strong drink he would not allow to be brought anywhere near him, and animal food he absolutely refused – fruit was all that he needed. The whole object of his life was to show evil in its true colours.

Josephus, Jewish War (Slavonic), JWF p.405

It is uncertain whether these passages in the Slavonic *Jewish War* – which do not occur in other versions – can be really be attributed to Josephus. But even if they were penned by some other hand and even if the details are somewhat fanciful and inaccurate, they still indicate that the traditional, non-orthodox account of John the Baptist had him as a vegetarian and teetotaller. And if John really was the Master of Jesus, then – considering the high esteem in which Jesus held John – it would be reasonable to suppose that Jesus followed his Master's example and was both vegetarian and teetotal, too.

Wine and Strong Drink

As with abstention from eating meat, there is no direct evidence that Jesus drank no alcohol. But anyone who has ever struggled sincerely with concentrated prayer or spiritual practice of any kind knows that the effect of alcohol or of any mind-affecting substance, legal or illegal, is to seriously disturb concentration. Such substances decrease will-power, determination, balanced judgment and self-control, often exciting lower tendencies in the mind. The entire range of human weakness is magnified by their use. Lust, anger, violence, jealousy, dishonesty, selfishness, vanity and all other such trends of mind come to the fore in one who has been drinking, even in small amounts. One has only to study law-court statistics to verify this fact. As such they are anathema to love, devotion and spiritual practice, and all mystics have instructed their disciples to give up their use entirely.

Alcohol, however, has been a planetary drug for as far back as we can trace our history and has become a habit firmly rooted in many human societies. One can hardly imagine Constantine, Justinian or many of the orthodox Christian authorities relinquishing its use. Hence, like vegetarianism, abstention from alcohol has vanished from normal Christian practice. This is only to be expected, but it does not mean that Jesus did not teach it.

Early Christians in Palestine

The Ebionites and Nazoraeans are the two names commonly associated with the Judaic Christians of Palestine, though the differences between the two are obscure. Some scholars have suggested that the Ebionites were Greek-speaking, while the Nazoraeans were their Hebrew- and Aramaic-speaking counterparts, but the two groups were probably not so very distinct, many people being bilingual in those days. Our knowledge of them is largely derived from the rantings and sparse accounts of the early Christian heresiologists, notably Irenaeus and Epiphanius.

The term 'Ebionites' (actually, *Ebionim*) was a self-designation meaning the 'poor ones', referring to those who were humble or "poor in spirit". It has been suggested that they were also poor in material goods, having taken vows of poverty, but the title also occurs in other literature of the period, as in the pre-Christian Dead Sea Scrolls,[7] where it definitely refers to spiritual 'poverty' or humility, rather than physical penury. Like the Judaic terms *Hasidim* (*lit.* pious ones) and *Zaddikim* (*lit.* righteous ones), *Ebionim* seems to have been used as a general name for spiritual and esoteric groups amongst the Jews, particularly those who gave their allegiance to a particular spiritual teacher or Master, though by the second century, the name was reserved specifically for one of the two main Christian groups in Palestine.

Epiphanius (probably following Hippolytus[8] and Tertullian[9]), however, speaks of a certain "Ebion" whom he proceeds to castigate as the

founder of their sect.[10] Ebion and his followers, he says, were all vegetarian and teetotal – they "abhor the eating of flesh, (and) take water".[11]
In this instance, scholars have commonly smiled at the presumption
of the heresiologists, but it is possible that Jesus may sometimes have
been called the *Ebion*, the 'Poor One', and that the ancient fathers
may at least be partially reprieved from their supposed error. The term
is certainly used in this context for the Teacher of Righteousness in the
Dead Sea Scrolls and may have been a general term for mystics at that
time.

Epiphanius is aware of the books we have as the *Clementine Homilies* and the *Clementine Recognitions*, though they are known to him as
the *Peregrinations of Peter*, and it is he who points out that these books
were used by the Ebionites. In them, Peter is also depicted as vegetarian and hence Epiphanius writes:

> They (the Ebionites) say he (Peter) abstained from living flesh and dressed
> meat as they do, and any other meat-dish – since both Ebion himself,
> and Ebionites, abstain from these entirely.
>
> *Epiphanius, Panarion I:II.30.15, PES p.131*

Epiphanius also relates that the Nazoraeans were "very like"[12] the
Ebionites in their beliefs, but omits to mention their diet. He does,
however, speak of another group – the Nasarenes – whom he describes
as pre-Christian. But the group is generally reckoned to be an invention of Epiphanius and to have been no different from the Nazoraeans.
The Nasarenes, he says

> forbid all flesh-eating, and do not eat living things at all.
>
> *Epiphanius, Panarion I:I.19, PES p.11*

And:

> They would not offer sacrifices or eat meat. They considered it unlawful
> to eat meat or make sacrifices with it.
>
> *Epiphanius, Panarion I:I.18.1, PES p.43*

Epiphanius also says that the Dositheans, followers of Dositheus, said
in the *Clementine* literature to have been a disciple of John the Baptist,
"abstain from meat".[13] And he refers to a number of other Judaic sects
who seem to have been very closely associated with the early Christians in
Palestine and were also vegetarian. These included the followers of
Elchasai, of whom Epiphanius says:

> He confesses Christ by name, if you please, and says "Christ is king".... He bans burnt offerings and sacrifices, as something foreign to God and never offered to Him on the authority of the fathers and the (Judaic) law, and ... he rejects the Jewish custom of eating meat.
>
> *Epiphanius, Panarion I:I.19.3, PES p.46*

In fact, from a variety of ancient and reputable sources, such as Philo,[14] Josephus[15] and Jerome, we learn that other sects of a similar character, including the Essenes of Palestine and the Therapeutae of Egypt, were all vegetarian. It seems to have been characteristic of the esoteric groups of those times – Christian or Judaic. It was also the accepted practice amongst Hellenistic esoteric groups such as the Pythagoreans[16] and was attributed to other Greek philosophers and mystics who had also taught transmigration of the soul, such as Empedocles[17] (c.490-430 BC). Indeed, it has always been the case that those following a spiritual or mystic path have either been strictly vegetarian or have had leanings in that direction. It is still true, even in modern times.

The vegetarianism of the Ebionites and the "Nazoraeans" or "Nazarenes"[18] is significant for these groups date back to the time of Jesus. Jesus himself was called the Nazoraean[19] and in *Acts*, Paul was described as a "ring-leader of the sect of the Nazarenes".[20] though the teachings that he took into the wider Roman Empire differed significantly from those of the Judaic Nazoraeans. Being descended from the direct disciples of Jesus who had lived in Palestine and the neighbouring area, the traditions they preserved are far more likely to reflect Jesus' real teachings than the groups that formed through the evangelical activities of Paul. The fact that the earliest Christians, directly descended from the time of Jesus, abstained from meat and alcohol is therefore a powerful testimony to Jesus having followed the same practice, for human nature being as it is, the general trend is to drop such restrictions as time passes, not to add them.

Peter the Vegetarian

Supporting this point of view is the fact that many of Jesus' well-known disciples are depicted as vegetarian in the apocryphal literature. We have already seen how Peter was said by the Ebionites to have abstained from meat and in the *Clementine Homilies* and *Recognitions* there are a number of places where Peter speaks out against the sacrificial slaughter of animals as offerings to idols and the subsequent eating of their flesh.

For instance:

> When you partook of meat offered to idols, you became servants to the Prince of Evil.
>
> *Clementine Homilies VII:III, CH p.131*

And as regards his own habits, Peter says:

> I live on bread alone, with olives, and seldom even with pot-herbs; and my dress is what you see, a tunic with a pallium: and having these, I require nothing more. This is sufficient for me, because my mind does not regard things present, but things eternal, and therefore no present and visible thing delights me.
>
> *Clementine Recognitions VII:VI, CR pp.340-341*

In another passage, Peter further commends a vegetarian diet and a simple lifestyle founded upon practical need – rather than a desire for luxury – together with a faith that God will provide all one's needs. He also points out that such a way of life is easy on the domestic budget:

> For what expense have those who use water and bread, and who expect it from God?
>
> *Clementine Recognitions IX:VI, CR p.405*

Demonstrating, too, that these Judaic Christians were by no means insular in their thinking and "poor of intellect" as the Christian heresiologists liked to deride them, there is a great deal in the Clementine writings concerning other beliefs and cultures. This includes a mystical interpretation of the Greek gods and their legendary exploits. The writer even has praise for the Brahmans of India:

> There are likewise amongst the Bactrians, in the Indian countries, immense multitudes of Brahmans, who also themselves, from the tradition of their ancestors, and peaceful customs and laws, neither commit murder nor adultery, nor worship idols, nor have the practice of eating animal food, are never drunk, never do anything maliciously, but always fear God. And these things indeed they do, though the rest of the Indians commit both murders and adulteries, and worship idols, and are drunken, and practise other wickednesses of this sort.
>
> *Clementine Recognitions IX:XX, CR p.413*

Whether he is correct that the "rest of the Indians" all behaved in such a reprehensible manner is doubtful, but the writer's reason for mentioning these cultural traits is to demonstrate that people practise and believe in those things with which they have been brought up. They thus perpetuate old beliefs and customs, good or bad, without really thinking too much about them.

James the Brother of Jesus – a Vegetarian

The first leader of the Judaic Christians at Jerusalem is always said to have been James the brother of Jesus, also called James the Just or James the Righteous. According to the fourth-century Christian historian, Eusebius, a certain Hegesippus, who lived a generation and a half after the martyrdom of James, described James as being vegetarian and teetotal:

> James, the brother of the Lord, succeeded to the government of the Church in conjunction with the Apostles. He has been called the Just (the Righteous) by all, from the time of our Saviour to the present day; for there were many that bore the name of James. He was holy from his mother's womb; and he drank no wine nor strong drink, nor did he eat flesh.
>
> *Hegesippus, in Eusebius, History of the Church 2:23, CHE p.125; cf. HC pp.99-100*

Jesus' own brother was vegetarian and teetotal, then. That, surely, is significant.

Matthew and Thomas – Vegetarians

There is as little genuine historical material concerning Jesus' disciples as there is of Jesus himself, and it is necessary to study peoples' traditional beliefs concerning them. From these sources, we discover that Matthew and Thomas were also said to have been vegetarian. Clement of Alexandria, for instance, who is not given to fabrication, comments in a discourse on not pandering to the palate:

> Happiness is found in the practice of virtue. Accordingly, the apostle Matthew partook of seeds, and nuts, and vegetables, without flesh.
>
> *Clement of Alexandria, Instructor II:1, WCAI p.197*

While the *Acts of Thomas* makes a number of references to Thomas as both vegetarian and teetotal. His friends relate of him:

> The simplicity and kindness of him and his faith do declare that he is a righteous man (Syriac: *magus*) or an apostle of the new God whom he preacheth; for he fasteth continually and prayeth, and eateth bread only, with salt, and his drink is water, and he weareth but one garment alike in fair weather and in winter, and he receiveth nought of any man (Syriac: takes nothing for himself from any man), and that he hath, he giveth unto others.
>
> *Acts of Thomas 20, AAA pp.161-162, ANT p.373*

And:

> That which he eateth is bread and salt, and his drink is water from evening unto evening, and he maketh many prayers.
>
> *Acts of Thomas 104, ANT p.410*

The stories in the *Acts of Thomas*, of course, are anecdotal and were never intended to be understood historically, but the teaching and tradition they impart was certainly meant to be taken to heart.

Bread, Herbs and Lentils which John Bought for Himself

In addition to his vegetarian diet and abstention from alcohol, it is also said of Thomas that he "takes nothing of any man for himself". The same is written concerning the apostle John in the *History of John*:

> His sustenance was, from the ninth to the ninth hour once, when he had finished his prayer, bread and herbs with a mess of boiled lentils, which he bought for himself as he went from town to town, eating, and drinking water only.
>
> *History of John, AAA p.8*

John was not only vegetarian but was very particular about living off his own income and purchasing his own food. This is another principle which all Masters have taught: both they and their disciples should earn their own living for themselves and their family by simple, honest means and should not be a burden upon others.

The reasoning behind this is partially based upon an understanding of the law of *karma* – that everything has to be paid for, sooner or later, and that there is no point in building up debts for the future. But begging also demeans a person, psychologically, putting them in an unsuitable frame of mind for concentrated meditation and for living a truly spiritual life. A person has to stand upright in their own eyes and before God before the mind can begin to focus at its natural head-quarters. Begging or living off others prevents the development of this attitude. And even though some religious orders advocate begging, it is an illusion that begging makes a person humble and dependent upon the will of God. It is not borne out by the evidence. Dignified and contented poverty, of course, is another matter, something quite different from begging.

This principle of earning one's own livelihood also receives a passing mention in the *Clementine Homilies* where Peter and his companions are travelling from Tripolis to Antioch. Since the background is entertaining, as indeed is the entire content of these writings, we include more than is perhaps required in the present context though it does demonstrate not only how the mystics like to lead a simple and straightforward life, but also prefer to avoid drawing the attention of a curious public. The unknown author relates:

> Therefore, starting from Tripolis of Phoenicia to go to Antioch of Syria, on the same day we came to Orthasia, and there stayed. And on account of its being near the city which we had left, almost all having heard the preaching before, we stopped there only one day, and set out to Antaradus.
>
> And as there were many who journeyed with us, Peter, addressing Nicetus and Aquila, said, "Inasmuch as the great crowd of those who journey with us draws upon us no little envy as we enter city after city, I have thought that we must of necessity arrange, so that neither, on the one hand, these may be grieved at being prevented from accompanying us, nor on the other hand, we, by being so conspicuous, may fall under the envy of the wicked. Wherefore I wish you, Nicetus and Aquila, to go before me in two separate bodies and enter secretly into the Gentile cities.
>
> "I know, indeed, that you are distressed at being told to do this, being separated from me by a space of two days. I would have you know, therefore, that we the persuaders love you the persuaded much more than you love us who have persuaded you. Therefore loving one another as we do by not unreasonably doing what we wish, let us provide, as much as in us lies, for safety. For I prefer, as you also know, to go into the more notable cities of the provinces, and to remain some days, and discourse.

"And for the present lead the way into the neighbouring Laodicea, and, after two or three days, so far as it depends upon my choice, I shall overtake you. And do you alone receive me at the gates, on account of the confusion, that thus we may enter along with you without tumult. And thence, in like manner, after some days' stay, others in your stead will go forward by turns to the places beyond, preparing lodgings for us."

Clementine Homilies XII:I-II, CH p.192-193

Peter, then, arranges for a quiet entry into the various towns he visits by sending his companions on ahead in separate parties and requesting that only the leaders of those parties should meet him at the city gates. So they enter Laodicea (now Latakia, Syria's chief port, in the northwest) and we rejoin the story after they had been there for some while, when Peter is asked if he would like to go on an outing:

When Peter had spoken thus, a certain one amongst us ventured to invite him, in the name of all, that next day, early in the morning, he should sail to Aradus, an island opposite, distant, I suppose, not quite thirty stadia (about three and a half miles), for the purpose of seeing two pillars of vine-wood that were there, and that were of very great girth. Therefore the indulgent Peter consented, saying, "When you leave the boat, do not go many of you together to see the things that you desire to see; for I do not wish that the attention of the inhabitants should be turned to you."

And so we sailed, and in short time arrived at the island. Then landing from the boat, we went to the place where the vine-wood pillars were, and along with them we looked at several of the works of Phidias.

But Peter alone did not think it worth while to look at the sights that were there; but noticing a certain woman sitting outside before the doors, begging constantly for her support, he said to her, "O woman, is any of your limbs defective, that you submit to such a disgrace – I mean that of begging – and do not rather work with the hands which God has given you, and procure your daily food?" But she groaning, answered, "Would that I had hands able to work! But they retain only the form of hands, being dead and rendered useless by my gnawing of them."

Clementine Homilies XII:XII-XIII, CH p.198

We must leave the story at this juncture, for the woman turns out to be the long-lost mother of the narrator, and the plot is too complex to enter into here. But the point in our present context is Peter's attitude towards begging. He does not countenance it and considers it a "disgrace".

The leading of a simple, industrious, self-supporting life was a common principle amongst the early Christians and in the *Death of Joseph*, one of the mythical writings of Coptic Christianity, the same ideal is attributed to Jesus' father Joseph. There, Jesus says:

> My father Joseph, the blessed old man, was working at the trade of carpentry, whilst we lived by the work of his hands. He never ate bread for nought, doing according to the law of Moses.
>
> *Death of Joseph IX, CAG p.133*

The potential in those ancient times for spongers to find a cosy place within a charitably-disposed community or for itinerant teachers, moving from place to place, to live off the hospitality of others, can readily be imagined. Indicating from the converse attitude that such people did exist, the unknown Addai insists that he has made no material profit out of giving Jesus' teaching or "word" to the world. His gain has been entirely spiritual, of the higher Word:

> I have not acquired anything with his word in the world. For his Word by which I have become rich was sufficient for me, and I have made by it many rich; for it lifts me up in this way (path) in which I go forth before Christ, who has sent after me, that I should go by it to him.
>
> *Doctrine of Addai the Apostle, DAA p.44*

By means of the Word, says Addai, he has been enabled to follow after Christ, "that I should go by it to him". This is more than sufficient riches for any disciple, for none would like to take material payment for giving such teachings to others.

Paul actually seems to have experienced criticism on this account and was certainly aware of the problem which he counters by pointing out that whenever he stayed in a community, he always put his hands to work and earned his own living. To the Thessalonians, he wrote:

> Now we command you, brethren, in the name of our Lord Jesus Christ, that ye withdraw yourselves from every brother that walketh disorderly, and not after the tradition (teaching) which he received of us. For yourselves know how ye ought to follow us: for we behaved not ourselves disorderly among you; neither did we eat any man's bread for nought; but wrought with labour and travail night and day, that we might not be chargeable to any of you: not because we have not power, but to make ourselves an example unto you to follow us.

For even when we were with you, this we commanded you, that if any would not work, neither should (they) eat. For we hear that there are some which walk among you disorderly, working not at all, but are busybodies. Now them that are such we command and exhort by our Lord Jesus Christ, that with quietness they work, and eat their own bread.

2 Thessalonians 3:6-12

He exhorts them by "our Lord Jesus Christ", according to his knowledge of Jesus' teachings, that they should earn their own living. Although Jesus must have been quite unequivocal on the subject, such matters clearly became issues not long after his death, with advocates on both sides of the fence. In the *Didache*, for example, the late first-century Christian manual of conduct for new converts – the same book that advocates fasting on other days of the week to the "hypocrites" so as to avoid being like them – we are amazed to find the instruction to give all the best food and produce to the "prophets, for they are your high priests".

This, no doubt, copied the Jewish custom of giving rich gifts to the priests, a practice which has been prevalent in all religions at various times in their histories. In this context, the "prophets" would be those who gave spiritual discourses and the justification for this point of view is Jesus' comment in St Matthew, "for the workman is worthy of his meat",[21] an obscure comment coming as it does on the heels of "freely ye have received, freely give."[22] The relevant extract from the *Didache* reads:

> But every true prophet who wishes to settle among you is "worthy of his food". Likewise a true teacher is himself worthy, like the workman, of his food. Therefore, thou shalt take the first fruits of the produce of the winepress and of the threshing-floor and of oxen and of sheep, and shalt give them as the first fruits to the prophets, for they are your high priests.
>
> But if you have not a prophet, give to the poor. If thou makest bread, take the first fruits, and give it according to the commandments. Likewise when you open a jar of wine or oil, give the first fruits to the prophets.
>
> Of money also and clothes, and of all your possessions, take the first fruits, as it seem best to you, and give according to the commandment.

Didache XIII:1-7, AFI p.329

While the recommendation to be generous and of service to others is in keeping with a mystic's teachings, it is very difficult to envisage Jesus advising his followers to donate their best to those who gave spiritual discourses or permitting those who performed such a service to accept donations from others. As he said elsewhere, "It shall not be so among you, but whosoever will be great among you, let him be your minister; and whosoever will be chief among you, let him be your servant."[23] A "minister" is one who serves or ministers to the needs of others, not one who takes.

So again we see very early evidence of the slow, inevitable decline of mystical teachings into the organized hierarchy of a religion, justifying human weakness in the name of a Master and obscuring his real teachings. For spiritually, the true begging is to become a humble beggar at the inner door awaiting the Lord's grace and pleasure in utter spiritual destitution and absence of ego. And the "workman" or labourer being "worthy of his meat" is possibly a saying set in the wrong context and whose true meaning is that one who labours at spiritual practice is worthy of the "Bread from heaven", a 'bread' which is given as a gift by God to the soul who truly begs and labours for it.

Paul the Vegetarian?

No one who has studied the matter denies that there was very early controversy in Christianity over the question of vegetarianism. There are a number of places in Paul's letters where he is clearly responding to opposition of his teaching that Christians could eat meat. He also writes specifically of his disagreements with Peter and James the brother of Jesus. As we have observed, James' exact relationship to Jesus' teachings is unsure, but he certainly seems to have been vegetarian and teetotal. And gleaning what we can from Paul's letters and from other sources, it appears that James also taught the Christians to practise all the Judaic laws, presumably as long as they did not conflict with Jesus' teachings as he understood them. There may have been good practical reasons behind this, for the Jews were very keen that all Jews should follow the many detailed observances and prohibitions of their religious law. To maintain social harmony, it may therefore have been the safest way for Jesus' Jewish disciples to have lived in Palestine at that time.

According to Paul, it was his rejection of Jewish customs which brought him into opposition with Peter, James and the other disciples of Jesus. The truth of this assertion, however, is difficult to assess for the disciples are far more likely to have been concerned about Paul's overall interpretation of Jesus' teachings and his inability to give the true mystic baptism and initiation instructions. In their view, Paul would have been a maverick who had not been appointed by Jesus and was not even one of Jesus' disciples. But whatever the reasons, there seems little doubt that Paul was responsible for the first major division within the Christian community. Coming at a time in the AD 50s when there must have been many of Jesus' original disciples still alive, this division would have been between the initiated disciples of Jesus and the converts of Paul.

Paul undoubtedly had problems with Christians who were Jesus' direct disciples and who understood Jesus' teachings differently from himself. This, together with the probable vegetarianism of John the Baptist, Peter, John, Thomas, Matthew and James, as well as the certain vegetarianism of the Nazoraeans and the Ebionites, seems to indicate that Paul was the one who began the move away from vegetarianism.

Paul believed in freedom from all Judaic observances and constraints. He often speaks of the "freedom we have in Jesus Christ", referring specifically to non-observance of Jewish religious laws. There was no need, he said, for his Gentile converts in Asia Minor and Europe to adopt them. No doubt he was correct, but at the same time he also threw out vegetarianism – one of the primary and cardinal tenets of mystic teaching.

Paul was interested in converts and in increasing numbers. In those days, as well as in present times, there was considerable prejudice against those who ate or lived differently from the majority. His potential converts would have felt this and it would have held them back from entering his fold. To overcome fear of public opinion, people must be acting from deep, self-motivated, inner conviction, something which is rare enough to reduce significantly the number of converts. Realizing this, Paul would naturally have been induced to waive as many restrictions as he could, including those on eating meat.

Nevertheless, the communities of converts formed by him came into contact with initiated disciples of Jesus or those who had heard of Jesus' teachings through these disciples. And since they taught both vegetarianism and abstention from alcohol, Paul's converts would have begun to wonder whether or not they were being given the correct teachings. Though we do not have a record of the communications that came from these communities to Paul, we can follow something of what was going on from Paul's replies. There is a hint of the controversy in *Colossians*, for example:

> Let no man therefore judge you in meat, or in drink, or in respect of an holy day, or of the new moon, or of the Sabbath days.
>
> *Colossians 2:16*

Paul is advising his followers not to feel concerned if their eating and drinking habits are criticized or if they receive adverse comment for failing to observe other customs such as the Jewish Sabbath or recognition of various holy days. The word 'meat', of course, is an old-fashioned term for 'food', as in "I have meat to eat, ye know not of" and in the *King James Version* it is generally used in this sense. What we would call 'meat' in modern English is normally translated as 'flesh'.

In *Romans*, Paul writes more specifically of vegetarianism, describing the eating of "herbs" (*i.e.* food from the plant kingdom) as weakness: *another interpretation*

> For one believeth that he may eat all things: another, who is weak, eateth herbs. Let not him that eateth despise him that eateth not; and let not him which eateth not judge him that eateth: for God hath received him.
>
> *Romans 14:2-3*

Clearly, some – if not all – of the Christians he was writing to were vegetarian and he is trying to forestall any quarrelling about it. The composition of the Roman community at that time is unsure, but it is likely that Paul's letter to them was written quite late on in his mission, when he was under arrest and on his way to Rome, never previously having been there or having met the Roman Christians on their own territory. It is likely, therefore, that there were very few of his own converts in Rome at that time.

Paul's letter to the Romans exhibits overtones of insecurity as he wondered how he would be received, and there are a number of places where he appears to be justifying his own point of view in advance of his arrival. For if Jesus had taught that only those whom he had chosen were his true disciples and also that they should be vegetarian, they would naturally tend to see Paul as a false apostle. Paul would have met this attitude on many previous occasions and would have been on his guard. It was still soon enough after the death of Jesus for the question to be one not of Judaic Christian or Gentile Christian, but of who was genuinely following Jesus' real teachings.

Later on in this letter, Paul seems to be anticipating disagreement when he writes:

> Let us no more pass judgment on one another, but rather decide never to put a stumbling block or hindrance in the way of a brother. I know and am persuaded in the Lord Jesus that nothing is unclean in itself; but it is unclean for anyone who thinks it unclean.
>
> *Romans 14:13-14, RSV*

The point that Paul is trying to make is that it does not make any difference what you eat, for nothing is pure or impure of itself. But if someone thinks that meat is impure, then for him it is impure and he is justified in not eating it. Paul is trying to be a diplomat and to please everybody. As he says elsewhere, "I am made all things to all men."[24] But in the process of pleasing everybody and gaining converts he is compromising with the realities of the mystic path. He then adds:

> If your attitude to food is upsetting your brother, then you are hardly being guided by charity (love). You are certainly not free to eat what you like if that means the downfall of someone for whom Christ died.
>
> *Romans 14:15, JB*

He seems to be saying that if one's eating habits upset another person, then one is not behaving "charitably" towards them and one should change one's diet for that reason alone. Elaborating the point, he continues:

> Because the kingdom of God does not mean eating or drinking this or that, it means righteousness and peace and joy brought by the Holy Spirit. If you serve Christ in this way you will please God and be respected by men.
>
> So let us adopt any custom that leads to peace and our mutual improvement; do not wreck God's work over a question of food. Of course all food is clean, but it becomes evil if by eating it you make somebody else fall away. In such cases the best course is to abstain from meat (food) and wine and anything that would make your brother trip or fall or weaken in any way.
>
> *Romans 14:17-21, JB*

Paul reckons peace and harmony to be higher realities than "eating and drinking" to the extent that he advises people to change their diet to mollify others, presumably for the meat-eater to become vegetarian or perhaps only when dining in vegetarian company. Whatever the situation, the issue is about "meat and drink" and it is clear that Paul does not teach that a vegetarian diet is essential – something which conflicts with the beliefs of other Christians. But he is prepared to adopt it if it keeps other people happy. Indeed, in an earlier letter to the Corinthians, he himself declares that he will no longer eat "meat" (meaning flesh) if it continues to upset people:

> Food, of course, cannot bring us in touch with God: we lose nothing if we refuse to eat, we gain nothing if we eat. Only be careful that you do not make use of this freedom in a way that proves a pitfall for the weak. Suppose someone sees you, a man who understands, eating in some temple of an idol; his own conscience, even if it is weak, may encourage him to eat food which has been offered to idols. In this way your knowledge could be the ruin of someone weak, of a brother for whom Christ died.
>
> That is why, since food can be the occasion of my brother's downfall, I shall never eat meat again in case I am the cause of a brother's downfall.
>
> *1 Corinthians 8:8-13, JB*

Paul again asserts his belief that it makes no difference so far as God is concerned whether or not a person eats meat. This he calls "this liberty of yours" – a freedom from constraint which others Christians did not 'enjoy'. He does, however, seem to agree that meat offered to idols is taboo. Therefore, he says, if someone happens to see you sitting down to eat in a such a temple (presumably of some other sort of food), he may be tempted to eat meat that has been offered to idols and thereby fall away. In this way, he says, "ye sin against Christ", and to avoid that he vows that from that day onward he will be vegetarian. "If meat make my brother to offend, I will eat no flesh while the world standeth, lest I make my brother to offend," as the *King James Version* renders it – though whether or not he stuck to his promise is unknown.

Paul's logic is characteristically convoluted, but these letters demonstrate the controversy he started by permitting his followers to eat meat and by teaching his own doctrine. In fact, whoever it was who told Paul's followers that his teaching on meat was wrong also seems to have pointed out that Paul was not a real apostle at all. This would explain why Paul immediately follows his comments concerning meat with:

> Am I not an apostle? Am I not free? Have I not seen Jesus Christ our Lord? Are not ye my work in the Lord? (Even) if I be not an apostle unto others, yet doubtless I am to you.
>
> *1 Corinthians 9:1-2*

He knows that he is not accepted amongst Jesus' original disciples. They are the "others" of whom he speaks, "If I be not an apostle unto others, yet doubtless I am to you," and he feels that the very existence of his group of converts proves that he is doing the Lord's work. Yet Paul's own words bear out that he had not been appointed directly by Jesus to give Jesus' teachings.

In fact, as discussed in an earlier chapter, so far as can be ascertained, he had never been taught the principles of Jesus' teachings. On his own admission, prior to his conversion, he was a violent opponent of Jesus' followers and is hardly likely to have taken the time to really study Jesus' teachings. Moreover, it was three years after his conversion experience that he went to Jerusalem, where he only met Peter and Jesus' brother, James, spending just fifteen days with them.[25] After that, he waited another fourteen years before again going to Jerusalem to see – in his own words – if his teachings had been correct:

> Then, fourteen years after, I went up again to Jerusalem with Barnabas, and took Titus with me also. And I went up by revelation, and communicated unto them that gospel which I preach among the Gentiles, but privately to them which were of reputation, lest by any means I should run, or had run, in vain.
>
> *Galatians 2:1-2*

But what they told him as regards his doctrine is not recorded. Indeed, there is very little from the other side of the fence concerning Paul's controversial apostleship, though what there is, is significant. Probably the clearest statement comes in an opening chapter of the *Clementine Homilies*, purporting to be a letter written by Peter to James. In this letter, Peter requests James not to make the books of his teachings available to all and sundry, but only to "our brethren, with the like mystery of initiation". In other words, they should only be transmitted to those who had been given the same initiation, so that those who wished to transmit the teachings could be properly trained to do so:

> Give the books of my preachings to our brethren with the like mystery of initiation that they may indoctrinate (train) those who wish to take part in teaching; for if it be not so done, our word of truth will be rent into many opinions.
>
> *Clementine Homilies, Epistle of Peter to James II, CH pp.1-2*

For if, he says, people are not properly so taught, then the teachings will be split into fragments by their "opinions" and interpretations. In fact, he says, this has already begun to happen amongst the "Gentiles" due to the unauthorized or "lawless ... preaching of the man who is my enemy" – an almost certain reference to Paul:

> And this I know, not as being a prophet, but as already seeing the beginning of this very evil. For some from among the Gentiles have rejected my legal preaching (my authorized preaching of the law), attaching themselves to certain lawless and trifling preaching of the man who is my enemy. And these things some have attempted while I am still alive, to transform my words by certain various interpretations, in order to the dissolution of the law; as though I also myself were of such a mind, but did not freely proclaim it, which God forbid!
>
> For such a thing were to act in opposition to the law of God which was spoken by Moses, and was borne witness to by our Lord in respect of its eternal continuance; for thus he (Jesus) spoke: "The heavens and the earth shall pass away, but one jot or one tittle shall in no wise pass from the law."[26] And this he (Jesus) has said, that all things might come to pass.
>
> But these men, professing, I know not how, to know my mind, undertake to explain my words, which they have heard of me, more intelligently than I who spoke them, telling their catechumens (new converts) that this is my meaning, which indeed I never thought of. But if, while I am still alive, they dare thus to misrepresent me, how much more will those who shall come after me dare to do so!
>
> *Clementine Homilies, Epistle of Peter to James II, CH p.2*

This is an extraordinary passage, for it speaks explicitly of the process we have mentioned so many times throughout this book. Moreover, though he is not mentioned by name, it links this first dilution of Jesus' teachings to Paul.

It is evident, then, that even from the times when Paul and Peter were contemporaneous, some years before the gospels were written, the process by which Jesus' teachings were to end up as a religion was already in progress. And amongst the first casualties, at the hands of Paul himself, were vegetarianism and abstention from alcohol.

It is unlikely, of course, that this letter was really written by Peter. All the same, the *Clementine Homilies* and *Recognitions* certainly capture much that is in accord with the universal mystic teachings, presenting it as the earliest tradition of Christianity. The writer speaks of the "eternal continuance" of the "law of God" given by Moses, "borne witness to" by Jesus. This "law" is the mystic path, not Jewish religious law.

So despite the uncertain history of these writings, it is likely that they still contain a strong element of truth regarding Peter's travels and teachings. Maybe there were actually three main camps – those of Paul and James both being breakaway groups from the teachings of Jesus as continued on by Peter until his death. But the available historical information is insufficient for anything more than speculation.

There is no doubt that the disagreement between the Pauline and the so-called Judaic Christians lasted for two or three centuries, maybe longer, until the Judaic Christians finally faded out. In fact, a number of scholars have expressed it as their opinion that some of the letters in the New Testament were written by the Pauline camp in order to try and persuade people that Peter had in the end come around to Paul's point of view. Probably *1 Peter* and certainly *2 Peter* come into this category. It has also been suggested that *Acts* was a late composition, forged with the same idea in mind.

There are also other apocryphal documents outside the New Testament canon which promote the same point of view, even suggesting that Peter and Paul met in Rome. It is from these stories that the tradition has arisen that Peter was executed in Rome. But historically, all of this material is extremely dubious, and some of these writings have been dated well into the second century.

2 Peter is the most certain candidate for forgery in the New Testament, speaking as it does of "our beloved brother Paul". With its long, wordy sentences, the style is also very different from *1 Peter,* and its concern with false teachers and the delayed end of the world identify it as pure polemic of a much later date, when these matters were occupying the attention of the Christian world.

Additionally, the two letters addressed to Timothy (*1 Timothy* and *2 Timothy*) and the one to Titus (*Titus*), written as if penned by Paul, possess a character and contents so different from all of the other letters attributed to him that many believe them to be forgeries. Their references to a well-established church organization of bishops and deacons, never mentioned by Paul and not otherwise encountered in the New Testament documents except for an odd introduction to *Philippians,* mark them off as early to mid-second century in origin. Doubts concerning their authenticity are aroused when we find 'Paul' recommending to his old friend Timothy:

> Drink no longer water, but use a little wine for thy stomach's sake and thine often (frequent) infirmities.
>
>

1 Timothy 5:23

This makes more sense if it is taken as coming from the pen of someone wanting to demonstrate to others that it is acceptable to drink alcohol. In fact, the drinking of wine is one of the primary issues in the *Timothy* and *Titus* letters, where even bishops and deacons are given the go-ahead to drink in moderation:

> A bishop then must be blameless, the husband of one wife, vigilant, sober, of good behaviour, given to hospitality, apt to teach; not given to wine, no striker, not greedy of filthy lucre; but patient, not a brawler, not covetous.... Likewise must the deacons be grave, not double-tongued, not given to much wine, not greedy of filthy lucre.
>
>

1 Timothy 3:2-3,8

And:

> For a bishop must be blameless, as the steward of God; not self-willed, not soon angry, not given to wine, no striker, not given to filthy lucre; but a lover of hospitality, a lover of good men, sober, just, holy, temperate; holding fast the faithful word as he hath been taught, that he may be able by sound doctrine both to exhort and to convince the gainsayers.
>
>

Titus 1:7-9

The writer then continues by identifying the particular source of his unease to be "they of the circumcision" – that is, the original Judaic Christians:

> For there are many unruly and vain talkers and deceivers, specially they of the circumcision: whose mouths must be stopped, who subvert whole houses, teaching things which they ought not, for filthy lucre's sake.
>
>

Titus 1:7-11

The style of these letters is distinctly unlike that of Paul's other communications and they are also far less compromising. However strong his feelings, Paul never speaks so divisively and critically, suggesting that the mouths of his opponents "should be stopped" and that they were only interested in money, in "filthy lucre". This is smear tactics, unworthy of holy men, and whatever his failings, Paul did not descend to that level. Rather, he usually tried to reconcile opposing sides. More-over, the expression that gets translated as "filthy lucre" is a favourite of the writer of these three short letters, for it occurs in four places. And apart from its tone being uncharacteristic of Paul, it never occurs in any of the other epistles attributed to him. These letters, therefore, almost certainly stem from a later period when the 'orthodox' Christianity that originated with Paul felt itself to be in direct conflict with the teachings of the Judaic Christians and needed to bolster its position.

That the conflict with other Christian groups occupies the mind of the writer of *1 Timothy* can again be observed when he has Paul 'fore-telling' the "latter times" when false prophets will come, commanding people to "abstain from meats":

> Now the Spirit speaketh expressly, that in the latter times some shall depart from the faith, giving heed to seducing spirits, and doctrines of devils; speaking lies in hypocrisy; having their conscience seared with a hot iron; forbidding to marry, and commanding to abstain from meats, which God hath created to be received with thanksgiving of them which believe and know the truth. For every creature of God is good, and nothing to be refused, if it be received with thanksgiving: for it is sanctified by the word of God and prayer.
>
> *1 Timothy 4:1-5*

Such specific 'prophecies' of the future are an almost certain indication of forgery, for they reflect the concerns of someone writing at that "latter time". In fact, we can see from his genuine letters that Paul was expecting an imminent end of the world. As far as he was concerned, he was already living in the "latter times", so futuristic prophecies concerning them would have been irrelevant.

The justification for eating meat – that God has made "every creature" to be eaten up "with thanksgiving of them which believe and know the truth" is a parody of logic and compassion. One could apply the same reasoning to anything in the world that one desired – that God had created it so it must be all right to eat it, indulge in it, possess it and so on. This comment is also quite the reverse of Paul's attitude in which he recommends vegetarianism if eating meat seems to upset someone.

The comment "forbidding to marry" provides us with a further insight into the nature of these 'dissident' groups, for this was not a characteristic of mainstream Judaic Christianity, but of more ascetic elements amongst the gnostics. Many of these, if not all, were also vegetarian, as we will shortly see.

All in all, then, both the authentic letters of Paul, as well as those of doubtful origin, tell us much of what was going on in Christianity at that time, but are quite unreliable as a guide to the teachings of Jesus. By this time, it seems that some of the Christian doctrines were quite the opposite of what Jesus had originally taught to his disciples.

Did Jesus Eat Fish?

It is likely that the gospel accounts of Jesus eating fish are also insertions stemming from the same controversy. Though the spurious nature of the stories does not in itself prove that Jesus was vegetarian, if it could be shown that the motivation behind their inclusion was to demonstrate that he ate fish, it would actually help to prove the converse! Based upon the evidence of the text itself, the last chapter of St. John, chapter twenty-one, is generally considered by scholars to be a spurious addition, as we discussed in chapter three. Nowhere else in John's gospel is there any mention of Jesus or his disciples being fishermen. Yet the first half of this chapter concerns a post-resurrectional miracle story devoted almost entirely to the subject of Jesus and his disciples catching, killing, cooking and eating fish.[27]

The story begins when Peter declares, "I go a-fishing". This they do and through the miraculous intervention of Jesus from the shoreline, they net a huge haul, "one hundred and fifty three fishes", we are precisely informed.... But one can hardly imagine the disciples, having just met the risen form of Jesus, and having netted such a miraculous catch, then possessing the presence of mind or even the inclination to start counting live fish in the dark while their Master looked on! Such details are the stuff of legend and anecdote. The story, which also records that the risen Jesus had a fire started on the beach on which he was already cooking some fish, then concludes:

> Jesus saith unto them, "Come and dine." And none of the disciples durst ask him, "Who art thou?" knowing that it was the Lord. Jesus then cometh, and taketh bread, and giveth them, and fish likewise. This is now the third time that Jesus shewed himself to his disciples, after that he was risen from the dead.
>
> *John 21:12-14*

A similar incident is related in one of Luke's post-resurrection narratives, where Jesus is made to ask pointedly for "meat" and is given some "broiled fish ... which he did eat before them". The writer seems to want to make a point of it:

> And while they yet believed not for joy, and wondered, he said unto them, "Have ye here any meat?" And they gave him a piece of a broiled fish, and of an honeycomb. And he took it, and did eat before them.
>
> *Luke 24:41-43*

The person or persons, then, who added these two resurrectional and – dare we say it – rather fishy stories was evidently doing so with a purpose at least part of which must have been to try and demonstrate that Jesus was not a vegetarian. The other motivation, of course, was to indicate that the resurrected form of Jesus was not a ghost or spiritual form but a physical body that needed physical food. But, like the controversy mentioned by Paul, the stories actually serve only to further the case that Jesus had indeed abstained from eating the flesh of any creature.

The same is true of the story concerning Peter's vision in *Acts*, a document evidently written by a Pauline sympathizer:

> On the morrow, as they went on their journey, and drew nigh unto the city, Peter went up upon the housetop to pray about the sixth hour. And he became very hungry, and would have eaten: but while they made ready, he fell into a trance. And saw heaven opened, and a certain vessel descending unto him, as it had been a great sheet knit at the four corners, and let down to the earth: wherein were all manner of four-footed beasts of the earth, and wild beasts, and creeping things, and fowls of the air. And there came a voice to him, "Rise, Peter; kill, and eat."
>
> But Peter said, "Not so, Lord; for I have never eaten any thing that is common or unclean."
>
> And the voice spake unto him again the second time, "What God hath cleansed, that call not thou common."
>
> *Acts 19:9-15*

The remainder of the story makes it clear that the meaning intended is that Gentiles should be included in Christian missionary activities. It is essentially support for Paul's activities. Yet the details of the vision lead one to think that there might have been a secondary motivation. Peter is hungry and is presented with a vision of every kind of specifically non-vegetarian food. He declares that he has never previously eaten anything "common or unclean" – but is instructed by Jesus to go ahead anyway. It seems that he is being told that although it was originally correct to have been vegetarian, this is no longer the case. This is more or less the same point that Paul had tried to put across in his letters.

Whenever the question of Jesus being vegetarian is discussed, people always ask, "What about the miracles of the loaves and the fishes?" We have already discussed Jesus' miracles in an earlier chapter, but it is of interest to observe here that early references to these two miracles characteristically omit all mention of fish.

A Coptic fragment of an unidentified gospel, for example, has Jesus speak of a number of his miracles, including the observation "I have parted a few loaves and satisfied many".[28] Similarly, the *Acts of Thomas* speaks of Jesus "satisfying many thousands with a little bread",[29] while the *History of John* says:

> He satisfied four thousand men, besides women and children, with five
> loaves of barley meal, and they ate and left some over, and carried and
> conveyed to their homes as much as they were able.
>
> *History of John, AAA p.15*

No mention at all is made of fish. But perhaps even more significant is the late second-century testimony of Irenaeus. On the two occasions where he refers to these miracles in his *Against Heresies*, he speaks only of "loaves", fish making no appearance whatsoever. His first description is in a long dissertation on the gospel miracles of Jesus, each one being mentioned with all its relevant details. Knowing Irenaeus' anti-vegetarian views, he is hardly likely to have missed an opportunity to put fish into Jesus' mouth. Yet he writes:

> Again, withdrawing from thence to the other side of the sea of Tiberias,
> he there, seeing a great crowd had followed him, fed all that multitude
> with five loaves of bread, and twelve baskets of fragments remained over
> and above.
>
> *Irenaeus, Against Heresies II:XXII.3, AHI p.199*

And again:

> Our Lord, after blessing the five loaves, fed with them five thousand men.
>
> *Irenaeus, Against Heresies II:XXIV.4, AHI p.209*

But even if the original stories did speak of fish, there remains considerable doubt as to their authenticity. The most likely explanation of these two miracles is that we are actually dealing with variants of one story, probably much exaggerated in the manner of all legends. And while the fish were the 'inspired' addition of a later hand, the bread which Jesus actually fed to a multitude in the desert was the "Bread of Life", the Word, which all Masters feed to souls who find themselves spiritually hungry in the desert of this world. Such an allegory would not have been without precedent, for the 'children of Israel' are said to have been fed 'manna from heaven' while crossing the desert on their way to the 'Promised Land'. Or maybe Jesus did sometimes make arrangements, with the help of his disciples, to feed the large numbers of people who flocked around him. That may in itself have seemed miraculous, providing the basis for later wild exaggeration.

Gnostic Vegetarians

The more mystically inclined somebody is, the more likely he is to be vegetarian. This is partially because the development of love and compassion go hand in hand with the development of true spirituality, and because one who has genuine tenderness of heart will always live in such a way as to minimize all suffering. But, in addition, those who really understand the law of *karma* and reincarnation, particularly those who can actually see it in operation from a higher level, will never kill other creatures if they can avoid it. No one would knowingly put himself into a debt he could have easily avoided.

It is for this reason that many of the gnostics of the early Christian period are reported to have been vegetarian. Marcion (*fl.*140-160), for example, is described by Tertullian (*fl.*190-220), Hippolytus (*fl.*210-236) and Epiphanius (*b.*315) as abstaining from meat. Echoing the letter to Timothy, Hippolytus writes:

> You, (Marcion, advise) ... the abstaining from meats which God has created for participation by the faithful, and those that know the truth.
>
> *Hippolytus, Refutation of All Heresies VII:XVIII, RAH p.297*

The second-century Saturninus is also said by Irenaeus to have taught abstention from animal food:

> Many of those, too, who belong to his school, abstain from animal food, and draw away multitudes by a feigned temperance of this kind.
>
> *Irenaeus, Against Heresies I:XXIV.2, AHI p.90*

And it is highly likely that other gnostics and their followers did so too, including Simon Magus, Valentinus, Basilides, Menander, Heracleon, Ptolemy and many more from the first two or three centuries after Jesus. For most of them taught escape from the domain of birth and death and the return to God by travelling the inner path of *gnosis* – and abstention from meat and alcohol are a natural part of this path. But so little is known of these great teachers. We only know that the Christian heresiologists did not like them for their beliefs and practices, which tells us more about the heresiologists and the wide spectrum of belief amongst the early Christians than it does about the individual gnostics.

There is little doubt that these gnostics had a profound influence on Christianity during the second and third centuries, spreading an understanding of mystic truths throughout the Roman Empire, bringing renewed life to those Christians and others who truly sought their Creator within. This we have seen in the examples of their writings quoted throughout this book. What their spiritual practices were is hard to tell, but some were undoubtedly of ascetic leanings, something not taught by the higher mystics but understandable nonetheless as an attempt to subjugate all bodily desires. Amongst them were the early desert fathers, famed for their austerity, abstinence and wisdom.

As a general designation, these ascetics were commonly termed Encratites, meaning the 'self-controlled' or the 'masters of themselves', one such group being founded in the mid-second century by the Assyrian, Tatian, who had his headquarters at Antioch in Syria. Tatian had been a pupil of Justin Martyr until the latter's death, after which he developed increasingly gnostic sympathies. Like their Jewish counterparts, the Nazirites, Tatian and the Encratites were also vegetarian and teetotal. According to Jerome,

> Tatian condemns and rejects ... meats which God has created.
>
> *Jerome, Against Jovinianum I:3, WTT p.48*

And:

> Tatian, the chief of the Encratites ... assert(s) that wine is not to be drunk.
>
> *Jerome, Commentary on Amos, WTT p.48*

Likewise, Irenaeus and Hippolytus assert:

> Others, however, styling themselves Encratites, acknowledge some things concerning God and Christ in like manner with the Church. In respect,

however, of their mode of life, they pass their days inflated with pride. They suppose that by meats they magnify themselves, while abstaining from animal food, (and) being water-drinkers, and forbidding to marry, and devoting themselves during the remainder of their life to habits of asceticism.

Hippolytus, Refutation of All Heresies VIII:XIII, RAH p.326

And:

Some of those reckoned among them have also introduced abstinence from animal food, thus proving themselves ungrateful to God, who formed all things.

Irenaeus, Against Heresies I:XXVIII.1, AHI p.100

Wherever we look, then, the sincere search for God goes hand in hand with a reverence for His creation and the consequent abstinence from meat and alcohol.

In the gnostic and apocryphal writings themselves, there are a number of allusions to vegetarianism in addition to those concerning the apostles. In the undoubtedly mythological *Acts of Matthew*, for instance, Matthew, meeting with Peter and Andrew, describes his journey to the "country of the Blessed" where every morning, Jesus appears to the inhabitants in radiant splendour. When he asks them why Jesus should have bestowed this privilege upon them, they reply by describing their country. It turns out to be a place of great purity, called "El Barbar" meaning 'the land of the Blessed', signifying that access to the inner realms where Jesus can be seen in such glory requires great purity of mind and conduct. The story, of course, is an allegory and amongst other things Matthew is told:

As for gold and silver we do not wish it in our country. We eat no flesh and drink no wine in our country; but honey is our food and our drink. We do not look on the faces of our women with desire.... Our country heareth no lying speech, and no one knoweth of it. No man weds two wives in our country; and no boy dieth before his father.... When winds blow, we smell from them the Scent of the garden of Paradise. There is no cold in our country, and no snow, but a Breath of Life; and it is temperate.

Acts of Matthew, MAA p.101

Upon which Matthew tells Peter and Andrew:

When I heard this from them, I longed to dwell in their country; and my
eyes were dazzled from hearing the sweetness of their speech.

Acts of Matthew, MAA p.101

Again, in the early Christian revelationary writing, the *Ascension of
Isaiah*, a book into whose narrative the author is in the habit of slip-
ping significant points of teaching, we find that a group of prophets or
holy men "who believed in the ascension into heaven" were constrained
to a vegetarian diet:

And they (the prophets) had nothing to eat but only the wild herbs that
they gathered on the mountains; and they cooked them and lived on them
together with the prophet Isaiah. And they remained on the mountains
and on the hills for two years.

Ascension of Isaiah II:11, AOT p.787

Similarly, in the early Christian allegory, *Joseph and Aseneth*, soon after the wealthy Aseneth has met and fallen in love with Joseph, a man
of renowned and extraordinary beauty who symbolizes the Master,
she happens to be brought her regular dinner:

Aseneth took her royal dinner, even the fatted beasts and the fish and
the meat, and all the sacrifices for her gods, and the wine-vessels for
their libations; and she threw them all out of the window as food for
the dogs.

Joseph and Aseneth X:14, AOT p.483

Such things are no longer to be a part of her diet. Again, in the allegorical tale of Peter, the apostles and Lithargoel, the man whose city
was called "nine gates", we find that on the journey to Lithargoel's city
"one who is anxious about meat ... the lions eat because of the meat".
Lithargoel says:

Concerning the road to the city, which you asked me about, I will tell
you about it. No man is able to go on that road, except one who has
forsaken everything that he has and has fasted daily from stage to
stage. For many are the robbers and wild beasts on that road.... The one
who is anxious about meat and green vegetables, the lions eat because of
the meat.

Acts of Peter and the Twelve Apostles 5-6, NHS11 p.215

And later, after they have travelled this mystic "road", Peter, who is the 'raconteur', says that they "evaded the lions because they did not find the desire for meat with us":

> I hurried and went and called my friends so that we might go to the city that he, Lithargoel, appointed for us. In a bond of faith we forsook everything as he had said to do. We evaded the robbers, because they did not find their garments with us.... We evaded the lions, because they did not find the desire for meat with us.
>
> *Acts of Peter and the Twelve Apostles 7, NHS11 pp.219-221*

Again, in the allegorical poem, the *Robe of Glory*, from the *Acts of Thomas*, which tells the story of the soul's descent from God, its sleep of death in the physical creation and its redemption through a Saviour, the soul is induced to sleep in this creation through the "food" that it eats:

> But in some way or other
>> they perceived that I was not their countryman.
> And with guile they mingled for me a deceit
>> and I tasted of their food.
>
> I forgot that I was a son of kings,
>> and I served their king;
> And I forgot the pearl,
>> for which my parents had sent me,
> And by reason of the heaviness of their food,
>> I fell into a deep sleep.
>
> *Acts of Thomas 108:31-35, AAA p.240, ANT p.412, HS p.17, RG p.15*

This "food" carries a double meaning, being both the food of worldliness and materiality, as well as the food that is eaten to provide sustenance for the body. And the food which causes the soul to "sleep" is that which entails the death of other creatures. The same double meaning is found in the Nag Hammadi text, the *Teachings of Silvanus*:

> Listen, O soul, to my advice. Do not become a den of foxes and snakes, nor a hole of serpents and asps, nor a dwelling place of lions, or a place of refuge of basilisk-snakes. When these things happen to you, O soul, what will you do? For these are the powers of the Adversary. Everything which is dead will come into you through them (the powers). For their food is everything which is dead and every unclean thing. For when these are

within you, what living thing will come into you? The living angels will detest you. You were a temple, (but) you have made yourself a tomb. Cease being a tomb, and become (again) a temple, so that uprightness and divinity may be restored to you.

Teachings of Silvanus 105-106, TS p.57

We are all seekers of life but are unaware of what it really is or where to seek it. The body is a temple of the Living God into which He can be found as the Source of all life and being. He can fill this temple with light, life and bliss, but not if it is already packed full of dead things: desires and thoughts of inanimate material objects and the flesh of dead creatures.

Mani the Vegetarian

Moving forward into the third century, the great mystic, Mani, is a further reliable witness to the abstinence from meat and alcohol so characteristic of the mystic path to God. There is absolutely no doubt about the fact that he taught this to all his disciples, though in later times, when his teachings too had become a religion, such abstinence was sometimes reserved more for the elite or the 'elect' than others. Vegetarianism and teetotalism remained an integral aspect of Manichaean practice amongst the Cathars, the Albigensians and others until the Catholic crusade of Pope Innocent III in the thirteenth century all but wiped them out.

According to the legend, during his mother's pregnancy, Mani's father, Patik, a resident of the twin cities of Seleucia-Ctesiphon in Mesopotamia, capital of the Persian Empire, heard a loud voice while worshipping in a temple of idols, instructing him to eat no more meat and to abstain from alcohol. As a result, it is said that Patik joined a 'baptismal sect', sometimes thought to have been the Mandaeans. Modern Mandaeans of the south are not vegetarian, but there is evidence from Mandaean legends that the Nazoraeans or Mandaeans of the north were vegetarian.[30]

Mani, as said before, stated that his teachings were the same as those of Jesus, Buddha and Zarathushtra, which means that he too believed that Jesus had taught abstention from meat and alcohol, and there are many references to this in the literature concerning Manichaeism. Amid the texts from Turkestan, for example, there is the verse:

The living masses, who devour flesh,
  have bodies like graves,
    or they are not unlike bottomless pits.
Numerous kinds of animals are unjustly slaughtered,
  in order to supply the arms
    of the three venoms and six robbers.

LSMH 104, BSOAS XI p.183

The "three venoms and the six robbers" are allusions to aspects of the mind and to particular human weaknesses – whichever may have been identified as such by the writer. Amongst a collection of notes and jottings of a Confucian official whose name was Chuang Ch'o, written in 1133, there is a lengthy record of the Chinese Manichaeans as "vegetarian demon worshippers", a sect "whose rules prohibit the eating of meat and the drinking of wine", and who referred to themselves as the "religion of light". They were also "strictly prohibited by the laws".[31]

According to St Augustine, at one time a follower of the Manichaean religion, the Manichaeans spoke of the "three seals" or vows – those of the "mouth, hands and breast" or, as Eastern Manichaean texts have it, the "mouth, hands and thoughts". These vows evidently covered the broad spectrum of outer conduct in life, including abstention from meat and alcohol. Samuel Lieu writes in *Manichaeism in the Later Roman Empire*:

The "Seal of the Mouth" forbids blasphemous speech, the eating of meat and the drinking of wine.... Wine is designated the 'bile of the Prince of Darkness' because its intoxicating effect induces forgetfulness of the divine message. A fragment of a Manichaean text in Middle Persian lists among the sins and harms of wine and drunkenness: unconsciousness, sickness, regret, contentiousness, fear (through falling), strife and punishment.

The "Seal of the Hands" enjoins the believer not to perform any task which might hurt the light particles (the souls) which are held captive in matter. This light is a deity because it is part of the Father of Greatness....

The "Seal of the Breast" applies to the carnal sins and by it the Manichaeans are forbidden to partake in sexual intercourse which is regarded as an imitation of demonic fornication and results in the procreation of matter and thus the further enslavement of the light.

Samuel Lieu, MLRE pp.19-20

Mani's precise teaching regarding sex is not clear from the extant documents, and the latter restriction relates to the Manichaean Elect of the
later religion who were expected to remain celibate and unmarried,
like the Catholic priests of Christianity. But fundamentally, the "three
seals" relate to purity of thought, word and deed – something with
which all mystics and indeed all religions would concur. And purity of
deed includes reverence for all life in the creation – by loving all expressions of life for the Lord who dwells within them, not by putting
them upon one's plate and eating them up. Only if a person pays full
respect to life without can they ever hope to find eternal life within.

We have seen, then, that there is considerable evidence that Jesus
taught and practised vegetarianism and abstention from alcohol. John
the Baptist, James the brother of Jesus, Peter and the apostles, the Judaic Christians, the gnostics, the ascetics, some of the desert fathers,
Mani – in fact, practically everyone except Paul and the branch of
Christianity that based itself on Paul's teachings – all seem to have
been vegetarian and abstainers from alcohol. Jesus' teachings also support the idea that he was, too, and that he taught this to his disciples.
And if he really did teach the path of the Creative Word, then – like all
the other mystics of the world who have taught this path – it is certain
that he would have been.

NOTES AND REFERENCES

1. *Deuteronomy* 5:17.
2. *Mark* 10:19, *Luke* 18:20.
3. *Numbers* 6:1-21.
4. Epiphanius, *Panarion* I.I.19.1, *PES* p.11.
5. *Luke* 15:16.
6. Epiphanius, *Panarion* I:II.30.22, *PES* pp.137-138.
7. *cf. DSSU* pp.15,186,233-235,244,270.
8. See Hippolytus, *Refutation of All Heresies* VII:XXIII, *RAH* p.303.
9. See Tertullian, *On the 'Prescription' of Heretics* X, *TTSPH* p.50.
10. See Epiphanius, *Panarion* I:II.30.2-3,18,24, I:II.31.1; *PES* pp.119-121,133,139-
    140,152-153.
11. Epiphanius, *Panarion* I:II.20.30, *PES* p.56.
12. Epiphanius, *Panarion* I:II.20.30, *PES* p.56.
13. Epiphanius, *Panarion* I:I.13.1, *PES* p.35.
14. Philo, *On the Contemplative Life* IV:37, *PhIX* p.135.
15. See comment on Josephus, *Jewish War* II: (8.5) in *SCO* p.176.
16. *eg.* Origen, *Against Celsus* V:49,VIII:28, *OCC* pp.303, 471; Clement of Alexandria,
    Instructor II:I, *WCAI* p.193.
17. *eg.* Hippolytus, *Refutation of All Heresies* VII:XVII, *RAH* p.295.
18. See earlier discussion, chapter 3, pp.133-136.

19. *Matthew* 2:23; Epiphanius, *Panarion* I:II.29.5-6, *PES* pp.116-117; *Gospel of Philip* 62, *NHS20* p.165.
20. *Acts* 24:5.
21. *Matthew* 10:10.
22. *Matthew* 10:8.
23. *Matthew* 20:26-27.
24. *1 Corinthians* 9:22.
25. *Galatians* 1:18.
26. *Mark* 13:31.
27. *John* 21:1-14.
28. *Gospel Fragments, ANT* p.31.
29. *Acts of Thomas, AAA* p.187.
30. E.S. Drower, *Haran Gawaita and the Baptism of Hibil-Ziwa*, p.viii.
31. Chuang Ch'o, in *Manichaeism in the Later Roman Empire*, S.N.C. Lieu, *MLRE* p.236.

CHAPTER TWENTY-SEVEN

Whithersoever Thou Goest

Satsang here to Jeff

The Yoke of the Master

In our exploration of his teachings, we have seen that Jesus taught some simple, fundamental mystic truths. God is to be found within, he said; the path to Him is that of the Word; the Word is to be contacted through the "Word made flesh", a living Son of God, by means of mystic baptism and spiritual practice. And, while practising these spiritual exercises, a certain way of life and mode of conduct is also required. This, in essence, is the mystic teaching of Jesus and of all the other great mystic Saviours.

Armed with this understanding and convinced so far as is humanly possible of the truth and efficacy of the path, and having received the gift of true baptism, there then remains only one realistic course of action for a sincere disciple: to follow the mystic path with all the energy, enthusiasm and commitment he or she can muster.

For those who are approaching this path, a Master explains its fundamentals, describing what it entails and expects of its devotees. For those who have already decided to follow it, he gives encouragement and guidance in every way he can to his flock of errant sheep, to inspire, cajole and love them into coming back inside the fold. Amongst the gospel writings, there are many places where Jesus does just this. Indeed, many such passages, where he was speaking directly to his baptized disciples, have already been encountered, and in this chapter we consider more deeply Jesus' teachings concerning the life of a disciple.

Jesus' various examples of the shepherd and the sheep are remarkably good analogies of the relationship that develops between a Master and a disciple. Sheep are nervous creatures, easily disturbed and frightened, with a tendency to follow each other to no good account. They can also get entangled in thorn bushes or fall into ravines and they have many enemies, especially in the Middle East of those times: there were thieves waiting to steal them and wolves eager to gobble them up.

Similarly, as human beings, we are easily disturbed by life in this world and have a tendency to imitate each other. Our attention is easily plundered or consumed by sensual attractions or stolen away by the many other seductions and allurements of the world. A disciple therefore struggles to overcome his normal human nature.

For his part, the shepherd sees to it that his sheep are protected as far as possible from all dangers. He has a power, an intelligence and a foresight which the sheep do not possess, enabling him to keep them safe. The good and diligent shepherd also comes to know all his sheep, caring for each of them individually, even going out of his way to save just one sheep in his entire flock from danger. In a word, the sheep are under the protection of their shepherd. If they had the wit, they might say that they had taken refuge with him, their powerful protector. In the care of the shepherd, they are safe. All this exemplifies the care of a Master for a disciple and the reliance that a disciple comes to have on his Master. The relationship develops into one of mutual love of a very high and spiritual order.

But to begin with, the disciple still retains his old habits and tendencies of mind. His ego makes him feel separate and on his own. Like sheep who wish to break away from the fold and the protection of the shepherd, the disciples do not take full advantage of the help that is offered. The Master, however, never uses force of any kind, but only love, gentle persuasion and the inspiration of his own example. Everything has to come from within the disciple, only then will it be of lasting value. Then, by degrees and through their personal experience, he wins the confidence of the sheep so that they willingly come to him and receive what he has to give. This is why Jesus says:

> Come unto me, all ye that labour and are heavy laden,
>   and I will give you rest.
> Take my yoke upon you, and learn of me;
>   for I am meek and lowly in heart:
>   and ye shall find rest unto your souls.
> For my yoke is easy, and my burden is light.
>
> *Matthew 11:28-30*

He extends an invitation and explains why it is worth accepting. He has no sins or *karmas* of his own at all. All other souls in this creation are carrying a heavy burden of sins from life to life. They are yoked to their sins and have to go wherever their sins take them. But by coming under the protection of a Master, they can find peace and the eternal rest of God even while still living in the body. And compared to the yoke of this world and the burden of sins that force us into situation after situation and life after life, the yoke of discipline imposed by a Master is very light indeed. It is a yoke of self-control and spiritual practice, leading to eternal bliss and beatitude. Inner peace and bliss are not, of course, the province of a Master's disciples alone. Many people of all time, races and religions have achieved such a state. But complete forgiveness of all sins, leading to salvation from birth and death, together with permanent and eternal rest, is another matter.

A yoke, incidentally, is the wooden piece which joins two oxen together so that they can work as a team, pulling a heavy plough or other burden behind them. The agricultural example is most apposite and Jesus is using a similar analogy when he observes:

> No man, having put his hand to the plough,
>   and looking back, is fit for the kingdom of God.
>
> *Luke 9:62*

Once having accepted the yoke of a Master and being joined to him through baptism, the duty of a disciple is to move forward with determination and faith, without regrets or doubts. A man who goes to plough a field but is always hesitant and looking over his shoulder to see if he is ploughing a straight line lacks confidence in himself and what he is doing. As a result, he takes a long time to plough his field and makes a poor job of it. The way to plough a field is to look straight ahead and to keep going. In this way, the task is well done and soon accomplished. The same is true of discipleship.

This is what it means to "follow" a Master, an expression commonly used in the gospels. In St Matthew, we read:

> And a certain scribe came, and said unto him,
> "Master, I will follow thee whithersoever thou goest."
> And Jesus saith unto him,
> "The foxes have holes,
>   and the birds of the air have nests;
>   but the Son of man hath not where to lay his head."
>
> *Matthew 8:19-20*

It is very easy and natural for a disciple, uplifted by his Master's presence, to get carried away by his own emotions and to express his willingness to do whatever the Master says and to follow the path laid out for him. But Jesus cautions such a disciple that the mystic path is not a bed of roses. It requires great self-sacrifice to learn the art of dying while living, to relinquish all vestiges of self, to overcome all weaknesses and to withdraw all attention from the body and the world. The mind has been going in an outward direction for millions of lifetimes and to change its habits is a tremendous challenge. The individual is greatly exercised and experiences a considerable struggle within himself.

It is not always so pleasant and easy to face up to what goes on within our minds, yet this is what following a Master entails, and a great deal more. The path of the Masters is the path of reality. No illusions will be permitted to remain. Emotional self-deception and justification, even in the name of spirituality, will all be exposed and eliminated. The disciple will be inwardly stripped naked of all artificiality and pretence. A Master may take nothing from a disciple, but he leaves no negative traits within him either.

So Jesus advises that while everyone else in this creation has a place to hide and to live in illusion, the disciple of a Master is ultimately denied all these escapes. He will be brought face to face with reality at every level. Ultimately, the reward is great, far exceeding anything that can be gained in any other way. But the effort required is correspondingly great. And then, too, the story is not ended, for the divine nostalgia takes hold upon the soul, a longing for God that grows within and never diminishes, night or day.

Everything of the world has to be inwardly relinquished. This is what Jesus means when we read:

> And another of his disciples said unto him,
> "Lord, suffer me first to go and bury my father."
> But Jesus said unto him,
> "Follow me; and let the dead bury their dead."
>
> *Matthew 8:21-22*

The disciple's statement is probably only Matthew's setting for Jesus' saying. The "dead" are the spiritually dead people of the world. From his other sayings, we know that Jesus cannot be advocating dereliction of worldly duties or disrespect of parents and family. He means that a disciple has to rearrange his inner priorities. He may have to lead a full life in the world, but by understanding its true nature, his inner attention is never really caught up in it. His first priority is his spiritual life, though he may keep this entirely to himself. It is more a question of inner attitude than of outward circumstances.

For this reason, Jesus advises his would-be disciples to sit down and really assess what they are getting themselves into, before they make any decisions. Masters are not interested in emotional conversions. They want sincerity and quality, not curiosity seekers or those who are just covering all their options. In Luke, he relates two parables to explain this point:

> Whosoever doth not bear his cross,
> and come after me, cannot be my disciple.
> For which of you, intending to build a tower,
> sitteth not down first, and counteth the cost,
> whether he have sufficient to finish it?
> Lest haply, after he hath laid the foundation,
> and is not able to finish it,
> all that behold it begin to mock him, saying,
> "This man began to build, and was not able to finish."
>
> Or what king, going to make war against another king,
> sitteth not down first, and consulteth
> whether he be able with ten thousand to meet him
> that cometh against him with twenty thousand?
> Or else, while the other is yet a great way off,
> he sendeth an ambassage, and desireth conditions of peace.
>
> So likewise, whosoever he be of you
> that forsaketh not all that he hath,
> he cannot be my disciple.
>
>   *Luke 14:27-33*

If somebody wants to build a tower, he first needs to make a thorough study of what is involved in case he finds at a later date that he has not got what it takes to complete the task. Similarly, a king, knowing that his army is less powerful than that of his enemy, has to study the situation very carefully before he decides to wage war. Otherwise, before he has even joined the first battle, he will have to press for peace and under such circumstances, the terms are unlikely to be in his favour.

A person who comes into the fold of a Master has engaged in a fight with Satan, the "king" of this world and the higher realms of the mind.

With his own resources, he could never hope to conquer such an enemy. The force that tips the scales in his favour is the Master. But he must be sure that he has faith in that Master before he wages war or builds a tower, else he is doomed to failure, at least until he gains such confidence.

A disciple can take nothing on the spiritual path for his personal credit. Having been accepted into the fold of a Master, he cannot then be proud of his 'achievement', exhibiting himself to others as a highly spiritual person or in any other way trying to gain some egocentric advantage from his discipleship, either amongst his fellow disciples or in the world. Jesus covers this attitude, too, when he relates the following parable:

> But which of you, having a servant ploughing
>   or feeding cattle, will say unto him by and by,
>   when he is come from the field,
>   "go and sit down to meat"?
> And will not rather say unto him,
> "Make ready wherewith I may sup, and gird thyself,
>   and serve me, till I have eaten and drunken;
>   and afterward thou shalt eat and drink"?
> Doth he thank that servant because he did the things
>   that were commanded him? I trow (think) not.
>
> So likewise ye, when ye shall have done
>   all those things which are commanded you, say,
> "We are unprofitable servants:
>   we have done that which was our duty to do."
>
> *Luke 17:7-10*

He says that a disciple should take no egocentric credit for following the path laid out for him by his Master. For one who has done what was his duty and was expected of him, the matter ends there. He cannot start feeling proud of what he had been contracted to do. Jesus, of course, is saying this for the disciple's own benefit. He does not want them to lose what they are struggling so hard to gain.

A disciple simply has to serve his Master by selflessly following all his instructions, implicitly. Then the Master will fulfil his side of the bargain and take the soul into his own lap. This is what Jesus meant when he said:

> If any man serve me, let him follow me;
>   and where I am, there shall also my servant be:
> If any man serve me, him will my Father honour.
>
>   *John 12:26*

To "serve" the Master means to follow what he says – to practise meditation and to live the life he advises. The highest service to a Master is meditation and when a disciple succeeds in that, "him will my Father honour". The blessings of God, through the divine Music of the Word, will be showered upon him inwardly, filling him with love and bliss. Then the Master will always be present with that disciple and the disciple will always be with his Master, for the real form of a Master is the Word, the Holy Spirit, which is omnipresent, omniscient and within every soul. This is what the author of the Nag Hammadi, *Teachings of Silvanus*, means when he says:

> Accept Christ for yourself, who is able to set you free.... For this King whom you have is forever invincible, against whom no one will be able to fight nor say a word. This is your King and your Father, for there is no one like him. The divine Teacher is with you always. He is a helper, and he meets you because of the good which is in you.
>
>   *Teachings of Silvanus 96-97, TS pp.37-39*

When the disciple accepts the Master, he takes protection from the highest Ruler of all. And that "divine Teacher is always with you" – he never leaves his disciples, but always helps them because of the "good which is in you", because of the divine potential that lies within every soul. And "he meets" them on the inner planes in his spiritual, astral form, derived from the Holy Spirit.

Persecuted for Righteousness' Sake

Though inwardly forsaking everything, relinquishing all attachments and desires of the world so that they become one-pointed in their devotion towards their Master, disciples are taught to earn their own honest living and fulfil their family obligations. Consequently, one of their most difficult tasks is to keep their inner orientation while faced with the everyday pains, pleasures and activities of life. The outer world is most seductive and weakens the will of the spiritual aspirant before he has even realized it. Even in the simplest processes of living, the mind has a tendency to move out into the world from its hidden, inner focus and its spiritual concentration is diluted.

The world may appear to have some comfort to offer through human relationships and in other ways, but such solace can actually dull the mind and distract the individual from the inner journey. Naturally, it is good to be positive and appreciative of what is of value in human life, being kind, loving and understanding, and accepting the same from others in the normal course of events. But if such human harmony, love and enjoyment is mistaken for the goal of human existence, then the individual has been deluded.

Many mystics have therefore observed that in this world the grace of the Lord is manifested as trouble and hardship, because these things tend to turn the mind away from material comforts and pursuits. They bring a person face to face with the illusory and transient character of things, sharpening up desire for the eternal and for real spiritual understanding.

In the time of Jesus, it seems that hardship was never too far away, for he and his disciples were persecuted by both the secular and religious authorities of the day. Perhaps, too, this is why John the Baptist and Jesus chose such outwardly difficult ways to die. If their disciples were to be oppressed, abused, imprisoned and even put to death, then they too could show by example that it was still possible to remain true to their spiritual ideals, retaining love for God and all men, while undergoing such extremities of suffering and persecution. In all things, a Master, like the Eastern shepherd, leads from the front, by his own example. Moreover, the *karma* that these Masters took upon themselves by undergoing execution would have helped to mitigate the similar suffering that some of their own disciples were destined to undergo.

Jesus was certainly aware of the hardship that his disciples would have to face if they adhered faithfully to his teachings. It must have been this knowledge which prompted him to say:

> Blessed are they which are persecuted
> for righteousness' sake:
> for theirs is the kingdom of heaven.
> Blessed are ye, when men shall revile you, and persecute you,
> and shall say all manner of evil against you falsely,
> for my sake.
> Rejoice, and be exceeding glad:
> for great is your reward in heaven:
> For so persecuted they the prophets which were before you.
>
> *Matthew 5:10-12*

He points out that this would not be the first time that followers of the mystic path had to face prejudice and persecution. A great many of the Jewish "prophets which were before you" had to bear a similar fate. So "rejoice, and be exceeding glad", he says, "for great shall be your reward in heaven" – such suffering will turn your minds away from this world and the spiritual treasure will become yours if only you remain steadfast and firm upon the mystic path. Whatever you have to endure, ultimately, it will be worth it. In St John, too, in the farewell discourses, he speaks in a similar vein:

> If the world hate you, ye know that it hated me
>> before it hated you.
> If ye were of the world, the world would love his own:
>> but because ye are not of the world,
>> but I have chosen you out of the world,
>> therefore the world hateth you.

John 15:18-19

Jesus makes it clear that his persecution is intended as an example for them, so that they can more easily bear such hardship. Worldly people love worldly people, he says, and they only hate you, "because ye are not of the world". People are generally alarmed by things they do not comprehend. Prejudice and intolerance can sometimes be intense against those who do not conform and, although the truly spiritual man understands the one who is worldly, the material mind cannot comprehend the spiritual. Perceiving such people as a threat, they will even imprison and kill them if social conditions permit, often in the name of God. Jesus continues:

> Remember the word that I said unto you,
>> the servant is not greater than his lord.
> If they have persecuted me,
>> they will also persecute you;
> If they have kept my saying, they will keep yours also.

> But all these things will they do unto you
>> for my name's sake,
>> because they know not Him that sent me.

John 15:20-21

If they have even persecuted me, he says, then you cannot expect any better treatment from them. If they will even persecute the Lord Himself, come in human form, then they will certainly not spare the disciples. But they only do this out of ignorance of who the Master really is. He then adds:

> If I had not come and spoken unto them,
>   they had not had sin:
> But now they have no cloak for their sin.
> He that hateth me hateth my Father also.
> If I had not done among them the works
>   which none other man did, they had not had sin:
> But now have they both seen and hated both me and my Father.
>
> *John 15:22-24*

If they had not heard Jesus speak and if he had not come and performed the task – the "works" – allotted to him by the Lord, then they could have taken refuge in the excuse that they did not know. But having heard him and seen him, they have hated him. And since he was one with God, they have effectively hated God also, whoever they may have been – even priests or otherwise religious people. Nevertheless, he concludes:

> But this cometh to pass,
>   that the word might be fulfilled
>   that is written in their law,
> "They hated me without a cause."
>
> *John 15:25; cf. Psalms 35:7*

This has been the common fate of all the prophets, he says – as he did in St. Matthew – and he quotes the thirty-fifth psalm where David speaks of his 'persecutors', which includes both the people of this world as well as the weaknesses of the mind.

Sheep in the Midst of Wolves

Being on the receiving end of persecution and prejudice is one thing, but learning how best to respond to it – both inwardly and outwardly – is quite another. In general, Jesus' advice was the same as for dealing with any other kind of anger. He recommended meekness, humility, love, turning the other cheek and so on. But there is a section in St Matthew where – according to Matthew's narrative – Jesus sends his twelve disciples into the world to give spiritual discourses to the people. And there he advises them more specifically on how to deal with persecution and rejection.

The authenticity of this setting, however, is dubious, for in Mark and Luke the sayings comprising Matthew's section are not found together, but in separate places. In Luke, some of the sayings are placed along with material that Matthew has in his Sermon on the Mount, while in Mark, some of them appear in his mini-apocalypse, which is probably Matthew's source for these particular sayings. This gives an apocalyptic flavour to Matthew's version of Jesus' advice to his disciples, which is unlikely to have been Jesus' original intention but suited Matthew's beliefs.

Studying the relationships between these passages, one concludes that Matthew has used Mark's story of Jesus sending his twelve disciples to preach to the people. But, from some other source, he has added considerably to Mark's version of Jesus' advice to them, collecting a number of Jesus' sayings together and presenting them as one continuous discourse because of similarity in theme. The result, however, is that they actually read unevenly, not as the unbroken expression of someone's flow of thought.

Moreover, while Mark and Matthew have Jesus send out twelve disciples, Luke – the Pauline supporter of Christianity for the Gentiles – has Jesus despatch disciples on two occasions – first twelve and later seventy. But lacking two appropriate speeches, Luke uses the same speech each time, editing it slightly for each version. The numbers sent out are significant for it was commonly believed that the twelve disciples signified the twelve tribes of Israel, which suggests that Jesus had only come for the Jews. Luke's "seventy", on the other hand, represent the seventy nations into which Judaism considered the Gentiles to be divided. Luke thus makes the story more acceptable to the Gentiles and especially to his Roman audience. If it is true that Luke was the friend and companion of Paul, then his desire to demonstrate a mission to the Gentiles is even more understandable. Luke may also have been attempting to account for the widespread distribution of Jesus' disciples throughout the known world, something which we have previously observed.

Matthew's 'discourse', therefore, is a hodgepodge of sayings taken from here and there, not all of which can be relied upon to have been the exact words of Jesus or even to have come from him at all. As we have seen so often and as scholars have spent so much time trying to disentangle, this has been the *modus operandi* of all the gospel writers. Editorial hands can once again be seen at work making us wish – as so many times before – that we had the real, unedited words of Jesus before us to dispel all doubt as to what he really taught. In this instance, however, as in others, despite the rearrangement of the text, the meaning for the most part is reasonably clear, particularly once Matthew's insertion of apocalyptic material has been recognized.

Beginning with the passage which Luke has in his equivalent of Matthew's Sermon on the Mount, Jesus says:

> Behold, I send you forth as sheep in the midst of wolves:
> be ye therefore wise as serpents, and harmless as doves.
>
> *Matthew 10:16*

Jesus advises his disciples that the world will be hostile to them if people come to know what they really believe and practise. They should therefore be as "wise as serpents" – they should quietly slip away from any situation which looks as if it might turn out to be problematic. Quite unlike the style of Paul, he advises against confrontation. After all, only those who are destined to come to a Master, will come to him, so there is no need to advertise the mystic teachings. Curiosity seekers, those who want to demonstrate their cleverness and those who only want to create a disturbance are best avoided. A perceptive person will spot them immediately and will refrain from being drawn into any altercation. This is what Jesus means by being as "wise as serpents", for snakes are very rarely aggressive. Mostly, they quietly get out of the way whenever they hear anyone approaching and nobody even knows that they were there.

Jesus also advises them to be as "harmless as doves" – never react or retaliate, whatever the provocation may be. Always pursue the most loving and most harmonious approach to any person or situation. This is quite in accord with his other teachings on meekness and turning the other cheek. He then continues:

> But beware of men:
> for they will deliver you up to the councils,
> and they will scourge you in their synagogues;
> And ye shall be brought before governors and kings for my sake,
> for a testimony against them and the Gentiles.

> But when they deliver you up,
>> take no thought how or what ye shall speak:
>> for it shall be given you in that same hour
>> what ye shall speak.
> For it is not ye that speak,
>> but the Spirit of your Father which speaketh in you.
>
> *Matthew 10:17-20*

This passage gives us an insight into the times and it must have been the way the Jewish and Roman authorities treated their 'dissidents', as indeed the Christians did until only a few centuries ago. But Jesus says, have no fear. The Spirit, the Word, is with you; the Master is always with you within and he will put the right words into your mind at the right time. You will be supported within, he says, so there is no need to start worrying about how to answer their questions and what answers you will give to particular questions. Just keep your mind centred and on the Master and if you can do that, then he will guide you in everything you say.

Matthew then inserts the apocalyptic sayings which are absent from Luke's version and come from the mini-apocalypse to be found in Mark:

> And the brother shall deliver up the brother to death,
>> and the father the child:
> And the children shall rise up against their parents,
>> and cause them to be put to death.
> And ye shall be hated of all men for my name's sake:
>> but he that endureth to the end shall be saved.
>
> *Matthew 10:21-22*

Again, we get a window into the nature of the times. Even family members informed upon each other. One can imagine how devout and strictly orthodox Jews or followers of the conventional Roman religions must have felt if one isolated member of their family became vegetarian, stopped drinking wine, started getting up early in the morning, began meeting with other followers of the same path and dropped everything whenever Jesus happened to be in the vicinity in order to go and see him.

Assuming that these words are really based upon something that Jesus said, he is pointing out that persecution does happen. Some disciples do have to face severe opposition from their own families. In some cases, hatred and intolerance must have been so high they were even handed over to the authorities for execution. But whatever happens, Jesus advises them, stick with it, because whatever the hurt caused to your feelings by ignorant people, nothing of this world is of any value at the time of death. All that a person can take with them is their spiritual treasure. Almost everyone in the entire world is running outward into materiality. Consequently, the true disciple has to buck the trend and make his life spiritually fruitful, whatever difficulties he may have to face. This is what he means by "he that endureth to the end shall be saved". We then read:

> But when they persecute you in this city, flee ye into another:
> for verily I say unto you,
> ye shall not have gone over the cities of Israel,
> till the Son of man be come.
>
> *Matthew 10:23*

This saying appears only in Matthew's gospel. The first part seems reasonable – Jesus advises his disciples to avoid trouble if they can, as he has said before. But the second half must surely be an interpolation based upon the belief in an imminent end to the world. But the end of the world so expectantly awaited by many of the early Christians never came. Matthew then continues with sayings that seem more reasonably attributable to Jesus:

> The disciple is not above his master,
> nor the servant above his lord.
> It is enough for the disciple that he be as his master,
> and the servant as his lord.
> If they have called the master of the house Beelzebub,
> how much more shall they call them of his household?
>
> *Matthew 10:24-25*

As he said in St John, if they can persecute the Master, then they can be expected to persecute his disciples. And if they can call Jesus "Beelzebub", the Devil, then they can hardly be expected to hold back their abuse from his disciples. He goes on:

> Fear them not therefore: for there is nothing covered,
> that shall not be revealed;
> and hid, that shall not be known....
> And fear not them which kill the body,

> but are not able to kill the soul:
>> But rather fear him which is able to destroy
>> both soul and body in hell.
>
> *Matthew 10:26,28*

Again he counsels them that they have absolutely nothing to fear. At the most, people can only destroy the body. But then the soul would be released, would meet the Master inside and continue its journey back to God, and there is no hardship in that. If anything is to be feared, it is Satan, who can keep a soul in the hell of this world, reincarnating in birth after birth. Jesus is giving his disciples encouragement to remain steadfast in adversity, for if they give way to self-pity, anger, frustration and hurt, their minds will turn back to the world and they will become liable to rebirth. He then adds:

> Are not two sparrows sold for a farthing?
>> and one of them shall not fall on the ground
>> without your Father.
> But the very hairs of your head are all numbered.
> Fear ye not therefore,
>> ye are of more value than many sparrows.
>
> *Matthew 10:29-31*

The Father knows everything, he says. Even the death of a sparrow or the number of hairs on your head all lie within the compass of His will. However strange it may seem, ultimately He is the doer of everything. So if the Lord is aware of all the tiny details of His creation, He is certainly aware of what is happening to the souls that have been initiated by His appointed and anointed Son and have been put upon the path of return to Him. Therefore, he concludes:

> What I tell you in darkness, that speak ye in light:
>> and what ye hear in the ear,
>> that preach ye upon the housetops.
>
> *Matthew 10:27*

Whatever a Master teaches his disciples is to be translated into action. Jesus did not mean them to go out and, finding people who were not the slightest bit interested in the mystic path, try to convert them. He means that a disciple should become so firmly rooted in his spiritual practice that nothing can disturb him, inwardly. Whatever the circumstances, he should go on living in the spiritual way he has come to know and understand. He therefore concludes:

> Whosoever therefore shall confess me before men,
>> him will I confess also before my Father which is in heaven.
> But whosoever shall deny me before men,
>> him will I also deny before my Father which is in heaven.
>
> *Matthew 7:32-33*

The disciple who is firm and secure within himself and has full confidence in his Master's teachings will not be shaken by adverse circumstances or by the difficulties of life. He will retain his inward balance and composure whatever the situation. He will remain a true disciple, true to his Master's ideals and teachings, not put off course by the attitude of other people. This is what he means by confessing "me before men". The disciple is not afraid or shy to "confess" or acknowledge his Master in public – either by word, if required, but also in his mind. He is not afraid to follow his Master's teachings, whatever others may say or do. Naturally, each situation is different and requires its own individual handling, but whatever the circumstances, a true disciple will never compromise with his Master's teachings in any way.

Such a disciple, Jesus says, will be acknowledged by the Master before God. He will be taken back to God. But a disciple who denies his Master before men – is easily influenced by public opinion or by the attitude of his family and associates, is weak within himself, compromising with his principles – the Master will "deny" him before God in the sense that the disciple will be unable to return to God until his faith has been considerably deepened.

These two sayings of Jesus are usually taken to be an exhortation to proselytize, and this may well have been the meaning which the compiler of Matthew's gospel intended to convey. But they have to be taken in the context not only of the advice that mystics generally give to their disciples, but also of Jesus' other sayings. He advised his disciples against confrontation, for example, counselling them to be as "wise as serpents" and – even more pointedly:

> Give not that which is holy unto the dogs,
>> neither cast ye your pearls before swine,
>> lest they trample them under their feet,
>> and turn again and rend you.
>
> *Matthew 7:6*

There is no point, he says, in talking to people who are not interested in what you have to say. Here, he is advising his disciples to keep quiet, quite the opposite of preaching "upon the housetops". This is what the writer of the *Gospel of Philip* means when he relates a parable:

> There was a householder who had every conceivable thing, be it son or slave or cattle or dog or pig or corn or barley or chaff or grass or ... meat and acorn. Now he was a sensible fellow and he knew what the food of each one was. He served the children bread.... He served the slaves ... meal. And he threw barley and chaff and grass to the cattle. He threw bones to the dogs, and to the pigs he threw acorns and slop.
>
> Compare the disciple of God: if he is a sensible fellow he understands what discipleship is all about. The bodily forms will not deceive him, but he will look at the condition of the soul of each one and speak with him. There are many animals in the world which are in human form. When he identifies them, to the swine he will throw acorns, to the cattle he will throw barley and chaff and grass, to the dogs he will throw bones. To the slaves he will give only the elementary lessons, to the children (of light) he will give the complete instruction.
>
> *Gospel of Philip 80-81, NHS20 pp.203-205*

A disciple who practises according to his Master's instructions becomes deeply perceptive, for no one understands the mind so well as one who strives to control it. He automatically assesses every situation and responds accordingly. In this way, he retains his own inner integrity, never compromises his principles and avoids disagreements with others.

Freely Ye Have Received, Freely Give

There is a part of this discourse of Jesus to his disciples which all three of the synoptic writers set as his advice to those who were being sent out to give his teachings. These sayings are certainly more specific to such a mission than the sayings we have already considered, although all three gospels exhibit variants on the same theme. It is Mark, followed by Luke, who tells us that Jesus' purpose in choosing twelve of his disciples was so that they could go out and give his teachings:

> And he ordained twelve, that they should be with him,
>   and that he might send them forth to preach.
>
> *Mark 3:14*

And when it was day, he called unto him his disciples:
and of them he chose twelve, whom also he named apostles.

Luke 6:13

This 'ordination' simply means being appointed, though in later Christianity it became the mandate which all priests were given when they were ordained by the church authorities. One presumes that these particular disciples were chosen because they had a good grasp of Jesus' teachings together with an ability to express things clearly. Some of them may also have been fluent in other languages such as Greek and Semitic dialects and languages other than Aramaic. Matthew's version, which provides far more material than Luke or Mark, begins:

And as ye go, preach, saying,
"The kingdom of heaven is at hand."

Matthew 10:7

The first and most important thing, he says, is to tell people that the "kingdom of heaven" is not very far away. It is "at hand"; it is right beside you and within you. Matthew then follows Mark who tells us that Jesus gave his apostles miraculous powers:

Heal the sick, cleanse the lepers,
raise the dead, cast out devils.

Matthew 10:8

But these are spiritual miracles, as we have seen. We are all spiritually sick, diseased, dead and possessed by the Devil and the powers of the mind. He continues:

Freely ye have received, freely give.

Matthew 10:8

Do not charge anybody for giving these teachings, he says. You have been given them absolutely free of any charge and you should pass them on in the same way.

Provide neither gold, nor silver,
nor brass in your purses,
nor scrip for your journey,

neither two coats, neither shoes, nor yet staves:
For the workman is worthy of his meat.

Matthew 10:9-10

This last statement seemingly contradicts Jesus' previous comment for he appears to be suggesting that his twelve apostles should live off others while they are travelling. In the context of Jesus' other teachings, this hardly seems likely, and we have noted in the previous chapter how, traditionally, the apostles provided for their own food. In the absence of the concluding line, his meaning seems to be that they should rely upon the grace and protection of their Master, not presenting themselves as rich and influential people, as some of them may well have been. They should just go from place to place in a very simple manner, without ostentation or putting on airs.

And into whatsoever city or town ye shall enter,
inquire who in it is worthy;
and there abide till ye go thence.
And when ye come into an house, salute it.
And if the house be worthy,
let your peace come upon it.

Matthew 10:11-13

It is normally presumed that Jesus is sending his twelve apostles to speak to the general public. Yet, once again, this does not fit with comments like not throwing holy teachings to the dogs nor casting pearls before swine. Moreover, to "enquire who in it is worthy" might be a difficult thing to do if they did not already know anyone in that town. Bearing in mind the multitudes that came to see Jesus and received baptism from him, it seems more probable and more practical that the apostles were sent on a mission to carry inspiration to Jesus' many other disciples, for Jesus is unlikely to have simply baptized disciples and to have then forgotten all about them, leaving them with no further support. And naturally, the apostles would have lodged with these disciples, since they were all part of one family or flock, the sheep of one shepherd.

So Jesus is probably suggesting that when they come to a town, they should stay with some good and sincere disciples. He also recommends that whenever they enter a house, they should be the first to greet the occupants, rather than permit themselves be given special treatment because their Master had given them some particular service to perform. He is, as always, teaching his disciples to serve each other and to be just like everybody else. So he says, "let your peace come upon it" – share your love with those brothers and sisters so that all may feel uplifted and at peace. He continues:

> But if it be not worthy,
>   let your peace return to you.
> And whosoever shall not receive you,
>   nor hear your words,
>   when ye depart out of that house or city,
>   shake off the dust of your feet.
>
> *Matthew 10:13-14*

If, by any chance, you stay with people who do not make you welcome, then he says, "let your peace return to you" – do not let your mind be disturbed by it. Just remain at peace within yourself regardless of what may be going on in the house around you. In fact, he advises: wherever you are not well received, when you "depart out of that house or city", just let all the disharmony or whatever has happened drop from your mind, like dust from the sole of your shoes. Do not carry it with you, letting your mind go over it again and again. Just forget about it. Matthew then follows Mark in ending with a reference to the punishment on the "Day of Judgment" given to those who receive them badly:

> Verily I say unto you, it shall be more tolerable
>   for the land of Sodom and Gomorrah
>   in the Day of Judgment, than for that city.
>
> *Matthew 10:15*

While Luke ends more simply:

> And whosoever will not receive you,
>   when ye go out of that city,
>   shake off the very dust from your feet
>   for a testimony against them.
>
> *Luke 9:5*

Luke seems to be uncomfortable with Jesus' words as he finds them in Mark and he changes them, though his addition – "for a testimony against them" – is not in keeping with Jesus' teachings on forgiveness and is anyway a somewhat futile gesture. Looking at the full context of

Jesus' teachings, it seems more likely that having advised his apostles that the best course of action was simply to forget about the incident, Jesus would have ended by saying that whatever other people do is their affair for which they will have to account when their day of reckoning comes, at their time of death. The overlay of eschatological expectations which is found in the synoptic gospels, especially those of Mark and Matthew, with 'Day of Judgment' comments tacked on to Jesus' sayings and discourses, is simply not in keeping with the rest of his teachings. But having lost the original ending due to Mark's apocalyptic zeal (or the editor of Mark's source of these sayings), the best that Luke can do is to make a rather ineffectual guess.

Let Your Light So Shine Before Men

The essence of Jesus' advice to his disciples when facing up to life in the world was to be living examples. In the discourse preserved in Matthew's Sermon on the Mount, Jesus describes this very beautifully:

> Ye are the salt of the earth:
>> but if the salt have lost his savour,
>> wherewith shall it be salted?
> It is thenceforth good for nothing,
>> but to be cast out,
>> and to be trodden under foot of men.
>> *Matthew 5:13*

Salt is the universal seasoning used by all people to bring out the flavour in everything. So if salt were to lose its flavour – what could be used to season the salt? You are like salt, he says to his disciples. The human form is designed by God with a purpose not possessed by any other form in creation. Only in the human form can the soul begin its journey back to God. But if while being in human form, a soul makes no attempt to return to God or to know anything about Him, then it is like salt without flavour. The very reason for its existence has been annulled. It is therefore "cast out" and "trodden under foot of men" – an allusion perhaps to being cast out into forms which are lower than that of man. Continuing, he says:

> Ye are the light of the world.
> A city that is set on an hill cannot be hid.

Neither do men light a candle,
> and put it under a bushel, but on a candlestick;
> and it giveth light unto all that are in the house.
>
> *Matthew 5:14-15*

Those souls who are travelling the path back to God are the light in the world. They are the "children of light", as they are called elsewhere. Such a light should not be hidden, in the sense that those souls who have received the true baptism should take advantage of that gift and learn to let the soul shine inwardly with its own great light. Then they will give "light to all that are in the house" – without their ever saying anything, they will become living examples to all those who come into contact with them. As he concludes:

> Let your light so shine before men,
> that they may see your good works,
> and glorify your Father which is in heaven.
>
> *Matthew 5:16*

When the light of the soul burns brightly inside, then people will see from "your good works" – from the way you live – that you have gained something of great value by following this Master. Then they, too, will be inspired to seek within and learn how to "glorify your Father which is in heaven".

This, then, is the other side of the picture. Jesus' times may have been violent and his disciples may have had to face much persecution, as did Jesus himself. But when times are difficult, people are more motivated to seek a way out and to find the true reason for living. Despite the hardships, "multitudes" flocked to see Jesus and their souls were set aglow with the divine Light.

There Am I in the Midst of Them

Disciples of a Master may be the "salt of the earth" and have the potential to be the "light of the world", but to begin with and even after many years they can still be very human. Were they not so, they would not have taken birth in this world. Souls take birth because of their sins and imperfections and, at the human level, this burden is observed as human weakness. Until a person has conquered the mind by going beyond the realm of Satan, they are still liable to human imperfection.

As a consequence, like any close-knit family or group of people, a community of disciples will have differences amongst each other, from time to time. Sometimes, this may even seem to be greater than in normal human families because disciples are playing for the highest stakes and life is sometimes lived with great inner intensity. Moreover, followers of the mystic path are often people of strong feelings. Those who do not care about anything can never be reached by a Master. Only a person who feels things deeply can be touched by him. Then their inner energies can be moulded. But those who are dull inside are untouchable. Sometimes, therefore, a person may have to be shattered and stripped of everything, his life taken apart by the seams, before he can begin to awaken spiritually.

With such children as his raw material, a Master has a busy job as a father and no small part of his energies can be spent in keeping love and harmony amongst them. In such a naturally hot-blooded area of the world, Jesus must have had many all-too-human situations to handle, and we glimpse this in some of the sayings and anecdotes that have come down to us. There are the sons of Zebedee who wanted special places in the kingdom of heaven much to the annoyance of the other disciples; the man who wanted Jesus to arbitrate between him and his brother over the sharing of their father's inheritance; Peter's asking how many times he should forgive someone – and so on.

All disciples are equal in a Master's eyes. Even if one disciple is physically closer than another to the Master, it is only due to the structure of human life. If a Master has hundreds or thousands of disciples, it is clearly impractical for every one of them to have a close personal relationship with him in an outward sense. Even if Jesus found a way to make personal contact once in a while with every one of his disciples, that would still have been very different from the closeness that the twelve apostles and some of his other disciples seem to have enjoyed.

All the same, a Master is present within every one of his disciples. Inwardly, all get the same love and attention, and all will ultimately be taken back to God, whatever they may do or think. In fact, those whom he keeps closest to himself may simply be those in greatest need of attention, just as a teacher may keep his naughty and inattentive students in the front row. Sometimes the deepest darkness is closest to the light. A Master knows how to ensure that he takes all souls back to God. As Jesus said, summarizing the parable of the shepherd and the sheep that went astray: "It is not the will of your Father which is in heaven that one of these little ones should perish".[1] And again: "Lo, I am with you alway, even unto the end of the world".[2] (though Matthew sets it as the final, apocalyptic, post-resurrection saying). And even more explicitly:

> Again I say unto you,
> > that if two of you shall agree on earth
> > as touching any thing that they shall ask,
> > > it shall be done for them of my Father which is in heaven.
> For where two or three are gathered together in my name,
> > there am I in the midst of them.
>
> *Matthew 18:19-20*

Even if disciples are physically at a distance from their Master, separated perhaps by hundreds or thousands of miles, or even if he has left this world, their Master is always with them. He goes wherever they go. And wherever and whenever they meet in his name, to remember him and give each other encouragement to follow the mystic path, the Master will be there "in the midst of them" to give them inspiration. Indeed, whatever they may ask collectively, or even individually, he will always be there to help them. But, being humble, as all Masters are, Jesus says that it is not he who will do it, but "my Father which is in heaven".

Understanding that the Master is within every one of his initiates means that a disciple treats all his fellow initiates with love and respect. Indeed, since the real Master is the Word, as a disciple advances inside, he comes to realize that the divine Music resounds within every soul and within every particle of creation. He then sees the Lord's creative Power everywhere and within everybody, and automatically treats everything and everybody with natural appreciation. This is why it has been said that far from becoming insular and short-sighted, the "chosen ones" actually become as universal as God Himself. It is the Master's presence within his disciples to which Jesus must have been referring when he said:

> He that receiveth you receiveth me,
> > and he that receiveth me receiveth Him that sent me....
> And whosoever shall give to drink
> > unto one of these little ones a cup of cold water
> > only in the name of a disciple, verily I say unto you,
> > he shall in no wise lose his reward.
>
> *Matthew 10:40,42*

A person who receives or serves one of his "little ones", his "chosen ones", is actually receiving or serving the Master and through the Master, God Himself. And since no action goes without its reaction or reward in life, they will receive the benefit of that service. Through that association, they will also be drawn to a Master, maybe not in this life, but sooner or later, and then they will receive the highest reward of all – that of being taken back to God.

The same idea lies behind another well-known passage attributed by Matthew to Jesus, and once again placed in an apocalyptic setting. The overall theme, however, being the judgment by the Son of man (the Messiah) at the end of the world when the righteous will receive their reward and the wicked will be punished, is mirrored in the pre-Christian, Biblical book of *Daniel* as well as *1 Enoch*,[3] a book now considered apocryphal but held in high esteem by many of the early Christians. The earlier Judaic belief in an apocalypse presided over by the Messiah has thus been projected on to Jesus by the compiler-writer of Matthew and, within this borrowed setting, he has placed some further sayings, attributing the entire passage to Jesus. At that time, Jews and Christians alike would have been very familiar with apocalyptic literature of this kind and the short discourse attributed to Jesus would have held no surprises for its audience.

Taking the embedded sayings on their own and assuming that Jesus really was their author, he would actually seem to have been talking about the time of death, not the end of the world. But unfortunately, this passage is unique to Matthew, so it is not possible to see how Mark or Luke have handled it and get an angle on how he has arranged Jesus' words. According to Matthew, Jesus says:

> When the Son of man shall come in his glory,
>   and all the holy angels with him,
>   then shall he sit upon the throne of his glory:
> And before him shall be gathered all nations (peoples):
>   and he shall separate them one from another,
>   as a shepherd divideth his sheep from the goats:
> And he shall set the sheep on his right hand,
>   but the goats on the left.
>
> *Matthew 25:31-33*

At the time of death everyone will be judged according to their *karmas*, on the one hand, and their spiritual efforts, on the other. At that time, a person's nationality will make no difference to them. It is how they have lived which will determine where they go next. The "sheep" are the initiated ones, while the "goats" are those who have followed the path of the mind. It is the same as the distinction between the "children of light" and the "children of darkness". Jesus then continues, and here – although the apocalyptic setting is continued – the words have no parallel in *Daniel* and *1 Enoch* and are more likely to have some degree of authenticity:

Then shall the King say unto them on his right hand,
"Come, ye blessed of my Father,
    inherit the kingdom prepared for you
    from the foundation of the world:
For I was an hungered, and ye gave me meat:
    I was thirsty, and ye gave me drink:
I was a stranger, and ye took me in:
    naked, and ye clothed me:
I was sick, and ye visited me:
    I was in prison, and ye came unto me."

Then shall the righteous answer him, saying,
"Lord, when saw we thee an hungered, and fed thee?
    or thirsty, and gave thee drink?
When saw we thee a stranger, and took thee in?
    or naked, and clothed thee?
Or when saw we thee sick, or in prison,
    and came unto thee?"

And the King shall answer and say unto them,
"Verily I say unto you,
    inasmuch as ye have done it
    unto one of the least of these my brethren,
    ye have done it unto me."

Then shall he say also unto them on the left hand,
"Depart from me, ye cursed, into everlasting fire,
    prepared for the devil and his angels:
For I was an hungered, and ye gave me no meat:
    I was thirsty, and ye gave me no drink:
I was a stranger, and ye took me not in:
    naked, and ye clothed me not:
    sick, and in prison, and ye visited me not."

Then shall they also answer him, saying,
"Lord, when saw we thee an hungered, or athirst,
   or a stranger, or naked, or sick,
   or in prison, and did not minister unto thee?"

Then shall he answer them, saying,
"Verily I say unto you, inasmuch as ye did it not
   to one of the least of these,
   ye did it not to me."

And these shall go away into everlasting punishment:
   but the righteous into life eternal.

Matthew 25:34-46

It is stirring stuff and when understood from a mystical point of view becomes even more vivid. For it is no hyperbole to say that the Lord and Master are present within every part of the creation and that to serve the Lord's creation is to serve the Lord Himself. To put oneself out in order to serve others is a great help, spiritually, for it softens and warms the heart, preparing the mind for spiritual practice and real worship and devotion of the Lord. A tender, kind, merciful, compassionate and loving disposition is essential if a person is to become sufficiently humble to enter the strait gate or the single eye. Moreover, one who sees the Lord everywhere and within everyone feels compelled to serve others as a humble and unostentatious servant.

Turning one's back on the suffering of others hardens the heart, turning the mind away from God. As all those who have lived a life of service to others can bear witness, there is far greater pleasure in giving than in taking. For the one opens up the heart and the other closes it down. And an open heart is open to God, becoming full of His love and bliss, while a closed heart is turned away from Him in selfishness, leading to depression and inner suffering.

So just as the Lord Himself is an ocean of mercy, love and compassion, so too should those who desire to truly worship Him imbibe His qualities. Jesus is comparing those who love his creation and those who do not. The true lovers ultimately find their way back to Him, while those who have helped no one but themselves "go away into everlasting punishment" – they are reborn in this world in life after life.

By This Shall All Men Know

It is all a matter of love. Whatever brings more love into the heart takes us closer to God. Whatever takes us away from love, takes us away from God. This is why Jesus lays so much stress upon love, as we have seen so many times. Love, indeed, is the hallmark of a true disciple. As he said:

> A new commandment I give unto you,
>   that ye love one another;
> As I have loved you, that ye also love one another.
> By this shall all men know that ye are my disciples,
>   if ye have love one to another.
>
> *John 13:34-35*

It may have been a new commandment for his disciples, but not for Jesus or any of the past mystics. The Lord has always been accessible and His nature has always been that of love. Again, according to John, Jesus says:

> As the Father hath loved me, so have I loved you:
>   continue ye in my love.
> If ye keep my commandments,
>   ye shall abide in my love;
>   even as I have kept my Father's commandments,
>   and abide in His love.
>
> These things have I spoken unto you,
>   that my joy might remain in you,
>   and that your joy might be full.
> This is my commandment,
>   that ye love one another, as I have loved you.
>
> *John 15:9-12*

Jesus repeats this message over and over again, because there is nothing so important as love. He says that those disciples who "keep my commandments", who follow the path he has described to them, "abide in my love" – they are cocooned inwardly by their Master's love. Just as Jesus swims in the ocean of the Father's love, so do they bask in Jesus' spiritual radiance day and night. Love is what makes both the Master and his disciples happy – "that my joy might remain in you, and that your joy might be full". He then says something that has been greatly misunderstood, over the ages:

> Greater love hath no man than this,
>   that a man lay down his life for his friends.
>
> *John 15:13*

While it is certainly an act of great unselfishness to save another person's life at the expense of one's own, this is not what Jesus means here. He is speaking of his own coming into this world of death, not of great acts of human courage.

In John's familiar style, the saying has a double meaning. A Master comes to this world out of love and compassion for its inhabitants. He was with God, the brightest of bright souls swimming in bliss and love. He was with the Source of all life, and he comes into this world of darkness, death, misery and suffering where people even sneer at human love and kindness, having no conception at all of divine love. This is the "greater love" that a Master has for his disciples, for "his friends". His life is dedicated to them.

The saying also means that by his physical death, a Master pays off some of the sins of his disciples, as did Jesus by his crucifixion. In this sense, too, he "lays down his life for his friends". He then continues, making it evident that by his "friends", he means his disciples:

> Ye are my friends, if ye do whatsoever I command you.
> Henceforth I call you not servants;
>   for the servant knoweth not what his lord doeth:
> But I have called you friends;
>   for all things that I have heard of my Father
>   I have made known unto you....
> These things I command you, that ye love one another.
>
> *John 15:14-15,17*

Through love he is going to make them just like himself. You will no longer be my "servants", he says, but my "friends" and equals. But only if "ye love one another". Jesus starts and ends with love.

Tares Among the Wheat

Love is nothing if it is not translated into action, both inwardly in spiritual practice and outwardly in human conduct. Jesus knew this well;

another of his many examples of love in action is to be found in the advice he gave his disciples on handling fellow disciples who are not really living the life of spirituality taught them by their Master. It is a situation encountered by many religious and spiritual groups, where the reaction to perceived 'deviation' on the part of others is often less than kind. In his parable of the tares, however, Jesus' counsels a tolerance and understanding that is born only of love and far-sighted wisdom. He relates:

> The kingdom of heaven is likened unto a man which sowed good seed in his field. But while men slept, his enemy came and sowed tares among the wheat, and went his way. But when the blade was sprung up, and brought forth fruit, then appeared the tares also.
>
> So the servants of the householder came and said unto him, "Sir, didst not thou sow good seed in thy field? From whence then hath it tares?"
>
> He said unto them, "An enemy hath done this." The servants said unto him, "Wilt thou then that we go and gather them up?"
>
> But he said, "Nay; lest while ye gather up the tares, ye root up also the wheat with them. Let both grow together until the harvest: and in the time of harvest I will say to the reapers, 'Gather ye together first the tares, and bind them in bundles to burn them: but gather the wheat into my barn.'"
>
> *Matthew 13:24-30*

And later, according to Matthew, Jesus explains his imagery, saying:

> He that soweth the good seed is the Son of man. The field is the world; the good seed are the children of the kingdom; but the tares are the children of the Wicked One; the enemy that sowed them is the Devil; the harvest is the end of the world; and the reapers are the angels.
>
> As therefore the tares are gathered and burned in the fire; so shall it be in the end of this world. The Son of man shall send forth his angels, and they shall gather out of his kingdom all things that offend, and them which do iniquity; and shall cast them into a furnace of fire: there shall be wailing and gnashing of teeth. Then shall the righteous shine forth as the sun in the kingdom of their Father. Who hath ears to hear, let him hear.
>
> *Matthew 13:37-43*

The parable occurs only in St Matthew, who true to his beliefs, has given Jesus' explanation of the parable an apocalyptic touch, but mystically the meaning seems quite evident. Jesus says that the "Son of man", the Master, comes and sows "good seed in his field". The "seed", the Word, is good and it has been well-sown by one who knows how to do so. The sower is a true mystic Sower and he has properly initiated the disciple. All the same, when the seed begins to sprout, the "servants", the fellow disciples, notice that certain weaknesses are also becoming evident in the disciple and seem to be choking the growth of the seed – his spiritual progress is being hampered by the "tares". They therefore ask their Master why this should happen and he explains that this is due to the activity of the "Enemy" – the Devil or the Negative Power.

The other disciples, therefore, being eager and zealous, ask if they should go and tell their brother about his imperfections and suggest that he relinquish them. But Jesus says, "Nay; lest while ye gather up the tares, ye root up also the wheat with them." Do not do that, he says, otherwise you might so offend him and hurt his feelings that he will relinquish the spiritual path altogether and want to avoid both the Master and his disciples. Now, although he is a victim of certain weaknesses, he is still meditating and struggling on the path. "Let them both grow together until the harvest" – let the situation continue as it is until the time of death. Then, the effect of his imperfections and the bad deeds he has committed will be weighed against his spiritual efforts and the balance will be to his credit.

The "children of the Wicked One" are the weaknesses of the mind, not the people of the world, as Matthew seems to be suggesting in the explanation he supplies, for it is weaknesses within a person that hamper spiritual progress, not other people. Similarly, the "end of the world" is the time of death, and the accounting is within the disciple. There is no preferential selection of the Christians against the rest of the creation in some final Day of Judgment. Likewise, while the "furnace of fire" and the "wailing and gnashing of teeth" may indeed refer to hell, they also describe rebirth in this world. And it is at the time of death that the "righteous shine forth as the sun in the kingdom of their Father" – they do not need to wait in their graves until the end of the world.

That the "tares" are the thorns or weaknesses which stand in the way of spiritual progress is clearly the meaning understood by the writer of the *Acts of Thomas*, where Judas Thomas says:

> I have fulfilled Thy will
>> and accomplished Thy work, O Lord....
> Let not my trust fail,
>> nor my hope which is in Thee be put to shame.
> Let not my labours be in vain
>> and let not my toils be found fruitless.

Let not my fastings and my urgent prayers perish,
    and my great zeal toward Thee.

Let not my seed of wheat be changed
    for tares out of Thy Land;
Let not the Enemy carry it away
    and mingle his own tares therewith;
For Thy Land cannot receive his tares,
    neither can they be stored in Thy mansions.

Acts of Thomas 145, AAA p.280, ANT p.428

Every disciple has only one battle to fight – against the powers of the Enemy, the mind. When this battle is won, the soul finds itself pure and pristine, shining "as the sun", ready to enter "Thy Land" – the "kingdom of the Father". The "tares" of the "Enemy" cannot reach that far; they cannot be "stored" in the Lord's high "mansions".

Labourers into His Vineyard

Probably one of the most common causes of friction in any community or family is jealousy and, while disciples of a Master may not be prone so much to jealousy over worldly possessions, they are certainly liable to jealousy over the things that matter most to them – spiritual progress and proximity to the Master. Slowly, of course, they learn to overcome it, but Jesus must have observed this tendency amongst his disciples, for he tells a parable to help his disciples understand what is happening. It is the well-known parable of the labourers.

We have already noted that Jesus and many others of this period used terms such as 'labouring' in reference to spiritual endeavour, particularly meditation. It is readily understood, therefore, that in this parable, Jesus' "labourers" are his disciples, working on the spiritual path, while the one who hires them is the Master. Jesus says:

For the kingdom of heaven is like unto a man that is an householder, which went out early in the morning to hire labourers into his vineyard. And when he had agreed with the labourers for a penny a day, he sent them into his vineyard.

And he went out about the third hour, and saw others standing idle in the marketplace, and said unto them, "Go ye also into the vineyard, and whatsoever is right I will give you." And they went their way.

Again he went out about the sixth and ninth hour, and did likewise. And about the eleventh hour he went out, and found others standing idle, and saith unto them, "Why stand ye here all the day idle?" They say unto him, "Because no man hath hired us". He saith unto them, "Go ye also into the vineyard; and whatsoever is right, that shall ye receive."

So when even was come, the lord of the vineyard saith unto his steward, "Call the labourers, and give them their hire, beginning from the last unto the first." And when they came that were hired about the eleventh hour, they received every man a penny.

But when the first came, they supposed that they should have received more; and they likewise received every man a penny. And when they had received it, they murmured against the goodman of the house, saying, "These last have wrought but one hour, and thou hast made them equal unto us, which have borne the burden and heat of the day."

But he answered one of them, and said, "Friend, I do thee no wrong: didst not thou agree with me for a penny? Take that thine is, and go thy way: I will give unto this last, even as unto thee. Is it not lawful for me to do what I will with mine own? Is thine eye evil, because I am good?"

So the last shall be first, and the first last: for many be called, but few chosen.

Matthew 20:1-16

The story is a very simple one. A "householder" employs a number of "labourers" at various times of the day. Hiring some of them first thing in the morning, he agrees their wages with them and sets them to work. And throughout the day, even up to the "eleventh hour", he goes on hiring labourers and putting them to work.

But at the end of the day, he pays them all the same wages that he had agreed with those whom he had hired first. On seeing this, the first ones become jealous and feel that having worked longer, they should be paid more. To which the "goodman of the house" responds that it is his prerogative to pay whatever he likes. He has given them what he had agreed with them, so there should be no cause for jealousy. And he adds, pointedly, "Is thine eye evil, because I am good?"

Jesus is referring to the fact that many people receive initiation from a Master. Some come to him in their youth, others in middle age, others only a few years before they die. Yet the Master's pledge to every disciple is that he will take them all back to the Lord. This is the wages that he pays.

But from a human standpoint, a disciple who has struggled with meditation all his life may feel jealous if someone comes to the Master towards the end of his life and immediately seems to be making good spiritual progress. Disciples, of course, are instructed not to talk about their spiritual experiences, but all the same it reflects to some extent in their conduct, bearing, understanding and the atmosphere they have about them.

This is what Jesus means when he concludes, "So the last shall be first, and the first last: for many be called, but few chosen." Many disciples are spiritually baptized by the Master – "many are called" – but "few are chosen" to return to God during that lifetime.

Every soul has its own unique history and *karma*. This is what makes each individual so different from everybody else. Everyone is carrying a different burden, even if they come to the mystic path at the same time and at the same age. Furthermore, some may have received initiation in their previous life or even in two or three previous lives. They may be 'old hands' and are just picking up the threads of their previous progress. As a result, much has already been accomplished and they may not have as far to travel as others. So even if they come to a Master late in life, they are already prepared and will seem to make rapid progress. Others may have been initiated in their youth, but if it is their first life on the path, they may have a great deal to overcome within themselves.

Only a Master knows the individual background of each soul, because he sees things from a higher perspective, from within. Looked at from the outside, it may seem unfair, but this is only because we do not have full knowledge of the hidden background. Every soul has a certain burden of *karma* to clear. The Master promises to help every soul that he initiates to clear that load. After that, the same wages of return to God will be paid to every soul. There is no unfairness about it at all, only human ignorance makes it seem so.

A Master is totally free. He also has unlimited spiritual wealth and can give that wealth to anyone he pleases, even if they have not earned it. Nobody can question his right to do so. As Jesus says, "Is thine eye evil, because I am good?" A disciple, therefore, can only be grateful for what he is being given. Everything that comes from a Master is, after all, a sheer gift. A disciple should count his blessings, not look at other people. The first *can* be last and the last *can* be first. That is the nature of the game.

In Such an Hour as Ye Think Not

All that a disciple can do is to labour at his spiritual practice and at living the spiritual life. Every effort is rewarded, for the mind records all trends and tendencies. Every positive effort develops a positive habit in the mind and every indulgence in weakness makes an old habit firmer still. Besides, as all mystics have said, whatever steps a person takes towards God, the Lord takes ten or a hundred steps towards him. As the Manichaean-Christian psalmist wrote:

> If I have turned to thee a little,
> thou oughtest to turn to me much!
>
> *Psalms of Heracleides, MPB p.188*

A disciple cannot really tell where he is on the mystic path, for there is no measuring scale by which spiritual progress can be gauged. Some souls may even be given mystical experiences because they are weak and need an inducement to generate faith, impetus and spiritual drive. Others may have great faith and conviction but also possess such curiosity that, if they were taken into the higher realms, they would want to explore so much that they would lose contact with the central current of the Word. They are therefore kept in darkness until their degree of purity is sufficient for them to be taken up beyond all potential distractions of the inner journey. Again, a Master knows that some of his disciples are humble enough to receive spiritual treasures, but he withholds inner experiences from others who would just waste what had been given through spiritual pride and a sense of superiority.

Nor can outer conduct always be a sure guide to inner spirituality, for even old and seasoned disciples can still be a prey to some very obvious human weakness owing to the strong mental impressions of such tendencies from past lives. Spiritual advancement does not always entirely preclude human weakness. For as long as a soul remains in this world, there will always be some degree of struggle.

Again, if somebody is in darkness, he cannot know how close he is to finding the inner light. Faced with such ignorance of himself and others, therefore, all that a disciple can do is to work sincerely and devotedly, keeping himself in readiness for the coming of the spiritual form of his Master and the start of the journey through the inner mansions. As Jesus said, using a short parable:

> Take ye heed, watch and pray:
> for ye know not when the time is.
> For the Son of man is as a man taking a far journey,
> who left his house,
> and gave authority to his servants,

and to every man his work,
and commanded the porter to watch.

Watch ye therefore: for ye know not
  when the master of the house cometh,
  at even, or at midnight,
  or at the cockcrowing, or in the morning:
Lest coming suddenly he find you sleeping.
And what I say unto you I say unto all, watch.

Mark 13:33-37

This parable and its associated sayings are placed by Mark in an apocalyptic setting, but they are independent of it and out of context with
the rest of the 'discourse'. Jesus is not speaking to his disciples about
the end of the world. The meeting he refers to is with the "Son of man"
within. No disciple knows when his Master will come to him in meditation or when he will come for him at the time of death. Therefore,
says Jesus, "watch and pray". Stay awake spiritually – and at night, too,
when the period required for sleep is over, stay awake in meditation.
For a disciple can never know when the Master will shower his grace
and show himself within.

An expanded version of what is evidently the same parable is found
in Matthew, where the essential message is the same:

Watch therefore: for ye know not
  what hour your Lord doth come.
But know this, that if the goodman of the house
  had known in what watch the thief would come,
  he would have watched,
  and would not have suffered his house to be broken up.

Therefore be ye also ready:
  for in such an hour as ye think not
  the Son of man cometh.

Who then is a faithful and wise servant,
  whom his lord hath made ruler over his household,
  to give them meat in due season?
Blessed is that servant,
  whom his lord when he cometh,
  shall find so doing.

Verily I say unto you,
 that he shall make him ruler over all his goods.

But and if that evil servant shall say in his heart,
"My lord delayeth his coming";
And shall begin to smite his fellow servants,
 and to eat and drink with the drunken;
The lord of that servant shall come in a day
 when he looketh not for him,
 and in an hour that he is not aware of,
And shall cut him asunder,
 and appoint him his portion with the hypocrites:
 there shall be weeping and gnashing of teeth.

Matthew 24:42-51

If a person knew the time of his death or when the Master would manifest himself inside, like a man who knew when a thief was coming, he would not be unprepared. But nobody knows when a thief will strike. The wise disciple, therefore, is like a servant who is always ready for the homecoming of his master. And when the master comes, says Jesus, he will reward such a conscientious servant by making him ruler over all he has. What a Master has is the supreme spiritual treasure of God – this will be the Master's gift to his patient, diligent and trustworthy disciple. Conversely, the servant who forgets that his master will return one day and who starts misbehaving will be caught unawares and will have to pay the price for it. He will suffer by being reborn in this world – "there shall be weeping and gnashing of teeth".

It is worth observing that this ending is a favourite with Matthew, one which he uses six times in his gospel. But the fact that it never appears in Mark and is only once found in Luke makes it seem likely that Matthew has doctored the endings of some of Jesus' parables in order to draw an eschatological meaning from them. The more probable ending to this parable is the one we find in Luke:

And that servant, which knew his lord's will,
 and prepared not himself,
 neither did according to his will,
 shall be beaten with many stripes.
But he that knew not,
 and did commit things worthy of stripes,
 shall be beaten with few stripes.

> For unto whomsoever much is given,
>   of him shall be much required:
>   and to whom men have committed much,
>   of him they will ask the more.
>
> Luke 12:47-48

Here, Jesus says that a disciple of a Master, one who knows the purpose of life and what his Master wants him to do, yet still does not do it "will be beaten with many stripes". He will have to pay for his dereliction of duty and his bad actions by suffering in this life or in another birth. But those people who have never accepted a Master, those "that knew not", although they undergo rebirth according to the law of *karma*, will be punished "with few stripes".

One who knows the law and wilfully breaks it is always punished more severely than one who contravenes out of ignorance. A judge or lawyer who commits a crime receives a stiffer sentence than a juvenile offender. Likewise, although a Master is compassionate and forgiving, he is also responsible for administering the *karma* of his disciples. Sometimes, his punishment may even seem more severe than that of the Negative Power, because he needs to turn the mind of his errant disciple away from the world. A mother may not hand over her child to the police, but her punishment may be more exacting than that of the law – not out of anger but out of her love and because she is determined to correct the child's behaviour in one way or another.

So the one to whom "much is given" – the one who has received the mystic baptism and has been put upon the path to God – "of him much shall be required", just as those people who have been given responsibility are expected to fulfil it. For this reason, too, a prospective disciple should consider the matter very carefully before getting himself involved with a perfect Master. He should feel very certain that he can take on such a lifelong commitment.

Therefore, staying with Luke's version of this parable, Jesus exhorts his disciples to strive as hard as they can. He says:

> Let your loins be girded about,
>   and your lights burning;
> And ye yourselves like unto men
>   that wait for their lord,
>   when he will return from the wedding;
> That when he cometh and knocketh,
>   they may open unto him immediately.

> Blessed are those servants,
>> whom the lord when he cometh shall find watching:
> Verily I say unto you, that he shall gird himself,
>> and make them to sit down to meat,
>> and will come forth and serve them.
> And if he shall come in the second watch,
>> or come in the third watch, and find them so,
>> blessed are those servants.
>
> *Luke 12:35-38*

He alludes to the parable of the ten virgins, five wise and five foolish. The wise "servants" or "virgins" – the disciples – practise their meditation and keep themselves in readiness for their Master's coming. They keep their "lights burning" and their lamps full of oil.

Such a high degree of spiritual vigilance is clearly a cardinal aspect of Jesus' teachings for he tells many similar parables to impress the same point upon his disciples. Here, in Luke's version, the Master actually prepares a table for his faithful servants, bidding them to dine while he himself serves. This is the role of the spiritual Master who manifests himself in this world or in the higher regions only so that he may give spiritual sustenance to his disciples. And the 'food' he serves is the Bread of Life and the Living Water. No one can be a greater servant or friend than he. "Blessed are those servants," says Jesus, whom the Master finds wide awake and absorbed in their spiritual practice during the second or third watches of the night, for he will shower an abundance of inner nectar upon them and show himself to them, inside. As he says in St John:

> Herein is my Father glorified,
>> that ye bear much fruit;
> So shall ye be my disciples.
>
> *John 15:8*

A Master wants all his disciples to "bear much fruit" by attending to their spiritual practice and returning with him to God.

NOTES AND REFERENCES

1. *Matthew* 18:14.
2. *Matthew* 28:20.
3. *Daniel* 7:9ff; *1 Enoch* XLVI, *BE* pp.63-65. See also F.C. Burkitt, *JCA* pp.21-25.

Many Mystics

Is This What Jesus Really Taught?

We have reached the end of our quest for Jesus' original teachings. Did Jesus really give these teachings, as we have presented them, or are we mistaken in our thesis? Yet if he did not teach the universal mystic path, then what did he teach? For it is beyond doubt that there is a great deal of mysticism in his extant teachings. And why, if he did not teach the mystic way, are mystics – like St Teresa, St John of the Cross, Meister Eckhart and a great many others – always considered to have been amongst the greatest of Christians?

Was Jesus narrow-minded, partisan and parochial like so many religious preachers and fanatics? Or was he broad-minded, all-loving, wise, full of understanding of all things and universal, truly one with the universal Father of all of whom he spoke so much and so lovingly? Were Jesus' teachings an isolated phenomenon or were they the same as those which so many other mystics, both before and since, have taught? And are we right in our suggestion that most religions have resulted from the decline and misunderstanding of mystic teachings when spiritual practice has been forgotten?

In the end, it is always up to the individual to decide what is true and what is not. If it be accepted that Truth lies within, then it is each person's right to seek it for themselves, wherever it may lead them, to assess everything within themselves, independently and with the greatest discrimination, intelligence and perception they can muster. Only sincerity of purpose is required. Searching beyond the conditioning of youth and culture, seeking to transcend prejudice and the habitual modes of thinking and belief that narrow down one's outlook, reaching always for the highest and most universal, each person must seek ... and seek. For if there is no seeking for a higher path or purpose, then life is reduced to no more than dry material survival and existence.

Many people, of course, accept the broad principles of mysticism and spirituality but have their own reservations or ideas on certain points. Or they see mysticism only within the framework of an established religion. Again, some like things to be expressed in one way, others prefer a different approach. These are all matters of individual personality and background. Ultimately, it is experience that matters most, rather than belief, for some degree of doubt and hesitation will always be present, even concerning the existence of a spiritual side to life, when faith is founded on belief and intellect alone. What is required, therefore, is practice – spiritual practice or meditation – in order to attain that experience. But how to know which practice will lead to it?

For somebody who only wants to talk and hold intelligent discussion, the problem of spiritual practice does not arise. Discussion and argument need no teacher. One who only reads and discusses recipes requires no kitchen nor the guidance of an accomplished cook. But one who wants to eat must find a place to cook and one who will teach him how to do it. This is why we have maintained that a mystic teacher is required before a person can enjoy his own mystical experience and actually find the mystic Truth within himself.

Charlatans and pseudo-teachers there will always be. This is the nature of the world and nowadays, owing to the unspiritual activities of a few, spiritual teachers are not so well regarded as they might be. Even amongst sincere teachers, it is difficult to find one who really *knows* what he is talking about and whom one feels convinced has actually reached the highest spiritual Reality himself. There are many mansions in the Father's house from which spiritual teachers can come and not all teachers are sent from the Father Himself.

Yet, the proof of the pudding, as they say, is in the eating. "By their fruits shall ye know them." And it is impossible to find someone who is travelling the mystic path who is not receiving help from one more enlightened than themselves. Anyone who gets anywhere has some sort of a teacher. A glance at history shows that this has always been the case.

From the earliest records of civilization until the present time we can find traces of the mystic teachings and often definitive treatises and other writings, too. The soul of man can never be suppressed for long, even by oneself. The spirit automatically rises and finds expression in every age and people. Jesus was not the only one who taught the ancient mystic path. He was only one in a long chain of mystics who have come and will continue to come into this world.

From Sumerian and other Mesopotamian cultures, three or four millennia BC; from ancient Egypt; from the Iranian Zarathushtra; from Buddha and the ancient Vedic seers of India maybe 1500 years BC; from the ancient sages of China and the Far East including Lao Tse and others; from the Greek philosophers and mystics such as Orpheus, Pythagoras, Heraclitus, Empedocles, Socrates, Plato and many more; from the Egyptian mystery schools; from the Semitic prophets of the Jewish scriptures that Christians call the Old Testament; from the writers of the Biblical Wisdom literature; from the Essene Teacher of Righteousness; from Jesus; from the gnostics; from the Mandaeans and Mani; from the tradition associated with Hermes Trismegistus; from the Neo-Platonists like Plotinus, Porphyry, Iamblichus and Proclus; from the Indian yogis and later mystics like Farid, Nanak, Kabir, Paltu Sahib and numerous others; from Rumi, Hafiz, Sa'adi, Mansur, al-Ghazali and the many Sufis of Islam; from Ramon Lull, St John of the Cross, Jacob Boehme, Meister Eckhart and the mystics from within the Christian fold – from all these and many more, we learn the same essential truths. And a greater number must there have been who have escaped the net of fame and passed away unheralded. The light has never been extinguished and, even in modern times, the same torch is carried high for those who seek the Way.

Each one of these mystics could have – and in many cases did – fill more than a volume with his teachings, and we could linger at great length amongst their writings to support the view that Jesus brought the universal and perennial message of all the great mystics. Indeed, we had collected together a great deal of such material from pre-Christian times, much of it fascinating for its insights into Christian and Jewish antecedents. It is also beautiful and often deeply inspiring. But in the end, there was too great a wealth of texts for a simple *précis* to do them justice and the reader's patience had already been presumed upon enough.

Before the Time of Jesus

So, although the full story must be left for another time, the reader may be intrigued to know that there are even hints of this ancient mystic teaching amongst the myths inscribed upon the clay tablets of the earliest Mesopotamian cultures, 4000 years or so BC. In the legend of Inanna's descent into the underworld, for instance, we find:

> Father, *Enki*, as the lord of Wisdom,
>> who knows the Plant (Tree) of Life,
>> who knows the Water of Life,
>> he will surely bring me back to life.
>>> *Inanna's Descent II:65-67, SL p.307, KTL p.33*

And there are also episodes in these myths which are clear precursors to the allegories retold in *Genesis*. The beautiful garden in which grows the Tree of Life, watered by the Water of Life were in use as mystic images long before *Genesis* was written.

The ancient Persian mystic, Zarathushtra, whom the Greeks called Zoroaster, of whose original writings only a handful now remain, also seems to have taught the mystic path of the Word, though as with Jesus and so many others, there is a divergence between his extant teachings and the religion which has formed around them.

From an analysis of his Avestan language, which resembles the earliest stratum of Sanskrit found in the Indian *Rig Veda*, Zarathushtra may have lived as early as 1500 BC. Yet his extant poems or *Gathas*, written in a clear and simple style, speak of the Word, the Sound, the Saviours, the immortality of the soul and its return to God, divine love, the Holy Spirit and the Evil Spirit or Negative Power, as well as other fundamental aspects of the mystic path. Amongst his terms for God's creative Power were *Sraosha* (meaning Sound), *Manthra* (meaning Word) and *Vohu Mana*, meaning Primal, First or Good Mind – a term akin to the later Greek and gnostic *Nous* and used synonymously by the Iranian Mani as *Vahman*. In one of his *Gathas*, for example, Zarathushtra speaks of the "path of the *Manthra*" and of being guided by "*Sraosha*'s Voice":

> When shall I find Thee, Lord of Truth?
>> when, wise in love, shall I find *Vohu Mana*?
> When shall I, guided by *Sraosha*'s Voice,
>> walk the path to mighty *Ahura* (Lord of Life)?
>
> Thy *Manthra* is the most sublime of paths,
>> ever, with its Voice, turning back
> the ignorant who have strayed.
>>> *Zarathushtra, Yasna 28:5; cf. CZ p.20*

There are a number of similar references, too. In another poem, he says that the soul has been given a choice between the path of Truth, led by a true or good Shepherd, a true Saviour, and that of deception and untruth, led by the false shepherd, the Evil Spirit. He suggests that the soul should choose the former:

> Between these two the soul should choose –
> as Protector and as Shepherd for herself –
> a Master, one possessed of Truth,
> a champion of *Vohu Mana*.

> For never, O *Mazda*, can the false shepherd,
> though dressed in pious mien,
> partake of the message divine.
>
> *Zarathushtra, Yasna 31:9-10; cf. CZ p.47*

And speaking more specifically of the mystic Saviour or Master, he writes:

> The Saviour, Lord of Wisdom,
> he who enjoys vision of the Divine –
> O *Mazda Ahura* (God), he becomes our Friend,
> our Brother, nay our Father.
>
> *Zarathushtra, Yasna 45:11; cf. CZ p.151*

The Greek mystics and philosophers, too, are well known to modern scholars and, emphasizing the mystical aspects of their teachings, some of the ancient writers even claimed that Zarathushtra was the disciple of Pythagoras, one of the earliest known of the Greek mystics, born around 570 BC.

The basic tenets of the entire universal and mystic path are present in the teachings of these ancient Greeks, fragmentary as the extant source literature may often be. One Supreme God, Source or Good (the Monad), the Negative Power as the source of all multiplicity (the Dyad, 'Strife' or 'Negativity'), the *Logos* or the *Nous*, the mystic Music or Sound, the idea of the enlightened Sage, meditation, reincarnation, vegetarianism, the pursuit of human virtue and perfection, along with other primary aspects of the mystic path, are all given prominence. Indeed, in the time of Jesus and for several centuries afterwards, followers of esoteric paths, especially in the Hellenistic world, were commonly regarded as Pythagoreans. Hippolytus, for instance, speaks of both Plato[1] and gnostics like Valentinus, Colarbasus,[2] Marcus[3] and Elchasai[4] as Pythagoreans, from which it is clear that they all gave mystic or esoteric teachings.

Prior to Pythagoras, the same tradition was coupled with Orpheus, a character who appears in some of the Greek myths and is probably more legendary than historical. If he lived at all, it would have been in the period 1430-1150 BC, but the tradition associated with him was undoubtedly mystic. Even in the early centuries of Christianity, Orphism and Pythagoreanism were commonly equated. The omnipresence and omnipotence of one God in His creation was also a fundamental Orphic doctrine, as was the soul's eventual return to Him and in one of the Orphic poems extant in early Christian times, we read that Zeus is the one Source, from whom arises all multiplicity:

> Zeus is the first-born, Zeus is the last,
>   the lord of all lightning:
> Zeus is the head, Zeus the centre;
>   from Zeus comes all that is;
> Zeus is the foundation of the earth
>   and the starry heavens; ...
> Zeus is the Breath of all things,
>   Zeus is the Spring of tireless fire; ...
> Zeus is king, Zeus is the Master of all,
>   the lord of the lightning.
> For He hid all men away,
>   and has brought them again to the lovely Light
>   from the holiness of His heart, working great marvels.
>   *Pseudo-Aristotle, On the Cosmos 6:400, SRCPC p.403*

As with Solomon, Jesus and many others, writings were pseudo-epigraphically attributed to Pythagoras. Hence, the Pythagorean sayings:

> God has not upon earth
>   a place more fit for Him to dwell
>   than in a pure soul.
>   *Pythagorean Saying, in Golden Verses of Pythagoras, CHGVP p.9*

And:

> Thou wilt honour God perfectly
>   if thou behave thyself
>   so that thy soul may become His Image.
>   *Pythagorean Saying, in Golden Verses of Pythagoras, CHGVP p.9*

And likewise from the elusive Sextus the Pythagorean, probably of the first or second century AD:

> You have in yourself, something similar to God,
> and (should) therefore use yourself as the temple of God.
>
> *Sextus, Sentences of Sextus, ILP p.192*

And from the fifth-century (AD) Pythagorean, Hierocles:

> What is the Law? ... The Law is the Intelligence (*Nous*) that has created all things; it is from the divine Intelligence (*Nous*) by which all has been produced from all Eternity, and which likewise preserves it eternally.... The Law is the immutable Power of God.... The Law is the Power of God by which He operates and brings all things to pass immutably and from all eternity.
>
> *Hierocles, On the Golden Verses of Pythagoras, CHGVP pp.7,8,10*

Similarly, amongst other Greek esoteric writings, we find:

> He, (*Nous*) is the Good *Daemon*.
> Blessed the soul that is most filled with Him,
> and wretched is the soul that's empty of the *Nous*.
>
> *Corpus Hermeticum XI:12, TGHII p.182*

Concerning human nature, to Pythagoras is attributed the axiom:

> It is impossible that he can be free
> who is a slave to his passions.
>
> *Pythagoras, in Stobaeus, ILP p.189*

And, from one of the pithy sayings preserved of Heraclitus (*c.*535-475 BC) of Ephesus:

> To extinguish *hubris* (pride, arrogance, ego)
> is more needful than to extinguish a fire.
>
> *Heraclitus, Fragment 88, HPW p.83*

Probably the most well-known of all the Greek philosophers are Socrates and his disciple, Plato. In *Phaedo*, Plato's account of Socrates' last meeting with his disciples before taking the cup of poison to which he had been condemned, Socrates is portrayed as facing death with

eager anticipation. Indeed, he points out that the real philosopher is
one who has sought all his life to understand the nature of death:

> I desire to prove to you that the real philosopher has reason to be of good
> cheer when he is about to die, and that after death he may hope to attain
> the greatest good in the other world.... For I deem that the true votary of
> philosophy is likely to be misunderstood by other men; they do not
> perceive that of his own accord he is always engaged in the pursuit of
> dying and death; and if this be so, and he has had the desire of death all
> his life long, why when his time comes should he repine at that which he
> has been pursuing and desiring?
>
> *Socrates (Plato), Phaedo 63e-64a, DPI p.414*

Socrates thus distinguishes between the philosopher as the lover of
true, divine wisdom – the seeker of the truly mystical experience – and
the sophist or quibbler whose approach is entirely intellectual. In fact,
there are many passages in Greek mystical literature where this distinction is clearly drawn. Later in the same dialogue Socrates says:

> The true philosophers, and they only, are ever seeking to release the soul.
> Is not the separation and release of the soul from the body their especial
> study?
>
> *Socrates (Plato), Phaedo 67d, DPI p.418*

And:

> It has been proved to us by experience that if we would have pure
> knowledge of anything we must be quit of the body – the soul by herself
> must behold things by themselves: and then we shall attain that which we
> desire, and of which we say we are lovers – wisdom.
>
> *Socrates (Plato), Phaedo 66d-e, DPI p.417*

And he goes on to speak about the reincarnation of the soul. These,
then, are only a very brief sample from the writings of the Greek mystics, showing that they, too, taught the same eternal truths.

Throughout the gospels, Jesus quotes or alludes to passages from
the Jewish prophets to reinforce his own teaching and to demonstrate
that they too taught the same spiritual truths. Extracts from the Old
Testament have been quoted throughout this book, and we present a
few more here which indicate that the Jewish prophets were, for the
most part, mystics. This is not a novel point of view, of course, for

there is no doubt that the later Jewish writers such as Philo Judaeus considered their earlier counterparts to have been holy men or mystics, while Jewish holy men throughout the ages have constantly referred to Biblical writings as the works of mystics. As we noted earlier, Clement of Alexandria even described Moses as a gnostic, one whose wisdom stemmed from mystic knowledge or divine revelation.

Proverbs, for example, is a fine source of spiritual teaching, and at one place the writer compares a Master to a fountain that gives divine or spiritual life to his disciples:

> The wise man's teaching is a life-giving fountain,
>> for eluding the snares of death.
>>>> *Proverbs 13:14, JB*

This is a fountain worth frequenting. As Jesus Ben Sirach advises:

> If you see a man of understanding, visit him early,
>> let your feet wear out his doorstep.
> Reflect on the injunctions of the Lord,
>> busy yourself at all times with his commandments.
> He will strengthen your mind,
>> and the Wisdom you desire will be granted you.
>>>> *Wisdom of Jesus Ben Sirach 6:36-37, JB*

Regarding the true place in which to worship God, the prophet Isaiah points out that if everything is the Lord's handiwork, what place can be built by man in which He will "rest"? No man-made house or temple can thus be suitable for His worship:

> Thus says Yahweh:
> With heaven my throne
>> and earth my footstool,
>> what house could you build me,
>> what place could you make for my rest?
>
> All of this was made by my hand
>> and all of this is mine – it is Yahweh who speaks.
> But my eyes are drawn to the man
>> of humble and contrite spirit,
>> who trembles at my Word.
>>>> *Isaiah 66:1-2, JB*

What pleases God is humility and dedication to His Word, the Judaic term for the Word or *Logos* being the *Memra*. And again, there are a great many references and allusions in Biblical writings to this creative Power of God, some of which we have already seen. It is His Wisdom, His Name, the Living Water, the Bread or Manna "which came down from heaven", the "Voice", the "Breath of God" and so on. In the *Psalms*, it is the Word which God 'spoke' for the creation to come into being:

> For He spoke, and it was;
>> He commanded, and it stood.
>>> *Psalms 33:9, JPS*

It can also be experienced by the soul:

> I rejoice at Thy Word,
>> as one that findeth great spoil.
>>> *Psalms 119:162, JPS*

And it is an ever-present guide:

> Thy Word is a lamp unto my feet,
>> and a light unto my path.
>>> *Psalms 119:105, JPS*

It is the "Light" and "Truth" sent out by God to guide the soul to the eternal realm, God's "holy Mountain", the "place where You live":

> Send out Your Light and Your Truth,
>> let these be my guide,
>> to lead me to Your holy Mountain
>> and to the place where You live.
>>> *Psalms 43:3, JB*

From a Christian point of view, one of the most interesting periods of Jewish mystical writing is that immediately prior to the time of Jesus. Prominent amongst the esoteric movements of that time were the Essenes, of whom, despite the wealth of twentieth-century apocrypha of dubious authenticity, very little is actually known. Apart from some references in the rabbinic (Jewish) literature and some passing comments by the Christian fathers, only three of the writers of antiquity ever speak of them, and that but briefly.

Philo Judaeus and Josephus both say that there were about four thousand of them living in the cities and villages of Judaea, while Pliny speaks of them as having a settlement or settlements near the Dead Sea, living "away from the western shore, far enough to avoid harmful things, a people alone, ... companions of palm trees."[5] It is unclear, however, whether the "harmful things" refer to the noxious breezes blowing off the Dead Sea or to the disturbances of the world! It is probable, then, that some Essenes lived in separate communities and others were more integrated with normal society, according to their bent of mind or the spread of opinion within their sect.

Josephus comments that "these men live the same kind of life as do those whom the Greeks call Pythagoreans"[6] from which we may presume that their beliefs were mystical or esoteric and that they were probably vegetarian and abstained from alcohol, like the Pythagoreans. He also writes:

> The opinion obtains among them that while the body is corruptible and its constituent matter impermanent, the soul is immortal and imperishable. Emanating from the subtlest *aether*, these souls become entangled, as it were, in the prison-house of the body, to which they are drawn by some natural spell. But when once they are released from the bonds of the flesh, then, as though liberated from a long captivity, they rejoice and are borne aloft. Sharing the same belief as the sons of Greece....
>
> *Josephus, Jewish War II:154-155; cf. JII pp.381-383, JW p.136*

Philo describes them as "not sacrificing living animals, but studying rather to preserve their own minds in a state of holiness and purity."[7] He also says that they were complete pacifists, not being involved in the manufacture of "arrows, or javelins, or swords, or helmets, or breastplates, or shields; no makers of arms or of military engines; no one, in short, attending to any employment whatever connected with war, or even to any of those occupations even in peace which are easily perverted to wicked purposes."[8]

With these three reports, the sum total of our knowledge might have rested but for the extraordinary discovery of a wealth of very ancient papyrus scrolls, many of them scattered into myriads of tiny fragments, lying in caves near the western shores of the Dead Sea, near the ruined remains of the ancient settlement of Khirbet Qumran. The story has been told many times and there is no need to retell it here, but one of the many theories concerning this community and the apparently associated library hidden in nearby caves was that this was the Essene site spoken of by Pliny.

Scholars are divided in their opinions, particularly because there is no reference in any of the papyri to the Essenes, nor indeed are these diverse documents representative of only one school of thought. From these writings, however, it is clear that the sect – whoever they were – did at one time have a great teacher. He is unnamed and referred to as the Righteous (Spiritual) Teacher or the Righteous One (*Zaddik*). And amongst the many scrolls are some devotional and often ecstatic psalms of great beauty, normally attributed to this teacher, which bear all the hallmarks of a mystic's pen.

Apart from the use of language and idioms common to the period, there is little to show any clear historical connection between the scrolls or the Essenes and Jesus or John the Baptist. In fact, it is generally reckoned that most of the texts predate Jesus by more than a hundred years. All the same, in these psalms is found – often couched in guarded metaphors – the same universal mystic teachings of which we have been speaking. And, interestingly, their style in places is very similar to that of the *Odes of Solomon* and the *Psalms of Solomon*, from both of which we have occasionally quoted.

Although there may be no clear historical evidence to link Jesus and the Teacher of Righteousness, it must be of significance that the early Christians in Palestine and the writers of the scrolls both called themselves the *Ebionim*, the 'Poor Ones'. It is likely, then, that the Teacher of Righteousness, John the Baptist, Jesus and the writers of the earlier Wisdom literature such as Jesus Ben Sirach, were all representative of the esoteric or mystic tradition within Palestine and Judaism at that time.

There is certainly no doubt that some familiar themes run throughout the hymns of praise and devotion found amongst the Dead Sea Scrolls. God's "Wisdom", also called "Thy Power", is accepted as the creator of all things. The fabricator of all evil and wickedness is Belial or Satan, the Devil, and there are even what seem to be veiled allusions to reincarnation using terms which we have seen before. The writer thanks God for having saved him from the lot of the wicked, from his own sins, from the pit of Sheol, for having been given life and for having opened his ear to divine mysteries. He is a "creature of clay" – a man – who feels he has been the recipient of God's special grace and mercy, far above that which he merited. He feels constantly guarded and protected from all the forces of this world which would otherwise pull him astray.

He has taken refuge in God's Name. He has been placed beside a "spring of water in a dry land" and has found souls who are like "trees of life beside a mysterious fountain" that draw their life from the "everlasting Plant" and "Living Waters", wishing to "be one with the everlasting Spring". He has found the "Plant of Truth", the "Plant of Heaven", the eternal Tree of Life. No wonder he is full of praise and thanksgiving for such blessings.

In fact, the entire mystic path that we have been describing is to be found in these rather beautiful and often poignant psalms or hymns, many of which are sadly fragmentary owing to the condition of the manuscript, and which scholars have admitted considerable difficulty in translating. There seems little doubt that they are the writings of a mystic who taught the path of Wisdom, as the following extracts indicate:

> I thank Thee, my God,
>> for Thou hast dealt wondrously to dust,
>> and mightily towards a creature of clay!
> I thank Thee, I thank Thee!
>> *Thanksgiving Hymns 17, DSSE p.194*

> I thank Thee, O Lord,
>> for Thou hast redeemed my soul from the Pit,
> and from the hell of Abaddon
>> Thou hast raised me up to (the) everlasting Height.
>> *Thanksgiving Hymns 5, DSSE pp.172-173*

> I thank Thee, O Lord, '
>> for Thou hast illumined my face by Thy Covenant, ...

> I seek Thee,
>> and sure as the dawn
>> Thou appearest as [perfect Light] to me.
> Teachers of lies [have smoothed] Thy people [with words],
>> and [false prophets] have led them astray;
> They perish without understanding
>> for their works are in folly....
> For [they hearken] not [to] Thy [Voice],
>> nor do they give ear to Thy Word....

Through me Thou hast illumined
　　the face of the Congregation
　　and hast shown Thine infinite Power.
For Thou hast given me knowledge
　　through Thy marvellous mysteries,
and hast shown Thyself mighty within me.

Thanksgiving Hymns 7, DSSE pp.174-176

These things I know
　　by the Wisdom which comes from Thee,
for Thou hast unstopped my ears
　　to marvellous mysteries.

And yet I, a shape of clay
　　kneaded in water,
a ground of shame
　　and a source of pollution,
a melting-pot of wickedness
　　and an edifice of sin,
a straying and perverted spirit
　　of no understanding,
　　fearful of righteous judgements,
what can I say that is not foreknown,
　　and what can I utter that is not foretold?

Thanksgiving Hymns 1, DSSE p.167

I [thank Thee, O Lord,
　　for] Thou hast placed me beside a fountain of streams
　　in an arid land,
and close to a spring of waters
　　in a dry land,
and beside a watered garden
　　in a wilderness.
[For Thou didst set] a plantation
　　of cypress, pine, and cedar for Thy glory,
trees of life beside a mysterious fountain
　　hidden among the trees by the water,
and they put out a shoot
　　of the everlasting Plant.
But before they did so, they took root
　　and sent out their roots to the watercourse

that its stem might be open to the Living Waters
    and be one with the everlasting Spring....

No [man shall approach] the Wellspring of Life
    or drink the Waters of Holiness
    with the everlasting trees,
        or bear fruit with [the Plant] of Heaven,
who seeing has not discerned,
        and considering has not believed
        in the Fountain of Life,
who has turned [his hand against] the everlasting [Bud].

Thanksgiving Hymns 14, DSSE pp.187-188

Thou wilt give to the children of Thy Truth
    [unending joy and] everlasting [gladness]....

And likewise for the Son of man ...
    Thou wilt increase his portion
    in the knowledge of Thy Truth,
and according to the measure of his knowledge,
    so shall he be honoured....
[For the soul] of Thy servant has loathed [riches] and gain,
    and he has not [desired] exquisite delights.
My heart rejoices in Thy Covenant
    and Thy Truth delights my soul.

I shall flower [like the lily]
    and my heart shall be open to the everlasting Fountain;
    my support shall be in the might from on high.

Thanksgiving Hymns 16, DSSE p.194

[How] shall I look,
    unless Thou open my eyes?
Or hear,
    [unless Thou unstop my ears]?
My heart is astounded,
for to the uncircumcised ear
    a word has been disclosed,
and a heart [of stone
    has understood the right precepts].

I know it is for Thyself
    that Thou hast done these things, O God;
for what is flesh
    [that Thou shouldst act] marvellously [towards] it? ...

And I, a creature [of clay
    kneaded with water,
a heap of dust]
    and a heart of stone,
for what am I reckoned to be worthy of this?

For into an ear of dust, [Thou hast put a new Word]
    and hast engraved on a heart of [stone], things everlasting.
Thou hast caused the straying spirit to return
    that it may enter into a Covenant with Thee,
and stand [before Thee for ever]
    in the everlasting Abode,
illumined with perfect Light for ever,
    with [no more] darkness,
    [for un]ending [seasons of joy]
    and un[numbered] ages of peace.

                              Thanksgiving Hymns 25, DSSE p.207

And so we end, fittingly, with the ringing words of an unknown mystic from the period immediately prior to Jesus. They exemplify so clearly that Jesus was only one in a long succession of mystics, true holy men, Messengers of God and teachers of the mystic Word or Holy Name. The teachings which he gave are to be found throughout the writings of his many predecessors, just as the mystics who came after him used the same manner of expression and gave the same teachings. And all of them, without exception, as if in order to demonstrate the unimportance of externals, have left us almost nothing by way of any life history. All that they have left has been their teachings.

Spirituality is not the province of one particular nation, one particular people or one particular religion. It is the common heritage of all humankind and lies within every single one of us, whenever and wherever we may be upon this planet. We have only to find the way by which we can experience, not just a part of it, but the whole of it, in all its glorious and liberating splendour.

NOTES AND REFERENCES

1. Hippolytus, *Refutation of All Heresies* VI:XVI, *RAH* pp.214-216
2. Hippolytus, *Refutation of All Heresies* IV:XIII, *RAH* pp.80-81.
3. Hippolytus, *Refutation of All Heresies* VI:XLVII, *RAH* p.259.
4. Hippolytus, *Refutation of All Heresies* IX:IX, *RAH* p.347.
5. Pliny the Elder, *Natural History* V:15.
6. Josephus, *Antiquities* XV:371 (10.4), *JCW* p.333.
7. Philo, *Every Good Man Who is Virtuous is Also Free* XII, *WPJIII* p.523.
8. Philo, *Every Good Man Who is Virtuous is Also Free* XII, *WPJIII* p.523.
9. *Thanksgiving Psalms* 14, *DSSE* p.187.

Abbreviations

The following abbreviations have been used (see Bibliography for full details). New Testament quotations are from the *King James Version,* unless otherwise indicated. When a reference contains two or more abbreviations, the first is to an original source or a foreign language translation while the second (and subsequent) abbreviations refer to the English translation used AND/OR to the different English language translations which have been collated to make the present rendering.

AA	*Apocrypha Anecdota II,* ed. & tr. M.R. James
AAA	*Apocryphal Acts of the Apostles,* W.R. Wright
AAGA	*An Aramaic Approach to the Gospels and Acts,* M. Black
AB	*Apocalypse of Baruch,* tr. R.H. Charles
AFI-II	*The Apostolic Fathers,* 2 vols., tr. Kirsopp Lake
AHI-II	*Against Heresies,* 2 vols., Irenaeus, tr. A. Roberts & W.H. Rambaud
AMC	*The Ascent of Mount Carmel,* St John of the Cross, tr. D. Lewis
ANT	*The Apocryphal New Testament,* M.R. James
AOT	*The Apocryphal Old Testament,* ed. H.E.D. Sparks
APAW	*Abhandlungen der Königlich Preussischen Akademie der Wissenschaften*
API-VI	*St Augustine on the Psalms,* 6 vols., tr. members of the English Church
APOTI-II	*The Apocrypha and Pseudoepigrapha of the Old Testament in English,* 2 vols., R.H. Charles
ASCPI-II	*Arnobius of Sicca, The Case Against the Pagans,* 2 vols., tr. G.E. McCracken
AT	*The Annals of Tacitus,* tr. J. Jackson
AuNT	*The Authentic New Testament,* tr. H.J. Schonfield
BBB	*Ein Manichäisches Bet- und Beichtbuch,* W.B. Henning
BC	*The Books of Jeu and the Untitled Text in the Bruce Codex,* tr. V. MacDermot
BCB	*Breviarium Chaldaicum,* 3 vols., P. Bedjan
BDB	*Beiträge zur Kenntnis der Religiösen Dichtung Balai's,* K.V. Zetterstéen

BE	*Book of Enoch*, tr. R.H. Charles
BSOAS	*Bulletin of the School of Oriental and African Studies*
CADUE	*Coptic Apocrypha in the Dialect of Upper Egypt*, ed. & tr. E.A.W. Budge
CAG	*Coptic Apocryphal Gospels*, tr. F. Robinson
CALNT	*Contributions to the Apocryphal Literature of the New Testament*, tr. W.R. Wright
CAN	*The Chronology of Ancient Nations*, al-Biruni, tr. C.E. Sachau
CH	*Clementine Homilies*, tr. T. Smith *et al.*
CHA	*The Constitutions of the Holy Apostles*, Clement of Rome, ed. J. Donaldson
CHE	*The Church History of Eusebius*, tr. A.C. McGiffert
CHGVP	*Commentary of Hierocles on the Golden Verses of Pythagoras*, A. Dacier, tr. N. Rowe
CIEKE	*A Critical Investigation of Epiphanius' Knowledge of the Ebionites*, G.A. Koch
CPM	*The Canonical Prayerbook of the Mandaeans*, tr. E.S. Drower
CR	*Clementine Recognitions*, tr. T. Smith
CS	*Conversations of Socrates*, Xenophon, tr. H. Tredennick & R.A.H. Waterfield
CSA	*The Confessions of Saint Augustine*, tr. E.B. Pusey
CZ	*The Chants of Zarathushtra*, tr. I.J.S. Taraporewala
DAA	*The Doctrine of Addai the Apostle*, tr. G. Phillips
DPI-IV	*The Dialogues of Plato*, 4 vols., tr. B. Jowett
DSGG	*The Dialogues of St Gregory the Great*, ed. H.J. Coleridge
DSSE	*The Dead Sea Scrolls in English*, tr. G. Vermes
DSSU	*The Dead Sea Scrolls Uncovered*, R. Eisenman & M. Wise
DYKG	*Do You Know Greek?* J.N. Sevenster
ESCN	*Ephraemi Syri Carmina Nisibena*, G.S. Bickell
ESR	*Ephraimi Syri Rabulae Episcopi Edesseni Balaii aliorumque Opera Selecta*, ed. J.J. Overbeck
ETCA	*The Excerpta ex Theodoto of Clement of Alexandria*, R.P. Casey
FAJT	*Fragments of the Acts of Judas Thomas from the Sinaitic Palimpsest*, F.C. Burkitt
FFF	*Fragments of a Faith Forgotten*, G.R.S. Mead
FGSO	*The Four Gospels: A Study of Origins*, B.H. Streeter
FNI-II	*The Fihrist of al-Nadim*, 2 vols., tr. B. Dodge
G12A	*The Gospel of the Twelve Apostles*, tr. J.R. Harris
GC	*Die Gedichte Cyrillonas*, G.S. Bickell
GG	*The Gnostic Gospels*, E. Pagels
GH	*The Great Heresy*, A. Guirdham
GIP	*The Graces of Interior Prayer*, A. Poulain, tr. L.L.Y. Smith
GJB	*The Gnostic John the Baptizer*, G.R.S. Mead
GOG	*The Gospels: Their Origin and Growth*, D.W. Riddle

GR	*The Gnostic Religion*, H. Jonas
GS	*The Gnostic Scriptures*, B. Layton
GSBM	*Ginza der Schatz oder das Grosse Buch der Mandäer*, M. Lidzbarski
GT	*The Gospel of Truth*, K. Grobel
GTR	*The Gnostic and Their Remains*, C.W. King
HC	*History of the Church*, Eusebius, tr. G.A. Williamson
HEDA	*The Hymns and Homilies of Ephraim the Syrian and the Demonstrations of Aphrahat the Persian Sage*, tr. J. Gwynn
HIMAI-III	*History of the Inquisition of the Middle Ages*, 3 vols., H. Lea
HJPI-III	*The History of the Jewish People in the Age of Jesus Christ (175 BC-135 AD)*, 3 vols., E. Schürer, tr. G. Vermes *et al.*
HPW	*Heraclitus*, P. Wheelwright
HRI-II	*Handschriften-Reste in Estrangelo-Schrift aus Turfan, Chinesisch-Turkistan*, 2 vols., F.W.K. Müller
HS	*The Hymn of the Soul*, tr. A.A. Bevan
IADSI-II	*Isaaci Antiochi, Doctoris Syrorum, Opera Omnia*, 2 vols., G.S. Bickell
ICM	*Interior Castle or the Mansions*, St Teresa, tr. Benedictines of Stanbrook
ILP	*Iamblichus' Life of Pythagoras*, Iamblichus, tr. T. Taylor
IMK	*Inscriptions Mandaïtes des Coupes de Khouabir*, H. Pognon
IPSO	*De Inquisitione Pacis Sive de Studio Oratione*, Fr. Alvarez de Paz
JB	*Jerusalem Bible* (1966)
JCA	*Jewish and Christian Apocalypses*, F.C. Burkitt
JCONT	*Jesus and Christian Origins Outside the New Testament*, F.F. Bruce
JCW	*Josephus, His Complete Works*, tr. W. Whiston
JDPW	*Saint Jerome: Dogmatic and Polemical Works*, J.N. Hritzu
JI-X	*Josephus*, 10 vols., tr. H.StJ. Thackeray *et al.*
JM	*Das Johannesbuch der Mandäer*, M. Lidzbarski
JPS	*The Holy Scriptures*, 2 vols., Jewish Publications Society (1955)
JRAS	*Journal of the Royal Asiatic Society*
JTS	*Journal of Theological Studies*
JW	*The Jewish War*, Josephus, tr. G.A. Williamson
JWF	*The Jewish War*, Josephus, tr. G.A. Williamson (first edn., 1959)
KI	*The Koran Interpreted*, tr. A.J. Arberry
KJV	*Authorized King James Version*
KTL	*The King and the Tree of Life in Ancient Near Eastern Religion*, G. Widengren
LATI-II	*The Life of Appolonius of Tyana*, 2 vols., Philostratus, tr. F.C. Conybeare
LBHS	*The Life of Blessed Henry Suso*, Henry Suso, tr. T.F. Knox
LHN	*The Liturgical Homilies of Narsai*, R.H. Connolly
LP	*The Ladder of Perfection*, Walter Hilton, tr. L. Shirley-Price

LRR	*The Life of Richard Rolle, Together with an Edition of His English Lyrics*, F.M.M. Comper
LS	*Leben und Schriften*, Heinrich Suso, ed. M. Diepenbrock
LSFY	*The Lives of Saints with other Feasts of the Year, According to the Roman Calendar*, P. Ribadeneira
LSMH	*Lower (Second?) Section of the Manichaean Hymns*, tr. Tsui Chi
LSTJ	*The Life of St Teresa of Jesus*, St Teresa, tr. D. Lewis
MAA	*Mythological Acts of the Apostles*, A.S. Lewis
MaL	*Mandaische Liturgien*, M. Lidzbarski
MCT	*Miscellaneous Coptic Texts in the Dialect of Upper Egypt*, E.A.W. Budge
MEL	*Mysticism in English Literature*, C.F.E. Spurgeon
MEM	*Mesopotamian Elements in Manichaeism*, G. Widengren
MENT	*The Making of the English New Testament*, E.J. Goodspeed
MFC	*Mithras, the Fellow in the Cap*, E. Wynne-Tyson
MHCP	*The Manichaean Hymn-Cycles in Parthian*, M. Boyce
ML	*Manichaean Literature*, J.P. Asmussen
MLRE	*Manichaeism in the Later Roman Empire*, S.N.C. Lieu
MM	*Mani and Manichaeism*, G. Widengren
MMI-III	*Mitteriranische Manichaica aus Chinesisch-Turkestan*, 3 vols., F.C. Andreas & W.B. Henning
MPB	*A Manichaean Psalm-Book*, Part II, ed. & tr. C.R.C. Allbery
MS	*Mysticism: A Study in the Nature and Development of Man's Spiritual Consciousness*, E. Underhill
NHI-X	*Natural History*, 10 vols., Pliny the Elder, tr. H. Rackham
NHL	*The Nag Hammadi Library in English*, ed. J.M. Robinson
NHS11	*Nag Hammadi Studies* XI: *Nag Hammadi Codices* V, 2-5 and VI, ed. D.M. Parrott
NHS15	*Nag Hammadi Studies* XV: *Nag Hammadi Codices* IX and X, ed. B.A. Pearson
NHS20	*Nag Hammadi Studies* XX: *Nag Hammadi Codex* II, 2-7, vol. 1, ed. B. Layton
NHS21	*Nag Hammadi Studies* XXI: *Nag Hammadi Codex* II, 2-7, vol. 2, ed. B. Layton
NHS26	*Nag Hammadi Studies* XXVI: *Nag Hammadi Codex* III, 5, *The Dialogue of the Saviour*, ed. S. Emmel
NHS28	*Nag Hammadi Studies* XXVIII: *Nag Hammadi Codices* XI, XII, XIII, ed. C.W. Hedrick
NJL	'Nazareth' and 'Jerusalem' in Luke Chs. I and II, P. Winter
NRI-II	*The Nestorians and Their Rituals*, 2 vols., G.P. Badger
NTA1-2	*New Testament Apocrypha*, 2 vols., E. Hennecke, ed. W. Schneemelcher, tr. R.McL. Wilson
NTD	*The New Testament Documents: Their Origin and Early History*, G. Milligan

OCC	*Origen Contra Celsum*, Origen, tr. H. Chadwick
OFP	*Origen on First Principles*, G.W. Butterworth
OG	*The Other Gospels*, ed. R. Cameron
OHL	*Origen, Homilies on Leviticus*, tr. G.W. Barkley
OLAG	*The Oxyrhyncus Logia and the Apocryphal Gospels*, C. Taylor
OPJG	*The Origin of the Prologue to St John's Gospel*, J.R. Harris
OPS	*The Odes and Psalms of Solomon*, tr. J.R. Harris
OSB	*The Odes of Solomon*, tr. J.H. Bernard
OSC	*The Odes of Solomon*, tr. J.H. Charlesworth
OTP1-2	*The Old Testament Pseudoepigrapha*, 2 vols., ed. J.H. Charlesworth
P	*Philebus*, Plato, tr. R.A.H. Waterfield
PACI-II	*The Philosophers: An Alternative Concept of Greek Philosophy in Light of Eastern Wisdom and Modern Science*, 2 parts, T.A. Richman
PB	*Plotinus on the Beautiful and on Intelligible Beauty*, tr. editors of the Shrine of Wisdom & T. Taylor
PE	*The Enneads*, Plotinus, tr. S. MacKenna
PEJCS	*Patristic Evidence for Jewish-Christian Sects*, A.F.J. Klijn & G.J. Reinink
PES	*Panarion of Epiphanius of Salamis*, tr. F. Williams
PhI-X	*Philo*, Vols. I-X, tr. F.H. Colson & G.H. Whitaker
PlEA	*Plato (Euthyphro, Apology, Crito, Phaedo, Phaedrus)*, tr. H.N. Fowler
PlSP	*Plato (The Statesman, Philebus)*, tr. H.N. Fowler
PL	*Pythagoras: A Life*, P. Gorman
PLI-II	*Pliny Letters*, 2 vols., tr. W. Melmouth & W.M.L. Hutchinson
PNC	*A Pair of Nasoraean Commentaries*, tr. E.S. Drower
PS	*Pistis Sophia*, tr. V. MacDermot
PSGG	*Pistis Sophia, A Gnostic Gospel*, G.R.S. Mead
PWJ	*The Principal Works of St Jerome*, tr. W.H. Fremantle *et al.*
RAH	*Refutation of All Heresies*, Hippolytus, tr. S.D.F. Salmond
REWA	*Reincarnation: An East-West Anthology*, J. Head & S.L. Cranston
RG	*The Robe of Glory*, J.H. Davidson
RMM	*The Revelations of Mechthild of Magdeburg*, tr. L. Menzies
RR	*The Ring of Return*, E. Martin
RSV	*Revised Standard Version* (1952)
SA	*The Secret Adam*, E.S. Drower
SCMP	*Studies in the Coptic Manichaean Psalm-Book*, T. Säve-Söderbergh
SCO	*The Scrolls and Christian Origins*, M. Black
SDMG	*A Study of the Doctrine of Metempsychosis in Greece*, H.B. Long
SECUC	*The Seven Ecumenical Councils of the Undivided Church*, ed. H.R. Percival
SESHS	*Sancti Ephraemi Syri Hymni et Sermones*, 4 vols., T.J. Lamy
SFMC	*A Sogdian Fragment of the Manichaean Cosmogony*, W.B. Henning

SI-II	*Suetonius*, 2 vols., tr. J.C. Rolfe
SL	*Sumerian Literature: A Preliminary Survey of the Oldest Literature in the World*, S.N. Kramer
SOL	*Sayings of Our Lord*, B.P. Grenfell & A.S.Hunt
SPAW	*Sitzungsberichte der Königlich Preussischen Akademie der Wissenschaften*
SPZ	*Syrische Poesian*, P.P. Zingerle
SRCPC	*On Sophistical Refutations, On Coming-to-Be and Passing-Away, and On the Cosmos*, Aristotle, tr. E.M. Forster & D.J. Furley
SSMI-III	*Studies of the Spanish Mystics*, 3 vols., E.A. Peers
SU	*The Symbiotic Universe*, G. Greenstein
SWN	*Syrische Wechsellieder von Narses*, F. Feldmann
TD	*Tusculan Disputations*, Marcus Tullius Cicero, tr. J.E. King
TGHI-III	*Thrice-Greatest Hermes*, 3 vols., G.R.S. Mead
TI-IV	*The History of the Peloponnesian War*, 4 vols., Thucydides, tr. C.F. Smith
TL	*The Laws*, Plato, tr. T.J. Saunders
TNT	*The Text of the New Testament*, K. & B. Aland
TS	*The Teachings of Silvanus*, J. Zandee
TTQ	*The Thousand and Twelve Questions* (*Alf Trisar Shuialia*), tr. E.S. Drower
TTSPH	*Tertullian: On the Testimony of the Soul and On the 'Prescription' of Heretics*, tr. T.H. Bindley
VIAF	*The Book of Visions and Instructions of Blessed Angela of Foligno*, tr. a secular priest
VJC	*The Vegetarianism of Jesus Christ*, C.P. Vaclavik
VMEI-II	*Vida* (Life) *and other works*, 2 vols., Marina de Escobar
WAF	*The Writings of the Apostolic Fathers*, tr. A. Roberts *et al.*
WCAI-II	*The Writings of Clement of Alexandria*, 2 vols., tr. W. Wilson
WGTDA	*The Works of Gregory Thaumaturgus, Dionysius of Alexandria and Archelaus*, tr. S.D.F. Salmond
WJMA	*The Writings of Justin Martyr and Athenagoras*, tr. M. Dods
WM	*Western Mysticism: The Teachings of Sts Augustine, Gregory and Bernard on Contemplation and the Contemplative Life*, C. Butler
WOI-II	*The Writings of Origen*, 2 vols., tr. F. Crombie
WPJI-IV	*The Works of Philo Judaeus*, 4 vols., tr. C.D. Yonge
WSI-VII	*Woodbrooke Studies: Christian Documents in Syriac, Arabic and Garshuni*, 7 vols., ed. & tr. A. Mingana
WTI-III	*The Writings of Tertullian*, 3 vols., tr. S. Thelwall & P. Holmes
WTT	*The Writings of Tatian and Theophilus*, tr. B.P. Pratten & M. Dods
ZDMG	*Zeitschrift der Deutschen Morgenländischen Gesellschaft*

Bibliography

This bibliography is not intended to be exhaustive of the vast literature covering the field. It is more of an (extensive) personal reading and reference list centred on the themes of this book. Emphasis is on primary source texts, plus a selection of other books of allied interest, spanning the last 150 years or so of early Christian and New Testament research. All texts referenced in the present book are listed. Subsections include both primary sources as well as studies, commentaries and so on. Editions referenced in the text are the ones listed below. Dates of first publication have been added in square brackets where significant. Books and articles are listed by their title, rather than by author or translator – in a selection such as this, it makes them easier to find.

Apocryphal Literature (Christian & Jewish)

Ante-Nicene Christian Library, Additional Volume Containing Early Christian Works Discovered Since the Completion of the Series, and Selections from the Commentaries of Origen, ed. A. Menzies, tr. J.A. Robinson *et al.*; T. & T. Clark, Edinburgh, 1897.

Apocalypse of Baruch, tr. R.H. Charles; SPCK, London, 1917.

Apocrypha Anecdota II, ed. & tr. M.R. James; in *Texts and Studies* V (1899); Cambridge University Press, Cambridge.

The Apocrypha and Pseudoepigrapha of the Old Testament in English, 2 vols., R.H. Charles; Oxford University Press, Oxford, 1913.

The Apocryphal Acts of the Apostles, tr. W.R. Wright; Williams & Norgate, Edinburgh, 1871.

Apocryphal Gospels, Acts, and Revelations, tr. A. Walker; T. & T. Clark, Edinburgh, 1870.

The Apocryphal New Testament, tr. M.R. James; Oxford University Press, Oxford, 1989 [1924].

The Apocryphal New Testament: A Collection of Apocryphal Christian Literature in an English Translation based on M.R. James, ed. J.K. Elliott; Oxford University Press, Oxford, 1993.

The Apocryphal Old Testament, ed. H.E.D. Sparks; Oxford University Press, Oxford, 1985.

Are These the Words of Jesus? I. Wilson; Lennard, Oxford, 1990.

The Book of Enoch, tr. R.H. Charles; SPCK, London, 1987 [1917].

The Clementine Homilies, tr. T. Smith *et al.;* T. & T. Clark, Edinburgh, 1870.

The Clementine Recognitions, tr. T. Smith; T. & T. Clark, Edinburgh, 1867.

Contributions to the Apocryphal Literature of the New Testament, tr. W.R. Wright; Williams & Norgate, London, 1865.

Coptic Apocrypha in the Dialect of Upper Egypt, ed. & tr. E.A.W. Budge; British Museum, London, 1913.

Coptic Apocryphal Gospels, tr. F. Robinson; in *Texts and Studies* IV, No. 2 (1896), Cambridge University Press, Cambridge.

Diatessaron of Tatian: A Harmony of the Four Gospels Compiled in the Third Quarter of the Second Century, S. Hemphill; Hodder & Stoughton, London, 1888.

The Diatessaron of Tatian: A Preliminary Study, J.R. Harris; C.J. Clay, London, 1890.

The Doctrine of Addai the Apostle, tr. G. Phillips; Trübner, London, 1876.

The Earliest Life of Christ Ever Compiled from the Four Gospels, Being the Diatessaron of Tatian, J.H. Hill; T. & T. Clark, Edinburgh, 1894.

The Ethiopic Book of Enoch, M.A. Knibb; Oxford University Press, Oxford, 1978.

Fragments of the Acts of Judas Thomas from the Sinaitic Palimpsest, F.C. Burkitt; in *Studia Sinaitica* IX, p.23*ff.,* C.J. Clay, London, 1900.

The Gospel of the Twelve Apostles, tr. J.R. Harris; Cambridge University Press, Cambridge, 1900.

The Infancy Gospels of James and Thomas, R.F. Hock; Polebridge, Santa Rosa, California, 1995.

Jewish and Christian Apocalypses, F.C. Burkitt; Oxford University Press, London, 1913.

The Lost Books of the Bible and the Forgotten Books of Eden, a compilation; World Publishing Co., 1963.

The Lost Prophet: The Book of Enoch and its Influence on Christianity, M. Barker; SPCK, London, 1988.

Miscellaneous Coptic Texts in the Dialect of Upper Egypt, E.A.W. Budge; British Museum, London,1915.

The Mythological Acts of the Apostles, A.S. Lewis; in *Horae Semiticae* IV (1904); C.J. Clay, London.

New Testament Apocrypha, 2 vols., E. Hennecke, ed. W. Schneemelcher, tr. R.McL. Wilson; Westminster, Philadelphia, Pennsylvania, 1963-1964.

The Odes and Psalms of Solomon, tr. J.R. Harris; Cambridge University Press, Cambridge, 1911.

The Odes of Solomon, tr. J.H. Bernard; Cambridge University Press, Cambridge, 1912.

The Odes of Solomon, tr. J.H. Charlesworth; Oxford University Press, Oxford, 1973.

The Odes of Solomon, tr. J.A. Emerton, in *The Apocryphal Old Testament*, ed. H.E.D. Sparks; Oxford University Press, Oxford, 1985.

The Odes of Solomon and the Johannine Tradition, J. Brownson; in *Journal for the Study of Pseudoepigrapha* 2 (1988).

The Old Testament Pseudoepigrapha, 2 vols., ed. J.H. Charlesworth; Darton, Longman & Todd, London, 1983.

The Other Gospels, ed. R. Cameron; Lutterworth, Cambridge, 1988.

A Popular Account of the Newly Recovered Gospel of Peter, J.R. Harris; Hodder & Stoughton, London, 1893.

Psalms of the Pharisees, Commonly Called the Psalms of Solomon, ed. & tr. H.E. Ryle & M.R. James; Cambridge University Press, Cambridge, 1891.

Bibles, New Testament Translations & Prayer Books

The Authentic New Testament, tr. H.J. Schonfield; Dennis Dobson, London (1956).

The Authorized King James Version [1611]; Oxford University Press, Oxford.

The Book of Common Prayer; SPCK, London, undated.

The Holy Scriptures, 2 vols.; Jewish Publication Society, Philadelphia, 1955.

The Jerusalem Bible; Darton, Longman & Todd, London, 1966.

The New English Bible; Oxford University Press, Oxford, 1961.

New Gospel Parallels, 2 vols., R.W. Funk; Polebridge, Sonoma, California, 1985-1990.

The New International Version; Hodder & Stoughton, London, 1973.

The New Jerusalem Bible; Darton, Longman & Todd, London, 1985.

The New Revised Standard Version; Oxford University Press, Oxford, 1962.

The New Revised Version; Oxford University Press, Oxford, 1989.

The New Testament: Revised Standard Version and King James Version in Parallel Columns; Thomas Nelson, New York, 1960.

The New Testament in Modern English, tr. J.B. Phillips; Geoffrey Bles, London, 1960.

The Revised Standard Version; Cambridge University Press, Cambridge, 1952.

The Scholars Bible, Vol. I: *The Gospel of Mark*, D.D. Schmidt; Polebridge, Sonoma, 1991.

Synopsis of the Four Gospels: Greek-English Edition, ed. K. Aland; United Bible Societies, 1970.

The Unvarnished Gospels, A. Gaus; Threshold, Battlebro, Vermont, 1988.

Christian Mysticism

The Ascent of Mount Carmel, St John of the Cross, tr. D. Lewis, ed. B. Zimmerman; Thomas Baker, London, 1906.

The Book of Divine Consolation of the Blessed Angela of Foligno, tr. M. Steegman; Chatto & Windus, London, 1909.

The Book of Visions and Instructions of Blessed Angela of Foligno, tr. by a secular priest (A.P. Cruikshank); T. Richardson, London, 1871.

The Collected Works of St John of the Cross, tr. K. Kavanaugh & O. Rodriguez; Thomas Nelson, London, 1966.

Complete Works of St John of the Cross, 2 vols., tr. D. Lewis; London, 1864-1906.

Complete Works of St John of the Cross, 3 vols., tr. E.A. Peers; Burns & Oates, London, 1935.

The Complete Works of St Teresa of Jesus, tr. E.A. Peers; Sheed & Ward, London, 1946.

The Fire of Love and the Mending of Life or the Rule of Living, Richard Rolle, tr. R. Misyn, ed. R. Harvey; Kegan Paul, Trench, Trübner, London, 1896 [1434-1435].

The Graces of Interior Prayer, A. Poulain, tr. L.L.Y. Smith; Routledge & Kegan Paul, London, 1950.

Interior Castle or the Mansions, St Teresa, tr. Benedictines of Stanbrook, ed. B. Zimmerman; 3rd edn., Thomas Baker, London, 1921.

An Introduction to the History of Mysticism, M. Smith; SPCK, London, 1930.

The Ladder of Perfection, Walter Hilton, tr. L. Shirley-Price; Penguin, London, 1988.

Leben und Schriften, Heinrich Suso, ed. M. Diepenbrock; Rari Rollman, Augsburg, 1854.

The Life of Blessed Henry Suso, Henry Suso, tr. T.F. Knox; Methuen, London, 1913 [1865].

The Life of the Servant, Henry Suso, tr. J.M. Clarke; James Clarke, London, 1952.

The Life of Richard Rolle, Together with an Edition of his English Lyrics, F.M.M. Comper; Methuen, London, 1969 [1928].

The Life of St Teresa of Jesus, St Teresa, tr. D. Lewis, ed. B. Zimmerman; 4th edn., Thomas Baker, London, 1911.

The Lives of Saints with other Feasts of the Year, According to the Roman Calendar, P. Ribadeneira, ed. & tr. W. Petre; London, 1730.

Luis de Leon: A Study of the Spanish Renaissance, A.F.G. Bell; Oxford University Press, Oxford, 1925.

Mysticism: A Study and an Anthology, F.C. Happold; Penguin, London, 1970.

Mysticism: A Study in the Nature and Development of Man's Spiritual Consciousness, E. Underhill; Methuen, London, 1948 [1911].

The Origins of the Christian Mystical Tradition From Plato to Denys, A. Louth; Oxford University Press, Oxford, 1981.

The Revelations of Mechthild of Magdeburg, tr. L. Menzies; Longmans, Green, London, 1953.

The Song of the Bird, Anthony de Mello; Doubleday, London, 1981.

St Augustine. See *Early Christian Literature*.

Studies of the Spanish Mystics, 3 vols., E.A. Peers; SPCK, London, 1951-1960 [1926-1960].

Vida (Life) and other works, 2 vols., Marina de Escobar; compiled from her writings, Madrid, 1665-1673.

Western Mysticism: The Teachings of Sts Augustine, Gregory and Bernard on Contemplation and the Contemplative Life, C. Butler; Constable, London, 1927 [1922].

Woodbrooke Studies: Christian Documents in Syriac, Arabic and Garshuni, 7 vols., ed. & tr. A. Mingana; W. Heffer, Cambridge, 1927-1934.

Dead Sea Scrolls

A Crack in the Jar: What Ancient Jewish Documents Tell us about the New Testament, N.S. Fujita; Paulist, New York, 1986.

The Dead Sea Scrolls, J. Allegro; Penguin, London, 1958.

The Dead Sea Scrolls, M. Burrows; Viking, New York, 1955.

The Dead Sea Scrolls: A Preliminary Survey, A. Dupont-Sommer, tr. E.M. Rowley; Basil Blackwell, Oxford, 1952.

The Dead Sea Scrolls in English, tr. G. Vermes; Penguin, London, 1988.

The Dead Sea Scrolls Uncovered, R. Eisenman & M. Wise; Element, Shaftesbury, UK, 1993.

The Essene Writings from Qumran, A. Dupont-Sommer, tr. G. Vermes; Basil Blackwell, Oxford, 1961.

The Jewish Sect of Qumran and the Essenes: New Studies on the Dead Sea Scrolls, A. Dupont-Sommer, tr. R.D. Barnett; Valentine, Mitchell, London, 1954.

The Meaning of the Dead Sea Scrolls, A.P. Davies; New American Library, New York, 1956.

The Monks of Qumran: as Depicted in the Dead Sea Scrolls, E.F. Sutcliffe; Burns & Oates, London, 1960.

The Scrolls and Christianity, ed. M. Black; SPCK, London, 1969.

The Scrolls and Christian Origins: Studies in the Jewish Background of the New Testament, M. Black; Thomas Nelson, London, 1961.

The Scrolls and the New Testament, ed. K. Stendahl; Harper & Brothers, New York, 1957.

The Scrolls from the Dead Sea, E. Wilson; W.H. Allen, London, 1958.

The Secrets of the Dead Sea Scrolls: Studies Towards Their Solution, H.J. Schonfield; Valentine, Mitchell, London, 1956.

Early Christian Literature

Against Heresies. See *The Writings of Irenaeus.*

Ancient Syriac Documents Relative to the Earliest Establishment of Christianity in Edessa and the Neighbouring Countries, W. Cureton; Williams & Norgate, London, 1864.

The Apocalypse of Adam: A Literary Source Analysis, C.W. Hedrick; Scholars, Chico, California, 1980.

The Apology of Aristides on Behalf of the Christians, J.R. Harris; Cambridge University Press, Cambridge, 1891.

The Apostolic Fathers, 2 vols., tr. Kirsopp Lake; William Heinemann, London, 1912-1913.

The Apostolic Fathers, J.B. Lightfoot; Macmillan, London, 1891.

The Apostolic Fathers: An American Translation, E.J. Goodspeed; Harper & Brothers, New York, 1950.

Arnobius of Sicca, The Case Against the Pagans, 2 vols., tr. G.E. McCracken; Longmans, Green, London, 1949.

Breviaricum Chaldaicum, 3 vols., P. Bedjan; Leipzig, 1886-1887.

A Christian Palestinian Syriac Horologion, ed. M. Black; Cambridge University Press, Cambridge, 1954.

Christology of the Later Fathers, ed. E.R. Hardy; SCM, London, 1954.

The Church History of Eusebius, tr. A.C. McGiffert; James Parker, Oxford, 1890.

Clement of Alexandria, J. Ferguson; Twayne Publishers, New York, 1974.

Clement of Alexandria: Christ the Educator, tr. S.P. Wood; Catholic University of America, Washington, D.C., 1953.

The Confessions of Saint Augustine, tr. E.B. Pusey, ed. T. Smith; Grant Richards, London, 1900.

The Constitutions of the Holy Apostles, Clement of Rome, ed. James Donaldson; T. & T. Clark, Edinburgh, 1870.

A Critical Investigation of Epiphanius' Knowledge of the Ebionites: A Translation and Discussion of Panarion 30, G.A. Koch; PhD thesis, University of Pennsylvania, 1976 (extracts appear in *VJC*).

Cyril of Alexandria: Select Letters, ed. & tr. L.R. Wickham; Oxford University Press, Oxford, 1983.

The Dialogues of St Gregory the Great, ed. & tr. H.J. Coleridge; Burns & Oates, London, 1874.

Early Christian Fathers, ed. & tr. C.C. Richardson; SCM, London, 1953.

An Early Christian Philosopher: Justin Martyr's Dialogue with Trypho, Chapters One to Nine, J.C.M. van Winden; E.J. Brill, Leiden, 1971.

Early Christian Writings: The Apostolic Fathers, tr. M. Staniforth; Penguin, London, 1968.

Early Liturgies and Other Documents, tr. W. MacDonald *et al.*; T. & T. Clark, Edinburgh, 1872.

Ephraemi Syri Carmina Nisibena, G.S. Bickell; Leipzig, 1866.

Ephraimi Syri Rabulae Episcopi Edesseni Balaii aliorumque Opera Selecta, ed. J.J. Overbeck; Oxonii, 1865.

The Excerpta ex Theodoto of Clement of Alexandria, R.P. Casey; in *Studies and Documents* I (1934); Christophers, London.

Die Gedichte Cyrillonas, G.S. Bickell; in *ZDMG* XXVII (1873).

History of the Martyrs in Palestine by Eusebius, Bishop of Caesarea, ed. & tr. W. Cureton; Williams & Norgate, London, 1861.

Holy Fire: The Stories of the Fathers of the Eastern Church, R. Payne; Skeffington, London, 1958.

The Hymns and Homilies of Ephraim the Syrian and the Demonstrations of Aphrahat the Persian Sage, tr. J. Gwynn; James Parker, Oxford, 1898.

De Inquisitione Pacis Sive de Studio Oratione, Fr. Alvarez de Paz, Vol. III of his complete works; Vivés, Paris, 1875.

Isaaci Antiochi, Doctoris Syrorum, Opera Omnia, 2 vols., G.S. Bickell; Glessae, 1873-1877.

Legends of Eastern Saints, 2 vols., ed. and tr. A.J. Wensinck; E.J. Brill, Leiden, 1911.

The Liturgical Homilies of Narsai, R.H. Connolly; in *Texts and Studies* VIII (1909); Cambridge University Press, Cambridge.

The Nestorians and Their Rituals, 2 vols., G.P. Badger; Joseph Masters, London, 1852.

Origen Contra Celsum, Origen, tr. H. Chadwick; Cambridge University Press, Cambridge, 1986.

Origen on 1 Corinthians, C.H. Turner; in *Journal of Theological Studies* X (1909), Oxford University Press, Oxford.

Origen on First Principles, Origen, tr. G.W. Butterworth; SPCK, London, 1936.

Origen, Homilies on Leviticus, tr. G.W. Barkley; Catholic University of America, Washington, D.C., 1990.

Origen: Prayer and *Exhortation to Martyrdom*, tr. J.J. O'Meara; Longmans, Green, London, 1954.

Origen's Treatise on Prayer, E.G. Jay; SPCK, London, 1954.

Panarion of Epiphanius of Salamis, tr. F. Williams; E.J. Brill, Leiden, 1987.

The Panarion of St Epiphanius, Bishop of Salamis: Selected Passages, P.R. Amidon; Oxford University Press, Oxford, 1990.

Patristic Evidence for Jewish-Christian Sects, A.F.J. Klijn & G.J. Reinink; in *Supplements to Novum Testamentum* XXXVI (1973), E.J. Brill, Leiden.

The Philosophy of Clement of Alexandria, E.F. Osborn; Cambridge University Press, Cambridge, 1957.

The Principal Works of St Jerome, tr. W.H. Fremantle *et al.* (1973); James Parker, Oxford, 1893.

Refutation of All Heresies, Hippolytus, tr. S.D.F. Salmond; T. & T. Clark, Edinburgh, 1868.

Sancti Ephraemi Syri Hymni et Sermones, 4 vols., T.J. Lamy; Mechliniae, 1882-1902.

Selections from the Commentaries and Homilies of Origen, tr. R.B. Tollington; SPCK, London, 1929.

Select Works of St Ephrem the Syrian, tr. J.B. Morris; John Henry Parker, Oxford, 1847.

The Seven Ecumenical Councils of the Undivided Church, ed. H.R. Percival; James Parker, Oxford, 1900.

Spicilegium Syriacum, Containing Remains of Bardesan, Meliton, Ambrose, Mara Bar Serapion, ed. & tr. W. Cureton; London, 1855.

St Augustine: Against the Academics, tr. J.J O'Meara; Longmans, Green, London, 1951.

St Augustine: The Writings Against the Manichaeans and Against the Donatists, tr. R. Stothert & A.H. Newman; W.B. Eerdsmans, Grand Rapids, Michigan, 1974 [1887].

St Augustine on the Psalms, 6 vols., *A Library of Fathers of the Holy Catholic Church*, tr. members of the English Church; John Henry Parker, Oxford, 1848-1857.

St Ephraim's Prose Refutations of Mani, Marcion and Bardaisan, 2 vols., C.W. Mitchell; Williams & Norgate, London, 1912-1921.

St Jerome: Dogmatic and Polemical Works, J.N. Hritzu; Catholic University of America, Washington, D.C., 1965.

Syrische Wechsellieder von Narses, F. Feldmann; Leipzig, 1896.

The Teaching of the Twelve Apostles, C.Taylor; Deighton Bell, Cambridge, 1886.

Tertullian Adversus Marcionem, ed. & tr. E. Evans; Oxford University Press, Oxford, 1972.

Tertullian Against Marcion, tr. P. Holmes; T. & T. Clark, Edinburgh, 1868.

Tertullian: Apologetical Works and Minucius Felix Octavius, tr. R. Arbesmann et al.; Catholic University of America, Washington, D.C., 1950.

Tertullian: On the Testimony of the Soul and On the 'Prescription' of Heretics, tr. T.H. Bindley; SPCK, Brighton, 1914.

Two Commentaries on the Jacobite Liturgy, R.H. Connolly & H.W. Codrington; Williams & Norgate, London, 1913.

Unknown Sayings of Jesus, J. Jeremias; SPCK, London, 1957.

The Works of Gregory Thaumaturgus, Dionysius of Alexandria and Archelaus, tr. S.D.F. Salmond; T. & T. Clark, Edinburgh, 1871.

The Works of Lactantius, ed. A. Roberts & J. Donaldson; T. & T. Clark, Edinburgh, 1871.

The Writings of the Apostolic Fathers, tr. A. Roberts et al.; T. & T. Clark, Edinburgh, 1867.

The Writings of Clement of Alexandria, 2 vols., tr. W. Wilson; T. & T. Clark, Edinburgh, 1867, 1869.

The Writings of Irenaeus, 2 vols., tr. A. Roberts & W.H. Rambaut; T. & T. Clark, Edinburgh, 1868-1869.

The Writings of Justin Martyr and Athenagoras, tr. M. Dods et al.; T. & T. Clark, Edinburgh, 1867.

The Writings of Origen, 2 vols., tr. F. Crombie; T. & T. Clark, Edinburgh, 1869-1872.

The Writings of Tatian and Theophilus and the Clementine Recognitions, tr. B.P. Pratten *et al.*; T. & T. Clark, Edinburgh, 1867.

The Writings of Tertullian, 3 vols., tr. S. Thelwall & P. Holmes; T. & T. Clark, Edinburgh, 1869-1870.

Gnosticism and Gnostic Literature

The Acts of Thomas: Introduction, Text, Commentary, A.F.J. Klijn; E.J. Brill, Leiden, 1962.

Bardaisan of Edessa, H.J.W. Drijvers, tr. G.E. van Baaren-Pape; van Gorcum, Assen, The Netherlands, 1966.

Biblical Interpretation in the Gnostic Gospel of Truth from Nag Hammadi, J.A. Williams; Scholars, Atlanta, Georgia, 1988.

The Book of Thomas the Contender from Codex II of the Cairo Gnostic Library from Nag Hammadi, J.D. Turner; Scholars, Missoula, Montana, 1970.

The Books of Jeu and the Untitled Text in the Bruce Codex, tr. V. MacDermot; E.J. Brill, Leiden, 1978.

A Comparison of the Parables of the Gospel According to Thomas and of the Synoptic Gospels, H. Montefiore; in *New Testament Studies* VII (1960-1961), Cambridge University Press, Cambridge.

The Complete Echoes from the Gnosis, G.R.S. Mead, ed. S. Ronan; Chthonios, Hastings, UK, 1987 [1906-1908].

Fragments of a Faith Forgotten, G.R.S. Mead; Health Research, Mokelumne Hill, California, 1976 [1906].

The Fragments of Heracleon, A.E. Brooke; Cambridge University Press, Cambridge, 1891.

The Gnostics and Their Remains, C.W. King; Bell & Daldy, London, 1864.

The Gnostic Gospels, E. Pagels; Random House, New York, 1979.

Gnosticism and Early Christianity, R.M. Grant; Columbia University Press, New York, 1959.

Gnosticism: Its History and Influence, B. Walker; Thorsons, Wellingborough, UK, 1983.

Gnosticism: Mystery of Mysteries: A Study in the Symbols of Transformation, J.J. Hurtak; Academy for Future Science, Los Gatos, California, 1988.

The Gnostic Mystery: A Connection Between Ancient and Modern Mysticism, A.G. Diem; Mt Antonio College Press, Walnut, California, 1992.

The Gnostic Paul: Gnostic Exegesis of the Pauline Letters, E.H. Pagels; Fortress, Philadelphia, Pennsylvania, 1975.

The Gnostic Religion, H. Jonas; Beacon, Boston, Massachusetts, 1963.

The Gnostic Scriptures, B. Layton; SCM, London, 1987.

The Gnostic Treatise on Resurrection from Nag Hammadi, ed. & tr. B. Layton; Scholars, Missoula, Montana, 1979.

Gnosis: An Esoteric Tradition of Mystical Visions and Unions, D. Merkur; State University of New York, New York, 1993.

The Gospel According to Thomas, tr. A. Guillaumont *et al.*; E.J. Brill, Leiden, 1959.

The Gospel of Truth, K. Grobel; Adam & Charles Black, London, 1960.

Heresy: Heretical Truth or Orthodox Error? J. O'Grady; Element, Shaftesbury, UK, 1985.

The Hymn of Jesus, tr. G.R.S. Mead; Watkins, London, 1963 [1907].

The Hymn of the Soul, tr. A.A. Bevan; Cambridge University Press, Cambridge, 1897.

The Hymn of the Soul contained in the Syriac Acts of Thomas, ed. & tr. A.A. Bevan; Cambridge University Press, Cambridge, 1897.

The Johannine Gospel in Gnostic Exegesis: Heracleon's Commentary on John, E.H. Pagels; Abingdon, New York, 1973.

Jung and the Lost Gospels: Insights into the Dead Sea Scrolls and the Nag Hammadi Library, S.A. Hoeller; Theosophical Publishing House, Wheaton, Illinois, 1989.

The Letter of Peter to Philip, tr. M.W. Meyer; Scholars, Chico, California, 1981.

Marcion and His Influence, E.C. Blackman; SPCK, London, 1948.

Marcion: A Study of a Second Century Heretic, R.S. Wilson; James Clarke, London, 1933.

Marcion: On the Restitution of Christianity, R.J. Hoffmann; Scholars, Chico, California, 1984.

Marcion: The Gospel of the Alien God, A. Harnack, tr. J.E. Steely & L.D. Bierma; Labyrinth, Durham, North Carolina, 1924.

The Path of Light, a translation and interpretation of the Askew and Bruce codices (ms.), C. O'Brien; Cambridge, 1995.

Pre-Christian Gnosticism, E. Yamauchi; SCM, London, 1973.

Nag Hammadi Codex I (the Jung Codex), 2 vols., ed. H.W. Attridge; E.J. Brill, Leiden, 1985.

Nag Hammadi Codex II, 2-7, 2 vols., ed. B. Layton; E.J. Brill, Leiden, 1989.

Nag Hammadi Codex III, 5, The Dialogue of the Saviour, ed. S. Emmel; E.J. Brill, Leiden, 1984.

Nag Hammadi Codices V, 2-5 and VI, ed. D.M. Parrott; E.J. Brill, Leiden, 1979.

Nag Hammadi Codices IX and X, ed. B.A. Pearson; E.J. Brill, Leiden, 1981.

Nag Hammadi Codices XI, XII, XIII, ed. C.W. Hedrick; E.J. Brill, Leiden, 1990.

Nag Hammadi, Gnosticism and Early Christianity, ed. C.W. Hedrick & R. Hodgson Jr.; Hedrickson, Peabody, Massachussetts, 1986.

The Nag Hammadi Library in English, ed. J.M. Robinson; E.J. Brill, Leiden, 1988.

Pistis Sophia, tr. G. Horner; SPCK, London, 1924.

Pistis Sophia, tr. V. MacDermot; E.J. Brill, Leiden, 1978.

Pistis Sophia, A Gnostic Gospel, G.R.S. Mead; Garber Communications, New York, 1984, reprinted from Mead's 1921 edition.

The Robe of Glory, J.H. Davidson; Element, Shaftesbury, UK, 1992.

The Secret Books of the Egyptian Gnosis, J. Doresse; Inner Traditions, Rochester, Vermont, 1986.

The Secret Gospel, M. Smith; Dawn Horse, Clearlake, California, 1982.

The Teachings of Silvanus, J. Zandee; Nederlands Institut voor het Nabije Oosten, Leiden, 1991.

Greek, Roman and Egyptian Literature

The Annals of Tacitus, tr. J. Jackson; William Heinemann, London, 1962.

The Art and Thought of Heraclitus, C.H. Khan; Cambridge University Press, Cambridge, 1979.

By Light, Light: The Mystic Gospel of Hellenistic Judaism, E.R. Goodenough; Yale University Press, New Haven, Connecticut, 1935.

Commentary of Hierocles on the Golden Verses of Pythagoras, A. Dacier, tr. N. Rowe; Theosophical Publishing Society, London, 1906.

Conversations of Socrates, Xenophon, tr. H. Tredennick & R.A.H. Waterfield; Penguin, London, 1990.

The Dialogues of Plato, 4 vols., tr. B. Jowett; Oxford University Press, Oxford, 1953.

Early Greek Philosophy, J Barnes; Penguin, London, 1987.

The Egyptian Arch-Gnosis, J. van Rijckenborgh; Rozekruis Pers, Haarlem, The Netherlands, 1982.

Empedocles, H. Lambridis; University of Alabama Press, Alabama, 1976

Empedocles: the Extant Fragments, M.R. Wright; Yale University Press, New Haven, Connecticut, 1981.

The Enneads, Plotinus, tr. S. MacKenna (1917); Penguin, London, 1991.

Great Books of the Western World: 17. Plotinus, ed. R.M. Hutchins; University of Chicago, Chicago, 1952.

The Greek Myths, R. Graves; Penguin, London, 1992.

Heraclitus, T.M. Robinson; University of Toronto Press, Toronto, 1987.

Heraclitus, P. Wheelwright; Princeton University Press, Princeton, New Jersey, 1959.

Hermetica, B.P. Copenhaver; Cambridge University Press, Cambridge, 1982.

Hermetica, W. Scott; Solos, Bath, UK, 1992 [1924].

The History of the Peloponnesian War, 4 vols., Thucydides, tr. C.F. Smith; William Heinemann, London, 1965-1969.

Iamblichus' Life of Pythagoras, Iamblichus, tr. T. Taylor; Watkins, London, 1926.

The Influence of Greek Ideas and Usages upon the Christian Church, E. Hatch (Hibbert Lectures, 1888); Williams & Norgate, London, 1914.

The Laws, Plato, tr. T.J. Saunders; Penguin, London, 1975.

The Life and Times of Apollonius of Tyana, Philostratus, tr. C.P. Eells; Stanford University, Palo Alto, California, 1923.

The Life of Apollonius of Tyana, Philostratus, tr. F.C. Conybeare; William Heinemann, London, 1912.

Myths of Greece and Rome, T. Bullfinch; Penguin, London, 1979.

Natural History, 10 vols., Pliny the Elder, tr. H. Rackham *et al.*; William Heinemann, London, 1961-1968.

The Orphic Poems, M.L. West; Oxford University Press, Oxford, 1983.

Philebus, Plato, tr. R.A.H. Waterfield; Penguin, London, 1982.

The Philosophers: An Alternative Concept of Greek Philosophy in Light of Eastern Wisdom and Modern Science, 2 parts, unpublished thesis, T.A. Richman; Stanford University, California, 1980.

The Philosophy of Plotinus, 2 vols., tr. W.R. Inge; Longmans, Green, London, 1923.

Plato (Euthyphro, Apology, Crito, Phaedo, Phaedrus), tr. H.N. Fowler; William Heinemann, London, 1966.

Plato (Phaedrus and Letters VII and VIII), tr. W. Hamilton; Penguin, London, 1973.

Plato (The Statesman, Philebus), tr. H.N. Fowler; William Heinemann, London, 1967.

Pliny Letters, 2 vols., Pliny the Younger, tr. W. Melmouth & W.M.L. Hutchinson; William Heinemann, London, 1915.

Pliny's Natural History: A Selection from Philemon Holland's Translation (1601), ed. J. Newsome; Oxford University Press, Oxford, 1964.

Plotinus on the Beautiful and on Intelligible Beauty, tr. the editors of the Shrine of Wisdom & T. Taylor; Shrine of Wisdom, Godalming, UK, 1984 [1932].

Pythagoras: A Life, P. Gorman; Routledge & Kegan Paul, London, 1979.

Select Works of Plotinus, tr. T. Taylor; G. Bell, London, 1909.

The Sentences of Sextus: A Contribution to the History of Early Christian Ethics, H. Chadwick; in *Texts and Studies* 5 (1959), Cambridge University Press, Cambridge.

On Sophistical Refutations, On Coming-to-Be and Passing-Away, and On the Cosmos, Aristotle, tr. E.M. Forster & D.J. Furley; William Heinemann, London, 1955.

Studies in the Platonic Epistles, tr. G. Morrow; in *Illinois Studies in Language and Literature* 18 (1935-1936), Nos. 3-4, University of Illinois, Urbana, Illinois.

A Study of the Doctrine of Metempsychosis in Greece, H.B. Long; Princeton University, New Jersey, 1948.

Suetonius, 2 vols., tr. J.C. Rolfe; William Heinemann, London, 1965.

Thrice-Greatest Hermes, 3 vols., G.R.S. Mead; Theosophical Publishing Society, London, 1906.

Tusculan Disputations, Marcus Tullius Cicero, tr. J.E. King; William Heinemann, London, 1927.

Jewish Literature

The Holy Name: Mysticism in Judaism, M.B. Caravella; Radha Soami Satsang Beas, Dera Baba Jaimal Singh, Punjab, 1989.

Jewish Mystical Tradition, B.Z. Bokser; Pilgrim, New York, 1981.

Josephus, 10 vols., tr. H.StJ. Thackeray *et al.*; William Heinemann, London, 1966-1969, 1981 [1927-].

Josephus, His Complete Works, tr. W. Whiston; Pickering & Inglis, London, 1963 [1867].

The Jewish War, Josephus, tr. G.A. Williamson, rev. E.M. Smallwood; Penguin, London, 1981.

The Jewish War, Josephus, tr. G.A. Williamson; Penguin, London, 1959 (first edn.).

Philo, 10 vols., tr. F.H. Colson & G.H. Whitaker; William Heinemann, London, 1941.

The Works of Philo Judaeus, 4 vols., tr. C.D. Yonge; H.G. Bohn, London, 1855.

Who Wrote the Bible? R.E. Friedman; Jonathan Cape, London, 1988.

Mandaeans and Mandaean Literature

By Tigris and Euphrates, E.S. Stevens (later E.S. Drower); Hurst & Blackett, London, 1923.

The Canonical Prayerbook of the Mandaeans, tr. E.S. Drower; E.J. Brill, Leiden, The Netherlands, 1959.

Diwan Abatur or Progress Through the Purgatories, tr. E.S. Drower; in *Studi e Testi* 151 (1950), Biblioteca Apostolica Vaticana, Città del Vaticano.

Ginza der Schatz oder das Grosse Buch der Mandäer, M. Lidzbarski; Vandenhoeck und Ruprecht, Göttingen-Leipzig, 1925.

The Gnostic John the Baptizer, G.R.S. Mead; John Watkins, London, 1924.

The Haran Gawaita and the Baptism of Hibil-Ziwa, tr. E.S. Drower; in *Studi e Testi* 176 (1953), Biblioteca Apostolica Vaticana, Città del Vaticano.

Inscriptions Mandaïtes des Coupes de Khouabir, H. Pognon; Paris, 1898-1899.

Das Johannesbuch der Mandäer, M. Lidzbarski (tr. in *MEM*); Alfred Töpelmann, Giessen, Germany, 1915.

The Mandaeans of Iran and Iraq, E.S. Drower; Oxford University Press, Oxford, 1937.

Mandäische Liturgien, M. Lidzbarski (tr. in *MEM*); Weidmannsche Buchhandlung, Germany, Berlin, 1920.

A Pair of Nasoraean Commentaries, tr. E.S. Drower; E.J. Brill, Leiden, 1963.

The Secret Adam, E.S. Drower; Oxford University Press, Oxford, 1960.

The Thousand and Twelve Questions (*Alf Trisar Shuialia*), tr. E.S. Drower; Akademie-Verlag, Berlin, 1960.

Water into Wine, E.S. Drower; John Murray, London, 1956.

Manichaeans and Manichaean Literature

Beiträge zur Kenntnis der Religiösen Dichtung Balai's, K.V. Zetterstéen; Leipzig, Germany, 1902.

The Cathars and Reincarnation, A. Guirdham; Neville Spearman, Jersey, 1970.

Gnosis on the Silk Road: Gnostic Texts from Central Asia, tr. H-J. Klimkeit; Harper, San Francisco, 1993.

The Great Heresy, A. Guirdham; Neville Spearman, Jersey, 1977.

The Great Vohu Manah and the Apostle of God, G. Widengren; Uppsala, Sweden, 1945.

Handschriften-Reste in Estrangelo-Schrift aus Turfan, Chinesisch-Turkistan, 2 vols., F.W.K. Müller; aus dem Anhang zu den *APAW* aus dem Jahre, 1904.

Lower (Second?) Section of the Manichaean Hymns, tr. Tsui Chi; in *BSOAS* XI (1943-46), University of London.

Mani and Manichaeism, G. Widengren; Weidenfeld & Nicholson, London, 1961.

The Manichaean Hymn-Cycles in Parthian, tr. M. Boyce; Oxford University Press, London, 1954.

Manichaean Literature, J.P. Asmussen; Scholars' Facsimiles & Reprints, Delmar, New York, 1975.

A Manichaean Psalm-Book, Part II, ed. & tr. C.R.C. Allbery; Kohlhammer, Stuttgart, 1938.

Le Manichéisme: Son Fondateur – Sa Doctrine, H-C. Puech; Civilisations du Sud, SAEP, Paris, 1949.

Manichaeism in the Later Roman Empire, S.N.C. Lieu; Manchester University Press, Manchester, 1985.

Ein Manichäisches Bet- und Beichtbuch, W.B. Henning; in *Abhandlungen der Königlich Preussischen Akademie der Wissenschaften* (1936), Berlin.

Mesopotamian Elements in Manichaeism, G. Widengren; in *Uppsala Universitets Arsskrift* 3 (1946), University of Uppsala, Uppsala, Sweden.

On Mithra in the Manichaean Pantheon, M. Boyce, in *A Locust's Leg: Studies in Honour of S.H. Taqizadeh*, ed. W.B. Henning & E. Yarshater; Percy Lund, Humphries, London, 1962.

Mitteriranische Manichaica aus Chinesisch-Turkestan, 3 vols., F.C. Andreas & W.B. Henning; in *SPAW* 1932, 1933, 1934.

The Religion of the Manichees, F.C. Burkitt; Cambridge University Press, Cambridge, 1925.

A Sogdian Fragment of the Manichaean Cosmogony, W.B. Henning; in *BSOAS* XII (1948).

Studies in the Coptic Manichaean Psalm-Book, T. Säve-Söderbergh; Uppsala, Sweden & W. Heffer, Cambridge, 1949.

Syrische Poesian, P.P. Zingerle; in *ZDMG* 17 (1863).

The Treasure of Montsegur: The Secret of the Cathars, W. Birks & R.A. Gilbert; Thorsons, Wellingborough, UK, 1990.

Mesopotamian, Zoroastrian & Persian Literature

Ancient Near Eastern Texts Relating to the Old Testament, ed. J.B. Pritchard; Princeton University Press, Princeton, New Jersey, 1969.

Avesta: The Religious Book of the Parsees, Spiegel, tr. A.H. Bleeck; Bernard Quaritch, London, 1864.

The Babylonian Epic of Creation, S. Langdon; Oxford University Press, Oxford, 1923.

The Babylonian Genesis: The Story of Creation, A. Heidel; University of Chicago, Chicago, 1951.

Babylonian Wisdom, S. Langdon; Luzac, London, 1923.

The Chants of Zarathushtra, tr. I.J.S. Taraporewala; D.B. Taraporewala Sons, Bombay, India, 1951.

From the Tablets of Sumer, S.N. Kramer; Falcon's Wing, Indian Hills, Colorado, 1956.

The Epic of Gilgamesh, N.K. Sandars; Penguin, London, 1972.

The Epic of Gilgamesh, R.C. Thompson; Luzac, London, 1928.

The Gilgamesh Epic and Old Testament Parallels, A. Heidel; University of Chicago, Chicago, Illinois, 1946.

The King and the Tree of Life in Ancient Near Eastern Religion, G. Widengren; University of Uppsala, Uppsala, Sweden, 1951.

Mithras: The Fellow in the Cap, E. Wynne-Tyson; Rider, London, 1958.

The Mysteries of Mithra, F. Cumont; Kegan Paul, Trench, Trübner, London, 1903.

The Mythology of All Races, Vol. V: Semitic, S. Langdon; Archaeological Institute of America, Marshall Jones, 1931.

New Light on the Gathas of Holy Zarathushtra, A.F. Khabardar; A.F. Khabardar, Bombay, India, 1952.

The Oriental Religions in Roman Paganism, F. Cumont; Open Court, Chicago, Illinois, 1911.

Pagan Christs: Studies in Comparative Hierology, J.M. Robertson; Watts, London, 1911.

Sumerian Literature: A Preliminary Survey of the Oldest Literature in the World, S.N. Kramer; in *Proceedings of the American Philosophical Society* 85 (1942), American Philosophical Society, Philadelphia, Pennsylvania.

Sumerian Mythology: A Study of Spiritual and Literary Development in the Third Millenium BC, S.N. Kramer; American Philosophical Society, Philadelphia, Pennsylvania, 1944.

Sumerian and Babylonian Psalms, S. Langdon; Luzac, London, 1909.

Sumerian and Semitic Religious and Historical Texts, S. Langdon; Oxford University Press, Oxford, 1923.

Tammuz and Ishtar: A Monograph upon Babylonian Religion and Theology, S. Langdon; Oxford University Press, Oxford, 1914.

Miscellaneous

An Anthology of Mysticism and Mystical Philosophy, W. Kingsland; Methuen, London, 1927.

The Chronology of Ancient Nations, al-Biruni, tr. C.E. Sachau; W.H. Allan, London, 1879.

The History of the Inquisition of the Middle Ages, 3 vols., H. Lea; Harper & Row, New York, 1955.

The Fihrist of al-Nadim, 2 vols., tr. B. Dodge; Columbia University Press, Columbia, New York, 1970.

The Koran Interpreted, tr. A.J. Arberry; Oxford University Press, London, 1964.

Mysticism in English Literature, C.F.E. Spurgeon; Cambridge University Press, Cambridge, 1913.

Reincarnation: A Study of Forgotten Truth, E.D. Walker; Houghton Miffin, Boston, Massachusetts, 1888.

Reincarnation: An East-West Anthology, J. Head & S.L. Cranston; Julian, New York, 1961.

Reincarnation in World Thought, J. Head & S.L. Cranston; Causeway Books, New York, 1967.

The Ring of Return, E. Martin; Philip Allan, London, 1927.

The Symbiotic Universe, G. Greenstein; William Morrow, New York, 1988.

Modern Apocrypha and Allied Material

The Alleged Sojourn of Christ in India, M. Müller; *The Nineteenth Century* 36 (1894).

The Chief Lama of Hemis on the Alleged Unknown Life of Christ, J.A. Douglas; *The Nineteenth Century* 39 (1896), pp.667-668.

Jesus Lived in India, H. Kersten; Element, Shaftesbury, UK, 1986.

Modern Apocrypha, E.J. Goodspeed; Beacon, Boston, Massachusetts, 1956.

Strange Tales About Jesus, P. Beskow; Fortress, Philadelphia, Pennsylvania, 1983.

The Unknown Life of Jesus Christ, N. Notovitch, tr. J.H. Connelly & L. Landsberg; G.W. Dillingham, New York, 1894.

The Unknown Life of Jesus Christ, N. Notovitch, tr. A. Loranger; Rand, McNally, New York, 1894.

The Unknown Life of Christ, N. Notovitch, tr. V. Crispe; Hutchinson, London, 1895.

La Vie Inconnue de Jésus-Christ, N. Notovitch; Paul Ollendorf, Paris, 1894.

New Testament and Early Christianity

After the Cross, H.J. Schonfield; Tantivity, London, 1981.

The Anatomy of the Fourth Gospel: A Study in Literary Design, R.A. Culpepper; Fortress, Philadelphia, Pennsylvania, 1983.

Androcles and the Lion, Bernard Shaw; Penguin, London, 1946 [1916].

An Aramaic Approach to the Gospels and Acts, M. Black; Oxford University Press, Oxford, 1967.

The Aramaic Origin of the Fourth Gospel, C.F. Burney; Oxford University Press, Oxford, 1922.

The Archaeology of the New Testament, J. Finegan; Princeton University Press, Princeton, New Jersey, 1969.

Behind the First Gospel, B. Lindars; SPCK, London, 1971.

The Birth of the New Testament, C.F.D. Moule; A. & C. Black, London, 1962.

Bread From Heaven: An Exegetical Study of the Concept of Manna in the Gospel of John and the Writings of Philo, P. Borgen; E.J. Brill, Leiden, 1965.

Born of a Woman, J.S. Spong; Harper, San Francisco, 1992.

Can We Trust the New Testament? J.A.T. Robinson; Mowbray, London, 1979.

Christianity in Talmud and Midrash, R.T. Herford; Williams & Norgate, London, 1903.

The Christian Platonists of Alexandria, C. Bigg; Oxford University Press, Oxford, 1913.

Colloquy in New Testament Studies: A Time for Reappraisal and Fresh Approaches, ed. B. Corley; Mercer University Press, Macon, Georgia, 1983.

A Complete Categorized Greek-English New Testament Vocabulary, D. Holly; Samuel Bagster, London, 1978.

The Complete Gospels, ed. R.J. Miller; Polebridge, Santa Rosa, California, 1995.

Coptic Egypt, B. Waterson; Scottish Academic, Edinburgh, 1988.

The Death of Jesus, J. Carmichael; Victor Gollancz, London, 1963.

The Debate About Christ, D. Cupitt; SCM, London, 1979.

Did Jesus Exist?, G.A. Wells; Elek/Pemberton, London, 1975.

Did Jesus Live 100 BC?, G.R.S. Mead; Theosophical Publishing House, London, 1903.

Do You Know Greek? J.N. Sevenster; E.J. Brill, Leiden, 1968.

The Earliest Gospel, F.C. Grant; Abingdon-Cokesbury, New York, 1943.

The Earliest Lives of Jesus, R.M. Grant; SPCK, London, 1961.

The Earliest Sources for the Life of Jesus, F.C. Burkitt; Houghton Mifflin, New York, 1910.

The Early Days of Christianity, F.W. Farrar; Cassell, London, 1898.

Early Eastern Christianity, F.C. Burkitt; John Murray, London, 1904.

Early Egyptian Christianity: From Its Origins to 451 C.E., C.W. Griggs; E.J. Brill, Leiden, 1990.

Edessa: 'The Blessed City', J.B. Segal; Oxford University Press, Oxford, 1970.

The Enigma of the Fourth Gospel: Its Author and Writer, R.E. Eisler; Methuen, London, 1938.

The Fall of Jerusalem and the Christian Church, S.G.F. Brandon; SPCK, London 1951.

The First Gospel: An Introduction to Q, A.D. Jacobson; Polebridge, Sonoma, California, 1988.

The Five Gospels: The Search for the Authentic Words of Jesus, R.W. Funk & R.W. Hoover; Macmillan, Riverside, New Jersey, 1993.

The Forgotten Beginnings of Creation and Christianity, C.A. Skriver; Vegetarian Press, Denver, Colorado, 1990.

The Formation of the Christian Biblical Canon, L.M. McDonald; Abingdon, Nashville, Tennessee, 1988.

The Formation of the New Testament, E.J. Goodspeed; University of Chicago Press, Chicago, 1926.

The Formation of the New Testament, R.M. Grant; Hutchinson, London, 1965.

The Four Gospels: A Study of Origins, B.H. Streeter; Macmillan, London, 1936.

Four Other Gospels, J.D. Crossan; Polebridge, Sonoma, California, 1992.

The Fourth Gospel and the Logos-Doctrine, R.G. Bury; W. Heffer, Cambridge, 1940.

The Genesis of John, A.Q. Morton & J. McLeman; St Andrew, Edinburgh, 1980.

The Gospel According to Jesus, S. Mitchell; Harper Collins, New York, 1991.

The Gospel Before the Gospels, B.S. Easton; Charles Scribner's Sons, New York, 1928.

The Gospel of Mark, B.H. Branscomb; Hodder & Stoughton, London, 1937.

The Gospel of Mark: Its Composition and Date, B.W. Bacon; Yale University Press, New Haven, Connecticut, 1925.

The Gospel of Mark (Red Letter Edition), R.W. Funk & M.H. Smith; Polebridge, Sonoma, California, 1991.

The Gospel of Thomas and Jesus, S.J. Patterson; Polebridge, Sonoma, California, 1992.

The Gospels as Historical Documents, 3 vols., V.H. Stanton; Cambridge University Press, Cambridge, 1903, 1909, 1920.

The Gospels in the Making: An Introduction to the Recent Criticism of the Synoptic Gospels, A. Richardson; SCM, London, 1938.

The Gospels: Their Origin and Growth, D.W. Riddle; University of Chicago, Chicago, Illinois, 1939.

The Gospels: Their Origin and Their Growth, F.C. Grant; Harper & Brothers, New York, 1957.

The Historical Jesus: The Life of a Mediterranean Jewish Peasant, J.D. Crossan; Harper, San Francisco, 1991.

The Historical Evidence for Jesus, G.A. Wells; Prometheus, New York, 1982.

The Historical Figure of Jesus, E.P. Sanders; Penguin, London, 1993.

The Historic Christ: An Examination of Dr Robert Eisler's Theory According to the Slavonic Version of Josephus and the Other Sources, J.W. Jack; James Clarke, London, 1933.

A History of Heresy, D. Christie-Murray; Oxford University Press, Oxford, 1976.

The History of the Church, Eusebius, tr. G.A. Williamson; Penguin, London, 1965.

The History of the Jewish People in the Age of Jesus Christ (175 BC-135 AD), 3 vols., E. Schürer, rev., ed. & tr. G. Vermes *et al.*; T. & T. Clark, Edinburgh, 1973-1987.

The History of the Synoptic Tradition, R. Bultmann, tr. J. Marsh; Basil Blackwell, Oxford, 1963.

Honest to God, J.A.T. Robinson; SCM, London, 1963.

The Human Face of God, J.A.T. Robinson; SCM, London, 1972.

The 'I am' of the Fourth Gospel: A Study in Johannine Usage and Thought, P.B. Harner; Facet, Philadelphia, Pennsylvania, 1970.

The Interpretation of the Fourth Gospel, C.H. Dodd; Cambridge University Press, Cambridge, 1953.

The Interpretation of the New Testament 1861-1961, S. Neill; Oxford University Press, Oxford, 1964.

Introduction to the New Testament, W.G. Kümmel, tr. A.J. Matill; SCM, London, 1970.

Jesus: A Life, A.N. Wilson; Sinclair-Stevenson, London, 1992.

Jesus, Aramaic and Greek, G.R. Selby; Brynmill, Doncaster, UK, 1989.

Jesus and Christian Origins Outside the New Testament, F.F. Bruce; Hodder & Stoughton, London, 1974.

Jesus and the Constraints of History, A.E. Harvey; Duckworth, London, 1982.

Jesus Christ in the Talmud, Midrash, Zohar, and the Liturgy of the Synagogue, G. Dalman, tr. A.W. Streane; Deighton, Bell, Cambridge, 1893.

Jesus in the Jewish Tradition, M. Goldstein; Macmillan, New York, 1950.

Jesus-Jeshua, G. Dalman, tr. P.P. Levertoff; SPCK, London, 1929.

Jesus of Nazareth: His Life, Times and Teaching, J. Klausner, tr. H.D. Danby; George Allen & Unwin, London, 1929.

The Jesus of the Early Christians, G.A. Wells; Pemberton, London, 1971.

Jesus on Trial: A Study in the Fourth Gospel, A.E. Harvey; SPCK, London, 1976.

Jesus the Jew: A Historian's Reading of the Gospels, G. Vermes; Williams Collins, London, 1973.

Jesus the Magician, M. Smith; Gollancz, London, 1978.

Jesus: The Man and the Myth, J.P. Mackey; SCM, London, 1979.

The Jew of Tarsus: An Unorthodox Portrait of Paul, H.J. Schonfield; Macdonald, London, 1946.

The Jewish–Christian Argument: A History of Theologies in Conflict, H.J. Schoeps, tr. D.E. Green; Faber & Faber, London, 1963.

John Wycliffe: A Quincentenary Tribute, J.J. Wray; James Nisbet, London, 1884.

The Life of Jesus Critically Examined, D.F. Strauss, tr. G. Eliot; Chapman, London, 1846.

Light on Saint John, Maharaj Charan Singh; Radha Soami Satsang Beas, Dera Baba Jaimal Singh, Amritsar, Punjab, 1985.

Light on Saint Matthew, Maharaj Charan Singh; Radha Soami Satsang Beas, Dera Baba Jaimal Singh, Amritsar, Punjab, 1978.

Living in Sin, J.S. Spong; Harper, San Francisco, 1988.

A Lost Edition of the Letters of Paul: A Reassessment of the Text of the Pauline

Corpus Attested by Marcion, J.J. Clabeaux; Catholic Biblical Association of America, Washington D.C., 1989.

The Lost Gospel: The Book of Q and Christian Origins, B.L. Mack; Harper, San Francisco, 1993.

The Making of Luke-Acts, H.J. Cadbury; Macmillan, London, 1927.

The Making of the English New Testament, E.J. Goodspeed; The University of Chicago Press, Chicago, 1925.

Marcion and the New Testament: An Essay in the Early History of the Canon, J. Knox; University of Chicago, Chicago, 1942.

A Marginal Jew: Rethinking the Historical Jesus, J.P. Meier; Doubleday, New York, 1991.

Moses or Jesus: An Essay in Johannine Christology, M.-E. Boismard, tr. B.T. Viviano; Fortress, Minneapolis, Minnesota, 1993.

The Messiah Jesus and John the Baptist According to Flavius Josephus' Recently Discovered 'Capture of Jerusalem' and Other Jewish and Christian Sources, R. Eisler, tr. A.H. Krappe; Methuen, London, 1931.

Myth and Miracle: Isis, Wisdom and the Logos of John, H.C. Kee; in *Myth Symbol and Reality*, ed. A.M. Olson, University of Notre Dame Press, London, 1980.

'Nazareth' and 'Jerusalem' in Luke Chs. I and II, P. Winter; in *New Testament Studies*, Vol. III (1956-1957), ed. M. Black, Cambridge University Press, Cambridge.

The Nestorian Documents and Relics in China, P.Y. Saeki; Academy of Oriental Culture, Tokyo Institute, Maruzen, Tokyo, 1951.

Nestorius and His Teaching: A Fresh Examination of the Evidence, J.F. Bethune-Baker; Cambridge University Press, Cambridge, 1908.

New Life of Jesus, D.F. Strauss; Williams & Norgate, London, 1865.

The New Testament Documents: Their Origin and Early History, G. Milligan; Macmillan, London, 1913.

New Testament Fundamentals, S.L. Davies; Polebridge, Sonoma, California, 1994.

New Testament Studies, C.H. Dodd; Manchester University Press, Manchester, UK, 1953.

The Origin of the Doctrine of the Trinity: A Popular Exposition, J.R. Harris; Longmans, Green, Manchester, UK, 1919.

The Origin of the Prologue to St John's Gospel, J.R. Harris; Cambridge University Press, Cambridge, 1917.

Orpheus: The Fisher, Comparative Studies in Orphic and Early Christian Cult Symbolism, R. Eisler; J.M. Watkins, London, 1921.

The Oxford Companion to the Bible, ed. B.M. Metzger & M.D. Coogan; Oxford University Press, Oxford, 1993.

The Oxford Dictionary of the Christian Church, rev. edn. F.L. Cross & E.A. Livingstone; Oxford University Press, Oxford, 1983.

The Parables of Jesus, R.W. Funk *et al.*; Polebridge, Sonoma, California, 1990.

The Passover Plot: New Light on the History of Jesus, H.J. Schonfield; Hutchinson, London, 1965.

Pattern of Persuasion in the Gospels, B.L. Mack & V.K. Robbins; Polebridge, Sonoma, California, 1989.

Paul, E.P. Sanders; Oxford University Press, Oxford, 1991.

Paul: The Theology of the Apostle in the Light of Jewish Religious History, H.J. Schoeps; Lutterworth, London, 1961.

The Priority of John, J.A.T. Robinson; SCM, London, 1985.

Q Parallels, J.S. Kloppenborg; Polebridge, Sonoma, California, 1988.

The Q-Thomas Reader: The Gospels Before the Gospels, J.S. Kloppenborg *et al.*; Polebridge, Sonoma, California, 1990.

The Quest for the Historical Jesus, G. Vermes; in *Jewish Chronicle Literary Supplement* (12 December 1969).

The Quest for the Messiah, J. Painter; T. & T. Clark, Edinburgh, 1993.

Rabbinic Literature and Gospel Teachings, C.G. Montefiore; Macmillan, London, 1930.

Redating the New Testament, J.A.T. Robinson; SCM, London, 1976.

Reincarnation and Christianity, a clergyman of the Church of England; Rider, London, 1910.

Reincarnation in the New Testament, J.M. Pryse; Elliot B. Page, New York, 1900.

Rescuing the Bible from Fundamentalism, J.S. Spong; Harper, San Francisco, 1991.

Resurrection: Myth or Reality?, J.S. Spong; Harper, San Francisco, 1994.

The Rise of Christianity, W.H.C. Frend; Darton. Longman & Todd, London, 1984.

The Setting of the Sermon on the Mount, W.D. Davies; Cambridge University Press, Cambridge, 1963.

The Seven Ecumenical Councils of the Undivided Church, ed. H.R. Percival; James Parker, Oxford, 1900.

The Sources of the Second Gospel, A.T. Cadoux; James Clarke, London, 1935.

The Sources of the Synoptic Gospels, 2 vols., W.L. Knox; Cambridge University Press, Cambridge, 1953.

Studies in Matthew, B.W. Bacon; Constable, London, 1930.

Studies in Pharisaism and the Gospels, I. Abrahams; Cambridge University Press, Cambridge, 1917.

The Synoptic Gospels, 2 vols., C.G. Montefiore; Macmillan, London, 1927.

The Synoptic Problem, W.R. Farmer; Macmillan, London, 1964.

Testimonies (Part I), J.R. Harris; Cambridge University Press, Cambridge, 1916.

The Text of the New Testament, K. & B. Aland, tr. E.F. Rhodes; William B. Eerdmans & E.J. Brill, Leiden, 1987.

The Text of the New Testament: Its Transmission, Corruption and Restoration, B.M. Metzger; Oxford University Press, Oxford, 1968.

Those Incredible Christians, H.J. Schonfield; Element, Shaftesbury, UK, 1968.

Trajectories Through Early Christianity, J.M. Robinson & H. Koester; Fortress, Philadelphia, Pennsylvania, 1971.

The Trial of Jesus of Nazareth, S.G.F. Brandon; Batsford, London, 1968.

The Twelve Apostles, J.R. Harris; W. Heffer, Cambridge, 1927.

Understanding the Fourth Gospel, J. Ashton; Oxford University Press, Oxford, 1991.

The Vegetarianism of Jesus Christ, C.P. Vaclavik; Kaweah, Three Rivers, California, 1986.

Who Was Jesus?, C. Cross; Hodder & Stoughton, London, 1970.

The Words of Jesus: Considered in the Light of Post-Biblical Jewish Writings and the Aramaic Language, G. Dalman, tr. D.M. Kay; T. & T. Clark, Edinburgh, 1902.

Oxyrhynchus Sayings of Jesus

Fragment of an Uncanonical Gospel from Oxyrhynchus, B.P. Grenfell & A.S. Hunt; Oxford University Press, London, 1908.

New Sayings of Jesus and the Fragment of a Lost Gospel, B.P. Grenfell & A.S. Hunt; Henry Frowde, London, 1904.

The Oxyrhyncus Logia and the Apocryphal Gospels, C. Taylor; Oxford University Press, Oxford, 1899.

The Sayings of Our Lord, from an Early Greek Papyrus, B.P. Grenfell & A.S. Hunt; Henry Frowde, London, 1897.

Index

The index is designed not only for general use but also as a memory refresher while reading the book. Consequently, references are to subject matter as well as to particular terms, metaphors, similes, names, places and so on. Index entries for particular individuals are usually followed by their dates, together with a very brief note on the person's significance relative to this book, often including works quoted. Abbreviations used only in the index are EC (early Christian writings), GT (gnostic text), MCT (Manichaean-Christian text), MT (Mandaean text), NH (Nag Hammadi gnostic text), NT (New Testament), NTA (New Testament apocryphal text), OT (Old Testament), OTA (Old Testament apocryphal text), *Aram.* (Aramaic), *Gk.* (Greek), *Heb.* (Hebrew), *Lat.* (Latin), *Md.* (Mandaean), *abbr.* (abbreviation), *lit.* (literally), and Bp. (Bishop). Book or text titles are followed by their author and/or an abbreviation (as above) identifying their general category. Foreign words are usually followed by their language and meaning. The index also contains a number of lists which readers may find useful. In particular, see Church fathers & early Christians, gnostics, apocryphal literature (NTA and OTA), early Christian literature (EC), gnostic literature (GT), Mandaean literature (MT), Manichaean-Christian literature (MCT), Nag Hammadi codices *or* library (NH), New Testament (NT), Old Testament (OT), and revelationary genre, plus lists of epithets and synonyms for God, the inner realms, the eternal realm, Masters, Satan and the Word. The index is not exhaustive for those entries or subjects where there would have been too many references (*eg.* Jesus, Father, light, etc.). In these instances, we have tried to give main occurrences only, especially in quoted texts. Endnotes are referenced with the endnote number in brackets. Space restrictions have meant the use of a small typeface. Anyone using the index extensively is welcome to enlarge it on a photocopier.

797 (*see also* prayer); "repent: for the kingdom of heaven is at hand", 29, 469 (*see also* repentance); "seek, and ye shall find; knock, and it shall be opened", 30, 746 (*see also* seeking); "seek ye first the kingdom of God", 20, 227, 863; "sheep in the midst of wolves ... wise as serpents, and harmless as doves", 965; "strain *at* a gnat", world's longest lived 'typo', 71; "strait is the gate, and narrow is the way", 744 (*see also* gate(s)); "take no thought for your life", 19-20, 225; "the very hairs of your head are all numbered", 227; "think not that I am come to destroy the Law, or the prophets", 547 (*see also* law and the prophets); "thou art Peter and upon this rock I will build my church", 569; "well done, good and faithful servant", 389; "where two or three are gathered together in my name", 35, 977; "who is my mother?", 879-80; "whosoever shall smite thee on thy right cheek", 45, 887-88; "whosoever will be chief among you", 35; "woe unto you, scribes and Pharisees, hypocrites!", 37, 101-2, 217 (*see also* Pharisees); "ye are the light of the world", 975; "ye are the salt of the earth", 974; "your Father knoweth what things ye have need of", 225, 798

Gospel of Mary (NH), 831

Gospel of Matthias (NTA), 65, 874

Gospel of Philip (NH), 135-36, 163, 265, 372, 389-90, 403, 445, 660, 675, 708, 799, 815-16, 852(10), 924(19), 970

Gospel of the Ebionites (NTA), 38, 65, 920

Gospel of the Egyptians (NH), 38, 65, 273, 666, 716, 852(4)

Gospel of the Nazoraeans (NTA), 920

Gospel of the Twelve Apostles (NTA), 704-5

Gospel of Thomas (NH), 37-38, 163, 194-95, 198-200, 214-15, 290-91, 348, 359-60, 404, 437, 539-40, 593, 692, 755, 799; sources of, 193

Gospel of Truth (NH), 222, 273, 343, 482, 696-98, 730

gospels (canonical), authenticity of, early Christian attitudes to, 14, 47-66, 124; collection as four gospels, 65-66; composition of, 14 (*see also* book production techniques; scribes); dating of, 66; early extant manuscripts, 59-62; historical accuracy of (*see* history writing); translations (*see* Bible); writing and copying (*see* book production techniques). *See also Gospels according to St John, St Luke, St Mark, St Matthew;* New Testament

gospels (non-canonical), 38, 65. *See also* apocryphal literature; *and individual gospels*

Grace (as Word), 284-85, 628

grace (of God, Word, Master, Jesus), in quotes, 146, 205, 249, 276, 294, 402, 432, 476, 511, 554, 562, 619, 639, 650, 692, 701-4, 786, 805, 846, 873, 883; in St John, 244, 513-14, 563; of baptism, 470, 703, 709

Graces of Interior Prayer, (*abbr. GIP*, Augustus Poulain), 22-23, 333-34

Gracious One (as Word, Master), 476

gratitude, 306, 353, 535-37, 704, 843, 855, 866, 889

grave *or* tomb, as physical body/existence, 218-19, 296, 417, 442, 592, 807-9, 815, 950-51; Greek funerary inscriptions, 119-20; Jesus empty tomb, 82, 93-94; "O grave where is thy victory?" 390. *See also* resurrection; rising from the dead

Great (as Word), Beam which is all Light, 673; Law, 543-45, 548; Mind, 452

Great Life (as God), 261, 710, 840

Greatness (as Word), 285, 628, 855

greed, 231, 396, 425, 443, 598, 610, 855, 864-66, 868-76, 886

Greek, as *lingua franca* and NT language, 14, 17, 44, 54, 60-63, 66-76, 81-83; did Jesus speak? 117-23

Greek philosophy and mysticism, 176-77, 179, 188, 238-39, 308, 415-16, 423, 442, 924, 914, 995, 997-1000; Christianity and, 124, 168, 419-23, 445-46, 550. *See also* Ammonius Saccas; Apollonius of Tyana; Aratus of Cilicia; Aristotle; Cleanthes; Empedocles; Heraclitus; Iamblichus; Orpheus; Plato; Plotinus; Porphyry; Proclus; Pythagoras; Socrates; *and also* Hellenistic philosophy; Hermes; Neo-Platonism

green pastures (as inner realms), 256

Greenstein, George (modern astronomer & writer), 187-88

Gregory of Nyssa (374-395, Bp. of Nyssa), on Origen, 423

Gregory Thaumaturgus (*c.*213-270, Bp. of Neo-Caesarea), 423

Gregory the Great. *See* Pope Gregory I

Grenfell, Bernard (found C2nd papyri at Oxyrhynchus), 67-68

Grotius, Hugo (C17th Biblical scholar), 111

Guide *and* guidance (of/as Master), 286, 321, 348, 350-51, 357, 429, 488, 512, 530, 533-35, 543-44, 561, 576, 598, 620-21, 696, 733, 750, 791, 794, 825, 854, 861-62, 911, 966, 1002

guilt, 371, 419, 892; of prodigal son, 471-73

Gutenberg, Johann (printed Bible, 1450s), 53

Hades, as hell, 440, 547, 714; as this world, 387, 391-92

Haguel (hell), 538

Hand of the Father (as Word), 664

harbour *or* port (of Life, of the Immortals), 306-7, 341-42, 619, 621-22, 624, 662, 713, 836

harmony and disharmony, 34, 147, 207, 237, 866, 880-86, 895, 932, 935, 961, 973, 976; in early Christianity, 15-17, 37-38, 160-61, 883

harp(s), harpers (as divine Music), 294-95, 297, 299, 790

Harran (in Persia), 175

harvest (spiritual), 274, 286, 314, 403, 785-86, 805, 842; parable of the sower, 328, 349; parable of the tares, 983-84

Hasidim (*lit.* the pious ones), 175, 535, 922

hatred, 18, 45, 271, 230, 281, 330, 359, 362-63, 396, 425, 443, 686, 858-60, 885-87, 962-63, 966

head money. *See* debt(s)

heavenly (as eternal realm), house, 297; kingdom, 908

heaven(s) (as inner realms), 31-32, 141-42, 153-54, 232, 259, 262, 349-56, 538, 815; as many mansions, 328-30; experience of, 333-34; location of, 319-23; Plant of, 1007; Word of, 476. *See also* angel(s); ascent of the soul; astral region; baptism: mystic; Bread from heaven; death; dissolution; door; five inner regions; gate(s); inner realms; kingdom of heaven; mysteries; seven heavens; treasure(s); Voice

Hebrew (language), terms and translations, 54, 119-20, 135, 142, 240-41, 263-64, 538, 568, 585, 663, 920, 922; in OT, 61, 68-70, 162, 286

Hebrews (NT). *See Epistle to the Hebrews*

Hegel (1770-1831), German philosopher, 27

Hegesippus (early C2nd Church father), 41(11), 41, 926

Height (as eternal realm), 307-8, 310, 342, 433, 435-36, 457, 491, 598, 604, 621, 666, 767, 777, 836, 839, 848, 853, 1005

Heimarmene (ruler of processes of *metempsychosis*), 485, 485(3)

Heli (Joseph's father in Luke), 657-58

hell, 320, 365, 397, 418, 434-36, 569, 678; escape from, 644, 714, 728, 778, 1005; of Abaddon, 1005; of this world, 295, 387-92, 397-98, 450-51, 455-57, 491-92, 600, 968, 984; worship God in fear of, 232. *See also* Hades; Haguel; Sheol; hellfire; pit

Manichaean Literature (MCT, *abbr. ML,* tr. J.P. Asmussen *et al.*), 298, 312, 449, 598, 728, 776-77, 836, 854

Manichaean literature, 171-72, 174, 539, 598. *See also Lower (Second) Section of Manichaean Hymns; Manichaean Hymn Cycles in Parthian; Manichaean Literature; Manichaean Psalm-Book; Sogdian Fragment of the Manichaean Cosmogony*

Manichaean Psalm-Book (MCT, *abbr. MPB,* tr. C.R.C. Allberry, includes *Psalms of Heracleides* & *Psalms of Thomas*), 171(11), 172(12), 181, 220, 258-59, 266, 270, 276-77, 293-94, 297-99, 438-39, 470-71, 513, 536, 541-42, 596-97, 600, 602, 604-6, 611, 619-23, 632, 642, 644-46, 666(30,31), 666-67, 668, 713, 716, 730, 732-33, 750-51, 753, 764, 769, 777, 784-85, 793, 809-10, 834-39, 845-49, 855, 871, 901, 988; languages of, translations of, 449, 776; Mandaean connection with *Psalms of Thomas,* 174, 732; sources, background, etc., 171-73, 449

Manichaeans and Manichaeism, as rival to Christianity, 172, 458-60; Cathars, gnostics as, 458-60, 950; in China, 951; St Augustine once a, 951

Manichaeism in the Later Roman Empire (Samuel Lieu), 951

manna, as Bread from heaven, fed to the children of Israel, 235, 247-50, 413-14, 920, 945, 1002

Man of Understanding, 538, 1001. *See also* Master(s)

mansions (as inner realms), 31, 141, 256, 327-30, 348-49, 358-60, 403, 586, 682, 713, 821-22, 830, 985, 988, 994. *See also* creation: hierarchy of

Mansur (Arabic mystic), 995

Manthra (*Avestan,* Word), 996

map of C1st Palestine, 84

Mar Ammo (disciple of Mani), 776

Marcion (*fl.*140-160, early gnostic teacher), 168, 365, 427, 474, 640, 814, 945; attitude to NT texts, 50

Marcus (early gnostic), 814, 997

Marina de Escobar (1554-1633, Spanish mystic), 25-26, 333-34

Mark. *See Gospel according to St Mark*

marked (souls), 684, 694, 709, 719

mark of the Beast on the forehead, 719

marriage, human, 86, 601, 881-82, 891, 895-99, 941, 947, 951; spiritual, 388, 593, 650-51, 695, 757-58, 843-50 (*see also* Bride; Bride-chambers; Bridegroom)

Marsanes (NH), 728

martyrdom, 171, 545, 809; *Depositio Martyrum* (chronology of Christian martyrs), 131; Ignatius, 228; James the brother of Jesus (*c.*62), 41, 926; John, son of Zebedee (apostle), 114; John the Baptist, 571; Mani, 171; Paul, 145; Polycarp (*c.*155), 114. *See also* death: dying while living

Martyrdom of St Thomas (NTA), 269

Mary Magdalene, 63; in *Pistis Sophia,* 433, 492, 707, 752-53, 799-800

Mary (mother of Jesus), 63, 94-96, 204, 560, 655-56, 804. *See also* virgin birth; Virgin Mary

Mary (sister of Martha), 107

Mar Zako (successor of Mani), 853-54

Master-disciple relationship, advice to attend to spiritual practice and lead a spiritual life, 534, 954-60, 987-92; advice to be living examples, 974-75 (*see also* twelve disciples: Jesus' advice to); all disciples equal, 976; among early gnostics, 39-42; attainment of the spiritual goal, 39, 713, 722-24, 912; bond between soul and Master, 532; disciples chosen, 445, 519-20, 523-24, 532, 551, 572, 679-89, 691-94, 722, 755, 976; happiness in a Master's physical presence, 552-53; inner presence of Master, 35, 533, 682, 966, 976-77 (*see also* radiant form

of the Master); inspiration and guidance of Master, 39-40, 533-38, 954; isolation in family, 966; love and harmony among disciples, 976; Master's help in clearing *karma,* 489-96, 533, 961, 987; meetings of disciples, 34-36, 975-77; rebirth of disciples, 722, 736

Master(s), approaching God through a, 513-15, 519-23; as exemplars of how to live, 532, 559; attitude of others towards, 400, 477-78, 514; descriptions of a living, 76, 244, 515-16, 503, 524-34, 538, 551-58; forgiveness, compassion, mercy and love of, 475-78, 496-502, 910; inner identity of, 865; living, 530-34; manifestation of, in this and higher worlds, 534-38; many names for, 538; motivation of, 503, 517-18; purpose of, 29-30, 35, 521-24, 533-38; response to criticism, opposition, persecution by, 503-4, 963-64; role and presence of, 509, 532-33; source of teachings, 517-19, 553; successors of, 40, 42, 563, 659 (*see also* Jesus; John the Baptist; Mani); summarized teachings of, 28-33; teachings sometimes secret, 319-23 (*see also* mysteries: secret teachings); true and false, 39-40, 42, 524-30, 532, 571-79, 713; "I and my Father are one", 515-16. *See also (also called)* Apostle (of Light); Arouser; Awakener; Bridegroom; Brother; Chosen One; Christ; Defender; Deliverer; *Ebion;* Envoy; Existing One; Exorcist; First-born (Son); First Guide, Man; First-begotten; Fishermen; Fisher of Souls; Gardener; Giver; Gracious One; Guide; Helmsman; Helper; Hidden One; Holy One(s); (Son of the) King (of Light, *Nous,* Peace); Liberator; Light; Living One; Man of Understanding; Messenger (of God); Messiah; Minister; mystic; Only-Begotten (Son of God); Paraclete; Peacemaker; Physician; prophet; Redeemer; Righteous One; Sage; Saint; Saviour; Shepherd; Son (of God, of Man); Sower; Standing One; Teacher of Righteousness; True Prophet; True Teacher; Word made flesh; *Zaddik*

Mathnavi (Rumi), 179

Matthew. *See Gospel according to St Matthew*

Matthias, 41, 65, 717, 874. *See also Gospel of Matthias*

meadows, 331. *See also* garden(s)

Mechthild of Magdeburg (*c.*1210-1297, German Christian mystic), 318, 766

Medicine(s) (as Word) 235, 254, 599, 602-6, 611, 644, 713, 850; of Life, 235, 391, 391-92, 467, 644, 603-5; of the Great Law, 544-45, 548; of the Spirit, 603-4

meditation. *See* contemplation; prayer; spiritual practice

meek(ness), 250, 379, 473, 859-60, 862, 867, 877, 886, 906-9, 955, 964-65

Melchior (*lit.* King of Light, one of the wise men), 132

Memoirs of Socrates (Xenophon), 189-90

Menander (early Samaritan gnostic teacher), 40-41, 308, 946

merchandise, 200, 206-7, 619

merchant(s), 206; Master as, 769; Peter as, 615; soul as, 200, 619, 726, 850

Mercury (Greek messenger of the gods), 429

mercy, 462, 805, 862, 869, 911; justice and, 445, 450-51, 455, 474-79, 493, 533; of God, Master, 242, 346, 457, 474, 478-79, 482-89, 496-97, 533, 544, 603-4, 679, 692, 698, 701, 704, 731, 751, 753, 755, 812, 834, 836-37, 847, 889, 916, 989, 1004

Mesopotamia, 79, 122, 167; ancient myths of, 179, 429, 995-96; Mandaeans in, 41, 151, 174-75; Mani in, 168-69, 171-72, 950; mythical antecedents to *Genesis,* 178, 274, 995-96; seven heavens in, 347

Messenger(s) of God, 29, 170, 244, 429, 454, 538, 781, 1008; in Islam, 138; John the Baptist as, 562; Mani as, 169; Mohammed as, 39. *See also* Master(s)

Messiah (*Heb.* anointed one), 103, 107, 170, 538-39, 548, 575

in Judaism, 97, 538-39, 180, 546, 595, 658-59, 978; Jesus as, 36, 91, 126, 135, 539, 584, 180, 269, 467-68, 476, 565, 584, 627, 711, 804; John the Baptist as, 565-66; political leaders as, 102. *See also* Master(s)

metanoia (*Gk.* repentance), 468. *See also* repentance

metaphor(s) and allegories, use of, 32, 153, 164, 178-79, 196-97, 207, 218, 224, 235, 260, 263, 304, 344, 348, 367, 387, 395, 509, 542, 592-94, 628-29, 641, 743, 826, 1004. *See also specific metaphors; and also* chastity; *Exodus; Genesis; Gospel according to St John;* Old Testament; parables and similes; Philo Judaeus

metempsychosis (*Gk.* transmigration of the soul), 442, 485. *See also* reincarnation; transmigration

Micah (OT), 94

Middle East in Jesus' time, *apostolos* (apostle) as mystic or prophet, 153; baptismal sects in, 673; belief in reincarnation, 15, 415-16; Buddhists in, 758; custom of blessing food, 637; Greek influence in, 17, 175-76, 323, 415-16; Mani in, 169-70, 259, 730; miraculous-birth stories, 662; mustard (coriander) in, 249, 581, 725; mystery schools of Greece and Egypt, 323-24; Nestorian Christians of, 391; papyrus, 50-51, 53; repository of mystic teachings, 175-77; use of metaphors in, 204, 207, 235, 244, 259, 273-74, 279, 342, 357, 562, 565, 623, 709, 730, 954; Wisdom literature of, 178-79; Zoroastrianism in, 169-70, 452, 806. *See also* Greek philosophy and mysticism; Hellenization

milk and honey, 255. *See also* sweetness

Milligan, George (C20th NT scholar), 109

mind, action and, 45, 190, 370; as agent of Negative Power, 32, 367, 374, 380, 404, 455, 530-34; as counterfeit spirit, 369, 433, 615 (*see also* counterfeit spirit); attention and direction of, 19, 29, 294, 478-79, 677, 697-702, 740-43; at time of death and after, 370, 406, 434, 436; conscience, 386, 851; constantly moving, active, 363, 741; control, concentration, stilling of, 24, 27, 30, 32, 42, 215, 263-64, 276, 288-89, 304, 414, 581-82, 725, 741-43, 746-47, 758-62, 798 (*see also* distractions: spiritual practice); critical nature of, 501-2; faculties of, 32, 367 (*see also* faculties); habitual and outgoing character of, 21, 32, 34, 42-43, 77, 208, 216, 231, 260, 282, 288, 321, 374, 406, 783; hell and, 397; impressions on, 370-71, 396, 435, 443, 498; inner experience(s), 292, 315, 317, 465, 773; in physical, astral and causal regions, 346-47, 367; like a stormy sea, 617, 621, 625; many meanings of the word, 446; Master and, 469, 604, 712; peace of, 788, 827; procrastination and, 783; purity and purification of, 32, 102, 123, 231, 277, 479, 546, 549-50, 588, 905; separation from God and, 32, 367, 437, 465-67, 533; slavery to senses, to sin, 369, 395, 468, 496, 781; Socrates speaks of, 190; soul and, 369, 393, 468, 494, 522, 530-31, 744; source of energy, 263. *See also* eye centre; eye(s) of the mind; single eye; *and also* externalization; literalization; *Nous;* Universal Mind; virtues; weaknesses

Mind, divine (*Gk. Nous*). *See* Nous

Mind of the Father (as Word), 696. *See also* Nous

Ministers of that drink (as Masters), 606-7

miracle(s), 89, 580-630; a huge catch of fish, 942-43; apostolic, 589-90; as fabrications, 14; as metaphors for spiritual truths, 592-631, 644, 971; at pool of Bethesda, 58-59; barren fig tree, 584; by concentration of mind, 581; casting out devils and demons, 583, 602, 608-16; faith and, 588; feeding the multitude, 584, 587, 641-45, 944-45; fishers of men, Fisher of souls, 624-31; greatest of all, 580; healing by Water, Vine and Tree of Life, 607-8; healing the blind, deaf, lame, sick, 584, 592-95; in OT, 89; in St John, 108, 410, 585-89; in synoptics, 81, 93, 582-85; man blind from birth, 410-11; of apostles, 589-92; of Christian saints, 545-46; of Masters, 588; of Paul, 147, 590-92; of Peter, 40, 589-90; of Simon Magus, 40; of spiritual Physician, 596-98; paralyzed man let down through roof, 480-82; raising a sardine from the dead, 589-90; raising Lazarus from the dead, 586; similar stories in different religions, 580-81; spiritual progress and, 581-82; walking on water, 616-25; water into wine, 649-51. *See also* blindness; devils; fish; Medicine (of Life); Physician

mirror (reflection), of God, 241, 283, 665, 900

Miryai (*Md.* mythical devotee), 730

Miscellanies (EC, Clement of Alexandria), 41(13), 48, 168, 181(32), 209, 324, 412, 426, 427(15), 874

Misdaeus, King (character in *Acts of Thomas*), 783, 893

missionary and proselytizing activity, 13, 34, 969

Mithras and Mithraism, birth of, 662; Christmas and, 129-33; early rival to Christianity, 130; eucharist and, 637-38; resurrection and Day of Judgment, 806

Monad (the One), 665, 997

monasteries, 42-43, 45, 53, 211

money. *See* wealth

money-changers, discrimination of, 48, 178, 463; Jesus in the temple, 205-208

monogenes (*Gk.* only-begotten), 510. *See also* Only-Begotten

morality and mysticism, 32-33, 851, 855

Moses, 71(5), 547-48, 902-3; at Jesus' transfiguration, 335-36; Clement on, 168, 1001; God as Father, souls as sons, 192, 203-4; infanticide of Pharaoh and Herod, 95; Jesus and, 192, 203-4, 281-82, 476, 518, 547, 576, 869, 881-82, 902, 917; Law of, 256-57, 291, 464-65, 494, 514-15, 547-48, 930, 938-39 (*see also* Law); miracles of, 581; on divorce, 881; on the Word, 253, 267-68, 286; Philo Judaeus on, 253, 262, 267-68, 271-72, 1001; ten commandments, 881-82; "man shall not live by bread alone", 246-50 (*see also* Bread); "thou shalt not kill", 44, 396, 494, 518, 917. *See also Exodus; Deuteronomy; Genesis; Numbers*

mosque, 201, 254, 289, 797

Most High (as God), 237, 265, 313, 391, 705, 790, 921; apostle of the, 710; knowledge of the secret of the, 623; Name of the, 624; Son of the, 778; Voice of the, 538

Mother (as Word), 332, 349, 454-55, 513, 543, 642, 650-51, 663-67, 716

Mother-Father (as God), 852

mountain, faith to move, 581

Mount(ain) (as eternal realm), Holy, 204, 331, 333, 336-37, 791, 1002; of God, 793; of myrrh, 792; of Yahweh, 332

mountain(s) (as inner realms), 204, 252-53, 255, 331-39 in Jesus' temptation, 339; in Jesus' transfiguration, 334-39, 830-31

Mount Tabor, 332. *See* map, 84

Mount Zion, 331

murder, 858-60, 882, 917, 925; Devil as a murderer, 380-81; religious justification for, 43, 49, 76-77, 201, 425

Music, divine (as Word), 287-318, 476, 565, 622, 630, 642, 678, 742, 748, 765, 773, 777-78, 790-91, 831, 846-47, 960, 977, 997; as singing, playing instruments, 294-99; changes in each region, 360; "bring all things to your remembrance", 824-25. *See also*